PERPETUAL MOTION

To Dear Colin and his guardian
colleagues of Royal Terrace,
with thanks and best wishes for
comming Christmas and New Year!

Yours #91 Mikhail

Translated by Judy Perraton.

ACKNOWLEDGEMENTS

In this biographical tale, the author attempts to illustrate, through his own example, the typical stages in personal and artistic growth and development from the first creative conception through the struggles in the realisation of his ideas; to the efforts to pass his experience on to the inquisitive new generations of creators and observers. This romantic ballad presents, in a subjective way, a host of international masters of music, drama, dance and the visual arts, each of whom impacted, one way or another, on the author's work in the performing arts, and had an influence on the author's life. Among the virtuosi mentioned are:

RUSSIA: D. Shostakovich, E. Khachaturian, N. Osokin, L. Feigin, A. Tseitlin, G. Firtich, F. Lopukhov, K. Goleizovsky, L. Yakobson, K. Sergeyev, A. Shatin, N. Tarasov, A. Lapauri, M. Rozhdestvenskaya, T. Tkachenko, S. Golovkina, P. Pestov, I. Sviderskaya, V. Panov, B. Pokrovsky, B. Chirtkov, Y. Lyubimov, I. Tumanov, R. Tikhomirov, A. Ginsburg, A. Dudkovsky, K. Müller, C. Andreyev, S. Shegelman.
UKRAINE: L. Tzhomelidze, G. Rels, Y. Lyuftgarten, I. Vishnyakov, I. Goldina.
UZBEKISTAN: B. Karieva.
TADZHIKISTAN: K. Nazarov, F. Zakhidova, M. Sabirova, M. Burkhanov.
BURYATIA: L. Linkhovoin, O. Krauze, L. Sakhyanova, V. Abasheyev.
GREECE: M. Merkury, S. Smailow.
ENGLAND: Dame N. de Valois, Dame B. Gray, M. Park, M. Clark, C. Gable, B. Glassman, D. Bird, N. Beriozoff.
FRANCE: C. Bessi, V. Verdy, I. Goube, V. Oukhtomsky, S. Golovin, L. Joffe,
GERMANY: J. Cranko, R. Nunez.
NORWAY: E. Frich, J. Kirkenaer. SWITZERLAND: M. Gorkin.
ITALY: Z. Prebil, M. Fusco, G. Penzi, P. Scisa, E. Terrabust, E. Piperno.
CANADA: L. Chiriaeff, S. Troyanoff, E. Von Gencsy, V. Warren, A. Wyman.
USA: A. Kramarevsky, V. Kin, M. Popovich, M. Svetlova,
ISRAEL: M. Kanterman, H. Levy, J. Ordman, S. Hoffman, G. Manor, U. Adoram.

Special thanks are due to Natalya Savitskaya, Liam Lorenco-Bone and Amanda Helm for their invaluable assistance with this work.
Whole 'catacombs' of those who represented the leading lights in science and culture in the former Soviet Union still lie hidden in unmarked graves in the Siberian tundra, awaiting rediscovery. The day will surely come when the clear minds of free men, together with the unstoppable progress of international civilisation, will raise up from beneath the deep permafrost layers of oppression and ignorance, the forgotten images and actions of these martyrs, to bring hope to present and future generations through recognising and acknowledging their self-sacrifice.

PERPETUAL MOTION

Mikhail Berkut

ARTHUR H. STOCKWELL LTD
Torrs Park, Ilfracombe, Devon, EX34 8BA
Established 1898
www.ahstockwell.co.uk

British Library Cataloguing-in-Publication Data.
A catalogue record for this book is available
from the British Library.

ISBN 978-0-7223-4591-7
Printed in Great Britain by
Arthur H. Stockwell Ltd
Torrs Park   Ilfracombe
Devon

CONTENTS

PROLOGUE

A sage may say: "A man is a plaything in the hands of Fate." Another may argue: "A human is the maker of his own destiny." Yet others may conclude: "Mankind invented 'destiny' as a mystical notion, to justify negative character traits, corrupt behaviour and other personal weaknesses and faults." Scientists (psychologists and biologists) attempt to determine a person's fate while still a foetus in its mother's womb, on the basis of its genetic heritage, socio-economic status and cultural environment.

Sometimes, however, the course of a person's life changes suddenly and decisively, because of some alien and uncontrollable force which has a fatal affect on that individual's future. Perhaps such a change could be attributed to fate, or more precisely, to a pirouette of fickle Fortune. It is not surprising that our ancient ancestors found it easier to explain natural phenomena by means of this or that religious or mystical fantasy. However, it is also true that an overly dogmatic belief in destiny will limit one's sense of intellectual freedom and hamper an individual's creative drive.

The oracles are right: 'You can't escape your destiny." But to dodge or sidestep it a little is within our capability. When we err in something for the first time, we readily excuse ourselves. However, when we repeat the error, we commit a serious offence. A well-wisher's advice on how to avoid such mistakes will often be fruitless, because no two people are alike. So, it is best to leave playful Fortune to her admirers, and instead identify the sources of our problems in our own character flaws.

Our world is, willy-nilly, made up of contrasting characters, each driven by competing principles of how to live together. In most respects, people are like animals: fighting for power, territory, or reproductive advantages. The difference is that people, with their intellectual ability, fight not only for their physical survival, but also for what they fanatically believe in, for Utopian ideals. In such a struggle, no measures or means are off limits, not even the mass extermination of their opponents. In the end, it is impossible to change this law of nature and stop the fatal advance of mankind's self-destruction.

VOLUME I

FINDING MY NICHE:
LESSER ORBIT

STAGE I: THROUGH TEMPESTS AND GALES

CHAPTER 1 WAR'S LEGACY AND MUSIC

The train was crawling slower than a tortoise. It seemed that either the train driver, or the locomotive, might be running out of steam. Some of the passengers were leaning out of the windows, yelling at the top of their lungs, trying to outshout one another, like vendors in an Odessa bazaar.

"Look, look! We just passed Lyubashovka!"

"It's not Lyubashovka. It's Beriozovka!"

"What do you know, blockhead!"

"Look at you, scumbag, calling me names. I'll come over there in a minute and smash your head in. See if you can go on goggling then with pretty black eyes!"

"Go on then! Just try me, you stinking insect!"

"Calm down, women, you're making the kids cry," the old conductor croaked, "and clear your backsides and bundles out of the passage – nobody can get past."

Mother would not let us out of our compartment until all the passengers had left the carriage. There was complete mayhem on the platform: people trampling on children, tossing bags aside, pulling one another's hair, pushing and shoving. Bagheera, as we dubbed Mother, observed these scenes with dismay. We had many nicknames for each other and our mother, my two brothers and I, depending on our moods. Bagheera, the black panther from *The Jungle Book* who protected Mowgli, suited my mother well.

"Ma'am, I'd let these savages scatter first if I were you. You've no need to rush. I'm not going to take you back to Kiev." The conductor had an Odessan sense of humour. Mother helped all three of us strap on our backpacks, gave each of us a small bag to carry, took my little brother Roman by the hand, scooped up the suitcase and then set off towards the exit. The conductor wished us good luck and we parroted back "Thank you" in unison.

On the platform, Mother called over a rough-looking old woman with a wheelbarrow. They haggled for a while before finally agreeing a price. We piled our stuff into the barrow and briskly marched off after the crowd. There were scores of horses with carts in front of the station. The Chief (Mother in command!) told us to keep our eyes open, stay close to her and watch our feet so as not to step into anything sticky and smelly. The old girl proved adept at handling the barrow at intersections, weaving in and out of the horses and pedestrians. We soon understood why she had threaded a rope through the handles of all our bags and secured the ends around the barrow's handles: the area was teeming with ragamuffins our own age, on the lookout for easy pickings. As we walked, we kept a protective ring tight around the barrow: Mother and Roman in the rear, my older brother Yosif and I on either side. The urge to look round was strong, but Bagheera's quiet growl held us in check.

Eventually, Yosif and I recognised our street and yelled in excitement. Startled, the old girl stopped abruptly.

"Have you lost your minds, or what?"

The Chief reassured her. "It's nothing. They're just happy."

We were jumping up and down around the barrow, and passers-by turned to look at us. Mother stopped the barrow opposite No. 26. While she and the old woman were settling up, we unloaded our bags and scanned the familiar surroundings. At the gate of our house, an old woman was sitting on a low chair, all bundled up in a shawl. An open sack of sunflower seeds was parked on the ground in front of her, with an aluminium mug in the middle. Her eyes were glued to us and her lips moved rapidly as she crossed herself. My heart skipped a beat. Being short-sighted, I could not see her clearly, but started towards her, as if under a spell. She stretched out a trembling hand, touching my shoulder, as if not trusting her eyes.

My voice came as though from beyond the grave: "Baba Sasha?"

She grabbed my head and pulled it to her chest: "Mishanya? Alive!" I helped her up. She kept muttering, "Lord be praised! Thank you, Lord, for letting me live to see this minute!"

Mother ran up to us.

"Aleksandra Vasilievna, darling!" she exclaimed. "I can't believe it! We're together again!"

Baba Sasha, our old nanny, took us to her place, on the second floor, where her daughter also used to live with her three sons, before the war.

Mother fired questions at her: "How is Volodya? Is he alive? What about Maria? And her children?"

"Due to return from evacuation any time now, just like you. Listen, Annushka, leave off doing anything else now. Get yourselves straight off to the Welfare Office. You need to register for a pension, and you should also try to secure the flat next to us, while it's still available. The annex, where your apartment was, was bombed. Come on, dear, now's not the time for tears. We'll talk about it all later."

While we were washing and changing, Baba Sasha made us some tea and then took a pasty stuffed with cabbage and potatoes out of the oven. We devoured it like locusts, not leaving a single crumb on the table.

Bagheera apologised, but the old lady blessed us and said: "Go in peace! Before it's too late. Don't forget the documents, Annushka. The Welfare Office is where it was before. You remember, don't you?"

"Yes, yes, Aunty Sasha, thank you! Please, take some money, and buy some essentials for us, just in case the store closes before we return."

Yosif, Roman and I were in a kind of stupor, overwhelmed with impressions and emotional at being back in our home city. We moved mechanically into line behind the Chief. I mused: *Looks like we're amongst the first evacuees to return to Odessa. A single mother, with three kids . . . Oy vey.*

At the Welfare Office, they first verified that we were indeed Odessans, and not Martians. They even checked the arrival date on our tickets. Then, after inspecting Father's papers, they gave us the OK. The Director, a one-armed invalid, went to the Residential Office and half an hour later handed Mother our residency entitlement. Just before the Welfare Office closed for the day, we were registered for pension benefits as family members of the war dead, added to the list of those eligible for American aid packages, given a cash handout to get us through the first few months and, finally, handed the keys and title certificates to our new flat. Mother warmly thanked the Director, shaking his hand. He, to my watchful eye, seemed to hold on to her hand longer than necessary. Bagheera finally freed herself and we hurried off to our new home, anxious with anticipation.

On the way, I asked the Chief, "What are these American packages they're talking about?" She explained that it was part of a generous aid scheme for the families of Soviet soldiers who had died in the struggle against fascism.

At home, 'Uncle' Volodya was waiting for us with a bouquet of daisies he had picked in the ruins of the backyard. A few of our neighbours had meanwhile learned of our return and of our father's death, but they greeted us warily, avoiding eye contact. I heard Baba Sasha explaining to Mother the reason for this cold welcome for returning evacuees. When the Nazis occupied the city, many of the residents looted the flats of evacuees, and now they were afraid of being held to account.

'Uncle' Volodya came with us and unlocked the door of our new, eagerly awaited home. It had a living room, a bedroom, a separate kitchen, and a long corridor. The toilet was in an outhouse at the end of the yard: we were clearly not going to be spoiled by excessive comforts. The flat also had a large balcony overhanging the main entrance to our building. An immediate clean-up was in order: the floors needed to be swept and washed, the walls whitewashed or painted and windowpanes replaced. Volodya tried to offer some words of comfort:

"Anna, you've no need to worry about any of this now. The district council will take care of refurbishment for all returning residents."

The Chief let out a wry laugh. "And when will that be exactly? In a week? Perhaps two? We need it now! Before the kids go back to school. So, my dear, here are 300 roubles. Go and find another helper, and fix this place up for us as quickly as possible. We're not going to just stand around here waiting. I'll pay for everything. Just do it without fuss."

"Boys, your mum was, and is, 'a general in a skirt'! Let's go and have supper, before another commander-in-chief appears on the scene."

Laughing, we trooped next door and knocked in unison. An intoxicating smell of Ukrainian borscht, spiced with garlic, drifted towards us from the inside.

"Come in, please!" Our nanny welcomed us in Ukrainian, an embroidered towel over her shoulder.

We washed our hands and sat around a table laid with enticing fare. Roman, who couldn't restrain himself, grabbed a spoon, but a quiet growl from Bagheera stopped him. We lowered our heads and waited until Volodya had finished mumbling grace – it was forbidden to say grace aloud, in the country of the Soviets.

At last, Volodya said: "Amen. Bon appétit!"

Some furniture and household items had been left behind in our new flat. While we were helping Volodya clear out the rubbish, Mother sorted out what to keep, what to throw away, and what we still needed to buy. We shuttled between the flat and the rubbish dump with junk. Within a week, however, Volodya and his partner had turned our neglected flat into a palace. The windows shone; the walls and the ceiling were bright white, and the floors planed and varnished. We boys celebrated while Mother paid. The men hauled in three small *couchettes* for us kids and a bed for mother. Each of us also had a small writing desk.

Roman was starting primary school this year; I was entering grade VI, and Yosif grade VII. All three of us were to be in the same school. The Principal was overjoyed to see us.

"Is this all of you, or is there someone else hiding behind the door?" Yekaterina Karlovna asked.

"Like all good things, we come in small packages!" Mother quipped.

Two elderly teachers were engaged in registering students and forming classes. This was to be the first school year in what had been Nazi-occupied territory. There were no new textbooks, notebooks or other school supplies. Of the seventh-graders, Yosif was the first to register. He offered to help sort the odd textbooks donated by parents. Mother informed the Principal that during the war he had worked in a village library and had developed a passion for reading. Then, in turn, she introduced me as an organiser of performing arts and Roman as a promising chess player.

There were only a very few boys attending the school at this time. Most of the young boys were homeless orphans who had lost their parents in the war and were now living in warehouses in the port or at a train station near the farmers' market. Shabbily clad, always hungry, school was the last thing on their minds.

Evacuees were slowly but surely returning, both to our block of flats and the Gypsies' house next door at No. 24. Before long, Baba Sasha's daughter, Maria Ilinichna, with three sons approximately our age, also returned home. Things were looking up. When the ten youngsters were around, we formed a 'Musketeers' Club' consisting of chess players, wrestlers, dancers, musicians and comedians. Our two families formed the core of the club with our neighbouring flats and the adjoining veranda as its base. Yosif was elected chairman, and Vitaly (the oldest of the neighbouring trinity of sons), deputy chairman. Our group became a kind of counterweight to the street hooligans and petty thieves. At first, we often found ourselves getting into fights with them, but then we gradually discovered a common language. Our mothers – Anna and Maria – would often feed, wash, and clothe these hungry vagabonds from the streets, and try to knock some sense into them, to leave their dirty alleyways and find shelter at an orphanage.

Life at school was gradually returning to normal. The Principal asked me to organise a New Year's concert with the first-graders, but we had no music. I asked Baba Sasha if, by any chance, she knew who had nicked our family piano during the occupation. Volodya gave me the address and suggested I take a policeman along. Mother agreed to lend the piano to the school for the time being if I succeeded. I made arrangements with the Principal, and she asked a policeman to join us, so the three of us set out to recover our stolen property. Volodya and two other men with a cart were waiting by the entrance. When the woman of the house opened the door and saw a representative of the state in front of her, she began to stutter. As the saying goes, a guilty mind betrays itself. Her flat resembled a furniture warehouse. I found our piano, but decided not to file an official complaint. This sort of crime, as the policeman stated, could land an offender in prison for three to five years. The porters carried our piano off to school and placed it in the gym. The whole of the following week I was hailed as a hero, and had my nose in the air so often that my neck hurt.

With sixteen girls from the first grade I staged an old dance 'Russian Dolls', and one called 'Kazachok' with twelve girls from the second grade. During the first rehearsals, I had to alternate demonstrating the steps with playing the tune on the piano until the Principal asked a teacher to help me. In fact, she was a better pianist than me and volunteered to continue rehearsals with both groups by herself, while I worked with the boys of both grades on a 'noise orchestra' that employed household items such as pots and pans instead of drums. There were also other participants, some singing, others reciting poetry. Altogether, a thirty-minute-long programme was shaping up, to be presented at a New Year's variety show before an audience of parents. This was a small, but decent, result, considering the difficulties of the post-war period. Costumes were minimal, but the performers' spirits were high, even though the technical skills were quite elementary. The noise orchestra of the Odessan ragamuffins was an absolute hit with the audience. Fortunately it was the last number in the programme, a tried and trusted practice, ensuring that we always ended on a high note. Yekaterina Karlovna warmly thanked the young performers and wished everyone a happy New Year for 1945.

Although the recovered piano helped me to prepare the school show, it didn't help me in my personal quest for music because it was usually out of reach, locked away at school. It happened that one of my friends, Kolya, owned a harmonica, which his dad had brought him from Germany during a home leave from the front. Not knowing how to play it, Kolya gave it to me as a New Year's present. I soon learned, alternately exhaling and inhaling, to produce a sound. But the harmonica was not much use for my work with schoolchildren.

Then, one day, while out walking in the park, I chanced upon an accordionist playing with a small instrumental ensemble. I stood transfixed, enchanted by his skill, unable to tear my gaze away from this musician 'blindly' controlling his magical instrument with perfect ease and virtuosity. Something truly momentous awakened inside me at that moment. It seemed like a turning point in my life: *I have to get myself an accordion and master it to perfection. Period.*

Mishutka, you're out of your mind. Where are you going to get the money?

I'll earn it over the summer. I'll slave for a couple of months, morning till night. And who will give a thirteen-year-old a work permit?

It's illegal. It'll be unofficial: wartime conditions. It's decided.

During the interval I asked the accordionist how much his instrument – or one suitable for a beginner – might cost in a flea market.

"One with 120 basses, 2,000 roubles; 80 basses, 1,500 roubles," he said, "German makes are cheaper than Italian."

I resolved there and then to buy an accordion. I'd get myself a small one for starters, and then see how things went. Working in the summer, for two months, or nine weeks, earning 200 roubles a week, I could save enough to purchase my dream.

The war was coming to a victorious end. Everyone was expecting the surrender of the fascists by 1st May. The school principal once again approached me for help. The parents of the third- and fourth-graders were complaining that their kids had been left out of the winter show. She now wanted me to involve these kids in the preparation of a May holiday talent show, with the help of the teacher pianist. We were to perform the same dances again, but also add new ones for the forthcoming grand celebration of the victorious end to the Patriotic War. There were to be public performances on the outdoor stages in the park. The Principal had promised to borrow costumes from the Pioneers' Palace and to invite an accordionist to play. This would be great practice for my professional future in the performing arts. I resolved to give it my all.

The organisers of the victory celebrations had envisaged multiple festive shows, simultaneously acted out in different parts of the city. The idea was to prevent overcrowding in any one place and enable the whole city to celebrate together. My chance of becoming famous was growing exponentially. I chose the Moldavian 'Khora' for the girls from the third grade, and the 'Sailors' Dance' for the girls from the fourth grade. The boys were unfortunately not very interested in dancing, but they were more than willing to serve as bodyguards for our female dancers in the event of any escapades on the part of the adventure-seeking gangs that always attended such outdoor performances. Meanwhile, I managed to make arrangements with a local bakery to work one and a half shifts there in the summer from 7 a.m. to 7 p.m. daily for 250 roubles a week. The earnings would be enough to buy both an instrument and a canvas carrying case.

By the end of the first week of May, all Soviet citizens were celebrating Victory Day. There was, in truth, at the time an overwhelming sense of the triumph of peace over war, of creation over destruction, of humanism over fascism. It was a day for paying tribute to the dead and for saluting the victors. Toasts were raised in every house and celebrations lasted through the night; wherever one turned there was music, singing and dancing. Still, on the following Monday, even the victors were expected to go back to their regular jobs or studies – life as usual. For me at school, final exams approached.

As soon as I had finished the last test, I showed up for work at the bakery without even waiting for the beginning of a new week. It wasn't complicated work, but it was very tiring: running back and forth with a metal baking tray piled high with freshly baked bread and bagels. At first, my calf muscles and back ached mercilessly but they quickly became conditioned. I also developed a more sensible way of handling the tray, which allowed me to conserve a good deal more energy. Still, I would come home at night barely alive from exhaustion. Immediately after supper I would collapse on a small couch in my mother's room, then wake up at 6 a.m., and by 7 o'clock would be back into the next day's cycle.

Demobilised veterans were now returning from the front with spoils of various kinds, often musical instruments, including many accordions. On the last Sunday in August, my friend Danny and I headed over to the flea market. There, in the musical section, we discovered several for sale. I tried out the keys of a few eighty-bass instruments with my right hand, and finally settled on a small and light beauty. It was in good condition, both in terms of its sound and mechanics. Danny got me a bargain for 1,600 roubles. Very tenderly we placed the instrument in its case and schlepped it home. It was heavy; however, as the saying goes, 'It's no effort to carry your own load."

It is difficult to describe what I felt at that moment: certainly enormous satisfaction at the way I had set about realising my dream and accomplishing on my own something that had previously seemed impossible, especially in the face of doubt and opposition of my family, who all thought my obsession with music and dance was mad. How could they foresee that from that moment on, fickle Mistress Fate was to turn me, irrevocably, towards music and dance; that the latter would come to permeate every aspect of my inner and outer worlds, bringing a little boy from Odessa into contact with the titans of art and culture? In truth, I myself at that moment had little inkling of what lay in store. Rather, I was driven by instinct.

I devoted all my spare time that year to teaching myself the accordion. The right hand progressed faster, thanks to my previous practice on a piano keyboard, but I faced a serious challenge with the left hand: trying to attain the necessary 'blind' mastery of the bass system in structure and harmony. Music schools did not offer courses at the time in the button accordion. Self-study manuals had disappeared from the shelves of bookshops during the war. Another possibility was to learn from a private tutor, but they would typically only be available on weekday mornings when I had to be at school. In the end, I resorted to teaching myself. Luckily, someone suggested I should see what help was available at the local House of Culture. There I was introduced to a *bayanist* (who plays a button accordion) who was available for private tuition on Sundays between 10 a.m. and 12 noon. We agreed a fee of twenty roubles an hour. I wrote down all his instructions for the left-hand movements. I learned a series of passages, scales and exercises for the coordination of musical phrases with the tempo/ rhythm of the bellows. We arranged to meet regularly, on the last Sunday of each month, for the next year. This was an invaluable piece of good luck in my musical studies.

Only six months after the end of the conflagration of the Second World War, a new Cold War began between the global capitalist and communist blocs. We children understood little of the difference between these ideological opponents, but painfully felt the end of the American aid packages and the disappearance of many staple foods from grocery aisles. Our mother, anticipating the coming famine, got herself hired in January 1946 to work part-time at the drinks counter of a bodega, a small bar and restaurant, which was located near our home and just across from my school.

In the morning, while we were at school, Mother would manage to clean the house, shop in the market and cook our lunch. Then she hurried to work. Coming home from school, we ate and then did our homework. At six in the evening we usually joined Mother in the bodega where we took our supper together. After that, we had time to ourselves until ten. My older and younger brothers would spend their time on the terrace of our house in blitz tournaments with the members of the chess club, while I set about perfecting my accordion technique in Mother's room, constantly widening my repertoire of popular songs and dances. By the time Bagheera came home from work, we were all snoring loudly, pretending to be fast asleep, because we had promised her we would go to bed on time. She, knowing our tricks full well, would go straight to the kitchen and do the washing-up. Then she'd take a shower, giving us a chance to fall asleep for real. Only then would she pass through our room to reach her own – where she would finally have a chance to unwind.

Every Sunday, while our mothers went off to a flea market in search of bargains in children's clothes and household items, our double trio of brothers (ourselves and Maria's boys) organised open chess tournaments. By then I was already enchanting the neighbourhood girls with my accordion playing and tonal singing in duet with my cousin David. My friends, Danny, Kolya, Syoma and Vitaly, provided a healthy interest for these girls, and everyone would happily sing and dance to my accompaniment, 'spin the bottle' for kisses, and generally have a good time together. Although we were only fourteen to fifteen years old, our interests and general behaviour tended to be quite advanced for our age.

My cousin on my father's side, Lenny 'Redhead', who was working as a mechanic at a local factory, introduced me to the director of a pioneer camp that was being organised for the children of factory workers. They wanted to hire a musician for two summer months to provide musical accompaniment for morning athletic exercises and for evening rehearsals of their performing-arts club. The wages were puny, but room and board were free. For an inexperienced beginner this was a decent start to a musical career.

The Director welcomed me warmly. He was surprised to find me already familiar with most of the common song and dance tunes. In previous seasons, his counsellors and youth leaders had had to teach pioneers everything themselves: songs, dramatic sketches and the most basic dance compositions (two taps and three claps). The counsellors were happy to learn of my arrival and heaved a collective sigh of relief. At the very first daily staff meeting, I outlined my position: I would be responsible for music alone. If the counsellors wished to include a special dance or a pantomime in the talent show that was to close the session, they would have to rehearse my choreography with the kids during the day on their own, and only in the evening have a rehearsal with musical accompaniment. Otherwise, I told them, there would no time for me to prepare the whole programme. The Director, who seemed quite pleased at this, looked around at the assembled crowd: "Any questions? No? Then, off you go."

Apart from sleeping in the same room, I had otherwise very little contact with my brother Yosif. We simply ignored each other beyond an exchange of a few phrases now and then on family-related subjects. He had graduated from middle school the year before and moved up to high school, so that, during the day, he was entirely off my radar. With my younger brother, Roman, on the other hand, it was a different story. There was warmth in our relationship that was to last for many years. Once in a while on a Sunday, nine-year-old Roman would visit me at the pioneer camp, and, to the delight of the camp's director, and in plain view of all the parents and important visitors, would stage a simultaneous exhibition in chess, playing on twelve boards against kids older than himself. A typical result would be three draws and nine wins, without a single loss. I was very proud of my younger brother. The Director loved him as his own son and took pleasure in losing one or two games to Roman after lunch.

The pioneers performed with great enthusiasm on the last night. I received compliments from the factory's administration and was invited to apply for the same job the following summer. Nobody appreciated what an effort it had been for me to coordinate the footwork of the performance while simultaneously playing the accordion strapped to my shoulders.

Roman passed on to me my mother's request to visit her at the weekend for a serious talk. We returned home together after the concert. In the tramcar, he laid out his pocket-size chess set with its magnetic base and explained to me various opening moves for professional chess games. The camp director had boasted to him that, after lunch, during the rest time while the kids were sleeping, he and I would play chess and he would beat me most of the time. "Misha, if you just memorise four of the most popular opening moves, six steps in each, you will beat your director in no time."

It was late when we finally reached home, but Mother was waiting for us with delicious borscht. After we had eaten, she sent us off to bed, warning me, "In the morning, after breakfast we need to talk about your future, following your graduation from middle school. You will need to be up by 8 a.m., and at nine I'll be waiting for you in my room."

Her formal tone did not surprise me. She was worried about my intentions to continue with school, given the impending economic crisis in the country. A wise woman, she would often repeat her mantra that an empty stomach needed bread first and foremost, not music. She could not see how music could provide a living, but I was determined to show her otherwise. Mother started the conversation with an outline of our financial situation and of the impending famine. Parents were stocking up on food supplies for their children. From 1st September, the government was going to revert to rationing food and basic necessities.

"Misha, what are you planning to do after your work at the pioneer camp finishes?"

"Continue with school, like my older brother," I stated.

"On 1st September," she said, "I'm going to go full-time at the bodega, 10 a.m. to 10 p.m. It seems to me that it would be sensible for you to take up a morning shift at the bakery, 7 a.m. to 1 p.m. Six hours is an allowable limit for a teenager. You could then eat lunch at my canteen, and do whatever you need to at home until 6 p.m.; and from 6 p.m. to 10 p.m. attend the Evening School for Working Youth, along with many of your peers. What do you think of that?"

"I'm sorry, Mum," I said, "but I want to do it my way. I want to study at the same day school as Yosif. In the evenings I'll work in clubs, and at private parties at weekends. I've already had invitations from the summer pioneers' families to play at birthday parties, weddings, and other functions. The camp director doesn't mind me doing that, provided it doesn't affect my work with the pioneers. I'm going to put up ads in public places, and you'll see how many offers I get for weekends."

"I just don't see how this can possibly be a stable job," she reiterated. "It's also not a respectable occupation if you're considering a serious career in the future. But it's your life and your decision."

At the end of August, I prepared the necessary documents and went to register for high school which was located just at the end of our short street. As he put my name on the list of the eleventh-graders, the head of admissions remarked that I'd be in the same class as my old friends, Danny, Syoma, Kolya, Vitaly and others. I was relieved to learn that. At least socially I would not be starting from scratch. An idea popped into my head. When I got home, I composed an advertisement: 'Accordionist/singer available, evenings and weekends to play at family celebrations. Reply to Annushka.' I gave the address and telephone number of the bodega. I then went to the Chief for approval. She consulted with her manager and he agreed, on condition that I played at his premises a couple of hours for free on major holidays. I had no choice but to accept and so my mother became my promoter. Having a telephone was a rarity at the time, but public enterprises like the bodega were required by law to have one in case of emergencies.

1946–47 went down in history as a year of a famine even more devastating than during the war. Bread was strictly rationed: 500g a day for adults, 350g for children. Money practically lost its value. On the black market only gold, silver and diamonds were valid currency. In the city, pigeons and seagulls were the first to disappear off the streets, then cats and dogs. A rat would go for half a loaf of bread. My friends rummaged among fallen houses and cellars in search of living creatures. At the cooking-oil processing factory where my father had worked before the war, we – as a family of a dead soldier – were entitled to receive once a week something called *makukha*, a block of compressed sunflower bran and chaff, left over from the oil-filtering process. This would normally be pig feed, but nobody could remember any longer what a pig looked like, and now it was us who were eating *makukha*.

The bodega's manager ran an 'under the counter' business, trading home-distilled spirits for dried bread. Mother cooked and offered the clients porridge, pasta, and mashed potatoes. These were the delicacies we usually had for dinner, washed down with fizzy water or tea. The situation in the city was indeed dire. Every morning on the way to school we watched as a horse-drawn cart would pass by, loaded with emaciated starving people, or even with dead bodies picked up in the streets and not even covered with sackcloth.

For the three years of the war, the earth had been so deeply contaminated by bombshells, mines and military machinery, that there was no way, according to the agronomists, that it could produce a harvest for at least another two years. The whole zone had to be cleared of mines and burnt-out hulks of tanks and trucks, but there was no one yet to do the job.

The summer of 1947 found me working again in the same pioneer camp. Meanwhile, the countries of the Soviet bloc lent a helping hand, through a system of 'compulsory volunteering'. At long last, the empty shelves of our stores were filled with longed-for foods and household items. It was their payment for the liberation from fascism by the Soviet Army. 'Better late than never.' Our matriarch rejoiced at this respite, but opted to continue full-time at the bodega for the time being, just to be on the safe side.

Then one day, at the end of the second camp session, as I was returning home carrying the accordion in its case, I stopped just for a moment to rest and shift the heavy weight of my instrument from one hand to the other, when out of nowhere, a dwarf with a really big head approached me and asked, "Are you still learning that or are you already playing?"

"I've been working all summer, playing. Just finished now," I said. "Is there anything else?" I was tired, and rather irritated with the idle chat, and I made to leave.

"Yes, as matter of fact. The 'anything else' is that I would like to offer you a gig at the Odessa Philharmonic. My name is Grisha, by the way. What's yours?"

"Misha!"

We both laughed.

"What's the gig?" I was getting curious.

"Musical accompaniment for the concert programme of the Ensemble of the Lilliputians – the little people. I'm their manager."

"Nice to make your acquaintance. Shall we pop into the bodega and talk over tea? My mum works there."

Bagheera was happy to see me and I introduced Gregory from the Odessa Philharmonic.

"We need to discuss some business, Mum. Can we step into the other room?"

"Of course. Grisha, would you like sugar in your tea?"

"Yes, thank you."

"No problem then, I'll bring it right over." The Chief had immediately grasped the situation.

Seated at the table in the corner, I began the conversation. "What exactly is involved here? And what are the conditions of employment: hours, payment, etc.?"

Grisha took out a sheaf of papers from his briefcase. They were programmes and photographs. I felt my knees weaken – *Mishenka, take it easy, relax, don't rush, don't sell yourself cheap . . . act like you know what you're doing, like you're an old hand at all this.*

"Yes," I said at length, "the programme is quite interesting, but the troupe appears to be rather small?"

"Just thirteen performers and myself."

"Have you worked with them a long time?"

"About three years."

"And what happened to the previous accompanist?" I pointed to one of the photos.

"Got drunk and couldn't perform," he informed me. "Lost us a gig. The management of the Philharmonic fired him. And now we have a new repertoire and new performers. It all needs musical arrangement: to be rehearsed with the master of ceremonies. After that we're taking the show on the road."

"When and where?" I asked.

"Mostly in the Odessa region," he said. "On weekends, there'll be two shows a day. At weekdays, from ten in the morning till two in the afternoon – rehearsals at the base. In the summer, during July and August, we'll be touring around the south of the country."

"What about the salary?" I asked.

"All depends on the number of hours you do," he answered.

"When can I attend a rehearsal of the ensemble?"

"Tomorrow," he said. "At the Railway Workers' Cultural Centre."

The next day, I went to this Cultural Centre. In order to look more impressive,

I took a notepad and a pen along with me to write down the names of performers, the theme of their acts, and the duration and character of their performances, etc. The night before, I practised variations by Glière for his ballet *The Red Poppy* and a waltz-caprice by Durall, just in case they asked me to play. These were in fact my party pieces. At 10 a.m. sharp, Grisha was waiting for me at the Cultural Centre. In the auditorium, he introduced me to the company's artistic director. Ilya Grannik was a bit taller than me, but two of his assistants, Margo and Carmen were little people and only reached up to my chest. I met the *conférencier* (master of ceremonies) and his singer wife, two pairs of acrobat-equilibrists (ladder, pole, monocycle, etc.), a pair of juggler-clowns and a music eccentric, Vasilisa (xylophone, bells). Altogether, not counting me, there were twelve performers for a full two-part programme. Two, including the musician, were of normal height. All the others were little people aged twenty-five to thirty-five. I tried to appear very confident, but in truth I was seriously nervous. I had no patron or recommendation, and so had to be my own agent, making sure I got a decent offer.

When asked about my age, I said, with a straight face, "Sixteen," adding over a year to my actual age. "I have four years' experience playing the accordion," I lied. "Before the war, I studied piano at music school. I also sing and dance a little." (Which was true).

I watched the entire rehearsal from the front row in the stalls. While the actors rehearsed their numbers repeatedly, I jotted down notes on the details of their performance. At the end of the rehearsal, Grannik asked me to play something. I first did a warm-up for both hands, playing some scales and then a dance from *The Red Poppy* (thirteen variations). There was an explosion of clapping behind my back.

I had just started on the waltz by Durall, when Grannik's clap interrupted me: "That's fine, thank you. Elvira, why don't you try your 'Gypsy Romance' with Mikhail?"

"Can I see the notes?" I asked the singer.

She shook her head. "Your predecessor took all the notes with him, and we can't get them back."

"Misha, can you figure out the accompaniment by ear?" Grannik asked.

"I can try," I answered. "I've played a Gypsy repertoire quite often before. Which songs, and in what key?" I asked Elvira."

"The song 'Dark Eyes' in B minor," she replied.

I got ready, probing the keys, and then looked up at the singer. She winked at me, and my fingers launched into a rousing introduction. After an extended pause, and as the little people in the audience grew quiet, Elvira carefully began to draw out the melody with her dramatic alto, but as confidence in my accompaniment grew, she soon took off without reserve, and finished triumphantly, in full harmony with the music. Grisha yelled: "Bravo!" The little people jumped to their feet in the stalls, applauding. Grannik came up to me, smiling.

"I would never have guessed!" he said. "You're hired. Go and get yourself sorted out with Grisha."

A contract between us was drawn up, signed and countersigned by the ensemble's artistic director. As the administrator of the ensemble, Grisha then had to take it for final approval to the Philharmonic. He promised to stop by at my house within two hours, with a signed and approved copy. On the way home, I visited Mother at work and reported on my success. She was very pleased that I'd finally found a practical outlet for my passion for music and theatre.

I explained that I'd now have to transfer to the Evening School for Working Youth.

"Mishenka, you've done really well," she said. "Congratulations on your first break. It looks like we won't be seeing much of you at home from now on."

"I doubt anybody will shed tears over that!" I riposted.

"That's not true! Roma and David ask after you all the time. So do our neighbours."

At home I held back from announcing this turning point in my life to anyone on the noisy veranda. Instead, I tidied up our rooms, and then laid out biscuits and jam on the table.

Suddenly, Roman burst into the room, his eyes round with terror: "Misha, there's a Martian out there, looking for you."

"That's no extra-terrestrial. It's an earthling by the name of Gregory, he's my new boss."

Coming out on to the veranda, I apologised and explained our chess club.

"I like chess," Grisha croaked in a sharp guttural voice, entering the flat.

"Welcome," I said and thrust the door open into the living room. "Will you have a cup of tea?"

"Thank you. I won't say no."

I went to put the kettle on.

Returning to the living room, I carefully studied the contract. It was quite a complicated document, but I understood it well enough. As we drank tea, I asked Grisha to fill me in on relations between the various members of the ensemble. I was anxious not to tread on anyone's toes. He described the group dynamics in some detail, emphasising that there was no connection between individual couples and groups, except through the annual contract with the Philharmonic, which was regularly renewed, unless something out of the ordinary happened. Having seen my guest off, I went to the evening school and applied for a transfer from the day school to enable me to continue my secondary education while pursuing a day job.

Grisha asked me to start work immediately: the performers had been without an accompanist for so long that they'd pretty much ground to a halt in the preparation of their show numbers. The following morning I began my work in the rehearsal hall of the Cultural Centre. The first artist was a singer. Here I encountered a serious problem: how to fill in, without the aid of annotated sheet music, all the details of an individual performing style of the singer over six compositions (two to three in each half of the show). There was a mass of detail for me to figure out and note down: the tonality of each song, the number of couplets in it, the number of bars in each couplet, metre and dynamics. It was almost impossible. It became clear why they'd not been able to find an accompanist for so long. I asked Elvira to make two copies of her repertoire in the library of the Conservatoire and bring them to rehearsals.

A similar, but even more challenging task awaited me in the musical accompaniment for the xylophonist Vasilisa. Her performance consisted of classical études on xylophone and bells. In spite of my musical genius (excuse my utter lack of modesty), I was still unable to reproduce a satisfactory accompaniment for her by ear alone. So I sent Vasilisa to the library along with Elvira. There were fewer problems with the remaining numbers. During the rehearsal, I selected musical backgrounds for each number to match the particular atmosphere of the repertoire. For instance, Moldavian 'Doyna' (traditional flute melodies), with their magical intriguing modulations were particularly suited to the illusionist; for the juggling clowns, there were waltzes and marches; for the acrobat-eccentrics, gallops and polkas. To accompany the satirical couplets performed by the *conférencier*, I proposed Volga river folk tunes in a comic vein.

Most of the performers approved my suggestions, just adding a few notes here and there according to their personal sense of each piece. After their amendments had been incorporated, we settled upon a final version of the accompaniment, with all the necessary details of pauses, changes in tempo, dynamics, etc. I immediately wrote down all the details of the accompaniment on separate sheets and asked each performer to check all the remarks, asking them also to put their signatures to these notes, both as a proof of their agreement and also to lend our communications a professional tone. Grannik really liked this idea. He announced that, from now on, once the final staging details of each number's conception had been agreed upon, each performer would sign them, so that nobody could afterwards blame the stage Director for their own mistakes. And so, as my 'employment log' would record, my professional career as a musician officially began at this point.

In the eighth grade of the evening school there were some twenty students, mostly girls, and only a handful of young men, all very serious and diligent, who worked during the day from 8 a.m. to 4 p.m. The girls were mostly there for a piece of paper, a diploma of secondary education, rather than for any real learning. They often whiled away their time in the classroom, giggling, flirting, writing little notes to one another, and distracting the teacher's attention. I sometimes had to raise my voice to hush them. Our form teacher was a modest, quiet chemistry teacher, Mr Kotlerman. He was also a chess master who was well known to my brothers. By the end of the second week of lessons I was elected head boy. Now I had an official reason, even a duty, to uphold good discipline in the classroom and to restrain the air-headed girls.

I did my homework each night between ten and midnight before going to sleep. In the morning I worked with the Lilliputians for two hours. We then had lunch at noon and afterwards rehearsed for two more hours. I decided it would be a good idea to improve my qualifications by attending courses in my lunch hour at the Performing Arts Centre. The lessons were in the form of seminars and included an introduction to the theory of music, dance, and stage acting. My musical instrument and other props were always kept locked at the Cultural Centre where the Lilliputians rehearsed. This allowed me to run over to the arts centre every day at twelve and participate in the seminars there until two. After work I usually had a bite at Mother's bodega, and at six went to evening school. This was a very tight schedule, but when one has a goal in life and a desire to reach it, one can overcome any kind of obstacle, however difficult. And so it was for me.

While working with the soloists, I drew Grannik's attention to the fact that their performances were rather static, and I asked his permission to allow me to teach them a few effective moves they could try out during the vocal pauses. He approved this idea for the satirical couplets and for Elvira's Gypsy repertoire. These added elements gave their performances extra impact.

When, a week later, the Philharmonic's artistic director reviewed the new programme of the ensemble, he noticed the changes in the presentation of the soloists and asked Grannik, "Why didn't you do this before?"

Grannik pointed at me. "Previously, as you know, we had a different concertmaster, more of a brawler-master, really."

There were bursts of laughter in the audience.

The artistic director congratulated me. "My compliments to you, young man!"

I nodded by way of acknowledgement. He, meanwhile, was whispering something into Grannik's ear, while the latter was staring at me, clearly intrigued. They were obviously speaking about me. Meanwhile, Grisha reported to the boss about the upcoming shows in the suburbs on the following weekend. The Director thanked everyone for the successful performance and wished us good luck with the new programme. Grisha informed us of the concert venues and distributed cards with detailed information on when and where. The master of ceremonies and his wife, the singer, thanked me for the extra help I had given them. He shook my hand, and Elvira kissed me on the cheek.

I prepared for the first tour with the Lilliputians with some trepidation. Early on Saturday, a specially equipped bus driven by Senya went round the city collecting the members of the ensemble. All their belongings and props were loaded into the back. The rest of the space in the bus was taken up by four rows of two seats on each side for passengers. Some people had their own designated seats. I was relegated to the back seat to join Vasilisa, the instrumentalist, because we were both single. Grannik and Grisha sat in the front row. It soon became clear that the bus was, for all practical purposes, the performers' second home, used on their frequent and sometimes lengthy tours.

Travelling in the most comfortable way possible helped us preserve and restore our energy levels on the long journeys between shows. In principle, our kind of ensemble had, temporarily, to function more or less like an extended family, in which the members helped one another on the road and on the stage – not because of any blood relationship or personal reasons, but purely out of mutual professional interest: *you scratch my back, and I'll scratch yours.*

I soon became close friends with Vasilisa. She eventually allowed me to shorten her name to Vasa, although she complained to Grannik that, following his lead as an illusionist, I had transformed her into a cat. This evocative new name stuck: Vasa Kalnichenko. I consoled her that in press interviews I would always call her Vasilisa the Beautiful (after the famous beauty of Russian fairy tales). In turn, she would call me Kaschey the Ugly Bug (after a no less famous fairy-tale villain). That way she got even with me. Vasilisa brought copies of sheet music for her repertoire from the library and I studied them at home. Instead of simply duplicating the melody of her xylophone or concert bells performance, I composed a special musical arrangement with accordion, using my newly acquired knowledge of symphonic harmony from the seminars at the Arts Centre. I was assisted in this by a professor from the Conservatoire who used me as a practical example in one of his lectures on musical theory. I accompanied sensitively so that rather than merely providing the backing, I was actively supporting the soloist's performance of the main theme. Vasa was irritated by this at first, but the end result was worth the problems it caused, and she eventually acquiesced.

Vasilisa's second number, performed in the second half of the show, was the reading of children's poems by Marshak, Barto (twentieth century Russian children's poet, well known to audiences), and other poets. She was dressed up as a girl of four or five, perched on a stool so as to be better seen by the audience, but she also tried to convey the content of the poems by means of a kind of mime. Unfortunately, acting wasn't her strong point, and it was clear that nobody had helped her. Sitting on the sidelines during her number and not playing an instrument, I had a rare opportunity to observe the audience's reaction. After our first concert, I asked Grannik if I could suggest some adjustments to her act. He agreed, but cautioned me not to overdo it, and also not to take offence if he later found it necessary to make his own changes to parts of the revised act. We shook hands on this, acknowledging the genuine understanding that had developed between us.

On Saturday, the first matinee for schoolchildren at three o'clock was a resounding success. The show was sold out; not a single spare seat in the performance hall of the local Cultural Centre. The audience was slightly smaller at the evening show and mostly adults, who were familiar with the ensemble and eager to see the new programme. Little people tend to arouse the interest of spectators around the world, because of a curiosity about both who they are and where they come from, but also because of the peculiar effect created by the stark contrast onstage between the diminutive figure of a human being and their normal-sized surroundings. Watching such a show, the spectators ask themselves: "Goodness, how can he, being so little, perform his somersaults or lift a partner over his head? How does this [please forgive my language] 'midget' manage to play the xylophone with such virtuosity? And most of all: where do these little people come from?"

At the arts centre, I discovered the following information in the *Great Soviet Encyclopaedia*: *'Dwarves* [such as Grisha] *are the product of a pathological development in the mother's womb, which results in a morphological disproportion of extremities: an overly large head, short arms and legs; a humped back and chest. Little people differ from dwarves because they are born with all the genetic characteristics of normal people, but at the age of five or seven, because of a breakdown in the proper hormonal functioning of the thyroid gland, their physical growth stops, proportionately, all over the body, while their mental and emotional development continues normally. In other words, little people are normal people, only in miniature.'*

After the second show, at dinner time, Grisha asked me if I wouldn't mind sharing a hotel room with Vasa for the night. Separate beds, and with toilet and shower in the corridor.

"It's not ideal, but I can cope. I doubt she'll agree though."

"Misha, single rooms cost us too much. I'm also sharing a room, with Grannik. Vasa is used to sharing a room with either me or Grannik. She only ever objected to the previous accompanist because he was rude to her and constantly drunk. She shouldn't have this problem with you, right?"

"Grisha, let's try it once. The only woman I've ever shared a room with previously was my mother. If the arrangement doesn't work out, I'll fork out for it from my own pocket and take a single room next time."

We all took our breakfasts and lunches at different hours, but we sat down to dinner together. This was our chance to hear Grannik's and Grisha's comments on the day's shows and receive information about the next venue in the nearby town. I came to dinner early and ordered a bottle of Moskovskaya vodka, instructing the waiter to bring it out when everyone had assembled at the table. Grannik and Grisha were the last to arrive. They'd just finished settling the account with the agent and were still gesticulating vigorously as they approached.

When everybody took their seats next to their partners, I found myself again next to the lonely Vasa. Fate was throwing us together.

"Evening, Vasilisa the Beautiful!"

"Greetings, Kaschey the Ugly Bug!"

Everyone laughed.

"How quickly you've got to know one another!" commented our *conférencier*.

"And what is vodka doing here?" Grannik asked the waiter. He pointed in my direction.

All heads turned to me.

"Today was my professional debut in your ensemble. The rule is: I pay for the drinks."

"Well, in that case, the next round is on me," interjected Grisha. "Another bottle to mark the start of the season with a new programme."

Everyone applauded noisily.

"Misha, I heard you were not too pleased with the prospect of sharing a room with me?"

"Vasa, I'm only sixteen and so far unspoiled by women's attentions."

"Don't worry, I'm thirty-two and happy to reform you. Ha ha!"

"Much obliged," I said. I tried to sound nonchalant, but felt the blood rushing to my face. We didn't notice that the appetisers had been served.

"Dear friends!" Grannik rose at the other end of the table. "I propose a toast: to the success of our new programme, achieved with the help of our new team members! Hurrah!"

It took a lot longer for us all to clink glasses than to empty them.

It turned out I was not the only debutant. It was also the first time for a pair of juggling clowns. Vasa spoke highly of them. They'd arrived in Odessa from Kishiniev (now known as Chisinau), just a month earlier, and were now living in the same block of flats as Vasa. After dinner, my companion took the keys to our room from the receptionist and I helped her carry the cases with her instruments to the room. Vasa took up the bed by the window, and I, modestly, by the door.

"In case of emergency, you'll be closer to the escape route," she joked.

"You cannot run away from your happiness," I rejoined.

Five minutes later we were both snoring in chorus.

In the morning, I got up quite early, did some morning exercises in the back garden, and, on returning, found Vasa already busy with her suitcase.

"Morning, how did you sleep?" I asked her.

"Hi there: Not enough."

I packed up quickly. We carried our luggage to the bus; returned the keys; had tea and biscuits in a hurry, and by eight o'clock were already seated in the bus, ready for the journey.

Grisha addressed everyone: "Keys returned? Got your money, watches, passports, props, and brains? Then, off we go!"

We headed for our next performance venue, an hour's drive away. Again, we had two shows that day, at noon and five o'clock. On Sunday, we always started two hours earlier than on Saturday.

At seven, having finished with work, we gathered our belongings and packed into the bus in thirty minutes. We bought some provisions for the road and were on our way back at eight o'clock in the evening. We were all so exhausted, that after a quick snack, we slept all the way back to Odessa. Vasa slept with her head on my shoulder, and I leaned back in the seat.

It seems this little woman has indeed decided to reform me. I smiled to myself in my slumber, sensing her warmth at my side.

Eventually, our theatrical chariot came to a stop. Grisha announced: "Tomorrow is a day off. On Tuesday we meet back at the Arts Centre, at ten o'clock sharp!"

When I got home, Mother was awake, waiting for her prodigal son.

"So, how was it, your 'baptism of fire'?" she asked.

"Excellent!"

"Congratulations!"

"Thanks!" I said. "Tomorrow I'll sleep in, go to the public baths for a good steam, and then to school."

In the spring of 1948, after two Saturday concerts at a cultural club in a small town, its director unexpectedly invited me to join him for dinner and to stay overnight at his place. He was a harmonica player himself and wanted to show extra appreciation to a colleague. Grisha had no objections. He just asked for the address and reminded me he would be picking me up there at eight o'clock in the morning. The Director's wife Julia and her younger sister Nina cooked up a feast. We all had a few drinks: raised several glasses, to our acquaintance, to music, to love, etc. After dinner, the young women sang Ukrainian folk songs, beautifully, in duet, while my host and I accompanied them on the harmonica and the accordion. Rather tipsy, we finally retired to sleep. In a small bedroom, two beds stood parallel to one another, just an arm's length apart.

My host explained: "This one is for me and Julia, the other room – for you and Nina. That is if you've no objections, of course."

My tongue being as unwieldy as his, I replied: "Always happy to oblige, provided she guarantees my safety."

We roared with laughter. I was sure that he was just kidding, and so was just answering like with like. Having gone to the loo, and rinsed my mouth, I finally lay down, with a deep sigh of relief. Dropping into slumber, I could hear some scuffling on the other bed. Sleep, at last. . . .

Just as I was beginning to drift off, I felt someone slipping under my bed sheet. I thought, *It's a sexy dream again.* But it wasn't. Opening my eyes, I saw above me the mischievous face of the lovely Ninochka. I tried to open my mouth to shout: "Shoo, you devil!" She, meanwhile, totally naked, pressed herself to me, covering my mouth with her own so I couldn't cry out. She began to caress my shoulders, chest, belly, and further down. . . .

At first, I tried to protest. Gradually, though, I gave in to fate and surrendered to the little minx. Nina was only a year older than me, but behaved like a seasoned vixen. Realising that I was totally inexperienced, she took charge, guiding me, and so I lost my innocence. I was only too eager to repeat the experience several times. In the midst of one of these exhaustingly long sessions, I heard a rhythmic creaking of the neighbouring bed. It wasn't hard to guess that, nearby, in the pitch-dark, the older couple was trying to compete in this marathon.

At eight o'clock, I was woken by the familiar honking signal of our bus. I floundered about in a panic, unable to locate my underwear. Wrapping myself in a sheet, I rushed about in search of my clothes; then dashed outside to pee, washed my face and rinsed my mouth. I even managed to kiss a laughing Ninochka. I thanked the host for his hospitality; grabbed my instrument case and headed out to the bus as slowly, and in as dignified a manner, as I could muster.

My colleagues greeted me with wolf whistles, clapping, and a great deal of laughter. There is something truly unique in the Odessan sense of humour!

I barely managed to open my mouth to ask about my suitcase, when Grisha pre-empted me, smiling, "Vasa took care of your luggage. Let's go!"

Passing by Grannik, I apologised.

"No problem, Misha. At least you are a real man now."

It was some time before the little people stopped laughing at the sight of the dark circles under my eyes.

While we were based in Odessa, I continued to attend seminars in music and folk dance at the Arts Centre. One day, the director of the Centre, Lyuftgarten, noticing me at both seminars, expressed an interest in my plans for the future.

"At present, I am working at our Philharmonic Society, as a concertmaster in the Lilliputians Ensemble. This is a temporary arrangement, of course, for a couple of years, until I graduate from high school."

"And then?" he asked.

"My dream is to train as a ballet master. I like staging theatrical performances that involve all genres of stagecraft, such as opera or a song-and-dance ensemble. That is why I'm attending different seminars here – to give myself the best grounding possible."

"Well, all of this makes good sense. If you should ever need any help, it would be my pleasure."

The regional Philharmonic Societies of Russia, Ukraine, Belarus, and other Soviet republics regularly exchanged performing troupes for summer tours around the country. Financially this was run on a 'break even' principle. After all expenses had been defrayed, whatever remained was divided between the actors. In 1948, our ensemble was put on the road for two months, to tour the Krasnodar region. This indicated a countrywide recognition of the Odessa Lilliputians Ensemble. In return, Grannik demanded a set of new costumes from the directorship, and approached me with a request to improve the staging for each number, making it visually more expressive.

"Misha, the management of the Philharmonic will pay you 3,000 roubles for this extra work, once it gets approved by the artistic director. What do you say?"

"I agree," I said, without hesitating. "When do I start?"

"Immediately. I'll let everyone know today."

I threw myself completely into the creative challenge of giving the programme a theatrical overhaul. What I wanted to do was to try to come up with a suitable visual motif for each of the different acts. For instance, the same pair of jugglers from the first half of the show would appear again, but in a completely different guise, in the second. The effect owed much to the different character masks (make-up) they wore, but was also due to a completely different type of movement and set of mannerisms. Even when the audience recognised the actors, they were none the less impressed with a new aspect of the talent displayed through a different kind of staging.

Working with Elvira demanded more time and patience than with the others. There were Russian, Ukrainian, and Gypsy songs and romances in her repertoire. Each song required a different approach, to convey its genre and mood. Elvira was not used either to moving onstage or to acting out the songs' lyrics. It was really difficult to get her to loosen up. She was convinced that all a vocalist needed was a voice and a musical ear, and that nothing else mattered. Instead of taking this to Grannik, I chose, to save time, to speak to Elvira's husband first. I explained to our conférencier (master of ceremonies), the problem with Elvira's delivery, and asked him to find out from her whether she wouldn't mind trying to improve her stage presentation, with my help. At the next rehearsal, the singer apologised for her stubbornness, and we went on to achieve great progress with her stylistic presentation in time for the summer tour. She learned and took on board all the basic choreography: the footwork, the dance movements, even the gestures and special poses. Our conférencier paid me a backhanded compliment, saying that I had the power to teach even an elephant how to dance. I didn't know what to say in return.

My school exams and the seminars at the Arts Centre were over by the end of June. I was free for a two-month-long tour with the Lilliputians. Roman saw me to the train station and received 100 roubles of pocket money from me. He promised to spend the money entirely on ice cream. In the morning, we were met in Krasnodar by the representative of the local philharmonic. He took us by coach to some students' halls of residence (vacant for the summer) that were to be our base for the duration of the tour, returning there every week. The coach driver, a native, and a descendant of the ancient Cossacks, doubled as our tour guide and bodyguard. He was fluent in three local dialects and knew all the country roads like the back of his hand.

In big cities and provincial centres ('*stanitza*' as they are called in the Don region) we were warmly welcomed by cultural representatives, and well received by audiences. For me, this was a journey of continual discovery, of things not found in Soviet textbooks: monuments of ancient Russian architecture, ethnographic museums, folk Cossack traditions. These artefacts were dubbed in the Soviet Union the 'cultural heritage of ethnic minorities'. They were not widely known about, but in terms of anthropological data, they represented a treasure trove of colossal value.

That summer, we came home laden with exotic souvenirs of local craftsmanship and we earned good money too. Grisha gave us a week off at the end of August. This worked out really well for me. The curriculum for the forthcoming year in the ninth grade of high school was promising to be more challenging than the eighth grade. I was also planning to register for the maximum possible number of advanced courses on folk dance at the Arts Centre, in order to develop my new professional role of choreographer. Many people I knew with years of theatrical experience repeatedly told me that I had an innate gift for dance and that I needed to dedicate myself to the study of this art. I wasn't so sure, but I trusted the Russian saying: 'When two mates tell the third he's drunk, the latter should go to bed." At seminars, female instructors would always pick me as their partner in order to illustrate to the others the dance elements of folk choreography. They could not help but wonder at how quickly I grasped the footwork, in precise coordination with the arm movements, and at my natural musicality.

After training for a year, I finally mastered the technique of coordinating playing on the accordion while performing dance movements with my feet, which I used in my solo number – the 'Sailors' Dance' from Glière's ballet *The Red Poppy*. During one of the performances for a children's audience, and without prior coordination with Grannik, I tried an experimental version. Finishing with an impressive finale, I could hear the applause coming not just from the audience, but from backstage as well. Clowns and jugglers were shouting: "Bravo!" For some reason, I thought they sounded ironic. I also suddenly felt a spasm of pain in my lower back.

After the show, at dinnertime, Grannik reprimanded me in front of everyone: "Misha, just for future reference, if you want to change or improve anything in your repertoire after it has already been sanctioned by the Philharmonic, make sure you tell me before going ahead with the new version; not afterwards! This, by the way, applies to everyone in the ensemble, because I bear ultimate responsibility for the content of the entire programme and the safety of the performers."

"I'm sorry, it won't happen again."

"All right," he said, "enjoy your meal then."

In the summer of 1949 we toured again for two months, only this time we were hired by the Stavropol Philharmonic to visit South Caucasus. These were quite exciting journeys along the Military-Ossetian road, winding between the mountain chains of the Caucasus. The shows took place in small towns, such as Dzau-Dzikau (now known as Vladikavkaz), and in large mountain villages (*a-ul*), where ancient traditions held sway. After a show, in the absence of hotels, all performers were typically quartered in private houses. Once, a chairman of the local council invited me to stay at his house. The privilege was extended on account of my reputation as a chess player.

Grisha, knowing my capacity for sexual escapades from previous situations, gave me a warning: "Misha, the Chechen-Ingush are still very observant of their ancient Muslim traditions. They are extremely hospitable hosts. If the chairman likes you, he will honour you with an offer to take one of his wives to bed. But don't get too excited. You first need to know and respect the conditions of this tradition. If you find in your bed a sword placed between you and the woman, you're prohibited from touching her. In the absence of the weapon, it's entirely up to you what you do."

I was certain our administrator was pulling my leg, and so, on hearing him, I just smirked. *You don't scare me,* I thought to myself, but just in case, I said: "Perhaps I can sleep at the Cultural Centre instead, so as not to inconvenience anyone?"

"Out of the question," he said. "First of all, it would offend the chairman. Second, the Cultural Centre is built into the foot of the mountain, and at night the place is teeming with lovely little creatures, like mice, lizards, and the like. . . . Better to sleep with a Caucasian beauty than with some rat or viper. No?"

After supper, the chairman and I played two games of chess. The first he won quite quickly because my mind was preoccupied with the thought of his many wives. In the interval between the games, after each of us had drunk a glass of Abkhazian wine, I gathered all my wits about me and remembered Roman's instructions on chess openings. Playing the white this time, I bluffed by starting with a seemingly standard move. My opponent, thrown off guard by an easy victory in the first game, made a wrong move immediately. By the time he had realised his mistake, it was too late to change the outcome. Shaking each other's hands, we moved to the guest room, where I discovered two arches hung with curtains: entrances to the male and female parts of the house. There was one oil lamp feebly lighting a wide stone ledge projecting from the wall and covered with a sheepskin. The host explained: "At night, it gets cold in the mountains. That door leads to the backyard and the toilet."

Leaving my suitcase and accordion by the wall, I resolved, as a precaution, not to change out of my clothes completely and went out to the toilet. Upon my return, I found myself in pitch-darkness.

So, I thought, *somebody has already turned the lamp out. This is a bit like a fairy tale: the further you go, the scarier it gets.* Groping with my hand in the dark, I managed to locate the bed, lifted the sheepskin, and, remembering Grisha's instructions, carefully slid myself in, perching at the very edge of the bed. *So, what now? Clearly, I can't sleep like this. Let's check who is next to me.* Gingerly sliding my hand along the covering of the mattress, I encountered the steel blade, and right next to it, somebody's hot thigh under a night slip. Jerking my hand back, I stammered an apology. I heard a woman's giggle in reply. A pungent aroma of perfumed oils emanated from my companion, filling my nostrils. I gave myself a good talking to. *No way, my precious! Not this time.*

How long I managed to sleep in this state, I'm not sure exactly. Suddenly, I woke up and sat bolt upright in the bed. I stretched my hand out towards the wall, but could find neither my companion nor the weapon. For my peace of mind, I checked that none of my body parts had been sheared off, following some ancient Caucasian rite. *So,* I thought, *I've managed to survive this time unscathed. Or perhaps I just had a bad dream?* I turned over and fell asleep again.

Waking up on time, I performed a series of morning exercises, and went into the kitchen. I had a cup of fresh Georgian tea with local feta cheese. Women in burqas bustled around me, offering various Eastern delicacies.

Coming in, the chairman enquired: "How did you sleep, my good fellow?"

"Excellent, thanks!" I replied.

"Very good then," he said. "Let's go!"

I decided to aim for the best possible marks in my last year in high school in order to increase my chances of matriculating at the Moscow Theatre Academy (MTA). Despite all my efforts, I received top marks in everything except Ukrainian. Unfortunately, that meant I was not going to be a gold medallist. In truth, this was only fair. In addition to studying at school, I was rehearsing or performing with the Lilliputians and attending courses/seminars at the Arts Centre. One can't do everything. Actually, according to MTA's published guidelines, all three areas of experience (good marks, performing experience, and knowledge of the history and practice of dance) were equally important criteria for admission. Extending my contract with the Philharmonic for another year, I warned Grisha about my plans to go to Moscow after graduation from High school and to apply to MTA.

He wasn't happy on receiving this news, and asked me not to say anything to the rest of the ensemble just yet. "Best not upset them ahead of time," he said.

Mother, for some reason, received the news of my plans rather badly. Yosif had just been admitted to the Department of maths and physics at Odessa Polytechnic Institute, and she was now concerned at how she would be able to make ends meet.

"It's quite enough that I should have to support one son in university for the next five years," she said irritably. For me, her reaction came like a clap of thunder in a clear sky.

"Mama, haven't I been giving you over half of my salary for my upkeep for the last two years? Now you want me to feed that egotist and moron as well?"

Mother quickly saw that she had been pouring oil on to the fire, but it was too late to go back.

"I see," I said. "It appears that for you, some of your children are better than others. I'm stuck with the role of Cinderella."

"Misha, you misunderstood me. I'm just tired of endlessly breaking my back, raising the three of you, and so I overreacted. I'm sorry."

"It's been a long time since you had to support me in any way. I've been bringing you 1,000 roubles every month, even when I wasn't at home for months at a time. And now you won't even have the burden of me being at home at all."

She was puzzled: "What do you mean?"

"I'm going to rent a room until my departure for Moscow. I will be helping you as much as I can."

It was bound to happen sooner or later. It had not been pleasant living and sleeping in the same room with an enemy, my brother Yosif, who threatened to hurt me. I made an arrangement with Vasilisa to lodge with her temporarily, paying half of the utility bills. I was content with the hard fold up bed she kept for visiting relatives. It was a long walk to school, but there was nothing I could do about that. At least I'd be able to sleep in peace at night. Vasa was like a dear sister to me. She took the news that I was planning to leave the ensemble very badly. I loved her dearly, and perhaps trusted her more than myself. She gave me much good advice, and often prevented me from making big mistakes. When the time came, Grisha was able to find a new accordionist quite quickly, and arranged a farewell party for me. The work with the Ensemble of the Lilliputians marked the beginning of my career in theatre.

In the early days of July, I went to Moscow to reconnoitre. As a high-school graduate applying for the ballet masters course, I was lodged in the halls of residence on Trifonovka Street near Rizhsky Railway Station. In the morning, together with my room-mates, I arrived at the institute. The secretary to the Ballet Masters Department gave me an appointment at eleven o'clock with the Dean, Anatoly Vasilevich Shatin. I had two hours of free time until then. I learned from other students that this old building near Arbat Square only housed the administrative offices of the Ballet Masters Department, while the ballet studios were at the Bolshoi School of Ballet, where the current staff members had once trained: Professors Zakharov and Lavrovsky and Docents (the rank between professor and assistant) Tarasov, Lapauri, Tkachenko, and Rozhdestvenskaya. Just hearing those names made my head spin. It occurred to me that perhaps I was aiming too high. I resolved that at my interview with Shatin, I wouldn't act like someone applying to the department, but rather as someone who was simply dreaming of a career as a ballet master, not as a teacher/trainer, but as a choreographer – in any genre.

Shatin turned out to be a very amiable and attentive dean. Any other instructor in his place, on hearing that I was only eighteen and still quite unschooled in dance, would surely not have bothered wasting any of their precious time on such a rookie. This wise sixty-year-old man, however, asked me a mass of questions, concerning all forms of visual and theatrical/musical arts; everything apart from dance. Who were my parents? What instruments did I play? What did I think of the opera and the symphony orchestra? Was I familiar with pantomime?

After an hour's interview which included the discussion of the academic and practical courses, seeing my eyes opening ever wider, the Dean concluded: "Misha, I'm not trying to dissuade you from pursuing your dream. On the contrary, you have come a long way only to discover the hard reality that lies ahead of you. But that also means that you have the most important thing that one must have when one is young – you have a clear goal in your life. You know what you want. And if this is so, my advice to you is this. Try to graduate from the Odessa School of Ballet in four to five years, working at the same time as an extra in opera/ballet and operetta. Continue to study European folk dances at the Arts Centre. Study the history of theatre and music, even from an encyclopaedia. As you can see for yourself, in the admissions guidelines for our department, you will not be admitted unless you have a diploma of secondary education, five years' work experience in a theatre, and an official recommendation from the Ukrainian Ministry of Culture, with a guarantee of work placement after graduation from MTA. We enrol students only once in five years. I am now selecting students for my next class, which will start in 1956. According to the quota, we are allowed to admit only six from the Soviet republics, and six more from countries of the Eastern bloc. Competition for places is fierce: there are thirty to forty candidates per place. That's all I can tell you at this point, Mikhail. I wish you success and good luck!"

I came out of his office in a state of shock. In the bathroom, I spent a long time splashing cold water on to my burning face, until the dizziness had passed.

On the train, all the way back to Odessa, I was wondering what the best strategy might be to get into the ballet school: to act independently or to use my connections at the Philharmonic?

Stretched out on the top bunk, in a compartment of the swaying train carriage, I turned over in my mind all the possible ways of finding youths interested in dance, as well as ways of potentially turning their interests towards classical ballet. In my daydream, I conjured up visions of home parties where I would play the accordion, images of dancing youths, the pioneer camp, little Gypsy kids from the neighbourhood. My dream of training as a ballet master had receded into an uncertain future, but my mind was set on trying every possible avenue to make it come true.

CHAPTER 2 DEVOTION TO TERPSICHORE

I had managed to save some money during my time at the Philharmonic – enough to support me for at least six months. After that, I would have to find a part-time job; work and study at the same time. Assuming a confident air, I went off to the ballet school.

The studios were empty as it was holiday time. I could hear a typewriter in reception. I knocked.

"Hello!" I said. "May I speak with the Director?"

"Just a minute."

The pretty girl got up from her desk and disappeared behind a heavy door. After what seemed like a rather long minute, a short, heavy-set man came out, not looking at all like someone who might once have been a dancer.

"What can I do for you, young man?" he asked, his eyes boring into me over his spectacles.

"I'd like to receive professional training in ballet, if it's not too late at my age."

"Come in, please, tell me briefly about yourself, and why you have suddenly decided to become a dancer at such – as you yourself put it – an advanced age."

I told him my story: my dream of working in music and choreography, my studies at the Performing Arts Centre, and my trip to Moscow.

"Would it be possible for you to give me some private lessons over the summer, so you can test out my abilities, and then, if possible, place me right away into the fourth or fifth year?"

The Director was stunned by my audacity. With a quizzical smile, he replied, "This is highly irregular. However, judging by the expression on your face, it looks like you actually mean it. You also appear to have faith in your future. In that case, only a physical test can help me solve the problem. Follow me, please." He got up and headed for the door.

Is he going to throw me out? I wondered.

The Director led me into an empty studio and shut the door. I became uneasy.

"Take off your shirt and trousers," he said, brusquely. "You can keep the underpants on." Before he had a chance to finish the sentence, I was already bracing myself to defend my honour. However, he stepped away and began to inspect me in a huge mirror that covered the entire opposite wall. "Stretch your arms out sideways! Up! Down!" And so on.

I followed my reflection in the mirror, not sure what he was after. Standing behind me, he studied my physique reflected in the mirror, first from the front and then from behind. He told me to stretch out the sole of my foot, stand on my tiptoes, arch my back, squat, jump as high as I could keeping my legs straight, and so on.

After the test, we returned to his office, and the Director gave me his assessment: "Your physique is good, but some of the physical attributes one looks for in a Classical dancer are insufficiently developed. Still, I'd like to give you a chance. I can work with you five days a week, from ten in the morning till midday, except for weekends when the school is closed. At the end of August, I can show you to the Admissions Committee, and then we can discuss your potential future in ballet. My name is Georgi Aleksandrovich Rels. We can begin tomorrow, if you like."

"Perfect!"

If you can imagine a gorilla dancing a ballet sequence, that was something like me during that first week. Rels wasn't playing games with me. In fact it seemed as if he had embarked upon an experiment, one any professional teacher would dream about: watching his charge, day by day, painfully trying to loosen up stiff knees and soles, stretching limbs to their absolute limit, and performing a full squat with a straight back and arms stretched upwards. I realised that for the instructor this was a trial too. But he never once raised his voice at my repeated mistakes; he would only patiently explain what I had done wrong, and say: "Please, once more, and with more precision. Also, do try to relax your face."

Without a doubt, Rels was a first-rate teacher. Intuitively, I let go of my habitual analytical approach and instead gave in to his hypnotic influence while memorising different poses, ports de bras (movements of arms) and the various techniques for moving feet and legs. Rels was impressed at my muscular memory and also at the self-discipline I showed in mastering the exercises. I was still far off the requisite performance standard but we continued to move along steadily, following the programme of year III, without trying to master every little detail to perfection.

At the admissions exam at the end of August, Rels reserved the demonstration of his special candidate for last. At our very first meeting he had become intrigued by my idea to bring together a group of overgrown teenagers, sixteen-to-eighteen-year-olds, willing to study ballet. For ordinary mortals, such a proposition would sound like a joke, but not for an artistic personality. I was fully aware that for Rels, the object of the experiment with me was to demonstrate to the Admissions Committee the genuine feasibility of a late start in the ballet training of boys, and thereby offer a potential solution to the pressing problem of a shortage of young men in post-war ballet. During my demonstration, the examiners often made notes on their notepads and exchanged remarks. When I came out to take a bow, they gave us both a warm round of applause.

My exam lasted twenty minutes, and the ensuing lively discussion behind the closed door a further forty, while I waited on tenterhooks for the verdict. Eventually the Director appeared, beaming. He apologised for my long wait and announced that the Teaching Board had approved the formation of an experimental class of late beginners, aged sixteen to eighteen, to number, after selection, no fewer than ten students, and to be ready to start no later than 15th September.

"The rest, Mikhail," he said, "depends on you. Congratulations!"

"Georgi Aleksandrovich, how much do I owe you?"

He waved his hand: "Forget it."

"Excuse me," I said. "I cannot. This is not what we agreed." I gave him 2,000 roubles in an envelope. "This is for your professional time," I said. "I never play the accordion for free."

The rest depends on you. Easier said than done. Where could I even begin?

For starters, I decided to establish a base for my operations at the school. I asked Alyona (the school's secretary) to assist me in relaying messages to potential candidates, and, with Rels's approval, she agreed. I wrote an advertisement: 'The ballet school is opening enrolment into an experimental male dance group for youths aged 16 to 18, from 15th September of this year. To register your interest, visit the school between the hours of 11.00 and 12.00, any day Monday through Friday. Ask for Mikhail.' Alyona typed it up using carbon paper and handed me a stack of copies and a box of pins. Meanwhile, I made a list of places where I might hunt for potential candidates and worked out a strategy for enticing 'those who like to move in rhythm with the music' into the net of the performing arts. I began with clubs and open-air discotheques, where classes of social dancing were known to take place on Wednesdays and Saturdays. I also posted flyers at the Performing Arts Centre, Cultural Centres and other public places.

In the last few days of August, I spent every evening at these hunting grounds, carefully and methodically singling out my quarry. Spreading the net of a conversation around a designated target, I would usually start off complimenting the dancer on his ability to move with the beat and to lead his partner. Then I would let drop, as if in passing: "You would make a really great professional dancer."

"Who me? You've got to be kidding!"

"Not at all. As it happens, I myself have already been studying dance for a year at the arts centre, and from September, I'm starting a special course at the ballet school, for late beginners like you and me."

"Ha ha! The idea of me doing ballet would be like trying to reach the moon!"

"Don't be so dismissive. You haven't tried it yet, have you? So you don't really know. I also used to think it was beyond my dreams, but now I'm very happy to have found my calling."

"How old are you?" they'd ask then.

"Eighteen," I'd say. "And you?"

"Seventeen and a half."

"Just the age!" I'd say. "It's just trying something new, that's all. It's not as though you're going to be facing a firing squad. What have you got to lose? Just imagine if it works out!"

"All right," they'd say then, "how do you get in?"

"There, on the wall," I'd say, "is the school's notice. I'm helping to register candidates. I'm there every day at the entrance to the school, between eleven and twelve. If you come during that time, I'll personally recommend you because I saw how you can move."

"Oh, that's better then," they'd say. "Otherwise it's embarrassing to come just like that, out of the blue: 'Hi, it's me, your Uncle Vanya!'" And we would laugh together. Sometimes, however, they'd respond with just a volley of abuse, apparently thinking I was making fun of them.

Several days after posting the ad, the first curious enquirers began to appear: what's all this nonsense about ballet? A whole ragtag assortment of characters responded: invalids advanced in years, young daredevils, thirty-something paedophiles, and other peculiar types. I endured all manner of abuse – taunts, swear words, threats – but stubbornly continued to sit by the entrance, next to an old granny on security duty. I weeded out the unsuitable ones by graciously and politely showing them the door, explaining that enrolment was already closed due to an overwhelming response. Those who were actually our best potential candidates would pause in the entrance, too shy to step over the threshold, so I'd have to keep watch on the steps of the school and invite them into the lobby, registering them then and there.

One day, three waifs arrived together: two of them were around my age, the third slightly older. All three were dirty, dressed in rags, and with bare feet. A bad odour hung about them. They launched into an energetic tap dance as soon as they entered the lobby. I had to stop them and explained that in the state they were in, there was no way they could be allowed even to enter the school. The lads were rather put out and went outside. The older one swore and left. The other two lingered.

The old granny on security duty tugged at my sleeve.

"Mishenka," she said, in a trembling voice, "my old man and me, we live nearby in a basement flat. He works as a janitor in our block of flats, and I work here. Our two sons fell in Stalingrad, but we still have their clothes and shoes. My husband is getting old. It's hard for him to sweep the courtyard and the street now and he needs help. If these lads fit the bill, we can offer them shelter, wash, clothe and feed them, in exchange for two hours of daily work at a time that suits them."

I went out to the disheartened lads and sat on the steps next to them. They scowled at me.

"There's no need to look at me like that. I'm one of this experimental group myself, and I'd like to help you. You're being given a chance to join the experimental class, provided it's what you genuinely want and you're ready to change your miserable way of living straight away."

They pricked up their ears: "What do we have to do?" Gleb, who was sitting closer to me, asked.

"I'll answer you, but only after you've told me about yourselves, briefly and honestly."

The second, Kostya, asked: "What exactly is it you want to know?"

"Well," I said, "are you brothers or friends? The truth, please."

"Brothers," he answered. "He's sixteen, and I'm seventeen. We lost our parents in the war. Now we're living in an abandoned warehouse in the port with some other mates."

"And how do you make a living?"

This drew a silence.

"Well," I said at length, "do you work, beg, steal?"

There was a long pause.

"A bit of everything," they admitted eventually.

"Had enough of that yet?" I pressed on.

"Perhaps," they said, "but what choice do we have?"

"Tell me, Kostya, if you were a director of this school, would you admit someone like you?"

"Nobody wants the likes of us!" Gleb bitterly fired back.

"Well, I wouldn't be so sure. It so happens that somebody does want you, only not in such a battered state. This old granny who works at security here, has just invited you to 'share her bread and salt'. She and her old man live nearby. He's a janitor, and the work is getting too hard for him at his age. If you don't consider it beneath your dignity to sweep the courtyard and the street around their block of flats, these old people will provide you with room, board, clothes, and hot water with soap. After the New Year holiday, you'll be able to join the theatre group, and, if you wish, rent a room of your own, as others do, including myself.

Listening to me intently, the brothers exchanged animated glances.

"You have half an hour to discuss this unbelievable piece of good luck. The granny will soon be taking her lunch break, and she can show you the room in her flat where her sons used to live before the war. If you agree, she'll cut your hair, clean you up and give you a change of clothes. After that we can present you to the Director. Think it over. If you decide not to do it, then good luck with your other plans!"

By the end of the first week of September, I had managed to put together a motley group of fourteen, including the two waifs who had settled at the old granny's. Obviously, not everyone had an equal chance of satisfying the requirements of the Admissions Committee. At a preliminary meeting of the candidates, I laid particular stress on the importance of their appearance, recommending that they cut their hair, take a shower, trim their nails, wear fresh underpants (for the inspection of their physique), and rinse their mouths to take away the odour of cigarette smoke.

One of my new friends, Sasha, made a joke: "Misha, it looks like you're getting us ready to be sold off."

"That's not too far from the truth. Only, it's more a case of getting ourselves ready for a long, but pleasant, enslavement. In any case, we have to make a good impression on the examiners."

When I turned up with my gang at the backstage door of the Opera Theatre the following Monday, the security guard, without asking any questions, immediately telephoned the police. Two police cars arrived almost instantaneously. I tried to explain to the officer that we were expected by the Admissions Committee upstairs in the ballet studio. But he cut me off: "If you and your gang don't clear off at once, you'll regret it. You wouldn't care much for the ballet I could show you—"

"But it's true, I'm telling you. We're expected, there, upstairs!"

"Don't give me that bullshit!"

At that moment, Rels came out and confirmed that we were, in fact, there for a good reason.

"So, what about the bullshit now?" I asked the Lieutenant.

"You'd better hold your tongue, lad!"

Sasha pulled me by the sleeve: "Drop it. Let's go."

The ballet instructors asked us to get undressed down to our underpants, and carefully studied our physiques. Rels commanded everyone, just as he had with me not so long ago, to squat, stretch out our feet to the maximum, and follow the other instructions of our examiners. They immediately weeded out those who were just too far off the mark in terms of their admissions criteria. Ten of us, however, who had successfully made the grade, were told to stay in the changing rooms. We dressed and remained there, waiting impatiently for the news. Finally, the Director appeared and invited all of the candidates into an empty studio. There, he thanked those who had not passed, expressed his sympathies, and asked the attendant to escort them out. Rels invited the rest of us to take seats on the floor in front of him.

"Your experimental group", he began, "has been approved on a temporary basis, for a trial period of the first term. If you succeed in passing an exam at the end of the term, then, in December, your group will be granted the status of permanent affiliation with the opera/ballet theatre as of 1st January 1951, for a maximum period of six years, depending on your progress at the school, at rehearsals, and in the performances of the theatre. You will be expected to work hard, and to follow the regime of studies at the ballet school and at the theatre. All your dance practice will take place in the theatre's workshop studios. You'll need to learn the norms of behaviour and personal hygiene expected of you here. You will also be expected to observe a strict code of student–teacher interaction and male–female professional etiquette. All this information is laid out in great detail for you on the public noticeboard at the school. The lessons start on Monday. In the remaining days before the start of the term, you need to obtain a theatre pass at the school. You will need to elect a group leader as your liaison person with the directorship of our school and of the theatre. You must treat the property of the theatre with care at all times, and you must never take anything away from the site. Your ballet teacher for the first term is Innesa Markovna Goldina. Her specialty is Classical dance, and she is so far the only one who has agreed to train you. Congratulations!"

After Rels had left, my classmates unanimously voted me group leader. I thanked them for the honour and told them I had an announcement of my own to make.

"Taking on the job of group leader properly and bearing responsibility for the group before the officials is no mean task – certainly not the picnic some might think. That is why, before I take it on, I need you all to promise to abide by the following rules:

"a) Nobody, except myself, will be entitled to represent the group before the administration, or before any of the teachers, either regarding our relations with ballerina partners, or any other negotiations, actions, protests, or the like.

"b) In the event of trouble within our group, I reserve the right to stop any offender and order him to leave the premises, pending further notice regarding his status within the group.

"c) All changes relating to our group as a whole, and all complaints and demands are to be settled by means of a vote, including the election of a new group leader and the appointment of a new teacher.

"All those who agree with these conditions, please raise your hands."

They all did.

"There's something else I need to tell you about, in addition to what Rels has told you about our project. The full curriculum of the experimental course contains four main subjects: Classical dance, Character dance, Historical court dance, and 'Pas de deux'. In the first term, which is also our trial period, we begin, as you've already heard, with Classical dance: this will be our chance to display our musical and dancing talents to the Admissions Committee. If we fall short of the expected level, our group will be disbanded. If we manage to make steady progress over the first two to three years, the length of our training might be cut by a year or two. It's up to us in the end. In the history of performing arts, there are many examples of individuals who, though endowed with only average ability, were still able to go further than their more talented colleagues because they had stronger will and the determination to succeed. Which is why it's important for us to show, at our first exam, not that we can dance perfectly (which is unrealistic), but that we have the potential to get where we want by dint of patience and determination, discipline, rigorous training, and belief in our ability to succeed."

In the few days remaining before the start of term, I needed to find myself a part-time job and somewhere to live. I recalled that at one of my summer gigs at the pioneer camp, I'd met a counsellor from the local orphanage who used to bring her charges to our campfires for singing sessions. At the time, she'd complimented me on my work with the pioneers, and mentioned that they were looking for a full-time musician/choreographer, with the possibility of living in the orphanage. But time had passed since and the chances were they'd found someone by now. *So what? Nothing ventured, nothing gained,* I reasoned with myself, *just go over there and find out. If all else fails, there are several more orphanages nearby. Maybe one of them will have a job for you.*

Things actually turned out better than I'd expected. The counsellor recognised me immediately.

"Hi! You want to work for us? Sorry, I've forgotten your name. I'm Maria, and you?"

"Mikhail. I'm looking for a job that provides accomodation, and I can only work after four o'clock."

"Perfect. We need someone starting straight away, first to prepare a New Year's concert, and, after that, on a permanent basis, for talent and variety shows. Come along, I'll introduce you to the Director."

Maria showered me with compliments when she introduced me to her boss, presenting me as a jack of all trades. The Director asked me some personal questions and warned me that the salary was small, but that board and lodging were included. Working hours were from four to seven in the evening, with a day off on Mondays. I could start the next day. I accepted the offer and left my passport and employment log with him. The secretary led the way to show me my living quarters in an annex building for the staff, in a corner of the orphanage's grounds, some distance from the noise of the children. The ground floor was occupied by a bursar and his wife; the first floor was for me with my accordion. It was a large, bright room. The toilet and shower were downstairs. It was perfect. The secretary showed him my documents and also asked me not to stomp too hard on my floor, just above their heads.

"For that purpose, we have a separate small theatre complex, with all the necessary equipment." Saying this, she took me to another building to reveal a small concert hall and two studios with a piano upstairs.

I said that I'd be moving in the next day.

"Great! We'll be expecting you then."

From the orphanage, I went to see Mother. I relayed to her my news about the ballet school, the theatre, and the orphanage where I was planning to live permanently. She was very negative about my new passion for dance, declaring that it was a shameful occupation for a man:

"I'm not trying to dissuade you. I only want you to know how I feel about it. Besides, Roman and I have now moved into the living room, to join Yosif. I've rented out the bedroom to two girls, students at the local vocational school. So, don't be surprised when you enter the flat. I can't rely on my children helping me in the near future, so I'm trying to fend for myself."

"You're right, Mother, and I'm just following your example. Say hello to Roma for me, and take care of yourself. Here is my address, in case my little brother wants to see me."

Having packed my meagre possessions into a suitcase, I left home with a heavy heart.

At the orphanage, my task as a choreographer was to create a special number for each group of children, first for the New Year concert, and then for the end-of-year performance. I asked for the student lists for all seven groups and, together with the counsellor, worked out a schedule of rehearsals. The orphanage had its own costume wardrobe, with ethnic costumes and shoes of various nations, in a range of sizes.

The following Monday, my first day off from the orphanage job, I visited Roman in Moldavanka (the area of Odessa where Mother lived). It turned out that the charming female flatmates had disappeared.

"Bagheera kicked them out because of Yosif," Junior told me, confidentially.

Investigating this intriguing game opening of our chess hero, I learned from the neighbours that the said eldest brother, who was a university student in applied mathematics at the time, had for some time, been engaged in training the female flatmates in sexual games, according to a strictly regulated schedule. However, for personal reasons, he rudely violated the order of sexual engagements established between them, saving the best gambits for one, but not the other. Naturally, the wounded pride of the slighted girl prompted her to kick her former girlfriend in the teeth and make a public scene for the stud, a scene that spilled out of our bordello, i.e. flat, on to the communal veranda and from there into the courtyard. The tongue-wagging neighbours lost none of their petty bourgeois time in spreading the news of these intellectual fillies far and wide. You can only imagine the reaction of the proud Panther, slandered and stained with gossip, to this session of simultaneous sexual chess performed by Yosif.

Natural sex drives inevitably played their part in my own relationships with girls. My closest friend, Lucy, from the Evening School for Working Youth, used to visit me after hours on Saturdays at the orphanage. Usually we would stroll down the seaside promenade and stay out till late, kissing and hugging, but never going beyond that. One day, however, Lucy arrived with a bag and announced that she had come for a sleepover.

I became nervous and asked her: "Why? Have you had a row with your mother again?"

"No! I just want you to become my first sexual partner."

I must have looked like I'd just been hit over the head with a hammer.

"You're kidding, aren't you? You can't be serious."

"No, I mean it, that is, if you've no objections."

Having had only limited experience with this sort of thing, I tried to explain to her the danger of pregnancy, the inevitability of disappointment, and the rest. She would hear none of it. Instead, the anticipation of possible intimacy drove us both to an almost unbearable state of excitement. To add to it all, given that my first woman had not been a virgin, I was rather nervous about failing in the surgical procedure of defloration. Although we were both only eighteen, Lucy acted like an adult, with confidence and full awareness. I, for my part, found myself caught between fear and desire, losing my sense of reality and self-control. What had to happen would happen – I gave in.

At midnight, moving as if in a dream, we went down to the beach and lay down in the nearby shrubs. I laid out my new sports jacket on the cool sand, and we commenced the ritual of undressing, kissing, and foreplay. To my shame, I have to admit that my girlfriend was much more active than I was in our intercourse. After a few failed attempts on my part, she, trembling all over, mounted me and, by applying her weight achieved what I could not. The whisper of rolling waves, the rustle of little lizards in the sand, and the laughing stars above, all in chorus, played an accompaniment to our short moment of bliss. I cannot remember how many times we repeated our intoxicating duet that night, burning as we were with the heat of desire. In fact, now I know it was not Ninochka, my first woman, but Lucy, who first turned me into a real man.

In the morning, we ran to the sea, in nothing but our birthday suits, to perform a ritual ablution. While I was washing away my sins, Lucy got dressed and waited for me with a towel. *So, that's what she had in her bag,* I realised, *pulling my trousers on. She must have thought all of this through in advance.*

Taking our seats on a bench under an acacia tree, we sat there in one another's arms, watching the morning fishing boats taking to the sea. Turning her face to me, Lucy relaxed and fell asleep in my arms. Admiring the angelic expression on her face, I kept asking myself the same difficult question: *What was it that motivated this beautiful clever girl to take such a serious step? A protest against attempts to limit her freedom? To get back at her mum? Or to tie me to her forever? This prospect was not funny at all. And if that happened, then what?*

On the way to the tram stop, I kept glancing at her sideways, feeling as if I had stolen something from her. She, on the contrary, only clung to me the more.

As if guessing my doubtful state of mind, Lucy confessed: "Misha, you have no idea how wonderful it is to give yourself away to a man that you love more than anything in this world."

"I'm sorry," I said. "I was just worried that I'd hurt you."

"My dear man, you acted like a true gentleman. I am so grateful to you!" Ignoring the understanding looks of the early risers out in the street, she embraced me with passion and pressed her lips to mine. Drawing her to my chest, I could feel her heartbeat and her whole body trembling with excitement.

The approaching tram interrupted our parting embrace. For a long time I stood there with my hand outstretched in a farewell gesture. *Is this all that a human being needs to be truly happy? But then, a human being is just another animal.*

In the first three months of studies at the ballet school, the experimental male group of late beginners followed a specially tailored curriculum and regime of training in Classical dance. In addition, we had to learn how to keep our competitive egos in check during practice sessions; how to maintain physical hygiene; how to treat our female teachers with proper respect, and, most difficult and important of all: how to keep to the rules of civilised and ethical conduct within the walls of the Opera Theatre. All of this turned out to be quite difficult for both the group leader and his peers, many of whom I had literally picked up off the street. It is said that it is easier to teach discipline and moral principles to young children than it is to adults, whose characters, views, tastes and social skills are already formed. In our group, we had it all: rows and fights; thievery and hooliganism; bad language and insults, alcoholism and dismissal from the group. There were moments when I had serious doubts whether my charges would pass the trial period of the first term.

Our first instructor was Innesa Goldina, a beautiful prima ballerina, who was now thirty years old. She taught us the basics of posture, positions of the head, arms, and legs; distribution of weight over the sole of the foot, and many other physical fundamentals necessary for the study of Classical dance. It was a titanic labour for her: to mould Neanderthal men into ballet dancers. We needed to stretch the soles of our feet to the maximum; to pull in the kneecap until the leg was absolutely straight; to turn out both feet and knees for pliés, to the limits of our endurance; to keep our shoulders down and turned out frontwards for better posture. We had to keep the stomach pulled in, and the chest pushed out, pulling the entire frame upwards, stretching the spine for a more effective visual presentation of the body. We had to maintain such control of our bodies throughout the duration of a dance, so as to keep up a consistent visual impression of the character onstage. It was not easy to absorb all this body science.

On top of having to endure, for years on end, the constant pain of the ongoing physical reconstruction of their body morphology, these overgrown youths would be subjected to the severe critique of teachers as well as the inevitable disdain of relatives and friends. Even neighbours would taunt them: "Look out, here comes our pretty ballerina!"

Personally, I did not mind such jibes. I had already gone through all of this during the war. My classmates, however, often came to lessons crushed by the prejudice and ignorance surrounding them on all sides. I had to expend huge amounts of energy and patience, persuading one or another not to pay attention to the sceptics, envious of his talent and good fortune in being able to work in an arts institution. This was not always true of everyone, because our group contained people of different levels of ability, and not everyone had the correct physiognomy for Classical dance. Nevertheless, everyone had a real chance at some point of being able to work in a musical theatre, or an ensemble of modern or folk dance. Above all, I was constantly afraid that if one of our group were dismissed, the administration might terminate our experimental course, and then all my plans for admission to MTA would collapse like a house of cards. I could not let this happen. So I'd often had to use Byzantine diplomacy in situations where personal and professional tensions erupted in the relations between students and teachers, or classmates and their ballerina partners.

Often forgetting that we were adults, Innesa would, without thinking, use the same educational methods on us as she did with children. Most of us were not really bothered by it, but some, particularly those who'd been dragged up on the streets, reacted badly to her occasional shouting, impatience, and her slaps on a humped back, one's disengaged knee, a dropping arm, a not fully stretched foot, and the like. In such cases, I would hiss the offender's name, trying to nip this trouble in the bud, while continuing to do my exercise as if nothing had happened. When this did not work and our insulted teacher left the room, interrupting that lesson, we would surround the offender and demand that he apologise before our teacher in front of the entire group. He, as a rule, would go off to find Innesa, and the lesson would continue, as if nothing had happened. Trouble over.

There were more serious incidents, however. For a long while after the war, young, physically attractive men would consider themselves sexually irresistible. One such was among us. Viktor was very popular among young women hungry for a man's caress. I was not at all interested in his after-school affairs. However, once, in the staff cafeteria at the theatre, Viktor began to speak indecently about our teacher in the presence of other members of staff. I approached him immediately and told him off. In response he called me a 'naïve ass' and told me to stay out of his personal life. I tried to explain to him that if rumours of his remarks reached the administration, we as a group would have serious problems on our hands, because we had, for the time being, no more than squatters' rights in this institution.

He just swore at me. At my signal, two other classmates who'd been sitting at my table drinking tea, got up and moved in our direction. Viktor continued to shout and swear, attracting the attention of everyone in the cafeteria. The three of us dragged him from his table and took him by the lift downstairs to the staff exit. The security guards knew me well and, hearing what had happened, turfed Viktor out, promising to call the police if he didn't come to his senses. Naturally, I immediately reported what had happened to the school's administration, promising that no such incidents would occur again in our group if we could help it.

Our trial period was to come to an end before New Year's Eve 1951. The latest incident with Viktor was extremely unhelpful.

The following morning, after barre exercises, Innesa enquired: "Misha, why is Viktor absent?"

"He might've been held up on his ship in the port," one of us said.

She raised her eyebrows.

"When fishing boats return from the sea in the morning, he hoses down the deck and other working areas on his boat," I explained.

"Please try not to miss any classes in the last two weeks before your exam – that is if you want to make a good impression on the committee."

We realised that Innesa had not yet heard about yesterday's incident or she would have shown it. Her professional intuition, however, told her something was amiss.

After lessons, we held a consultation in the changing room. Half of the students demanded that we dismiss Viktor because he had endangered the very existence of our group. Using my double vote as a group leader, I insisted that we give him a second chance, arguing that it was his life as an orphan and the rough environment he lived in at the port that caused him to act bullish at times. We also discussed presenting him with our demand that he apologise before the cafeteria staff, and adopt a professional attitude of respect towards the female teacher, or else leave the group voluntarily and immediately.

Leaving the theatre, we found Viktor at our favourite haunt on the boulevard. I informed him of the group's decision and gave him three days to decide what he wanted to do. "Think hard about our ultimatum and about your future," I told him. "If you accept our conditions and are ready to follow them, come back on Tuesday. Otherwise, we all wish you good luck and goodbye!"

As I rushed over to the orphanage for a rehearsal, I could not stop thinking about Viktor. *Have I overplayed my hand, trying to help a buddy? Will he appreciate it?*

When Chief Ballet Master Vronsky came to inspect our course and saw the young men, he told us: "If you meet our expectations in this exam, then, as of 1st January, we'll give you two more teachers, in Historical and Character dance. If you master these, you'll be contracted to dance in the current opera/ballet repertoire where they desperately need male partners in both these genres. Everything will depend on how you progress, your determination, and creative discipline."

I realised this meant that at the end of this school year I'd have to leave the orphanage and find a job in the centre, not far from the theatre, to work between the hours of 3 and 7 p.m. This would give me a chance to take classes in the morning, and to perform with the ballet troupe in the evening. It also meant I'd have to live at home again until I found a room in the same district, so that I didn't have to spend so much time commuting.

At the orphanage, meanwhile, fate dealt me another blow. During a lunch break, while all students and staff were eating in the main canteen, someone stole the accordion from my room. I was floored by this. Without a musical instrument, I'd be out of a job. The Director called the police. The detective discovered adult footprints on the staircase and concluded that this theft had been carried out by professionals. They wrote down the make and brand of the accordion as well as all the details of its condition and I signed the complaint. It occurred to me that if I didn't launch an immediate search on my own, I might never see my musical partner again. I recalled that the chief of police in Moldavanka knew me well. He was the father of Tonya, a friend from my teenage days. I had sometimes played accordion at their family parties. Collecting my meagre possessions together, I immediately went home to Moldavanka, where I stopped by at the local police station and asked to see the chief. I told him of the theft and asked for his help in recovering my accordion. His deputy carefully wrote down all its particulars and told me to be at the central flea market, in the musical instruments row, on the following Sunday at 10 a.m.

There were masses of people at the Odessan flea market as usual. In the musical section, I walked up and down every row of instruments and could not see mine anywhere. For two hours I braved the chaos of the bazaar and then returned home exhausted and empty-handed. At home, I found a note from the chief of police stuck into the keyhole of my door asking me to come to the police station as soon as possible.

"You're a lucky one, Mikhail. Must have been born with a silver spoon in your mouth. Come here and see! This is yours, isn't it?" The chief greeted me with a smile.

In the open cabinet, there stood what looked like an accordion, wrapped in a flowery bed sheet stolen from my bed at the orphanage. *So, that's where it went, I thought, recalling that I'd not been able to find the bed sheet when packing up at the orphanage.*

Carefully unwrapping the instrument, I confirmed that it was mine. To check its condition, I played a few chords. The police station's staff, gathering around, congratulated me on the recovery of my precious object. Naïvely, I thought that I'd be able to take it straight home. The chief, however, explained that any stolen and recovered object had to remain in police custody for up to three months, until the trial of the thief. When I asked whether they'd been able to catch the thief, the chief explained: "While you were pushing through the crowds at the flea market, our thief was busy selling your accordion behind your back, offering it at half-price."

"So, you were using me as a bait, to distract his attention?"

"Precisely."

"That's very clever! Bravo!" I applauded them, and went out, but came back almost immediately and asked the man on duty to pass on my heartfelt thanks to the chief for having saved my artistic life.

Meanwhile, back at the orphanage, panic had ensued after my departure. The counsellor found me at the theatre and begged me not to abandon them. We agreed that I would borrow an accordion from a friend for several rehearsals and finish preparing the New Year's programme for them. The directorship of the orphanage was very pleased with the performances of individual groups around the New Year tree and with a joint finale, involving all the performers. Every negative event has its upside. Thus it was that the incident with the accordion precipitated my liberation from an impossible load of responsibilities for the forthcoming year. I now had an opportunity to focus on achieving my goal: amassing the maximum amount of knowledge and experience in all forms of dance.

Every day after our Classical dance class, I would rush over to the Arts Centre for seminars on the folk dances of Europe between noon and three o'clock. Over three months of intensive studies, I'd gained a thorough grounding in the national repertoires of the various Soviet republics and, from January, I was getting ready to start on the dances of the European countries of the Soviet bloc. The teachers at the Arts Centre were quite pleased with me, and often used me as an assistant in practical demonstrations of duet dance sequences. At one such lesson, the Director, Lyuftgarten, who had observed me in action, asked me to see him in his office. While I changed, I was busy wondering what I might have done wrong.

It turned out, however, that he had recommended me for the position of leader for a children's dance ensemble, at the Mariners' Cultural Centre. This was one of the top ensembles in the city and was subsidised by the Trade Union of the Black Sea Fleet. This was a great honour for me, a nineteen-year-old youth. Their huge Cultural Centre, with its two theatres for summer and winter, was a well-known architectural landmark on Primorsky Boulevard, between the Opera Theatre and the Potemkin Steps. After all the misfortunes of the previous year (leaving home for the orphanage, Viktor's departure, the theft of my accordion), my luck suddenly seemed to be changing. I felt as though the powers above were finally blessing me on the path I'd been dreaming about since childhood.

During my meeting with the director of the Mariners' Centre, I realised the person I was dealing with wasn't just a prominent administrator, he was also a broad-minded intellectual. An assortment of creative enterprises flourished under his protective wing: an art studio, a library, a drama theatre, a chamber orchestra, an adult song and dance ensemble, a modern ballroom dance studio, and, finally, this children's ensemble. The last of these, whose long-serving head had recently retired, was the weak link in this otherwise successful cultural centre. The Director was looking for a young enthusiast, able to work with the youngsters. After looking over my CV sent by the Performing Arts Centre, he'd decided to meet me in person.

The first thing he asked looking through the papers was: "Where did you study the soldiers'/sailors' repertoire?"

"At seminars with soloists from the state dance ensembles."

"The ones given by Lyuftgarten, you mean?"

I just nodded, unsure how to address him properly: he looked like an ex-officer.

As if reading my thoughts, "My name is Plakhov," he said. "Viktor Vasilyevich."

"And mine's Mikhail, or just Misha."

"At the Centre, and with the children, you will be known as Mikhail Semyonovich. According to these papers, you are an adult, and so your obligations and remuneration will be that of a regular adult staff member. My deputy will sign a contract with you for a six-month trial period, starting on 1st January 1951. If you succeed in building a strong group and creating an interesting repertoire, and if you manage to perform with distinction at a festival of volunteer performing arts groups – as befits the good name of our Centre – you'll be given a contract with us for five years. There will be the potential for your salary to grow in proportion to the results of your efforts, and there will be bonuses. All the other details you can discuss with my deputy. Any questions?"

"What about advertising, and other ways of announcing new enrolment into the ensemble?"

"Our in-house agency will deal with all that. You can agree the text with the head of recreation."

At the meeting with her, I expounded on my plans for the reorganisation of a children's dance ensemble in some detail. I set out the necessary components for working with thirteen-to-sixteen-year-olds, including the need for an accompanist, changing rooms, costumes and shoes for future performances, special uniforms for rehearsals, first-aid kit, etc.

She enquired: "How does one as young as you come to know so many of these details?" I suggested she flip through my employment log, but she nonetheless expressed a doubt. "You're proposing to work with thirteen-to-sixteen-year-olds. The normal practice is to start with younger kids."

"You're right," I said, "it is more logical: 'Slow and steady wins the race.' However, our director is already expecting concrete results from me by the end of the season. He wants us ready to perform at the regional festival, and I'm determined to meet these expectations of his to the full. If we do manage that, then we can enrol the nine-to-twelve-year-olds in the following year, and so initiate a junior troupe of the ensemble. That way we get an opportunity to make ourselves known, and then ensure the continuity of our creative growth and development."

The head of recreation was listening to me with wide-eyed amazement: "Is every ballet master as experienced as you are at your theatre?"

"I'm not a ballet master yet, although I am planning to become one. But I do have some experience in working with children, and I hope you will have a chance to see that for yourself at the end of the present season, that is, if you accept me into your artistic family."

"Mikhail Semyonovich, I find your project very appealing, and, on behalf of our Department of Public Recreation, I promise to lend our full support to the children's ensemble."

"Thank you!" I said, with a small bow, shaking her hand. Something in the conversation with this woman had left me with an inexplicable sense of unease.

Viktor did not show up for the meeting with me by the backstage door on Tuesday, and I had to tell our teacher that our ranks had dwindled. She merely shrugged her shoulders. It seemed she had already heard rumours about the cafeteria incident. So then, it was meant to be. After the lesson, Innesa positioned us at the barre relative to our physical abilities, and, in centre practice, she divided us into three groups of three. She then decided on our order of appearance. Throughout the whole of the final week before the exam we rehearsed our exam demonstration in a carefully worked-out order. Certainly many of us were nervous: the following Saturday would decide the future of our experimental male ballet group. I got my colleagues to trim the excessive growth in their armpits, and to wash other tight spots so as to eliminate any sweaty smells; to launder their uniforms; to mend their worn-out ballet shoes; to cut their tangled hair and dirty fingernails; to repeat every procedure they had had to perform at the original examination.

My colleagues, of course, teased me again: "Daddy Misha, are you grooming us for marriage?"

"No, worse," I said. "It's for a career in ballet."

Considering that some of them were older than me, my patriarchal approach could easily ruffle some feathers, but I persisted in accordance with the Russian saying: 'When you first meet someone, you're judged on appearances, but when you part, it's all about wits.'

The long-awaited day finally arrived. Twenty chairs were lined up along the mirrored wall in the exam studio for the members of the Examination Committee.

"Why so many judges?" my peers asked.

I numbered the guests:

a) the directorship and pedagogical council of the ballet school: our alma mater;

b) the administration and creative directors of the theatre, who supported us financially;

c) ballet masters and coaches who would be our potential future instructors.

"The last thing they're interested in", I said, "is our technical skill or acting potential. They want to see what can be made of us in the future, given our overripe physical condition: they're going to look for balance and coordination, a musical ear and the height of our jump, spatial awareness and awareness of group dynamics, concentration and memory, stage discipline and suchlike. The most important thing at today's demonstration is to deliver to the committee a strong impression that what they're seeing before them are not Odessan yobs from the street, but real artists, with a sense of dignity, manners, and self-control."

The exam lasted about an hour. Silently, we took our places before the committee, one after the other, following a quiet cue from the teacher, occasionally drying our faces with towels or rubbing the soles of our ballet shoes with resin. After a customary bow, we stood before leaving the room, expecting individual questions; but they never came. We left the studio to a thin round of applause. In the changing rooms of the ground floor, we let ourselves breathe freely. I proudly announced that I had never expected such a unified display of good order and self-discipline throughout the entire demonstration: "If, they don't admit such talents as ours after this, we should apply to the Bolshoi!"

My patter provided the necessary release of tension. Everyone cracked up, until the Director came in with congratulations, saying that our group had been transferred to the permanent care of the theatre administration. He also informed us that, starting in January, we would have a new curriculum and new instructors:

Classical dance – Ludmilla Tzhomelidze: daily, 9.30–11.00
Character dance – Ivan Vishnyakov: Monday, Thursday, 11.30–1.00
Historical dance – Innesa Goldina: Tuesday, Friday, 11.30–1.00
Stage rehearsal for mime extras: Wednesday, 2.00–4.00

We were also happy to hear that two sixteen-year-olds from the ballet group at the local Pioneers' Centre were to join our team in the second semester. This meant that the stability of our group was now assured.

After taking a shower, we all marched off to a nearby cafeteria to celebrate our success.

After moving out of the orphanage on the day the accordion was stolen, I stayed at my mother's place for a short while. The administration at the theatre provided me with a list of rooms to let in the city centre. I chose three that more or less met my requirements, and went hunting. I finally settled on a flat on the mezzanine floor of a two-storey house. We agreed on terms, and I received a set of keys in return for the payment of the first month's rent. In view of the impending holidays, we set the moving date for the afternoon of 3rd January.

In the evening, I went to visit Mother at the bodega. I waited till she had finished her work and then shared my news with her about the ballet school and the new flat.

She reacted coolly: "It's no use trying to dissuade you. You're old enough to make your own decisions now, whatever you think is best for you. I hope you'll at least see in the New Year with us."

I nodded in affirmation.

"Remember: as long as I'm alive, this flat remains yours equally with your brothers. I always knew that sooner or later your path would lead you away from your family."

"Mother!"

"Misha, this is normal. Your father warned me even before the war that by the time I was old, my boys would all have gone their separate ways. You're just the first to do it, that's all."

In order to make it up to my mother somehow, I stopped by at the police station and asked the chief to release my accordion for just one night, New Year's Eve, in honour of the holiday. He refused, saying that he had no right to do this before the trial.

I offered him a compromise: "Your driver will bring the instrument over to my place at 11 p.m. I will play for my family for three hours. Then, at 2 a.m. he will pick me up, with the instrument, and bring me over to your place, and Tonya and I will play and sing for you until five in the morning. Then your man will take the accordion back to the police station, and I will go home to bed. Please, I'm asking you to do it for my mother."

Tonya's father laughed: "Misha," he said, "with your knack for compromises, you should be a diplomat in the foreign service. Fine, I'll take the risk, for your mother's sake. All right?"

"Huge thanks! You can't imagine what a big help this is."

It was as if a heavy boulder had been rolled off my chest. Now I could turn to preparing for my removal with a clear conscience, having resolved how to pay my dues on the family holiday. Mother was very pleased with the news of the accordion. As a result, she invited all father's and her own relatives to our New Year's Eve celebration. I asked Mother to keep the accordion secret from our guests for the time being. I also procured a small fir tree and decorated it with Roman's help for a very Christmas-like Soviet celebration of New Year. The relatives came in and out, trying to do their best in preparation for the holiday. Even neighbours were involved, supplying chairs, tables, and dishes. Only Yosif either kept to his room or was absent all day long. This suited us quite well – reducing the chances of some nasty surprise.

The guests began to arrive from ten o'clock. Right on the dot of eleven, a police car drove up to the house. The neighbours, seated on our richly decorated veranda froze with their mouths open, seeing a policeman carrying a baby wrapped in a flowery bed sheet. At every step the baby would let out strange squeals, breathing heavily.

The newcomer asked: "Where does Misha, the musician, live?"

Everyone had suddenly lost their powers of speech.

The Sergeant repeated his question, now with an edge to his voice. Somebody pointed at our open door. He knocked, but with all the noise in the flat, nobody could hear him. Then, carefully holding the wrapped-up bundle with both hands, he attempted to squeeze through the double door. Naturally, in his clumsy-rough male claws, the 'poor babe' began to whine ever more hysterically in a strange squeaky voice.

The slightly tipsy neighbours on the veranda were about to jump on this tyrant and save the babe from mutilation but, just then, the sweet voice of Annushka hostess pronounced: "Please come in! Welcome! Thank you so much for your consideration and care!"

"No worries, ma'am. I'll pick it up again, together with Misha, at two."

At this point our 'granny' Sasha could not restrain herself any longer and plunged into an attack in Ukrainian: "Will you all just take a look, dear folks, at the ungodly things going on here? Will somebody explain what is wrong with this poor child?"

"What child? This is Mikhail's accordion!"

Fortunately, 'Uncle' Volodya, who was standing next to her, reacted instantly, catching his eighty-year-old collapsing wife in his arms. The remaining neighbours had expediently dispersed. Mother brought the New Year surprise into the flat and handed it over to me with a radiant smile. Everyone's jaws dropped at the sight of the bundled 'baby'.

"Excellent! That's just what we needed today – a foundling!" pronounced Yosif.

"The name is Apollo," said I, slowly unravelling the bed sheet.

Seeing my 'Apollo', the guests broke into a round of applause, anticipating a jolly night. Naturally, all my relatives, unlike the neighbours, were in on the pantomime with the 'baby', because Mother had informed each of them in secret that Misha was going to bring an accordion. But this just made it more fun to play along. I took the instrument into the bedroom to get it ready. My cousin David asked if we were going to sing a duet as we used to do. I reminded him of a few of our favourite tunes and then we joined the others at the table.

It was the first time I'd been free of musical engagements on a New Year's Eve. Typically in the run-up to this holiday, I'd earn more at private functions than in six months' work at the Mariners' Centre. But at the latter I could look forward to professional recognition, a welcome from the audience, and some prospect of a creative future that could not be bought at any price. After the war, David and I had devoted much time to singing in duet. He had a good ear for music and a pleasant lyrical baritone. I would harmonise, as necessary, within a wide range, between bass and falsetto, accompanying his main melodic line. I have to say that we were a big hit, not only with girls, but also with elderly women, nostalgic for their youth. Our repertoire mostly consisted of folk and contemporary songs in Russian and Ukrainian. Guests often joined in, forgetting their shyness under the influence of drink.

At the high point of the evening, the policeman returned to pick me up. Saying goodbye to the guests, I marched off with the smiling cop through the ranks of applauding neighbours on the veranda. The celebrating guests accompanied us with a cappella singing all the way to the car.

Tonya's family greeted us warmly, imposing the customary fine for being late – a shot of vodka – according to an old Russian custom. We quickly tuned up – the host on a guitar, and me on my accordion. Tonya stood between her father and me and launched into one popular folk song after another in her strong mezzo-soprano voice, while the guitarist and I played along and tuned in with each other. Our trio worked really well. The audience howled and cried with rapture, not forgetting to refill their glasses now and again. Suitably warmed up, the guests gradually began moving into the garden at the front of the house, the winters in Odessa being mild (10–12°C). The men lifted me up with my accordion in the chair I was sitting on, and carried us outside. The bug had gotten to me as well, and I played a number of folk dance tunes with abandon, including Gypsy rhythms and the sailor's dance 'Yablochko'. Neighbours from the surrounding buildings listened at their open windows, applauding and joining in the singing, yet with some restraint, afraid of appearing to interfere with the family party of an important official.

At five, the driver pulled up at the house. Warmly exchanging farewells with everyone and, of course, getting to kiss both mother and daughter, I handed the carefully wrapped instrument back to the host. We were each grateful to the other. Even though the distance between our houses was minimal, the driver insisted on taking me right to my door and waited to see me in. Only then did he drive off to return the instrument to the police station. The guests at my mother's place had all left by then, but Mother and my Aunty Faina were still clearing up. Mother impressed a grateful kiss upon her sleepy musician, who immediately collapsed into bed.

On the first day after the winter break, I found the two new members of our group from the Pioneers' Palace sitting waiting for me in the changing rooms. I introduced myself, and explained that when it came to any questions that weren't related to the academic process, they should come to me first before taking the matter up with the teachers.

"As group leader, I'm here to liaise on your behalf with both students and teachers. Welcome to the experimental male ballet team!" They thanked me and moved to get up, but I stopped them: "Your good manners will stand you in good stead in the classroom, but amongst ourselves we can be informal. By the way, we lost one talented guy recently because of specific ethical issues. I suggest you pay due respect to the teachers here and show sensitivity to the older classmates. But now it's time for a warm-up before the teacher arrives."

When we entered the classroom, our peers greeted us noisily with Happy New Year wishes.

I introduced the newcomers: "Our ranks have grown! Meet the new recruits!" To the question: what about Viktor? I merely criss-crossed my wrists, letting them know the matter was now closed. When our pianist appeared in the doorway, everyone rose at my signal. The pianist introduced our new instructor of Classical dance – Ludmilla Alekseyevna Tzhomelidze, and then presented each of us to her individually, stating our names. The newcomers were introduced by me, with a note that this was their first day with the group. For good measure, I also mentioned that they'd had previous experience in dance, having studied at the ballet group of the Pioneers' Palace. Ludmilla acknowledged my explanations and began to whisper something animatedly to the pianist.

Ballerina Tzhomelidze had been a soloist dancer in the opera and ballet theatres of Tbilisi and Odessa for twenty years. She began her teaching career after retiring at the age of forty, and soon afterwards became the right hand of Odessa's head ballet master. In the Soviet Union and other countries of the Soviet bloc, ballet artistes typically retired after working for twenty years in the field, regardless of their actual age at the time. From an early age (girls at eight, and boys at ten), the workload of dancers far exceeded the norms approved by the state health-and-safety regulations for those under the age of eighteen. Daily lessons, rehearsals, and performances inevitably take their toll on the body over the course of thirty years. During the first ten years, the exercises intensively strengthen and remodel the natural muscle-bone structure of a ballet student; but then, gradually, over the next twenty years, they start to destroy the physical condition of the dancers, unless they retire in time. Not every soloist is able to cope with that.

At the beginning of our first lesson, Ludmilla explained that different teachers have different approaches to the training of a professional dancer. Their methods of teaching may vary significantly.

"Because of your mature age, your teachers have had to come up with a new system of training. We're having to reshape what are almost, or already developed, male bodies to make them more elastic. We need to straighten your knees and stretch out the soles of your feet; stretch the muscles and tendons all over your bodies, strengthen your spines to enable you to lift your partners, etc. None of this is easy for either teachers or students. When Mikhail succeeded in getting your group together last summer and presented it to the directors of our school and the theatre, many of my colleagues were sceptical. Yet we chose to give it a go, partly because, since the war, there's been such a dearth of male dancers.

"Being an experienced coach, Innesa Goldina managed to refit you with new 'ballet' legs instead of your old 'street' legs. She got your joints into shape for a new regimen of movement in space. Judging by the results of your demonstration, which I attended myself at the end of December, it was clear that you'd somehow managed to achieve in three months what younger boys take a year to do.

"I will also be working with you on a temporary basis, just until the end of this term. At this point, however, now that you can firmly stand on your feet and realise how much patience and self-discipline is required in ballet, we're going to start studying the alphabet of Classical dance: the main exercises at the barre and in centre practice. Gradually, we'll be increasing the complexity of these exercises, until you're ready to use them in sequences, and at the normal performing tempo. The latter you'll learn under the direction of another, male teacher, in the next academic year.

"I should warn you that I don't intend to cut you much slack, as I would with young children. There's no time for any foolery. If any of you feels he doesn't have the strength to stay the course in spite of the difficulties, I suggest he looks for an easier profession. And now, take five minutes for a warm-up."

"Please excuse me," I piped up, "but might I ask a favour?"

"Yes, what is it?" Ludmilla was surprised.

"You see, in this group of ours, we aren't always that quick in our grasp of the subjects being taught, so we often feel quite ashamed of ourselves, in front of both our peers and our teachers, which leads to people getting tense and frustrated. In short, if a situation arises, please allow me to deal with it. It will be better for all those involved."

"Of course, Misha, this sounds good to me."

"Thank you, madam!"

Innesa, who was now teaching us Historical Dance, began her class with a lecture on the origins and popularity of this social genre of dance in royal/ aristocratic circles. Half an hour later, at the end of this introductory lecture, a group of senior girls from the ballet school suddenly turned up in the studio. They were already dressed in sleeveless tops and long wide skirts. This was a pleasant surprise, because it was hard to imagine how Innesa was going to partner eleven dancers at once. Forming pairs according to height, we began with the study of different ways in which a bow was taken in thirteenth-century Europe. Traditional poses, modes of interaction with a female partner, and also simple walking steps were next on the list of our subjects for that lesson. The girls had taken the same course a year earlier, only without male partners. Their experience helped us a great deal in the study of this unusual ceremonial style of Court dancing. It goes without saying that our fourteen-year-old partners from the sixth grade giggled quite a bit as they interacted with us 'hippopotamuses'. Nevertheless, by the end of our lesson, we'd finally got the gist of the medieval style in Branle and had even begun to amuse our partners with our grotesquely mannered bows, like circus monkeys. In spite of these difficulties, we were quite pleased with our first introduction to Court dancing (the roots of ballet), and to our young female partners. Innesa concluded that, in light of the fact that this was our first exposure to such unusual material, we hadn't done too badly.

She had been bracing herself for something much worse.

Historical Dance was destined to play a leading role in the formation of our inner spiritual world as future ballet dancers. Without overly exerting ourselves physically, we were not only being introduced to classical music, but were imbibing its aesthetic influence with every fibre of our beings, transforming this or that characteristic/stylistic note into its appropriate manner of movement and interaction with our partners. Paired promenades and salon reverences in Estampie (a popular medieval dance and instrumental style of the thirteenth and fourteenth centuries) and Allemande (a processional couple dance with stately, flowing steps, fashionable in sixteenth-century aristocratic circles) had transformed the behaviour of these former waifs so dramatically that even Goldina could not hide a smile during the rehearsals. Our female partners from the ballet school were an inspiration to us. In spite of their shyness at the close contact with these pseudo-suitors, they authentically preserved the style of the epoch in Sarabande, or jumped energetically with a dancer's support in Saltarello. Innesa usually partnered me to demonstrate the individual 'pas'. Then afterwards we would all practise them for a while, my usual student partner and I dancing at the front, with the other pairs following our lead. In this manner, our learning seemed to progress faster under Innesa's supervision from the side.

Our teacher barked out her comments: "Dancers, where is your aristocratic bearing? Pull your stomachs in! And don't 'sit' on your thighs! Raise your heads! And straighten your backsides! Look at your own female partner, not someone else's! Remember that you are now dancing at a Royal Court, not at a discotheque in Luna Park!"

At the end of each class, we would drop down on one knee to express our gratitude to Innesa and her girls. Thanks to their patience and perseverance, our success in this subject was noticeable not only in the classroom, but in everyday situations as well. We learned not to drag our feet, even when we were tired, but to hold ourselves erect, and to walk elegantly with proud gait. Even our coaches paid us compliments during stage rehearsals. The main achievement of these lessons was a transformation of our male world view to a higher regard for the representatives of the 'weaker' sex.

From literary sources on the history/theory of ballet, we know that the original 'Character Dances' (performed some 300 years ago) consisted of various set movements relating to particular dramatis personae, stock characters, such as a master of ceremonies, a queen, a chambermaid, a priest, a court jester, etc. Later (a century on), the term 'Character Dance' was applied more broadly to refer to any form of 'occupational' dance, such as those of warriors, pirates, sailors, haymakers, gendarmes and children, as well as to ritual forms of dance. The last to come under that umbrella term, were various folk dances of different ethnicities, refashioned, for theatrical effect, along the lines of classical choreography. Unfortunately, Ivan Vishnyakov did not bother to explain the background to students who were entirely unschooled in such matters. Since I had some knowledge of the subject from my seminars at the arts centre, I was quite tickled to be playing the teacher's substitute, answering their torrent of questions.

Vishnyakov always kept me at the front in his classes, both at the barre, and in the front line in centre practice. He came to rely on my multi-ethnic knowledge of folk moves, and my quick grasp of new sequences. Unlike Ludmilla, who always kept me at the back during her classes, embarrassed by my 'saxauls' (crooked legs), Ivan had no problem at all using me for the demonstration of old routines from Lopukhov and Chiriaeff's textbook *The Fundamentals of*

Character Dance, which I also happened to have in my private collection. For me, this singling out was not only a matter of professional prestige in the group, but also offered me the opportunity to work later on as Vishnyakov's substitute at our ballet school, on those occasions when Ivan was busy rehearsing at the operetta, where he held a permanent position as a ballet master.

Vishnyakov was a good specialist in dances used in the musical-comedy repertoire, and he was particularly skilled in working with singers. He kept an eye out for those among us who had limited abilities for classical ballet, but were potentially good candidates for the lighter genre. The prospects for a dancing career, especially for men, in theatres of musical comedy in the 1950s were almost unlimited. Ivan was in great demand in all four theatres in the city. In reality, he had no time for serious teaching. As a result, he didn't so much teach, as show us the movements, and then get us to repeat them, correcting our mistakes as he went along. But some of my classmates who were a bit slow on the uptake, weren't able to learn the choreography presented in such a way, and they found it very difficult.

Working for the most part with professionals, Vishnyakov had little patience, or interest for that matter, in going over and over the same elements of a new movement, before asking students to reproduce it in its totality. He could see that his methods were not working but he was also concerned about delivering academic results in accordance with the programme of training that he himself had presented to the school. Which is why, after a lesson, he would often ask me to go over the difficult elements or sequences he'd just shown us, but at a slower tempo, with those who needed help. I responded willingly to this call, because it gave me the opportunity to practise the movements further. But those who needed my help often felt uncomfortable taking up my time, knowing that I'd had to dash off after our lessons to my job at the Mariners' Centre. The upshot of all this was that the students became somewhat disaffected. I had to explain to them that it was in our interests to bear with Vishnyakov because there was no one else who could replace him. I promised to give them all the extra help they might need, and told them not to feel any compunction about turning to me for help. I was taking this on, not out of charity, but for pragmatic reasons. If weaker students were allowed to fall behind they might decide to leave our group at the end of the school year, as Viktor had done. In that case, our group could be disbanded, and that would mean the end of my professional future in ballet. Without a graduation diploma from the ballet school I would not be able even to submit my application for admission to MTA. I felt this sword of Damocles suspended permanently over my head.

I had an unpleasant surprise on 2nd January, my first day at the Mariners' Centre. I arrived a little early for the registration of novices who had come in response to the advertisement and, contrary to my expectation, discovered that they were kids, aged nine to twelve years old. The head of recreation assured me that this was all out of her control: the notice about additional enrolment had been composed before my arrival and it hadn't been possible to change it.

"Why didn't you tell me this at our first meeting then?"

"After speaking with you and seeing your point," she said, "I immediately changed the text of the ad, indicating the age as fourteen to sixteen, but it was already too late."

"I'm sorry, madam," I said, "but you must see what a ridiculous position I find myself in. For the moment, I'm ready to consider this incident a 'regrettable misunderstanding', but in future, I hope that you will discuss everything connected to the children's ensemble with me in advance."

"Absolutely, Mikhail Semyonovich, you may have no doubt on that account."

"Thank you, madam!"

With the junior group came their tutor, Oksana, a former soloist of the senior group of the ensemble. She was twenty-eight and had her eight-year-old daughter, Lyuba, with her. Because of the younger than expected ages of the participants and the presence of the tutor who was to become my assistant, I had to revise the repertoire I'd originally prepared. I wasn't excited about 'folk dances of the Soviet republics' as the choice of programme for the festival because all the other studios in the city would be doing the same. With the juniors I decided to stage a choreographic composition 'Pioneers' Summer', and with the senior group, a dance suite 'Celebration on Board Ship'. I composed two distinct scenarios based on my own knowledge and experience, with meticulously developed details in each of the contrasting subjects. Then I turned to the selection and compilation of the musical material from well-known tunes by popular modern composers. This done, I handed the finished scores to the accordionist of the ensemble to do the musical orchestration.

I would run to the Cultural Centre three times a week at four in the afternoon to coach both groups in the choreography I had worked out beforehand at home. I delegated to my assistant Oksana the job of coaching each successive episode of choreography. Without this system I would not have been able to complete the staging of two such large-scale compositions in time. I had to insist on getting a second accordionist for our parallel coaching sessions – one for me and one for Oksana. To my great satisfaction, the kids loved the choreographic compositions they were asked to learn and, with the help of Oksana and parent volunteers, we maintained a good working discipline.

Only now could I appreciate why the head of recreation had gone against my wishes and organised a junior group, and foisted an assistant from the senior group upon me. In those early days of my budding career, I really was too young to bear the responsibility for individual youngsters in the ensemble and to get involved in their personal issues with parents. Oksana turned out to be the precious missing link in the chain of control and command of the children's collective, being both an experienced dancer, and mother of an eight-year-old. One could not have imagined a better candidate for this work with my young charges. And there was another factor as well. The previous children's ensemble had died out because it had been in direct competition with the senior group. The management of the Cultural Centre had had to close the less well-known, and less successful, junior group, because of the rivalry between the choreographers of each. This story, relayed by Oksana, served as a lesson in professional ethics for me.

In my case, there was no danger of a conflict with the senior group, mostly because my assistant was able to act as a bridge between us. But it also became clear to me, that if I succeeded with the children, the directorship would be likely to offer the leadership of the seniors to me as well, as soon as their prominent former head retired. When that happened, Oksana would, without a doubt, become head of the junior group. Since we had already established a common professional understanding, it was clear to both of us how useful we could be for one another in that situation. She, for her part, was not able to do choreography on her own, and I, for my part, desperately needed her as a coach, particularly for the girls. Thus an unspoken mutual concern for our respective professional futures became a fruitful stimulus to our formal relationship.

At the theatre, academic training and stage practice grew steadily more intense. In Classical dance, Ludmilla kept our noses to the grindstone, not moving on to the next stage of training until we had exhibited technically spotless mastery of the previous programme at the barre and in centre practice. Both parties would exert themselves to the limit to ensure a precise, though not necessarily outstanding, articulation of this or that exercise for legs and feet: slowly, but correctly; in harmony with the movement of arms, head, and torso; pushing off energetically with the entire surface of the foot to launch into a jump, but then moving down gently from tiptoes to the sole of the foot in pliés. We had to learn all forms of port de bras by heart, like a multiplication table. For most of us this was a gargantuan task.

There was not a lesson when our adorable Ludochka did not scream at us hysterically:

"Misha, when will you ever straighten out those 'saxauls' of yours?" This remark usually referred to my legs, which always put my teacher in mind of twisted tree trunks.

"Sasha, raise your chin, pull your backside in! You're a dancer, not a gorilla!"

"Tolya, pull in your stomach! Have you gotten pregnant from my corrections?"

And so it went on, for half an hour at the barre, and as much in centre practice. If, after a triple repetition of the same correction, the student still made a mistake, she would remove a fashionable high-heeled shoe from her lovely foot and launch it in the direction of the offender. He would catch it in mid-air, run up to the furious beauty and restore the shoe to her bare foot. Everyone would applaud, and the lesson would continue as if nothing had happened. Once, in centre practice, I became the victim of our enchanting Fury. My head in the clouds, I had missed her comment addressed to me. The next moment the shoe flew past my ear and was caught by the classmate standing behind me. Approaching the pale Ludmilla, I apologised, bent my knee and attempted to replace the cursed shoe on her foot with trembling hands.

"Misha, what's your problem, have you never seen a woman's foot up close?"

"Such a beautiful one as this, madam, I have never had the pleasure to see." Rising from the knee, I backed away with a musketeer's reverence, not turning my back on her, for which I was rewarded with a blown kiss.

Tzhomelidze was for us an Aphrodite: strict and fair, kind and fearless. Like all Georgians, she was highly emotional. After the lesson, Ludmilla asked me to come to her office. I thought that this was, as usual, to do with the rehearsals or with some issue of discipline.

"Misha, please forgive me, I forgot that you have poor vision. This 'shoe-shooting' won't happen again."

The goddess stretched her hands towards me. I tried to kiss her hands, but in a fervour of guilty conscience, she hugged me instead, pulling me to her divine chest with such passion that my head began to spin. I wound my hands around her waist, and thought to myself: *One can only dream of dying like this!*

Sensing my excitement, she pushed me off at once, and said: "Run along now!"

On Wednesdays, from two till four in the afternoon, during the stage rehearsals for the mime extras, we were gradually entrusted with more important and difficult roles: kings and dukes, priests and gendarmes, innkeepers and pirates, and other characteristic roles in a play. Working as extras at the theatre not only provided us with good practice in wearing heavy medieval clothes, shoes and personal weapons, but also allowed us to experience mannered interactions with other subjects in group episodes onstage. Until our experimental group joined the theatre, such roles would often be played by women dressed as men. Naturally, the producers preferred young energetic guys who could run, fall, wrestle, roll over, etc. We were paid a very modest sum for each show, but it was still helpful in meeting our basic subsistence needs. The most important benefit though, was that through such practice we began to experience direct contact with the audience, to gain spatial awareness of the stage, and, above all, to grow accustomed to the supernatural atmosphere of the theatre.

Modest though they were, our acting skills began to get noticed by audiences, who were able to distinguish individual characters from the crowd. The directorship promised that, in the next academic year, they'd appoint a coach in stage movement for us: acrobatics, fencing, hand-to-hand wrestling, throws and tripping. Because of this work as mime extras, many of my classmates were able to surmount their financial difficulties, and almost everyone now lived in rented rooms in the city centre. This relative comfort and a growing confidence in their ability to support themselves had a positive effect on the psychological and physical state of these former waifs. The social mores of the group were gradually evening themselves out. Looking at those young men who had found their way to the theatre from street corners, I felt a quiet pride at having helped them leave behind their post-war deprivation, and opened up to them the world of the Arts.

My own flat was now transformed into a musical, choreography lab, where I engaged in arranging popular tunes on my accordion: polkas, marches, waltzes, gallops, and other characteristic genres for the composition 'Pioneers' Summer', and well-known songs about the Black Sea and its pearl, Odessa, for the 'Celebration on Board Ship'. The next task was to produce sheet music for each of the two compositions. I was also preparing musical scripts for each episode and the overall staging for both compositions. Yet another task was to select some movements from the existing canon and then come up with new and original ones to typify a specific character, animal or plant.

I had nearly completed the choreography for both performances. Following my advice, Oksana started training the second cast of girls to act as substitutes for the main one, in case they were needed. It was harder to do that with the boys because there were fewer of them on the whole. Nonetheless, a healthy sense of competition drove the young dancers to learn the solo performances of others, which in turn motivated the main performers to perfect their own technique and expression. If, in a rush of creative fantasy, I devised a piece of choreography that was too difficult for children, Oksana would approach me after the rehearsal and ask me to simplify it. I was truly grateful to her for such input. She was impeccably ethical in her conduct, always supporting my authority within the group. And I, in turn, would always make a point of showing full confidence in my assistant in front of the directorship and parents. Without such mutual respect and recognition we could never have succeeded as we did.

In February, I was eventually summoned to a hearing in the case of the stolen accordion. Fortunately, the hearing was in the afternoon, so I would only miss one lesson. There were a lot of people in the small courtroom. I was invited to take a seat in the front row because my case was to be heard next. When the Judge asked about the theft of my personal property, the detective briefly confirmed the facts: that the item had been stolen from the orphanage and the thief apprehended at the flea market. The Judge asked me to describe in detail the instrument that was wrapped up in a flowery bed sheet. I named the make, the number of basses and octaves on the keys, and described the colouring of the mother-of-pearl on the straps. Two witnesses confirmed my descriptions.

Then the Judge asked: "What else was stolen that day?"

"My linen suit, which is now on the defendant."

There was laughter in the audience. Someone sitting to my right swore under his breath. I had the impression that the majority of those present were siding with the thief, not the victim. I became alert. The Judge asked if I had any other complaints about the defendant. I said that I had not, but that I had a request.

"Please." The Judge nodded.

"Two months ago I was deprived of my instrument, which I need and use to earn my daily bread. I need to get it back immediately, and my linen suit as well."

The audience buzzed in response, and my neighbour to the left hissed menacingly: "You boy, just cool it. He'll remember you for this, once he's served his term."

I turned round to look at him. He had the face of a typical felon. "What do you mean?"

"You'll understand when you get a 'pen' ['knife' in prison jargon] in your back!" he said.

The Judge announced the verdict to the defendant Kravchenko: five years behind bars for a series of thefts, including my accordion, which would only be returned to me after a month. I met the chief's eyes and gestured to him: What was I supposed to do now?

He waved his wrist: You may go now.

I left the courtroom depressed, rather than satisfied that justice had been done. All the way home I kept looking over my shoulder, expecting the thrust of a knife in my back at any moment. That, I suppose, is what the felon sitting beside me must have intended.

The head ballet master at the theatre was aware of my creative ambitions with regard to ballet, and so let me sit in on rehearsals. I was to keep quiet, and not draw attention to myself. Hiding behind the grand piano on Wednesday afternoons, I would spend hours, observing different stages of rehearsal and learning about various styles of Historical and Character dance by 'corps de ballet'. I would jot down old and new interpretations of various compositions, using my own system of shorthand. I tried to memorise by ear the main musical themes and leitmotifs of familiar scores. At home I would transcribe these memories on to sheet music before going to sleep, checking them against the live sound on the accordion. Sometimes I would go through the same exercise on the piano at the Mariners' Centre. I would analyse the musical structure of every dance, phrase by phrase, and bar by bar. Then I would compare that with my notes on movements, made at rehearsals. Thus my familiarity with Historical and Character dances grew. I used this collection to learn about the nature and development of these genres; the principles of their composition; styles of a particular historical period and their cultural context; musical metres; tempo/rhythms and musical dynamics; reprises, variations, elaborations; pauses (fermatas), and other forms of dramatisation used in choreography.

Every day I discovered something new for myself. I tried to record it in my head, in my muscles, or on paper, as much as was possible to do. In that period of active self-education I would feel an almost painful yearning to learn everything there was to learn about the art of theatre. Twice a month I took seminars at the Arts Centre: 'Stage Design and Costumes' and 'Critical Analysis of Stage Performance'. They were intended to provide additional background education for the heads of performing arts groups, and were designed to introduce us to the nature and specific features of individual forms and genres in performing arts, in ways that could be of use to us during our careers.

It's hard to imagine now what a vast amount of knowledge a nineteen-year-old beginner had to assimilate both in theory and in physical practice, and through what was, in effect, an inner transformation, in order to be given a chance to be considered for admission to MTA in six years' time. Yet it was the source of all my yearning at that time: not merely to master the academic programme of the ballet school, but also to familiarise myself with the functioning of theatre, in all its creative and production-oriented modes; to establish a rapport with audiences, even if only through participation in the mime scenes and as part of the chorus. Most importantly, I believed in my musical and choreographic abilities, and believed these could be the areas where I would score points in any competition with the soloists of the Bolshoi and Kirov at the admissions exams, whatever titles and special contacts they might have that I didn't.

I knew full well that in the matter of performing skills my competitors would be way ahead of me. The only way I could get the Examination Committee interested in me was by displaying special traits of character and talent not typically found even in the soloists of the ballet theatres. I had to convince the great masters seated behind a table draped in red velvet that I had not only the creative potential to compose and direct original dance compositions, but that I also possessed an innate aptitude for leading a troupe of ballet dancers in all aspects of theatrical performance. I had to convey the image of a goal-oriented personality, one prepared for the relentless acquisition of professional knowledge, not somebody looking for special privileges due to an important position or a distinguished title.

The time came for the regional festival of amateur performing arts groups. Among the judges were some of my teachers: Goldina, Vishnyakov and the director of the Odessa Performing Arts Centre, Lyuftgarten. They all knew me in the context of the classroom. It might have seemed that my personal connection to the judges was a guarantee of success. In fact, the opposite was true. The moral and professional stakes were only raised, especially at such a public event. In the eyes of these people – my teachers – any directorial error on the part of their pupil would reflect badly on them, exposing a failure in their teaching methods. So I had to leave no stone unturned. I terrorised my assistant and the head of public recreation, double-checking that I had not overlooked any possible slip-up on the part of the staff at the Cultural Centre or by interfering but misguided parents. I had already had plenty of opportunities to become acquainted with the working principles of Soviet employees: 'It doesn't matter where you work, as long as you don't have to do any work," and I wanted to prevent any possible failure that might result from bureaucratic bungling.

Both our junior group with 'Pioneers' Summer' and the senior group with 'Celebration on Board Ship' made it to the final round of the competition at the Opera Theatre. The former was to be the opening number of the first half, and the latter was to conclude the show. They both won. After a traditional award ceremony, the performers went to change, while the manager and technicians came down to drink a bottle of champagne provided by me, in honour of our double victory. This was my introduction into the world of Odessa's performing arts, as a young debutant choreographer and head of a dance ensemble. The staff of the Mariners' Centre warmly congratulated me on this double debut: the birth of a new children's ensemble and of their new leader.

My social and personal life was almost non-existent: "Hi and bye." I only just had time to drop in at Mother's bodega on Mondays, my day off, to see her and have a bite. I would also see Roman there and engage him in one of our chess duels. He would usually sacrifice his queen at the start, but still manage to defeat me within a mere five minutes of any game we played, whispering: "Checkmate."

On rare occasions, my cousin David would also stop by when I was there. Sipping *kvass* (a popular non-alcoholic drink made from fermented rye) and munching on *pirozhki* (meat pasties) we would sing old romances to the delight of inebriated customers. Any of my childhood friends who wished to see me would come to the bodega on Mondays for a couple of hours in the evening. We would noisily exchange news and the latest gossip; sing, laugh, and play dominoes until Mother chased us out.

By this time, Yosif and I had completely gone our separate ways, but he still tried to get at me whenever he had an opportunity to do so, with remarks like, "Mother had three sons: two were clever, and the third was a ballerina."

I never took the bait, only responding, "A barking dog was never a good biter."

My girlfriends considered me a lost cause, accusing the muse of dance, Terpsichore, for having stolen me. I missed their company too, but no more than that. Once, on the street, I ran into Lucy and froze on the spot. She attempted to walk round me, but I thrust out a leg, blocking her path.

"Oh, it's you!" she growled, "How's life?"

"Come to my new abode near the Opera Theatre and see for yourself."

"Why would I do that, after you've been AWOL for six months?"

"Just to spend some time together, as in the good old days under the stars."

"Oh, so now we call it 'spending time together'? I thought it was just 'screwing'?"

"Why so rude?"

"Farewell, you wretched clown!" this one-time friend of mine said, cutting me off, and walking away.

I stood speechless with my mouth open, watching her go.

While in Moscow the previous summer, I had popped into a second-hand book store opposite the Bolshoi. Not believing my luck, I'd picked up three books there by the great masters of ballet:

A. Vaganova's *Fundamentals of Classical Ballet* (Leningrad),
F. Lopukhov and A. Chiriaeff's *The Fundamentals of Character Dance* (Leningrad),
B. Ivanovsky's *Historical Dance of the 13th–19th Centuries* (Leningrad).

These 'sacred writs' not only fed my creativity and helped my teaching, but also lit a lasting spark of interest in research. At MTA, Dean Shatin had warned me that, after the official exams, members of the Admissions Committee, which typically consisted of the leading masters of stagecraft in all genres, would conduct a personal interview with candidates who had passed the first round of admission. At the interview, applicants would be asked about Russian performing arts, and about the widely known details of its social and cultural development. A good result at the interview could decide the fate of a future producer/choreographer.

This was the stumbling block which I had to negotiate over the next few years. Naturally, I had no idea, even in very general terms, what the sociopolitical ideology was in the spheres I would have to operate in. The issue was not simply being able to name composers and ballet masters or to name the places and times of their creative output. The state Admissions Committee would want to evaluate the general educational level of each candidate, assessing his/her analytical ability as well as his/her social and cultural background. I sought advice from Lyuftgarten. He listened to me very attentively, making notes and asking questions periodically to clarify various points. Then he looked over his schedule.

"Misha, I've been thinking about this very subject for some time. I'm convinced the leaders of our Performing Arts groups would be very interested in deepening their professional understanding. Thanks to you, I've discovered a way of conducting three-month courses on the history of Performing Arts, inviting speakers from the Conservatoire and the university. It is simply unacceptable that our members of performing groups should know more than their directors."

I sighed with relief. There's a Russian saying: 'The prey often runs towards the hunter.'

I spent a long time with Lyuftgarten, discussing the schedule of courses for the next three years, grouping together related subjects into six consecutive seminars: musical instruments and ensembles; vocalists and choral singing; mime and drama; dancers and ballet troupes; clowns and circus; figure skating and artistic gymnastics. Even in very broad terms, such a rich programme could fill in the gaps in the professional education of the leaders of amateur Performing Arts groups. But for anyone looking for more, it could also open up the scientific and aesthetic secrets of the relationships between the different forms of audio and visual expression.

At the school, everyone was preparing for final exams. In early June, we had to take the exam in Classical dance. The guys were worried, not just because this was our first official examination, but also because Ludmilla had slightly overloaded the finale of the allegro with exercises that were still too technically difficult for our level. We understood that the teacher wanted to present her students and her work in the best possible light, but it was too much too soon. Physically, we were capable of performing anything with ease: we could jump high, and we breathed steadily. At the same time, exercises that demanded a higher level of technical training, did not look very good when we tried to execute them. Only the two young men who had studied for three years at the the Pioneers' Centre ballet studio were able to perform them adequately. As for the rest of us, it all looked rather shabby.

At the request of my classmates, I went to the teacher with the suggestion that only those two younger guys took part in the display of these technically difficult numbers, at the end of the main programme. It was not a request I wanted to make, but I had to try.

To my surprise, as she looked into my frightened eyes, Ludmilla did not attempt to scratch them out, but instead kissed each one and smiled back sweetly, saying: "Mishka from Odessa, if you could only see how funny you look at this moment!"

Two lessons prior to the exam, and without any comment, Tzhomelidze scrapped the technically difficult elements from some two or three exercises, as if she had planned to from the start. It was a wise move: not to place some of the students in the group above the others.

After the lesson, looking over all her troublemakers, she concluded with satisfaction: "Boys, you truly are much better performers than you think you are."

We sighed with relief. Ludmilla burst out laughing in her Georgian contralto, and we applauded her.

The Examination Committee consisted of Chief Ballet Master Vronsky, our coaches from the theatre, and the director of the ballet school, Rels, together with our teachers. The demonstration lasted an hour, and proceeded at a good tempo. It began with a somewhat heavy set of exercises at the barre, followed by an array of different combinations in the centre, all without any of us making a single sound. We exhibited our spatial awareness individually, each of us according to his own technical abilities; with impeccable tempo/rhythm, in harmony with the pianist. We displayed a clear gradation of technical difficulty within the framework of such an introductory course. Everything we did bore out the logic and method behind the sequence of exercises we were doing, in respect of both their physical and their technical difficulty. It was as if our teacher had put a spell on us.

Our level of concentration, as well as our control in the execution of these movements, enabled us to achieve what would have been impossible for kids to achieve. When we heard the final command: "Take your bows!" we were surprised that we had already come to the end of the demonstration. A round of applause from the committee at our ceremonial exit served as the best evaluation of the teacher and her students. When Ludmilla came out of the examination hall to congratulate us and say goodbye to her 'slow-thinkers', I presented her with a bouquet of eleven roses on behalf of the group, one from each of us, and a card with each of our signatures. We gave her a big round of applause, while she gave each of us a kiss. Rels came out as well, and introduced our new teacher of Classical dance and 'Pas de deux' for the following year, Nikolai Yegorov. He had been a soloist of ballet for twenty-five years before retiring.

The exam in Classical dance behind us, we now switched our attention to Character dance. Daily, for three hours before lunch, we would work alone with the pianist, and then, for two hours after lunch, with the teacher. In the morning we would spend an hour at the barre, polishing the elementary technique of movements, coordinating them with positions of the head and free hand. In centre practice, I would first dance facing the mirror before the two rows of my classmates, then I would correct them, or work with them on their weaker elements. It was hellish work. Afterwards I would have to rest for half an hour on the floor, during the lunch break, recovering my energies for the next session of work with the teacher. Vishnyakov rarely interfered with the practice at the barre, only doing so if there was a serious mistake to be corrected. He corrected small details individually and on the go, without stopping the music. In centre practice, we would drive our teacher mad, not so much with our poor technical execution, but with our stony faces, which were merely the result of our efforts at concentration. But to perform a Character dance without expressing its emotional content is pointless. The impact of this form in the staging of a show lies in the degree of expression one brings to the role.

It was not Vishnyakov's objective to show a wide range of Character dances in different styles at our exam. Rather, he was trying to graft on to the classical base we had just acquired the potential for performing the technical elements of a completely different genre. It was hard for my colleagues to understand, let alone accept, the demands of our teacher: to turn the knees in rather than out; to contract, rather than stretch out the sole of the foot, and so on. The problem was that these contrasting techniques (of classical versus Character dance) were being taught far too close together in time. It made the task of digesting and absorbing the principles of each much more difficult. It also gave rise to a good deal of resentment and frustration among the students.

The truth was it was not easy, even for me who had been studying various dances for some eight years by then, to switch from one style to another. I tried to put this challenge into perspective for my colleagues: "There'll be even more contrasting styles we'll have to learn, when moving from the medieval epoch to the Renaissance, and from Renaissance to Baroque, in Historical Dance. The broader our range of knowledge and the richer our dance vocabulary," I argued, "the higher our qualifications as ballet dancers will be." Only the super-fit could endure our training marathon. Observing the state of my classmates I seriously wondered whether we would all manage to get past the finishing line.

For the examination routine at the barre, Ivan placed me first in line, right foot front, so that my peers, standing behind, could observe me and follow my lead. For the same reason, he also placed me strategically in the middle of the front line in the demonstration of centre practice. He saw that I stood out in the class thanks to my technical skill and capacity for expression, and so he assigned to me a few additional elements in centre practice, which were more difficult, both technically and stylistically, than those assigned to the rest of the group. Not wishing to break away too much from my colleagues, I asked Ivan to alternate my solo demonstrations with those of the whole group. During the exercises at the barre, many members of the Examination Committee smiled to themselves sarcastically or condescendingly, noticing our hopeless attempts at performing something that we were as yet incapable of executing. Innesa and Ludmilla would nod to us from time to time by way of encouragement.

The atmosphere in the hall was tense. Those twenty minutes by the barre seemed like an eternity to us. It was clear to everyone in the room that our demonstration had only confirmed a well-established axiom: in art, there is no room for miracles. The acknowledged geniuses of ballet, such as Nijinsky and Nureyev, Karsavina and Plisetskaya, had achieved success only thanks to constant, systematic and unrelenting practice. Without that, as history has amply shown, even a brilliant natural talent runs the risk of remaining undeveloped in practice and 'rotting in the bud'.

During the break after the barre exercises, I hissed at my colleagues who were wiping sweat from their faces in the corner of the room: "Wake up, you sleeping beauties! It looks like you've all pooed your pants in fear!"

They all cracked up with laughter.

"Come on, Odessans! Let's show them what we're made of! If we're going to go out, let's do it in style!"

"Misha, what is it? Are you telling some fresh anecdotes there?"

"Oh, no, Ivan Nikolayevich," I replied. "Our group itself is the freshest anecdote in town."

All the examiners burst out laughing. The tension in the room relaxed a bit.

In centre practice, we were as if transformed. At the start of the first étude, standing in the centre of the first line, I looked over my shoulder and winked at the guys, scowling with a scary face. They nodded in understanding. Our manly air, and the relaxing effect this break in tension had on our bodies, produced, for some inexplicable reason, and to the astonishment of all those present, a small miracle. With composure and confidence, we moved through one cascade of combinations after another, deriving pleasure from our own performance. The committee members sat with their mouths open, unable to understand what had happened to us. Vishnyakov himself could not believe our transformation. The last étude, a shortened version of the 'Sailors' Dance' from Glière's ballet *The Red Poppy*, just knocked everyone off their feet. The guys let out shouts; I whistled. We finished and froze, looking at Vronsky. He held a pause, making a decision. Then got up and applauded. This is rare in exams. The rest of the committee also stood and applauded, while Vronsky shook Vishnyakov's hand.

Turning to us, Vronsky said: "I hope to see you soon on our stage. Good luck to you!"

It was, we knew, not the quality of our technical execution that had drawn the applause and the commendation of the theatre's director and the committee, but our sudden, and unexpected, spiritual transformation in the course of the exam.

On the morning after the exam, I couldn't get out of bed. All my muscles hurt so badly, it was as if I had been pounded all over with clubs the day before. When my landlady came knocking on my door at midday, I could barely drag my feet over to open the door. Seeing me in such a state, she got a fright at first, but then, upon hearing my explanation, insisted I come downstairs to take a hot bath with salts.

I protested: "Do you intend to marinade me, and without spices?"

"The spices you can have later," the old woman smirked. "By the way, dear, a pretty young woman came by yesterday with her daughter and left a love letter for you here. Trust me, women like her do not want marinated men. So, get your pyjamas and come downstairs in fifteen minutes, and meanwhile I will heat up some buckets of water for you, and brew a special herb for a healing bath."

It was only when I read Oksana's note that I realised, being so absorbed in the exams at the ballet school, that I had completely forgotten about my job at the Cultural Centre. The kids had a break at the end of June for school exams, but the heads of the ensembles were still expected to show up for work, or make an arrangement with the administration regarding their temporary absence. *Oh, my God, what an idiot I am! I could so easily lose my job that way.*

I started cleaning up in my room and had forgotten all about the bath when I heard Maria Ivanovna shout from downstairs: "Misha, it's all ready! Come now!" She reminded me of my mother, whom I had not visited for a while.

On the way down, I suddenly remembered that I had forgotten my soap and sponge in my room and I turned to run up to get them, only for some reason all I could do was crawl on all fours, like a tortoise. Every step was accompanied by a sharp piercing pain in one side or the other. *Catastrophe! How am I going to be able to work?*

The water in the bathtub was green and smelled of forest. Seeing my doubtful grimace, the hostess explained: "This is pine needles and rutabagas, both excellent for sore muscles. After this soak, I am going to give you a massage with olive oil, as I used to for my young footballers. Now they have all left the nest and don't need my help." While my hostess was busy in the kitchen, I was able to relax completely in the tub and began to feel the pain in my back and legs receding. My physical system was returning to its normal state. When the hostess returned, I was standing with my back to the door, all soaped up, and working hard with a sponge all over my body.

"I've brought two containers for you here. Mix the hot water with the cold and rinse yourself. When you've finished, come out into the hallway, and I'll rub your back and feet there on the bench."

I began to protest, but she was already out of the door. *She is like a fairy godmother! I've been living here for half a year, little suspecting that behind that severe mask of hers lay the kindness of a mother with a big heart.*

During her massage, I asked if she liked ballet.

"Before the war, my husband, may he rest in peace, and I often attended the opera. He was a professor of medicine at the university, the one on Olgyeva Street."

"Well, if you're interested in seeing your patient in action, dancing onstage, please come next Sunday to the Opera Theatre. There will be a concert of the Odessa School of Ballet at 1 p.m. It's free to get in. If anyone stops you, tell them that Misha from the ballet is your lodger. I'm the only Misha there, and everyone knows me." I couldn't resist boasting a little to my landlady.

CHAPTER 3 BAPTISM OF LOVE

At the end of the performing season, I met with my assistant, Oksana, at the Mariners' Centre to discuss our imminent plans for the summer. She informed me that the Director had extended our salary to include the month of June because we had been working overtime in the previous six months. This was a great boon. We decided to start rehearsals with the senior group of the children's ensemble from 1st July in order to prepare for the performing tour in August. The group were supposed to learn two new dances over three weeks: one for girls and another for boys. They were also supposed to rehearse the 'Marine Suite' with a reduced number of performers (sixteen girls and eight boys). For the tour, our group was combined with a vocal ensemble from the naval college: twelve youths with their leader/accompanist. Their repertoire was broad and varied, and included solo numbers, duets, and trios. To match their contribution, we needed to add a couple of numbers to our own programme.

Then I remembered the two youths from the Pioneers' Centre and proposed to Oksana that we use them in two duets, which I could choreograph on an impromptu basis. They would not look very different from our sixteen-year-olds and would also bolster the male component of our ensemble. At this moment, a warden entered the office where we were sitting and asked us to leave because she had to lock the building at six o'clock. We took the lists of the ensemble members and went down to Luna Park across the street from the Mariners' Centre.

In a cosy niche under the acacia tree, I remarked to Oksana: "We should have come here from the start." Our eyes met. "Oksana, do you think Plakhov [director of the Mariners' Centre] would agree to let in two soloists from the outside?"

"I will ask him tomorrow," she said.

"You will probably come with Lyubanya to the school's concert at the Opera Theatre on Sunday. Please, let me know then what he says, so that I can make arrangements with the boys right away."

"What is this? A new way of asking a girl out?"

"Oksana, dear, I'm sorry, I've been so busy lately. I value you as a colleague. I also respect you a great deal and like you, and yet I know so little about you: only that your daughter was accepted by the ballet school, and that her father was killed in action. But that's all." The widow's eyes misted over. "Please, forgive me," I whispered, giving her a hug.

She clung to me silently, and I felt her tears rolling down my neck, and was afraid to stir. After what seemed a very long pause, she lifted her head.

"Mishanya, you are a decent man and an acknowledged talent. I would love so much to bear you a son, who would be just like his father, down to the smallest detail. But forgive me, I'm daydreaming. . . ."

Another Lucy? I thought.

Oksana gently tried to free herself from my embrace, but I only wrapped my arms around her more tightly.

"Oksana, like any woman, you must be able to tell that I am attracted to you. At present, I have no one closer to me than you, in every sense. I'm not bothered at all by our nine-year difference in age, or by the fact that you have a daughter. But you also know about my plans to 'sail away' in five years, once and for all, returning to Odessa only for short visits to see Mother, friends and old teachers."

Pressing her head to my shoulder, she nodded, not demurring from anything I'd said.

"You already have one child growing up without a father. Why would you want another in the same situation? Please understand: I could never forgive myself this mistake, my dear."

"I love you, and want to have a son who would be a living image of you."

"But how can you know it would be a boy?"

"I'm certain of it."

"And what will your friends, colleagues, relatives think?"

"Mishenka, does it matter when you really love someone? I am twenty-eight. Who will take me, with a child on my hands? And what husband is going to tolerate my passion for dance? Please, forget everything I said."

"How can I forget what you said, when I love you too? Only I did not wish to show it, or lead you on, or ruin your already difficult life."

"My dear magician, you have already broken my heart. If you have a mind to glue it back together again, then please take me to your nest."

She pressed her lips to mine under the thick canopy of the acacia. Half reclining on my lap, she curled and stretched her body against mine, exciting me to the very limit. A metronome was ticking in my head: *To be or not to be?*

Straightening up on the bench, I whispered, looking into her sparkling eyes: "Come with me, sweet temptress. No one can escape one's fate."

She smiled happily, fixing her hair and buttoning up her blouse.

"Just one thing, my dear. I need to stop off at the cloakroom for a minute to pick up a bag."

She curtseyed. "As you wish, my Apollo. Only tell me if this is really happening, or am I just dreaming?"

I pinched her playfully to prove she was not dreaming.

I was only gone for a minute, but when I came back outside with my laundry bag, she was nowhere to be seen. It was embarrassing to call out, and in the dark I could not make out her familiar form anywhere. *She must have changed her mind,* I decided, *so then that solves my dilemma.*

Entering my house, I ran into the landlady, and asked her about the show. She confirmed that she would be coming with her granddaughters. I reminded her about the young woman with a daughter who had left a note for me a few days before, and told her that the said person might be coming to visit me from now on.

"Well, if it's just that one, I don't mind. You are young. I understand."

The dress rehearsal of our Historical dance the following morning was threatening to turn into a complete disaster. The girls, in floor-length dresses, were busy practising how to move about without stepping on their hems, but kept tripping up and falling over, getting up and giggling, then falling over again with their next step. We, their partners, in tights, velvet breeches and embroidered vests, looked (in the absence of wigs and make-up) like patients who'd recently escaped from an asylum. Thirty minutes of valuable time was lost in getting used to our costumes. The men's footwear – soft velvet shoes with long curled-up toes – was simply killing us. The shoes made our feet longer, which in turn made movement awkward and difficult when dancing with a partner. We kept catching the hems of the girls' dresses with our pointy toes and lifting their skirts up to the knees. The ladies were squealing, the men cackling, and Goldina was sitting there going very pale, completely regretting the very idea of a dress rehearsal.

At the sight of this chaos, my comic mood instantly changed, sensing impending disaster. I approached our teacher with a tentative request: "Innesa Markovna, may I try?"

She raised her hand in protest: "No, Misha. I can see for myself . . ."

"Please, let me speak directly with everybody, but without you in the room. I might be able to salvage some of what we managed to achieve earlier."

She looked me straight in the eye, got up and left the room. The noise behind me gradually subsided. Everyone was looking at me in anticipation.

I turned to my colleagues: "Dear friends, if these costumes were given to monkeys in a zoo, they would create less of a hullabaloo than ours."

"Yes, but we are not monkeys!" the leader of the girls protested, clearly piqued.

"That's just my point," I raised my voice, staring her down.

"There's an old Arab proverb which goes: 'In every new undertaking there hides a snake.' In the Middle Ages, it would take years for dancers to get used to such dresses, while we're being asked to do the same in a few hours. It's no wonder these inconveniences irritate us, obstructing our movements and distracting our attention. But we're not apes! Surely we're capable of overcoming these inconveniences and taking a mature approach to the challenge? Goldina is now considering removing our suite altogether from the concert programme, because she has lost faith in our ability to make it work. I propose that we instantly adopt a professional attitude and, without any further farce, help each other deal with the stumbling and falling-over. I am going to call Innesa, and we're going to act as if nothing had happened. Is that agreed?"

Everyone returned to their dancing positions without a word.

I explained to the teacher the issues we were facing, and the dress rehearsal then continued in a heightened emotional atmosphere. The teacher patiently bore with our stumbling, and we, with equal patience, helped each other in the dance. This might seem strange, but the guys behaved much more maturely than the girls. Perhaps, this was indeed due to the fact that they were older. They adapted to the unusual costumes faster, apologising to their partners for poor turns, and taking care not to step on the hems of their dresses. Unfortunately, the girls (fifteen to sixteen years old) were used to giggling at the slightest provocation. And now, they were bursting into nervous laughter at every stumble or mistake, not so much because they were enjoying themselves, but because they were unable to control their clumsiness in such cumbersome dresses. The guys were barely able to hide their irritation and shot exasperated glances at me, each time another girl stumbled and then giggled.

The school rules dictated that only a group leader could speak in the classroom. Following one such breakdown in discipline, I came up to the girls' leader, Galina, during the musical interlude, and hissed at her with a smile, making sure everyone could hear: "We are human beings, not monkeys! This behaviour is intolerable and needs to stop right now."

Her face turned red, while I returned to my place, continuing to smile sweetly at the teacher. The girls' leader approached her giggling colleagues and told them off with some force. From then on, the stumbling and falling-over magically ceased. Apparently, our senses had become sharpened from nervous shock. Our self-control and attention to our partners greatly improved. The last run-through went off without interruption. Innesa, with a contented smile on her face, thanked everyone for the outstanding work and reminded us not to be late for the dress rehearsal onstage the next day. As if on cue we sank into a deep curtsey in the style of the thirteenth century. All faces glowed with satisfaction. The pianist patted me on the shoulder as he left.

On Saturday, at the full rehearsal for the school concert I helped Innesa work out all our entrances and exits through the wings. In the process, I pointed out to the teacher the uneven surface of the wooden stage floor. As a result of repeatedly nailing props to the floor, it was full of bumps and holes. The hems of dresses would surely catch on the splintered wood and ruin the performance.

Goldina was horrified: "What are we to do?"

"Perhaps we could ask the artistic director to have some linoleum laid over the original rough floor?"

"Good idea. So then this afternoon, we won't do the demonstration onstage, but fully dressed, in the ballet studio. Last time, the run-through didn't go too badly. And, Misha, thank you! Your help is invaluable!"

With this she ran off to warn the members of the Examination Committee about the change of the exam's location. Meanwhile I gathered my colleagues together and told them that the next rehearsal would take place onstage, but without costumes.

Just then, the stage director came up to us, asking what the change of plan was all about. When he heard what I had to say, he gave his own appraisal of the situation:

"Stagehands are off until four in the afternoon, so we cannot do anything about the linoleum now. Tomorrow, they'll prepare everything in the morning, which gives us from ten till twelve to rehearse the entire programme. Your group opens the concert, and I can give you ten minutes to orient yourselves, but not more than that."

With this, we hurried off to change.

Goldina was already waiting for us in the make-up/wardrobe area. She apologised for the problems with the costumes and, to our great relief, reported that today's exam at two could not be moved from the stage to the ballet studio because the latter was being used at that time for a ballet rehearsal. Therefore, the school director had agreed to count our performance in the concert the following day as the exam in Historical dance, since all the examiners would be present in the audience anyway. The artistic director called us back on to the stage urgently and asked us to check the plan of all entrances and exits one more time before the start. Seeing the disoriented expressions on the faces of some of the girls, I sensed that they were experiencing stage fright at the prospect of performing on the real opera stage for the first time. The men, by contrast, after a year's practice in mime scenes felt totally comfortable onstage. I suggested that they lead their partners, rather than follow them in all the movements, and delicately apply pressure to direct them, if they should lose their confidence and bearings.

By nine the following morning, we were already in our make-up/dressing rooms. All costumes and shoes had been made ready at eight. Two costume coordinators, one female and one male, checked that each set of clothing was complete, in good order and the right size for each of us. This time round, we were also handed headgear and instructed on how to use it. At nine-thirty, Innesa called us to the stage, to inspect our costumes and shoes. We marched, without music, up and down the stage, rehearsing our entrances and exits through particular wings, and adjusting to the newly expanded spaces between ourselves and our partners, created by the bulk of the costumes, and the limited space available in the areas of the stage that were lit. In principle, both the artistic director and Goldina were satisfied with the progress we had made, although we ourselves were keenly aware of the weakness of our artistic expression, as we concentrated on the dancing technique and the spatial patterns of our choreographic figures. Certainly, such stage qualities are important in ballet. But we didn't want to end up looking like stiff puppets. In the end, what mattered in a performance was the way we interacted with our partners.

After our rehearsal, I asked Galina to gather all the girls together in the lobby for an important announcement. When all the 'historians' (a nickname for those studying Historical dance) had finally arrived and carefully settled themselves in their chairs (so as to avoid ruining their dresses), I began by expressing my sympathy for their tiredness. I then enquired: "What do you think of our first joint performance on the stage of the Opera Theatre? Is this all we are capable of, for the presentation of the Medieval Historical dance?"

The girls' leader burst out: "Misha, what are you asking? When we're onstage, how do we know what's missing from our performance?"

"I would agree with you, if it was all just a matter of dancing technique or following the choreography onstage. But these are only the external means by which we give expression to our inner state of being. If that inner content is lacking, then all that is left is just a decorative empty shell. I happened to overhear a conversation backstage between our dance masters. He said, 'It is an interesting suite, but these "walking corpses" have no idea what characters they are supposed to be playing. This is a pitiful caricature of the Middle Ages.' She replied: 'You are being too harsh. This is just a school concert, not a professional performance. They lack stage experience.' And he said, 'If that's the case, let them dance at their school and gain stage experience at cultural centres. To allow such poor quality on this stage is an insult to art.'"

Both my male and female colleagues shouted in protest:

"What do we care what these theatre snobs think of us!?"

"If it had been that bad, Innesa would have told us."

"And actually, Misha, you are overreaching yourself a bit, choosing to criticise us like this."

At this point, Sasha from Peresyp, who had been silent up to this point, cut in: "You, little whippersnapper, why don't you just wipe your nose and shut up, and think before you go attacking our head? So, we are sitting and wasting time here, and no one has yet proposed what we can do today to improve our performance tomorrow. I'm normally quite a sceptical person, but I can tell you that in the Character dance exam, Misha managed to whip us into shape in ten seconds, and with a positive result too. And now he seems to have a piece of useful advice for us as well, and we are acting like haggling countrywomen at Privoz market."

Galina looked enquiringly in my direction. Everyone was waiting for my reaction.

I paused for a moment before responding: "I understand everyone's frustration, and take no offence. Sasha, thanks for your confidence in me!"

"You owe me one," he said. "Don't think you can get away with just a simple 'thank you'."

Everyone laughed, and the atmosphere in the lobby lightened up.

"As far as dance technique goes, and our spatial orientation, there is little chance of us improving on these by tomorrow. But in terms of style and emotional expression, we can make miracles happen in just a couple of hours today and tomorrow morning during the final rehearsal. In Historical dance, the key is not to imitate the teacher, me, or the dancing figures depicted on the paintings in the lobby, but to express our own personalities and modes of behaviour. What I have in mind is to try and fix our mechanical movements, which are hampered by heavy costumes which are rather uncomfortable for dancing. In our Conservatoire library, I have read several books about the specific style of movements dancers employed at the balls, as well as the affected, exaggerated manner of interaction between partners during dances and in the intervals in between. I could demonstrate a few examples and you will see that they are not difficult to memorise and perform in your own style.

"The main thing is to liberate our imaginations and to transport ourselves into that distant and foreign social milieu, one where a dancer cannot just tell his lady to shut up and wipe her nose. At the same time, in that society, a lady would never embarrass her partner. We could still surprise our guests tomorrow, if we make the effort now to get acquainted with the principles of this dancing style."

"Well, if what you are saying is true, why haven't we heard it from our teacher?" the same girl as before piped in.

Sasha raised his hands in a gesture of silent wrath. I pressed a forefinger to my lips to signal silence to him.

Galina went over to the girl and told her quietly: "I think you would be better off keeping mum. Innesa spoke about this at the very beginning of the course. Only you paid no attention. You chat during lessons too much, and you distract others."

"Misha," she turned to me, "we are ready to work. Girls, let's move to the corner lobby and practise there."

Using the prim processional steps and curtseys of the thirteenth-century branle, I demonstrated two contrasting versions of that dancing style.

Ahead of the demonstration I spoke to my partner: "Sonia, do you feel shy with me?"

"A little."

"Are you afraid of me?"

"No."

"Do you trust me?"

"Depends in what."

"Are you comfortable dancing with me?"

"Very much."

"Why?"

"Because you are always confident in your moves and patient in correcting my mistakes."

I bowed before her in the medieval style. She, without hesitation, responded with a beautifully executed curtsey. Everyone clapped.

"Now, pair up, and try the same thing. Only, please, in all seriousness, before doing this, try to transport yourselves into the thirteenth century. Imagine that you are in a huge assembly room, where guests are waiting to participate in a high-society ball. Men rapidly scan the room in search of a companion for the evening. Having fixed on their object of interest, they proceed to their targets in a most stately manner. Locking eyes for the briefest of moments, he and she assume the classically prescribed poses of that epoch: she of a waiting lady, he of an approaching gentleman. He, with exaggerated attention, invites his chosen lady with a stylish bow. She, with a played-up shyness, either shows her assent by a formal curtsey, or declines the invitation with a gesture, signalling a previous engagement."

The walls of the lobby were hung with huge eighteenth-century mirrors. Checking their reflections, my colleagues strove hard to transport themselves into the thirteenth century. Seeing how difficult it was for them to do that, with giggling girls at their side, I approached Galina to express my concerns and asked her permission to address the girls separately. She gathered her colleagues in the corner once more, and I embarked on one last attempt to appeal to their sense of reason and propriety.

"Charming ladies, it so happens that when a person laughs incessantly, he, or she, inevitably loses their self-control. This is a well-known phenomenon, and you've now had an opportunity to see it for yourselves. You are only fifteen or sixteen years old, but you are no longer kids. You are young women. Were you living in certain other countries, you would be getting married and bearing children by now."

My audience shuddered involuntarily, but Galina motioned them to be still.

"Very understandably, your mothers warn you against obnoxious males and premature sex. But the way you are acting now is quite out of order. We are not rehearsing some scene of physical intimacy from Chekhov or Dostoevsky here; we are merely trying to express, in an ironic way, the mannered flirtation that would take place at medieval balls. None of you would think twice about playing the coquette in front of a mirror or with whomsoever you like, but all of a sudden here, in dance, you strike a pose: 'I am not that kind of a girl.' In three months, in September, we will all be starting a training course in partnering. In the lifting curriculum of that course, there will be much more physical contact between us. Do you imagine that our instructor is going to tolerate your giggles every time a partner has to lift you up by the waist and then hold you above the knees with your bottom pressed to his chest, to prevent you from sliding down during the dance movement? Do you really think that a ballet artiste, dancing in step with you, and out of breath, thinks of the pleasure of touching Vera, Lyuda, or Zhenya, as he is lifting a heavy girl up in the air at the limit of his strength? After six years of studying ballet, I can assure you the answer is 'no'.

"I'm sorry, ladies, but those of you not yet ready for physical contact with your dancing partner, should consider changing profession. You now have a brilliant opportunity to overcome your hang-ups and these attacks of nervous giggling. In the court dances of the Middle Ages, physical contact between dancing partners is minimal. If you cannot overcome your psychological barrier now, your career in ballet is doomed. If you have any sense at all, you must try to change your infantile behaviour now, so you don't end up undermining our entire collaborative learning venture in the future. Why should the dancers waste their time and energy because of a few immature girls? Galina, please speak to your colleagues as well. If they really don't want to look like 'walking corpses' tomorrow, we're going to have to practise today, after a bite at the cafeteria, for a couple of hours in the time slot of the cancelled exam. I'm going to demonstrate some standard elements of mime, to be used in paired sequences onstage between dancers. It's intolerable of you to be acting out medieval high society during the dances, and then acting like petty vendors from a bazaar during the silent promenades onstage between dances."

At the end of the rehearsal, I asked the artistic director for permission to stay a little longer in order to practise silent promenades onstage. He relayed my request to the stage manager.

"Is this for your soldiers, commander?" he asked.

I nodded in assent.

"That's fine with me, but only for two hours. Do you need the curtain down?"

"Yes, please."

The stage manager waved to the stagehands, while I gathered my colleagues together.

"Let's work only on the silent promenades from the end of one dance to the beginning of the next. Focus on paying maximum attention to one another, and be very cautious of the heavy dresses during interaction."

"Yes, it's a much better idea, to move across the stage openly, in full view of the audience, than to go stumbling in the dark, with the lights off," commented the artistic director.

Yet it was still very difficult for us to make the transition from branle to farandole, or from sarabande to saltarello. Not only did these dances use different musical measures (4/4 or 6/8, 3/4 or 3/8) and various tempo/rhythmic configurations, but they differed starkly in their different types of stylised steps, each according to its own historical era. Even professionals would have had a hard time performing such different Historical dances in sequence.

By the end of the rehearsal we were all very tired, but pleased with our creative effort and the satisfaction of a difficulty overcome. I complimented the girls on their efforts, and their partners joined in the applause. We resolved to practise the mimic dialogues by ourselves with an imaginary partner, at home in the evening, in front of a mirror, and then to test these out during the morning rehearsal at 10 a.m. Naïvely, we hoped that the audience, admitted free of charge, would be forgiving of our mistakes.

Galina was smiling as she approached me: "My mother is inviting all the 'historians' for a dinner at our place tomorrow, after the concert. This is to celebrate the end of the school year and my birthday, which is on Monday."

I told her that I would discuss this with my colleagues and give her an answer in five minutes. The guys naturally unanimously welcomed an opportunity to relax and have a good meal.

I proposed to contribute a rouble each to buy flowers for the hostess, but a more experienced Sasha corrected me: "Two roubles each, one more for a box of chocolates for the birthday girl."

"Good thinking!" I nodded in approval and then ran off to report our acceptance to Galina.

Innesa had left the rehearsal in low spirits the day before, not realising that, later on, we had embarked on an additional corrective rehearsal. The following morning, she visited boys and girls separately in their dressing rooms to find out how we were feeling. Without any prior agreement, we all uniformly answered: "Fine." She wished us good luck, invited us to meet up in the cafeteria after the rehearsal for a final round of instructions, and went to the stalls to observe our performance from there.

Just before the start of the rehearsal we gathered in the centre of the stage, joined hands in two concentric circles, girls on the inside, boys on the outside, and following a prearranged cue, shouted together: "On, to victory!" and then took our positions onstage. The stage director and musicians were amused by this display, but didn't pause to question us, taking up their own assigned positions for the start of the final run.

A signal was given from the production manager's panel: "Historians, stand by!"

We were already in our designated positions onstage, and dropped into bows and curtseys to one another. The music started, and the curtain floated upwards. The bright light flooded us on every side, but we had got used to this the day before. There was nothing to stop us now.

During promenades between dances, while passing other pairs, I would quietly remind everyone: "In Branle – with measure, without affectation; in Farandole – attention, the skirt is on the floor; in Sarabande – emphasis on stylised movement and grace; in Saltarello – take care in lifting."

By the second dance, our nervousness had disappeared, and we began to enjoy the performance. Finishing the last dance, we froze in an impressive bow.

The artistic director exclaimed, "Bravo, well done!"

We responded with a loud "Hurray!"

The girls ran off to change for their ballet numbers, and the guys went down to watch them perform.

After the rehearsal, Innesa asked the artistic director: "Did you help them with the promenades?"

"No, they stayed after the finale yesterday, and practised on their own. I'm seeing these changes for the first time myself. I think, Innesa, these students of yours show promise. Just give them time."

Meeting us in the cafeteria after this conversation, Innesa enthused, "What a pleasant surprise! I can guess who initiated this."

"My apologies, Innesa Markovna. I wanted to ask your permission, but unfortunately could not find you after the rehearsal yesterday."

"And for this crime I am now going to punish you!"

"I beg you, please have mercy!"

She came up to me and pecked me on the cheek, gratefully. "Misha, I can see now how you earn your kisses."

The guys roared with laughter; and the girls exchanged surprised glances.

"Yesterday, I was aware both of my own and of your failures, but did not wish to upset you before the concert. In Historical dance, the greatest amount of time and patience is required, not to learn the choreography, but to understand the performing style and manner of behaviour in that society. Patience we could find, but time was against us. That is why I decided to leave these mistakes to be corrected next term. I must admit that I have no idea how you managed to turn around the entire psychology of intimate relations in life and onstage in just two hours. But be that as it may, I have no worries about your performance now. Take a rest, relax. And 'break a leg!'"

"To hell with it!" I hurried superstitiously to respond on everyone's behalf, and added, "Sorry, ma'am!" stepping back and raising my hands over my head in mock terror.

Laughing, everyone took off to the dressing rooms. Innesa and I stayed behind and ordered tea.

"Misha, you and I need to get together before 1st July and discuss with the teachers of Character dance and 'Pas de deux' the programme and schedule of joint classes with the girls for the next academic year. Rels has asked me to find out what time would be good for you next week?"

"Well, on Mondays I am at the Arts Centre, and on Fridays at the Conservatoire library. The rest of the week is fine until lunchtime."

"Very good, I'll tell them. But you try to relax now, you look very tired."

Before the start of the show, I called Galina out of the dressing room and asked her to try to instil an upbeat spirit among the girls, in spite of the fact that everyone was tired. She reassured me that everything was going to be fine, and passed me a note with her address on.

"My family are all here for the concert. My mum was really glad to hear that you are all going to come. She promised to have a table for thirty people, including my family, ready in the garden by 5 p.m."

"It's really kind of her. Thanks!" I gave her a quick kiss on the cheek and ran off to my colleagues.

For the hundredth time we checked every part of our costumes and shoes: the security of our belts, so that we did not lose our trousers; our shoelaces, so that we did not fall over during the movements; the elastic on our hats, which could fall off during a jump. All was well, and we were ready to make our stage debut.

The manager's assistant asked me: "Misha, are you all here?"

I looked around and nodded to her.

The stage manager's command sounded on the intercom: "Historians, stand by!" And after a short pause: "Music!"

The curtain began to rise.

In an instant, I switched into a different mode, counting seconds under my breath, without moving my lips: One-21, Two-21, and so on. After making sure that everyone was keeping a uniform tempo/rhythm, I stopped counting, and concentrated instead on my partner. The audience gradually fell silent. The spectators, surprised by the unusual sight before them, stopped munching and coughing, straining instead to recognise their family members under the covering of the strange headgear. The audience were completely silent all the way through the Branle. The dim light of the hanging candelabra, against the backdrop of ancient fortress walls conjured up the gloomy, depressing atmosphere of the early Middle Ages, with its social rigidity, religious Inquisition and lack of artistic freedom. Our faces, lit by the side projectors, looked like theatrical masks. At the finale, the audience was afraid to clap, surmising that perhaps we were representing a funeral procession. When the music had stopped, a few hesitant claps cut the air, but the rest were waiting for what would happen next.

During the first silent transition, I gave a voice signal for Farandole, and made an emphatic gesture to the 'walking corpses'. They quickly got the point, and in a matter of seconds, while the backdrop and lighting were being changed for the next dance, affected a miraculous transformation, coming to life with coquettish smiles. Our playful jumps and gallops produced an animated reaction in the audience and onstage. Then the chains of dancers began to intertwine in variegated patterns, as though in a kaleidoscope. The energised movements onstage, the zigzags, spirals, and figures of eight, so impressed the audience with their quick and varied progression of ornaments executed by us with such spirit and feeling, that the dance's finale was met with loud and enthusiastic applause from this suddenly awakened crowd.

The eccentric interaction of pairs in the next silent transition provoked bursts of laughter from the audience, and our mood lifted visibly. In contrast to the Farandole, the flowing music of the Sarabande introduced an intimate lyrical tone into the romantic interaction between the dance partners. This was a difficult test for our pious maidens, but they passed with flying colours, much to everyone's surprise. The audience was charmed by the dance. We, in turn, inspired by the warm reception, began to overdo our role playing a little during the next transition. I had to send a 'telegram' through my teeth again: "Don't overdo it." But at the approach to the pompous Saltarello, it was no longer possible to restrain my fired-up colleagues.

In a gesture of support for the vigour and energy of our performance, the artistic director sent a drummer, armed with a tambourine, into the midst of our musicians. The charming ladies, who had all mellowed down during the Sarabande, perked up in an instant. They decided to show their partners and the audience, the fiery Italian side of true Odessans. Moved by this, the dancers appeared to forget their fatigue and, propelling their own partners into the air, caught others in turn; then catching and holding the girls in their arms, one arm on the waist, and the other under the knees, they spun on the spot like a tornado. The girls squealed but did not give way, playfully slapping their partners in duet combinations, or turning under their partners' arms, while the latter galloped around them. The audience were beside themselves. Children were screaming from the rush of emotion, while the dancers' mothers shed tears of parental pride. This was truly a small but fitting climax to the tremendous amount of work we had put in. We had not expected such a furore of an ending, especially given the rather mortifying beginning.

At the end of the show, all the school's teachers and the artistic director joined the performers onstage for a bow. When the curtain fell, the artistic director thanked the staff and remarked on the successful 'overture' of the 'Hysterical' – that is, 'Historical' – group. Everyone chuckled, and congratulated us. The men went to stand behind their partners, squatted down, and then, placing their hands on their partners' hips rose, lifting them in the air. The girls placed their own hands over those of their partners to perform this jump. This was a promising sign for our future work together in the 'Pas de deux' course. The girls, landing on their feet, turned round simultaneously to face their partners, giving each a kiss on the cheek. The guys were stunned by this gesture, which was doubtless Innesa's idea; she, at this moment, was clapping louder than anyone else. This small token of recognition was greatly appreciated by the men, who typically felt constrained next to their female partners.

Saying goodbye until September, Goldina congratulated us sincerely, and also gave each of us a kiss in front of everyone, as a way of underlining both her appreciation for our efforts and her approval and support. Overall, we were well pleased with the results of the first year. Then I suddenly remembered that Oksana was waiting for me by the staff entrance. I dashed downstairs and seeing mother and daughter, asked the security guard's permission to let them in. While the warden was talking with Lyubanya, I whispered to Oksana that I would be expecting her, with my landlady's blessing, tomorrow at seven, on the corner by my house. She acknowledged the invitation and in turn relayed to me Plakhov's approval of two soloists for the August cruise. After saying goodbye to my visitors, I went to inform the young soloists about the project. They were to let me know of their decision the following day, between five and six in the evening, at which time, if they were interested, I would give them further details. Both were intrigued by the idea of the cruise.

After showering, we ran home to change for our visit to Galina's house. We arranged to meet at the final tram stop at 4.30 p.m. Sasha was entrusted with buying flowers and chocolates.

"If the collected money isn't enough, I'll make it up out of my own pocket," I told them. "No need for your charity, Mr Millionaire! We'll all contribute equally."

Weighed down by the accordion, I arrived a few minutes late. The passengers on my tram were shocked to see me surrounded by such a riotous gang, whistling and waving their fists. The tram driver tried to scare off the rowdy gang by loudly honking his horn, just as the hooligans were attempting to beat me up. But then he noticed a bouquet of roses among the gangsters and realised it was safe to move off.

Meanwhile I addressed the gang: "So, who loves music here?"

The first sucker to raise his hand, was handed the heavy accordion to carry and complimented by howls of derision from everyone present.

At 5 p.m. we approached the only noisy house on a quiet country road, and were greeted by the young hostess: "Hi, guys! Long time no see! Come on in."

Giving Galina our best wishes, I presented her, on behalf of the class, with a box of chocolates and a kiss on the cheek. After me, all ten vagabonds repeated the procedure.

Watching this, I exclaimed: "Galya, now I see how you earn your kisses."

Everyone laughed.

Galina's mother agreed, "That is exactly why she invited all of you. No need to blush, my dear. You'll have to give each one a goodbye kiss later on as well, in accordance with the demands of thirteenth-century court etiquette."

"Madam, and these twentieth-century flowers are a gift from the multi-tasking male team of the Ballet Department. We pledge to laugh, eat, and sing all night long, if you please."

"Well, you are most welcome! Boys, why don't you sit down?"

"We are confused by the empty chairs between the girls. Let them cast lots or choose who to have as their table companion."

"How will the lots work?" the birthday girl asked.

"We'll cut up strips of paper and write our names on them. I'll hold the strips in my palm hiding the names and girls will pull a strip at random. The name on the strip will indicate her companion at the table."

"I like this idea!" Galina chimed in animatedly.

Mama Vera interjected, "Boys, while your ballerinas are playing Russian roulette here, let me show you our garden, and if you find any fruit still hanging after my kids have combed every inch, feel free to pick it. Galyusha, we'll be back in five minutes, and then we'll start on the food. If we don't, your grandmother is going to kill me."

I was scanning the rows of girls in front of me. Galya said, "Misha, what's wrong?"

"Ahh, just wondering which of the beauties here present is the grandmother. . . ."

The girls chuckled again. I presented the strips of paper with the names evenly fanned out in my hand, but with my own slightly sticking out. I winked at Galina.

"The first draw is for the birthday girl. We'll announce the names as soon as the guys come in."

The girls were animatedly whispering to each other, and passing strips of papers under the table. The little brother wanted to catch the cheats out, but seeing the warning look on his sister's face, swallowed his remark. Returning from their inspection of the garden, the guys seated themselves accordingly and the two hostesses went to the kitchen to fetch the main course.

After stuffing themselves with homemade delicacies, the exhausted dancers soon began to feel sleepy and mellow. Everyone started remembering who had made what mistakes, and how we had all got disoriented at the start of the suite. I explained that the lighting designer had forgotten to warn the artistic director that he'd changed the lighting for the opening of the Branle, to illustrate a transition from the gloom of the Middle Ages to the light of the Renaissance. And the artistic director had then had to adjust the script on the spot. He'd asked me to pass on his apologies to all of us.

Mama Vera raised her glass: "Dear artists, congratulations on your wonderful triumph at the concert today and on your successful completion of the first year of studies! Hoorah!"

We toasted each other with paper cups full of lemonade.

"Let's sing something native, Odessan."

The grandmother came out of the kitchen to hear us sing. I began with 'The

Pearl Odessa', then we sang 'Shalandi' (boats), 'By the Black Sea', and so it went on until sunset.

Saying goodbye, Mama Vera hugged me and said: "Misha, Galya has told me a lot about you. She is going to help the girls prepare themselves mentally for next year's class on partnering. I hope that the guys will also be patient with their female partners. You make a good team. At the concert today you really made your case for becoming professional artists."

On the way home, I mulled over the end of the school year and thought about plans for the period ahead. Our theatre's creative team were on holiday until the end of June. July and August were the most active months of the year, because of the mass onslaught of tourists visiting the city. Everyone wanted to see the Opera Theatre, a famous architectural landmark, and also to see a show there. Vronsky, the chief choreographer, via the personnel manager, urged us to familiarise ourselves with the theatre's repertoire as quickly as possible if we were interested in performing there the following season. We would join the 'corps de ballet', performing Historical dances. Naturally, it was in our interests to grab this chance. July and August were holiday months at the school. The administration of the Ballet Theatre were offering us the chance to attend all rehearsals and shows at the theatre during July so we could learn the Historical and Character dances by watching the professionals. From the beginning of August, they would provide us with two instructors for morning and afternoon training sessions in the choreography of both genres, ably assisted by a demonstration duo who were retired former soloists. For those who completed this intensive training course successfully, the administration would offer a contract from 1st September: rehearsals would be paid for by the hour, and the sum total of performances would be paid by the month. Upon graduation from the ballet school, those who made the grade would be enrolled in the permanent troupe of the Ballet Theatre. Participation in this training course, could mean a transfer from playing as extras to 'corps de ballet', and open up great prospects for a professional future.

Picking up my post in the entrance hall, I noticed a large three-leaf screen standing by the main door. It was not new, but very clean and without holes. A note pinned to it read: 'Dear Misha, this is for your room, for the convenience of guests. Thank you for a wonderful concert. M. I.'

By five o'clock I had finished my tasks for the day, and, while waiting for my visitors, began picking out on the accordion a number of military tunes that might serve for a 'Soldiers' Dance'.

Hearing the triple ring of my doorbell, I dashed downstairs and let in my two classmates.

"We could hear the music from the opposite side of the street, half a block away from your attic."

"How dare you call this an attic! Your head is an attic, and with a hole in the roof too!"

They laughed as we climbed the stairs.

My landlady opened the door on to the landing: "Misha, are these clowns with you?"

"Yes, madam. Yesterday you had the privilege of observing them onstage."

"Ah, fine."

The boys could barely hold back their laughter until we reached my flat.

"Wow!" they exclaimed in one voice, "these are royal apartments all right!"

"An experimental ward for the deranged," I corrected which made them laugh again. "Sit down, kids, and tell me what you've decided."

"Our parents are OK with us going on the cruise. We're just concerned about missing two weeks of August when we could have been observing the rehearsals and shows at the theatre, and whether that will have an impact on our studies."

"Well, I have the same problem, but you and I are somewhat more experienced dancers than the rest of the group, and I think the remaining two weeks will give us enough time to get the range of the Historical/Character dance repertoire of the theatre. The main course on the contract starts in September, so August should give you sufficient time to prepare for that. That's why I specifically invited you two for this cruise. As a prize for participating in the cruise you'll get two original duets from me as a gift. I'll choreograph them myself, and the Cultural Centre will cover the cost. I'll also give you a written authorisation to perform these compositions wherever and whenever you wish. The two pieces will be a 'Soldiers' Dance' and 'Cossacks' Games'. You'll be performing them on cruise liners and at cultural centres along the Black Sea coast.

"If you agree to the conditions in principle, we need to start working on the compositions immediately. I'll let the personnel manager and artistic director know that we'll be absent for the first half of July. You will need to sign a contract with the Mariners' Centre for the period of rehearsals and for the cruise. Think it over again and consult with your families. If you agree with everything, come to the Centre tomorrow at three. But if you decide not to do it, there's no need for you to come. Also, don't worry if you decide not to do it; I won't hold it against you. But if you do agree and we begin working together, you won't be able to back out. That's the deal. Otherwise you'll be standing up the whole project. Nobody in Odessa will want to work with you after that."

After seeing the guys out, I decided to sit on a bench on the boulevard and have a good think over whether *to be or not to be* with Oksana. This woman continued to be a mystery to me. We worked together really well. My trust in her had grown over the last six months, as my assistant and colleague. She'd been in a position to work against me if things had gone awry, as had happened before with the senior group, but she'd followed all my instructions without argument, had actively helped me, both as a choreographic tutor and a disciplinarian, and had unequivocally upheld my authority in the ensemble. Her loyalty had won me over and given rise to warm feelings of sympathy. For my part, I was scrupulously polite to her, listened to her practical advice, and was always careful not to patronise her in the classroom.

She had more than once caught me admiring her beautiful statuesque figure. I wasn't a womaniser, but as a normal man I was moved by female beauty.

Emotionally ruffled, I arrived at the meeting place five minutes early. I was certain that Oksana would have changed her mind again, for much the same reasons, but suddenly somebody behind me placed their hands over my eyes. Covering them with my own, I felt a wedding ring on one finger and relaxed a little.

I forced her hands down over my long nose to my mouth and began to kiss her fingertips one after the other. Feeling the body behind me beginning to shake, I realised that she was laughing. This encouraged me further, and I quickly raised the two pairs of hands in the air and swung under them to face the flirt. I was taken aback, barely recognising Oksana in a short skirt, with a new haircut, glowing with youth and beauty, and looking at least ten years younger.

"I am sorry, mademoiselle, but I don't make acquaintances in the street!"

"But I DO!" she interrupted, wrapping her bare arms around my neck and latching on to my lips, as if to a wine jug. I let go of her and began to shake my wrists, while the passers-by stared at us and commented with a chuckle: "Poor guy! – That's a lethal grip! – Peace be with him! Amen!"

Finally, running out of breath, Oksana unlocked our lips. Then she picked up a bag at her feet and, grabbing my hand, tore off down the street, on the winds of love, covering the short stretch to my 'palace of happiness'. Stealthily we mounted the staircase, so as not to disturb my landlady, and quietly entered my bachelor's nest, carefully shutting the door behind us.

Suddenly Oksana burst out laughing at the thought of our childish behaviour.

"This is all so unreal," she whispered in my arms. "Please forgive me, sinner that I am."

"Never!" I said, drying with my lips the tears of joy that had welled in her eyes. "I've been waiting for this moment for so long. . . ."

She looked long and hard into my eyes, as if trying to read my inner thoughts and feelings, plans and aspirations. Then, she sighed with relief, stroking my shoulders.

"How come you have such developed muscles?" she wondered.

"During the war, I worked as a loader on a collective farm, then, after the war, in a bakery. I've also been playing the accordion for a long time."

"You can see straight away that you are a hard worker. That's what I love about you."

"Darling, let's drink a toast to our meeting. While you are getting settled, I'll set the table for a little meal. Behind the screen, there's a chair, and a water basin. A fresh towel is by the sink, and there's a shelf there for your toiletries."

"Do you expect me to live here?"

"No, not to live! But sometimes you may want to stay overnight. Tomorrow, at work, I'll get a set of keys made. You can then come up here without bothering the neighbours, any time that Your Highness condescends to a meeting with her humble servant Mikhail."

"Enough of this, chatterbox!" exclaimed the queen, closing my mouth with another intoxicating kiss and sending my head spinning.

Opening my eyes, I discovered an Aphrodite sitting in front of me, a colourful bathrobe over her naked body, with a wineglass in her hand.

Noticing my dropped jaw, the goddess of love laughed out loud: "How long am I to sit here with an empty glass?"

"This moment, my fair lady." I bowed low, pressing my lips to her naked knee.

She ruffled my curls. The bottle tipped in my hand, filling up the glasses.

I dropped on both knees right next to my goddess: "To this meeting!"

"And to love!" she added.

Slowly draining the wine, we threw the glasses (paper cups, really) theatrically behind us.

Green lover that I was, I got up to pick up a sandwich, but Oksana rose, snatched it out of my hand, and seated herself on my knees, wrapping her arms around my shoulders.

"I am going to be your appetiser!" she announced, kissing me.

Undoing my shirt, my goddess began to cover my shoulders and arms with kisses. I could not bear this torture any longer. I carried her to the bed where we collapsed together laughing. I managed, not without some difficulty, to wriggle free from my clothes, causing the bed to squeak and rattle.

Eventually she shuddered, pressing me to her chest and shivering like a leaf in the wind. She suddenly began to sing:

> *"Do not hurry, when it's not right to hurry!*
> *Do not hurry, when eyes gaze into eyes!*
> *Do not hurry when eyes are moist with tears!*
> *Do not hurry, please don't hurry!"*

She shouted out loud to the whole world.

Are there words in any language which accurately describe that extraordinary merging of physical and spiritual satisfaction? I very much doubt it. Only through visual or performing art can some faint echo of the true sensation of sexual intimacy be reached, but nothing more. Oksana lay quietly on her side, with her back pressed to me, tenderly rubbing her face against my hands crossed in front of her. Then she playfully placed her breasts into my cupped palms and tossed her head back on to my shoulder. Such unquestioning trust is a priceless gift for a man.

After a short while, my beloved slipped out of my arms. "Wait here!" Aphrodite commanded, and throwing a bathrobe over her shoulders, disappeared behind the screen.

I could hear splashing in the water basin and humming 'A Gypsy on Horseback'. I picked up the well-known tune in the second voice. Continuing to sing, Oksana threw me some pyjamas, and ordered me to wash my hands, and sit at the table.

"Yes, my beloved tigress/queen."

"And now, my dear bear, I am going to treat you to your own sandwich, but only after a glass of wine." My goddess was in high spirits now.

Laughing, we drank *Brüderschaft* and turned to the food.

She prepared to wash the plates, but I pulled her away from the kitchen, declaring that in my house I could not let anyone else do this job. While my guest was busy at her toilette in front of the mirror, I turned on my old record player, with a no less ancient record of an Argentinian tango.

We came together again, this time in a different mode. Wrapping my hand around her waist, I pressed my stomach to hers, in my favourite of ballroom dances. She opened her beautiful flashing eyes, surprised by my confidence and skill in handling a partner.

"And I thought you were only a master of stage dance."

"Madam, in tango, we don't talk, but focus on enchanting one another."

At last she put her face against my chest, and we tenderly caressed each other, until our joint breathing slowed, and we both fell into a blissful slumber.

After an indeterminate time, my girlfriend rose suddenly: "Oy, Mishanya, I must run home. My parents must be wondering what happened."

While she was washing behind the screen, I collected our clothing from around the room. Then I washed, got dressed and combed my hair like a good boy. My knees were shaky, though, and seeing my rather battered appearance in the mirror, I got a bit of a shock, not recognising myself.

"Let's go," commanded my now made-up and powdered queen.

"I could use some of that stuff," I mumbled, locking the door behind us.

We went downstairs on tiptoe. I was determined to see my mistress all the way to her place, but she stopped at the corner of the street, and pressed her cheek to mine: "Thanks, my dear, but I'll be fine from here on. See you tomorrow at the Centre at three o'clock. Don't forget. Goodnight!"

"Bye!" I mumbled again and stumbled home.

Shutting the entrance door behind me, I only now noticed a note in my pigeonhole. Rels, the director of the ballet school, was inviting me for a meeting on Wednesday at ten, to discuss the schedule of classes for our experimental group for the next school year.

Well, well, Misha, I thought to myself, *you are keeping busy all right. Forward, lovers, that is, musketeers!* On shaky legs, I climbed the stairs to my attic.

In the morning, I had a headache from the previous day's strong wine. There were other aches elsewhere from active love making, but a cold shower restored me to some state of normalcy.

I arrived at the Mariners' Centre ahead of time, to discuss with the manager the specifics of the upcoming tour: dates, participants, the repertoire of the naval college, the cruise's tourist programme, schedule of stops, people in charge, etc. The wardrobe manager was back from her vacation and getting ready for the cruise. The accordionist was already waiting for me in the studio. Together, we turned to compiling a potpourri for a 'Soldier's Dance'. When the 'soldiers' appeared, I introduced them, and asked Oksana to find each a pair of boots in the wardrobe department. The accordionist promised to finish preparing the compilation at home, working to our script and the marks I'd made in the music booklet.

At ten in the ballet school, a heated debate was in progress on the subject of our experimental group, behind the closed door of the Director's office. I tactfully held back from entering and was about to leave the waiting room, but the secretary gestured me to stay and disappeared behind the Director's door. After a minute, she invited me to enter. I greeted everyone with a bow. Rels, Goldina, Vishnyakov, Yegorov, and Tzhomelidze were all in attendance. I modestly seated myself by the door.

Rels opened the conversation: "Misha, we're discussing the future schedule of your group in joint courses with our senior girls. According to Innesa, you've already helped them in the preparation and execution of the last school concert, and we are grateful to you for this."

I bowed my head again silently.

"We are also aware of the fact that, besides training at the theatre, you are also directing, rather successfully, the children's ensemble at the Mariners' Cultural Centre. This suggests to all of us that you are not only interested in dance, but in the profession of choreographer/producer as well. Which is why we hope that you, as a future colleague, will be able to understand our predicament, and also appreciate the teachers' confidence in you, in spite of your still very young age."

"Thank you."

"As you know, there are almost no boys in the school. The Ballet Theatre, like many other theatres in the country, badly needs male performers. From 1st August, you and your male colleagues are going to be invited to train in the Historical and Character dance repertoire of the 'corps de ballet', to replace women dancing male parts. Thanks to your persistence [here I bowed my head again], your ten guys have turned out to be potentially quite useful both for the school and the Opera Theatre. We realise that one shouldn't count one's chickens before they're hatched. At the same time, you and your colleagues are naturally impatient to perform on the stage of the Opera Theatre, even though you're not yet fully ready for it.

"You also realise, of course, that, for our senior girls, it's absolutely essential to train with a male partner, in particular in Historical, Character dance, and 'Pas de deux', in order to acquire the skills necessary for professional ballerinas. Your training with the senior girls has clear benefits for you as well. What concerns us, as teachers, however, is whether it is practically possible for your male group to combine even a partial workload in 'corps de ballet' with your studies at the school? We very much hope that you will help us find a positive way out of this rather delicate situation. After all, you are a product of our school and we are all proud of your achievements."

"Georgi Aleksandrovich," I said, "You're so right. At our age, we are impatient at having to learn 'slowly, but surely', though I personally am not so averse to that. I would say, however, that for everyone in the group, myself included, it has not been easy to adapt either to the new physical culture, or to the ethics of relationships in this new artistic world. As you know, not everyone survived the four-month trial period. Some had to leave. But those who did stay on, will, I'm absolutely sure, go through to the very end. My confidence in this is simply based on the conversations that we have each day after classes, discussing our mistakes, difficulties and plans for the future. The school concert turned out to be a more serious test for all of us than any type of exam at the school, since what our teachers might excuse for understandable reasons, an audience would never forgive. That is why it is so important that the training in the theatre goes on while we're still at the school. The artist's life onstage is far too short to be starting it at the age of twenty – another reason, by the way, why six years of studies are too long for us. We need to have completed the programme of studies (even if nominally) and have begun putting it into practice by the end of three, or a maximum of four, years. Otherwise, we'll be wilting on the vine. All the guys think this way, including myself. But obviously the last word is yours.

"As far as joint classes with senior girls go, this has been, without doubt, very useful to us. One small problem, though, has been the physical contact between fifteen-year-old girls and twenty-year-old guys. The girls often giggle nervously during training, causing us to feel unsure about the propriety of our conduct. Either at home, or at the school, somebody needs to sit down with the girls and have a preparatory conversation on this subject with them. Otherwise it will slow down the work in class and rehearsals. Despite this, I can assure you that if you're planning on introducing one or two additional groups of senior girls for joint training in historical, character, and 'Pas de deux', we'll be able to take them on as well, provided the timing accommodates our schedule."

"Well, that's just what we're talking about: coordinating the two schedules, that of the school, and that of the theatre. What do you think are your physical capabilities, in terms of participating in both on the same day?"

"I would say, two classes at school, one rehearsal, and one performance."

While the Director and I were talking, the other teachers were listening intently and making notes in their pads. I responded to some of their questions, and then Rels asked whether I had any questions of my own, on behalf of the group. I said that we did have one, for the Director.

"Then please wait in the lobby for ten minutes, while we finish consulting here," the Director asked. He thanked me for my input, on behalf of all the teachers.

With a bow of my head, I left the room and went out into the street to take some air. Sitting on the steps of the grand entrance I began thinking about the sensitive situation that had arisen in the relations between the school and the theatre around our experimental group. Each side clearly wanted to use us for their professional ends, both as soon, and as much, as possible. We would need to be on our guard not to take too much on ourselves, and to protect our own interests.

The secretary called out to me through the window. The door to the Director's office was open. On seeing me, Rels shut a file lying on the table in front of him.

"Misha, let's get a cup of tea. I'm so worn out from these constant hassles. By the way, the teachers hold you in great esteem. Tzhomelidze promised to help, exclusively for your sake. Watch out for that woman, she is known for breaking young men's hearts."

Sitting down in the nearest tea rooms, Rels enquired, "So, what additional cares have you invented for my ripe old age?"

"The guys are all asking that you keep the promise given by Vronsky, to provide us with a trainer in stage movement. Once a week, on Monday afternoons. The stage director often ridicules us at the rehearsals of the mime extras, because we don't know how to tumble, fence, 'fall down dead'; or how to use the hand props, or weapons; or how to do hand-to-hand combat, etc. With a proper instructor we could learn all this in a year. You know how useful these skills are for male dancers."

"All right, all right! I take your point. I'll see what can be done. I also have something to ask you about. It's about Character dance classes at the school. Vishnyakov is strongly recommending you as his substitute for Saturday classes, on those occasions when he cannot absent himself from the Operetta, when there's a premiere or something like that. It doesn't happen all the time, but it still happens often enough. The schedule would be 2.30 to 4.45 p.m.: two classes, of an hour each, for the girls of the third and fourth years, with a fifteen-minute break in between. For barre exercises you can use your own approach; for centre exercises – polish the technique already introduced by Ivan. The pay will be hourly. The benefit to you: a note in your employment log about this professional experience. But we'll need to get permission from Plakhov for you to combine this extra work with your job at the Centre."

"Thanks for your trust in me. In principle, I'm game. I'll need to familiarise myself with the educational programme of the two classes at the barre, so as not to interfere with Ivan Nikolayevich's method. Are there no boys at all in the school?"

"There are, one or two in each grade, but Vishnyakov has refused to train them because he has no time."

"If you like, I could give all of them a joint lesson, by way of a compromise, on Saturdays, after the girls, from 5 to 7 p.m."

"How do you imagine this working? They have different levels of training."

"In cases like this, I usually give everyone the same intensive exercises at the barre, and for centre exercises, I divide them into groups and work on different études with each group according to their level. I have some experience with that."

"Misha, you've been squeezing me dry today!"

"Sorry, Georgi Aleksandrovich, it was your idea!"

"Yes, but your plan of action, which 'unfortunately' suits us very well!" We both laughed.

At the Cultural Centre, I found the two soloists already practising their variations. The accordionist had finished compiling the music and played it through for me. He had produced a perfect arrangement of military tunes, earning a sincere compliment from me. I only corrected the tempo and fermata/pauses here and there, in order to enhance the effect of handclaps and of the tapping of feet. I could see that the boys were really enjoying this Character dance: giving an impression of a gun by aiming with one leg at an opponent, and imitating a gunshot with a synchronic tap of the heel; or, holding each other's arms criss-crossed in the front, and performing high jumps to simulate hand-to-hand combat; and also performing acrobatic tumbling sideways to 'escape a wild bullet'.

On the last Saturday before our departure of the cruise, a dress rehearsal was held in the presence of some administrators from the Black Sea Fleet. The directors of the Arts Centre and the Ballet School were invited to provide their professional opinion on the ideological and artistic contents of the children's repertoire. Naturally, I gratefully acknowledged all comments of the administration on the choreography and the props, and, in return, got the go-ahead for all our public performances.

Before he left, Rels asked me, "Misha, wherever do you dig up these talented boys? In May, at the regional competition, I observed the junior group on the stage of the Opera Theatre, and now the senior group here. Altogether, twenty youngsters, eyes burning with excitement. How do you manage to get them interested in dance rather than football?"

"You will have a chance to observe my methods next year at the school, if I get to work with the boys on Saturdays. But for now, this is a professional secret."

We both chuckled.

I hurried off to greet Lyuftgarten and to introduce Oksana to him.

"She's my right-hand person in the ensemble: a teacher and a counsellor/ nanny at the same time."

"As a former footballer, and as a dancer, a more accurate description would be your 'right foot'. And, by the way, I knew your partner from the senior group long before you appeared on the scene. Misha, you have not visited us in a long time. Forgotten us?"

"How can one forget one's alma mater?"

"Good answer. I hope you remember our project – a course on the history of performing arts?"

"I do! In fact, I'm encouraging my colleagues [I pointed at Oksana] to sign up for this unique seminar."

At this moment, a secretary invited Oksana and me to see Director Plakhov, for a consultation with the representatives of the Black Sea Navigation Authority. We were introduced to Fyodor Ivanovich, a temporary administrator of our two ensembles – dance and vocal. All organisational questions were to be directed to him. We also received official mandates confirming our identity and status with the navigation authority, for presentation at the border zones of the Black Sea coast. Without being given the reasons, we were also warned to be careful how we conducted ourselves in the ports of Sukhumi and Batumi, and also to look after the tour crew there. The Director and representatives wished us good luck.

When everyone had left, I asked Oksana, "Could we dine together tonight, somewhere near my place and then . . ."

"Fine!" She looked at her watch, "At six, in a Georgian tavern, on the corner of your street."

"See you there," I answered, feeling that all my cares had suddenly dissipated into thin air.

How little indeed one needs to feel happy! I mused, running off to attend to some errands.

For a Saturday night, the Georgian tavern was relatively empty. I took a seat and asked for a menu.

"Wat menu? You've fallen fram ze sky, or wat?" – a waiter with a moustache jumped on me. "All ze kitchen in here!" The Caucasian man tapped himself on the head. "You kun order me whole head if yah like!" he roared, baring his toothless gums, and shaking his moustache.

Looking at him, I thought: *What a picture! Like a character from a Charlie Chaplin film.*

"Wat you looking at me for? I ain't your missy!"

"When she comes, then we'll order. Thanks."

"Wat you thank me for? Why 'thanks'? Funny man!"

At this moment, Oksana entered, and instantly taking in the situation, turned to the 'moustache' and sharply ordered: "One mutton soup, and two portions of fried *boukeras*!"

"Ah! Zat's clear now. Wat menu, funny man!"

Oksana, smiling sweetly, asked: "First time here?"

"And probably the last," I remarked glumly, feeling the unkind stares of other visitors on my back.

Oksana took my hand in hers, and squeezed it gently to calm me down.

"I have good news for you."

I raised my eyebrows, wondering what she was going to say.

"If you're amenable to the idea, I'll stay over tonight, and tomorrow we can go and visit my aunt at her summer house in Luzanovka. She's invited us for lunch."

Listening to her, and grasping hold of her wrist, I could not believe my ears. I was in seventh heaven.

"I thought you didn't want to make our relations public," I blurted out.

"At work – no, but it's impossible to hide it from relatives and girlfriends."

After the meal, we hurried home. I offered to carry Oksana's bag and almost collapsed under its weight.

"What have you got in there, bricks?"

She only touched my lips with a forefinger, which I immediately and hungrily licked. Like mischievous children, we sneaked into the flat, and fell into each other's arms as soon as we'd shut the door.

"I missed you so much, my dear, I could barely hold myself back from kissing you at work."

"Darling, we need to see each other more often."

We merged again in an endless kiss, until we were out of breath.

"You'd better see what gift I brought for you, before I change my mind and take it away."

Holding my breath, I started impatiently unwrapping the package.

"Hey! Clumsy bear! Take care not to drop it!"

I couldn't believe my eyes. In front of me was an almost brand-new record player, one of the latest improved models, such as I had recently spotted in Plakhov's office. I was speechless, and out of embarrassment, joked flatly: "And it spins on three speeds, in both directions?"

"No, dear, this machine works on two speeds, and only in one direction, while your head spins the other way on a third speed."

"Oksanushka, darling, this must have cost you a fortune! I don't deserve such a gift."

"This is not some souvenir to accompany night-time love making. This is a tribute to your talent, to help it develop, and blossom more fully and effectively."

I began to say thank you, when the woman covered my mouth, as before, with her juicy lips. I realised that my goddess had total power over me, and succumbed to my fate. I don't remember how I lost my clothing; how I found myself on the bed of love; how many times I soared to the skies with my Aphrodite, or how many times I collapsed on the ground from exhaustion. I only remember a sweet drunk feeling that repeatedly flooded me in this intoxicating celebration of the joy of human existence.

Sometime around midnight we woke up and sat at the little table arranged like a still life, with wine, fruit, and cream pastries. Oksana put on one of her favourite records that she had brought along. We cooed like two doves over the food and sang in tune with the record. Then my girl seated herself on my lap, wrapping her legs and arms around me.

In the morning, I showered, and then approached the bed to wake my Sleeping Beauty. But then, peeling back the sheet, and seeing my divine Aphrodite lit by the rays of a rising sun, I pounced on her like a lion. She was too quick for me though. Spotting me through her thick lashes, she rolled from under me just at the moment of my lunge, and in an instant disappeared behind the screen. I landed face down on to the warm bed. Peering from behind the screen, the naughty girl tittered brightly, just like her daughter. I feigned a fit, slapping the treacherous bed with my hands and feet, while Oksana, sticking her tongue out, gleefully shook her head at me. It was pure pleasure to see a mature woman acting like a child, in the carefree abandon of the happiness she felt in my company.

I quickly made the bed and got dressed. I was about to make tea, when I saw her, already looking picture perfect, with a tea kettle in her hand, and a smile on her face. I simply stared at her: how beautiful she was!

"What's up?"

Oksana raised her eyebrows. I could only let out a deep sigh.

"Breakfast is served!"

It turns out to be pure pleasure to obey the woman you love, I acknowledged to myself.

"Mishanya, focus on breakfast. If we set off late, the trams will be awfully crowded."

"Yes, ma'am! Will be done, ma'am!"

"Don't forget your swimming trunks and sunglasses. We may have time for a swim before lunch."

"Yes, not to forget!" I hugged her from behind and kissed her on the ear.

"Ay, I didn't mean myself, you mischief!"

"Guilty! Won't do it again. Not until we reach Luzanovka!"

There are few words to describe, or adequate colours to paint what an Odessan tram, bound for the beach, is like during the summer season. Half-naked, fleshy shapes pressed up against one another, like sardines in a tin, grabbing on to the railing under the roof with one hand, while hanging on to a netted sack full of bottles and jars with the other, their sweaty bodies glued to those of their neighbours. As the tram jumps and jerks, the sacks of bottles and jars smash into the surrounding knees and shins. At every abrupt start, the packed mass takes a step back on to the feet of those behind them, and at every halt rolls on top of those in front. When two trams meet at a junction, the tram drivers stop and chat for fifteen minutes, exchanging news, until finally a passenger loses patience and shouts: "Shall we get a move on, or what!"

"Shut up, you scum, or I'll smash your face in! You wouldn't want any time at the beach then!"

The exhausted passengers become incensed: "Scandal! Outrage!"

The driver, in turn, shuts off the engine, locks his cabin and announces: "This tram terminates here! Get off and wait for another one!"

Oksana was not going to put up with this: "Folks, hold on, don't get off!" She pulled me after her to approach the driver. He reeked of vodka, clearly the aftermath of last night's party. Coming right up to him, my enraged tigress questioned him with a veiled threat: "Does the name Yevgeni Alekseyevich Vorobyov sound familiar to you?"

The smile slid off his face.

"The director of the Tram and Trolley Authority?"

"Yes, why?"

"Because I am his personal assistant! You don't remember me?" Oksana thrust into his face the red-coloured authorisation document we had received in the Cultural Centre the day before. "If you don't stop your nonsense this minute, and deliver us to our destination, there will be a report on Vorobyov's table tomorrow morning, telling him all about your drunken sabotage, signed by a dozen witnesses. Under the Ukrainian Criminal Code, that will be worth three years' detention, minimum."

The Odessan thug recoiled under her glaring stare and returned to the driver's seat. The tram took off, and sped along to Luzanovka. The passengers were in awe, whispering, and pointing at us. They must have taken Oksana for some VIP, and kept silent all the way to the end of the journey.

I needed some explanations too: "How do you know this Vorobyov?"

"Ah, we're just neighbours."

As the Russian saying goes: "To live with wolves is to howl like wolves."

Oksana's aunt greeted us warmly. She had a small house, with a flower and vegetable garden. All was neat and well taken care of, indicating the good pension of an officer's widow. Her daughter would usually bring her family here on weekends in the summer, but since the kids were in a pioneer camp at the moment, their parents went to visit them, instead of coming to her. On the way to the tram, we had stopped at Privoz (the main market in Odessa) and bought groceries and beer. Unloading all the provisions on to the table, we left the aunt to cook and ran off to the beach.

We took lounging chairs under an umbrella near the bar, where an assortment of ice creams – the weak link in Oksana's diet – was on offer. An Odessan summer can be a blistering affair, and we made sure to apply plenty of sunblock to our backs, so as not to turn ourselves from pale-skinned maggots into bright-red boiled crayfish. We spent hours in the water, diving from the board and playing ball. It had been a long time since I'd derived so much pleasure from being out in nature with someone I loved, and without any witnesses to boot.

"How was the beach?" enquired the aunt in the same cordial manner.

"Perfect! It's been a long time since we relaxed so much. Been too busy lately," Oksana replied.

"Wonderful. Then, wash your hands and sit at the table!" the hostess urged.

After swimming, we hungrily devoured a fresh salad with crab and another with aubergine, washing it all down with cold beer from the cellar. After dessert, Oksana ruefully admitted that we had to run, because we were leaving on a cruise the following day.

We warmly thanked our hostess for her hospitality and hastened to the tram stop. Sitting opposite each other, we immediately launched into the discussion of operating procedures for the duration of our sea cruise.

"Misha, from tomorrow and for the next two weeks we will need to revert to our original relations, i.e. putting things on a purely professional basis."

"Agreed. Only we shouldn't overdo it: the kids will think that we've quarrelled."

"The wardrobe manager and myself will be supervising the girls; you and the accordionist, the boys."

"Agreed. And we should avoid even accidental meetings in private."

"Yes. If we need to discuss something, we must do it in public."

"We'll also need to keep close tabs on the goings-on between the senior girls and the guys from the naval college. At their age, any excessive curiosity of either party for another will only draw the unwanted attention of Administrator Fyodor Ivanovich."

"Oksana, from 1st August we are starting intensive study of the theatre's repertoire in Historical and Character dances. Do you by any chance know when the new season opens at the Cultural Centre?"

"Nobody knows yet. The head of the senior ensemble is still in hospital after surgery. There was a complication and he won't be coming back to work. He retired. I heard that the directorate is urgently looking for a replacement, but I think that Lyuftgarten might be able to give you a fuller account. As far as I know, there are two veterans, my age, in the senior ensemble that have been assisting the choreographer, so there is no immediate crisis. A new choreographer might ask for different days and hours of work, which we'd then have to accommodate. That's why they are waiting, before putting together a new timetable. In any case, Plakhov will give us two weeks off after the cruise for the overtime we're putting in."

"Much obliged for this; it's important information. I didn't have a chance to mention this to you earlier, but I've been offered the chance to substitute for Vishnyakov at the ballet school from 1st September, and also to teach Character dance to a boys' group on Saturdays. I think they're giving me a trial period at first, but if I manage this group, Vishnyakov will probably want to transfer to me all the Character classes at the school. He's extremely busy directing at the Operetta, and often has no time for teaching. For me, this opportunity would be an important step on the path to my ultimate goal."

"Congratulations, my dear! This is the first serious recognition of your talents in the professional world."

"Thanks, darling!"

"What if Plakhov asks you to take on the senior ensemble? Would you agree?"

"It would be interesting, and also useful for me personally, but it might be unfair to the members of the ensemble to have to lose a choreographer again in four or five years. Also, what would that mean for you?"

"I could take over the children's ensemble from you, if you continued to choreograph all the dances."

"But when I leave, what then?"

"The same, even if you don't take on the seniors."

"I don't believe Plakhov would agree to such a compromise in any case, so the discussion is pointless at the moment. Also, don't forget I've engagements at the school and the theatre."

"If you have responsible assistants, it can all work out. You would be the choreographer for both ensembles. I would continue as your assistant with the children, and the two veterans will assist with the adult group. A very convenient arrangement for everyone, at least for the next five years."

"Well, darling, your brain is just like parliament: you have found a place and a job for everyone. All that remains is to find out what Plakhov thinks about all of this."

We chuckled and gave each other high fives, as we reached our stop.

At 8 a.m. the next morning, a tourist bus was waiting at the entrance to the Mariners' Centre. The bus driver and the accordionist were loading aluminium containers with our wardrobe and shoes, musical instruments and props. I checked every container's label against the list in the hands of the wardrobe manager.

"Mikhail Semyonovich, why are you so suspicious?" she asked.

"When you've burned yourself on a hot drink, you blow even on cold," I joked, and walked over to the administrators standing at a distance.

Greeting me, Plakhov enquired: "All well with the luggage?"

"Yes, all in order," I reported. "I'll go and check to see if everybody is here. Don't worry, Viktor Vasilyevich. Your travellers are in good hands."

"Well, Fedya, on you get! Good luck and safe return!"

"Thanks, Viktor. Mikhail Semyonovich, are all of yours here?"

"Yes, Fyodor Ivanovich. Twenty-six ruffians and four adults."

"Goodbye, we'll see you all soon!" I said, addressing the group of tearful mothers and smiling officials from the Centre. Oksana and I wished each other 'happy trails'.

Near the cruise liner, the cadets of the naval college were already waiting, and standing to attention. Their head greeted us and ordered the cadets to help us unload the heavy luggage from the bus and take it to the loading dock to be transferred on board. While Fyodor Ivanovich was talking to the conductor of the vocal ensemble, I introduced the ten youths, Oksana, the wardrobe manager, and the accordionist to the cadets, and finally gestured towards the sixteen girls, issuing a warning (just in case):

"Even such fearless sailors as yourselves would do well to stay away from these young predators since each one of them is at best a cat, and at worst – a tigress."

Naturally, the 'pirates' smirked, but got the message. The conductor approached us at this point and introduced himself. While the loading continued, Fyodor Ivanovich concluded all the introductions and informed everyone what sort of conduct he, in the capacity of manager, would expect from all personnel and participants in the tour.

At last, we climbed on board, proudly displaying our personal mandates with photographs to the first mate who met us at the top. The two seamen next to him held up a banner: 'Dear Laureates of the Festival of the Black Sea Fleet. Welcome on board the cruise liner *Victory*!' This was a nice gesture that we all appreciated. The first mate showed us where to line up for a meeting with the Captain. When all fifty honoured guests had stationed themselves, the first mate's whistle announced the arrival of the Captain. Naturally, all officers and seamen on duty, including cadets, stood to attention. We, dancers, feebly copied them, remembering some practice at assemblies in pioneer camps. But our efforts were a caricature of the seamen's performance. When the Captain appeared on the bridge, all the servicemen and cadets saluted him at the first mate's signal. All the dancers in turn looked at me to follow my example. I'd not served in the army, but intuitively felt that we shouldn't imitate the servicemen. In such situations, it's always better to keep to a neutral position than to act like clowns.

"Dear guests, on behalf of the crew I welcome you on board our ship and congratulate you on your triumph in the Festival of the Black Sea Fleet. We are very moved by your honourable mission to entertain the crews of our ships as well as the residents of coastal towns at the local cultural clubs of the navy with your performances. I wish you every success in your studies and creative endeavours."

The first mate whistled again, and the Captain departed. Fyodor Ivanovich asked us to stay behind. Handing the keys to our cabins to me, the conductor, and Oksana, he gave us the timetable for that day and the next, as well as telling us about the transfer to another ship after that:

12 noon Lunch in the staff dining room on the middle deck.
4 p.m. Thirty-minute concert for the crew on the upper deck by the pool.
7 p.m. Dinner, rehearsal, and free time.
9 a.m. (next day) Bus excursion to the town's places of interest.
7.30–9 p.m. 1.5 hours' concert at a local cultural club.

The same two-day cycle more or less repeated itself six times. Our performances were a huge hit in the port cities of the Black Sea coast. And the cities themselves left us all with memorable impressions: fortresses, museums, parks, historical monuments of the past. It was an unforgettable excursion into the mysteries of the past and the present around the Crimean Peninsula and the ridge of the Caucasus. Finally we returned to Odessa directly from Batumi.

Upon arrival into our home port, we said our goodbyes to the crew, and thanked the Captain for their exceptional hospitality. It was sad to part with the naval cadets, our faithful partners onstage. At the Cultural Centre, we were greeted heartily by the parents who had missed their offspring, and by the administration, pleased with our performance and our safe return. Oksana and I took our trophies to the Director's office. On the way, we made arrangements for how we were going to communicate with each other over the next few days: if there was something urgent, we decided to leave a note for the other at my house on the shelf for the post in the lobby.

"From Tuesdays I will be at the opera all day, with the experimental group."

"And on Mondays?"

"Doing household chores during the daytime, and then dreaming about my beloved in the evening."

"Won't you go to see your mother tomorrow?"

"If I can hope to see you tomorrow, then I will go and visit my mother today."

"Lyubanya will be in the pioneers' camp for another week, so I could help you while she is away."

"Then, as always, at 7 p.m. Thanks for offering to help your humble admirer."

My girlfriend graced me with a promising smile and we parted.

"You've completely forgotten us," Mother chided when I got there. "Your old friends ask about you all the time, and I don't know what to tell them."

"Mum, I've only just got back from a tour. We took the children's ensemble on a tour of the Black Sea ports and ships. I am sorry to have been out of touch: it won't happen again."

"Just like in the old days: today you apologise, and tomorrow you'll do what you like."

"Mum, how are you? Is the work here becoming too much for you?"

"Not too much," Mother sighed.

"But enough, all the same," I added.

Mother smirked. "Chatting, as always? How is your work?"

"Yes, work is great. The studies are taking a lot of time and effort."

"That's what you wanted, no? Too late to complain about that."

"I don't know what 'complain' means. On the contrary, I only regret that I don't have more time for my professional training. That's why I only rarely see you and Roma. And, unfortunately, I don't see many more windows of opportunity in the near future either."

"People have been saying that you were seen, with a woman. I hope you'll invite us to the wedding."

"Of course, in ten years perhaps, not before."

"Why, do you have it all planned out, years ahead?"

"Well, we all live according to Stalin's five-year plans, no?" I blurted out, without thinking.

"Don't joke about it!" Mother warned, looking round apprehensively. " 'A chatterbox is a gift to the enemy,' you never know who might be listening in."

"I'm sorry, you're right. Send my love to everyone. Be well!" I kissed her and took off.

What an idiot! In a public place too! A sure way to land myself behind bars and bring others under suspicion.

On Monday morning, I began the day, as always, with a trip to the laundry. The warden at the staff entrance to the theatre gave me a note from Rels to come to the school immediately. *Ooh la-la! I completely forgot about getting permission to combine my two jobs.* I tore off to the Cultural Centre.

Plakhov wasn't in. The secretary promised to prepare my letter by lunchtime the next day. At the cashier's I ran into the head of the Public Recreation Department. She reminded me that they were planning new announcements to run in newspapers throughout August for an additional enrolment into the ensemble. She wanted to know what my enrolment requirements were.

I replied: "Boys for both groups," I stressed, "only boys! Girls, and their mothers, are interested in dance as it is; they don't need additional encouragement."

"That's true, and there's nothing wrong with that." She remembered her own daughter. "I saw your trophies from the tour. My compliments!"

"Thanks, but some credit for our success must go to you as well, as our administrator."

"Mikhail Semyonovich, as ever, you are always so charming," she pronounced ambiguously.

On my return home there was a sudden loud knock on the front door.

That's just what I need now: a visitor! Who is it? Landlady? Neighbour from downstairs? A policeman, on account of the loud music?

At the sound of the knock, I approached the door, and asked sweetly: "Who's there?"

Silence. The knocking came again.

My inner bull (my star sign is Taurus) reared itself: "And who might it be in such a hurry?" I growled, yanking the door open aggressively.

Who should be standing there in front of me, but my beloved, with a bottle of her favourite champagne. Grabbing hold of them both, I dragged them inside my castle and began to spin them round until we collapsed on to our throne.

"Madam, may I ask, to what do we owe the appearance of this champagne?"

"To the occasion of your appointment as new artistic director of the Mariners' Dance Ensemble, consisting of three groups: adults, youths, and children."

"What, already?"

"It turned out the administration had been discussing your candidature for a while. They were only waiting for you to get back from the cruise to make a final decision. Today, at the cashier's office, the secretary relayed to the Plakhov's request to come and see him. At two, there was a meeting between Plakhov, the head of the Public Recreation Department, as well as Yuri and Valya – tutors of the adult group, and myself, as a representative of the children's group. There, Plakhov informed us that you had been recommended for the post of artistic director, and that the groups would now be changed. Yuri would remain as assistant/tutor for the adults; Valya, as tutor for the youth group (formerly the senior group of the children's ensemble), while I would continue assisting in the junior group. Everyone is happy with this arrangement. It gives you an opportunity, as joint choreographer for all three groups, to have the freedom to mix and match the dancers from the different groups, and transfer them to more advanced group levels according to their personal development."

"This is what they'd call 'marrying me off in my absence'. What if I don't like the bride?"

"I warned them that you might be leaving in five years to go to Moscow or Leningrad for further education, and that you didn't want to tie yourself down to obligations in Odessa for the long term. Everyone knows about this anyway – at the theatre, at school, and at the Arts Centre. Plakhov also said he knew about it, and that your aspirations for higher education were most commendable. So the last word is yours. You will now have three assistants, responsible for the technical quality of productions, and for organisational and educational work with members. Mishanya, such trust is not easy to earn. By the way, the secretary told me that the resolution had already been signed by Plakhov and was waiting for you."

"Thank you, Oksanushka. You are my good fairy, and I don't know how to thank you enough. But I must also think very carefully about my physical capabilities and timetable. The offer is very attractive, but it is also a heavy responsibility, considering that both the theatre and the school are central to my plans for the future, and I cannot afford to lose them. In any case, some trial period will be necessary. One aspect of the proposed scenario which I'm concerned about (otherwise it's ideal for a budding choreographer) is Yuri and Valya: their personal qualities, and their ability to work as part of a team with a leader much younger than them. Unfortunately not everyone is like you, my loyal friend and partner. I will have to present very rigid conditions to Plakhov if we are to keep our reputation and the high standards of our work."

"Perhaps you're right, my dear. Maybe it is a bit premature to drink champagne. Let's have a bite to eat first and then discuss in detail the prospect of working with potential partners. I brought along some stew that my mother cooked for us. I'm going to warm it up, and you will set the table, please."

"So, about this pair of veterans. Even before I met you, at the regional arts centre I was warned not to have anything to do with these two. They were already known for their dirty schemes and machinations. People like that, with a lot of ambition but little or no talent, tend to go about with an inferiority complex, in constant fear that their ineptitude will one day be discovered and they'll be replaced by more competent professionals. While the old and sick director, their former teacher, was still around, they were OK. They'd simply change his choreography to suit their own vision, without even asking for his agreement to the changes. You know I won't put up with that. I'm not planning on changing the repertoire of the adult group for now, but I am going to gradually introduce my own choreography. That is only natural, but they're not going to like it. And if I discover alterations being made to my choreography, I'll immediately put a stop to it, and return the dance to its original composition. The same goes for the choice of cast, music tempos, choice of costume, etc. At the first sign of intrigue behind my back, between them and the members of the ensemble, I'll put an end to our joint work. If I were you, I wouldn't appear on the scene while they're around. If predators like them were to find out about our intimate relations, they'd not hesitate to use it to destroy us. They did the same with my predecessor when they tried to steal the children's group from her. You know this. I've also experienced this kind of thing with others more than once before."

"So what do you propose to do, Misha?"

"Unfortunately, I'm not able to give you a proper answer yet. Six years ago, Vronsky was invited from Tbilisi, where he was also the chief ballet master, to be the artistic director at the Opera Theatre here. Accepting this post, he brought along his assistant Tzhomelidze, who taught us Classical dance in the second term at the school, while continuing to tutor at the theatre. Every minister, director, leader, head of an enterprise brings along some of his former close associates whom he trusts to his new job. That's normal. If he/she doesn't, there's a risk that the new project will fail."

My partner was listening to me in shock, her hand over her mouth.

"I've only just now realised what happened between these veterans and the previous head of the children's group," she said. "I'd been helping him out while Lybanys was in his group. So, what's going to happen now? Everyone was relying on your accepting the offer."

"It was a serious breach of etiquette to involve secondary parties in the discussion of the future structure of the place, without first discussing it with the main candidate himself. The head of the Public Recreation Department is clearly on the side of the veterans, and has misled Plakhov. By the way, what's your relationship with her like?"

"Coolish."

"Why so?"

"I suspect because of my support of the former head of the children's group in his dispute, and also because of my complete financial independence, with my military widow's pension."

"Well, the picture is becoming clearer by the minute, while our chances are decreasing."

"Mishanya, perhaps there's room for compromise?"

"I can't quite see it yet. On both fronts, veterans, internally, and the head of recreation externally, those involved won't have to exert themselves much to destroy us."

"Tomorrow, if the secretary passes on to you Plakhov's invitation for me to come and see him, tell her that in August I'm at the theatre daily, from ten to five. If there's anything urgent, they can leave a telephone message for me at staff reception."

My partner's eyes became moist with tears. I gave her a hug and reassured her: "Please don't be distressed, my dear. All is not lost yet. Plakhov is a clever fellow, and he owes nothing to this triumvirate. If he listens to my arguments, I'll offer him a compromise: a trial period of one year, on condition that, if there's any attempt, be it direct or indirect, on the part of the veteran assistants or the head of recreation to sabotage my leadership, I will formally, in writing, absolve myself of all responsibility for the consequences. This will mean that, after my warning, the administration of the Cultural Centre will bear direct responsibility for any potential failure of the ensemble. Plakhov is not going to stand for this. If anything happens he'll make the head of recreation responsible."

In the morning, we parted: Oksana went off to the Mariners' Centre, and I to the theatre. After a month-long absence, I was happy to see my colleagues from the experimental group again. In the absence of the two younger soloists and myself, they had been attending rehearsals and performances of the current repertoire of the theatre, observing the style of Historical and Character dances, of the earlier and later epochs, of this or that nationality; familiarising themselves with the musical genres of both classical and modern composers. On some days, they performed in the mime troupe twice a day, earning some extra money in July to sustain them through the jobless month of August.

At ten, we attended a compulsory tutorial with the artistes from the 'corps de ballet'. After that, the manager introduced to us our head tutor and a couple of retired dancers who were going to be doing demonstrations for us. The scheme for our introduction to the repertoire was as follows:

11–1: The study of poses, curtseys, steps in the style of a certain epoch – copying the demonstration pair from behind, and dancing with an imaginary partner, or with each other. Then, Maria Andreyevna would tutor us until we had learned by heart the choreographic script for each musical-dance phrase. Through endless repetition, we would memorise the sequences of the learned phrases for the entire composition.

2–4: During the rehearsals of the 'corps de ballet', we would observe the female ex-dancers doing male parts – the roles we were eventually supposed to take ourselves. After that we would practise performing the same composition ourselves, and with our own partners.

When she saw Oksana, the secretary of the Mariners' Centre asked where she might find me. When she found out I was at the theatre, she immediately telephoned the staff reception and asked to deliver to me Plakhov's invitation to get in touch with him most urgently. Then Oksana delivered the approval for my dual employment to the ballet school, where a different secretary informed her that the director of the school also wanted to speak with me urgently. Even from the street, while running home for dinner, I could make out the unmistakable potent, delicious aroma of garlicky borscht. I dashed up the stairs, not at my usual dawdling pace, but on the wings of a growing appetite. A steaming plateful of that inimitable, red vegetable soup was already waiting for me on the table. My sweet cook refused to share in the meal. While I was downing a second helping, she shared with me all the news, and congratulated me, with some irony and jealousy, that I was becoming too popular in Odessa. Everyone wanted me, and at that very moment. *This is not a good sign!* I thought to myself, but said nothing.

"All right, dear, you can run along now! While I conduct a major clean-up here. Don't forget to check your post regularly."

For dessert, I received a kiss.

"Such a lucky bastard you are! Sh-h, don't scare off your good fortune!"

By 5 p.m., I was already at the Cultural Centre, sitting in the Director's waiting room, while he was busy finishing with his visitors. Wrapping up her own work for the day, the secretary allowed me to use her desk to spread my papers around. I had got into the habit, using a special system of notation, of recording the dance learned that day with the tutor at the theatre. Now, to really get to grips with it, I was periodically executing the movements and poses of the dance in the middle of the waiting room. The working day was over, and no more visitors could be expected. But at that moment the Director's door suddenly opened, and the official guests were confronted with the sight of me, bent over in a deep curtsey, and with my back to them. The surprised guests hastened to take their leave.

"Mikhail Semyonovich, have you been waiting long?"

"Not to worry. I was busy."

"You've probably already heard about our new dance project?"

"Yes, I knew that you'd been looking for a new choreographer for the adult group for some time. But I've unfortunately not had a chance to acquaint myself with the latest developments at the Centre: I've been too busy trying to catch up at the theatre after being away for two weeks."

"By the way," he said, "you, Oksana, the accordionist, and the wardrobe manager all received an official commendation from the navigation authority for the success of the cultural-educational programme for the communities of the Black Sea coast. Fyodor Ivanovich, in his report, particularly noted how disciplined and well organised the dancers were.

"And you're right," he went on. "For some time now, we've been looking for a new choreographer for the adult group, but without success, for a number of reasons. Experienced choreographers aren't easy to find, and we're also not interested in the mediocre and untalented ones. Both our administration and the regional arts centre strongly support your candidature. We know you have your obligations at the school and the theatre. And you also have personal plans for the future, and they will take you beyond Ukraine. We have been considering a number of possible scenarios, were you to take on the post, which won't undermine the present successes of the children's ensemble, but at the same time strengthen the currently shaky foundation of the adult group. A compromise, suggested by the head of recreation, was in principle approved by your assistant and the veteran tutors whereby these would all remain in their current positions."

Then Plakhov explained the details of the scheme, already known to me from Oksana.

"I talked this over with the director of the arts centre. He expressed serious concerns about the possibility of it working, in light of certain objective factors. I thus find myself in a dilemma. On the one hand, as I already mentioned, I don't want to slow down the progress of the children's ensemble; on the other hand, we must act urgently to prevent the dissolution of the adult group, which will be inevitable if we don't get in a professional choreographer. It's this which has compelled us to try, even if only temporarily – let's say for five years – a merging of the two ensembles under your joint command, encompassing all three groups and all three assistants, with each assistant being responsible for their own group, but reporting to the one choreographer. It's important for me to know what you think about this, and also that you speak candidly."

"First of all, Viktor Vasilyevich, I would like to thank you for the trust you have shown in me. May I ask which assistants will be responsible for which group?"

"Oksana – for the children's group; Valya – for the youth group, and Yuri – for the adults."

"What are the personal relations between the assistants?"

"Yuri and Valya are a couple. They've been dancing with Oksana for many years."

"What is the composition of the adult ensemble at the moment?"

"As far as I know: a minimum of eight men and twelve women. When there is a need for particularly important shows, they invite some veterans to complement the group. If you like, I can ask the head of recreation to join us. She has all the details."

"No, thank you! Please excuse me if I overstep the mark here, but you did ask me to speak candidly. I observed a rehearsal of the adult ensemble onstage here, after my group's rehearsal, and saw their performance in the Opera Theatre earlier this year. I even had a chat backstage with their old choreographer. So

I have some idea about that group. Just as you did a background check on me before giving me a job here, so I did on the children's ensemble. In the process I came across details of an unseemly conflict between the previous heads of the dance groups. Sorry, may I continue?"

"You have my full attention." The Director was looking straight at me.

"I'm not interested in gossip, but since we are talking about a very serious project, it is natural that a potential leader should be curious about the members of the team he has to work with. I don't have all that much life experience, but I do have some, and I have also already made enough mistakes to be wary of making new ones. In general, your idea has definite attractions for me, both professionally and personally. I can see myself staging dramatic and comic suites on military–naval subjects, or on a pirate theme, with the adult group; an athletics Olympiad or an international festival with the youth group; and winter tales and pioneer games with the children's group. Unfortunately, I seriously doubt it would be possible to create such a repertoire with the present veteran assistants.

"They've probably been blackmailing everyone around them, saying that, if they leave, the rest of the adult group will follow. This is possibly why the head of recreation proposed such a compromise. However, the end result might well be the failure of the children's ensemble, in addition to, rather than instead of, the salvaging of the adult group. When someone suffers from gangrene, we treat it by amputating the affected part of the body. So why not announce a new enrolment into an Odessa Mariners' Ensemble, under a new artistic director? Our youth group by next year will be ready for a transfer to the adult group anyway, so that, if the veteran assistants and a couple of their supporters were to leave, our Centre would only gain by that: there would be room for new young enthusiasts to take their place. That's just the law of progress.

"We can always find another pair of experienced retired dancers who would be more than willing to devote the second half of their artistic life to the training of the next generation of dancers, especially at such a prestigious establishment as this. Otherwise, any new choreographer will always have to watch his own back, for fear of being stabbed by his own assistants. Last year in December I promised you that I'd restore the children's ensemble to health, and I kept my word. Give me a green light for next year, and you will have the best dance ensemble in the city. I won't fail you."

Plakhov listened to me with rapt attention, making notes in his agenda book. At the end of my impassioned speech, he said, with deep concern in his voice: "Thanks, Mikhail Semyonovich. I will think about this and let you know what I decide."

I wasn't sure if I'd succeeded, but I knew that I had done all I could to convince him. From the Mariners' Centre I went to the school and fortunately caught Rels still in his office.

"Misha, hello! I was just thinking about you. We were going over the schedule with Vishnyakov today and decided that it would be best if you took both younger groups of girls for Character dance. He also approves of your scheme of working with the boys of different ages in one group, as an experiment for this year. After the exam at the end, we'll see how to continue with that idea. The snag is that, according to our curriculum, the kids are supposed to have Character classes twice a week, but you seem to be engaged at the Mariners' Centre."

"That's not a problem. From September onwards, I'll change my free evening from Monday to Wednesday. In any case, I need to see the detailed curriculum for the first two years of Character dance training, so that I don't end up repeating with the senior groups what they already learned with Vishnyakov, both at the barre, and in centre practice."

"I'm not sure if Ivan has this information on paper, but I will try to put that material together for you, or at least write down his explanations of what he does in which class."

"The exercises at the barre and in centre practice, I can develop myself. I only need to know the names of dance movements and their national origin."

So now, if, as a result of my last talk with Plakhov, I ended up losing my job at the Mariner's Centre, at least I'd have some creative and financial compensation at the school to fall back on. It would be sad to leave the place where I'd already invested so much time and energy, but it would not be my fault. If the administration of the Mariner's Centre violated the terms of our agreement without even consulting me beforehand, they would have to bear the full consequences of a fallout.

However, when, later at the theatre, I saw our demonstration pair, both of them forty-year-old veteran dancers, professionals, still brimming with energy, I started thinking: why not offer the assistantship at the Mariners' Centre to them? During the lunch break, I presented the idea to them and asked if they liked the idea of working with me at the Mariner's Centre. At first they were rather taken aback, but then, when they realised that the Mariners' Dance Ensemble wasn't some folk-dance troupe, but instead a serious choreographic collective, they promised to give my proposal proper consideration and to get back to me the next day at the rehearsal. I felt they were sufficiently intrigued by my proposal that no additional pressure was necessary. Such prestigious workplaces as this were not that easy to find in Odessa.

Meanwhile, Plakhov consulted with his superiors; discussed the matter with Lyuftgarten; and insured himself against a counter-attack by the pair of veteran assistants. Meanwhile, I received provisional agreement from the demonstration pair at the theatre to join me as assistants at the Cultural Centre. When I informed him of this new development, Plakhov asked to be introduced to the couple immediately. The next day I brought Valery and his wife Irina to the Mariners' Centre, showed them round our dance studios, with changing rooms and showers; the main indoor stage, and the summer theatre with its shell-shaped roofed stage structure. They were genuinely impressed by the high standards, and also by the scale of operations of the organisation.

At the meeting with the Director, they showed him their diplomas and employment logs; told him about their current work at the theatre in their capacity as tutors on an hourly basis. They also showed him their credentials for specialising in Historical and Character dance (court/ballroom and stage/folk). They had never worked with children before, but were ready to try their hand. Plakhov told them that he would be able to inform them about the administration's decision in a few days' time.

When Oksana learned about the latest news, she became distressed and even panicky.

"Misha, you have no idea what this couple of schemers are capable of!"

"Maybe I don't, but Plakhov does. He was going to discuss the situation with Lyuftgarten. I am sure the two directors together can find a Solomon-like solution to this. Most likely the Arts Centre will offer the veteran assistants one of the smaller collectives linked to some Odessan trade union, where they'll be able to choreograph and also bear full responsibility for the productions. The Mariners' Centre will pay them compensation amounting to one month's salary, and that will be the end of the story."

"My dear, this is wishful thinking. In reality it might all turn out quite differently."

"No, dearest! In fact, this is the most popular formula for solving professional conflicts like these to avoid negative publicity. An ancient Eastern proverb says: 'Put a lamb shank into the wolf's muzzle, and he will stop growling at you.'"

"I'm afraid that in this particular situation, these two will care more about getting their revenge than getting compensated. The problem is that, like me, they're not capable of choreographing their own repertoire, and it's too late for them to learn. The same wise men say that 'A true artist is born, not made.'"

"So what do you think I should do in this situation, Oksana?"

"Misha, I don't know and cannot decide for you."

"So then, let's put these speculations aside, and trust in our good fortune. The bottom line is this: I don't see any gain in working with potential enemies. It also goes against my principles."

Plakhov succeeded in convincing most supporters of the veteran pair at his Cultural Centre and in the administration of the navigation authority, not to risk losing the children's ensemble a second time, and instead to reinforce our adult group with professionals from the theatre. As I had predicted, Lyuftgarten offered my 'senior colleagues' from the old Mariners' Dance Ensemble two options: a) an adult collective, one well established in the city; or b) organising a new children's dance studio at the cultural centre of one of the large factories, both from 1st September. Thus it was that, thanks to a compromise decision by the higher administration, a model of a new tripartite dance ensemble in our Cultural Centre was launched with great potential for the future.

Naturally, my first challenge in stabilising a collective made up of different age groups and abilities was to organise the educational and creative processes separately, for each group. I also needed to establish a framework for advancing from one group to the next. In the end, I developed an array of easy, but effective, exercises for the barre for three consecutive levels of the technical development of dancers, as well as three different repertoires for each of the three groups. At the same time I defined, in detail, the creative, educational, and organisational responsibilities of each tutor-assistant. I wrote these down in the form of a memorandum, in order to prevent misunderstandings, and had all my assistants sign a copy. They did, all along marvelling at my bureaucracy. But I wasn't bothered. I was absolutely certain that such pedantry was for the best, for clean professional relationships.

The next important item of business was advertising. I composed an enticing text for a poster and for a newspaper advertisement, both announcing the enrolment of young men and women into a newly redefined Mariners' Dance Ensemble. I entrusted the head of recreation with the task of publicising the ads and the posters as soon as possible, because there were only three weeks left to September. In a rather dry manner, she promised to do what she could. I could understand her disappointment at the dismissal of the veteran pair. Nevertheless, I continued to behave with her in an emphatically polite way, and she made sure not to crack so much as a false smile. The Director's secretary handed me four contracts for our entire creative team and suggested that we fill them in, sign them, and return them to her as quickly as possible. Our accordionists were being contracted as part of the orchestra.

Seeing me in his waiting room with the contract forms in hand, Plakhov launched into some good-humoured banter: "Aha, our head choreographer is busy with paperwork. Excellent!"

"Yes, as far as paperwork is concerned, I would like to show you the text of the poster and advertisements that I've prepared for publication. What do you think?"

"Has the head of recreation seen it?"

"I gave her copies, but she is very busy at the moment." He held my glance for just a while longer than necessary, and read the unmistakable signal there.

The study of the Historical/Court repertoire of the opera and ballet performances progressed at a brisk pace. Our greatest difficulty consisted in having to retain those dances we had already learned, while at the same time learning new compositions, every day, intensively, throughout the four weeks of August. This would have been quite enough even for mature professionals. Everybody understood this, and sympathised with our lot, trying to provide additional help during rehearsals to those boys who were slow learners. I pleaded with their more capable colleagues to devote half of their lunch break and half an hour at the end of each two-hour rehearsal to giving individual instruction to those falling behind, so as to maintain the uniform level within our group. The guys who were falling behind suffered more emotionally than physically, keenly aware of their lack of ability, and of the fact that they were slowing down the entire experimental group. At the rate we were going, we would learn only half of the forty required compositions by the end of August. These were Historical dances and processions for the balls and royal assemblies. It was obvious that we had to change the way we learned the material, or we would lose half of our group by the start of the new academic year.

Catching Rels at the school, I explained our predicament to him in great detail, and he promised to speak with Vronsky. Rels then invited me into his office to confirm the schedule of classes for the new academic year. I was happy to see that there was instruction in stage mime and stage combat on Mondays. Rels also supplied me with a list of names for the exercises at the barre and centre practice used by Vishnyakov in senior groups. He particularly emphasised the importance of joint classes at the theatre with the senior girls of years VI and VII. The Director had also allocated four hours on Sunday for my choreographic work in Character instruction with junior groups, which was to prepare them for a New Year's concert. In addition, each junior group was also to be trained for the year-end school concert. I could not refuse any of this because I was about to ask for a favour myself.

Rels asked: "What is it, Misha?"

"It's an idea for helping some of the guys in my group who are falling behind, but I am uneasy about bothering you about this, on top of everything else."

" 'What is not easy is 'putting your trousers on by way of your head', as we say in Odessa. Tell me!"

"There are two windows in our group's schedule at the moment: on Wednesdays and Saturdays. What if we were to schedule additional rehearsals in these three hours, from 3 to 6 p.m. not with 'corps de ballet', but with the senior girls (years VI and VII): one and a half hours, tutored by Maria Andreyevna and the demonstration pair, Irina and Valery? The latter could go over everything that was learned in the morning rehearsals slowly and meticulously, and our senior girls would get a chance to become familiar with the Historical dance in the theatre's repertoire. Perhaps you can insert a couple of extra hours into their schedule as well. For us, it would be a huge help: it would allow us to absorb better the new choreography which we're having to take in on a daily basis; at the same time, it would restore our self-confidence and prevent a potential dissolution of the group."

Listening to me, Rels was already busy making corrections in the schedule, and then he exclaimed: "Where were you with this idea earlier? And, by the way, are you trying to do my job for me? Or perhaps you would like to be my assistant?"

"Georgi Aleksandrovich, 'Appetite comes with eating.'"

"If I understand you correctly, you are asserting yourself in this case exclusively on behalf of your colleagues. You yourself would not benefit from this arrangement because during these hours you will be working here at the school."

I only shrugged my shoulders.

"Well, the idea is a good one, and I will get to work on it, without delay."

In the morning, after the session at the theatre, I dropped by at the ballet masters' office and asked to see Maria Andreyevna. She immediately came out and asked what the matter was.

Briefly, I described the issue and the proposed solution to her: to engage the senior girls from years six and seven as our partners in thorough study of the Historical dance programme. This would relieve the female 'corps de ballet' in the theatre from assisting us.

"We are very grateful to you for your patience and help, but we are unable to digest so much new information so quickly. Half of us are not coping, the rest are falling behind and losing faith in themselves. If we aren't able to bring them up to speed, the weakest among us will break down and leave, unable to cope with the sheer physical and mental pressure. In order to prevent the collapse of the group, we would like to ask you to support Rels' proposal to the theatre's directorate: to allocate two extra hours per week, a studio, a pianist, and a demonstration pair, in order to improve our learning of the theatre's historical repertoire. Rels has promised to arrange the participation of the senior girls in this. The days are Wednesday and Saturday, 3 to 6 p.m."

"That's fine, Misha. I will speak with the boss after the rehearsal."

Naturally, Vronsky could not refuse his protégée this rather reasonable favour. He not only allocated a studio, pianist, and demonstration pair, but also found the money to pay the latter for the extra hours, and entrusted Maria Alekseyevna with overseeing our collaborative work with the senior girls. Everyone involved in this project was highly appreciative of the Director's patronage, especially in view of the theatre's rigid financial set-up. My colleagues were happy because they now had the chance to chew over the new elements of the Historical/Court repertoire thoroughly, and at a reasonable pace. They also felt much better working with their old and familiar partners, rather than the ballerinas who could sometimes be impatient. At the same time, Maria Andreyevna relayed to me Vronsky's doubt about the practicality of investing the theatre's resources in training those students who would anyway most likely end by signing up with the Operetta rather than the Opera and Ballet Theatre. But Vronsky knew as well as anyone: 'You can't make an omelette without breaking a few eggs.'

Still, I decided to discuss this issue with my colleagues. The temptation to work at the Theatre of Musical Comedy, aka the Operetta, was very real: the attractions were easier work and better pay. After discussing this danger, we decided to maintain our loyalty to the Opera Theatre for at least five years, till the autumn of 1955. All the guys promised to behave themselves, in my absence, at the additional rehearsals on Wednesday and Saturday. If there were any problems, they were to communicate via my deputy, Sasha. Another problem was solved. But not for long.

Climbing up to my attic, I caught the strong smell of fried fish, and realised that my favourite cook was at home.

Knocking on the door, I heard a guarded call: "Who is it?"

"A passer-by, attracted by an appetising aroma from your window."

I cut my chatter abruptly, seeing the red eyes of my beloved, smeared with mascara. Shutting the door, I took her into my arms and kissed each eye in turn, smearing the black even more. At the sight of my black lips, she giggled, and proceeded to rub the black off with her fingers, each of which I kissed in turn as they touched me.

Hugging me tightly, she whispered with a threat: "I am not giving you up, whatever they say!"

I instantly grasped the situation and proclaimed, by way of comfort: "Even if you wanted to give me up, my dear, I can promise you, you would not succeed."

"Ah, so you have already been considering this?"

"No, Oksanushka, but to put it simply: I've been expecting this to happen at any moment. Fortunately, it's happening a week before the opening of the season."

"Before or after, the result is the same."

"Not at all, my darling. In two weeks' time, everyone will have forgotten all about this, provided we just ignore the slander, and continue to behave at work as if we know nothing and wish to know nothing about it. No explanations or apologies are needed! We should interact in public warmly and professionally, just as we did during the cruise. Nothing sentimental. We are adults, and outside of the workplace, nobody has the right to interfere in our private lives, neither morally, nor legally."

"Why are you so sure of that?"

"I'll explain, but after we've had dinner, all right?"

The fried gobies from the Bay of Odessa were sailing into my mouth, helped on their way by the tide of fresh beer. I almost swallowed my tongue along with these delicacies.

"And where, pray, did you procure this charmer of a fish, woman [Odessan slang]?"

"Well, where else, of course, at Privoz!" Oksana joined in my banter.

"And would it count as a criminal offence in this house, to ask for seconds?"

"Not in general, but for *you*, a show-off from Moldavanka, it will cost a dear penny!"

We had both become somewhat tipsy by then, and my beloved's equanimity was almost restored.

"You really don't know anything about a letter to the Cultural Department of the navigation authority?"

"No, but I can easily imagine its contents."

Oksana's eyes widened in surprise: "Really? Let's hear then."

"When you came to the Cultural Centre today to arrange for the testing of new candidates for the ensemble, the head of recreation innocently asked if you'd heard anything about an anonymous letter charging you with moral corruption, subverting the image of a Soviet educator, and allowing yourself to get intimately involved with the artistic director of the children's ensemble. Horrified, you asked her who had this letter? She replied, 'I passed it on to the Director, as was my duty.' You hastened to Plakhov, but the secretary told you that he was at the head office of the navigation authority, and that she hadn't heard of any anonymous letters. You almost collapsed senseless at this point, but then, being a practical woman, decided to drown your sorrows in a sea of beer and gobies."

"You're laughing, but I warned you not to cross these people!"

"Oksana, that pair of bastards have turned out to have even less sense than I initially gave them credit for. They would make very poor chess players, incapable of thinking several moves ahead, or of calculating their opponent's, i.e. Plakhov's, moves. First of all, you may rest assured that everyone at the Cultural Centre and at head office knows about our extracurricular relations. And all are of the opinion that it's none of their business, provided it doesn't begin to affect our work. The father of my cousin and friend David is the head of human resources at the Odessa Academy of Sciences and a lawyer by training. I described our situation to him and asked what he thought the risks were. He confirmed the possible risk of being fired, but only if we made a public exhibition of ourselves, or used our personal relations to the detriment of the ensemble's members or of our colleagues at work. The best advice in such a situation as this is simply to ignore the disparaging remarks, and the ridicule, and any insults that could get us to lose our cool. If the administration values our work and has confidence in our position as educators, they will protect us from such attacks, and the intrigue will be blocked by an administrative action from within, namely, by the dismissal of the initiators or by their transfer to another workplace.

"So, my good fairy, you should calm down and give the administration a chance to deal with this matter. Our head of recreation is forgetting an important maxim: 'Never spit into the wind!'"

"This sounds too good to be true!" commented my girlfriend, seating herself across my lap, with a wine glass in hand, "Mishanya, I am so happy with you. I cannot imagine my future without our son."

We took turns sipping from our glasses, caressing each other, and then gradually undressing, until we fell into a rapturous oblivion of carefree love. I clung to her tender fragrant body in a deep harmony of spirit and flesh, thanking the powers above for these rare moments of bliss and calm.

"How little one needs to be happy!" I kept repeating this mantra. "So why then, does the Almighty sometimes destroy what He has created?"

"Darling, it's time for me to go."

Oksana clung to me so passionately that she squeezed the breath out of me. I rubbed my face against her fragrant breasts, as if trying to store up the memory until our next meeting.

"Alas, my dear. Time to come back to earth, into the world of cares, hustle and bustle."

Running off to the theatre, I once more reminded Oksana not to react to any assaults of the enemy but to focus entirely on the testing of potential recruits to the ensemble and on the preparation for the season's opening.

Lyuftgarten, seeing me at the arts centre, exclaimed, "Misha, hello! Glad to see you here. How is the training at the theatre going?"

"OK. Slowly but surely."

"Are there any new recruits in the Mariners' Ensemble?"

"Yes, for the children's group. The situation with the adult group is less clear at the moment. As you know, we had problems with the former tutors there, but thanks to your help we should soon have that situation under control."

"Very good. To turn to our own business, I asked you here to let you know that the only time a professor from the university can be available for our lectures on the history of performing arts is Saturday, eleven to one. As a young specialist and a newly appointed member of the Artistic Board of the Regional Arts Centre

– I raised my eyebrows in surprise – you are invited to attend a meeting with the lecturer in order to finalise the programme and the order of topics to be covered in the course. Have you thought about the programme, and also how to get the audience interested in this seminar?"

"Thank you for the honour of giving me a membership in the Artistic Council. With your permission, I would like to suggest the following:

"a) issue in writing, a personal invitation to all the heads of amateur performing groups, explaining to them the need periodically to raise their professional level, as educators, so as not to fall behind their charges;

"b) the invitation should go out to every registered director of a semi-professional dance group, with the programme of the seminar attached, for their information; and

"c) we should promise every participant in the seminar an official certificate of completion. It should be something like a diploma, framed, with a glass covering, to be hung on the wall. The proposed timing of lectures – right before lunch – should work well for the participants. I will try to register for this seminar together with my whole team."

"Misha, thank you for your help in this project! Your meeting with the lecturer will take place on Saturday at 11. He wants to understand the range of specific interests of his future audience."

The Professor, when he came, had the appearance of a typical academic: past middle age, with a bald spot on his head and thick glasses on his nose. He had a well-trained voice, with clear Russian pronunciation, without any Odessan cadence. His conversation was measured and weighty, punctuated by faint gestures.

At my appearance, Lyuftgarten rose: "Professor, this is the Mikhail I was telling you about, a representative of the future generation of choreographers, with advanced training in theatre and choreography. It was his idea to invite you to contribute to the cause of professional/academic enlightenment. He can explain better than I what a contemporary dance teacher needs by way of aesthetic training."

I detected a note of sarcasm in Lyuftgarten's words, but did not quite catch its target, and so resolved to be cautious in my dealings with the lecturer.

"Periodic seminars at the Arts Centre have provided a good deal of material to the leaders of performing arts groups, enabling them to design the choreography of ethnic dances. Over the last five years, since the end of the war, the general educational level of our artistic directors has risen significantly. Many of them attend universities, or even schools of drama. But often faced with a question about the nature or history of a dance, the teacher doesn't know, or tries to improvise something unsatisfactory on the spot. That is why we have come up with the idea of improving the cultural and aesthetic level of the educators."

"Unfortunately," the Professor remarked, "in the university Drama Department, dance is studied only as a subsidiary means of artistic expression. From your personal experience, can you tell me which period of the history of dance your colleagues would find it most useful to focus on, and which would also be of potential interest to their young students?"

"From what I know," I said, "the forms of dance can be grouped into three categories: first, dances that express emotional states, performed for personal pleasure; second, ritual dances connected with special occasions such as weddings, childbirth, funerals, harvest, hunting, war; and third, dances for social occasions and entertainment: street performances, carnivals, processions, etc.

"If we start at that primary level and show how the later folklore of specific ethnicities developed, this will generate lively interest among the professional audience. If the lectures can be accompanied by illustrations and slides, it would help us understand and memorise better the development of poses, gestures, and facial expressions. Personally, I'd be very interested in a comparative study of compositional harmony between motion of dance movements, aural vocal/instrumental accompaniment and the visual expression of the decorative elements of performance, and how they function in different cultures."

"Mikhail, what you are listing sounds fascinating, but you are forgetting that I am an historian, not a ballet critic. Dance comes last in the hierarchy of performing arts, after music, singing, drama and pantomime, which is why there is a dearth of competent literature on the subject. Only dancers or choreographers are really in a position to communicate in words the nature of movements so familiar to them; to analyse a dance's capacity for emotional expression; to describe the laws of interaction between these two aesthetic categories."

"I fully agree with you, Professor, yet to enable choreographers to approach dance compositions and their performers critically, they do need to equip themselves with some theoretical/historical knowledge. This is precisely what we are trying to provide here."

Lyuftgarten who had been listening in silence up to this point, apparently recording our dialogue in shorthand, now intervened: "May I interject here? As far as I can see, both sides agree on the main thing: the directors of our dance collectives need to receive a minimum of some general background on the history of dance: origins, primary forms and genres; information on the interdependence between music and the decorative elements of performance; distinctive national colour; forms of dramatic expression; physical and aesthetic importance as a whole. Professor, if you agree in general with that, then we can work out the details as we go."

On the way home, I was beset by doubts about this professor of history. He was clearly puzzled by my questions about the origins and evolution of dance and pantomime. Perhaps because he wasn't particularly competent in the theory of choreographic composition? Or perhaps he was concerned about the religious underpinning of ancient ritual dances? This might be an unpopular – even dangerous – subject in the Soviet Union. The lecturer also apparently did not expect that, in addition to dance, he would have to shed light on the earliest forms of sound/rhythmic accompaniment for dramatic performances (clapping, the use of rattles, sticks, etc.) and decorative elements, such as body paint, masks, headgear, etc. To cover all these subjects he would probably need to invest much more time and energy in the preparation of lectures. Yet this was precisely what the teachers of dance, working on original compositions, badly needed. The Professor was probably anticipating that amateur choreographers like myself would be asking him difficult questions at every turn, and that he might not always have a decent answer. After all, he couldn't know everything.

Oksana greeted me warmly, but I could nevertheless read a hidden worry in her eyes.

"More bad news?" I pricked up my ears. These days I was always expecting some new stab in the back on the part of my enemies.

"Mishanya, you look very tired and preoccupied. And probably, not eating well . . ."

"Which is not good for our offspring!" I concluded.

My girlfriend jumped at me with a ladle in her hand. I thought, *She is going to smash it against my forehead,* and raised my hands in the air to simulate complete surrender. But my darling aggressor instead wrapped her arms around my waist and as usual covered my chatty mouth with her lips. I placed my longing hands over her two perfectly shaped breasts and rapturously pressed myself to her in a long fermata/pause. Only the borscht, which was now starting to boil over on to the stove, induced me to let go of my sweet prisoner.

To the greatest satisfaction of my girlfriend, I not only devoured a large portion of her divine concoction, but also asked for seconds. And so, having eaten our fill, we finally turned to the long-awaited satisfaction of our most immediate needs.

"What new land mine have our 'friendly' plotters laid for us now?"

"Over the last three days, I've been visiting my old classmates from the adult group of the old Mariners' Ensemble, and none of them have received the flyers inviting them to join the new collective. Last week, however, I did see piles of these flyers by the cashier's window and also the posters at the entrance to the Cultural Centre."

"Yes, I saw them too. The head of recreation simply did not comply with the Director's instructions."

"My dear, calm down! I'm going to clean up here and change the bed sheets, and you, meanwhile, can sit down and write an official report addressed to Plakhov recounting this matter, asking him to forward it to the appropriate administrative officials. More than that we cannot hope to accomplish today."

"My sweet, you are a wise adviser. I'm proud of your philosophical approach."

At 10 a.m. on the last Sunday of August, I was at the ballet school, attending a parents' meeting where the new students were being introduced to their teachers, and where I was being paraded as proof of male representation among the teachers. Indeed, at my appearance – being the only person there with a flat chest and dressed in trousers – the faces of the ten lads showed an almost tangible relief. I had to leave almost immediately, however, and waved them all goodbye. At 11 a.m., in the Summer Theatre at the Mariners' Centre, Oksana and I were already selecting candidates for the beginners' group of the children's ensemble. Those who had had some experience with stage performances were immediately assigned to the senior subgroup. We were pleasantly surprised to see among them three boys, between twelve and fourteen years old, who had come with a recommendation from their teachers. They were looking through the photographs of our summer cruise with great interest.

While my assistant was speaking with the parents, I informed the kids about the programme: preparations for a winter concert and for a review performance at the end of the season, in May. At my initiative, all the new members of the ensemble received postcards with a photo of the Cultural Centre on the front and a return address and a schedule of classes on the back. Parents and offspring departed in high spirits. The head of recreation was supposed to show up for the procedures, but had failed to put in an appearance. After lunch, with some trepidation, we awaited the candidates for the adult group. There were many more fifteen-to-seventeen-year-olds than we had expected, and only a handful of adults from other cultural centres. The former members of the adult group had either not received invitations or had decided to boycott it.

We were rather eager to learn what had happened with my report to Plakhov, but it would have been inappropriate to ask his secretary. There was nothing to do but wait for events to unfold. Everyone knows it is easier to fight than wait for a fight. My star sign is Taurus, and I find it best to stay out of the diplomatic games, because I lose my temper too easily if I feel slighted. This was why I had asked Oksana to see the head of recreation about the enrolment into the adult group. Oksana was startled to learn that the head of recreation was no longer employed at the Cultural Centre. She had been urgently transferred to the post of director of a cultural club in the port of Ilichevsk, not far from Odessa. Sworn to secrecy, Oksana was told what had happened. On receipt of my report, Plakhov had invited the head of recreation to explain herself; in particular, why she hadn't complied with his explicit instructions to send out flyers about enrolment into the new ensemble. She'd said that she hadn't been able to find the addresses of the former members.

"Why didn't you ask for a copy from the head office where you sent the information two years ago, before the ensemble's tour abroad?"

She'd had nothing to say to that. This had all happened on Thursday. Twenty-four hours later, the head office of the Black Sea Fleet had issued the order for her transfer to a new post.

The first week of a new season is typically the busiest in the year. Everywhere (theatre, school and the Cultural Centre) classes were starting for new groups, with new instructors, following new programmes, and with new problems. Without Oksana's help, I doubt I'd have been capable of getting through that week without ending up in a mental hospital. At the theatre, from the very first lesson on Classical dance, good, strictly professional, relations were established with our new teacher, Yegorov. A former lead dancer, he knew his art down to a tee and trained us without any show of emotion, like a surgeon in an operating theatre. After a thirty-year-long career onstage and sixteen years of training male dancers, he knew exactly what he was doing.

With him also, we began an introductory course in 'Pas de deux': classes twice a week, held jointly with our partners from the previous year's Historical dance course, now the senior girls from year VII. We started on the technique that did not involve any lifting: balancing on two feet en pointe in all five positions; then, on one foot: in all standard poses of Classical dance. Later we began working on light lifting: holding the girl by the waist and lifting her to the level of one's chest, head, and on outstretched arms, lowering her on to the shoulder in the sitting position. With the group of girls whom we already knew, we had no problems. Their leader, Galina, had clearly done a good job with them.

On Monday, after Classical dance, we had our first lesson in stage movement. The night before, stagehands had brought several rolls of carpet to the ballet studio and stacked them under the grand piano, without any explanations as to who, or what, they were for. We were guessing that they were for the next day's ballet rehearsal. Suddenly, an athletic-looking man in a tracksuit walked in. We thought he had lost his way and offered our help.

"Are you Mikhail?" he asked, shaking my hand.

I froze with my mouth open.

"I am your instructor in stage movement. My name is Anton Andreyevich. Is everyone here?"

"We are only eleven representatives of a rare species."

"I love training animals," he rejoined in the same ironic manner. Introducing himself to each of us individually, Anton Andreyevich tried to memorise all the names. "Vasya, Kolya, Petya, Zhora! Unroll those carpets stacked under the grand piano. Misha and Sasha, go to the storage room on this floor and bring a container marked 'no. 17'. It has props for your group. Here are the keys for the door and the container. After the lesson, you will take it all back and return the keys to me. Without them, the warden won't let me out of the building."

Smiling, we followed his orders without demur. There was something spellbinding in his voice and in the expression of his eyes, instilling an unshakeable regard for him and a desire to submit to his will, like an apprentice collaborating with a master. He seated us on the carpet in a semicircle with legs crossed in front and palms down on our knees. When we were all sitting like this in front of him, the animal tamer finally began his magic show.

"Relax! Breathe deeply and evenly! Focus your attention only on the exercises we are going to perform, in order to warm up the muscles quickly and effectively. Copy me in mirror image. Don't hold your breath, and don't interrupt the tempo of continuous movements."

The ten-minute cycle began slowly, with a warm-up for the head, shoulders and torso; then it focused on different sections of the arms and legs, and concluded with an active and fast workout for bones and muscles, balancing on the buttocks, and still sitting on the floor.

The programme of the intensive course consisted of four segments and was planned to take place over the course of one year.

a) Work with hand props: glasses, bottles, trays, towels; walking stick, crutch, staff, umbrella; chair, table, stool and ladder; knife, sword, shield, sabre; sickle, fork and axe.

b) Elements of hand combat without weapons: body grabs; lifting and throws, rollovers, etc.; the handling of weapons: knife, sword/sabre, shield, spear, etc.

c) Facial expressions for the various emotions: joy–sadness, threat–fear; laughter–crying; confidence–doubt; adoration–contempt; surprise–caution; anger–kindness, etc.

d) Imitation of behaviour and actions: children, old people; birds and animals; eating and drinking; labour; love, quarrels; search and hiding; hunting and fishing, etc.

The programme was intended as a general introduction, compressing into one year what would normally be studied over three in the schools of dramatic art. For us, however, it was to form the basis for our own, further, self-education. Each of our sessions with the trainer produced in us an enormous sense of satisfaction, both physically and emotionally.

The first public lecture by the history professor at the regional Arts Centre attracted many directors of amateur performing groups. There were even some teachers of dance who had travelled from far away to be there: some out of curiosity, others to further their knowledge. After the registration for the course, Lyuftgarten officially launched the three-month-long seminar on the subject of 'The Origin and Evolution of Ethnic Dance in the Sphere of Theatrical Performances'. Because I was short-sighted, I sat in the front row during lectures and performances. In front of me were two rather stern-looking women, clearly from the Ministry of Culture or from the Department of Public Education. For the first forty-five minutes, the lecturer spoke about the corrupt methods by which capitalist ideology influenced scientific research into the origins of the world; about the only true and correct position of the followers of the Marxist–Leninist teaching; about the misguided views of ancient educators and the incomparable work on the subject of the nationality question by the great Soviet leader. Instead of addressing the audience, the lecturer kept addressing the two official figures sitting in front of me. These rather odious censors, for their part, kept up a constant stream of audible remarks to one another during the Professor's introduction, making it difficult for others to hear him.

During the break, I naïvely asked two colleagues what they'd thought about the first half of the lecture. Both seemed shocked by my sarcastic tone, each of them giving an unambiguous endorsement of the lecture as a quite normal introduction to any seminar on a sociocultural topic. I bit my tongue, realising that I had displayed a complete lack of political correctness. In my mind's eye I could see my mother's face, warning me about speaking without thinking. Returning to my seat, I stared at my notebook, without looking to right or left, still feeling the heat of embarrassment in my face.

Once the two officials had left, the Professor turned to the main topic on the programme. He spoke in an accessible way, about primitive forms of communication between humans, emphasising that facial expressions and dance were the primary and most effective forms of communication between tribes, serving both as a way of expressing their practical needs in daily life, and as a way of giving expression to their spiritual aspirations. Unable to understand and explain natural phenomena, or his own weaknesses and defects, primitive man invented supernatural idols who could both solve his daily problems and also be blamed for his personal failures and losses. These idols needed to be placated with regular sacrifices, accompanied by dance and drumbeat, which were intended to ensure that a tribe was blessed with food, water, fire and successful reproduction. The pantomime and ritual dances that are still familiar to us today, were born from such primitive practices.

STAGE II: A BUMPY ROAD IN EDUCATION

CHAPTER 4 NEW LINE OF EXPERTISE

It was September 1952. I was full of excitement on the way to the ballet school to meet my new pupils in Character dance. In the first lesson, I explained briefly to them the meaning of the subject. The girls of the third and fourth years were intrigued by the unusual style and rhythm of the exercises and the basic technique of finished movements. Both groups were suspicious of a new, unusually young, teacher at the start of the lesson, but all finished the class with bright, shining eyes and broad smiles of satisfaction produced by their creative efforts. I must confess that, for me as well, as a new teacher, the first lesson with the ballerinas posed a serious test, notwithstanding all my considerable previous tutoring experience. Everywhere in schools, pupils start off by putting a new teacher to the test, to see what they can get away with. Here too, the girls asked silly questions to distract me, chatted behind my back and made faces at me, forgetting about the mirror-walls of the studio.

By contrast, I instantly established a rapport with the boys of the mixed group. They turned out to be just nine teenagers, of different ages, heights and levels. The oldest was fifteen. He had graduated that summer from middle school and had already set his mind on finding a job, rather than continuing with his ballet training. Hearing about a special course for boys, however, he became interested and answered the call. In his middle school, he'd been teased incessantly for four years by his peers, and at the ballet school he was plagued by girls' taunting. I appraised his physique: tall, well built; sad and intelligent eyes. *This one will work,* I thought.

"Come with me!"

"Where?"

"You will know in a moment. Wait here!" I commanded, and knocked on the Director's door.

Rels raised his head from a pile of papers: "What's the matter?"

"It's about Andrei from year V. It would be better for him if he joined our experimental male group. He doesn't fit in with the other boys, but with us he would flourish. Please, speak to him, and please excuse my interfering with your authority."

"You never cease to amaze me, Mikhail! Call him in!"

"Thank you, Georgi Aleksandrovich. I knew you would agree with me."

I seated the rest of the boys down on the floor and began my usual 'overture'. Although it was a mixed bunch, as a group, the boys looked quite good. I explained to them the situation at the school: the small number of boys, the difference in their levels of training, and our common goal of studying together and performing Character dances onstage. In concerts, they would be dancing on their own and possibly with girls. The boys shifted about restlessly, impatient to get started on something more captivating than the never-ending classical exercises at the barre and in the centre. I promised to choreograph two dances for them, something appropriate to their levels of training, and another dance, jointly with the girls of year III.

The start of the new season at the Mariners' Centre was challenging. In addition to regular classes, the first week was full of organisational matters, mostly connected with the arrival of the new head of recreation, who was still trying to get a handle on the new job. Oksana was set upon by the parents of fresh recruits to the children's ensemble, and by new participants in the youth and adult groups. She had to explain to the kids the rules of behaviour, and what was expected of them, during lessons and in the changing rooms. She also had to organise parents' invigilation of classes and rehearsals.

At 5 p.m., I led the excited kids to their classroom and began teaching them the basics of stage movement: how to move in a specific direction onstage, and how to create spatial patterns of a straight line, a zigzag, a spiral, etc. Then I demonstrated to them the difference between running onstage and running after a departing bus in the street. The children laughed out loud, trying to outrun each other. To finish, boys and girls separately, all of them competing with one another, performed various types of jumps: on two feet, on one foot, from one foot to the other, etc. Thirty minutes later, tired but happy, the little dancers returned to their parents. They were too exhausted for any fooling around.

After observing the warm-up of the youths, Oksana and I decided who (the tallest and strongest) among this group were ready to be moved up to the junior subgroup of the adult ensemble. At the same time, we added new recruits from other youth companies in the city who had come to join our dance ensemble. This approach enabled us to refresh and expand the contingent of the newly combined Mariners' Ensemble. The first lessons in the youth group went off without a hitch and on a high note. Irina and Valery brought the group into line from day one. Meanwhile, I began working with them on a dance suite, 'Moldovan Rhapsody'. I fashioned combinations of individual movements, passing them on, as I went along, to Irina or Valery who could then teach their proper execution to the girls' and boys' groups. Oksana worked on finalising the casts for each number. The accordionists, meanwhile, were busy producing sheet music for musical arrangements. Overall, the place was buzzing with activity, like a professional theatre. When Plakhov peeked into the room during one of my demonstrations, I could only signal to him with thumbs up, and the Director nodded in approval.

Sunday was the day I had set aside for my creative work. From morning till evening I worked out staging plans and composed choreography for my two main clients: the ballet school and the Mariners' Ensemble. Altogether, there were eight to ten compositions: for different levels of students, with different themes, different styles of music (classical or folk), different ethnic flavours and personalised manners of performance. It helped that I had developed a method of finding and creating a dance text, which would be unique to each production. The same elements of footwork, when performed in a different style, or tempo/rhythm, and when combined with clapping and tapping, squats and jumps – depending on the personal abilities of performers, and accompanied by contrasting tonalities of music – can produce endless varieties of combinations, and can look completely different when applied to different kinds of subject matter, particularly when dealing with folk culture, or with characters onstage.

The process of using the same basic elements to create something unique is common to all forms of art: whether it's composers who create timeless symphonies out of twelve musical tones and halftones; or poets who weave sonnets from the letters of the alphabet, or artists who paint unforgettable pictures from seven basic colours. When asked where I find, or steal, the endless combinations of movements that make up my choreographic vocabulary, I joke that it's a 'trade secret'. The truth is that it is not always possible to explain the creative process in words. Sometimes I'm not aware myself how I compose, how the muse guides my imagination. On such days it is best to leave me to myself.

In any creative process, the key is to grasp the moment of discovery, of realisation. The rest is merely the technical and artistic means by which such initial ideas may be brought to fruition. Over the years I diligently studied Slavic folklore and stored away in my experimental piggy bank many colourful samples for future choreographic interpretation, to be used in the staging of Character dances. For example, such traditional ethnic characters as Ded Moroz (Grandfather Frost) and Snegurochka (Snow Maiden), Matryoshka (Russian Doll) and Jongleur, Swan Princess and Zmei Gorynich (Dragon of the Mountain), all work well as subjects of children's dances for a young audience. If a choreographer understands child psychology, the way their imagination works, and how they perceive action onstage, he/she can successfully employ these fairy-tale characters in dance compositions. What may seem naïve or silly to an adult, can leave a deep impression on a youngster's mind, and encourage him on the right path. A choreographer has all the traditional characters at his disposal. By using Russian folk dances, and by varying basic movements and the dramatic interpretation of character types, he is capable of creating memorable performances. It is precisely this artistic pulling-together of dance elements from a particular ethnic lexicon, which underscores the entire creative process.

Rels transferred Andrei into our experimental group. I had warned my colleagues about his arrival and they received him warmly. This fifteen-year-old lad had excellent abilities for Classical dance. If he didn't make any mistakes and if he concentrated all of his attention on training, he would be guaranteed a successful career in ballet. He could never have foreseen then, that a decade later, he would become the leading soloist of the Odessa Ballet. His four previous years' studying at the ballet school had not been in vain: Andrei was quick to pick up the theatre's repertoire, surprising the choreographer and his dance partner.

The boy became as attached to me as to an elder brother, and shadowed my every move. In the intervals between classes I advised him on how to behave with colleagues, or with the theatre's employees and with the schoolgirls and ballerinas.

A week later, I presented him, as an official member of the experimental group, to the personnel manager of the theatre as a candidate for the extras. Andrei nearly jumped for joy on hearing that he would be earning a little money. I had to dampen his excitement by telling him that he could not be under contract with the theatre until he was sixteen in a few months' time. Until then, his mother would be given his salary. Andrei decided to wait until December to sign a contract with the theatre.

Vronsky pressured the tutors, and they in turn pressured us, to learn the Historical dances in the theatre's repertoire as quickly as possible. We were supposed to finish this tutorial before the winter holidays because, during the winter break, our group was scheduled to perform two shows a day – something that would improve the financial situation of all the participants. I asked Maria Andreyevna to have the debutant substitute for me in these performances owing to my engagements at the Mariners' Centre. She recommended that the ballet manager sign a contract with Andrei from 15th December. As they say in Russia, 'The wolves are sated and the sheep are safe.'

The organisation and training of the children's ensemble was a matter of great concern to me. It was set to perform in the New Year pantomime at the Cultural Centre where the girls were to dance as snowflakes and the boys as little animals. Oksana was assisted by the wardrobe mistress and two committed mothers. The main group of dancers and reserves were taking turns performing every other day. Oksana's daughter Lyubanya had the role of the Snow Maiden while I was Ded Moroz (Grandfather Frost). As the main characters of the show, we had to perform two matinees every day, one hour before lunch with the little kids (three to five years old) and one hour after lunch with older kids (six to eight years old). For this work, Plakhov promised Oksana and me a two-week vacation at the resort city of Yalta in the first half of August: two separate rooms with a shared bathroom; therapeutic mudbaths; excursions and entertainment, everything paid for by the Trade Union of the Black Sea Navigation Authority. Oksana voiced her intention of taking Lyubanya along so that we could all go together. I was unsure about the idea, but my lady friend stressed the positive side of such a family enterprise.

"All the girls at the ballet school, both those you dance with and those you teach, are all talking about you. My daughter is really proud to be working with you."

"Lyuba is just a child. What does she know?"

"I'm sorry, Mishanya, your naïvety astounds me. This child is almost nine. She sees everything, she knows too much, perhaps, and understands human relations perfectly. When my mother asked her if she was jealous of me, she replied, 'Grandma, I'm proud that Mother has such a dedicated friend and lover. When I grow up, I would also like to have such an admirer.' My mother almost fainted hearing this, and you're saying she's just a child. She is reading novels I wasn't allowed to touch before I was sixteen. And there's more. When I stayed over at your place for the first time, Lyuba asked her grandma in the morning: where is Mum? 'She was out late with her girlfriends and stayed the night with one of them.'

"That evening the girl asked me: 'Mama, do you love Mikhail Semyonovich?' I went weak at the knees but she repeated her question.

109

'Of course I do, very much, he is my colleague.'

'No, I mean romantic love, not respect.'

'You mean do I love him as a person?'

'Yes!'

'Very much!'

'Why?'

'Because he is a decent man, a loyal friend and a talented artist.'

'And as a man?'

'Darling, you need to go to sleep. Have sweet dreams about Goldilocks and the Three Bears.'

'And you too – about your favourite bear!'"

As we had expected, the three pairs of veterans from the adult group of the ensemble never reappeared after the first rehearsal. Irina, Valery and I had to reshuffle the groups a little, transferring two of the more mature lads, together with four of the girls, from the youth group to the adults. The reshuffle created a more balanced male/female ratio in both groups. My strategic choice of dance number for the mixed-ability adult group was a 'Sailors' Quadrille'. I chose it because of the simplicity of technique and the emphasis it placed on playful male bravado, female coquetry and exaggerated flirtatiousness. It was an intriguing choice for the experienced dancers of varied ability, but it also gave them the opportunity to get used to each other: eight pairs of dancers in the quadrille periodically changed partners, displayed their virtuosity in solos, teased the slow ones good-humouredly, and jealously tripped the show-offs. The dance concluded with a complex sequence, performed in harmony by the entire group.

For the remaining nine girls, I choreographed a humorous composition, 'The Odessan Market'. In the dance, vendors and buyers haggle for five minutes, unable to agree on a price. Starting with an impatient queue snaking across the stage, erupting into small scenes of argument between chatterboxes, the composition moves to a fist fight between offended peddlers who chase after each other. It finishes with a whirlpool of female figures frozen, at the end, in a pile of bodies, with limbs sticking out in all directions.

With the youth group, I first reintroduced the previous year's repertoire from the Black Sea tour, replacing those members of the cast who had been transferred to the adult group with new recruits. Irina and Valery began coaching the youths in this repertoire while I turned to the choreography of the 'Moldavian Rhapsody'. The latter consisted of a suite of dances: Khora, Bukuria, and Jok. At this time the youth group was my pride and joy in all aspects of creative discipline and productivity. Oksana missed her former charges and readily helped me with introducing them to the new repertoire. She also reintroduced the composition 'Pioneers' Summer' to the children's group. Only then did I turn my attention to choreographing the 'Russian Maslenitsa' (a celebration of the imminent end of winter). This was quite a complex suite, consisting of round dances, virtuoso displays and clown acts. The youths learned the suite with enthusiasm, engaged by the artistic fusion of a complex dance technique with mime.

The true delight, however, was the children's group. We changed the age parameters of enrolment for the year, admitting ten-to-eleven-year-olds into the junior subgroup and twelve-to-fifteen-year-olds into the senior subgroup. This was Oksana's idea and it proved to be a good one. At the very first lesson, I began training the little ones in the choreography for the New Year show, learning the body motion and steps of snowflakes with the girls, and forest animals (wolf, bear, fox, hare, etc.) with the boys. My demonstrations of the characteristic behaviour of these animals greatly amused the kids.

In the corridor parents would ask Oksana: "What are they doing in there? Why are the kids squealing and laughing?"

"The choreographer is mimicking how the children dance the fox's part, as if it were a goat, and the squirrel's part as a bear."

So what other urgent business was on my agenda? All was well at the theatre. At the school, the young ballerinas were not yet up to speed. At the Mariners' Centre, everything was under control. At the Arts Centre, the seminar participants would ask the Professor many questions, most of which he was either unwilling or unable to answer. I personally thought that the Professor knew more than he was letting on about the sociocultural history of dance through the ages, but was concerned about how to present it within the framework of Soviet ideology.

When I shared my concerns with Lyuftgarten, he shut his office door, and then, resting his hand on my shoulder, said: "Misha, stay focused on your strengths and leave alone what may ultimately hurt and disappoint you."

I looked into his sad eyes, sighed, shrugged my shoulders, and walked out of his office, eyes downcast. I felt the Director's heavy stare on my back.

When children are upset, they run to their mothers for comfort.

"Oh, bright star on our horizon!" exclaimed my mother, turning her face towards me for a kiss.

There was a noisy group of youths in the next room. I raised an eyebrow, nodding in their direction.

"It's your little brother celebrating with friends."

"What's the occasion?"

"Shame on you!" Bagheera joked. "Everyone but you in Odessa knows. Your brother was just awarded the title of 1st Category Chess Master. At fourteen, it's a huge achievement. Go and congratulate him!"

I looked in and waved to Roman.

He shouted brightly: "Misha, come on in! Everybody, this is my almost best brother," and he introduced me to his friends. "He dances, and teaches ballet."

"Congratulations, little brother! What a success! I toast your future victories as well!"

"Thanks!" We clinked our mugs of kvass, drained them, and then hugged each other.

"Take a seat, Mikhail, and tell me, what's up with you?"

"No, thanks, you go on celebrating with your friends, and I'll go and chat with Mum."

"She talks about you all the time, and considers you the most practical of the three of us."

"Take care of yourself, Junior!"

I saluted the whole company, and went to sit next to Mother.

"Mama, how've you been?"

"I'm holding up OK, thanks."

"Why isn't Yosif with them?"

"Better not ask. . . ."

"They still don't get along?"

"Like cat and dog. With every year that goes by it only gets worse."

"When does he graduate from the university?"

"He's to be a burden around my neck for two more years. . . . But I would rather hear about you."

"No news with me, I'm just studying and working. Mama, you look tired, you must take better care of yourself," I said, getting up. "See you soon!"

"Be well, my dear!"

On Sunday at 10 a.m., Oksana brought her daughter to the Mariners' Centre for a rehearsal of the New Year pantomime. According to the script, Lyubanya as the Snow Maiden was supposed to assist Grandfather Frost and two clowns (Pat and Patashon) in greeting guests; dance solo in the composition 'Winter Waltz' with snowflakes and in the 'Forest Polka' with the animals; she was also to dance the duet with Grandfather Frost in the show's finale. Simply put, she was to be the star of an hour-long show. At the enumeration of these duties, the girl's eyes shone ever brighter, and her mother's gradually widened.

"Misha, are you sure she can handle all this?"

"Absolutely! And I'm sure she will be brilliant! Aren't you, Lyubushka?"

"I don't know, but I'll try my best. I love this programme."

Over the next two hours, the Snow Maiden learned three solo variations of the waltz, and all the main sequences of the polka, which she would be performing with the animal characters. She was to rehearse this part of the dance with her little partners at the Mariners' Centre. I complimented Lyubanya on her dedicated work, and told her to come again on Thursday for the rehearsal of the waltz and polka. She answered with a curtsey, and ran off to change. Together with Oksana, we quickly went over all of the Snow Maiden's numbers that involved two clowns. Then, I hurried off to the ballet school for my first choreography meeting with the girls of years III and IV.

At one o'clock, I entered the studio of the ballet school accompanied by a pianist, where, according to the schedule of the rehearsal, the girls of year III should have already been warming up, ahead of the teacher's arrival. They weren't there. The accompanist proposed going to the changing rooms to call the girls in, but I said no. Instead I gave her an adaptation for piano of the ballet score for Rimsky-Korsakov's *The Tsar's Bride* and asked her to play the 'Yar-Khmel' dance originally accompanied by a choir. The sounds of music must have reached the changing rooms, because the head of the girls soon appeared in the studio and began warming up. Five minutes later, I looked around:

"Is that everyone?" (Out of eighteen students barely half were present.)

"The others are still in the changing rooms. Shall I call them?"

"No, thanks. Continue with your warm-up, sitting on the floor, and listening to the music. Its structure is not square, as in typical ballet dances. Try to memorise the motifs of an ancient song, where phrases alternate with a different number of bars: 4 + 6 + 9, etc. I'll be counting the measure, 4/4 or 6/8, and you'll be bending one finger for each bar of music in a measure. Maestro, we are ready!"

While we were practising the aural reading of the piano score with those present, one by one the other girls kept appearing at the door. As they did so, I gestured to them to stand to one side. When the music stopped, I conducted a roll call, noting down in a register those who were late. Their behaviour was a blatant breach of discipline, which called for immediate inoculation against the spread of the disease.

"Dear pupils, I'm not interested in hearing your excuses, be they genuine or false. Such a brazen demonstration of disrespect towards your teacher and the accompanist is simply not acceptable in a professional school. I was under the impression that we had already worked out the ethical principles of our interaction. It would appear that I was mistaken. Judging by the angry expressions on your faces, it appears you considered yourselves to be doing your choreographer a great favour by merely turning up here in the studio, instead of staying in your warm beds. Let me remind you that the Director of your school specially requested me to come here during my free time and choreograph a dance for you to ballet music, in order to expand your knowledge of stagecraft as well as your knowledge of the Character dance repertoire. Perhaps you thought you would be dancing only what you liked when you joined the ballet troupe, and not what your artistic director told you. Because of your lax attitude, we've already lost twenty out of 120 minutes of the valuable time allotted for today's rehearsal.

"Next time, if you have any self-esteem, you will make sure to come to Sunday rehearsals twenty minutes before, not after, the start of the session; you will then warm up like students intending to become professional dancers, and you will greet the arrival of your teacher and accompanist with a conventional bow. If any of you fails to show up at the next stage rehearsal without a note of explanation to the school's administration, you may consider yourselves discharged from participation in my choreography sessions. Anyone who is late for the start of the session will have to sit and observe the others dancing for the rest of that rehearsal. I do not intend to complain to the administration because this is extracurricular work, not paid for by the school. When you get home today, however, be sure to share with your parents the news of your appalling behaviour in the professional ballet school, and also notify them of the possibility of your being excluded from participating in this number in the New Year show.

"Please, come to the middle now! 'Yar-Khmel' is a scene from an ancient wedding ritual. The composer Rimsky-Korsakov created this piece based on Russian folklore, loosely bringing together folk motifs in a classical symphonic stylisation. This unusual musical arrangement for an orchestra and choir requires dancers to be particularly attentive listeners, because the compositional architectonics of the accompaniment are different in this piece from the square arrangement familiar to you from other dance practices. Today we'll begin with an introduction to the ethnography of Russian dances: traditional positions of arms and feet; poses and bows; walks and foot-tapping; jumps and turns, etc. We'll focus on the style and manner of performance. After that, we shall look at specific dance techniques, such as footwork coordinated with the movement of hands holding kerchiefs, each following a different tempo and using various measures: 4/4, 6/8, 2/4. Your ability to listen out for the musical architecture here will be further complicated for inexperienced ears such as yours, because of the polyphony of the choir singing against the background of a symphony orchestra.

"This is why I ask you not to talk during the rehearsals and to focus your attention to the maximum on the tempo/rhythm and melodic modulations of the accompaniment. At the beginning, I am going to count the metre out loud, but after that you will need to understand the piano accompaniment on your own. My choreography contains a number of episodes that involve acting and mime, providing an expressive background of movement for the main dance action, all in concord with the choral polyphony and the orchestra. I recommend that you listen to a record of this opera at home, while revising the choreographic compositions in your head."

The year IV girls arrived for their choreographic rehearsal at 3 p.m. sharp, apparently after being given a warning by the previous group. While I was discussing the piano score with the accompanist, I could hear them whispering behind my back, warming up by the barre and on the floor. Five minutes later

I turned round and greeted them. They jumped to their feet and answered with some poorly coordinated curtseys. I asked the head girl to tell me who was missing from the class and noted them down in a register. Asking my permission, she ran off to see if anyone had got stuck in the changing room. I exchanged a meaningful glance with the pianist.

"Girls, please come closer. Sit down for a few minutes and stretch out your legs. As you perhaps already know, your dance is based on my interpretation of some themes from Tchaikovsky's opera *Cherevichki*. Rich classical music, saturated with symphonic renditions of Ukrainian folk tunes, provides a mine of opportunities for choreographic representations of contrasting characters using dance and mime.

"In a Museum of Fairy Tales, there is a shelf with twelve pairs of colourful magic shoes lined up around a music box. While the gong is striking twelve times, the twelve pairs have to be put on, each pair to fit the right-sized feet of those wishing to participate in the dance competition. Following a signal, the music turns on automatically, and the feet wearing the magic shoes start dancing uncontrollably of their own accord, for three minutes. Then, over another sequence of twelve strikes of a gong, the shoes have to be returned to their original positions on the shelf or they will lose their magical power. The fairy dance starts and ends with the dancers facing the shelf with the magic shoes and with their backs to the audience. They take up this initial position, when either the lights or the curtain goes down."

The boys from the Character dance class arrived, as usual, ahead of time, impatient to attend their first-ever choreographic rehearsal. While the pianist familiarised herself with the score of 'Khorumi', I helped the young dancers with a warm-up and, counting out loud, instructed them in the unfamiliar music metre 5/4, alternating with 6/8 in the central part of the opus. I told the boys about Georgian folklore, and laid particular emphasis on the historic-ritualistic character of the bellicose male dance they were about to learn. Their faces lit up with excitement at the description of the various episodes of mime (reconnaissance, attacks, chases, etc.) showing their keen anticipation of fighting, danger, and victory, all things deeply rooted in their male psyche.

I was slightly concerned about the physical capabilities of these youths in handling some of the elements of the choreography, such as mock fighting and lifting. For example, in one episode, five of the taller and stronger dancers form a circle by placing their arms on each other's shoulders, while supporting three lighter dancers, who stand on the shoulders and intertwined arms of their supports, and who also have their arms linked with each other. This two-tiered group of spies moves fluidly clockwise in a circle on the stage on the lookout for an enemy. The dance also involved acrobatic elements in an imaginary hand-to-hand combat. I realised the students were neither physically nor technically prepared for such an advanced level of choreography. I explained to them the danger of practising these dance movements on their own, without a coach. As a result I had to spend half the working time during sessions on doing workouts for their weak muscles so that they would be able to perform the excessively difficult and intricate wrestling moves, rollovers, and throws required. Fortunately for this purpose, I was able to make use of the repertoire of my own morning training sessions with the school's instructor in stage movement. Nevertheless, thanks to their tireless enthusiasm, the boys made good progress in mastering the elements of stage hand-to-hand combat, together with the elements of Georgian folk dance.

At the theatre, we were finishing the study of Historical dance from the foreign opera repertoire. Because I was sharing a dance partner with young Andrei for half of the time in dance rehearsals, I had an opportunity to record old choreographic compositions in shorthand, thereby adding new material to my own archive. I would find it easier to analyse on paper the specific characteristics of the timeless notation model of choreography. Naturally, when looked at using modern aesthetic criteria, many of these ancient compositions could seem archaic: either because of a rather minimalist pattern of spatial sequences both in the movement of pairs and in the contact between partners, or because of rather monotonous and repetitive elements altogether, characteristic of such a type of dance, which often lacked dynamic variation or development of tempo/rhythmic expression.

The intimate dialogue between partners in such dances as Sarabande, Galliard, and Volta, was supposed to develop rapidly, producing an effect, over a period of three to four minutes, which would give its participants a sense of spiritual satisfaction from their brief physical interaction. It would appear that the point of aristocratic balls of that time, especially at the time of Catherine de' Medici, Elizabeth I and Louis XIV, lay in this erotic lyrical duet. My young colleagues often felt embarrassed when their professional female partners passionately clung to them with their breasts and stomach or when their legs intertwined in a dance. In such cases, my substitute, the sixteen-year-old Andrei, would usually step aside, while I took such sexual fire upon myself.

Our afternoon classes with the senior girls at the ballet school were reasonably productive. The professional relations between us men and these girls also gradually stabilised thanks to our female partners from the previous year, now students of year VII. During the first week of classes, I became aware of several animated and tense clashes between the girls of years VI and VII, who were clearly discussing their working relations with us. We, the guys, immediately felt in all classes and particularly in 'Pas de deux', a new tension in our physical contact with the new/younger partners from year VI. I could only repeat to my colleagues: "Patience and hard work will overcome anything."

At the same time, there were some incidents of unethical conduct on the part of our guys. To deal with them, we made an agreement with the head of the girls that she would report any such incidents to me immediately. In dealing with such cases, I typically began by making an announcement about the complaint at the weekly Saturday meeting of our experimental group. I would never mention the girl's name, but would demand that the offender apologise and work out the situation with his partner. If a complaint were repeated, the offender would have to be punished: his name would henceforth be tainted in the professional world. Such a blemish on one's reputation, once acquired, is almost impossible to rectify. Even if an incident is the fault of an inexperienced female dancer, it is the man's responsibility to apologise and straighten out the situation so that it doesn't recur.

We had no personal problems in the Historical and Character dance lessons at the theatre. Teachers and students worked with such intense creativity that there was absolutely no time to think of anything else, except to observe the teachers' demonstrations and repeat sequences of dance elements time and again. It was clear to us that Goldina and Vishnyakov were going out of their way to present the results of their work with us to the exam board at the mid-year exam in December in the best possible light. We did not mind the intense schedule of work, even though, after four hours of non-stop movement from morning till lunchtime, we were seriously tired, both physically and emotionally. Still, we did not wish to fall behind our professional ballerina partners at the sessions of

'Introductions to the Theatre Repertoire'. Usually, our female partners from the school would themselves be exhausted after a previous ballet class, and would often have a hard time coping with the intensity of rehearsals, and lose their self-control. Time and again, I had to remind the guys of the difference in age and physical stamina between themselves and the girls. They always promised to be patient and help their younger partners learn the choreographic texts, so that they would not have to repeat the whole dance an extra time. The girls truly appreciated that.

I finished the choreography of eight new compositions at the school and at the Mariners' Centre before November, giving the dancers ample time to memorise sequences of movements in choreography, and also to get used to the artificial behaviour of characters onstage. There were a number of other things they had to get used to as well: the exaggerated expression of their feelings and emotions; new partners; unusual costumes and footwear (snowflakes and little animals), and the props. I wrote a report for Plakhov about our readiness for the New Year pantomime, and presented a list of requirements that had to be met in order for the matinee to be a success. One of the last items to be taken care of were costumes for performers, for which I gave a list to the wardrobe mistress, along with the sketches of costumes that had to be produced by the theatre's Costume-Making Department. After intense preparations, the New Year's show went smoothly, as did my studies, and work until the summer continued according to plan.

We had exams at the ballet school every Saturday in June. Our experimental male group took the first exam, in Classical dance, on our own, and then the rest of the exams with female partners. Exams in 'Pas de deux' and Character dance took place at the school's studio, and Historical dance at a graduation concert in the Opera Theatre. All the while, I was myself presenting the first results of my work as the school's instructor in Character Dance. This involved presenting each class individually for an exam according to their specific curriculum, and in addition, presenting them onstage in the common graduation concert of the school. It meant I had to keep running back and forth between my colleagues at the theatre and my students at the school. Colleagues in my experimental group dubbed me Figaro, because I was playing the roles of both student and teacher. I didn't mind this. On the contrary, I felt flattered. The most important result of these exams was that our impressive performances finally convinced the committees of the theatre and the school to reduce our educational programme from six to four years. This was a well-deserved victory and one which imbued us with a renewed belief in our ability to achieve what we had set out to do.

In our experimental capacity, we knew we were a group of over-aged pioneers, and we also understood that our successes in ballet were only relative. Normally, the study of, and training in, classical ballet would begin much earlier: no later than eight years old for girls, and ten for boys, not eighteen-to-twenty-year-olds like us. By our age, the human skeleton is fully formed, so any attempt to reconstruct it artificially is doomed to failure. This need not have precluded our making it as excellent dancers in any other genre (Character/Historical, Operetta, Pop, Modern, Jazz), but not in Ballet.

That is why, out of the twelve students in our group, only half had any real chance of becoming Classical dancers and performing ballet numbers onstage. The rest were destined to dance in Historical and Character genres of the opera/ballet repertoire only, or in musical comedy theatres. Still, the grounding provided by a classical education would always distinguish a true dancer from the mass of non-professional performers. Perhaps it was the rigid notion of an age limit in ballet education which moved both Vronsky and Rels to cut down the period of our enforced physical reconstruction from six to four years, as well as to take my advice – treating us as a case study which could show what a strict regime of training could achieve. They could test it again, by enrolling another experimental class, this time for fourteen-to-fifteen-year-olds, for an express course of ballet training over six, rather than eight, years, and meanwhile, a generation of ideal ballet candidates would have time to grow up.

Up to the end of July I paid regular visits to the university library, trying to read up on the history of the first socialist state in the world and on the birth of proletarian culture. I was more attracted, however, by colourful encyclopaedias on the subjects of the visual arts and theatre. I enjoyed this type of research: writing out the names of famous artists and important dates; learning to distinguish between historical periods in the development of arts and culture, with their characteristic aesthetic principles, styles, and genres, defined according to scientific-philosophical criteria. I did all this by way of giving myself a general education, trying to fill in the gaps in my knowledge.

One day, at 6 p.m., I had just laid out my books at home for a study session when the doorbell rang downstairs using my coded signal. *Who could that be, coming without an invitation?* At the main door I saw a familiar face from the theatre box office: she had a note for me from the stage manager urgently pleading for me to come and substitute for a missing cast member.

It's always like this at the start of a season, I reflected philosophically, running upstairs. Fifteen minutes later I was sitting in the make-up studio of the theatre. While I was being made up and bewigged, Sasha told me what had happened with Andrei – whose substitute I was. I asked him to remind me of the choreographic episodes of tonight's performance: what exactly I had to dance, and with which of the ladies; and from which sides I had to enter and exit the stage. Sasha spun around in the small room, waving his arms in the air and getting in the way of the make-up dresser. While Sasha was doing this, I had to keep jerking my head up and down, trying to follow the movement of his feet in the mirror. The result was a match for any Shakespearean tragicomedy. Finally, the wardrobe master stuffed me into a medieval costume and passed on to my first lady.

Olesya sighed with relief: "I was getting myself ready to dance without a partner today. There's a twenty-minute interval coming up now, and that's all we have to review all your entrances and exits for each dance of the court ball. During the performance I'll guide you through the labyrinth of choreographic figures and let you know each of the next moves as they come. It's a piece you have already danced with me before. All right?"

"Yes, ma'am, I'll follow your lead!"

Olesya laughed in response and slapped me with her fan.

"Then, let's go."

A story of my outrageous performance that night was to remain a favourite anecdote in the theatre's circles for quite a while. The trouble was that I couldn't quite remember the order of sequences in the dance suite, but at the same time did not wish to appear like a complete incompetent in front of my colleagues. So, I decided to act like a scatterbrain admirer of the female sex, and at every turn, when I did not know what to dance, I would improvise a sudden attack of affection for my lady: feigning surprise at her grace, whispering compliments in her ear; brushing off dust from her dress with a kerchief. Making a bow, I would drop the kerchief and then rush to pick it up and present it to her; I would kiss her bare arms and shoulders, and so on. The problem was, at the beginning, that

Olesya could not understand what was happening and would express her dismay at my behaviour with the falsely polite smile of an aristocratic socialite. Soon, however, she could see that I was resorting to clowning only when I couldn't remember the order of the elements. Meanwhile, the audience, noticing my repeated bouts of clumsiness, had decided it must be the deliberate expression of my character, and began to respond to my farce with bursts of laughter, and even looked forward to each new little spectacle. In a suite consisting of three separate dances, my reserves of comic and mime variations were already exhausted by the end of the second duet. What was I to do in the third?

Of course, I was happy to save the show, and to help my colleagues and tutors out. All the time onstage, my buddies and my partner Olesya would quietly hiss their instructions for the upcoming movements (dance figures, poses, and turns) through clenched teeth and smiles. I never once upset the spatial scheme of the dance or found myself out of sync with the music. It must have been a natural instinct for self-preservation, coupled with good reactions, acute perception of the logic of intervals and the geometry of direction, that got me through. My female partners and male colleagues were more anxious than I was in these impromptu episodes.

After the show, the producer's assistant came over to thank me and shook my hand. "Today you passed another important test: learning how to act on the spot and discovering an important part of theatre mores. Andrei wasn't able to come today because his mother locked him up. It was a good thing his sister brought a note from him in time for us to get in touch with you. By the way, in the note, Andrei is asking for help in finding a place to live. If your landlady has a room, perhaps you could recommend him to her. When he turns sixteen, Andrei is allowed to live on his own if he is engaged in a course of studies or has a job."

I promised to help out my 'brother in arms'.

Only when we were on board ship on our way to Yalta, did Oksana and I realise that we were truly free for the next two weeks, and could forget about the daily hustle and bustle, and relax completely. 'Completely' was a somewhat relative notion because I did take a stack of sheet music along with me, to think about choreographic compositions for the following year. These two weeks in August were in fact my only chance to think through the first seven or eight choreographic ideas for the three classes of the ballet school and the four dance groups at the Mariners' Centre. In each case, the choreography had to suit the gender of the troupe, and, in addition, their level of skill, whether to a professional or amateur standard. Oksana and I decided that I would work in my room from eleven to one and from two to four, while mother and daughter sunbathed on the beach and took an afternoon siesta. The rest of the day we would spend together: excursions, games, walks, cruises, etc. We had two luxury rooms with a joint veranda, as well as all the amenities and comforts of the resort at our disposal.

The two weeks zoomed by all too quickly, and we were back again in Odessa in the second half of August, engaged at the Mariners' Centre in interviewing new candidates for each of the groups of the ensemble. At the theatre, I also had to catch up with my colleagues, who, in my absence, had been learning new Character dances from the theatre's opera repertoire. At the staff meeting of the school I again presented my vision of a programme for the upcoming academic year, and proposed a list of new compositions for the end-of-year concert to be staged in the Opera Theatre. At the regional arts centre, Lyuftgarten asked me what I thought would be the next most useful subject

118

from the history of arts from which the teachers of dance could benefit, as he needed to contact the university about a new lecturer.

I suggested two topics: 'Elementary Theory of Music' and 'Vocal or Instrumental Accompaniment for Traditional Folk Dances Adapted/Stylised for Stage'. The first would be of use to choreographers of folk ensembles, getting them to look at the metrical foundations and melodic structures of music; and the second would teach them how to exploit more fully the potential of tempo/ rhythm and dynamic musical resources in their choreographic compositions. The second topic could introduce them to a wide range of possibilities in the use of musical accompaniment, helping them to identify the most suitable solutions for each style and genre of choreography, enriching the quality of performance and the audience's emotional engagement with the action onstage.

My studies at the ballet school, and my work at the Mariners' Centre, continued at the same intense rate for the next two years. The only memorable event of that historical period was the death in 1953 of the notorious theoretician and practitioner in the fields of mass social engineering and 'final solutions' for ethnic minorities – Joseph Stalin. Although the monster was dead, condemnation of Stalin's cult of personality was still three years away. In the Soviet Union, anniversaries of our victory over fascism gradually acquired the status of the greatest state holiday on a par with the anniversary of the October Revolution. In 1955, at the finale of a regional festival celebrating the tenth anniversary of the great victory in the Second World War, the children's ensemble of the Mariners' Centre had an opening number, performing a cheerful dance suite 'Young Naturalists at the Zoo', while the youth ensemble concluded the entire show with a dramatic composition, 'Victory Day'. A government representative from Kiev who had attended the show, approved the ensemble's choreographic programme for a performance at the republic's main official concert, on 9th May 1955, in the capital of Ukraine. There were to be thirty-four performers and six assistants going to Kiev for the occasion. I must admit that, without the help of the tutors and administrators of the Mariners' Centre, I could not possibly have brought my grandiose ideas to fruition, and our ensemble could not have achieved the success it did. As it was, Plakhov, who was in the audience, could rightfully take pride in his collective. At the final meeting, he was presented with a laureate's certificate, and the whole ensemble was invited for a farewell dinner for the winners of the festival. Our victory was featured in the Odessan newspaper The *Black Sea Commune.*

The same article announced the appointment of a new chief ballet master of the theatre. The ballet manager explained to me that Vronsky and Tzhomelidze were being transferred to the central Opera and Ballet Theatre in Kiev in a week's time: he, as chief ballet master, and she as teacher/répétiteur. I told him that I wanted to say goodbye to my former teacher. I waited for Ludmilla's return from her ballet class by the staffroom. She was genuinely happy to see me:

"Ah, here is my favourite pupil, come to say goodbye to his 'tigress'." 'Tigress' was Ludmilla's nickname among the experimentals. Kissing me on the cheek, Tzhomelidze asked: "What can I do as a farewell gift for the head of my 'band of rogues'?"

I explained to her about my plans for higher education and about my predicament of having to get a guarantee from the Ukrainian Ministry of Culture of future employment in the republic, upon graduation from the academy. I also asked her to assist me in obtaining a reference from Vronsky in support of my application to MTA.

"Oh, yes, of course! I've heard from Rels about your achievements at the school, and I also heard about the recent jubilee concert in Kiev. Vakhtang Ivanovich will not deny your request, even though we are very busy with preparations for our departure at the moment. I will leave an envelope for you with the ballet manager. You will find your reference letter there, as well as my contact details in Kiev. Give me a call when you are there. I will always be happy to see the future ballet master."

We kissed each other, and I followed her departing figure with a look of sadness and hope.

In June, when I was examining students at the school, the secretary passed me an envelope delivered from the theatre. Inside was a recommendation signed by Vronsky: Ludmilla had kept her word.

The following autumn, while still working at the theatre, school and the Mariners' Centre and simultaneously following an evening course in the history of arts at the university, I began getting the necessary papers together for my application to MTA. It turned out to be much more difficult than I had expected. All administrators were preoccupied with their own business and I often had the hardest time cutting through the bureaucracy. My documents had to reach the Admissions Committee of MTA by 1st January, in order for them to be reviewed in good time and ranked vis-à-vis other candidates'. I had finally assembled everything except for two items: a list of government awards and titles, and a paper from the Ministry of Culture guaranteeing my post-graduation employment in the Ukraine. The former I did not have and I had to go to Kiev as soon as possible for the latter. Lyuftgarten wrote an effusive letter on my behalf addressed to Deputy Minister Shabli. It was as if he were recommending me for the highest state honour, the Lenin Prize. His effort produced an appointment for me at the ministry's Theatre Department in early January 1956.

Lyuftgarten personally reviewed all my papers being sent to Moscow; instructed me on how to behave diplomatically with the Deputy Minister and his staff, and also advised me to speak Ukrainian at the ministry. He cared about my future, as a father would for a son, and I did not know if I would ever be able to thank him adequately. It seemed that the two directors were jointly deciding my fate. Through Oksana I received a letter of instruction from Plakhov authorising me to travel to Kiev to take part in a three-day choreographers' seminar. The assignment came complete with a hotel booking and a train ticket.

I couldn't believe my eyes, but Oksana explained it in simple terms, "Without a reference letter from the Ukrainian Ministry, your application will lie dead in the filing cabinets at MTA. In spite of all your talent and professional experience, your success as a choreographer at the last republican festival, and the laureate's certificate, you are still not a Ukrainian by nationality, you have no honorary state titles, and you are not a member of the Communist Party. With all these 'nots' in evidence, only such prominent figures in the field of culture, as Chief Ballet Master Vronsky, the director of the Arts Centre, Lyuftgarten; the director of the ballet school, Rels; and the director of the Mariners' Cultural Centre, Plakhov, have the political gravitas to convince the officials at the ministry in Kiev that you are worthy of their support and worth a guarantee of future employment in the republic.

Seeing me off at the train station in the evening, Oksana expressed her philosophical conviction: "If the people at the Theatre Department are sensible, they will not oppose the four Odessan masters, not least because, as of last year, Vronsky heads the ballet troupe of the Kiev Opera Theatre. Plakhov deeply respects and values you. Not only did he arrange a train ticket and hotel for you, he also made sure that you receive per diem remuneration for this business trip. People like Viktor V. do not throw money to the wind. He has faith that one day his investment in your future will be fully repaid by your contribution to culture and the arts, even if he is no longer around to see it. The important thing is to remember not to cower in front of the ministry aces in Kiev. Be clever, reserved, tactful, just as you normally are. Be careful how you answer their potentially provocative questions. One wrong word may decide your fate."

"Darling, you speak like my mother."

"Every mother feels deeply the trials of her children. You are used to being in charge, and, as a natural leader, you do not like being upbraided; you get provoked easily in polemics, and you are prone to saying too much, without caution. You need to be alert on this occasion. I'm sure my beloved hero will return from Kiev victorious. You should also know I will be supporting you every inch of the way."

Lying on a narrow bunk in my train compartment, I was unable to sleep for a long time, thinking about the next day, and turning over Oksana's warnings in my head.

At seven thirty in the morning, the conductor announced the train's arrival in Kiev. So as not to wander around aimlessly in an unfamiliar city, I took a cab (that is a horse and cart) to my hotel. Once installed in my room, I first took a shower; then, after checking my papers and wishing myself 'break a leg', I stepped out. At the hotel reception I found out how to get to the ministry, and boarded a tram. Arriving at my destination, I passed security at the main gate with my head held high. Inside the ministry building I quickly found the Theatre Department and walked gracefully into the reception. My appearance caused no surprise. The secretary knew who I was, and why I had come. She smiled sweetly:

"Please wait a minute!"

Taking my file, she entered one of the four doors with the sign 'Opera/Ballet'. Soon afterwards, the door opened, and the secretary invited me to enter.

I found myself in a spacious room, where a grey-haired bespectacled man was sitting behind a heavy desk, studying my file. He answered my greeting with a nod and gestured to me to sit down on a chair by the window.

"Mikhail, I see here that you have excellent recommendations. Do you know Vronsky personally?"

"Yes, Vakhtang Ivanovich was my patron at the theatre for five years, where I knew him both as the artistic director of the ballet and as head of the jury at shows and festivals."

"Yes, yes, I do remember your composition 'Victory Day' with slides and visual effects at the tenth anniversary concert last year. Your choreography was highly commended in the press. It's a pity that it wasn't performed by professionals such as those in the Veryovka Choir or in Virsky's Ensemble. Are you familiar with these names?"

"Most certainly! These are the best folk collectives in Ukraine! How could I not know them? One can learn a lot from them, both from their repertoire and their performing technique."

The official pierced me with his eyes, assessing whether my answer had been genuine. I hastened to add, "Even Classical dance and so-called 'modern' dance have to be constantly nurtured by the living roots of ethnography, whatever the genre of theatre or musical stage performance, and in folk dance ensembles, this goes without saying."

"I am happy to hear you think so. I will present your case to the Deputy Minister today, and you'll have an answer by tomorrow, midday. Goodbye!"

At the staff entrance of the Opera Theatre, I asked for Tzhomelidze, lying that I was her nephew come from Odessa. The ballet manager called me back and said that Ludmilla Alekseyevna was at a rehearsal. She was asking me to meet her at the staff entrance at 1 p.m. to go for lunch together. I was glad of the opportunity to take a stroll down Kreschatik Street, and to pop into the famous cathedral. At the appointed hour, I was waiting with a bouquet of white roses by the staff entrance.

At the sight of me, Tzhomelidze ran forward to kiss me, while I exclaimed: "Dear Aunty Lucy!"

Her deep contralto laughter was so contagious that the security guards joined the laughing chorus: "Ludmilla, you are so young! How come you have such an elderly nephew?"

"I have a dozen such nephews in every republic! Ha ha ha!"

Taking the flowers from my hand, and me by the arm, she hastened to the exit, kissing me on the way.

"How long are you here for, *Toptygin* (Clumsy Bear)?"

"Just for two days. The day after tomorrow I have to be with my young charges at the ballet school and at the Cultural Centre."

"How is your mother?"

"She is well, thanks. And how are you, in your new place? Do you miss the beauty queen Odessa?"

"There is simply no time to be nostalgic, Mishenka."

Over lunch in a nearby eatery, I explained to Ludmilla the purpose of my visit to Kiev: about the morning appointment at the Theatre Department in the ministry, and about my dire need for a special ministerial paper assigning me to a course of study at MTA, a document without which all the other application papers would not even be considered.

"The head of the Theatre Department promised to present my request to the Deputy Minister today and told me to come back for an answer tomorrow. Ludmilla Alekseyevna, I am most grateful to you for the recommendation that Vronsky wrote for me last summer. At the same time, knowing our bureaucratic system as you do, you also realise that just one telephone call from Vakhtang Ivanovich to the Deputy Minister could be decisive. I am sorry if I'm overstepping the mark."

"Misha, there is no need to apologise. I am sure that you also help your students when they need your support. It shouldn't be a problem for Vakhtang to ring the ministry and confirm his recommendation, but there is always a possibility that the Deputy won't be in to receive his call. I know the head of the Theatre Department well and will give him a call when I am back at the theatre, but of course he does not make the decisions. Don't you worry, my dear, I will do everything in my power."

On the way back to the theatre, Ludmilla asked me to notify her about the Deputy Minister's decision tomorrow and promised me a seat for the evening performance of the ballet *Shurale* by Yarulin.

That night, the ballet's themes invaded my sleep with nightmares: one moment, I was dancing the lead part of the Forest Demon on the desk of the head of the Theatre Department, jumping and twisting my body in menacing poses, forcing him to sign my papers; another, I was abducting his seductive fifty-year-old secretary, but unable to decide what to do with her, and trying to stuff her into my suitcase in case of a bad day ahead. . . . I woke up in a cold sweat and had to admit to myself: *Mishenka, this bureaucratic hassle of signatures, and recommendations has driven you a little loony. Stop wallowing in delirium! Get up and 'storm the Winter Palace', that is, the Ministry of Culture!*

Packing my suitcase, I ran down to the reception to pay for my stay, swallowed a sandwich on the way, and then made my way to the ministry to find out what fate had in store for me. In the lobby of the Theatre Department, I placed my coat on a coat stand in the corner and pushed my suitcase under it; then I combed my hair in front of the mirror, straightened up and approached the very secretary who had featured so prominently in my nightmare. I decided that if it were my fate to suffer defeat, then I would accept it with my head held high.

Without betraying any emotion, the woman nonchalantly passed me my file, asking me to sign for the receipt of a letter and the rest of my papers. Only then did she hand me an official envelope with my name on it. I thanked her, put on my coat, and stepped out into the corridor. In the main lobby of the ministry, I sat down on a marble bench and carefully removed the letter from the fatal envelope: in it, in black and white, were the very words required by MTA. I could not quite believe it was real: I kept turning the precious piece of paper over and over in my hands, even smelling it and looking through it at the light, finally stroking its glossy surface with affection.

My emotions still in turmoil, I found a notary's office on the lower floor of the same building and made three copies of the historic letter, sending one copy by registered mail directly to MTA. I then wrote a warm thank-you note to Ludmilla and Vakhtang, expressing my heartfelt gratitude to them for safeguarding my future. I bought another bouquet of roses and left it, along with the note, with the security guards at the theatre 'For dear Aunty Lucy from her adoring nephew'. I went gift-shopping afterwards and found the perfect gift for my Odessan patrons, an administrative desktop calendar for 1956: now, even if they tried, they would not be able to forget my farewell year in Odessa. I also found treats for Mother, Roman, and my landlady, and even bought a cute souvenir for Lyubanya. The best gift, of course, was reserved for my beloved. In my joy, I had not noticed how I had spent all my money: there was only some small change left, just enough to pay for a cup of tea on the train. On my return journey, I kept thinking, *Why am I so lucky?* This was a remarkable confluence of good fortune, large and small: the continuation of my friendship with Tzhomelidze after her transfer to Kiev; Vronsky's interest in my career; the patronage of three Odessan titans over the course of many years, and the invaluable support of Oksana. Such luck was almost worrisome.

Oksana was waiting for me next morning on the platform of Odessa's central train station. I gave her the thumbs up from a distance. She understood straight away, and pushed through the crowd to me, and hung on my neck, drawing stares from passengers passing by.

"Oh, my dear! I was so worried! Is it true then: the Deputy Minster himself has signed your papers?"

"With some assistance from Vronsky, I believe."

"Naturally! The Deputy wouldn't know you personally," my girlfriend rejoined.

On the trolleybus, Oksana shared the latest news with me and we discussed plans in terms of my work at the Mariners' Centre as it was to be my last semester there. We decided not to tell anyone but the three directors about my impending departure. There was no reason to upset my charges ahead of time. After the end-of-year concerts and exams in June, I would inform everyone, thank them for their collaboration and wish them success for the future. At home, presenting the mother and daughter with their gifts, I announced that I was going to make another present to Lyubanya, something to remember me by when I was gone: a solo dance 'Ganzya', based on the music of a Ukrainian ballad of the same name, but in the modern style.

Oksana was very touched and let a tear drop: "Mishanya, all these five years I was hoping you would do something like this, but never dared ask for such an extraordinary favour."

I inscribed the gift calendars with warm words of gratitude and best wishes for each of my patrons. They were touched by such an unusual sign of attention, and also agreed to keep my eventual departure secret for the time being. In turn, I promised to assist in finding a replacement from 1st July. I had a list five pages long of all the things I needed to get done before my departure. Every day I crossed off two or three, but added four to six new ones. I was getting concerned that this merry-go-round would never end.

Mother, hearing that I would be leaving Odessa in six months, sank on to a chair in shock: "This means I won't see you again?"

"Not until the following summer holidays," I confirmed. "I would like to invite all relatives and friends for my birthday on 7th May, to a party at our place. It will be a good opportunity to say goodbye to everyone as well. Do you mind?"

"That's a very good idea. But wait. What if you don't get into MTA?"

"Then I'll move to Leningrad, and stay with Cousin Sofia for the time being, until I figure out what to do next. In any case, I intend to visit Odessa only during the summer holidays." During the following months, weekends were dedicated to farewell visits with relatives and friends. The first Sunday in May, from 12 to 4 p.m. was designated as the day for my going away party. Visitors came and went over the course of twelve hours. Two accordions, mine and Danya's, were in constant use, either separately or together. Guests ate, drank, sang and danced, offered congratulations and shed the odd tear. Moldavanka was seeing her prodigal son off in style. Neighbours stopped by with drinks, drowning out the sadness of the impending separation with their indomitable compatriot.

On Tuesdays and Fridays, after her classes at the ballet school, Lyubanya regularly came to the Mariners' Centre to work with me from 3 till 4.30 p.m. on the choreography of her 'Ganzya' romance. It was my original interpretation of a well-known tune sung by the soloist of the opera, Galina. A three-minute-long composition was built around the couplet structure of a Ukrainian romance, stylised for a coloratura soprano with periodic changes of tempo and rhythmic patterns during the arpeggio.

A capricious, impatient young woman comes for a date with her lover who, for some reason, has been delayed. Passers-by, in an imaginary park, tease the waiting girl, whose reactions reflect the nature of their comments and help the audience visualise the scene. Their scornful remarks further wound the girl's pride, but finally she sees her lover approaching from a distance and dashes off the stage to fall into his embrace. In this semi-character genre, Ukrainian folk elements are stylised by means of the Classical dance vocabulary into a particular language of expressive choreography that helps present the heroine's character. I had envisioned an ideal framework for the performance of this composition to be a simultaneous, synchronised vocal performance by a singer, positioned to the side, downstage, and a dance, performed by Lyubanya upstage in the middle.

In the last five years I had somehow lost track of how the capricious eight-year-old Lyubanya had turned into a thirteen-year-old young lady, perfectly suited to the execution of my choreographic ideas. For the final rehearsals, Oksana privately arranged for our accompanist to come along with his accordion and play for two hours, while Lyubanya danced. Observing her daughter's progress, her mother hid her face behind the accompanist's back to conceal her tears of joy. Her emotions were understandable. The girl was not only brilliant in her dance technique, but she also infused her every step, every pose and gesture with so much spirit and feeling, conveying the content of the composition with ultimate precision, that she gave the impression of a true talent that had matured early. It was the product of her mother's genes and of my friendship with her, a rare synthesis of physical and spiritual association.

I corrected the young soloist very gently, rarely complimenting her, and often asking her not to overdo the effects of facial expressions, rather to concentrate on the motion of her body as the best way to present her stage image. She absorbed all my corrections like a sponge. Running into the vocalist Galina at the theatre one day, I shared my vision of a joint vocal/choreographic performance of 'Ganzya' with her and suggested that she come to see my unusually talented pupil in action. Galina agreed to come to Lyubanya's rehearsal for half an hour. I brought her to the Mariners' Centre, introduced her to Oksana, Lyubanya, and the accordionist. Then Lyubanya danced the romance twice in a row, and I asked Galina what she'd thought of it.

"This is a very attractive idea. Since the girl is a student at the ballet school, she is in any case on her way to joining the theatre's ballet troupe eventually. I'll speak with the artistic director. If he's interested in this joint vocal/choreographic duet of 'Ganzya', we would have to present the number to him. Personally, I am taken with the idea, but I don't make the final decisions."

"You see, Galya, the fact is I will be leaving Odessa soon. Would you please keep in touch with the school? I teach there and I'll inform the Director of this potential project."

I had sketched out most of the choreography for the current year at the school and the Mariners' Centre before the New Year. The task in hand was to finish up the compositions; to polish the technique and national characterisation of each dance; to line up costumes and shoes for the performance; and, finally, before my departure, to hand the repertoire over to a new leader.

Over the previous two years, the ensemble had grown in size, joined by new talented members, and its repertoire had also grown, now representing a wide range of European folk dances. This often allowed us to combine several of them in one part of a show under the umbrella title of an 'Olympiad'. Starting the following year, Plakhov intended to book the theatre at the Mariners' Centre for the last Sunday of every month to put on a public concert prepared exclusively using his Arts Centre resources – drama, choir, and chamber orchestra – in the first half of the show, and the united Mariners' Dance Ensemble in the second. The Director's dream was finally to become a reality. I advised him to appoint Valery to the post of artistic director of the ensemble, retaining Irina and Oksana as tutors, to ensure continuity of the present repertoire, while inviting an outside choreographer only on an ad hoc basis, for particularly complex productions, in order to maintain a healthy professional climate in the collective. At my last rehearsal, Plakhov ceremoniously presented me with a monetary prize and an honorary certificate of recognition awarded to me by the navigation authority. I heartily thanked them and confessed that the Mariners' Cultural Centre would always occupy a special place in my heart.

I held a warm farewell dinner for my patrons, Rels and Lyuftgarten, where I expressed my lifelong indebtedness to them for their faith in me and their unwavering support. They simply acknowledged my contribution to the cultural upbringing of young Odessans and wished me further success. Parting with them was difficult. To say goodbye to my colleagues from the experimental group, I made a booking at the Tide restaurant, where we celebrated in style.

To say goodbye to Mother, I came home. Roman was, as always, happy to see me, but Yosif was absent. The neighbours poured out on to the veranda and stood, clapping and chanting: "Mi-sha! Mi-sha!"

Mother could not let go of me for a long time, and kept repeating, "Take care of yourself! Don't forget us! Be well!"

Only Oksana and Lyuba came to see me off at the train station. The girl gave me a hug:

"Thanks for everything you have done for me. I shall treasure our 'Ganzya'."

Oksana and I had said all that needed to be said the night before. She held herself together in front of her daughter, only nervously clasping my wrists. She pressed me to her, looked deep into my eyes, and tenderly kissed me on the lips.

"Farewell, my idol! May all your dreams come true!"

The train began to move. Lyubanya ran alongside my carriage for a while, waving her handkerchief.

Farewell, Odessa! Forgive my betrayal: I am leaving you for an uncertain future.

CHAPTER 5 CATCHING THE FIREBIRD

Once again, six years down the line, the train was taking me to Moscow where I was to try my fortune at the ultimate educational destination for all those seeking to become professional choreographers – the Moscow Theatre Academy. It was a long shot, but I had to try it, despite the odds. I cannot pretend that I was not afraid: my decision to leave the comfort and promise of Odessa was akin to jumping off a cliff with the chance of landing in a pit of vipers and scorpions. The step I had taken in this new direction was a reckless gamble, with every chance of ending very badly. But it was too late to turn back now. Kievsky Railway Station was already coming into view ahead of us, in the glow of the rising sun.

Greetings to you, Moscow, queen among cities! Please be gracious to me, bring me luck in the world of theatre and forgive my failings should my uncompromising nature get me into trouble.

Loaded up as I was with heavy books and sheet music, I took a taxi from Kievsky to Rizhsky Railway Station, from where a porter helped to carry my 'bricks', as he called them, two blocks down the road to Trifonovka. At the students' halls of residence, the warden, Shura, familiar from my previous visit to MTA, assigned me to a room with seven other ballet students, who were also applying for the ballet masters course. The only arrival so far was a fifty-year-old Chinaman. I was the second. The Chinaman spoke Russian badly, but this was better than my Chinese. As a result we mainly communicated by facial expressions and gestures. The only element of misunderstanding between us was in the matter of farting. The Chinaman broke wind loudly and unapologetically. And whenever he did so, I could not help but snigger. He seemed baffled by my reaction, and I had to explain that in Russian culture, breaking wind in public and loudly, was a sign of bad manners.

"Why?" he asked. "Isn't this a natural bodily function for a man?"

"But it creates a bad smell!" I grimaced in response.

"The quiet ones smell bad!" Ye-yan exclaimed indignantly. "The loud ones don't smell at all!"

"No, they only stink," I agreed, concluding this international conference on farting.

This was my first lesson in sharing living quarters with someone from a very different culture. My dreams that night were full of booming foghorns and the screeching of tyres on wet gravel.

A warm welcome awaited me at the MTA Admissions Office. A staff member looked through my papers and told me that I needed to get a medical form signed by a doctor from the hall of residence, confirming that I was in good health. On receiving a passport-sized photograph from me, the secretary, Lena, instantly produced a temporary student pass, entitling me to use the library of the Museum of Theatre and any empty studio at the Bolshoi School of Ballet, if I needed to practise my dance routines. These classrooms were also to be used for our examinations. I also received an information pack containing a timetable of upcoming examinations, the names of teachers on the Board of Admissions and an explanation of the criteria for candidate evaluation. Only five places were available for the candidates from Soviet republics and a few more for our friends from Korea, China and the European countries of the Soviet bloc. The foreign candidates, however, were admitted without exams.

At 2 p.m. the chair of the Ballet Masters Department held an introductory meeting for the candidates from the Soviet Union. He greeted the candidates and wished them good luck in the exams. Dean Anatoly Shatin, briefly outlined the examinations and the set-up for practical tests. He read out the names of our future teachers of specialised subjects and answered candidates' questions. Shatin suggested that, immediately after the meeting, we find ourselves a partner with whom to work on preparing a two-minute dance to demonstrate our skills as potential choreographers for the exam in dance composition. This routine could be in any genre or style. At the end of the meeting, his assistant Nina Chefranova announced the names of the seventeen candidates who would compete for those five places. Most of them were the leading soloists from different ballet troupes around the country.

She informed us that we should refer all organisational or administrative questions to her. Any questions of an artistic or creative nature were to be addressed to the Dean, Shatin.

After the meeting, I paired up for my dance composition exam with twenty-two-year-old Masha Karaban from Moldova's Chişinău Theatre. Like me, she too had little experience of performing onstage and was dreaming of becoming a ballet master. She agreed to dance in my lyrical-comic miniature composition called 'A Meeting in the Port' and I, in turn, agreed to perform in her melodramatic duet, 'Antony and Cleopatra'. Each composition was to last two and a half minutes. Mine was based on semi-character movements and hers was in the style of modern Classical dance. In addition, I decided to perform a solo dance, with my own choreography: 'Trepak', from Tchaikovsky's ballet *The Nutcracker*. This was to last a mere one and half minutes.

The first trial for all applicants to the ballet masters course was the assessment of individual musical abilities by Aleksander Tseitlin. It involved assessments of hearing (sensitivity to rhythm and metre), the ability to memorise and reproduce melodies, and also to break down a polyphonic structure into its component parts. In addition, we were required to play an instrument of our choice. I performed my favourite piece, the 'Gypsy Rhapsody', on the piano passably, and without frills. The rest of the exams followed daily, one taking place each morning. These were group exams in classical, Historical and Character dances. They were assessed by the staff of the department, and presided over by Rostislav Zakharov. In the afternoon, the Board of Examiners discussed our performances, while we rehearsed our solo and duet compositions. The practical part of the examinations finished with the test in dance composition. There then followed a series of individual interviews with the State Examination Committee, on the subjects of history, education, philosophy. The concluding stage was a personal meeting with the head of the Choreographic Faculty of MTA, Professor Zakharov, for the final assessment of the candidate's ideological views, sociocultural background, ethnic background and creative ambitions. Everyone knew this was the final hurdle.

The Professor opened a folder containing my personal records and enquired, suspiciously: "Did you actually work directly with Vakhtang Vronsky at the Odessa Theatre?"

"Not with him directly, I worked with his assistants. However Vakhtang Ivanovich had the opportunity of seeing my choreography performed at various festivals over the course of five years."

"Who were your teachers at the ballet school and theatre?"

"Ludmilla Tzhomelidze, Nikolai Yegorov, Ivan Vishnyakov, Georgi Rels and others."

"What do you like about the profession of choreographer?"

"The opportunity to work creatively, to teach others, to see my productions onstage."

"What are your parents' professions, I mean your biological parents?"

"Before the war my father worked in a factory and my mother was a schoolteacher."

"Your records indicate that you are a Jew by nationality. I find it hard to believe that the Deputy Minister of the Ukrainian Ministry of Culture personally signed your recommendation."

The blood rushed to my face and I caught my breath. Zakharov could not believe that a Jew had been approved to study at such a prestigious institute and was therefore implying that the Deputy Minister's signature recommending my application was somehow not genuine. *Is this a provocation?* was the thought that raced through my mind. *How should I react? Probably best to let it pass.*

Zakharov realised that he had crossed a line.

"I have nothing against Jews, you understand. I'm just surprised by this extraordinary fact!"

Seeing the expression of shock on my face, the Professor irritably motioned for me to leave. I got up, without a word, made a polite bow, and departed, holding my head high. When I came out of his office, my competitors who were waiting outside, did not even bother asking me how my interview had gone. The answer was written all over my face.

I would record this Saturday as a black day in my life. That morning, the secretary Lena had reminded all the applicants to wait until after all the interviews with Zakharov were over at 5 p.m., to find out the names of the five successful candidates. The other non-successful applicants would vacate the halls of residence the following day to make room for the newly arriving applicants for the course in ballet education. In spite of Lena's reminder, I was so wounded by Zakharov that I did not wish to wait a minute longer in that despicable institution. This appeared to be a place where the personal qualities and talents of a future student were not determined by the results of examinations, but by his ethnicity. On my way back to the halls of residence, I recalled the advice given to me by Lyuftgarten, my dear Oksana, and other close friends, who, since well before my departure from Odessa, had been advising me to change my family name to a Ukrainian-sounding one. I, for my part, had found it difficult to credit their arguments at the time. I also did not wish to insult the memory of my dead father who had fallen in the war. It had been no secret for a while now that the Central Committee of the Communist Party and the Supreme Soviet had placed a 5–10% quota on the acceptance of Jews to higher education institutions. I just did not wish to believe such discrimination really existed, until reality slapped me in the face.

Reluctantly, I began packing my suitcase in the halls of residence with the bitter tears of defeat rolling down my face. My slightly tipsy colleagues returned to the halls at 6 p.m., and, on seeing my packed case, promptly launched into noisy congratulations. I grudgingly replied that their mean jokes were most unwelcome. This seemed only to add to their raucousness. They guffawed loudly, until the warden, Shura, appeared, asking what all the commotion was about. She pulled the list of the successful candidates from her pocket and with a grubby finger pointed to my name on the list. In a fit of elation I grabbed her by the waist, lifted her in the air and whirled her in between the beds until we collapsed on one of them in a heap. She squealed, and the other residents who had gathered in our room attracted by the noise, joined in the chorus of hysterical laughter. There was nothing left for me to do but to give a 'tenner' for a crate of beer to my defeated colleagues to console them, and to celebrate my victory.

First thing next morning, I ran to the nearest post office and sent telegrams to my mother and to Lyuftgarten: "Accepted to MTA along with four other Soviet candidates. My huge thanks and love to everyone." Then I rang my cousin Sofia in Leningrad, informing her of my arrival in two days' time. Nobody could believe that I had been accepted to MTA without connections or bribes. I could hardly believe it myself until I received official confirmation of it in writing with a student ID card entitling me to various concessions on transport, in museums, theatres, etc. At the halls of residence, our warden, Shura, transferred me to the third floor, to a room with three other room-mates: Ye-yan (Chinese), Joseph (Lithuanian), and Stefan (Bulgarian). Overall, eleven students were enrolled in our course: three women and eight men, six of whom were foreigners.

In Leningrad, my cousin Sofia gave me a warm welcome. I spent the entire second half of August before my return to Moscow visiting museums and exhibitions, attending festivals and theatres (the student pass was a big help). I spent the last of my money on books on the history of ballet and international guides to folk dances. My well-to-do cousin lent me some money to buy some decent clothes and a training suit, so that I did not look like a *sharyga* (Odessan slang for a street urchin / petty thief) among my foreign colleagues. I promised to pay her back on my next visit to Leningrad. She didn't yet know that I had received an offer to teach a seminar on the 'Sailors' Dance Repertoire' at the Leningrad Performing Arts Centre in early January. The director there knew his Odessan counterpart, Lyuftgarten, very well, and the latter had contacted him to recommend me. I was offered fifty roubles a day for five hours of work, and a free return ticket from Moscow to Leningrad. This promised to be a much needed source of financial assistance during the winter break.

The first day of the term at MTA, as in most colleges, was devoted to organisational matters: we were handed copies of our schedules and proceeded to familiarise ourselves with the locations of classes, libraries, research facilities, training studios, etc. Our lessons were to take place at two main locations: in the morning, all practical subjects were to be taught at the ballet school on Pushechnaya Street, near the Bolshoi Theatre. All afternoon classes were at MTA on Sobinovsky Lane, near Arbat Square. Evenings were to be devoted to individual learning: we could return to the studios of the school and work on our dance compositions, or attend one of the three opera and ballet theatres of the capital, for a visual study of their repertoire. This was a six-day working schedule.

Among our classes were:

Methodology of Classical Dance – Nikolai Tarasov (three times a week)
Methodology of Historical, Character Dances and 'Pas de deux' – (once a week)
Choreographic Composition – Anatoly Shatin (three times a week)
Traditional Classical Repertoire of Ballets – Leonid Lavrovsky (Mondays)
Marxism–Leninism, History of the Communist Party – Sergei Gusev (twice a week)
History of European Ballet and Drama – Nikolai Elyazh (twice a week) Musical Analysis of ballet scores – Aleksander Tseitlin (twice a week)
Acting; Stage Scenery – Krause Müller (twice a week)

The financial situation for most Soviet students was often quite desperate. A regular stipend was twenty-four roubles a month, and the Stalin Prize stipend (for straight A marks) was thirty-seven roubles. Unless one had parents or state aid providing financial help, it was impossible to live on eighty kopecks a day: paying for transport, food, books, stationery, and other household items. One week into the term the need for a part-time job was already imperative. The problem was that the institute's schedule did not leave much time, or energy, for extracurricular work. It was also essential to put all one's efforts into the studies at this initial stage, so as to get into the rhythm of classwork and individual study, and also to make a positive impression on teachers, colleagues, and the administration.

On Shatin's recommendation, I was immediately elected as the trade union student representative for two subdivisions: ballet masters and ballet teachers. Irrespective of my own wishes, I could not decline such an appointment. I fully understood the strategic move of my patron who wanted to bolster my social credentials by putting me in a position of student leadership. Shatin's sense of decency caused him to be troubled by the fact that a talented student could be obstructed in his professional growth simply because of his ethnic origin. Shatin also knew that I could handle such an extracurricular assignment. It could also work in my favour in the long run. Because of the sensitive issue of my Jewish ethnicity, I needed to strengthen my position in the institution with a view to future prospects. I could only guess that, behind my admission to the course lay a smouldering conflict of egos and authorities between Dean Shatin and the head of staff, Zakharov. The personal signature of the Ukrainian Deputy Minister on my recommendation must have kept Zakharov awake at night. For my part, I was well aware of the difficulty of the situation I found myself in: caught between the hammer and the anvil. I would have to exercise fierce control over my propensity to rush blindly into conflicts in my defence.

A test of this came about soon enough. In the autumn of 1956, an International Youth Festival was scheduled to take place in Moscow, organised by UNESCO. At the end of September, the assistant to the Dean, Chefranova, invited me to her office and told me that our institution had been allotted the task of appointing three students (one from each department) to help in organising the rehearsals of the out-of-town collectives on the stages of local Arts Centres during the month of October. The catch was that, although this task was by appointment, it operated according to volunteer principles, that is, a person was asked to devote their own free time and resources to fulfil the assignment. At first I accepted the offer as an honorary mission and an opportunity to learn first-hand about the folk dances of foreign cultures. Then, hearing that the rehearsals would be taking place in the afternoon and would require me to miss my own classes in specialist subjects, I began to have second thoughts. In the end I decided to accept anyway, on condition I was provided with a travel card for that month. Chefranova thought my request outrageous. She declared it was none of her concern how 'volunteers' were to travel while carrying out their social missions. I tried to explain to her that my financial circumstances were now so dire that I had had to give up using transport on a daily basis and was instead walking from the halls of residence to my classes in order to save money. She didn't even want to hear my arguments. Only then did it occur to me: *Why me? Why was I asked to take up this task? Whose idea was it?*

After classes I went to see Shatin, but as he was out, his secretary Lena offered her help:

"What is it, Mikhail? Perhaps I can help, if it's not personal?"

I conveyed to her the gist of my conversation with Chefranova and asked whether Shatin knew anything about the matter.

She said: "He's in a meeting with the Rector just now, but, speaking personally I can tell you this is the first I've heard about this. Shatin will be back at 5 p.m. to sign some papers, so if you come back in half an hour, you'll be able to catch him."

Lena told me that Shatin was back and waiting for me and was already informed of the matter.

"What would you advise me to do in this situation?" I asked him.

"Misha, do not distress yourself on this account. In every institution, as you know full well, it is often the case that 'The right hand doesn't know what the left is doing.' A very apt description. Just now, at a meeting with the Rector, we decided to assign this honorary 'voluntary' mission to Professor Zakharov's student, Sasha Udaltzov: he is currently working on his MA dissertation and will be glad to help in the festival preparations. You are free to carry on with your programme of studies. If you don't mind, I would ask you not to discuss this matter with anyone, so as not to cast a shadow on Chefranova's reputation in the eyes of the students. She simply made a rash move. Regarding your financial difficulties, which I heard about from Lena, I suggest you approach the nearby Moscow State University and offer your services in coaching their semi-professional dance group. This should help you out until next semester, and then you might get a prize stipend if you do well in the exams in December. If the part-time job doesn't impinge on your studies and other responsibilities, we would not object."

My financial situation was indeed catastrophic. I was gradually losing weight, and with such a poor diet could even become ill. There was nothing left for me to do but to telephone Mother and plead with her to send me a food parcel as soon as possible, to be sent with the attendant on the Odessa–Moscow express. This was a common method of sending food parcels in those days: starving students in the cities of Moscow and Leningrad were fed by their families from the south of the country, and the regular express train service between north and south provided the means. A private arrangement between a train attendant, who would be paid either in money or in kind (food), made the transfer of parcels possible. I gave Mother the telephone number of my halls of residence, so she could give me details of the delivery over the telephone. Several days later, returning home from the theatre one evening I found a note about the parcel delivery on my bed. What a sight I was the next morning, dragging a 15 kg box on my shoulder from Rizhsky Railway Station and staggering under its heavy but welcome load. Students in the halls of residence, getting a whiff of the contents, cheered me on, offering help and threatening to come for a party in the evening. Stuffing my precious treasure under the bed, I went to the Bolshoi School.

Our pianist Clarissa paid me a compliment: "Misha, you seem as bright as a new penny today!"

I whispered into her ear: "I got a food parcel from home today."

"Aha, now it's all clear. Congratulations!" and she played the footballers' victory tune.

In the 'treasure chest' sent from Odessa I found a hunk of cured pork fat, pink and garlicky; a dozen cans of cod fillets in tomato sauce, and 6 kg of various cereals. *This should last me a while!* I thought with satisfaction.

On Sundays, I usually did my laundry and made provisions for the rest of the week: I cooked a vegetable soup, poured it into glass jars and placed them into a specially constructed container attached to the outside of the window, which served in place of a refrigerator. This soup, which I would normally warm up in a common kitchen, served as both breakfast and dinner.

With the receipt of the food parcel, I could now add lunch to my daily meals, consisting of two slices of rye bread interlaced with a thin slice of pork fat. As a result, nobody wanted to sit next to me in afternoon lectures, and even lecturers made faces at the pungent smell of garlic. They patiently tolerated it, however, believing that it was coming from my Chinese classmates sitting behind me.

With Mother's food parcel stored safely under my bed, and with Shatin's promise of a part-time job at Moscow State University (MGU), I was able to look ahead with more confidence. I could focus my energies on studying and getting good marks, aiming to pass my exams with flying colours and getting myself the Stalin Prize stipend. My motivation was not only to get the invaluable extra thirteen roubles a month, but also, and more importantly, to prove to my detractors that, in addition to my proven choreographic skills, I was also academically able. I became seriously interested in the history of European ballet, as a result of perusing the rare old books I had recently acquired in Leningrad. I spent a good deal of time making notes on important names and events, as well as comparing the publications on this subject from different time periods and by different authors. Even though the evolution of European culture was not represented by those authors uniformly, the family tree of European ballet gradually began to take a more distinct shape in my mind: from the court dances of Catherine de' Medici in Italy, via the systematisation of classical forms of dance under Louis XIV in France, to the full-scale ballets of Petipa in Russia. Such was the trajectory of ballet's genesis in the historiography of the European theatre.

Leading philosophers of the seventeenth to nineteenth centuries confidently predicted the death of classical ballet in conjunction with the disappearance of royalty and aristocracy. Despite their predictions, however, the art of ballet survived. Its survival was not the result of the numerous attempts, either to conjoin the symbolic language of ballet with the method of social realism on the Soviet stage, or to adapt its forms to suit the avant-garde tastes of modern audiences. Rather, the opposite is true. Over the course of three centuries, it was those classics of ballet, which had for the most part retained their original choreography, that had survived the test of time, by analogy with the masterpieces of Leonardo, Michelangelo, and Raphael. The unadulterated original copies of such ballets as *Giselle, La Bayadère, Don Quixote, Coppélia, Raymonda*, and *Swan Lake* should be kept in video archives of theatre museums, alongside other examples of the cultural anthropology of dance.

I learned the history of the Communist Party by heart, as if it were a poem of Pushkin's. During her lectures, Professor Yampolskaya addressed all her remarks primarily to me, because the rest of the students either did not have very good Russian being foreigners, or, as was the case with the locals, were so exhausted from the morning training sessions that they succumbed to a lethargic slumber, even if they looked like they were still awake. Mina Yakovlevna had a knack for painting the ideological battles between Lenin, Plekhanov and Trotsky and other minstrels of the Bolshevik revolution in intriguing dramatic colours. When, on occasion, I asked her a problematic question, she would ruefully drop her grey-haired head and look at the audience over her spectacles with a sense of nervous apprehension. I usually sat in the centre of the front row, exactly opposite her lectern. Once, in a fit of irresponsible light-mindedness, I dangerously touched on a sensitive subject. Yampolskaya fixed her eyes on her notes and said very quietly: "Misha, cool it, or you'll end up in a bad way."

After the lecture, I came to her with an apology. *What an idiot! These aren't innocent games, and the teacher's stakes are much higher than yours.*

By contrast, in the music analysis lessons, taught by Aleksander Tseitlin, I felt like a pig in clover. During the lessons, Tseitlin either played the scores of the nineteenth-century ballets on the piano, or let us listen to the reels of modern recordings: orchestrated ballet repertoires of Shostakovich, Stravinsky, Prokofiev and others. For me, those were unforgettable moments uncovering the mysteries of a beautiful terra incognita: the musical thinking of a composer, his transformation of a literary drama into a musical symphony with the help of musical instruments and human performers. At that stage of my aesthetic development, the analytical expositions of Alexander Naumovich appeared to me like a form of fairy-tale magic. For my mastery of choreography I am largely indebted to this brilliant musician.

A no less significant element of our curriculum was 'Stage Scenery and Costume Design'. Professor Müller knew his subject inside out. He kept us engaged, not only by vividly presenting to us the modern technology for stage transformation, but also by making us sketch and draw our own visual perceptions of the dancers' spatial sphere. Students had a genuine respect for their aged professor. He was always available for consultations and gladly provided feedback on individual projects, both for costumes, scenery, and various 'magic' onstage: the disappearance of figures from a dance floor; flights over the stage, lighting effects, and the use of shadow projections. Professor Müller's generous attention to our individual needs and the information he conveyed to us, all ensured we were well versed in his subject when it came to applying it in our own professional capacities.

By contrast, the class on acting was a bit of a disaster. Nina Chefranova had taken acting during her own studentship at MTA and had even written an MA thesis on the role of mime and gesture in ballet, but she chose to structure her course simply as a series of lectures on the methods of Stanislavsky, without giving us any opportunity to try them out. My colleagues were constantly complaining that Chefranova's lectures were a waste of our time and of MTA's resources because we could easily obtain the same information by reading a book in the library. What we needed was practice: to test, in real stage settings, the principles and concepts developed by the great theoretician of dramatic arts. For some obscure reasons, however, the designers of the ballet masters' programme did not assign much importance to acting skills, although one could argue that those skills were indispensable for the choreography of ballets based on the works of Shakespeare, Goldoni, or Balzac. Had I not had the opportunity of undergoing an active course of training in stage movement and pantomime at the Odessa Theatre prior to MTA, there would have remained a gaping hole in my professional education. All specialist disciplines (Classical, Historical, Character and 'Pas de deux') were grouped under one umbrella term, 'Methodology of Choreographic Composition' (or 'Dance Composition'), supervised by Shatin, taking us through all the steps of choreography training, up to and including the concluding step: the stage choreography of a full-scale ballet. The term 'methodology' did not imply a syllabus of technical dance elements, or a pedagogical approach. Instead it referred to a step-by-step process of creating a choreographic composition according to the following model:

1. *Idea*: theme, genre, number of dancers, size and type of stage, type of audience.
2. *Choice of music*: duration, instrument, architectonics, accompaniment.
3. *Cast*: age, technical skills, acting skills.
4. *Expression of movement*: style and character of body motion, facial grimaces, gestures, poses.
5. *Spatial design*: graphic modelling of travelling onstage.
6. *Composition*: of dance episodes within a context, or of loosely connected dances.
7. *Stage scenery*: scene painting, set construction, props, projections, costumes and make-up.
8. *Author's critical analysis of the finished composition and its perception by the audience.*

A course on the 'Methodology of Classical Dance' expected students to be familiar with the ballet school's programme of training in this subject: either according to Vaganova's system, followed by the Mariinsky School, or according to Tarasov's system, followed by the Bolshoi School. In this course, Alexander Lapauri would devote the morning sessions to joint instruction for the whole group, filling in the gaps in our general education. This would be followed by individual tutorials with each student, where we were supposed to come up with our own choreography for ballet fragments selected from the current theatre repertoire. The compositions were to be assessed in an exam in December. Tarasov suggested that I prepare my own rendition of the 'Waltz of the Snowflakes' from *The Nutcracker*. For the exam, I was to present a written outline of my choreography in shorthand, and demonstrate any part of it indicated by the examiners in a personal performance with piano accompaniment.

The courses on Historical/Court dance with Margarita Rozhdestvenskaya and on Character dance with Tamara Tkachenko, both followed a similar pattern to Tarasov's course on Classical dance. The only difference was that these types of dance vocabulary far exceeded European ballet in the number of dance elements and characteristic ethnic features that had to be learned. Most of the foreign students in our programme only had a very vague idea about these ancient forms of dance. Among the Soviet students, there were two women from ballet schools, two men from folk ensembles, and me – a hybrid of Ballet and Folk training, thanks to my six years of specialisation in Historical and Character dance at the Odessa Performing Arts Centre, ballet school and Opera/Ballet Theatre.

Rozhdestvenskaya and Tkachenko were experts in their field: they had taught these disciplines for many years at the Bolshoi School of Ballet and at MTA. Both were preparing textbooks on their subjects. Both had a lot to offer their students. I was so hungry for every new piece of information (dance or mime) they introduced, that they both soon recognised and appreciated my familiarity with, and deep interest in, the subject. Due to an uneven level of previous training in these subjects among the students of our group, both teachers needed to go back to basics. This was too boring for the Soviets, who had studied all of this at ballet schools ten to fifteen years previously, so they stopped coming to classes, hoping to catch up just before the exams. Rozhdestvenskaya and Tkachenko quietly accepted this, but they were puzzled as to what to do with me, who continued religiously to attend their classes. They finally offered me the job of their assistant in classroom demonstrations, a post which I readily accepted, having a lot of prior similar experience.

In the technique of 'Pas de deux', Lapauri (a former leading soloist of the Bolshoi) taught us the elementary principles of interaction between partners in close physical contact with each other: during action onstage and in static poses (holding hands, embracing, supporting ballerinas under the knees, or by the shoulder). This class was scheduled only for the first semester to give students a general introduction to the physical dynamics of duet compositions and to the universal principles of partnering techniques in all genres of dance. The subject matter included catching, rolling over, carrying, and different kinds of lifting (on to the shoulder, on outstretched arms, etc.) Such types of support are common in Historical dances, such as Galliard, Volta, Mazurka, and others. They are also common in many Character pair dances. This was not a regular course in 'Pas de deux', rather, it was an auxiliary class, to assist us in understanding the duet technique as employed in the choreography of all genres of dance.

The most interesting subject by far was Shatin's 'Methods of Narrative Dance Composition'. The teacher not only knew in great detail all genres and styles of dance, with a deep understanding of music, he was also familiar with the related forms of performing arts: pantomime, drama, music, singing, sculpture, graphics, etc. In his classes, theory went hand in hand with practice: we were given an opportunity to apply theoretical principles to practical tasks, and employ our bodies as instruments of expression. Individual études of improvisation were subjected to collective analysis and constructive critique under the Professor's close supervision.

In Shatin's analytical lexicon, there were no designations 'good/bad', 'nice/unpleasant', or 'positive/negative'. Instead of such subjective and emotive evaluations, we were encouraged in our critiques to employ only objective statements, related to the author's original idea and method of implementation: logical or unconvincing; successful or incomplete; in-depth or superficial; clear or unclear, etc. Moreover, in order to support our critique, we were required to reproduce the element we had found wanting, in an improved version of our own. This approach eliminated ad hominem attacks, and focused everyone's attention on the quality of the work and on a collaborative approach to learning. We often had a hearty laugh trying to imitate someone else's choreography.

The first exam in dance composition consisted in creating a dance monologue on the topic of one's choice, approved by the Professor. With Shatin's blessing, I chose 'Liza's Arioso by the Winter Canal' from Tchaikovsky's *The Queen of Spades*. A performer in my miniature composition was Rasuk-Hi, a student from Korea. I decided to use contemporary choreography because it better suited Rasuk-Hi's personality and also because she was not trained in Classical dance. In the second semester we were planning to work on a duet with a subject plot. We would again have the freedom to choose the subject and the music, and would be able to use as performers graduating students from the Bolshoi School taught by Sofia Golovkina. Shatin always made sure that the students in his programme had the optimal conditions for creative work. It is no surprise then that his classes were infused with creative energy, a productive tempo and discipline, and a healthy collaborative atmosphere. The students loved and deeply respected him.

My hard work in the first semester paid off. In December I passed my exams with flying colours, securing a Stalin Prize stipend for the next semester. In the lobby of MTA, they posted a list of the best students with my name among them. Both teachers and students congratulated me, and only Zakharov and Chefranova ignored my success, not returning my greetings when we ran into each other in the corridor. I had to live with that. Two of my creations for the dance-composition class were noted as particular successes and recommended for the students' New Year concert: 'Medieval Branle with Torches' for four pairs (Historical dance) and 'Sailors' Joke' for six men (Character dance).

In early December, I was invited to the office of the university's trade union and asked to take charge of the students' New Year concert, traditionally held after the winter exams, on the stage of the MTA theatre. A twenty-year-old beauty from the MTA Drama Faculty, Valeria, proposed playing the Snow Maiden if I agreed to be her Grandfather Frost. I accepted the offer, on condition that they supplied an accordion for the show. The student activists were alarmed:

"And who is going to play? We haven't any money for a musician."

"Well, I could play, on a voluntary basis," I proposed.

They accepted my condition with some apprehension, believing, perhaps, that I was kidding them. Still, they procured an instrument and had me sign a receipt for it. We made arrangements with Valeria to begin rehearsals in a week's time, to take place at 8 p.m., in the lobby of MTA, under the vigilant eye of the security guards.

The concert opened with an official address by the Rector who wished everyone a happy New Year. The rest of the thirty-minute-long programme consisted of various numbers performed by students. During a short intermission, Valeria and I changed into our costumes, while someone placed an accordion under a New Year tree in the lobby. The head of the trade union's committee announced on the mic that some honorary guests from a different planet had arrived with gifts for those in the audience, but would deliver them only if the audience shut up immediately and greeted the guests with a round of applause. The pianist played a triumphal march, while the Snow Maiden and Grandfather Frost made it up the stairs from the lobby. The audience were racking their brains over the identities of the actors.

There were a few outside guests at the concert. One of them, the director of Moscow's Central Music School, situated next door to MTA, approached me and Valeria after the concert and invited us to perform in our 'alien' roles at two matinees for kids at her school, the following week, during the winter vacation. I shouted a loud *Hooray!* in my head because I was sorely in need of cash. My other efforts to earn some money consisted of regular visits to the Trade Union Office of the History and Law Departments of MGU where I was trying to organise a local dance ensemble. By mid-December, thirty students (mainly women) had signed up for the group, and it was decided that the rehearsals would begin on 10th January, taking place twice a week in the evenings in the university's halls of residence on Presnya. The cost was five roubles an hour, about 130 roubles a month, and the accompanist was to be paid separately. I signed a contract with them for a year, with the possibility of renewal. For the 'alien' appearances at the Central Music School, Valeria and I received fifty roubles, and I immediately bought myself a train ticket to Leningrad.

My cousin Sofia's husband greeted me with open arms:

"*Nu*, Mishka, you rock! Congratulations on your achievement at the institute! My folks are still asleep – been decorating a New Year's tree till late. So, tell me how you managed to earn the Stalin Prize stipend, with your damaging 'fifth point' [the question about ethnicity in the Soviet internal passport] and without personal connections?"

"Due to a strong optical distortion of the examiners' oculars."

"Ha ha! I get it. At the sight of your oversized Odessan nose the examiners went cross-eyed!"

"Enough, Borya! Give him a chance to breathe! Also let him take a shower and have a cup of tea. Then you can chat to your heart's content."

Sofia gave me a warm hug and whispered: "Don't listen to him. We're all extremely proud of you."

Boris worked as a director of a big textile factory, and was accustomed to using a patronising tone with his subordinates.

Their three-year-old son, Arkasha, woke up and ran out to join us: "Uncle Misha, where is my gift?"

"Tomorrow, you will find it under the New Year tree."

We celebrated New Year's Eve with Boris's mother, sister and family. In the morning, while everyone was sleeping in, I began preparing the programme for my seminar at the Leningrad Performing Arts Centre. It was scheduled for 2nd –7th January.

The following day, Sofia and her family left for a resort on the coast of the Gulf of Finland. This worked out well for me, because I had the flat to myself. It was also useful for Sofia to have someone looking after her home. Before leaving, Sofia asked me not to bring anyone over as the flat was full of valuables. I promised her that my only visitor for the duration of the seminar would be the immortal beauty – Terpsichore.

"And who is that? I don't recall her among your lovers?"

"Unfortunately not. She keeps company with the patron of the Muses, Apollo."

"Well, in that case, she can stay over. I have no objections."

My intensive seminar at the city's arts centre was for the most part attended by ex-ballerinas from the Mariinsky Ballet, who were now working as choreographers of semi-professional dance ensembles. Our personal introduction was coloured by a touch of scepticism on the part of the seminar participants. However, once they had heard the music from Glière's *The Red Poppy*, their attitude changed completely. In a matter of six days, we practically finished the 'Sailors' Dance'. I offered the participants two extra hours for free in order to do a shorthand recording of the learned choreography. At the end of the seminar, my elderly pupils presented me with a bouquet of flowers and invited me to come back with another seminar the following year. The director of the arts centre paid me for the seminar and also gave me a letter addressed to the rector of MTA with a positive reference about my work. This was both pleasant and possibly useful for the future.

After the enjoyable winter holidays, I was naturally met with some unpleasant surprises upon my return to MTA: life is made of stripes, where white and black alternate in a regular sequence. In the jargon of material dialectics which all Soviet people had wired into their brains at the time, the alternation of fortunes is called 'the law of unity and struggle between opposites'. In accordance with this law, I discovered a number of unwelcome changes in the new schedule of classes, for semester II: the second part of 'Partnering Technique' (methodology of duets) had been replaced by 'Classical Ballet Repertoire'; 'The History of the Communist Party' had been replaced by 'Political Economics'; and, in 'The History of European Ballet', we were now to cover the Russian/Soviet period. As a rule, the tuition of every specialist subject in our programme of studies would be stretched over a three-year period, and the subject taught in a progressive series of modules. This was perfectly understandable, and acceptable to both foreign and domestic students. However, we objected when it came to subjects that did not contribute in any way to our education. Whether because of the mature age of the participants (twenty-five to forty years) or because of their professional experience, there was a good deal of resentment felt at having to study such subjects.

A case in point was the course of 'Ballet Repertoire', taught by the chief ballet master of the Bolshoi Theatre, Leonid Lavrovsky. Out of the twelve students in our group, only three Soviet students and one Czech had had any classical ballet training. The rest, who were foreign students from China, Korea, Bulgaria and Albania, and also two students with a folk dance background, were simply physically incapable of dancing solo parts of swans in threes, fours, or even in group scenes of 'corps de ballet'. In addition to this, there was the fact that Professor Lavrovsky was consistently late for morning classes, and sometimes came with a face swollen from drinking, and smelling of alcohol. He was mean and irritable in the way he communicated with us and the poor Chinese and Koreans were afraid of him, especially when, in his drunken state, he would try to demonstrate fragments from the second act of *Swan Lake*, and then scold them for their imprecise performance of classical sequences. In the changing rooms, everyone was brave enough to state their true opinion of him, but nobody dared to make an official complaint.

This shameful situation was damaging the reputation of the Ballet Masters Department and of MTA as a whole. The students could not understand the rationale for the presence of this course in the curriculum at all. Why did they, as future choreographers, need it? In the MTA library, there was an archive of professional film recordings of all the best-known ballets from the Mariinsky and Bolshoi repertoires. Using these films, it was easily possible to learn the choreography and transfer it to any stage of any theatre if need be. My colleagues approached me, in my capacity as student trade union representative, to speak to the administrative officials about our dissatisfaction with the course. My first response was that I had no such authority. But thinking the matter through, I realised that my social post actually did entitle me to speak up on behalf of the members of our trade union. I knew that I was in something of a bureaucratic bind, and was taking a big personal risk. Given this, I decided to consult with the head of the institute's trade union committee. He heard me out and advised me not to take any action on my own. Instead he promised to speak to the dean of the department himself.

At the next lesson on dance composition, Shatin announced that Professor Lavrovsky had gone away on a business trip to Europe to stage a ballet there and would be back only in May to conclude his course. In the meantime, Sasha Lapauri would again teach us 'Technique for Duets'. The Chinese students, unable to restrain themselves, suddenly broke out into loud applause. The rest of us, however, tried not to show any reaction to the news. Anatoly Vasilyevich also preferred to act as if nothing had happened and went on teaching his class 'The Composition of Choreographic Dialogue'. It was none the less clear to everyone that, behind the scenes, a serious clash of titans was taking place within the department, the details of which we would probably never know.

In January, I began working with the dance ensemble of the Moscow University Club, and my financial situation significantly improved. I was both eating and dressing better now. At the same time, new items of expenditure presented themselves. First of all, I had to buy myself a used reel-to-reel audio player to use at home for the preparation of choreographic compositions for my courses at the academy and for work at the university club. In addition, their accordionist often demanded sheet music with a full accompaniment score, which was not always readily available. As a compromise, I had to revive my piano skills in order to demonstrate the tunes to the accordionist. My Sunday was given over entirely to self-study and household chores. There was no time left over for my personal life. The girls in the club were eagerly learning a choral dance 'Russian Barynya' and their enthusiasm allowed us to finish the choreography in time for a performance on the occasion of International Women's Day, 8th March, on the stage of the university's main auditorium.

After the concert, we had a male enthusiast join our otherwise all-female group. This gave me an idea to stage a comic dance, 'Yurochka', with him and the girls on the model of eight brides and one groom. Of the eight girls, two were experienced lead dancers, and both were called Emma: one (Emilia Ivankova) was from the law programme, and the other – from history. Both were twenty years old, beautiful, smart and competitive: they each fought tooth and nail for the only available male partner, even though he was gay. All the members of our dance group, however, were required to know the choreography of both dances: 'Russian Barynya' and 'Yurochka', so as to be able to substitute for one another if need be. 'Yurochka' was ready for performance by 1st May and we presented it at a student concert with immense, and unexpected, success. Another concert for Victory Day, 9th May, attracted two more guys to our enterprise, and they also quickly learned the male part for 'Yurochka'. To keep these two interested in staying with the ensemble, I quickly had to come up with a dance for three males, a 'Sailors' Dance', to be staged by 1st June. With the girls, I began work on the dance elements of our next production, 'Kazachok', to be worked on fully in September, after the summer vacation.

The two female soloists of the ensemble were rivals not only in dancing. Both girls were interested in me, and I flirted lightly with each of them in turn, though without much thought for the future, walking them home after classes or concerts. Fortunately, the two lived in different halls of residence. Since parting with Oksana the previous summer, I had not seen anyone for a year, and naturally was sex-starved, no less than my dancing sirens. At the same time, both common sense and a sense of responsibility kept me from intimacy with either of them, although I knew it would not be for long.

In May, Professor Lavrovsky returned from his European mission, and the compulsory study of the classical repertoire resumed in all its glory. Two Soviet students from the professional folk ensembles and four Chinese and Korean students made a show of ignoring this subject, leaving the studio even before the start of the class. The tensions in the department were coming to a head. We were hearing rumours that Zakharov and Lavrovsky were in cahoots against Shatin, blaming him for the change of the curriculum in midterm, after it had been approved for the whole academic year. As a Ukrainian proverb says, 'When masters fight, slaves feel the blows.' The six students decided to leave the programme altogether, right before the midterm exams, on the grounds of dissatisfaction with the curriculum. This amounted to 50% of the entire enrolment for that group. For MTA, the incident was a serious institutional failure, and Dean Shatin was deemed responsible.

The remaining six students in our programme passed all the exams, with the exception of 'Classical Ballet Repertoire' and 'Stage Acting', with the highest marks possible. The final exam, in 'Dance Composition', was held in the presence of all the teachers and the MTA rector. Three Soviet and three European foreign students demonstrated their achievements in composition and staging (personal performance) of a plot-based choreographic dialogue, on the topic of their choice. Prior to the demonstration, each student gave a detailed presentation on the choreography of their duet from the original idea, to the storyline and the trajectory of its dramatic development, down to the sketches of costumes. After each presentation, the members of the Examination Committee asked professional questions about the project and invariably received competent answers. This exam was not merely a test of the students' competence in dance composition. It was, in actual fact, a test of Anatoly Shatin's methodology of training future choreographers in the Ballet Masters Programme, founded and supported by him.

While we were washing and changing, the committee discussed each individual's personal results for the first year of their specialist studies. Returning to the studio, all six of us presented ourselves to the committee again. Significantly, the examiners were seated in characteristic groups of allies and opponents: Zakharov, Lavrovsky, Gusev (secretary of the Communist Party) and Elyazh to one side of the Rector, and Shatin with his supporters, Tarasov, Lapauri, Rozhdestvenskaya, Tkachenko, and Tseitlin to the other. The Rector stood up and proclaimed that we had all passed with flying colours. He congratulated us on our excellent results and wished us all a good summer holiday. He also shook Shatin's hand demonstratively and thanked him for his outstanding work with such a mixed Soviet–international group. Everyone, including the opponents, gave the Dean a round of applause.

When the committee had dispersed, Anatoly Vasilyevich invited the 'perfect six' to dinner at his home the following day. It was truly special to meet his wonderful family: his wife, Elizaveta, and their twenty-year-old daughter, Alyona. He lived in a small flat, consisting of two rooms and a kitchen, in a second-rate suburb of Moscow. In view of his social position, this dwelling was way too modest. He explained, however, that his wife's parents had lived all their lives in this flat and that Elizaveta was reluctant to abandon it and move to another part outside the city. Over dinner, the host asked each of us to talk a little bit about our artistic careers so far, and then diplomatically answered our own questions about the original rationale and structure behind our programme and its prospects for the future, particularly given the current disagreements between its leaders.

"You are all mature professionals, and it is natural that you should be concerned about your future. I can assure you, however, that as long as our present rector remains in his post, we should not fear any negative developments. Our programme is still in its infancy. What is happening at the moment is merely the programme showing the normal symptoms of a growth spurt. The original idea, twelve years ago in 1935, was to create a Ballet Masters Programme at

MTA, reflecting all forms of post-revolutionary dance culture, including its propagandists, Isadora Duncan, Fyodor Lopukhov, Kasyan Goleizovsky and other avant-garde theorists of the time. After the ideological plenary meeting of the Communist Party Central Committee in 1937, the situation in the country changed, and the representatives of the so-called new movement, 'drama-ballet', such as Sergeyev, Chabukiani, Zakharov, Lavrovsky, and others, ushered in a new era of Soviet repertoire, categorically rejecting any modern influences that deviated from the strict party line.

"Six years ago, when I invited Professors Zakharov and later Lavrovsky to join the programme, we all had a clear and solid agreement to promote modern types and forms of choreography for the future theatres of the Soviet Union. My colleagues' position has changed radically since then, however. Hence our disagreements about the methodology of training future ballet masters. They seem to think that we should be training choreographer-tutors who would mechanically transfer old choreographies from one stage to another. I believe we need to be training professionals, able to come up with their own, original, compositions. Our disagreements don't mean that our course will be terminated and the students turned out, however. Our fights and disputes are in fact useful because they present opportunities for the right approach to prove itself in practice. What happened yesterday at your exam starkly illustrates the need for personal freedom in any form of creative activity, and the sheer inadequacy of the copycat approach. A choreographer should be allowed to interpret any idea through the prism of his own personal artistic vision, by implementing his ideas onstage in a way that he or she finds most suited for their articulation, and also in a way that is most consonant with his or her personality and individual world view."

As we were saying goodbye to our host, we were suddenly shaken by the sound of thunder and the din of shattering glass. Shatin rushed to shut the window.

"Sounds like a storm! If you run, you will make it to the metro station before it starts pouring!"

The darkness over Moscow was suddenly lit up by a bright light, like daylight, and the red glow of fire. At the same time, the lights went out and the noise of traffic on the Novoslobodskaya Highway suddenly ceased. We hurried outside. The city looked dead, like something out of a science-fiction film. Trees, buses, cars, everything, lay overturned, upside down, and the ground was carpeted with a layer of broken glass. In shock, we were staring at motionless figures on the ground, pedestrians and passengers, on the pavements and on the road. This moment of frozen silence lasted no more than a minute, but it seemed like an eternity.

Suddenly, sirens from fire engines and ambulances pierced the air. The figures on the ground, probably recovering from slight concussion, stirred in silence, many of them covered in blood, cut by shards of broken glass. It all looked like a nightmarish dream. Our group scattered in different directions in panic, each unsure what to do – whether to help others, or save ourselves from some unseen and unknown danger. An innate survival instinct ordered me to hide from the piercing rays of the steadily diminishing glow in the sky. People all around were wandering aimlessly, stumbling, bumping into each other, their eyes wide open.

At the entrance to the metro, I started feeling nauseous and slumped on to a bench.

Later that night, I found myself lying on a hard wooden surface. I could not understand where I was. Scenes of wartime bombing in Stalingrad hovered in front of my eyes: the screeching of sirens, broken glass on the tram's floor, fountains of spurting blood . . . At first light, I felt somebody touching my shoulder. Ungluing my eyelids, I could dimly make out a nurse's face.

"Alive!" she exclaimed in disbelief.

I was stuffed into an ambulance full of other victims which took off, accompanied by the hysterical blaring of sirens. I was certain that I had already seen such episodes in some documentary films. I remember being undressed and, together with other patients, sprayed with cascades of water directly from a hose. I cannot tell how long that procedure lasted, but my mind gradually cleared. When I came to and was able to move around, I found my clothes, not without some difficulty, but my bag, with some small change, my student ID and my house key in it, was nowhere to be seen. It was useless trying to look for it in that chaos. I asked the nurse where I was and how I could get back to Trifonovka. There was no overland transport operating then, and so I had to walk to the nearest metro station. Doctors advised me to drink milk and to take cold showers for three days.

Incomprehensibly, there was absolutely nothing about the events in the newspapers or on the radio. It was as though nothing had happened. Most people had their theories, but were too afraid to speak out. Only later, it became clear that the cause of the blast was an explosion at an underground nuclear facility in Podlipki (later Kaliningrad and now Korolyov), a suburb of Moscow. It is hard to guess how many victims (dead and wounded) there may have been in Podlipki and in the surrounding boroughs of Moscow. While I was lying in bed in my halls of residence, recovering from my recent shock, the warden appeared with a note for me.

"Misha, here is the doctor's name and room number in the Sklifosovsky Clinic. They just called to say that your friend Emilia Ivankova's operation was successful and that she is expecting you."

I sprang to my feet: 'Trouble looks for trouble,' as the saying goes. Moscow's streets had not yet been cleared of traces of the recent catastrophe, but in a central supermarket on Mayakovka Street I was able to buy fruit, biscuits, sweets and even a small bouquet of flowers, though I did stop to wonder whether the latter was a good idea.

With some difficulty, I managed to reach the clinic. The reception area presented a depressing sight: dozens of wounded, hastily bandaged, were sitting or sprawling on the floor, waiting for medical attention. Moans, sobs and calls for help intermingled in this tragic choir, full of pain, fear and helplessness. There were not enough medical staff to deal with the constant flow of new patients still arriving three days later. I climbed to the third floor where the corridors were also overflowing with the wounded. It took me a few moments to distinguish Milia among the patients all similarly attired. I noticed her only when she started waving to me with a free hand from the opposite end. Apologising left and right, as I stepped over and around the wounded, I finally reached the object of my journey. She had one arm in a sling.

My friend demonstratively swung her healthy arm around my neck with such passion, as if we had been lovers for a long time. I did not object.

"Mikhail Semyonovich, please forgive me: I tell everyone here that I have a very jealous husband, otherwise I couldn't keep all the local admirers at bay. Let's go to the staircase landing: we can speak there in peace. I have half an hour before the next injection. I hope you weren't affected by this incident: I was worried. I am also sorry to disturb you with this request for a visit."

"Milia, you may drop the formalities. We are friends. What happened to your hand?"

"The day before yesterday, I was studying, as usual, in the library, sitting by the window. Then, at about 8 p.m., there was the sound of thunder, and a huge windowpane shattered over my head sending down a shower of glass that cut my hand to the bone. They rushed me here, braced the arm above the wound to stop the bleeding. But there were hundreds of other victims here already, and I had to wait for four hours before I could be seen. I was afraid that gangrene might set in, so I started kicking up a fuss in triage, threatening to sue them for negligence, under Article 48B of the Russian Criminal Code (sometimes it helps being a law student). They immediately rushed me to the operating room: washed and anaesthetised the wound, and then stitched it up. The surgeon said that he'd been able to restore the artery, but could not reattach the severed ends of the main nerve. Since nerve cells do not regenerate easily, there is a risk that my left hand will be permanently paralysed. What they should have done was to sew it up in one hour not four."

"Anyway it's not true! Any cells can be regenerated, even brain cells. The surgeon was conservative in his prognosis. It all depends on your strength of will, discipline and the quality of your physiotherapist."

"I won't be able to dance in your ensemble any more."

I saw bitter tears welling up in her eyes and carefully put my arms around her, letting her head rest on my shoulder. *Let her cry it out,* I thought to myself. After a minute, Milia stirred and tried to free herself from my hug, but it was too late for retreat. I was kissing every little tear rolling down her face, and pressing my lips to her eyes. This course of medical-sexual therapy concluded with a long mutual kiss. Finally, out of breath, the 'patient' took a step back and turned away in embarrassment:

"Mikhail Semyonovich, I'm sorry, I lost control."

"First of all, not Mikhail Semyonovich, but simply Misha, for the purposes of our out-of-office communication. Secondly, no one has lost control. It is a natural expression of our feelings. If two sensible people begin feeling an affection for one another and have serious intentions, such feelings should not be stifled or rejected, rather, they should be guided along their proper course. In support of such a romantic premise, let me present you with these flowers and sweets. Please let me come and see you daily, at a convenient time, at least until they check you out of this hell."

Milia listened to me as if hypnotised, stunned by my confession, unable to believe it was real. Staring at me through the veil of flowers she was trying to decide whether I was serious, or joking, as was my wont: "You can visit between 2 and 4 p.m., it's a good time because everyone takes a nap."

During my subsequent visits, I just entertained Milia with funny stories, avoiding physical contact. On Saturday, her hard cast was replaced with a light one, and I helped her to return to the halls of residence. On the way, I asked permission to test again the sensitivity of the fingers on her damaged hand. She could feel my squeeze a little more than before, but she could not move her fingers. When she checked out, the doctor confirmed that paralysis was unavoidable because of the damage she had suffered to a radial nerve. My friend gave me a look of despair, and we looked into each other's eyes for a long time, as if reading one another's thoughts.

"Misha, what are you after? I cannot dance in your ensemble any longer, and you don't need a disabled wife on top of all the other challenges in your life. You will be better off with the other Emma now."

"That might be so, but there is something there, drawing me to you, something I cannot explain."

"You are simply sorry for me. But this is not enough for mutual happiness. It's like in Shakespeare only the reverse: *He loved me for the dangers I had passed, and I loved him that he did pity them. You owe me nothing. I set your conscience free."*

"Thank you, but I would not be able to live and create in peace until I have helped to return full functionality to your injured hand. Because I know I can do it. Please indulge me in this. As time goes by, we can see how our personal relations pan out. You will always have the final say on this."

Tears ran down Milia's face and fell on her cast. I dried her cheeks with my lips, then bent down and kissed each finger of her injured hand.

We exchanged addresses and agreed that if she wanted to see me for her birthday on 2nd August, she would let me know. If not, we would see each other in September, at the first meeting of the dance ensemble. I walked her to the train station and we said goodbye without any show of emotion. I just wished her a safe journey and reminded her how important it was that she do the exercises I had prescribed, at least two or three times a day. Milia promised to follow my course of physical therapy faithfully. The next day, I left for my summer vacation on the Black Sea where everybody was waiting for me.

Just before I left, I telegraphed home: 'Mum and Roma, don't forget to roll out the red carpet from Privoz to Moldavanka!'

On the way home from the train station, I was absorbed in sweet reveries of the future and working out my immediate plans for the stay in Odessa. Reaching an all too familiar intersection in Moldavanka, I slowed down, combed my hair, brushed off the dust, and straightened out the shirt underneath my backpack. Right: now I can appear before Mother.

The bar at the bodega was crowded as usual, and I had to elbow my way through to place my order: "Woman, a shot of vodka, this instant!"

"What's the matter: are your pants on fire?"

"Zhora, assist this friar out with a gentle kick up the backside!"

"Misha!" the barmaid shouted. "Let him through! It's my son!"

Mother's boss, Fedya, came out on hearing the commotion: "Aha! Welcome, Mr Artiste!"

"I can't believe you are here!" Mother sobbed.

"Anna, you can go with him to my office. I'll stand in for you."

Fedya took up his stance behind the bar: "So, who's next to jump the queue?"

Drunken customers roared in unison.

In Fedya's office, I took off my backpack to present myself for a full inspection.

"Thin as a rake as always," Mother complained.

"But in good spirits," I added.

"Yes, that much is clear. I was just about to tell you off for your obnoxious 'Shot of vodka, this instant', when I spotted my dear 'happy medium'," she chattered, stroking my head. "How long will you stay?"

"A week or two. It's not up to me."

"Whose decision is it then? You don't believe in God, which means you are your own master."

"How is Roma, Mum?" I changed the subject.

"Studying at the polytechnic, playing chess, and dating his girlfriend, Lyuba. He found a temporary job in a factory for the summer, covering for those on vacation. Yosif has graduated from the university and got a job at a refrigeration factory. We are at war."

"What's going on?"

"He doesn't want to pay his share for the flat and utilities."

I changed the topic once more, unwilling to get into family issues.

"Mamulya, may I invite all our relatives tomorrow night to celebrate my visit? I'll buy all the necessary provisions at Privoz, if you give me your list."

"Why such haste?"

"I am spectacularly tired. I'd like to go to Bugaz for a week to rest."

"Fine."

I felt my pulse quickening as I approached No. 26. This is what 'missing home' means. By the gates the eternal Baba Sasha was still there, with her sack of sunflower seeds in front of her. She was nodding in her sleep. I thought to myself, *She must be over eighty.* I felt a lump in my throat.

Coming right up close, I squatted in front of her, and said very quietly, so as not to frighten her: "How much for a cup of seeds?"

She began to babble, as she had done years earlier, on our return from Stalingrad.

"God bless me, it's Mishanya! I've been waiting for you all day and still missed you." She kissed me on the forehead. "Annushka showed me your telegram. Thank God, you are well!" She was crossing herself and me in turn: "All the neighbours know about your arrival, and my grandchildren have been asking about you. Go, darling, have a rest and come to see me in the evening. I made your favourite borscht with garlic for you. Volodya and Maria are in Bugaz and don't know about your coming. Promise me you'll go and see them while you are there. Let Maria tell her boys about your successes."

That evening I went over to Baba Sasha to indulge in her borscht and present her with a box of her favourite chocolates. She categorically declined the gift, and then expediently put it out of sight in case I took her seriously and took it back. She told me the news about her grandchildren, my childhood friends, all of whom happened to be out of town at the moment. No one was married yet. All were doctors, like their father, and worked in different towns. I swore Granny to secrecy and shared my plans to marry a Russian Cossack woman from Kubany.

"What will your mother say when you bring a shiksa [non-Jewish woman] into the house?"

"Nanny, it doesn't matter: I am not planning to live here. What is more important is how the girl's provincial parents will react to their daughter's union with a Jew."

"What do you know about them? What is their background? Are they decent folks?"

"Her father is the director of a collective farm, a Cossack, and a party member. They own a house with a big orchard and vegetable garden, as well as farm animals. Her mother is also from an old Cossack family, has raised five children and runs the household."

"If I were you, Misha, I would not be in such a hurry to get married. Not until you finish at the academy."

"Objectively speaking you are right, but the circumstances suggest otherwise."

Our dialogue was interrupted by Mother's appearance.

"Where were you? I was starting to think I had dreamt up your return."

"I was at Baba Sasha's, eating her heavenly borscht and hearing stories about her grandchildren."

"Aha! And I meanwhile brought you some pirozhki with liver and your favourite kvass. By the way, the grand reunion with the relatives has been moved to Sunday: they want to come to Bugaz. That would be the best option for everyone: we can spend all day swimming and sunbathing. You invite Uncle Volodya and Maria

Ilinichna, and we will bring all the food and drink, so you won't need to worry about anything. Fedya gave me a day off to celebrate your return."

"Mum, can you explain to me what's going on between you and Yosif? Perhaps I can help resolve this family conflict? Otherwise, how can you live together?"

"Soon it'll be a year since Yosif started seeing Polina. They have decided to get married in the autumn and they want to live in our flat. Roman protests. He says that Yosif can get a new flat, allocated to them by the factory as 'young specialists'. But Yosif prefers to stay in our flat because it is close to his work, and so he is doing everything to turf Roman out. He even suggested that I exchange flats with Polina's mother so that she could live with them. But I am not going to give in without a fight. Roman, in turn, is dating Lyuba, and is staying over at her place at the moment, to avoid bloodshed. Yosif meanwhile has lost all sense of decency: he's demanding that you and Roman give up your rights to the flat on the grounds that he is the eldest brother."

"That's bollocks. Where is he now?"

"He'll be home soon."

"Mum, I am not going to deal with him tonight. I'll talk to him tomorrow, before work."

Early in the morning, hearing Yosif's footsteps, I got up and followed him into the kitchen.

Seeing me, he uttered: "Hello to the prodigal son! What brings you back to our parts, after such a long absence?"

"Hi! We need to speak on a matter of great importance. It won't take more than five minutes."

"I can't, I need to go to work. And, by the way, I have nothing to talk to you about."

"It's in your interest to talk to me. You may go on getting ready for work. I, meanwhile, will outline my offer to you. I hope you recognise the profit to you in it. I'm quite aware of your conflict with Roma and Mother over the flat: you're planning on getting married and are worried about the limited living space. There are already four people registered as residents in the mere forty square metres of this property. Since the minimum living space allocation per person is nine square metres, a fifth resident cannot be registered as living in this flat, not, at least, until someone moves out. Naturally, you're interested in staying in this flat because it's close to your work; otherwise your factory may allocate a flat for you and Polina somewhere far off, say in Cheryomushki.

My elder brother tried several times to interrupt me, but I continued with my prepared monologue, unperturbed by any of his nasty remarks and threats.

"You have a real opportunity to remain in this flat, provided you accept my conditions."

"Go on, I'm curious to hear what a half-baked whoremaster can propose to a qualified engineer."

"Roma will not vacate the flat unless you pay him off. I could vacate it immediately, but only in exchange for a document signed by you, and specifying your agreement to the following: to pay two-thirds of the utilities and house maintenance fees from here on; to allow Mother unimpeded access to all common areas of the flat: living room, kitchen, toilet, balcony, etc. Finally, you must build a permanent partition wall in a corner of the living room, creating a separate room for Mother's personal use, thirteen square metres in size, with a window, private entrance and electricity. We will need your response to this offer within five working days. If you reject it, Mother and I will be forced to contact the trade union leadership of the factory where you work. In addition, we'll file a claim with a People's Court to protect Mother, an invalid of the Second World War, and Roma, a family member of a serviceman who died in the line of duty, from your aggressive actions against them. If you have any sense at all, you'll accept this reasonable offer, rather than face the prospect of being disgraced, both at work and in the public eye."

The first thing I did, immediately after speaking with Yosif, was to go to Passport Services at the local police station and file an application for a change of name from my Jewish one to Ukrainian. I put down, as my reason for change, the fact that Berkut was my professional theatre name, which I had been using for the previous seven years, ever since my work with the Ensemble of the Lilliputians at the Odessa Philharmonic. I left all the necessary documents with a girl at Passport Services and presented her with a poster of an old performance I had choreographed. It had my picture and credentials on it. She was pleasantly surprised, and impressed to be in the presence of a 'celebrity', and so promised to turn the paperwork around in less than a week. I blew her a kiss, in recognition of her goodwill.

That same day, I paid brief visits to my local patrons and gave them my Moscow and even Leningrad addresses (just in case). It should be noted that not one of them was at all surprised to see my name changed. Indeed, they approved of it as it was a common practice in the theatrical world, and not regarded so seriously. It turned out that I had been wearing myself out on this account for nothing. My fears that the state officials would discover and condemn me for a crime proved unfounded.

Karolina-Bugaz is a three-kilometre-long strip of land separating the mouth of the Dniester river from the Black Sea. It is about fifty metres wide, stretching out into the sea to the west, under which flows the Dniester, dumping its waters into the sea. On the other side of the bridge is Belgorod-Dniestrovsk, an ancient fortress on the border of Ukraine and Moldova, which at some point in history was once Romanian territory. Bugaz is essentially a country road. On the side facing the sea stands a row of substantial brick houses with gardens and vineyards. On the other facing the river is a string of fishermen's huts. One of the seaside houses was the summer residence of our closest Odessan neighbours: old Uncle Volodya, the husband of Baba Sasha, and his daughter Maria, Mother's friend. Across the street from them, on the riverside, a small cosy hut with a cement cellar for storing fresh fish, vodka, and other foodstuffs, was to be my home for the coming week.

After a year's absence, my first item of business in Bugaz, was to clean up my little hut and organise my Gypsy lifestyle out there. I had only two days to prepare my dwelling for the arrival of guests on the Sunday. In the evening, I went across the street to say hello to Uncle Volodya and Maria Ilinichna. Strategically calculating the time, I arrived just as they were sitting down to dinner: in my own hut, there was not a crumb to be had on that first night.

Knocking on their door, I heard: "Kolya, come on in!" They took me for their next-door neighbour, and suddenly, Maria recognised my prominent nose, and shouted: "Oy! I can't believe my eyes! Is this Mishka from Moldavanka? Have you fallen out of the sky?"

"No, he couldn't have!" Uncle Volodya rumbled. "Look, there are no wings on his back. Plus, he's got a bottle in his hand."

I placed in front of him a bottle of Armenian cognac, and presented his daughter with a box of soft meringues, a well-known Russian delicacy called *zefir*.

"Papa, look! He still remembers my favourite sweets." She hugged and kissed me warmly. "Look at you, darling, you've turned into a skeleton! You're nothing but a bag of bones! But not to worry – we're going to fill you out with borscht and fried fish. You'll grow some flesh in no time. Your girlfriends in Moscow won't recognise you."

I was smiling broadly. It was such a pleasure for me to hear their unforgettable Odessan voices again.

On Sunday, at eight thirty in the morning, I heard the noise of an approaching crowd. The night before, I had attached a piece of paper on to my gate saying: 'SHUSH! Beware of Dog! Enter in single file, don't smash the bottles.' By the way the crowd reacted to my humble message, I could tell that the new arrivals were my relatives. What followed is impossible to describe. The roar of joyful greetings was louder than the shouts of vendors in Privoz market. There were only twelve of them, but they made the noise of 120. I ran out to greet them. There wasn't a part of me that was not kissed, hugged, squeezed, or slapped. My brother Roman lifted me up in the air, shook me up slightly, and lowered me back on to the sand. Mother, with her three sisters, quickly unpacked the bags with the food and drink they had brought and put them away into the cellar, while my cousins questioned me about Moscow. By nine, everyone had gone off to the beach on the seaside, to claim the best spots. We spent three hours sunbathing, swimming, playing ball, chatting, and having a good time.

At midday, Mother and my aunts returned to the hut to prepare lunch, while the younger generation stayed behind for another hour to enjoy the fresh air, away from the smog of the industrial city. My cousins crossed over to the riverside and caught some crayfish with hand nets. We boiled the crayfish with seaweed and served them as appetisers. At one o'clock, Uncle Volodya and Maria joined us. They brought along four three-litre bottles of red and white wine of their own vintage. The table was buckling under the weight of fried fish, fresh salads, cooked aubergines, pirozhki, and other home-made delicacies. Elderly guests sat at the table hiding from the burning sun under an umbrella, and the younger ones lounged on blankets on the ground, while I couriered back and forth between them like Figaro. Roman warned me that at 6 p.m., when everybody left, he and Mother wanted to stay behind in order to discuss with me the situation with Yosif. They intended to return to Odessa in the morning. I was glad of this opportunity to help resolve a family conflict. As they left, the guests informed me, in secret, that everybody would reassemble at Mother's bodega on 11th August to celebrate Roman's twentieth birthday.

When the guests had finally left, Mother, Roman and I cleaned up our humble hut and seated ourselves around the 'table of judgement'. Before leaving for Bugaz, I had given Mother the copy of a sample letter, addressed to the trade union of Yosif's factory, and had asked her to discuss with Roman the details of his proposed pay-off in exchange for giving up his entitlement to one-quarter of the living space in our flat. I had also asked them to consider what part they would like me to play in the negotiations. They had met at the bodega and discussed the matter. Mother had showed Roman a draft of her agreement with Yosif obliging him to carve out a separate room for her within the flat. Now, it was Roman's turn to play 'a gambit with four knights'. Our wise Mother naturally did not wish to air our dirty laundry in public, but she also realised that it was impossible to let Yosif continue in his aggressive ways. My younger brother, with his non-confrontational nature, was unable to stand up to Yosif on his own and protect Mother, so they had to use the fact of my temporary presence to exert some useful pressure on the eldest.

"Roma, what compensation do you want from Yosif in exchange for vacating the flat?"

"A minimum of 2,000 roubles, and that's only for Mother's sake, believe me."

"I fully appreciate that. We must reach a compromise. I personally am not able to produce such a sum. Mamulya, do you think it might be possible to borrow about 1,000 from your sisters and from Fedya (the bodega's manager)? I will add another 1,000, and then Roman could give up his residential title to this property. If we don't reach a settlement between us and appeal to the People's Court, they will most likely recommend that we exchange our two-bedroom flat for two one-bedroom flats, possibly somewhere far out, and this will be inconvenient for everyone. Mama, you need to decide now whether you wish to go ahead with this ultimatum or not."

"After a long pause, Mother pronounced that she would pay half of the pay-off sum, so that Roman could have some reserve money set aside for a wedding.

I continued: "Roma, if you agree to our proposal, then you should write a statement now, which I will dictate to you, indicating your readiness to vacate the flat and waive your entitlement to it as of 1st September on condition that Yosif meets our demands for accommodating Mother's needs for living together. You will also write me a receipt for 1,000 roubles, and Mother will keep this money and give it to you on the day you move out and get a stamp in your passport confirming that. We need to keep this arrangement secret. Neither Lyuba, nor Mother's sisters must know about it until after we have put it into effect. Do you agree?"

They both nodded.

"I'm going to write a letter to Yosif, while you, Roma, make a clean copy of your personal statement, so that I can show it to Yosif, if necessary, to prove that we have made such an arrangement. Mama, you will take my letter to Yosif. Both you and Roman can read it. On Thursday, I'll come back specifically for the talks with Yosif. If he refuses to talk to me, then be ready to activate plan B.

On Thursday 2nd August, I took a bus to Odessa. First of all, I sent a telegram to Milia: 'Happy Birthday. Best wishes for the speedy recovery of your hand. Kisses. Misha.' Then I went to see an attorney at the district People's Court. After studying the papers, she immediately drew up a draft of a letter in Mother's name, asking for protection against unfair treatment on the part of her son, Yosif, in wanting to bring his future wife to live in a flat of just forty square metres, when there were already four people registered as legal residents at this address.

"Have your mother copy this letter in her own hand and sign it. She should also mention that she is a Second World War invalid, and provide her ID number."

"How much do I owe you for the service?"

"There is no fee for the disabled."

I then hurried over to the bodega. Between 11 a.m. and midday, there were typically very few customers, once the morning needs of hung-over alcoholics had been met, and Mother had a chance to take a few minutes' break from the bar. I explained to her that she was risking nothing by composing the letter suggested by the attorney. On the contrary, it could be very useful to have it to hand in a conflict, to show to Yosif that we were not bluffing, but ready to defend our interests.

"Mummy, dear, 'If you're going to run with wolves you have to howl like wolves,' says a Russian proverb. I am absolutely sure that, once he believes we are in earnest, Yosif will come round and accept our conditions, which are actually rather advantageous for him. I am sorry to be saying this, Mum, but over the years you have nurtured a cruel, but not a stupid man. He indulges in emotional abuse. At the same time, he is sensible enough to appreciate the seriousness of our intentions, with all the official papers we are ready to file. He will see that it's not just empty talk. So, I'm sure he'll accept the deal. I'm more concerned about what he might try to do afterwards, when I'm not around any more. Let's just say that he does keep the promise to provide you with a separate room in the flat, and that he pays maintenance fees and the cost of utilities for a while. Then, when he gets married, he will bring his wife to live in the flat. Then they will produce a wonder-baby and the same problem with the shortage of living space will surface again, only this time in a more aggressive form. You don't need a degree in space science to work this out.

"Besides, he probably has his eye on another room in our communal corridor, which is presently occupied by a sickly old granny. When she passes away, he'll arrange an equal exchange of flats, and transfer his mother-in-law to that room. And they will be one happy family, while you will feel even more isolated. You know this is a real possibility because Yosif has already proposed that you exchange flats with Polina's mother. It's an unbelievable affront on the part of a son vis-à-vis his own mother."

The Panther quietly wiped away her tears. She took out a piece of paper and copied the statement drafted by the attorney. Then I made copies of both Mother's and Roman's statements, for safekeeping.

Yosif did not show up all day. Mother was very agitated, while I kept repeating to her like a parrot: "Mum, we cannot show our agitation to Yosif. He is trying our nerves on purpose, to show his independence. But he has nowhere to go. He is cornered. His bravado works only against people like you who would compromise to their own detriment in order to avoid a conflict. He's been playing on your emotions all his life. Please, calm down. Don't appease his sadistic nature. Let's go to sleep, and we'll see what's what in the morning."

Mother began to cry again.

"Your father is probably turning in his grave right now. If he were alive, this would never have happened. He always told me, before the war, to be strict with you boys."

I felt a lump in my throat and couldn't say anything, only hugged her. She went to bed, and I placed the copies of both statements (Mother's and Roman's) on Yosif's desk. At 11 p.m. I too fell asleep.

I heard Yosif coming in at around midnight. I woke up in the morning when Yosif opened a door into the living room where Mother and I were sleeping. My older brother came up to my bed, and I instinctively prepared myself for a fight.

He kicked my mattress and said in his unpleasant nasal voice: "Here is your document and your stinking papers. You need to thank Polina. It was she who convinced me to accept this temporary compromise. Read it, and tell me if all is in order. You have ten minutes."

He threw a stack of papers on the table and went to the kitchen. Mum was already up and sitting on the couch combing her hair.

"Good morning, Yosif!"

There was no reply. I looked at her, raising my eyebrows.

Mother only shrugged in response: "Every day I say 'good morning' and 'goodnight' to him, and he never replies."

"Thank God that not all your sons are like him. Good morning, dear Mamulya!"

I came up to her and kissed her. She sighed and shook her head with sadness.

Yosif had thrown down two copies of the agreement in which everyone's responsibilities were laid out in detail, including dates for the construction of a partition wall. They were signed and dated by him with a blank space left for Mother's signature. I gave her a pen and showed her where to sign on both copies. When Yosif again marched through the living room on the way to his own one, I gave him a copy of his and Mother's agreement, with Mother's signature, and a copy of Roman's statement.

Before she left for work after breakfast, Mother suddenly broke down: "Mishenka, I don't know how to thank you for everything!"

"You don't need to. Any normal son would have done the same in my place. A woman theoretically can have many children, but every child has only one mother. Go and work in peace today! I'm not going to get off Yosif's back until your room is completely ready for use. The work should start on Monday. Meanwhile, Roman and I will move all the furniture out to the balcony, except for your couch and my camp bed. Get some old bed sheets ready to cover up the furniture."

After I had seen my mother off, I went to Roman's factory to make arrangements about the furniture.

At the security check, the guards were surprised: "We only know two brothers, both chess masters."

"Now you have a chance to meet the third one – the 'happy medium'."

"Why? Also a chess master?"

"No, worse: a dancer!"

"Ha ha! So are we, after a drink or two."

To convince them, I performed a striking dance move from the Gypsy repertoire: a squat with a jump and a tap. Arriving on the scene, Roman interrupted the guards' applause.

"This is my middle brother, a 'great artiste from a bankrupt theatre' [a Russian saying]."

The youngest was happy to hear about the positive outcome of the negotiations and promised to be at my disposal at the weekend to deal with the furniture.

"How did you manage to convince Yosif?"

"I left the copies of Mother's and your statements on his desk in the evening. In the morning he signed, accepting all our conditions though of course not without a scene."

"Misha, how did you know that everything would actually pan out just the way you predicted?"

"Yosif is a mechanical engineer, he deals with machines; you are a mathematician and a chess player, and you deal with plastic figures; I am a teacher and an artist, and I deal with people. Over the twenty years of living with Yosif I've managed to study the psychology of our elder brother so thoroughly, from my own, personal, painful experience, that I'm able to predict his thinking and subsequent actions under any circumstances now, with almost 100% accuracy."

At home, I found a telegram waiting for me: 'Thank you. Broken arm is missing you. Come and visit in the middle of August. We'll return to Moscow together. Emilia 900 3 VIII 1957.'

"Good news! Well then? On Monday the 13th, we'll head for Kubany."

I hurried to the post office and sent a reply: 'Thanks for the invitation. Will arrive in Slavyansk evening August 13th. Flowers and ovations are unnecessary. Misha.' This would put the cat among the pigeons!

When the construction work in the flat began on the Monday, I moved back to my hut in Bugaz, to enjoy the ascetic life of a hermit. On the Friday I returned to Odessa to check on the progress of the construction. All was in order, except for the installation of electricity. In the evening, I impressed upon Yosif once again that without this condition being met, Roman and I would not waive our title as residents. Yosif promised that he and our cousin David would install electricity in Mother's room over the weekend. David confirmed the arrangement. On 11th August, we celebrated Roman's twentieth birthday in style. We booked the back room at the bodega and partied hard with all our relatives, including father's red-haired lot, just like in the good old days. Roman's celebration was both a house-warming party for Mother, and a going away party for me. The music didn't stop until two in the morning. Daniel and I took turns playing the accordion, trying to outdo each other in Russian/Ukrainian and Gypsy/Moldovan repertoire. The Odessans had not seen such hearty celebration in a while. My former colleagues from the theatre came over after their evening performance, and the partying resumed with renewed energy. Soon the guests were out on the street, dancing and singing at the famous Moldavanka intersection, cheered on by a tipsy crowd. Mother and Roman were pleased with the celebration.

On Monday 13th August, I left my beloved Odessa once more, bound for uncertainty.

CHAPTER 6 A FATAL CHOICE OF PARTNER

I left Odessa at six in the morning, and two changes later I finally reached Slavyansk by 6 p.m. Milia had calculated the time of my arrival perfectly and was waiting for me at the entrance to the station with her brother Alik atop a horse-drawn cart. They saw me first and drove almost up to my nose, while I was still looking around.

Suddenly I heard the groom's polite invitation: "Dear Mr Visitor, sir, your carriage awaits! Step in, if you please!" The sixteen-year-old youth had a sense of humour.

My girlfriend hastened towards me, with her arm still in a sling, although no longer in bandages. She hurriedly threw her arm around my neck and planted a kiss on my cheek, as she had done in the Moscow clinic after the accident.

"Misha, please excuse us, but we must rush: my family is waiting for us at the dinner table."

The mare halted of her own accord in front of an impressive wooden house with a large adjacent plot of land. Behind the tall fence was an orchard of fruit trees, a vegetable garden, a barn, chicken coop, and sauna. Alik whistled, and his parents came down the porch staircase: Mother with bread and salt on an embroidered towel, and Father with a bottle of home-made vodka and two glasses.

Greeting me with a triple kiss, Milia's mother declared, "Welcome, dear guest!"

Her father added, "Well done for coming to our part of the world!" according to the old Cossack tradition.

I clinked glasses with her father; we downed half-filled glasses in one and followed up with bread and salt. The alcohol went straight to my head, but I managed to hold on to Mother Earth, even grunting like a seasoned alcoholic from Mother's bodega. The whole female crew on the porch broke into applause. Even Milia banged on the railings of the porch with her good hand. I answered with a deep Russian bow, touching the ground before me with my fingertips.

After this ceremonial introduction, Milia presented the members of her family. She then took a fresh towel and led me to a place to wash behind the porch.

There were ten of us around the dinner table. Her father naturally sat at the head. On one side sat Alik, on the other, myself and Milia. In between toasts, Sergey Andreyevich kept asking me personal questions. Most of the time I answered him briefly, and sometimes I deliberately avoided answering altogether, changing the subject when he touched on my relations with my family or with Milia. She had told me that her father was an agronomist. During the war, he rose to the rank of major in the Intendant [superintendent/manager] Service, and after the war, he returned to Kubany to help restore the country's agricultural production.

"Mama, we are going for a walk to the pond, we'll be back by 10 p.m. All right?"

Milia grabbed my hand and pulled me from the table. On the porch, she inhaled deeply looking up at the crescent moon and the bright stars over our heads. It was calm and quiet all around us.

I gently touched the fingers of her injured hand and met Milia's questioning stare. So, she felt my touch. This was encouraging.

"May I see your scar and assess the sensitivity of your hand?"

"If you insist."

Milia took off the sling and turned to the moonlight. A thick scar, about ten centimetres long, half a centimetre wide, ran from her shoulder down to the elbow. There were stitch marks on each side, and the arm looked quite disfigured. Nevertheless, assuming the role of a medical specialist, I decided to reassure my first ever patient:

"It doesn't look half as bad as I had expected," I commented.

"You should have seen the scar when they had just removed the stitches and painted it all over with iodine as antiseptic: you would have fainted."

"Yes, and collapsed into your arms, my dear."

She giggled and futilely tried to free her hand from mine by moving her shoulder.

"Milia, you should treat with due respect the doctor who has come from far away to treat your poor hand!" I kissed the scar.

She goggled at me, and I immediately kissed her eyes one at a time. She seemed to think it was impertinent on my part.

Quickly easing her arm back into the sling, she pulled me with the other hand away from the porch and towards the gate. I feigned resistance and protested that I would never do that again.

"Have no fear, Mishenka! We'll just walk to the pond to hear the frog choir. I guarantee your complete safety, as your personal attorney and bodyguard."

"But what if the frogs decide to dance 'Pas de deux' with me or – even worse – kiss me?"

"First of all, it's me who is going to dance with you, and secondly, it is you who is going to kiss me."

"Thank God for the miraculous transformation of the virtuous Emilia from a frog into a princess!" and I advanced, with my arms wide open, towards her.

"Not so fast, dear. I thought I had made it clear when and where we are going to do all this."

I froze with my arms stretched out, like the Saviour on the Cross.

"Mikhail, don't blaspheme. Leave your Odessan sarcasm for the frogs."

"Your orders, mistress. I am your humble slave, O Frog-Princess!"

I dropped on one knee and placed her injured hand on my head. Just at that instant, the frogs began their evening concert and we both chuckled.

"Comrade Director, are we staging a play by Shakespeare or Goldoni?"

"Neither of them! This is simply a humble plea of a love-struck clown pleading with his enchantress for an intimate moment in the presence of frogs."

"May I consider your plea over there, on a bench by the pond? You won't have to wait long."

I was putting on an easy tone in our conversation, but in reality I was beset by doubts, after the inspection of Milia's monstrous scar, whether I would be able to restore the functionality of her hand. I saw myself as a complete charlatan and my feeble attempts to cover up my confusion with silly jokes only made me feel worse. When we reached the bench, I took Milia's lifeless hand from its sling and rested it on my lap. She did not protest, only stared at the moon in silence. It was essential to test the surface of the hand and its muscle tissues for sensitivity – for any sign of reaction from the central nervous system.

"Milia, I would like to determine the sensory state of your entire hand. I am going to press very lightly and briefly each of your fingers, and if you feel my touch, say 'yes' once. If you feel me brushing your skin with my fingertip sideways, then repeat 'yes' twice. Is that clear?"

I began by massaging the numb fingers of her injured hand, and then tenderly pressed them to my lips. Suddenly I felt a very faint vibration in her wrist.

"Milia, were you trying to remove your wrist from my hand, or am I mistaken?"

"Yes, I was thinking that it's already time to go back. My people go to bed early."

"Wait a minute! Try to do the same, only stronger," and I pressed my lips to her fingertips again. The vibration in her wrist was real.

"Hooray!" I shouted so loudly that the frogs fell silent.

"Misha," Milia asked cautiously, "do you really think it's possible . . . ?"

"Do I think? I know! Somewhere in your left arm life is awakening again. My dear Frog-Princess, congratulations on your inevitable rebirth in the form of Emilia Sergeyevna Berkut! Sounds good, no?"

She stood there, intent on turning back home, and suddenly froze in shock, hearing my words.

"In our Cossack clan, we don't joke on this subject."

"I am not joking. You know that I like you very much and so I am asking you to become my wife."

I went down on one knee to await a fatal response. Milia lifted her head and looked me straight in the eyes, trying to ascertain the seriousness of my intent. Delicately, I pulled her towards me and firmly seated her on my lap. Raising her healthy arm I wound it around my neck. She was not objecting.

"Milia, let us speak openly, as good friends, if possible. I understand your doubts. After a year of professional interaction in the dance ensemble, and after only one month of a more personal contact, we do not yet know each other well and we do not yet have a deep understanding of our characters. But we are both very sensuous people who respond quickly. We owe each other nothing as I intimated at the clinic, but there is no doubt that there is an attraction and feeling between us. If that were not the case, I wouldn't be here. You don't have to answer me now. Let us try, over the course of this week, to get to know each other better. In any case, please allow me to finish my medical experiment with your hand. Then we shall see how our relations develop.

"If you reject my offer, this would not affect my feelings for you and would not deter me from wishing to help return your hand to life. The least you can expect from me is that I would assist you in getting back to your halls of residence and we would continue our dance classes at the university club as if nothing had happened. I could carry on with my course of physical therapy for you in the evenings, after work. Tell me: do you think that this might work? My only advice is this: don't consult anyone else about this. Try to think it over and decide on your own. After all, I will have to live with you, and not with your mother."

"Misha, I am very happy to hear your proposal. And I agree with your suggestion that we get to know each other slowly. Thank you for your attention to such an ordinary person as myself. But now it's time to get back to the house."

All of a sudden she dug her lips into mine, pressing her virginal chest against mine, passionately without restraint. This was blissful – a nectar-sweet moment of love.

Milia's anxious mother was already looking out for us at the gate. She took me up to the attic where a mattress decked out with fresh bedding was laid out by the window. Next to it were my suitcase and backpack and a clean towel hung from a plank under the ceiling. She apologised in advance that she might wake me up early in the morning when she let the cattle out. Then she wished me goodnight and descended the steep ladder with admirable ease. In half a second, I was out for the count.

In the morning, I was indeed woken up by the farmyard choir of clucking chickens, bleating sheep and mooing cows. All my surroundings, including smells and sounds, vividly reminded me of our country life as evacuees and the recognition sent a sense of deep nostalgia through me.

The morning rhapsody over, I went down into the garden for my morning exercises and then took a shower in the log sauna (Russian *banya*) where cold water made me dance and shiver as I attempted to wash off oily soapy lather from my body. The pleasure of drying and rubbing myself with a starchy towel was almost as authentic as in the Odessan sauna.

Seeing that I was up and already washed, Alik called me inside for breakfast. He then invited me to join him on a tour of the collective farm.

"Then, at one this afternoon we'll get on the bikes, and shuttle between farmsteads and little villages in the vicinity until five o'clock. Now, in the summer, I work as a courier carrying messages in lieu of telephone calls between the chairman of the collective farm (my dad), the agronomist, and team leaders in the fields. It's a large area, so our legs are going to have a serious workout."

If only he knew how many hours a day my legs worked out on a regular basis!

After breakfast, I gave Milia a fifteen-minute session of massage therapy. She then went on to study the latest edition of the Russian Criminal Code, while I turned my attention to the choreography of the coming academic year. Milia's mother complained that her husband had been working twelve-hour days, except for Sundays, for the last twelve years.

Sounds like a voluntary labour camp, I thought to myself. *He's put himself into shackles and now cannot find a way out of the trap.*

There were two men's and one woman's bike under the porch. Alik prepared his father's bike for me and, right after lunch, we took off to the collective farm's headquarters. I was not a good cyclist. At every turn I veered widely to the right or left, inducing uncontrollable laughter on the part of my future brother-in-law. I threatened to give him a dance lesson in the evening to see who would be laughing then. He promised to compose his last will before he began dancing.

Sergey Andreyevich greeted us warmly and introduced me to his subordinates. He gave his son a stack of papers with instructions and enquiries addressed to the team leaders of various subdivisions of the agricultural complex. Alik tuned up my bike, adjusting the chain, a few nuts, and whatever else had loosened up on the road. He also kindly offered me his well-worn old straw hat to protect my uncovered head from heatstroke. Thanking him for caring for the weakest part of my body, I reminded him that I had grown up in Odessa where every babe learns to boil in the sun from day one. Milia had provided me with a water flask and some fruit in the bike's basket to ensure my creature comforts until evening. We stopped about every ten to twenty minutes at one area or another of the collective farm, and while Alik exchanged communiqués, I explored barns with agricultural machinery and silos with freshly harvested vegetables. Most of the produce was carefully packed in open boxes made of wooden planks, but there were also heaps of produce piled up directly on the ground outside between barns: cucumbers, tomatoes, cabbage, squashes. Some of these vegetable pyramids were beginning to rot. I picked up one such cucumber and a tomato. Alik explained the reason for these, as he tossed them back.

"The sorting facilities at the regional centre don't have enough storage boxes of sturdy construction, and they also run low on trucks that could transport the produce from the fields to the sorting points. When we deliver containers with our produce to the storage centres, we are supposed to get back an equal number of empty boxes in exchange. The problem is that the storage facilities often don't have those boxes ready because they are busy delivering perishable produce to consumers. This is a vicious cycle, and in the end, badly needed containers stuffed with produce lie idle at storage facilities, while delivery trucks return to collective farms without the necessary boxes. As a result, because of a lack of packing containers and transport, tons of precious vegetables grown with back-breaking labour, rot in piles on a farm or at the regional sorting/ storage facilities. The same sort of losses happen during fruit and grain harvests: basically during all harvesting. What good worker can watch such a waste of his labour with equanimity? That is why the chairman takes to heart the failures of the production process that occur thanks to a lackadaisical attitude on the part of the local administrative leadership. He fights with the regional authorities, but without noticeable success. Every year the productivity and output increase, while the distributive system and its logistics remain the same, if not worse. Packing materials and means of transportation deteriorate, but there are no replacements."

Hearing this account, I felt my hair bristle with indignation. The reality was incomprehensible. I had just passed an exam in political economy, where a textbook clearly stated: *'The socialist system of public economy in the Soviet state is the most progressive and most developed in the world with regard to the production and distribution of objects of mass consumption for the population of our great country.'* It appeared that what the textbook said and what took place in real life were two different things. Was what I had seen a case of intentional falsification? Or was it simply the case that the right hand didn't know what the left was doing? One way or another, the economy of any political system cannot function or progress properly in the face of such contradictions between theory and practice. Rather the opposite is true: sooner or later, if the situation doesn't change, such an economy would begin to degrade. This would be obvious even to a schoolchild. Could it be a case of intentional malpractice? Now I understood why the chairman/agronomist of the collective farm was so preoccupied. He could be blamed for all these malfunctions, a typical scapegoat. And even without that worry, it must have been hard to watch the labour of the whole collective going to waste.

In the evening while I was giving Milia her massage, I asked, "What's going on in the farm with the rotting vegetables?"

"We don't speak about this at home. Let's go to the pond and listen to our favourite frog choir."

I realised that her father's position was even worse than it had first appeared.

On the bench by the pond, Milia tried to chase the clouds away. She put her head on my shoulder and her arms around me, and whispered, almost touching my ear with her lips: "I am very happy that you have come. My parents didn't believe that I had such a kind friend as you."

Listening to my dove cooing, and admiring the reflection of stars in the pond, I gradually forgot the cares and hassles of the distant world and relaxed into the surrounding quiet. My girlfriend continued to play with my hair and brush her lips against my ear.

"Thank you for your help with my hand. Your confidence is contagious, and now I am also beginning to hope that it can be cured. I often dream that I am drawing water from a well, or holding a branch in that hand and prodding Krasotka (a family cow) into the cowshed. Will I really be able to do that?"

I turned around and kissed her lips. She held me tight a long time, then sprang up, and walked around me to seat herself on my other side. I looked at her in surprise, not sure why she had moved.

"What's wrong? Did I offend you?"

"Yes, very much!" she feigned displeasure coquettishly and then swung her leg over and landed on my lap gripping my thighs with hers, and wrapping her good hand around my back.

Such initiative caught me off guard: I froze.

She sweetly pressed her head to my chest and whispered: "Now I can hear the beating of your heart, so don't even try to deceive me!" This Cossack maiden gazed at me with burning eyes and waited for a reaction.

I was not about to rush, however. This was a decisive moment for either intimacy or rejection. Trying to interpret the intentions encoded in her pleading look, I realised that I could no longer be passive under such intense pressure. I began to remove her sling carefully from her shoulder, finally hanging it on the back of the bench. The same chaotic thoughts rushed through my head: *to be or not to be?* I lifted her injured wrist to my face and pressed it to my right cheek. Then I began to plant kisses on to each finger, the wrist, the forearm, the scar and the shoulder. I smoothly moved on to kiss her neck, ears, and every inch of her face, concluding with a passionate kiss on her half-open mouth. I could hear a warning bell ringing in my heart, but I could not stop. Milia was trembling with excitement, rubbing her cheek against my chest. She was clearly ready for anything.

I delicately untied the strap of her sleeveless dress on one shoulder and pulled the top down under her breast. Impatiently I then unclasped her bra and slid the strap off her injured arm. I then repeated the procedure on her other side, replacing her good arm around me. Milia cooperated in this magical striptease without resistance, with her face burning, eyes closed, and breath quickening. I was touched by her trust in me. In the moonlight, the half-naked Venus appeared a real goddess of attraction and love. I was captivated. First I kissed her shoulder and then made a chain of kisses down across her breast and stomach. She trembled with every kiss, and when my lips touched her nipple, she moaned deeply, clinging to me convulsively with her whole frame, and triggering my instant arousal.

It needed a huge effort for me to stop. I kissed her lips and then lifted the dress back up, covering her naked breasts. I let Milia sit up and press her burning head to my shoulder. She didn't want to let go of me. Her lips were glued to mine again for a long moment.

We got up and walked back through the jumping frogs on unsteady legs. They croaked hysterically, "ribbit-ribbit" to warn each other of approaching danger. It seemed to me, however, as if they were congratulating me on this new era in my personal life. Milia's hand on my shoulder brought me back to earth. We reached the house in silence, arms around each other, and parted each to our own quarters.

During the morning therapy session, I had a faint sensation as if I could feel Milia's thumb moving. Holding the other four fingers together, I asked her to try and move her thumb alone.

She suddenly screamed: "Mama, Mama, look, it's moving!"

Her mother ran in, fearing that something terrible had happened and then burst into tears: "Merciful God, thank you for your kindness!"

"What has it got to do with God? It's Misha who is a miracle-worker!"

"That's not true," I protested. "It's Milia who made it happen. I only helped her in the healing process."

The excited mother paid no attention and continued in the same vein: "Thank you, dear God!" She then hurried off to inform her sisters about the miracle.

Meanwhile, I proceeded to check the mobility of her other fingers which she could not yet move in isolation. Then I asked her to move pairs of them: forefinger with the middle, and index finger with the little. This manoeuvre produced better results. Now I knew what course of therapy to follow.

At dinner time, my host congratulated me on the progress of the medical treatment and asked: "Mikhail, what are your impressions of our collective farm? Be honest."

"Sergey Andreyevich, I am not an agronomist so I am not familiar with agricultural economy. As an amateur I was impressed with the high level of organisation of collectivised labour. At the same time, I was surprised to see mounds of harvested produce rotting on the ground. Alik tried to explain to me the difficulties that the regional sorting facilities are experiencing with packing containers and transportation. I must confess, as I have already told Alik, that after a recent exam in political economy, I have a hard time confronting such a contradiction between theory and practice in the production and distribution of consumer goods in our country. I am ready to believe that there are very good explanations for this paradox, and that I am simply not competent enough to draw correct conclusions. All I can say is that I am really sorry to observe such waste of produce."

"My friend, I am sure your intuition serves you well here: not to pass judgement over the professional sphere that is unfamiliar to you. In any case, I would like to thank you for helping my daughter."

After dinner, the family gathered around Milia to witness her progress. I demonstrated in three steps the success of the therapy. Relatives hugged and kissed the patient whose face was wet with tears, and they applauded the self-taught healer from Odessa. They were wondering how it was that I knew methods of physical therapy and I explained that in the world of ballet, injuries were common, and professionals had to consider and develop the optimal ways of recovery.

"Enough!" pronounced Milia. "Good things – in small doses." And she again led the way to the pond.

I sat on the bench and motioned Milia to join me. She halted, however, and unexpectedly started pulling off my T-shirt.

"Mama!" I yelled, raising hands in the air. "People, save a poor clumsy bear!" I continued to howl, inwardly praying that she would not change her mind.

"Mishenka, don't waste your breath. Nobody will hear you anyway. Yesterday you were undressing me, today it is my turn to undress you. That is only fair," she concluded, pulling her summer dress off and hanging it on the back of the bench.

She stood in front of me in a swimsuit and worked on freeing her injured hand from the sling. She ended up playfully wrapping it around my neck, and laughed like a child. I liked that.

"Milyusha, are you planning to take a plunge with the frogs?"

"No!" coquettishly chirped my Venus. "I wish to tame my favourite bear."

To be honest, such a major change in Milia's attitude worried me slightly, but as usual in such circumstances, I decided to play along and let Fortune lead the way.

Meanwhile, Miss Venus seated herself comfortably on my lap, and announced with some authority: "As a future attorney, I cannot allow discrimination in the sexual arena!"

This was too much, and I just burst out laughing. My girlfriend paid no attention to my outburst and proceeded to stroke my hair, cover my face with kisses, and apply her lips to mine with force. Interrupting, I wrapped my arms around her and drew her to my bare chest. She cried out softly and slid to the bench. Like a cat she began to rub her face against my chest. Delicately I moved to slip her swimsuit down to her thighs. Now we were indeed equally attired. At first we only caressed each other's breasts and stomach, but libido soon took over our senses. She kissed my chest with abandon while my hands wandered over her legs, buttocks, stomach and thighs. Miss Venus gripped my hand between her thighs and growled with pleasure. Suddenly, the cat shook with convulsions, sticking her nails into my back, and then slumped and rested still on my chest.

I took her dress and covered her shoulders and breasts with it. Then, rocking her like a baby, I began to sing softly: *"There was a Gypsy riding on a horse. He saw a girl with a pail in her hand. The pail was empty, empty of water. This bodes ill for the girl."*

Milia responded in Ukrainian: *"My dear mother told me many times not to invite young lads into the orchard."*

We both smiled ironically.

Venus jumped up, indeed remembering her mother: "Oy, Mishanya, we must go back at once."

On the way back to the village, I halted. "Milia, what do you think of the idea that I ask your father for his daughter's hand tomorrow?"

She took it as a joke: "Which hand, the healthy or the injured one?"

"Actually, I am quite serious," I assured her.

Milia covered her mouth in shock. "Are you sure about this?" she whispered through the fingers.

"I have thought about this for a long time, and I want us to walk through life together – if you agree."

"I was only dreaming of it, but I was not sure if I could burden another person with my—"

"Milia, but I am not 'another person', I am a friend and—" She quickly closed my mouth with her hand.

"My beloved friend and magician, I will be happy to become your wife!" She launched into one of those intoxicating ambrosial kisses.

When Alik came out to look for us, we were already at the door.

The brother looked us up and down: "What's up with you? You look like there is a special occasion."

"We are going to the cinema." I blurted out the first thing that had come to mind.

"There is no cinema in our village."

"Well, then we are going to the village club."

"The local Cultural Centre is open only on weekends."

"Oh, well then, we'll just have to celebrate at home. Fine."

The people around the table stopped talking to see what it was about. Milia and I rose from our seats.

"Dear Sergey Andreyevich and dear Klavdia Ivanovna! Milia and I have decided to get married and we are asking for your blessing."

A glass of vodka trembled in the host's hand while his wife wiped away tears. The rest of the crowd sat silent in shock, their jaws dropped. The parents stood up at the opposite ends of the table:

"This is delightful news, and we give you our blessing," the head of the family declared. "Klava and I have chatted about this possibility several times. In other circumstances, this step might have been premature, but in this case it seems to us to be right. Crops need to be harvested in time or they go to seed. Mother and I give you our blessing! We wish you a peaceful and productive life together for the joy of all your relatives! Hooray!"

The noise and shouting that followed were so loud that Milia's aunts who lived in the house next door thought there was a fire and came running in with buckets. Everyone was congratulating us, wishing us health and happiness. Milia's parents decided that we would celebrate with a small private wedding ceremony on Saturday because in a week's time we were due to return to Moscow. The father invited me for a man's talk, face-to-face, before dinner next day to discuss our next steps.

Only two days remained until the famous wedding and everyone was panicking. The father set up stools from the *banya* in the middle of the garden for our private meeting, and got down to business without further ado.

"You are both students and this raises several issues, so please forgive me if I tread on your toes."

I gave a nod and prepared for a predictable talk.

"Milia is graduating from university next year. You – in three years. How do you plan to live together in the meantime? Where will you live and who will pay for it? Will you have a residency permit for Moscow?" The questions went on.

"After graduation, Milia is planning to apply for a course of graduate studies in law at Moscow University. This might take two to three years. While she is working on her dissertation, she will take classes in the Art History Department at MTA at the same time. During my final year there she could join an MA programme, and then defend a dissertation on the same subject of copyright, but this time in its application to stage arts. Thus, Milia could become a unique specialist and work in the same field as me. A common professional interest gives a young couple more chance of staying together if they can work together."

"That's fine. But what about your financial situation? Art alone is not enough."

"In principle, my income could be quite decent. I already teach at the university twice a week and fully provide for myself, and this is not counting a miserly stipend. In the future, working full-time, I expect to be able to provide a comfortable life for my family. Plus, I think your daughter does not intend to be a housewife after earning two graduate degrees. Yes, it would be a struggle for the first three years, but after that we should be financially secure."

"When do you plan to have children? I apologise if I'm being tactless."

"Not until we are finished with studies, although you, as a father of five, would know there can be no full guarantees in this matter. If Milia gets pregnant, we'll deal with the consequences."

"We haven't much money in our family. For the duration of your studies, we could only send you food parcels once a month, if you wanted."

"Thank you, Sergey Andreyevich, for being willing to help, but I am sure there would be no need for that. I hope that in future we would be able to reciprocate in kind."

In spite of the small size of the affair, the father was still compelled to invite his vice-chairman and wife, the head of the Village Soviet, and the head of the local Communist Party branch. For reasons of space, the wedding table was therefore set up in the garden by the porch. To my surprise, Milia's aunts hired the village concertina and balalaika players for the occasion, in lieu of a wedding gift.

Milia looked wonderful in her wedding outfit: a lace dress and handmade golden crown, with the profile of a frog on the front. A short white veil was attached to this crown. The bride herself cut out the profile of the frog from cardboard and attached it to the crown, as a symbol of our happy love. I also smartened up, digging out my only tie from the suitcase. In honour of the event, a piglet was roasted whole on a spit in the garden.

The wedding feast was a smashing success. I danced several improvisations from the Russian/Ukrainian repertoire with my wife. Tipsy family members and guests sang together in two or three voices so that the whole village could hear. The tables creaked under an excess of food and drink, much of which was new to me. This was a rare occasion when the mother was relieved of kitchen work and sat peacefully chatting with the women, sharing in her daughter's happiness. The bride walked over to the women from time to time and satisfied their curiosity about me and our plans for the future. I was doing the same for the men's side. At 6 p.m. a horse-drawn village coach arrived to take the guests home. The chairman proposed the last toasts 'for the road'. The guests and musicians all wished us luck before departing.

After all the dancing and hustle and bustle of the wedding celebration, I felt quite tired and decided to take a shower in the *banya*. Alone in there, I recalled yesterday's talk with Sergei Andreyevich and for the first time realised that from that moment on I was not only responsible for myself, but also for my wife and our future progeny. I got dressed, combed my hair, cleaned my ears and teeth. Spotting me from the porch, Milia and her mother came down to meet me:

"'Light steam to you,'" dear son in law!" [The Russian wish of 'light steam' goes back to the days when taking a steam bath (*banya*) was the only form of full-body washing in Russia.]

"Thank you, my sweet Mother-in-law!" I responded.

All the relatives who were, by then, drinking tea and eating pudding (a layered cream cake), chuckled and invited me to join them.

Milia's aunt, Aleksandra Ivanovna, enquired: "Misha, would you like a piece of cake?"

"No!" I riposted, "I would like two pieces!"

The hilarity continued, and I decided that that was a perfect moment for telling Odessan jokes. After a minute, everyone was laughing so hard that the neighbours' dogs started howling. Milia's poor father woke up after a two-hour nap and appeared on the porch in underpants:

"What's up with you? Why the noise?"

Everyone cracked up again.

Another of Milia's aunts, Anna Ivanovna, squealed: "Sergei, what is up with us is a wedding. What about you?"

Confused, the father turned around, scratching his head and muttered to himself.

Aunty Shura (Aleksandra) added to his back, "Next time you make an appearance, don't forget your trousers!"

The youngsters guffawed. The chairman went back to bed to sober up.

Appearing from the *banya* with her mother, the bride also demanded: "What's the cause of such merriment?"

Interrupting each other, her relatives told her: "It's your freshly baked husband who is telling us his Odessan jokes."

"What husband? Since when 'husband'? I am a free girl and have no plans to marry."

Once again, a burst of laughter exploded over the Cossack village.

To enter our marital chamber we had to climb a stepladder and then draw it up behind us. The procedure was reversed when going down. This was quite a romantic set-up: to spend our first wedding night under the roof like two doves. Milia's experienced mother had prepared everything her daughter might need to be comfortable. Having some previous experience myself, I was in no hurry. I suggested to Milia to go up first, and then to call me when she was ready. The bridal chamber was a real surprise: the floor was strewn with garlands of fragrant flowers. On a stool by the window stood a water jug and two upturned glasses on a napkin; a flashlight, a comb, a washing basin, and even Vaseline. The loving mother had thought of everything to ensure the success of the ritual.

A minute later, wearing nothing but my birthday suit, I lifted wide the sheet. My naked bride was there, with her eyes closed and arms folded on her chest. I knelt in front of her and in the dusk admired her athletic figure. The moon was almost full, and its light from the window bathed my Venus's body in magical colours. I first kissed her injured hand and lifted it off her chest, then repeated the same with her good hand. I touched my lips to her eyelids and the tip of her nose, finally making my goddess smile. I only then gathered enough courage to place my palms on her wrists and stroke her arms, shoulders, breasts, belly, legs, feet and toes. Placing my cheek to her soft belly, I extended my arms to their full length and embraced her trembling frame. My mouth moved over her legs, thighs, breasts then back to her lips, and Milia quivered at every new touch. Kissing her, I carefully lowered myself on to her and let go of her right hand. She immediately wrapped it around my neck and clung to me feverishly.

I moved my hand to the secret place between her legs and involuntarily she squeezed my caressing fingers hard in response and her good arm tightened around me.

I whispered, "Hold on, my love" as I entered her with an energetic thrust.

She cried out from the sharp pain and for a moment held her breath, eyes and mouth wide open. Then there was no stopping us as we moved together, faster and faster, until we at last merged in a union of spiritual and bodily ecstasy. Finally, we lay still without speaking, catching our breath. I kissed away her salty tears with my lips.

She asked with touching naïvety: "Mishenka, am I a real woman now? Thank you for this happiness, my beloved! Please excuse me, I need to tidy up. Wait by the window, I'll just sort myself out. This will be best."

Through the window I looked up at the moon, and sensed its magical pull. *How little a man needs for happiness. As people say: the power of Mother Nature is immeasurable.*

Milia and I having agreed on this, I told everyone at breakfast that we had to return to Moscow without delay because there were only four days left before the start of the academic year. We needed a couple of days for travelling and a couple to find a place to live.

"For the winter holidays, we are planning to go to Leningrad where I am scheduled to give a seminar to the heads of local dance ensembles. Milia meanwhile can do some sightseeing there. We can stay at my cousin Sofia's, near the Opera Theatre. In the summer, we plan to visit Odessa, and then, with your permission, come here, or vice versa."

Mila's father poured me some vodka, heaved a deep sigh, and on behalf of the whole family concluded: "Congratulations on your civil marriage! Good luck, good health and happiness to you in your life together! Consider our place as your own home. We will be always happy to see you here!"

We clinked glasses and downed the vodka. The mother was drying her eyes again on a corner of her headscarf.

At 5.30 p.m., Milia's brother and father drove up to the house in the same village cart pulled by Vorchunya. We had said our goodbyes ahead of time, and Milia's relatives now stood in one line from the porch to the gate, with the mother at the head of the line. Milia and I bowed deeply (in Cossack style) and marched to the gate under a shower of flowers and hail of good wishes. At the station, the father removed me from the cashier's window and paid for the tickets himself. He gave me the telephone number of the collective farm's headquarters, to use in case of emergency. I thanked him once more for his hospitality. I also wished him luck in resolving the farm's problems and promised to cure Milia's hand by the time of our next visit. When the train arrived, Alik helped us with luggage and then said goodbye warmly, quietly noting that he was now going to be alone in an all-female battalion.

The evening before, to everybody's delight, Milia had demonstrated the controlled movement of each individual finger, as well as the ability to half bend the wrist of her injured hand. Over the next two days on the train to Moscow I inexorably continued the course of physical therapy, in spite of the journey's inconveniences. My patient followed my instructions, but was embarrassed by the other passengers watching.

I drafted a letter addressed to the dean of the Law Department of MGU (Moscow State University) from a student who had been a victim of the June explosion in a Moscow suburb, when she was preparing for the exams at the university library: 'Due to the injury received on the premises of this University, I request an allocation of a double room for me in the University's halls of residence where my husband (a student at MTA) will take care of me, as well as supporting me when I travel on public transport. I attach the medical report, marriage certificate, and other documents.'

Having read my draft, Milia was terrified: "I can't sign this!"

"Why not?"

"I don't feel comfortable asking for preferential treatment."

"'Uncomfortable is sleeping on the ceiling because the blanket keeps falling down.' It is your constitutional right to demand compensation for the physical trauma received as a result of the government's negligence and on public premises. My dear, you are soon going to be a certified lawyer, and I shouldn't have to teach you about the laws regulating social insurance for Soviet citizens."

"You are right. I never had to do anything like this before, and I am ashamed of my helplessness."

"There is no shame in asking for what is rightfully yours. Everything is crystal clear here. They won't dare refuse you because they wouldn't want to risk a public scandal. My sweet wife, trust me. I am an old hand in these matters. And I promise to accompany you on all visits to the authorities."

We were alone in our train compartment on the way from Dnepropetrovsk to Moscow, so we were free to discuss our immediate plans without witnesses. My wife was clearly upset by the prospect of having to tackle the authorities. Nevertheless she listened to the advice of a more experienced leader and copied out the letter to the Dean three times, adding useful corrections, and earning three kisses in exchange. Now we could outline a plan of urgent actions to be taken upon our arrival in the capital.

With the enumeration of each subsequent point of the plan, my wife's pretty eyes opened wider and wider. Smiling evilly, I placed my open palm to her chin.

She crossly demanded, "What's that for?"

"If your pretty eyes spring out of their sockets, I will catch them before they drop to the dirty floor."

The cat angrily slapped my hand: "You are joking, while I in all honesty do not know how to beg for help. And I hate all the bureaucracy of the official institutions. And why are you so sure that everything will turn out according to your plan? How do you know their reaction? Explain this to me, if you please."

"My dear, you have spent all your life under the protection of your wonderful parents, while I have been living independently since the age of sixteen, earning my own living. Life has taught me to think through every situation with all its possible developments, in order to avoid unnecessary losses, of which I've had more than my fair share. I don't want to quarrel with you or repeat my old mistakes. If you aren't interested in trying to arrange better living conditions for both of us together, then I can take you straight from the railway station to your halls of residence, and I will return to mine. We'll continue to see each other at the university club, during dance classes, and you will recover your freedom, without any sexual discrimination."

I climbed to the top bunk and turned my face to the wall, pretending that I had been offended. A minute later, the beaten cat began stroking my hair and purring pitifully: "Forgive me, O severe husband. Truly, I continue to behave like a Frog-Princess, unable to shed my frog skin completely and become a worthy partner for an eagle [Berkut]. You are right again. I have to learn how to conduct myself with all kinds of people: of different ages, professions, character, etc. I solemnly swear to obey you until the New Year in everything that concerns our daily life, my left hand, and dances at the club. Please kiss me, my wise ruler!"

I turned to her, smiling, and complied with her wish.

"O women, who has created you for men's troubles?" I grumbled, descending from the top bunk.

We then resumed the long and laborious discussion of our action plan. I convinced her not to tell anyone about the successful healing of her hand until after we had put our living arrangements into place. On the contrary, I suggested that she should put her arm into a sling and display its complete immobility whenever we went to visit various institutional offices. I threatened Milia with a discontinuation of my therapy if she refused. In the end, she had to agree to all my conditions. I also felt awkward proposing such compromises, but 'To live with wolves is to howl like wolves." The local authorities should have offered help to all the victims of the nuclear disaster rather than pretend that nothing had happened.

We were surprised to find no queues at the Register Office. We arrived at 10 a.m. and were the first to be seen. A clerk gave us a form to fill out, took our passports and checked our student IDs. She wrote down our addresses and asked us to come back in half an hour. We went to a nearby cafeteria for a cup of tea and then returned. The Director invited us into a special room for the ceremony. She called the secretary in as a witness because we had not brought one of our own. She asked us whether we were getting married of our own free will; then demanded that we kiss each other to prove that. This was such a welcome part of the ritual to us that the Director hastened to pronounce the entwined couple husband and wife. She handed us the long-awaited marriage certificate, and her secretary kindly agreed to type up three copies of the same for three roubles, the student rate. We then waited half an hour while a notary verified those copies for us in exchange for six roubles (no student rate). However, with these documents in hand, we were now an officially married couple, and no one had the right to separate the happy Berkuts, even in the absence of wedding rings.

We sped to the Sklifosovsky Clinic on the wings of joy for a medical form to support Milia's disability. There we were met with more intransigent bureaucracy. I warned Milia in advance to be as aggressive as possible, or we would never get her document. When an administrator told her to come back tomorrow, the soon-to-be lawyer went into action so quickly that she even scared me!

"Don't you feed me tomorrows here! It's thanks to your irresponsible organisation that I am disabled today. You will produce the document I have come for at once, because according to the law (she gave the number and date) of the Civil Code of the Russian Soviet Federal Socialist Republic, you are obliged to present this document to every patient you check out. If you do not, I shall instantly instigate a criminal investigation against your administration on the grounds of intent to obstruct a patient's civil rights."

People in white appeared from nowhere and nurses stood around waiting for the administrator's instructions to restrain the psychopath. The administrator kept glancing in my direction, suspecting that I was either someone from the ministry or a journalist. I calmly observed the situation from the sidelines, now and then writing something down in a notebook. Milia continued her attack on the hospital bureaucrat.

"Call the police right away. Let us see who they'd arrest: a wretched victim of your professional incompetence, or *you*, you medical executioners?"

While my wife continued to rage in her assumed role, her medical file was delivered to the front office. They typed up and offered to the raving patient a copy of her medical report.

She showed the paper to me, and I whispered back after taking a glance at it: "Compare it with the original and demand to have it stamped."

When asked to sign the copy of the medical certificate, the lawyer-to-be insisted on seeing the original and on having the surgeon's signature verified with an official stamp. The administrator held two documents in his hands while Milia compared them. At last, Milia thrust the copy into her bag and promised the poor functionary that she would see to it that his actions were properly investigated. I had a feeling that Milia had slightly overplayed her cards, but it was forgivable in an inexperienced actress.

The next prong of the attack was the Law Department at MGU. In the Dean's office, a secretary carefully read through the letter and disappeared behind the door.

Three minutes later she reappeared with it, but authorised for action and addressed to the head of the Accommodations Office: 'I urgently request that you provide all possible help to this injured student from the Law Department," signed by the Dean. Milia's face shone with delight.

At the Accommodation Office, the person in charge went over our documents and telephoned the halls of residence to find out whether there was a spare room for graduates and ordered to have one booked for Emily Berkut from the Law Department. He pencilled an order and had his secretary type it up.

At the trade union's office they recognised me at once thinking that I had come about some dance-related business. Reviewing Milia's application, the union's representative enquired why she had not appealed to the Social Security Office of the Moscow Soviet immediately after checking out from the hospital, but hearing her explanations, she signed her resolution without further ado and told us to hurry to the Social Security Office before it closed at 5 p.m. We had two hours at our disposal. I sighed ruefully as my guts had long been growling with hunger.

My wife looked at me questioningly, but I only urged: "Into battle, musketeers!"

"What was that?" she demanded.

"Nothing, just something from my youth."

Holding hands, we ran all the way.

At four thirty, out of breath, we reached the Social Security Office. Here a clerk asked to see all our documents, including a letter to the Dean and a resolution from the union's office. She asked us to fill out yet another form, and told us to come back in a week to hear the decision of the Committee for Work Disabilities.

Milia asked her: "May I ask what the subsidy is and how soon can I receive it?"

"The subsidy depends on the degree of disability assigned to your case: first, second, or third. In effect, the sum ranges from eighty to 110 roubles." In those days, that amount was as at least the double of a student stipend, which was very handy. "You will need to re-register your disability every year because your physical condition may change with time. In August of next year, at least a week before the current medical report expires, you will need to present us with an update from the local hand specialist."

The superintendent of MGU's halls of residence was already waiting for us, intent on finishing his working day as soon as possible. He quickly familiarised himself with our papers, and invited us to come and take a look at our new accommodation. On the way, he enquired whether Milia was that student who had been injured by the falling glass in the library.

"Rumours have wings," Milia confirmed.

"More than twenty students of the university were affected that day, and many of them live here."

The superintendent introduced us to the warden of our block, Margarita Ivanovna, and wished us luck. An elderly woman handed us the keys with a smile:

"Welcome to your new haven!"

We instantly felt better at this display of such goodwill. She took us to a two-bedroom flat on the third floor, one bedroom of which was to be ours, with a shared bathroom and kitchen, and a storage room in the hall. In our room, there was a writing desk next to a huge window, two beds, a wardrobe, and many bookshelves. The room was set up for the convenience of graduate students working on their dissertations. We thanked Margarita Ivanovna and confirmed that we would be moving in next day.

"Well, my dear wife, you've done brilliantly!" I kissed her the way I used to in the old days. "Well, my dear husband, the credit is all yours: you planned every step of the way."

"Not quite. I forgot about the possibility of appealing to the Social Security Office in such cases. But it turned out well in the end, except for the scene at the clinic."

"Without you, I could have never got it all done in one day. Never. That means you've earned a celebratory supper and dinner combined."

Milia took me to a luxurious student canteen resembling a restaurant, where we had a filling meal. We then went to visit our club and found the head at his desk who greeted us with "Perfect timing!"

We confirmed the timetable of classes for the new academic year: Monday and Thursday, and composed a notice to be posted in the halls of residence announcing the date of the first performance to be 7th November (anniversary of the October Revolution). He also passed on an invitation from the trade union's representatives of the History and Law Departments to play Grandfather Frost in two New Year matinees for the children of their staff. I agreed on condition that a Snow Maiden from the academy would be paid fifty roubles, Grandfather Frost seventy-five, and an accordionist twenty-five, for each performance lasting two hours. Other expenses (costumes, prizes, etc.) would be covered by the trade union. The head of the University Club wrote down all the conditions and promised to bring a contract to the first meeting of the dance ensemble.

On the way to Trifonovka, Milia pointedly asked, "Mishulya, since when do you play Grandfather Frost and who is this mysterious Snow Maiden? Why haven't I heard anything about this, and what other secrets do you keep from me in your capacity as a professional entertainer?"

I laughed heartily at her questions and her tone of wounded jealousy.

"You are laughing and that hurts me. Tomorrow I'm filing for divorce."

"O my saint Emilia! Don't be angry with your no less saintly husband, Mikhail! He has been playing Grandfather Frost since he was seventeen, sometimes accompanying himself on the accordion. The Snow Maiden is Valeria, from MTA's Drama Department. She paired up with me for the New Year performances last year at the Central Music School and at MTA. You don't know the half of your virtuous husband's performing talents. Constant surprises are in my nature, and also supplied by capricious Fortune."

Now it was Milia's turn to laugh: "So, I see, you are a jack of all trades then. Bravo!"

When we reached Trifonovka, we found our friends at the halls of residence noisily celebrating their reunion after the summer holidays. Everybody joined in a chorus of congratulations for the newly-weds. I gave two of my young colleagues ten roubles and asked them to buy beer and pretzels for the party. Among the girls were Valeria (the Snow Maiden) and Lyuda Gurchenko, future megastar of Russian cinema, who was then a student at the Film Institute. I introduced Valeria to my wife and mentioned the invitation to play two New Year matinees at MGU, for fifty roubles each. She readily agreed. In the Drama Department, the majority of students were women, but mostly men in choreography. The two groups complemented each other perfectly.

We left for our own room at midnight, absolutely exhausted from the day's activities, but still with enough energy to take a shower together and rub each other's backs. After some very satisfying intimacy in bed, we finally collapsed senseless.

Our first morning was a difficult one. Milia had a hard time waking up. She had not prepared her clothes, bag, or brains the day before, and was now taking a long time, so that I was afraid we were going to be late for the start of classes at 9 a.m. I was irritated and could barely conceal it as I helped her to get dressed, blaming myself for not checking on her state of preparedness before going to bed. As a result, we had no time for hand massage, my morning exercises, or even breakfast. I sat by the door silently, waiting for my wife to finish her preparations. Finally we left our happy nest. On the way, I kept silent.

"I am sorry, but I cannot move any faster in the morning."

"If you get everything ready in the evening, you wouldn't have so much to do in the morning."

"Well, we were out last night, weren't we?"

"In such cases, you need to get up earlier."

"It's easy to say 'you need', but what if I cannot?"

"You are not a child, and I am not about to re-educate you. It won't work between us like this!"

At the doors of the Law Department, I reminded her, "I will wait for you here at 7 p.m., for fifteen minutes at the most. If you don't show up, I'll know that you have already left for the halls with someone else, and I'll go home."

As I had expected, Milia did not show up. She wasn't at home either.

I decided to begin working on the new choreographic repertoire and went to bed at midnight, but didn't have time to fall asleep. A noise in the corridor announced the arrival of my spouse. She hammered on the door, and I sprang from the bed as if the fire alarm had gone off.

"This is my mean husband!" shouted my drunken wife to her friends. I apologised to them and closed the door behind her. I dragged my tipsy wife to her bed, took off her shoes; changed her into a nightdress and took her to the toilet for a pee: I did not fancy waking up in the Frog-Princess's pond. I finally put her to bed and started to drift off to sleep.

In the morning, I followed my regular routine, wrote a note to her, saying that I would be back at 8 p.m. and that I categorically demanded that she didn't bring any visitors back to the room. I left home with a heavy sense of having made a mistake. I hadn't planned to spend time that should be dedicated to my studies on babysitting someone too selfish to consider me. But: *'If you pick up a load, don't say it's too heavy.'* I will put up with it until the New Year. If in these four months Milia does not adjust to her new status as wife and partner, I will return to my bachelor's room on Trifonovka, and that will be the end of our marriage.

During a break between classes I sat down and made a list of household chores: shared and individual chores for each of us. I also wrote down our morning routine and some rules for living together. I made a copy for Milia, so that she could make changes and amendments. My hope was that by laying it all out in written form, Milia could organise herself effectively and we could live together harmoniously. Returning home, I found my wife at her desk. The room was cleaned up. There was a bouquet of fresh flowers on the night table, and Milia's face shone with a smile. She hurried to meet me with a hug and a kiss.

"I am sorry, my dear. Friends got me drunk last night: we went to celebrate my recovery and my getting married. There was no opportunity to let you know."

"I understand and I am not angry. We have more serious problems to deal with, however, in communicating and living with each other. I have prepared a list of our shared responsibilities and I am asking you to look it over, while I make dinner. Please feel free to add or change what you find necessary. Please take this seriously if you want us to build a family together. Otherwise you may as well chuck this piece of paper in the bin."

I was busy cooking in the communal kitchen for half an hour, but when I came back, Milia was still working on the draft of our family constitution. She responded to my proposal to eat first and then discuss our family issues with a request for another minute to let her finish it. After dinner, we sat on the couch to talk, and following long discussions, Milia declared:

"Misha I do see that formally you are right, but it is hard for me to put aside my friends and my former views. I need some time to adapt. I must figure it out for myself."

"Very well. You can have three days to think this through, and if we do not sign this memorandum of social/domestic life by Sunday, I am going to return to Trifonovka, and we will both consider ourselves free of our marital obligations, to my utter chagrin and regret."

"What about my hand, though? Will you leave me in this state without helping me any more?"

"Excuse me, this smacks of blackmail. First of all, it is not me who is turning away from you. On the contrary, it is you who prefers your friends and freedom to your husband. Secondly, your hand is well on the way to recovery, and you can easily continue the treatment by yourself or with the help of friends. I only want to give you a piece of advice: don't listen to your jealous girlfriends. This is about your future, and you should use your own head in deciding what is best for you. If you do need advice, then take it from a married woman who would not mislead you about the challenges involved. I realise that I have probably made a big mistake in my life, and am already full of regret."

In the morning, my wife woke up ahead of time. She took a shower and then spent a long time drying herself with one hand. I pretended to be asleep, affording her a chance to enjoy her precious freedom. She finally approached me, placed her injured hand on my chest and began moving the stunted fingers so that I could feel them.

"You're devious," I mocked her.

She kissed me tenderly: "Good morning! Time to get up."

While I was washing my face, Milia applied ointment to her scar. The rest of the morning unfolded according to schedule. At eight thirty we parted by the building of the Law Department, confirming our rendezvous at the same spot in the evening. My practical classes were due to resume that day on Pushechnaya Street, next to the Bolshoi Theatre. I had to hurry to make it there on time.

Six of the remaining students in our group (four men and two women) had joined forces for the purposes of the ballet class with seven students training to become teachers of ballet. Thus, a normal-sized group for a morning warm-up with Lapauri was formed.

At the start of the class, Lapauri approached me and quietly enquired: "Where are the rest of the choreographers?"

"They left the programme."

"For what reason?"

"You will get more satisfactory explanations at the Dean's."

After the Ballet class, we had Composition with Shatin. It was another top class with a master, yet we sensed a thunderstorm brewing. It was an unprecedented case of institutional failure in MTA's history – to lose half of the enrolled students at the end of the first year because of their dissatisfaction with the academic programme. Naturally, everyone was looking for a scapegoat, and the Dean was the most suitable candidate because he was not a communist. Students at the Choreography Department were for the most part mature individuals (twenty-five to thirty-five years old) with enough work experience to be able to distinguish positive from negative in their education, yet they all preferred to keep quiet, to finish the course of studies without upheavals and revolutions and gain maximum knowledge even from such pseudo-professors as Leonid Lavrovsky. The latter was invited by the 'Chair of Staff', Zakharov, out of political considerations: in order to have among the faculty the head ballet master of the Bolshoi, even if he was to be no more than a nominal figure in the curriculum.

In historical literature, Lavrovsky's life is presented in rather contradictory terms. He was an excellent dancer in his early days and he knew the classical repertoire very well and could transfer it without much effort from one stage to another. He was assisted by colleagues in choreographing his unique ballet *Romeo and Juliet*, and in practical terms, the stage adaptation of Shakespeare's drama was carried out by the opera director of the time, Radlov. This was the same Radlov who had helped the young Zakharov with the dramatisation of his first ballet *The Bakhchisaray Fountain*. While Zakharov became interested in choreography and continued, if with only marginal success, to produce original drama-ballets for over a quarter of a century, Lavrovsky limited himself to spreading someone else's choreography around the world. And why not? It was popular and easy to digest. He became famous as a first-rate copycat ballet master who had no particular talent for original compositions. His own ballet *Fadetta* was not a great success, and his choreography for the ballet *Paganini* was, according to the Western media, stolen from someone else's repertoire during one of his tours abroad. While Zakharov at least attempted to write an autobiographic memoir *The Art of a Ballet Master* on the basis of his professional experience, Lavrovsky who had no pedagogical or choreographic abilities, had no professional right to teach at the institute named after Lunacharsky, a man who had made great contributions to the advancement of Soviet culture. Due to his amoral personality and tactless behaviour in the classroom, MTA lost six talented students and undermined its international reputation.

Notices announcing new enrolment in the Dance ensemble at MGU were posted in the halls of residence and produced impressive results. Over twenty freshmen, living mostly in the same halls, signed up. I had reported to the club director that it was impossible to teach over fifty people in one group, so we decided to introduce a beginners' group that would meet for an hour and a half on the same days right before the main group. This meant that our working time would be extended by one hour, and I immediately realised that without Milia's help I could not manage this. 'Every problem presents an opportunity' is a common proverb.

"Mikhail Semyonovich, here is your contract for this season, only we need to change it in accordance with new arrangements."

"Excellent. We can deal with formalities next time."

I hastened to inform Milia that she was going to be my assistant in coaching the beginners. She was pleasantly surprised by the news.

"You can give them an introduction to the main positions of feet and arms for ten to fifteen minutes, describe the order of classes, training suits, and hygiene: hairstyles, towels, and what to do during menstruation."

At first, Milia was shocked by this sudden demand on her cooperation, but she quickly appreciated the situation and said that she would tell the beginners to assemble at five thirty for the introduction.

"Now I believe in your ability to surprise, O respected teacher!" pronounced my assistant and went off to the changing rooms to address the beginners.

I met them in the studio. After short greetings, I congratulated them on their initiation into the world of dance, introduced my assistant and soloist of the ensemble and left them in her care, saying goodbye until Thursday. In the hallway, the main group and three new guys were already waiting for me.

Saluting the veterans, I counted everyone and addressed the three newcomers: "Excuse me, are you here to escort your darling girlfriends?" I gestured towards the line of girls who were smiling with satisfaction.

"No. We came to join the ensemble. We would like to learn to dance if possible," one of the three answered for all of them.

"If you have a good head, well-tuned ears and eyes, and healthy arms and legs, there is every chance of success. All the more so because our girls need partners. In dance, I mean."

Everyone chuckled.

"So: welcome!"

The rest of the group broke into applause.

"There are more of us now. To date, we have twenty-two female and six male dancers. Emilia Berkut, formerly Ivankova, is unable to dance at present due to an injury, which you have probably heard about at the university. She will be helping me with the beginners for now. Their class will run from six till seven thirty. Then I will work with the guys separately for half an hour, and at eight the whole group will train together until 10 p.m. After the New Year break, we will resume our normal schedule. As far as the repertoire goes, we will need to revise 'Barynya' and 'Yurochka' for the October holidays. Simultaneously we'll be learning the choreography for two new compositions: the 'Sailors' Dance' for the guys, and 'The Moldovan Suite' for the girls. Both dances should be ready by the New Year. Then, by March the whole group will learn the 'Ukrainian Gopak'. There will be a lot of work. Try not to miss any classes."

After the rehearsal I explained to Milia that I could not warn her about the assistantship with the beginners because I had not known their numbers.

At bedtime, in the evening, I demonstrated to Milia through a series of exercises how much the flexibility of her wrist and hand had increased: she was able to open and turn her palm without assistance, and to bend and straighten her arm at the elbow.

My girl was bright as a penny, kissing me, and crooning, "My wonderful magician, my beloved husband, my noble teacher, thank you very much!"

Even though those compliments were not entirely deserved, I was still pleased to hear them.

"Milia, if you are going to do this, then we need to work out a programme for your training in methods of choreographic work with young people. We also need to establish our respective responsibilities in the beginners' group of the ensemble, so far as to airing our differences in front of others. My intuition rarely betrays me. I can see that according to many parameters you would make a good teacher, if you are provided with the right information and refer to your own experience. Expertise will come with time and regular practice."

"I like this idea a lot, but I am less confident of success than you are."

During the third term of the academic year, our MTA curriculum changed. Methods of Classical dance with Nikolai Tarasov, was now available only in the form of personal consultations, on the basis of need. The study of classical repertoire with Lavrovsky was entirely transferred to the Ballet Teachers' Division, where the students were happy with the option. For them, it was valuable to know the stock Classical repertoire well because they would be tutoring and coaching dancers in that repertoire for the rest of their professional lives, working at opera and ballet theatres. With these changes, a happy compromise was finally achieved at the department, whereby both the 'sheep were safe, and the wolves sated'. To the relief of the Ballet Masters' Division, instead of Classical repertoire we resumed training in methods of *'Pas de deux'* with Lapauri. At that time, the Ballet Teachers' Division was conducting an intensive course for ex-ballet dancers from European countries. Several of the younger participants in that division chose to attend with us, once a week, a course in Partnering Technique, mainly for their own benefit: they could later use the knowledge in their respective home theatres. This added contingent gave us an opportunity to address the technique of 'Pas de deux' in greater detail.

In Historical Dance, taught by Rozhdestvenskaya, we moved on to the study of the Renaissance. The dances included in the third term: Courante, Pavane, Galliard, and in the fourth term: Volta, Rigaudon, Passepied. Our former female partners from the Bolshoi School implored their director, Golovkina, to allow them to practise with us once a week. Our productivity grew exponentially due to this contact with professional performers. In Character dance with Tkachenko, we began to study the European repertoire: in the third term, Albania, Bulgaria and Romania; in the fourth, Germany, Czechoslovakia and Yugoslavia. In this course, we had to manage on our own, without the partners from the Bolshoi School of Ballet, and because of that, even though, as the Professor's assistant I had to repeat the same elements time and again, the retention of the new material progressed slowly. The subject seemed to be undervalued both in ballet schools and at theatres, and, as a result, Character dances were often a weak link in the professional training of Classical dancers.

With the help of Nikolai Elyazh, in the History of Ballet, we successfully progressed from the eighteenth into the nineteenth century. Courses in Music Analysis with Tseitlin, and in Stage Scenery with Müller continued in the same productive rhythm as before. The only subject in the curriculum that instilled panic and fear into all students, wherever they were from, was 'The Fundamentals of Marxism–Leninism', taught by the head of that department, Sergei Gusev. This was an indispensable subject in the curricula of every university in the Soviet Union. One cannot deny the fact that Gusev knew his subject and how to teach it. At the same time, he was merciless with us poor students who were confronted with figuring out the intricacies of different socio-economic formations for the first time. Luckily, I had taken this course once before at the University of Odessa, and still I did not always catch the real sense of some postulates expressed in flowery convoluted language by a professor who liked to flaunt his lecturing virtuosity. He had a way of stupefying us first with ideological slogans and then listening to our puzzled questions with an expression of disdain on his face. Everyone feared and hated him, calling him a sadist and scorpion behind his back. Gusev had no compunction about destroying a politically illiterate Azerbaijani student in front of her peers only because she had misquoted one of Lenin's pronouncements.

Not wishing to be Gusev's next victim, I spent hours memorising texts and writing out ideological theses long into the night, knowing that the next day he would certainly ask me about some controversial detail from Lenin's *Historical Materialism or Empirio-Criticism*. If I failed to give a precise formulation of this or that ideological notion, he would make me a laughing stock: "In Philosophy, you need to think with your head, not your legs! Ha ha ha!"

Most of the time, my colleagues simply lowered their heads and did not react to his sarcasm. That Gusev had a personal grudge against me I had no doubt. He didn't attempt to hide it. I was at pains to understand the reason. The Professor was a ruthless atheist and anti-Semite. Everyone knew that. Once, at a seminar, he lost control. At that time, in the 'countries of people's democracy', even under socialist rule, churches were not turned into stables and stripped of golden domes, as was the case in Russia, Ukraine and Belarus.

At a seminar on Marxist–Leninist Aesthetics, the Bulgarian communist Stefanov once expressed doubt that religion was 'the opium of the people'. The Professor exploded with rage and howled like an animal stung by a hornet: "How dare you deny this truth when even the false Messiah, Jesus Christ, was a puny Jew by birth and only later in life styled Himself as a great martyr!"

Our jaws dropped in shock at the Professor's cynicism. The religious student turned white, a notebook clutched in his trembling hand. After a loaded pause, Stefanov got up proudly and said: "Excuse me, Professor. I must go out."

Gusev's argument derived from a well-known fact of gospel doctrine, but it was chilling to hear how this head of the Philosophy Department in a major Soviet institution framed the matter: he pronounced the words 'Jew' and 'great martyr' with such vehemence that we could see saliva spraying from his mouth.

Czech Karl rose from his seat: "Professor, excuse me! I am a member of the Communist Party of Czechoslovakia, and Stefanov's a member in Bulgaria. In our countries, as you probably know, the government and the party have a slightly different attitude to religion than here. Thousands of practising Christians are members of the Communist Party, and the two affiliations do not conflict with each other. I agree with Stefanov on this. Please excuse me, I have to go and check on him," and he left the classroom.

This measured and dignified response from our colleague landed like a ticking bomb ready to explode, but the ringing of the bell announced the end of the class. Gusev left, but the four of us stayed in our seats, immobilised with shock.

Albanian student Kanaccio broke the silence: "Comrades, let's just forget about this!" But I could not calm myself.

By contrast with Marxist–Leninist Philosophy, lessons in Dance Composition with Shatin were a breath of fresh air. Shatin's tone was always pleasantly calm, never dictatorial or insulting, demonstrating with quiet confidence how this or that choreographic solution could produce the most colourful and convincing result. He always offered us an opportunity to analyse and critique colleagues' work, which made perfect sense as we acted as performers in each other's compositions.

The curriculum for that year included a trio composition in the third semester, and a quartet or quintet in the fourth. The key requirement for the composition was the presence of a storyline, but the theme and genre (drama, comedy, tragedy, grotesque) were left up to us. The time allotted was three to four minutes. We were meant to follow Stanislavsky's dramatic schema: introduction, motivation, development, culmination, resolution. At the same time, we were given full freedom to apply our creativity. We didn't have to follow this schema dogmatically, but could change the order of components, even order them backwards if that were expedient and beneficial for the implementation of the choreographer's idea. The Professor was a fine psychologist: he stimulated our imagination and then delicately channelled the realisation of our ideas along the lines of individual vision and professional quality. This he did without the pressure of censorship according to the principles of social realism in *Marxist–Leninist Aesthetics*. Anatoly Vasilyevich was a brilliant guide for his students in the artistic depths of the poetry of dance, coaching us in every stage of choreographic composition: from initial idea to implementation onstage.

In the spring of 1958, I began teaching Character dance at the Performing Arts Centre in Moscow. The first Sunday class attracted many people. The seminar was an intensive course attended mostly by former dancers, now forty-to-fifty-year-old retirees, from ballet theatres or folk ensembles such as Beryozka, Moiseyev's ensemble, or the Red Army Ensemble. They were now leaders of non-professional dance groups in the suburbs of Moscow and nearby towns. Half of them actively engaged in learning while the others just watched and made notes. This seminar turned out to be a second academy for me, in terms of teaching experience. While in Leningrad, at the first seminar, several snobs had begun by clowning around and showing off but had finished by shaking my hand with respect; in Moscow, the retired dance professionals sat about in corners, making tactless remarks and laughing out loud. As a professional teacher and choreographer, I could not launch into the actual dancing without an introduction to the specific style and character of sailors' dances: the marching step, rocking on the waves; imitation of rowing, swimming, diving, working with tackle and sails, etc. About twenty women, former ballerinas, were attentively listening and writing down important information, but several older men continued brazenly to show disrespect. I purposefully lowered my voice, so that the participants could not hear me very well.

One of the women interjected: "Could you please speak up?"

I shrugged: "I'm sorry you cannot hear me well, but my voice is not strong enough to talk over our respected colleagues chatting away in the corner."

A middle-aged ex-ballerina walked over to the troublemakers and showed them the door. I don't know what she said to them, but they shut up at once and subsequently sat quietly or joined the rest in practice. I continued the class as if nothing had happened.

The practice began with simple elements: a rocking from side to side as if on the deck of a sailing boat. Then I added foot tapping, clapping, turns, etc. The main working group (about sixteen women and eight men) was doing well in following my demonstrations. It helped that I demonstrated on a small stage, while they practised on the studio floor. Observing the pace of their progress, I gradually enhanced the technique and tempo of performance. Suddenly, I noticed that the former troublemakers in the corner were trying to imitate the footwork, while sitting down. I walked over and politely invited them to step into the centre of the dance floor and join the others.

"Girls, please go easy on these shy lads."

Everyone cracked up.

I gave a signal to the accordionist to slow down the tempo and repeated the dance sequences with the 'lads' from the very beginning. After a ten-minute break, I introduced more complicated claps, tapping, and squats. I could see from these snobs' eyes that their professional appetite was awakening, but now the ex-ballerinas were having a hard time with a complex rhythmical syncopation of male technique, and needed extra help. I instructed the guys to carry on, and joined the women to work on the nuances of rhythm and technique.

In three hours we had learned all the group choreography, apart from solos. I made an effort to emphasise that the main purpose of the seminar was not to encourage them to copy someone else's finished compositions, but to give them a chance to become familiar with the style and character of performance involved in this genre, so that they could come up with their own original compositions.

"All the sequence elements and particular ports de bras (motions of arms) that you are learning here, you would be able to implement using a standard pattern of composition, in line with the technical ability of your performers. To conclude our first session, I am going to show you several men's solo variations on the theme of sailors' contests."

Choosing the music with my accordionist, I demonstrated three different types of solo parts which the audience found impressive and responded to with ready applause. Thanking everyone for their attention, I approached the woman who had earlier assisted me in establishing a healthy workspace on the studio floor. Ludmilla introduced herself as an ex-soloist of the ensemble Beryozka, and presently the head of the Moscow Dance Ensemble of Labour Reserves.

The treatment of Milia's hand steadily progressed. While we were still in Slavyansk I had given her a tennis ball to exercise her wrist, but only now was she finally able to hold it with all fingers and squeeze regularly using the whole palm. On Wednesdays and Saturdays we visited the swimming pool at the halls of residence, where I insisted that Milia swim with my support. Trying to stay on the surface, she was forced to imitate the movements of the healthy arm with the impaired one, like it or not. Naturally, this technique did not have an immediate positive outcome. Milia often lost patience, helplessly slipping sideways underwater. Invariably, whenever that happened, I insisted on the continuation of torturous procedures, convinced that any living creature possesses an instinct for survival and the means of adapting to any unusual conditions, even seemingly unbearable. A paralysed hand, buoyed up by water, is lighter than a healthy hand, and has a greater potential for mobility. My thinking was that such physical therapy would stimulate the two severed ends of a nerve to rejoin in order to restore the original functioning of the tissue.

Thanks to my new assistant's support, running two groups of the university dance ensemble was soon under control. Milia participated with great enthusiasm in the production of the 'Russian Dolls' dance with the junior group. After an hour and a half of joint practice, I usually switched to coaching the guys in a separate room, while Milia continued with the girls, polishing up their technique. She later joined the main group of the ensemble as a soloist. Milia usually did exercises at the barre and learned the new choreography on her own in order to keep up with the main group and dance with them in the upcoming concert. For me, working for four hours straight was a habit, but I was concerned about my wife's condition. She was so absorbed by creative activity that she wouldn't even hear of a short break. At the same time, it is possible that such intense activity helped her to think less of her physical disability and motivated her body to fight to heal naturally.

I had finished the staging of all three dances by the end of November. The director of the club invited the head of the university's trade union to observe the performance and to organise the production or rental of costumes. Milia presented the junior group, and I the 'veterans'. The 'sailors' produced the greatest effect. This was the first male solo dance in the history of the university variety shows. The guys were on brilliant form, and the administration was generous with applause while the girls stomped their feet backstage. All three dances were approved for inclusion in the programme of the New Year concert. There was no money, however, for the second accordionist, and I had to step up to the plate and play together with our accompanist in order to give the performance a richer musical texture.

Milia and I decided not to risk the progress of her hand, so agreed that she would not perform. Instead, she willingly took upon herself the organisational responsibilities for the whole ensemble during the pre-concert rehearsals in the central auditorium of the university and in our club. All members of the ensemble treated her with great respect and sympathy. She also was pleased with an opportunity to obtain valuable professional experience, but nobody was in a better position than me to appreciate how much courage and self-control dealing with her predicament had cost her.

Lectures and seminars in Marxist–Leninist Philosophy with Gusev continued in the usual way. After the 'religious-utopian' incident, all three foreigners in our six-strong group failed to appear for the seminar. They must have received instructions from their embassies.

Taking the register, Gusev called my name and without looking at me, asked: "Mikhail, can you state the conditions necessary for the socio-economic formation of socialism?"

"Unity and struggle between opposites, transformation of quantity into quality, from each according to ability, to each according to productivity."

"Very good. What is your opinion on each of these theses? Be brief without any of your Odessan vagueness."

"I am in full agreement with the genius conceptions of our ideological leaders."

Gusev twisted his lips into a caustic smile and, looking at me over the tops of his glasses, ruefully shook his head.

"Maria?"

"I am of the same opinion, Professor."

"Galina?"

"Sorry, Professor, that's also what I think. Nobody could put it better than our leaders."

Gusev stared at us over his glasses, apparently trying to make up his mind.

"Well then, I am pleased to see such solidarity among you, in terms of political loyalty to our great thinkers. This ends today's seminar. You are free to go."

Maria, the former leader of the Moldovan Komsomol, let out a sigh of relief, and pronounced with a smile: "Phew, now he's going to show us who's boss!"

"But why? We've done nothing wrong!" Galina from Baku began to whine.

I preferred to keep shtum, remembering Mother's advice. It was clear: if any one of us dared to step out of line, he would devour us. But all three together? Too much to swallow. At the end of term, Gusev examined us via written tests in which we wrote our answers to a number of questions relating to the course. We undertook similar tests in other subjects, academic and practical. Dance composition required special preparation. We were supposed to dance in each other's compositions, three trio miniatures, in the presence of members of the department and other official guests, including the director of the Bolshoi School, Sofia Golovkina, who was interested in new ideas for the practical curriculum repertoire for her school and performance numbers for the graduation concert.

Each student's performance lasted about ten minutes and included presentation of the idea (two minutes), performance (three to four minutes) and analysis/ discussion (four to five minutes). The last segment involved questions and answers between the teachers and the performer. What impressed the audience most was not the originality of dance movements or complexity of choreography, but a clear storyline in dramatic triangles and the precision of its individual components. The main goal of the students was to find an unconventional solution for their idea, while moulding each individual dance character from material commonly found in typical human behaviour. Such stereotyping of dance characters, even if they represented a specific literary personage (e.g., Othello), impressed the audience much more than the idiosyncratic expression of personality by whichever dancer happened to be performing the role. In each miniature, the diagram of dramatic relationships between characters onstage was outlined not by symbolic gestures of pantomime, but by the dynamics of dance and choreographic flexibility. The compositional development of each subject-based trio revealed the unique aesthetic influence of a great artist and masterful teacher.

The swimming therapy produced incredible results. Milia was able to bend her arm at the elbow and slightly lift it this way and that, but the fingers of her closed palm could not hold any object unsupported for any length of time, other than, briefly, an empty handbag. Her left arm was twice as thin as her right. She began to regrow the muscles on the left arm and hand through regular exercises with a tennis ball and light weights (gauntlets).

Milia's winter examinations went well, as usual. Law students were meant to spend the last term of the academic year as interns working in a professional capacity in the geographic area of their permanent domicile. During the previous summer, Milia's father had arranged, just in case, for her to intern at the district attorney's office in Slavyansk. At the time, because of her disability, Milia's family had doubted whether she would return to university at all, let alone graduate. Last summer, Milia's plan had been to take a year off from her university studies and then see what happened. She had never told me about those plans because no one could have known what would happen as a result of my August visit. Everyone was waiting to see how our relationship would develop.

In December, after the winter concerts, my wife brought me up to date with some startling news, which she had not disclosed earlier, not wishing to interfere with the course of my work at the club and the Performing Arts Centre.

"Misha, unfortunately, from January until April I will need to be in Slavyansk for my internship. I will come back to Moscow for the final and bar exams. It's a pity that I can't come with you to Leningrad, but the doctor has confirmed that I am in my third month of pregnancy. I am sorry for causing you all these troubles." The news rushed out of her in one breath, and she turned away waiting for my reaction.

I was not entirely surprised by the last piece of news because neither of us had been careful enough about contraception. The news not only did not upset me, but on the contrary, made me happy: it was better for this to happen now, while we still had two years at least ahead of us when we could be together. After that, fate could order us in different directions. My wife stared at me with fear in her eyes. In response, I smiled broadly and tenderly kissed the mother-to-be.

"My precious wife! Congratulations on this wonderful event in our family life. I wish you well in shaping the tangible fruit of our love."

An hour later I was helping Milia on to a train heading to Dnepropetrovsk. I asked her companion in the compartment, an elderly woman, to assist Milia with her injured hand if need be. Then I telegraphed Alik in Slavyansk asking him to meet his sister at the change of trains in Dnepropetrovsk and accompany her to Slavyansk. I was sad not only at being alone in Moscow, but also about going to Leningrad by myself. I also anticipated difficulties in managing two groups at the club on my own from January on. What could I do? Once more, capricious fate had taken a hand without any regard to my wishes!

This was not, of course, the first time I had had to arrange things on my own. The next day I was scheduled to conduct the last lesson/show at the Performing Arts Centre. The Director had invited representatives from the Ministry of Culture, press, and personal guests. I began by explaining the purpose of the seminar, its programme, and expressed my satisfaction with the participants' professionalism. The group then went ahead to show separate movements and combinations on the marine theme. In conclusion, we demonstrated fragments of three compositions, with alternating performers.

The audience was thrilled with our performance. The Director addressed warm words of gratitude to me, wished everyone a happy New Year and good luck to the participants in the seminar for the next term and the programme of Gypsy repertoire with Mikhail Berkut. This surprise announcement was met with a thunder of applause. Tikhonova presented me with a bouquet of flowers on behalf of the group. She also introduced me to her director from the Labour Reserves' ensemble. He gave me his contact details and asked me to visit him in early January to discuss the possibility of my working for them as a choreographer for special events. The director of the Performing Arts Centre paid my salary for the previous term and offered a contract for the next. I thanked and congratulated him in turn, promising to return in January. Tikhonova was waiting for me at the exit with my bouquet of flowers which I had forgotten onstage. On the way to the metro, she asked if I might find some free time for choreography work in her ensemble from the September of next year.

"If the job involves working under your personal supervision, ma'am, I will make the time, especially if there is room for creative opportunities with appropriate compensation!"

We both chuckled and wished each other all the best.

On 30th December I took an overnight train to Leningrad, but I could not sleep. Drawing up a balance sheet of my activities for the previous year, I was coming up with an ambiguous result: half positive and half negative. As far as my professional life was concerned, my plans had been realised with acceptable results, but my personal life, if I were to be completely honest with myself, had been a bit of a roller coaster. For both Milia and me, the losses occasioned by our marriage, turned out to be both unpredictable and irreversible. There was no doubt about that.

In Leningrad, my cousin greeted me with an indignant accusation: "Where is your devoted spouse? Have you already divorced her before we even had time to meet? You didn't even give me a chance to see her. Do you really need this?"

If only Sofia knew how closely she had hit the target! I thought with sadness. All women have a fine sense of intuition. Still, I decided to keep quiet about Milia's pregnancy and just explained that her absence was due to the need to start her internship in Slavyansk. Dropping the bags in the hallway, I rushed to the Leningrad Performing Arts Centre to register my readiness to begin a seminar on Gypsy dances from 2nd to 8th January. The Director was already waiting for me in order to finalise the schedule and programme of classes.

In the last two days of the year the streets were crowded with people searching for New Year presents. I also hurried to the Gostinny Dvor on the Nevsky Prospekt to pick up some gifts for my generous hosts. Leningrad has always been my favourite city in Russia. I have never ceased to admire its architecture, canals and, of course, the art collections in palaces and galleries. My dream was one day to live and work in this legendary and romantic city. After a traditionally noisy family celebration for New Year, Sofia and her family, as usual, departed for a resort on the Gulf of Finland, leaving me alone in her flat.

Seminar participants greeted me like an old friend. Following a short introduction about the characteristic style of Gypsy folk dances and their sources, we launched without further ado into the technique of using various accessories such as tambourine, whip, long skirt, shawl, etc. Then we turned to the main steps. After a break, we focused on a series of claps and the Gypsy tapping technique, which was so different from that used by sailors. I had considerable experience in the methodology of breaking down the complex sequences of Character dance into their component elements, and so I patiently explained to my retired ballet dancers the technique of syncopated claps and fancy footwork that relied on the parallel positioning of feet instead of the familiar turnout position typical for classical ballet. To be frank, it was not easy either for them or for me. For a long time they mechanically continued to employ the turnout position, like so many Charlie Chaplins. One had to hope that with time and patience, old habits would be overcome. Soon, however, after doing some critical analysis at home, the heads of non-professional ensembles came to see the need to reform their performance tool, i.e. their feet, and more importantly, adjust their aesthetic world view: the art of dance is not only classical ballet, but is much broader and more varied – it has been a form of sociocultural communication between people from early times.

By the end of the week, we had completed the programme of Gypsy dances, including individual elements from different categories: solo variations, group excerpts and united finale. The Director and official guests accepted our work with approval.

Many of them wondered how I had managed to engage the elderly snobs who had typically been mere armchair students, but here they were taking turns dancing in group excerpts. I explained that I had had them practise in a separate room away from hypercritical women, and had also promised to keep to a slower tempo for the performance. The Director introduced to me the head of the Dance and Song Ensemble of the Leningrad Trade Unions. Like his colleague in Moscow, he also invited me to do choreographic work with them. Thanking him for his interest, I explained that for the next two years my programme of studies at MTA required me to engage in choreographic practice at a theatre, so I could not be sure of my availability.

After Milia's departure to Slavyansk, I had had to vacate our couple's flat immediately and return to my room in the halls of residence on Trifonovka where the warden, Shura, had kept a place for me. The day after my return from Leningrad, I was instantly plunged into the familiar whirlwind life in Moscow: the fourth term of studies at the academy; seminars at the Performing Arts Centre; work at the university ensemble; and, most importantly, preparation for the final exam in dance composition. This time the subject was a multilevel choreography of a quartet/quintet. This type of assignment entailed a significant step forward in terms of 'symphonising' the creative idea of a dance. Shatin confidently continued to lead us to what had seemed unattainable heights in the staging of simultaneously acting character types in all their combinations, both qualitative and numerical.

It was a pleasant surprise to learn that from January onwards lectures on 'The Fundamentals of Marxism–Leninism' for both ballet divisions, of teachers and choreographers, would be given not by Gusev, but by one of his colleagues. Apparently, he opted not to engage in further disputes with foreigners since he could not behave as tactlessly with them as he did with their Soviet peers. This was a great boon for us since our footing in that subject was rather shaky. In Historical dance, we were completing the Renaissance period, and in Character dance, the repertoire of Eastern Europe. This was also to be the last term for 'Partnering Methods'. Next year we were supposed to apply our knowledge of *'Pas de deux'* in our choreographic work with students from the Ballet school and with dancers from the Bolshoi. The courses in Music Analysis with Tseitlin, and Stage Scenery with Müller were also to end. In the next academic year we were expected to select plot lines or themes from theatrical drama in order to produce original choreography using Character and Historical dances for the plays of Ostrovsky, Chekhov, Dostoevsky, Gorky, etc., as well as for the operatic and musical comedy repertoire.

The first week at the University Club was a challenge, due to the absence of my assistant. I had to oversee the maintenance of the last term's repertoire, including the 'Russian Dolls' Dance' with the junior group, and at the same time work on the new repertoire for the concert on 1st May. A compromise was inevitable, and I chose to teach the junior group last year's 'Belorussian Dance' with the help of the veterans. This saved us time and gave an opportunity to work on the 'Ukrainian Gopak' with eight guys and sixteen girls from the main ensemble. These cheerful dances infected the participants with such high spirits that they often didn't want to part after rehearsal, continuing to practise in the lobby, the corridors, and even the changing rooms. By mid-April we completed both compositions: 'The Moldovan Suite' with the junior group, and the 'Ukrainian Gopak' with the main group. The director of the club, reviewing our finished performance, approved and issued instructions for the rental of Ukrainian and production of Moldovan costumes. My ensemble participants performed beautifully in concerts on 1st and 9th May. The administration showered us with compliments, but I had a heavy heart as my time with the ensemble was coming to an end: next year I would have no time for them, and I had promised to turn the repertoire over to a new choreographer without compensation.

At the Moscow Performing Arts Centre, my course in Gypsy dances was designed for twelve, not six, sessions as in Leningrad. In practice, it was to stretch over three months. Because of that, I expanded the programme by adding two extra dances, so that altogether we studied:

a) 'Bagatelle' – solo, a popular miniature with a shawl for female dancer.

b) 'Spring Night' – love story for a duet: man with a guitar and woman with a tambourine.

c) new version of 'Gypsy Rhapsody' – a group dance, in expanded format.

Work with the Muscovites progressed much more actively and productively than in the previous year. We repeated the same procedure: starting with elements of footwork and port de bras with props, followed up by more technically difficult elements using the whole body in a complete dance phrase and closing with large sequences of characteristic music and choreography. As in Leningrad, much of our time at the beginning was spent learning the technique of rhythmic clapping, so alien to Classical dancers, as well as learning to keep their feet aligned instead of turning them out as they had been trained to do. Curiously, men overcame this physical Rubicon quicker than women.

On Saturday I visited Tikhonova's dance ensemble. Her group performed three dances for me: one dance each for guys and girls separately, and one with the whole group.

In the Director's office, I remarked on the good level of preparation and discipline among the participants, and asked, "What are you looking to have in your repertoire: national dances of European countries, or subject dances from factory/workers, sports and festivals or other contemporary settings?"

Tikhonova and the Director exchanged glances, and Ludmilla replied, "If possible, we would like to have something unusual in our repertoire, with an original staging idea, something that would make us stand out among other dance groups at the regional festival. Let's say something like a 'Youths' Suite' or 'Scenes at a Factory', with many funny episodes and surprises."

"I could come up with such compositions, but only for the next season. Let's say [I parroted Ludmilla] one composition for a New Year's concert, and another for the 1st of May, if you please."

The Director's face brightened with a smile. "If we please! We've been dreaming of this for years, but our choreographers usually gave us something used and reused from their old repertoire, while we wanted fresh and colourful new creations for our youngsters. How much time will you need to compose these dances and what will be the cost?"

"Each of my sessions in the dance studio is usually three hours long, at twenty roubles per hour. This also includes the time I spend at home preparing the choreography. At the moment, my Saturday afternoons are free till 6 p.m. The rest of the time I am engaged at the university and theatre."

"That's perfect. If the artistic director is happy, I am going to prepare a contract for you to sign to start the second Saturday in September. Welcome to our working family! I know you will be happy here. Lyusya, will you please see Mikhail off and come back here. Goodbye!"

Parting at the door, Tikhonova spoke warmly, "Mikhail, our trade union is a generous patron: there should be no problems with the provision of costumes, props, and musical accompaniment. Thank you for your interest in our Ensemble!"

Practical examinations, in the second term of the MTA course, typically took place at the end of the exam period. We had 'Methods of Historical and Character Dances' in the morning and 'Dance Composition' in the afternoon. That was one long and unforgettable day. Members of our small team, numbering six, in spite of being a rather contrasting, colourful lot representing four Soviet and two Euro-Slavic republics, had become so close over the two years of studying and working together that we understood each other at half a sentence, and could read silent signals in a blink of an eye. In the dance-composition exam, we had ten to twelve minutes at our disposal. Keeping to the time limit was one of the assessment criteria. We were all dressed in neutral black, and only sported brightly coloured sashes for each new dance, in accordance with the choreographer's creative ideas. Groups of one type (two to three performers) used sashes of the same colour; individual performers used differently coloured ones which contrasted with those of the group performers. The colour scheme helped the audience to follow the polyphonic and choreographic logic of a dance that often involved a storyline developing along parallel tracks. Final rehearsals were accompanied by two pianists who performed four-hand pieces by famous composers: sonatas, plays, études. The professional piano performance of complex scores enabled the examiners to distinguish more clearly the melodic and harmonic interweaving of leitmotifs and auxiliary themes characterising this or that personage in a theatrical dance piece.

At the beginning of the exam, Shatin explained that the main objective set before the students was to 'symphonise' their choreographic ideas, and he asked the examiners to ignore possible imperfections in the performance due to the fact that all students were engaged in dancing each other's compositions, six altogether, without a break. He introduced our pianists with gratitude and suggested that the teaching staff would be able to address questions to the students. We had not expected that such a potentially difficult trial for the second-year graduates would go off quite as smoothly and effectively as it did. Even Zakharov remarked on our coordination and creative discipline. The success of this exam was a serious achievement for the master and his pupils.

Later, at a dinner in Shatin's home, we were able to relax and joke good-humouredly about little mistakes known and noticed only by the authors and performers themselves. The results of the exam propelled us forward along the path of our professional development.

On the day of the exam, the legendary choreographer Kasyan Goleizovsky was working on the third floor of the same building with the graduates of the Bolshoi School. He was staging a concert for the performance at the theatre. Running into him at the local cafeteria, Shatin had invited the Great Maestro to attend our exam. Goleizovsky readily agreed and patiently observed the entire show. At the end, the Dean introduced his pupils one by one to the seventy-year-old colleague. I had never dreamed of ever meeting this genius, whom I had heard so much about in the ballet world. The Soviet press had long been forbidden to write about him. According to the stories told by the retired theatre staff, the ballet master at the Bolshoi, Kasyan Goleizovsky, had been exiled in 1937 to Tadzhikistan for ten years, on trumped-up charges of overtly erotic choreography and a corrupt personal life, without the right to future work in the theatre. He had only recently been allowed to return to Moscow. A great choreographer of the twentieth century had fallen victim to sordid intrigues among the ballet's big shots of the time. It is debatable whose loss was greater as a result: his own or that of Soviet culture.

My train arrived in Slavyansk on time. Alik was already waiting for me with the cart, parked under an old chestnut tree.

"How is my darling wife?"

"Can't wait to see her wayward husband."

"What news with your dad?"

"He is taking over as a head agronomist at a nearby state farm."

"Why? Is there more order there than at the collective farm?"

"Milia was wondering if you had remembered to bring a box with her textbooks and notebooks."

"Aha, I hear you: paying me back with the same currency!"

Alik chuckled: "I am only following the elders' advice."

"I hope the women's battalion is in good order?"

"Oh, yes, even more so: we've added a she-goat. The day before yesterday I was cleaning up in her corner and she butted in the butt, if you excuse the pun, that's all the thanks I got from her."

I snorted, and Vorchunya, the mare, neighed, in sympathy for the goat's unpardonable behaviour.

The carriage driver whistled as we approached the house. I remembered my arrival first time with the bread and salt ritual and vodka, but this time the porch was empty. Alik and I picked up the bags and entered the noisy house. The reunion with Milia was a happy one, but there was tension in the air. I decided to ignore it for the moment and instead chatted away:

"Dear Mother-in-law, you have been feeding your daughter well, I can see, she's as round as a barrel."

She fired back: "No, dear Son-in-law, it's you who have stuffed her, so be sure to take care of the rest." Her words were crude but true.

We carried on joking, kissing and hugging, and only after a while remembered that I might like to freshen up and change clothes after a long journey. A very pregnant Milia looked rather well for her condition, but there was something furtive in her eyes, as if she had stolen or broken something. She was able to move her injured hand quite freely now, but it was still rather emaciated compared to the other one. I asked Milia to squeeze my left hand as strongly as she could with her injured hand and saw that she had not been regularly exercising with the tennis ball.

The question in my eyes was answered with a plea to be excused: "Misha, it's been hard keeping to my regime without you, especially in this current state."

Smiling, I caressed her large, taut belly.

"Don't worry, my love, this month I'll be taking care of you. You can rely on me fully day and night."

"In what sense?" my wife smirked.

"In every sense but the one you had in mind."

After a snack of fresh milk and home-made bread, we moved to the middle of the garden where a chair and table were set up for Milia to study for her state exams which she had missed. Due to pregnancy she had not been able to sit the exams with the rest of her peers the previous month, but instead was allowed to sit the exams in September. This snag in the smooth progression of her studies had not only dented her self-confidence, but also threatened her plan to start a graduate course at MGU in parallel with an undergraduate course at the Art History Department of MTA.

Meanwhile I decided I needed to radically change my manner of communication with Milia's family. I sensed their displeasure with Milia's premature pregnancy. As was to be expected, they blamed me for a lack of contraceptive care and I had to admit they were right. Nevertheless this did not give them the right to interfere in our family life. Although I continued to be outwardly polite and friendly, I exchanged my clown's mask for a serious role as a future father and head of the family. I did not react to their jokes and avoided discussions of our future plans, making it absolutely clear to them that these were strictly a matter for Milia and me. My wife was caught between a rock and a hard place.

The last six months of pregnancy she had spent in a sort of family collective, in which all personal issues were decided by everyone rather than individually, and as a result, she had completely lost her self-confidence under the domineering influence of her parents and relatives. Such herd-like behaviour on her part was unacceptable to me. I made numerous attempts, all to no avail, to persuade her that she was misguided, and that we had to decide our future ourselves without external interference. It was obvious that 'habit was second nature' to her and I stopped fighting and withdrew into myself. I set up my own study area next to Milia and began preparing the choreography of the 'Youths' Suite' for the Labour Reserves' ensemble. I could do it because I had all the melodies for the composition stored in my head and was able to compose mentally, recording in shorthand all the dance steps and spatial patterns.

On 13th July Milia and I took our usual afternoon walk to the frog pond. On the opposite bank of the pond we could see a bulldozer dragging out muddy algae and spreading it on the shore to dry. A second worker collected up algae which had already dried into his truck to be taken for chemical processing. They'd been working on the pond in this manner for two weeks now, eight to five every day. We usually took our walk to the pond after five when it was cooler and the noisy machinery had stopped. That day, however, it was overcast and we came earlier. Just as we had settled on our favourite bench, Milia suddenly grabbed me by the wrist:

"Mishanya, my waters have broken!"

"Broken what, love? Are you not well?"

"It's starting! Call an ambulance!"

I jumped on the bench: "Milechka, what ambulance? We are two kilometres away from home, three kilometres from Slavyansk."

"You're a man, aren't you? Think of something!"

"Man/van, van/man," I mumbled in panic, looking around. "Wait a minute here! Don't give birth without me!" I pleaded and tore off like a bullet to the other side of the pond to the men still working there. I located a ten-rouble note in my pocket, stored there for just such an emergency.

I almost ran into the truck driver in my haste. He was startled, possibly thinking that he was being attacked by a runaway maniac. He grabbed a heavy tool from under his cabin seat and kept brandishing it in front of my nose while I explained the matter to him and asked him to give my wife a lift to the hospital in Slavyansk.

The agitated driver shouted, "No hospitals! We finish work in half an hour and don't give me this bullshit!"

I pulled out the ten roubles. The amount was equal to five bottles of vodka. He extended his hand to me, but I retracted mine as quickly.

"You will get the money at the hospital. My wife's father is Sergey Ivankov, chairman of the local collective farm, and a former colonel, now retired. If either the mother or child should die thanks to your refusal, you will end your days in prison. The chairman will dig you up from underground if necessary. Let's go before it's too late!" I showed him the ten-rouble note again.

"Vasya!" he shouted to his partner. "Wait for me here, I'll be right back! OK, let's go!"

We helped my moaning wife into the truck's cabin. I took off my T-shirt and handed it to Milia, so she could use it to staunch the flow. I then seated myself between her and the driver and commanded, "Until we get to the main road, go slowly, carefully, otherwise she might deliver right here in the cabin." With my right hand I supported Milia's back and with the left I pressed her legs to the car seat.

At the hospital, they took Milia off at once. I briefly described the events of the last hour to a doctor on duty and asked for a nurse's robe to cover my mighty chest. The hospital reception staff promised to telephone her father at the farm right away and tell him where Milia was. An hour later, Alik appeared on his bike, then Milia's father arrived in a horse cart a little later. The doctor informed us that with a first pregnancy, delivery might turn out to be a protracted affair, possibly until midnight in our case. I asked Alik to let me keep his bike, while he would return home with his father.

"I will need to stay around to find out whose daddy I am."

My father-in-law took me to a nearby eatery and asked his acquaintance, the manager, to feed his starving son-in-law, promising to repay him in kind. I had had no idea how difficult waiting is when one can do nothing. Every two hours I left the hospital to take a walk in the town, and then returned to learn the news. After 11 p.m. I settled on a couch in the waiting room and dozed off. At exactly midnight a nurse woke me up to say that Milia had given birth to a boy. I hugged the old woman with such force that her bones cracked. She took me to the room. I could see Milia through a glass window, lying on a bed with a baby next to her. A nurse picked up the baby and brought him to the window for me to see. He had a wrinkled blue-red face and black hair.

Did I look like this at birth? I wondered, now such an Apollo! My expression gave nothing away as I blew a kiss to his pale-faced mother. She smiled sideways, and winked in response.

Apparently giving birth is harder than having sex, I concluded sympathetically as I rode Alik's bike back home, barely seeing my way in the dark. On the main road there were no cars and all was quiet, no howling wolves. Still, I felt uneasy alone in the night and had to check my pants periodically for signs of weakness. Riding out on to the main street of our village, I discerned the flicker of a flashlight in the distance and understood that someone was waiting for a prodigal son-in-law. I thought it was Alik, but coming closer I recognised my mother-in-law.

She rose heavily from a bench by the gate, came up to me and grabbing my wrists, demanded impatiently, "So, what is it?"

"All's well! Congratulations on the birth of your first grandson!"

The poor woman dropped on her knees and burst into tears. She was touching her head to the ground in front of her, thanking her God. I leaned the bike against the fence, waited a minute or two, then approached the praying woman and helped her to her feet. I wanted to lead her back into the house, but she thanked me and instead turned to the neighbouring house to share the news with her sisters. I took the bike inside and climbed up to my attic.

We named the boy Dmitri. The boy had been a little too big for his mother and she had had a hard time delivering him. She needed time to recover her health. Fortunately, the house was full of helpful free hands, and the new grandmother took the care of the baby upon herself. This certainly helped Milia to recover more quickly from the first shock of motherhood. She only breastfed the baby periodically, otherwise his care was shared between Dmitri's aunts under his grandmother's close supervision. My duty consisted in taking my son out in a pram and safeguarding him from bugs and domestic animals. Sometimes I dropped off myself while rocking him to sleep in the pram. Milia felt much better after a week and began to smile and shower me and the baby with kisses. I closely monitored the number of kisses bestowed in order not to allow any discrimination between father and son in this young Soviet family! Sometimes I caught Milia kissing even the soles of Dmitri's feet, which unfortunately she never did for me.

During one of my vigils with the pram in the garden, a car drove up to the porch, and a man in a dark green suit emerged asking for Emilia Berkut.

"I am her husband. And you?"

"I am a detective from the General Prosecutor's Office. I've come regarding an incident at the Slavyansk regional office."

"Just a minute, I will call her."

Milia came out and invited the detective in, apparently not surprised by his visit. I thought that it must be something to do with her internship at the office and didn't pay much attention. I was still waiting for an explanation two days later, when I finally heard an exchange with her father over the dinner table. He certainly seemed to think that there were no secrets between us. I continued to eat my borscht pretending I hadn't noticed anything, while a somewhat tipsy father ignored all alarm signals from Alik and the others around the table. It was a perfect scene from cheap vaudeville. Milia's father continued to question his daughter about the outcome of the investigations at the General Prosecutor's Office, and the visit of a detective from Krasnodar, indignant that his daughter was refusing to discuss the matter. A scandal was brewing.

"Sergey Andreyevich, please excuse me. I think it would be more appropriate for you to discuss family secrets without me," and I left the house.

Sitting on a bench outside the gate, I could hear my angry father-in-law shouting. He was enraged by the rest of the family's tactless manner. Finally, the door slammed and Alik appearing on the porch and called me inside. I decided to teach them a lesson and did not respond. A few minutes later, Alik found me and relayed his father's request that I return to the table.

"Tell your dad that I regret to have become an unwitting cause of trouble to your family. I can now see that your family consider me an outsider, and you will not see me again in your house. It's a great shame, but I can't force you to like me."

I got up and took off into the garden to work on choreography. Soon my wife appeared with the baby's pram and positioned it next to me. I collected my papers, waiting for her explanation or apology. For some reason, she remained silent.

"Milia, we need to return to Moscow in the middle of August to organise our affairs and prepare for the start of the academic year. I am going to Slavyansk to get tickets now. Are we returning together or are you staying here for a while?"

There was no reply.

"Fine, see you later."

"Wait, we need to talk."

"OK, but not here and without Dmitri. I'll be waiting for you by the pond until 10 p.m. If you don't come, I'll go to the station and buy one ticket to Moscow."

"What's the hurry?"

"If it wasn't for the baby, I would have left immediately, in order to relieve your family of my presence. I have no desire to remain here a day longer and endure you and your family's demeaning treatment of me. In fact, I think that it is better for you to stay here, where everyone is cleaning up your shit after you. That would be much easier for you than doing anything to help yourself or your husband and son. So, I will be waiting for you by the pond."

My beloved appeared at the pond in a furious mood, and took a seat at some distance from me.

"Respected wife, may I enquire as to the reason for your anger with me? What have I done or said to you to incur such hatred?"

"You are taking away my freedom and forcing me to divulge personal matters."

"Are you referring to the incident at the General Prosecutor's Office, or are there some other sins, of which I am unaware?"

"During my internship there, my boss sexually attacked me. I complained to the head prosecutor who opened a criminal investigation, but meanwhile my offender hanged himself in his office to avoid defamation and prison."

"You can't be blamed for that, unless you had given him cause."

"That's what I am suspected of – that in the seventh month of pregnancy I was flirting with him."

"There must be grounds for such an accusation."

"They have witnesses saying that they had seen us chatting on daily matters at an eatery and that he had often given me a lift home after work in his official car. So, it looks as if in spite of my pregnancy I had given him a reason to attack me."

"Calm down, you are not to blame for what happened. You naïvely put your trust in that man and without thinking of sex, flirted with him, while he misread your intentions. You either didn't know or forgot that you were dealing with the predatory side to human nature. Any man could have taken advantage of such a situation, but not with a pregnant woman. This one turned out to be a sex maniac. Now you can see yourself how naïvely and carelessly you had behaved with that consultant at the General Prosecutor's Office, chatting away, showing off your learning, displaying your trust and femininity, typical of the weaker sex. This is natural."

"From what you say, one may conclude that I was the cause of his death."

"No, I didn't say that. This could have happened between him and any other woman. He was playing Russian roulette with his life and finally lost. His end was predictable, but it had to happen sooner or later. So, you shouldn't be castigating yourself, but you can learn a few lessons here."

"Misha, I am sorry for not having told you about this earlier. It was a mistake to follow the advice of my family who have a very poor understanding of human relations. When you are not with me, I am unable to make the right decisions. You are right, I am used to having all decisions made for me. This is how I was brought up, and only thanks to you have I understood this, after all these mistakes and failures. Please forgive me, if you can. I must leave here as soon as possible, not to lose you and myself."

At dinnertime, my father-in-law poured me a shot of vodka and declared, "Misha, on behalf of my whole family, I want to apologise to you for our blatant violation of an old Cossack tradition of hospitality, and I hope that henceforth nobody in my house is going to interfere in a young couple's life, or tell them how to live. Let's drink to peace between our families!"

We drank, and turned to our food. After the meal, I informed my host that I had bought tickets to return to Moscow on 17th August.

"Why so soon?"

I explained our reasons. "With the baby, it will be hard for us to find a flat to rent, and we need time to prepare for our studies. Besides, for some reason, from the first moments of my arrival here and in spite of all my good intentions towards and respect for the hosts, I have been feeling a bit of an intruder, which I greatly regret. So, the sooner we leave, the better for everyone. I am sorry! Thank you very much for the bread and salt. Goodnight!"

I headed for the door.

"Misha, wait for me by the gate. I'll feed Dmitri and we'll go for a walk."

Behind my back, I heard my father-in-law's menacing voice. "So? All happy now? Managed to insult a new member of our family. Put shame on my head.

Set your sister against her husband and her son's father. What's this with your arrogance and lack of feeling?"

"Sergei, enough already!"

"Klava, don't provoke me to do something I'll regret! It's your upbringing, what else?" He got up with a crash and left to go to his room.

The sisters began to bicker between themselves. The baby started crying. Alik shushed them all and went outside.

While Milia was dealing with the baby, Alik sidled up to me and ruefully summed up. "Can you imagine now what life is going to be like for me now, with this women's battalion, to bear their squabbles and gossip? As soon as I graduate from high school, I'll go to university somewhere far away."

"Good luck, my friend."

At that point, Milia came out of the garden: "Misha, let's get a breather, away from this bedlam."

I sighed. "A year since I came here for the first time. What a sad anniversary! Who would have thought that such a fiasco was in store for me."

"No matter, my dear! You have shown them today. I have also reached some conclusions."

On the very same bench by the pond, we sat recalling our wedding last year and a romantic return to Moscow. Milia sat on my lap and cuddled up to me like in the good old days. With her right hand she played with my curls, and slid her injured hand, now on the mend, under my T-shirt to caress my chest. It had been a long time since we had kissed like that. I had begun to think that our love was all but gone.

"Mishanya, I beg you not to leave me alone for any length of time. Without you, I wilt, I lose my confidence and fall under the influence of others. I need your strong character and your knowledge of people. I had thought that my sisters were trying to help me with their advice, but I can see now that you were right. They envy my happiness and maliciously try to undermine it. I can't understand why?"

"My pretty Frog-Princess, according to statistics I have read, 90% of young couples experience problems with their parents after marriage. Most of them have to do with sharing living space and finding the means to live independently. So, in each case, it's down to the young couple and their families to prevent problems."

Upon our arrival at Kievsky Railway Station in Moscow, I left Milia and Dmitri by the information booth and went to look at a noticeboard advertising accommodation. I found a one-bedroom flat near the metro, on the second floor of an old house, with a balcony and all amenities. I waited for Milia to finish up with Dmitri's feeding, run to a bathroom and a snack bar, and settle with our bags in a corner to await my return. After grabbing a snack myself, I hurried off to look at some possible rentals. At my first stop, the door was opened by a young woman, with the puffy face of an alcoholic.

"What do you want?" she wheezed.

"I've come about a flat for rent."

"For how long?"

"Until the New Year, and possibly longer."

"That's four months or something?"

"Yes."

"Fifty roubles a month, 200 altogether, pay all up front!"

"For one month?"

"No, for all four!"

"I don't have that much money at the moment," I lied just in case. "I can only pay monthly."

"Fine, money – on the table!"

"First, a receipt – on the table."

"You're quick! Where from?"

"From Odessa."

"I see. Should've said so."

"You hadn't asked."

Smirking, she shook her head.

While the woman was signing a receipt, I checked on the condition of the kitchen, toilet, and heating. Everything seemed to function properly. The only room in the flat was rather run-down and dirty, but there was a balcony: always handy for drying out laundry and setting the pram outside so that the baby could sleep in the fresh air.

"Here is your receipt."

"And the keys?"

"In the lock."

"And for the balcony?"

"Same place."

I checked the locks and then asked: "And where are you going to live?"

"At my sister's."

"Please write her address on the back of the receipt."

"What for?"

"Well, where will I find you if something happens?"

"You're really anal, you know that?"

"Once you've burned yourself on hot milk, you blow even on cold water." I verified what she had scribbled on both sides of the paper. "Where is your signature?"

"Didn't I write down everything you wanted?"

"All but the signature." I smiled knowingly and thought to myself: another one of those clever cookies. Must be thinking that I am the green one.

I wrote down our names for her and the address of MTA. We exchanged my money for her receipt. I locked the door behind the woman and hastened to the railway station.

In twenty minutes, we were back and started cleaning the place up, while Dmitri slept in his pram on the balcony. We spent the whole day setting up house, and in the evening went to one of the numerous eateries near the railway station. We also bought some groceries.

Upon our return home, Milia went to the bathroom to give the baby a wash, and suddenly I heard her scream at the top of her lungs: "Misha, look who's lying here!" The drunk flat-owner was asleep in the bathtub.

The baby began to cry. I took him to his pram, and then asked Milia to help me. Together, we yanked the woman out of the tub and dragged her out to the landing. Milia found in the bathroom a second set of keys which the drunkard must have used to get back into her flat while we were out. I suggested that Milia should keep the keys in her purse until the woman returned our rent money. I gave Milia the receipt I had procured from the drunkard and instructed her how to report this to the police at the railway station, and what protection to demand from them for the sake of the baby. At first she protested that it should be me going out there to fight, but she soon realised that as a mother and a lawyer, she had a better chance of securing the baby's protection than me. I advised her not to be shy and claim that the baby's survival was at stake.

"Don't forget to mention that you have been on internship at the prosecutor's office all spring."

Half an hour later, I heard a noise on the landing and went outside. The drunkard was still on the floor, unable to get up. Neighbours from all around were lodging complaints about her with the police concerning the constant racket and filth.

The senior officer entered the flat with Milia and explained: "We cannot detain her for more than three days in a pre-detention cell without charging her with something."

"Tomorrow I will bring you a paper confirming that this woman had defrauded us of our money. In accordance with article XXX of the Russian Criminal Code you must take measures to protect the well-being of a child against violators of public order in a communal dwelling."

The officer promised to report the incident to his superiors immediately. The drunkard was taken away to the police station. I stepped out on to the balcony to let Milia compose a claim to the local Police Department. Rocking my son to sleep, I came to a sad conclusion that I had made a bad mistake in my search for accommodation. When my wife joined us on the balcony to enjoy the panorama of Moscow's night lights, she also acknowledged with regret that we would have to look for another place to live. We decided that in the remaining ten days, we would try our luck at the halls of residence on the Vorobyov (Leninsky) Hills, base of the Moscow University Research Centre. If we could get accommodation there, it would be very convenient for Milia's research work, and as a mother, she could probably get a room there, on the condition that I live elsewhere.

In the morning, collecting all necessary documents, we went without the pram to storm the Vorobyov Hills. We were greeted with emphatic politeness at the central Human Resources Office of MGU. They praised us for appealing to them while there were still vacancies for single mothers. I showed my student ID for MTA, and confirmation of my residency in their halls of residence. Milia presented her passport and resident's pass for the halls of residence on Presnya. She also presented the timetable of her exams for September and an application for graduate studies here at the research centre. We were told to come back in two hours to find out if there was a vacancy in a children's day-care centre. We went for a walk, got a bite to eat, and then sat on a bench in Lomonosov Park, while Dmitri slept, enjoying the fresh air. We returned to the Human Resources Office where the news was discouraging: a place for a child under twelve months old would only become available on 1st January.

"What we can offer by means of a compromise is a separate room in the halls of residence, but only if you can guarantee that the mother would spend most of her time with her son while preparing for the exams. And also we could offer this only for four months, until the New Year. If you are happy with this option, you could move in on Monday."

There was not much else we could do but return the keys from the ill-starred flat and say goodbye to the rent we had paid in advance. I had learned another hard lesson.

On Monday, I first took my things to my hall of residence on Trifonovka, then took a taxi and went with Milia and Dmitri to the Vorobyov Hills. The living conditions for the graduates here were of the highest standard. Most of the inhabitants were foreigners who spoke very good Russian. We had to leave the pram in a crammed hallway and bring it into the bedroom at night. For the first three or four months, the baby could easily use the pram as a crib. Then? All's in God's hands. I supplied my family with food and toiletries, spending a few nights there illegally. Luckily we had two sets of keys, so I was able to come and go without problems, which eased our communication.

On the third day after our return, I took Milia and Dmitri to the Dean's office at the Law Department of MGU, and then went to MTA to say hello there.

Secretary Lena exclaimed at the sight of me: "Hi! We've been searching for you all over Moscow. Where've you been, migratory bird?"

Shatin answered her ring, and came out. "*Nu*, Mishka from Odessa. You produced a son and are keeping it secret! Congratulations!"

"Thanks. It's been announced on the radio, no? The thing is that we have just settled in."

The warden from the halls of residence informed me that you are spending your days at the Leninsky Hills. You like it better there?"

"That's not quite how it is. Milia and the baby are there, and I am on Trifonovka. In theory."

"Well, well, come on in. We also have news for you. We've had a request for sessional choreography work at the Youth Theatre, under the directorship of Boris Chirtkov. I recommended you for this temporary work from 1st November, in accordance with the programme for this term: dance in a drama/opera. I hope you are interested."

"Of course – very much so. Thanks for your faith in me. In September and October I will gather the necessary information on this subject from your lectures, and I promise not to fail you."

"Excellent. Lena, please reply to the Youth Theatre that the aforementioned candidate has agreed. By the way, how is Milia managing her studies with a baby on her hands?"

"She is sitting the exams *post factum* and will then continue with a graduate course writing a thesis on 'Author's rights for theatre/stage performance'."

"Say hello to her and send my best wishes!"

At midday I went to MGU to meet up with Milia and take them home. I was about to introduce myself to the secretary of the Law Department, when she said: "I remember you, from last year. You are a choreographer, Emilia's husband?"

"Yes. But I had no idea I was famous all over Moscow," I said coquettishly.

"I don't know about 'all over Moscow', but here at the university, your dances are very popular with the audience whenever we have a concert. That's a fact."

"Thanks for your kind words. May I ask who is sleeping so sweetly in the armchair next to you?"

"Emilia has just gone in to speak with the Dean about the exams. There will be a special examination period in the first half of September specifically for all those who had missed the one in the spring. Your wife should sit the exams with this group. If she doesn't, she may have problems. She is expecting her husband to help."

"Excuse me. Is it possible to find at the university a woman who could look after the child for the two to three weeks during the exams? I am sure there must be some student who would not mind earning some extra cash."

"You would be better off with an older, more experienced woman than with a student. Less risky for the baby. In Human Resources, they should have some contacts for retired women offering room and board or babysitting services."

"Thanks a lot for this. You are very kind."

At this moment, Milia emerged from the Dean's office with a stack of papers and a frown on her face. "Thank you, Raisa Lvovna, sorry for troubling you with my little one. Ah, you are here already? Then, pick up your cuckoo's egg and let's go!"

I exchanged a glance with the secretary and smiled. "The world is not without kind people."

My son woke up in my arms and began grizzling.

"Let's find the bathroom," commanded his mother.

While Milia changed and fed the baby, I waited patiently in the lobby, working out our next step. At lunch in a students' canteen, the baby slept on her lap, while she worked on her soup with the other, attracting everybody's attention. I only helped her a little. Nevertheless, we exchanged information and made a plan of action. The first matter of business was to enquire at Human Resources about a possible babysitter for three weeks. We were immediately supplied with several local names and addresses and allowed to leave the sleeping baby in one of the empty rooms, for two hours maximum, while we looked for a nanny. Milia supplied the human resources associate with some expressed milk and extra nappies (just in case) and we took off. We rushed like mad from one address to another, like actors in a film. Only the third candidate appeared suitable: a retired woman in her sixties, mother of two grown-up daughters with their own families and grandmother of four. We were satisfied. The grandmother had a two-room flat on the ground floor. Her husband had fallen in the war. She had too much time on her hands and wanted to earn some cash to save for New Year's gifts for her grandchildren. Milia signed an agreement with her for three weeks, starting from the next day, 9 a.m. to 5 p.m., for five roubles a day. Milia would come to breastfeed at 1 p.m., and would provide expressed milk for in between feeds.

Milia was allocated a one-off subsidy of 100 roubles by the Human Resources Office, on the basis of the agreement with the nanny. She was on cloud nine. We returned together to the academy (it was only two blocks away), to show off our progeny. Fortunately, Shatin was in. He bestowed a kiss on Milia and congratulated her. He also expressed his support for her interest in the world of ballet and theatre and for her wish to earn a degree in Art History at MTA. He offered to advise her any time in the course of her research studies if she should need professional help.

"The subject of 'the author's right to a work of choreography' has troubled many specialists from different countries for centuries, and if you, dear colleague, could manage to shed some light on this murky and still unresolved matter, you would be making a huge contribution, not only legally, but aesthetically, to the history of stage arts. I give you my most heartfelt blessing for this difficult task!"

On the way home, we continued to discuss the details of our plan. I promised to come and visit the baby at the nanny's during my lunch break, on the way from the Bolshoi School to MTA, and to pick up special baby milk from the pharmacy on the exam days. I looked at my son and felt my heart bleed as I pondered the travails of this little fellow, the blame for which I laid squarely upon myself. It took us forty-five minutes to reach the Vorobyov Hills. This meant that every day the round trip would take two hours. After the state exams, Milia would need to spend a lot of time working in the library, attending supervisions and writing her dissertation. At the same time, she would need to take care of the baby, tidy the room, etc. I attempted to show Milia the virtual impossibility of carrying such a huge load, of research work and of motherhood, simultaneously. She, however, insisted that she would manage.

"Misha, give me a chance to try and organise myself in the halls on the Vorobyov Hills. There, I have all the resources, academic and household, at my disposal."

"But the challenge is not only in the availability of resources. It's about the human ability to combine such different occupations without help. It's like trying to hold two watermelons in one hand. As a result, either you will fail in your studies, or the baby will suffer. Quite possibly, both could happen."

Even after a heated debate, I was unable to convince Milia to send our son to the all-day nursing care for babies.

I spent the last few days before the beginning of the academic year organising family life and preparing for the third-year practical programme of Character and Historical dances, with a focus on methods of stage composition for drama theatre. Over the summer holidays I was supposed to have picked out a theme, either from literature or folklore, to implement onstage. I had to choose a scene or episode for a possible choreographic presentation, not imitating a text by means of naturalistic pantomime, but offering a creative interpretation, through flexible movement and dance. The latter were meant to express deeply the nature of the characters and strengthen the impact of stage presentation upon the audience. We were free to choose any genre: mystical ritual, lyrical drama, tragicomedy, abstract grotesque, etc. At a preliminary meeting with Chirtkov at the Youth Theatre, we compared our artistic visions with regard to stage body motions of theatre actors. He expressed his personal view of how the choreography of the play might look, and provided me with useful information about the play, actors, and stage scenery.

On Saturday, I visited the Labour Reserves' Ensemble, where Tikhonova introduced to me the entire collective and pointed out the particular characteristics of each subgroup. We identified and appointed soloists in technical and style categories. In passing, Ludmilla also informed me that from the following Sunday, there was going to be a seminar on Indian dances at the Moscow Performing Arts Centre, led by a choreographer from Calcutta. I was intrigued and asked if I was eligible to attend.

She explained: "All professionals are eligible, if they have the time to attend."

I promised to come to the seminar and asked Tikhonova if she would be my partner.

"There are women who are much younger than me here."

"Yes, but it doesn't mean that they are better dancers. Besides, I am afraid of contact with women."

"Yes, I can tell," she chuckled.

After the meeting with the Labour Reserves' ensemble, I ran to MTA to copy the timetable for the new term. I was handed an invitation from Golovkina to come for talks about practice sessions for her students with choreographers. Lena also asked me if I were going to the Bolshoi School right away, to take along and pass on to the Director a schedule of our practice sessions on Pushechnaya Street for both streams of the department, the ballet teachers and choreographers, to be coordinated with the school's timetable. In gratitude, my kind fairy rewarded me with a freshly typed copy of the choreographers' timetable.

In Golovkina's reception, I was asked to wait because the Director was meeting with Goleizovsky. *This is a chance to speak to the Maestro, I shouldn't miss it,* ran through my mind.

When Kasyan came out, Golovkina called her secretary. I greeted the Master. He looked at me thoughtfully, trying to remember where he had seen me before.

I reminded him: "You came to see the final choreographers' exam at MTA last spring."

"Ah, yes, now I remember. You are Shatin's pupil."

He offered his hand. I shook it and nodded in response.

"Excuse me, Kasyan Yaroslavovich, I wanted to ask your permission to sit in on your rehearsals at the school occasionally if possible. I am a great admirer of your talent and would like to get to know your methods a bit better, if you wouldn't mind."

"You are welcome, from 1st October, on the third floor."

"Thanks so much!"

The secretary emerged from Golovkina's office and motioned me to enter. I nodded.

"Sit down!" Golovkina invited.

"Here is a schedule from the academy which I've been asked to pass on," I said.

"Misha, for our programme of performance repertoires in different genres, we require a number of miniatures and short compositions similar to the ones you demonstrated in Shatin's exam last June. There are more than enough classical compositions in our programme, but we are most of all interested in contemporary themes, and not in the traditional ballet style."

"Can there be anyone better suited for this task than Goleizovsky?" I paid tribute to the master.

"Kasyan is a brilliant choreographer, but for more senior students. He works only with graduates, while we need practice sessions for our year V and above. Anatoly Vasilyevich mentioned that in your previous life you had choreographed graduation concerts for the Odessa School of Ballet on their Opera Theatre stage and that you have a lot of experience in working with children. Please consider this opportunity and take a look at our years IV to VII. Perhaps you will have some ideas. Come along, we'll discuss them. We cannot pay you, but we can give you the go-ahead to fulfil your creative ideas, and we can provide willing performers. I'll advise our tutors and teachers of your possible visits."

By 5 p.m., I finally reached the nanny's flat. My six-week-old son lay on a sofa, without swaddling clothes, kicking his feet in the air and purring. At the sight of me, he smiled (or at least I wished to think he did) and asked for a bottle of vodka (well, one day I was likely to hear that). I sat down next to him, lifted him up, and supporting his little head began purring in duet with him. At this point, his mother rushed into the room, all out of breath.

"Oh, great, you're here. I'm late."

"Yes. No 'hello', no kiss, no 'how're you?'" I complained to our son, "And all because of you."

The baby loudly passed wind in response.

"Aha, that's how you show your respect for Daddy? You son of a bitch. Oops, sorry, Milia, I forgot that you are his mother."

The nanny laughed, and my wife fumed.

"Instead of wasting your breath, why don't you wrap him up, while I pack his bag?"

I lowered the baby on to a sheet, wrapped it criss-cross around him and slung the package carefully on to my back. The nanny cracked up again, the baby crooned happily, and his mother was having a fit:

"Are you out of your mind? Striped monster! This is a baby, not a doll!"

"Hey, that's a bit too much, don't you think? A monster, might be, but 'striped', that's slander! Take it back this instant!"

Re-swaddling the baby, the mother pushed his smelly bag into my face and hissed: "Let's go!"

I blew a kiss to the broadly smiling nanny and trudged along after the commander, keeping the smelly bag as far away as possible from my not so small, but highly sensitive nose.

At the halls of residence on the Vorobyov Hills I showed my pass to the porter, which he pointed out was due for renewal. I promised to sort it. Milia's room was a right mess. I gave her a look, but didn't say anything. Stepping over things scattered all over, I quickly changed and without a word, started to clean up. I began with the filthy toilet and dangerously dirty bathtub. In half an hour I collected the soiled nappies that had been used by the son in the last three days and put them to soak in a tub. I spent an hour in the kitchen, washing dishes, taking out the trash, and finally washing the floor. My wife tried to launch into explanations several times, but I deliberately ignored her excuses. I washed dirty bed sheets and nappies and put them on the line to dry in the bathroom and kitchen. Only after all that, I took a shower and sat down at the desk to work on the choreography for Tikhonova's ensemble. Milia gave the baby a bath, and put him to sleep in his pram. She spent some considerable time doing something in the kitchen and bathroom, as well as picking up scattered papers and things from the floor.

"Misha, what are the plans for tomorrow?"

"From eight till twelve, I am going to take our son to the park. Meanwhile you can study for exams. Give me some milk and sweet water for him. I'll lunch at a snack bar. If I smell the familiar aroma from the baby, I will come for help to you. At midday sharp, I must leave for a seminar at the Performing Arts Centre. Daily, except Saturdays, we'll be meeting at the nanny's at 1 p.m. On Saturday, we'll pick him up from her together at 5 p.m., do our shopping and return here. We'll maintain this routine until you are done with your exams. On Monday, my classes at MTA resume, and I'll be spending nights on Trifonovka. Also, next week I am starting to work with the Labour Reserves' ensemble on Saturdays. The income should help with our daily expenses. I am also going to do work-practice at the Youth Theatre and the Bolshoi. On Sunday, I am at the Arts Centre from 2 p.m. If you should need my help urgently – and I don't mean to clean up your room – then ring Shura, the warden at my halls of residence, and leave a message. The unsanitary conditions you live in are dangerous to a baby's health. If this is the state of your place after three days when he's mostly been away from you, what is it going to be like when he is with you all day? As a mother, can you picture the scene?"

CHAPTER 7 CHAUVINISM IN ART

Everyone was surprised to see me attending the seminar on Indian Classical and Folk dance at the Performing Arts Centre. The Director personally introduced me to the teacher from Calcutta, and the interpreter relayed to him my professional interest in the course: a plan to stage a ballet on the subject of the Mahabharata. In the class, I positioned myself in the last line of participants, in order not to confuse the others by my quick grasp of new movements and musical rhythms. The guest teacher often cast encouraging glances in my direction, but never voiced any corrections of my mistakes, conscious of upholding my authority in the eyes of others. This was a good lesson in teaching ethics and filled me with respect for the Professor. At the end of the session, the Director led our Indian guest to his office, while we went to change. As I was leaving the building, I received a message from the Director to wait for him for ten minutes. I told the messenger that I would be outside, on a bench by the entrance. An embassy car with a small Indian flag on the wing was parked across the street. While waiting, I occupied myself with a revision of the Indian mudras – hand and finger gestures – which we had learned in the class that day, noting their meaning on my notepad.

"Aha, that's where you are! Mikhail, our guest wishes to speak with you. Come along!" The director of the Performing Arts Centre led me to his office and then left.

The interpreter explained the reason for summoning me: "Professor Shapura is the head of the Dance/Mime Department at the University of Calcutta. He is interested in practical information about folk dances of Europe. What he learns from books is not sufficient. He is looking for a specialist who could teach him two to three times a week, for a month, here in Moscow. He would be ready to pay for this service. The director of the Performing Arts Centre highly recommended you. What would you say to such a proposition? Can your academy authorise you?"

"I am a big fan of Indian dance and music. Currently I am a third-year student in the Choreography Department at MTA, and have been working with European Historical and Character dances for ten years. There can be no talk of money. However, on the basis of equal exchange, I would be happy to trade my knowledge of European material for that of Indian dance. I will immediately report to our dean about this short-term project and am almost certain to get a positive response. As you know, as a private individual I am not allowed to engage in communication with foreigners. The Indian Embassy would have to put in an official request to MTA, probably via the Ministry of Culture, for a professional exchange of information about folk dances of India and Europe between two specific individuals from two institutes of higher education."

The interpreter conveyed this to Shapura who nodded in enthusiastic ascent: "Mr Berkut, thank you so much. Goodbye! All the best!"

My third year at MTA had begun. At the first lesson in dance composition, we presented our lists of episodes and scenes from popular dramas of Russian and European authors that we were considering as subjects for our graduation projects. Shatin addressed further questions to each of us aimed at illuminating the theme, genre and style of choreography, categories of performers, etc. The night before, I had changed my mythological theme from Scythian to Indian, an episode from the epic Mahabharata. Noticing this change, my mentor raised his eyebrows:

"Misha, since when are you a fan of Hinduism?"

"Since yesterday, Professor."

"So, why aren't you wearing a Sikh headdress?"

"I left it in the changing room so as not to alarm the kids."

My colleagues cracked up.

"May I explain the reasons for this change after the class?"

Shatin nodded and continued inspecting the project ideas of other students. Then he began his lecture:

"In a theatre play, the dance is not a plug-in number, as in a variety show or an anniversary concert. Instead, it is shorthand for a broader concept, 'stage movement', which is one of many tools in the expressive arsenal of Dramatic theatre. A choreographer's vocabulary includes gestures and poses, separate movements of head and body, of upper and lower limbs, short sequences as well as complete fragments of a potential dance. At the same time, none of these can be subject to a choreographer's whim. Every tiny gesture or grimace onstage is not a product of the choreographer's spontaneous improvisation, on the contrary, it is a result of careful consideration and is based on the production's script developed by the play's director, who in turn works from the author's script. In this way, a choreographer becomes a co-author of the performance, along with the playwright and the director. A choreographer is therefore required to familiarise himself with the play and the director's production notes, to assess the physical and technical parameters involved in the stage movement of actors and dancers; to work with an artist on the design of costumes and props; to maintain constant communication with the play's director concerning the development of actors' motions and the performance in general. The success of a given production often depends on a fruitful collaboration between the choreographer and the show's cast, director, and stage crew."

The third-year curriculum in Historical dance was dedicated to the Baroque period: Polonaise, Gavotte, Gigue in the fifth term, and Minuet, Bourrée, Contredanse in the sixth. In Character dance, we turned to the West European repertoire: Irish, British and Scandinavian in the fifth term, and Italian, French and Spanish in the sixth. By the end of the year we were supposed to finish the curriculum in both disciplines in order to have all the necessary information at our disposal for the course in Dance Composition, and for our work-study practice in Moscow theatres, as well as for cinema, television, philharmonic societies, and athletic organisations (such as figure skating or artistic gymnastics). Out of the academic disciplines, only three remained on the agenda: Marxist–Leninist Aesthetics, History of Drama theatre, opera and Ballet, the last two dedicated to the twentieth century and the Soviet period respectively in the fifth and sixth terms. This trio was to be a concluding chapter in our historical-philosophical education. In the Dean's office, we were given special passes entitling us to attend stage rehearsals at the Bolshoi Theatre for our educational benefit. The Bolshoi School was to provide us with students to use as performers in our final projects for dance composition. The load of classes and practice continued to be so heavy that we had no time for eating or sleeping.

Once, after a lesson in Historical dance, I approached the Professor. "Excuse me, Margarita Vasilyevna, may I ask you a question?"

"Yes, of course."

"When is the expected date of publication for your book, if it is not a secret? I was hoping to get a copy before graduation, if possible."

The author smiled sadly: "Not any time soon. The illustrator has just finished with the drawings and diagrams. I now have to sort out this chaos of papers with page numbers and headings for illustrations. Only then will I be ready to give the manuscript to the publisher. The production process will take at least six months. So, you can work it out."

"Margarita Vasilyevna, you know my passion for Historical dance. I would be most happy to help you out with the illustrations: to fix their position in the book in accordance with the text, and to mark their numbers and headings on the back of each. For example, twice a week, Tuesdays and Thursdays, five to seven in the evening, after classes. Would that suit you?"

"But this is not part of your student workload, Misha." The elderly professor was looking at me over her glasses, in surprise. "Why would you wish to waste your precious energy and time on this?"

"Excuse me, but I don't see it as a waste of time. It is in my professional interest to help speed up publication of the material that I sorely need for my work. The only book in Russian on this subject, by Ivankovsky, presents

Historical dance in a rather limited and one-sided fashion. Working with you, I have a chance to fill in the gaps in my education. Is this not sufficient reason for a student to wish to help his professor?"

"Thank you, Misha. You are very persuasive. Here is my address and telephone number. See you on Tuesday."

Margarita Rozhdestvenskaya lived in a building for employees of the Bolshoi Theatre on Gorky Street. She had a large bright flat furnished with antiques and her office room was unusually neat for a creative personality. In spite of her venerable age (late seventies), Margarita retained a sharp mind and good memory. At the same time, a full load of teaching at MTA, both in the ballet masters and ballet teachers programmes, and her research in European Historical Court dance demanded a lot of energy and attention. Household and personal matters as well made the life of this elderly woman quite full. Before me, Margarita had had another girl from the department assisting her with the book, but she had recently left to take up a job elsewhere. Over the previous three years, I had often supported Margarita in class and sometimes substituted for her when she was ill. This fact rather than my eloquence was what must have convinced her to take up my offer of help with the book. I immensely enjoyed working on the montage of illustrations, while learning new information about the dances that had been left out of the MTA curriculum.

When this project was finished, Margarita Vasilyevna confessed: "Misha, I don't know how to thank you enough."

"I do. When the book is published, I would love to have a signed copy."

Pecking me on the cheek at my departure, she added, "I am confident that in the future you will continue my legacy in Historical dance."

Milia passed her state exams with flying colours and was admitted to a graduate course at the Law Department of MGU. I must give her credit for this: she was brilliant at accumulating and memorising the necessary information. She also had good speaking ability and could dispute a subject of any material she'd studied with ease. At the same time, as a mother and housekeeper, she was completely hopeless. As a graduate student at MGU, she already had a few lectures to attend. In addition, Milia had applied for and been accepted on a course in art history at MTA, on the basis of her graduate diploma from MGU. This included an automatic transfer of all credits for the philosophical and historical subjects that she had just passed at MGU, and an opportunity to complete a four-year programme in two years. Even so, it was impossible to 'embrace the infinite', i.e. to handle such a load of studies, while at the same time caring for a two-month-old baby who needed constant attention.

One day, a bad premonition sent me flying to the Vorobyov Hills. Entering the lobby with its soaring stairwell, I heard a baby crying, and without waiting for the lift, I rushed upstairs. Once inside the room, my hair stood on end in horror. I ran up to the pram, scooped up my son who had turned blue from prolonged crying and instantly closed his mouth with a bottle of milk. It is possible that I simply panicked at that moment, but it is better not to say what I thought and felt towards his mother at that moment. I washed and changed my soiled baby who, fed and dry now, fell asleep instantly after all the stress and commotion. Meanwhile, I rolled up my sleeves and turned my attention to a clean-up operation: bathroom, toilet and kitchen. I didn't touch the dirty laundry scattered all over on purpose, and only opened the window for ventilation. My wife appeared fifty minutes later. She frantically burst into the room and froze at the sight of me.

"How long have you been here?" she asked apprehensively.

"You'd do better telling me what time you left! I've been working here for almost an hour."

Milia slumped on to a chair like a beaten dog, and glanced at her watch. "Three and a half hours ago."

I nearly choked from rage, but pulled myself together and calculated out loud: "This means that our two-month-old baby slept for about two hours after you had left, and then has been screaming for his mother for at least an hour until I appeared. Dear wife, this sort of thing cannot continue. I am not in the least interested in visiting you in prison after you have been convicted for infanticide. Stubbornness is not a proof of intellect. You are totally incompetent as a mother and housekeeper. If it were not for the child, I would not spend my time and energy trying to retrain you. I would leave you to drown in your own excrement. There can be no excuse for a mother treating a baby in the way you have treated our son. Tomorrow, I am going to apply for a place for him at a social services Infant Care Centre. It's on Sretenka, three stops by trolley to Hertzen Street. You must write a letter of application this very instant. Give me his birth certificate, your ID and confirmation of your residency with him at this address. It would be best if we met at the Law Department at 2 p.m., together with the baby, and went to look at this social services facility. I hope you have no objections to this idea any longer."

Milia sat at the table and drafted up a letter. She gave it to me to check, then made a clean copy after my corrections. All this she did without uttering a single word. I looked through a stack of required documents and suggested that she visit her Trade Union branch tomorrow, no later than midday, and get a letter of support from them, requesting a place for her son at the Infant Care Centre, and providing a confirmation of her status as a graduate student.

"If for any reason, you do not come to the Law Department at the appointed time, I will immediately report you to all relevant authorities, including your dean and your Trade Union branch, exposing your dangerous behaviour towards a child. I warn you not to drive me to these extreme measures!"

"May I ask why you refuse to hear my explanations?"

"No, they will have no effect on my decision. They will only produce additional stress for both of us. The negative sides of your personality are well known to you."

"What are you implying?"

"You are incapable of looking after yourself and others. Your tendency to get absorbed in chatting with friends, showing off what you know, and forgetting your responsibilities as a mother, wife, and housekeeper. I'd better stop here. I am deeply disappointed in you as a friend, woman, and person. Every new incident like this that reveals your egotism and lack of character drives me further and further away from you. I beg you to acknowledge the problem before it's too late. So, then, tomorrow at 2 p.m. at the Law Department."

The day before I had relayed to Shatin what had taken place in my meeting with the Indian dance master at the Performing Arts Centre. He took the brochure and business card presented to me by the Indian professor and asked me to come by the next day for a chat. The following day he informed me before the lecture that the rector of MTA had already approved the idea of cultural contact with a friendly state and invited me to meet with the officials in his office in a day's time. To be frank, I had not anticipated that the Indian episode would produce so many complications in my already 'entertaining' life, but it was too late for retreat. I went to the library and discovered a couple of books in English on

Indian folk and Classical dances in the 'foreign languages' section. I pored over them in the study room of my halls of residence until late at night, making notes on various forms of ancient choreography reflected in temple art and sculpture. I was deeply impressed with the ancient monuments of Indian visual arts, illustrating a school of Indian Classical dance through the performers' flexible gestures and poses. It was an overwhelming discovery for me. Our professors at MTA taught that the origin of choreography and theatre lay in Greece, 2,000 years before our era, but it seemed that in India it had happened 2,000 years before that.

In my head, I again heard my mother's voice: "Mishenka, take care! Silence is golden."

Shatin and two officials from the Ministry of the Interior attended the meeting in the Rector's office. When I turned up, Rector Gorbunov introduced me in a rather one-sided fashion and asked me to relay how I had met Professor Shapura, who was the initiator of this cultural exchange, what were the names of his interpreter and the director of the Performing Arts Centre. I answered factually, and added that I had been specialising in Historical and Character dances of Europe for some years and that I was rather interested in learning the Asian art of choreography, as well as that of other continents. The Rector asked me to wait for a few minutes in the corridor. Ten minutes later, I was invited back inside and the door shut behind me. I thought that I was about to be arrested for unauthorised contact with foreigners.

To my utter amazement, however, the two officials affirmed the proposed project, with a proviso: "India is a friendly country, and the ministry approves the expansion of cultural connections with it, provided the Ministry of the Interior has full oversight. Here are the telephone numbers that you should use to inform us about your communications with Shapura, his interpreter and any other foreign representatives during your visits to the Indian Embassy. If you agree to these conditions, we wish you good luck in you creative work."

This was the beginning of my Indian saga at MTA. Lena, Shatin's secretary called the embassy and invited Shapura to MTA for a meeting with the Dean to flesh out the organisational details. At the appointed time I was waiting for our guest by the entrance. I saw him in and introduced him to Shatin. With the help of his interpreter we agreed to meet twice a week during October, on Thursdays, four to seven at the Bolshoi School to study the Indian material, and from ten to one on Sundays at the embassy to study the European programme. I reminded the Professor of his other commitment.

"Excuse me, Professor, would it not be too tiring for you to have our morning study session, and then to give a seminar at the Performing Arts Centre on the same day?"

"Actually, that course has been cancelled. It proved too physically difficult for the retired teachers."

"It's all for the better then," I commented in a jolly tone.

The interpreter scowled: "Perhaps you are right."

We moved to a performance hall and discussed the repertoire for both programmes of cultural exchange there, fixing the first meeting for the coming Sunday.

Choreographic rehearsals at the Labour Reserves' ensemble progressed on a high professional level. I was pleasantly surprised to see that fourteen-to-sixteen-year-old teenagers were capable of paying close attention to lengthy explanations about imagery in dance composition, and bearing with my pedantic demands for technical precision and clean execution of complicated sequences onstage. The choreography was difficult and totally unfamiliar to many of the kids. I treated them as adults and expected them to meet the challenges seriously. Sometimes I had to tease the girls who mimicked their male partners by performing their female roles in a similarly rough manner:

"While you try to maintain the precision of technical performance, please remember your innate femininity at the same time. Otherwise the audience will not be able to see the difference between you and the guys. Of course, you should not overplay the girly part, but it is quite legitimate to give a playful wink to your partner or shrug your shoulders capriciously now and then."

The girls giggled and cast questioning glances in the direction of Tikhonova who was coaching the boys on the other side of the training hall.

I should like to note that the Labour Reserves provided me with a kind of creative breather and a laboratory for my artistic experiments. The 'Youths' Suite' had been conceived as an ethnically neutral piece and was musically based on a selection of tunes taken from Soviet composers and, choreographically, on a free association of various techniques from the Character dance repertoire. Specific groups of youths and girls, as well as the soloists, each had a category or leitmotif of sequences and a style of performance corresponding to the tonalities of the music. In different combinations, these subgroups either created visual harmonies or contrasts, while the rest of the Ensemble acted as an accompaniment on the sides of the stage, expressing through gesture and movement their emotional reaction to the main action. In such a polyphonic choreography, inexperienced dancers that had been used to following veterans in much simpler compositions, often felt disoriented in space and in music, and had to learn for themselves how to hear the music and to follow the simultaneous development of action on several fronts at the same time.

In September, we focused on the main episodes of individual and group performances. In October, we worked on the choreographic text of presentation by specific groups in various compositional segments. In November, the Ensemble rehearsed first small and then large components of a multilayered composition, and finally, we took up the run-through of the whole suite. Here we ran into a problem. According to my choreography, the dancers were supposed to act in multiple roles in the composition, changing places between thematic subgroups in the course of the performance. This was meant to produce a great visual effect. The beginners, however, were not yet used to such a brisk change of positions, partners, or emotionally diverse images. Ludmilla and I worked patiently with individual dancers, explaining, demonstrating, and repeating their parts with them. Still, many of them lacked confidence and continued to look at the more experienced dancers and, as a result, often stumbled or fell, causing some chaos. To address the problem, I proposed to remove, temporarily, one girl and two guys from the final part of the suite, at least until they became confident of their parts in this complex choreography. This allowed the performance to stabilise, and the 'Youths' Suite' was run without a hitch in front of the ensemble's directorate and approved for inclusion in the current repertoire.

Milia collected all the necessary papers confirming her status as a full graduate student from the Law Department, and together with our little son, we went for a visit to the Infant Care Centre on Sretenka. The Director there met us coolly at first, with a hint of suspicion, but after looking through our passports and a letter of support from the Human Resources Office of the MGU, she warmed to us and explained how the centre operated:

"We are only able to accommodate babies up to twelve months of age here. Mostly, they are children of parents who are here temporarily and are not Moscow residents. We have no vacancies at the moment, but there is a possibility that one will open up on Saturday. A single mother from Hungary was planning to take her baby away. If she doesn't change her mind, then you have a chance to place your baby with us from Sunday, 1st October. That is, of course, if there are no medical reasons as to why he should not be here. Give me a call on Saturday morning to confirm the availability of a place. Here is the number. My name is Klavdia Petrovna. I am the head paediatrician. And now let's take a look at him. Can you please undress him?"

At the end of a five-minute check-up, the Director summed up, "Overall, the boy is in good health. He only has a little bit of irritation between his legs."

My wife and I exchanged glances.

The doctor picked up a tube of lotion and applied some ointment to the irritated skin around the baby's private parts. "This is quite common with newborns, and it can be easily treated if you change and wash him often enough. Take this lotion and apply twice a day."

On Tuesday and Fridays, Milia had two lectures on the History of Art at MTA. She made arrangements with the babysitter for half a day, for three roubles. It was I, of course, who was paying these expenses. On these days we usually met at MTA, lunched together, but parted at night to sleep in our own halls of residence. I gave Milia the telephone number of the Labour Reserves' Ensemble and asked her to leave me a message about the vacancy with the Infant Care Centre.

"If the answer is positive and they have a vacancy, then I can come over in the evening after the rehearsal, and help you get him ready. And at 4 p.m. on Sunday, we'll move him there. I will check with Shura today whether they could give us graduate student's accommodation, since you are also a student at the academy now. I hope Madam Berkut has no objections?"

"Well, I'd started to think that you'd left me out of your personal life plans."

"You were wrong then, weren't you? Had that been the case, we wouldn't be sitting in a cafeteria together now, giving an impression of a happy couple. By the way, let me bring you up to date with my plans for this semester. Write it down in your diary. Up until 1st December, I will be working with the ensemble. In October, I am exchanging lessons with an Indian professor from Calcutta and choreographing miniatures at the Bolshoi School for Golovkina. In November, I will be working at the Youth Theatre with Boris Chirtkov on the stage movement for his play. In December, I have exams at MTA, and then will work in my traditional capacity as Grandfather Frost at winter shows. It would be great to go to Odessa for the winter break, so that I could finally introduce my beautiful wife and mighty son to my relatives and friends. That is, of course, if you agree?"

We were unbelievably lucky, because the Infant Care Centre offered us a place, from October until mid-July of the next year. I booked him a place at a nursery (near the halls of residence on Trifonovka) from 16th August for a six-day week, because Milia and I were living in graduate student accommodation, and could bring the baby in only on Sunday, and even then, illegally. Thanks to the round-the-clock care provided by highly qualified nurses and doctors, the baby was soon thriving at the Infant Care Centre. I visited him daily, during my lunch hour, gobbling my sandwich on the way there. His mother visited at 6 p.m., after her classes at MTA and MGU, and played with him for half an hour before he was taken away for sleep along with the other babies. The Almighty must have sent this miraculous salvation to us to reward us for our patience. To change residence three times in one month, with a two-month-old baby in tow, was no mean feat. I am typically a doubting Thomas, but I have to admit that without this miracle, neither Milia nor I could have studied or worked productively. And no less importantly, thanks to this routine in our baby's life, our conjugal relations also returned to their former warm state. With the new arrangements in place, each of us punctually and willingly performed the duties of a parent and a partner, even though we were both grossly overloaded with work and study.

On my way to the first meeting with the Indian colleague at the embassy, I felt slightly nervous because I had never before found myself in close contact with a foreigner. I took along my accordion for musical accompaniment, and was stopped by the policeman on duty at the entrance to the embassy.

He checked my passport and then demanded, "And what is this luggage?"

In response I opened up the case.

"Fine, come through!" he barked.

I was greeted by the interpreter, Nata, in the hallway. She welcomed me warmly and led me to the basement gym.

Shapura shouted to me in broken Russian, *"Privet!"* and shook my hand. He led me to the changing room and addressed some remarks to me in English. I didn't understand a word, so he switched to the universal language of gestures. The Professor waited for me to change and then led me back to the gym. Nata helped me to discover where he would like to begin. He asked for a stage version of the Russian dance 'At Moiseyev's'.

I smiled back my understanding.

Nata sat opposite us and translated simultaneously our conversation, my explanations and corrections. I kept it simple, repeating slowly one after another the elements of movements, first for the female role and then, after a ten-minute break, for the male role for another hour and a half. The last thirty minutes of each section I accompanied our practice on the accordion. Shapura was ecstatic about the results of the first lesson. He thanked me with a traditional Indian gesture – two palms together drawn to the chest. I showed him how to perform the Russian bow with an outstretched arm. Nata suggested keeping the accordion at the embassy for the time being, so I would not to have to drag it along every time.

On Thursday, I waited for the Professor at the appointed hour by the entrance to the Bolshoi School on Pushechnaya Street. At his approach, I greeted him in English, and he me in Russian. We climbed to the fourth floor and I took the Professor to the changing room. He appeared with a small tambourine but without his bag which I gestured to him to fetch. He nodded and shrugged. I was dressed in a training suit and ballet slippers. The teacher made an approving gesture. I took out my library books in English and explained through his interpreter that I was interested in the Classical dance 'Bharatanatyam'.

The Professor applauded with enthusiasm: "OK, let's go!"

He began by explaining, with Nata's help, the physical sensations associated with the proper positions of the body, head, arms and legs. Then he demonstrated the staccato rhythm of the sound accompaniment by the clicking of his tongue and lips. Next he explained the principles of balancing on one foot, while making spherical movements with the other. He also suggested exercises for neck muscles. The last thirty minutes of the first half he dedicated to a methodical elucidation of hand gestures – mudras – focusing only on a few main signs made by hands and fingers. After a break, he showed me first the elementary footsteps, then, separately, arm movements. At the end of the lesson, he combined the footwork with the arm and hand gestures in short sequences, all along accompanying himself with tongue and lip clicking to articulate the tempo/rhythm. Only at the very end, he ran through the whole sequence with the accompaniment of a small drum.

In contrast to the flat illustrations in print, the gestures and poses came alive in the performance of a master, leaving a deep aesthetic impression. Every small body motion, in tune with a facial expression, conveyed a specific meaning in the behaviour of a character or his/her emotional reaction to the action onstage. A human body endowed with the rich language of physical mobility holds infinite potential for the expression of minute philosophical nuances of thought or erotic sensibilities, through the medium of gesture and dance. Personally I do not believe in mysticism. Yet I cannot deny that in the midst of studying the vocabulary of Bharatanatyam with Professor Shapura, I sometimes felt myself almost hypnotised by the spiritual, psychic presence of my teacher. With every session, I was drawn ever deeper into the magnetic field of his magical influence. Of course, I was not planning to stage my diploma project in the style of 'Bharatanatyam', but I considered it quite legitimate to incorporate its spiritual tone, dramatic emotions, and ornamental figures in my work.

I started to look for a popular Indian subject that would be readily digestible and suitable for a stage and visual presentation by means of choreography. The images of Krishna, Shiva, and Rama were too well known and overused in world literature, drama and cinema. I wanted something fresh, original, and different. Reading the myths and legends from the epic Mahabharata in a Russian translation, I stumbled upon a poem by V. A. Zhukovsky, 'Nal and Damajanti', an Indian version of *Romeo and Juliet*, and I knew that I had found my theme. The poet's romantic interpretation of this ancient story of love and loyalty instantly won me over. After a month-long introduction to the classical school of Indian dance, I decided to use this theme for Shatin's assignment: to create a theatrical presentation of a mythological story using choreography. I selected the music for my production from the works of Russian composers (Borodin, Rimsky-Korsakov), as well as from other admirers of Oriental tunes.

The overall result turned out to be so successful that my mentor urged me, "Misha, why don't you use this fable as a basis for your final diploma project in the fourth year?"

"I am a little nervous about that, Anatoly Vasilyevich."

"You should be, if you were a shameless plagiarist, but in our creative lab, your friendly peers, with their constructive analytical critique, would help you to polish and perfect your model before you take it to a theatre where possible mistakes would have a much more serious impact than here."

"Thank you, teacher. I will go ahead and gather the necessary information in the embassy library, and also ask Mrs Menon if she would agree to be my consultant on the project."

In early November, I started my choreographic practice at the Youth Theatre, assisting the director Chirtkov in the staging of a drama, *With Red Hot Iron*, based on the novel *How the Steel Was Tempered* by Nikolai Ostrovsky. Pavka Korchagin was one of the most popular heroes of the revolution. In my youth, I had also sympathised with this fighter and martyr for a great cause. And so I put a small part of my heart into the work on that play. Boris Chirtkov had by then finished the design of his artistic vision for the production and he was now expecting me to complement his design with my choreographic ideas. In my mind's eye, I had the images of Golovin's and Deineka's artwork, as well as *Windows of Growth* by Mayakovsky. For the most important third act, I developed a choreographic script of mime poses alternating in a kaleidoscopic fashion behind the lit-up screen at the back of the stage. The sculptural pyramids of shadows and the moving silhouettes of figures were meant to reflect the flow of memories of a blind and paralysed hero, creating either a lyrical or a tragic atmosphere for the action onstage. The mime scenes were designed to intensify the emotional and dynamic expressiveness of actors and to aid in the delivery of the Director's vision.

The constructive criticism of colleagues helped me to identify problem elements in the choreography and after their corrections had been implemented, Shatin approved my composition for stage production. On my request, Chirtkov arranged with the Shchukin Theatre Institute to provide freshmen, wishing to display their artistic potential, to act in my mime sequence. Both MTA and the Shchukin Theatre Institute were located in the same building, only on different floors, so that our collaboration was natural and convenient. I soon found seventeen young and eager youths and girls willing to work with me on the choreography for the play. I conducted all the preliminary work in the rehearsal studio of the institute, and then gradually transferred individual fragments to the Youth Theatre for stage rehearsals of the corresponding episodes of the play. Seated in the auditorium, Chirtkov first observed the silhouetted actions and poses of my group behind the screen, checking them against his production script. Then, after his corrections, our mime group was usually joined by the main cast acting in front of the screen in order to coordinate the timing and actions of both parties with the meaning and emotional impact of a given scene. Once the lighting design for the mime scenes in the third act had been finished, my choreography began to show with a greater effect against the chromatic background.

In the first two acts which contained live action rather than the hero's remembrances, I had to work with the main cast and extras (consisting of retirees and students). In this capacity I felt much more confident thanks to my personal experience at the Odessa Theatre. Nevertheless, I used the opportunity to reinforce the Director's ideas with additional gestures and more emphatic poses in the climactic moments of the drama. I kept offering new ideas along these lines, and Chirtkov either accepted or rejected them, depending on his vision of the whole. Sometimes Chirtkov himself approached me with a request to develop a particular episode, either of a duet or a duel, to bring out, through stage movement, the physical/bodily interplay between violence and love. Naturalism never appealed to my aesthetic vision, because theatre is not life, and it requires an exaggerated expression of emotions to make a dramatic statement. Therefore, in working with extras, I followed a middle course, somewhere between the realism of the main cast (who acted in accordance with the principles of Stanislavsky) and the grotesque silhouettes of the third act. Every appearance of the extras in the first and second acts, either at the back of the stage, the sides, or on the upper tier of stage scenery, I choreographed in the manner of an ancient Greek chorus. Silent actors used static pantomime not to represent the monologue or dialogue taking place centre stage, but to reflect the emotional reaction of the surrounding crowd (e.g. disapproval or support, disappointment or satisfaction, joy or sorrow, etc.) to the dramatic state of main actors, or to display the potential or actual effect of the main protagonists' interaction. Intentionally slow transitions of extras from one mise en scène to another resembled the changing of slides in a projector, depicting either the civil war, the building of a railway, property confiscations during the New Economic Policy, or other historical events in accordance with the script.

With the Director's permission, I invited my colleagues and teachers from the

Ballet Masters Department to the dress rehearsal and received many positive as well as negative comments. As I was wont to reassure my beginners in dance: "A new debut is always difficult." My name was listed in the production's programme: 'choreography by M. Berkut'. It was also pleasant for me to read in a review that had appeared in the newspaper *Soviet Culture* that 'a student from the Ballet Masters Department at MTA found an effective approach to the choreographic dimension of the play directed by talented actor and director B. Chirtkov'. Shatin congratulated me on my theatrical debut and announced that my success in the production would count towards a solid pass mark in dance composition in the upcoming exams. He also approved Zhukovsky's 'Nal and Damajanti' as the libretto for my diploma project. I needed this permission to go ahead in my search for a composer next term, in order to begin collaborative work on the musical score. At the embassy, I requested an interview with Mrs Menon who was the wife of the Indian Ambassador to the USSR. She was very happy to hear about my plans to use themes from the Mahabharata in my diploma project and promised to provide all help necessary in organising practical lessons with Indian dancers on tour in Moscow, as well as to act, in general, as a cultural consultant for my project.

In early October, I presented to Golovkina my repertoire of contemporary choreographic miniatures for students of the Bolshoi School in years V, VI and VII. The finalists, from year VIII, however, worked directly with Kasyan Goleizovsky. My compositions for the first semester included:

'Future Pilots', based on a painting of the same name by A. Deineka, and using
  'Mimoletnosti' by Prokofiev (for three boys);
'Snake Charmer', from the Mahabharata, using Scott's 'Indian Suite' (solo);
'Martians', with Shostakovich's music, 'Fantastic Dances' (for two boys and
  three girls).

All three compositions were designed and staged for students in contemporary/classical (non-traditional) choreography style, with the use of natural body language and Character dance, as well as acrobatic elements interspersed with grotesque poses, gestures and facial expressions. After five years of professional training, young dancers easily handled the technique of avant-garde choreography. Overall, the unusual manner and style of all miniatures were so strikingly different from the common standard that they could be an eyesore for a traditionalist choreographer and audience. The Director, Golovkina, laughed heartily, watching her 'Martians', performing eccentric anti-classical sequences en pointe.

"Misha, personally I like your choreography, but if I end up behind bars because of it, you will be the one to bring me parcels from the free world. Ha ha!" she declared. Sofia Nikolayevna could afford such jokes because her husband, as rumour had it, was a big shot in the KGB.

Two to three times a week, after my classes at the Bolshoi School, I dropped in to watch Goleizovsky's rehearsals. He typically worked with the final-year students at least an hour longer than all the others. I would sit quietly in a corner behind a grand piano and watch the master in action, in a state of enchantment. He was a good pianist himself and often demonstrated to the accompanist the desired tempo-dynamic shades in music. It could appear that he improvised his choreography on the go, because he was not using any sheet music, as many of us often do. Kasyan, it would appear, often nursed the main outlines of a choreographic scenario in his mind for a long time and in a rehearsal studio simply finalised the details of that vision, using the live material of performers' bodies. Every time I observed the creative process of this genius at work, I perceived the magic of a shaman who circles an enchanted dancer in a quiet and concentrated trance and then pounces on them with an outburst of revelation, fixing any imprecision in physical posture or spiritual content. With the emotional agility of a young man, he moved his old body to demonstrate to the pupils the required intensity of expression, hypnotising his receptive audience in the process.

I always left Goleizovsky in a state of creative ecstasy. I was set in motion and wanted, while still under the spell of his enchantment, to compose, improvise, dance, its influence was so powerful. If Kasyan had been invited to teach at MTA, it's not hard to imagine how many more students would have been inspired by his creative potency. The head of staff, Zakharov, however, did not even want to hear of Goleizovsky, this seventy-year-old titan of Russian ballet.

Once, after a rehearsal, Kasyan approached me in the studio and asked: "Misha, what are you up to this Sunday?"

"In the morning, I am taking private lessons in Indian dance at the embassy."

"Would you like to come over for tea at four o'clock? My wife Larissa (a teacher at the Bolshoi) would like to meet you. I am writing a book about dance and would be interested to hear the objective opinion of a young specialist. I hear that your wife also studies at the academy?"

"Unfortunately, our little son is with us on Sundays."

"Even better. Come, all three of you, including the offspring. We'll be glad to see you."

I relayed his invitation to Milia, who welcomed an opportunity to go out as a family. My wife's mood improved even further when she had heard that on Saturday we were going to a matinee at the Bolshoi to see a production of *Stone Flower* by Yuri Grigorovich, music by Sergei Prokofiev. Finishing up the rehearsal at the Labour Reserves a little earlier that day, I hurried to the premiere of the new ballet.

Milia was already waiting for me by the entrance: "I was worried that you would get carried away with your production and forget about our rendezvous."

"You are right, I could have, but not when the rendezvous is connected to a ballet premiere."

My wife slapped me on the hand with the tickets: "Moron Semyonovich, you are failing the gentleman test miserably."

"Pardon, ma'am. I shall reform myself immediately."

Both my wife and I were deeply impressed by the contemporary choreography of a classical ballet that was inspired by Prokofiev's modern music, but based on an old myth. Grigorovich's approach was in fact quite close to my idea of reinterpreting a legend from the Indian Mahabharata. Not so much in the choreographic style, as in the principle of stylising Russian folklore to the level of classical forms of ballet. Wretched 'dramatic choreographers' such as Zakharov and Lavrovsky, performed astonishing backflips of criticism in their attempts to discredit Grigorovich's creation, calling his ballet a buffoonery, a perversion of Russian ethnography and of the venerable tradition of Classical European dance. Unlike his venomous colleagues, the public and the press received this turning point in the history of Russian Ballet theatre with huge enthusiasm.

After the show, we hurried off to the Infant Care Centre to pick up our son.

He had begun to recognise us and even smile at his mother. I promised to remind him of this parental discrimination when he grew up and asked his daddy for five kopecks to buy an ice cream. The baby was, in general, on great form; he just missed his parents.

Goleizovsky lived near MTA and not far from Arbat, in an old house in a rather shabby quarter of Moscow. Larissa turned out to be much younger than her husband. She was very happy to see a baby among her visitors. She took him from my arms and began to play with him as if he were a doll. For my part, I turned to gazing at a stupendous collection of various wooden sculptures fashioned from tree trunks and stumps. There were also numerous ballet-themed drawings and lithographs on the walls.

"Kasyan Yaroslavovich, are all these creations the product of a choreographer's imagination?"

"Yes. During one particular period of my artistic life, I discovered that I had a huge amount of unexpected free time. All that you see here is a result of a vacuum in my Ballet career."

Moving dexterously around the kitchen, Larissa quickly served us tea with honey biscuits. Five minutes later she had already learned all our individual and combined life stories thanks to a talkative lawyer. Meanwhile I described to Kasyan my impressions of Grigorovich's ballet.

The host asked with a smile, "Which of you two is the art historian and which the choreographer?"

"We both dabble in this and that. More specifically, Milia in art history, and I in ballet. For now, my wife dominates in academic study, and I try to prevail in dance, but I don't always succeed."

"Why is that?"

"Her Cossack upbringing gets in the way."

Kasyan got up. "Misha, let's leave our women to chat and turn our attention to business."

The choreographer's office was dominated by a piano, while the walls were lined with bookcases from corner to corner. It was an impressive sight.

"Have a seat."

"Thank you."

"Many choreographers turn to writing in their old age: either about themselves or about dance. I heard from a number of respected colleagues, Rozhdestvenskaya and Tkachenko, that you personally dedicate much of your time and energy to the study of Historical and Character dances. Even that you have become enthralled with ancient Indian choreography, which is to your credit, as a thinking ballet master. This is not so common in our profession."

I nodded in grateful acknowledgement of his compliment.

Goleizovsky continued musing: "Like those others, I have also given in to the mania for writing. For many years now, I have been nurturing an idea for a book, *Images in Russian Choreography*. Larissa is negative about this idea because she is convinced that the book would never be published, at least during my lifetime. Trusting my own intuition and hearing from Rozhdestvenskaya about your voluntary help with the montage of her illustrations, I feel that I can share with you an outline for my future book, in order to receive a second opinion about the prospect of publishing it. Could you do me such a favour? I would truly appreciate it if you did."

"Maestro . . . May I address you this way?"

Kasyan smiled in reply.

"I wouldn't see it as doing you a favour, on the contrary, it is an honour to earn the trust of a deeply admired colleague. I would be most happy to give you what is, I am afraid, likely to be a rather incompetent opinion on your book. I suspect that such historians and critics of ballets as Solertinsky and Slonimsky, as well as other experts could do a much better job."

"Misha, your objections are reasonable, of course, but I don't trust those opportunists. As you probably know they have been marinating Nikolai Tarasov's book on the male technique in Classical dance for the last ten years, and nobody is able to break through the bureaucratic armour of their censorship without the agreement of Rostislav Zakharov. You are lucky that he has not yet destroyed you, mainly thanks to the overwhelming majority of supporting voices in your favour. But you should be wary of those sharks, and the dangers they pose to you and your family."

"You are right," I sighed, "please tell me the main idea and theses of your book; what historical periods it covers, how it is structured, etc."

"In this work, I would like to tell readers about the history of Russian dance culture, starting from the primordial conceptions of ritual choreography, through the social and folk development of national dance, to its culmination in stylised classical form of a ballet show, like that of *Stone Flower*. By the way, the originator of this style was George Balanchine in the USA in the 1930s. I envisage a book in seven chapters, about 500 pages in total. I would supply my own illustrations (line and colour). The composition: contemplations and conclusions reached after fifty years' practice."

"Excuse me, Maestro, for this personal question: are you a member of the Communist Party? Do you have state awards and titles?"

"No. It would seem that I have always been on the list of disloyal citizens. Larissa also brought the ideological side of this project to my attention. I did try to join the party, but was told I'd been too long about it."

"Judging by what you have told me, your most vulnerable spot is the earliest historical period. It will be quite easy for your ideological opponents to accuse you of theological propaganda, even if you describe ritual dances in a most objective scientific way. I ran into this problem in historical courses at the University of Odessa, where a professor did not even mention the ritualistic mime in liturgies in his lectures on the origins of theatre. In response to my question 'Why?' he coldly replied: 'Because it is not in our programme. Religion is not popular in the Soviet Union.'"

"So, Larissa is right. I should forget about this idea, once and for all."

"Excuse me, Kasyan Yaroslavovich, but I cannot agree with you. Your brilliant idea to highlight the poetry of Russian choreography should not be dismissed. If you would like to know the objective opinion of a specialist from the new generation of ballet masters, then write your book, by all means, just like your colleague and my teacher Tarasov have done. These books will serve a great purpose even if they reach their readership only when their authors are no longer around to witness it. Nonetheless, your creative spirit will continue to serve as an example of professional integrity that did not bend under the pressure and will continue to inspire generations of younger choreographers."

"Dear Misha!" exclaimed Larissa. "What a sweet talker you are! Kasyan, did you know that Milia is writing a dissertation on the subject of 'Authorial Rights of Choreographers in the Sphere of Stage Arts'. Now you have a personal attorney against your plagiarists."

Milia dropped into a curtsey with a smile. "Please excuse us, but we have to go now. Thank you for the tea. It's been a great pleasure to meet you. As a lawyer, I am at your service. Misha, get your child out of here!"

"What did I tell you? Not a woman, but a Cossack in a skirt."
Everyone chuckled.

The ambassador Krishna Menon invited my wife and me to an official pre-New Year dinner in honour of cultural representatives in Moscow. It was a pleasant surprise for us to see our rector, Matvei Gorbunov, among the guests. Also attending were many other important figures from Moscow's cultural life: Obraztsov (Theatre of Marionettes), Chirtkov (Youth Theatre), Khrennikov (Composers' Union), Moiseyev (Ensemble of Dance), Golovkina (Bolshoi School), and of course the Deputy Minister of Culture, Kuznetsov, with his head of Theatre Department, Vartanyan. The Indian side was represented by the cultural attaché and chairman of the Society for Indian–Soviet Friendship and Cooperation. Mr Menon opened our gathering by introducing the guests and then wished us all happy New Year. He also thanked the rector of MTA for their interest in Indian folklore, as it concerned an adaptation for theatre of the legend of Nal and Damajanti from the Mahabharata. The selection of guests seemed to have been tailored specifically for the promotion and advancement of my diploma project, in which the hostess of the evening acted as a consultant. Now and again, during conversation over dinner, she mentioned my studies with the professor from Calcutta, and dropped hints about future plans to train with touring dancers from India and about lending costumes from her wardrobe for the performance of ballet excerpts at the embassy and at the Bolshoi School. Milia and myself were the youngest there and conducted ourselves with extreme modesty.

During the winter examination period, Milia agreed to attend a holiday performance of the Labour Reserves' ensemble with me. This was meant to give both of us a short break from the stress of exams. My composition 'Youths' Suite' was the closing number of the show. Ludmilla Tikhonova had refined it, so it was now at a proper professional level of technique and artistic quality. The kids worked very hard to do their best in the presence of the choreographer and their success was uncontested.

That month I would once again play Grandfather Frost in matinees for the Central Music School, MGU, and MTA. The Snow Maiden (Valeria) and I had developed a winning routine together over the previous two years and could now perform it with unfailing success. We also both appreciated an opportunity to earn some extra cash.

After the exams, Milia and I were hoping to make a trip to Odessa, in order finally to introduce my better half and a quarter to the people at home. This was not to be, however. The director of the Infant Care Centre warned us that if we took our son out for a week, she would not be able to take him back due to medical quarantine. Because of this complication, we decided to go, just the two of us, to Leningrad instead of Odessa. After a year of learning how to be a family, and after the hard term full of work and studies, we were indeed exhausted and needed good rest. Just before the departure, we swung by the Central Department Store (TsUM) to shop for new clothes for ourselves and to buy gifts for my cousin and her family.

As was her wont, Sofia greeted us with an effusive tirade. "Aha, so I finally get to meet our Odessan ugly duck's beautiful wife."
"Why duck?" I feigned offence.
Hearing our noisy conversation, the rest of the family, who had been

decorating the Christmas tree in the living room, poured into the hallway. After introductions, we were finally given a chance to shower and change after the journey.

As had been the case in previous years, my precocious nephew ran up to me demanding, "Uncle Misha, where is my gift?"

"Under the tree."

"Ah, all right then."

My cousin immediately besieged poor Milia with hundreds of questions, worried that she would not have the time to ask her about everything before their departure for a winter resort on the Gulf of Finland – we would be gone by the time they returned. The head of the household, Boris, had procured an accordion somewhere, and in the evening the whole extended family arrived for the festivities. We saw the old year out with a bang and joyously welcomed in the new one, partying until 2 a.m.

Sofia woke us up in the morning to say goodbye before their departure: "Muscovites, here are the keys to the flat and the telephone number of our resort. Enjoy your holidays!"

"Mishanya, I cannot believe we are going to have this huge flat to ourselves for a whole week! It's got all the amenities, and the location is perfect, right next to the Opera Theatre!"

"I can hardly believe this luck myself. By the way, dear wife, if my memory is not cheating me, we never had a honeymoon. What would you say to having a honey-week now?"

Milia embraced me passionately and kissed me like she used to in the 'good old days'. Right away, I felt a deep sense of relief from a build-up of tension. We set about arranging a programme of tourist activities. First of all, we headed to the Kirov Opera and Ballet Theatre, where I proudly displayed to an administrator my pass for the Bolshoi. He meticulously checked the details and compared the photo with the original.

"I am sorry, comrade, my nose came out much longer than it is in real life."

"I am afraid, the opposite is true," returned the bureaucrat and, smiling, offered us two reserved seats for the ballet *Spartacus* by Leonid Yakobson, with music by Aram Khachaturian. Like my previous visits, there were no tickets of any kind for the Kirov available through the box office which is why I had never before had a chance to see this ballet that had achieved such fame. At the Maly Opera Theatre we were also able to get student tickets for Bizet's *Carmen*. Having secured the theatrical part of our programme, we could turn to the gourmet delights of a famous eatery on the Nevsky Prospekt. A cup of hot chicken broth accompanied by two pasties (with chopped liver and with cabbage) was traditional student fare. It was so delicious that we nearly swallowed our fingers along with the food. Our honey-week had begun. Over the meal, we made plans for each day of the holiday week. We also counted our savings three times over, but for some reason found no hidden reserves. All I could do was to make a resolution not to buy any books this time.

The first item on the programme was a visit to the Hermitage. Milia was in a state of hypnotic stupor for four hours. Slowly we moved from one room to the next. Original paintings, known to us until now only through illustrations, sailed before our bewildered eyes in a kind of an endless procession, leaving deep impressions. Greek and Roman sculptures particularly engaged my imagination, as I considered the potential of interpreting their sense of movement in choreography. I caved in and bought a photographic catalogue of that part of the exhibit. We didn't leave until the museum closed. My wife was emotionally and physically spent after the Hermitage:

"Mishenka, can we go sit down somewhere and watch some funny light operetta?"

I answered her with a sardonic smile, but resolved to try my luck one more time: 'If the Almighty is on vacation, perhaps the Devil can be of assistance.' We headed towards the theatre of musical comedy. Kalman's *Silva* was starting in thirty minutes on New Year's Day. I assumed an important air and knocked on the administrator's door. There was no answer, yet I could hear somebody's voice. I decided that desperate measures were required.

"Happy New Year! Please accept the warmest wishes of happiness from your Moscow colleagues!"

A woman in a black suit smiled sweetly: "You're wasting your ingenuity: there are no tickets."

"I am sorry, madam, but we are not after tickets."

"Really? Then what are you doing here?"

"Oh, you are from Odessa," I declared, handing her my pass for the Bolshoi.

"Interesting. How did you know?"

" 'It takes one to know one.' We would be most satisfied with two added side seats in the stalls. Today is the first day of our honeymoon."

She chuckled, amused by my cheek. She looked over a list of reservations.

"You must have been born with a silver spoon in your mouth! There are, in fact, two no-shows, so congratulations on your marriage. Here is a wedding gift for you from a fellow Odessan. Good luck!"

I was holding two 'special reservation' tickets in my hands and couldn't believe my eyes. Shaking off the shock of my own success, I blew a kiss to our kind fairy.

After the brilliant show, on the way home, Milia remarked, "Misha, you must be a magician of sorts. She was totally bewitched by you."

"Who, Silva?" I feigned innocence.

"You know who. The administrator. If I hadn't been standing right next to you, she would've given you not only the tickets, but herself in addition."

"Well, well, that's the first time I've heard you to be so jealous. Please continue, I beg you."

My wife threw her arms around me: "Thank you, my dear, for the first honey-day."

The rest of our holiday week was filled to overflowing with museums, theatres, excursions, and other entertainments. On top of that, we were fired up, stimulated by a return to intense physical intimacy.

For me personally, the emotional highlight of our marathon was *Spartacus*, which had by then been running for three seasons with overwhelming success. Its tremendous impact consisted in changing the visual perception of choreographic action onstage by abolishing the use of the stiff ballet slippers, *pointes*, in favour of *demi-pointes* technique. For me, as for many others, this approach was like a clap of thunder in a blue sky. By deliberately rejecting *pointes*, Yakobson proved to the whole world that there was another form of ballet that had a right to contemporary existence, a form that relied upon the dramatisation of the vivid expression of the body's natural motions instead of conventional arabesques and mime gestures. My feeble brain could not cope with the idea that a theatre such as the Mariinsky, one of the cradles of Russian Classical ballet, could allow such a profanation of the century-old tradition of a conservative art. That could mean only one thing: that in terms of Soviet cultural progress, the city of Lenin was miles ahead of Moscow, in fact it was ahead by a whole historical epoch. Since the early twentieth century, 'dancing sandals' had been outlawed by the Bolsheviks as a bourgeois fetish. One can better understand why the choreographer and composer of *Spartacus* had to wait a very long time for permission to present this controversial ballet to the public. This also explained why the Bolshoi was ignoring Yakobson.

The week flashed past like lightning. We'd accumulated enough cultural impressions to last us a whole year. I was wondering what the New Year would hold in store for our fragile family life and upcoming creative endeavours. I was suspicious of how smoothly the last year had ended. Was it a good sign? I wasn't used to a peaceful life and was wary of possible new developments in the future. On the way back to Moscow, I was haunted by the images of Yakobson's ballet: the vivid choreographic motion of each mise en scène.

"Misha, are you still thinking of *Spartacus*? Try to get some sleep. We have a lot to do tomorrow."

"I cannot fathom why the Bolshoi is not inviting Yakobson to stage his ballet there. After all, it's about slaves fighting and dying for their freedom. Perfectly in tune with Marxist–Leninist Aesthetics."

"Because Lavrovsky is like a dog in a manger: he doesn't eat hay, but won't let others eat it either."

"No, I suspect there's another reason. His style is more intelligible and appealing to a broad spectrum of audience than the classical style. It may therefore turn out to be a more effective form of ideological propaganda for Proletarian culture and could eventually displace Classical ballet altogether."

Upon arrival in Moscow, we immediately dropped off our bags at the halls of residence and ran to see our little son. He was in great form and received a nice new outfit from his vagabond parents in honour of his imminent six-month birthday to be celebrated the following Sunday.

The head paediatrician reported, "He eats for two and poops for three, so we have no problems with him at all."

We spent the rest of the day hastily preparing for the beginning of a new term at MTA. For ballet master students, the sixth semester was the last in terms of academic subjects. Practical courses in Historical and Character dance, as well as piano were to come to an end. In the previous term, in response to my official request and thanks to the Dean's support, I was assigned to an English teacher once a week for two semesters as a matter of exception, because of the need to communicate and use research materials in English. In dance composition, the focus of my attention at the time was the structuring of a libretto's dramatic composition and of a ballet's musical-choreographic scenario. In addition to the MTA curriculum, I had four additional foci of professional engagement at the time:

1) Training in Indian classical and folk dances with the touring dance groups and soloists from India.
2) Choreography for the May concert in the Labour Reserves' ensemble.
3) Learning English.
4) Second half of the programme of miniatures for the Bolshoi School of Ballet.

Altogether, my daily programmes were loaded to the limit.

In my personal preference for smaller forms of Ballet, I particularly found myself drawn to two models: Goleizovsky and Yakobson. I continued my occasional practice of dropping into Kasyan's choreographic rehearsals with the graduating students of the Bolshoi School, and studied his improvisational/ emotional style, trying to work out the source of the master's powerful spiritual influence upon the performers. I was not successful in my efforts. Walking the exhausted choreographer home, I asked about his former creative activities.

In the course on the History of Soviet Ballet, Professor Elyazh more or less ignored the contributions of Goleizovsky and Yakobson, branding them rebels against the centuries-old venerable tradition of Classical dance, and barely mentioning their contemporary ballets without even basic critical analysis. As far as I was able to find out, in 1923 Kasyan had organised a Chamber Ballet Theatre in Moscow, where in 1925 he staged his original ballets *Teolinda* and *Joseph the Beautiful* (on a biblical subject). Two years later he also staged *The Whirlwind* in symbolic/abstract form. For ideological reasons, his ballets were prohibited and his Chamber Ballet Theatre dissolved. Only in 1947, in exile, after twenty years of interruption, he staged his new ballet *Du-Gul* (Two Roses) at the Tadzhikistan Opera. Another ten years passed, and in 1957, Goleizovsky was finally rehabilitated and allowed to stage the ballet *Scriabiniana* at the Bolshoi. The ballet consisted of choreographic miniatures to Scriabin's music. They became instantly famous. In 1962, Goleizovsky would stage his final full-scale ballet *Leili and Medzhnun*, also at the Bolshoi. In the world of theatre, especially abroad, his name as a choreographer was widely known. European ballet companies invited him constantly, but the Soviet authorities just as consistently refused him an exit visa. There is no doubt that the cultural world lost a great opportunity for enrichment as a result of this ideological stand-off, both in terms of Ballet repertoire and in the development of Stage dance.

The artistic fate of Leonid Yakobson was in many ways similar to that of Goleizovsky. In 1930, because of his nihilistic attitude towards Classical dance, the young choreographer was flayed by conservative critics, fierce patriots of the old school of ballet, for his avant-garde staging of the second act of the ballet *Golden Age* to Dmitri Shostakovich's music. After that, Yakobson was barred from the Mariinsky Theatre. Three years later, however, the talented ballet master proved his innovative vision with a futuristic ballet *Till Eulenspiegel* at the Leningrad School of Ballet. In spite of such future stars as Natalya Dudinskaya, Olga Lepeshinskaya, Inna Zubkovskaya, Konstantin Sergeyev, Vakhtang Chabukiani, performing his early popular/athletic miniatures, his professional isolation lasted for twenty-two years, similar to Kasyan's exile from Moscow. Leonid's activity was reduced to staging small concert numbers and miniatures. In 1936, he created *Pictures at an Exhibition* to Mussorgsky's music at the Sverdlov Theatre. In newspapers, he was branded a 'choreographic pirate'. In 1944, Yakobsonstaged one-act ballets *Spanish Capriccio* and *Romeo and Juliet* at the Vaganova school. In the West in the 1940s and 1950s, contemporary ballet was already in full bloom with Martha Graham in the USA and Marie Rambert in Britain. In Leningrad, however, a new innovative production by Yakobson, *Shurale*, to music by Yarulin, was released only in 1952, but was then staged practically in every opera and ballet theatre of the Soviet Union. The stubborn choreographer remained true to his credo, continuing to combine classical forms with naturalistic movements. In 1953, he staged *Solveig* at the Maly Opera Theatre. Finally, in 1956, Yakobson came out with *Spartacus* to music by Khachaturian. Once again, his ballet signalled a revolutionary turn, and once again was met with critics' disapproval and insults to his talent. A six-year-long isolation from theatre followed the triumph of *Spartacus*, during which Yakobson created similarly unforgettable images in his choreographic miniatures of 1959. The last output of this irrepressible creative genius came in the 1960s: *Bedbug* based on Vladimir Mayakovsky's poem, and *Twelve* based on Aleksander Blok's poem. Each evoked a wave of further rage on the part of critics.

One day, at the end of the term, I was invited to come and see Shatin. He excitedly announced, "Misha, it looks like we have found a composer for your diploma project. Lena has his details. His name is Nikolai Osokin."

"Thanks! This is good news."

Shatin's secretary dialled the number and handed me the receiver. I introduced myself to the composer and agreed to meet him at MTA the next day. Osokin was a professor at the Gnesin Musical Institute. At out first meeting we briefly introduced ourselves and outlined our spheres of interest. The sixty-year-old composer presented me with a hefty list of his compositions (symphonies, piano concertos, preludes, etc.). I could only show him a rather brief list of my choreographic miniatures, with a reference to the music's composers for each. I also explained to him the idea for my diploma project and gave him a copy of Zhukovsky's poem. In addition I left with him until our next meeting a photo album on Indian Classical dance that I had borrowed from the embassy and a library copy of the Mahabharata. I asked if he could look through the material quickly and let me know if he saw potential for collaboration.

"If, in principle, the Indian theme and the specific subject for a libretto captured your imagination, I would be able to present you with a full choreographic scenario for a ballet in three acts, requiring about an hour and a half of music. The first duet and group scenes would need to be shown at the Bolshoi School and the embassy in the next (seventh) semester, that is, before the New Year. If the music and the choreography should prove successful, there is a plan to stage the ballet in an opera theatre in one of our Central Asian republics. How do you feel about this proposal?"

"I'll be able to tell you in a week's time. Come to my place at 7 p.m. Here's the address."

Osokin's flat in the House of Composers had a spacious studio, with a fortepiano, and was well equipped for composition and recording of audio scores. His wife, the director of the Central Music School had known me in my role of Grandfather Frost in her New Year shows for kids, and now greeted me as an old friend. I was at first embarrassed to be revealed in such a lowly capacity to my potential collaborator, but it soon became clear that it was exactly due to this connection that I now found myself in their home. Shatin had a close professional relationship with Maria Osokin, asking her to recommend pianists/accompanists, and providing choreographers or tutors for her school's events in return. Following Shatin's request this time, Maria Osokin persuaded her husband to consider the possibility of collaborating on the new ballet. Nikolai Vasilyevich taught composition at the Gnesin Musical Institute and was a master in the theoretical analysis of music, in teaching methods and musical instrumentalisation.

"Mikhail, I've carefully studied the materials you provided, and am ready to try my abilities in this genre. I have not previously worked for the theatre, but have always been drawn to the magic of stage productions. I have a few questions, however, about the technical side of our collaboration."

We spent quite a long time honing the practical details and were in the end satisfied with my musical and choreographic score. Over the summer, Osokin promised to prepare two solo variations (Damajanti and Nal), their lyrical duet;

temple dance for girls and mystic dance for demons (men). We made a plan to meet again at his place, at the end of August.

Both Milia and I did well in the spring examinations. In addition, according to my personal tutor's unofficial assessment, I had also made significant progress in English. I was now reading the Indian manuals on onstage art a bit faster and could converse on a basic level with the touring dancers who came to the embassy. Milia, meanwhile, had completed the curriculum of the first and second years at the Art History Department of MTA, and moved on to the second half of her dissertation project in the graduate course at MGU. Her rapid progress with the latter meant that she had a possibility of finishing her curriculum there in two years instead of three. If so, she would be trying to finish her studies at two universities at the same time and that, in turn, would, in a year's time, allow her to dedicate her full attention to completing her project on author's rights. She had indisputable talent as a student and showed every promise of becoming a serious researcher.

In early July we checked our son out of the Infant Care Centre and finally departed for Odessa. Three days of travel in a private compartment proved comfortable. The only challenge was to look after our toddler who was already confident on his feet and went on explorative expeditions up and down the train carriage, putting himself in constant danger of falling off the step on to the platform or getting stuck in the links between coaches. Because of the summer heat, and in the absence of air conditioning, all the doors between the coaches were open for ventilation. Our boy was bouncing with energy and eager to communicate. He patted seated men on the thighs and hid from us under women's skirts. All in all, he was the centre of attention. By then, he knew three words: mama, papa, and *dai* (give). In Odessa, we were met on the platform by a crowd of relations, including my cousin Sofia from Leningrad who had come down for a holiday. Her husband Boris drove us home in his car. Neighbours greeted me in typically Odessan manner as one of their own, even after a two-year-long absence. Baba Sasha couldn't contain her tears when she saw my son, and surreptitiously made the sign of the cross over him, glancing at my wife with apprehension. Remembering that Milia was Russian, she sighed with relief. I had made sure that our arrival fell on a Saturday, so that my relations could stay with us till late to celebrate the family reunion. Danny came with an accordion, and for hours our house was filled with the music and half-forgotten tunes of our youth. On Sunday, a steady stream of visitors, relatives and friends, continued unabated.

After dinner in the evening, I picked up two bottles of vodka and a three-litre bottle of Baba Sasha's wine, and went with Milia, Dmitri, and Danny to our neighbours, the Gypsy house at No. 24, to visit my old friends. The howl of greeting was so loud that all the neighbours around appeared in their windows to determine the cause of the commotion. The ancient matriarch of ninety-three was still alive, but had completely lost her hearing. She recognised me and was happy to see me. She welcomed both the wine and my son, giving him a blessing. Danny launched into 'Dark Eyes', and we once again immersed ourselves in a storm of music and tears of reminiscence. The women surrounded Dmitri and his mother, and declared that the little one was a typical Romanian Gypsy. Indeed, he was black-haired, dark-skinned, smiley and fearless. Upon hearing that my mother was originally from Bessarabia (Moldova) they unanimously proclaimed that my Moldovan grandmother must have had a Gypsy lover, from whom my son had inherited his looks.

After some drinking, a guitar and a tambourine appeared, and everyone took to the floor. Seeing how Milia and myself were flaunting our Gypsy dance style, our friends made a circle giving us space and cheered us on with clapping and shouts. Our son, who was sitting on the old matriarch's lap and clapping along, finally fell asleep exhausted. She raised a hand with a kerchief over her head and everybody fell silent. She said something to her family in Gypsy dialect and then handed the baby to Milia. They saw us off all the way to the gate.

We spent a happy week at Bugaz, holidaying on the Karolina promontory. I whiled my time away fishing, and Milia then fried the mackerel for our dinner. In between we took turns looking after our little rascal. Dmitri caught the sun. He spent his days playing with live crabs, chasing lizards, building sandcastles and swimming on an inflatable ring, tied with a string to a moored boat. Milia was intent on leaving by 1st August, in order to make it to Slavyansk by 4th August, her birthday, which she wanted to celebrate with her family. To my regret, in the light of what happened last year, I did not consider it right to spoil her celebration with my presence. So we decided that I would accompany them to Dnepropetrovsk and put them on a train to Slavyansk there. I would then return to Moscow and prepare for the next term. I had in mind to do some work on the ballet score with the composer Osokin, and to develop a staging plan of selected excerpts to be choreographed in the course of the coming year. I also needed to prepare a programme of European dances to study with the professor from Calcutta.

At the end of August, I was back at the railway station, waiting for the arrival of my family from Slavyansk. I hastened to the railway coach indicated in a telegram. The porter had already unloaded the baggage on to the platform. My little son shouted in excitement: "Papa, Papa!" Milia, however, only coolly touched my cheek and with an insincere smile headed straight for the exit. I picked up a lead-heavy backpack, a suitcase and another bag, and on buckling legs, staggered behind. In the taxi, we sat in silence for a long time.

As a matter of politeness, I asked, "How was your journey?"

"Perhaps you would instead like to tell me what you've been doing here alone for a whole month?"

The driver turned around with a grin, thinking that madam was joking, but seeing his mistake, he apologised and quickly returned to his driving. I ignored the question, playing with Dmitri. It was clear to me that my wife's relations had set her against me again. It was to be expected.

"Let's not have this personal talk in a taxi," I reasoned.

At the halls of residence, the security guard was surprised to see a baby with us. I had to explain, "Tomorrow morning, we are going to check him in at a twenty-four hour nursery, for six days a week. Warden Shura knows about this."

We kept Dmitri's old baby carriage in the hallway. It was a bit small for him now, and I would've thrown it out, but he had to sleep somewhere on Sundays when he was with us. *I'll have to figure something out,* I made a mental note, dragging their luggage inside.

Milia stopped by the window, next to a night stand with a bouquet of flowers.

"In honour of your arrival, madam."

"I am not interested in flowers. I am waiting for an answer to my question."

"Tomorrow or the day after, when Dmitri is at the nursery, we'll have a talk, if you like, but now, would you please not make a scene and start doing something around the house? I'll get out of your way now and come back later this evening. There is food on the window sill and in the cupboard, and money in the drawer. You know the rest and can figure it out without me."

"No, wait, don't go."

"Sorry, my dear! I have waited for you for a month and this is your welcome. Please forgive an excessive show of sentimentality on the part of a husband." I grabbed the flowers and chucked them into a bin.

Pricked, my wife yelled, "May I ask where you are going?"

"To see my girlfriends! Where else?"

Behind the door I could hear Milia screaming something to my back, but I was already down the staircase, and trying to switch to another mood.

I went to MTA to find out the timetable of classes for this semester. Lenochka, just as last year, informed me that the Dean was waiting to speak to me. I saluted like a young pioneer 'Always ready!' and heard a familiar voice from behind the door:

"How was your holiday? Is the Black Sea blue yet?"

"Thanks. During the two years of my absence, both Odessa and the sea stayed the same. The natives reckon that I haven't changed, only I have become too much of a Muscovite for their taste."

"Come on in and take a seat. As you can see in the timetable, there are no longer group studies in dance composition. Instead every student will have thirty-minute consultations with me on a weekly basis, regarding their diploma projects. Some extracts from the final production need to be shown during the winter examination session, and the whole thing at the spring exam. Performers can be drawn either from the acting ballet troupes or from the graduating class of the Bolshoi School. What are your other professional commitments for this year? If I am not mistaken, last year you were choreographing for the Labour Reserves' ensemble, with our consent?"

"My contract with them ended in May. Golovkina, however, is expecting six miniature compositions this year, to the music of Russian composers. And except for the Indian contacts, there is nothing else."

"You see, Misha, the Central School of Athletics (CSA) has approached us with an official request to recommend them a choreographer who could help with creating the Olympic programmes for artistic gymnastics and figure skating. Are you familiar with these areas?"

"A little, but I can also learn quickly, if necessary."

"In that case, if you are interested in this sports project, we will recommend you, on condition that it takes no more than two afternoons of your time a week. It could be good practice for you in an unusual genre, as well as some financial help to your family. By the way, I hope that Milia and your son also had a good summer."

"Anatoly Vasilyevich, thanks for your confidence in me. You won't regret this recommendation."

"I have no doubt. Lena, please get in touch with the Central School of Athletics and let them know that we give consent to Mikhail's temporary collaboration with them, on the standard conditions that apply to all graduating university students. Good luck, Misha!"

I answered my mentor with an Indian gesture of thanks. Lena typed up my recommendation and telephoned the director of the CSA.

"They expect you today, after 3p.m."

I thanked Lena and hurried to MTA library. They quickly supplied me with the required literature on artistic gymnastics and figure skating. I leafed through several books, noting down specific terminology from both disciplines and a list of their accessories: hoop, jumping rope, ribbon, scarf, ball, club and torch. At least, equipped with this minimal knowledge, I would look somewhat competent.

When I met the director of the CSA, she confessed that she had just got off the telephone with Shatin who had given me a very positive recommendation. She expressed a wish to sign a contract with me immediately, for ten months, from 1st September till 30th June. They would pay me on the highest pay band, three roubles an hour, that is, thirty-six roubles a week. In those days, this sum was equal to the average salary of a blue-collar worker, or the monthly stipend of a graduate student. I didn't hesitate for a single moment and promised to bring the necessary documents and a photo for the completion of paperwork to my first lesson.

"Let us go and meet the athletes and their coaches."

Veronika Grigoriyevna, the Director, led me to the athletic gymnastics hall first and introduced me to the coach. She noted down the schedule for their floor work and beam exercises. Then we went to the section of artistic gymnastics trained by a female coach. Here, in bins on the floor, we saw balls and clubs as well as ribbons and jumping ropes hanging on hooks in the wall. I asked the Director's permission to come to work an hour ahead of time to practise working with the accessories. She promised to prepare a pass for me at once. Finally we went to an indoor stadium with an artificial ice-skating rink. It was used for practice by hockey players and figure skaters. I expressed an interest in coming there daily for the rest of the week to observe the technique and character of figure skating, in order to draw a comparison in my mind with dance techniques on the ground. After obtaining my temporary pass for the CSA, I hastened back home.

Passing by the halls of residence on Trifonovka, completely absorbed in thoughts of my new job, I did not immediately recognise my wife and son walking along the path.

Carefully walking around them, I was intent on continuing on my way, when I heard from behind: "Excuse me, mister, would you be Mikhail Semyonovich Berkut by any chance?" *Blind toad!* I thought to myself, but salvaged the situation on the spot. "Sorry, I do not make street acquaintances, but in this case, I accept your invitation."

Dmitri had been playing with a wooden car, oblivious to his surroundings, but hearing my voice, he looked up and stretched his hands out towards me. I picked him up together with the toy and sat down on a nearby bench. Milia sat next to us. Dmitri helped me to fish out a new contract from my bag.

"Dear Emilia Sergeyevna, you might possibly be interested to learn that your, excuse my language, so-called 'husband' has secured a profitable gig for this year, at the Central School of Athletics, to replace his job at the Labour Reserves' ensemble."

Milia carefully read the contract and pronounced: "Dmitri, your father is almost a millionaire. It looks like you might get a new pram."

"I hoped this news would compel the angry cat to reward a poor mouse with a kiss?"

In the morning, getting Dmitri ready for his nursery, I asked Milia as a favour to check out for me at the MGU library some books on figure skating, artistic gymnastics and athletic dancing, so that I could prepare for my new job by 1st September.

"Why didn't you get them at MTA?"

"I asked, but they don't have anything of relevance. Besides a manual for folk dancing, I need university teaching materials on these subjects, even if they are in English or German. Could you please do this for me? We'll go together, but if you could check them out under your name to work in the reading room, I could stay and study there."

"This is a husband exploiting his wife and an example of male chauvinism in the family."

"And what do you call a case of eating, dressing, and holidaying paid for by a husband?"

My wife stared at me in dismay. She wanted to argue, but choked and turned red from a wave of anger. Confused Dmitri stared in surprise first at his mother and then at me, trying to understand whether we were joking or having a proper row.

"It's all right, sweetie. Look, there is a horsey pulling a cart over there." But Dmitri turned around to his mother and took her by the hand.

On the first day at the nursery, Dmitri threw a fit, unhappy with unfamiliar surroundings and new carers. He wailed and asked for his mum. I asked Milia not to show her face, but to stay in the cloakroom, in order not to add oil to the flame. The elderly head of the nursery came up to Dmitri with a brightly coloured ball. She bounced it a couple of times in front of him on the floor and Dmitri immediately turned his attention to her. Picking him up and carrying him to the group of other kids, she explained over her shoulder: "This is a well-known trick with the boys. Isn't that so, sonny?" and she gave him the ball. "Your parents have no clue about children. They are busy with their work and have no patience for you."

Milia was sitting in the cloakroom and shedding bitter tears. It had been a long time since I had seen her in such a state. I took a clean hanky from my bag, handed it to her and sat down nearby. I softly put one arm around her, stroking her shoulder with the other.

She clung to me and moaned: "The child needs a real mother, not some substitute nannies. And he needs a proper mother, not a helpless one like me. How do we get out of this vicious cycle? Tell me!"

"Calm yourself, my dear. People are staring. Everything will be all right. You'll see."

I helped her off the bench. Milia went off to the bathroom to wash her face and then we left for the university.

I found several books in English and French on the subjects I wanted in the main reading room of the university library. All the books were by unfamiliar authors. Milia supplied me with dictionaries and promised to return in two hours. I was so deeply absorbed in my reading that I didn't notice how the time passed. I read, translated, made notes and sketches. Sometimes, in my oblivion, I even waved my arms in the air, drawing pitying smiles from the library staff. Milia showed up at the agreed time. We had a bite to eat at a student canteen and returned to the library. We worked together until dark, while Milia researched her dissertation project. She reserved the selected books for our use until the end of the week, promising to be back in the library at 10 a.m. daily. We left the library with a sense of satisfaction from knowledge acquired and a sense of certainty about the well-being of our child.

We went for a spot of supper and then to the Metropol cinema to see a new movie. The day that had started with stormy clouds on the horizon ended with dearly awaited intimacy.

At the end of the first week of term, Shatin informed me, during our first consultation, that Osokin had called Lena to ask me to visit him today at 7 p.m. "Apparently, he has prepared something for you over the summer."

We discussed the most effective schedule of rehearsals with the ballet dancers from the Bolshoi to work on solos and duet episodes as well as group rehearsals with students from the Bolshoi School. My mentor also recommended a recent art-school graduate, Cyril Andreyev, as a specialist in theatre design for my project.

"Misha, at the pre-diploma exam in June, it would be good to show at least the sketches of costume design and stage design of the key scenes as well."

I reminded Shatin, "Mrs Menon has kindly offered a huge collection of female and a limited assortment of male costumes from her personal wardrobe."

Shatin recommended getting in touch with my 'friends' from Internal Security to ask for permission to take the artist to the embassy to select the costumes.

Nikolai Osokin and his wife gave me a hearty welcome. Maria complained that I had spoiled her summer vacation, because Nikolai spent all his time composing ballet music, and what is more, in several compositional variations.

"I am very sorry, but I didn't ask him for that extra work."

"You don't need to ask him," grinned his wife. "He always composes like that, so that there are alternative possibilities in case of some misunderstanding. Anyway, have a productive session. I am off to do some shopping. Good luck!"

From the maestro's studio I could already hear the sounds of the fortepiano, drawing out exceptionally melodious tunes and drumming dance beats. I felt goosebumps on my skin. Quietly, I stood in the doorway, afraid to stir. I didn't want to break the musician's concentration as he played.

At the end of the piece, I asked, "Excuse me, Professor. What were you playing?"

"This is the girls' dance from act one – four and a half minutes, as indicated in your scenario. Take a seat! I will play for you all five episodes that I promised, in several variations."

That was my first collaboration with a professional composer. It is impossible to put into words the elation I experienced in the half-hour of music that followed.

Once, during a regular visit to one of Goleizovsky's rehearsals at the Bolshoi School, I heard oriental tunes and quietly asked the pianist what it was.

"*Du-Gul*," she whispered.

In Kasyan's Tadzhik ballet (Two Roses), I could clearly hear Arabic intonations, but in the choreography of the duet, which I was observing at that moment, I could not see any elements of Tadzhik dance. The choreographer schematically generalised the sculptural lines of poses, Oriental movements of the head and arms. Such stylised personal calligraphy was sufficient for a ballet stage. Goleizovsky followed this principle of choreography not because he did not know Tadzhik folklore, but because it was his artistic credo. Every human body is a unique performance instrument, capable of expressing, independently of its ethnic origin, universal themes and subjects using performing arts. The effect upon the audience is proportionate to the degree of talent and professionalism of the performer in question.

Walking the master home, after the rehearsal, I asked him: "How is your book going?"

"I am working on the final part. How is your Indian ballet?"

"I am working with the composer Osokin. Do you know him?"

"Only in symphonic music. I've not come across his work in theatre. Still, I wish you the best of luck!"

At the Bolshoi School, I learned a staggering piece of news. The administration of the Bolshoi had invited Igor Moiseyev to stage *Spartacus*. Why was the head of a USSR Stage Folk dance ensemble asked to do this and not the actual choreographer, Yakobson? Was it indeed possible that the competing antagonism between the two leading theatres was so strong that the Bolshoi's directorate was prepared to take such a serious risk, in order to curtail a transfer of the Mariinksy's production to the capital? What was happening behind the scenes at the Ministry of Culture? Everyone only shrugged their shoulders. All my colleagues from the Ballet Masters Department went to see the dress rehearsal of Moiseyev's *Spartacus*. There are successful productions and then there are others, where a viewer, unfamiliar with the avant-garde forms of theatre, is not sure what the message is. This creative experiment by a well-known specialist in folk dance led to him being totally discredited in the sphere of Classical ballet. His production consisted of separate plug-in numbers of pop-art style and group scenes executed in the naturalistic maner of cheap pantomime. Some included chariots with real horses who, unnerved by bright lights and the noise of the orchestra, left picturesque green piles all over the stage, on which both valiant warriors and beautiful hetaerae periodically slid and fell. In Moiseyev's choreography, there was no clear artistic style or genre, logic of dramatic plot, or any theatrical atmosphere. Instead, his ballet was a totally eclectic production. In fact, the whole thing looked like an act of provocation, skilfully engineered by seasoned saboteurs. After the premiere, the ballet was removed from the Bolshoi's repertoire, and the likes of Zakharov and Lavrovsky celebrated Moiseyev's aesthetic destruction.

The negative criticism in the press directed at Moiseyev's failed production of *Spartacus* on the one hand, and various supporters of Yakobson within the world of theatre, on the other hand, finally succeeded, as a result of fierce debate, in persuading the Bolshoi's administration to invite Leonid Yakobson to stage his one-act ballets and choreographic miniatures. Once again, our whole group attended the dress rehearsal of a choreographic *Triptych* produced by the irreverent Ballet Master.

The first act presented a class concert of Character dance, and not in the *traditional academic* form of a ballet school's curriculum, but as an *artistic theatrical* interpretation of the genre in Yakobson's original manner.

The second act was a Contemporary ballet 'Night City', which both in content and choreographic text, was unique in the theatre repertoire of the time. Colourful scenes of American life, in grotesque genre, were strung one after another in a contrasting kaleidoscope of social types from bourgeois society.

The third act, in the assessment of critics and many ballet aficionados, was a masterpiece of world choreography. In an exhibition of Rodin's work, the sculptures of the great master come to life: duets, trios, etc. All different in subject matter and in the number of dancers, but bound by the unique style of Yakobson's choreography. The leading soloists of the Bolshoi, including

Ulanova and Vasilyeff, dressed in marble-coloured tights and leotards, presented to the enchanted audience, through the language of choreography, a hitherto unknown world of poetic beauty, spiritual and romantic love, and the physical happiness of intimacy. In the art of Socialist realism, such erotic 'profanation' of established norms could not be forgiven. The production's run was soon terminated, but not indefinitely.

My work at the Central School of Athletics (CSA) turned out to be much easier and more comfortable than I had expected. At our first meeting, the Director explained my responsibilities as a teacher/choreographer in exhaustive detail. Every two-hour-long class with younger and older girls (twelve to fifteen years old) in artistic gymnastics should start with a thirty-minute warm-up at the barre, just like at ballet school, but with a heavier load on the arms and emphasis on the elasticity of the torso. The next thirty minutes were to be spent in the centre: polishing the known and learning new technical elements of Classical dance. The remaining hour was dedicated to practice with accessories and to the mastering of new sequences of dance elements for feet and hands, using ribbons and scarves.

During the second lesson of the week, the head coach usually joined us after the warm-up and selected from my dance vocabulary those elements and figures that corresponded best to the standards of Artistic gymnastics. She tactfully pointed out to me which kinds of moves were particularly promising in creating a visual effect that could impress the jury. The selection, of course, had to take into account the limitations imposed by the programme and the need for maximum technical precision in execution. The routine was more or less the same with the older group of gymnasts, only their level of practice was more advanced. The gymnasts were supposed to perform in several groups, each group using a different accessory (duets with hoops, trios with balls or scarves, etc.). Typically, all members of one group would perform the same synchronised choreography. It was impressive, but also predictable.

I decided to offer an idea to make the senior gymnasts' presentation more interesting, varying the sequence of elements required for each individual within their respective group, but in polyphonic harmony with each other and concluding with a united coda. The coach liked the potential that this idea held for giving them an edge in competition with other schools, and she convinced the Director to allocate one more hour of training for me with the older group, with corresponding remuneration for this extra work.

In my work with figure skaters, I felt almost 'totally at home'. The age groups were the same as those of the gymnasts. I worked once a week with the girls, and once with the boys. Their first half-hour was also a warm-up. The following hour was dedicated to learning new elements in the Classical and Character dances, and the final half-hour to the choreography of specific sequences on the basis of the learned material. The absence of accessories freed up my imagination to choreograph short, finished variations. Sometimes I brought my own sheet music and at other times I used the pianist's collection. My vocabulary of dance elements, derived from various genres and styles, had expanded so greatly over the previous few years, that I had no difficulty whatsoever in selecting the most suitable elements to match the music, for static or gliding movements on the ice. Thanks to my innate adaptability to new study and working conditions, I quickly acquired a taste for choreography on ice and at every training session provided the coach with multifaceted combinations of new dance elements from every style and genre. The coach integrated my land-bound choreography into dance routines on ice, relying on her own taste and factoring in the skaters' ability. I was quite content with this partnership. After all, I was acquiring invaluable skills for working in the field of athletics, and financially I was well rewarded for my efforts. For those reasons, I sometimes stayed behind with the stronger pairs and tutored them, free of charge, in the basics of pair dancing. I would demonstrate the technique of supporting on the gym floor, and the coach would then transfer those principles to the ice.

After the May competition, the Director presented me with an official certificate of appreciation, on behalf of the City Committee of Physical Culture and Sports, for excellent work in training young champions.

In the middle of September I received an invitation from the embassy to visit Mrs Menon on a Saturday morning. At the meeting, she informed me that they had received an invitation from Delhi for me to come to India for a year to study dance at the University of Calcutta with Professor Shapura. The invitation was issued as part of a cultural exchange but also at the personal request of Mrs Menon's husband. I enquired about the arrangements for my wife and child. It turned out they were included in the invitation, but only for a month, sometime in the middle of my tenure there. My ballet consultant assured me that in two to three weeks' time MTA would receive an official letter through the Foreign Office of the Ministry of Culture. To be honest, I did not know what to say. I expressed my gratitude to Mrs Menon. I asked if it would be all right to introduce the ballet's composer at the embassy and to present a few excerpts from the future score. She readily agreed and immediately invited us all for dinner the next Saturday. I passed all this on to the Dean and the 'security agents' and received their approval for a visit to the embassy with colleagues.

Mrs Menon and the Cultural Attaché were waiting for us in the library room. I introduced the composer and his wife, as well as the designer who had brought along a folder of sketches. Cyril was taken to the wardrobe room right away to select clothing samples and accessories for the temple dancers and demons. The costumes for soloists would be sewn by an in-house seamstress, but would only be used in demonstrations of ballet extracts at the embassy and in the winter examinations at the Bolshoi School. While Cyril was absent, Osokin sat at the piano and played his first compositions for the ballet *Nal and Damajanti*. Maria Osokin assisted her husband by turning the pages. I gave Mrs Menon a copy of the libretto in Russian to follow and added a few words of explanation before Osokin played each piece. She listened very attentively, and once in a while asked him either to repeat the whole piece or a part of it. The ambassador's wife was an accomplished sitar player and knew a great deal about European music. After Osokin's demonstration, she offered a brief assessment.

"These are very unusual and interesting compositions, especially for a European ear. I imagine that with an orchestral accompaniment, they will sound even more impressive and colourful. Good luck! And now let us move to the living room where we can continue our meeting."

Andreyev and the Attaché had meanwhile set out the first colour sketches of costumes and stage design on chairs all round the sitting room. The images of dancing demons, dressed in extravagant costumes, were the most visually effective. It is worth noting, however, that Cyril had also very skilfully stylised an Indian sari for the temple dancers' ballet tunics, richly adorned with accessories. The most challenging task for the artist was to find effective renditions for Nal's and Damajanti's stage appearances, in their solo and duet entries. He had deliberately come up with two to three versions for each character, in order to get valuable feedback from a knowledgeable audience, intimately familiar with the mythological subject. Cyril asked those present not to mince their words in expressing their opinion, because any criticism would help him create a more convincing and effective design.

Over dinner, the ambassador listened with great interest to his wife's and the attaché's report of our first steps in composing the ballet score and stage design. At the other end of the table, the Osokins and I were debating with the chairman of the Society for Indian–Soviet Friendship the challenges of an artistic fusion of a centuries-old religious philosophy of Hinduism with modern European culture. The stumbling block was the need to find a successful modern theatrical and choreographic interpretation of a well-known legend while preserving the spiritual essence of the Mahabharata. I was well aware that my task was not easy, which was why I readily agreed to immerse myself in the study of Indian ethnography, history, and philosophy for a year at the University of Calcutta. Mrs Menon raised the last toast of the evening to a successful collaboration of all participants in the project, including the absent ballet artists, and said she was looking forward to the presentation of excerpts from the ballet before the New Year. We didn't throw glasses over our shoulders, but there was a chorus of applause.

One fine morning in early December, at a review of diploma projects, the students of dance composition showed their works in progress, me included. Among the guests were Mr and Mrs Menon, Nikolai and Maria Osokin, as well as Andreyev, Goleizovsky, Golovkina, and Mironov (from the ministry). Shatin himself introduced the guests and asked them to direct their questions to the choreographer and author of the libretto at the end of the performance. The soloists' presentations went without a glitch. I was, however, concerned about group scenes. Unnecessarily so, as it turned out. Following a pep talk, Golovkina's students delivered a brilliant performance and earned a round of applause.

Mr and Mrs Menon thanked Shatin for the invitation and told him how much they had enjoyed the presentation. Saying goodbye to me, the ambassador asked if I had received the invitation to India yet.

I shook my head.

"Just in case, check with the Dean's secretary," he advised.

"I will."

Mrs Menon invited Milia and me for a pre-New Year's dinner at the embassy.

Kasyan shook my hand before leaving: "Well done, Misha! Keep it up!"

After the guests' departure, I was waiting for the head of staff, Zakharov, to launch a scathing attack on me, but he apparently chose not to fight in the open, but to stab me in the back. It would have been unlike him not to. The other teachers had very positive feedback for me. Tseitlin remarked on the original and rich musical score. Tkachenko congratulated me on the brilliant rendition of Character dances. Müller approved Cyril's sketches of costumes and set design. Overall, I was happy with the result and thanked everyone for their help and support for my project.

The day after the exam, I was called to MTA's Human Resources Office. The same familiar security agents were waiting for me there.

They began with a bit of small talk: "How did the exam go?"

"Excellent."

"What did Mrs Menon tell you before their departure?"

"She invited my wife and me to a dinner at the embassy. Next Monday, 6 p.m. It's a traditional event they host at the embassy."

"What did the ambassador talk to you about?"

I relayed to them the contents of my conversation with Mr Menon.

"Do you know Vera Bokadoro from Paris?"

"Yes, she is a first-year student in our Ballet Masters' Department."

"Your pigeonhole is next to hers. Whenever you notice letters in her mailbox, we would like you to copy down the names of her correspondents from the envelopes. Would you be able to do that?"

"I would like to, with all my heart, but it is simply physically impossible for me: I am terribly near-sighted. Besides, from nine till six daily, I am usually at the Bolshoi School, and don't check my pigeonhole on a regular basis. Also, in six months' time, I will be graduating and going to another republic for a year."

"It looks like you are not so keen on helping your country in matters of security."

"My deepest apologies."

"Well, we hope there is no need to remind you about confidentiality."

Afterwards, in the library, I tried hard to concentrate on the figure skaters, but the encounter with the KGB agents had seriously shaken me up. The trouble was that I had no one to consult.

At the Indian Embassy's New Year reception, we met the same familiar faces: the Deputy Minister of Culture, Kuznetsov, the head of the ministry's Theatre Department, Vartanyan, the rector of MTA Gorbunov, Golovkina and others. A festively decorated fir tree stood in the centre of the living room, and a coffee table in front of it was loaded with drinks. After a few, the guests loosened up and congregated around the tree with their glasses, chatting away. The ambassador opened his dinner with a toast for genuine peace and friendship between nations.

In the middle of conversation during dinner, Mr Menon suddenly addressed the Deputy Minister: "Mr Kuznetsov, please excuse me, but do you know anything about an official invitation from the government of India to Mr Berkut for an exchange course at the University of Calcutta? Your Theatre Department must have received it in May. Here is a confirmation of receipt."

At this moment, all conversation around the table ceased. Milia squeezed my knee hard under the table. A wine glass in the Deputy Minister's hand visibly trembled.

He looked at Vartanyan, who, with a straight face, returned, "Yes, we passed that invitation on to the rector of MTA about six months ago."

Honest-hearted Gorbunov raised his bushy eyebrows in surprise. "As far as I know, we have never received such a document."

The revelation was like a bomb. The Soviet bureaucratic system had clearly failed in this case.

Kuznetsov concluded: "Apologies, Mr Ambassador. There must be some mistake here. I will personally look into this and let you know what I find out."

"Thank you, Mr Deputy Minister. By the way, an exchange student from Delhi has already started her course at Moscow University, while Mikhail is still here."

Mrs Menon moved in to deflate the tension: "Ladies and gentlemen, a New Year cake!"

The guests made a show of good humour as they said their goodbyes, pretending that nothing had happened. For me, however, the whole episode clearly signalled the beginning of my downfall, even before I'd had time to soar. Bureaucrats like Vartanyan would never forgive public humiliation of the sort he had experienced today at the table. It was obvious that he had told blatant lies, but the embarrassment he had caused to the Deputy Minister and the Rector would cost him dear, even if he was only following the instructions of higher authorities to ensure a block on my invitation to India. Krishna Menon, however, was apparently determined to see this case through to the end, and that could lead to a cooling of relations between our friendly countries. Naturally, those same authorities would start looking for a scapegoat. And what better candidate could they ask for than me? In fact, my crazy project and I were the real reason for the ministerial blunder in the eyes of the foreign diplomat. To punish the culprit would be a double whammy: it would relieve the leadership of personal responsibility for the scandal and would teach other eager students to keep their heads down.

In this disaster, I was particularly bothered by one question: what had compelled Mr Menon, who had had the benefit of a ten-year tenure as ambassador in Moscow and therefore knew the Soviet system inside out, to put everything on the line in this high-stakes game with the ministry? He had to know that it would not end well. What was he hoping for? That his popularity and influence in international diplomacy would tip the scales? That the new Indian Government would be willing to exert some pressure? I went to see Shatin to get his advice.

He listened to my report with sadness: "Misha, judging by everything that took place at the embassy, it would appear that you and I have suffered a defeat. Apparently, the ambassador learned some time ago that someone had cut the lifeline of support for your diploma project, but it is possible that he had no way of sharing the news with us. Being the professional diplomat that he is, however, he decided to make absolutely clear to you who was behind the obstruction of your plans for a creative future in theatre. You know full well now what bureaucrats like Vartanyan and his ilk are like. It's best to stay away from them!"

I listened to my mentor with dismay, unable to get my head around what had happened and to comprehend the motives behind the blocking of my project.

"You should not commit professional suicide right at the start of your career," Shatin continued.

I just grimaced with bitterness.

"We'll find you different material for the diploma project. The most important thing right now is not to panic. Focus on your work at the Bolshoi School this spring semester and finish the second instalment of those miniatures that Golovkina likes so much. In your situation, it is important not to lose confidence in yourself as a choreographer. Don't discuss the incident with anyone. Accept the fiasco of the Indian project philosophically. As far as your professional investment in the project is concerned, I see no mistakes, either in preparation or production. You may like to consider the incident as a rough start to a productive future career. I often repeat in my lectures to students: an artist's faith in his own abilities is a 50% guarantee of success. I am deeply saddened to witness your loss, but I believe in your talents. Sooner or later, wherever you find yourself, your talents will find expression in one or another genre of choreography."

"Thank you, teacher. Not to worry. I survived the war, I'll survive this as well."

When I went to the embassy to return the costumes and accessories, Mrs Menon softly enquired, "Mikhail, is it true that you yourself had declined the invitation to Calcutta, on account of your family?"

I stared at her, appalled at such shameless misinformation.

"Do you know that last August your invitation was used to send Kunakova, a dancer from the Kyrgyz Opera Theatre, to Calcutta?"

At this, I was simply dumbstruck, and could only shrug my shoulders in response. 'So, that's where the dog is buried', as the Russian saying goes. Now I could understand the ambassador's behaviour at the dinner table. Everything fell into place in an instant. I could see tears on Mrs Menon's face. I took her hand that was holding a handkerchief and kissed it. Then took a step back and bowed with an Indian gesture: hands drawn to the chest. "Madam, thank you for everything. And I am sorry for this fiasco."

As I left the embassy, my friend the policeman on duty at the door, asked, "What's the matter?"

I only waved my hand.

That day was one of the darkest of my whole life. It felt as though a close relative of mine had died. I had not only lost good friends in this ordeal, but my dream of my ballet *Nal and Damajanti* had turned to ash, burned like a moth that had flown too close to a flame.

I was naturally devastated by the debacle of my diploma project, but following the advice of my unbelievably loyal patron, I forced myself to switch my attention to the New Year matinees in which I played Grandfather Frost with the Snow Maiden Valeria, in the same old venues. My mood was as far removed from clowning as you can imagine, but the signed contracts and sense of responsibility prevented me from reneging on my promises to entertain blameless children during the holiday season.

On Saturday and Sunday, Milia brought Dmitri to two of my performances at the Central Music School and MGU. Both times I took him up for a couple of minutes and presented him with a snack. He was a little scared by my white beard and moustache, however, and preferred to dance with his peers around the New Year tree, while trying to hold the Snow Maiden by the hand. He must have inherited his father's sexual genes.

Over the New Year's holiday period, Dmitri spent three days with us in the hall of residence. On 1st January, Milia took him to the circus, and on the 2nd I took him to the zoo. He was beside himself with excitement at both events.

Our son returned to the nursery the next day and his exhausted parents took a train to Sosnovy Bor, on the outskirts of Moscow. There, in a pine forest, lived an old mate of mine from Odessa, Nikolai Golovchenko. Having moved to Moscow, he became an inspector of public transport on the Moscow river. Before my marriage, I used to visit him on all major holidays. Now, after a three-year gap, I decided to restore that lost connection: my frayed nerves required a quiet break, and my mind an escape from heavy thoughts. I turned to physical activities. As in the war, I chopped wood for the fireplace and shovelled snow. Milia ferried provisions from a grocery store on a sled and cooked our meals. We went skiing together in the forest, and before we had time to say 'hop', the winter idyll was over and it was time to return to work.

I was deeply grateful to my wife for never mentioning my Indian trauma once during the holidays. Instead she tried to distract me with gossip from MTA and MGU, with new family plans, and recollections of our trips to Leningrad and Odessa. Out in the fresh air of a pine forest, we rested well and recharged our batteries.

I spent all my free time in January in the sound library at MTA, listening to numerous three-to-five-minute musical pieces which I could use for the choreography of possible miniatures: bagatelles, preludes, romantic ballades, études-tableaux, classical suites of dances, etc. I analysed each piece thoroughly for its suitability for staging, and if I thought it had potential, would proceed to outline a libretto and choreographic scenario. I worked out a cast for each piece, and a plan of stage rehearsals. I now had something to take to Golovkina.

The Director read through the programme with visible interest, nodding in approval now and then, raising her eyebrows or smiling. My programme included four piano pieces by Shostakovich, and two études for children by Mussorgsky:

1) 'Ugly Duckling': solo for a boy, fifth grade (Scherzo – Shostakovich).
2) 'Pierrot and Harlequin': duet for boys, fifth grade (Polka – Shostakovich).
3) 'Three Piglets': trio of girls, fourth grade (Waltz – Shostakovich).
4) 'Forest Ball': sextet (3 pairs), fourth grade (Gavotte – Shostakovich).
5) 'Ballet of Unhatched Chicks': girls, third grade (Mussorgsky, arr. Ravel).
6) 'Little Cossack Children': boys, fourth grade (Gopak – Mussorgsky).

Sofia Nikolayevna was fascinated by the proposed programme:
"Misha, how many choreographic rehearsals would you need to complete this programme by 1st May? After that, our tutors can continue rehearsing your repertoire on their own."
"Three times a week, two academic hours each, 2 to 7 p.m., with two fifteen-minute breaks. Provided that we start on 16th January and that students do not miss any rehearsals."
The wretched end of my Indian project struck a blow not only to my professional prestige, but also affected the composer who had spent so much time and effort composing the music. I had failed him, and Osokin would probably never get involved in theatre again. As far as the artist Andreyev was concerned, I could at least compensate him with a new commission to design costumes for my twelve miniatures at the Bolshoi School. He was happy to take on this project and produced some very nice designs. Golovkina approved his original sketches and sent them off to production in the Bolshoi's wardrobe department.

Shatin, for his part, took the whole Indian saga to heart. He could not even properly explain to Maria, Osokin's wife, why the work on my project had been stopped. The heads of MTA whispered about the matter in corridors, never bringing it up in public discussion. The Dean became ill from worry. Lena said that he had heart problems and would return to work in a week's time. Milia promised to find out, using her own channels, what had happened in relations between India and the USSR in recent months. She visited the House of Friendship, where her acquaintance, the head of the Society for Indian Friendship and Cooperation told her in secret: "Due to a recent change in government in India, our relations with that country have cooled for the time being. This can't be for long, however, and only affects the spheres of culture and economics."

Naturally, Shatin's opponents were not asleep. How could Zakharov pass up a chance to accuse the Dean of political myopia? Milia learned about this from her friends at the Art History Department. A cold war between the supporters of Shatin and Zakharov at MTA flared up with renewed vigour. The students of both divisions (the ballet masters and ballet teachers) felt the fallout. Zakharov's first-year students did not speak to Shatin's graduates. It was easy to imagine what their leader told them about us. It might be hard to believe, but this is how it really was.

When Shatin returned to work, he had a piece of good news for me. The Deputy Minister of Culture in Tadzhikistan, Nazarov, and the artistic director of their Opera/Ballet Theatre Valamat-Zade were inviting me to work as chief ballet master for the upcoming 1961–62 season. This would qualify as my final year's practice towards the award of a diploma. Their current repertoire and plan of new productions had already been approved by the Artistic Council. The salary would be in the top category, with living accommodation and a nursery place guaranteed.

"Misha, Nazarov also promised a place for Emilia, at the republic's Museum of Fine Arts, in accordance with her professional expertise. I am now preparing your file for a presentation to the Theatre Department. They will be able to provide you with an official mandate for Tadzhikistan."

I felt reinvigorated at this welcome news, but decided not to celebrate until I had the paper signed by Vartanyan in my hands. After everything that had happened over India, it was 'Better to have a sparrow in the hand, than a crane in the sky."

To my utter amazement, Milia reacted to my news very badly. She categorically declared: "I am not leaving Moscow. What is there for me in your godforsaken Tadzhikistan?"

"Are you serious? No, you can't be. Let's talk about this when you are in a better mood."

"I am not going to sacrifice my career for the sake of your wild schemes."

"Where did you pick up such ideas – in Slavyansk? Or have you found some other well-wishers here?"

"Do you expect me to follow you everywhere, as a thread follows a needle?"

I decided to terminate our conversation at this point, took a shower and went to bed. Milia continued to make a din with dishes in the kitchen for much longer, and mumbled something indignantly under her breath. I ignored my wife's arguments, determined not to rise to the bait. My hope was that 'it would all look better in the morning.'

Next day I left at 8 a.m. as usual. Milia deliberately lingered in bed, waiting for me to shut the door behind me. I was trying to control my emotions, in spite of the storm raging inside my Taurean mind. I didn't want to get upset before the stage rehearsal at the Bolshoi School, but was already feeling antagonistic. Instead of preparing for a session of choreography, I was breaking my head trying to understand the psychology of my wife, a woman I loved, who was nonetheless set on breaking up our family's future.

On Saturday morning I stayed at home in order to have a talk with Milia about the immediate future. She stayed in bed, waiting for me to leave, but I didn't as I was waiting for her to get up. Finally, she got up and over breakfast, asked if I would pick up Dmitri from the nursery in the evening because she would be busy.

"Sorry, but tonight I have a demonstration of the final programme at the Central School of Athletics, at 7 p.m."

"You never have time for your son. I also need time for myself!"

"Let's talk about summer plans instead, so that we arrange them in time."

"My plans are clear. I take final exams at MTA and MGU, and finish my thesis on author's rights. Then I will take Dmitri from the nursery and go to Slavyansk for the rest of the summer. At the of August, we will return to Moscow."

"You are saying this, as if you have already divorced me. If you no longer wish to maintain a family and want to live alone, I won't stop you.

"Shatin actually had you in mind as well when he was making arrangements for me. He recommended you as a highly qualified specialist in Art History and in jurisprudence. Nazarov promised to give you a job as inspector/assessor of new acquisitions at the republic's Museum of Fine Arts. Next week I will go to the Theatre Department at the ministry to get a mandate for Tadzhikistan and I need to fill in the form, which asks about family status. You need to think through, seriously, without hysterics, all the pros and cons of our living together that occur to you, because your decision will affect not only our personal lives, but also the fate of our son. My contract with the Tadzhik Opera is valid only for a year. After that we will have some options: to stay on for another year, to go to another republic, or to return to Moscow. You have forty-eight hours to make up your mind. The fate of our family is in your hands.

"If you refuse to come with your husband, to his new place of work, I will file for divorce immediately, and ask for full custody of our son, citing your psychological and physical ineptitude in taking care of him. I will not deal with you directly – you will have to deal with my lawyer. I will have to present details of your criminal negligence of our son at your hall of residence, drinking parties with your friends, and your behaviour at the Slavyansk Prosecutor's Office. A court will decide with whom our son would fare better: in Dushanbe, with his father, or in his mother's inadequate care in the students' hall of residence. I am really sorry that I might have to resort to these extreme measures, but I would do so for the sake of our son. This is not our first conflict about his well-being, but I hope it will be the last. You have the casting vote. The day after tomorrow I will visit Shura and inform her about the end of our courses and that we will vacate the room at the end of July."

On Sunday, we walked in the park as usual. When Dmitri fell asleep in his carriage, we sat down on a bench, and Milia announced that she was ready with her answer.

"You know full well that you are blackmailing me with your threats. At the same time, I believe that you genuinely care for your son and wife. I did not know that the Tadzhik adventure would last only a year and I jumped to conclusions. Having thought about everything I agree to a temporary stay in Tadzhikistan. I take back calling it 'godforsaken' and I apologise for my unacceptable reaction to your sudden announcement of changes in our life and in our place of residence."

"That's fine. Let's consider this misunderstanding resolved. We have two months to play with. During this time, we need to finish all academic projects; prepare clothing for a hot climate; collect the necessary materials for work in the theatre and museum; make copies of personal documents; stock up on supplies of medication for the child, including insect repellent and other such remedies. At the end of July I will put you on the train to Slavyansk, and then I will wait for you in Dushanbe in mid-August. There is no doubt that your relatives will try to dissuade you from going to Tadzhikistan. If for any reason, however plausible, you should fail to come, I will immediately give instructions to my lawyer in

Moscow to launch divorce proceedings, in accordance with a letter I will leave with him."

At the end of May, Milia and Dmitri came to the closing ceremony of the Russian Federation's Children's Olympics. Moscow Central School of Athletics (CSA) took first place. Dmitri was very excited about the children's performances with various accessories, and particularly enjoyed the children's figure skating. During the interval, he ran between the rows of seats, trying to imitate the skaters, eliciting laughter and applause from the audience. When I was called out to be presented with an honorary certificate, my son shouted brightly, "Papa! Papa!" His embarrassed mother didn't know where to look.

In June, the graduating Ballet masters presented extracts from their diploma works, in two groups, three students in each, two before and one after lunch. Theatre workers, Ballet teachers, and other professionals sat in the performance hall of the Bolshoi School behind the two rows reserved for the Examination Committee. Because of the young age of my performers, I was given a slot in the afternoon: the first twenty minutes for the children's programme, then the second twenty minutes for the six miniatures staged last year with the high-schoolers. The costumes designed by Cyril Andreyev were prepared for the graduation concert of the school. Golovkina and her tutors did a great job polishing up the dance technique of their charges, while I worked with them on acting and emotional expression. After my short introduction, the school's principal announced each piece of the programme with the names of the composer and performers. The demonstration went off very well. Rozhdestvenskaya and Tkachenko kissed me and showered me with congratulations me on successfully completing my studies. After all the tribulations, I had somehow managed to scrape a perfect mark in the exam.

By 1st July, my wife had also taken all her exams in academic subjects taught in years III and IV of the Art History Department. She had three more exams to take in the first half of July. Meanwhile I was prepared for the big move: getting our papers ready and waiting for the official invitation from Tadzhikistan. At last, Lena, the secretary, informed me that I was invited to come to the Ministry of Culture's Theatre Department on Friday at 10 a.m. I was nervous going there, as the tragicomic scene to match Gogol's *The Inspector General* that had taken place around the embassy table was still fresh in my mind. The head of department, Vartanyan, would be unlikely to forgive me for the public embarrassment that my Indian project had cost him, nor would Zakharov miss a chance to cause me trouble. They would certainly try to teach me a lesson. But what kind? In spite of doubts and concerns, I felt confident in my mission and went bravely to face the music.

Inspector Mironov greeted me with dry formality. He took my documents and gave me a form to fill in. He studied my CV for a long time and finally disappeared behind the chief's door. Ten minutes later, a secretary called me and led me to Vartanyan. Mironov was standing in front of the table, enumerating the stages of my personal profile. Zaven Gevondovich lifted his eyes from my files:

"I am puzzled as to why the Tadzhik Deputy Minister Nazarov is interested in you. You have neither a strong background in dance, nor in choreographic work at a theatre. The only seriously positive references are those from Vronsky at Kiev Opera, and Golovkina, the director of the Bolshoi school. I wonder what you used to enchant them? Your Indian spices? Ha ha ha! By the way, about your ballet on the Mahabharata: if you plan to work in our theatres, my advice to you is not to forego your service to the Soviet audience in favour of foreign themes. In our country, such an approach is not appreciated by either the audience or the authorities. Remember that!" Vartanyan was provoking me, pricking my pride and patience, but I managed to hear him out in silence and bear all his jokes and deprecations with stoic dignity. It wasn't easy.

At the end of July, I sent Milia and Dmitri off to Slavyansk. Saying goodbye, I warned Milia: "You have another trial ahead of you. This time, it's going to be a trial of your will and determination. Remember that there is no way back if you go off the rails. Listen to the voice of reason!"

One day later, a train delivered me to Dushanbe. Once again, like four years earlier on my way to Moscow, I was approaching an uncertain world. Only this time I was not heading north, but south, and into the embrace of a completely different geographic and historical culture. I wondered whether I would be treated according to my personal and professional qualities, or with regard to my national and religious background. According to Goleizovsky, the natives treated him much better during the years of his exile than the Russians from the administration of the republic ever did. Kasyan advised me to respect local customs and sensibilities and not to make a fuss about alien elements of their daily life, which were unfamiliar to Slavic peoples.

Tadzhikistan borders Afghanistan. On the train to Dushanbe, there were a lot of military men from the Border Service (as I thought) returning from their summer holidays. In my compartment, there were three officers in green uniforms, who broke into whispering about something whenever I left the compartment and returned to silence whenever I stepped back in. Hearing that I was a choreographer going to Dushanbe to work at the Tadzhik Opera, they asked for my passport. I also showed them my contract, confirming that I was going to Tadzhikistan for the first time and that I didn't know anyone there. After this, the officers became a little more open in discussing their business. I asked if I had made a mistake moving there from Moscow? They explained that they had been sent on assignment to restore order in the republic, and advised me not to mention my meeting with them to anyone.

"I never saw or heard you," I assured them.

They chortled. "But we could still come to your premiere!" The KGB agents got off in Tashkent and wished me luck as they said goodbye.

All compartments, apart from those reserved, were now filled with local passengers, carrying bundles and pots. Our coach was detached from the Moscow train and attached to another. Lying on the top couchette, I looked out of the window and admired the changing landscape: the savannah pulsing with heat, exotic jewels of mountain villages, silhouettes of mosques, colourful mosaics of bazaars, endless caravans of camels and donkeys. I only now understood why 'Baroness' Milia was so terrified by the prospect of moving to this frontier of Asian civilisation. Nonetheless, I was keen to learn a new musical and dance ethnography, applied arts and, most importantly, the daily life of this little-known region, the home of Omar Khayyám. There was enchanting mystery in the monotonous landscape passing before the windows of the moving train, accompanied by a rhythmic clanking of wheels. The future was hidden, a yet unknown reality in the daily life and spirit of my new surroundings.

The conductor announced our arrival in the Tadzhik capital, Dushanbe.

VOLUME II

EVER MORE SCARLET EAST:

MEDIUM ORBIT

STAGE I: IDEOLOGY AND CULTURE

CHAPTER 1 YASHMAK OR TUTU

I was met on the station platform in Dushanbe by the theatre's chief administrator, Aaron Efimovich. He waved a friendly welcome and rushed over to meet me:

"Welcome to the capital of the Republic of Tadzhikistan and its opera house!"

"Thank you! How did you know which carriage I was in?"

"Usually officials and stars travel in the only sleeper carriage of the train."

"It's nice to hear that people working in the arts are held in such high regard here."

"I wouldn't go that far. But it's usually the case everywhere that 'Beauty may open the door, but only virtue enters.'"

"That sounds more realistic already, and somewhat ominous, don't you think?"

We both laughed at our black humour as we walked along to an old banger.

"Excuse me, Mikhail Semyonovich, but this is the only car we had available. In the town centre we go everywhere on foot."

"In that case, let's get the driver to drop my luggage off at the hotel, and we can go on our own two feet. I hope you won't mind being my guide?"

"On the contrary, it'll be my pleasure to show you the cultural gems of our local heritage."

As Aaron helped me climb to the first floor of the arrivals hall with my luggage, he apologised once again for the lack of a lift, which had not been included in building regulations for local three-floor buildings. Their limited height was due to frequent earthquakes in this area. This news lightened my mood. I was curious to know what my next surprise here would be.

My room with its balcony looked really smart. Even the lack of an en suite toilet and shower did nothing to spoil the favourable impression of comfort. *But what on earth is this?* My wide eyes settled on four metallic cups on the floor, each containing some kind of liquid. The bed legs were positioned neatly inside them. The administrator explained that this was the norm here in all homes as defence against scorpions and *phalanxes* (giant spiders). That's why there was also a sheepskin on the floor, as both insects and reptiles were repulsed by the smell of it. *So, that's the second 'pleasant surprise'. I wonder what the third will be?*

"By the way, Aaron Efimovich, could you explain why the poor spiders and snakes have such a strong dislike of fresh lamb? Surely what they eat is all the same to them?"

"As a ballet master, you would be interested to see goats and sheep dancing in Asiatic pastures! Occasionally, when the grazing herds destroy spiders' or adders' nests by accident, the latter assume that they are being threatened by predators, and fiercely defend their territory. In turn, the grass-eaters, not wishing to receive a fatal bite, leap up and down at the sight of spiders and snakes, until finally they trample their opponents under their hoofs. Unfortunately, this kind of 'mutual understanding' often occurs with people too. Yes, sadly, that's how it is. But don't worry, dear guest. This presents no threat to you. Relax. Valamat-Zade has asked you to visit him in his office with your plans at 6 p.m."

"My dear guide, thank you for your help and useful information. See you this evening."

My hotel, the opera house and state departments were all in the town centre, in close proximity to each other around Lenin Square. The city's residential district was just beyond this collection of architectural gems. Irrigation canals in little narrow streets ran with dirty green water, probably only to moisten the sweltering air. The small, single-storey houses all had large gardens. Alongside were several old mosques which had sprung up all around Dushanbe about a kilometre from the centre. All in all, the town resembled a large village. However, this turned out to be a misleading impression. In fact, trade in anything here was pretty brisk using the Asiatic republics' tradition of barter, both in the state and private sectors. Groups of men were busy debating something in every *chaikhana* (tea room), smoking long pipes with God knows what kind of tobacco, which gave off a sweet, heady aroma. Subsequently, when studying the history and customs of these people, I recalled several times my Moscow friends' words of warning prior to my departure. One had the feeling that in all areas of life, things functioned in two modes: the demonstrable/external versus the conspiratorial/internal. The theatre's artistic director, Gafar Rustamovich, greeted me with open arms.

"My dear chief ballet master! How was your journey and how is the hotel?"

"Thanks, it was a long journey, but it gave me the chance to think about my plans. The hotel room is fine just for me, but my wife and son are coming in a couple of weeks, followed soon after by my mother, and then it will be a little tight and we'll be short of a few essentials."

"Ha ha! 'a little' – you're obviously a bit of a jester as well as a choreographer!"

"No, just Misha, born and bred in Odessa."

"Don't worry, we'll find you a big house with a garden. Let's talk about your plans instead. As I understand it, you showed an interesting children's programme in your Moscow institute. Can you incorporate it in the children's New Year's show? For nearly thirty years we've been putting on an annual performance of *The Nutcracker*. The boys are 'a tad' (to use your expression) fed up of seeing the same dancing tutus and grey mice in tights all the time. We need something to make a fresh impact."

"Shostakovich's music was written for piano. Can you orchestrate it?"

"We'll ask the composer himself, and he can arrange it for our theatre. You just need to give me the whole piano score in the right order of chosen pieces. The orchestral director will prepare a commission for the composer. In addition, we have planned Mikhail Glinka's opera *Ivan Susanin* for the first six months, and Georges Bizet's *Carmen* for the second. As you well know, both shows feature rich prospective material for the choreographer. What do you think?"

"I like this programme, and I'll gladly take part in the production, if the Ballet troupe is up to the technical rigours of this project."

"A week ago, nine graduates returned as first-category soloists after eight years of studying in Leningrad. You are in luck." (St Petersburg was renamed Leningrad after the revolution and since perestroika it has become St Petersburg once more. During my years in the USSR it was always known as Leningrad.)

"In that case, during the current season I would also like to prepare *Poem of Man*, a ballet-concert in two acts involving a group of soloists consisting of fourteen to sixteen dancers."

"Isn't this a lot for a new ballet master to take on single-handedly?"

"You may be right. However I'm counting on help from a friend and colleague from that Faculty of Dance Teaching methodology at MTA, who, as far as I know, is here on pre-diploma practice before the beginning of the season. Pyotr Pestov is a very talented teacher and répétiteur."

"Yes, I've heard of him. Nikolai Tarasov gave his pupil an excellent reference. I will confirm this programme with the theatre's Artistic Committee, and wish you luck with it all!"

The next day, after Gafar had officially introduced me to the Ballet Department as their new leader, I got the troupe on side right from the off. I didn't want to give them the false impression that I was a novice choreographer straight out of school. I asked the répétiteur, Zakhidova (a retired former prima ballerina), to divide all the artistes into three groups: soloists, 'corps de ballet' and those heading for retirement, with more than twenty years of stage experience in their field. I suggested to the manager Maxim (the administrative head of department) that he draw up a list of all the dancers by category. I also announced the proposed repertoire for the coming season. I reminded them that the new teacher/répétiteur from MTA, a former leading soloist with the Perm Opera/Ballet Theatre, would not accept in his practice classes/rehearsals any wide-legged trousers, robes or jerseys or similar unprofessional items in the traditional dancer's uniform.

Everyone looked in astonishment at Gafar, the smiling Artistic Director of the State theatre, who simply shrugged: "Real art demands real sacrifice."

When I met the troupe, I noticed that the artistes looked bored and arrogant. In the break I asked Maxim about this.

"Why is it that lots of the dancers seem disinterested in their art, and why are they surprised by the expectation of discipline at work, both in the studio and onstage?"

"Mikhail Semyonovich, we haven't had any new ballet productions or a proper ballet leader for a long time. People have got out of the habit of professional rigour. Now, along with strengthening the soloists, and with you and Pestov joining us, I'm sure that many of them will see it as a positive impetus in improving the atmosphere in the department overall, and a return to the previous high standard of training and conduct in performances. Now we have all the conditions and opportunities we need to achieve this."

"I'm banking on it. Can I count on Zakhidova, the répétiteur, as well?"

"Absolutely. It was particularly difficult for her to carry the burden of this mess on her own."

"Dear colleagues, may I have your attention? [The noise and laughter in the studio did not reduce.] This is how we are going to work. Maxim, what's the surname of that ringleader/joker in the old, scruffy jeans?"

"Nikolai Kryukov. He's due to retire soon."

We both headed towards him.

"Comrade Kryukov, forgive me for interrupting your rowdy behaviour in work time. I understand that you have completely lost any sense of professionalism and can't wait to retire."

The cheery group around him fell silent and dispersed in all directions. He was shocked by my boldness and opened his arms towards his mates, calling on them for solidarity. But they preferred to save their own skins.

"Dear Nikolai," (I spoke sarcastically, assuming the well-recognised role of a public prosecutor) "in ten years of staging productions, I have never come across such buffoons, who claim to be heroes in everyday life but just clamber about everywhere onstage. You think you're a first-class clown. But in my eyes you are merely a pathetic self-taught amateur jester."

Guffaws resounded around the studio.

"If you don't start behaving in a professional manner immediately, then I will ask you to leave the studio for good. Tomorrow we will discuss your undermining conduct in Valamat-Zade's office. So, dear colleagues, let's agree as friends: three claps from the teacher/répétiteur or ballet master/choreographer, as you know very well, indicates a prompt command for silence and attention. Enough! I have come here not for a one-off production, but on a permanent basis, provided conditions are palatable to us all. We have outlined a varied repertoire of small-scale productions for the coming season, which will make full use of the whole troupe in a range of various dance styles and genres, including group Character and Historical compositions from the operas *Ivan Susanin* and *Carmen*, a children's ballet/concert for the New Year and concluding with the Balletic mosaic *Poem of Man* for the troupe's leading veterans and young soloists from Leningrad. To put it into perspective, the new season offers a unique full-length ballet with participation from the whole troupe. There is plenty of work for everyone. The rest is up to you."

The theatre administrator told me that Valamat-Zade was on the case looking for suitable accommodation for my family. The Artistic Director kept his promise. Aaron collected Emilia and Dmitri from the station – she was tired from the long journey and he was jumping for joy at arriving – and drove them to the fairy-tale, luxurious house that had belonged to a certain government agent, 'repatriated' once and for all to Eastern Siberia. Three bedrooms, a sitting room, dining room, kitchen, bathroom with shower, etc.: more of a fantasy than a house. A huge courtyard with additional rooms, a summer kitchen, hammock, armchair/rocking chairs. Bunches of grapes hung from the trellis roofing over our heads. We had never seen such sophistication, even in films.

My wife could not believe her eyes: "Can all this really be just for us?"

"And for Mum too, who will be arriving soon from Odessa."

The administrator was astonished at the effect the house had on my family.

"Well, you can arrange everything to your own taste here. If you should need anything, please don't hesitate to ask."

"Aaron Efimovich, thank you for everything and come to our house-warming once Pestov has arrived, on the last Sunday in August. You must bring your wife but not the children, ha ha!"

"If I've understood correctly, Pyotr is going to live here with us?" asked the mistress of the house.

"Yes, and he will share a room with you, and I'll sleep in another with our son, with Grandma and the cat in the third. Pyotr won't be any trouble, even if you talk to him non-stop."

"No, Daddy, I will sleep with Granny Anna, Mummy really loves cats, and you can sleep with your friend Petya!" Dmitri proclaimed confidently as his crazy parents chuckled.

This marked the end of our happy overture and the beginning of our unpacking and sorting out the house, which we tried to complete before darkness fell. The canteens in state institutions closed at 5 p.m. A woman could not go into a *chaikhana* (tea room) without a yashmak or scarf covering her head and half of her face, so I had to take a few glass jugs with lids and a teapot from our house. My son and I ran to the nearest *chaikhana*. While he, with some trepidation, surveyed the men seated on cushions smoking in semi-darkness, I got what we needed and we hurried home.

In the second half of August all the ballet artistes were obliged to come back to work after a month's leave. However, they were in no hurry, knowing that it was still early, as apart from the morning classes with Zakhidova, there was nothing to do. They didn't know about the new reinforcements, and Maxim had to call them in individually from their 'absence without leave'. I consciously turned a blind eye to this, understanding the repercussions of long-standing anarchy in the Ballet Department. Although Valamat-Zade promised all kinds of support to strengthen creative discipline, I nevertheless patiently took charge of the group's mental recovery, bringing psychological influence to bear on each individual. I asked the inspector not to report the artistes' illegal, long absence to management (for which I would be answerable), at least not until they all came together the following Tuesday, when I planned to begin staging the new choreography. At the same time, I held an introductory discussion with performers from the Vaganova school to establish their Dance profile based on their practical stage experience. Potentially, I envisaged experienced roles/ images in the children's New Year show and in the adults' spring programme of Ballet miniatures. At the same time, Zakhidova, the répétiteur, started to bring them into Solo roles from the current repertoire of Classical and National ballets with the help of veterans who were slowly 'awakening'. Patience was essential in everything.

Each morning, after Zakhidova's warm-up class, I taught the steps and movements of Historical and Character dances from *Ivan Susanin*, at first just with the women. Then Zakhidova took them into another studio to polish up technique, and I worked in parallel with the men, who had only limited conception of the way a 'Mazurka' could be staged, and no knowledge of the 'Krakoviak' dance. I tried my utmost to impart the bravura and complacency of the Polish national character, so as to prepare them for rehearsals with Pestov, who would not be as patient with them as I was. He would usually end up shouting in annoyance. In these situations, Pyotr would stutter a bit but persist until they met his standards for professional performance. After my technical and stylistic training of the performers, who were unfamiliar with the nature of European Character dances, I assumed it would be easier to work on subsequent stages of producing a new repertoire. However, my hopes were not justified. The professional damage inflicted on the artistes by the long break in artistic creativity, had distorted their physical form, and ruined their intellectual interest in theatre and spiritual belief in their capabilities.

Unfortunately, this became all too clear at my first production rehearsal, as we began our preparatory study of the technical elements with the "corps de ballet" (the regular group of dancers – not the soloists), for the new choreography to come. In essence, the Dushambe theatre company was in a tragic state of moral and physical disintegration. The fat and unwieldy behinds and stomachs of the ballerinas could be reduced significantly in a month by dieting and stepping up the training regime. But what to do with the poisoned mindset of an idle, spiritually paralysed artiste? Such alienation doesn't lend itself to quick repair. Internally I was in shock, but didn't let this show. I continued to give patient explanations, demonstrations and corrections, as if nothing was wrong. Finishing the rehearsal early, I invited everyone (about ten men and twenty women) to sit on the floor in front of me for a chat.

"Regardless of the fact that I am younger than many of you, I still have considerable experience as a producer and sober/objective judgement as a leader. I don't mean to judge you for losing your professional shape and spirit. On the other hand, I can't imagine the Opera Theatre will allow ballet artistes to perform in such unprepossessing condition, both physically and spiritually. We need to take urgent, effective measures to restore your physiques and self-belief. Without these qualities, the art of ballet is unthinkable. We all understand this perfectly."

"How do you propose to achieve this?" asked Zakhidova.

"Firstly, to go on a strict diet and lose the excess weight you're all carrying. In any case, I'll leave the inspector a list of recommended foods and a diet sheet, in line with our work schedule. Secondly, three times a week, but not on performance days, répétiteurs will follow my instructions and lead a half-hour course of intensive physiotherapy with men and women separately, over one month, beginning on 2nd September.

Thirdly, each of you must quickly decide for yourself whether you will participate in this difficult – in all aspects – programme of psychophysical rehabilitation to attain a professional standard of ballet in the Opera Theatre. Those who decline this charitable and practical help, will not be included in the numbers for new productions. They can continue their former way of life and work towards retirement, if the management decides to carry on paying their salary. Any questions?"

People left the studio in silence, noisily discussing the latest in the corridor. Zakhidova and Maxim stayed behind. They were happy at this new direction, but doubtful about the reality of putting such progressive ideas in place. I suggested that we go to see Valamat-Zade about this project together.

It took Mum almost a week to get from Odessa to Dushanbe by train, changing at Volgograd. She was fortunate with her travelling companions, and I met 'the frog traveller' in bright spirits. Aaron wouldn't hear of a taxi, and took us straight home in the theatre's prehistoric car. My mother's jaw dropped: she was dumbfounded at the sight of this luxury. Ten minutes later, Milia returned from the nursery with our son. Seeing his grandmother, Dmitri bounded into her open arms with a shriek.

Our guest naturally shed a tear: "My favourite grandson! Heavens, how you have grown in the two years since I last saw you. Misha, I have dreamed about him so often recently."

"Granny, Granny, we have got a little trolley in our yard. I'll take you for a ride on it, OK?"

My mother really liked the house, with her own room, the garden and, especially, two kitchens. My put-upon wife could now relax. From Monday she was planning to work in the museum, and had worried about her mother-in-law's impending arrival. Milia would, of course, take our boy to nursery and pick him up after work. On Mondays (her day off), both women would go to the market together with the trolley. Mum would look after the kitchen and yard, and inside the house, each of us three would clean our own rooms. Mum willingly took charge of her grandson's room. My duties included sweeping up fallen leaves in the yard in the mornings.

Pyotr Pestov finally arrived on the last Saturday in August. Aaron set him up in the best room in the same hotel. The next day I took him to meet Gafar. Valamat-Zade received Nikolai Tarasov's star pupil respectfully. He called in Maxim and asked him to show Pestov the ballet studios, stage, canteen; and to arrange for the whole troupe to meet their new teacher/répétiteur at 12 noon the next day.

"Misha, stay a little longer. We need to make an urgent decision on something in their absence."

I realised that he had already got to hear about my project, and wasn't surprised by his request.

"May I know the details of your ideas for restoring the Ballet Department's morale?"

In detail, I set out the problems I had observed at the first production rehearsal and my idea to restore the 'corps de ballet' urgently to standard form.

"Everything you have described is true, and everyone here sees it and knows it. For this reason in the search for a ballet leader, we asked the dean of MTA to send not only a choreographer, but also an enthusiastic leader who would be capable of reinstating the Ballet Department in its fitting role as Opera Theatre partner. Judging from all of this, you potentially possess the necessary attributes of a leader. But clearly you have been in a rush, not consulting with me and have set part of the group against you, even before you have started your practical activity. You have breached working hierarchy and theatre etiquette."

"You are right, Gafar. Please forgive my hurried reaction. I assure you that this will not happen again. I sometimes find it difficult to delegate. But in this case, not having had personal experience as chief ballet master in a theatre, I should have outlined my doubts and plans to you."

"I'm pleased that you understand this and believe that you are genuine in your intentions to improve the status of the 'corps de ballet' and the company's work as a whole. That's why I'll overlook your error and will back you this first time. But next time you slip up, don't bank on that. When you go to meet Pestov tomorrow, I will stay behind for a tête-à-tête with my former apprentices. I'll explain to them in straightforward terms your positive motives and ethical errors. I will demand from them complete compliance with theatre regulations, the ballet work regime and progress into working shape throughout September, and all the attendant consequences for anyone sabotaging the professional demands made by management."

My mother, Anna, organised a celebratory supper in Pyotr's honour, and we marked his arrival in sunny Tadzhikistan in suitable style. She was very upset that my friend lived in a hotel room by himself, with no kitchen, toilet or shower. The matriarch of the house ordered him to come for lunch no less than three times a week (Mondays, Wednesdays and Fridays) and regale himself with fresh Ukrainian borscht and dumplings.

Pyotr started to stutter from embarrassment: "Anna Da-Da-Davidovna, thank you! I'm used to living on my own and am not afraid of the Big Bad Wolf."

"That's wonderful. Now you can get used to living with others in your new family."

We all laughed, but my son cackled the most, even though he didn't get the joke.

"Pyotr Antonovich, perhaps I could call you Petrus, and address you as 'ty'[familiar form] as if you were another son?"

"That makes sense, that's what my g-g-grandmother used to call me."

Our guest was really struggling now.

"Petro, you are worrying for nothing." I decided to diffuse the charged atmosphere. "Mum is simply lacking a fifth son to qualify for a Heroine-Mother's title and pension."

At this point we all came down to earth with a bump, apart from Dmitri, who was struggling to get half a dumpling into his mouth. But when the old woman thwacked me with a napkin for my impudence, the little one burst out laughing, spraying dumpling and curd cheese all over the table. Now the circus began.

The adults laughed uncontrollably, and the little boy's convulsive giggles turned to tears.

After supper, holed up in my study/room, Pestov and I spent a long time discussing our plans and working methods for the Ballet Department. I outlined to him in detail the moral and physical condition of the neglected company, and told him about my premature attempt to bring about a 'revolution', which would no doubt either be thwarted by Valamat-Zade or supported through my professional demands on his own terms. In this theatre he was both God and king. No one here dared to go against the theatre's artistic director in anything.

"Then why did you recommend me to him and sign my summons to this, forgive me . . ."

"Petro, I myself was still unaware of the state of the troupe during this holiday period, but I don't consider our coming here a mistake for one moment. On the contrary, these fundamental difficulties in pre-diploma work practice will give us useful experience for a future career in any theatre in the country. I don't want you to go in tomorrow and make exactly the same mistake as I did yesterday. That's why I felt I had to bring you up to speed on what to expect in this situation."

"I could easily work in Moscow with Golovkina in the Bolshoi School with no problems at all."

"Petya, I saw your classes at MTA and in school. You have a much wider range as a teacher/répétiteur in a ballet troupe than as simple trainer/instructor in a school. You have successfully performed jester roles in *Swan*, Mercutio in *Romeo* and Shurale himself. You have Character dancing in your blood, which is not something any old classical teacher can boast about. That's why I called you here."

"OK, you've persuaded me. What compromise did you want to warn me about?"

"This is already a business discussion. Here is a pen and paper. Make your own notes:

"a) The day after tomorrow most of the artistes will come in gowns, baggy trousers and similar glad rags to your lesson, to disguise the fact that they have put on weight. In the studio and onstage they will practise the whole opera/ballet repertoire in this attire with Zakhidova, not wishing to display their graceful, but ugly shape. You must give them a straightforward warning to attend the following lesson in appropriate uniform.

"b) All latecomers to your lesson must warm up by themselves in the corridor, so as not to disturb the rest of their colleagues' concentration at work.

"c) I am warning you not to allow anyone to leave the rehearsal for any reason, without checking with the teacher/répétiteur so as not to interrupt the music and the ballet troupe's established regime. You, Zakhidova, the inspector and I equally, will insist on these and other essential conditions in creative discipline. Otherwise repertoire plans will remain only on paper."

"Misha, these demands are quite harsh, but I'm with you completely: 'Like cures like,' and I will implement these conditions gently but insistently."

At the troupe's general meeting, the artistes greeted us with applause. Valamat-Zade introduced the new teacher/répétiteur and asked me to summarise his creative biography.

"Pyotr Antonovich danced in the Perm Ballet for ten years as lead soloist and taught in the Ballet school. The Theatre management enthusiastically recommended Pestov to MTA's Teaching Department in the Ballet Master Faculty, where we studied together for four years under the same dance professors. Last month, Golovkina invited my colleague to take up a permanent job in the Bolshoi Theatre School. However, I managed to persuade my close friend and comrade-in-arms to come here to Alisher Navoi Theatre to collaborate on our creative plans. I hope that we will achieve success, with the blessing of the artistic leadership, through shared professional cooperation."

"Mikhail, please introduce Pyotr to the theatre management team and department leaders, while we exchange opinions here. Let's meet up in half an hour in my office," concluded Gafar.

After meeting the theatre's director and artistic elite, we drank some green tea in the canteen and went down at the appointed time to see the artistic director. Petya fired questions at me, most of which I was unable to answer. One thing was clear: we had stirred up a hornet's nest in the Ballet Department, which would be difficult to quell. Valamat-Zade came back with Zakhidova and Maxim, and asked his secretary to bring a blank copy of the working agreement with ballet artistes. Underlining the division of duties of hired staff in theatrical art, he then gave this copy to the ballet inspector. He ordered it to be copied and hung up in a glass frame in both male and female cloakrooms. He then called the chairman of the Theatre Trade Union Committee and arranged a meeting. Everything happened efficiently and quickly without any emotion. Zakhidova fortunately turned out to be the Ballet Department's Communist Party secretary. So, all the management cards were in Gafar's hands. We waited patiently for his preparations to end.

"Sorry, colleagues. Now let's talk about the situation. There is nothing surprising about what was going on in our company, as I have already explained to Mikhail. Before we could restore the creative working capability in our ballet troupe, it was essential to strengthen its leadership. There are dozens of enquiries to the Personnel Department from young specialists/performers graduating from city ballet schools this year, wanting to work for us. But we couldn't resolve even this problem without a chief ballet master. We have funds for twelve to sixteen additional ballet artistes. Unfortunately, we don't have our own ballet school in the republic, and are forced to hire dancers from elsewhere. Some of them are naïve and have put on weight (about to retire), working twice a month on the stage, and have decided that they are irreplaceable and run the show here, sabotaging both the inspector's and the répétiteur's work. The theatre management has waited a long time for the right moment to rejuvenate the ballet company. As far back as ten years ago, we tried in vain to open our own ballet school (as our neighbours in Tashkent have done) with Fatima Zakhidova. To our great disappointment, we failed in this because of local prejudice. For this reason we sent twelve hand-picked children to the Vaganova school in Leningrad, who have now returned as nine soloists, hungry to take up dancing professionally. That is the situation today, my dear friends. We urgently need to do something new with the troupe. I am ready to send a telegram without delay to inform the candidates who are interested in competing to fill the vacancies for ballet artistes on Monday 21st September. Ages: under twenty for women and twenty-five for men. We will pay travel expenses and provide hostel accommodation for participants. What do you think about this, and what would you add to this project?"

"Personally, I fully approve of this proposal, but on condition it remains completely confidential until the day of auditions, to avoid any sabotage of the company's current work."

"It'll be a real challenge to keep this important operation under wraps for long, but I agree."

"As an inspector, with good knowledge of my subjects' characters, I suggest laying off the main instigators/saboteurs for two weeks. They have systematically breached their contract conditions in more than enough ways, despite repeated disciplinary penalties to justify doing so. Otherwise they will do everything to spoil the auditions, as happened at today's meeting."

"Good, Maxim. Prepare the materials for all three and give them to the Personnel Department. I personally will take charge of organising the auditions. Any questions? Thanks for your time!"

Every first non-working Monday in September, the Central Communist Party and government of the republic, required the male theatre workers to put in one day's obligatory work in collecting the cotton harvest in the Tadzhik fields. They all looked forward to this with impatient enthusiasm. It was a unique opportunity to relax freely away from female surveillance and endless household or family worries. At 6 a.m. several buses transported noisy choristers, dancers, musicians and technical workers to the nearest agricultural centre. Then, at the bosses' instruction, various vehicles distributed the willing forced labourers from the arts around the cotton warehouses in surrounding villages. These 'highly intelligent' male representatives of the Soviet intelligentsia had to transport bales of raw cotton, picked beforehand and carefully packed by the skilful hands of 'unintelligent' female collective farm workers, from the fields to the storehouse on a two-wheeled cart. We – the elite of socialist society – coped with this 'unbearably laborious' commission without any problem for six hours, including long snack breaks. Then, remaining loyal to our brigade, we visited the local tea house en masse in different villages, where they had already prepared 'bread/salt' in advance – this being pilaf and shashlik for the honoured guests. From 12 noon to 4 p.m. the fragrant Tadzhik wine 'flowed like a river' – or rather a canal. At the end of this unforgettable, productive working day, the half-dead theatre enthusiasts were dropped off home in a state of alcoholic oblivion.

The instigators of such responsible sociopolitical measures naturally did not overlook the administrative/artistic leadership of the theatre and its separate departments. Firstly they took us around the snow-white cotton fields serviced by our workers. At the sign of approaching management, the animated grafters grabbed three bales of cotton in each hand. They piled and pulled them simultaneously with both hands on to two carts, managing periodically also to wipe the sweat (which was running thick and fast off the joyful, beaming faces on to the parched earth) off their forehead with their knee. We, the management, proudly smiled with tears in our eyes and couldn't wait until we, the quintessential, spiritual embodiment of the theatre collective, were taken to a mystical lunch with the director of this model farm. His huge estate and the way he managed several hectares exceeded all our expectations.

Our host, dressed in a colourful gown and sporting a turban, was already standing on the threshold in anticipation of our arrival, waving his arms to each side and shouting: "Welcome to my modest abode, dear guests! Please don't be shy, leave your dirty footwear outside. Thank you!"

Petya and I exchanged glances. Aaron Efimovich, who was next to us in the bus, had forewarned us, "Lads, be careful. Don't blurt out anything tactless in this house, through ignorance of local or ceremonial customs. Consult me first if you don't want to put your foot in it."

"Thanks for the advice. Pyotr Antonovich is generally a silent type. But I love to chat, and because of this, often come a cropper. I'll gladly take you up on your censorship today, chief administrator."

Either side of the entrance stood two boys, most likely our host's sons, each holding a small basin of water with a towel over his shoulders. Following the example of those in front, Pestov and I took our shoes off and rinsed our hands, bowing our heads in thanks.

There was a fireplace in the middle of the large sitting room and, in the centre of the cupola-shaped ceiling was a huge hole to let steam and smoke escape. Large cushions were scattered on Persian rugs around the hearth, where people sat, semi-reclining, or with crossed legs.

A group of women in long black dresses with veils fastened on their heads, busied themselves behind us, organising drinks and snacks. Out of curiosity, I looked round and noticed that a few of them, judging by their movement and voices, must have been quite young. After fulfilling my obligations to the master of the house, I became bold, and decided to show my respect by demonstrating how educated I was.

"Excuse me, Khakim-Pasha, could you tell me which of your daughters likes to dance local folk dances?"

A blow from Aaron's elbow to my side interrupted my question. The host kindly pretended not to have understood my chatter, and turned to Valamat-Zade.

The administrator, not looking in my direction, and with a false smile, whispered: "These women are all his wives! Don't ask risky, naïve questions."

I realised that I had messed up again, and subsequently confined myself to discussing with Pestov the flavour of the next dish or exotic fruits. Following the two-hour lunch, Khakim-Pasha invited us to have a look at his chickens in their various enclosures. I stayed by a newborn lamb, stroking its unusually black wool.

Once seated in the bus, I suddenly saw one of the host's sons with a black lamb in his arms, heading straight towards me.

"This is a gift for you from the head of the household."

I held the bleating animal on my knees and was flummoxed at how to react in this situation.

"Aaron, what should I do with it?"

"Shashlik or *lulya* kebab," he replied.

Everyone burst out laughing, and Pestov scoffed at me, with his stammering: "Make him a s-s-soloist in your New Year's programme, otherwise he'll shit all over the place."

Valamat-Zade turned out to be a great strategist in the conflict within the Ballet Department. He issued a final warning to the three main protagonists (one woman and two men): if there was no improvement in their conduct, and if they refused to abide by the new working conditions, they would have to leave. The troublemakers decided that the theatre's artistic director, as before, was simply bluffing, and resumed their former boycott positions in the group. The inspector then handed them a pre-prepared notice of dismissal in accordance with contract terms, with two weeks' pay, and passed on Gafar's instruction: from the following day these sacked workers would not be allowed into the theatre. The management, Party Committee and Professional Committee unanimously supported this albeit harsh – for these three – but fair decision in relation to all the rest who wished to see the Ballet Department progress professionally. This was an exceptional case in the entire history of the Tadzhik Opera Theatre, and warmly welcomed by many of the workers. The four-strong ballet leadership team started to act assertively, immediately taking the bull by the horns. As soon as the next day, the morning warm-up and training classes (soloists with Pestov and the 'corps de ballet' with Zakhidova) took place in a new atmosphere of discipline and productivity. Naturally, it was a challenge for everyone after such protracted lethargy, to start working in the necessary, normal regime straight away. I urged the teachers not to put too much pressure on them at first, but to be patient and let the artistes rediscover their lost courage.

The system we had devised earlier in Odessa for carousel work between two studios simultaneously/in parallel, with two répétiteurs, helped me to impart my choreography to the performers more quickly, easily and precisely. Valamat-Zade removed rare ballet shows from the repertoire for two months until the new dancers from the competition could be included in them along with the Vaganova soloists' group. As well as the intensive performance rehearsals, the 'corps de ballet' artistes who had got out of shape were forced to undergo a special course of therapeutic exercise every night, following my programme. They worked tirelessly and visibly lost weight. As a result of the successful September auditions, the Ballet Department was enriched by fourteen young artistes in the 'corps de ballet' and two mature soloists. The emotional and creative mood in the troupe lifted dramatically. In the evenings I completed choreography for the Polonaise, Waltz and 'Krakoviak' in the whole act of Glinka's opera but got rather bogged down in the particularly refined style of the Mazurka. Many dancers from the sticks found it torturously difficult to adopt, quickly and accurately, the aristocratic manner of interacting in the most complicated Character/Historical dance in the Court repertoire. At times it cost us an enormous amount of patience to turn these 'bears' into graceful and confident members of a nineteenth-century Polish court. However, by the end of October, I managed to give the répétiteur the complete choreography for the Polish act of *Ivan Susanin*.

At 6 p.m., the whole collective worked in parallel in two studios again. Zakhidova introduced the newcomers to the current opera and ballet repertoire, while Pestov and I worked on the children's ballet for the New Year: *Dancing Dolls*, to music by Dmitri Shostakovich. In one half of the studio I reproduced these miniatures with young soloists. In the other, Pestov rehearsed pieces familiar to him as I had choreographed them recently in Moscow's Bolshoi Theatre School. These were images of amusing little animals in a humorous choreographic style, incorporating subjects well known to a children's audience. The performers and répétiteur themselves often laughed at the fanciful, unique movements of the 'animals' and their mimicking/eccentric elasticity. Work on this one-act ballet-concert was moving quite quickly and was finished by the end of November. At the beginning of the season I had had to demonstrate my credentials in classical vocabulary from the off. At the preliminary meeting with the Leningrad soloists' group in September, I had discovered a talented couple: Malika Sabirova and Muzaphar Burkhanov (eighteen to twenty years old). I decided to cast them in three trial miniatures, including:

1. 'Song of the Black Swan' (music by Hector Villa-Lobos) Malika Sabirova, as a solo.
2. 'Snake Charmer' (music by Cyril Scott) from an Indian carving Muzaphar Burkhanov, solo.
3. 'Amour and Psyche' (music by Jules Massenet) to Canova's sculpture of the same name – duet.

Gafar sometimes wandered into our rehearsals and sat with a contented smile near the pianist. He didn't say anything, just waved goodbye as he left. Work in the Ballet Department got into full swing to such an extent that we barely had time to rush home to Mum for a bowl of borscht in our lunch break. Petya would collapse in the yard on the stove-bench, half dead during 'feeding time', and I would go into my study to get ready for the evening rehearsal. This was an agony of sublime creativity. The young recruits from the auditions gradually assimilated the old repertoire and successfully adapted to the general work regime, as well as to the individual nuances of the recovering company. The new soloist couple from Kharkov, Ukraine, knew the whole classical repertoire well and really valued Pestov's qualification. We could count on their loyalty. Potentially this merited a change of répétiteur, as necessary.

Milia adapted slowly and without interest to the conditions of her new job. She had her own separate office in the Museum of Fine Arts and everything in place to undertake successful critical analysis and evaluation of original works by local painters and sculptors. However, this head of department preferred to spend most of the day chatting about nothing with her colleagues, explaining away her negligence by saying that everyone here was used to doing nothing, and she didn't consider it expedient for herself 'to pretend' in front of them, like Pestov and I did in the theatre. My wife shocked me with her social parasite's cynical philosophy, after receiving such a comprehensive education.

How did she get to be so conceited and nasty? She grew up among workers/ peasants, in a family of genuine labourers. It would seem that the university atmosphere of the student intelligentsia had had a dramatic influence on Milia's outlook, inculcating in her a cynical moral code: 'It doesn't matter where you work, as long as you don't work hard.'

At the beginning of December my wife and I flew to Moscow at the ministry's expense: she was attending a month of lectures for her postgraduate course at MTA to 'upgrade her qualification', followed by another month to present her findings on proving authors' rights for choreographers and stage producers, and I was organising an orchestral score by Dmitri Shostakovich of his piano pieces for the ballet *Dancing Dolls*, and with the added aim of purchasing hand-stitched, elastic costumes (tights/breeches, swimming costumes/jumpsuits, etc.) for the performers for their animal roles in the miniatures.

Grandma reluctantly agreed to do the nursery-school run for her smart grandson single-handedly in our absence. I would do it myself on my return to Dushanbe. In the plane on the five-hour journey to Moscow, Milia and I discussed the possible complications with her work, with regard to the neglected registration of subscriptions and analysis of new works of fine and applied art. Authors were waiting weeks for a response from the museum's art critic, and had begun to complain to the ministry board.

Before we left, Nazarov had telephoned: "Mikhail, what's going on with Emilia? She's not complying with the conditions of the contract she signed: she's neglected the order book; is not responding to enquiries, etc. If the head of department doesn't use government funds for the museum, then they will be cut from the organisation's budget in the next financial year and be redistributed. Our inspector offered her practical assistance, but she has declined. We need to know why she's neglecting her duties. Find out from your wife and come back to me as soon as you can."

Milia sat next to me, her face bright red and shaking with rage. I hardly recognised her. She looked like she was going to throw herself at me and tear me apart: "If only you knew how much I hate you!" my wife screeched and spat in my face.

Given that I am a Taurean, it's amazing that I didn't give her a bloody nose right there and then. Some kind of internal counterbalance, atypical of this zodiac sign, restrained me from my customary reaction to such an insult. I merely wiped my face with a handkerchief and with enormous restraint, answered: "Thank you, that's the last time you complain about this event in your miserable self-centred life. And because all I did was to pass on Nazarov's query. He's the one who gave you your first solid job in your profession, is paying for your trip to Moscow to complete your dissertation, and is putting up with your destructive conduct in the museum. As a thank you for his undeserved kindness, you let down the Deputy Minster, disgrace your husband and publicly insult him by spitting in his face."

In the plane toilet I spent a long time washing my face in cold water to calm myself down.

Shura, the warden at the MTA halls of residence, had reserved us a room at Trifonovka as usual. I warned her that I would be going back to Dushanbe in a week's time, but that my wife would stay on another week, and emphasised 'and no longer'. My old friend understood the allusion and assured me that she would book this room out to other postgraduates beforehand. With gratitude and warmth I kissed the good fairy and draped a fashionable scarf around her shoulders. At first she refused, but realising that I might present this gift to another woman, she quickly changed her mind. God, these women are all the same! I had to sort out another gift for the composer Shostakovich on behalf of our theatre management for orchestrating his music. This was a set of national garments: gown, skullcap and bedroom slippers.

When Gafar handed me this package, I had asked him tentatively: "What if Dmitri Dmitrievich doesn't accept this souvenir, but wants payment for his arrangement?"

"He's welcome to send his bill to the Alisher Navoi Theatre. We'll pay him for his work."

I was apprehensive about meeting the legendary composer in his private studio. The elderly secretary (most likely his wife) carefully read through the theatre management's letter with the note designating the choreographic objectives.

"Just a moment. I will show this letter to Dmitri Dmitrievich."

But to my delight, the composer himself came in a few minutes later, and shook my hand vigorously. Realising immediately that I was a spontaneous choreographer/chief theatre ballet master, he invited me to sit down for a couple of minutes, apologising for being busy. I explained to him briefly that in the past I had already put on a series of miniatures to his piano pieces in the form of a New Year's show for children, and later a ballet-concert in similar style for adults. I gave him a file containing the summary content and cast in each composition.

"This is extremely sensible!" the composer exclaimed.

"Sorry, maestro. May I ask, how long will the arranging take? I am here in Moscow for seven days for this sole purpose."

"Are you joking? It's 1.30 p.m. now. Come and pick up your commission at 6 p.m., no later." And with a toothless smile, Shostakovich left and closed the door. I was transfixed in disbelief.

"Mikhail, don't forget your package!" the secretary reminded me, bringing me back to earth. "Don't be late! We close at 6 p.m. Best to come half an hour early – in case anything needs clarifying or correcting. If you wish, you can leave your package here in the meantime."

"Sorry, it's a souvenir for the composer."

Seeing the contents of the gift, the secretary promised to put it in the composer's personal museum. I returned at 5.30 p.m. with a smile ready, prepared to forgive a delay. The secretary offered me a folder with music written in pencil. She apologised for the fact that there was nowhere to make a clean copy, assuring me that this would be good enough for a competent conductor.

"Take a seat and check the notations/indications against your list of piano opuses while you're here. Please give this bill to the theatre director, with grateful thanks from the orchestrator."

I noticed a figure of 700 roubles and remarked with some surprise, "Why so little for such a big score? There must be at least one zero missing here."

"The composer was impressed with your theatrical dance interpretation of his music."

I kissed her hand, and asked her to pass on my sincere and warm thanks to Dmitri Dmitrievich. Then I hurried off to the nearest photo studio to make a copy of all twenty pages with the writer's priceless personal original markings in pencil, which I decided to keep for myself as a souvenir.

While Shostakovich was orchestrating his music, I had managed to call in next door to the All Russia Theatre Society shop on Gorky Street, and order all the required jersey/hand-stitched items on the theatre's list. The familiar sales assistants promised to complete the urgent order over the next three days. While I was there, I picked up the monthly programme for the Moscow opera/ballet theatres.

There was nothing suitable on that evening so I decided to check the musical arrangements in the hostel, to check for any mechanical omission or chance mistake by the composer. However, back at base, I found a noisy bash going on in our room. Excusing myself in front of the unknown guests, I asked them if they could make their way off promptly so that I could get to work urgently on Shostakovich's orchestral score, and laid the folder of music down on the dirty table under my intoxicated wife's nose. She tried to stop her friends from leaving, but seeing my expression, they thought it best to disperse in silence, so as not to provoke a scene. My wife followed them out, slamming the door.

Sometime around midnight her friend knocked at the door and reported that Milia was staying with her on the first floor, so I shouldn't worry. *Things are going from bad to worse,* I thought, before going back to sleep.

In the morning, without waiting for my other half, I hurried to MTA for a meeting with my mentor. In the Dean's office, Shatin and Lena (his secretary) greeted me cheerfully, asking me which resort I had come from to have such a great tan. I just smiled back.

"Lena, I have to join Misha for half an hour – you understand. So come on, reveal 'the peace breaker'! What sort of revolution are you bringing about with Pestov? He wrote a detailed letter to Tarasov: four pages long. Nikolai Ivanovich brought it to me so that I could refute negative rumours with actual facts, also to confirm your significant successes in rejuvenating the troupe and its active creative endeavours, the improvement in artistes' qualifications and the expansion of the opera/ballet repertoire with your choreography. Is this actually the case?"

I gave my spiritual father a potted summary of my errors and achievements. I explained the whole underlying cause, which it was best not to highlight in the letter, and voiced my doubts about the realistic possibility for any professional ballet master to work in this republic because of the growing influence of Islam on local social and cultural life, and on the older generation in particular. I explained that Gafar was between a rock and a hard place. For this reason, over the last few years, ballet in this theatre had been deteriorating before all the presiding Ministry of Culture officials, and no one from the area could make up their minds to strike a progressive blow against primitive, religious trends, which forbad women's faces to be uncovered onstage, or any performers to have bare limbs, even when dancing in close-fitting costumes.

"In his letter, Pyotr pays you many compliments, both as troupe leader and choreographer. He also expresses serious concerns about the presence of classical ballets in the theatre's future repertoire, with regard to the growing religious aggression against socialist culture in the republic. Surely this is quite dangerous? Perhaps you young specialists are exaggerating it all?"

"Anatoly Vasilyevich, I give you just two examples of this genuine problem. In the group from Leningrad from the Vaganova School, the two soloists, Sabirova and Burkhanov, are extraordinarily talented in the art of dance. Muzaphar, who left Tadzhikistan as a child to study in Leningrad, somehow didn't manage to be circumcised when he should have done as prescribed by Muslim tradition. On his return to Dushanbe, local fanatics demanded that he urgently rectify his 'errors'. The nineteen-year-old Komsomol [young persons' communist society] member categorically refused this ritual, as the next day he had to dance the leading role in the ballet *Chopiniana*. Islam's faithful servants made the guy drink some kind of potion and when he was unconscious, right then and there on the table, they cut off part of his male equipment. The next day, after hearing of this event, Valamat-Zade was forced to cancel the show, as there was no understudy.

"Burkhanov's partner, Malika, aged seventeen, now found herself in a more tragic situation. Because of her diminutive stature, this ballerina with a glittering future was forced to dance either solo roles or duets with a male partner, as even on pointes she was out of sync with the group of girls. However, Gafar realised that to his great disappointment, ballets such as *Swan Lake*, *La Bayadère*, *Raymonda*, *Don Quixote*, *Paquita* and so on, would be unlikely to see the light of day again on the stage of the Alisher Navoi Theatre with their revealing, short ballet tutus. They expose too much of the female performers' 'depraved' fleshy frame, which offends the traditional taste of local audiences and fundamentally goes against the grain of Tadzhik cultural aesthetics. So it follows that there is no place for someone like Malika Sabirova here."

Shatin listened to me attentively without interrupting, just making notes in his file. "Misha, a similar ill wind is blowing from Afghanistan next door. Valamat-Zade is feeling edgy at falling between two stools. If it's as serious as you and Petya describe, then neither of you is going to stick it out there. Try at least to take all worthwhile opportunities to finish your pre-diploma placement."

My week in Moscow was so productive, packed with a programme organised in advance, that it flew by in a flash. I hardly saw my 'almost better half', as I came home late every day after a show at the Bolshoi or the Nemerovich-Danchenko Theatres to avoid any kind of scene at the hostel. She too seemed to be busy all day at MTA, preparing for her term in the last week. I was ridiculously lucky to see *Carmen* performed by Arkhipova, and Yuri Grigorovich's latest ballet, *Legend of Love* by Kara Karayev. Without a doubt, this choreographer would surpass Zakharov/Lavrovsky with the Bolshoi Ballet. The rich language in his contemporary Classical dance came close to giants like Vassily Lopukhov, Mikhail Fokine and (judging by the films) George Balanchine. I took my hat off to him. But the choreography in the Asiatic *Legend of Love* didn't always match the music by a long way. That's most probably how it is and how it should be. It's not without reason that artistic stylisation is an effective and specific method of composition in the ballet master's creative endeavour, rather than a natural duplication of movements from the folk dance repertoire.

Listening to *Carmen* gave me lots of new ideas for my own choreography for this opera in Dushanbe: not only for all the dancers but also for the accompanying chorus. I happily paid a visit to my teacher Rozhdestvenskaya and recounted to her my Polish act in *Ivan Susanin*. She was intrigued to know how I had decided on the choreography for the ball repertoire. Her book about Historical and Social dance had just been published, and my patron reminded me that she had promised to present her temporary assistant with a signed copy. I acknowledged that the course I had done with her at MTA was a vital ingredient in my training as a professional choreographer. When we said goodbye, the elderly muse of dance kissed me as if she knew that we would never see each other again. Before leaving for another world, she left in the Dean's office for me a signed copy of her book, which over many years has remained one of my perennial, creative bibles.

My next visit was to my undisputed idol Goleizovsky, who had also completed his work, *Images in Russian Choreography*. However, he couldn't get his book published as the Soviet censor delayed its publication for an indefinite period. Nevertheless, our time together was warm, and our conversation went on till late in the evening. Kasyan Yaroslavovich asked endless, curious questions about the place of his previous 'aesthetic' exile. I had to describe in detail all the innovations, most of which were old hat for him, merely updated. It turns out that in Tadzhikistan, active practice of Islamic beliefs has never ceased, with all its prejudices – backward to 'civilised' eyes. At various times it has gone deep underground or risen openly to the surface of everyday life, depending on the leadership of the Soviet Union Communist Party. The experienced master often smiled sarcastically at his memories on hearing my tales about the problems in the theatre today.

"Dear Mikhail, it's so strange for me to hear you repeating episodes from my own past, thirty years on, as if it were yesterday. There is truth in 'perpetuum mobile'. Our respected Ilich was right when he asserted that the history of man usually moves up in a spiral staircase. Sometimes conflicts between life and death are so organic that it's not worth trying to control them. It's in our interest to go somewhere where they are not, and start something new in a fresh place."

For a couple of days before returning to Dushanbe I reminded Milia about my flight back on Sunday and suggested to her that we meet up after her classes at MTA on Saturday night, to have a serious discussion about her work at the museum and about the future of our family, as Nazarov was waiting for an answer from me, and Mum had to go back to Odessa for New Year.

She grimaced in irritation, but took herself in hand and mumbled: "All right, at 6 p.m. sharp in the institute foyer. If you're not there after five minutes, I'm leaving."

For the whole of my last day I charged from shop to shop to purchase specific items: new collections of folk dances, records of opera and ballet music, photo albums and similar essential resources for choreographic compositions. The All Russia Theatre Society shop had already sent two parcels of stretch-jersey items to the Alisher Navoi Theatre as per my order. I waited a little while for my wife at MTA. We decided to have supper first in a nearby kebab place, so as not to spoil our appetite with the bitter taste of conflict. Then we withdrew to the Arbat arcades.

"What shall I tell Nazarov about your work in the museum?"

"In view of everything, I can't get out of the trouble I've caused myself. It's best for the coordinator to help me to clear what I've neglected, and then I'll resign. This work obviously isn't for me, and it was a mistake to take it on."

"In that case, so as not to let yourself, me or Nazarov down, give me your resignation addressed to him, and ask him to release you from your duties from 1st January. It would be a decent gesture to give him notice well in advance."

"I'll give you that tomorrow morning. I'm more anxious about your mum leaving for Odessa. I won't be able to work, study, look after our son and clean the house without help. We'll have to take someone on from outside."

"Sorry, but I don't see the sense in you continuing your postgraduate studies at MTA, if this work in the arts field is not for you. Bringing up our son and looking after the house will be enough work, without you putting the time in somewhere else as well."

"So you're suggesting that I become a housewife and clean up after you?"

"Firstly, I always clean up my own muck. Secondly, you are making yourself unemployed. Thirdly, most mothers in the world would rather be a housewife than do a banal job."

St Emilia looked into my eyes with such hatred, as if I had wounded her deeply or humiliated her. She wouldn't permit anyone to suggest anything of the kind.

"I hope that you really don't think so badly of me after supporting my education for so many years. Otherwise, what was your reward after all your personal efforts?"

"To get a load of disgusting spit in my face from my beloved wife on a plane for all to see."

Milia winced nervously again, probably from the force of my blunt accusation. She remained silent for a long time with her head down. Finally she looked up and turned to me.

"I was wrong, and ask you to excuse my behaviour, although I'm sure that you will never forgive me for this. We are just not made for each other. We are just too different."

"I repeat that you're a free agent and have the right to live alone or with another husband. Yesterday I met with my lawyer who suggested revising our divorce application to mention the latest incident in the plane. If you have decided not to come back to Dushanbe, so be it. I will confirm my decision quickly by telegram. He simply can't believe that a lawyer of your calibre is capable of so stupidly biting the hand that feeds her. He believes you should see a psychiatrist."

"Again you're provoking me to do something I will later regret."

"You are simply confirming your friend's good advice with this. For our son's sake, I'm only interested in one thing: is his mum the way she used to be, or do I need to find a replacement for her? On my own I won't be able to give him a normal life."

"I will come home in a week's time. Six months later I will leave Tadzhikistan with our son."

"Thank you for clarifying the situation and don't forget to leave your notice for Nazarov."

On the way back to the hostel later on, we were the only ones on the trolleybus.

I asked her: "Sorry, but I've been trying to understand for a long time: what are you really aiming to achieve in life?"

"I don't know myself. It's as if a lot of the things I dreamed of turned out to be an impossible illusion in practice with partners, colleagues, relations and people in general. I get caught up and will probably never shake it off.

"Why are you afraid of seeing a psychiatrist? It might help you to find yourself, examine your personal belief system in making life decisions so as to avoid fatal mistakes, which can sometimes be absolutely irreversible. Think about it for a while."

"I never stop thinking and always come to the same conclusion. Nature has created my psychological make-up in such a way that it skews my perception of how to behave properly and realistically with people. I constantly do the opposite of what people expect of me. Clearly it's my destiny, from which I will never escape, and fighting against it is senseless."

On my return to the theatre I quickly handed the musical director Shostakovich's score for *Dancing Dolls* so that he could work with the orchestra. The stage designer and I defined details for the painting and appliqué work on the jersey costumes for both animals and space creatures. I checked in the shoe department how the 'hooves' and imitation paws with claws were coming on, the wigs, half-masks with beaks/noses in headdresses; wings, tails in the Props Department, etc.

This one-act ballet was set to be performed on 21st December along with a one-act opera (without any dances) *Nasredin in Bukhara*. The *Ivan Susanin* dress rehearsal was two days later. There were different ballet dancers in these shows. But the répétiteurs and pianists were the same – as was the producer. It is easy to imagine the agony, felt both in the rehearsal studios and on the main stage. Gafar quite successfully coordinated the parallel output of both premieres. I had to give him his due. He took his work very seriously. His subordinates knew this and quickly and precisely obeyed all his instructions. Zakhidova with the 'corps de ballet' and Pestov with the soloists had rehearsed my dance programmes to a high standard in my absence, just as much technically as in the musical aspect. All I had to do was to refine and polish the emotional and stylistic nuances in the Polish Character/Historical dances and the imaginary dolls' acting skills.

Both premieres went off very successfully with showings over several days: the children's programme was matinees, and *Ivan Susanin* was on in the evenings. The press made a huge song and dance about Moscow specialists bringing about a rebirth in Tadzhik ballet. Special mention was given to the Leningrad school graduates in *Dancing Dolls* and the 'corps de ballet''s young 'novices' (from various schools in the neighbouring Soviet republics) in the Polish act of the new opera. Artistes from the Ballet Department worked truly selflessly, and deserved all the plaudits they received. Even my son shouted and stamped his feet in delight at the sight of the 'dancing dolls'. On a Monday at the beginning of January, my mother organised a farewell lunch, to which I invited all of the theatre management team. Naturally the musical and artistic directors did not appear. The remaining guests: the stage manager, designer and choirmaster came with their wives, and we had a wonderful evening. Mum made a fabulous borscht and baked her famous pirozhki with liver or cabbage and egg. I got an appetiser for the theatre barmaid, and asked her to help my mother serve the guests in our garden as I wasn't going to rely on Milia.

The meal was glorious. I was unanimously voted top funny storyteller/joker. Pestov was on good form. He forced me to get out the accordion and to my surprise improvised a Russian dance tune to the accompaniment of female guests along with the mistress of the house. Milia dragged the singing women into the middle around Petya, who after a glassful was doing crouches and pirouettes and steps with claps. The chief choirmaster, wisely and in timely fashion, covered his ears to avoid hearing the off notes as the dancers' choir performed 'Korobushka' (a Russian folk song). The stage manager gradually emptied a second bottle. Dmitri was skipping, hopping and running around the accordion player. Mum and the barmaid were sitting together at the table and wiping away tears of laughter. Only one designer was focused on taking photos of the winning tableaux for the following day's press. At the centre of his attention was a frightened cat in a tree, who, taking fright at all the mad activity happening on his territory, had his tail up like a bottlebrush, and was arching his back, screeching wildly and baring his teeth, threatening to pounce on his aggressors.

The New Year's celebrations caused a great stir. My mother left. Milia was busy bringing up our son and looking after the house. Meanwhile I notified the Deputy Minister of her resignation. Over the two remaining weeks of the old year, the inspector of the Applied Arts Board succeeded in restoring order to the abandoned Museum Department. He used the available funds in the budget to settle all the artists' debts built up during Milia's negligent tenure. When I collected her personal things from the office, I asked the inspector to convey my apologies to Nazarov for his futile assistance to my wife.

"That's why we don't send our wives out to work. They have much more important responsibilities in the family and at home. We consider that the female mind and character is not made for serious male service."

I decided not to get into a philosophical debate, and just spread my hands and shrugged my shoulders. But inside I wondered: *Perhaps he's right. There's no smoke without fire.*

As expected, once Mum had gone, everything went to pot. My son went around with a snotty nose in dirty clothes. You couldn't go in the kitchen or toilet as they reeked of rotten stuff and human waste. My wife sabotaged her duties as a mother and housekeeper. On Mondays (my day off) she entrusted me with taking Dmitri to nursery and picking him up in the evening, instead of doing it herself. I refused, asserting that parents have no right to take their child into a group of young children from such dirty, unhygienic conditions. At this she jumped off the bed, using foul language to me in front of our son, who naturally started crying. I led him outside, set him up with the trolley, and asked him to play in the garden for a bit while his mum and I had a chat indoors. He was distracted by the toy, and I went back into the bedroom with a jug of cold water to 'cool things down'. Milia, understandably, had returned to bed, assuming that Dmitri and I had gone to the nursery. I put the jug of water on the bedside table and sat down on the bed at a cautious, safe distance.

"Milia, you can't go on like this. I don't know what you're hoping to achieve, but to speak to our little boy's father in front of him using such obscenities is criminal. You can do away with motherhood today if I bring him up. So, let's have a calm discussion about the difficulty we have in living together and come to a constructive decision about our parental and household responsibilities for the next five months before we divorce once we're back in Moscow, so as not to traumatise our child or each other for nothing."

My wife childishly hid under the blanket, ignoring my suggestion. With foresight, I laid one hand on the bedside table next to the jug, and with the other, pulled the blanket towards me. As anticipated, my furious wife threw herself at me with arms wide. Meeting an unexpected stream of cold water in her face, my 'unwell' wife fell silent in shock.

"You beast! If you spit at me again or lay a finger on me, I will break this jug over your stone head. I will put you in prison for hooliganism, but I will not allow the rabid creature that you are, to insult our three-year-old son or his father."

There is some truth in the adage: "Like cures like." Struck dumb by my counter-attack, she dashed to the bathroom. Milia took a shower, did her hair, spruced herself up, got changed and went outside, where our son and I were already having breakfast. While the lady of the house was sorting herself out in the kitchen, I quickly got Dmitri washed and dressed in clean clothes, sat him on my shoulders and we hopped off to nursery, leaving his mum drinking tea in the garden, looking downcast like a beaten dog with its tail between its legs.

"Bye, Mummy," my rider repeated over and over as we got further away from home.

In the nursery I asked the leader to excuse us for being late, explaining that Dmitri's mother was ill, and promised to pick him up at 6 p.m.

At home I found the housekeeper cleaning the rooms. Without saying anything, I busied myself with cleaning the yard, handling the broom like a true caretaker. I put the rubbish out, watered the bushes and overhead grapevines with the hose, then gathered all the dirty bed linen and towels from the shower room for washing at the theatre laundry. With the cleaning finished, Milia made lunch – for the first time since Mum's departure. Meanwhile I prepared some dances from *Carmen* for the next day's rehearsal in my studio.

After lunch I carried on working on opera choreography, and the mistress of the house cleaned both the kitchen and toilet, freshened up again in the shower, and only then invited me to come and talk to her in the fresh-smelling sitting room. *Thatch your roof before the rain begins,* I thought, accepting my smiling wife's invitation.

"Dear, terrible husband, thank you for my latest 'almost holy resurrection'! I am ready to talk and put in place all the realistic, necessary conditions to continue our family together, in the interests of our son and your prestige in the theatre, for our time in Tadzhikistan, in spite of the deep antipathy I have to this country with its wild traditions of sexual and male chauvinism and hypocritical society."

After the lawyer's opening tirade, we successfully and rationally divided up our parental and domestic duties, keeping our emotions under strict control. We vowed not to traumatise our son with scenes, but to demonstrate our respect for each other in front of him and others around us in public, even if we had already lost it in private. We would not give our enemies the pleasure of witnessing our airing of any personal issues in public.

It was my secret ambition to stage dances in *Carmen*. In my favourite Character genre, my choreographic fantasy had taken flight on the creative wave of the winged Pegasus, high into the stars. For many years I had studied (in school, the Creative Folk Centre, MTA, and privately with Violeta Gonzalez) Spanish folklore: Khabanera, Jota, Farruca, Flamenco and many other ethnographical tributes. The 'corps de ballet' artistes failed to master one series of movements, as I had already overloaded them with the technical elements of another. Zakhidova complained about all this 'quite a lot of' and 'quite fast' for both the young and more experienced dancers. However, I carried on putting the pressure on gently and insistently as I couldn't get down to the choreographic staging until the performers had learned all they could about the synchronised rhythm of legs and snake-like movements of the arms with or without castanets. I had to second Pestov to the male 'corps de ballet' group, removing him temporarily from rehearsing new choreographic miniatures with the soloists. In this way, learning the choreography became more productive.

In the evening during the opera shows I continued to work with Pestov in parallel in two halls on my ballet-concert *Poem of Man*. This programme included, in addition to the three above-mentioned compositions, six more miniatures motivated by sculptures, pictures and mythological images of the same subjects, to music by contemporary Russian and foreign classical composers.

1. 'Planet Morning' (music by Scott) – to an anonymous antique engraving.
2. 'Three Graces' (music by Claude Debussy) – to a sculpture of the same name by Antonio Canova.
3. 'Satyr and Nymphs' (music by Claude Debussy) – to a picture of the same name by Nicolas Poussin.
4. 'Eternal Gauls' (music by Sergei Rachmaninov) – to an ancient Roman sculpture.
5. 'Serenade Grotesque' (music by Maurice Ravel) – to Carlo Goldoni's poem about unrequited love.
6. 'Stormy Petrel' (music by Sergei Rachmaninov) – to Maxim Gorky's poem.

Such was the content of miniatures in the first act on themes of an earlier historic era of humanity. The programme for the second act offered a representation of a later historic period and included staging of contemporary monuments of fine and literary art through artistic musical/dance composition. However, the local social and cultural problems delayed its completion.

After visiting my production rehearsal with the soloists, Valamat-Zade invited me to his office for a 'heart to heart', warning his secretary that he needed to be undisturbed for fifteen minutes. Sketches of costumes for the ballet miniatures were laid out on his couch and chairs. He asked whether it was my idea that the patterns on display were to be the decoration on performers' attire. I nodded affirmatively. He gestured to me to sit down.

"Misha, from time immemorial we have observed a strict moral tradition on the Asiatic theatre stage: not to show respectable women with bare legs in public, even if they are only outlined in close-fitting jersey tights. Ladies absolutely must dance in wide-legged trousers or long skirts. Usually only courtesans are depicted in paintings or indulge men by being half naked in the tea house, and then expose themselves in ecstasy from intoxicating drugs. To avoid any unpleasantness with regard to our responsibilities, I strongly recommend you to revisit the artistic decision for your decorative/pictorial presentation following the example of the ballets: *Du-Gul*, *The Bakhchisarai Fountain*, *Scheherazade*, *Gayaneh*, *Seven Beauties* and other Asiatic ballets."

I thanked him for his advice and promised to think about the complex situation. Only now, after six months of working in this theatre, did I finally understand why classical shows had been practically frozen in the ballet repertoire danced by women in short tutus with conventionally bare backs and legs, and men in tight breeches with their organs on show between their legs. All this was offensive to the conservative local audience. Women laughed naïvely and loudly in the theatre at the music, shamefully turning their heads away from the dancers. Men reacted indignantly to this obscene spectacle with disgusted grimaces and spat on the auditorium floor with contempt. During the performances in similar ballets, the morally wounded Tadzhiks of both sexes unceremoniously left the show as the orchestra started up, without waiting for the interval. It was hard for me fully to understand and evaluate what exactly was the more significant moral crime in this situation in the realm of Marxist–Leninist aesthetics: the defilement of age-old social and spiritual traditions of the Central Asian peoples by celebrated European progress of global civilisation? Or the cynical ignorance of contemporary forms of theatrical art by ossified, learned advocates of conservative religion?

I couldn't visualise the living sculptures by Canova or Rodin in baggy trousers, nor think of suggesting to Sabirova that she dance 'Song of the Black Swan' (Villa-Lobos) in a long gown with a yashmak instead of a ballerina's tutu. Naturally, after the conversation with the theatre's artistic director, I was in deep shock and couldn't see a way out of this deadlock. It was useless to argue with Gafar. To continue the planned staging, knowing it to be all wrong was also senseless. My sponsor, the chief theatre administrator, counselled me to seek Nazarov's advice, as he was considered one of the most modern proponents of Tadzhik culture in the republic. The Deputy Minister saw me without delay. Knowing the reason for my visit, he shook his head in discouragement and recounted his story.

As a student during the thirty-year evolution of the Producer's Faculty at the Moscow Theatre School, Nazarov translated Anton Chekhov's *The Cherry Orchard* into Tadzhik. Coming home to Dushanbe after completing his education, he took up the post as the capital's theatre artistic director and immediately began a production of Chekhov's play, which was popular the world over. The local press gave the premiere a positive critical review overall, but unambiguously expressed the hope that next time they would see a play by an Asiatic writer staged in the republic's theatre. Apart from two children's shows which had already been running a long time in the current repertoire (*Nasredin in Bukhara* and *Aladdin and the Magic Lamp*), essentially there were no other Russian plays which had been translated into Turkic. For this reason almost all the drama pieces were performed by a Russian-speaking company. The young producer turned out to be without a portfolio of personal creative work, and was merely fulfilling the functions of an artistic director. When the Turkish government invited Nazarov to produce in Ankara, he gladly signed a contract with the capital's dramatic theatre for three years. He was preparing to extend the arrangement, but received an invitation to the post of Deputy Minister of Culture from Dushanbe and was compelled (willingly and by obligation) to return to his homeland.

"Mikhail, as you understand very well, I can't offer you any practical help with anything, apart from off-the-record, friendly advice. If you have the courage of your convictions in your creative credo and are not minded spiritually to adapt your personal and artistic principals to the local traditional conditions in the arts, then find another theatre, free from confused prejudices, where you have not acquired powerful enemies in your fledgling career. Nonetheless, these are dangerous, difficult times for the whole republic, which as you know, shares a border with Afghanistan. Unfortunately, Islam's conservative influence is taking a hold on our people ever more broadly and deeply from our near neighbours, which Moscow is not very pleased about. Confidentially, in all probability, things could start to get serious here in the near future. I myself, as a non-believing party member, offend many people just by being here. My enemies would be happy not to see me in this government."

"Taking everything into account, I won't be able to finish production of my miniatures?"

"On the contrary. If you can't or don't want to change your convictions, complete this programme to your original plan and show it to the theatre's Artistic Council in May at the reception for *Carmen*, when ministry officials, the public and the press will all be present. They will all get to see your controversial compositions and you will get to hear their opinion. This will give you the moral right to end your contract in June and decide 'to be or not to be'! Whatever happens, I wish you every success!"

"Thank you for your candid advice, Karim Nazarovich. I'll keep this conversation between the two of us."

As I left his office, my heart felt lighter and I could think more clearly. Now I knew how to conduct myself with Valamat-Zade and was ready for the opening move. If it's not my personal problem, but the general situation in the republic, it means that I will play the proposed game with him by local rules, and won't become a Don Quixote tilting at windmills or waving a red flag at a bull. At the theatre, the porter gave me a request from the administrator to pop in and see him after the start of the performance.

As soon as he saw me Aaron asked curiously: "So how are you doing?"

"Your recommendation turned out to be really useful. Nazarov spent half an hour chatting with me, 'putting my thinking straight'. After this, my position in today's theatre has become significantly clearer. Under newly applied circumstances, I will complete the first act of sculptural miniatures and stage it for the official guests immediately after the public showing of *Carmen*. Let them decide what to do with me."

I knew that Aaron would report back to Gafar about this visit, making his knight's first zigzag chess move.

At the end of May, Dushanbe's cultured society and the ministry's theatrical directors, under Nazarov's leadership, accepted a new staging of *Carmen*. Artistes from the creative departments revived Bizet's convivial music with great enthusiasm on the capital's stage in Tadzhikistan. At the same time, while members of the reception committee were discussing the operatic premiere in the conference hall, stagehands had lowered the silvery-velvet backdrop and the wings, covering up the *Carmen* stage set. They removed the architectural props and cleaned the floor ready for the miniatures from *Poem of Man*. When the discussion was over, Valamat-Zade invited the guests to light refreshments in the theatre canteen. This gave Petya and me the opportunity to have an hour's run-through of the stage presentation with minimal lighting. They put a grand piano next to the control panel in the wings, from which I would conduct. During tea, Gafar gave out a crudely printed type-written programme for the miniatures to members of the jury, listing the performers' names. He gave a brief explanation of the anthropological idea for *Poem of Man* and naturally, put up for discussion the question of theatrical costumes. The stalls and boxes were closed. But artistes from the 'corps de ballet' and choir, and colleagues from other departments gathered in the upper galleries of the auditorium.

Prior to the viewing, the Artistic Director requested the audience in the gods to remain quiet, and not to applaud between numbers, so as to maintain a conducive working atmosphere in the pit. At his signal I gave the command for curtain-up.

The first miniature was 'Planet Morning' to the musical étude by Claude

Scott. Two pairs of primitive *Homo sapiens* illuminated in silhouette by the rays of the rising sun, depicted the spring of humanity in a ritual dance glorifying the abundance of nature. Their bodies (in tights) were partially covered in animal skins, acquired on a hunt.

The curtain came down after each number in the programme. The lighting was low in the auditorium, allowing guests to make notes in their programmes and Pestov to get his next performers ready onstage.

The last miniature to be shown was 'The Proud Stormy Petrel' (to Rachmaninov's 'Prelude'): a symbol of man's eternal struggle for cultural progress and intellectual creativity. After this the whole group of this programme's performers (with the house lights on) came out to take a bow. They were treated to a standing ovation. Some of the artistes pulled the pianist, répétiteur and choreographer on to the stage. The excited audience started to chant. Valamat-Zade signalled for the curtain to come down. Essentially, this was my public farewell to the Tadzhik theatre. I thanked all the participants onstage, including Zakhidova, who had been actively helping Pestov behind the scenes.

The next day, the city's newspapers lavished congratulations on the Opera Theatre for their creative victory in their production of *Carmen*, and praised the artistes for a dazzling performance of Spanish dancing, restraining themselves from naming the choreographer and répétiteur. However, 'a spoonful of tar spoils a barrel of honey' as the critics remarked on an additional showing of a one-act ballet *Poem of Man*, in a production by the chief ballet master. 'With his experimental choreography, Mikhail Berkut has quite simply outraged centuries of traditions in Classical dance, with his impertinent imitation of the famous modern dance form in Western Bourgeois art. Not only were his miniatures full of sexual, erotic elements described as "fluid," but he added yet more to this naturalism by putting half-naked dancers on the Soviet stage, defiling the spiritual, aesthetic essence of our National culture. Such a vulgar, dangerous spectacle cannot be permitted within the walls of the capital's Theatre.'

At the entrance to the office, Valamat-Zade met me with a false attack: "Misha, I warned you, but . . ."

"Yes, Gafar. It's true. Nazarov also predicted a negative reaction from the local public for flouting ancient Asiatic traditions." I gave him a broad smile. "But not all creative people can compromise their artistic principles. For this reason I have decided to spare you any unnecessary trouble. Here is my resignation from 1st June. Thank you for everything!"

Milia was on cloud nine. Her postgraduate term was starting on 1st July and she absolutely had to be at MTA a month in advance for the appropriate exam preparation. Pestov's and my pre-diploma placement came to an end officially at the end of May. The state exams for both apprentices and defence of their diplomas were planned for a month's time in MTA. Everything was falling into place. Nevertheless, Pyotr was disappointed that his epic work with the soloists had not been valued by the theatre management. Over the few days prior to my resignation from the post of chief ballet master, I wrote a detailed report on Pestov's diploma work, commenting on his high level of professionalism as ballet teacher and répétiteur. Valamat-Zade, himself an MTA graduate, did not dare to argue with this conclusion. He allowed his secretary to type up this document on headed theatre paper with my signature. In turn, I received from the Deputy Minister of Culture, Nazarov, an official report of my productive work as an MTA diploma student in my post as ballet troupe leader. He remarked on my exceptional talents as a choreographer in the operatic shows *Ivan Susanin* and *Carmen* and on my successful creative quests for contemporary styles in classical ballet, and in particular, in the miniature compositions *Poem of Man*. The Deputy Minister thanked the Dean for recommending both practitioners to the Alisher Navoi Theatre.

The fast train whisked us away from Dushanbe to Moscow like lightning. At least that's how it seemed to me. In actual fact, the express trailed across the sands of Tadzhikistan and Uzbekistan like a snail. The June heat was unbearable. The four of us including Petya fitted comfortably into one compartment. Pestov played patiently with Dmitri all the way, while the child's parents traded goods at the big shops. Passengers paid fatherly compliments to him, not me. Milia laughed, but I was filled with jealousy, and itched to defend my parental rights. My wife found a gracious audience for her stories of writers' plagiarism in theatrical art. A few times I had to stop the impassioned lecturer when I noticed how poor Petya, tortured with legal theses and anti-theses, was beginning to lose consciousness. I would take him out for a smoke on the carriage platform, where he would report the latest news from life behind the scenes in the theatre, of which I had no knowledge.

"Did you know that the review of your miniatures was written by someone Gafar had sacked?"

"'The moon pays no heed to the barking of dogs.' Still, it helped us to get out at a good time."

"Sabirova and Burkhanov got lucky as well. Nazarov signed a placement for them – a year at the Bolshoi in Galina Ulanova's soloists' class, regardless of the fact that Valamat-Zade had already refused them."

"Of course, the artistic director understands that after Moscow they'll never go back there."

"By the way, the Deputy Minister has signed a contract as a producer in Turkey again."

"Listen, how do you know all this gossip? And why didn't you tell me before?"

"Precisely because I am not a gossip, and unlike you, an inoffensive audience. For example, it was explained to me that you and I turned out to be sacrifices in a shoot-out in the long war between the Ministry of Culture and the artistic director on the one hand, versus Nazarov and the theatre director on the other. Moreover, in August, Gafar is being transferred to become director of the Philharmonic Society."

"How could you keep this to yourself for so long? Is that what you call being a best friend?"

"Tell you, who with your 'bull's horns' have messed up so many times? Best not to."

"Where on earth did you get to? I keep having to drag Dmitri out of the next-door compartment. Some young Muscovite girls on their way home from a competition in Tashkent have seduced him there. Your son has already told them all about our family and friend. 'Mum's writing a serious book and Dad and Uncle Petya are busy with their dancing. Only Granny used to play with me and read me stories at bedtime. Now she's gone home to Odessa and I haven't got anyone to play with.' Each time I bring him back from the giggling girls, he cries that he wants to stay there with them. You can imagine what your son's going to be like in twenty years' time! That's your influence!"

Listening to the mother's complaint, Pyotr laughed uncontrollably, and I added fuel to the fire: "It's not funny, it's sinful! A child is enjoying himself with girls to kill time in the train. I don't see anything wrong with that. It's better than squashing flies on the window all the way."

Eventually the conductor announced that we would soon be arriving in the capital.

Pestov and I defended our diplomas based on our placement in the Alisher Navoi Theatre: he in his capacity as ballet teacher/répétiteur, and I as choreographer/ ballet master. Pyotr passed both state exams with flying colours: Philosophy of Marxism–Leninism and Pedagogical Methodology. In addition to analogical pedagogy, I had to complete a test on methodology of dance composition and staging. I got top marks in both state exams in my specialism. But, to my delight, presiding on the state commission on the philosophy course was my old friend and enemy, deputy chair of Marxism–Leninism, the respected Sergei Gusev.

After my impeccable answers to the exam questions and supplementary clarifications on ideological theses on the very same theme on the side of commission members, the Professor unexpectedly asked me, with a sarcastic smile: "Mikhail, what do you think about socio-economic politics in Israel?"

The judges at the table looked around, astonished. Having thought for a moment, I responded calmly: "Forgive me, Professor, at lectures and seminars on Marxist–Leninist philosophy we never had any information or discourse on this subject, so I'm unable to answer your question as it's not on the syllabus."

"Surely you read the papers or listen to the latest news on the radio?"

"Unfortunately, the Choreography Faculty's full curriculum does not allow students to extend our professional attention to everything that's going on in the world."

News of this event at the State exam spread around MTA. In the hostel, some students shot hateful glances at me while others regarded me with sympathy. Nevertheless, after defending my diploma, the lecturers in the department, with the exception of Professor Zakharov, congratulated me on completing the course and wished me well.

Shatin, passing me in the corridor, quietly uttered (rather than congratulating me): "Well done, you didn't rise to the bait. Go and see the Philosophy Faculty Dean. There's some news for you."

"Thank you!" I replied in the same neutral tone of polite interaction. All the same. I struggled to understand in my naïve, primitive mind why a professor, head of the Philosophy Faculty and secretary of the MTA Party Committee, felt the need to stoop so morally low in the eyes of his colleagues and students, to wreak such small-minded revenge against a wretched, insignificant figure like me. To do this, he had to be a deep-rooted anti-Semite, to express his racist sentiments so cynically and openly in public, crushing 'internationally democratic principles of socialist society in the USSR' in his own shit.

In the list of diploma exams I had taken, all six in my specialism were graded 'excellent' and only the seventh – Marxism–Leninism – received 'satisfactory'. This clearly demonstrated the creative wastage imposed by the straitjacket of Soviet ideology. I realised that I was blacklisted and would never be free of it in the future.

Yet again, my spiritual father, Anatoly, had prevented me from reacting impulsively against my own self-interest in spite of his position as Dean of the faculty. He had enough trouble besides me in defending himself against constant persecution by the 'Zakharovs', 'Gusevs' and 'Vartanyans'. But he decided on principle to prove his case to all his progressive, principled detractors in creative pedagogy in selecting a system of artistic education for future choreographers.

261

That's why the Dean, again, recommended me to the Buryat-Mongolian (from the Buryat Autonomous Republic) Minister of Culture's enquiry, for the post of chief ballet master of the Ulan-Ude Opera Theatre, with potential responsibility as artistic director of the arts festival to mark the republic's forthcoming fortieth anniversary. Once the necessary paperwork had been completed, they would be expecting me at the Buryat Theatre in a month's time for the beginning of the season in September.

My wife had no wish even to hear about this project, and announced that this time she would not leave Moscow until she had finished her dissertation and completed her postgraduate study. So instead of the once promised family cooperation, I had run into a brick wall. But my vivacious son, despite being small, was of an animated disposition requiring both parents' input. His so-called mother suggested that I took our child with me to Ulan-Ude for a year, so that she could finish her second academic degree. I couldn't believe what I was hearing, but couldn't find the emotional energy or moral incentive to go against her suggestion. I felt totally conflicted: if the child stayed with her, he stood the risk of dying; with me, the four-year-old boy would be a ball and chain around my choreographer's feet. As wise men say, 'He that would eat the fruit must climb the tree.' Yet again I was filled with bitterness that my unfulfilled dream of a lifelong healthy and strong family was falling apart before my eyes, like a house of cards. Our split was inevitable and there was nothing I could do to prevent it. I was conflicted: feelings of creative excitement about the forthcoming work warred with an awareness of the sacrifice entailed in safeguarding my child, created and nurtured against the odds over the last five years.

For the entire six days of the train journey, Dmitri never stopped asking about his mum: "Why hasn't she come to Mongolia with us? Why did we leave Moscow? When will I see Mummy again now? How much longer will she be studying for her exams?"

My heart ached from all his questions. We had company in the compartment. An elderly Buryat couple were chatting in their own language, no doubt commenting on my conversation with my son. I read him stories endlessly, and taught him to play chess, fed and dressed him. But I could never completely take his mother's place in this four-year-old child's life, and feared for his emotional well-being in a new nursery with friends who spoke in other tongues.

"Daddy, why are you crying? Are you missing Milia too?"

"I miss her, but I'm not crying. I've just got a bit of dust in my eye."

"How much longer will we be in this horrible train? I'm already really fed up with it."

"We'll be arriving in Ulan-Ude tomorrow, sonny. Sleep well, my darling."

"You too, Daddy . . . Ulan-Ude, Mula-Zade," (nonsense word rhymes) the exhausted 'sapling' mumbled sleepily.

CHAPTER 2 PERMAFROST IN BALLET

"Wake up, sonny, time to get up! We'll be arriving in Ulan-Ude soon."

"Again: Mula-Zade, luna-mude! Daddy, when will we stop moving about all over the place?"

"Sleepy boy, you're like a grumpy old man, dreaming of a peaceful life."

"Mummy says that too, she's 'fed up of rushing about here and there all over the world'."

"That's understandable. She is a home bird and prefers being in one place. But you and I are migratory birds from the eagle tribe, aren't we, my boy?"

"Then why haven't we got wings like birds have, so that we could fly?"

"Sorry, darling, we're already here. I'll explain later. There's no time now, OK?"

We were met at the station exit by the theatre administrator, Galina Rodionova and her driver Victor. On the way to our accommodation we paid a visit to the special nursery, where the little ones were off for the week. While the doctor was carrying out a medical examination of Dmitri, Galina and I defined the terms of my accommodation in the house for theatre staff, and the possibilities for my son's care at weekends.

Tired and lethargic, the newcomers dozed off before long, ready to make an early start on their new life in the Buryat capital. Dmitri was happy to sleep with his daddy in the double bed. In the morning, depositing my son at nursery, I promised him that I would drop in for ten minutes every evening at 7 p.m. with news about Mummy. I explained that I would take him to Nanny Masha's on Saturday.

"She will give you a wash and feed, my little golden eagle. Then at 9 a.m. on Sunday, Daddy Berkut will whisk his little bird off to the theatre, where he will stay with him the whole day. In the evening, we will go and eat our favourite pasties again and go to sleep together."

"So what will I do at Nanny Masha's house? Swat flies on the window again?" my son whined.

There was laughter from the other mums dropping off their children at nursery around us. I explained to them, "He's picked this up from me during our five days in the train coming here from Moscow. Sonny, you won't be bored with your nanny. She's got grandchildren you can play with."

A teacher came along in a multicoloured car, and took Dmitri to his group. I lingered, watching him go off, and let out a heavy sigh.

One of the mums sympathised: "Dad, don't worry about your son. This is the best nursery in town. He will be all right here."

Rodionova was waiting for me at 10 a.m. at the theatre. En route to the director, she asked how my son and I had settled into our new place, and how he had taken the first parting from his dad at the nursery. I thanked her for her concern about these two 'desolate wanderers'.

Belyayev, the Director, welcomed me extremely good-naturedly. With arms wide open theatrically, he came towards me, exclaiming, "Dear Mikhail Semyonovich, welcome to the Buryat temple of art! How was your journey? How have you settled in? What are you inclined to create in our country?"

"Thank you. The chief administrator organised everything much better than we had anticipated."

"The Minister of Culture is expecting us after lunch. Now our artistic director, Lar Linkhovoin, will hold 'a five-minute meeting' with his posse of principals. Rodionova will help you to find him. We'll meet up again here at 1 p.m. and go to the ministry together. Good luck!"

"Galina, is everyone in your republic this warm and friendly towards people from elsewhere?"

"Buryats by nature are extremely sincere in expressing their feelings in all situations."

The Artistic Director's secretary apologised when she saw Galina and me and quickly hurried off behind an oak door, through which a tall and stately man emerged with heavy tread, surprising for a Buryat. He smiled cordially and yet again opened his terribly long arms wide, came close to me and took me by the shoulders:

"Good to have you with us, dear servant of Terpsichore, in Apollo's sacred chamber! Dear colleagues, our numbers have grown! Chief ballet master, Misha Berkut!"

As I got up from the armchair in Linkhovoin's office, I was met by applause from the theatre's leaders: the Artistic Director, stage manager, choirmaster and designer. Lar ceremoniously introduced each one of them. He explained that the season opened in a week's time and they were just determining the final programme for the first four months up to the New Year. He said it would be interesting to hear the latest opinion of a new comrade-in-arms, if it were not too premature for someone who'd just arrived.

"On the contrary." I smiled, mirroring the artistic director. "I like to take the bull by the horns."

Shatin had told me in Moscow about the universally celebrated talent of the 'central bass' Linkhovoin. He was a Stalin Prize winner as USSR Honoured Artiste, deputy in Russia's Supreme Soviet and so on. The sociopolitical figurehead of Linkhovoin in the republic placed him on the same footing as the local government chiefs, which was why he was so self-assured with his subordinates, while possessing personal tact and courtesy at the same time. Both within and beyond the theatre, Lar enjoyed sincere respect and recognition from a wide circle of theatregoers, and deservedly so.

"Mikhail, on 25th December, we are planning the forthcoming premiere of a new version of the opera *Prince Igor*. In response to my telephone enquiry to MTA for a ballet master, your mentor declared that they had no better candidate in Historical and Character dance choreography today. We are also au fait with your pre-diploma practice through a copy of a report from the Tadzhikistan Deputy Minister of Culture, where you put on dazzling dances in the operas *Ivan Susanin* and *Carmen*. I'm curious: do Asiatic dances also come into your creative repertoire? In addition, we would like to see your choreographic Classical dance gems in the first six months. Is there anything unique in your creative treasure chest that would be of interest to us? I'm sorry if I'm expecting too much from the Ballet Department leader right from the start."

"In theory, your enquiries regarding repertoire are entirely realistic. I'm ready and willing to take on and bring to fruition the proposals you've highlighted, but you see, no one buys a pig in a poke. It would be flippant and unprofessional for any ballet master to promise something without having first become familiar with the make-up and technical capabilities of the troupe. Nevertheless, in principle, both your projects are of interest to me creatively. But I'll only be able to give you my official agreement once I've got to know the company."

"Bravo! We'll continue this business discussion after meeting with the Minister of Culture. Dear colleagues, thank you for listening. Unless you have any questions, you may go. Mikhail, please stay."

Lar accompanied the department leaders and stayed behind with them for a few minutes in the corridor, probably clarifying their first impressions of the new chief ballet master.

"Mikhail, I must bring you up to speed on affairs in your department, so as to avoid any unnecessary complications. As you know, your predecessor Misha Zaslavsky worked here very successfully for several years and was also the theatre's Communist Party secretary. Naturally it was difficult for him to combine these two responsible positions. For this reason, the ballet company was essentially neglected, not in terms of his choreographic abilities, but because of the lack of energy and time to resolve the issues of a complex creative troupe, in both a professional and a biophysical sense. I'm talking about the natural incompatibility of the Mongols' morphological structure – square build, short limbs, nomadic horsemen with crooked legs, etc. – with the requirements of Classical dancers. At the beginning of the '50s we tried to create our own Ballet school based on neighbouring models – Irkutsk, Khabarovsk, Novosibirsk, and others. But a group of Classical dance experts categorically declined this idea as profaning classical ballet in the Opera Theatre. In return for this, our department leaders helped to pick out more than sixty musicians, singers and dancers from local amateur talent shows, who became the republic's School of Performing Arts' first students. Their building is on this same square, opposite the Opera Theatre. We enjoy good relations with them.

Our leaders teach there two to three times a week, by recommendation of the Minister of Culture, preparing their best students for future careers in choirs, 'corps de ballet' and sometimes even our theatre's orchestra. Zaslavsky invested a huge amount of work in training local Character dancers who already take part in opera/ballet shows straight from college. Naturally, we are forced to invite Classical dance soloists from elsewhere in the Soviet republics. We have limited funds for this. Just to organise and achieve everything calls for reasonably large financial subsidies from the Buryat and USSR governments. Above all, Zaslavsky deserves respect for the strength of his intense public activity but he didn't know how to develop our ballet to an adequate level with the opera. We hope very much that as a young and experienced enthusiast, you will be able to create that which eluded your predecessor. I guarantee you my full support in all your endeavours to strengthen the Ballet Department: inviting soloists, professional teachers/répétiteurs, composers, designers/ producers and similar specialists from the capital's theatres, educational institutions, wherever. Take up Zaslavsky's Pedagogical baton in the School of Performing Arts. Sell your creative vigour to the Minister of Culture. Then you'll have a green light for your future ballet productions both here and in other Siberian theatres.

In Ulan-Ude (as in Dushanbe), all the main departments were situated around the central Lenin Square, including: the government, theatre, hotel, university, school and other establishments. It took literally all of five minutes for Belyayev, the Director, to take me to the Ministry of Culture. On the way, I tried in vain to understand: why is it necessary to introduce me, not such an important bird, to the top brass in the republic? I didn't have to wait long for an answer. After my introduction to Sadykbayev, Minister of Culture, the latter asked if I had managed to have a chat with Linkhovoin and was interested to know from Belyayev about my living arrangements and my son's nursery. Following positive responses from us both, the Minister got straight down to business. He spread out a map of Buryatia on a nearby table and invited me to have a look at it, while listening to his commentary.

"Mikhail, we have a serious and responsible mission for you, which you are within your rights to decline, if you feel that you are not sufficiently competent to complete it appropriately. It concerns a Festival in honour of the 40th anniversary of our republic in May next year. We are planning to celebrate our anniversary with a Festival of Folk Arts in these three regional Buryat centres, which will put forward folk groups and professionals of all genres from which to select the best for a Gala concert in the Opera Theatre, after the Republican government's ceremonial conference. We propose that you take on Artistic leadership of the festival and stage the final show, beginning on 1st November this year. Belyayev has been appointed overall Administrative director of this event."

"How does one get around these mountainous areas in the country's out-of-the-way places?"

"A six-seater plane, Jeep, horseback and on foot. Ha ha ha!"

"In the Festival working party, in addition to the Musical director and Ballet master, it's essential to have a sound/cine operator, a journalist and an authorised Government representative for communication with local authorities. In all, the minimum number for a functional group is five people. Do you have the budget for this?"

"Absolutely. Give Belyayev a list of the required conditions and items to cost the project. He will write the contracts with your assistants, and my Department of Arts Board will write up an agreement with the festival's Artistic Director. Do you have any other questions?"

"Lar Akimovich asked me to continue my predecessor's mission in the School of Performing Arts. As far as I know, this is your 'baby' and I wouldn't want to be misunderstood. To work successfully in the theatre, I need to take part in training local staff, and I'm prepared to teach the students the Art of Dance. However, for any specialist, to be productive in three areas of responsibility is quite a lot to take on. Would it be possible to hand over the teaching to our ballet teachers and répétiteurs?"

"Unfortunately, it's illegal without an official diploma in higher education. They can only work as your assistants, not as Principal teachers. One solution to this difficulty would be for you to train them once a week, on your day off, and they would work (as assistants) with your learning resources on the other days. Everyone would be happy with a division of labour along these lines."

"I agree. There's just one last request to make this heavy programme easier for next season. Unfortunately, travel around outside Ulan-Ude is made more complicated by the presence of my four-year-old son, who is struggling enough as it is without his mother here. Once we have put on the premiere of *Prince Igor* on 25th December, I'd like to take my son to Moscow to be with my wife, so that I can be free for the Festival and at the same time purchase scores of Rachmaninov's symphonic works for our orchestra in the Moscow Conservatoire bookshop, in time for our ballet *Splintered Lilac*. I'd appreciate your help in organising the return flight tickets to Moscow for a few days, as the train takes ten days. Those are my wishes."

"Mikhail, if I have understood correctly, you agree, in addition to the theatre, to take on the duties of Festival artistic director for six months, and stage the Gala concert from 1st November to 3rd May, also, to teach once a week in the School of Performing Arts and act as a consultant to your assistants on the other days. On these terms, I promise to fund a business trip for you to Moscow for a week (plane there and back) to prepare your new ballet. Belyayev, you are Berkut's partner rather than his boss, in organising the festival and the Gala concert in the theatre. Both of you have equal rights, make sure that you draw up over the next week costings, a work plan, and a monthly programme for district and regional bases, jury members and a technical group. Both of you can sign monthly accounts on my behalf. Is that agreed? Let's get stuck in! Mikhail, excuse me, I need to talk further with Belyayev. All the best!"

In the evening I listened attentively to a Buryat version of Tchaikovsky's *The*

Queen of Spades. All soloists and vocalists obviously belonged to the Slavic race and sang without local accents. However, visually, with their oval-shaped skulls, they were barely distinguishable from their historic brothers in arms in the Mongol racial group. It seems that this genetic heritage was assimilated in the period of the Tartar–Mongolian yoke, and hundreds of years later, the external racial contrasts of both groups had faded considerably. A similar phenomenon arose even with local dancers at the Imperial ball. Dressed in the same court attire, they looked like a complete assortment and made a pleasant impression through the refined manner of their performance. Choreography was important in Zaslavsky's production. I recognised my mentor, Margarita Rozhdestvenskaya's method. But although their singing was really pure and harmonious, I found the choristers quite static. Physical expression in the dramatic scenes featuring the choir and mime artistes was severely limited.

In the interval, the ticket lady popped in to the Director's box and gave me an invitation to call in at the management. When I appeared, Rodionova got up to meet me with an envelope in her hand and officially introduced me to the guests and friends present:

"This is our new Chief ballet master from Moscow, Misha Berkut. Please show him your love and favour."

Unfamiliar faces, looking around, nodded their heads deferentially.

In a note, Linkhovoin asked me to call in to see him tomorrow at 10 a.m. before meeting the troupe at 11 a.m.

Then, someone unexpectedly pulled me down by my jacket flap and squeaked playfully: "So can you dance on one leg? Or do a headstand?"

"For tipcats like you, I can do more than stand – I can dance on my head."

"Timon, come here quick!"

"Granny, Granny, tell me, what's a tipcat?"

"Mikhail, please excuse my grandson. He pesters everyone he doesn't know. I am Galina's mum. Very nice to meet you. We visit my daughter every evening during the interval. She's so busy in the theatre that she doesn't see her son for days at a time and he misses her."

"Mikhail Semyonovich, there's the third bell. Go and watch the opera, don't miss the start," the administrator reminded me.

I couldn't sleep that night. So many new impressions and proposals! There wasn't enough time to digest and break them down in my head or file them in date order.

By 9 a.m. the following morning, I was already at the theatre, where I asked the doorman for the key to the ballet master's room. Next to me, a middle-aged man was removing a letter from the letter box inscribed with the word 'BALLET'.

Hearing my request, he turned round quickly and greeted me: "Hello, Mikhail Semyonovich! I am your troupe manager, Demyan Kadyrov. I've got all the keys to the building. We're expecting you after class at 11 a.m. I've informed everyone of the meeting with the new chief ballet master."

"Tell me a bit about the make-up of the troupe, the teachers/répétiteurs, pianists and yourself."

"I've been retired for twelve years already, and for nine of those I've been the manager. I've outlived four ballet masters."

"Why do they change so frequently, if it's not a trade secret?"

"I don't know. Zaslavsky was here longest of all, around five years before he also left. He practically transformed our classical repertoire. He was offered better terms at the Lvov Theatre in Ukraine, and he accepted gladly."

"Is the morning class a general one for everyone? Or do the soloists warm up separately?"

"Just the one class, but not everyone comes."

Next to the writing desk in my personal office were a piano and electric record player. The shelves were stacked with records of opera and ballet music, photo albums and books. This must have been where Zaslavsky prepared his theatrical productions and lectures for the school. The window of the top floor offered a broad vista of the square with its modern buildings and exotic fir trees. In the distance stood a temple to Buddha – naturally, non-functioning – an ancient architectural monument. A knock at the door interrupted my musings on religion and history. Demyan introduced to me the répétiteur Alfred Fotiyev, former leading soloist with Kharkov Ballet.

"It's a pleasure to meet a fellow countryman so far from home. Correct me if I'm wrong, but after the meeting you are rehearsing *Sleeping Beauty* for an evening performance. Please come and have lunch with me in the break, then we can have a chat. I don't want to hold you up any longer. I wish you success in your work. Demyan, stay on, please. After you've taken the register in class, help me to find in these boxes a complete list of the current repertoire with details of performers, a monthly work schedule to the end of August, creative biographies of all the ballet artistes taking part, both permanent and sessional; a list of those about to retire (by work stage) over the next four months, and a list of casual students from the School of Performing Arts. Thank you. Linkhovoin is expecting me."

The secretary advised Linkhovoin that I had arrived.

Lar emerged. "Hi! How was your meeting with the Minister? I hope he didn't scare you off by putting the pressure on."

"Lar Akimovich, I may be young, but I've been around the block a bit. I'm not easily shocked. Sadykbayev was pushy and politely patient. He loaded me up gently and unhurriedly. In principle we agreed on everything."

"Before you arrived, they suggested that I took on Artistic direction of the Festival, but I declined, since as deputy, I have to sit on the presiding council during the creative process and then sing in the second section of the concert. As you'll understand, those things are incompatible."

"May I ask you, as leader of the Buryat Theatre, to help me in the final choice of items for inclusion in the Gala concert? It'll be clearer to you which of them after selection will reflect more fully the forty-year development of Buryat culture in folklore aesthetics and political, ideological aspects. Films and audio-recordings of all the competition winners – candidates for the Gala concert – will be available to you before they actually arrive in Ulan-Ude. Your objective, professional opinion will help to reduce any unnecessary transport and accommodation costs and participants' concerns."

"Misha, you're not as young as I thought you were from our first meeting, and you know very well that I have no right to refuse you, so I have to give you my consent."

We both burst out laughing, high-fiving each other.

"Prior to meeting with you, I managed to see the Ballet troupe manager and répétiteur this morning."

"Wonderful! Actually I wanted to talk to you about this before the meeting with the Ballet troupe, to avoid any potential surprises. Over the last ten years, as you probably already know, we have got through five different ballet masters, which has had a detrimental effect on the company in all respects. The ballet artistes hold the Theatre's management and Artistic leadership responsible for this. Zaslavsky lived amongst us and ran the department quite productively, but after his departure, the leading soloists made known their dissatisfaction to the Minster of Culture in a letter to the Theatre leadership. However, the actual reason for the instability in ballet masters stems not from the fact that their salary is lower than that of other department heads, as they have complained about in writing, but in their creative dissatisfaction when working with unprofessional artistes in the 'corps de ballet', even including several of the soloists. Ethically, we cannot make this known to the company, although teachers/répétiteurs experience the very same difficulties in work and other professionals understand this full well. To be honest, I don't know how to get out of this organisational impasse. One thing is clear: the new department Leader really must take great pains to gain an in-depth knowledge of the real artistic paradox, and very delicately, like a plastic surgeon, cut and sew – cut off and stick back the distinct groups or individuals with patience and diplomacy, so as not to destroy the whole organism. This is a complicated operation, alas, which has fallen largely upon your shoulders, for which you have my apologies."

"I sensed something yesterday during the performance of *The Queen of Spades*, and asked the manager to collect information for me on the creative biographies of the ballet artistes and details of the performers' repertoires. To use your metaphor, I've had an idea for a 'psychosurgical' operation to bring together the various groups into one combined, solid creative body. But we need financial resources to ensure a positive outcome to this. I'm talking about recruiting additional dancers urgently to the soloists' group as well as the 'corps de ballet'. An unhealthy organism needs a 'transplant' of healthy bio-cells, i.e. fresh blood, to eliminate ulcers infected with harmful bacteria and open the way to potential progress in the renewed ensemble's creative functioning. After lunch I will have a look at the materials I've been given. In the evening I'll sit in the auditorium to watch *Sleeping Beauty*, and tomorrow morning I'll let you know whether it's 'to be or not to be'. I'm sorry; we probably need to get to the Ballet Department meeting now."

"Misha, I'm sorry to keep you. After I've introduced you to the troupe, I must get off to my own rehearsal straight away. I'm sure that you'll sort things out with your apprentices. I'll expect you at 10 a.m. tomorrow. If you need anything urgently, just pop in."

The artistes were sitting on the floor in the ballet studio, and there was a sudden hush as we appeared.

"My dear friends, allow me to introduce your new Leader, Mikhail Semyonovich Berkut, young teacher and ballet master with eight years of choreographic experience. In common with his predecessor, Zaslavsky, he is also an MTA graduate. He has come to us with great creative plans, approved by the Theatre management team and Ministry of Culture. Mikhail is appraised of our specific challenges, and is ready to work on these issues with your cooperation. I assure you of my support. I have great hopes for your professional and aesthetic development. Good luck!"

Wild applause echoed around the room, followed by a deathly silence.

"Lar Akimovich, if possible, can we meet at nine thirty rather than ten tomorrow, before ballet classes?"

"Sure! Come along with Demyan and he can get hold of the information you need about the troupe."

The troupe manager, répétiteurs and pianists were sitting on one side. I went over, shook hands with each of them and returned with Demyan to my position in front of the seated dancers. I waited for them to stop talking, looking around at their curious faces.

"Dear colleagues . . ." I began very quietly as usual, forcing them to strain to hear me, and to focus all their attention on their new leader.

The manager tutted at someone and got ready to make notes in his pad following my orders, remarks, requests, etc.

"I'm not going to tell you about myself just now. I'm more interested in hearing your thoughts about the difficult working conditions in the current circumstances (I was being ironic): the poor studios and substandard facilities, the overwhelming rehearsals and performances [there was an 'ahem' from somewhere in the room], the harsh or severe reproaches of the manager and répétiteurs, the unpleasant sound of the piano or pianist, the extreme deductions from your salaries for being late or not turning up to rehearsals or shows, the un-called-for reprimands which become personal business, for the punch-up in the Wardrobe Department, or appearing onstage drunk. I think it's better not to go on.

"I'm sure that it's not the tiny salary that has drawn us all into ballet, but boundless love of the art of dance. Without a doubt, all of you artistes here, from leading soloists and prizewinners through to new graduates from the School of Performing Arts, are ready to commit your energy and emotion to our Muse Terpsichore, in return for creative satisfaction onstage. And when you don't get these opportunities, the Ballet Department will inevitably see discord, squabbles, affairs and other problems between people, which will curtail our artistic ensemble's successful cooperation. As a matter of urgency, we need to examine our personal positions in the company and refresh the working atmosphere at rehearsals. Anyone who can't or won't take on the standard conditions of his/her profession in this season's new productions will not be used. What this means in practice for those people is voluntary retirement or compulsory dismissal in the end. Belyayev, the Director, asked me to remind you of your contractual obligations:

"a) to attend morning classes, all rehearsals and shows as set out in the timetable;

"b) lateness and absence during working hours without appropriate notice or valid reason will result in penalties from the management; and

"c) the manager is required to bar drunken artistes from work.

"In my five minutes with our Artistic Council, I notified them of my rehearsal plan for the Ballet Department's forthcoming season, on condition that essential reorganisation of the company's work is undertaken.

"By the New Year, the 'corps de ballet' and I will devise new choreography for the opera *Prince Igor*, including: 'Polovtsian Dances' (warriors, housemaids, rent boys/boys); 'Russian Dances' (girls, captured warriors); crowd scenes with the Choir and Mime artistes. In addition, moving images of the main heroes, and at the same time, we will prepare a Ballet-Concert, *Poem of Man*, with a group of soloists – a minimum of twelve professional performers – in three acts, to classical music by Russian/Soviet and European composers. In all there will be nineteen choreographed miniatures in contemporary style on the theme of man's anthropology (from our primitive forbears through the origins of civilisation to today's ideas). Most of these compositions were tested out on the graduates from the Bolshoi Theatre School in Moscow.

"For the second half of the working season, alongside Operatic repertoire unfamiliar to me, planned by the theatre's Artistic Council, I propose a unique double bill in honour of the ninetieth anniversary of the great Russian composer

Sergei Rachmaninov: a one-act opera *Aleko* and *Splintered Lilac*, a ballet in two acts to his music, including: 'Youth Symphony', a dramatic sonata, 'The Cliff' and 'Symphonic Dances'. The idea of my libretto/scenario is centred on an artist's longing for his homeland, from which he had long since parted irreconcilably. (Rachmaninov left Russia after the first revolution in 1905). Lar Akimovich, here is my manuscript. If this project is of interest to you, then I, as the writer, will allow you to print off a copy and distribute it to members of the Artistic Council to peruse and discuss. Now I must go and have a look at my artistes in their ballet class. After that I'll report back to you on the outcome of our meeting yesterday and my viewing of *Sleeping Beauty*, and about today's class. Then we can have a chat about the situation."

I only viewed the second half of the ballet class. The Soloists were training by the right-hand barre, and the 'corps de ballet' by two others. Fotiyev ran the general class and managed the group of professionals, while Tyzhebrova took charge of the school apprentices. To the observer it looked quite sparse, without any commentary. In contrast to yesterday's show, *Sleeping Beauty*, the dancers were without heavy costumes, so it was impossible to conceal their physical flaws in their stretchy uniforms (swimming costume and tights or football shirt and breeches). The contrast between soloists and the 'corps de ballet' brought tears to my eyes. This is the reason Zaslavsky had not combined both groups into the same episodes in his versions of 'state' ballets.

The longer I watched the school dilettantes' absorbed faces, dripping in sweat before me in the middle of the studio, alongside the professional soloists (even at different stages of completing the exercises), the more deeply I became aware of having fallen, once more, into a creative trap. At the end of the class I gave generally positive feedback of yesterday's show, recalling sarcastically that the leading soloist Dambuyev, in each of his variations, was reeling about so much, as if he were dancing at a school friend's wedding.

"Thank God he didn't fall into the orchestra pit! I suppose for this achievement he deserves another honour."

Once we had collected together all the archive materials on the artistes' professional categories and general information on the ballet dancers, Demyan and I went down to the artistic director. Linkhovoin and the manager agreed the numbers in the different categories and potential pensioners with more than twenty years of service. Lar identified possible vacancies and asked me what was the minimum number required on the permanent staff to restore normal functioning in the Ballet Department.

"Instead of the standard numbers common to Opera theatres, the Soloists' group is twenty, and the 'corps de ballet', forty. We'll be able to fulfil the current and planned repertoire with fifteen soloists and thirty 'corps de ballet' artistes. So we need another twelve people, six in each group, excluding replacements for those who'll soon be retiring.

"Demyan, not a word to anyone about this project, please! Write a memo to the Director about Dambuyev. You can go!"

"Mikhail, please explain your reckoning and reasons for asking to recruit an additional twelve permanent staff?"

"In the first place, there are a few dancers in the pensioners' group who are over forty (both men and women), who are no longer able to maintain the physical load on their bodies and, quite understandably, are working at half strength even onstage. I understand that at this age it's unpleasant to be unemployed, and a meagre pension is insufficient to keep a family.

What usually happens is that ballet artistes run dance clubs in schools and organisations in all capitals and large cities across the USSR. In any case, it makes no sense to keep them as ballast in the department when our position has become more complicated.

"Secondly, you yourself noticed the marked contrast in natural and physical structure between Soloists and the "corps de ballet". For example, I can't use soloists of high and low stature in the same group, as this would evoke misplaced laughter from the audience and demoralise the performers. It's the same with the "corps de ballet". We also really need to have roughly five tall ones and ten of average height in the group of Soloists, and in the "corps de ballet", similarly: ten average and twenty shorter. This will enable the choreographer and répétiteur to shape (in their substitutions) the performers into the most positive, harmonious make-up, as required by their roles.

"Thirdly, most of the "corps de ballet" have transferred from the School of Performing Arts and lack a specialist ballet qualification. In the group historic and Character dances they fully correspond in technique to the opera/ballet repertoire. But in the staging of episodes from traditional ballets by Tchaikovsky, Glazunov, Pugni, Delibes, Chopin, etc., some need to perform Classical dances in harmony with leading soloists. This eclectic presentation looks completely absurd in today's theatre."

"Misha, I completely agree with you in all of this, and even warned you about this on your first day. You understand that I can't guarantee you new staff that quickly, but can promise to do everything in my power to hold auditions over the next month. Set out in writing all your grounds and reasoning without delay. My secretary will type a letter to the Minister of Culture with your attachment. We will both sign this petition and tomorrow it will be on Sadykbayev's desk. Despite the fact that you, my dear friend, are raising my blood pressure, I'm happy that we have found a Ballet Master who is sufficiently sure of his convictions and brave enough to instigate radical action in his department, and not avoid essential problems, leaving your charges behind to the mercy of fate. I have to admit that Zaslavsky repeatedly took up the question of refreshing the group with the Artistic Council. But in his party position he decided not to make an assault on the bureaucratic fortress and chose instead to withdraw. Meanwhile, the Artistic Council members are impressed with your plans for the ballet. If they agree to the auditions, we will have to discuss the libretto for *Splintered Lilac* in detail, i.e. the music and staging."

The meeting with répétiteurs turned out to be a turning point in the troupe's internal revolution. Both over forty, and with a wealth of performing experience under their belts, they became teachers only in the last season, before Zaslavsky's departure, which prepared them specially for their replacement both within the troupe and in the school.

Hearing about my simultaneous productions of *Prince Igor* and *Poem of Man*, both répétiteurs held their heads in their hands, looked at each other, then at me, and beseeched me: "Mikhail Semyonovich, you are obviously overestimating the capabilities of our dancers, both physically and technically. The way they are used to working is 'Slow and steady wins the race.'"

"Unfortunately that's how it has to be. That's why (between us) I explained to management that it would only be possible to undertake the planned repertoire by recruiting additional young graduates from ballet schools in the surrounding Siberian towns with opera theatres. In all, twelve permanent colleagues, six in each group category. From 1st October, after our respected veteran dancers have retired, we will refresh the Soloists and "corps de ballet" with young, new enthusiasts, who will also stimulate creative activity amongst a few ballet artistes who've got a bit lazy. This project is under discussion with those on high at the moment, and I'm almost sure of a positive outcome, through my past experience and on the strength of our particular circumstances.

"I came here not to rake it in, or 'wait for my ship to come in'. To my delight, in the run up to the anniversary of the republic, as you'll understand later on, the Ministry of Culture needs me more than I need it [I strutted before my subordinates], and I'm obliged to make the best of this situation to safeguard my work in the theatre. Similar 'blackmail' [I was justifying myself] is just one of the forms in the struggle for existence in the harsh world of the arts. I agree with you. My planned repertoire is slightly too heavy for a substandard company, taking into account also the reintroduction of the ballet *Coppélia* for children's matinees for the New Year. With your help, I'm planning to finish the choreography for *Prince Igor* in November. While you're both busy with *Coppélia* in December, I'll work with the soloists individually in the evenings on choreography for the solo and duet miniatures. If we succeed in replenishing through auditions, I'll easily finish staging for *Poem of Man* in parallel with *Prince Igor* over two months with the soloists' group, and keep up their creative interest. If we don't manage to recruit, then I'll have to postpone *Poem of Man*.

By 7 p.m. I was usually running to meet my son. On the way to the nursery I always bought some chocolate, which he happily tucked into after supper, while I told him the next story of Scheherazade. Later, once we had finished the episodes in this series, I started to make up five-minute tales about Aladdin, Nasredin and the Thief of Bagdad. It was the only way he would let me go back to work. All through the first week, Dmitri would ask after his mum every day. I would lie to him, saying that she had called and said hello. Eventually the boy realised that I was not being honest with him, and stopped asking about his mother. He really enjoyed the nursery. His teacher informed me that on his second day there, Dmitri had had a fight with the former 'gang leader' and had taken over his position as leader in all games, marching and participatory activities. Observers considered him to be too advanced for his four short years, and he knew more about people's private lives and misdemeanours than children in the older group. I reminded him once again that tomorrow, Saturday, he would be going to Nanny's.

"Sonny, she'll clean you up, feed you, and wash your dirty things."

"What? Why? What are you on about now?"

"Sorry, I meant your pants, vests, socks . . ."

"Oh, now I understand. Daddy, don't speak to me in Buryat: things, springs . . . Ha ha ha! Half the children don't understand each other here. We often use sign language, like the deaf. Our tutor Nina Karimovna is always laughing at us."

Rodionova caught up with me between rehearsals to warn me that at 5 p.m. Dmitri's nanny was coming to see me at the ballet. I needed to give her two to three sets of clean clothes for my son, so that after his shower she had something clean to put him in.

I arrived at the nursery just as parents were collecting their little ones. Dmitri bounded up to me and happily slapped me on the arm. I was really struck by this.

"I was frightened that you would be so busy with your dancers that you would forget to take me home today."

"No, little one. Now we're going together to Nanny Masha's. Tomorrow I'll pick you up in the morning and take you to the theatre, where you will spend all day and all night dancing with me! Ha ha!"

"Daddy, that's not funny. You can dance with Nanny Masha, and I'll clap."

At this, all the mums around us burst out laughing.

Dmitri pulled his arm out of his coat sleeve and with his arms akimbo, announced: "What are these fools laughing at? I do want to watch you and Nanny dancing *Swan Lake* onstage. Mummy said that this was the best ballet in the world. Isn't that so? And I also want to see the *Pant-cracker* ballet, with grey rats dancing around the huge Christmas tree."

The parents were in hysterics and rushing to leave the nursery cloakroom with their children, before they ruined their reputation with their uncontrolled laughter, thanks to my son.

"Dmitri, stop! First of all: *Pant-cracker* is when you were a little boy and used to wet your pants. The ballet you're thinking of is called *The Nutcracker*, where mice are dancing, not rats! And secondly, a nutcracker is a tool you use to crack hard nuts. Is that clear? Let's go, my love! Nanny is already waiting for us. You'll watch your favourite circus at the theatre tomorrow."

On the last Monday in August, after dropping Dmitri off at the nursery, I rushed into the theatre. In the four hours before lunch I put together a choreographic score for the Polovtsian figure in the second act of the opera. After lunch I handed to Zina and Alfred a syllabus for 'Polovtsian Camp's' Character dance (barre) and centre practice, for them to teach in the school. After a cigarette break, there were two hours left to study the course of European Historical dance, from the Middle Ages, Renaissance and Baroque periods. By the end of classes they were coming together.

"Mikhail, do you always work yourself to death like this? We're not used to this in Buryatia."

"For some it would wear them out, but for others it's just limbering up," I boasted, swaying with fatigue.

"We've got a short meeting with the school's director at 9 a.m. tomorrow. By nine thirty you'll go off to give your Ballet classes in the Theatre, and I'll stay with him to discuss the project in more detail. I'll be available to you in the evening, after rehearsals. If you need to clarify anything after today's 'gallop through Europe', please don't hesitate to ask. We start the new school year the day after tomorrow. We are really up against it."

The school Director welcomed us with curiosity, astonished at the Minister of Culture's generosity and my enthusiasm. I explained our general interest by saying that Sadykbayev was killing two birds with one stone in this project.

"The first of these is that theatre ballet masters must prepare future leaders of artistic activity in the school, which is necessary for the aesthetic development of people living in the Buryat area. The second bird is to ensure that the theatre attracts the most talented graduates, to the choir, orchestra and "corps de ballet" on an annual basis, to replace those who are retiring. That aside, the creative camaraderie between the school and theatre enables the senior students to receive hands-on, qualified experience onstage. Finally, competent graduates in stagecraft have a good chance of getting to sing or dance with the Buryat or neighbouring republics' Folk ensembles. The Minister of Culture is adopting an extremely astute policy and tactic. If you agree the financial/

administrative details of our enterprise with him, tomorrow we'll be ready to start our teaching marathon together."

"Mikhail Semyonovich, thank you for your interest in our school. You have presented your programme and methodology on a highly professional level. Today, we'll decide the project details in our meeting with the Minister, and I'll let you and Rodionova know the outcome."

At the morning five-minute meeting with the Artistic Council, I presented Linkhovoin with the completed drawing of the choreographic score for *Prince Igor*, including individual mise en scènes for the soloists during their arias and duets, promising in any case to have this work finished by the end of November. I also handed him the detailed programme and contents of *Poem of Man*, based on contemporary Classical dance: three sections (in agreement with anthropological eras), comprising six miniatures each in every act. But I emphasised that the implementation of this ballet-concert would only be possible exclusively with the presence of performers from the professional school of Classical dance.

"Unfortunately, as it stands, our troupe of ballet artistes numbers only six dancers who meet the category's criteria by dancing on pointes. As any opera theatre needs a minimum of sixteen Classical dancers for such ballets as *Giselle*, *La Bayadère*, *Chopiniana*, *Swan Lake* and so on, not counting leading soloists, I suppose there's no point in continuing. For this reason I'm tabling an amendment to the Ballet Department's planned repertoire for the forthcoming season at the next Artistic Council. The unique, new productions of *Poem of Man* and *Splintered Lilac* will be postponed for an indeterminate period, while we restock the troupe with suitable staff.

"In the Opera Theatre we benefit from a stage producer, choirmaster, ballet master, but even with the Seven Pillars of Wisdom, these people are working in a void without performers. So I've decided to make a public statement: if, in September, my plan for recruitment to the troupe has not worked out, I will fulfil the promise I made to the artistic director for Borodin's opera, after which I will go and seek my fortune in another theatre. Please excuse me."

"Mikhail Semyonovich, the Minister has received our memo and is giving this matter his urgent attention. I understand your disappointment and doubts. But it's too early to panic."

"Forgive me, Lar Akimovich. Above all, I have the greatest respect for you and the members of the Artistic Council. When I discovered that this question had been raised previously by Zaslavsky and his predecessors, I doubted the ministry's ability to resolve this problem."

"Circumstances have changed now, in connection with the fortieth anniversary of the republic, and we have more opportunities to receive subsidies from the anniversary fund to organise auditions. The school director advised me of your plans with the répétiteur to prepare future "corps de ballet" artistes. You know how much I support the idea to expand and strengthen the Classical part of the troupe. I'm convinced that we can pull this off this year more quickly than before. I ask you not to jump to any rushed conclusions. I'm meeting with the Minister today regarding this problem. He's taken an interest in you and will do everything possible to hold auditions in September. Now off to work!"

I left the Artistic Director's office with my face burning.

The secretary was alarmed: "Mikhail Semyonovich, would you like a glass of water? It's from the spring."

"No, thank you. I feel OK. Just got myself a bit worked up."

I popped to the toilet and freshened up with some cold water on my face. I took a few deep breaths.

Going back up to the ballet troupe, I got together seven soloists from Alfred's class; two of whom, after 'Camp', were stretching their legs out on the floor; the rest were working with the teacher on centre practice. I asked the manager to send the pair of lazybones to my office.

"Dear ballet artistes, explain to me why you are not doing the whole class?"

"The girl, embarrassed, looked down, but he smiled insolently and fixed me in a stare: "We find Fotiyev's classes too hard going for the morning warm-up."

"That's your personal opinion. How can you dance in these rags?"

"Why are you picking on us about this?" she snapped. "Everyone dances like that here!"

"Because you are qualified Soloists, and youngsters will copy your example. Look at your colleagues: Sakhyanova and Abasheyev, Gurova and Baranov are dressed as required, only with leg warmers on. If you don't train daily for centre practice, you definitely won't be able to meet the technical challenges of new productions. I have no intention of educating you or coming into conflict with you, but by lying on the floor for a long time, you will inevitably degrade and lose skills. Your muscles will atrophy, your blood will cool down leading to poor circulation, your reactions will become feeble and your fat deposits will increase, etc. I advise you to take a look at your professional attitude in class and onstage. You are free to go."

I put in place a timetable for work in September with Demyan and discussed with him all the important organisational/administrative questions in the department. I asked him delicately to 'put the screws on' creative discipline: to put the information up on the board with a request from the troupe leadership, during class and rehearsal, to adhere to the approved standard of training uniform, so that ballet masters would be able to correct dancers' mistakes effectively. And for those wishing to retire in the near future, could they please complete a survey for the theatre's trade union.

"Mikhail Semyonovich, wouldn't it be better to wait until the auditions for the pensioners?"

"If you consider that it's safer for our work, then I have no objection. Take into account that from tomorrow (1st September) Zina and Alfred are starting combined work in the school on Wednesdays and Fridays, from 4.30 to 6.30 p.m. During these hours I will be working every day on the production of *Poem of Man* with soloists, to fit in with their free time from evening shows.

Belyayev (the theatre director) called me on urgent business. He was happy to tell me that the USSR Ministry of Culture had just sent a telegram confirming the use of anniversary funds to supplement the Buryat Ballet staff, to comprise no more than fifteen permanent employees in first and second categories. So, we could continue with the festival.

"Mikhail, congratulations on your success! I hope now that we'll have some good fortune and opportunities to celebrate our fortieth anniversary appropriately. At two thirty today, Sadykbayev is gathering all the heads of the leading cultural institutions in the capital to form an Anniversary Committee for the festival and celebratory concert in the theatre. My secretary is already typing up the project plans, expenses, programme and staging that you presented to me last week. I didn't give these materials to the Minister as I wasn't sure of getting the funds for the extra dancers, without which you openly refused to work after showing the authorities the opera premiere. Off you go, get ready for your presentation to the ministry at 2 p.m. I'll check your letter and project on behalf of Sadykbayev. You can sign it, and we'll go down to the reception office together. I suggest you put on a clean shirt and tie."

I finally tracked Linkhovoin down at an opera rehearsal and told him the latest news.

He exclaimed smugly, hugging me: "I told you this time we'd get there! And you didn't believe me."

"It's true, I was panicking. Guilty as charged. Thank you for your support."

A dozen leading specialists from the world of entertainment and music in Buryatia were gathered in the small conference room at the ministry. Sadykbayev came in with his managers. At this point the Minister invited me to the presidium table with a wave of his hand. An official from the Department of Dramatic Arts emphatically and respectfully shook my hand. The Minister introduced me to those assembled and quickly listed the attending leaders: the principal of the university Faculty of Music, the director of the School of Performing Arts, the Artistic Director of the Buryat Folk Ensemble of Song and Dance, the director of the Stage Circus, the chairman of the Republican Committee of Physical Culture and Sport, the director of the Centre of Folk Creativity, and so on. He informed all the leaders about Belyayev's authority as Director of the festival administration, and clarified for me the role of the leaders in the project:

"These respected cultural officers are official members of the Republican Committee for the Fortieth Anniversary and make up the jury for regional auditions in the Festival of Folk Arts, helping you, as chief producer, to select the best items in the area for the first section of the Gala concert in the Opera Theatre, on 3rd May at 3 p.m. In front of me is a rough draft of the festival proceedings and concert production. I'm assuming, Mikhail Semyonovich, that you can talk us through the general outline much better than I can.

"Dear friends and colleagues, as you know, the aim of this celebration consists of three fundamental conceptual, *artistic* aspects.

"First: a representation of the republic's general development over the last forty years, both *socially* and *industrially*, as well as in its *cultural* and *educational* spheres (films, photo documentaries and so on).

"Second: to tell a wide audience about the origins of ancient Buryat culture and art, *defined* in the ethnographical arts of *dance*, and rich folklore (exhibitions/expositions in museums and galleries).

"Third: to delight visitors from Soviet republics with our professional accomplishments in the field of musical/dramatic arts, achieved over the forty years in which Buryatia has flourished in the multinational family of brother nations in the Soviet Union. In the first section of the Jubilee Gala, we will show ritual forms of ethnography, preserved in the inner heartland of the area, and go on an historical excursion into the past with the Buryat Folk Ensemble of Song and Dance. The second section will include the university orchestra and choir, the Performing Arts School Dance Ensemble, the circus acts, artistic gymnastics, opera and ballet extracts, the 'Polovtsian Camp' from *Prince Igor* and a Grand Finale, with the participation of all companies performing in the concert. We envisage combined choirs and dance/sports compositions onstage, also, a simultaneous parade of participants from the *first* section in the auditorium with festival accessories marking the 40th national anniversary."

Bringing the meeting to a close, the Minister asked if there were any general questions and thanked me for my contribution. He asked the leaders for all project programmes for the Gala concert, with exact names of the writers of the song texts and composers, to present to the Arts Board no later than 1st October this year, to be ratified by the special department of the Ministry of Culture. I went over to the group of Directors and Leaders talking animatedly, and shook hands with each of them. The Board official invited me into the office and asked what my fee was for preparing and running the festival, including stage-managing the Gala concert.

"The standard fee for this kind of project in capital cities for six months' work is exactly 6,000 roubles. In view of the current circumstances, I am willing to work for half of this amount."

"Great! I'll send a contract for you to sign through Belyayev. Good luck!"

Both directors, General and Artistic, were waiting for me to work out a plan for organising and running the ballet auditions in the middle of September. I offered a text of the telegram to be sent to all the nearby opera/theatre ballet schools (from Perm to Vladivostok), specifying the details of age, duration and other audition criteria. I persuaded Belyayev to pay not only the auditioning artistes' travel expenses, but also the approximate equivalent of two weeks' salary as an incentive for them to come. Linkhovoin backed my idea, in view of the last-minute publicity and included this point in the telegram. Now it looked like a solid invitation. All day long on Sunday 15th September, Rodionova, assisted by students from the school, met and settled the candidates as they arrived. The following day, fourteen dancers were taken on by the troupe out of twenty-seven hopefuls: six into the soloists and eight into the 'corps de ballet'. I hadn't expected this kind of experiment to be so successful. Obviously not all audition winners were of high calibre. However, with their professional preparation, they too played an active role in motivating the weak members of the 'corps de ballet'. For two weeks before the auditions I managed to put on three group compositions for 'Polovtsian Camp' and even four choreographic miniatures with soloists:

1. 'Autumn' (to 'Waltz Triste' by Jean Sibelius) – duet.
2. 'Fugitive' by Mikhail Lermontov (to Rachmaninov's 'Prelude') – solo.
3. 'Maidens' Reverie' (to the waltz by Villa-Lobos) – solo.
4. 'Duel' by Nikolai Ostrovsky (to Rachmaninov's 'Musical Moments') – trio.

The soloists were both very struck and fascinated at the same time by the unusual style and technique of Contemporary Classical dance. Each Miniature was learned by both casts, so that with the limited number of soloists, they all benefited from the necessary commitment. This was 'the touchpaper' for the stagnating dancers. Sometimes they looked helplessly at me with eyes wide, not understanding how to execute a particular technical move or support in Duet in the air, genuinely at a loss:

"What is it, a dance or acrobatics?"

"Both, in the sum total of movement." I smiled.

Once they'd got used to my *signature* choreography, the performers quickly embraced the style found in the Neoclassical Art of dance (without stereotyped arabesques or attitudes at every turn). The répétiteurs put their heart and soul into it, content to begin working productively in the department. The pianists enjoyed playing half-forgotten classics by foreign composers, and avant-garde contemporary works.

On our next day off from the theatre, I carried on with my choreography for 'Polovtsian Camp' from first thing. After lunch I 'stuffed' the répétiteurs with new sequences of Historical and Character dances. At 4 p.m. the three of us went to school. It was our first meeting with students from the Dance section. The Director introduced us to the third grade. He advised them that I would be staging a special composition so that they could participate in the anniversary Festival, and if they got through the public showing in the city, then the school's 'Young Suite' would be included in the programme of the best items for the Gala concert in the Opera Theatre. He demanded 100% attendance and rigorous creative discipline from students. Costumes and shoes for this production would be ordered specially from Opera Theatre sources and would remain in the school after the concert for future performers' use. Zina and Alfred were to study the academic programme for all three grades so that they could cover me and each other.

The new ranks of the Ballet Department soon got into a creative rut. Naturally, when fourteen new, young artistes turned up in both group categories, a few of the veterans 'had to bite their tongue' at the loss of their position and the increased risk of their potential replacement in the body of performers. I no longer dropped hints to anyone about retiring, but neither did I conceal my principle for allocating roles not based on hierarchy in the troupe, but in line with candidates' personal qualifications. By the end of September I had produced four more miniatures for *Poem of Man* with new soloists in the main *section*.

1. 'Song of the Falcon' by Gorky (to 'Étude' by Medtner) – solo.
2. 'The Young Guards' by Fadeyev (to 'Impromptu' by Muravsky) – *quintet*.
3. 'Mother's Loss' (to 'Prelude' by Sergei Prokofiev) – solo.
4. 'In the Name of Life' by Polevoi (to 'Étude' by Rachmaninov) – *quartet*.

Zina and Alfred were active in acquainting the newcomers with the current ballet repertoire. The troupe had work coming out of its ears. But the old ones didn't say a word; they knew full well what my response would be.

I found many of the orchestral scores for miniatures in the university library. Nevertheless, we still had to orchestrate the piano works by Rachmaninov, Prokofiev and Medtner. With Belyayev's permission, I sent a telegraph to Moscow to Leonid Feigin, whom I'd worked with successfully in the past, and asked him urgently to orchestrate seven pieces for piano, as per the itemised list. He replied that he would only be able to meet this commission by mid-October. Our chief conductor Maimeskul gave the go-ahead for this timescale, on condition that our premiere would not take place before the end of December. So there was no going back. I consciously took on the risk of getting *Poem of Man* ready in time.

I decided to go cap in hand to that same potential retiree, who scowled at me following my request to take a whole class with Fotiyev. In *Poem of Man*, Nikolai was the second cast in two miniatures and had waited a long time for his turn to rehearse them. He was one of the best in the Character genre. I asked Demyan what he thought about putting Nikolai forward in this new plan.

"He's an experienced dancer, though as a person he's a right pain. But for a répétiteur this could be a good thing."

I made the suggestion to the veteran, in terms of a trial period to help Zina rehearse the men's repertoire for 'Polovtsian Camp', in the aim of building a career as a répétiteur in future.

"You've got twenty-four hours to think it over: you can either become my assistant (until the curtain goes up), and learn a new profession. Or I'll look for another candidate for this lucky position."

"Thank you for considering me. I'll have a think and talk to my wife about it, and get back to you tomorrow."

In the ballet world, any artiste coming up for retirement would be mad to turn down this kind of opportunity. Once Nikolai had agreed, Demyan and I reorganised the rehearsal schedule. Now Alfred and I could work on the miniatures in the evenings with artistes who were free after the show. As usual, I worked out the new choreography in one studio, while he polished up the finished compositions in the other. In this way, the production process for *Poem of Man* went at twice the speed. Both principal assistants worked calmly in the school as well as the theatre. Before his meeting with the 'corps de ballet', I gave Nikolai summary information on teaching, rehearsal methodology and the specifics of Character dance in the opera. I advised him not to display his authority and personal emotions in front of young dancers, but to focus on their errors and be patient when correcting the distorted form of their warriors from the half-wild horde. He promised to consult me for clarification of choreographic details if he had any doubts. I now felt confident to prepare both shows in time.

On theatrical stages, linen slips and backdrops are fixed to the floor with cast-iron bricks, which stagehands transport from one spot to another in small two-wheeled barrows with metal baskets. I asked the stage manager to lend me (in exchange for half a litre of vodka) a trolley on Sundays to go to the market with my son. He agreed, as long as we returned it by midday. I picked Dmitri up from his nanny at 9 a.m. He was already dressed and waiting for me with her outside, and ran to the 'tsar's carriage' with a whoop. I tried to rein in his emotions, but at four and a half, this was impossible and I had to regress to my own childhood. My son sat in the basket, jerking his legs and driving a thirty-year-old stallion with a stick, laughing hysterically. I skipped along, pulling the trolley to market, not paying any attention to the stupefied passers-by and frequent acquaintances from the theatre.

How could I deprive my 'foundling' of the joy he deserved in spending time with his father just one day a week, which he looked forward to impatiently all the rest of the time?

Every evening, when I rushed to see him at nursery for five minutes, he would ask: "How many days are there until your day off?"

Galina, the administrator, seeing my full programme on Sundays, suggested I take Dmitri to her house for a few hours after the matinee, where he could play with her five-year-old son. After supper, his grandma could take my 'seedling' to his nanny's, where he would spend the night in a familiar setting. In the morning Daddy would collect Dmitri from Nanny Masha's and take him to the nursery.

"That will be better for everyone!" Galya concluded.

I just let out a heavy sigh and after a long pause, uttered in despair: "Madam, why are you taking on this burden? Haven't you got enough of your own worries?"

"The boys have become good friends. It was Grandma's idea: to help you both out in a tricky situation. Please don't take it the wrong way. Everyone can see how hard it is for you on your own."

"I still haven't managed to thank you for the huge amount of work you've done to organise the ballet auditions, and here you are coming to my rescue again with a lifeline. I don't deserve this. I'll be indebted to you my whole life."

"Oh, Mikhail, you can have your little joke!"

I kissed her hand ceremoniously, camouflaging with humour the shame I felt as a father.

The triumvirate system of teaching through the carousel system at college was highly successful. With the third grade, we studied almost all the sequences from 'Polovtsian Dances': 'Warrior-Spear Carriers', 'Harem Wives' and 'Kolchakovna's Maids', also the dance of the Russian girls in Yaroslavna boudoirs and the slave captured by the enemy. With the second grade and best students from the first grade I produced a 'Young Suite': 'Friendship', on a theme about two brother peoples: Russia and Buryatia, comprising thirty-two participants. The problem was that there were very few genuine Buryats in the college. To get the right balance, I had to add in Chuvashes, Bashkirs, Tatars, Tuvinians and other similar racial types, to achieve a suitable racial proportion of Slavs and Mongols. Along with soloists from third grade, this group dance made an effective impact, which was crucial for the Festival Gala. In addition to this, in recompense for the overtime Alfred and Zina and I had put in, I obtained the Director's agreement to use students from other sections for the mime scenes in 'Polovtsian Camp' and in the grand finale of the anniversary concert.

I tracked down Valery Merkulov, the chief designer, in the theatre, and told him about my problem with the staging of the festival Gala concert. I asked, "Would it be possible to draw a veil over the weak numbers?"

"My dear Misha, don't think of yourself as the great Buryat discoverer. This problem has existed here quite happily for many years before your time and will persist for a lot longer to come. Make a note of these 'cancerous growths' in the programme. The lighting designer and I will make them look like rosebuds. So, now that you've brought me up to speed, have a look at the sketches for costumes for Polovtsian and Russian characters in *Prince Igor*. The decoration sets will be restored. We'll update the old weapons and shoes or replace them with new ones.

Merkulov and I went through each refined model of ballet costumes one by one, to my enormous satisfaction. He had exceptional flair as an artist in conveying the character image of dance movement. He would often stop by our production rehearsals and draw in his notebook. He never asked any questions, and disappeared as imperceptibly as he had arrived. I was intrigued by his decisions on costumes for the contemporary classical choreography of *Poem of Man*, in contrast to the historic subject of the opera. He promised to show me all his costume sketches for the miniatures the following week, after submitting the patterns for *Prince Igor* to the sewing department.

At variance with other choreographers, like Mikhail Fokine, Kasyan Goleizovsky, etc., I devised my compositions for 'Polovtsian Dances' not as isolated fragments of the opera, but with the participation of surrounding characters, in line with the relevant episode. Usually these were: ancestral aristocracy/nobility or Buddhist monks; a crowd of onlookers or children playing, somehow or other reacting to events taking place or playing an indirect part in the fundamental dance. This made the onstage action more animated and reinforced the comedy or drama of the clashes taking place. I knew this opera very well from my time as a young man in the Odessa Theatre. This helped me to make the soloist singers change their poses, and employ more examples of meaningful gestures and even move into the mise en scènes. The opera stage producer sat in the auditorium and most diplomatically corrected my choreographic diversions in creating fluid images of the central heroes, in keeping with their personal characteristics and the relevant dramatic situation. Now and again the vocalists grumbled, but the Artistic leader would make them see reason.

As usual, difficulties arose in working with members of the choir, who had always sung standing on one spot in the corner or by the stage backdrop in a concert arrangement. A static scene of this nature would impoverish the emotional impact of the action playing out in front of the choir and limit the audience's emotional perception of events. We eventually managed to break the choir's customary immobility and make them sing on raked benches, sitting down when ballet soloists were depicting in silhouette behind a screen the captured prince's patriotic dilemmas as the choir sang above their heads. In the Russian scene with Yaroslavna, I choreographed instead a smooth promenade of female choir members with arms joined around the heroine, performing the traditional, dramatic round dance with added singing. These and other slow transitions from one mise en scène to another, set to the orchestra's musical intermezzo, created (depending on their vocal range) new fluid group tableaux onstage. In principle, the conductor and stage producer approved of these innovations, though they would often smirk behind my back.

Rodionova continued to look after me, on a more frequent basis and more intensely. On Saturdays I had to visit festival locations in town to look through their programmes, and issue my corresponding instructions for combined compositions in the Gala concert and also to have a hand in strengthening the presentation of some isolated weak items, which needed doing for the jubilee programme. One day I just didn't make it back to collect Dmitri from nursery at 5 p.m. I asked the nanny to do this for me, but she refused outright, even for a supplementary payment, not wishing to encounter the other mums there. I couldn't see any way out of this mess. Masha reported the problem to the administrator, and Galina invited me to see her in the office. I hadn't even managed 'hello' before she began admonishing me gently, but warmly:

"Misha, I considered the two of us to be friends in adversity, thought we understood each other. My mum has just collected her grandson from his nursery and it's no trouble at all for her to take Dmitri to his nanny on a Saturday. Why didn't you take me up on this?"

"Madam, why must you break a man's heart with your kindness?"

"Firstly, you're not a man, you're a choreographer. Secondly, musketeers went out of fashion ages ago. Thirdly, I'm older than you so please listen to me otherwise I'm going to get cross!"

I sighed deeply once more, looking reproachfully at her, and on reflection, asked her cautiously: "Aren't you afraid that everyone will start gossiping about our strange relationship?"

"Rumours about us have been going around for ages."

The Opera Theatre in Ulan-Ude, for all its limitations and complications, towered as a unique citadel of Classical Art throughout Buryatia. For many local aboriginals a similar conditional, refined form of theatrical/stage imagination of life and being of people was inaccessible to their artistic perception on the basis of their Buddhist upbringing, preserved in provincial families (in secret) over the course of the last forty years. Such a period seems like a mere 'drop in the ocean', in comparison with forty centuries of spiritual influence of Buddhism on people's consciousness down through the generations. Above all, Buryatia made a gift to Soviet culture of pearls of dramatic art such as Linkhovoin in opera, and Sakhyanova and Abasheyev in ballet. In the last week of November, progressive audiences from the far reaches of the republic attended the premiere of *Prince Igor*. The Russian/Mongolian motifs in the opera delighted representatives of both major nationalities making up the Buryat population. All six evenings in the theatre were a complete sell-out. At the end of each show, during the standing ovations, Linkhovoin/Konchak would escort me and the other producers on to the stage. The papers vied with each other in trumpeting about Borodin's timeless music and the show's central heroes. There wasn't a word about the stage producer, choreography, artistic production or other elements of the theatre's presentation. The artistic director explained this by saying that the press didn't see the difference between the new and old versions of the opera. Regardless, the Minister of Culture gave a stylish reception for the leaders, to celebrate this creative triumph.

Following our free Monday, we began intensive rehearsals for *Poem of Man*, with the orchestra as well. In my ignorance, I hadn't appreciated how much trouble I would cause the musicians in learning the score, differentiated by the composers' styles. Thankfully, the chief conductor Maimeskul had, over the last few years, found reasonably qualified musicians from the conservatoires in the country's capital cities, for the top concert-master positions in all the instrumental orchestral groups, who set a confident precedent for their colleagues to follow. At the first stage run-throughs, the ballet soloists were slightly taken aback by the unaccustomed orchestral sounds of the now familiar piano works by Rachmaninov and Prokofiev. The instrumental arrangement by Leonid Feigin of the widely known 'Musical Moments' and the preludes breathed new artistic life into these genial masterpieces with their unique choreographic interpretation of *Poem of Man*. I was achieving my dream.

Dancing two to three solo or duet miniatures in an evening on a bare stage without decoration, puts as much mental/physical pressure on professional artistes as a feature-length show. The slightest inaccuracy during their performance is acutely visible to a demanding public, and no entourage will ever divert the audience's attention from solitary masters in action on the ballet stage. The premiere of *Poem of Man*, to my huge delight, reached a high level of artistry. Naturally I didn't expect such plaudits as for 'Polovtsian Dances' from Borodin's opera. However, the press (this time) was surprisingly positive about this event, remarking on 'the huge cognitive meaning/significance of the Ballet-concert in the public's aesthetic development'. Special compliments were paid to Sakhyanova and Abasheyev for their performances of the dramatically contrasting duets 'Autumn' and 'Eternal Gauls'; Gurova, for 'Song of the Black Swan', and Dambiyev, for 'Fugitive'. The choreographer was not forgotten either, in his 'successful search for new creative ideas and fluid forms of their embodiment onstage'. The critics rapturously acclaimed the orchestra's leading role in the show under the baton of the talented and sensitive conductor, Yuri Novikov.

Rodionova was sad at passing on my flight ticket to Moscow for New Year.

"Mikhail, my Timonya is quite sorry that Dmitri is going away. They've become really firm friends. Are you sure it's a good idea to leave your son in Moscow?"

I just smiled in response, and wished her a happy New Year in advance. She wished my son and me a good flight and buried her head in papers. I realised that there was no point in hoping that this good-hearted woman would look at me with a twinkle in her eye. Walking away, I felt uncomfortable turning my back on her continuing concern for us both. But I always remained at a distance from her, not wishing to encourage a more intimate relationship. Nevertheless, the administrator didn't give up, and continued gently and determinedly to draw me into her enchanting web. I thought about Galina the whole time on the plane while Dmitri slept, not understanding what it was that she found attractive about me.

Shura, the warden of the halls of residence, greeted us cheerfully and straight away told me quietly, "You're just in time. Yesterday Milia's room-mate went off on holiday, and you can sleep there for the whole week. I've changed the bedding and have put a camp bed upstairs for your son."

"Thank you, my good fairy. I'll pop in to see you this evening with a New Year's gift, OK?

My wife was unaware of our arrival. In my telegram from Ulan-Ude, I'd asked Shura not to tell anyone about our visit, as I wanted it to be a nice surprise for everyone. Milia, of course, was at MTA. Dmitri and I settled in and I sorted out everyone's New Year presents, then we went to have lunch. Moscow is five hours behind Ulan-Ude, so our usual routine was turned upside down. After lunch my little son fell asleep again, while I worked out a plan to purchase copies of Rachmaninov's orchestral scores soon for *Splintered Lilac*. I devised a programme of activities for the whole week and didn't notice the time passing. A noise in the keyhole caught my attention. I was in the habit of leaving the key in the lock on the inside as I was always afraid of losing it in the chaos of the room. I went to open it.

"Oh Misha! When did you get here? Why didn't you let me know in advance by telegram?"

"We got here at lunchtime and didn't want to tear you away from your studies. We decided to give you a happy New Year surprise, but it looks like I got it wrong. Excuse us, madam."

Dmitri woke up and threw himself at his mummy. Holding each other close, they were both crying tears of happiness. Milia was kissing her son, not believing her eyes.

"Mummy, you've finally come. I've been waiting for you for such a long time, I really missed you."

"No, little one, you're the ones who have flown to Moscow to Mummy on your Berkut wings, and now I will never let you go. After the holiday you and I will go to Granny's."

"To the one who lives in Odessa, or the one with chickens and a cock, a cow and goat?"

"Milia, don't make any promises to Dmitri until we've had the chance to talk about family matters!"

"First you deprived me of my son. You never wrote anything about how he was. You turn up like a bolt out of the blue and try to dictate to me again how I should live and how to act."

"No, my dear. You are the one who walked away from your son in favour of your personal freedom; you broke up our family. . . . And where has your education gone – to explain parental relations to your four-year-old son? I suggest, it's not too late for us all to go down to the grocer's. We can get something to eat somewhere and once Dmitri's asleep, we can talk about everything quietly, without any fuss."

As expected, after supper Milia was still not ready to clarify our relationship. She clearly had other plans for this evening.

Dmitri held on to her arms and burst into tears: "Mummy, please don't go! I want to be with you and tell you about my friend. Please!"

"There you go, Mummy dear. Your son has made a decision for both of us. You stay here, and I'll go and do what I need to do."

My poor spouse's jaw dropped. I gave Dmitri a kiss and made my escape from this farce. The enraged Emilia, already out of the habit of parental responsibilities, made some angry threat to me as I left, but I wasn't bothered at this stage. I recalled Rodionova's question about the wisdom of taking my son and leaving him in this mess.

There were two days to go until the New Year. I resolved not to put up with any conniving from my estranged wife. Early in the morning on 30th December, I went to MTA for the whole day. I wished everyone a happy New Year and gave out the exotic gifts. Shatin was pleased with the rave press reviews of both premieres, *Prince Igor* and *Poem of Man*. My mentor looked indifferent. I asked the Dean's secretary why this was. Lena told me sadly that Gorbunov, the rector of MTA, would be retiring in the next academic year, to be replaced by Gusev (my sworn enemy), head of the Marxism–Leninism curriculum. This meant victory for Zakharov and the end of the road for Shatin. A tremor ran through my whole body at this fateful news. *Now they'll finish him off for good.* Anatoly Shatin had founded the Choreographic Faculty and been its backbone for about twenty years, and was invulnerable to his enemies with Gorbunov as rector to shield him. Without him, the clique comprising the Zakharovs and Gusevs would make short work of a non-party dean of faculty. Superstitious people would say, "Trouble begets trouble."

In the Conservatoire library I ordered copies of Rachmaninov's piano and orchestral scores: 'Youth Symphony', 'The Cliff' symphonic poem, and 'Symphonic Dances'. The head of the Archive Department promised to supply the order urgently by 3rd January, if it could be paid for in advance. I had no funds left to complete the transaction with her. Then I left Lydia Popova in the All Russia Theatre Society Ballet Department a set of Buryat press articles about my two last premieres, and caught up on the latest news from the ballet world. Kasyan Goleizovsky was out when I called, but I posted my acclaim through the letter box for him too. I felt like blowing my own trumpet and making the old master happy that he had had such a positive influence on young choreographers. All the academic departments had already shut down for the winter holidays. Passing the Bolshoi Theatre School, I popped in on the off chance and to my surprise, came across Golovkina, literally closing the door to the Director's office. Sofia Nikolayevna was genuinely pleased to see me and gladly accepted both programmes of my Buryat productions. Going down Pushechnaya Street, I asked cautiously what she knew about Malika Sabirova, former soloist with the Tadzhik Ballet.

"Oh, Malika is doing really well at the Bolshoi with Ulanova. Galina Sergeyevna is getting her ready for an international ballet audition in Varna [a Bulgarian resort] next August."

I didn't know how to kill time that evening, to avoid returning prematurely to the inferno. Traditional New Year's shows were playing in all the theatres. Then all of a sudden, a poster stood out in front of my half-blind eyes: 'Goleizovsky's Ballet Miniatures. 8 p.m. on 30th December. Tchaikovsky Concert Hall. Soloists from the Bolshoi and Leningrad Theatres."

This was why I hadn't found him at home. He would have been rehearsing onstage all day.

For me, this was a gift from the Almighty in return for my hard labour and endless patience. Without further ado, I rushed off at top speed to Mayakovsky Square. There was a small queue at the ticket office. Leading couples had come specially from Leningrad's Mariinsky Ballet to take part in this concert: Dudinskaya/ Sergeyev and Zubkovskaya/Kuznetsov. It was an anniversary tribute to mark seventy-five years of the great Master of Dance. Representatives from the ballet world and faithful devotees of Terpsichore were assembling in the auditorium. Pure classical miniatures alternated in the programme with compositions of the 'avant-garde movement' from the choreographer's recent repertoire. The venue thundered with applause: 'Mazurka' by Maximova, Narcissus by Vasilyeva, 'Habanera' by Plesetskaya, 'Waltz and Romance' by the Leningrad guests. It was a storm of success and delight on both sides of the footlights.

With difficulty, I forced my way through the wings to pay my compliments to my mentor. Kasyan was surrounded by a dense ring of his fans. I stood modestly at the side, happily watching his success. Exiting the stage through the escorting crowds, the man we were there to celebrate caught sight of me and called out my name.

I rushed over and hugged him, exclaiming: "Maestro, my heartfelt compliments! Bravo, *bravissimo*, my dear teacher!"

His wife Larissa kissed me and whispered: "Come round to our place on the evening of the 2nd for his birthday!"

I got back to the hostel quite late, and automatically straightened my sleeping son's blanket, which had slipped off. As usual I locked the door, leaving my key in the lock to guard against unexpected visitors. Around 6 a.m. I was woken by some commotion outside the door. Assuming that Milia was in a hurry for the toilet, I opened my eyes to see her sound asleep in her bed. The situation was clear: I crept towards the door, turned the key quickly and pulled it towards me. The trespasser's key dropped with a clink at my feet. Before me stood a flabbergasted, familiar-looking twenty-year-old student from the second grade of the Drama Acting Faculty, in complete shock, holding out a bouquet of roses. I thanked him brusquely for the flowers and locked the door. My wife could not avoid waking up due to the noise. She jumped out of bed, wrapping her dressing gown around her. Seeing the bouquet, she made a run for the locked door, but the key was in my pyjama pocket. The woman was lost; she covered her face with both hands, moaning like a wounded animal, and flopped down on the bed. Sadly, I pulled a little envelope with a message out of the bouquet. In silence, I stuffed the unfortunate flowers head down in the waste bin. I picked up the spare hostel key and hid the trophy in my bag. My dumbfounded wife waited on guard for an attack from me. However, I deliberately and calmly rinsed my face at the sink, got dressed and began to pack my suitcase. The disgraced muse of Art History lay down again on her bed, her face to the wall, thrusting her head under the blanket. This comedy could have been penned by Shakespeare.

Before leaving I approached her bed, sat on the edge and quietly but sternly announced to her: "I'm going to the station now to buy tickets for both of you for Slavyansk, for the evening train on 2nd January. All the timetables will already be back to normal. You'll be able to finish off all your course formalities in the morning and at 5 p.m. should be ready to leave. You can send Alik a telegram about meeting you at the change of trains, in line with the timetable. I'll be back with the tickets in a couple of hours. If you're out, I'll leave the tickets on your table. If you refuse to comply with my requests, on the morning of 2nd January the illegally copied key from the MTA student hostel, the note from your fancy man and my accompanying letter about turning the student hostel into a brothel will be on the MTA trade union Chairman's desk, with a copy to the principal of Art History. If you have any sense of reason and reality left – not to mention maternal abilities – you will do everything I ask, without the usual deceitful shenanigans. You've got what you wanted in your personal life. It's a pity you have paraded your moral decline so disgustingly with your public whoring. You forgot about the chief rule in any hostel. In the civilised world, 'You don't shit on your own doorstep.' You have disgraced yourself, our son and me. You have shown your true colours – a street tart."

It was difficult to get tickets in a general carriage for the fast train on this date. As I expected, my wife wasn't in the mood to see me again on what was a black day for her, let alone on New Year's Eve. I promptly fetched my bag, locked the remaining suitcase and rushed to Serebryanny Bor (a forested Moscow suburb) to my old friend Nikolai Golovchenko's for a 'wee dram' just like the good old days.

"So where's your better half? No way you've got divorced? You haven't been at it for long, mate!"

"No, not long, it's relentlessly bitter. Where would you like the starters? And where's your Christmas tree?"

"Starters are by the window. And bloody hell, we've got more than we need. I'll go and get some firewood."

"No, don't, my dear host! I'll bring some wood from the barn, and you lay the table."

"Misha, first of all, let's pop down to the shop. I actually didn't expect such important guests."

This park was always a delight to me, both in summer and in winter. It was a surprisingly beautiful, fairy-tale corner of Moscow, which by some miracle had remained unspoilt. Two-storey houses between pale pines, under a blanket of snow were reminiscent of the world-famous Russian souvenir boxes and eggs made by craftsman skilled in this ancient tradition. Snow crunching underfoot, pure air that carried all sound – it was simply delightful!

At 11 p.m., two (or perhaps only one and a half) bachelors sat down at the festive table. Saying goodbye to the old year, we didn't notice that we had downed the first half-litre of vodka. Kolya was recounting his news, bitterly critical of the party and government. I was amazed by the fact that he, such a prominent anti-Soviet propagandist, would be trusted to drive the personal car belonging to the Deputy Minister of Inland Water Transport. He explained that he always kept his head down at work, and didn't interfere with anything, just listened out for the polemics behind the bosses' backs. He was deeply respected and sometimes even given incentives for his unassuming ways. They gave out government parcels of delicacies at festival times.

"Have they seen the cross around your neck? And at work as well?"

"One day in the summer, when it was really hot, I was pumping up a flat tyre, and took off my jacket and tie. The boss was surprised to notice my cross and asked if I believed in God. I replied glibly that I believed in the bottle, money and sex. But this was a memento from my late granny! The King of Heaven for her! The boss laughed but warned me that in executing my professional duties, I should not show my trinket to anyone, otherwise I'd be finished for good. I explained to the chief that in case of an accident, for this gold 'trinket' containing a diamond, they could get a new Volga (car) off the assembly line and deliver it to my house. I'm a dark, non-party member, a non-believer and a sinner. As you know, not far from here is a closed zone of government country houses. In summer their families take up permanent residence here. In winter, they come for weekends. They can call me up at any time of day for an urgent dispatch to anywhere they like and for any length of time. I'm single, so there is no one to make a fuss. I am a godsend for them."

Suddenly we heard the Kremlin clock chiming. During the USSR national anthem, we stood and sang, and poured vodka down our dehydrated throats. I slept on the sofa, in a sleeping bag, dead beat. In my sorrowful state, I'd clearly had a skinful. In the morning (or rather, at midday), we were both hung-over, and polished off the leftovers from the New Year's dining table. Kolya saw me to the trolleybus stop, where we said our goodbyes, probably for another few years.

For the whole of the journey to Trifonovka I was deep in thought: should I divorce my unfaithful wife or not? It would be more convenient to see my lawyer now while I was in Moscow, and tell him about the latest events, which could serve as an essential motive in any divorce.

Our room was empty again and total chaos reigned. Milia had evidently begun to pack her suitcase, as her things were strewn everywhere. I put everything into a pile on her bed and sat at the table to write (just in case) a note to the trade union. I wasn't intending to give it in just yet, but wanted my wife to see how serious I was about my ultimatum, if she should refuse to go to Slavyansk. I pulled out of my case a present for the manager (warm, embroidered mittens and a scarf), and went downstairs. The key lady told me that Shura was not there. She would be back in an hour. I asked her to put the package in her office, and hurried off to finish the official letter before my loved ones returned. Outside our room I found Milia's friend from the first floor, knocking insistently on the door, apparently assuming that everyone was asleep inside.

"Young lady, if you're looking for me, then I already have one wife." *You can have too much of a good thing!*

"Oh, I'm sorry, doesn't Emilia live here any more? I wanted to give her a letter."

"I'm her lawful husband and can deliver your letter direct. What's your name?"

"No, thank you, better for me to do it once she's back." The young woman began to get fidgety.

"In the hostel you're probably known as a matchmaker or madam!" I spat out.

The poor student ran off without a backwards glance, like a dog, who's stolen another dog's bone. With my dirty tale-telling letter completed, I went down to the warden again. She greeted me with a kiss for the nice gift, and declared that I spoiled her too much.

"Excuse me, Shura. Just out of interest, up until what date did you give Milia this place?"

"Hold on, I'll tell you." She took my wife's personal card out of a box. "Last August when you went to Buryatia with your son, she was only here until 1st September. Then she was granted permission to live in the hostel from 1st to 31st December this year."

"As you know, she refused to go with us to Ulan-Ude and now doesn't want to take the child, and I can't find anyone to replace her. On 5th January I must get back to the Buryat Theatre, and I'm really worried about what will happen to my son. I have bought them two tickets to Slavyansk to go to her parents. But I'm not convinced that she will forsake this paradise for anywhere else."

"Misha, one way or another, I give everyone advance warning of the end of their term here."

When Milia and Dmitri came back, she found on her table two train tickets and a copy of my letter to the trade union.

My son clung to me with a happy cry: "Daddy, Daddy! Mummy and I went to see the Dolls' Theatre. They had scary demons and a witch with a bone leg and a furious hag. But the good fairy beat them all in the end."

"I'm very happy that you went out with Mummy today. Tomorrow it's my turn, and in the morning you and I will go and dance around the Kremlin Christmas tree with Father Christmas and the Snow Maiden [his assistant]."

"And Mummy too, yes?"

Milia, reading my note, looked up quizzically.

"No, little one. Mummy needs to pack your suitcases as in the evening you're going to go to your Slavyansk granny, and I'm going to stay here for a couple of days and work."

A knock at the door interrupted our theatrical scene. The warden came in with a piece of paper.

"Misha, excuse me, another postgraduate student is coming from Poland to take Emilia's room on 2nd January."

"Thank you for reminding us. Could she please stay here till 5 p.m.?"

"Yes, I'll suggest that she leaves her bags in my office in the meantime. If you yourself need somewhere to stay in Moscow, as a former hostel resident, I can let you have a room up to 5th January, with authorisation from the management."

"Shura, I'm not sure what I've done to deserve such a generous reward. Once again, thank you for everything."

Dmitri was sitting on his mother's lap. The latter was wailing quietly, her voice flooded with tears, "Forgive me, little one, for not going with you to the ends of the earth and for not seeing you for so long, my beloved. I missed my little bird so much. I often dreamed about you."

"Don't cry, Mummy! We'll come back here again soon, or Daddy will come to ours, and we will all play hide and seek together again, like we did in Slavyansk, remember?"

I couldn't endure this trial any longer, and went to the ballet master's room to find out if any of the students I knew in Moscow had stayed there for the holidays. There were just two Polish chaps of my age playing chess. A third was leafing through a *Soviet Ballet* magazine.

"Berkut, how did your premiere go in Ulan-Ude? It said in the advert 27th December."

"Thanks, it went better than expected. Would you like to stretch your brains with a game of chess?"

"Always!" shouted the colleague. "Take a seat on the bed, don't be shy!"

After a few games, I went back to my place. My family were already asleep. Undressing in the darkness, I groped my way to the couch. Milia was lying on my bed. As soon as I came near her, she moved towards the wall. I turned around silently and, moving carefully around my son's fold-up bed, lay down on her bed. I didn't even want to analyse my wife's surprise move, so sickening was it to me.

Unsurprisingly, there were no tickets left for the Kremlin Christmas tree. I had to pay twice the price for them from someone. But my son and I had a great time seeing in the New Year on our last day together. In the enormous Palace Hall stood two luxuriant fir trees, a Grandfather Frost with a microphone in between them. Each tree had its own Snow Maiden and several little wild animals. The children were beside themselves with curiosity and surprise. After the dances and marches with the Snow Maidens around the trees, parents collected their tired little charges and led them into the theatre auditorium, where a magical half-hour show was presented. At the palace exit, the Snow Maidens handed each child a beautiful package from Grandfather Frost. Everyone was in transports of delight, parents and children alike. The impressions of such a grandiose display would remain in the memories of those small children for a very long time. Dmitri jumped up and down all around me, his present in his hand, twittering non-stop about the Christmas tree.

After lunch in a canteen, we hurried back to Trifonovka. Milia was already home from MTA and was finishing off the packing. Dmitri couldn't wait to tell his mum about the show, acting out the various characters' parts. I got my suitcase together and took it to the ballet master's room. My wife wrote a goodbye note for someone while I tidied up our room. Then we took down our son's fold-up bed and the dirty bed linen. I asked the key lady to call a taxi. My wife left the key lady an envelope for someone and I returned the room keys. Both en route for the station and on the platform itself, Milia and I completely ignored each other. I loaded the things into the carriage, and sat them in their seats. I gave Dmitri a kiss and wished him bon voyage. I didn't even look at my wife. I was moving as if in a trance. It felt like my heart was going to leap out of my chest. My eyes were blurred.

I had so little trust in my wife that I remained on the platform for a full ten to fifteen minutes behind the porter's booth, watching her carriage to see if she and our son might run out at any moment. Only after the train had disappeared from view did I sigh with relief, feeling confident about Dmitri's favourable treatment under the protection of his Grandma Klava and her sisters. Even so, the combination of inner emptiness and the loss of my family depressed me no end. I couldn't reconcile myself with the thought that I would never see my son again, that mischievous face with crafty eyes. I decided to record 2nd January in my diary as a day of mourning in my life, and could think of nothing better than to go to the bar and drown my sorrows. In all this family drama, I had forgotten that I had been invited to a reception for Goleizovky. So instead of popping to the snack bar, I made my way home. I freshened up in the shower, spruced myself up and raced off to Kasyan's.

I got so carried away in self-criticism that I nearly missed my stop at Arbat Square. Music and laughter could be heard from Kasyan's home. As I rang, there was a sudden hush. The hostess opened the door.

"Mishka from Odessa!" was how she introduced her guest, as she thrust a glass of vodka into my hand. "Sorry, darling, we are all just meeting our obligation to declare a toast in honour of the name-day boy."

Goleizovsky was sitting at the head of the table, grinning widely. I went over to him and asked, to a roar of laughter, "Maestro, would I, as an Odessan, be permitted to propose two toasts?"

"You have my permission, on condition that one toast is a Moscow toast; the other can be Odessan."

"Dear colleagues, I propose we drink to the eternal Great Master. Hip hip hooray!"

Someone topped up my glass again during the second hip hip hurricane.

"Fellow drinkers, Odessan toasts are usually brief and demand intellectual concentration. Dear name-day boy! May I always be in good health for you!" (No laughter.)

After the second glass they sat me down at the table and fed me. The doorbell went again. The whole ritual repeated itself with the next guest.

A taxi brought me home. I had trouble finding my new room. I just managed to get the door open before falling into an unfamiliar bed.

For the whole of 3rd January, I mooched around the book and audio shops. I picked up copies of the Rachmaninov scores in the Conservatoire, and bought a gift for Rodionova, without knowing why. I justified this step as token of gratitude for her help with my son, although my actual motives were entirely different. After the goings-on with my wife in the hostel, I now considered myself released from our marriage, even before a formal divorce. Naturally, these circumstances opened up broad sexual prospects in a land of hungry women and sex-starved men. I deeply regretted that my working situation in the theatre placed moral ties on my hands/feet and other extremities.

On my return to Ulan-Ude, I became so immersed in the affairs and problems that were waiting for me right from the start, that for a while I completely forgot about my worldly needs and desires, until I handed Galina her present (a fashionable set of toiletries). In a gush of thanks, she rewarded me with a long kiss on the lips, pressing her magnificent breasts too passionately (as it seemed to me) against my (for some reason) quickening heart. I extricated myself from her clutches with some effort, feeling some vibration in my trousers. After this event, I avoided seeing her all week, but alas . . . my fate as a criminal male with crystal-clear morals in the theatre was decided, and not in my favour. I turned out to be unable to resist the call of nature any longer.

On Monday, Alfred, Zina and I worked in the school, as usual, on the forthcoming programme of Gypsy dances for the new opera *Aleko* by Rachmaninov. For teachers and students this was a unique opportunity to study something that did not feature on the official list of nationalities in the USSR. I was also engrossed in my popular subject and demonstrated the technical elements of Gypsy movements of the feet and ports de bras using a shawl or tambourine, to the point of exhaustion.

After work I still had to call in at the grocers, take a shower, make supper and finish off: check new choreographic episodes for the first picture of *Splintered Lilac*. I'd just got settled down to work and was intending to switch on the record player, when suddenly there was a knock at the door, forcing a sigh from me, so unexpected was it at such a late hour.

"Who in the Devil is coming to mess with my head now?" I said out loud in annoyance.

I opened the door. Vaguely, I made out in the gloom of the corridor, a lady proffering an envelope.

"Forgive me, madam; you probably need the next door. I'm not expecting anyone here."

"Except for me! Ha ha ha!" announced Rodionova, and embraced me in a deadlock grip, biting my lips greedily, which were dry from sexual fasting.

I took hold of her automatically, and lifted her up while kicking the door shut behind me with my foot.

"Galyusha, this is called 'invading someone's space'. I categorically and irrevocably protest."

"I agree. But these are just 'flowers'; 'berries' will be juicer, just you wait! Your pianist insisted that I gave you this note. So how could I let her down? 'Mikhail Semyonovich, I beg you to check the tempos in the Rachmaninov score after tomorrow morning's class, in the break before the start of the first production rehearsal. Excuse me.'"

"Oh, these women! They always stick together, for good or bad."

"So what about it, dear Mishenka? Cherry flavour, you must be grateful to me, but don't . . ."

This time I didn't let her finish her moral reprimand. I closed her mouth with my kiss in response, tenderly caressing her extremely appetising bottom from behind.

Further events unfolded in silence and with lightning speed. Both sex-starved partners impatiently tore off each other's unnecessary coverings and flung them furiously in all directions. I had scarcely turned off the light when the crazed Galka pulled the no-less-wound-up Berkut on to her on the long-anticipated couch. Two trembling birds were kissing, touching and rubbing against each other in the release of sex, taking this agonising duet to unbearable limits. The burning woman, not anticipating any initiative from the male, jumped on to her 'stallion' and cried out once she was astride him. The first flight was unfortunately short, as a result of my almost year-long break from practice in intimate relations. But after swapping roles, we took the next gallop on a long marathon distance without a break. Galina's agonised moan became a hysterical shriek. I had to cover her mouth with my palm, so that the female neighbours didn't run to form a queue at my door. Finally, one last gallop through the final barrier and the racing couple collapsed in oblivion.

From this fateful evening on, Galka would visit her Berkut every Monday when he was in town. I tried not to advertise our intimacy in the theatre, but she responded calmly to the 'knowing smiles' of friends and colleagues. The woman was even proud of the fact that she had a man free from family obligations, who paid her attention and treated her with respect on an ongoing basis. Over time, people lost interest in our 'defective' closeness, which failed to arouse their interest with its open nature. In actual fact, our friendship was a warm one, and turned out to be happy and fortuitous for us both. My lady friend, seeing how time-limited I was, willingly helped me with things around the house. I showered Galina's family with gifts, in spite of her protestations. She made a copy of my house key to avoid having to knock at the door when she visited, and during my rehearsals, stocked up on food items using money from the box. These domestic details saved me time and energy to put into creative projects.

At the first rehearsal of the new Ballet I told the artistes briefly about Sergei Rachmaninov, the talented Russian pianist/composer living in America. The international music world would celebrate on a big scale to mark the great musician's forthcoming ninetieth birthday. My libretto for *Splintered Lilac* presented the idea of the Russian intelligentsia's futile struggle for freedom of democracy and press in Russia's social and cultural life at the end of the nineteenth century, against the backward stagnation of the tsarist regime. These far sighted activists from the upper echelons of society, joined together in an association under the code name 'White Lilac', hoping, through literary and artistic means, to change the centuries-old history of feudalism. The abortive revolution in 1905 destroyed their belief in the socialist re-education by peaceful ways, and the avant-garde union was disbanded. This served as a motif for the basis of Sergei Rachmaninov's future ballet *Splintered Lilac*.

The first picture of the first act in the scenario to the music of 'Youth Symphony', deals with the musician's early education and his student years: a charmed youth with toys and games, favourite diversions and disappointments, the joy of success and bitter taste of defeat; the professional development of a promising pianist and composer.

The second picture, to the music of the symphonic poem 'The Cliff', reveals a campaigner for creative freedom in art, resisting canons and traditions in vain. A symbol of 'eternity in creativity', the unshakeable 'cliff' of progress towers over a calm or raging ocean, which often dashes ships' wreckage on to another shore, leaving the barely surviving seafarer half dead.

The third act illustrates the contrasting life of a musician, forced by the shipwreck to leave his tortured motherland for a foreign continent full of promise. But neither universal glory nor material wealth, nor creative satisfaction could destroy his nostalgia. The musician's love for his homeland remained fated.

Naturally, soloists performed the principal roles: the hero, his lady friends and rivals at auditions. Artistes in the 'corps de ballet' were comrades-in-arms or opponents in clashes in protest demonstrations; or, in artistic imaginings the ocean and orchestra; also the contemporary crowd of good-for-nothings and passers-by. The choreography for individual characters was put together on the basis of fundamentals of contemporary Classical dance. Symbolic images of water, wind and fire (in the second picture) presented themselves as group compositions of abstract rhythmic movement, revealing the symphonic structure of the music in polyphonic form. The staging of choreography for the musicians, playing various instruments, and their conductor, was decided in pantomime/dance register, according to the orchestral group playing at that moment. Street and general dances (in the first two acts) in celebratory episodes were performed in the Character genre by diverse races and nationalities or professional associations in the relevant location. The 'Symphonic Dances' of the third act were projected in contemporary ballet style.

By the end of the next three months, in line with the Festival calendar, I had to select the best performers in artistic terms for the first section of the Gala concert, for regional shows. The working group consisted of: the Ministry of Culture's authorised representatives, the Director of the Centre of Folk Creativity, a film/sound technician, a journalist and me. At our disposal was a six-seater plane, which transported us to regional centres and large towns. The first two short-distance trips were extremely productive. Fans of all types of performing arts assembled in the regional arts centre. Amateur musicians, playing old Buryat instruments, accompanied exotic 'Round' dances. Ritual/ceremonial dances alternated with acrobatic slapstick, and so on. In the club hall, the audience usually numbered 500 people in 300 seats. The public would give the masters of folklore a tumultuous reception on entering and leaving the stage. A festival of this nature only took place once every five years in these outlying areas, so it was no surprise to witness such a response from the locals.

The third trip to the most far-flung region of Buryatia, held particular interest for me. Many elderly participants could not attend the show in the main arts centre from backwaters of the mountainous landscape. The working group had to go to them in a Land Rover, from one village to the next. Our torturous travels usually more than justified the exotic nuggets of dramatic art, offered as masterpieces in the anniversary programme. Our Buryat journalist from Ulan-Ude was struck by the hitherto unknown ancient ethnography. However, an even bigger surprise was yet to come for me: a visit to a modern European settlement built in a low-lying area (about the size of the central Luzhniki stadium), surrounded by a thick ring of mountains. Everyone in our group had been here before, apart from me. Ironically, the settlement was named Raivadu (Heaven in Hell).

The small white, identical houses mirrored the mountain ring in a double, circular line, facing each other, thus creating a unique street without end of (approximately) thirty-five to forty fairy-tale cottages. Inside the residential circle were four public two-storey buildings housing a library, a secondary school, medical centre and arts centre, all in the same architectural style. A statue to Karl Marx, festooned in flowers, stood in the little central square. It turned out that the inhabitants of Raivadu were settlers from the German autonomous district in the Upper Volga river area. I unwittingly winced at this discovery, having witnessed the evacuation twenty or so years ago (during the Second World War) and the apparently tragic exile of German immigrants and communists who had fled fascist repression in Germany to come to the USSR. When Hitler's troops started to get near the Volga, Stalin ordered his compatriots out of their perfectly habitable homes and sent them off to Siberia within twenty-four hours.

The chairman of the village council settled the visitors in the two closest houses for guests, where we were looked after by local women active in civic life. The village inhabitants lived here as a small but crowded community, looking out for each other like members of a large clan. A reception was laid on for us in the evening in the basement of the village council building, where the host introduced the council members: the school head, the senior doctor from the hospital, the club leader and his deputy Communist Party organiser. I sat at the table next to Otto Krauze, a cultural worker. He turned out to be a former artistic director of the Leningrad Philharmonic Society, about fifty years of age, who also fell into the group of those who had been exiled. Over supper, Otto recounted his story about losing his family, after his Russian wife refused to accompany him to 'some godforsaken place'.

"Everything we see in Raivadu was built and equipped by the hands of settlers. There are virtually no Buryat people here. The only Russian is the divisional policeman, a serving village council member. Everyone else derives from the original emigration from Germany to Russia. Although the state supports us here, we are completely isolated from the outside world, apart from radio, newspapers, post/telegrams and occasionally, rare visitors from elsewhere, like you. Nonetheless, tomorrow we'll show you our artistic achievements."

At 9 a.m. I knocked at the door of the club, which opened slowly and by itself. A smiling Krauze greeted me in the hall with a mini remote-control device in his hands. Beside him sat Betty, a huge – scarily so – German sheepdog.

In response to my quizzical, raised eyebrows, my host explained: "I named my guard dog in memory of my wife Elizabeth in Leningrad."

"Does everything in the club function on the wizard's signal?" I made a stupid joke.

"Almost: the alarm system for uninvited guests; fire sprinklers; stage and auditorium lights; moving the slips; curtains, overhead decorations and lighting equipment, etc."

Betty came gently over to me. She sniffed my shoes and trousers, then went to lie down in her bed by the entrance. I poignantly recalled our Julebars, the same breed, who had guarded our family during the war in the empty village of German Povolzhya, where the people of Raivadu had come from.

At 10 a.m. I began the overview of local activity with my assistants:

a) Vocal ensemble of teachers, two school choirs (younger and senior classes) with a classical repertoire in German and Russian (a capella and with piano accompaniment);

b) Chamber and symphony orchestra including teachers and their former pupils.

My astonished eyes nearly popped out of my head, forcing a smile from Krauze. He clarified: "For many years, singing and playing any chosen musical instrument has been a compulsory subject in the school curriculum. Many of our talented graduates (with special permission) are working in opera houses in Siberia, including Ulan-Ude. Unfortunately there are no sports, stage or circus venues. That's why the only entertainment we have is classical music and theatre: Sunday concerts and competitions or performances of Brecht, Shakespeare and other European playwrights. These diversions complete our social and cultural life and help us to preserve our social networks. Without these activities we would all have died here. We live in hope that our punishment will soon come to an end."

I had a lump in my throat at the injustice of it all. I confessed to Krauze: "It is hard to make a definitive selection from all the demonstrations that you've shown me today, but categorically everything that we have seen and heard is way above the level of the other performers in the republic which make up the first section of the Festival Gala concert. Professionally speaking, the high calibre of the school choir and orchestra allows us to use these groups only in the second section, along with the university and Opera Theatre. Personally, I have a high regard for the work of your school leaders – both collectively and individually, I've got my sights on the teachers' vocal ensemble before the final part of the concert. But I can't promise anything, you realise."

"Dear Mikhail, you're not the first specialist to be impressed by our participants' achievements. But in spite of your wishes, you are unable and powerless to change our political status as 'exiles'. In terms of land, we relate only to Buryatia, but essentially are governed by the USSR, which, for many reasons, will never let us out of Raivadu."

"But why not? The war has been over for a long time. Stalin is not around any more. East Germany is flourishing."

"Forgive me, my dear colleague. The foreign press has reported worldwide time and again on the legal exile of the Pri-Volga Germans and their inhuman confinement in a mountainous enclosure more suited to packs of wolves and jackals. After these announcements our social circle became even smaller. Don't worry about it, maestro, and don't try to bang your head against the wall of justice."

On my way back to Ulan-Ude, I pondered my last conversation with Otto Krauze.

Our little craft touched down in Ulan-Ude, like a sparrow hopping over a pothole.

At the end of March I had completed the programme for the Gala concert and showed it to Linkhovoin for 'reconnaissance in force'. As promised, he listened to a few recordings of unfamiliar tunes and a few days later, gave me his opinion.

"On the whole, the programme is extremely inspiring, diverse and effective. But if I were you, I would remove one of the numbers. Not due to the quality of performance, but . . ." the artistic director stopped short.

"I expect you're talking about the German Teachers' Vocal Ensemble from Raivadu. I'm up to speed on the political situation with this group. But I really need it before the final curtain, after 'Polovtsian Camp', so that we can prepare the stage in the seven minutes of their performance: the benches, decoration and combined-choir finale."

"I realise that, but I'm really not convinced that our ministry will go for such a compromise."

"Lar Akimovich, there is no more deserving 'crowning glory' in the whole of the republic to lead into the grand finale. You obviously underestimate your opportunities and influence in Buryat art."

"Misha, I agree with you, but you are pushing me into conflict with my boss. Other stage producers – your predecessors – have tried to drag them into the spotlight, and always been refused."

"Times were different then. They didn't have the backing of a figurehead like Linkhovoin."

"I can see that you were born under the sign of Taurus. I will try, but can't promise you anything. Our only hope is the Russian Minister of Culture, who's a personal friend of mine."

Everyone involved in the first section of the Gala concert came along on 1st May. On the morning of 2nd May, I rehearsed their performances onstage with lighting effects. After lunch, I perfected the finale and climax of the concert with participants of both sections, including the combined choir (on benches) under the direction of the theatre conductor and group dances/processions (in the auditorium) with the help of my assistants. In the evening I pushed on with two amended run-throughs. In the lunch break following a half-hour polishing-up of the finale, we ran through the whole programme again and at 4 p.m. produced a successful performance of the Gala concert. At the official celebration (before supper) the Minister of Culture handed out certificates of honour to all the group leaders who had played a part in the gala.

Krauze caught up with me in the foyer and passed me a box with a crystal bear as a souvenir, with an inscription expressing thanks from all the Raivadu residents. I was touched by such gratitude and embraced Otto in farewell, promising to remember them all.

He whispered in my ear in response: "Don't refuse any souvenirs from the Buryat leaders. They will be offended."

It was only then that I noticed that we were standing in full view of the winning anniversary show. They came up to me applauding, and reciting something in Buryat. I bowed in different directions, pressing my hand to my chest and repeating "Thank you" over and over. Krauze broke through the crowd with a canvas bag. Laughing heartily, my colleagues packed it with parcels and boxes bearing people's comments. The men shook my hand, and the women gave symbolic kisses, cheek to cheek. It appears that for Buryat people, this is the highest sign of respect and gratitude to their leader.

The boss of the Arts Board appeared in time, took me into his office and handed me an envelope containing my fee. He shook my hand and congratulated me on my success.

"Mikhail Semyonovich, leave your pile of souvenirs here for the moment. The Buryat people are very straightforward. The attention you have enjoyed from group leaders here has to be merited. You have also earned our trust. Thank you."

I made another bow, shaking him by the hand, and answered that I had acquired a wealth of information on the ethnography of local folklore, which I would draw on in future. The Director led me into the banqueting hall and showed me to my seat next to Linkhovoin.

Following a few words at the opening reception from the Minister of Culture, Linkhovoin expressed his wishes for a happy fortieth anniversary of the republic to all the official representatives from the different districts and the leaders of their prize-winning groups, and congratulated them on their creative endeavours.

Drawing near home, I noticed a light in my window and realised that Galina was waiting for me. The table was graced with a bouquet of flowers, a bottle of champagne and a box of chocolates.

"My beloved bear, congratulations on your achievement. This was a grandiose spectacle. I know what's in this bag. Souvenirs from the Buryat victory show."

We sat up till late discussing the concert's exotic numbers, and slowly but surely, emptied the bottle and box of chocolates. It was the first time that my lady friend spent the night at my place, as we all had the following day off. We revelled in our intimacy almost all night long. When I awoke at midday, there was no sign of my good fairy in the house. Just a note poked into the flowers: 'I love you and want you, lots of love, Yours always, Galka'. It was lovely to know that I had someone close alongside, who was constantly thinking and caring about me.

"We don't need much to be happy," this bear repeated, longing for a caress.

I enjoyed many compliments about the success of the Gala concert at the theatre. Even so, despite the glow of success, I was not myself. Something was bothering me and grating inside me, leaving me ill at ease, and putting me on my guard.

"Mikhail Semyonovich, they're waiting for you at rehearsal," Demyan, the ballet manager, reminded me.

The production and working out the new choreography of the second act of *Splintered Lilac* was taking place, as usual, in two studios with both répétiteurs. The process set up for the artistes to learn the technical elements of the movements and compositional sequences enabled the stage producer to complete a rough draft of all the separate components over the course of May: group and solo dances, fluid extracts and theatrical mise en scènes. For the remaining three weeks before the premiere at the end of June, I was hoping to mount the whole ballet, including the stage rehearsals with artistic lighting, decoration, and orchestral accompaniment. Almost all the costumes were in the final stage of completion. The artistes were looking forward to the dress rehearsals, so that there was time to adjust any inevitable miscalculations in size or discomfort in their stage gear. All theatre departments were working at full capacity on schedule in preparation for the premiere of the opera *Aleko* and the ballet *Splintered Lilac*.

That week, the June plenum of the Central Committee of the Soviet Communist Party was taking place in Moscow to address ideological questions, and was also attended by a party/government delegation from Buryatia. As he was singing a central role in *Aleko*, Linkhovoin was released from participating in this plenum, with Belyayev, theatre director, attending in his stead.

After reports from party leaders of all the republics, the Soviet Communist Party decreed: 'In connection with systematic deviation from the Marxist–Leninist line in the aesthetic education of Soviet youth in favour of bourgeois ideology, it is for workers in Literature and the Arts to cut short this pernicious influence on our Socialist morals without delay.' Cited as one of the depraved examples of similar influence by Western culture, the Buryat Opera and Ballet Theatre was singled out: 'whose repertoire included a show to music by Rachmaninov, a composer who shamefully fled from Russia to America in the

Great October Revolution. Traitors of the Motherland have no place in our art of Socialist Realism.'

At this point, Belyayev, as ordered by his superior, sent a telegram to Linkhovoin: 'Stop preparing the show with Rachmaninov's music right away. The Soviet Communist Party is issuing a decree regarding the popularisation of Soviet composers rather than those overseas who have betrayed the Motherland. We can discuss details on my return. Sadykbayev, Minister of Culture.'

In the evening, during preparation with Demyan for tomorrow's dress rehearsals of the second act, the ticket lady brought me a note from Rodionova. Galya asked me to pop into the Administration Office on important matters as soon as I was free. I concluded that this was her next female ruse.

Seeing me, she locked her door and reported in a half-whisper: "Misha, I received a telegram from Sadykbayev in Moscow addressed to Linkhovoin. I beg you, please don't take this to heart! Knowing that you are a Taurean, I've decided to show it to you first, so that you don't lose your temper and 'shoot the messenger'. Sit down and get ready for a shock."

I scanned the text and returned the telegram to her. Galina was shaking all over.

"Don't worry, darling. This decision will hit Linkhovoin rather than you. He won't give up his position that easily. Lar will think of something. Don't jump to conclusions."

"Thank you, Galya, you're a real friend. All the same, I need some time alone now."

On the way home I stopped off at the chemist and bought some valerian just in case. My chest was pounding. I felt a bit better after taking the drops, but the pain was still there.

Don't rejoice, 'members of the jury'. My time has not yet come. We can still win!

I continued my work in the theatre and school for two days as if nothing had happened, to the surprise of some colleagues, who were in the know about the telegram. On Tuesday morning my five-minute meeting with the artistic director did not take place, as he was at the ministry for a conference. After classes we went through all three ballet scenes with both casts, apart from the students. Before checking the evening performance of *Le Corsaire*, Demyan got the troupe together in the studio and invited me along to keep everyone in the loop.

"Dear friends, no doubt you've already heard about the thunderclouds over our new ballet. As company leader, I consider it my duty to keep you informed that the premiere may be cancelled at the last minute, for political reasons. Moscow believes that music by Sergei Rachmaninov, a 'traitor of the Motherland', should not be heard in the Buryat Opera and Ballet Theatre. I have no authority to comment on the grounds for this. I hope that there will be a positive decision from local government today or tomorrow. In any case, thank you for excellent work on this (alas, my) production. From the bottom of my heart I wish you success in your personal and creative lives. Thank you. Alfred and Zina, let's meet as always at four thirty in my office. Demyan, you too."

"Dear colleagues, you will have deduced that the situation is a lot more serious than I outlined earlier to the troupe. Last night I telephoned MTA from the post office. I was told that Leningrad, Kiev, Minsk and other theatres are also suffering just like us: shows by foreign writers/composers have been cut from the current repertoire and plans for the year are being changed. Naturally, the Buryat Government has no power to go against decrees from the Soviet Communist Party. It is impossible to be creative and productive in such working conditions. It's not in my nature to keep receiving the salary as department leader. So, to my enormous disappointment, I am leaving you. I am sure that you will understand my reasons and not pass judgement. We have worked fantastically well together, and your help and solidarity has been invaluable to me. I expect Alfred will take over from me for the time being, until a new ballet master comes along. I advise the school to leave the first two grades as they were, but to lead the third (on Monday) jointly. Please convey my apologies to the Director. Demyan, please cancel all rehearsals for *Splintered Lilac* tomorrow. As far as *Aleko* is concerned, I'll find out the situation from Linkhovoin. Thank you. You are free to go."

At 7 p.m. the Artistic Director summoned me to his office. Lar looked like a lost puppy, if not worse.

"Misha, you probably already know about Rachmaninov, 'traitor of the Motherland'. I must warn you, your stage rehearsal on Tuesday will receive a visit from . . ."

"Forgive me, Lar Akimovich. I have to interrupt you. I have changed all rehearsals for the premiere. As I am still leader, I can't allow any further trauma to the troupe, either spiritually or in terms of morale, in relation to *Splintered Lilac*. As regards *Aleko*, as the author, I give you permission to use my choreography and stage movements in the opera, under my supervision. Please receive this as a gift from me for your help and kindness towards me. Here is my resignation 'for special family reasons', from tomorrow. Could you kindly forward my employment log and salary to the address indicated."

"Mikhail, are you sure that you are making the right move in relation to your troupe?"

"Absolutely. They already know about my decision. I am also sure that you as an artiste (rather than artistic director) understand me completely, and would not have derived any pleasure at seeing me being lynched in public. What's happening now is, to put it mildly, inhumane. Please don't make me change my feelings of respect and admiration for you. I'm not sorry that I came, as I've learned a huge amount here. Thank you for everything. Remember me fondly!"

Coming out of the Artistic Director's office, I tore along to the station for a ticket to Leningrad (via Moscow). The next express was at 8 a.m. I had twelve hours to spare. At this point I called Sofia from the station and advised her of my arrival in a week's time, then made my way straight back to the theatre. I put all my work and home clothes into two bags and carted them home. Galina was already waiting for me with a tear-stained face. News of my resignation had spread through the theatre like wildfire.

"Mishenka, what are your real reasons for having to punish the dancers?"

"Galochka, you must know better than me; you are always out and about with your bosses."

"I speak Buryat and overheard some comments. But they didn't make any sense to me. Belyayev was saying to Linkhovoin, that in Moscow you are considered guilty of cosmopolitanism: connections with the Indian Ambassador, you hobnob with exiled Germans, popularise American immigrants from Russia. But what does all of this have to do with Opera and Ballet?"

"It just does, my darling! All of it comes into ideology, controlled by the 'proletariat's dictators', in this way: 'We'll pave the way for you with bayonets and shrapnel'" (A line from the party's anthem.)

"OK, you need to get on your way. I'll pick you up at 7 a.m. Wait for me."

On the platform it took a long time for Galya to release me from her embrace, convulsing with sobs. She just couldn't conceive that our friendship and close bond was ending so abruptly.

At the last minute before the train moved off, I declared: "Farewell, my love! I will never forget you!"

Five days alone in the compartment was time enough to explore my real reasons for inflicting such a harsh punishment on the whole troupe, when the artistes themselves were completely innocent, not to mention their leader. To discredit my deputy, a state prizewinner?! More than anything, the essential cause of this was initiating the show to commemorate ninety years since the birth of Rachmaninov, the 'outcast/traitor'. In edifying others, one ignores the Soviet establishment in the art of socialist realism. I had forgotten Vartanyan's warning about this (from the USSR Ministry of Culture) in connection with my diploma work on an Indian theme: "Don't look overseas! Use our home-grown creative resources!" It's possible this was a fateful coincidence for me. Fortune had turned her back on me.

Endless alternative plans for the future filled my head. It was a scorching summer and stuffy in the carriage. I was looking forward to changing trains in Moscow, the city of my hopes and disappointments. For all that, Moscow had put me on the professional track and given me a path into a creative life. She was always a second nurturing mother for me, and I hoped she would remain so forever.

Arriving in the morning at Kazan Station, I made my way quickly to Leningrad Station. I punched my ticket for the 'Red Arrow', which would be leaving at midnight. Leaving my luggage in the cloakroom, I hurried off to MTA. Lena (the secretary) was happy to see me and confided that Shatin would be finishing a composition class on Pushechnaya Street (opposite the Bolshoi) at 1 p.m. This gave me the chance to look around the city centre's music/ballet shops and to buy the latest interesting collections: sheet music, folk dances and academic, historical works about ballet. Waiting for the end of the lecture, I was glad to meet my mentor and invited him to lunch. On learning that I was only passing through Moscow on my way to Leningrad, he telephoned MTA to alert his secretary that he would be late back to the principal's office. My patron was sorry that I couldn't have a look at this third-grade exam.

I updated Shatin on recent events and asked him to explain, if he could, why Vartanyan and his clique were persecuting me, even in the Siberian tundra? The Dean smiled and sadly outlined the same old reasons: the eternal conflict between devotees of Classical dance and avant-garde contemporary choreography on the one hand, and the contrasting training methodology used by ballet masters at MTA on the other. These contradictions create fertile ground for bureaucrats in theatres run by the USSR Ministry of Culture for endless intrigues against successful choreographers and ballet artistes, as they themselves are by their very nature totally undistinguished, and unable to come up with anything creative. Such green envy pushed them regularly to get involved in amoral action and even crime, following the rule of dogs in the manger: unable to eat the hay themselves, but not allowing anyone else the pleasure.

"Anatoly Vasilyevich, you have already realised that I am moving to Leningrad to try my luck there. I'll keep you posted on my creative adventures. Mind how you go!"

Back at the ballet school, I left my shopping with the secretary and went to watch some classes given by my old teachers: Lapauri's 'Pas de deux' and Tkachenko's Character dance. Unexpectedly and unforeseeably, I bumped into my old friend Pestov, who was doing very well, leading classes for Golovkina with the senior boys. He had some happy news to share: Malika Sabirova had included my 'Song of the Black Swan' (to music by Villa-Lobos) in her 'free' programme at the World Competition for Ballet Artistes in Varna and was rehearsing it with Ulanova at the Bolshoi. At the beginning of June all grades in the school were preparing for exams in their specialist subjects as usual. So there was lots to see. Pestov's class of 'Male Variations' made a particular impression on me. Pyotr had managed the whole group impeccably, and also each student in turn, according to his individual abilities and personal problems. In the evening I just had time to watch the new programme given by Igor Moiseyev's folk dance ensemble.

After this, I happily boarded the night train to Leningrad. Worn out, but satisfied with my visit to Moscow, I collapsed on to the lower bunk and slept till morning. I woke up just as the conductor announced that we were arriving in the legendary city of the Revolution.

STAGE II: LURE OF SPIRITUAL NOURISHMENT

CHAPTER 3 AESTHETIC PEARLS FROM THE PAST

It was only one and a half blocks to Sofia's from Moscow Station. I heaved my considerable luggage (rucksack, suitcase and bag) there like a camel, attracting attention from all the people out that morning. Nevertheless, I survived the weightlifting and ten minutes later I was there. My cousin directed me by telephone to collect the keys from the housekeeper and said to call her immediately at work as soon as I got in. With all the housekeeping instructions from the woman in charge, I duly got myself organised in the flat. After the long journey it was sheer joy to relax in a scented bath. I got together the necessary paperwork and set off to the College of Performing Arts as a matter of priority.

It was a broad, old-fashioned building on two floors, with high ceilings and spacious studios, suitably equipped for this type of institute. The key lady took me to see the deputy director of the student section.

Introducing myself as a ballet master from Moscow, I outlined my qualifications, and spread out my personal certificates, theatre programmes and press cuttings on the table in front of her. She scanned through the information presented and asked about my employment log, which had been left behind in Ulan-Ude. I explained that up till now I had only worked on an agreed basis as choreographer/producer, and that unfortunately I had had to make an urgent return to Moscow from the Buryat Theatre for family reasons. I promised to provide my employment log within the next two weeks if necessary. Alternatively, I could supply a folder containing my contracts and references, including my teaching practice in ballet schools and the College of Performing Arts, as well as the general 'Art of Dance' course which I had delivered during the last ten years, and seminars at the local Arts Centre.

"Wait here a moment, please. I'll have a word with the Director and come back to you in fifteen minutes regarding our requirements and the opportunities at the school for the coming academic year. Have a look through our programmes and brochures."

Quarter of an hour later, the deputy invited me in to see the Director. He was an elderly, grey-haired man who looked like a typical bureaucrat. He gestured to me to take a seat, and studied my features for a relatively long time.

"Mikhail, I have just called my colleague, the director of Leningrad Arts Centre. He gave you a glowing reference and recommended that I take you on as a specialist in choreographic composition method. We'll have a vacancy for a post like this on 1st September. Four and a half hours a day, three times a week, to start with. If you can provide your employment log for continuing professional development as a member of the college staff, and you deliver promising results with students' learning over the first four months, we'll be in a position to offer you a full timetable as deputy head of the Choreography Department, as our current leader Yana Sadovskaya is retiring. We will also be needing copies of all your documents. We will pay you the standard teacher's salary without any special grading or bonus. Think it over, and if you decide to accept, come in to complete the paperwork as soon as you can. There's no time to lose."

I rang Galina straight away in Ulan-Ude and requested the necessary references from Linkhovoin and the Director of the College of Performing Arts in relation to my creative and teaching work. She promised to do all she could, although she was dubious about how realistic it was to expect a positive outcome from such a request as I had been made a scapegoat since leaving. I'd expected nothing less after my flight, so this was no surprise. I sent a telegram direct to Belyayev, asking him to forward my employment log urgently. I was aware that I was taking a sledgehammer to crack a nut, and knew full well that, in my situation, lying down with my paws in the air was not the best form of defence. However, a provocative counter-attack could sometimes stun an uncertain opponent. Who knows what kind of action this crazy choreographer has thought up following his fall from grace? 'Best to steer clear of trouble!'

While 'the jury was out', I decided to visit Ginsburg, director of the Philharmonic Society, who knew Otto Krauze from Raivadu very well. As soon as I mentioned his name, the secretary rushed in to her boss and a moment later invited me into the office. Alexander Naumovich looked artistic, and was a player (of the mature variety) on the cultural scene.

He leaped up from his desk and, indicating the sofa, asked quietly while looking over his shoulder at the closed door: "Mikhail, excuse me for being so familiar. When did you last see Otto?"

"A month ago. In Ulan-Ude, at the fortieth anniversary celebrations of the Buryat republic."

I told Ginsburg how Krauze and I had come to meet, and about my support for his vocal ensemble at the festival's final concert.

"Young man, you may experience some difficulties as a result of the courage you have shown. It's already been twenty years since his name was uttered out loud in the Philharmonic Society. But how can I be of service to you?"

I explained that I had moved here to my cousin's from Moscow and was trying to find permanent work as a choreographer, and showed him my programmes and posters from the Odessa Philharmonic Society and the Mariners' Ensemble, as well as the Buryat Opera and Ballet Theatre.

"Within the mixed groups that make up our staff is a youth ensemble. "Leisya Pesnya' [Flowing Song] comprises: a vocal octet, instrumental quartet, six dancing couples and a master of ceremonies/team leader in charge. Sviridov, our artistic director, plans and refines the programme with them. Their repertoire needs updating in October. They are currently on tour for the summer in Belarus and the Baltic States, and will be on leave in September. If you have time to compile a new review for them in October with Sviridov, I'll gladly draw up a contract with you, once I've confirmed the proposed project with the Artistic Council for Leisya Pesnya's next production.

"Last year our regular choreographer was seriously ill and virtually out of action. It's not easy to find a new ballet master in the variety/popular genre. All the candidates were from classical or folk backgrounds. So, fortune is smiling on us to send us you. I'll put you in touch with Sviridov right now and off we go!"

"Alexander Naumovich, I didn't manage to tell you that I've been offered a permanent job at the College of Performing Arts starting on 1st September. I expect I'll need to get their agreement for this temporary position. I'll be tied up there for three mornings a week, but will be free the other days up to 31st December. So . . ."

"Don't worry, I know Strizhachenko very well. We're from the same department at the regional Cultural Board, and always help each other out in our work."

When I got back to my cousin's place, I found a full house with the whole family present.

"Where did you get to, Misha bear? I've been calling you all day, about ten times in all. I wanted to find out what you like to eat and bring you some delicacies from our Elysian supermarket. Now you'll have to eat what's on the table and don't you dare complain!"

"Boris, how do you cope with this tigress? Share your state secret with us."

"Mummy, Mummy, who on earth is this Teddy?" asked my six-year-old nephew, Arkady.

"He's a great big bear, like your favourite Uncle Misha. He teaches dance. So: listen up, you bow-legged man! Where is your family? Why did you come without them?"

"It's a long story. I'll tell you later. 'Fine words won't fill a belly, especially a big one.'"

"Sofia, why are you pulling his leg? Let the hungry man eat in peace!"

Boris and I bonded over a few glasses, swapping football news.

After supper Sofia marched me into my room and ordered me impatiently: "So come on then, my little artiste, out with it! What catastrophe has happened in your family down there?"

I gave her the broad outline of how incompatible we were in our life as a couple, our moral codes and personality differences. I told her about today's work opportunities in Leningrad and asked if I could stay there till the end of June, until I got myself registered for work from 1st September and could look for accommodation in the city centre. She gave me a bunch of duplicate keys and went through the details of how the household was organised.

Boris was getting ready for a trip to Odessa on 1st July. He asked how

303

my permit was coming on at the police station and advised me to give their address as my permanent place of residence in preparing my papers for the school. He promised to help me get set up as necessary. I decided to cover myself and ask his advice as a factory director, on the most effective way of retrieving my employment log from Ulan-Ude. I recounted my creative disaster with Rachmaninov and the circumstances of my abrupt flight here.

Then Boris rang a lawyer friend of his in a legal consultancy. He outlined the situation in brief and asked him to send a telegram urgently to the director of the Buryat Opera and Ballet Theatre director with an official request to forward by return for his attention the employment log for Mikhail Berkut, which he was retaining illegally in breach of employment law.

The next day I decided to try my luck at the Mariinsky Theatre in dance for opera with my choreographic miniatures. In general, large theatres don't bother with small forms of stage ballet for commercial reasons. But 'while the cat's away, the mice will play.' On my way upstairs to Konstantin Sergeyev, in the artistic director's reception, I noticed a door bearing a small plate: Fyodor Lopukhov. I knocked, and the door was opened by none other than Fyodor Vasilyevich himself. I was so shocked that I lost the power of speech.

"Were you looking for me, young man? Do come in. Will you take a cup of tea?"

I couldn't believe my eyes – I had only gone and found my way in to the living Lopukhov's home!

"Forgive me, Fyodor Vasilyevich, I assumed that this was an exhibition about your work."

"Ha ha ha! You're not the first to fall for that one. Have a seat! The tea's getting cold. Tell me, which theatre are you from? What do you dance? What are your plans? I live a very solitary life so am always really interested to hear the latest about our world from my rare visitors."

I introduced myself briefly. I reported that my specialist field was small-form choreography. I showed my host opera posters and programmes: *Ivan Susanin*, *Carmen* and *Prince Igor*, as well as the illustrated brochure/libretto for *Poem of Man* (forty-six pages), a review with photographs and a programme of the concert given by Bolshoi Theatre School graduates.

The old master was impressed and rang Sergeyev.

"Kostya, I have an unexpected visitor from Moscow. Have a look at his materials. You might be interested in some of Mikhail's miniature repertoire for soloists during their secondary performances on foreign tours."

A few minutes later the Ballet Department secretary arrived with an invitation for me.

"Fyodor Vasilyevich, I don't know how to thank you for your hospitality and for the recommendation."

"No, thank you, my dear colleague, for coming, and for telling me about the Tadzhik and Buryat Ballet. If ever you're passing, please do drop in, don't hesitate at all. Good luck!"

The secretary led me to the artistic director's reception and asked me to wait until Konstantin Mikhailovich had finished with his visitors. She offered me some theatre programmes and biographies of leading ballet artistes to look through. When his visitors had gone, Sergeyev himself came to meet me, curious about how I knew Lopukhov. After hearing my explanation, he brightened up, and asked about my specialist education. Going through my materials, which had been brought to his attention by Lopukhov, the artistic director's attention came to rest on the miniatures: 'Autumn', 'Eternal Gauls', 'Song of the Black Swan' and 'Fugitive'.

"Mikhail, as you realise, work is already under way. Sometime in November we will be starting to update our repertoire. What I'm interested in is these four miniatures, which we need for our performances at friendly receptions on our American tours. If possible, leave me the materials for *Poem of Man*. The Artistic Council will discuss this project, and by November will let you know the outcome of our decision to the address you've given."

"Konstantin Mikhailovich, please allow me to pop in to your stage rehearsals and shows to do a visual appraisal of the specifics of your leading soloists."

"I'll ask the chief administrator to order you a temporary one year pass."

My next task was to find suitable accommodation in the city centre, between the work bases. The private rental-sector flats seemed to be illegal in principle, and the prices in the area I needed were crazy, even for a small, one-room studio. I had to make do with a 'communal' flat (with six neighbours along the corridor). There were only seven light switches: by the entrance, kitchen, toilet, and shower. There were seven gas rings with numbered, lockable lids (to avoid flies falling into boiling borscht). I decided for now to stick with this option, on the strength of its central position opposite Kazan Cathedral in a dead-end street. I would have to sacrifice all my comforts, just spending the night in this ugly building and trying to maintain an acceptable human standard of sanitary hygiene.

In the last week of June I finally received a registered letter from Galya in Ulan-Ude. My employment log read: 'Left of his own accord.' Naturally, the only reference given was from the director of the College of Performing Arts, and fortunately, it was extremely favourable, in both professional and personal aspects alike. Galina mentioned in her accompanying letter, that all the ballet artistes and students were sorry that I had left so suddenly, and wished me well for the future. This was still a raw wound. I found it strangely sad and painful to read about unfinished creative work in the theatre. But over the last ten years I had already beaten my head against the wall so many times, it felt as if there was no space left for any new blows. My head splitting, I rushed to get my paperwork sorted out with Strizhachenko in the college and Ginsburg in the Philharmonic Society. Both directors copied the documents and asked me to pop back in a few days' time to complete the formalities. By the end of the month I was ready to leave for the Black Sea.

I telephoned my mother at work in Odessa to tell her that I was coming. She was delighted to hear my voice. She was upset with me as relatives and friends were always asking about me, but she never had any information for them. I apologised, blaming it on my heavy workload.

"Misha dear, your wife sent me a telegram to say that she's arriving with Dmitri on 9th July and could I meet them at the station at twelve thirty. I would happily have you all to stay, but as you know, I don't have enough room for three guests."

How could that be? I listened to my mother in silence, pretending to know about this turn of events. But my head was spinning and my knees were shaking at the very thought of such a surprise.

"Mum, Nanny Sasha has two free rooms. Talk her into giving up one of them for Milia and Dmitri, and I'll sleep at yours on the fold-up bed, until we leave for Karolino [seaside resort]."

"This would work for a week, as in the middle of July her daughter is coming with her husband."

"Great! We'll all be in Bugaz till then. Love you."

This news was really eating me up, but I managed to get a grip on myself in time. The new family circumstances forced me to change my original plan to travel with Boris in the car.

I promptly bought a ticket for the fast train to Odessa via Kiev, and left for my mother's the very next day, much to my cousin's surprise. On the way south, I analysed the unforeseeable situation, in an effort to understand my 'opponent's' next move.

Judging by the evidence, my wife had just finished her postgraduate course at MTA, and defended her candidacy for the History of Art Faculty. She had returned to Slavyansk, the town of her birth, with her second academic qualification. Rather than taking her in with open arms, they taught her how to fight with me. Had she decided to take Dmitri and leave him with Nanny in Odessa? "Let Dad look after his son now." She could then disappear back to Moscow.

Odessa greeted me with the scorching, suffocating heat of a south-coast summer. On the way from the station to my old house I popped in to see Mum at the bodega on the corner of Mayasoyedovskaya and Khvorostina streets. Our joy at meeting up again was boundless. It was two years since we had seen each other. Time flies.

"Misha, you have matured so much and are the spitting image of your dad. Only you have my eyes."

"What's happening with Roman? How are things between you and Yosif? I hope the family are all alive and well?"

"Roman and Lyuba got married. They have a daughter, Sana. Yosif battles with me as always. After our communal neighbour died, his mother-in-law moved into her flat, now the three of them give me a hard time in the kitchen. But I'm tired of fighting now. I assert my rights as mistress of the house. Your aunts sort out our arguments."

"Mum, how did Nanny Sasha react to my suggestion for her to have Milia and Dmitri at her place?"

"She agreed to it for forty roubles a month, plus all communal expenses to be split between them."

For three days before my family's arrival, I put a lot of effort into arranging my former nanny's room to make it as comfortable as possible. I bought a child's bed for my son. I strongly suspected that Milia would go to Odessa on the specious pretext of leaving him in my care, thus getting revenge on her husband for insulting her in Moscow due to her public debauchery and the disgrace she had caused me. This was so typical of her faint-hearted character: her envy, feelings of inferiority, her inability to cope with the practicalities of life, her lack of willpower and self-control. Nonetheless, on her arrival she floored me with her news, to a much greater extent than I had expected.

When I met my wife and son at the station, the conductor initially lugged their luggage along the platform. Then she carefully lowered Dmitri into my arms and finally, Milia was helped down from the step. Turning round, I saw my spouse in a voluminous gown with straps, in roughly her seventh month of pregnancy.

Already on edge in anticipation of a surprise, I wasn't at all shocked. I carried on chatting with my son, as if I hadn't noticed anything strange about my wife's appearance. Most likely she was expecting the logical response of a zodiac bull from me, and had been rehearsing for some time in Slavyansk the forthcoming public scandal on the platform in Odessa, which to her extreme annoyance and disappointment didn't materialise. Poor Shakespeare! How often had I cause to recall him in dramatic scenes in my life! I whistled for the porter and asked him to carry our luggage to the taxi rank. I sat Dmitri on my shoulders and the three of us slowly strode off towards the station exit. In the car, my wife settled in the front seat next to the driver, while my son and I sat in the back. He fired questions non-stop about the trolleybuses and trams whizzing past us. Nanny Sasha met us at the gates and walked us to her flat. Milia was silent, following behind in a complete quandary. I lugged two enormous suitcases up to the first floor and our old nanny carried my wife's bag over her shoulder. Dmitri brightly stamped upstairs.

Eventually, St Emilia lost patience: "Where the hell are we going? You can't have rented us a flat, as per your telegram?"

"Madam, you're not in Slavyansk now. Please keep your voice down in a communal home!"

Mum had heard about Milia's pregnancy and was overjoyed at the prospect of another grandson.

"Mummy dear, how do you know it'll be a boy rather than a girl? You're not a sorceress after all!"

"I can tell by the shape of her belly. Your brothers will all have daughters, but you will have only sons."

Dmitri didn't move from his grandmother's lap, when we went to see her at the bodega. Mum loved her grandson to death and was always lamenting his bad luck with his actual parents.

"Where do women get this flair? They always hit you right where it hurts."

My Aunty Faina (one of my mother's six sisters) worked as chief nurse in the Children's Department at the local hospital. She confirmed Mum's prediction.

"It's definitely a boy; she's about six to seven months gone. Get a second fiancée ready for this one."

"Misha, are they all magicians in your line? I want a girl, not a boy. It's a mother's right!"

We laughed at this joke, but my wife was actually upset about the prediction. The next day we all travelled safely to Bugaz.

Volodya (Nanny Sasha's husband) woke me up at 6 a.m. They had a large house and garden on the other side of the avenue, on the sea side of the spit. The two of us set off to do some fishing in my rowing boat, cruising along the Dnieper estuary for a couple of hours. As a rule, we would catch gobies and sardines, which would be enough not only for our families, but for the coastal cats and seagulls, who would meet the fishermen with lots of noise. With a smile, Milia accepted her son's living catch to prepare fresh fish soup, smoked in the sun and marinated with bay leaves. My mother had taught her this culinary skill in her last visit to Odessa, when Dmitri was still little. Now, when he awoke from his afternoon nap, we would fish with rods from the boat no further than 100 metres from the shore, to allow Milia to rest and sleep on the trestle bed.

On Sunday it was traditional for our whole clan to get together with Nanny Sasha's family to celebrate 14th July – Dmitri's birthday – and at the same time we exchanged news of the two families from Mum's and Dad's sides. We went for walks and relaxed in both houses by the sea and estuary. So as not to repeat the eccentric circumstances of the first birth, we all returned to Odessa together on the last bus. Sofia took my wife and son in her car, and Boris gave them a lift home. We put on a concert with our guests in the bus. After seeing Mum home, I went to my cousin's to collect my family – it was only two blocks away. I laid the sleeping 'sapling' in Sofia's old trolley and pushed him home to ours.

"Misha, thank you for a lovely day in Bugaz and for your consideration towards your wife."

"I'm happy that you've retained some positive feeling towards my family after all the rows."

"We need to talk about the future of this child, which you don't count as yours."

"When I asked you about it in Moscow, you refused to clarify our relationship. This is neither the time nor the place for a conversation of this nature. Let's try to clear it up tomorrow."

The following day, we went to the park near the old church after breakfast. While our son was playing in the children's playground, my wife and I were involved in close negotiations.

"Misha, how do you justify the assertion that I'm carrying someone else's child? Just before New Year, on the first evening when you and Dmitri came back, we had sexual relations. I was in shock at that unexpected meeting, and didn't take any precautions."

"It happened just the once, about six months ago. Based on what you say, you are gearing up to give birth at the beginning of August, i.e. around seven months after our contact. Judging by what I've heard from the hostel, you started meeting your lover in October, which makes nine months to the due date. What would you be thinking, if you were me?"

"In the first place, it's a coincidence of fate. Secondly, seven months is also a normal period for an unusual pregnancy. Any paediatrician would tell you that. Thirdly, even if I had been unfaithful to you, it doesn't give you the moral or legal right to turn your back on the child."

"On this let's cut short our argument for the time being. In mid-August I must go back to Leningrad to set up some new work. Until then I will try my best to ensure more or less normal living conditions for you during your pregnancy in Odessa. I will fund your accommodation costs until the end of the year, and will leave Mum some money for your expenses, around fifty roubles a week. These conditions may change, depending on your conduct and relationships with the children."

"How is this possible? You can't be trying to educate me again? It's beyond me!"

"I'm talking about your maternal obligations in the immediate future. In a year's time when your second child is stronger, you will get him into a crèche and go back to work, just like most women with postgraduate qualifications."

"Just out of interest, how am I going to organise all this without a permanent permit for Odessa?"

"Before I leave, I'll try to get you and Dmitri registered at Aunty Faina's, as she has some free floor space because her children are now living in Cheryomushki. I'll come down at New Year and hopefully will move you three into her flat next to Privoz for the same price. Whatever happens, I suppose it'll be better for you to live among relatives for the immediate future, for your own security and help with the children. On 1st September, Dmitri will go to kindergarten to Mum's youngest sister, Aunty Dora (next door, around the corner), and you will be with the little one at Aunty Faina's 'in the lap of luxury'."

"As always, you have got it all planned for everyone. What if I don't accept your conditions for my life?"

"No one forced you to come here. You can go back to Slavyansk or Moscow. No one is muscling in on your freedom. That said, in a year's time, if you go off somewhere else, I will file for divorce. What'll probably happen is that they'll split the children between us, so you'll get another chance for your amorous adventures. Your fate is in your hands or as they say: 'Each to his own.'

"Dmitri, it's time to go home. Can you see the communal steam baths opposite the church? Tomorrow morning you and I will go in there to wash away all your dirt and all my sins for the whole week."

"Mummy, Mummy! What are sins, and what do you eat them with? Is it potatoes, macaroni or rice?"

"Let's go, chatterbox. I'll tell you when we get home. You're a mucky pup, all dusty, and you've ripped your trousers."

Milia was clearly perturbed by our tricky conversation. She had naïvely assumed that all men were lechers. Catch them by the tail and they'll chase you to the ends of the earth. My wife was probably not well versed in the type of men who are squeamish (even at times of sexual cravings) about sleeping with a prostitute. They are mentally unable to share their partner with another.

Not long before, I had organised a trip to Privoz market in the car with Sofia. After the conversation with Milia, Boris was already waiting for me by our gates with the motor. We left the two boys with Nanny Sasha. The elder taught the younger to play chess while Sofia and I jostled with others among the crowded market stalls. Loaded up like donkeys, we gradually struggled to the car with bags full of fruit, vegetables and other foodstuffs. But we had secured ourselves the freshest of the lot! Nanny could now prepare Ukrainian borscht for three families. Uncle Volodya, our neighbour, brought a pail of grapes that he had grown himself in Bugaz, on which we gorged ourselves. Mum, coming straight from work, also sampled the borscht, while quizzing me about our plans for the immediate future. She was struck by the fact that her daughter-in-law and her grandsons would be living as her neighbours here in Odessa, and she would be seeing a lot of them in this house.

My mother promised to organise temporary registration with the police through her sister Faina, and for Milia and the children to stay in her flat. My aunt worked in the hospital from morning till late at night and on her days off went to see her children and grandchildren in Cheryomushki, so it suited her to have a tenant to look after the house. We were talking from 1st December (around four months after the birth), when the 'Madonna and child' would get acclimatised to life on sinful earth. Mum arranged it so that family members could drop in at Milia's on their way to Privoz every other day, to negotiate her shopping order. This would alleviate the isolation felt by this mother and her two young charges. The aunts worked things out between them to clean Aunty Faina's flat on their days off. Outsiders may find it hard to believe there was such close cooperation between our relatives. All her life, my mother helped her sisters to organise their family celebrations: baking day and night, stuffing, marinating for seventy or eighty appreciative mouths. They were more than happy to reciprocate when required for her selfless devotion to the clan.

On 4th August we were woken in the middle of the night by Nanny Sasha knocking on the wall.

As I was in my underpants, I jumped up instantly, with Milia's pregnancy on my mind.

Nanny shouted: "Misha, your wife's waters have broken. Run down to the Food Production College [the building next door]. There's a twenty-four-hour security guard on duty there. Ring the doorbell or knock on the window. Get him to call an ambulance."

309

Five minutes later, my wife was ferried off to hospital, just two blocks away. For the rest of the night I sat and waited in the Children's Ward reception until Aunty Faina arrived at 8 a.m.

"Misha, wake up! It was a straightforward birth, but the boy is very feeble, he doesn't move much and is refusing to breastfeed. The charge nurse has just arrived and is personally monitoring his health." Aunty Faina advised me to go home and not to worry. I could see from her face that the child was in a critical condition, but kept quiet.

The following morning, the chief paediatrician explained to me very patiently that they would need to keep my wife in for a week due to the newborn's immature development in her womb. This was not the first time they had seen this pathology in a premature birth. Milia was doing everything she could to get stronger and resume active functions. My wife was feeling relatively normal and had plenty of milk.

"Sorry, Doctor, is this problem down to her seven-month pregnancy?"

"I don't think so. Whether it's seven or nine months, these are standard timescales for foetal development. Eight months is worse."

I returned home completely dispirited and confused about what had happened. Perhaps through her slapdash nature she had damaged the baby during her trip from Slavyansk to Odessa a month before the birth? Had she carted heavy suitcases about or lifted them into the carriage? The chief paediatrician's explanation didn't quite add up.

During this time, Nanny Sasha took it upon herself to look after Dmitri. I supplied her with food and funds. Every morning and evening I went to the hospital. Alexander (as we named the boy) was not making much progress. On the fifth day after the birth, Aunty Faina reported that our son had been transferred to an isolation ward for the seriously ill, as he was exhibiting symptoms of pneumonia. This could only end badly.

"Your wife is ignoring the advice of our medical staff. It's very hot on the wards. There is no ventilation, so the windows on all sides are left open. Nonetheless, your son must be kept constantly swaddled because of his low blood pressure and generally weak circulation. Every time Milia breastfeeds him, she sees sweat on her son's face and decides to cool him down and strips him naked. The duty nurse noticed that the little one was turning blue, raised the alarm and took him to the doctor. The child's temperature went up during the night. In an effort to justify her actions, Milia started a row. I asked them to call my wife to reception for a very serious, important matter."

"I've heard your criticism, sir, about everything that's been said about me."

"I have no reason to argue with you. I just want you not to cause any problems in this hospital, so that you and the child are OK. By behaving in this way, you are alienating the very people who are trying to help you both. Once again, you are 'shitting on your own doorstep'. You are letting Faina down and undermining her authority as senior ward sister."

"I've had it up to here with all your moralising. I'm fed up of hanging around here! I want to go home."

"Weren't you the one moaning to me that 'it's amoral for a father to abandon his child to the mercy of fate'? And now you want to leave your ill son to his lot. What's wrong with you?"

"The chief doctor is telling me I have to go and get disinfected, and they will feed the little one themselves."

"That's because you've lost your self-control and present a risk to the baby.

Apologise to the chief doctor and Faina for your outburst. Have a little patience!"

By the end of his first week, Alexander's condition was life-threatening. The chief doctor said that the only thing that could save him was plasma (a new remedy), which was only available in hospitals in capital cities, and then only for a fee. On Aunty Faina's insistence, the deputy director of the regional Health Department rang Kishinev – the nearest capital, in Moldova – and arranged an urgent courier delivery of this prized substance. Mum put out an SOS and in an hour, our relatives had amassed the necessary fee for the delivery of life-saving plasma. The hospital surgeon inserted it into the baby's head in two sessions (due to his young age), with a long interval between each one. In the first few hours after the procedure, it looked as though Alexander was improving. But in the night his condition worsened again. The impending tragedy was keenly felt by the whole of the Children's Ward staff. Milia was beside herself and Mum and Aunty Faina were crying. The child was wasting away before our eyes. The chief doctor acknowledged that he had received the plasma too late. They could do no more to save the boy.

At this, I consulted with Aunty Faina and announced: "In that case, let our son end his short life at home rather than in hospital."

My wife and I signed to take the sick baby away, and took him home in an ambulance.

When she saw the boy, Nanny Sasha went right up close to him and took in the smell of his breath. Hearing the story of the plasma, she let out a deep sigh and shook her head.

"They have worried the life out of your son with pills and needles. Misha, let's go out on the terrace! Your son is dying, as you know. I might still be able to save him. Give him this chance! I have treated my grandsons successfully more than once. We are all doctors in our family."

"Nanny, you know that irrespective of all my gratitude and love for you, I don't believe in miracles."

"It's not miracles, but ancient folk medicine, which has saved many lives from the brink. Go with your other half to the grocer's and buy milk and honey. Give me half an hour!"

"No, Nanny Sasha! Milia will go with the eldest to have lunch at the bodega with Mum. She'll tell her about her sick grandson. On the way back, she can buy what you've asked for. I want to see your medicine."

"Good, go and get them organised. In the meantime, I'll get ready for the old family procedure."

I popped into our room again. My wife was sitting on the bed crying, our ill son at her side.

"Milia, you wanted to call into the chemist for some women's things. Could you buy a bottle with a teat while you're there? Have lunch with Dmitri at Mum's and bring me back a sandwich. On the way home, buy some fresh milk and honey at the grocer's."

I called to the eldest playing outside. I washed his face and hands at the sink, then walked him to the gate with his mum and returned to the witch doctor. Nanny was boiling some kind of grass, and left the medicine to cool by the window. She scalded a teaspoon with boiling water, then folded a blanket into four, and spread it on the table. Unswaddling this pale, slightly blue two-week-old mite, she undid and threw out his wet nappy. She wiped him with a dry towel and set about her sacred ritual. I sat there in a trance observing Nanny Sasha, seeing her in a completely new light. First she smeared the little one's skin with

311

goose fat to keep him warm. Then her old fingers began delicately massaging the front and back of his tiny body, turning him from one side to the other with diamond precision. This tiny invalid made no objection at all, neither kicked nor whined. On the contrary, judging by appearances, he was enjoying the massage. Nanny carefully moved his little arms to one side and crossways, and his legs up and down straight. The boy's misty eyes pensively followed the old nanny's movements. Individual parts of his body moved convulsively now and again, as if his nervous system were coming out of hibernation.

Eventually, Nanny Sasha unwound the flannelette swaddling and wrapped the boy up in it. She sniffed his breath again and stuck her lips to his forehead to gauge the sick boy's temperature. Next, she quickly put yellow (unbleached) cotton wool all around him, and pulled a towel soaked in vodka out of a basin. She squeezed it out carefully and wound it around my son, who gave a little squeak at this point. But Nanny Sasha hurried to conserve the alcohol content, neatly slipping this 'snow white doll' into a plastic bag from the chemist, just leaving his head out. To finish off, she wound a clean sheet around the poor patient and lay him on the bed between pillows. They served as sound barriers against the nerves of those present. At first the poor child just moaned. Then he started his heart-rending wailing. No doubt, once all the spirit vapours began penetrating the towelling and goose fat, the little one was starting to react to the burning irritants on his delicate, tender skin. Nanny Sasha was rocking gently as she pressed the sick child to her bony chest, quietly whispering something in time with her movement. My son's cries gradually lessened. The healer mopped up the sweat on his face with a towel. Two or three minutes later, Alexander fell silent, then breathed noisily through both nostrils. Horrified, I looked at the sorceress, too frightened to ask if her charge was alive. Nanny Sasha gently placed the boy on the sofa. She took a few steps back and crossed herself. She removed from the table all her instruments of torture (Heaven help you!) so that his mother wouldn't see them on her return and then there wouldn't be any trouble.

Turning to me, she said: "Misha, run and buy a pram for your son. He'll only wake up in the night or early tomorrow morning now. Don't tell anyone about this healing, or they'll send me to Siberia."

"Nanny, I don't know how to thank you for saving my son. Tell me."

"Your trust in me is the greatest honour that I could ever earn."

Nanny Sasha showed Milia her sleeping son with his pink cheeks. On waking, he drank a whole quarter of a litre of boiled milk with honey (all mixed up with the pre-prepared potion). I happened to notice a shortage of food and sanitary items for the boy, so I dived into the chemist just before they closed. I bought ten bottles of special milk for newborns, a dozen nappies, children's cream and dummies. I popped in to see Mum and relayed the good tidings. Noticing the milk in my bag, she rushed into the kitchen and brought back a bucketful of ice.

"Take this home, mix it up with the bottles and put it out on the balcony. The little one should drink three times as much and pee twice as much now, to make up for what he's missed. Thank God he's come round!"

I lugged all the shopping home, and was sorry that my children had such an irresponsible mother. She was in the chemist and only bought one dummy and an empty bottle for her son, while purchasing a pile of cosmetics for herself.

That night, Nanny Sasha took the little boy off to her room, promising to return him to his mum in full health in the morning. Milia was too scared to object and agreed to everything, as long as her son was alive. I realised that Nanny Sasha wanted to complete her mission and remove all traces of sorcery. In the morning, she told us that the boy had woken up in the night, and she, the healer, had put in his hungry mouth a dummy dipped in honey-milk. Then she wiped him over with a hot, damp towel and changed his swaddling. After downing half a bottle, Shurik (diminutive of Alexander) fell asleep again. The crisis had clearly diminished, but the fragile state of his weak body demanded his mother's special, undivided attention, which, realistically was not going to happen. For this reason, leaving money for accommodation up to the New Year, I asked Nanny Sasha (tactically, in relation to Milia) to manage Shurik's condition, for a substantial reward at Christmas. She promised to help my wife to look after both 'saplings'.

Before I left for Leningrad, the whole clan got together belatedly with Mum at the bodega to celebrate Alexander's birthday and bid me farewell.

My six-week 'holiday' in Odessa had been a nightmare. Mum remarked that I had lost weight and looked strained. Hardly surprising after these '1001 nights'. By the time Alexander was born, Aunty Faina had succeeded in getting Milia and Dmitri registered at her address. So my wife now had the right to live and work in the Black Sea town. During my last two days I introduced her to my former guardians/directors: in the Ballet School, Arts Centre and the Mariners' Centre, in case she could be useful to them as a lecturer for candidates studying the history of art in connection with the theatre and ballet. Milia was very sceptical about this. Still, I fulfilled my obligation, though I had strong doubts about her inclination and ability generally to work anywhere at any time. One way or another, I left my mother 1,000 roubles from the money I'd earned at the Buryat Festival.

"Mum, once I've gone, please give Milia just fifty roubles a week every Sunday evening, for all her family expenses apart from the rent. One condition: she must sign a book with you to confirm receipt every time. That's important."

I thanked Nanny Sasha; the youngest was obviously on the mend. The nursery right next to the house accepted the eldest. I bought the little one a large folding pram. In fact, I thought of everything and provided the minimum items required until I came back in December. Nevertheless, I left feeling depressed about my split family, and worried about Emilia's behaviour in my absence. I realised that she was not content with her social situation as a housewife and mother feeding her kids – on her own.

I was far from convinced that Alexander was my biological son, after an eight-month pregnancy. However, to avoid disgrace, I chose to put up with the uncertainty and bit my tongue. Having said goodbye to everyone the night before, I set off for the station early the next morning.

Once back in Leningrad, I prioritised moving into the communal flat and setting up my living quarters. In the last week of August I attended the college daily, taking part in teaching councils to organise the new academic year. After lunch, I checked exercise programmes for the barre and centre, for all three grades, and worked with the concert master on musical accompaniment for my classes. Sadovskaya, the head of department, was eager to hear about my professional concepts on the methodology of teaching choreographic disciplines. I set out teaching plans for her in writing for my subjects, which she approved without even looking at them. This confirmed my subsequent work in the college. Students in all groups were inevitably more cultured than the Buryat people, in the sense of general education and level of preparation in music, dance and acting skills. I found it significantly easier and more enjoyable to work with them than in Ulan-Ude.

It was tough for candidates to get into the Dance Department, with between five and seven people competing for every available place. Each group consisted of up to thirty students, and each of them in turn was obliged to select a musical instrument to learn, or to sing in the vocal ensemble. Students in their second or third year of study ended up with me: the younger ones attended three classes a week lasting two school hours (forty-five minutes), while the seniors had six. In all, three days from 9 a.m. until 2 p.m.

The first task in my subject was to establish a professional teacher–student relationship. We defined the stage etiquette between all parties, and agreed class and home tasks according to composition type. I warned the participants from both grades: "The harder and more intensively we work, the more practical material you will take away from this class for your future professions as choreographers/producers of Folk and Theatrical dance. Otherwise, you could have an easy going job as a librarian in the club, which is an equally respectable profession."

To my satisfaction, I noticed that almost all of the students really appreciated my professional competence and creative discipline. If anyone began clowning around, I would stop the music. I would go over to the offender and gently warn them that if it happened again, I would exclude them from the class. As a rule, this sufficed, even for the most obstinate.

At the end of September, Ginsburg introduced me to the artistes in his ensemble. Following a month's leave which marked the end of the holidays, they were keen to resume work on the new repertoire. In my four free days from college, I rehearsed with them from 10 a.m. until 6 p.m. – we ate snacks on the go. Naturally, with the men, I put on 'Jolly Marines', a sailors' suite for five performers; six girls and one guy learned the mischievous dance 'Flirtation on the Neva'. I also produced 'Baltic Quadrille' using the whole team. All three compositions were in the style of *musical comedy*, based on Russian Character dances. The abundance of Solo sequences and lifts in Suets called for additional practice and training in partnering lifts, as they clearly lacked the relevant technique and experience for a secure staged performance. Two nights a week after school classes I had to teach them the 'Pas de deux' technique for Duets. A few of the girls needed to lose weight fast. Nonetheless, the whole group responded favourably to the production task in hand, beyond my expectations.

I also managed to work a little with the vocal octet, enriching their performance through accompanying motion of the arms, legs and head, to suit the character of the repertoire at hand: cross-steps, stamps and claps (to musical interludes), or gentle shoulder and leg shakes (during the singing). As usual, when faced with unaccustomed change, the singers would occasionally groan in a sign of protest. But the artistic director lent his enthusiastic support to this Theatrical artistry, and rigorously put a stop to all attempts to sabotage the group's creative progress. Ginsburg, in his evaluation of the new programme, made special mention of the stage movements in the vocal octet's delivery, and personally thanked the producers/choreographers. Leisya Pesnya's premiere was organised for the anniversary of the October Revolution, and took place to great acclaim at the Philharmonic Society on 6th November. During the interval, Ginsburg introduced me to the Director of the regional Cultural Committee. He informed him of my involvement in the festival to mark the fortieth anniversary of the Buryat republic in May that year, and of my permanent work at the college.

In their practical test during the winter term, my students demonstrated to the Committee the elementary principles of 'choreographic composition' in their studies, and executed very effectively my choreographed forms of national Theatrical dances of the USSR. Stepanyan, head of the Drama Department, remarked that the dancers had advanced significantly in their acting ability, and congratulated me on my successful debut in the College of Performing Arts. After the review, the Director called me into his office. He expressed how pleased he was with my display, and asked how I would react to his suggestion of taking over the running of Sadovskaya's department from 1st August, in line with her retirement. I thanked him for his faith in me, and explained that I was more interested in working creatively as a teacher/choreographer in a position with artistic freedom. I apologised for turning down his offer, and acknowledged that I would shortly be agreeing supplementary hours in elementary partnering technique in duets, in which the department's students were really in need, although it would only be one class a week with second- or third-graders.

"Mikhail, I appreciate your candour. I will consider your wishes, and you may revisit my proposal. Sadovskaya's departure could complicate matters for you if she is replaced by a specialist from outside, who immediately starts telling you how to do your job. Perhaps you and Larisa (a classical teacher, Sadovskaya's assistant) could work out a compromise solution that would suit all of us? The Cultural Committee telephoned and asked me to tell you that they are expecting you tomorrow at 10 a.m. to discuss a People's Artistic Festival in May of next year. They no doubt need specialists of your calibre to make up their panel. Good luck!"

I was met at the Cultural Committee by the head of the Popular Culture Department, R. Bokov. He had a look at my portfolio containing materials about the Buryat Festival, and singled out several points from my biography: my origins, education, and professional roles.

"Mr Berkut, we invited you on the insistence of our Philharmonic Society director, Ginsburg. Every two years, as you're probably aware, we hold a regional showcase of performing arts. We need an experienced specialist in this category of art to select the best groups for a Gala concert where (according to the judges' decisions) prizes will be awarded for distinction. If your file is anything to go by, even though you are quite lacking in experience in this arena, you have the fundamental skills to undertake the proposed project. Do you have the creative interest and time available to take on this proposal? We're talking about a contract from 8th January to 9th May. What would your fee be?"

"At present, I'm occupied at the College of Performing Arts three mornings a week. It would be interesting to have other work of this nature, and I usually charge in the region of 1,000 roubles per month. My terms would be as follows:

"a) a Musical Director for combined choir and orchestra;

"b) a Deputy/Administrator, responsible for organisational issues;

"c) my own Personal Assistant, to take charge of contact details and printed documents;

"d) a large stage for the Gala concert, with a Festival production team: artist/designer, my assistant producer, technicians, etc."

"This is all acceptable. I will update the Committee Chair regarding our discussions. If there is a positive outcome, you will need to come back again to sign the contract. Call me tomorrow between 4 and 5 p.m. on this number, and I'll let you know."

Two days later I signed an agreement with Bokov for the Festival. There was a week to go before New Year. I was not going to make it home to see the family in Odessa. It was a five-day round trip on the train. College classes were due to start on 2nd January. Unfortunately, it was clear that I needed to cancel my train south. I went to the post office to ring Mum.

"Fedya, hi! It's Misha in Leningrad. Sorry to disturb you. Can I speak to Mum, please?"

"Mishenka, my son. How are you doing up there? Freezing, I expect. When are you coming to Odessa?"

"Mummy dear, forgive me. It's not going to work out this time. I've only got a week between jobs."

"It's not the end of the world. What matters is that you're well, and it's great to hear your voice. Shurik's on good form. Dmitri, as always, is giving us all the run-around, but he is unfailingly obedient towards me. Milia and I argue occasionally but as you know with me, 'you make your bed so you have to lie in it', as you would put it. So don't worry."

"Mum, I'll send you another 500 by postal order for Nanny and the family. Sorry about the extra work. Give the kids a kiss from me and keep well! Take care of yourself."

Next I ordered a second call to Shura, the warden in Moscow, and asked her to reserve me a room in her hostel (during the holidays) for the week beginning 30th December. Once she'd confirmed, I rushed off to the station for a ticket on the night train. There were no seats left in the general carriages so I had to make do with a compartment (twice the price).

It took me two hours to pack. On the way to Sofia's, I stopped off at Gostinny Dvor Shopping Centre to buy New Year's gifts for everyone, then got to my cousin's in time for supper.

Seeing me with my suitcase and half a dozen gifts in my arms and teeth, she clasped her head, exclaiming: "You homeless tramp! Are you moving back in with me now?"

"No, my dear cousin, I've come to wish you Happy New Year before I head off to Moscow, to thank you for the supper invitation, and to tell you my news."

Her husband laughed on hearing our conversation, while my nephew, Arkady, the eldest, was already straddling me.

"Uncle Misha, where's my present? I bet you've left it at home. Go on, tell me, where is it?"

"Hey, sonny Jim. Stop shaking my shoulders. They'll come out of their sockets. Look, my little hare, just wait a moment!" And I chased the six-year-old scallywag around the table, knocking over chairs in the way, waving my arms and stamping my feet.

"Mum, save me from this giant bear! Daddy, what are you laughing at?"

Suddenly, I accidentally caught my foot on the table leg and went flying across the sitting-room floor. The chief of the redskins promptly took advantage by coming at me from behind and grabbing hold of my hair.

"Poor Toptygin! Give me my present now, or I'll scalp you."

"Stop racing around now, stripy features, it's not a racetrack you know!"

After supper, I updated my hosts on the news about my job and forthcoming plans in the city. At 10 p.m. we exchanged New Year's greetings and I hurried off for the midnight train.

Shura, the warden, welcomed me to the hostel like family. She led me into the ballet masters' room, where only one of the six beds was taken. The rest of the lodgers had all gone off for the holidays. I threw my case under my bunk and decided to try my luck at the MTA library in the last few days of the year. I desperately needed to find some information on foreign shows and contemporary ballroom dancing, which were not very popular at that time in mainstream practice. There was no sign of Shatin in the Dean's offices. Lena, the secretary, confirmed that he would only get back from leave on the morning of 3rd January.

A whole day's work in the reading room resulted in my finding in the catalogues of foreign literature, details of a periodical published in English: a monthly collection *Modern Ballroom Dancing* and *Spectrum of Contemporary Social Dance*. Looking through the few copies left on the shelves, I was fascinated by their photographs, excerpts from scores and references. The librarian lent me (as she knew me) six collections for four days, and asked me to leave my passport as collateral. There was no photocopier at MTA, unlike the Conservatoire next door. I dashed in, an hour before they closed. In the collections of interest to me I noticed names of African and Latin-American dances. I paid up front for the copies, as I had done for the previous orders for Dushanbe and Ulan-Ude. In return, they guaranteed that the work would be ready for the morning of 3rd January. I thanked my lucky stars.

Now I could relax with a clear conscience. On the way out of the Conservatoire, I grabbed a few leaflets detailing the theatre/concert programmes for this week. As in previous years, the capital's stages were dominated by children's matinees and performances of old, classical operas and ballets in the evenings. The only item that caught my eye was a Barcelona Flamenco Ensemble, on at the Hall of Columns at 8 p.m. I decided to devote this evening to the Gypsy classic. The following evening was 31st December, so I needed to consider how, and with whom to see in the New Year. First I popped into the Hall of Columns ticket office and bought a ticket for the flamenco ensemble. Then I paid a visit to my old friend Cyril Andreyev in the Arbat next door, a theatre designer from my student days at MTA.

I rang the bell and the door was opened by his mother. She asked tentatively in a whisper: "It can't be Mikhail Berkut, can it?!"

"Madam, I'm sorry to intrude, it's good to see you looking so well."

"Now I know it's definitely Misha from Odessa! Cyril! There's a visitor from your ancient world! Come here!"

"Where did you disappear to this time? Odessa, Dushanbe, Ulan-Ude?" the young man enquired as he came out.

I had heard on my last visit that his father had died of a heart attack.

"Tell me, which wind has blown you to Moscow for New Year?"

"I'm living and working in Leningrad at the moment. I've come here for a week to update my knowledge in the MTA and Conservatoire libraries. I missed my old friends."

"Where are your family? I hope you're not divorced like the rest of us sinful artistes and painters?"

"On the contrary, I've been growing the ranks. My second son, Alexander, arrived recently, and they're living with my mum in Odessa. Once I've sorted out a place to live, I'll move them up here to be with me."

"Lads, supper is served. Wash your hands and carry on your conversation over food."

"Thanks, Elena Viktorovna, but I couldn't eat a thing, i.e. yes. I mean, perhaps I will, for your sake. They say: 'It's rude to decline food.' Me, as an educated . . ."

"Misha, stop larking about – you know what my mum's like. She's a female version of Commander Chapayev."

"Cyril, it's six thirty now. I've got a ticket for the flamenco ensemble in the Hall of Columns at 8 p.m."

"Oh great, we can go together. I adore Gypsy stuff. Mum, we've only got an hour."

"Bravo. Now they're rushing me. Oh these boys! How on earth do we put up with them?"

The Barcelona Flamenco Ensemble performed with first-class artistry. Two singers, two guitarists and six dancers gripped the audience in a continuous two-way emotional incandescence of theatrical reflection and delight. True performers in this genre possess a spiritual, magic strength which pervades the auditorium. The various male and female artistes not only entertained the public, but with each performance, went through the traditional range of gestures, movements and rhythm. In a unique artistic transformation, they often brought themselves to a state of natural ecstasy.

During the interval, Cyril asked me where I would be celebrating New Year's Eve tomorrow. Learning that I had not yet resolved this dilemma, he suggested that I spent it with him in the company of single men from Moscow's theatre world. We arranged to meet up tomorrow evening at Arbat metro station at 10 p.m., with our overnight bags.

On 1st January, after a night on the tiles, I lay in until lunchtime. I used what was left of the day to set the programmes for the College of Performing Arts. As promised, the Director had put in an extra class on Duet technique for second- or third-graders. Then I added one unwanted class on Friday based on Stage folk dance for first-graders. In this way, my timetable increased to eighteen hours a week (six hours a day). In line with the creative demands of my various posts at the opera, Philharmonic Society and running the regional festival, this was more than enough to be getting on with. I clearly didn't have sufficient time to get myself organised for all these projects. Times like these called for help from a person qualified for the role of wife or partner. But alas! I was destined to complete my marathon by myself.

On the morning of 3rd January, I paid a visit to Shatin at MTA. He looked worse than last time. I cheered him up with my contracts and plans for the opera. My mentor was very complementary about his senior students. He complained that it was becoming impossible to work at MTA. At every turn, he was plagued by his enemies, blocking his development of the faculty to incorporate modern principles of professional education.

"If you decide to come back to Moscow, I will try to set you up as my assistant."

"Professor, I would be honoured. But it's unlikely that the new principal would confirm my appointment. He would rather fall in battle, than let me near a job at MTA."

"Time is moving on, things are changing. After a series of complaints from teachers regarding the Principal's lack of knowledge, I've heard that the ministry wants to promote him."

"Whatever happens, I'm already contracted in Leningrad for the time being. If any definite opportunities come up in MTA, please give me a call on this number at my cousin's. We might be able to come up with an unforeseen compromise." Getting back into Leningrad early in the morning from the night train, I had planned to complete programmes for all grades in the last two days of the winter holidays. There was a note with the previous day's date stuck on my bachelor's-pad door from the college director, summoning me on urgent business. I quickly gathered my working things together, changed the contents of my travelling bag and was already at the College of Performing Arts by 9 a.m. The secretary informed Strizhachenko of my arrival and invited me to go through.

"Mikhail Semyonovich, we have suffered a huge loss. On 2nd January, during a complicated operation in hospital (from which she never regained consciousness), Sadovskaya has passed away. Five years ago they found she had a cancerous tumour. They tried treating it, but it was unsuccessful. In August last year, while you were on holiday in the south, the doctors insisted on operating. However, the patient herself categorically declined it, allowing the illness to become even more incurable. She was planning to retire on 1st September, but was worried about abandoning her 'baby'.

"For the last seven years, Sadovskaya has worked with Larisa as her assistant, whom she had fostered from schooldays. After four years of practice in the Maly Opera Theatre, the young ballerina (demi-character profile), heard about her former teacher's illness and came back to her as her assistant. Over this period, Larisa has virtually completely assimilated the method of work with preschoolers, after which she started to lead first-graders in this field completely off her own bat. In addition, she has taught all students in the department the basics of Classical dance (using the Vaganova system), depending on their level of training. In the hours she had free from her own classes, she supported Sadovskaya in all her classes. You have not yet met Larisa, as you both work on different days of the week. Also, she is quite shy, particularly with men, though she is active, emotional and precise in her work. Recently Larisa has actually taken charge of all the paperwork and administrative functions in the department, in view of Sadovskaya's seriously deteriorating health. I concede that I did not have the heart to take this work away from her, as she had lived for it over so many years without a break.

"Mikhail, I'm telling you all of this because I find myself in an awkward position as Director, not wanting to lose a valued specialist and unable to support a large/complex department in our academic establishment, without a Leader at its head. So, could we compromise by dividing the leadership duties between you? We'd leave the administrative/organisational part to Larisa, as she's been managing this recently, and you could take on the artistic/teaching lead. I understand that the least important element to you in this situation is the financial side. Nevertheless, the Accounts Department is obliged to pay everyone overtime. Larisa and I spoke about this yesterday. In principle, she is interested in learning from your experience in choreography and teaching, although she is quite anxious about your temperament at work. Still, this is a temporary thing. If you also agree in principle, let's get together to discuss this collaboration. I'm sure you'll work it out between you."

"Artyom Savelich, if I understand you correctly, I will have to supervise her beginners in my free days and she will help me as necessary with the senior students. Under these circumstances, I request your permission to use (on a voluntary basis) another second-grade student, Valery Kuchinsky, as an assistant for demonstrations and to work on male technique under my direction. I will also need Larisa's help as a partner in the Partnering course. I assume that, pedagogically speaking, you can't use a student for this purpose. Now, after our professional 'betrothal', in your office, it's best if you determine all the subtleties of our 'joint leadership'. I can only promise to follow full pedagogical etiquette with my colleague and assistant."

"Come in, Larisa. It's my pleasure to introduce to you your new Artistic sponsor and fellow teammate. And to introduce you to him as his Head of administration and organisation, plus his assistant in all dance/teaching programmes."

Initially, my colleague looked astonished, but by the end of the introduction, she was laughing.

"That's called 'marrying me off in my absence', so, we're engaged! Let's hope it works out."

"They've done the same to me. I'm certain we'll make a successful creative partnership."

I shook the Director's hand, kissed Larisa's hand, and took my leave with a bow.

The next day, after visiting the Cultural Committee, I studied the Festival schedule in the area's regional centres, and obtained a list of the panel members and contact details for the final concert's production team. A minibus had been arranged for the first trip out to a regional presentation in the town of Lomonosov on the coming Saturday. The panel comprised specialists in various genres, Chairmen from the local Arts Centre and the Cultural Committee, and a photojournalist. The head of the Popular Culture Department gave me the Artistic Director's brief for the Regional show, and reminded me that all organisational issues (allowances, lodgings, food, transport, etc.) were dealt with by his subordinate. My responsibility was to evaluate the performances and select numbers for the final concert. This suited me fine.

Of course, there were more art lovers in just one district of the Leningrad region than in all the regions of Buryatia put together. We were listening to and observing groups and individual performers from 10 a.m. to 3 p.m. and from 4 p.m. to 9 p.m. Many of them were working at professional level. It was lovely – in comparison with Ulan-Ude – to experience advanced appraisal. The Lomonosov Town Council had taken such care to organise the show with scrupulous attention to detail, that we managed to process (as on a conveyor belt) the whole programme in one day without staying over, to the great astonishment of the panel and show hosts. During a belated supper, the deputy chairman of the local Communist Party Committee thanked us for our tireless endeavours and presented us with souvenir gifts. We were deposited back in Leningrad towards midnight, and dropped off at our homes.

Following the compromise in our production 'betrothal', Larisa and I met at the college and worked together on the next term's course syllabus. Of below average height, and in excellent, fit condition, the twenty-seven-year-old colleague was blessed with the ability to grasp new movements quickly, a good musical ear and demonstrably high technical ability in performing a routine. She described to me in detail her programmes (preschool and beginners), invited me to observe her first-grade classes, and asked my permission to make a note of my exercise syllabus for senior students, in case she needed to stand in for me. I gave her a 'good' and in turn, offered her the opportunity to learn with me the basics of

'Duet technique' in Folk and Theatrical (character) dance. Larisa had apparently not come across this genre before and felt 'out of her depth'. She quivered every time I took her hands or put them on my shoulders; when I took her by the waist and spun her around, lifted her up, pressed my elbows against her hips, she would blush, embarrassed. This was either because she had already forgotten her practice at the Maly Opera Theatre, or due to the strength of the antagonism she felt towards men. One way or another, I pretended not to notice her natural reactions. I gave her time to regroup psychologically and get used to my hands.

After lunch I gave Larisa the basics on introducing Duet technique to Beginner couples. She wrote down the general parameters for both partners.

"Lara, in our individual preparation, please address me by my first name (without the patronymic). I find this a much more comfortable way of interacting with a partner. It's a different matter in public. So, on Tuesdays and Thursdays I suggest we meet here, after your classes with the first-graders, plus the lunch break from 1 to 4 p.m. I need to give you the programme for Character dance training (exercises at the Barre and in the Centre) rather than Classical. This will warm the students up sufficiently to give them a stronger technical basis for Stage Folk dance in subsequent years. In Moscow I trained young artistic gymnasts from the Central School of Athletics for the Olympics, and they won first place in this type of sport. I'll gladly give you the series of sequences with objects (ribbon, hoop, ball, skipping rope, flag, etc.), which you can include in the programme for preschoolers and young children as you wish. It's my choreography and I give you the right to use it in exchange for your help on the Duet technique with serious students (two classes a week). Larisa, you must try to have your pupils ready for Character training by 1st February. You need to let me know how I can help you with this. As regards Duet technique, I hope you have nothing against us doing joint training and demonstrations to students in the senior classes. The Director has allowed me to make use of Kuchinsky, the best student in second grade, as a volunteer assistant, in the aim of monitoring as closely as possible the mastery of partnering and sequences on the side. Valery is older than the others in this group and has more dance experience. This will only work if you don't mind demonstrating lifts with him too."

"Of course not. This is normal academic process in a class in any school."

"Thank you. See you tomorrow at 9 a.m."

Sofia (my cousin) worked as manager of the ordering department in the Elysian supermarket on Nevsky Prospekt. Every time I did my shopping, I would call into her office to find out if there were any urgent telephone messages for me. In mid-February, my mother called from Odessa, asking me to contact her. I made my way swiftly to the post office.

"Hi, Mum. What's up? How are you?"

"I'm fine, don't worry about me. Mishenka, your wife is living it up all over the place. When she found out that you won't be back until summer, Milia gave up taking care of the children. She swears at your nanny and terrorises all the family. Every morning she leaves the house for the whole day, saying that she's looking for a job. We don't know how to manage her. Milia needs you home."

"I'm really sorry that she's giving you so much grief. But I can't come as I'm contracted till 1st June to make enough money for a cooperative flat for the family. Please give my wife my emphatic advice: if she has such an acute need for her husband in Odessa in the bosom of his family, then she can go back where she came from without being invited. Give Nanny Sasha some more money for her troubles. I'll send you some money in the post for my wife's train ticket to Slavyansk and a few other expenses. Don't worry, my dear, and say hello to everyone. I'll sort everything out when I come."

Every call to Odessa knocked me off my creative track to such an extent that I would need a few days afterwards to get back to my normal working rhythm. The best way to achieve this was to throw myself completely into new choreography. I started listening to the Western-produced audio cassettes bought recently in Moscow. I drew up a musical/choreographic plan including three compositions for the Philharmonic ensemble and went to the nearest recording studio to put down copies of the orchestral accompaniment for these. Now I could call on Ginsburg and present him with my plans for a new dance programme for the Leisya Pesnya ensemble.

"Hi, Mikhail! What have you been up to? People have already been asking about the choreographer."

"Sir, I have brought you a project for a new ensemble programme and would like to hear your opinion. I managed to find recordings of the rarest music.

" 'Graduation Ball' (student rhapsody) – for six couples – 8 minutes of sound;
" 'White Nights' (lyrical quartet) – for two pairs of soloists – 5 minutes of sound;
" 'Visitors from Havana' – for four couples – 7 minutes of sound.

"This is a working copy of the original music and an outline of the new programme. If you're interested in these ideas, please let me know by the summer, so that I have enough time to work on the choreography in Odessa. I don't want to delay you."

"Respected ballet master, wait a moment! We have one more group, 'Stage Circus', who have been asking for choreography for a long time to reinforce the movements in their display. I've noticed from the photos of your posters in the Odessa Philharmonic, that you are mentioned as choreographer of the circus review with the Lilliputians (clowning, juggling, acrobatics, musical tomfoolery, etc.) Can you help our circus artistes?"

"Alexander Naumovich, I am only available after 4 p.m., and this will only be until 1st February."

"That's why I'm offering you this work on a temporary basis (between tours). They are only occupied between 9 a.m. and 3 p.m. in training or performing in town at school matinees. For each three-hour rehearsal you will be paid seventy-five roubles (at the rate of twenty-five roubles an hour), in line with your category. They need at least ten sessions with you over a two-week period, from 15th to 28th February, before they go off on their next trip."

"Comrade Director, this is what's known as a voluntary/compulsory invitation."

"I agree, old friend. Come by tomorrow and we'll sign the contract. Thank you. You've really helped me out."

"If you confirm the new programme for the whole ensemble, we'll have to reset the sound recording for a live performance by the instrumental quartet."

"Our Artistic Director does this regularly for all the Philharmonic musicians."

In the middle of February I started work with the Philharmonic circus group. First I observed closely the full programme in two departments, noting their ideas and comments. Sometimes I asked them to repeat some of the clowns' or acrobats' reprises, keen to single out the imperfections in their stage delivery. We drew lots to continually rotate/alternate numbers at rehearsals, allocating thirty minutes to each. The first day we worked on the artistes' entrance and exit from the stage in the style of their genre. I asserted that this was their weakest point in the run-through. Each performer had to maintain their Artistic form onstage continuously.

"It's no coincidence that I asked before you started your display, that you put your heart and soul into everything to give me a true picture of your professional potential and to evaluate the stage production. How can I help you if I don't understand it: today, either you worked half-heartedly, or is this your actual level of ability? We're not going to get very far like this! Either we work at maximum output, or we go our separate ways now."

"Maestro, excuse us," interrupted the troupe Leader, "we want to work with you."

"Good! You'd be well within your rights to ask what these intricate movements in the entrances and exits are all about.

"a) Today's audience is more culturally sophisticated than in the last century.

"b) Audience members usually cough between numbers, have a look around and chat about their impressions. For you, it's crucial to redirect their attention to the stage, especially the children.

"c) To get the public in tune right from the start with the specific Artistic perception of the genre being performed, it's essential to exaggerate the elements of your individual presentation style as soon as you come on, to fill the vacuum left by the break between numbers, thereby focusing the audience's attention.

"Similar criteria need to be applied to the audience reaction in the theatre even as you leave the stage. To ensure that his performance makes a lasting impact on the public, the artiste must take a bow (to applause) and withdraw from the stage also in the style of this genre, not in a different way to the entrance. You must remain imprinted for as long as possible in the viewer's subliminal memory. You will definitely have learned all these secrets of success from the circus-school stage. But the crystal grains of art lose their sparkle with time and need a jeweller's hand to restore their lustre. There is nothing shameful in this natural corrosion.

"So, who's first: you clowns? Please take the stage. Don't be shy, we're all friends here."

Every year on 23rd February I wished my favourite cousin a Happy Birthday. This time, without a particular invitation I surprised her in pirate style, with a ship sailing to the ball. The entire crowd shouted greetings to me, hoping that this kind of welcome would curb my appetite. Nothing of the sort. After a three-hour rehearsal with the circus asses, I fell on my precious food allowance like a hungry camel. I stuffed myself to the gills with rare delicacies, cramming them into all the corners of my elastic stomach, to last the whole of the following week. My stomach swelled by the minute rather than by the hour. To my relatives' general mirth, Boris (Sofia's husband) gradually dragged me away from the table. In the kitchen, helping the hostess to dry the dishes, I asked for her advice:

"My dear cousin, have you heard from my mum about the problem in our family? If you were Emilia, what would you do, if you had given birth to your lover's child and hadn't seen your husband for ten months?"

"You've shocked me! I didn't know this. That's why she took the risk of travelling to Odessa, taking three days and having to change trains, when she was seven months pregnant, all on her own with a four-year-old already. It's hard to understand!"

"As a mother, you obviously realise that giving birth at eight months is not without consequence. The chief doctor of the Children's Ward in Odessa Hospital and Aunty Faina (senior nurse) knew about the pathological cause and kept it from me. But this didn't bother me any more as I'd decided not to live with her any longer. The issue is the children. I didn't bank on Milia getting pregnant in my absence and coming to give birth at my mum's place."

"All the family in Odessa suspected that something unpleasant was going on between you. But no one wanted to get involved in someone else's family business. 'Lovers' quarrels are soon mended.' What usually happens in these situations is that couples get divorced and often share the children between them."

"Although she's a highly educated woman, in actual fact, Milia is unable to manage everyday life. Her psychological and physical make-up prevent her from looking after the children or the home. Other people have done this for her all through her life. She knows that I will look after the children's material needs. My wife is used to living as a parasite and never intends to get a proper job anywhere. But at the same time, she wants to live in Moscow or Leningrad and be the centre of attention. Her bilious envy of her husband's success and personal ambition in unproductive academic projects push her to the limits. Even though she acknowledges that the differences between us are completely irreconcilable, she has to prove to everyone else that she is living in the same (if not better) conditions as her former husband and on the same social rung as him. Milia is capable of sacrificing her children, their father and anyone else for that matter to these ends. So right now in Odessa, she's wearing out Mum and Nanny Sasha, demanding that I move them here immediately. This is the advice I need from you. Sofia, your guests and their children will soon be returning to their own homes. Ask Boris, once Dmitri is asleep, to consider my problem with you and let me know what the system is for purchasing cooperative accommodation in this city."

"Misha, Sofia has given me a brief summary of your problem. As far as cooperatives are concerned, it will cost you dear in the city centre. It's much cheaper on Vasilyevsky Island. It's illegal to have four people living in a three-room flat (two bedrooms). How much have you got available now for a first deposit, and how much will you have in six months' time?"

"At the moment I've got 3,000 roubles, and in June I'll have 7,000. This is almost definite."

Sofia's husband did some calculations on a piece of paper and five minutes later gave an accurate summary: "Today, a three-room flat in the Vasilyevsky Island area costs about 23,000 plus 10% overheads, plus electricity/gas (inside) and furniture – another 1,500. In total, this comes to roughly 27,000 roubles, out of which you must forward a minimum up front of 15% of the value of the flat on signing the contract, and it's the same everywhere. Plus, over the next twenty years you will be obliged to pay back a monthly loan of approximately 150 roubles. It's a serious undertaking. If you stop payments, the flat will have to be sold. Do you have any guaranteed means to protect your home? If you have definitely decided to buy a cooperative flat, and are confident that you can maintain the financial commitment, then now is a good time to do it, as they've just started building a block of co-op flats in four seven-storey buildings on Vasilyevsky Island. I'm good friends with their chairman and could guarantee you a recommendation on condition that you keep your money in a savings account or in my safe, as you prefer. Ha ha!"

"Boris, if I've got this right, then I would only be able to move into this flat in a year and a half. Not this summer, or the following one?"

"Yes, if you can put in 12,000–13,000 roubles by then. Good luck!"

"Sofie dear, I have a favour to ask of you. Please call my mum tomorrow at work and ask her to invite Milia to the bodega at 8 p.m. the day after tomorrow to have a chat with you about them moving to Leningrad. I'll come here and in my presence you can explain to my wife the situation with the cooperative flat, that it'll only be possible to move there in a year's time, once they've finished building it. Tell her that I'm working in several places from morning till late at night to get the money together for this flat. If Milia is not prepared to wait in Odessa till then, pass on my advice to go back to Slavyansk."

"Misha, it's really awkward to be in the middle of you two, but I'll do it for your children's sake."

"Thank you. I'll come and see you at work tomorrow to find out how it went."

My mother promised Sofia that she would organise the discussions and asked her to wait for her call at an appointed time. If Milia didn't turn up after half an hour, we were to call the bodega. I would explain to Mum all the circumstances and conditions for buying the flat. She would note the main points and relay them in person to my wife in the evening. If my wife sabotaged the situation, I had decided that I would stop sending her money and instead I would ask my aunt (Mum's sister) to buy the children what they needed from my account. In principle, Sofia approved of this scenario. But my wife showed up on time. My cousin went through the details of the move with her. Milia was about to get difficult, but from the tone and nature of the conversation, I understood that Sofia had managed to change my unbalanced wife's mind, at the very least until I got to Odessa this summer. She also reminded Emilia that for any mother, the well-being of her young children should always remain paramount: they were to be prioritised above herself, her husband and everyone else.

At 10 a.m. on 8th May, there was a gathering of the regional prizewinners who would take part in the final Festival concert. We spent two hours going through the staging with them, half an hour prior to curtain-up. Judging by the general consensus of the guests and specialists, the concert was of a high standard, to my relief. Lydia Grishina, Cultural Committee chairwoman, congratulated me and expressed her thanks for an excellent gala. She introduced me to a colonel from the deputy political commander's headquarters, within the Leningrad Military District.

"Mikhail, in July this year, we have to start preparing for the twentieth anniversary of victory over fascist Germany. We need a specialist of your calibre to oversee our command's anniversary presentation, which will span the zone from the Belorussian border to the Arctic Ocean, including the Baltic States and the Karelian–Finnish Autonomous Soviet Socialist Republic. Here are my personal contact details, in case this proposition is of interest to you. You can then get in touch with me through the City Military Centre, so that a contract can be signed promptly. Your managers at the Leningrad Cultural Committee have nothing against your involvement in this project. Thank you for your interest."

I turned the Colonel's sparsely worded card over in my hands until I was escorted to the table. Grishina praised everyone for a successful show. She thanked the regional leaders for their hands-on help in developing local Performing Arts and the aesthetic education of Soviet young people. I was so tired that everything seemed to be just a pleasant dream. But I remembered to thank my technical stagehands and with a joke, gave them all the promised bottles of 'elixir' to celebrate our conquest, as a sign of gratitude for their excellent work.

On Monday morning before the start of classes at college, I brought Larisa a huge box of chocolates and Tkachenko's (my MTA teacher) freshly published book *European Stage Folk Dances* for Valery Kuchinsky. It was quite difficult to resume teaching without a breather, irrespective of the plaudits coming my way from all directions following the successful show. Sofia, Boris and my nephew pushed their way on to the stage through the crowd of group leaders. My cousin handed me an unrivalled bouquet of flowers, gave me a kiss, and shouted through the noise: "Happy birthday!" It was only at this point that I recalled that I was born on 7th May. The director of the college congratulated me on my creative triumph, and advised that the committee were expecting me. After work, I popped in to the manager of the Popular Culture Department and picked up my fee. I dropped in to see Sofia at the Elysian to do a bit of business, and wanted to give her my next instalment for Boris. But my cousin stopped me in time, shaking her head.

"Hang on about fifteen minutes for me. Boris will give us a lift home around 6 p.m."

In the car, I apologised to my cousin for my blunder with the money.

"Mishenka, it's hardly surprising. You're shattered and have let a few things slip. Don't beat yourself up about it."

Boris pulled in to the nursery to pick up his son, Arkady, who jumped into my arms in the back seat and started fighting with me. I put up no resistance, just held my hands up."

"Daddy, why doesn't your 'Giant Bear' want to play with me today?"

"Leave him be! He's tired from yesterday's concert and needs to rest."

"I didn't see him dancing. How can he be tired? Is it from bossing people around?"

"Your uncle wasn't dancing. He put on all the choreography for simpletons like you."

"What did he put on? Where did he put it? Daddy, tell me, what language is Mummy speaking to me?"

Boris kept quiet, shaking with stifled laughter. The car began to weave from side to side.

"Toptygin, I'm asking you nicely: let's fight! Or I'll shut you in a cage."

"For making threats like those, I'm going to take your trousers off now, and smash your face in!"

"I don't understand. Why do you need to take off my trousers for that? Mummy, you know everything, tell me!"

But Sofia could not endure these 'torments' any longer, and was doubled up in hysterics.

"Look, you guys, if you don't stop your philosophical debates right now, I'm going to explode!"

"Strange people, these old men. Now you've invented some other kind of debates. To Hell with them!"

"Oy, you pirate! Confess your sins. For that, you will get one from me now."

Arkady and I resumed our arm-to-arm combat while we were parking near the house.

"Misha, let's fill out an enquiry form for the cooperative and a contract for a three-room flat so that we can reserve it well in advance. The problem is that nearly all families would prefer a large amount of floor space. As a rule, you need to have your 'foot firmly in the door' (i.e. a contact) for this. My friend on the cooperative promises me a 'favour' in exchange for my 'kindness' to him. But the deputy director of the Executive Committee Housing Division has the final say about the flat, a Mr Lashchenko. To guarantee a flat, he usually requires a 'reward', but I'm not going to get involved in any dealings of this kind with him, in my position as factory director."

"Boris, thanks for the information. I must have a separate room to work in. If it doesn't work out straightforwardly, then we'll go for a smaller flat. Milia and the children will live in the cooperative at my expense, and I'll stay where I am at the moment. There's no point in us both risking our good reputations."

After ten rehearsals in February, as was to be expected, I failed to complete my improvements on the artistic presentation of Philharmonic circus group artistes. They were so used to their old, banal routines, that even though they were willing, they struggled to yield to the new canons of contemporary, theatrical art. We consulted jointly with the society director, artistic director and troupe leader, and decided to extend the second half of this project to the end of May, when the circus artistes would be back from their next tours, and I would have completed my District Festival. All week, the Circus artistes and I worked intensively to come up with new expressive frameworks for their old reprises. Through continual, dogged reworking of the external presentation of their long-since-run-in technical moves, each number looked slightly different. Whereas once a seasoned theatregoer could predict the next surprise, now, what the familiar numbers promised the public, in most cases, was a stunning effect or something to intrigue or perplex them. The Philharmonic leaders applauded the changeover to the new presentation of the old programme and addressed their compliments direct to the stage producer/choreographer. Ginsburg was happy to double my fee, and I (thanks to my natural modesty) did not argue with him.

In the break between classes in College, the secretary passed me a telephone message from the manager of the Military Cultural Centre, requesting me to call in and see him that day at 5 p.m. regarding the show. I presented myself, in true military fashion, on the dot. The secretary announced my arrival. A Major from the Politburo Division came promptly out of the office. He gave me a warm, civic welcome, shaking my hand and inviting me in.

"Hello, Mikhail Semyonovich. Welcome to our peacetime domain. To the best of my knowledge, you are already acquainted with the Colonel, deputy head of the district.

The latter got up to meet me, shook my hand and waved me to a leather armchair by a writing desk. Both officers were holding some sort of brochures and programmes.

"If my memory serves me right," the Colonel reminded me, "in our initial discussions two months ago, you agreed in principle to take on Artistic leadership of the military Performing Arts competition in the Leningrad district, and to act as stage producer for the Gala concert. Today we would like to confirm the basic parameters of this project and finalise a contract with you to complete it over a ten-month period, starting on 8th July. As I've already indicated, we have a large area. Travelling to military quarters with panel members will only be possible once a month, and will often involve an overnight stay."

"What will your fee be for conducting the Festival and staging the Gala concert?"

"It will be 7,000 roubles for ten months' work (based on 700 roubles a month) plus: payment of all production expenses (against invoices): copies of audio-recordings and texts for the leaders, hire of a film-reel operator with camera, films and similar accessories."

In mid-June, the Head of the Military Cultural Centre invited me to sign a contract for the Gala. In his office, he introduced me to Maria Ivanovna, head of his Popular Culture Department, who was responsible for all the administrative and organisational procedures in preparing the shows across the Baltic garrisons and the Gala concert within the Leningrad Military Academy itself. She would also be supervising the timetable and the jury's work schedule.

"Mikhail Semyonovich, we've been through the information you provided at our last meeting, with the commanding officer of the District Political Department, and we've decided to hold a small banquet in our conference room after the concert, and invite you and the panel to share in our glory. Chairmen from the Ministry of Defence will be attending. With this in mind, Maria Ivanovna will take a hand in overseeing the work of the show's chief stage producer and Artistic Director in the interests of security."

"Comrade Major, I understand your concern and obligations regarding the event, and have nothing personal against this vigilance. But the Colonel did not mention this condition when we first spoke. There can only be one Master responsible for the professional, creative leadership of such a complex, large-scale activity, and you must place your trust in him. Otherwise we can have no further dealings with each other. This is a question of principles and we cannot compromise. No one can tell the Artistic Director how to plan and complete his stage project. On the contrary, your administrative representative, whoever he may be, would, in actual fact, be obliged to carry out all the professional wishes and instructions given by the show's Artistic Director as far as this is workable and logical. I am very sorry, but on this basis I cannot sign the contract, as I am of the mind that 'Too many cooks spoil the broth.' I suggest we postpone the final signing until we're clear about the Colonel's position."

"Mikhail, in the meantime, please familiarise yourself with the content of the contract, and Maria and I will go and call the management to clarify how things stand with the agreement."

I read through all the terms of work carefully, underlining the unacceptable point about my administrative assistant/organiser. The Major returned without his colleague and asked me to pick up the telephone on his desk.

"Best wishes for your health, Comrade Colonel. . . . Yes, all the terms are acceptable apart from the authorised person. In spite of the respect I have for Maria Ivanovna, no female candidate can meet this obligation for a number of reasons, including communications and military service etiquette. For this position I need a person capable of taking orders and discussing and demanding that the garrisons' political representatives complete essential actions/activities:

"a) the Administrator will often have to go backstage to men's dressing rooms to discuss the show with participants in their 'coarse' soldiers' lingo;

"b) the male organiser is frequently expected to provide physical assistance in transporting elderly panel members or equipment to meetings in the hall."

"All right, Mikhail! You have convinced me. Your assistant will be a young captain from our department, with the authority to resolve the issues you've outlined. Please sign the contract and pass the telephone back to the Major. Good luck!"

A minute later, I had signed the contract. I received a list of jury members and the timetable for outings with them to the District's garrisons, beginning on 19th July. This time things were sorted.

I apologised to the college secretary for bothering her with the telephone messages for me.

"There's no need to worry, Mikhail Semyonovich. It makes me do some extra exercise."

For New Year, I decided to take her a cake and card by way of thanks. I had only just got home when there was a ring at the door. I went to open it in surprise.

"Misha, I'm sorry. You'd only just left when the Mariinsky Theatre rang. The secretary passed me a note. I thought that this was important and decided to bring it to you as a matter of urgency."

"Thank you, Larisa. You are a real friend. It's an invitation from Konstantin Sergeyev, the Artistic Director at the Mariinsky."

My colleague was amazed at my extremely modest abode. I explained that I was not allowed to invite guests into the communal flat, and suggested a coffee on Nevsky Prospekt.

"I assumed that you lived here with your family. Forgive me for intruding, please God."

"You have nothing to feel guilty about. My wife and I have gone our separate ways. The children live with their mum in the south."

"In that case, if you don't mind, let's go and have coffee at mine, and we can sort out our plans for the next academic year while we're at it. My place is not far and I live alone."

"Larisa, are you sure it's a good idea to invite a single man to your home?"

She flushed, but insisted on her plan, naïvely trying to change my mind.

"You're not someone off the street; you're my senior partner and friend, as far as I understand our relationship. It's Sadovskaya's old flat, where I've been registered for many years now. So after her passing, thanks to Strizhachenko, the authorisation transferred to my name, something I could not have dreamed would be possible."

"Wonderful! Now you are a rich bride-in-waiting, and just need to find a worthy suitor."

"Oh no! Why are you wishing that on me? I have never done anything bad to you. This is my home and fortress, on the first floor, with a balcony looking on to the courtyard. Be kind to me!"

The flat was indeed luxurious; there was no comparison with my kennel. I enjoyed a cup of aromatic coffee, taking in the paintings on the walls.

"Misha, what dates do the entrance exams start this year?"

"On 3rd August. First and foremost, we need to check the physical attributes of all the individual candidates. Only then will I be able to determine their feeling for rhythm, balance, coordination of movements, memory for choreography, etc., find out about their motivation for choosing this profession, and learn about their past experience, so that we can eliminate 'accidental lightweights'."

"The timetable will probably stay the same. Or will you change it again as you did in January?"

"I don't think so. But I will need some free time to visit these Regional shows and for the one-off productions at the Mariinsky Theatre and Philharmonic. So I would prefer to pass my experience and knowledge on to you not on your working days, but during my regular classes. In your capacity as permanent assistant you will master the genres, methods and techniques that interest you more quickly and thoroughly in one stint with me."

"Misha, that's exactly what I wanted to ask you after the exams, but I was a bit shy. You can't imagine how interesting and enjoyable it is for me to work with you. Before, under Sadovskaya, I was fearful and avoided men. They only saw me as a female. You are the first person to open up other aspects and feelings towards your gender. I am so grateful to you. I hope you understand that . . ."

"Lara, don't be fooled! All men are the same. Excuse my frankness. Attractive young women can inspire natural desire in me too. It's a problem of self-control.

Combining work and personal relationships between colleagues you have ongoing dealings with, even if they are husband and wife, often ends in tears, for many reasons and in different circumstances."

"But, you see, not everyone is the same. I want so much to be with you! Don't push me away!"

"Lara, I don't want to lose you as a workmate and friend, someone I feel a real affinity with. I also feel bad about wounding your female pride and human worth. Forgive me, my dear. It's best that we remain on the same footing as before. Analyse my arguments in the cold light of day. If you change your intentions, we will consider that this conversation never happened. You will never have to regret displaying any weakness. You will not be despising me for taking advantage of you. . . ."

"But what, if, in spite of everything, I keep to my former opinion? What then?"

"Then in August, once we've selected the new recruits, just let me know. I will come to you for a whole night, going against my principles. Promise me this summer that you will seriously weigh up the pros and cons, so that you won't regret what's happened later. Bear in mind that I am not planning to give up my children or, more to the point, get married again. For me, creative freedom is inviolable."

"I have no wish to settle down with a family. But being alone forever is just as wretched a prospect. By the way, why are you so sure that I would regret intimacy with you?"

"Because I've experienced moments like this several times, but for you it's the first."

"Allow me to kiss you to thank you for being so open."

Lara clasped my neck with her burning hands and drew me to her in an outpouring of virginal passion. I realised that she was a flower yet to be plucked. After an intoxicating first kiss, I determinedly but delicately released myself from my colleague's trembling arms and took several steps back towards the exit, bowing as I went.

"I wish you happy holidays. I'm off the day after tomorrow. See you in August."

I could feel Lara's eyes on me from her balcony as I made my way across the garden in the courtyard. I consciously did not turn around so as not to get her hopes up, but continued my steady pace towards the cast-iron gates in the old St Petersburg style. Only when I got to St Isaac's Square did I turn around.

Setting off for the Mariinsky Theatre the next day, I tried to change my mindset from Teacher to Ballet master. I recalled the list of miniatures which had been of interest to the artistic director, and the proposed make-up of soloist performers. I paused on the stairs by Lopukhov's door, but decided to call on him later, after speaking to Sergeyev. I was asked to take a seat in the ballet company's main office. A few minutes later Konstantin Mikhailovich cordially invited me into his office.

"Misha, our troupe is going on tour to America in September. Before then we need to prepare a small programme for official meetings in embassies, the United Nations, and so on. If, as before, you would like some unpaid work to put on three miniatures selected by us from your collection, we would be very grateful for the opportunity to include them in our concert repertoire. We are currently planning work for the ballet company in August. Can you rehearse with the soloists after lunch, from 2 p.m. for a few days a week, over the month?"

"In principle, I'm free in the afternoons in August. I'll be away in July. Please send a schedule to the College of Performing Arts to this address."

Lopukhov was not in. A passing ballerina explained: "Fyodor Vasilyevich is in hospital. He's had an operation, but he's doing OK."

"Thanks for letting me know, Natalya Mikhailovna. It's very kind of you, madam."

Because of my poor eyesight, I only recognised Dudinskaya at the last minute – Sergeyev's partner and wife. She was already in the corridor, and waved to me without turning round. I just about managed to apologise for my rudeness.

I resolved not to waste time pointlessly before my departure, and buy gifts for my loved ones in Odessa. In two to three weeks both my sons and my wife would celebrate their birthdays. After Gostinny Dvor, just as I was nearly home, it suddenly dawned on me that I had promised Nanny Sasha a special souvenir. So I popped into the restoration workshop in Kazan Cathedral.

Ignoring the sign 'No Entry to Unauthorised Personnel', I asked the painters: "Where can I buy a small icon as a present for my ninety-year-old grandma?"

They looked me up and down suspiciously, assuming that I was an undercover KGB officer, or worse.

"Dear comrade/citizen, where have you appeared from? Clear off to your beloved while we . . ."

I showed them my pass for the Mariinsky Theatre and promised to make it worth their while.

"Hey Vasya, I noticed an old painting in the rubbish in the crypt. Perhaps that would do? I'll go down and get it. Let him have a look and make his gran's day."

It turned out to be a small, shabby representation of the Virgin Mary and Child on old, cracked wood, covered in a thick layer of dust and grime.

"You can take it as it is for twenty-five roubles, or I can restore it for fifty roubles."

I looked around furtively. I paid him quickly and stuffed the icon into my bag.

As ever, Odessa welcomed her prodigal son with a sultry summer. The platform was loud with the customary, familiar noise and scrum. I didn't have the strength to carry my heavy suitcase, and called a taxi. Nanny Sasha met me like one of her own, with tears in her eyes. She crossed herself in honour of my safe arrival and went into the room where Alexander was sleeping soundly after his lunch. My wife and the eldest were at the beach. While we were alone, I fetched the icon from the suitcase and tentatively presented Nanny Sasha with her gift, worried that she would refuse it. Curiously, Nanny Sasha unwrapped my football shirt . . . and froze.

"Mishenka, where did you unearth such treasure? It has been blessed in an Orthodox church!"

"Some friendly restorers in Kazan Cathedral gave it to me in great secrecy. Leaning on a chair, Nanny Sasha fell to her knees, pressing the icon to her breast. Seeing her frenzied prayers to her Lord and God, I went out on to the veranda, feeling that I had committed a kind of sacrilege, and that Nanny Sasha was praying to the Almighty to absolve me.

As usual, Mum burst into tears when she saw me. The Panther shouted to Fedya to take over from her.

"Mishutka, you've lost so much weight! Are you feeling OK? Never mind, we'll feed you up."

"Mummy, how are you? Are you still working from morning till night every goddam day?"

"Son, as long as I can still stand, I don't want to be stuck at home! I'm better being out with people."

"We can talk about everything this evening at Nanny Sasha's, after you finish work. OK? See you later!"

I walked to the Opera Theatre to take in my native streets and squares, cobbled carriageway and green acacias. Pleasant memories came to mind in waves, and then disappeared into the mist of the irrevocable past. All the same, Odessa in comparison with other cities, is the Belle of the South. Even the splendid Leningrad comes second to her flirtatious charm and happy inhabitants. In the theatre I left my friend Syoma Kogan (concert master of the first violins in the orchestra) an invitation to my son's fifth birthday party on 14th July. I did the same for a soloist with the ballet in the operetta, Sasha Sandler (a course-mate from ballet school).

Picking up some fresh fruit from the market at Privoz, I hurried home. Nanny Sasha was sitting at the gates as usual with an open sack of sunflower seeds. She was selling them, despite her eighty years, not to earn money, but so that she too, like my mother, would be involved, and interact with neighbours and old acquaintances who happened to pass by. As I drew near she beckoned to me with her crooked finger. I gave a bow.

Nanny Sasha kissed my forehead and whispered quietly in my ear: "Thank you for the present, my son. It's a sin to remove a consecrated icon from a church, without permission from the Father or senior priest. But I have atoned for your sins by praying to the Higher Powers."

Inside, my children and well-turned-out spouse were already waiting for me. Dmitri jumped into my arms with a shriek. Milia was anticipating my first step with Shurik (Sasha) in her arms. I approached them gently and soberly. I kissed the surprised 'sapling' and inclined my head towards my wife.

"Hi! How are you getting on without Dad? I hope you're not going hungry, and not missing me?"

"Daddy, the teacher in our group doesn't let us swear or fight, even . . ."

It was already impossible to stop the eldest until he had got out of his system all the news from nursery, which had now moved to its summer residence at 'The Fountain' by the seaside. The children would be there continuously for eight weeks from the following Sunday. Parents had to visit their children every weekend, to give them a change of clothes and remind them of their existence. My feisty Aunty Dora recommended Milia as assistant to the manager to keep an eye on the older children's safety on the beach and to help with the extended care of them during their round-the-clock presence. As my wife had to stay there for two months, Shurik was accepted into the crèche for the younger group ahead of schedule, as an exception. This was fortuitous for Aunty Dora. I was happy to hear the positive news:

a) my sons would spend all summer at the seaside close to their mother;

b) Aunty Dora would not tolerate any negligent behaviour on my wife's part;

c) Milia's being occupied at work and away from me, would allow me to get some rest.

I spent two weeks in Bugaz. Friends and family came over on Dmitri's birthday. Aunty Dora stayed behind to work. Boris and his family also brought the birthday boy and his mother. Before lunch I caught up with Milia and confirmed the situation with the cooperative house that was in the process of being built, where a three-bedroom flat on the fifth floor had been reserved for us. I explained to her in simple terms that I needed to work in several places to pay the necessary instalments. I tried to assure her that it made much more sense to stay in Odessa during the last year of the cooperative building project, rather than renting a room for the family in Leningrad for that period, with all the additional expenses and inconveniences.

"If you tried to get some temporary work here, that would help me to pay the cooperative costs sooner, so that you could move there."

My wife listened suspiciously to what I had to say, and announced categorically: "I don't believe a single word you say. All of you are against me here. Even your mad nanny."

All day long, during Dmitri's name-day celebrations, his mother avoided any part in the festivities, coarsely flouting the basic norms of hospitality. In response to all my drinking companions' bewildered looks I simply waved, saying, "Don't pay any attention." Inside, I was consumed with shame.

Before sunset Boris and Sofia took Dmitri and Mum to their summer lodgings. I imagined that my cousin (being a Communist Party Leader at her place of work) was imparting legal knowledge to the young communist, on the essence of maternal morals, on the way to Odessa. Once again, I was seized with a feeling that I was trying in vain to put a round peg in square hole.

I returned to Leningrad for the first trip out to a garrison show, in the middle of July. Not all jury members arrived at the departure point on time, as they were not convinced that the project was going ahead. It turned out that the Military Cultural Centre had not signed a year's contract with a few of them (for ten trips and two Leningrad shows in military quarters and academies). It was made clear to me that the famous Maria Ivanovna was already handling working arrangements. At this point I advised the Major (the head of the Military Cultural Centre) of the criminal sabotage by his member of staff, and announced that I would report in writing to the Colonel, the deputy of the District Politburo, concerning all further detrimental actions undertaken by his schemer. I asked him to put in place urgent security measures for the district show. The Captain, authorised from the district headquarters, who was present during this exchange, confirmed the lack of contracts with three members of the panel. I consciously exaggerated the negative significance of this fact, to cover myself against future attempts to undermine my work.

We arrived at the Selection Committee an hour later than scheduled. The Captain explained to the local management the reasons behind such an unacceptable incident in military circles, and asked them to excuse us for getting off on the wrong foot. We spent all of the second half of Saturday and Sunday morning going over instrumental and vocal ensembles, dances and comic sketches from soldiers' lives (training, field kitchens, leave, etc.) Many numbers were similar to each other in their type, but differed in content and quality of performance. With considerable patience, we offered arts enthusiasts the chance to show off and develop their talents while they were busy defending the motherland. I asked candidates for the Gala concert to stay behind after supper on Saturday and after lunch on Sunday. All specialists from various genres (choirmaster, musical director, ballet master and stage manager) worked for two hours individually with prizewinners from the latest auditions on perfecting their performance technique and stage presentation. In the majority of cases these genuine raw talents had no professional leaders of their own. The talented enthusiasts were happy to receive consultations and be in a creative space with well-known theatre masters.

I found an envelope under my door in Leningrad with the Mariinsky Ballet's rehearsal timetable for the following week and a heart-rending note from Larisa:

'Dear Misha, "I love you, what else is there to say?" (From *Eugene Onegin* by Pushkin.)

"Oh la la," I uttered.

Although such insistent directness frightened me a little, it was nevertheless nice to know that someone thought well of me, and needed me personally.

I made an appearance at the College of Performing Arts on 1st August, and then only after lunch. The school lobby was choked with students wanting to register for entrance exams. I managed to force my way through the crowd to a desk with the sign 'Dance Department'. The young people reluctantly let me through, indignant at my impertinence.

Someone shouted: "Hey, old man, where are you off to? The end of the queue's on the other side, there by the doors."

Everyone around me started laughing.

Raising her head from her papers at the noise, Larisa exclaimed: "Mikhail Semyonovich, welcome back! How was your journey? Come here, here is your chair. Take a seat!"

The laughter and comments stopped abruptly. Larisa got up and gave me a squelchy kiss on the cheek.

"I had already started to worry that you wouldn't get back on time. Here are all the registrations for July in the diary. So far a total of forty-seven, and around thirty today. Valery is helping the entrants to get changed and follow the correct order."

All departments were obliged to let contestants out by 5 p.m., as many of them faced a long journey home to far-flung areas of the region: Valery, the assistant, had already left with them. Larisa and I had to stay behind to tot up the results of the recruitment drive, and leave all the audition paperwork for the director of studies. After a hectic day's work, we followed each other home.

"Misha, I hope you remember your promise and received my note (under your door) detailing written confirmation of my decision to enjoy intimate contact with you."

"My dear friend, why have you selected me in particular for this sacred mission? You are surrounded by so many gorgeous young men! What is it about me specifically?"

"It's because I admire, trust and love you. Is that so little?"

"Sorry. As before, I'm sure that I'm just the object of your passionate nature."

She took my arm and pressed against me as we walked, like an innocent child.

"I beg you, don't push me away again. You are a noble man."

"OK, wait here. I'll pop up to mine, grab a few things and come straight down."

Once inside, I threw into a bag a nightshirt, clean underpants, condoms and aftershave. I nearly forgot the souvenir from Odessa for the persistent assistant, who was every inch as 'odd' as me. I sighed heavily and rushed back down. *What's to be will be*, I resolved.

"Lara, we haven't had any lunch today. Let's grab a bite to eat in the kebab place opposite."

"Now I understand why they say, 'The way to a man's heart is through his stomach.' All the same, I'm pretty hungry too and wouldn't mind something to eat on this occasion."

Spreading the table with our decadent feast, we decided to start by drinking to a successful intake of students; to our friendship; to fruitful cooperation and to love. I expressed my desire to take a shower. But Lara preferred to run a deep bath and promised to scrub my back, 'as a punishment for her suffering'. I didn't like to refuse, fearing that the mistress of the house might change her mind. While she was preparing the ceremonial bed, I closed my eyes and luxuriated in the hot, steamy bath. Opening my eyes, I saw a beautiful naked woman with an enchanting smile on her lips and a bristly loofah in her hands.

"This is the first time I've ever seen a man in the nude. Sir, be so kind as to stand up and turn your back to me. Lean forward gently with your hands against the wall!"

I followed Aphrodite's instructions without a word, wondering how we could have sex in this position.

"Spread your legs as wide as your shoulders. Not mine, yours! Now, breathe deeply and evenly."

"What's the matter? Have you had enough?"

"Don't even think about looking round, or I'll remove a layer of your skin with this loofah."

First, the lovely enchantress tenderly rubbed my shoulders and elbows with soap with her left hand. Then, using the loofah, she began skilfully rubbing my aching back. This experienced masseuse was working miracles. I was almost groaning with pleasure. Suddenly, the chaste young woman threw down the loofah, hopped into the bath and embraced me from behind, pressing her firm bosom against my tingling back. I let out a sigh, as if experiencing an electric shock. She laughed, and started to caress my chest and stomach, forcing me down into the water. In a spin, I turned over and took the trembling girl by the waist, biting on her hungry lips. Squatting, she pulled me down and, lying on her back underneath me, clasped my thighs with her legs, splashing water out of the bath. We wriggled like fish that had just been tipped out of a net and thrown into a small reservoir. Lara unexpectedly froze, boring into me with an intent look of adoration. I gently disentangled myself from the weave of her embrace, and helped her up in the slippery bath. We clung to each other further in a protracted kiss in the shower, threw on some gowns and took our places at the table. I filled our glasses neatly with cognac. My friend sat down astride my legs, and proposed another toast to love. Each gulp was sealed by a deep kiss of probing tongues, as we tenderly squeezed our chests up against each other. Putting our glasses down, we eventually made our way to the sacred bed. I noticed a towel on top of the bed and Vaseline on the bedside cabinet, and felt reassured by her forethought.

Lara asked me to leave the light off. The light from the half-moon through the wide bedroom window was sufficient for us to determine the objects of our desire in our endless kisses. I kissed her body, causing the chaste virgin to wriggle like a snake, especially when I planted long drawn-out kisses on her erect nipples. She was squealing with sweet delight. When I used my finger to check whether she was sufficiently wet, my friend became rigid, grabbing hold of my elbows. I asked her to loosen her grip. I caressed her 'secret entrance' with my instrument of love and confidently penetrated her 'hidden treasure'. Lara cried out, squeezing my elbows. I restrained my animal instinct, giving her a chance to take charge of herself. Then I carefully, delicately, went deeper into sexual ecstasy. My friend moaned and held me to her as if we were on a trampoline, until we simultaneously came to climax and the ensuing void of emotional devastation.

Assuming Lara to be asleep, I went to the toilet. I removed the condom, had a wash, took a shower and carefully snuggled up next to Sleeping Beauty in the bed.

Suddenly I heard: "Mishenka, there's no need for you to use contraception. When I was young, my Mum taught me how to protect myself from unwanted pregnancy. Sorry, I forgot to tell you about this. Come here, darling. I'm already missing you."

"Aphrodite, I'm sorry if I hurt you. I loved it so much with you that . . ."

"Don't worry, my beloved. You were very gentle with me, and I'm grateful to you for that. Today you've reinforced my belief that I chose the right man as my first lover."

Taking my hand, Lara laughed and pulled me to her, and we were transported to paradise once more.

This time the little pioneer decided to go on top and take control of the love act herself. At first she slowly took pleasure in her own inner experience. But after the next climax, she flew into such a passion that I began to worry about her extreme state of arousal. My friend was riding me furiously, getting out of breath at times, and whinnying like a winded horse. Her orgasms came thick and fast one after another. At the last shared release, Lara collapsed motionless on my chest and lay in the same position for a few minutes. I just caressed her back, bottom and legs tenderly, humming some tune, until she came back from her happy oblivion and lay down under my wing. We slept in each other's embrace like that until late morning. I didn't notice as the newborn woman slipped out of my arms to perform her ablutions. I awoke to the noise of the shower, and was just thinking about getting myself together for breakfast, when Venus came out of the bathroom with her dressing gown undone. Only then, in daylight, did I realise just how beautiful she was.

"Mishenka, don't you recognise me? I'm your number one lover these days."

My friend gave me a hug, and kissed me so sweetly that I changed my mind about breakfast.

I edited all three miniatures for the leading soloists in one of the top ballet theatres in the world. I strengthened the weak sequences of movements, and enhanced the fluid motion of the arms, defining dramatic nuances in the duets, as well as adding musical refinements to 'Song of the Black Swan'. Every Tuesday, Thursday and Saturday (up to lunchtime) I put on and rehearsed my best numbers from the series *Poem of Man* with the Mariinsky Ballet stars in turn:

1. Inna Zubkovskaya and Vyacheslav Kuznetsov in 'Late Autumn' were unique
2. 'Eternal Gauls' to music by Sergei Rachmaninov, in a performance by Kaleriya Fedicheva and Nikolai Budarin, was a suitable tribute to the great composer's music
3. But 'Song of the Black Swan' gave rise to a serious problem. My original choreography to Villa-Lobos's refined music was beyond this ballerina. Fedicheva's unimaginative interpretation with her athletic build, lacked innate, lyrical inspiration. She neither understood nor had a feel for the spirit of this 'hymn to triumphant love'. Kaleriya blindly copied 'The Dying Swan' in Mikhail Fokine's contrasting cliché, as performed by Anna Pavlova.

I shared my pessimism about 'Song of the Black Swan' with Sergeyev, and asked his permission to use Nataliya Makarova in this miniature.

"Misha, that's impossible. Kalya is 'good friends' with Rachinsky, the theatre Director. It's best not to rub her up the wrong way, otherwise your numbers will 'not see the light of day'.

I exhaled deeply and thought: *It's the lesser of two evils.* Wrapping up work on the mini programme, my heart was heavy as I headed for a creative compromise with 'Song of the Black Swan'. I closed my professional eyes to the ballerina's performance, which lacked any musicality, and her spiritual impotence in internal imagery. At the Artistic Council's official viewing of the new compositions, Sergeyev thanked me and committed to rehearse my miniatures himself: duets with the piano; 'Song of the Black Swan' additionally with the orchestra's first violinist. As we parted, he expressed his regret about 'Song of the Black Swan' and hoped that we would continue to collaborate on creative projects in future.

At the College, Larisa handed me a letter from Ginsburg, confirming the production of the new programme for the Leisya Pesnya ensemble in the second half of October. He requested me to go down to the Philharmonic to sign the contract as soon as possible. My young colleague completed the academic programme for the senior grades as part of her assistant duties in my classes, by studying the Theatrical Folk repertoire. She and Valery demonstrated tirelessly new sequences and duet techniques for partnering in front of all the participants, while I 'cut out' students' errors and corrected them in the presence of the assistants. In this way, we killed two birds with one stone in my classes:

a) we maintained excellent theatrical/stage form thanks to repeated demonstrations;

b) by helping me, they picked up the Character repertoire by themselves for both grades;

c) they got to know the Composition method for Theatrical Folk dance.

This suited them and me equally. But I urgently needed to train up cover for myself in case I obtained supplementary production work, and got held up on my out-of-town Festival trips.

The Philharmonic Director was happy to see me as usual. He had paid all my expenses in Moscow for copying music to choreograph the new repertoire, and proposed a contract for a substantially larger sum than the previous year. He was up to speed with my cooperative problem and tried to help me out, knowing that his generosity would result in buying 'my scalp'. Even so, I was very grateful to him.

The Ensemble's artistes greeted me with embraces at the first rehearsal. They proudly showed me a few positive reviews from Belorussia and the Baltic States, which included compliments addressed to me. They were really curious about the new programme and impatient to start production. Before each new piece of choreography, I explained to the dancers the idea behind the number, which audience the given composition was aimed at, and in which artistic manner it would need to be danced.

1. 'Graduation Ball' – in academic style for schoolchildren and students
2. 'White Nights' – in romantic register for a conservative, more mature age group
3. 'Visitors from Havana' – in free, emotional manner for your own pleasure.

The movements in the first composition featured playful elements, and at times frivolous young people, happy to have completed their long and meandering road of secondary education. The next miniature in two dimensions projected the affectionate, lyrical relations between both couples in endless emotional interactions. The third suite depicted the bravura and hot-blooded mosaic of Afro-Hispanic traditional movements in Cuban dances, reflecting the life-affirming character of the island residents.

My dancers in these 'fiery' rhythms of rumba, Mozambique and so on, were going out of their minds. Their exceptionally advanced techniques and emotional saturation in this 'tourist review' frightened me, even though I dressed the girls in national dress, and the guys in proletarian overalls with 'hammers and sickles' on their chests. I was hoping that combining folk costumes with work uniforms would save me from the Soviet censor. At the presentation of the programme, all members of the Artistic Council applauded thunderously, with the exception of Ginsburg. The Director was puzzled by the unexpected success of these 'bourgeois influences' which had been criticised on ideological grounds in Moscow by the June plenum of the Soviet Communist Party's Central Committee. Among the guests at the regional Cultural Committee was the director of the Culture Department for Leningrad trade unions, Vladimir Rubinov. Ginsburg introduced me to him and asked me to come to his office.

The head of the Culture Department congratulated me on a successful event and asked whether I would like to take on Artistic leadership of their City Song and Dance ensemble from 1st January. I was astonished at such an abrupt change of leader.

"Thank you for your consideration. I have heard a lot about this group and even worked with them for a while during preparations for the Gala concert in the last Festival this year. What happened to their highly esteemed leader and extremely experienced specialist?"

"He'd been seeking retirement for a long time, but in the dance world it's difficult to find a suitable replacement – not just professionally speaking, but on a personal level as well. Judging from your work in the Philharmonic Society, and the show you've managed, you bring both talent and patience to your work, which is important in this field."

"Unfortunately, as you know, I am officially signed up on the staff of the College of Performing Arts, and am not permitted to take up permanent work elsewhere, without approval from the management. In addition, I have been hired until May next year by the Military Cultural Centre to oversee the Baltic District Festival in honour of the twentieth anniversary of victory."

"Please don't worry about this issue. You are only busy with Strizhachenko three mornings a week. If you are free the rest of the time, then this would suit us, if you agree."

"In principle, I'm interested in your offer, as long as this doesn't cause any problems in my main place of work, which I hold dear."

A few days later, Strizhachenko summoned me and reported that the management of the Regional Board had been singing my project's praises with the Trade Union Ensemble.

"Mikhail, you know that I have no objection, as you and I agreed on this point when we drew up your contract here. As I can't give you a full timetable here, and you never ask to be paid overtime, I am morally and legally obliged to give you a reference for supplementary work in the time outside your main place of work. I hope that this won't reflect on the quality of your activity here in the college."

"On the contrary, you are establishing a fantastic base for students from all departments to practise, in the aim of developing their experience in diverse genres of theatrical art under the leadership of the best specialists in the city in the Vasilyevsky Island Cultural Centre."

I telephoned Mum in Odessa, who told me that everyone was well. Aunty Dora (thank goodness she was in good health!) had got Milia a job in her nursery, where Dmitri was already in the oldest group. My wife was running eurhythmics classes three times a day and teaching the little ones of various ages singing, dancing and mime sketches based on well-known fairy tales. Everyone was pleased with her. I asked my mother to pass on to my spouse that I would not be able to come for the winter holidays for the second time, as I would be starting work with the Leningrad Trade Unions' Song and Dance Ensemble on 1st January. This meant that my time was completely full, so that I could manage the initial payment on schedule to guarantee the cooperative flat. Building was due to be completed in June. Once I had received authorisation for our apartment, I would come to Odessa immediately and move the family to this city of European culture and white nights.

"Send my thanks to Dora for finding Milia a job and getting my son into the nursery."

This time, I saw in the New Year at Sofia's as a respectable citizen. My cousin passed on a note from Fedicheva, the ballerina, requesting me to go and see her. While the guests were gathering, Boris took me aside into his bedroom and showed me the instalment reports for the cooperative. To my enormous satisfaction, I had completely cleared the advance payments in the contract. Now I needed to save money for furniture and household items. I only had six months to play with. Boris advised me to rent a flat from 1st July, where we could live as a family while we were getting ready to move into the cooperative, to safeguard us against any delays.

In the New Year, before doing anything else, I called into the Mariinsky Opera Theatre to see Kalya Fedicheva, the prima ballerina. She came out of the make-up and dressing room in a dressing gown to see me, and, wishing me a Happy New Year, handed me a package: a souvenir from New York, which she had brought back recently after the troupe's tour to America. I thanked her for the beautiful tie and read with interest a short review of the Mariinsky Ballet's performance in the USA, including a positive critique of the original miniatures by the leading soloists. Just then, the director of the Vaganova Ballet School walked past, and took an interest in the photograph of his former student in the foreign press. Kaleriya introduced me to Boris Shelkov and nipped back into her dressing room. The Director asked me if there was anything in my repertoire for young graduates from their Vaganova school. I answered in the affirmative (the Devil had my tongue!). I recommended that he sought a reference on me from Sofia Golovkina, director of the Bolshoi Theatre School, where I had put on many ballet compositions for her students. I wrote down Sofia's and Larisa's telephone numbers for him, and asked him to come back to me, if he was still interested.

During the whole of the first week of January (from 5 to 10 p.m.) I took combined groups from the Trade Union Ensemble (choir, ballet and orchestra), and got to know the conductors, répétiteurs and accompanists. I was aware what a huge responsibility it was. For this reason, I asked Rubinov to include the Ensemble's administration in the Cultural Centre management team, as I physically did not have the energy to take charge of it all single-handedly. About a week later an organisational assistant appeared: Yefim Friedman. Following my predecessor's departure, his duties had been carried out on a temporary basis by Gelya Vonskaya, répétiteur for the younger group. With my arrival, she remained in charge of the older ones, and in her place I was planning to put Valery Kuchinsky from the college.

I already knew most of the dancers from the recent show. I began on a wide scale by putting both groups on simultaneously in three choreographic pictures on contemporary themes, and musical rhythms with the participation of the vocal sextet.

1. 'Naval Service' about Baltic sailors, for twelve older men (veterans).
2. 'Beauty Contest', humorous piece for fifteen more mature female dancers with ballet master.
3. 'A Night in the Club', an entertaining impromptu for younger ones: sixteen girls and eight boys. Plus: a vocal sextet, with solo and mixed (with dancers) presentation.

The Principal and Artistic Director of the Vaganova Ballet School approved the list of my miniatures for production:

1. 'Future Pilots' to Alexander Deineka's painting; music by Prokofiev: 'Mimolelnosti' (trio).
2. 'Stormy Petrel', to Gorky's poem; music by Rachmaninov: 'Prelude' (quartet).
3. 'Martians' to music by Shostakovich: "Fantastic Dances" (quintet).

This programme was due to be completed over March/April, so that the teachers had enough time to rehearse the new productions for their pupils before the traditional school concert at the end of the academic year. At my first meeting with Shelkov, the Director, he had asked me specially to use more boys in the miniatures, because mostly the invited choreographers naturally preferred to work with the girls who were less problematic in terms of discipline and concentration.

At the first rehearsal for 'Future Pilots' (fifth grade), the boys behaved well enough, while they worked on the different characters intended by the choreographer. At the next meeting with them, I was forced to stop the music due to bad behaviour from the performers during my explanation and demonstration.

"Guys, if you continue to behave in this way, we will stop here."

The pianist also tried reasoning with them and advised me to report back to Shelkov. But I didn't want to begin my production work by complaining to the Director. Feeling that they were all as bad as each other, I completed my choreography of the miniature in question. At the rehearsal for the next production 'Stormy Petrel', with the pre-graduate class of boys (sixteen to seventeen years old) and a graduate girl (eighteen years old) it was the same story. The young soloist girl, a very strong ballerina, was conducting herself in an entirely professional manner. Right from the start, a group of three wasters started to fool around. To make the image of a bird in choreographing 'Stormy Petrel', there were naturally some high lifts. Shelkov had guaranteed that these pupils had been studying 'Pas de deux' for several years on their course, and knew the fundamental technical holds in Duet ballet programmes. I tried repeatedly to impress on them that their attitude to their soloist partner was dangerous and could end badly. But they were ignorant, and just carried on larking about in the studio. I had no choice but to go and see the Director.

"Boris Ivanovich, I'm sorry. I absolutely refuse to work in such risky conditions."

I explained the situation to him and announced that I didn't want to be held responsible for an inevitable accident to their partners due to their lack of discipline in overhead lifts. Shelkov called them into the ballet studio and gave the young men a serious telling-off. Ten minutes after he had left, while executing a complicated lift – a throw, flight and catching the partner – three blockheads were laughing and dislocated the soloist's shoulder. It was fortunate that I had not yet started production on the composition, but had only provisionally worked out the technical difficulties in the choreography. The female student could have come off much worse. Even so, I was shocked. It was very hard to witness such slackness in future ballet artistes in spite of their healthy intellect. The elderly pianist was beside herself at the students' barbaric conduct in class. In Shelkov's office, I expressed my deep alarm at the unprofessional attitude of the participants to their duties in the school, and stated that it was a direct result of weak training by their Principal classics teacher.

Larisa met me at the college the following day, and asked, worriedly, "Mikhail, how are you feeling? You don't look yourself. Has something happened with your family?"

I asked if we could defer this conversation until after work. On the way home I told my friend what had happened, and shared the doubts tormenting me about the boys' conduct.

"I've seen male ballet classes countless times in ballet schools. Boys are far from attentive at all times in class, but generally their behaviour is tolerable. For some reason, at my rehearsals they relate to me and the soloist girl with palpable disrespect. Even Ekaterina, the pianist, noticed how aggressive they were. What's behind this sabotage?"

"Misha, I haven't visited the school for a long time. I'll go and touch base with my old friends and find out the latest. I expect I'll get some up-to-date news. If I find out anything important, I'll come and see you this evening."

A few hours later, a ring at the front door interrupted my choreography for the Ensemble. Grabbing my bag, I went out to meet Larisa, and we popped down to the nearest snack bar. I could see by her face that there was some serious news about the ballet school.

"My dear boss, your fears turned out to be justified. Everyone in the school is talking about this event. Yesterday after you had gone, Shelkov and Balabina, the Artistic Director, called in the three culprits in the incident and had them up against the wall, promising to exclude them instantly unless they explained the reasons for their yobbish behaviour. The lads acknowledged that they had heard their principal classics teacher Mansour Karimovich in conversation with the pianist several times in breaks, and the former was amazed that the ballet school's Artistic Director and Principal had chosen an 'unqualified Ballet master from the amateur world' as an experiment, rather than using his choreography. The pupils thought of your productions as inferior, and as a mark of solidarity with their teacher, decided to sabotage them, without a thought for the possible consequences. Mansour received a reprimand for breaching the pedagogical code."

"However, this does nothing to change the damage to the soloist and my professional name. I can't forgive myself for agreeing to work under such conditions."

"Accidents happen in sport and ballet all the time. It's not your fault. The poor female student has had her shoulder reset in hospital, but will be in plaster all week. As for the stupid boys, no one knows what will become of them."

"Larisa, thanks for telling me all this. Now it's clear to me where the fault line is."

"All boys are thoughtless, and their stupidity makes them dangerous. What surprises me is their teacher, stripped of the most basic prudence, gossiping within earshot of his students, or purposely setting them against their personal rivals."

Following the first outings to the military competitions in the Northern Garrison, it became clear that it would be impossible to hold the Gala concert in the small, open Maly Arena of the Military Academy for a variety of artistic and technical reasons. I persuaded the Colonel and Politburo representative to use the Soviet Army Drama Theatre premises for this. I could unleash all my powers of production on such a large, wonderfully equipped stage. As usual, the first section of the stage show was devoted to folk/genre-based repertoire comprising diverse autonomous, ethnic representatives from the many nationalities in the district.

The Second section was made up of Artistic forces from Leningrad's military learning establishments: the advanced 'seafarers', the Air and Infantry School, Women's Schools of Communication and Nursing, and so on. With each of these performing groups I devised a short presentation on their work, using choreography and imitation through movements of these elements: handling weapons or techniques of hand-to-hand combat; flying jumps – by pilots or tightrope manoeuvres by paratroopers, and more. For the finale, I brought them all together in one composition, a victory suite in a kaleidoscope of changing episodes of the distinct types of troops – culminating in a united climax with the combined choir and orchestra of the military academies.

Nevertheless, I had underestimated my enemy once again. During the gala, in the interval between the two sections, I bumped by chance into Maria Ivanovna from the Military Cultural Centre on the stage. So I asked the Political Department's authorised representative, in the interests of ensuring the production, not to allow her backstage until the concert was over. But this request was not complied with. My assistant stage manager directed the whole show from the control board behind the wings, where an exercise book containing a score of signals and cues for the whole programme lay on the table: for the lighting technicians, scene changers, artistes' exits, curtain-up/ down, and so on. While the film was being changed on the screen in front showing 'shots of the fall of Berlin and hoisting of the Soviet flag over the Reichstag', the finale's participants were getting ready behind the curtain. The assistant stage manager managed this process as you'd expect. Suddenly, he called the Director's box under which I coordinated the whole concert from the central control board, and in a panic reported that someone had taken his whole score from the operations desk. I nearly had a heart attack. I went mad, and rushed along the corridors around the auditorium and into the wings, bringing the concert to a successful conclusion by myself using my own manuscript.

The perplexed Colonel's political representative asked me: "Why was the finale delayed?"

Following my explanation, I didn't envy the fate of this serving officer from the Military Cultural Centre, who had ignored my warning.

Production on the new programme in the trade-union Ensemble was going at full pelt. The Premiere was scheduled for 2nd May at the Leningrad Concert Hall. All the leaders: choirmaster, musical director, ballet master and répétiteurs were working to full capacity so as not to fall flat on their faces at the May Day festivities. Gelya was working with the senior girls on their acting and sequences for the humorous 'Beauty Contest'. Its dancers never stopped laughing at themselves during rehearsals. The big question was whether the audience would be amused. I rehearsed with the 'sailors' on perfecting their technique for meticulous presentation. Kuchinsky was working up a sweat with the youngest on the composition 'A Night in the Club'.

The Ensemble's Premiere came off a lot better than everyone expected. We barely wore in the new costumes and shoes. As required, we rehearsed assorted numbers with vocalists and the orchestra. But I was worrying for nothing. My colleagues and their pupils had much more experience of theatrical appearances than I realised. Mobilising themselves for the last stage of preparation, they took the premiere by storm.

The papers said: 'Finally our Trade Union Ensemble has awoken from its winter slumber and found its own Artistic style in the contemporary repertoire.' Rubinov, our chief from the city council, took pride in his pet project, and onstage after the show, congratulated the whole group on their creative triumph. We were also invited to take the new programme to Peterhof for the traditional White Nights Arts Festival. It was a great honour for the Trade Union Ensemble to perform alongside the city's professional theatres and orchestras. For me personally, it was part of the ongoing rehabilitation of my name following the production downfall in the ballet school, and I felt that I was back to the appropriate level.

As a result of the charge of profanity levelled at me by a teacher from the Vaganova school, I decided to reshape my creative profile towards Balletic art. In my free moments I thought up three new ideas for future shows in a Contemporary, Classical vein, for professional performers in Ballet schools and theatres from large cities across the Soviet Union.

1. *Thumbelina* – to themes of the eponymous tale by Andersen (to music by Shostakovich 'Light Pieces for Piano'). A two-act ballet with twenty-five to thirty Ballet dancers.
2. *Meeting the Stars* – a libretto incorporating themes from the history of Soviet cosmonauts, music by Georgi Firtich.
3. *Gadfly* – to Ethel Lilian Voynich's novel.

I offered the music and choreographic scenario of this one-act ballet to Georgi Firtich, a young composer and author of Yakobson's ballets *Bedbug* and *Twelve*. I was fascinated by the contemporary, extravagant language of his music – stylistically it was very thought-provoking. After acquainting himself with the suggested project, Firtich agreed in principle to work with me on this ballet without an official contract, on an experimental basis by verbal agreement, with no reciprocal obligations. There were no other terms on which I could agree.

Sometime later in my creative work with Firtich on the fantastical topic of 'Heading for the Stars', I decided to chance my arm in another genre of choreography.

My third idea for a dramatic ballet (which had been my dream for many years) was *Gadfly*, based on the novel of the same name by Voynich. I took my time in writing it, and painstakingly edited the libretto on this theme, until I was satisfied that its concise, dynamic dramatisation of a popular subject, would be specifically digestible to open romantic images onstage using Contemporary, Classical dance and Artistic presentation. It took me a long time to make up my mind to show the completed version of this libretto to Leningrad Ballet theatres or individuals, such as Firtich, Slonimsky (critic/historian) and others of their ilk. I preferred to take my time with this pearl. It was already painfully easy for my rivals to steal this idea from me and bring it to life in a theatre themselves.

With the second-graders in the college I completed a programme featuring National (Folk) theatrical dances of the USSR nations. That particular repertoire included first of all Caucasian and Central Asian republics. Students were interested to learn about the lifestyle and mentality of these peoples, national elements and sequences from Buryat, Uzbek and Georgian choreography. The third-grade students showed an even greater thirst for discovering the dances of foreign countries such as Poland, Hungary, Italy and Spain. They hungrily soaked up examples of the Mazurka, Czardas, Tarantella and Jota. They took notes in their exercise books and constantly pestered me for more information, realising the temporary nature of this source. At their final graduation exam for the Composition class, the third-graders had to show two-to-three-minute études or miniatures, whose subject matter could be on any theme, using Duet technique (without national characteristics). The subjects of work could be: distraction of love, competition, solidarity, a struggle, sporting games, and so on. These were my first graduates from a two-year syllabus tailored specially to their profile, comprising practical mastery of a course of composition and method of instruction in the disciplines of dance.

The exam period was approaching. In this academic year students from all years of the Dance Department had made such significant progress in comparison with the last year, that even teachers from related disciplines noticed the difference and at the final Teachers' Committee meeting, unanimously celebrated (to my delight) the successful results in choreographic education of future leaders in the stage arena. Many of our recent graduates had received diplomas with distinction and invitations to work in the field. My reputation as a teacher grew noticeably.

Still, these pleasant indications shrouded an uncertain future, now that my family had arrived in our new permanent place of residence. My wife had long been intolerant of her lack of advancement and opportunities compared to my active life in this city, and would start needling me for certain to her own self-destruction in her home town. 'As you sow, so shall you reap.'

In spite of my misgivings, relations between Larisa and me continued most favourably, both personally and professionally. We did not advertise our intimacy and didn't appear in public together, outside of work. However, the truth will out. Sooner or later, Milia would find out about this and force me into a corner. I confided my worries to my friend during one of our Saturday meetings. Naturally she was upset about the impending changes.

"Mishanya, how are you planning to go about things once your family is here? Is our close friendship and productive working relationship really going to burst like a bubble?"

"Lara, over these last two years I've become very attached to you. I will really miss my close friend and comrade, whom I've trusted with personal and professional matters without a second thought. Nevertheless, it's for the best for both of us: the academic year comes to an end on 1st July, and we will have to stop seeing each other by September. Let's see what transpires with my cooperative flat, and my children in the crèche and nursery, and what my former, but still undivorced wife, has in mind. I'm sure that even without knowing anything about how close we are, she will find many ways to destroy my career, as she has before in other cities. I'm sorry things have to change."

"All right, darling, don't upset yourself. I have no claims on you, either morally or legally. Do what's best for your career and family. I'll be waiting for you."

At the beginning of June I called in to see Sofia for the latest news. Boris cheered me up with some pleasant but disturbing developments: building on the cooperative complex on Vasilyevsky Island was now complete. New inhabitants would be allowed to move in from 1st July with the official authorisation from the city authorities. To obtain these documents, those moving in had to relinquish their old accommodation to the Housing Office or re-rent it to other family members. Boris alerted me that Lashchenko, deputy director of the Leningrad Executive Committee Housing Division, had his eye on my flat, as he had a more 'grateful' client than me. My cousin's husband urged me again to move my family here as a matter of urgency, rent them a temporary room and get a glowing reference from my main places of work sent to the director of the city Housing Department. Then Emilia and I could obtain authorisation from the Leningrad Council Executive Committee.

I wired Mum some money straight away, called her at work and asked her to help Milia and the children to make their way urgently to Leningrad. I rented a one-bedroom flat (plus kitchen and bathroom) for them for two months from 1st July in the centre of town, not far from Vasilyevsky Island. I received two references for the cooperative-flat purchase; one from the regional Board of Culture, and the other from the Trade Union Committee. I swallowed my wounded pride and went cap in hand to the director of the Philharmonic, who had once promised to help with a residence permit for my family if necessary. Ginsburg gave me a somewhat cool, but respectful reception. I asked about the Ensemble. He was full of praise for their successful tour and was sorry that my suite 'Visitors from Havana' had had to be cut from the repertoire for reasons I was aware of. I updated my former mentor about my family coming and reminded him of his promise. The Director asked me to pay him a visit once they had arrived and he would gladly help to organise a permit for the new flat.

At the end of June, in line with our plan, I moved into Sofia's for a while. Mum told me on the telephone when Milia and the children would be arriving in Leningrad. On 2nd July I met my family off the train at Minsk Station. To my huge surprise, I was as nervous as a schoolboy about to sit his first exam. It was as if fate were smiling on me. Alexander now had black hair, whereas last summer in Odessa he had been a little blond boy, who resembled his mother's lover. However, my father had also been fair-haired with grey eyes. Mum assured me that Shurik looked like his grandfather, only his eyes were different. I was completely preoccupied with my youngest son's paternity. Fortunately, Boris had been on annual leave since yesterday, and came to the station with me to help move travellers into their temporary rented apartment. Sofia left me the keys for their home, and asked me to water the flowers on their balcony while they were away on their customary three-week break in Odessa, and to collect the post from their mailbox downstairs, where there could be something for me about the flat. I promised to comply with my cousin's requests and to let them know how things went with getting the authorisation and permit via my Mum. Boris and I hadn't noticed the train come in, and had to hurry to the designated carriage.

"Daddy, Daddy, Uncle Boris! We're here! And Mum and Shurik. Come here!" cried Dmitri.

The next day, we went to Vasilyevsky Island to have a look at our first flat. The manager showed us the three-bedroom flat that been assigned to us on the fifth floor. He pointed out where all the meters and controls were for gas, electricity, heating, water, etc. On Boris's advice, I showed his old friend my reference for the authorisation from the City Cultural Authorities and Trade Union Committee. He approved these documents, but insisted: "In view of the fact that Lashchenko, deputy director of the Leningrad Executive Committee Housing Division, is currently on holiday, you will have to go and see Ms Nezhdanova, director of the city Housing Department. You'll have to take the whole family, but it's best that your wife speaks to her rather than you."

Before we went to meet Nezhdanova, I decided to prepare my spouse for this delicate mission, as I understood full well the cooperative manager's strategy. When the boss found out how this mother was currently living with her two little boys, moreover with two academic qualifications, plus a husband who spent the night at his cousin's because he had nowhere to sleep, etc., Nezhdanova could be deeply moved, and write out the authorisation, without waiting for her deputy, Lashchenko, to return from leave. I decided to tread carefully and began by asking my wife if she liked our future flat.

"This flat is the stuff of dreams. I didn't actually believe this fairy-tale project would come off."

"Why's that? After all, it's private rather than state ownership, which has cost me an arm and a leg. All the documents have been signed (and stamped) by both parties."

"That's not important. It's people who decide everything here, not papers. If the authorities want to give this mansion to another, more deserving client, then no one's going to stop them. That's what happened with my father, a genuine communist, who refused to give regular bribes to the manager on behalf of the collective farm members. After twenty years as chairman, they sacked him illegally, regardless of all his service, and caused him to have a fatal heart attack. You, my dear, are not a party member, nor an official, nor a war veteran, and you have no money for bribes. Sorry to be so frank."

"I agree. But you are a mother with two children, a Soviet Communist Party member, and have two academic titles. They can't treat you in the same way as a retrograde like me. As it turns out, you have been blessed with all the rights and opportunities to speak to the manager."

"I don't know the details of registering for the cooperative and haven't even read your bosses' references. As a rule, the man should take care of all these affairs."

"Where are your pride and principles? Before, you used to go on about equality between men and women. You fought for women's freedom in family life. I'm not suggesting you work in a mine and dig for coal or defend your homeland from enemies. But as an educated lawyer, fight for your rights as the mother of two small children. That aside, you are legally entitled to additional floor space as a qualified member of the workforce. As a professional lawyer, you know this better than me – I'm just a frivolous, flighty dance master. If they turn us down, it will be on your head."

"OK. Tell me, how should I act and what should I say to the boss?"

"Just tell it like it is. Show her your academic qualifications and my official Leningrad documents. Tell her that ever since we met at Moscow University, we've dreamed of living and working in this glorious city – the centre of Soviet culture. Bring all your diplomatic skills and logic to bear to get the authorisation for this cooperative flat."

After lunch in a health-food cafeteria, we set off home together. While the children were asleep, I wrote a declaration addressed to the head of the Leningrad City Housing Department: 'With regard to the need to move people into the cooperative building promptly, we request your urgent authorisation to purchase accommodation at the above-mentioned address.' Milia made two clean copies of the letter. We both signed it and arranged to go to the housing office at 9 a.m. the following day.

In the evening I popped in to Sofia's in advance to consult with Boris one more time about any possible complications with the authorisation before he left for Odessa. My cousin was sorry that she hadn't got to see my children.

Early in the morning, I helped to load the holidaymakers into their car, and having wished them a happy trip, rushed home to wake up my loved ones. By 9 a.m. our harmonious family unit was already waiting at the Leningrad City Housing Department. The policeman on duty at the entrance glanced in surprise at my ruffians and asked to see our identity documents, then indicated where the cafeteria and toilets were. Dmitri saluted the policeman with his left hand, as he was holding Shurik's hand with the other. While Milia was having breakfast with them in the cafeteria, I got copies of all our documents certified by the notary.

After checking our 'marks' in the toilets, we went up to the Housing Office reception. To my astonishment, there were no townspeople present. All on my own, I approached the battleaxe of a secretary, and asked, with a sweet smile: "How do we register with Nezhdanova's reception to obtain authorisation?"

Without looking at me, she snapped: "Yesterday was the last day you could come. There will be another visiting day next week."

"Excuse me, but our cooperative building has been available since 1st July. All the inhabitants are fitting out their flats already. Unfortunately, we didn't manage to get our authorisation in time, and without this, the cooperative chairman won't allow the workmen to finish fitting out our flat to the owners' requirements. He said that if we didn't provide him with the authorisation quickly, then the workmen would be leaving the following day, and we would have to finish off the incomplete bits ourselves. I'm a ballet master/choreographer and can teach you to dance in no time. But I'm not so familiar with technical matters. I beg you to give this file to the Director and ask her to make an exception and see us urgently."

The secretary looked at me, shaking her head in distress. With a deep sigh, she said, "Where do such tiresome people come from to give me a hard time?"

She grabbed my folder of documents, shoved it under her arm and disappeared into her boss's office. A few moments later she emerged, disgruntled and growled in my face, "The Director will expect you and your wife at 10 a.m. on Friday, the day after tomorrow. Don't be late."

Milia had overheard my conversation with the sullen secretary and didn't understand how I had broken through her bureaucratic armour and been granted an audience. I explained to her that my gentle harassment of the poor woman had irritated her to such an extent that she had decided to get rid of me and leave me in Nezhdanova's hands. However, the latter did not conform to her expectations, and found something of interest in our folder. That's why she had decided to check the information provided by these inopportune visitors herself.

We all went to Vasilyevsky Island again, to take a closer look at our home. The supervisor went along with my suggestion to have a quick look at the internal completion of our personal fixtures and fittings. He left us alone for a busy half an hour in the empty flat to work out where the furniture and individual family members would fit in.

On Friday, as we walked past the policeman at the Housing Department, Dmitri saluted with his right hand. To our astonishment, the policeman responded in the same way, looking very serious. Going upstairs to the hall, I encouraged Milia and reminded her of our strategy for the impending conversation. In unison we said good morning to the now familiar battleaxe. She alerted the Director that we had arrived. Leaving my wife in reception, I told her that I would wait for her in the cafeteria, and the three musketeers headed off to have breakfast. I attended patiently to the firebirds at the table, catching each other by the tail, interrupting my thoughts about Milia's visit.

Finally, my wife appeared and sat down, beaming like a Cheshire cat, exultant: "I'll have to go back for that authorisation in an hour's time. You were right. It's so good that you and I rehearsed the forthcoming chat with this cog in the bureaucracy. It's exactly as you predicted: the Director checked our passports and residence permits first. She asked where we lived at the moment, and what attracted us to Leningrad. In actual fact, Nezhdanova didn't ask much about you, as she had a lot of information about you from your references. The old woman fired questions at me: about my work in the public prosecutor's office in Slavyansk and the Buryat museum; what my dissertation was on, and what my career plans were. I confirmed that as a double master of science, I am entitled to an extra twelve square metres on top of the usual floor space for four people: $9 \times 4 = 36$ m^2, so 48 m^2 in total. The flat we are requesting authorisation for measures 45 m^2. This means that we have 3 m^2 in reserve. The Director explained that her assistant usually dealt with cooperative accommodation, but he's on holiday until the end of the month. As an exception, thanks to the two little ones, she is going to write me out an authorisation for our flat which will be ready in an hour. She wished us a happy life in our new home. As I was leaving, she shared that she also has two sons, but much older than mine."

"Darling, well done on winning your first duel! I owe you one!"

"I owe you too, my esteemed husband, for sending your wife into battle ahead."

My wife and I arranged that she wouldn't look for permanent work until the New Year, in order to focus on the children's well-being. The youngest needed time to get used to new teachers in his new nursery. The eldest had to adapt to a new school system in the murky atmosphere of unfamiliar classmates, and obey the instructions of his first-ever form teacher. This was a tough time for our strained 'saplings', as they developed their individual personalities in various peer groups. This was different to what they were used to: they were caught between a rock and a hard place, where Mum insisted on one thing, Dad on another, and Grandma yet another. There was no point in complaining. The nursery and school system ran in a specific way as the teacher saw fit. This was exactly what our long-suffering children needed.

Once our children were set up, I threw myself into my two jobs at the college and the Ensemble. In my free time I continued to work on ideas for potential ballet productions on a professional stage. The libretto and musical score of *Gadfly* were ready for the Ballet Theatre. Firtich, the composer, – on the black market – had almost finished the score of the one-act ballet *Meeting the Stars*. The score of *Thumbelina*, the children's show, was ready for production: it was completed by a recording of piano extracts of Shostakovich's works, half of which he had already orchestrated earlier for the Tadzhik Opera and Ballet Theatre. I was certain that he would orchestrate the remaining instrumental scores of his works. The main thing now was to find a troupe of performers and a stage to bring these creative projects to fruition. In my situation this was no easy matter, and carried associated risks. But also you can't go on waiting in vain. The time had come to decide: 'To be or not to be!'

Milia got all her diplomas and educational certificates together in a file, and summarised her jobs in a CV. She made a list of all the potential ways to apply her skills: academic research, teaching, reviewing and other fields requiring a knowledge of art. Her daily mission, after sending the children off to school each day, was to visit the central library to check the latest vacancies in culture and academia, as well as talking to people and leaving them a copy of her CV. I counselled her endlessly to remain patient, as she was an 'outsider' (not from Leningrad), and a 'harassed' mother of two. Several residents considered her overqualified. Such 'negative' traits in most experienced individuals can put people on their guard and even frighten them off. Still, 'help yourself and others will help you.' It was essential to be persistent and continue with the job search, until Milia came across someone who was looking for just that kind of specialist skill, with an unusual profile and determined nature.

Eventually, she was offered a series of presentations about authors' rights at the Academic Centre, on origination, publishing/printing, fine art, theatre, etc. Every other Saturday she was to give a lecture for an hour and a half, then spend half an hour on a question-and-answer session from 10 a.m. to 12 noon. The pay wasn't great, but when it went well, it was great publicity for Milia. I agreed to take our sons for a walk on her lecture days: to the zoo, visit the Dolls' Theatre, or enjoy the 'Children's World' department store. We would have lunch with Milia, and then I would rush off to work in the Cultural Centre, while the 'pirates' would head home for a well-earned rest. On the way home, they would vie with one another for their mother's attention, recounting their impressions from the morning. Milia would listen with a happy smile. I was just as pleased as my wife about her good fortune at the Academic Centre. This was exactly the kind of place where she could show herself in all her glory. Milia was hugely knowledgeable, her language was of a high standard, she put feeling into her presentation, and didn't have any problems in connecting with her audience, as was often the case in teaching dance: it was good clean work 'at arm's length'.

'Live' publicity like this can easily lead to a lecturer's position in some university, academic research centre, and suchlike. It's just a matter of pitching it at the right level, and not coming a cropper. Those attending the Academic Centre were highly qualified in their own fields, certainly to an equally elevated level as the lecturer. So preparing for these lectures was a serious affair, and they had to be delivered not in the style of a sermon, but rather with feeling, intelligence and consideration, with pauses in the appropriate places. There was a screen in the small conference room (capacity: fifty people) with an automatic projector, to illustrate examples of plagiarism. I had to purchase a compact portable screen and a fairly expensive auto-projector for Milia's use. My wife ordered copies from the central library of all the slides she needed to use in her lectures. For the first time in our life together, Milia asked for my honest opinion on how she sounded and looked on the podium. She asked how best to deliver her presentation, how to pronounce specific terms, what the tempo and cadence of her speech was like, her impersonations and actions, etc. Suspecting that she was teasing me, I kept quiet.

"Why don't you believe me? I actually need your help."

"I'll agree on one condition: no arguments! Hear me out then try out my suggestions in front of the mirror. Decide for yourself whether to include them or not. If you're interested in this kind of support, let me know, I'm only too glad to help."

After much angst, I decided to show my libretto *Gadfly* to Igor Belsky, Artistic Director of the Maly Opera Theatre. He read through three pages of my interpretation of Voynich's famous novel, in front of me. He nodded his approval and promised to present this project for discussion at the Artistic Council. I advised him that there was also a musical/choreographic scenario to work on with a composer, and that I was ready to stage a personal ballet production in the theatre. Igor promised to let me know what the council decided. I left Belsky, with an awareness of how naïve I was in my dealings with the amoral world of scheming and deceit. It felt like I was jumping into the predator's gaping jaws of my own free will. I had been ready to give birth to *Gadfly* for a long time: I had to decide to go for a risky labour. 'What will be, will be.'

The next day I had a call from the Mariinsky Ballet secretary, who put Sergeyev on.

"Mikhail, we are currently preparing the programme for a festival concert on our stage here, to mark the anniversary of the October Revolution. Fedicheva would like to dance your 'Song of the Black Swan'. Could you come in on Wednesday at 5.30 p.m. to rehearse with her for half an hour?"

"Konstantin Mikhailovich, I'd be delighted to accept this delectable mission."

In addition to the ballerina and pianist, the show producer and director also attended the rehearsal in the ballet studio. Watching the whole miniature straight through, I perceived some core alterations to my choreography, which ruined the main image of life-affirming love, replacing it with the clichéd dying swan. With great tact and diplomacy, I pointed out this paradox to Kaleriya, which was at odds with the character and genre of Villa-Lobos's music. The ballerina responded by having a fit of hysterics, and insulting me in front of the concert producers. I went up to Sergeyev's office. Shaking all over with indignation, I relayed what had happened at the rehearsal.

"How can such blasphemy go on at the Mariinsky Theatre?"

"Last year, before the USA tour, I rehearsed your 'Autumn' and 'Gauls' myself, as I'd given you my word. Naturally, Natalya Mikhailovna (Dudinskaya) agreed to rehearse 'Song of the Black Swan'. But Kaleriya refused any help from her, and this is the result."

"I'm not on your staff, and haven't received a penny from your office for my miniatures. As you must realise, you have no right to use my work. For this reason, I demand – rather than request – that you remove this number from the concert programme immediately and do not put it on anywhere at any time in the future."

"Misha, as a fellow ballet master, I understand how you feel, and you have my sympathy. But in making this decision, you would be consciously closing the door of this theatre forever, which would be really sad."

"I am deeply sorry about that. But my professional honour is worth more to me than this."

"Your will is my command. Your 'Song of the Black Swan' has been cut from the programme. Here is a pen and paper. Confirm this demand in writing addressed to me."

At the beginning of October the cooperative chairman invited me to come and see him urgently.

"Mikhail, I'm afraid I have some bad news for you. A month ago, Lashchenko, deputy director of the Housing Department, sent me an official enquiry: 'On what basis did we sign you up into the cooperative for a three-bedroom flat totalling 45 m^2, when your family only consists of four people and according to state norms, each person is entitled to 9 m^2. You are allocated 36 m^2 in total.' I replied in writing: 'As far as I am aware, the clients have academic status (through your wife) so are legally entitled to a supplementary room measuring no more than 12 m^2 in order to undertake academic work in the home. If this is not the case, then you did not need to grant this family authorisation for an unlawful claim to the space.' Mikhail, I understand that you are an artist. But as a lawyer, your wife is clued up on Soviet law, and understands full well the commercial motives of the situation. Nevertheless, you must expect a serious attack from the city Housing Department. Have a chat with your cousin's husband. You met all the legal criteria when you moved in here and no one has the right to evict you."

"Thanks for letting me know and for your help."

I decided beforehand not to worry Milia and waited for Lashchenko's next move. While the jury was out, I rang Boris. He refused to discuss the issue over the telephone and promised to come back for lunch with the whole family the following Sunday and have a look at our flat. Prior to that, I received a second letter from the Housing Department, addressed to me personally now. The Deputy Director demanded that we vacate our illegally occupied flat within thirty days. Attached to the letter was a list of three cooperative two-bedroom flats on the outskirts of the city, where we could choose to move to. Milia opened the post before me and was understandably in shock. I got home later from rehearsal. We shut ourselves in the office so as not to wake the children. My wife was in no condition to understand what was going on around this flat. I had to explain to her the system of bribes for granting authorisation for highly sought-after three-bedroom apartments in cooperatives, and how they were thereby controlled by the Housing Department.

"What are you on about? The Director was so generous with me."

"That's right. But you told me yourself how Nezhdanova doesn't have any dealings with private cooperatives as a rule, and gave you the authorisation as an exception because of the children. When Lashchenko came back from his holiday, and found out that we had moved into a three-bedroom flat, he realised that he had lost his chance to feather his nest, and kicked up a fuss. Following a month-long conflict with the Housing Department, this self-promoter decided to move us out to the back of beyond, with the backing of the top brass (higher than Nezhdanova)."

"I'm not moving anywhere. They can drag me out of here feet first."

"Don't let it get to you. I've had a chat with the cooperative chairman, and he has assured me categorically that we have a legal right to live here based on our family make-up and your academic status, in line with the cooperative rules. Lashchenko was banking on uneducated idiots. As a lawyer, mother of two and a party member, you can write a letter of protest against the breaches of confidence made by his subordinates, supported by the relevant article of the legal and moral code on your legal rights. We will get Boris to read through this on Sunday and give us his opinion, and you can make any necessary amendments. We'll take copies of all the letters attached to Lashchenko and dispatch it all to the man himself."

I had to ask Boris to come a bit earlier on Sunday in connection with the letter from the Housing Department, which was best discussed before lunch. He promised to bring everyone at midday. To minimise my wife's stress in preparing the said lunch, I took the boys downstairs to play in the playground. When our guests arrived, we started off with a quick tour of the lovely surroundings outside, and then went up in two lifts to our home. Sofia and Boris really liked the flat.

"Why don't you have any furniture along this wall? Is it where you punish the little upstarts?"

"No, dear cousin. It's . . . I'm waiting for the opportunity to move your wonderful piano here."

"You've got a long wait, my dear! How will I sing Leshchenko's romances without it?"

"Sofia, can you give Milia a hand in the kitchen? The children can play on the balcony. Don't worry. There's a high net on the fence. Misha and I will go and catch up in his office for ten minutes."

"Show me what this 'goose' has sent you. I was right about him."

Boris took the envelope from me, and read the official missive through twice.

"Looks like this bureaucrat is worse than I thought. He's not just bluffing. He's obviously got robust 'protection' from above, much stronger than Nezhdanova's. Otherwise he wouldn't be coming on so heavy, like a tank. Can I just give the cooperative chairman a ring?"

I left the office cautiously, deciding to check on the scallywags on the balcony.

"Misha, I'm just going to pop in and see your chairman for quarter of an hour. I'll be back for lunch at 1 p.m."

"Toptygin, why have you got this high net? Is it for catching pigeons?" my nephew Arkady asked.

"No, my little hare, it's so that my lovely monkeys don't fall from the fifth floor and land on people's heads."

"I don't get it. What monkeys?"

"These two in front of you, who often climb up the grille, not realising how far it is to fall."

After lunch Sofia took the initiative and got started on the washing-up. The children went for a rest. Milia, Boris and I got together in the office for a clandestine business meeting.

"I showed Lashchenko's letter to the Chairman. Everyone's of the same opinion."

"Milia, your written declaration is on the whole quite intellectual and makes a good case. But I would suggest making indirect reference to Lashchenko's official breaches in a few places, without accentuating his personal attributes. You will make more of an impact in standing up for your rights as a citizen, mother and professional person if you refer to legal clauses by number. Neither the cooperative chairman, nor me, are officially involved in your dispute, as he and I are part of this social welfare system. You would do well to keep us on your side without publicising it, or risking our positions. As you can see, three-bedroom flats are always in short supply, as they are earmarked for the city's bigwigs. That's why by paying extra to the cooperative for preference of the highest order on these establishments, their owners are 'obliged to show one's gratitude' to Lashchenko (via the senior Director) in order to be conferred with their privileged authorisation. You are the only ones not to have done this."

"A smart operator in Lashchenko's shoes would have left those in breach of the criminal code in peace. But judging by appearances, he is forced to cause a scandal so as to prove his loyalty to the corrupt system of state organisations. I expect Lashchenko will send you a more threatening letter in thirty days' time. Don't panic. We'll discuss it together and plan the next stage of the dispute. Whatever he uses to frighten you with, no one has the right to physically evict you from this flat, which you are occupying legally. Still, you need to get ready for bureaucratic ripples. Get all your documents copied and notarised. Don't stoop to levelling personal insults or accusations at your enemies. If it comes to it, go to the city prosecutor's office, right up to the Russian state general prosecutor, the International Child Protection Board, etc. If the worst comes to the worst, buy the same flat in Moscow for a fraction of the price. Move your money from this cooperative to another, then you won't have the sword of Damocles hanging over you."

The Trade Union Ensemble's production team managed to complete the vocal/ choreographic composition *Happy Cruise* in two months. This was a forty-minute review portraying episodes of life on a passenger ship, sailing around the Baltic coast. The Sailors' songs and dances took the form of Character style representations of Northern European peoples: the Latvian choir 'Seagulls over the Sea'; Lithuanian dance 'Klumpakojis' (in wooden clogs), Estonian 'Baltic Joke', Finnish 'Cross Step Polka', and more. The concert programme concluded with the 'Nevsky Quadrille' performed jointly with their choir. All vocalists in their mini ensembles (trio and quartet) did not sing standing stock-still on one spot, as was their usual custom. I made them either pose or do some actions in their repertoire, or move around, changing their stage positions in a collaborative performance with dancers of the Finnish polka and Estonian waltz. As a genre, this show was close to operetta, as it was bursting with cheerful and lyrical episodes from sailors' lives and tourists' youthful experiences. We timed the Premiere to coincide with celebrations for the October Revolution anniversary in the Kirov Palace. All elements of the ensemble coped brilliantly with the tough task of bringing their performance together in an artistic harmony of song, dance and orchestral sound for the first time. Our chief, Rubinov, took to the stage during the final curtain calls. He thanked all the artistes and leaders, and wished us happy 'Great Revolution' celebrations. It was noticeable that he didn't give me a mention. I took the hint, and didn't react to it.

Larisa managed not only the teaching work in first grade, but also the administrative functions of the whole department with a high degree of competence. As before, she was assisting me in Duet Technique, and had become more active since Kuchinsky had graduated. She regularly attended my course on Dance Composition and was always willing to help out as a partner with production work on the repertoire. As always, I invited the management, and all teachers and students to the Trade Union Ensemble concert. From then on, we would use for critical analysis, examples from my concert programme that they had seen recently. It was nice to see the impact of my teaching, when students found the execution of my choreographic conception weak or vague, or infringements in the vocals or dance. Larisa and I no longer discussed our relationship or my family. We resolved any work issues quickly and straightforwardly. Only one day, she asked me rather awkwardly, whether I had changed my address and telephone number, as she was worried about losing touch at work.

I asked: "Lara, why are you asking? If anything like that happens, you'll be the first to know."

"Yes, of course, I understand. I thought I'd heard that. I'm sorry, goodbye."

"Surely the lynching has not started already? I had expected this to happen much later."

In the middle of November, I arrived home to find my wife in tears. In response to my question, she outlined Lashchenko's next demand: "We have a week to get out of this flat, or they'll get the police to help evict us."

I burst out laughing, so ridiculous did this letter seem to me.

"I'm writing to Seryozha Prokhorov in Moscow. He is currently working as assistant to the Russian State General Prosecutor. You know him from the Law Faculty and the Moscow State University Club."

"That's the right way forward. But a personal letter to a former classmate is one thing. An official statement about a violation of socialist law by a member of staff in a state organisation, is quite another. You must not 'cry into your pillow' but let it be known that this bribe-taker is unlawfully putting a mother and her two children out on the street in winter, and you demand your rights. Quote clauses from the Citizens' Code. Use their language. Better still, send a second copy of all the documents to some kind of social, populist organisation in Moscow, making both addressees aware of the existence of the file copy. In this case, they won't be able to put this off in the pending tray. To avoid looking like bureaucrats in each other's eyes, they will be forced to take action following your contact. Send everything by registered post."

About ten or twelve days after we had sent the letters off to Moscow, to the Russian State General Prosecutor and International Child Protection Board, we got a call from the Smolny Palace (Leningrad Regional Party Committee) and for some reason, they asked to speak not to my wife, a party member, but to me.

"Mr Berkut?"

"Yes, who am I speaking to?"

"It's the regional Party Committee here."

"I'm sorry, I'm not a party member. You probably want to speak to Emilia Berkut."

"No, Mikhail Semyonovich. The second secretary of the regional Party Committee (Ideology Department) wishes to speak specifically to you about the epistle you sent to Moscow. Can you make tomorrow at 10 p.m. in Smolny?"

At this point the line went dead. I suddenly recalled an episode with the Gestapo in a war film, where a Soviet secret agent had been captured and the tone of his interrogation was like this last telephone conversation with Smolny, to the point of absurdity. Fortunately, Milia was running a bath with the children and did not overhear this conversation. To be honest, it was a shock. I hadn't anticipated such a turn of events, so I didn't know how to react to this 'knight's move'. I needed to calm down first, then analyse the senseless threats. Holed up in the office, I tried to put all the pieces of this game in position, to get a clearer view of the situation with the letters.

"Misha, I heard the telephone ring from the bathroom. Was it something for me?"

I shook my head and went to put the children to bed. I told them a bedtime story about the adventures of Dobrynya Nikitich, expressing my sadness that we couldn't buy a sword and shield at this time. Life was so good in the olden days. If you don't like the evil ruler, just chop his head off! Now you need to think up other ways to achieve this purpose. I felt completely devastated, but kept myself in check all the same. For the morning, I prepared my cooperative file, a clean shirt and tie. I even polished my shoes to such an extent that you could smell me from a distance. I thought: *If I'm arrested, at least I'll look intelligent.* I wrote a half-page farewell letter to my wife and hid it in a particular place. When Milia visited me in prison, I would tell her where to find this pre-death missive. I felt so sorry for myself that I almost shed a tear. My wife walked into the office just in time and asked for my help in organising her lecture for Saturday. I had to change tack.

I was at the entrance to Smolny at 10 p.m. The duty police officer looked through my passport, checked his watch with some surprise and rang through to confirm my arrival. A few moments later, a man in a black suit asked my name and invited me to follow him. Two men were standing with their backs to me, spreading out some papers on a long table in a meeting room). I said hello. They did not respond. I repeated my greeting more emphatically and a little louder. No reaction. A familiar technique to express contempt towards someone. *They are trying to break my spirit. How little they understand, that such cheap tricks are known to any theatre producer from the word go.*

Turning about, I shouted, "Goodbye!" and made for the exit.

A sarcastic voice rang out halfway behind me: "Comrade Berkut, where are you rushing off to? You've got time to send vengeful letters to Moscow, but not for a chat with us, eh? You've slandered the best member of staff in the city Housing Department without any proof, and taken advantage of his absence to move in illegally."

"I've already told your assistant on the telephone that you need to discuss this issue with my wife. As a law graduate, she is certain that we bought the flat we are living in legally, after refusing to pay Lashchenko a bribe via his director. We protest against his inhumane demands regarding our move, and his threat to throw a family with two small children on to the street in winter, assisted by the police, as is customary in New York's Negro ghetto. And you think that a normal mother should put up with all of this and wait for the lawbreaker to carry out his threat? Forgive me, esteemed leaders, but clearly you are either badly informed, or are consciously covering up your lackey's criminal actions to avoid a public scandal.

"This file contains all the materials from the last two years relating to our membership of the cooperative. If you read it, and judge that my wife or I have committed a crime, then arrest us. In any case, a justified complaint from the mother of my children does not give you the moral right to summon me to an interrogation in the middle of the night and deride your visitor."

"Can you leave us a list of names of the people who have paid bribes to the Housing Department?"

"Of course not. We agreed with our witnesses that they would testify in court. If you have no further claims against me, permit me to go home to my family at 10.30 p.m."

"We recommend that you consider your position with your future in mind."

"Thank you, and you can take advice from a producer: next time you feel like having some fun, buy yourselves a cockerel and, instead of a guest, shake some bells at him."

Both officials had a brief chuckle. I waved goodbye and left.

In the lobby, the man in black accompanied me to the palace exit without a word. I was expecting a KGB officer to come round every corner and arrest me for insulting public servants in the course of their work."

One way or another, they had it all worked out beforehand. They were looking to amuse themselves, and I had given them some entertainment. Bowling along Nevsky Prospekt, I couldn't stop thinking about the second secretary at the regional Party Committee (Ideology Department), and realised only then, why it had been necessary to go through this farce with me in the night.

No doubt on the go-ahead from the International Child Protection Board, the officials from the pertinent section of the Soviet Communist Party had requested the Leningrad Regional Party Committee to 'sort it out and report back' on the risk of danger to the children, in connection with corruption at the city Housing Department. So he asked about a list of witnesses so that he could formally let Moscow know what measures were being taken, and naturally did not wish to meet with the complainant: a mother with a legal background. The situation was clear: we had upset the anthill, and the unforgiving insects would not rest until they had driven us out of their territory.

By December, Milia was coming to the end of her talks at the Academic Centre. The sixth and last lecture was on the following theme, 'Authors' Rights in Choreographic Work'. She ordered several versions of the ballet *Sleeping Beauty* (music by Tchaikovsky) from the film rental shop, performed by ballet troupes from the capital cities of the Soviet Union, so that she could show the same excerpts to compare the different choreographic interpretations. This was absolute proof of the brazen mutual plagiarism engaged in by ballet masters, who had justified similar crimes over the years through the lack of a fixed text in the language of dance, even with the old stenographic system of recording choreography by Lisizian, Benesh, Laban and others. The film-maker alone had resolved this problem. It's easy to imagine what would have happened in the Conservatoire Concert Hall, had the orchestral conductor suddenly changed the leitmotif of a famous symphony written by Prokofiev, or one of Glinka's operas, and named himself as the musical editor in the publicity. In ballet, this is almost always the case. The lecture in the conference room at the Academic Centre was attended by Lopukhov, Yakobson, Slonimsky and other famous ballet luminaries. This was a dazzling finale to the cycle on authors' rights. The lecturer received a standing ovation. We had left the children with Sofia, which gave us the chance to have lunch in a local restaurant afterwards, to celebrate Milia's achievement. I offered her my heartfelt congratulations on her professional acclaim in her specialism of art appreciation.

After collecting the children from Sofia, I linked up with Boris for an update. He was upset about the potential consequences following what had happened at the regional Party Committee, announcing: "Misha, you've burned your bridges with this visit. You need to get out of here before it's too late."

"I know, Boris. That's why I'm asking you to help me sell my flat after the Christmas holidays, when I will be leaving my posts. My wife will remain here with the children until 1st April. This will give me three months to find a cooperative flat in Moscow, as well as a permanent job at the beginning of the season. In the meantime, I'll get to work on my former production projects. Apart from organising the transfer of money from one cooperative to another, I want to leave you some funds to support the family, so that on Sundays, you or Sofia can give Milia enough to feed three people and cover everyday expenses. This can be signed for so that we all keep track of it. I'll pay for the cooperative instalments and communal accounts on my visits here at the end of every month.

I'm sorry to burden you with extra worries. Milia might try to extort money from Sofia, as she did with Mum in Odessa, but she won't try that with you. Here's the telephone number of my friend, Nikolai Golovchenko in Moscow, where I'll be staying. If anything urgent comes up, ring in the morning at my expense. Once again, thank you for everything."

Back home, after putting the children to bed, my wife, who was in a good mood, confessed her sins, which she had been keeping from me over the last two weeks.

"At the beginning of December, I was summoned to the office of the city prosecutor about my complaint to Moscow. The prosecutor's assistant spent a long time chatting to me, clarifying how things worked, and was surprised that I had gone straight over his head rather than approaching him first. But I explained that Lashchenko's threat to forcibly evict me and the children in winter had forced me to take extreme action against such inhumane aggression and corruption. Any mother would have done the same in my shoes. This hooligan is a true bandit. He belongs in prison.

"The prosecutor's assistant confessed that he had known about the practice of taking bribes in this section for a long time, but without witnesses and direct evidence, they couldn't make any accusations and were forced to be patient."

"Milia, from my side, I too have to own up that I hid from you my visit to Smolny following a telephone summons, when you were giving the children their bath before bed."

After I'd recounted the incident in the regional Party Committee, my wife exclaimed indignantly: "God, what's happening to the Russia we know? I thought things like this only happened in Slavyansk. And these little people living in the city of Lenin, consider themselves members of his party? Misha, we need to get away quickly, to escape the plague. I beg you, let's go back to our beloved Moscow."

I told Milia how Operation Moscow was going to unfold over the next three months.

"I'm afraid it's going to be tight money-wise as a result of losing my jobs. Boris has agreed to help with the sale of the flat and give you seventy roubles every Sunday to live on until you move to Moscow. You will have to manage on this budget. I'll take care of all other costs. Be frugal! Otherwise we'll end up in serious financial difficulty."

"I'm with you all the way, on one condition: can we sleep together today? Please give me this New Year's gift after our three-year gap."

I peered at my wife, not knowing if she was being serious, and joked: "It's a bit snug with two in a single bed. Two can only sleep there in a sandwich position."

"We can put the mattress on the floor in the office, as we've done more than a few times."

"That's a different matter then. An honest man is not going to say no to sex."

Milia sat on my lap and hugged me, nuzzling my shoulder with her nose.

"Thanks, darling," she whispered. "I've been waiting for this for such a long time. I'd already given up hope."

Her tears of longing and happiness trickled on to my collar, tickling me unbearably. But I remained sufficiently stoic to withstand this great experience of love and mutual forgiveness.

Immediately after the Smolny visit, I wrote a farewell letter to Rubinov.

'Dear Vladimir Pavlovich, I am unable to extend my annual contract with you from 1st January as I am moving to another city on a permanent basis for reasons known to you. Thank you for everything that you have done for us. Yours fondly.'

The winter term was going well in the school as usual. At the last test on the composition of dance, the secretary passed on an invitation from the Director, to call in and see him after work. Saying my goodbyes to Larisa and the pianist, I kissed them both and wished them all the best, and headed for the Director's office.

"Mikhail Semyonovich, I'm sorry to cause you distress on New Year's Eve."

"Don't worry, Vladimir Petrovich, here is my letter of resignation. I completely understand. You are an excellent director, and I enjoyed working with you. Sorry, and goodbye."

We spent my last evening with the family at Sofia's, seeing in the New Year and a change of fortune for me. A luxuriant Christmas tree, presents, the boys, delicious food and joy across the land. My cousin was in tears when we said goodbye, sympathising with my plight.

"Dear Sofia, whatever happens is for the best. Things will turn out right for us in the end!"

Boris took us home at 2 a.m., and told me not to worry about my family. On 1st January, the whole herd of Berkuts went to see *The Nutcracker* at the Mariinsky Theatre. We celebrated the New Year around our beautiful tree at home that evening. The children and Milia received quality gifts from Dad wearing a Father Christmas mask. Our sons went to bed. My wife cried as we parted. Everything was as normal life should be in a normal family, with the exception of one thing: my heart was haemorrhaging all the way to Moscow Station.

CHAPTER 4 THE GOLD CHAINS OF FREEDOM

My old friend Nikolai had promised to meet me at Leningrad Station. Would he wake up in time after a heavy Saturday night?

I was just disembarking when a strange-looking porter rolled up in a non-uniform peaked cap and asked: "Dear passenger, would you like some help? I don't charge much, just one bottle."

"Oh, hi! I didn't recognise you after my sleepless night on the train. Where did you come by that trolley?"

"Great, my friend! I'll tell you later. Let's go before I'm arrested for theft."

Kolya pulled the luggage along briskly, deftly manoeuvring his way through the crowd of travellers.

"You're such an innocent Leningrader! I've borrowed the trolley without asking. I've parked my boss's car on double-yellows, and need to get it back by 12 noon. That's the deal!"

We got there in time to avoid a fine for breaking the rules. The main ring road to Serebryanny Bor took no time at all. On the way home, we stocked up on things that would keep outside on the covered terrace. We returned the car to the garage punctually and presented the manager with a bottle of vodka.

Over lunch I recounted the sorry saga of the Leningrad cooperative.

"Misha, you've got a bad memory. How many times do I have to tell you: 'If you're going to live with wolves you have to howl like a wolf'! But you stubbornly persist in pissing in the wind. I'm amazed they haven't sent you off to hard labour by now. You'll go through another learning curve in Moscow. Put that in your pipe and smoke it! I hope you don't experience anything negative in the capital: it's not luck, but a part or consequence of a system devised by the state over the last fifty years. At this stage no one individual can change anything. With all your intelligence and talent, 'If you can't beat 'em, join 'em.'"

"I agree with you, mate. I will try to apply the lesson I learned in Leningrad here in Moscow."

"Here are the keys. You know the drill. Make yourself at home. If you spend the night with a beautiful woman somewhere in town, give me a ring so that I don't worry."

First and foremost I paid a visit to MTA, and let Shatin and his secretary know that I had moved to Moscow on a permanent basis. I left my contact details with Lena. Then I went to the Bolshoi School to meet with Golovkina, the Director. There I came across my former colleagues: Andreyev, the designer, and Pestov, now a leading teacher of men's classes in the ballet school. I took pains to spread the word that I had moved back to the capital. I also visited the Moscow Central Palace of Culture, and got to meet Isabella Sviderskaya, formerly a Bolshoi soloist, and now the new head of the Dance Department. She said that she remembered me from previous seminars with leaders of choreographic groups and my displays at concerts in the State Academy of the Bolshoi Theatre School. This was when Isabella had recommended me to panel members for the amateur show to commemorate the fiftieth anniversary of the October Revolution. She had persuaded Tumanov, the festival's Artistic Director, to take me on as one of his assistants, as a choreographer on contract for ten months with a commensurate salary. That marked the beginning of my second Moscow epic ten years later.

Between lectures in the Academy I met Shatin. My mentor was thrilled about my move to Moscow, and offered me the opportunity to head up courses for amateur choreographers for a year from September, as a spin-off of the MTA Ballet Masters Department, which was currently being run by Sasha Kudryavtsev, Zakharov's assistant. Classes took place on Mondays from 9 a.m. to 1 p.m. in the MTA sports hall within the establishment.

"As well as Artistic leadership, you will have to teach all the special disciplines (method and practice): Classical technique, Theatrical Folk, Historical (Court), Duet and Dance Composition, in a range of elementary fundamentals for each subject. The work is hard and unpaid, but rewarding. It is great publicity for your career in the capital and there's a good chance (if you do well) of being taken on by MTA as my official assistant. You could also do a postgraduate correspondence course, something you've been dreaming of for a long time."

"Anatoly Vasilyevich, you know what an honour it is for me to work with you. But as before, I don't hold out much hope that Gusev, the MTA principal, and Professor Zakharov, will approve this project. I will accept your proposal on condition that it is only for one academic year, to prove to our 'friends' what I'm capable of."

Sofia Golovkina, the director of the Bolshoi School, was also pleased to see me on her turf.

"Misha, we've consulted with the opera director, Boris Pokrovsky, and Isabella Sviderskaya from Moscow Central Palace of Culture, and we've decided that you are the most suitable candidate for the post of Artistic Director of the Bolshoi People's Opera/Ballet Theatre-Studio affiliate, based in the ZIL (Likhachov car factory) Cultural Centre."

"Everything's in place with the Opera. The ballet leader, Zhenya Valukin, left to work in Cuba on 1st January, and we're recommending you as his replacement. The salary is small, but it's a prestigious location to start with, after a long break from Moscow. Making up this unique company are young men and women who didn't get through the auditions for the capital's ballet troupes. In the main, these are already professional dancers aged seventeen and above, who are perfecting their technique by studying the current repertoire. Regular classes are held on subjects familiar to you, and there are productions of one-act ballets, separate compositions and dances in opera, plus stage rehearsals and public performances on Saturdays. It's an excellent creative hothouse for people like you, who are always in pursuit of innovation. The affiliate is subsidised by the wealthy Central Committee of the Car Manufacturers' Trade Union.

In the main, the affiliate staff team includes production directors, music conductors, Choirmasters, Ballet teachers and pianists from the Bolshoi Theatre and school, all working in collaboration here. All in all, the theatre studio comprises eighteen people including you, the local administrator and wardrobe mistress. There are around 140 artistes: twelve solo singers, forty-six choir members, twenty-four musicians and sixty-something dancers. In reality this group is the same as the famous Ballet studio in Leningrad's Maxim Gorky Palace of Culture. Both are (unofficially) branches of the Bolshoi and Mariinsky Theatres. Shows such as Grigorovich's ballet *Stone Flower* to music by Prokofiev or the opera *Stormy Petrel* to music by Vasilyev grew on the strength of avid lovers of art, gaining wide public acclaim in Theatrical circles throughout the country. Now the affiliate is in urgent need of a choreographer for the Ballet studio's part in the Festival Gala show and to take up leadership on a permanent basis."

"Thank you, Sofia Nikolayevna. May I have a look at how their groups are made up, have a chat with the leaders and theatre administration, and check the terms of work?"

"I'll ring Zhilin, the Palace director, and he'll set it all up for you."

My first meeting with the affiliate leaders was arranged for the following Monday (a day off at the Bolshoi Theatre) in the Director's office at the ZIL Cultural Centre, and subsequently with the Ballet studio teachers. After the introductions and a brief presentation about the content of the Gala show *Stormy Petrel*, Pokrovsky, the production directors, asked whether I'd be interested in choreographing this opera, to include: Character street dances for students and sailors, court dances at the imperial palace, adjusting the movements for soloist singers and choir members, and crowd scenes on the Winter Palace square.

"The timescales for all this are really tight, as the deadline is extremely short. The rough draft of stage production on the opera has been completed; the same for the vocal, orchestral part. Just the ballet master's work remains. Do you have time for this?"

"The project you've outlined is really tempting for a professional choreographer, with a Ballet troupe on board. It's no mean feat to get this load off the ground in three to four months, even in a State theatre. But a lot depends on how well organised the administration is and the enthusiasm of the artistes. On this basis I am willing to give it a go."

"Mikhail Semyonovich, if I've got this right," the Director addressed me, "given the above-mentioned conditions, you guarantee to put on the required dances and meet the stage production directors' requirements in deciding the choreography for the whole of *Stormy Petrel* by 1st June."

"Absolutely, as long as I can start work with the artistes by 1st February."

"Boris Alexandrovich, you have the final say on this."

"Vasily Ignatyevich, there is no time to lose."

"In that case, Mikhail Semyonovich, you can sign up for your new commitments tomorrow and be fully fledged Artistic leader of the affiliate from 1st January."

"I'm sorry, but today is already the 17th."

"It counts as future overtime." We all laughed, and cemented our agreement with handshakes.

"Elena Fyodorovna, please introduce the new Artistic Director to his colleagues and sign the authorisation for him to get a front-door key. Mikhail Semyonovich, I am at your disposal any time. Here is my personal telephone number. I wish you well!"

"Please excuse me, sir. I didn't expect things to move so quickly from your side, and promised my two young soldiers who are four and nine years old that I would visit them in Leningrad between 22nd and 24th February. At the same time, I need to bring over all my choreography materials."

"No problem, I'll authorise your creative trip to Leningrad for four days."

"Thank you. I'll make up those days another time."

"No, thank *you* for taking on the choreography for the Opera."

After taking on the Bolshoi affiliate, I noticed that discipline and numbers needed to be restored in the Ballet studio. The Director of the Bolshoi School gave me a list of graduates over the last two years who hadn't found work, singling out those whom she had already persuaded to come and work in the Affiliate, so as not to lose their physical shape or nerve completely. We sent invitations out to the rest.

Turning the crisis situation in the Ballet studio to my advantage, I pressed Golovkina and Zhilin to strengthen the male group using Pyotr Pestov, a teacher from the Bolshoi School, for the Soloists. We knew each other well from working together at the Tadzhik Opera and Ballet Theatre. The patrons didn't dare refuse, and took full responsibility for the consequences. After discovering that Pyotr Pestov, the Bolshoi School's pre-eminent teacher, was starting off his supplementary teaching post by teaching Classics in the Affiliate, many of the young ballet artistes (both former and new) registered at the ZIL Cultural Centre. While my three teachers and répétiteurs were whipping their charges into balletic Opera, the stage producer and I worked with the solos and singers, vocal ensemble and choir members, on the fluid forms of movement for characters in *Stormy Petrel*.

At the same time, on 1st March I got down to work on production of the Street dances with the ballet soloists: twelve girls dancing the 'student parts', and eight young men dancing the 'sailor roles'. In parallel, I gave the 'corps de ballet' an intensive course on forgotten or unfamiliar manners of Court-Historical dances and after only a month, choreographed ballroom suite, including: Pavane, Courante and Galliard. Clearly there were not enough male partners. Once again, I had to ask Golovkina for urgent assistance. The trouble was that it was still a long way off to her graduate exams in the Ballet school, which could have topped up our reserves. The Director suggested to me that foreign students could join in the performance of historic dances in *Stormy Petrel* to gain some practice. For us, this turned out to be the best way out of a critical situation. In line with my promise to Pokrovsky, the Opera choreography was duly completed by 1st June.

After the premiere, he shook my hand, congratulating me on a successful outcome, and confessed: "My dear colleague, I must admit, at first I didn't have any faith in your .frivolous bravado. But over the course of rehearsals, I realise that I underestimated you."

On my days off I would call Leningrad regularly. I told Milia how I was advancing my career and updated her on my search for a cooperative flat. Most new builds were a long way out of the centre, or in Moscow's industrial zones. Just by chance I found a place near Rechnoi Vokzal metro station, where work on the inside was due to be finished by May. On 23rd February I arrived in Leningrad for Sofia's fortieth birthday and to re-register my cooperative credits while I was there. My wife and I agreed that they would move to Moscow at the beginning of May. There was a delay in the cooperative building at Rechnoi Vokzal, and we had to vacate our Leningrad accommodation by 1st May, so we had to rent a one-room flat in Moscow for two months in the Krasnaya Presnya district. I persuaded the director of the nearest primary school to take Dmitri for a couple of months so that he could finish second grade. In return, I promised to put on a performance with the Matryoshkas in their dance club, at a concert to mark the completion of the school year. Dmitri played the Jester role again.

After the luxury of the Leningrad cooperative, my wife had naturally forgotten the bleak conditions of temporary rental flats and started to nag me continuously. I continued to live at Nikolai's as the three of them could barely fit into the one room in Presnya. There was no question of a fourth family member being there. At this time of year I was up to my eyes and only saw my family on Sundays. I picked up the boys for the whole day to give their mum the chance to clean the flat, do the washing, go shopping, etc. Instead of this, she would go and visit friends and come home late at night. The round of scandals and hysterics started up again, and I was in no fit state to argue with her. I had to change tactics. I would run in for five minutes, leave some money for the following week and then disappear, not giving Milia the opportunity to go out. These tragicomedies played themselves out in front of the children. But I had underestimated my opponent.

At the beginning of June, Golovkina invited me to the graduate exams for her girls and Pestov's boys. In the break, Yuri Grigorovich, chief Ballet master at the Bolshoi, having heard that I was now a Moscow resident, invited me to put on a series of my miniatures with ballet soloists at private receptions given by the Soviet Embassy on its foreign tours. We agreed a rehearsal for the coming Tuesday, after the morning class at 11 a.m. He knew my repertoire from concerts in the Bolshoi School and with soloists from the Mariinsky Theatre. To start off with, Yuri Nikolayevich picked three duets and two solo numbers, which would go down well with Western audiences. I was all fired up in excited anticipation of this work. On Sunday I was busy on the production of *Stormy Petrel*, and unable to go and see my family, so I postponed it until Monday afternoon.

I bragged to my wife about starting to produce my own shows in the Bolshoi. I hadn't yet got my bag open when she grabbed the envelope of money and tore out of the house like a madwoman. The boys and I could hear her hysterical laughter and comments in the stairway. The children looked around in alarm, not understanding what was going on. I calmed them down by suggesting an outing to the park. Back home after supper, I told the kids the story of Mowgli in the jungle from Rudyard Kipling's *The Jungle Book* and put them to bed. Expecting my wife to return in the small hours, I prepared my rehearsal for the Bolshoi. Milia didn't show up. When the children asked where their mum was in the morning, I didn't know what to tell them.

At 10 a.m. I was on my marks by the door, ready to fly out as soon as she came back. My wife turned up at ten thirty. I spat in her face without a word. I pushed her out of the doorway and charged out to flag down a car to get me to rehearsal on time, arriving at the stage door of the Bolshoi at eleven twenty. The doorman called the ballet manager. The latter answered through gritted teeth that they had cancelled my rehearsal. It felt like someone was emptying a pail of hot water over my head followed swiftly by cold. Only a complete cretin could bugger up this fantastic opportunity of working at the Bolshoi.

I left the Bolshoi with my professional status in tatters. I wanted to stand in the shower and wash off the scum associated with my spouse.

At my next meeting with the administrator of the Bolshoi affiliate, Golovkina asked: "Misha, is it true that Yuri Nikolayevich invited you to put on your miniatures with the soloist ballet dancers and you didn't turn up to the rehearsal?"

I recounted the reason I had been twenty minutes late.

She replied, "People in our profession shouldn't settle down with a family and children."

"Alas! I realised my mistake too late and have paid a high price for it."

"In this case I'll pass on to Grigorovich the reason you messed up. You've let him down as a leader and he has lost hope and professional confidence in you."

"If I were him I would feel exactly the same and would have done exactly the same thing. Nevertheless, I implore you; please convey to him my sincere and heartfelt apologies."

By mid-June, the cooperative flat was ready to move into. Thanks to my references from ZIL and the Moscow Cultural Centre, I registered my family with the police at the new address without any problems, and obtained authorisation from Moscow City Council in my name. Picking up the keys from the cooperative Chairman, I took my family to view their future home. The kids ran around the empty rooms, knocking into each other. A stretch of the Moscow river could be seen from the balcony, with its barges and boats. This was a beautiful, panoramic cityscape. I showed my wife the floor plan marking where the furniture would go.

"If there's anything you don't like, speak now before we work to this plan."

After checking the interior of every room in detail, she muttered sceptically: "Everything suits me fine apart from one thing – living in the back of beyond, miles from the centre of town."

"If you can find something nearer and better, we'll move there. But for now, until Shurik and I have measured and made a note of all the furnishings, you and Dmitri can pop down to the closest school and register him for third grade. Here are fifty roubles for all the textbooks, exercise books and things like that, plus the new school uniform, shoes and PE kit. I'll need the receipts in case we need to change anything. Best to bring everything here, then we'll have less to carry when we move in with the children.

"How are we going to get all the stuff back here?" The incensed mother was exasperated.

"With your feet and hands, in one or two trips. It's only 200 metres from the metro station."

I decided to use my day off for a total chill-out. The little one and I went down twice to the home-ware shop over the road by Rechnoi Vokzal. First we bought a small fold-up bag on wheels. We filled it up with various crockery, utensils and toiletries, and wheeled it home. Then we went back to the shop and bought a tough nylon rug in green for the balcony and a roll of thick, transparent plastic for the balcony fence. The shop assistant hoisted the second roll on to my shoulder. I nearly collapsed under the weight.

He led Shurik to our side of the busy avenue and ordered him: "Keep a firm hold on Dad's waist and show him the way home, or he'll get lost or fall over."

We made the remaining 200 metres to our front entrance comfortably, but bent double. The doorman helped to take the heavy load off my shoulder by the lift. Dmitri and his furious mum were sitting on the floor in the corridor opposite our door.

Shurik threw himself on her with open arms, but the good and wise mother barked at him: "What kept you? To hell with you! We've been sitting here waiting for ten minutes!"

"Milia, stop it! Here are your keys to the new flat, just don't yell at the child!"

Dmitri helped me to spread the green flooring on the balcony and attach the protective plastic covering to the external side of the fence.

"Now you and Shurik can happily play chess or whatever you like out here. Nothing and no one will fall down or climb up the balcony trellis."

"Comrade Superior, I have put all the shopping away. Please can we all go out to eat somewhere?"

An hour later, friendly relations had been restored and we were all tucking in to *pelmeni* (ravioli) on Komsomol Square.

"Boys, in the few days you have left, please give Mum a hand packing everything you need to take to Slavyansk. Use your rucksacks and the manageable suitcase. Also, put into boxes, bags and the remaining suitcases everything that is to be moved to the new flat by taxi. I've already given notice to the landlord that we are leaving here on 30th June. On that evening, you will go off to Granny Klava's in Slavyansk.

"Daddy, what will you do in Moscow without us? Dance with little tarts?"

Dmitri jumped right up on to his chair, nearly overturning the table and full plates with it.

"Idiot! What are you on about? Eat your *pelmeni* without talking and keep your mouth shut."

The poor little mite nearly choked. Milia lowered her head towards her plate. I pretended that nothing had happened, preferring not to react in a public place.

"Kids, don't annoy your mum. Do as she says. You've worked hard today. I will pick you up in a taxi at 10 a.m. on the 30th. Everything must be ready for the move. I need to go and buy your tickets at the station now. Dmitri, if you need anything, you have Uncle Kolya's telephone number, where I'm staying temporarily. Call from a telephone box."

At the station, at the last minute as always, and as it was still summer to boot, I paid through the nose for a compartment. Though this made it possible to send the boys off to be cared for by their grandmother for six weeks and during this time, I could prepare for the new season. Now I would be able to collect my thoughts.

In the arts world, the whole of that year was devoted to the fiftieth anniversary celebration of the October Revolution. I asked the publishers, Soviet Russia, if they would be interested in a compilation of contemporary dance suites under the heading *Heroism through the Generations* which they confirmed they wanted as early as March. But I just didn't have any time to make the said project a reality. After dispatching my family to Slavyansk, I spent all of July writing at Serebryanny Bor. I drew outlines of dancing figures and diagrams of spatial patterns in modernist Character style. In this way I fixed the movements for the stage positions in pantomime scenes. The album included notation of choreographic compositions, united by the theme *Heroism Through the Generations*:

1. 'The Glow of Revolution' – striking workers at the May Day celebrations in Petrograd
2. 'Young Guards' by Alexander Fadeyev – young fighters in the Patriotic War
3. 'Space Saga' – Soviet astronauts, conquering the frontiers of space

A compulsory clause in the contract with the publishers was to use a red silhouette of a dancer on a white background (in poster style) on the whole outer cover. I didn't dare to argue with such a definite, primitive decision by the designer. Still, I assumed that at least the content of the opus would demonstrate the writer's loyalty to 'socialist realism'. I submitted my work to the editor on 1st August. To my enormous surprise, at the end of October (just before the holiday), my first series of choreographic compositions appeared in print. Shatin took pride in his student's achievements, hoping that this would help to bring our MTA project to fruition.

When I met Andreyev, the Bolshoi School designer, I asked my friend to find out whether there were any pensioners in his building who would like to rent out one of their rooms to a bachelor, including all utilities and telephone. After losing my job at the Bolshoi, I had no intention of living under the same roof with my unhinged wife on a permanent basis. Cyril's mother found me an excellent alternative among her neighbours, where the female owner lived with her sister in her country property most of the year and agreed, for a modest sum, to rent out her large bedroom/office with a desk, like the one I'd had at Rechnoi. At the end of June I moved out of Nikolai's and into Cyril's, not far from the Arbat. I promptly got on with furnishing and equipping the cooperative flat. The basics were in place by the time the family returned from Slavyansk. Only the finer points needed attention, which the lady of the house would have to finish off to her taste. I refrained from putting in a telephone.

My sons were happy to be back in Moscow. They were curious to see how the interior of the flat looked now. They moved their personal things, toys and school items into their room. There were two plastic chairs and a small table on the balcony. Milia came back from Slavyansk with her sister Tanya, ten years her junior, who was hoping to get a place in MTA. We all went to the supermarket together to buy bed linen and clothes for the children. Once I'd paid for all the purchases, I helped them home and wished them a happy time getting moved in. My wife asked whether I was prepared to give her funds for her own personal needs.

I took her into the office and stated: "Here are 100 roubles for the children up to the end of the month, and 100 to get things organised in the new flat. Since you intentionally lost me my job at the Bolshoi, you are now dead to me. You can get the children settled at school and nursery now. Look for a part-time job and provide for your personal needs through your own resources and means. I will continue to support the children and pay for the accommodation as long as I can. I want nothing to do with you."

"You are legally obliged to provide for the mother of your children, not to mention the moral side of things."

"Apply for a divorce and maintenance, which I will gladly pay you. In this case, your sister could help you with the monthly instalments on the flat. You have always bitten the hand that feeds you, so just carry on in the same vein. I'll leave my office permanently locked as I've lost all trust in you. The rest of the living space will remain available to you. Please leave it alone!"

Sviderskaya, having honed her skills at the Moscow City Cultural Centre, was the official tutor in the MTA Ballet Masters Department within the affiliated branch, and had handled all documentation for the yearly courses since 1966. As in all higher-education establishments, during the first week of August, she and I ran a recruitment drive for new students from former dancers of ballet theatres and state folk ensembles, who nowadays are leaders of amateur choreographic groups in the capital and Moscow region. In total we signed up thirteen students (of mixed gender), who were versed in classical or stage folk dance technique, had a musical ear and were no older than forty. Once we had decided the course candidates, Isabella gathered them all together for an initial discussion. The tutor explained the class regime, their responsibilities and accepted uniform. I listed the special subjects in the academic programme for the next ten months.

Stormy Petrel took place on the stage in the Palace of Congresses on the eve of the celebrations for the October Revolution, performed by artistes of the ZIL Cultural Centre affiliate. As a result of the group's industrious efforts, this was a monumental performance in the Kremlin, and highly acclaimed in the press. Of course, ballet had a subsidiary function here, but nevertheless, in between the bursts of pompous praise for the opera soloists and choir, the critics occasionally fêted in passing 'the professional choreography of Street dances and crowd scenes, and the accurate/precise performance of Historical dances at the court by young Ballet artistes'.

On 6th November, hot on the heels of *Stormy Petrel*, and following the Creative Government Conference, we gave the Gala Festival concert in the Kremlin. Sviderskaya and I rushed around like headless chickens to ensure the next Dance groups made timely entrances from their designated wings on the huge stage, and exited promptly after their performances. Fortunately, all creative groups and technical services worked well together under the direction of the experienced Producer. We all knew only too well what the slightest error or inaccuracy could cost us in observing the sequence of the numbers. The concert was impeccable, to a high standard, much to everyone's great relief.

The contingent of students from the MTA affiliate was complex. Former dancers of pensionable age (thirty-five to forty) took an interest in understanding the history and theory of the Art of dance. The younger members, more impatient, who were used to thinking with their feet (instead of brains), attended only the practical classes, with dubious excuses. I warned Sviderskaya that if these individuals didn't make the grade in theory during the winter term in December, then they should be dismissed. She concurred, and the following Monday before classes began, she made everyone aware of this. One of the doormen made a point of leaving the studio. From this day forward, no one missed a single class without a valid reason.

Isabella rationalised to her colleagues: "If we don't maintain our own creative discipline, how can we demand this from others? The teacher's personal example is an important quality in leadership."

At the end of December Sviderskaya observed me for two hours as I tested students on their theoretical and practical programme. The students expressed themselves extremely well. Those who had got their results remained in the studio and in the spirit of competition, gave competent answers from their course mates to my occasionally tricky questions.

During our report to Shatin on the tests in the affiliate, Isabella admitted: "Anatoly Vasilyevich, today I witnessed and evaluated the positive results of our project to raise the qualifications of amateur choreographers, which is down to Berkut's arrival five months ago. I thank you on behalf of the students."

As we approached the New Year, Milia went away somewhere with her sister for five days. I handed her written notification that if she failed to return within her promised timescale, I would take the children to their grandmother in Odessa for an indefinite period until the divorce came through. The boys and I spent the last three days of the old year in a marathon of trips between the Kremlin Christmas tree and *The Nutcracker*, or the zoo and the circus. Four-year-old Shurik slept on my lap on public transport, while the excited eldest recalled images of the fairy-tale episodes of animals and villains he had just seen, scaring the poor passengers in the metro. His natural theatrical genes shone through at an early age. We went to see Nikolai in Serebryanny Bor in the New Year. Each of us had a rucksack on our backs with a pair of ice skates and personal toiletries. Dad also carried a huge suitcase of clothes for all the musketeers. It was no small miracle that we arrived safely at the right place on the right day.

Nikolai gave us a really warm welcome with a little Christmas tree in the corner, under which intriguing packages beckoned. The main surprise was a small accordion which he had acquired in the government country homes club, on condition that I played a matinee free of charge for their children, dressed up as Father Christmas. It was an unforgettable holiday. We sang for ages and everyone danced in the crowded room while I played on. The musketeers slept side by side on the floor in sleeping bags on airbeds by the hot fireplace. The next day, after the matinee, we learned how to ski and slither around on skates. On the third day we went tobogganing down the hill and cantered through the snow on horseback. The fourth day saw us return home excited, refreshed and happy. Milia was already waiting for us with lunch, picking up the parental baton from me. The boys vied with each other to regale their mother with tales of their adventures. I declined to eat with them and hurried home to my place, so that I had time to prepare for resuming work after the winter holidays. I wasn't even interested to know who my wife's companion had been during the festive season.

A New Year's gift was waiting for me in the house near the Arbat. 'The Young Guards' publishers were now publishing my choreographic compositions on a contemporary theme every other month in their monthly magazine *Youth Stage*. Kaminskaya, the editor, had signed a contract with me for six miniatures a year.

1. 'Song of the Falcon' – from a collection of Maxim Gorky's poems.

2. 'Duel' (Inner Duel) – about Pavka Korchagin from *How the Steel was Tempered* by Nikolai Ostrovsky.
3. 'Future Pilots' – on a painting of the same title by the artist Deineka.
4. 'In the Name of Life' – about a War hero, the pilot Maresyev, on the story by Boris Polevoi.
5. 'Baltic Fleet Sailors' – on the Peacetime passenger cruise ship (forces and leisure).
6. 'Soldier's Friendship' – in military study and cultural pursuits.

After the second piece of work on Pavka Korchagin, an unfounded heckling comment appeared in the newspaper *Soviet Culture*, written by one Mr Rogozin, the author of Folk Dance descriptions for another rival publisher, which referred to his colleagues: 'Respected Choreographers, describe your fantastical, romantic ballets using fairies and princes, but don't bring shame on the names of Soviet heroes of the revolution and war!'

Kaminskaya, my editor, responded swiftly in the same newspaper: 'To the author of the last criticism of respected Choreographers: before displaying your impudence in Art, you should first acquaint yourself with the Ballet 'Youth' in the current repertoire at the Nimerovich-Danchenko Theatre (Burmeister's production) about the revolutionary hero, Pavka Korchagin. Please accept our sincere condolences.'

I knew nothing of this duel until I received information from my friend Isabella Sviderskaya. In her twenty-five years in ballet she had learned almost all the tricks of the theatrical world. Isabella then got in touch with the editor whom she'd known for a long time, and asked, "Since when have contemporary themes become unpopular in the Soviet press?"

Kaminskaya confided to her, "After the first work came out in January, a call came in for me from the Press Department of the Russian Ministry of Culture, recommending that I find a more established choreographer for this important project. Both party members from the paper and censors repeatedly consulted each other and sent in a joint official enquiry to the ministry: 'In connection with the fact that it is difficult to find a professional choreographer in Moscow who handles contemporary subjects, and taking into account the fact that there is an official contract with the writer for the current year, the editor must continue to honour the terms of the agreement.'"

Of course even a stupid bureaucrat wouldn't take on that kind of responsibility.

On learning that Milia was not working in her specialist field, Shatin organised for her to give a two-hour paid lecture at MTA on 'Author's Rights in Theatre Arts Production'. It was so well attended that they had to move the presentation into the assembly hall. The faculty's teachers/professors and future stage producers/ballet masters, as well as theatre critics, were keen to absorb some new information over the course of an hour. Then they put a range of questions to the lecturer, not always gaining the best response. The fundamental problem in establishing an author's right to a stage composition lay in the lack of any visual record of the original: in the stage producer's and actor's treatment of the image or movement and spatial patterns in choreography. Without convincing evidence of plagiarism, the law had no teeth in the face of the offenders. I changed the slides throughout the lecture, following Milia's signal. Summing up, Shatin thanked the lecturer to thunderous applause in the auditorium and wished her well in publishing as soon as possible her academic, legal ideas, which were so vital to creators of stage drama, opera, ballet and other theatrical genres. My mentor expressed his sadness at the family discord Emilia and I were currently experiencing.

"Misha, two talented personalities from different arenas cannot be on the same team."

"Alas! My dear teacher, I realised this a long time ago. But you can't turn back the clock!"

On our way home from MTA, my wife remarked sadly that Shatin didn't look well.

As the season came to a close, the whole of June was wildly busy. My first graduates from the Ballet Masters Department in the affiliate sat their exams at MTA with great ceremony. At the composition test by class some students brought participants from their own amateur activities, achieving a diploma production within five to seven minutes. The theme was 'Subject Dance, Ceremonial or Contemporary' (wedding, harvest, birthday or family drama, comic training, sports competitions, etc.). Upon successfully completing the year's course, the graduates received an official certificate of qualification as a leader of a performing dance group with the right to teach children professionally in clubs and general schools, on equal terms with colleagues on the academic curriculum. The diplomas were signed by Shatin and Sviderskaya.

Taking advantage of the favourable conditions created by the affiliate's successful graduation, Anatoly Vasilyevich gave the Principal another glowing reference about me, in the aim of getting me enrolled as his assistant, and once again, his request was denied. Zakharov had two assistants in his team, and Shatin did not have one. This was blatant discrimination regarding my candidacy and a deliberate and malicious continuation of the vendetta by the head of MTA against the Dean of faculty. I observed bitterly to my mentor that it would be better for both of us if I relinquished my role as Artistic Director of the affiliate in favour of a less troubled successor. It was clear to me that it was better to forfeit my pride and prestige than prolong the agony of disappointment endured by my dear and close friend and sponsor.

As the salutes resounded in celebration of the October Revolution at the end of the past year, I began a new programme with those assembled in the ZIL Cultural Centre ballet studies, not giving the dancers a chance to cool off following their achievements. In June, after six months of intensive preparation we put on two premieres at the Bolshoi affiliate ZIL: the opera *The Tsar's Bride* by Nikolai Rimsky-Korsakov and my ballet-concert *Poem of Man*. In the opera, our group from the 'corps de ballet' performed various dances, including the celebrated ceremonial suite, 'Yar-Khmel' (Spring Overture), accompanied by and with the participation of, the choir. A group of soloists presented my choreographic miniatures in three sections, under the energetic and highly competent direction of the répétiteurs Pestov and Lebedeva. Both shows/performances were repeated on Sundays on the Cultural Centre's large stage with an hour's interval between the opera and the ballet. However, dancers from both groups performed equally enthusiastically both times in the different productions to a rapturous reception from the public. Our work was quite highly acclaimed in leading theatrical circles and by the Cultural Professional Council. The director of the ZIL Cultural Centre asked me to come and see him before I went on leave. He thanked me for my excellent input and for achieving such great heights with our group.

With the backing of his leadership, Zhilin asked me if I would agree to head up the forthcoming All-Russia Amateur Artistic Show by workers in the car construction industry to celebrate fifty years of the homegrown patriotic car manufacturing giants: ZIL, GAZ, Rostelmash and others.

"The Central Committee of the department's trade union is offering you a ten-month contract, August to May, including flights on your free days to the main centres of industry with your panel members, and the production team for the final Gala concert. Your fees and business expenses will be covered in the contract. If you accept, you will be required to present a list of your collaborative partners in the various genres, and the total remuneration for you and them. It means considering important practicalities in making a success of this project."

I gave my agreement in principal, and promised Zhilin the necessary information for preparing and conducting the Gala show and concert in a couple of days.

Lena (Shatin's secretary) rang from MTA in March to report that Boris Chirtkov, former director of Moscow Youth Theatre (MYT), was looking to get in touch with me. I had assumed that he had already retired, so it was nice to hear that a veteran of the stage had remained in his post and was now doing occasional work in television. The Ideology Department of the Soviet Union Central Committee of the Communist Party, through the All-Union Board for Radio and Television, had offered him the opportunity to create a programme of satirical sketches, *Biting Times*, which would pillory the 'bourgeois vices' of drunkenness, yobbish behaviour, theft, and so on which were detrimental to socialist society. Boris Alexandrovich had discovered by chance that I was in Moscow, thanks to the negative comments directed at me by Rogozin in *Soviet Culture*. It's not for nothing that people say, "Every cloud has a silver lining."

My former production director and I greeted each other warmly after a ten-year gap. Flushing, he revealed to me his vision of this delicate, dangerous project. I confided in him my doubts relating to public criticism in the aspect of creativity which was out of sync with the method of Socialist realism demanded by the Soviet censor.

He responded: "Some people get away with not playing by the rules! The radio and television are the state organs for communicating with the masses. We are not planning to deride party, government or trade-union bodies, but just moral and ethical distortions in individual conduct and social flaws in society in various spheres of productivity and being: low levels of discipline, covering up infringements and bureaucracy, grovelling or palm greasing, personal insults, violence, and so on."

I listened to him and smiled broadly at this honest citizen's naïvety and innocence.

"Dear colleague, I agree with you. But I must tell you that I'm not a party member."

"I'm aware of that. I would take on all the political responsibility. Your task would be to work with my stage producer, using the screenplay to create a comic, ironic choreography to light music by a composer of your choice, and to help me select young actors who've been well trained in dance and mimicry, and to find the right style. I'm amazed that the three of us with the composer Yan Frenkel, have successfully put together the first *Biting Times* for over three months without being arrested for it!"

In presenting Zhilin with the information pack on the car-manufacturing festival for the Trade Union Central Committee at the ZIL Cultural Centre, I expressed my hope that he would oversee the event under discussion.

He nodded affirmatively and asked: "Mikhail, may I ask, why you haven't joined the party?"

"Vasily Ignatyevich, this is a serious step in the life of any artiste. It's not in my nature to be a card-carrying party member and call myself a communist, without being heavily involved in sociopolitical activity. It's impossible for me to combine this kind of activity with my overloaded creative practice. Both things would result in an inferior outcome. That's already been proven through my personal experience with the Komsomol. Working in the Odessa Philharmonic Society with the Lilliputians from 1949 to '50, we would be on tour for three to four months in different republics. I was expelled from VLKSM due to irregular payment of my membership subscription over two years.

In addition, I am a bull by nature and too straightforward: I speak as I find. I would be thrown out of the party after my first negative criticism of social disorders or national discrimination and they would be right to do so. People like me don't belong there. I prefer to remain a non-party patriot of my homeland, and do an honest day's work in my job, shouting about the achievements of the socialist system and images of Soviet people in my choreographic compositions, like *Stormy Petrel*, 'The Young Guards', 'Inner Duel', 'In the Name of Life', and so on."

"Well, that's your right. I'm often asked by the factory management and the trade-union committee, why Berkut isn't a party member. Now I'll know what to say to them. But if you change your mind, I will give you my personal recommendation as a member of the factory party committee. Misha, it's clear to both of us that working in a leadership position within the ideological arena of art and culture in a large company (around 140 people), half of whom are party members, without being a communist yourself, looks a little strange to say the least. You're off to Odessa on three weeks' leave the day after tomorrow. Think about what I've said at your leisure."

"Thank you for your advice and recommendation, sir. I'll reconsider my position. If the Trade Union Central Committee accepts my terms for Artistic Director of the Festival and of the Gala concert, I would like to sign a contract before I leave, so that I can start work on the project in Odessa. Please call me at home tomorrow and ask the Central Committee for some brief information for me about the history of Soviet car manufacturing with photographs of the construction models."

"I'll lend you my copy of the outline for the last celebrations, on the fortieth anniversary."

After my meeting with Zhilin, I went to explain the holiday situation to my sons. I waited on the balcony until they'd finished supper. The party membership situation was running through my mind.

The sound of my wife shouting and children crying from the kitchen/diner interrupted my musings. When he saw me, Dmitri tore himself away from his mother's grip and threw himself at me, his nose dripping blood on the floor.

"Daddy, Daddy! Take me with you to Odessa. I don't want to go to Slavyansk with Tanya."

"First let's get you cleaned up. Then we'll sort out our family business."

I shepherded my eldest into the bathroom, and wiped away the blood, squeezing his nostrils. I held a cold, damp towel to his nose and laid him down on the sofa in the sitting room, with his head tipped back.

"You can come to Odessa with me, if you can keep still until I come back from the kitchen. Otherwise, all your blood will run out and instead of going to Odessa, you will be taken to the cemetery. OK?"

My trembling son blinked affirmatively. My wife was comforting Shurik in the dining room.

"Why did you hit him? Why? Dmitri was right. I want to go to the seaside with Daddy too!"

"Milia, please tell me what's going on. Why is Dmitri's nose bleeding?"

"It's none of your bloody business! Or mine; we'll let the court decide. Just carry on doing your thing with your fucking ballet dancers, and we'll bring the children up here without any help from you."

Tanya was washing up in silence.

"If you don't stop swearing in front of the child, and don't explain your assault on our eldest, then I'm calling the police downstairs right now. I'll set up an official system with them to monitor your extreme behaviour with the children. I'll take a photo of my son's bruises. Shurik will attest to your vulgar language in front of him. I will demand that you are removed from them in the interests of their safety and well-being. At the same time, I'll report your sister for living illegally in this flat on an ongoing basis all year without a Moscow permit. So, I'll wait for one minute. You will have only yourself to blame for what happens next."

"Milia, explain to him. Things will get nasty for us otherwise, if he calls the police."

"Don't worry, sister dear. He's always bluffing like that, it's the pot calling the kettle black."

I returned to Dmitri to pick up my bag, and told him to wait for me without getting up, until I came back with the policeman to get a statement about his mother's thuggish behaviour. My wife, who had calmed down now, caught me in the doorway and invited me to take a seat in the living room.

"Let your son explain why he is rude to Tanya and calls her a bitch. I warned him that I would smack him in the mouth if he carried on swearing like that in front of Shurik. So today he got it in the face. But it was hard for me, punishing him like that."

"Dmitri, do you know the meaning of the word you used to your aunt?"

"That's what the older boys at school call the women who wait for their husbands on street corners."

"And have the boys explained why they are waiting there on the junctions?"

"Of course, to go to the cinema and then a restaurant with them, and spend all night kissing."

Milia's eyes nearly popped out of her head. She was clearly expecting a different answer.

"Sonny, Aunty Tanya doesn't wait for anyone on the corner. Why do you call her that?"

"Because at nine o'clock in the evening, when Shurik and I go to bed, there are men waiting for her opposite our house, across the road. Tanya waves to them from the balcony, like Romeo and Juliet in the film. Sometimes Mum goes out with Tanya and leaves us on our own. Shurik goes to sleep, and I watch them from the balcony until they go into the metro station."

My wife sat down, wringing her hands, white as a sheet, ready to explode at any second. Tanya stopped clattering about in the kitchen, eavesdropping on our conversation.

"Dmitri, it's not nice to watch other people. It's called spying on your parents."

"So is it nice for parents to wipe blood off their children's noses? Why do

Mum and Tanya always say nasty things about you and my Odessa granny? I miss Grandma."

"All right, lie still just a little longer until the blood congeals. Then we'll talk about Odessa."

"Milia, let's finish this conversation in the office in private, please."

"We can do that up to the point when you start criticising me; I admit that I lost control. I overestimated my capabilities, thinking that I could bring up my sons by myself."

"There's no point in criticising you, as you're incorrigible and not in a fit state to correct your mistakes even when you're aware of them. You continually use foul language in front of the children, then you're surprised when they swear. Today you gave your son a bloody nose. In a few years' time he'll do the same to you. We both need to take radical measures to avoid the moral and physical destruction of our children. If you have even the slightest drop of maternal sense left, don't bring your sons up to be against their father, who in the face of all the negative family circumstances, continues to care for them even at arm's length. It's cheap and vulgar on your part to use our children in the conflict between us, and enlist your sister's help with this. They are already mature enough to understand everything."

"You have thrown us to the mercy of fate and now you're blaming me. Do you call that fair?"

"There is no point in trying to resolve our relationship now. For the last ten years it's been pretty clearly defined. Tanya is stirring up your children against their father because she has none of her own. She lost her father at a young age, and wants your children to grow up as semi-orphans as well. Are you really so blinded by your hatred of me and my family that you can't see how we can affect our children in future?

"I have provided you with housing and possessions in Moscow. What more do you need? I turned a blind eye to my enemy living like a parasite in my house on my account, only because of her assistance to you in looking after the children and flat. Even this was of no value to you, and you carried on insulting me in front of our sons, due to my refusal to live with you. As a lawyer, do you call this justice? Accept the fact that we are incompatible and thank your lucky stars for their blessings in supplying you with a man that you hate. I didn't come here to argue but to collect the children for a three-week break at the seaside in Odessa. You are within your rights to come with them or stay here, as you see fit. But there is nothing for them to do in Slavyansk. I will release you from your maternal duties for your pleasure on one condition: don't bring men off the street in here. This is in breach of cooperative rules, not to mention morals. I will let the chairman know that we are away and ask him to let all the keyholders in the foyer know about this potential risk. You must tell me your decision today so I know whether to buy three or four tickets to Odessa.

"After consulting with her sister, my wife stated that she would not be coming to Odessa. I asked her to pack the necessary things for both boys into one suitcase and two rucksacks.

"I'll come tomorrow afternoon to check the contents and leave you your share of the monthly payment of 100 roubles for the time we're away from 10th to 31st July."

"This isn't enough. I need to buy some clothes and a train ticket to Slavyansk."

"I'm sorry, but I don't have any spare cash. I've suggested more than once that you set yourself up as a cultural worker in local children's organisations and cover your personal expenses, as you did before in Odessa and Leningrad, but you have not taken my advice."

"I don't need you telling me what to do. You are legally obliged to support me 100%."

"One hundred roubles is the average monthly salary for a school teacher. Take me to court and you'll soon find out how much single mothers get in maintenance compared to what you receive. I'm off to the station now to buy our tickets for Odessa and for my children's sake, will buy their mum a ticket to Slavyansk for 11th June, coming back on the 30th, if you are prepared to agree to that."

"Get your own ticket. I'll get by without your help. I've found someone who'll support me."

I advised the boys that tomorrow we were going to the Black Sea. A friendly 'hurrah' resounded in response.

Then Shurik asked: "Daddy, what makes the sea black? When we've had a bath the water's black too."

I remembered in time that Zhilin was expecting me at the ZIL Cultural Centre at 5 p.m. to sign the contract with the Trade Union Central Committee. He confirmed that he had designated an administrator for the duration of the Festival and Gala concert in the Cultural Centre. I left him contact details for members of the production-team staff: the Musical director Emin Khachaturian (All-Union Radio Orchestra), the producer Boris Chirtkov (Moscow Youth Theatre), Choirmaster Mikhail Kanterman and the Moscow City Cultural Centre specialist Isabella Sviderskaya. After securing their agreement in principle over the telephone, I proposed that they come to see Zhilin soon to sign a working agreement with the Trade Union Central Committee. My creative colleagues were happy at the opportunity to earn 1,500 roubles each for eight visiting consultations in car-manufacturing centres of the Russian Federation, and to prepare the Festival's Gala concert in May the following year. It stands to reason that my scope of work and corresponding fee were significant. Nevertheless, the high standards in the capital, on the one hand, and my non-party status on the other, required me to take on a serious weight of responsibility.

The kids and I had a fantastic break on the Black Sea. We caught the sun and returned to Moscow full of vim and vigour after our three-week estrangement from our usual world. As expected, our house was empty. Milia had not kept her word to come back from holiday in time for the children's arrival. That being the case, we went to have lunch at Rechnoi Vokzal.

"Have you been to Turkey to get that tan?" the key lady for the Cooperative building asked us downstairs.

"Almost. Opposite, across the Black Sea in sunny Odessa. By the way, would you happen to know where there's a children's summer camp in this area?"

"Of course. It's bus No. 7, the second stop. There's a pioneer camp and nursery for workers of the River Fleet. It's right by the river in the woods, it's a lovely spot. Your boys will love it."

"Thanks for the information. Follow me, musketeers!"

But there was no sign of them. The door woman laughed, looking towards the exit, where both warriors were hiding between the doors.

"Aaii, sonny boys. Where are you, stripy features?"

I walked towards the ambush like an elephant. Fearsome predators fell on me with wild cries from both sides. Terrified, I sank to my haunches with my head in my hands and began squealing immediately: "Help!"

The key lady was laughing louder than anyone, wondering who was in charge: the children or their father?

After lunch we caught the bus to the children's summer camp. A fairy-tale vista over a corner of the Moscow river extended in front of us, with white blocks of buildings between the pines and fir trees. The guard directed me to a small cottage, where I obtained all the necessary information. The last shift for children on holiday was due to start in a few days. I telephoned my friend Nikolai in Serebryanny Bor from Rechnoi Vokzal, the personal chauffeur of the deputy minister of the River Fleet, and explained the situation. I persuaded him to send a reference for me via his boss to the manager of the complex, with the aim of enrolling my sons for the last session. In return, I would train his pioneers to dance at the end-of-season concert.

"Misha, my boss and I are on leave from yesterday. I'll give him a call at his country house now and try to make an exception for my 'nephews', along with your choreographic offering. I can't make you any promises. Call me in half an hour."

We were in luck. Thanks to Nikolai, both rascals were accepted by the complex without any obstacles. Pending my wife's return, I was now free to get on with preparing the repertoire for my creative projects and organise the academic process in the affiliate ballet studio: timetable of classes, syllabus, students' locations and so on.

A week later on Saturday, the mother, who had now taken up drinking, reappeared.

"Where are my children?" she snarled menacingly, using attack as a form of defence.

"Where they should be in the summer holidays: having time out and enjoying themselves at camp."

"Don't bother to explain any further! I'm calling the police now to tell them that you have abducted my children."

"In the first place, they are 'our' children, not 'mine' as you refer to them, and secondly, I didn't 'abduct' them, rather, you abandoned them by refusing to come on holiday together in the south. And thirdly, I'd be only too pleased to have a meeting with a representative of the authorities to show them how we go about our parental duties."

"I need maintenance for August urgently; you are obliged to pay this on time."

"How does 'on time' work in relation to a mother returning from her gallivanting to her children who are waiting for her? I'll bring you the money after lunch today, at 2 p.m., and we'll have a serious talk about everything. Tanya, please go for a walk somewhere for half an hour. Milia and I need to talk in private."

"She's not going anywhere! I have no secrets from her and you can't boss her around!"

"In that case, I'll go off and if you need my help, you can come to me."

"Milia, don't make your life more complicated on my account. I'm happy to go for a wander near the house."

"You, my dear, need to learn some life lessons from your younger sister."

"I've had enough of your moralising. Leave this for your . . . I want to know, where are my children?"

"Our children are in the River Fleet pioneer camp, not far from here."

"You're lying. They are still in Odessa with your stinking relatives."

I paused for a moment until the stream of insults had washed over my poor head.

"Have you exhausted your putrid reserves of what you have to say? Maybe now we can have an intelligent discussion?"

Enraged, she sat down at the table, looking dishevelled in her dirty clothes. Her face was puffy, with dark circles under her eyes. I had never seen her looking such a mess.

"So, I repeat: the boys are spending time in the children's complex until 27th August. Like all parents, you can visit them on Sundays up to 12 noon or after 4 p.m. Naturally, they've been asking after you frequently, and were upset that you weren't at home when they returned from Odessa. I explained that Mum had got held up in Slavyansk. You didn't even make the effort to leave a note about the change of plan, or telephone the key lady downstairs. I don't ask you to account for your personal activities, but I cannot accept your lack of maternal care for the children. This can't go on. This is plain for all to see, but for the time being no one has said anything, either at home, school or nursery. I was naïve enough to assume that your sister would help you with the children so that you might be able to work mornings in your specialist field, but I was wrong. Tanya has had the opposite effect: turning you into lushes and putting the children at risk. I'm not trying to re-educate you, but I'm warning you for the last time: be careful!

"Here is your share of the maintenance for August: 100 roubles. I spent the children's money on their food, summer clothes and shoes, school stuff for Dmitri – everything that you were responsible for, as per our agreement. You, 'God's gift to men' preferred to join the young tarts. Look in the mirror and see what you look like. I hope that our sons will recognise their mother when you meet up with them tomorrow. Bus No. 7, second stop."

At that moment the keys scraped in the door. I grabbed them from Tanya's hands.

"My dear sister-in-law, you can't stay in our flat any longer, as you are an evil influence on the mother of my children. Over the next week you will have to move into a different place or go back to Slavyansk, either of your own free will or with police assistance."

"But I don't have any money for a ticket. Milia, what's going on? What have I done?"

My wife turned to stone at the table, her face in her hands. I hurried off to work at the camp.

At the ZIL Cultural Centre the Director unexpectedly summoned me to ask whether I knew Azarov.

"Yes, if you mean Azarov from the 'School of ballroom dancing' within our Cultural Centre. I even took some classes with him to gen up on Latin dancing while I was preparing choreography in the Contemporary Ensemble."

"Do you know the story of his conflict with Shkolnik, a ballroom teacher in Moscow?"

"Oh, he's a really unpleasant person. I overheard that he had slandered Azarov, as a rival in his field, and the latter was suspended from teaching for a while. This happens quite often in our theatrical world of dirty tricks."

"In 1962 after the June plenum on ideological distortion, on the basis of a school pupil's statement, Azarov received a two-year prison sentence for malicious propaganda of bourgeois culture (Latin dancing) in socialist society."

"Vasily Ignatyevich, I wasn't aware of this. But he still works with that Latin programme of Ballroom dancing, and is confirmed as competent by UNESCO. I have even included his ten-minute presentation on ballroom mosaic, comprising a Latin section, in the concert scenario for the Gala Festival. Perhaps I shouldn't have done this?"

"Mikhail, that's why I wanted to see you as a matter of urgency. Yesterday I was approached by representatives of our security forces, who know you from as far back as your studies at MTA. They asked me to arrange a meeting with you in my office tomorrow at 12 noon, without anyone else present. I suppose that it's about loyalty to Azarov again. Can you make it?"

I delayed my response, studying Zhilin's eyes carefully. My mind was racing.

"I agree. I'll come to your office at midday with a packet of biscuits and my will."

The Director ignored my joke, but shook my hand warmly. I left feeling flushed, a typical reaction in such circumstances.

One day I had asked Azarov in the Cultural Centre canteen: "Would you be able to put together a short suite of ballroom dances from the twentieth century?" I explained to him what I wanted to achieve, and Azarov had willingly taken up the challenge.

Zhilin introduced me to two KGB officials in civvies, and left us to it.

"Mikhail, we are sorry to be disturbing you again after ten years. We urgently need your objective, professional opinion on the historical nature of ballroom dancing. We are not art specialists. To avoid repeating mistakes we've already made in evaluating the ideological influence of choreography on the socialist cultural education of Soviet youth, we are asking you to explain to us in everyday language the origins of Contemporary Ballroom dances. In particular, we are interested in such modern examples as the Twist, Shake, Rock 'n' Roll, and suchlike."

"Usually a course of lectures on this theme is ten or twelve hours long. Instead, I'll try to summarise the essence of this form of social contact between people in ten or twelve minutes. I'd recommend taping this information on your audio tape so that it's easier to remember. Don't be shy, you can lay your microphones on the desk."

The men, smiling, exchanged glances and complied with my strange request.

"The basis of many Historical, Social dances is in the ethnic roots of Folkloric choreography in the form of ceremonial rites or entertaining contests. In the second form, besides sport and the circus, a particular type of intimate entertainment has gradually come into being at social festivities over the last century: dancing in *couples*. Not for the spectators, but for your own enjoyment in close physical contact with a partner like in the Waltz, the Tango and other similar dances. Yes! The stimulus for such close proximity is sex, and there is nothing wrong in this: it's just one part of human nature. In Europe and Central America, the relatively cold conditions force people to dance in costumes, which are very limiting of their partners' movements. In hot countries such as Africa and South America, ceremonial and socially entertaining dances are naturally performed in light loincloths or tunics. Even in compositions for couples, close contact between the dancers is out of the question due to the heat and moisture on the skin. That's why, in non-ceremonial entertainment, everyone improvises as a rule in dance, i.e. each in his own way, and this is natural for the conditions in the southern hemisphere.

"The movement of southern settlers to America and Europe in the nineteenth and twentieth centuries has, over the years, gradually levelled out the aesthetic foundations of cultures which have stagnated in both hemispheres of the planet. The assimilation of contrasting rhythms in music, vocal technique, dance movement and painting, has thrown a wide audience into confusion with regard to evaluating Artistic criteria of the arts in all spheres. Something similar has happened even in isolated Soviet culture. Naturally liberal expressions of emotion by African tribespeople who, paradoxically, were in harmony with the classical canons of Europeans, shocked the conservative critics and residents who were listening and watching. And as is always the case in such situations, anyone breaching the established moral code was subjected to repressive measures on principle: it's better to be over-vigilant than under!"

"Mikhail Semyonovich, thank you for the information. As Artistic Director of the car-manufacturing Festival, may I ask you to write us your personal critique of Azarov's current professional ethics, in his capacity as ballroom dancing specialist, with reference to his participation in the Gala Festival concert."

"I'll be happy to be of service to you in this way, if it will help my colleague."

At this point I wrote an official reference on the professional and personal attributes of the elderly master and talented teacher. After reading my account, Zhilin judged that Azarov deserved a gold medal. I had three chances to shape my associate's destiny:

1. Send him to Siberia again for longer.
2. Save him from further disgrace and suffering in his pensionable years.
3. Act like a prostitute: be on both sides, like a lot of people did at that time.

I chose the second path as I was certain that the KGB officials needed a 'scapegoat' to blame if the management was not happy. The fact that they were coming back to me after ten years, meant that I was the best person to justify their doubts about Azarov's political status. 'Might as well be hanged for a sheep as for a lamb.'

The Director considered my story. "Mikhail, you are playing with fire."

I had been celibate for almost a year and a half. My first tentative steps on returning to Moscow and the fiasco with the Bolshoi, the split with my wife, and emotional, psychological instability, put paid to any interest in women for a while, and as I suspected, the potential for intimate relations with them. Only after the successful debut in the affiliate theatre studio did I calm down enough to notice the second choirmaster in the opera, Yekaterina Ilinichna, who often looked at me with hungry eyes. She was intelligent, self-confident, and though not very beautiful facially, she had an extremely appealing figure, and was about five years younger than me. She was a loner, and didn't mix with anyone at work on a personal basis. One day after the show, we bumped into each other on our way out of the Cultural Centre, not altogether by chance, as it seemed to me. Nevertheless, as we were walking past the bar by the metro station, I stopped and made a chivalrous proposition:

"Madam, would you like to celebrate our successful show with a glass of wine?"

"I'd love to, but not here. Why give the students something to gossip about?"

"In that case, we can do this at my place. I live really close to here."

She looked into my eyes quizzically and remarked with a smile, "Mikhail, you are a dangerous womaniser. I am in your hands."

That marked the start of our mutually enjoyable romance, which lasted longer than I anticipated.

On the way to my house we popped into the late-night supermarket. I invited Katya to choose any eats and drinks that she fancied. I picked up a box of liqueur chocolates and we licked our lips in anticipation of the meal, hurrying back to mine. We laid the table together and without further ado, got down to eating and drinking. We joked and laughed as if we'd been close friends for many years. The lady proposed a toast 'to brotherhood', probably to check if I knew how to kiss properly. Both of us were skilled and practised in breathing techniques from class. For this reason, our first kiss extended into a lengthy fermata (pause). Finally, with much laughter, we tore ourselves away, spilling the prized drink. I carefully sat my guest on my lap, and she leaned tenderly towards me.

"Well, you're quite a mischief-maker, Misha the dancer. You've won Catherine the Great's heart with one glance," my languishing colleague kept saying in a velvet contralto between sips and kisses. Picking up on her female longing, I carefully removed her blouse. But she then stopped me gently with a kiss and commanded me kindly: "Mishenka, it would be better if you got the bed ready for love, while I take a shower, if you don't mind."

There was nothing for it but to follow the Empress's command without complaining.

My guest came out of the bathroom in my dressing gown, with tousled hair. I was clearing the table, and the sight of this charming fairy made my jaw drop and I stood stock-still with the plates in my hands. Katya inserted her vibrating tongue into my mouth, holding my neck with her bare hands. This was a mind-blowing kiss, sucking me in. The gown slipped off her shoulders. Venus pressed her virginal breast to her Cupid so tenderly that my outstretched 'wings' nearly dropped the crockery.

Katyusha (a diminutive of Yekaterina) caught the shaking plates from my hands just in time and kindly gave me another command: "Come on, heavenly slave! Now it's your turn to wash away your sins from the ballet."

I was convinced that this was a sweet dream, as all these goings-on seemed so unlikely. I pinched myself in one place and squealed with pain, assuring myself that what was going on was real. My visitor turned off the main light, just leaving the table lamp on.

Semi-reclining, (like Rembrandt's Danaë) the Tsarina stretched her arms out to me and sang quietly from Leshchenko's romance:

"Come to me, come to me quickly me dear! You are far away."
"I'm flying to you. I'm flying on the wings of burning love, my commander!"

Thankfully, the show at the Cultural Centre always took place on Saturdays, so we didn't need to rush off anywhere the following morning. My lady friend and I were paralysed by the delights of our intimacy, forgetting everything else, apart from one thing: to join together in the fruitful ecstasy of love again and again. In between, we drank wine and sang famous arias from Vertinsky's romances. Without words, I hummed the accordion part with the choirmaster, surprising the singer with my vocal ability.

"Misha, you've got an excellent ear for music. Do you play any instruments?"

"I play the accordion a bit, and am even rustier on the piano. It's all a very long time ago."

"I noticed a case in the corner. Is it a musical instrument or a sewing machine?"

We laughed, and clung to each other again, not wanting to let go, for fear of missing each other too much: two beings of the opposite sex with equal hunger and a natural need for spiritual and physical interaction. After this unforgettable night of impromptu love we started seeing each other regularly on Saturdays at my place near the Arbat, both feeling happy beyond measure.

The Director of the Bolshoi School sent a few young people to the affiliate who had not got through the auditions because of their ages (sixteen to eighteen). Musa Lebedeva (women's teacher) was delighted that her girls were receiving additional partners. Pyotr Pestov (men's teacher) was disappointed that he would have to torture himself again with retrograde material. I reassured him by filling him in on the decision of the director of the Cultural Centre to assign an additional number of staff to the ballet studio to work with a group of young adolescents combined with the younger boys (fourteen to fifteen). I managed to convince Zhilin that we needed to strengthen the male contingent in the studio in relation to the forthcoming centenary of Lenin's birthday. In a year's time we were scheduled to put on a one-act ballet to Beethoven's 'Appassionata'. Nikolai Rakhmaninov, the new teacher, was required to smooth off the rough edges of the raw granite of live dancers to perform the roles of revolutionaries over this period. I conceived this ballet as an anthem to the October Revolution, based on motifs from the French painter Delacroix's *Liberty on the Barricades*, using all of the men from the ballet studio.

At the same time, dramatic events were unfolding in the pioneer camp. I had arranged with the senior (youth) leader to do supplementary hours on Sundays at the usual time, only with the two eldest groups, due to the technical complexity of their repertoire. The parents were interested in watching what their progeny were up to at the camp. These rehearsals were not compulsory. Basically they were for those needing individual help to maintain the quality of the whole performance. Dmitri tried as hard as he could and even helped his classmates with their dance. After yesterday's confrontational discussion with my wife on her return home, I suggested that she visit her children today on parents' day.

Shurik asked me in the nursery: "Daddy, where's Mummy? You said yesterday that she had come home already and would be here today."

"Don't worry, sonny! I expect you'll see her after your quiet time."

My spouse turned up in the nursery during my rehearsal. Naturally, Shurik started to play up when he saw her, stating that he didn't want to stay there without her. She decided to take him home. The experienced manager invited Milia into her office and told her that she had no right to remove Shurik without his father's consent, as he was the signatory on the official documents for the children's enrolment here.

"This is the first time we have met you, and we have no wish to interfere in your relationship with your husband. You both need to come and see the camp manager tomorrow and leave a signed slip so that you can take your children out as you wish. As a lawyer, you will understand these formalities. Goodbye. Fyodor Ivanych, please see our visitor out," the manager said to the security guard, waiting in the doorway.

Stunned, Milia followed the doorman. On the way out she expressed the wish to say goodbye to her son, but it was explained to her that he was in class now and couldn't be disturbed. She had to take herself home.

After the rehearsal I was called in to see the senior teacher, the deputy camp manager. She asked her assistant to bring Dmitri from the second group.

"Comrade Berkut, one hour ago, your wife visited the nursery and tried to take Alexander home. But our colleagues refused to hand over the child and recommended the mother discussed this issue with the centre manager tomorrow. What's going on?"

"Your colleagues were right to act as they did. I'm sorry about what happened. My wife is psychologically unstable, and because of this she finds life difficult and causes unpleasantness to those around her, and her children in particular. Please forgive the inconvenience."

At that moment, Dmitri was brought in. He ran to me, grabbed my hand, and shouted: "Daddy, I don't want to go anywhere else at the end of the session. I'd rather run away into the woods."

"Hold on, my dear! If you're going to go to the woods, then let's run off together. I love the forest too . . ."

"You're always joking. I don't want Mum to give me a nosebleed again!"

"Calm down, no one is going to kidnap you. It's just a misunderstanding. In the worst-case scenario, if someone *did* want to take you away from here without my knowledge, you're already a big strong boy and know how to look after yourself in that kind of situation."

"Yes, I remember all the defence moves that you taught me when I was little."

With a smile, he and I exchanged glances. The senior teacher struggled to wipe the smile off her face.

"Dmitri, wash your hands, go and have supper and then off to bed. Goodnight!"

"Thank you, Daddy!" my son pressed his head into my shoulder and skipped off. I thanked the teacher for her prompt response and summed up: "I'll have a word with my wife now. She probably won't turn up tomorrow. It would be best if she came to the concert at the end of the season. Once again, please accept my apologies."

I was ashamed at washing my dirty linen in public. But Milia's behaviour was becoming so unpredictable that urgent action was needed to safeguard the children from her next outburst and the potential risk. I decided to take definitive and official action and fight fire with fire. As expected, the gallivanting sisters were nowhere to be found at home. I left my wife a note about my visit.

In mid-August I had a call from Boris Chirtkov. He asked if we could meet up to define the next subject for *Biting Times* which was going to be broadcast on television twice a year in May and December. I read out the screenplay to him and voiced my anxieties: "Don't you think that we're a little harsh about our shortcomings?"

"I've already been summoned by the party's Central Committee and expressed dissatisfaction about the extremely negative presentation of satire in the last programme. I explained to the censor that the title of our review is *Biting* and not *Good-Humoured Times*."

"Then change the name. Is that too difficult? Do it!"

"Misha, the prevailing wind at the Soviet Communist Party Central Committee has changed direction now. Mostly it's our last contract for the following year thanks to Lenin's anniversary. Let's say a gentle but firm goodbye by ridiculing state misappropriation and bribes."

"I'm not afraid of the Big Bad Wolf. I'll choreograph your whole dramatisation."

The ZIL Cultural Centre introduced itself to the Gala Festival of Car Manufacturing with four major groups: the Academic Opera Choir and

Symphony Orchestra with classical repertoire, the Ballet studio with Glinka's 'Waltz-Fantasia', Azarov's 'Ballroom Mosaic' and the Vocal Dance Ensemble TechNet's (technical staff club) 'Factory Suite'. All of these took part one way or another in the combined Overture and concert Finale. In the middle of September I began putting on 'Waltz-Fantasia' with both Studio groups which had a more complex choreography for the professional ones, and a 'corps de ballet' function for the pre-professionals. All four Teachers and Répétiteurs (two men and two women) sweated buckets, trying to teach the students waltz technique. As it turned out, this was no mean feat: eight months to master the style and manner of freestyle Waltz, and moreover in the 'symphonised' choreography of spatial patterns onstage. As the New Year approached, I put together a rough draft of all the separate parts of the ballet to Glinka's thirteen-minute symphony. I also completed a choreographic set of the 'Factory Suite' in the 'TechNet club'. Now the répétiteurs were required to test out thoroughly the synthesis of dance techniques with specific rhythmic sequences. Only after this groundwork could I get down to working on the symphonised choreography and the dancers' artistic expression.

At the next stage rehearsal for 'Waltz-Fantasia', one of the directors of Mosfilm (Moscow Film Studio) introduced himself to me and offered me (on Chirtkov's recommendation) the opportunity to choreograph the film *Pyotr Ryabinkin*. I agreed, but requested a meeting at his studio to find out about it in more detail. Grigory Finkelshtein scheduled a meeting for Monday at 11 a.m., and asked me to bring materials from my latest productions.

Around this time I also drew up a contract with Chirtkov for televising the next episode of *Biting Times*. The composer Yan Frenkel wrote a piece of expansive variety music for this occasion, using modern harmony in places, with syncopated rhythms in a satirical characterisation of a negative personality. This enabled me to present their stage forms more distinctly through choreographic devices, on top of the vocal quartet. The Director of television coverage was really satisfied with our creative trio's output, and passed on his sincere compliments during the broadcast.

Before the New Year, during a visit to the children, my wife announced that she and Tanya needed to go to Slavyansk as a matter of urgency, as their mother was seriously ill. She asked me for some money for the ticket. We looked at each other. I suspected that this was just another ruse to extort money, and said: "I won't give you any money but I'll buy a return ticket for you, and a one-way ticket for Tanya."

"I need extra funds for the holidays. I am a living human being, you know."

"I give you enough every month, including the cost of clothes for the boys. Look at them: dirty and ragged. Why don't you wash their underwear? Dmitri, when did Mum last wash you in the bath or shower?"

"I can't remember exactly. Last Sunday probably. Shurik is even dirtier than me."

"How many times a week or a month do you change your socks, pants and vest?"

"Every time we wash. Why are you asking me? Mum knows best."

The eldest left the kitchen, perturbed. Milia looked at me savagely, with red marks on her face. I went up to her and threatened her: "You are a criminal and don't deserve to be called Mother. The money I give you for the children, you spend on going out. It's beyond belief. What a disgrace! I will go and buy your train tickets now as promised: for one week from 28th December. If you don't appear on 3rd January, I'll apply for a divorce and put both boys in boarding school pending the court's decision. You have lost all sense of shame and pride. I'll bring the tickets in the evening and give you them once you've washed the children and put them in clean clothes."

When saying goodbye to us two years before in Leningrad, Sofia had generously offered: "Misha, if you ever want to spend a week somewhere with the children at New Year, remember the flat is at your disposal while we are on holiday in the Gulf of Finland."

I called her and stated that the three musketeers would arrive at her flat for the winter holidays on the morning of the 30th. So it would be better for her to take herself off somewhere during this time.

She screeched with delight, frightening her husband and son with her impetuous reaction: "Guys, did you hear that? Mishka is coming with his rascals for a week without his wife. You big-nosed devil! What have you been up to?! We were only talking about you the other day. We can't wait to see you. As always, I'll leave the keys with the caretaker and make up the children's beds."

I charged off to the station again (Leningradsky this time), and was just in time to buy tickets for the sleeper for the evening of the 29th. As soon as the boys found out that we were going to spend the New Year in Leningrad, they were so happy that they bounced almost as high as the ceiling. We went to Detsky Mir (Children's World) department store together to buy gifts for ourselves and our Leningrad family. Naturally I spruced the hungry beggars up and took them to the barber's for a haircut. To cut a long story short, I transformed the scruffy monkeys into neat and tidy little boys. At the same time, I made myself look more youthful just in case. Who knows?

After some consideration, I telephoned Larisa.

At the sound of my voice, she asked guardedly: "Misha? I thought you'd forgotten all about me. Where are you phoning from?"

"From Moscow at the moment. Tomorrow I'm coming to Leningrad for the holidays with my sons. I would love to meet and catch up, if that suits you?"

"I'll be available from 30th December and of course I'd love to see you. Is your wife coming with you?"

"I'm living separately from my family, and just visit my children once a week. Write down my telephone number. If you change your mind, please just telephone my cousin. I won't be upset."

"Why don't you just telephone from your cousin's when you get here and we'll sort out a place to meet. See you soon!"

I replaced the receiver with an unpleasant feeling that I was intruding boorishly into a stranger's life.

At 9 a.m. our relatives welcomed our invasion with warm embraces.

Sofia was astonished: "My little boys, you're so tall already! You're growing like billy-o."

"Aunty Sofia, what's 'billy-o'? A tsar's carriage with horses or . . ."

But our hosts' friendly buzz drowned out Shurik's curious enquiry. Arkady took the young visitors off into his room to regale them with his stamp collection. I made the most of a free moment to call Larisa from the sitting room.

"Misha, if it's OK with you, let's meet at mine today at 8 p.m., like we used to in the good old days. I hope you remember the address. The bell is at the front door, No. 4."

"Great! On condition that I bring something to drink and some goodies from the Elysian shop."

"Misha, who do you think you're dealing with here? Breakfast is included."

The three musketeers were trying to outdo each other around the table, telling their stories about ballet, television or the River Fleet pioneer camp. After breakfast, my cousin explained the sleeping arrangements during their absence over the next week, apologising for the inconvenience.

"The two nights while we're still here, Toptygin, you will have to sleep on the floor on a mattress."

"My dear cousin, you already know that I've always enjoyed sleeping on the floor with some beauty or other. So today I'm partaking of it in another location, and tomorrow I'll be with you if Boris has no objection."

"You are so rude!" The hostess thwacked me with a tea towel and threatened to tell her husband on me.

Hearing his name, he came out of the office smiling.

"Sofia, why are you attacking the man after his long journey? Give him a chance to get his bearings!"

"He's already got too many of those; he's just told me that he's spending tonight somewhere else."

"That's how it is for a single man. He should know where and with whom to spend the night."

"You men are all the same, as soon as a woman shows you a bit of leg."

Once the boys and I had finished decorating the Christmas tree, I asked the lady of the house where the zoo was. She explained that it was a long way away and difficult to get to.

"Boris is just going off to check on his factory [he was factory director] for a few hours. He can take you and my Dmitri to the zoological gardens and pick you up from there at 5.30 p.m."

The kids had a fabulous time looking at unfamiliar insects and reptiles. They returned home worn out, but happy. On the way, Boris took an interest in the Moscow cooperative and seemed satisfied with its financial status. I thanked him again for transferring my credit from one cooperative to the other, and invited him to come and stay.

Sofia was working as deputy manager of the Elysian shop. She called her assistant and asked her to have my order ready for 7 p.m. Before going out for the evening, I told my sons that I was going out on an 'urgent task' and would be back by lunchtime the next day. They promised to obey Aunty Sofia and not to be rude to her son Arkady, who had a tough dad with a big belly. They chuckled in response, and Boris shook his fist at me.

Crossing St Isaac's Square, I recalled my first amorous encounter with Larisa. The details of that memorable evening came flooding back as if it were yesterday. The four years since then had flown by. We had both changed. A female figure 'like a vision of pure beauty' appeared in the doorway at my timid ring.

Taken aback, I feasted my eyes on this fairy-tale sight, and after a significant pause, asked: "I'm sorry but may I please see Larisa, my former bosom pal and true friend?"

She laughed and opened her arms to me. We kissed three times on the cheek as Russians do.

"Welcome, my former master and kind-hearted protector!"

My hostess accepted my gifts and took them into the kitchen. I put my bag down and wandered around the sitting room, taking in the photos on the walls. Suddenly, I caught sight of my own portrait next to Sadovskaya, an enlargement of a small photo. I froze.

"Those are the leading lights in my life," Larisa explained, laying her head on my shoulder.

I was rooted to the spot, and put my arm around her waist. I was suddenly engulfed by sadness for all that I had lost.

"Misha, today is the first day of the holidays and I've been cleaning all day and missed lunch. Let's go to the Pelmeni café next door for a hot snack and then come back here."

As we enjoyed the dish that I hadn't tasted for some time, I was interested to hear all the news about the College of Performing Arts, Mariinsky Theatre, Maly Opera Theatre, Trade Union Ensemble, etc.

"After you'd gone, I continued as deputy head of the Dance Department in the College of Performing Arts. They took on a ballet master/teacher from the Institute of Culture as the new artistic director. The Director only realised at that point what we had lost in you. He made desperate efforts to develop my qualifications, sending me on summer courses with choreographers in the Conservatoire, and seminars with leaders at Leningrad City Cultural Centre and the Institute of Culture. He insisted that I took over completely as Head of Department from 1st September. You gave me more hands-on input than any of my teachers, not just in terms of professional knowledge, but you helped me to consolidate my own spiritual foundation, which was completely missing before."

"I imagine you're exaggerating. No teacher would have been able to make you into what you've become without the talent, energy and sense of purpose that are there in you."

"Thanks for your kind words, Misha. Let's carry on talking at home."

The champagne made us a bit lethargic. As we sat on the sofa, Lara turned over and lay down across my knees, her face towards me, and gave me a puzzled look.

"My wise master, you have more experience than me. Please tell me why life happens like this? A woman spends half her life looking for a suitable friend and colleague. But when she finally finds him, she loses him to circumstance?"

"Darling, I've been searching for the answer to this question for a long time, without any conclusion. Most likely, fickle Fate enjoys playing with people in this way, and no one has the strength to counter her. Somewhere in the depths of truth this is how things have to be. Sometimes it is better to have loved and lost, than not to have loved at all."

"I missed you so much at first. I thought I was going mad. Making a portrait of you made it easier, as it looked like you were here next to me. When times were tough I complained to you or asked your advice, and this was helpful."

Throughout the evening she kissed me on the lips just like before. I purposely didn't take the lead, not wanting her to think that I had only come here to sleep with her, although I did want to very much, I have to admit.

Lara understood that I was being delicate in my approach after a long absence. She carefully took off my jumper, unbuttoned my shirt and unexpectedly, proposed a toast. I recharged our glasses and we clinked them together.

"I want to drink to love rather than loss. Even if it's short-lived!"

And we came together again in a honeyed kiss. We had broken through the barrier of our protracted break. The partners enjoyed intimate relations on their lovers' bed for what seemed like an eternity. At midnight we took a shower together as we used to and sat down at the table to refuel after our energetic orgy.

We ate and drank, laughed and joked, forgetting all about our circumstances. We just had a great time together. Once back in the sacred bed, we repeated the different moves of our sensual duets over and over, until finally holding each other close and still for several hours.

On waking up, Lara asked: "Excuse me, but who are you, and how did you get here?"

"I'm a portrait from your wall that's come to life. And who are you?"

"I'm the owner of this portrait and now I'm going to hang him back up on the wall."

"I beg you; don't do that, my dear lady. I prefer to hang on you."

We laughed and romped like children, until we could resist each other no longer.

Over a late breakfast, Lara looked so tranquil, but was suddenly serious: "Mishanya, why can I still feel something big and hard inside me?"

I nearly choked on a piece of tasty cheese. We giggled so much that the windows vibrated. My friend sat on my lap and slapped me on the back, until the cheese flew out and landed right on the plate. Wiping away tears with a serviette, I confessed: "Now I know why I love you so much."

"I'm curious: why?"

"Because you're a maniac from Leningrad."

"And you're a clown from Odessa. That's how it is."

This was a lovely release of our professional and personal tensions over the last few years. I left Larisa my home address in Moscow and invited her to come and visit in the next holidays, promising that I would treat her like a queen: take her to shows, museums and other diversions. She promised to think about it. As we said goodbye, we looked each other in the eyes for a long time, not knowing when, or even if, we would meet again. I sighed deeply and stepped out of the doorway with a bow. Just like the first visit five years before, I crossed the courtyard without looking back, feeling her eyes on my shoulder blades.

I got back home in time for lunch with the family, and asked my cousin how the children had been.

"They were asking me about your 'urgent job', and when it would be finished. I told them that it depended on how attractive and appealing the 'urgent task' was."

"Aah, we get it now. Only once he's speared his enemies with his sword."

"Where are my musketeers now?"

"Boris, go down and get them from the games store! Misha, your little one was asking after his mum today. Dmitri reassured him, saying that she will get back from Slavyansk on the same day as you do from Leningrad."

"Sofia, forgive me, I'll be in your sitting room for half of tomorrow night."

"The Christmas tree's in there. You can sleep in Boris's office, my little tramp! Look, your boys are back."

"Dad, Dad! How did you get on in yesterday's battle with the crusaders? Who won?"

"As you can see, I am still in one piece. It's just that my legs are giving way for some reason."

My hosts burst out laughing at once. My cousin took the children off to wash their hands. Boris poured us a glass each. While the boys were splashing each other under the tap in the toilet, he and I indulged in the hair of the dog.

"Misha, sorry to ask, but have you joined the Communist Party now?"

"No, Boris. I'm not going to do so now. I've picked up some additional work and have to confess that I'll barely manage to get it all done for everyone on time, without taking on an extra burden in the community."

"Sofia and I have been thinking about you. You are gaining in status in Moscow, just as you did here, and sooner or later, in order to maintain your position, you will have to join the ruling party, otherwise you could find yourself in a Leningrad situation all over again. If you need it, Sofia will recommend you, in her capacity as party organiser at the Elysian."

After lunch I decided to take a nap along with the children, to freshen up for New Year's Eve, but I couldn't get to sleep. My conversation with Boris was preying on my mind.

After a noisy New Year's Eve, my hosts went off to the Gulf of Finland for their customary holiday. The kids and I entertained ourselves by doing the tourist trail in the winter holidays. Thanks to our good fairy, the fridge was stuffed with all imaginable treats for breakfast and supper. During the day we had lunch in the city and came home for an hour's snooze. Naturally, at this time, as ever, I took advantage of the chance to prepare my Moscow programmes in Boris's office. At 4 p.m. we would go out again and would have completed our 'working day' by 8 p.m. The boys were tired but not worn out. Dmitri was so used to looking after Shurik, that he often anticipated my reminders and sometimes my forgetfulness. Shurik respected the eldest. He complied unconditionally with his advice and requests. Dmitri exerted a kind of patriarchal power over the youngest. But sometimes I had to stop him from behaving aggressively as his patron. I said to him more than once, "It's six of one, half a dozen of the other."

We got back to Moscow without any hassle. This time their mother was ready and waiting for her little guys. I left her some money, and reported back on what I'd bought the children. I reminded her that the boys would need a bath in a day's time. In answer to this she gave me a snide smile and nodded. I felt that all my paternal efforts were evaporating into thin air. I had such a lot of work lined up for the next six months that I had to draw up a finely tuned timetable of my activities.

Naturally, the Gala Festival concert absorbed most of my attention. I raced from the TechNet factory club to the ZIL Cultural Centre Ballet studio at 6 p.m. At 8 p.m. I left there for a rehearsal with the opera vocalists or the choir with the affiliate orchestra. Only after that, at 10 p.m., did I meet up with Azarov in the Ballroom school, to help him with the choreography for his ten-minute review. My colleague and friend Katya (the opera choirmaster) could see how overloaded I was, and tried to help me with domestic chores at weekends: housework, shopping, etc. I was really grateful to her for such friendship and care.

At the Mosfilm studios they helped me to find the film crew for *Pyotr Ryabinkin* and the Director's office. Grigory Arkadyevich introduced me to Kirilenko, the regisseur (Production Director). They had gone to some lengths to swot up on my file, and asked whether I had worked in film before.

I answered that I hadn't: "Only in television: two years on the series *Biting Times* with Boris Chirtkov."

"Yes, the TV guys recommended you, as did Pokrovsky and Sviderskaya. We've been looking for a choreographer for a long time, and have compared various candidates. We liked your 'Waltz-Fantasia' by Glinka, who is similar in spirit to the hero of the film *Pyotr Ryabinkin*. We'll present these materials to our management and let you know their decision. In any case, we'll return your resources to you, with the reel of *Biting Times*."

One week later, the film people left an envelope for me at the ZIL Cultural Centre.

I read through the film studio contract a few times. I noted a few questions I was unsure about. The legalities didn't always make sense to me. Prior to meeting the film crew, I popped into a legal firm to see a lawyer I knew. He clarified the terms I didn't understand and only charged me twenty-five roubles for half an hour, as a favour.

As we were about to sign on the dotted line at Mosfilm, Grigory Finkelshtein warned: "Mikhail, from your experience of contracts in your group productions, you are no doubt aware of the 10% compensation for the unforeseen costs of your administration during preparation for the Festival. I am banking on your prudence and our shared understanding on this issue. Of course this is strictly confidential, just between us."

I was stunned by such a cynical demand for a bribe, but replied after a moment's reflection, "Evidently I'm no novice in the show production and often pay 'unforeseen costs' from my own pocket, such as the post-concert meal. But what you're asking for, just to avoid any misunderstanding between us, could be construed by authorities' inspectors as a bribe, and you and I would be behind bars."

"Misha, it's not done in film studios to lay on a thank-you meal once the film's made."

"I'm not a party member. If I break the law, it's easy to make mincemeat of me. I have no intention of risking my name or liberty. Come up with a safer version of compensation for unforeseen costs for me, and I'll gladly sign the agreement, under which you will be obliged to: pay me an advance of 25% of my fee on signing the contract, 50% on completion of my basic choreography for 'Waltz-Fantasia' (according to the producer's wishes), and the balance of 25% on finishing the film. On that note, let's sign."

The film director laughed openly at my lack of business sense. He asked: "Mikhail, you weren't born in Odessa by any chance, were you?"

"Not by chance, no, but on purpose, yes!"

"How's that? I've been to Peresyp countless times and never came across Mishka from Odessa?"

"Because I was actually born in Moldavanka and lived there for twenty years. Anyway, let's get back to business!"

"OK, Comrade Ballet Master. You've convinced me. I propose that we sign the contract."

We shook hands and sorted out our copies of the agreement. Then Grigory took me to see the film equipment, Stage Design Department, and other parts of the film studios. He introduced me to the main production committee. An elderly secretary wrote me out a pass for the year and wished me luck. I bowed in grateful thanks.

"Grigory, where do you find such polite young people these days?"

"From Privoz in Odessa, if you're acquainted with the pearl of southern aristocracy."

In the last episode of *Biting Times*, Chirtkov included family conflict, street fights and the bribery system. He directed the last mimic scene in a comic genre himself. I choreographed the rest in grotesque style: a sentimental quartet with two couples, flirting with other peoples' partners in secret, plus an altercation between policemen and yobs, alternating with a dance contest between them. Yan Frenkel was on good form, and had written a fantastic piece of music for the farewell review. We were sad to leave all those in the production team. We had found a way of bringing *Biting Times* to a smooth end, and were amazed at how long our creative friendships had endured. This was a blatant contradiction of the socialist realist method in art, and sooner or later, I would have to give up my fragile existence as a satirist and troubadour. Alas, that's when critics of social disadvantage learned the hard way. We all gave the artistic director, Boris Chirtkov, a standing ovation, for his courage in swimming against the tide.

I was certain that my personal file in the security services was full of unremittingly negative information. For this reason, I went to great pains to demonstrate in my work the positive principles of socialist morals in the subjective sense of the term. But it didn't always tie in with what was happening on the ground around me, which was full of social vices: falsity, corruption, embezzlement, and so on. A party membership card in my pocket would have forced me to take on everything as part of my formal role, and like other society members, become an active part of this totalitarian system of state management and learning, cultural education and social life. This went beyond my spiritual principles in life. I decided not to change anything about myself for the time being. In the overture and finale of the Gala concert I passionately proclaimed the achievements of Soviet car manufacturing over the last fifty years, both in the text of the lead readers, to the accompaniment of the academic choir and symphony orchestra, and in the dance movements of the entire show. The grand finale embodied the triumph of heavy industry in the country of socialism and drew forth a thunderous response from the ZIL Cultural Centre audience. At the end of the concert, Zhilin organised a decadent buffet for the management (which came out of my fee). The company leaders and members of the cast congratulated me in the foyer and were pleased with their success, which was a great honour for me.

The last year, as a result of overwork, a punishing routine and poor diet, had aggravated my stomach ulcer. I was tortured by heartburn. I went to my doctor, stating that I was being burned alive, and asked him to put out the fire inside me.

"I can't see any smoke yet. I advise you to drink a bottle of Borzhomi (soda water) every day."

I decided to go one better than the doctor and drank not one, but three bottles of this mineral water daily. A month later, the heartburn in my stomach had developed into acute pain. I returned to the doctor. He sent me for all sorts of tests and said to come back in a week's time.

In reception, he asked: "How many bottles of Borzhomi are you drinking a day?"

"Three," I announced proudly.

"But I only prescribed one. You are killing yourself! By adjusting the doctor's orders, you have reduced the acid in your stomach to zero. Now you must reverse it and increase your acidity to normal levels, which will be much more complicated in restoring your health. Here is a prescription for Bull's stomach acid, which is not exactly pleasant, but please take just one and not three tablespoons per day. And don't get any wild ideas about choreography! 'A little knowledge is a dangerous thing.'"

The doctor was right. From that moment on, my stomach would not accept anything apart from cream cheese with milk twice a day. I was wasting away by the hour rather than by the day. Thankfully this happened in June, after all the shows. I telephoned Mum in Odessa and bearing in mind my illness, apologised that it would not be possible to come for the summer holidays. She insisted that I leave the children with Milia and follow a course of treatment in a local sanatorium.

"Your nanny will have you back on your feet again in no time. Do as your mother says and you will always feel better." During the war this was her favourite declaration to her sons.

We both laughed.

When I saw my family on Sunday I decided to advise them of a change of plan. But my wife was a step ahead of me, announcing that she was going off to Slavyansk with the children for the whole of the summer. I was surprised and pleased in so far as this fitted in with my need to recover. I was anxious that all my creative projects, which had to be completed in the autumn, would fall apart, and as a result, I would face scandal and disgrace. Initially, the children were disappointed at the prospect of a holiday in the country, but cheered up when they heard that near the house was a lake that they could cycle to and swim in. It's true that every cloud has a silver lining!

Before my departure south, the Artistic Council of the Bolshoi and affiliate studio convened in the ZIL Cultural Centre. The scores for the opera *The Decembrists* and the ballet *Appassionata* were ready for the orchestra. The soloists and choir had learned their vocal parts. The 'Ballroom Mosaic' had been arranged for the opera. After my holiday I was planning a choreographic montage of excerpts from the new ballet. Both premieres were scheduled to be completed over two months ready to be performed at the celebrations of the October Revolution in the first week of November. I wasn't worried about this timescale, as I had already put on all the episodes from *Appassionata*: solos, duets and groups, in the spring. The teachers/répétiteurs had perfected them quite well to piano accompaniment. But the orchestral rendition of the piano original always requires the Ballet master to make some adjustments to the choreography and execution. I was confident that I would be able to resolve this issue with the help of my assistants. The director of the ZIL Cultural Centre asked me to stay behind. Aware of my treatment in Odessa, he wished me well and reminded me again about the problem of my not being a Communist Party member.

"Mikhail, I will defend you as far as I can, but you must understand that I am not omnipotent. Senior management above me has warned that if you don't make the right decision by the time of the celebrations for Lenin's birth, I will have to look for a new ballet master for the affiliate."

I only slept one night at Mum's place in Odessa. Nanny Sasha invited me to hers for the evening.

She listened carefully to my account of my illness and declared: "Mishanya, I think I can help you if you can have faith in folk medicine and find enough patience in yourself to continue the treatment until it is finished."

"My dear Nanny, I am in your hands. Just tell me, what does this course of treatment entail?"

"Tomorrow you and I will go to Bugaz together. Volodya [her husband] will order approximately 200 kilograms of fresh cabbage. They will deliver it to us in a van straight from the field and put it in the cellar. We have an old juicer, which Volodya will use regularly to make you cabbage juice. This course of treatment will take two weeks. On the first day (let's say, Monday), you will take one glass of juice in two sittings: half in the morning and half in the evening. Each day you will increase the dose proportionately by one glass and the number of sittings during the day. In this way you will get up to seven glasses per day.

"On the following Monday you will start to reduce the dose by one glass every day, until you get back to one glass in two sittings on Saturday. In these two weeks you can continue your normal diet: cream cheese with milk three times a day, on condition that it's one hour after drinking the juice. The treatment ends there. All through the following week you can eat pickled cucumbers and fresh fruit in addition to the cream cheese with milk, but in small portions. During the course you must not do anything strenuous or lift heavy weights. You must lie down more and walk slowly on the seafront or paddle in the sea. After the third week you can go like the clappers."

"Nanny, here is some money to cover expenses. I'll pay you and Uncle Volodya for your labours later. Let me know when they're bringing the cabbage and which day we will be starting the treatment. You know how much I appreciate your endeavours to get me back on my feet."

"And you, my son, also know, how happy it makes me to treat my surrogate child."

Once back in Moscow, I made a beeline for my doctor, as I had promised I would.

Seeing how radiant I was, he asked in astonishment: "Is that make-up or natural?"

I took a paper napkin from his desk and wiped my face carefully.

"How strange!" joked the doctor. "You left green and you've come back brown! All right. Let's do some tests and have a look at what's changed internally. Come back in two days' time. Don't eat anything apart from cream cheese and drink a lot of water – natural rather than Borzhomi."

I was frightened to tell him about the treatment I'd followed, as homeopathy and alternative medicine was not officially recognised by the Soviet authorities. When we next met, the doctor apologised for the negligence of the lab assistants, who had got my results mixed up with those of another patient. He asked for them to be done again and a day later telephoned me in a panic, telling me to present myself at the polyclinic as soon as possible, with an empty stomach. I understood that I was not long for this world!

At the sight of me, the doctor asked when I had last eaten.

"This morning, tea and a biscuit."

"Is that all?"

"Yes!"

"Bloody Hell! Then here's where you go for an X-ray. They are expecting you. The radiographer will give you a photo for me and you must bring it here right away."

In the X-ray room I was given Milk of Magnesia to drink. They took the photo and five minutes later handed me the film for the doctor. The doctor turned the negative over impatiently and hung it on the screen next to the old photo. He spent ages comparing the two negatives.

"Where has your ulcer gone? Own up, who have you given it to?"

"I'm sorry, Doctor! I'm guilty for not telling you about my course of homeopathic treatment in Odessa last month. You would not have believed me."

I recounted the details of Nanny Sasha's old folk remedy. The elderly doctor listened attentively to my account, continuing to study the X-rays. Suddenly he slapped his forehead, finally finding the answer to this tricky riddle.

"In all probability, at first the strong acid in the cabbage gradually licked the damaged mucous membrane off the stomach walls, forcing the organism to create a new, protective and stimulating plasma through its naturally healthy immunity, as in the stomach of a newborn baby. Dear Mikhail, I will forgive your dishonourable behaviour towards me, if you allow me to carry out a gastroscopy of your stomach in the university Medical Faculty, as an educational exercise for the students, where I teach diagnostics of internal organs."

Naturally I agreed. Fortunately, I had forgotten all about my ulcer (physically speaking, at least).

At the beginning of August, Finkelshtein from Mosfilm called and invited me to a meeting with the production team for *Pyotr Ryabinkin*. Seated around a large table were the screenplay writer, operator, designer, composer and other members. Kirilenko, the Director, informed those present about the progress on preparing the film sets, completing casting, and confirmed the timetable for the film's release in May of 1970, i.e. in twenty-two months' time. He defined the timescale of work for the actors and film crew at the base and on location. From 1st September, I was down to work five days a week from 9 a.m. to 1 p.m. with the producer on the stage positions for leading characters and the spacing of auxiliary groups. Included in my basic brief was the creation of individual moves and forms for the central heroes, following the script and the stage patterns the Director gave them, plus the rhythmic/mimicking choreography for the entourage of leaders taking part in their dynamic crowd scenes. I have to admit that I was fascinated by such creative improvisation at rehearsals. The actors had spent all spring working at the table on the script with Kirilenko. Now they were collaborating with the regisseur (Production Director) and choreographer, incorporating their own personal register and style in the graphic design of characters before those or other suggested circumstances and taking into account individual physical attributes.

Over the next three months, the producer and I completed a rough first version of rhythmic movements in the studio for scenes in the film. I could only attend the location shoots on Sundays, which was rather inconvenient for the Director. He only called me in on weekdays on exceptional occasions and only if absolutely necessary. At the beginning of December, Finkelshtein asked me (by telephone) to come in with my passport.

Naturally I was wary, and asked as I entered his office: "Director, what has happened?"

"It's nothing to worry about, my dear ballet master. I've authorised 50% of your fee. When you signed the contract six months ago, you asked for an advance of 1,000 roubles of your agreed fee. As you will recall, I did not have the authority to satisfy your request and as an alternative, offered you this sum as a loan from my personal funds on condition that you would return it on receipt of your fee."

You're a rogue, I thought.

"You are giving me a backdated receipt now for the total amount owing. Each time you receive part of the fee (advance or payment) you will pay me back half of the debt and I will confirm this with a corresponding receipt in your name. Will this be acceptable to you?"

"Absolutely. I must say, Comrade Director, you are an excellent businessman."

"Thank you. I'm putting the invoice in the safe. You know where it is."

I came away with the money. We exchanged receipts for the payment and went our separate ways without further pleasantries.

As I left the film office I felt a bit sick, as if I'd trodden in some muck.

I felt that I was becoming psychologically unwell. On the one hand, it was clear even to a fool: 'One cannot conquer alone.' On the other, I didn't have the strength to trample on everything that I'd held dear for thirty years.

I remembered that in similar difficult circumstances, the best way out of a spiritual impasse is to plunge yourself into work, to avoid having time for unproductive and dangerous thought. From the first week of September, I threw myself into the depths of creative activity: Mosfilm in the mornings, and the ZIL Cultural Centre affiliate after lunch.

My friend Katya paid me a compliment: "Misha, the Black Sea has a positive influence on you. You've come back to work with excess energy. Sometimes I think you've brought back a little bit of aggression too. It's probably just something specific to your character and the Taurus sign."

"Thanks for your kind words, Katya."

At the beginning of November 1969, the Bolshoi affiliate 'sputnik' celebrated the anniversary of the Revolution in two ways: with the one-act ballet, *Appassionata,* to music by Beethoven, and a two-act opera by Boris Shaporin entitled *The Decembrists.* We performed this combined programme several times to great acclaim from the press and gala judges. Sviderskaya gave her official endorsement of *Appassionata* for the Gala concert in April 1970, on the stage of the Kremlin Palace of Congresses. The general management of ZIL expressed their thanks to all affiliate leaders for the excellent aesthetic education provided to their young ZIL employees. Zhilin was presented with an award for 'Excellence at Work'. Mosfilm contacted him to seek official permission to use Berkut's production of Glinka's 'Waltz-Fantasia' from the film recording of the Gala Festival of Car Manufacturing, for their new art film *Pyotr Ryabinkin*, guaranteeing to include the ZIL Cultural Centre in the credits. The Director naturally consented to the free advertising for the Cultural Centre's activities, and confirmed this in writing. This is how I secured my author's rights for services to Mosfilm.

When I next visited my family, I warned my wife that in relation to the forthcoming Lenin anniversary, I would have to stay in Moscow for the winter holidays, and could take the children to Nikolai's in Serebryanny Bor just for five days, from 30th December to 3rd January.

She replied, disgusted, "Anything's better than nothing."

The inquisitive Shurik asked, puzzled: "Mummy, I understand that you are the female sheep, so does that mean that Dad is the wool?"

Dmitri fell on to the sofa with a thud and laughed as he pulled his legs up. I could barely contain myself. Milia opened and closed her mouth a few times. Instead of giving the youngest a response, she moved into the kitchen. Poor Shurik didn't understand why everyone was reacting so strangely to his question. I went up to him, slapping the eldest on the bottom on the way.

I explained: "It's just an old folk saying: for a hungry man even a hunk of black bread will seem like gingerbread. Kids, do you like the idea of spending the New Year with Uncle Kolya in the woods?"

"Yes, yes! We went sledging there and learned how to skate and ski. Hurrah!"

I telephoned Nikolai to let him know we were coming. He apologised for not being able to have us, as his cousin and her daughter were coming to visit. A friend of his offered me the use of a holiday home in the closed zone of government country houses, where his boss lived. It didn't cost much. If I agreed to play Father Christmas for them at the children's matinee, I would probably get the accommodation and food for all of us free of charge. He asked me to call back in half an hour. Following discussions between Nikolai and the deputy manager of the Club and chairman of the village Council, I was offered a room with three beds for five days including food, in return for not one, but two, matinees for preschoolers and school-age children in the role of Father Christmas. I was happy to agree. The government zone included a luxurious children's playground with hills to sledge on, figure skates – everything you needed for a action packed winter holiday with young children. Kolya noted my measurements for the Father Christmas costume and footwear, and I promised to bring my accordion. He reminded me to take my passport and the children's birth certificates, work permit and residence details. Knowing how bureaucratic the system was in the zone inhabited by members of the government, I drew up a list of telephone numbers for my places of work, school and nursery. Armed with all this, the kids and I set off for the resort. I didn't believe that I, with my complicated personal life, could be so lucky. We were welcomed with open arms at Serebryanny Bor.

Only now did I understand the essential difference between the lifestyle of government ministers' families and us – mere mortals. I guess that's how it has to be. For this reason I didn't mind too much about such comfort and luxury.

During the morning of the 31st, to the delight of all children in the settlement, including mine, I played my accordion around both Christmas trees in my role as Father Christmas and distributed festive gifts to the noisy children with a charming Snow Maiden. After lunch, while my little chaps were sleeping, I washed away all my sins from the old year. Only then was I in the right mindset and physical condition to see in the New Year, 1970. The club and children's playground were 150 metres from our cottage. The kids were running in and out without a coat, in ski suits and hats and scarves. For a few minutes I enjoyed watching the musketeers amusing themselves with the various attractions, until the cold suddenly propelled me into the bar to warm up. During our frequent outings, I would always find in my pirates the same inexhaustible enthusiasm for diversion. Then I would get fairly tipsy in the bar from multiple warm-up sessions. At 6 p.m. the cafeteria assistant announced the start of the children's New Year's supper. The adults were saving themselves for their midnight feast. After their food, I washed and changed my sons, then we made our way to Nikolai's house across the forest.

"Are there any wolves here?" asked the youngest.

"Only pigeon-toed teddy bears," the eldest replied.

"Are you talking about me, Dmitri?"

"No, they don't dance like you. Much better."

Shurik burst out laughing, forgetting to be frightened. I shone the torch on the path in the darkness.

Five minutes later my old friend met us in his hallway with sparklers. Shurik was shy and hid behind me. Dmitri had already come across this phenomenon and accepted the sparkler from Nikolai unperturbed. The youngest watched warily from behind my back. I introduced the lads and myself to the guests, and Kolya produced his cousin Agrippina and her twelve-year-old daughter, Masha. Dmitri placed the gifts we had brought for everyone under the Christmas tree. Our host offered us tea and cream cakes. The boys looked at me, waiting for the signal to start. Masha smiled, observing their behaviour. Mother Pina (diminutive of Agrippina) poured tea for us all. Kolya poked the wood in the open fire. It was a veritable 'country idyll', just like one of Perov's paintings. I put a pastry on each son's plate in timely fashion, and kept a close eye on both rivals to make sure that they were not sneaking a bite. They kept their heads bowed modestly in an effort to conceal their hungry eyes.

Finally, our host gave the long-awaited command: "Ladies and gentlemen! Tuck in! Happy New Year!"

We had barely managed to clink our glasses of champagne before both troglodytes on 'ready, steady, go' had gulped down their 'prey' whole, licking the cream off the end of their noses with long tongues. It's easy to imagine the challenge the young brothers had set themselves, watching other people's leisurely pace in devouring the pastries.

In fact, Nikolai had had the foresight to make a booking for four at the banqueting hall in the club. After the tea we popped into our residence in the village. Kolya and I had to show our passes to the policemen on the gates. In unison we wished the strong arm of the law a happy New Year. I put the children to bed and suggested that my friend showed his relatives the local sights until my little 'saplings' were asleep.

I took Pina to one side: "If Masha gets tired after seeing in the New Year, bring her here and put her in my bed. There are clean sheets and towels in the cupboard. Make yourselves at home."

'Thank you, Misha, that's very kind. We'll see how she goes."

After seeing my friends off, I sat down on the edge of Shurik's bed in the darkness and reflected again.

The officials were all seated at individual tables in the banqueting hall, separated from the others. Their families, friends and personal guests, apart from me, were dispersed around the banqueting hall at long tables of twenty people. The flow of hors d'oeuvres and drinks continued non-stop until midnight. When the Kremlin chimes rang out at midnight, everyone stood up and wished each other happy New Year to the clink of glasses. While we were waiting for the hot dishes to arrive, I excused myself and ran out to check on my 'Sleeping Beauties'. Pressing my ear right to the keyhole in the cottage hallway, I could hear even, heavy breathing, and raced back to the dinner table. An hour later, after the gluttony had got under way, some of the guests started to sing in different harmonies. The club director approached me and asked if I would accompany the singers and those wishing to dance. Nikolai held up his hand in protest, but I stopped him with a look and asked for an instrument, on condition that I would play for two hours at the most.

"The complete menu is available to the four of you, free of charge."

The Director signalled to the waiter to bring an accordion. Pina and her daughter were amazed to see me as musician. But once they heard 'Korobushka', they joined in the popular Russian tune with everyone else around the table. So I played requests, moving from one table to another, and accompanied singing guests between toasts until they cleared the tables away.

At 2 a.m. Agrippina asked me for the keys and took her daughter home to bed. Kolya explained to me why she was single, and asked me not to bring it up with her.

"Her husband was a policeman. He was killed in a clash with an armed gang. She can't contemplate getting married again. She's devoted herself entirely to her daughter and elderly mother. I've talked to her about you many times. I even offered to get the two of you together once I discovered that you were living apart from your family. But she just waved her hand, saying: 'I'm not interested in chance encounters with men. There's only one man on my mind.'"

They had started dancing to recorded music in the hall. When Pina came back and returned the keys to me, I asked her for a tango. She declined, on the pretext that she had forgotten it all.

"Pina, what are you worried about: Misha is a decent man and won't embarrass you."

"But I'll crush all his toes. How will he be able to dance his ballets after that?"

I took her hand and led her into the throng of dancers. I held her by the waist and pressed my abdomen to hers, as is the style in tango. Pina just sighed. My timid partner was light on her feet and a smooth mover. She picked up my sequence of moves and pauses. She quickly became accustomed to being in close contact with me, and stopped feeling inhibited. Friends took Nikolai off to the bar. Pina let herself go. Occasionally in a slow dance she would press up against me or lay her head on my shoulder. I assumed she was remembering her late husband.

She glanced at her watch: "Misha, I'm sorry, it's time to go. If Kolya's friends are getting him drunk, I won't get him home."

My friend was already 'merry' in the bar. His cousin pulled him away from the counter and asked: "How much does he owe you?"

"Nothing. The Director gave him the nod today."

Kolya and I waited outside while Pina woke, dressed and brought out her sleepy daughter. I saw them to the gates and wished them a happy New Year.

The woman embraced me, kissed me three times and whispered: "Thank you very much, I enjoyed it so much."

"Misha, come round for some borscht tomorrow afternoon with your musketeers!"

"OK, we'll attack your fortress at 1 p.m. Best to surrender to captivity now!"

On 3rd January the refreshed boys returned happy to Rechnoi Vokzal. Complete chaos was waiting for us at home. I purposely didn't touch anything in the flat. I fed the boys and put them to bed. Tanya's suitcase had reappeared in the kitchen.

After midnight the sisters showed up completely drunk. I went to leave without saying a word.

"Where's my January money?" the mother started yelling, getting all worked up. Naturally, the children woke up.

Dmitri came out of the bedroom: "Dad, what's happened?"

"Nothing new, sonny. You are back in your dirty, disgusting home. Go to sleep. As for you, respected mother, from today you will get your money by post."

"You fucking scum! I hate you so much!" screeched my irresponsible spouse.

I went downstairs and asked the key lady to call the police urgently regarding a rioting drunken woman, who was a threat to her children's safety. Then I sat at her desk and wrote a statement addressed to the chief of the local police about my former wife's systematic failure in her maternal duties, leaving the children unsupervised for the night, hitting them until they bled, and mentioning the fact that her sister had been living in the flat illegally for the last two years. The duty police lieutenant checked my passport and sons' birth certificates. The key lady confirmed that I owned the cooperative flat and that the drunken women had returned home recently. He took my statement and went up to our home with a colleague.

I was shaking in the taxi home. I couldn't believe what was happening.

In the morning, I called a lawyer I knew, and briefly outlined the crisis in my family. I asked for his urgent advice on how to proceed.

"Mikhail, it's not in your interest to file for divorce now. Let's wait for the outcome of the police intervention. She has the upper hand over you: two children, problems in finding work, superior legal education and your absence from the family home."

As a Moscow City Cultural Centre specialist, Sviderskaya did not include me in the jury for the current competition to commemorate Lenin, as I was presenting my own production for judging, and consequently, not entitled to criticise others. Again, she strongly recommended that the director of the Gala concert include *Appassionata* in the programme, which had been created specially in honour of Ilich, and which had received glowing reviews in the press. The first planned version of *Appassionata* featured as the prologue. In the second version, it had vanished completely from the programme for unknown reasons and without any explanation. Isabella decided to involve the director of the Cultural Centre in this exceptional case; he was a member of the ZIL Party Committee on ideology.

A few days later, Zhilin called me in and anxiously imparted some news: "Mikhail, we were due to show the committee *Appassionata* again and at the same time, your three miniatures on a contemporary Soviet theme, in case we needed to replace the unwieldy *Liberty on the Barricades* with a more light-hearted composition like *Stormy Petrel* to Rachmaninov's music. When's the best time to show this in our Theatre?"

"Vasily Ignatyevich, forgive me, but who is this whole fiasco for? 'No to this, no to that!'"

"Well, it's not all about you, it's about the reputation of your group and the factory too, for that matter."

"You are right. Mid-February, if that's convenient, in line with the agreed plan."

"Good, I'll check the theatre schedule and let you know once the regional committee has confirmed."

The dancers took this news quite calmly. They were even happy about revisiting the miniatures that they hadn't performed for a long time. I was perturbed by their anxious looks, which followed me around the Cultural Centre.

At home, Katya asked me in a state of panic: "Misha, what's going on at the Centre? Lots of people are spreading rumours and there's a hush when you pass by, like in some cheap vaudeville. Are you having problems with the management?"

"No, darling. I guess it's just the usual tittle-tattle and hot gossip. Still, Katyusha, I'm afraid that under these circumstances it will be better for us to stop seeing each other for a while until things die down in the Cultural Centre. It looks like my wife has written a complaint to the Professional Committee about my lack of consideration for the children, and been keeping an eye on our time together. I don't want to put you in the spotlight of public opinion."

"I suppose you're right. This is unpleasant news to me. I will miss you."

I accompanied my upset lady friend to the metro station and expressed my regret again.

The teachers/répétiteurs and dancers at the affiliate understood the responsibility in showing the group's choreographic work to the committee. On 17th February, the fateful viewing started with miniatures, followed by *Appassionata* twenty minutes later. Sitting in the box by the producer's control panel, I was genuinely proud of my semi-professional artistes and their highly qualified trainers. The show went off impeccably, in spite of the empty auditorium, which was closed to the public. Making up the specialist committee were Golovkina and Sviderskaya, the artistic director of the private view and chairman of the Ideology Department of the Soviet Communist Party Central Committee, and the leadership team of the ZIL Cultural Centre. They all headed into Zhilin's office to discuss the display, and invited me to join them. The first to share their highly professional opinion on the choreography and its performers were the director of the Bolshoi School and the Moscow City Cultural Centre dance specialist.

The Artistic Director of the Lenin Commemorative Festival stated: "Without a doubt, the compositions that interested me, *Appassionata* and *Stormy Petrel*, conform to the idea of the Gala concert and are extremely impressive aesthetically. The problem is that the first is too big for the concert programme, and the second – with four dancers – is not substantial enough for the prologue. I can't make a conclusive decision right now, I need to give it some consideration. I'm sorry, colleagues, you can only use the third part of the sonata – four and a half minutes – for the prologue."

Next, the chairman of the Ideology Department of the Soviet Communist Party held the floor.

"Mikhail Semyonovich, in the programme's epigraph for your miniatures *Poem of Man*, you use the poetic appeal from the German philosopher Goethe: 'A man is only worthy of life and freedom if he fights for them every day!' In the ballet *Appassionata* to music beloved by our Great Leader, you have set motifs from the painting by the French painter Delacroix, *Liberty on the Barricades*, which has nothing to do with the Great Leader's activities. Please explain: for what or whose freedom are you battling for with such fervour?"

"It's Potskin from the Central Committee's Ideology Department," whispered Zhilin, who was seated next to me.

"Comrade Potskin, I am no broadcaster or researcher, I'm a Ballet master and choreographer. I express myself artistically not through words, but using the human body in movement. Everything that I sincerely wished and tried to convey in my productions, I have completed quite confidently through choreographic means, resulting in critical acclaim from the press. If you didn't see this in the work we have presented today, then please accept my deep regret at the pointless waste of your time. Forgive me, but I have to leave you as my ulcer is flaring up. Thank you for your time, comrades. I wish you all the best!"

As I left the office, a deathly silence from all those present followed me.

Once I was home, I lay on the sofa to collect myself after the shock in the Director's office. My thoughts were racing, preventing me from focusing on any conclusions.

So, I need to find a new job from September (permanent or temporary) outside of Moscow.

A telephone call penetrated my musings. Sviderskaya was concerned about my health. "How are you feeling, free thinker? You scared everyone, leaving like that. The artistic director of the festival said that in view of such uncertainty, he can't use the ZIL ballet at all. Your opponent was content with this decision. Golovkina admitted that she didn't understand anything that was going on. She asked me to say hi. Zhilin has decided that every Saturday from 1st March until the end of April, he will introduce opera and ballet on to the large stage at his Cultural Centre. I too, following his lead, am organising regular concert dance ensembles in the capital in honour of Lenin's anniversary, featuring prizewinners from the last show on the city's top stages. So don't be miserable. There is lots of work on offer for you and your charges over the next two to three months in the Bolshoi affiliate."

"Thanks, darling. Sorry, but I can't talk to you on the telephone, particularly about personal matters. Let's meet up and I'll fill you in on what you still don't know about my work."

"OK. Pop in and see me at Moscow City Cultural Centre at 6 p.m. and we'll go and sit somewhere in some godforsaken place."

"Right, Misha, out with it! What are you keeping from me?"

I told her about the repeated attempts by Zhilin, under pressure from those on high, to sign me up to the Communist Party and about my being out of sync with the theatre/studio manager, where many of the cast were communists. "Obviously we're talking about permanent work as a member of staff, not a one-off event."

"What nonsense! Most of my leaders in Moscow are not party members. Perhaps there are some other reasons at play: family, staff, personal? Have a think."

"Over the last two years at MTA, Zakharov has reacted aggressively to Shatin's efforts to take me on as his assistant. Vartanyan from the Ministry of Culture hates me, from way back during my diploma ballet at MTA on the theme of India. Yesterday at a meeting in the ZIL Cultural Centre, Potskin from the Soviet Communist Party labelled me an enemy of the Soviet people. My wife is plotting against me because I don't want to live with her."

"That will do. That's already a colourful bunch of enemies, desperate – I'm afraid – to drop you in the shit. Nevertheless, you have a solid circle of friends and colleagues, including Shostakovich, Khachaturian, Pokrovsky, Chirtkov, Shatin, Zhilin, Golovkina, Goleizovsky and me. Don't panic! If there weren't any scandals in art, no one would ever get born."

"That's why I don't want to expose my friends, if I am going to continue to work in Moscow."

As I still bore the scars of being personally lynched, I decided to stave off becoming financially bankrupt as a result of the creative embargo in the capital. The closest boundary to Moscow remained a possibility. Boris Chirtkov promised to recommend me to his friends/colleagues in the drama theatres in Suzdal, Pskov and Novgorod, as choreographer for new pieces at the beginning of the following season (in three months' time).

My next problem lay in securing my cooperative flat. The chairman assured me that it was possible to pay the monthly instalments immediately for the whole year in advance, to avoid any breaks in payment. My entire film-studio advance went into this. I didn't panic. On the contrary, I surprised myself with my self-control and rational approach. But panic would no doubt set in sooner or later.

It never rains but it pours. At the beginning of February I had a call from Lena, Shatin's secretary, who passed on some tragic news: Anatoly Vasilyevich had died yesterday of a heart attack. This was a crippling blow to me. I couldn't move. My eyes misted over.

"Bastards. They still had to finish off a real diamond: an honest and good man."

"Yes, Misha. You have lost not only your faithful mentor and sponsor, but a close friend, spiritual father and teacher. Hang on in there, my old chap! Have a glass of water."

I telephoned his widow to give my condolences.

"Thank you, Mishenka, for your warm words and for sending us your book. Anatoly always took great pleasure in his students' achievements. You know very well how long they'd been persecuting him. These last few years he had designed his next course which was due to start in September. Around New Year, the Principal warned him that he should retire on 1st August, while specialists older than him were working on the senior staff. Anatoly really struggled with this scandalous injustice, until his heart gave up."

At the public memorial service in the MTA theatre auditorium, I approached the deceased and lightly touched his arms crossed on his chest.

"Farewell, my dear teacher! Your soul will never die in the consciousness of those for whom you illuminated the creative path in your eternal search for truth and perfection."

Arriving home, I wrote an obituary for the *Izvestia* newspaper:

> We are in deep mourning for the malicious murder of a dear teacher, Anatoly Shatin, at the hands of enemies of the people. He founded the Ballet Masters' Department of MTA in 1950. His blessed memory and his invaluable contribution to Soviet culture will live on forever in our hearts.
> Your students kneel before you.

I asked the cooperative secretary to type it up in return for a small payment and send it by telegram. She carried out my request and brought back the receipt from the telegraph office. I realised that I was making a dangerous mistake, but at that moment, was unable to act in any other way.

By 1st March I had been working for a further three months at the film studio. Paradoxically, I found my safety valve here in refining the actors' movements and choreographing the group scenes. I was so engrossed in my work that I forgot about the pressing problems in my personal life during that period. Dmitri learned my telephone number off by heart in secret and would telephone me from a call box at the metro station on Sundays. He was eleven and a half years old. He would pop out for bread and milk by himself now, play football with the boys and eye up the girls. My closest neighbours would laugh, warning me that I would soon be a grandfather. The eldest told me about the visit by the police in the night following my statement.

"They quoted the law about Mum's drunken state and the dirty flat. They asked me how often my mother left us alone at night. I answered: nearly every Saturday. The policemen confiscated Tanya's passport and took her off to the station. Mum had a row with them. It was only because of us that they didn't lock her up."

The opera and ballet shows in the ZIL Cultural Centre were an exceptional success. The Director finally achieved his dream of initiating car workers into the world of classical art, and giving members of the working class an aesthetic education. He was proud of this. Zhilin was in my eyes an exception to the many party, administrative leaders around me.

When we said goodbye, he admitted: "Misha, I seriously understand your disappointment as an artiste and your reasons for declining my recommendation of you to the party. Nevertheless, I am surprised that with all your patriotism and capabilities, you haven't found a route to political compromise on this issue."

"Vasily Ignatyevich, it's hard for me to convey in words how grateful I am for your understanding of my spiritual perspective. I take pride in the fact that I was able to work with you. I will always remember how kind and patient you were with regard to my personal difficulties. My sincere thanks to you for everything that you have done for me. Goodbye."

As I was clearing out my literary textbooks from my office at home, I chanced upon a strange, non-standard publication of Boris Pasternak's *Doctor Zhivago*. I had heard about this banned book, which had won the Nobel Prize, but had forced its author to leave his great motherland. Before kicking up a stink, I familiarised myself with the content. Over two or three evenings I avidly devoured 250 pages and understood why the writer had provoked such indignation from the censors and global interest from readers in the new novel.

I asked my wife: "How could a forbidden piece of literature be in my office without me being aware of it?"

"Tanya brought it over last year. There's nothing terrible in it. Don't go on about it!"

"What other kinds of diversions has this piece of trash organised with your help against our interests? Return this book to her and let me in on your secret about other banned things in our home."

"I'm tired of your suspicious mind. Leave me alone."

"If your sister turns up here again, I will take this book to the police station as I am not prepared to take responsibility for your crime and disorder."

When Dmitri asked me what was up with me, I explained that I was going to Odessa to recover. The sleeper train was a good place for self-analysis, my search for new creative objectives and potential pathways to for achieving them.

During my stay in Odessa I decided to devote my time to completing the extended project for publication of my next collection of choreographic compositions, *Dancing Girls*. The art publishers had officially commissioned this book from me the previous year. But because of all the preparations for Lenin's anniversary, I hadn't as yet had time to write it. The editor had postponed the printing deadline by six months. Now circumstances were forcing my hand. I had planned to include a description of three folk stage dances with drawings of figures and diagrams of their spatial patterns onstage.

1. 'Ganzya' – Ukrainian solo dance, to the music of a popular romance.
2. 'Katyusha' – A Russian dance: quartet to the well-known tune from the Second World War.
3. 'Lyana' – Moldovan group composition to music from the song of the same name.

These dances were conceived and produced in various genres: lyrical poems, dramas and comedies. All three works at festivals were celebrated as prizewinners or competition winners. On my return to Moscow, I spent a week working on the graphic design of the book, and this time submitted my work to the editor on schedule.

The good news was that my book *Dancing Girls* came out in print at the end of 1970. I have to admit that I hadn't imagined that the censor, following such political faux pas, would allow my work to be published, let alone with a print run of 100,000. How could my 'good sponsors' permit such a slip, after I'd 'made an enemy of my homeland' at the same time as enjoying such popularity in the Dance world across the country? They probably just included me on the blacklist of practitioners circulated to local Theatre boards, but had forgotten about the danger of 'anti-Soviet propaganda by the damned choreographer' in the press. It was easy to envisage what sort of 'incentives' the poor art editor had received for publishing me, and the spreading of creative output by a banned author. They could not have foreseen the sheer volume of sincere complements and gratitude I was to receive from professionals and dance aficionados in years to come for this piece of literature, addressed to Moscow City Cultural Centre from all the union's European republics. Sviderskaya rang and began to congratulate me, but I interrupted her, reminding her that my birthday was only in May. She chuckled, realising that I didn't know yet that my book had been published. When the penny dropped, I shouted out "Hurray!" and promised to bring a bottle of champagne into Moscow City Cultural Centre. My sons were very proud of my success. My wife chose to ignore it. I dashed into the bookshop and bought all the twenty-odd copies they had. At home I signed them all and sent them to all my closest friends and colleagues.

Eventually I was invited to meet the chief producer of the Suzdal Drama Theatre. I signed a contract for one production in the first instance, on a trial basis. After getting to know the troupe at rehearsal, viewing their show in the evening and making the last train back to Moscow, I was feeling a bit more relaxed. During the hour-and-a-half-long journey, I read through the materials for the work I was planning, and familiarised myself with the musical accompaniment, visualising how the forthcoming production would look. The drama in question was on the contemporary theme of Soviet astronauts' conquest of space. Fantastical creatures from other planets also featured in the play. The production was planned for a children's/young people's audience and did not present any particular difficulties for me in terms of choreography as I had already amassed a wealth of stage experience on the theme of space. I just decided to supplement the existing score by adding Shostakovich's music for fantastic dances.

There were a few days left before beginning work in Suzdal. It was impossible to prepare for it in my domestic set-up so I decided to go to Kolya's for this period in Serebryanny Bor. His cousin Agrippina answered the telephone.

"Misha, Nikolai is no longer with us. We buried him the day before yesterday. I'm here to sort out his things, as the Housing Office needs to take back the flat by 1st September."

I listened in shock, unable to say anything. Finally I managed, "Pina, would it disturb you if I came over for a couple of days to visit his grave?"

"Of course not. On the contrary, it would make it easier to have someone here with me."

I grabbed a bag and hurried off to the metro station, reappearing less than two hours later at the cottage that I had known for so long. Pina greeted me without saying anything, holding back tears, and offered me some tea. Pulling herself together, she recounted the tragic event.

"Kolya had been drinking a lot recently. Because of this, he was sacked as a chauffeur a year and a half ago and resumed his former duties as a signalling technician for the River Fleet. He was on his way home one night in the staff cutter, when he fell into the water in a drunken state and drowned. They found him three days later. He was buried with honours in the local cemetery. After lunch we'll go and see how he's settled in there. May he rest in peace!"

On the terrace I set myself up to prepare my new choreography. But I couldn't concentrate on composition due to thoughts of my lost friend. With enormous difficulty, I forced myself to programme the scripts/scenarios, analyse the new music, and carry out the preparatory technical work to compose the movement narrative. Pina was cleaning the flat behind me, and packing up boxes of rubbish and possessions. I could hear telephone calls through the terrace windows and her conversations with those who were ringing. In the end, she invited me to have lunch with her.

I proposed that we drank to his memory, but she declined, shaking her head: "Not now, thanks. It would be better in the evening, after the cemetery. I still have work to do."

We walked the two kilometres to the cemetery along the forest path. My friend's cousin laid flowers on his grave with its temporary sign. She poured some water from a bottle, crossed herself and got up off her knees.

"Let's go, Misha. It'll be dark soon and there are no electric lights here, or candles."

The grieving woman took my hand. We advanced silently along the compacted path, nervous of treading on the squirrels that darted between our feet. The stupefying aroma of pines and fir trees provided an ironically lyrical note. I wanted to express my delight in the nature around us, but didn't dare to disturb her mourning. As we drew near the house it was completely dark.

Agrippina turned to me unexpectedly. "Mishanya, hold me, please, like you did when we danced the tango together."

For a moment, I was taken aback, but feeling warm hands on my shoulders, I held her around the waist and squeezed her tightly towards me: one palm in the small of her back, the other on her buttocks.

She sighed deeply and stuck her cheek to my neck, cooing tenderly like a dove: "God, that's so lovely! Don't let go, my dear! Hang on to me a little longer!"

We walked the rest of the way home like a young couple, embracing and holding each other tight.

Together we quickly laid the table and drank to the dead man.

"May God rest his soul! Though actually his short life was good for nothing."

His cousin was referring to the homosexual side of Kolya's existence. At first she had thought that I was batting for the same team. But in the dances at the New Year's ball, with my strong legs intertwined with hers, she felt something different, and realised she'd been mistaken.

"Mishanya, take a shower while I clear up here, and then I'll be right behind you, OK?"

This woman was clearly used to being in charge in her home, and so it was here too. However, I was happy to obey her instructions. After freshening up, I transformed the already open sofa bed into a bed of pure white. I pulled my pants out of my bag and lay down in anticipation of the dessert to come. Agrippina came out of the shower room wearing nothing but what she was born in, with her hair let loose, She had the fine figure of a mature woman: average-sized, bouncy breasts, a plump, round bottom, a comparatively slender waist, which made me move towards her. Looking at her body, I would have had her down as a sportswoman rather than an office worker.

As she came nearer to me, the Amazonian smiled so sweetly that a Satyr almost jumped on to her. But I pressed my indomitable weapon of love between her legs, an aristocratic gesture to invite the charming lady to share the love bed with me. She no less graciously surrendered to my embrace. We progressed further as one indivisible whole to paradise on the wings of Cupid or the Devil. Women think that only men always want to, and that they are doing us a great favour by giving themselves only after showing some resistance, without any particular desire for intimacy in sexual contact. I'm willing to swear that it was the other way round that night. Starved of sex after a break of several years, she broke free of the chain imposed by long abstinence. She could not satisfy her hunger for passion and ecstasy. After her husband's death, the poor recluse thought that she would never again experience happiness as a woman and resigned herself to chastity. But nature had reclaimed one of its own as she made up for lost time. She demanded sexual satisfaction over and over again until completely exhausted. It's best not to remember how the poor satyr kept his reputation.

My little dove cooed on my chest: "Mishenka, I beg you, stay another night. Don't cut short my sweet dream."

"I can't stay for one, but two is no problem. How can I refuse the goddess of love?"

When we said our goodbyes in the metro station, Agrippina shed a tear for Kolya.

Then she hugged me and made a sincere declaration of love.

"Mishanya, you have made me happy. I am indebted to you. When things get tough, just come! I am yours."

Fortunately nothing had happened at my place. I rang Suzdal and advised the theatre secretary that I was coming on the fast train from Moscow that evening at 5.30 p.m. She read out the name and address of the hotel. She confirmed that they had rented a flat for me for two months from 1st September, which could be extended if necessary. The premiere was scheduled for 5th November. I had a couple of weeks' grace, should the production director wish to make any unforeseen adjustments. Once in Suzdal I took a taxi, dumped my things in the hotel without unpacking, and rushed off to the theatre. I asked the administrator for a comp (complimentary ticket). She already knew of my arrival and asked the ticket usher to take me to the directors' box. The latter offered me a printed programme, in which I learned that they had a special youth group to do the mimicry and crowd scenes. But I couldn't find the name of the choreographer. This meant that the kids themselves must have cobbled together any old thing. In the interval I noted down the key questions and wishes for tomorrow's meeting with the artistic director, including: a thirty-minute class in the morning for everyone who wished to attend, then instruction in elements of cosmic moves and dance movements to a recording of the orchestral music by Shostakovich and the Leningrad composer, Firtich. I asked for the group manager to put up posters in the two-minute interval, to announce that work with the actors would start immediately after the weekend, on Tuesday morning. He was amazed at my speed.

"Mikhail Semyonovich, why the hurry? We still have two whole months ahead of us."

"Dear colleague, that's how it is in your department. But I'm working with inexperienced dancers, so it's much less."

In the morning I told the Artistic Director about my plans for the show and training programme for actors in the dance/movement technique of 'cosmic' choreography, to the futuristic music 'Fantastic Dances', including: short phrases of mime dialogues in the Martian language of pantomime or group poses that changed periodically into silhouetted shapes behind an illuminated, multicoloured screen, to match the content of the interaction onstage, etc. The Chief listened to what I had to say and smiled, writing something constantly in his notebook.

"Now I understand why Boris Chirtkov recommended you so highly."

He called up the production assistant, whom I knew already, and asked him to pass on to the youth group (former students from the local College of Performing Arts) the body motions for the mime. These were to be done completely as I directed, for two months, up to the premiere. And also to arrange a pianist and répétiteur for this period from the college who could work as my assistant. As it turned out, the Chief himself taught acting skills in the College.

I usually went to stay in Moscow on Sunday evenings and took the last train back to Suzdal on a Monday. At home I checked the post and Dmitri's answerphone messages. Milia asked me to set up a line for outgoing calls if I could guarantee that they wouldn't last long. She also offered to pay half of the telephone expenses.

"You've got to take what you can get." I returned the phrase she had addressed to me in front of the children.

She just gave a wry smile and thanked me for getting the telephone line put in.

I feared that the Suzdal show could be my 'swansong' in Russia. For this reason I went about the choreography with all guns blazing. If I was destined to fall, then better to fall a long way and not have to get up again. How could I carry on after this, like a snake crawling on its stomach the rest of my life? This is exactly how Maxim Gorky thought of himself in 'Song of the Nightingale', fighting valliantly for his idea.

I continued to work in close collaboration with the production director. I made adjustments based on his observations at rehearsals, and suggested alternatives in decisions open to question on the style of movement of this or that character. Occasionally the inexperienced kids got carried away with the grotesque element in their performance of cosmic phantasmagoria and instead of peace-loving Martians, portrayed terrifying devils. In these situations, I had to restrain their energy and re-channel it into a more cosmic genre. The foundation of my work was completed by 1st November. All that remained was to fine-tune the whole choreographic score, to check how well it fitted with the extravagant costumes, with occasionally fancy accessories worn by representatives of other planets. At the premiere, the young audience screamed, laughed or froze with shock in nervous anticipation of the next feat of stage technology. The actors were superb in their unaccustomed roles and with a new producer. The local press was fulsome in its praise of the theatre's new work.

At the modest post-premiere meal, the chairman of the local Cultural Board congratulated the actors and production team on their success. When the feast was over, the theatre Director came over to me and thanked me for my excellent work. He reminded me that my fee was ready in the accounts office, and wished me well. I took my leave of the Artistic Director and left quietly without any fuss.

On Monday I came home to find my wife drinking tea at the table in our sitting room with an unknown man. Evidently they were not expecting me back, and in their shock, made no reply when I greeted them.

I went over to the young man who was in his early twenties – about ten years younger than Milia – and asked: "Whom do I have the honour of addressing?"

"It's Sergei Nikolayevich, my ballroom dancing partner."

"Respected dancer, may I have a word with you in private, man to man?"

My wife jumped up and grabbed my sleeve, in an effort to avert a scene. I shook her off on to the sofa and made a beeline for my spouse's partner.

"After you!" I gestured towards the door. "See yourself out! Don't you ever come back here, unless you want to lose the most treasured part of yourself that makes you a man!"

Milia launched herself at me again with her claws in my eyes. I grabbed her hands and pushed her on to the sofa again. At the same time, the visitor rushed around the other side of the table and left.

"You bastard!" screeched my wife, "you are so going to regret this!" and ran out.

Milia had left her notebook on the telephone table. I found her unlucky partner's details easily, and copied down the valuable information. My sons came home from school about this time. Shurik did long days in first grade at primary school. The eldest was in sixth grade. He usually finished classes at 3 p.m., picked up the youngest and brought him home. Back in the spring I had given him Tanya's keys and tied them inside his satchel with a long shoelace, to use only exceptionally when they came home from school and their mother was out. They were not to give these keys to their mother for any reason!

My sons were happy to see me and both talking at once, shouted out: "Mum lied to us. She said that we would have a new dad now, but you're here. . . ."

"Wait! Calm down! Dmitri, tell me what you're talking about, but without all the noise."

"On Friday Mum got us together and told us that you were not going to live with us any more, because you are divorcing her once and for all, and that we would have a new dad now, much better than you. He is the son of a general who was a war hero and a very rich man. We will now live a life of luxury. No one will force her to work, and we will go on holiday to Crimea, Riga and even abroad. Wherever we like, like free birds. . . ."

"Thank you, Dmitri. You stay here and don't let anyone into the flat, even Tanya. Shurik and I will go on a recce. Not a word to anyone! If Mum comes back and asks about your brother, tell her that we have gone out for a walk. But I'm sure that she won't be back tonight. We'll be back by supper time. Don't worry about us, just get on with your homework. Shurik, are you ready for battle?"

"Yes, Dad!"

"Then off we go, musketeers!"

I checked on the map to see where our hero lived. The youngest and I set off at a march. As we could have expected, it turned out to be some out-of-the-way place on the outskirts of Moscow: the last station on the metro line. After eventually finding the address, we went up to the top floor of a two-storey, old and dirty building.

An elderly man of pensionable age opened the door to my knock and asked warily: "Who are you looking for?"

"Does Sergei live here?"

"Yes, come in. What do you want to see him about?"

I looked around. In one corner of the small room was a pram containing a six-month-old baby. One bedroom, a kitchen and toilet. No table or chairs, that meant that someone slept on the floor in the middle of the sitting room (on a mattress), as I did at Mum's in Odessa.

"I am Emilia Ivankova's husband, and she is your son's lover, and the mother of two children, eight and thirteen years old."

The poor war hero's face fell. He heard me out, without interrupting my account with the story of his heroic conquests and his worthy rank as a general in the air force. I gestured to the pram quizzically.

"Unfortunately, my son is a charlatan, an impertinent liar and base person.

This is his child, whom my sick wife and I have to feed and care for. The child's mother fled from her dregs of a husband. You're not the first to come here complaining about this swine's extortion and destruction of someone else's family. Take him to court."

"Shurik, did you hear all that?"

"Yes, Dad. Let's get out of here, please. I want to go home."

"I'm sorry to have disturbed you. I'm pleased to have met you and found out the truth."

Shurik was dragging me towards the door. The youngest and I didn't say a word all the way home, each lost in our own thoughts. He obviously felt sorry for his mum who was up to her eyes in shit.

It goes without saying that my wife was not home. I told the eldest all about what we had discovered. His eyes glazed over like a fish. He couldn't believe how naïve his mother was, with all her learning. Shurik sat on the sofa and cried. Dmitri went to reassure him and I got supper ready. After putting the children to bed, I rang Agrippina and asked if she knew of anywhere near her where I could rent a bachelor's room. I explained the situation to her. She asked me to give her five minutes. I pulled both additional telephone sets out of their sockets and locked them in the cupboard where the main line remained. I called the cooperative technician to come as soon as he could to put in a second lock (cash in hand). My fortress was defended. Pina rang back and said that she was named on her mother's behalf in relation to her parents' old flat, where her mother was virtually not living any more as she was always in the big flat with her daughter and granddaughter.

"Officially, my mother doesn't have the right to let her accommodation. If you agree to cover all the costs, she will happily bail you out, and come and live with us. We'll free up a wardrobe, my late father's writing desk and cupboard for you. She's even kept Dad's telephone, which you would also have to pay for. Her flat is five minutes' walk from my place. If you agree, Mum and I will remove all her personal items now and clean up your new pad. You'll be able to move in after 9 a.m. tomorrow."

"My good fairy, Pinochka, I don't know how to thank you."

"I'll tell you later."

As I'd imagined, Milia did not come home that night. In the morning I sent the children off to school, and collected up my things. I called a taxi and moved into the address Pina had given me on the telephone.

A grey-haired, intelligent-looking woman opened the door and smiled kindly as she invited me in: "You're very welcome, Mikhail! This is now your mansion."

I kissed her hand and thanked her for providing a practical solution to my problem.

"No need to thank me. It was our instability in the family, which has righted itself thanks to you. How about a nice hot cup of tea to start off with?"

"Thank you."

After we had taken tea together, the lady of the house showed me around the flat.

"The costs come to about thirty roubles a month (plus the telephone). If you wish, my neighbour Dusya can come and do the cleaning here once a week for three roubles. At the end of every month, you will need to pay Agrippina all the communal expenses. I hope you'll be happy here in your new place. If you need anything, just ring."

I returned to Rechnoi Vokzal at 3 p.m. to see if Milia was home for the children. When she saw me instead of the children, she made a point of turning her back on me and going into the kitchen.

"Yesterday Shurik and I paid a visit to your partner Sergei's house. He lives the life of a parasite with his parents, on their pension, in primitive conditions with his six-month-old child, whom the mother has abandoned. His elderly father, a sergeant-major by rank, told us that several women had been round before me, having been promised marriage, just like you, by his son, and all trying to extort money from the supposedly rich father. Congratulations on your wedding!"

"You're lying as usual. He is a nobleman from an upper-class family; you are no match for him."

"I'm glad that you have finally found a suitable partner in life, who will look after you better than I can, both materially and sexually, as you have already promised our children. From 1st January I will suspend payment of the cooperative instalments and your maintenance pending the judge's decision. You no longer need my help, now that you have such a rich sponsor. With all my heart, I wish you well. I'm taking the children to Odessa for New Year and will leave them there until the court's judgement. I cannot live under the same roof as you. So until the flat is sold, I will live somewhere else. You will get your quarter share from the sale of the cooperative flat. The remaining three-quarters will stay with the father and children."

"How dare you! It's against the law. No court will allow that."

I heaved a heavy rucksack full of books on to my back and left the house without another word.

Agrippina had arranged for her daughter to attend a school sports camp in the winter holidays, so she and I went to Riga for a week, where one of her cousins and her family lived. I think God had sent me a reward to compensate for the ordeals in my personal life. We had a wonderful break at the Riga seaside, among cultured, good-natured people. Happy, plentiful suppers and dances with a beautiful lady. It would be a sin for anyone to wish for greater happiness. But I was tormented constantly by the same thought: where and how could I escape the encroaching threat obstructing my creative activity. I decided to make one final attempt, and send my professional details to the regions nearest the capital (with the exception of Pskov and Novgorod). Perhaps some theatre would be interested.

"My dear cavalier, who are you thinking about all the time on holiday by the bay of Riga?"

"About you, my good and wonderful fairy. I'm scared of losing this gift from God."

"Thank you, my crafty troublemaker. Let's go and dance my favourite tango."

Back home, I asked Pina for her help with a particularly personal, major issue in my life.

"This power of attorney is in your name, and has been notarised as authorisation for you to receive my payment from the film studio following the Artistic Council's release of the film *Pyotr Ryabinkin*. Finkelshtein, the Director, will pay you 5,000 roubles on my behalf, out of which you must pay back my historic debt of 500 roubles against a receipt. Keep the rest safe for when you need it, should anything unexpected happen to me, e.g. hospital, abduction, etc."

I gave my lady friend a brief outline of my wife's threat to take revenge on me.

We came back to the capital under a blanket of snow, refreshed and rested. But not for long. As I opened my door at Rechnoi, I heard familiar shouting inside: "Give Tanya her keys back, or I'll smash your face in with this frying pan!"

I snatched the pan from my wife's hands, and pinned the violent mother against the kitchen wall.

"If you don't stop this, I will call the police immediately just like last time. You and your sister will have to explain yourselves at the station. Tanya, I'm giving you five minutes to disappear with your suitcase. Get out of my house! I know all I ever want to know about you."

"Let go of me, you scum! You don't live here and have no right to boss me about."

"We'll hear what our police friends have to say about that! Kids, come with me. As for you, sister dear, I've warned you more than once. You're going to get what's coming to you now."

I took my sons into the office. Locking the door, I let out a heavy sigh and asked: "How were the holidays? Are you ready to go back to school?"

"We stayed at home the whole time."

"We went to look at a Christmas tree once," added Shurik.

"The day before yesterday, we didn't have any clean shirts for school. Our socks stink. Sometimes I take a shower, but Shurik probably doesn't remember the last time he had one."

"Sit here a moment. I'm going to talk to Mum in the kitchen. Don't break anything!"

Tanya and her suitcase were nowhere to be seen. Milia was writing something at the table.

I apologised: "Finally you have taken the wise decision to file for a divorce."

"This is a request to the cooperative chairman not to let you into the building, because you don't actually live here, and are interfering with the way I bring up my children."

"What's the chairman got to do with anything? This is a police matter. While you're at it, don't forget to mention that these children are going around dirty and smelly, haven't had a bath for weeks on end, and have no clean clothes. They go to sleep at midnight when their mother gets home from cruising, and eat whatever they can find whenever they get the chance. No one checks if they're doing their homework, and so on. I gave the keys to Dmitri. Otherwise the children could be left out on the street after school, the way you organise things. I'm going to speak to the cooperative chairman now and will be back in half an hour with officials from the police and local council. They will write a report about the state of the children and your parenting capacity."

I didn't get a single reply (either positive or negative) to my enquiries to theatres in neighbouring capitals over the next two months. There was a complete embargo. I was backed into a corner and like a red rag to a bull, went for the kill. I wrote a statement regarding the Soviet Communist Party Central Committee secretary's political repression on ideology. I itemised the services I had provided to four Soviet republics. I made no criticism or complaint. Only in the final sentence did I express my bewilderment at the creative vacuum surrounding me.

'I cannot believe that all these repressive measures against an individual teacher and choreographer have been provoked by my undue respect for nationality and the principle of non-membership of the party.'

I enclosed copies of my diplomas and awards. I packed up my printed programmes, posters, books, critical reviews, etc., and forwarded the valuable parcel to the relevant address.

My official contract with the film studio ended in January. But the release of *Pyotr Ryabinkin* was delayed, predictably, by a couple of months. The producer called me in from time to time for some fine tuning or for a final say in deciding dramatic movements. Eventually, the private screening was scheduled for 5th March 1971. As people were applauding at the end of the film, a member of the auditorium staff came up to me and invited me into the administrative office to take an urgent telephone call. Naturally, I assumed that something had happened at home, and was quick on the woman's heels.

I grabbed the receiver from the administrator's desk and feeling panicked, shouted, "Hello, hello!" only to hear short pips.

Suddenly, someone behind took me by the shoulder.

"Weapons on the table! Now!"

In the theatre, some well-known actors often messed about with each other in this fashion. So I took it in my stride and automatically fought back, sending the joker back where he'd come from. At this point my arms were twisted behind me and bound with handcuffs. Looking around, I saw two bruisers in uniform and a woman with her back to the door, blocking the way to any surprise visitors. As they carried out a personal search, I stated that I'd left my briefcase containing important documents and money in the auditorium, and that my winter coat was in the cloakroom.

"Your briefcase and coat are in safe hands, don't you worry. Don't talk to anyone and don't try to run! You'll just make things worse for yourself."

On their way out of the auditorium, the audience stepped aside to allow me through – I was the one who had choreographed the film they had just watched – with his hands cuffed behind him. I was pushed roughly into a car and the door slammed; the cuffs were still on.

"May I ask where you're taking me?" I asked the chap sitting next to me.

"You'll find out soon enough. For now just sit still and be quiet!"

"It's minus twenty-four degrees outside and you haven't let me put on my coat or hat. Are you nice and warm in your fur coats? It's not fair on the one you're arresting."

The car drew up at the police station. They dragged me out of the car and bundled me into the reception. The elderly man on duty made a note of the arrested person arriving. My briefcase was on his desk. He made a description of the contents. I pointed out the token and ventured that I needed my coat and hat from the studio cloakroom. They took me off to the holding cells and clapped me behind bars.

STAGE III: INTO THE BLACK HOLE

CHAPTER 5 THE DECAPITATED MUSE OF DANCE

For the next few hours, I found myself standing cheek by jowl with a group of people who had breached the peace, and some who had committed more serious crimes, arrested and crowded into a cell. We all faced the prospect of being reshuffled in future, in line with the charges against us. While there was a constant influx of new people, some were being taken away, so that the approximate total of fifteen to twenty criminals of varying ages combined with cops, remained roughly the same. Those who were unable to withstand the physical demands of this experience and had passed out, were unceremoniously dragged out and thrown into the basement, where the regional Department of Internal Affairs' medical unit was situated. Those left carried on breathing out stale alcohol and putrid cigarette fumes into each other's faces, while they waited for their criminal trial to come up. It was clear that most of my companions had already experienced a similar ordeal, and patiently endured the punishment they deserved.

My mind was racing: how should I behave among these pickpockets, yobs and miscreants? How could I let Agrippina know of my whereabouts? What offence were the officers planning to pin on me? I began a careful study of the faces, looks and habits of my closest neighbours. Some of them looked wary and furtive, others like professional bandits. A third group were panicking, frightened of the possible consequences of their excessive drinking, etc. I spotted near me a definite plant, an informant, with eyes darting everywhere. He tried to make conversation with me, but I kept quiet, not wanting to respond to his false curiosity. On my other side was a drunk muttering something under his breath, obviously suffering from chronic alcoholism.

I addressed him: "Excuse me, mate! Were you asking me something, or did I just imagine that?"

"No, I'm cursing myself for taking my eye off the ball again and overdoing it with my mates."

"Were you driving, then?"

"What happened was that I clipped a kiosk selling baskets on the bend."

"Was anyone injured?"

"Just me. Now I'll have to pay another fine."

"Is it a lot of money?"

"Not really, fifty roubles. But it's not the first time."

"If you telephone my wife and tell her where we've met, she'll pay your fine for you. Will you remember the number? Or have you got something to write it on your hand with?"

"I've got an indelible pencil in my pocket somewhere. Give it to me then, slowly."

Discreetly, I dictated Pina's telephone number and checked what he'd written on his hand.

"Who should I ask for?"

"Pina. I'm Misha. What's your name?"

"Fedya. But will she definitely pay?"

"If you say hello from me, it's a dead cert."

We shook hands to cement our arrangement, and turned away from each other.

I realised that the officers were testing my endurance. The next time a guard came in, I asked to see the duty officer. He asked me my name and went off. A few minutes later I was taken to see the Lieutenant.

"What are you complaining about?" asked the duty officer, sternly.

"How much longer are you planning to keep me in these inhuman conditions without explaining why you're holding me? This contravenes the basic statutes of the Russian Code of Criminal Procedure."

"Hey, old man, take him to the seventeenth! Let him use the toilet in the corridor first."

This turned out to be a solitary confinement cell for particularly dangerous and disturbed 'clients': 3 × 4 m, with a platform to sleep on. There was no side table, nor slop bucket, nor light. The only meagre light came through the grille from the corridor. The guard shoved me in and threw my winter coat and fur hat on to the platform. He made me sign for my things.

A short time later they brought the drunken chap on a trolley and bundled him on to the same platform where I was sitting. I had to move aside, closer to the wall. Coming to, the boozer started bothering me. I got up and went around him to the door. But my companion would not desist. Realising that all this was intentional, I tried to avoid a confrontation. When my persistent cellmate grabbed my chest, I repulsed him with such force that he passed out or pretended to, after hitting the back of his head on the wire mesh. I yelled hysterically for the duty cop. I threatened them with court for getting someone else to make an attempt on my life, in blatant breach of the laws of the Code of Criminal Procedure. Of course I put on this noisy show at midnight, hoping by such means to force the guards to empty the stinking cell of this unnecessary threat to my (even without him) unsavoury state. Sure enough, thanks to the noise I was making, disturbances kicked off in the neighbouring cells. The guards dragged my unconscious hero away. Their response to my request for the duty officer was that I should wait till morning. I told them that I urgently needed a Validol tablet for heart problems from my personal things in my briefcase, as my heart was pounding. No one answered.

I lay on my back in my winter coat in the centre of the platform and rested my head on my fur hat. Crossing my arms across my chest in an effort to calm myself down, I looked, without intending to, like a dead man. I tried to pinpoint the least risky way of behaving in my new situation as a prisoner, and the most likely responses to my written protestations. Fully aware of my powerlessness in the face of the evil deeds by these 'Soviet gods', I nevertheless was naïvely banking on their ignorance that I was informed about the Soviet laws pertaining to the Code of Criminal Procedure. I had begun studying this procedural bible of Milia's from the legal library as far back as the Leningrad threat at Smolny. I was still usefully acquainting myself with criminal legislation when I sent off the devastating article about Vitali Reznikov to the *Literary Gazette*, in response to his attack on me for the contemporary theme in my choreographic miniatures. Following a complaint to the Ideology Department of the Soviet Communist Party's Central Committee about the embargo against me by the creator, I had decided – anticipating arrest – to study the code in depth, certain that I was going to need it before long.

I must have lain in the same position for a long time, without moving or making any noise with my breathing, weighing up the battle in store for me. A guard making his second round noticed that I had been in the same position for a long time and decided that the prisoner had gone to meet his Maker. As the key sounded in the lock, I tried to see through my eyelashes, to check who they were going to put in with me this time. When I saw only two of them (one inside, the other outside the cell), I realised that they were worried, and so pretended that I wasn't breathing. The policeman inside came right up to the platform, reached out to my boots and carefully moved the 'dead' foot. I sat bolt upright on the platform, as if I'd been stung, staring at him wildly. The poor sergeant leaped out of the cell in an instant, and his old pal slammed the door behind him. It was a long time before the Pretrial Detention Centre regulars who'd woken up in the cells next door settled down. I felt a little sorry about giving my guard such an unwarranted shock.

The following morning I was taken to see Colonel Kolesnikov, the head of the District Police Headquarters which was situated within the vast car-manufacturing plant. I could see that my case was more serious than I had imagined.

"I've been told that you've made a complaint about your treatment in our Pretrial Detention Centre."

I described to him the events that had taken place, and asked to be kept in an individual cell until I was charged. I stated my wish to call my wife or a lawyer that I knew.

"You no longer have a wife. Yesterday, after hearing about your arrest, she unilaterally petitioned for divorce in the interests of safeguarding the children and herself too. Everything has been completed through proper legal channels. This can hardly come as a surprise to you! You will be provided with a solicitor once criminal proceedings have been instituted against you. Show some patience and don't forget that you are not in the Metropole Hotel now, but in the Pretrial Detention Centre run by the police station."

"I worked in the Law Faculty at Moscow State University for three years and lived with a postgraduate in legal science for fifteen years. I am familiar with the Russian Criminal Code. Forgive me, Comrade Colonel. You don't need to remind me of your obligation to charge me within three days or release me due to lack of evidence of any crime."

A knock at the door interrupted our conversation. An elderly colleague came into the office.

"This is Captain Skvortsova, who will be investigating your affair."

I spent two hours in the investigator's office, patiently answering her questions on personal and professional matters. Skvortsova wrote everything down, highlighting specific information in detail. To my question, "What am I being charged with?" she clarified briefly: "Administrative and financial irregularity according to article XX of the Russian Criminal Code."

It was about the illegal receipt of salaries over the last two years by a few specialists in the Bolshoi's opera-ballet affiliate under my artistic leadership. Working in conjunction with the ZIL Cultural Centre, they had, over the course of a few years and in line with an annual contract, been supplying the administration at the Cultural Centre with written permission for work from the Bolshoi Theatre or school. Lately, for unknown reasons, they had not attached these yearly permissions to the signed contracts. Naturally the Cultural Centre management refused to agree an official contract with them without such confirmation from their main place of work. Obviously, without these specialists the theatre faced collapse.

In a panic, Slonimskaya, deputy manager of the Group Activities Department, had suggested engaging two Ballet studio students under false pretences on the same salary, which they would then have to pass on to their unregistered teachers from the Bolshoi. This kind of fallacious practice was fairly commonplace in establishments because of the need to find a compromise for staff. This was common knowledge to everyone in the department and no one was concerned about it. I too was completely aware of this falsification, as officially, I confirmed my team's working hours in a monthly time sheet for the Accounts Department. During the time I was away at festival locations, colleagues' hours were signed off on my behalf by Nadia Sychova, our theatre administrator. Neither of us had ever signed official agreements with the ZIL Cultural Centre. Behind bars, it dawned on me just how lightly I had taken my professional responsibilities as artistic leader, with blind trust in my Bolshoi affiliate management.

In the main, our Ballet studio at the People's Theatre was made up of talented young men and women, scrupulously selected in annual auditions every August. On rare occasions, by a process of elimination, we took into the troupe candidates who were not entirely suitable: children of top officials (by request of the Cultural Centre's management). As a rule, I only worked with these untalented girls in the 'corps de ballet', and then only in the back row of performers. One of the seriously unsuccessful girls in Musa Lebedeva's class demanded a solo from the ballet repertoire, much too advanced for her technical abilities. Lebedeva naturally politely refused the student's request, at which she was subjected to an undeserved stream of abuse in front of the whole group. Looking into this occurrence, I dismissed Vorobyova from the studio when she refused to apologise for her rudeness in class. The following day, the disruptive girl's mother came into the Cultural Centre and created a scene, threatening to take us to court for discriminating against her daughter. A week later an inspector from the local financial management auditors for the car factory region turned up at the Cultural Centre with a statement from Vorobyova about Berkut's financial embezzlement by registering fictitious staff in the Bolshoi affiliate's People's Theatre. I could never be certain whether this was a chance event in Lebedeva's class, or a prefabricated act of provocation by my enemies.

The well-known facts of persecution and punishment brought to light by the Soviet regime's many detractors confirmed again and again that the KGB ran an organised system of operational control:

a) censorship in printed matter: literature, photolithography, advertising and so on;

b) fabrication of reasons for charges, having nothing to do with a free-thinking person's actions;

c) spreading false rumours about a popular free spirit.

However, I had never considered myself a member of the militant category of Sakharovs and Solzhenitsyns or similar ideological champions. I tried my best to avoid political, national and religious influences in my art. Nevertheless, by refusing to join the party, I added fuel to the fire, from the point of view of the Soviet censor, who assumed without any grounds: 'Whoever is not with us is against us.' As a result of their harsh victimisation, the Gusevs/Zakharovs and Potskins/Vartanyans forced me on to the other side of the ideological barricades.

The investigator reported that during her interrogation, Olya and Alla, my ballerinas from the ZIL studio, had insisted on a meeting with me on behalf of the whole company. At first I refused this idea outright on pedagogical grounds.

"But why?" Skvortsova was amazed. "They are your pupils and hold their ballet master in very high regard. Not everyone who's been arrested can say that. You should be proud of your charges, and not turn your back on them."

"My charges are not used to seeing me in such an unprepossessing state."

"If you like, I can organise a shower and shave for you as an exceptional case."

I agreed and thanked the investigator, although I was surprised by her enthusiasm which seemed highly suspect. Most likely she was counting on getting a statement that would land me in it, from the tape recording of our conversation with the two ballerinas. For my part, I was interested to find out how my colleagues and the deputy manager of the Cultural Centre, like Slonimskaya, had reacted. I would also take the opportunity to pass on important information for Zhilin, the Director.

I had no trouble imagining the shock and commotion caused by my arrest within the ZIL Cultural Centre and the powerful echo that would reverberate through all the Moscow institutions associated with my name. For me, this persecution did not just limit me physically in depriving me of my liberty.

Highly placed opponents undertook to destroy my morale, just as they had with Lopukhov, Goleizovsky, Yakobson and Azarov, by rubbishing all my small contributions and broad ambitions in developing contemporary choreography, in teaching dance, in historical research and printed publications. I had to admit that so far they had succeeded. I could only tip my hat in deference to the victors and reap the fruits of my own actions and failures.

It was painful and shameful to see the fear and confusion in the eyes of my best students, but getting a grip on myself, I half whispered to them while looking to the door: "Did you know about Vorobyova's mother's statement about me?" The girls shook their heads in silence.

Olya asked timidly: "How are you feeling? Everyone is worried about you and they all send their regards."

"I'm still alive. Tell Zhilin personally: Slonimskaya is friends with the troublemaker."

"No one at the studio believes the vicious rumours about you. Look after yourself!"

On my fourth day in the detention centre, I called for the duty officer and told him: "In accordance with the Criminal Code, if you don't officially charge me today with my lawyer present, then you will have to release me from detention. Otherwise I will make a complaint to the Russian state prosecutor's assistant, under the supervision of Sergei Prokhorov, my former student at Moscow State University, on the basis that you are breaking socialist law – with all the consequences that would ensue."

For some reason I 'forgot' to specify to the officer that I had only been Sergei's dance teacher in a university club. Still, in the evening, I was transferred in a Black Maria police van to the prison on Matrosskaya Tishina in Moscow, where I was to be detained awaiting trial for up to two months.

Here, at Matrosska, the supervisors were impassive as they accepted me as one of a group of criminals. They sorted us mechanically according to the type of crime committed: robbers, yobs, drug addicts, rapists, swindlers, etc. Fortunately they put me into the last category of the least dangerous offenders. They made us strip naked. After a quick medical examination they shaved our heads, armpits and pubic area, then shoved us into the shower. We were issued with prison garb, and then sent to different cells. All this took place quickly and efficiently using a long-established system. If anyone started acting up, he received a physical 'reprimand', and consequently kept his mouth shut for ages. After such a clear lesson the remaining recruits decided to keep quiet and follow the thugs' orders. By the time the final siren sounded, all newcomers had been allocated to their places. I ended up in a 'family' of four fellow inmates. In the centre of the small cell was a table while three bunks stood along each wall. There was a single small window behind the grille just below the ceiling and a commode in the corner, next to the door. The four prisoners played dominoes, not paying me any attention. I said hello into nothingness, and waited for them to finish the next round of dominoes. Then I pushed my way through to the second free bed on the left-hand side of the table.

"Take a seat, mate! Relax after your journey! We'll finish our game in another ten minutes and all go to bed. Then you can take up your lodging for the night in our luxury hotel."

At 6 a.m. we got up to the bell; 6.30 a.m., check everyone is present and correct; 7 a.m., breakfast; 8 a.m. until noon, appointments with lawyers, investigators, medical staff, etc.; 1 p.m., lunch; 2–5 p.m., free time (letters, reading; visitors were allowed on Sundays); 5 p.m., exercise; 6 p.m., supper; 7–9 p.m., free time; 9 p.m., night bell. During the morning inspection I asked the duty officer to provide me with a copy of the Russian Criminal Code, along with a pen, ink and paper.

"You can order the code by leaving a note through the little window in the door in the evening. The librarian collects the orders before the night bell and supplies them by 8 a.m. He will provide you with paper and writing equipment on request."

"I'm sorry; no one had told me this. Thanks for letting me know."

The officer made a note in his record book of the new prisoner who would occupy the spare bed in the cell. I was gradually getting to know my cellmates. I learned the daily regime thoroughly. Cautiously, I asked the more good-natured inmates about the unwritten code of relations between prisoners and about communication with the outside world. I wrote a letter to Agrippina explaining my new location. I asked her to come and see me in visiting hours the following Sunday.

All week I pored over the code in my free time and made notes of essential information on the articles of law that the MIA (Ministry of Internal Affairs) staff had contravened during my arrest, the transfer to the police station and four-day detention in the Pretrial Detention Centre. I addressed a letter to the state prosecutor of Moscow city. I wrote out a copy and handed it to the officer on his morning rounds, whom I had already got to know. He promised to send it off promptly to the person in question. Sunday came and I waited impatiently for Agrippina to visit. When we met, she couldn't hold back happy, yet bitter tears. I tried to comfort her, but she found it really difficult to control her emotions.

"Don't worry, darling. I survived the war, so I'll survive something like this. It's not the first or last time the authorities have manipulated things to subjugate suspicious people."

"Misha, I'm sorry. I had to call on Zhilin as I was worried about you. He said that he is doing everything he can to improve matters for you in the future."

"Pina, act on my power of attorney with Mosfilm, and keep everything until I get out of here. Find the telephone number for that lawyer I know in my notebook and give him a quick hello. Pay your mum from the apartment expense fund for six months in advance. If I'm not back by then, put my stuff in storage."

At the end of the first month of my time in the 'rest home' at Matrosskaya Tishina, I received a response to my complaint to the prosecutor, in which it was duly noted that investigation into the facts outlined in my statement was under way. They promised to inform me of the outcome within three months (by which time I would already be God knew where). This provoked universal laughter in the cell. I admit, I hadn't expected anything else. I had to ask myself: who or what could I count on if my situation worsened significantly? A few days later, I was summoned to the next interrogation with the investigator. Skvortsova introduced my defence counsel, Rubin Goldberg, and questioned me for an hour in his presence. In response to the question: "Why haven't I been charged yet?" the investigator didn't even deign to reply. The lawyer said that he would explain later, when we were on our own. I realised that my trial was not going to go smoothly. As she concluded her interrogation, Skvortsova promised on her way out to come back the following month. My lawyer who was over fifty, had, it turned out, been injured in the war, when he had lost his left arm and acquired a scar on his face.

"Mikhail, I hope you realise that you have made a serious error, by participating in a cover-up operation to provide the salaries of important Theatre specialists. Notwithstanding your most noble intentions to keep the group together, this counts as a crime in the eyes of the law. We will have to prove formally that you did not enter into a contract with them and thus do not bear direct responsibility for this administrative, financial infringement. But as teacher and supervisor, you involved your young students, Olya and Alla – seventeen and eighteen years old respectively – in a swindle, which was very demoralising for them. Essentially, you may be charged on legal grounds with misappropriation of funds for mercenary purposes as a leader in a superior working position. The remaining financial, administrative details are just ways to stir things up. You must stick to your position of formally following the instructions issued by the deputy department manager, A. Slonimskaya, no matter how naïve such justification may be. In the chaos of your everyday life in the arts, you didn't attach enough importance to this, which you deeply regret, and are ready to fulfil any punishment for your professional negligence."

"Rubin Borisovich, to some extent that's exactly how it was. The manager explained that leaders of many factories and educational establishments often went in for compromise measures like these, to help them achieve their aims and keep functioning successfully."

"Still, this makes you no less guilty. There's one rule for them and another for everyone else. Fortunately, all the witnesses at the Cultural Centre, with the exception of Vorobyova and Slonimskaya, spoke very highly of you. This has confounded the investigator's strategy, which in turn has delayed the trial."

I returned to the cell feeling puzzled by my lawyer's last remark. It was becoming clear that they wouldn't keep me here for long now, thanks to the lack of direct evidence for my crime or insubstantial witness statements. I was 100% convinced that my devious detractors would not be satisfied with a light punishment for my error.

Indeed, on closer observation, the suspicious Arno (as he called himself) displayed rather strange ways of interacting with his cohabitants and the duty officer in the mornings. Also, judging by the tone of his voice and expression in his eyes, it was clear that he was not who he made himself out to be. To my stage manager's eye, he performed his prisoner role too lightly.

One day, perturbed, he suddenly asked me: "Why are you always watching me and sniffing around me?"

"You really remind me of one of my colleagues in the theatre," I extricated myself.

He stared at me for a long time with a snide smile, and said finally for all to hear: "When I was a child I would injure people like you with my catapult. You fucking Jew!"

I didn't rise to the bait. The men playing dominoes instantly turned to look at us in astonishment.

The old man Georgi jokingly enquired: "Why can't you play nicely? It's no coincidence that they say: 'Wherever you find an Armenian, there's a Jew with nothing to do.'"

Arno understood immediately that I had exposed his cover and clenched his fists in rage. The next day, as we were walking around the prison yard, he asked the guard to take him to the medical wing as a matter of urgency. He didn't return from there.

Georgi joked again: "Misha, how did you piss your 'friend' off so much that he left us so soon?"

"I let him know that it was no secret to any of us that he was an agent planted by the MIA."

My fellow inmates had a good laugh at my naïvety. It turns out that they had guessed before me, but kept it to themselves to avoid any trouble.

This latest event brought me closer to my companions. In answer to their asking: why I had got myself shacked up with them, I told them briefly about my administrative, financial offence. My mates looked from one to the other without a word, smirking through their moustaches. I realised that they didn't believe me, and kept quiet.

"You don't get put in prison here for a little crime like that," the old man asserted. "For example, I got into hot water with currency. Everyone else is in for con tricks with the savings bank, forging documents, stealing cars, etc. There must be something more serious underlying your article of law."

I didn't want to get into it. I just confirmed that my lawyer had said the same thing.

"Why are you studying the Criminal Code? Your complaints won't do you any favours. The more you're in their faces, the quicker they'll do for you."

These wise words of warning gave me the creeps.

To allay the boredom, I began work on a textbook about Character dance in two parts:

a) Syllabus for technical exercises at the barre (supported exercises in the classroom).

b) Elements and combinations of movements for centre practice (similar exercises and other routines in the middle of the studio) including: ports de bras (sequences of arm movements) and studies of various national dances.

Everything was based on traditional folklore, but in the style of classical ballet. This teaching aid was aimed not only at professionals, but also at amateur lovers of choreographic art. This project was an ambition of mine. I hadn't imagined that I would start to make it a reality so soon. Work and life in general had filled my time to such a degree up until my arrest, that even thinking about this was unimaginable. And now it seemed unrealistic to try to create anything worthwhile in these conditions. Perhaps it was just a way of distracting myself from negative thoughts and exercising my brain cells.

As the second month of incarceration drew to a close, most of my original cellmates were transferred following trial to a holding prison at Krasnaya Presnya. Only one was left out of the original residents. I asked the duty officer on his morning round to organise an urgent meeting for me with my lawyer. A few days later, Goldberg reported some bad news regarding the trial.

"After discovering the lack of any evidence of your crime in your file, I requested that the area prosecutor cut short the overdue investigation, close the case and release you from prison. He refused, on the grounds that on the strength of particular circumstances the court has granted the investigator a further two months to gather evidence against the person charged, and to look into the testimonies of new witnesses for the defence. I protested against this biased decision, but to no avail. The prosecutor and judge insisted on their way of doing things, despite the fact that it's illegal."

"Still, according to the Criminal Code, they don't have the right to keep me in prison for more than two months under investigation, without sentencing me."

"Even so, the court has the power to extend this time in exceptional cases.

So get ready for your transfer to Butyrka [a detention centre in another part of Moscow] 'sanctuary' next week. You'll have to do another two months there before you get your sentence. Hang on in there!"

Further ordeals awaited me in Butyrka. I was put in a cell of recidivists: professional muggers and burglars. At first they welcomed me cautiously, assuming that I was a police 'grass' (spy).

Tim, the eldest and a strapping bear of a man with a vivid tattoo, asked: "So, tell us about yourself! Who have you 'written off' [killed] of your own free will, and for what reason? Only don't muddy the waters!"

"I'm waiting for the court decision on an administrative, financial clause for fiddling staff."

The young prisoners looked at Tim quizzically, and he screwed up his eyes and clarified: "Was that for sham workers or something? Then why have they put you in with us?"

"Probably for poor behaviour at Matrosska."

The group expressed their scepticism as one. "We'll talk you through our Butyrka system. What sort of work do you do?"

"I'm a ballet master/choreographer."

"What do you eat that with?"

"I teach dance."

"I've got it now."

The criminals laughed, taking me for some kind of clown. Tim silenced them with a look.

A couple of days later, I had a visit from my lawyer. Once Goldberg learned that I'd been placed with a group of repeat offenders, he wrote something down in his pad, and warned me to "be on your guard" and "keep your eyes peeled" just in case.

"The court hearing for your case is scheduled for Monday. We have to establish the usual exchanges with the prosecutor and the potential tricks he could use with witnesses. Keep yourself calm and confident, and don't rush your answers to tricky questions. I am not aware of any surprises in the investigation, but judging by all the material they have, the criminal suit against you doesn't hold water."

The lawyer and I went through my defence in painstaking detail, admitting guilt only in the unethical use of students to falsify papers for paying teachers on the ZIL Cultural Centre staff. Goldberg listed all the extenuating circumstances. Nevertheless, the forthcoming court appearance and the other world of my former colleagues did not make me feel very positive. Rather, the converse was true.

On the day of my court appearance, I was let out in the morning through the furnace of purgatory, and then, with my head shaved, wearing my civilian clothes, I was brought into the citadel of justice. My defence lawyer turned out to be a legal executive. After the prosecutor had read out the criminal charge, and the witness Vorobyova had been cross-examined, Goldberg forced them both into a corner with his arguments and depositions from the witnesses for the defence. Monday was a day off at the theatre. The Bolshoi teachers, working additionally at the ZIL Cultural Centre, and artistes from the affiliate People's Theatre, occupied the public benches in the court as if following the defendant's script, and essentially, played the role of troubadours for the accused. Their comments on my professional and personal attributes in response to the prosecutor's questions made it sound as if they were recommending a candidate for the Lenin Prize. The judge and both sworn witnesses at his sides, looked around in bewilderment, seeking clarification from the prosecutor. As a result of a brief whispered exchange between the guardians of the law, the two hours allocated for my criminal court trial were cut short. Due to insufficient evidence, my case was adjourned for a hearing on the following Monday.

By all accounts, I should have been pleased with a short-term victory. But my intuition as a beaten dog told me the opposite: imminent danger. But from which side? Prisoners were usually afraid to discuss details of their proceedings in the cells.

"Hey, artiste, what are you looking so pissed off about? Did you lose your case?" the ringleader, Tim, asked.

"The hearing was adjourned. I got all psyched up for nothing. Now my heart's thumping."

"Knock on the peephole and ask the guard to call the doctor."

"It's late now. The medical office is probably shut. I'll make it till morning somehow."

"Holding on won't do you any good, mate. We don't need any bodies in the cell."

I knocked several times on the peephole. Finally it opened. "Who's looking for a thump?" bellowed the short-tempered guard.

I peeped through the opening: "I need a doctor or nurse urgently . . ."

Before I could finish, a huge fist punched me in the face and the door slammed shut. I rushed over to the sink to stop my nosebleed with cold water and toilet paper. Seeing the state I was in, Tim was furious, and punched his fist through the cell wall into the corridor outside. At this point the alarm bell went off and armed guards rushed to the scene. The thug filled them in on what had happened. Without looking into the incident, they took me off to the medical quarters, and Tim to solitary.

Once back in my bedchamber, I discovered that Tim had been transferred to another cell, and was being punished for damaging state property.

"Well, at least I wasn't asking for anyone's help," the victim tried to justify his action.

The prisoners demonstrably turned against me in contempt. After the fight in the cell, all that remained was a weak, emergency light to be used at night 'as needed', with the guards periodically monitoring the condition of their sleeping charges in the cell. Every time the neighbours used the commode I woke up terrified, anticipating a possible attack. In an effort to get back to sleep, I reassured myself with the knowledge that I was exaggerating the danger. *These prisoners need you and your fate like a hole in the head. Sleep well!*

In the morning, the duty officer making his rounds asked me, "What happened last night?"

I recounted the incident briefly and said I was sorry to have disturbed the neighbours. I asked his permission to keep on me some analgesic Validol for my heart.

"It's prohibited to keep any tablets in the cells. The medics bring pills and water as necessary to those who need them during their rounds, or take them to the infirmary."

The next day, Tim's bunk was occupied by a new client by the name of Stas (short for Stanislav). I suspended writing my book for a while, to allow him the opportunity to settle into the neighbourhood.

During our walk, Stas sidled up to me. Trying to make conversation, he asked spitefully: "What are you writing while you're under arrest? You should do your writing at home, not in the joint."

"It's nothing of interest. Better, you tell me what's brought you here to Butyrka?"

The newcomer rolled his eyes and went off whistling into the crowd of smoking prisoners.

Stas's bunk was the closest to the door, while mine was on the same side, the next one along the wall. Behind me was the elderly currency speculator. At night we seldom got up to urinate in the corner, so as not to wake the others by elbowing our way between the beds and long table. We all lay with our feet towards the door. In this way, I could also keep watch on Stas as he slept, while he couldn't see me. That night I woke up at every odd rustle and checked through my eyelashes what my dangerous neighbour was up to. By 3 or 4 a.m., sleep engulfed me. Suddenly I heard a chair scrape and opened my eyes. A figure of some kind was leaning over me, one hand on the table and the other holding something shiny. From my childhood during the war, thanks to my poor vision, I had developed an acute reflex and response to surrounding danger. With lightning speed, I drew both legs up under my blanket and shoved them into the attacker's chest, and pushed him away from me with all my might (dancers have strong legs). Leaping backwards with his arms outstretched, Stas lost his balance and crashed to the floor on his back, hitting his head on the door. My howl of hysteria woke up everyone in our cell as well as the neighbours. There was a great commotion. The guards came running at the sound of the alarm. I shouted out that this bandit had tried to knife me. The blood dripping from his fingers was evidence of this. They took Stas away.

Setting the bed straight, I noticed a bloodstain on the brown blanket and the glint of a razor blade from a shaving kit. I took it carefully to the sink. My eyes hunted feverishly for a safe place to hide the attack weapon, which undoubtedly would mark me out as one of the criminal fraternity. Sitting on the commode out of feigned necessity, I just happened to pick out a barely noticeable slit between wooden boxes of toilet paper and the wall. I had a job to stuff the blade into it from the other side of the strut, and pushed it deeply in with my nails.

Now they would have to unscrew the box from the wall to get at this material evidence. Not surprisingly, I couldn't get back to sleep after such extreme stress. So I mulled over all the possible options of the charge against me, and my defence until it was time to get up.

After breakfast, each person in our cell was called in for questioning. I described to the member of staff the details of the night's events and initial conversation with Stas during our walk. The investigator told me about the 'victim's testimony, in which he had asserted that I attacked him with a razor blade. He had tried to wrest it off me to defend himself, and cut his fingers as a result.

"Hand over the blade immediately; otherwise you will face serious consequences for this."

"He's lying. You can see his blood on my blanket. That's proof that Stas attacked me with the razor in my bed, and not the other way round."

"For disturbing the peace at night-time and concealing a weapon in your cell, you will be severely punished. In addition, a criminal action will be brought against you for attempting to maim an inmate. Give us the blade before it's too late!"

"I demand an urgent meeting with my defence lawyer in line with the Russian Criminal Code."

Back in the cell, my four room-mates fired questions at me: "What actually happened between you last night?"

"What razor blade is the investigator questioning us about as witnesses?"

"How did you shit on them so much that they are trying to get rid of you all together?

"And in any case, why the fuck do we need all this hassle because of your problems?"

I sat silently on the bunk listening to them and simply shrugged my shoulders in reply.

After lunch I was taken back to the prison officer.

He asked coldly, staring at his papers: "Have you brought the blade?"

"I'm waiting to see my lawyer."

The investigator nodded to the guard. The latter put me in solitary confinement. Right inside of the place by the wall were three cubicles the height of a person, roughly 1 × 1 m in size. Red stains resembling blood could be seen around one of them, and a moan was audible from within. I was just trying to work out where I was when I was shoved into one of them.

A blow to my back propelled me with one knee and both hands straight on to the sharp concrete spikes covering the whole inner surface of the cubicle and the door. I had anticipated hunger, cold showers, and fights. But punishment like this, meted out by these 'fascists', was beyond my wildest imaginings. Nevertheless, somehow I managed not to panic, and in complete darkness, I licked the blood off my palms to disinfect them and even tried to reach my bleeding knee with my saliva-covered fingers, but without success. I gave a heavy sigh and thought about my situation.

I heard them cart off my already silenced neighbour to Calvary. He had obviously passed out, unable to withstand the strain of slow torture. Contrarily, this thought only made me stronger-willed. I even began singing quietly, using counterpoint as usual to express my critical emotions. "This is our final, decisive battle . . ." (from the Communist Party anthem). Poor Lenin, ideological, political author of this tragedy. If only he could have seen what his secret ambition had turned into, he would certainly be turning in his mausoleum. Could he really have imagined how much these ignoramuses and cretins could distort his noble and progressive ideas of socialism for mercenary purposes?

A short while later the door to the gas chamber (as the inmates called the cell) flew open and the long-awaited order rang out: "Get out!"

I shuffled out, and was bundled into the shower room. The medical attendant bandaged my knees and put some 'brilliant green' antiseptic cream on my palms, to cover up any trace of legalised crime. He flung me a clean robe and sent me back to the guards, who showed no let-up in the tempo of my 're-education', and led me into another cell. I protested, demanding that they return my academic jottings, which had been left in the previous place. You should have seen those goons laugh, clutching their fat stomachs, and rolling around like clowns:

"Professor, while you were relaxing in the 'quiet room', they turned your old bedchamber upside down in a search. All your papers and other rubbish were taken to the trash ages ago. This isn't a university, you know. Ha ha ha!"

On Friday morning I reported to the officer making his duty rounds:

"The next hearing on my case is taking place on Monday. I really need writing materials to prepare for the meeting with my defence counsel tomorrow afternoon."

He duly offered me a sheaf of paper with some pencils, and made a note for himself about my meeting with the lawyer. In no time I had made the most of the opportunity to record in writing the facts of the Butyrka workers' crime in breach of the Criminal Code, underlining their intent to maim me at the hands of criminals and my unlawful confinement in the bloodstained cell. When Goldberg heard about these latest events at our meeting, he told me to sign on the bottom line of ten clean sheets of paper. He made a close examination of the cuts on my palms and knee, and promised to type out my complaint to the assistant of the Russian general prosecutor for the attention of Sergei Prokhorov. He would take it to him personally and send a copy to the relevant department of the Ministry of Justice (as back up). Then we went through all the possible peculiarities of the trial hearing in painstaking detail. The defence informed me of a change in the make-up of the jury. Goldberg was certain that a new charge would now be brought against me: moral and destructive rather than administrative and financial. He promised to appeal if the case became extreme.

On Monday my case was heard personally by the Chairman of the Regional Court with two jurymen at his side. Without any introductory formalities, the new prosecutor introduced two witnesses for the prosecution and aggressively interrogated the two fictitiously enrolled students from the ZIL Cultural Centre. The judge coarsely silenced the defence counsel, not allowing him to express arguments in favour of the accused. This was (in Goldberg's words) a cheap farce in a prearranged scenario, with a conclusion fixed in advance by the higher organs of power. Thirty minutes later the court adjourned to consider its verdict. For over an hour, the lawyer and I waited for the fateful decision in the isolation unit. He reassured me, explaining that the delay must be due to disagreement in the judge's threesome. The longer and more deeply they argued, he continued, the better it would be for the defendant. At long last we were invited into the conference room without any members of the public or witnesses. The judge and one jury member (in contravention of the article in the Russian Criminal Code) delivered their verdict.

'Following two hearings of the criminal matter, for amoral involvement of participants of the Ballet Studio in financial manipulation at the ZIL Cultural Centre, the Artistic Director Mikhail Semyonovich Berkut is on trial for criminal responsibility according to article X, part X. The accused is sentenced to eight years' imprisonment, serving time in the Labour Correction Colony [in the uranium mines in the Kirov region].' Once I was free, I would only be allowed to work in the manufacturing industries, and would have no right of abode in the capital or major cities in Russia. (Signed by the judge and just one of the two jurymen.)

I was prepared for something like this. My defence lawyer stated that he would appeal.

At the end of the week the duty officer warned me of a meeting after lunch, for which I would need to tidy myself up. I didn't ask any further questions, just nodded my agreement. In the empty staff office, without the usual mesh gates were just two stools, in opposite corners. A minute later the officer brought in a thickset man in civilian clothes and introduced him as a colleague of the Russian state prosecutor. I stood up and made a formal bow.

"Please sit down, Mikhail Semyonovich!"

"I'm already 'sitting down'. It's been four months already."

Prokhorov smiled. "Milia and the children send their regards."

"Thank you. Forgive me, I don't know what to call you now."

"Sergei Fyodorovich at work. But, just like fifteen years ago, you can simply call me 'Seryozha'."

We were sitting five metres apart, eyeing each other up and down warily. My interlocutor nodded to the guard, who left. I sighed heavily.

"Mikhail, I haven't come here to interrogate you. The leadership of ZIL and the Bolshoi Theatre are insisting that the regional court reconsiders your sentence, in relation to your indirect involvement in the recent breach of administrative and financial discipline. I have come as a result of your complaint."

"Sergei, I understand that I have committed a misdemeanour at work, and admitted my guilt on the first day of the investigation. However, I haven't found mention in any of the articles of the Russian Criminal Code of prison officers' authority to persecute or mock the defendant in conditional, preliminary confinement before the trial. Or to subject me to the risk of physical mutilation or unwarranted punishment through severe torture. Look at my shredded palms and knee from the lock-up. I want to know: what have I done to deserve all this?"

"I assure you that I will look into these facts and regret any possible extremes in the prison administration's dealings with your trial. Along with this, I strongly recommend you not to get so worked up about short-term problems. Do you want me to pass anything on to your family?"

"Say hi and give them my best wishes. Thank you."

From what Prokhorov had said, I realised that people on the outside at the highest level were fighting a bitter battle for my future and Zhilin, director of the ZIL Cultural Centre, was playing a leading role in this defence party. He quite rightly considered that I had essentially taken the blame for everyone. The friendly advice from my former student to 'stay patient', was nothing other than a signal from Zhilin: don't upset the Justice Department workers with your complaints, because they will only use them as a weapon against your 'malicious breach' of socialist law and social morals. Depriving a citizen and professional of his legal right to work in the field of culture and reside in the major cities of Russia for such an insignificant crime is actually an incomprehensibly impudent witch-hunt against an artiste for his endeavours in non-party, free creativity to celebrate his contemporaries' heroic spirit and the romance of classical heritage.

Pitiful torchbearers for socialist realism, sin and shame on your ignorant heads! This was an example of the kind of curse I sent into the Butyrka darkness. And every time, bouncing against the thick walls of the Ministry of Justice, they came back to my cell unchanged like a boomerang with a distressing echo, to beat me mercilessly into enlightenment.

A week later, Goldberg reported back happy news on the positive outcome of my appeal. My previous sentence had been changed from eight years to three years of forced, corrective labour, not in the uranium mines, but in the

Gorky car factory, with the possibility of parole six months before the end of the period. But the removal of my civil rights, in restricting the work I could do and the areas I could live in on a permanent basis, remained as before. On the one hand, I was preserving my biological life, living up to the ZIL management's testimonial about me, and on the other, a bone was thrown to the bloodthirsty jackals, desperate to deprive me of my creative life in my homeland, i.e. the very essence of existence altogether.

The lawyer also informed me that I was to be transferred in a few days to a third prison in Krasnaya Presnya, a transit prison for dispatching convicted prisoners to their intended destinations. He warned me to be prepared for much worse conditions and not to take my eye off the ball. I thanked Goldberg warmly and embraced him in farewell.

On arrival at my new 'state home' I was taken straight from the car to the medical room. The guard stayed and waited by the door (as I understood) of the new prisoners' customary medical examination. A strange doctor with a shaved head looked like a prisoner himself.

He commanded me coarsely: "Strip! Well, what are you waiting for? Need me to help you? Ha ha ha!" He looked me over from all sides and barked again, "Get your clothes on! Sit down here! Open your mouth!"

Something about this absurd scene disturbed me. The doctor felt my forehead for a long time, and peered underneath my eyelids.

Finally, he yelled decisively to his assistant orderly: "Syphilis! Two pints!" and started to prepare a syringe with a tube for a jab.

"Excuse me, Doctor. May I ask, what is going on?"

The latter was exasperated.

"Don't you know that you've got syphilis? Cut the pretence! You can't get away from it."

"That's curious, how have you diagnosed that without a blood or urine test?"

"You've got some raised bumps on your forehead – it's the first sign of this venereal disease."

Naturally I took a symptom like this as a joke and asked the doctor in the same tone: "But what about my third nipple? Maybe it's gonorrhoea personified?"

"Roll it up."

"What exactly?"

"Your sleeve, of course."

"What for?"

"Don't kick up a fuss! You know, for a blood test," and he looked at the guard.

The latter came away from the door in our direction. The doctor pumped roughly a pint of blood out of me into a glass receptacle, as if actually using a pump. My head was spinning. This gave me an idea of how to stop the bloodsucker. As soon as he had applied cotton wool to the puncture from the syringe, I squeezed it with my finger, rocking from side to side. Seeing another syringe in the doctor's hand, I rolled my eyes and fell off the chair on to the floor in a faint, banging my head on some metal scales nearby. Here is where it actually went dark, from the blow to the head as well as the loss of blood. I felt the alarmed doctor scoop me up by my shoulders and slap my cheeks, but I decided to play the role of the 'dying swan' to the very end. Only after a stream of cold water was splashed on my face, did I finally come to, imploring the doctor with wild eyes: "What happened?"

"It's nothing to worry about," he growled, writing something in his daily journal.

The attendant and guard sat me on a chair. I thought the doctor was fully intending to carry on with his session of forced blood donation, but the orderly and guard simultaneously grabbed me under the arms and walked me to my base.

On the way, barely moving my heavy, unsteady legs, I asked my escorts icily: "Where are you taking me?"

"To solitary," the orderly replied. "You'll be comfortable there."

The assistants exchanged meaningful looks. I realised that further ordeals were in store for me, but wasn't sure if I had sufficient strength to overcome them ad infinitum.

A huge 'banqueting' hall, roughly 80 × 90 m, was graphically decorated with complete square cages with brick partitions along three walls – each protruding half a metre into the spaces for solitary cells. It was just like a zoo for criminals. Each cage contained a table in the centre and a couple of two-storey bunk beds. In the corner was a slop bucket and at the front a mesh door. In the centre of the high hall was a circular arrangement of sanitary inspection stations. All the workers were wearing white gowns and surgical gloves with an anti-infection face mask around their necks. Three inmates in one of these cages greeted me without turning around, playing a game of chance with dominoes. I said hello and lingered by the door, not knowing which place was available to a newcomer. At the same time, the bump above my ear was hurting from my fall, my head was spinning and I felt sick.

One of the players turned to me in a break: "Is this your first time inside?"

"Yes, but I've already done four months: two in Matrosskaya and two in Butyrka."

"So how come you're so pale, like an anaemic sausage? I suppose you've got syphilis as well?"

"No, the doctor in the medical room just drained a pint of blood from me for no reason at all."

All three looked around at the same time and shook their heads in disgust.

"Look, mate, there's no place for you here. Do your time in another zone before it's too late."

The guys carried on with their game and I thought: *There are good people in this world.* Nevertheless, I decided not to take up the free mattress and called the duty officer. I recalled my lawyer's and Prokhorov's exhortations. Without causing a fuss in my usual manner, I sat quietly on the floor by the mesh door. Clasping my knees, I rested my head on my arms and decided to wait for a suitable opportunity. During the next round, the guard asked me through the grille: "What's up with you?"

"I need to speak to the duty officer urgently."

"He's not here."

At this point the three men kicked up a stink about them not following the rules regarding chronically ill prisoners. They had in mind those with tuberculosis, venereal diseases, eczema and similar. The noise brought the officer and two thugs rushing from the medical station. Hearing about my situation, he explained that they could only move me to another zone the next morning. But he warned that it would be a lot worse for me there.

"What could be worse than contracting syphilis or tuberculosis here?"

Without a word, the duty officer noted my personal number and returned to his station.

I chose to spend the night on the floor rather than lying on the infected, stinking mattress.

After breakfast the guard and medical orderly took me to the zone for convicted prisoners awaiting transfer as per their sentences. This was a wide, square space, approximately 20 × 20 m, full of rows of two-bunk beds, covered not with mattresses, but with sheets of plywood. The smell of disinfectant penetrated my nostrils. Most of the bunks were free. Exhausted after a sleepless night, I sat down on the nearest of them and watched the movements of the guards with individual prisoners in an endless stream: back and forth. It turned out that prisoners were only allowed to be transported by train during the night. So in the daytime they were sorted into groups for prison wagons going in the same direction. I was so tired that I didn't notice myself collapse on to the plywood and fall asleep.

I was woken by a working prisoner shouting with a bowl of broth and a hunk of bread in his hands. Completely wiped out, I tried to doze again, but this time my slumber was interrupted by the officer, reminding me that sleeping during the day was not acceptable. Having found out where I should be going, he glanced at his notes and informed me that I would be transferred to the Gorky group after breakfast tomorrow. He took me to fill in some form and told me to bear with it. I wanted to ask, "To what end?" but stopped myself. The old man was clearly being sarcastic, although there was something he wasn't telling me. I felt as though someone outside of me was in control of my destiny. The officer looked severely at me and at the same time seemed to sympathise. As if he knew more about my case than he should in his position, or had received special instructions.

Surely my previous sponsors can't still show that they care about me?

Those departing that night were sorted into groups by supper time. There were only a few of us left in the banqueting hall. Following the evening meal the guards in surgical masks gathered all tomorrow's 'tourists' into one corner and disinfected the remaining part of the room.

I asked the bloke nearest me about the resort we were going to.

"Why do they do this? It's impossible to breathe like this."

"You'll find out soon enough."

Once they'd finished spraying chlorine on the floor, bunks and slop buckets in the other corners, the poisoners moved off, slamming the door shut behind them. Inevitably, a minute later an acute stench of chemicals surged our way. Without any ventilation this was an echo of the fascist gas chambers of the Second World War. Shielding our noses and eyes with our sleeves, we tried as much as possible to minimise the effect of the assault on our senses. But hardly five minutes had passed before all of us in turn began running to the close-stool in our corner to vomit or rinse our eyes under the tap. This went on for several hours until it was over. In my innocence, I assumed that all the prisoners would have to be disinfected before their departure the next day, so as not to pose a risk to the outside world, which would be only fair. Alas, once again I had underestimated the situation and overestimated the humanity of the public health services.

As soon as the main lights were switched off following the spraying, leaving just a weak night light, we settled into our bunks to sleep. Within fifteen minutes of drifting into a light sleep, my hands began to itch unbearably, followed by my whole body, including my back, chest, head and other delicate areas. Waking up, I noticed dozens of bedbugs on me, sucking blood all over my body. I jumped up in horror, bashing my head on the upper bunk. The hungry bugs were frantically tearing my poor body to pieces. I shook them off me and started stamping my feet. Here I saw on the floor hundreds of uninvited masseurs, crawling aggressively in my direction, towards the smell of fresh blood. I thought I was having a nightmare. But turning around, I caught sight of the remains of last night's blood-sucking sacrifices in the corner. We all stamped wildly, bent double, spun around, and jumped on the spot, all in an effort to get rid of the small, virulent predators. To an outsider, this could have looked like a dance of devils in Hell, waving their arms and legs in chaotic rhythm: with shaking heads, open mouths and bulging eyes, reminiscent of my choreography for Mussorgsky's – *A Night on the Bare Mountain*.

Some of the prisoners took off their coats and whipped each other with them, trying to scare off the greedy parasites. But with limited success. Under our boots ever larger bloody blisters from blood-sated bedbugs were bursting with increasing frequency. Hordes of their mates streamed towards them, crawling out of the cracks between the floor and the wall in a swarm. The weakened prisoners started shouting, calling for help. But no one from the outside came to our aid. I decided to endure this new trial of inhumane blasphemy in silence, whatever may happen. Continuing my convulsive stamping and shaking, I began to think where and how I could protect myself in the most effective way from a mass of attacking insects, and finally I found the solution. In our panic during the bug invasion, we had left everything in the same corner, fearing that we would poison the disinfected area in the other part of the room. Shaking my robe out carefully, I trod the brown parasites into the opposite corner. I clambered up on to the top bunk and sat cross-legged, Asiatic style. Removing my boots feverishly, I emptied them out. My bare head and face were still crawling with the disgusting bugs, creeping into my ears, nose and down my collar. I struggled to get rid of them, aware that this was only a temporary phenomenon. The plywood underneath me was still wet from being sprayed with bleach, leaving my brain stupefied. I didn't know how long I could tolerate this smell and the pain in my eyes, but it was a case of choosing the lesser of two evils.

I confess that my enemies were much more robust than I was. Half an hour later, boldly overcoming the disinfectant, they interrupted my drowsiness again with their evil bites. I squashed them on the plywood with both boots from all sides, and threw them down. But these insects, like cockroaches and ants, were so tenacious, that nothing was beyond them. They worked out the defensive movement of their sacrifice sooner than the last victims had evaluated their strength. Five inmates were surprised by my unwise preference for self-destruction by bleach. Yet the canny bugs were wide awake. Noticing their dead comrades on the floor beneath me, they changed their strategy. After climbing up the metal bunk supports until they got to where I was, my predators attacked me from behind, from under the plywood, on which I was sitting. But I was waiting for them with arms at the ready, and turned around 180°. When they became too numerous, I jumped on to another bunk. The great carnage raged until morning. My lacerated cellmates sat with their boots in their hands on the floor by the door, where there was more disinfectant, crushing all the merciless assailants around them with the last of their strength. Only now did I understand the officers' warning on the eve of the night battle. It's not without reason that Mayakovsky and Yakobson paid homage to their poetry and Dance in the Mariinsky Ballet production of 'Bedbug'.

Immediately after the wake-up call, a group of cleaners came quickly into the battle hall with buckets and mops to clean away the debris of the bloody trials. We were taken all together to the medical station for treatment (shower, shave, ointment for bug bites, etc.). They gave us a clean robe, warmer than the last, and disinfected boots. The whole day was eaten up in preparing for our departure: documentation, instructions, medical reports and the return of our personal effects.

After supper, the Black Marias took us to the central trading and sorting base for Moscow. There, a whole guard of sub-machine-gunners with Alsatians – our personal guard – awaited the 'guests of honour'. Naturally all prisoners' hands were handcuffed in front and each group of six to eight 'tourists' heading for the same destination were chained together. They spent ages pointlessly sorting us, until eventually I ended up in a hermetically sealed prison wagon in the middle of a goods train. Inside the lodgings were a total of four cages lengthwise, mounted on the wall. There was straw on the floor and a hole in the metallic hoop instead of a slop bucket. The sliding door of the cage had a padlock, and on the ceiling was one small window per cage behind a grille on each side of the carriage. Two bodyguards to four convicts – one in each cage. It could have been worse. These wagons were clearly meant for the privileged few.

For two days during the journey I gave serious thought to my principles in life and moral conduct. It had become apparent that they did not tally at all with what was going on around me. I couldn't and shouldn't go on like this. I faced a stark, uncompromising choice if I could only survive this considerable trial:

1. Accept the Soviet Communist Party's conditions of ideological control which were repellent to me. Become a creative puppet of socialist realism and pretend like the other champions of the arts in the Soviet Union. Or:
2. Carry on fighting for my professional and artistic convictions. Or:
3. Try to make a break for freedom from this mire of lies and violence, by leaving my homeland. Or:
4. Take it to the limits, to the world of eternal peace and inactivity, satisfying the interests of my sworn enemies.

After my long and torturous ramblings, I worked out a plan of action:

a) to see out the two and a half years of forced labour at the Gorky car factory with all my strength;

b) to study the social customs, cultural life and systems of state education in the developed countries of Western Europe, North America and even Australia, if necessary;

c) to escape or emigrate (via Israel) by myself initially. Then, if that worked out, to bring my sons.

This was no philistine's sweet fancy, but a principled survival strategy. I swore on the spirit of my mentor Shatin and my father's ashes that as long as I remained on this earth, I would complete this sacred project. Or I would give up life without regret, as many more-significant beings had done before me.

We pulled into Gorky at midnight on the third day. We were unloaded one by one. One guard stood below, by the open door to the carriage, while the other remained above. A vivid picture from wartime films came into focus before my eyes. The beams of bright projectors illuminated two lines of machine-gunners with Alsatians from our special train right up to the gates of the goods station. I jumped down on to the sleepers and in shock, waited for an order. My wrists were trembling with trepidation in the handcuffs in front of me.

A voice on the loudspeaker boomed a warning about following instructions precisely: "Move slowly, along the specially lit corridor! Keep your hands in front! Don't look round! If you try to run, we will shoot without warning."

I was greeted on both sides every five metres by the Alsatians' spiteful snarls. Despite the fact that I understood the need for such precautionary measures, this ridiculous presentation of me as a dangerous criminal made me smile inside. But picking my way carefully over a dozen railway lines with half-blind eyes, I was scared of falling and getting a bullet in the back. Through the gates policemen shoved me into a Black Maria and drove me into town.

I awoke at sunrise in a detainee's cell in Gorky Police Station.

Lying on the floor I asked a prisoner cleaning up rubbish in the corridor behind the grille: "What time is it?"

"Six thirty. You can sleep a bit longer. The bosses don't come round until 8 a.m. They won't forget about you."

"How do I call the duty officer? I need the toilet before it's too late."

"Look, there's a white knob on the wall outside the grille there. Call him, and he'll take you."

A moment later, the officer appeared and welcomed me. I thanked him. He took me to the toilet and told me to come over to him once I'd finished. I was so accustomed to being supervised outside the cell that I was amazed at my freedom of movement. After a wash, I adjusted my baggy clothes in the mirror, and smoothed the non-existent hair on my head. I rinsed my mouth out, and cleaned my boots with toilet paper. Once I'd finished the enjoyable task of cleaning myself up, I then stood to attention before the officer in charge. He smiled into his moustache.

"Berkut, Mikhail Semyonovich? Dance teacher from Moscow?"

"That's correct, Comrade Senior Officer."

"You will meet the manager and his work-placement chief after 8 a.m. Breakfast is at 7 a.m. Here are the latest newspapers. Have a read in your cell. You know the way. Off you go."

"What if I run off?"

"Where would you go? This is a closed zone. And there's no point in adding to your time."

My chief turned out to be an intelligent commander. He supervised all administrative, economic and financial lawbreakers who were serving time with unskilled labourers in various departments of this factory.

The manager stated: "See Artyom Nikolayevich about any issues to do with work and everyday life. Your personal well-being during your time here depends on your conduct and output, as does the likelihood of your parole after two years. So it's all up to you."

The chief called me into his office and invited me to take a seat.

"You'll be working in the wheel department, punching semi-finished products. The work is physically demanding but cleaner than in other departments and there are fewer inmates. In the main, they're local residents from the town or surrounding villages. You will be living in the workers' barracks within the factory. Every morning on the way to work and back you must sign the register with our duty police officer. Failing to register is punishable by law and you will be subject to an immediate search. I alone have the authority to permit any infringement either in the department or barracks. Any 'taking your eye off the ball' will be considered a breach of discipline, and this will have a negative impact on your parole. And vice versa, social activity will count positively towards your fund of privileges. In three months' time, you may be permitted to visit your family in Moscow for New Year. Now we'll go to the warehouse and you'll choose some civilian clothes for yourself: a work uniform, shoes, pyjamas, toiletries and other items which will come off your future wages. You are obliged to keep the barracks clean, follow the routine, and obey the rules of communal life."

To finish off, Artyom Nikolayevich left me a pack of vouchers for three meals a day in the factory canteen for the next month, until my first wages. The money would be transferred to my name in the local savings bank to repay my debt to the state and the personal costs for my keep in the three prisons.

On my first morning at work, the chief introduced me to the department leadership and left me his telephone number. The foreman led me to the stamping section and gave me clear instructions regarding the technological process of the work to be undertaken:

"a) take a 17 kg wheel frame off the overhead conveyor;

"b) carry it carefully to the stamping press (so as not to drop it on your foot);

"c) put the wheel precisely on to the arm of the press like a ring and secure it with the claw;

"d) press the pedal down (the hammer will automatically bash out an opening for the bolt and mechanically move the piece into the next position; by following this sequence you will stamp a total of six holes around the core);

"e) take the wheel off the bench arm and take it over to the overhead conveyor a few metres away;

"f) lift the item to head height and hang it on the passing empty hook on the conveyor;

"g) take a step back immediately and wait for the next wheel frame to come to you (without holes for bolts).

"You will repeat this whole five-minute process from the beginning again. The norm in our production is ten wheels an hour. Any questions?"

"Not for the moment."

"Think you can manage it?"

"I hope so, once I've had a bit of practice."

"Have a look round today and tomorrow, and try it a few times with your colleagues' help. From Monday on I'll start writing you an order for your own work. I strongly recommend that you fatten yourself up and build up your strength."

"I'll try."

Of course, on my first working day without help from anyone else I only produced eight wheels an hour before lunch, and six afterwards. My back was killing me. I was amazed. *How can this be? I've been lifting my partner over my head regularly for fifteen years and have never experienced such unbearable pain. The wheel weighed less than 20 kg to boot.*

Of course, I had overrated my capabilities. Nevertheless, I wasn't inclined to give up. While walking around to familiarise myself with the department, I had noticed the medical office. During the lunch break I ran in and asked for a wide elastic girdle out of my salary. In exchange for a receipt, the nurse gave me a sports corset designed for weightlifters and advised that I was not the first prisoner to come to her with this request. I breathed a sigh of relief. When she heard about my profession, Marina shared with me that as a young woman she used to dance at Gorky University. I asked whether she had seen the ZIL Ballet on our tours to Gorky two years earlier on the Drama Theatre stage.

"Oh, yes! The girls and I went to see your operas and ballets almost every night. Mikhail, if you need any medical help, just call in. Feel free! This is snake cream. When you've finished your shift, take a hot shower and drop by. I'll massage your back. Rub your aching muscles before work in the morning."

Marina asked me to sign for the corset and cream, and wished me well.

Thanks to the nurse, the aches and pains throughout my body calmed down. But clearly I lacked the necessary energy and physical power. Such biological deficiencies in the body do not restore themselves that quickly. I just about made it through the first week. Thanks to workers in the Soviet Union's industrial plants over the last few years, we had two free days.

On Friday, the foreman came up to me after lunch and asked sympathetically: "How are you doing?"

"Not great."

"Do you want to stay here next week or move to another department? They could find you lighter, less risky work there. What do you think?"

"Give me another week to get settled in with everyone, please. I really want to get through this experience. And the people here are nice, they're trying to help me out."

"OK, Mikhail. But be careful not to do yourself any damage. Otherwise I'll be in trouble."

"Thank you for your trust and understanding. I promise not to let you down!"

All Saturday and Sunday I took time out for myself. I did some exercises, ate well, rested and went for a walk in the evening. I couldn't stop thinking about my burning soul and the 'snake' massage.

I felt hale and hearty on Monday morning and decided to attempt nine wheels in the first hour of work. It was difficult, but I managed this extra load to the original normal limit (eight out of ten). But with each passing hour the ninth wheel became ever heavier. My colleagues nearby could see me struggling with the last wheel before each ten-minute break, but had no authority to absent themselves from the machine tool without the foreman's permission, even though they wanted to give me a hand. On the last stage, before breaking for lunch, during many futile attempts to lift a finished wheel on to the conveyor, I crashed on to the floor with it, making such a noise that both the foreman and department manager came running. The workers, feeling sorry for me, were exasperated at the management's cruelty. I was taken straight off to the medical quarters. Marina made me up some kind of injection and made me take some medication. I felt more shame than pain. As the lunch break came to an end, the department's trade union organiser arrived, and discussed something very animatedly with the nurse. An ambulance appeared and sped me off to the factory hospital.

The chief was already waiting there to give me the once-over. He had heard from Marina what had happened, and asked if I had been forced to carry out this work that was beyond my capabilities. Naturally I denied that the department manager had put any pressure on me. I confirmed that it was my personal initiative to attempt to achieve the working norms on an equal footing with everyone else. I expressed my regret at my unsuitability for the work, and for causing them unnecessary inconvenience.

"On the contrary, 'Every cloud has a silver lining.' We've just received an enquiry from the factory's Trade Union Committee for permission to transfer you from this department to the Cultural Centre, so that you can continue your sentence within the factory. But the police-station chief noticed in your court sentence a condition about potential future activity 'only in the arena of goods manufacturing'. The Factory Committee chairman has sought assistance from the general director of the Gorky car factory. In collaboration with the Party Committee secretary, they have decided the issue in your favour and personal interests. They have called us, you and the director of the Cultural Centre in for negotiations on Friday. The project in question was originally planned for January, in three months' time, but now the situation has changed and they are talking about your immediate transfer. As a matter of urgency, you must draw up a list of essential conditions to prepare Cultural Centre groups to take a successful part in a forthcoming amateur competition. Unfortunately, you will have to remain in hospital for a few days to explore the repercussions of this incident. Following the X-ray, the doctor has confirmed that your lower disc is compressed in your spinal column. He said, 'You are lucky. This fall could have made you an invalid for life.'"

We were met at the Factory Committee by the chairman and director from the Cultural Centre. The chief introduced me to his leaders. It turned out that I knew them both well from the recent tours of the ZIL People's Theatre in Gorky.

The chairman got straight to the point: "Mikhail, we are offering you a full-time schedule in your specialist field in the Cultural Centre: six days a week, apart from Mondays with the three main groups at the Cultural Centre."

1. Russian Folk Choir under the direction of Levanov (dances and suites)
2. The ballet studio, artistic director/teacher Volgina (excerpts from the repertoire)
3. Dudkovsky's variety ensemble (staging of movement for the programme)

You will work as a choreographer with each group two to three times a week. We will pay one and a half times your rate into your account in the savings bank, so that you can pay off your debt to the court. We are fully aware of everything that went on at the ZIL Cultural Centre, and you have our deepest sympathy for everything you have been through. Zhilin passed on his regards and was happy about your transfer from the wheel department to the Cultural Centre. Do you have any questions for us about the project in hand?"

"Firstly, my thanks to all of you for your help. I will do my best to repay your trust. Secondly, to work successfully, I need to rent a room next to the Cultural Centre. Thirdly, I must bring from Moscow some of my production materials, or will need someone to do this for me from the address indicated, and on my telephone confirmation. I'm talking about music scores, audio tapes, books, notations, tape recorder, etc. On top of this, I will need a pass to move freely around the zone, some cash in hand to pay for the apartment, food, clothes, professional bits and pieces and toiletries, internal transport costs (bus, taxi) and so on. I would also like to have a look at the groups you've mentioned as soon as possible and get to know their leaders, as well as studying the rehearsal and stage restrictions of the work spaces within the Cultural Centre. I'd like to settle the timetable for future classes and the potential or desired repertoire, plus meet the Director with the leaders of the three groups to discuss my proposed productions, etc."

"Mikhail, thank you for this. You will resolve all creative issues in the course of your work with the Cultural Centre's artistic leadership, and the administrative details with the general director. We are counting on your successful work to win prizes. Good luck!"

From the Factory Committee, the chief and I headed to see the superior police officer to complete the necessary documents for accommodation in the private sector and work in the Cultural Centre within the grounds of GAZ. Artyom gave the Colonel an official order from the car factory's general director, who in this zone was lord and master, under the auspices of the Ministry of Defence.

Signing my new pass, the policeman asked Artyom with some alarm, "How has this come about? We take on responsibility for changing a court sentence in your protégé's case, but we don't stand to gain anything from this?" He shook his head, discontented, looking at me reproachfully.

Sensing his irritation, I turned to my custodian, not knowing how to react to this kind of statement. The latter merely shrugged his shoulders and kept quiet.

"Excuse me, comrade. Have I understood correctly that I'm preparing your amateur activity for the forthcoming competition on an unpaid basis?"

"That's absolutely right, Mikhail. There are more than 300 staff in the car factory, including guards and operatives. They even have their own club. Every year we take part in an amateur show, but we have never been lucky enough to win the competitions. That's why having the opportunity to train once a week with them for a winning programme would be invaluable."

"Right! Who will be able to bring my accordion and working materials from Moscow?"

"Let people you trust send all that from the capital with someone and we'll receive it here and hand it over to you. You can't imagine how happy our artistes are going to be."

Over the weekend, the leader moved me from the barracks to a private flat, which he had rented on my behalf. As before, I had to report daily to the police station, but this did nothing to wound my pride. I couldn't believe that I now had two rooms: one to sleep in, the other for creative work. Could these living and working conditions really compare with past ones – in prison and in the department? Even taking into account that I would have to work in three Cultural Centre groups and now the Police Club, I considered myself extraordinarily lucky. Of course it would mean working with the guards free of charge. Still, it was worth it. I sighed with relief, and spent all of Sunday preparing programmes and presentations of creative projects for the approaching meeting with Cultural Centre leaders the following morning. Lieberman, the Director, made all the introductions. He summarised the decision of the factory trade union and GAZ Party Committees to use my talents and experience as a stage producer/ballet master in the next two years to prepare them for amateur theatrical productions. Without any particular formalities, I proposed to each colleague two to three alternatives for unique projects according to their individual choice, based on the ensemble's artistic profile and their performers' technical abilities. After a face-to-face meeting with the leaders, we decided the repertoire in collaboration with the management.

I started off with a variety review, comprising: a compère, vocals, dance, music, comic sketches and the like. Alexander Dudkovsky himself, the Cultural Centre mouthpiece and administrator, was actually a young and adventurous leader. He happily took on board all my production ideas for the ensemble and developed them subjectively in his unique, satirical way, without worrying about the reaction of the censor or critics 'from on high' to his poisonous attacks 'from the ground up'. I warned him that my status as a pseudo-prisoner could invoke complications with those overseeing, which was the last thing we needed. He and I agreed that the choreographer's name would not be printed anywhere on the programmes and posters. With the leader's help, I managed to complete this review by mid-December. Dudkovsky was an excellent administrator. In a comparatively short time, he arranged for the stage props to be ready. I rehearsed the programme under my own direction with audio and light effects, accurately recalling and reproducing all the subtle movements in the production. I gladly shared with him the benefit of my experience in the theatre, and as a token of his gratitude for this collaboration, Sasha supported me in my work with other groups and with my personal problems.

He helped me to make a telephone call to Agrippina in Moscow. My friend was delighted to hear my voice and learn of my new workplace. She promised to pack up the materials I listed and send them with my accordion to the appointed address with the train conductor. She agreed to call my son Dmitri and give him my address, so that he could let me know about his achievements and how the youngest was doing. Pina invited me for New Year. I promised to try, commenting that I would be lucky, before phoning Mum in Odessa. She started crying with joy, saying that she wanted to come to Gorky for a few months after the New Year's celebrations, to be with me and help her 'happy medium'. I undertook to ask the management about getting permission for her to come, and to let her know the outcome. The last call was to Sofia in Leningrad, leaving Dudkovsky's telephone number, and asking her to ring me.

The next focus of my professional attention in the Cultural Centre was the Russian Folk Choir, which consisted of a dance group: twenty-four main performers and an orchestra of folk instruments: eight musicians with their conductor. A retired former soloist led the dance group, and he was a good répétiteur and organiser. But they usually invited a choreographer from the Ural Folk Choir. From a choice of three, Levanov selected my propositions from the old ceremonial 'Russian Easter': a thirty-five-minute programme involving the whole group in a general composition for theatre. The choir sang from time to time using the spacing and movements of round dances; orchestral soloists danced with a pipe, balalaika or concertina. The dancers echoed the choir with a recitative or danced with tambourines and wooden spoons. This huge piece of work was like getting blood out of a stone. Each separate part of the ensemble produced excellent work, but they were not used to being onstage in joint, interwoven acts of traditional rituals and were clearly opposed to the principle of working as an ensemble in ancient, folkloric festivities. Levanov, his wife (the second choirmaster) and I often had to battle with inertia and laziness from the elderly choir members, resistant to progressive change in the group. Still, thanks to the leaders' enthusiasm, the new production advanced slowly but fruitfully for all that.

The most neglected area was the ballet studio. Yana Volgina, a middle-aged retired former ballerina, instructed children and adolescents in the Vaganova technique, but lacked any creative spark. Occasionally she put on excerpts from ballets without taking into account the performers' technical and emotional capacity. She simply wanted to satisfy their mothers' demands to see their little ballerinas onstage in tutus. In response to my suggestion that she reorganise around 100 dancers to take part in a production more suited to their age, physical attributes and abilities, Yana arched her grey eyebrows as if I'd fallen out of the sky.

"What for?"

"How else can I satisfy the Director's request to put on something nice with your learners in time for the competition, which will catch the jury's attention?"

"Mikhail, we've got by just fine without you for nine years and we'll survive another nine years!"

First I consulted Dudkovsky, to explain the delicate situation with the ballet.

"If I don't keep my word to the Factory Committee chairman and the director of the Cultural Centre, this could influence my chance of parole. Tell me, what should I do?"

"For the last few years our ballet studio hasn't generally played a part in shows. It's not the first time the question has been posed about new management, but we haven't found a worthy successor. I'll bring Lieberman up to speed on this problem. He's been looking for a way out of this ballet impasse for ages. I'll ask him to ring the director of the Gorky Regional Cultural Centre."

Back home I found a note from Dudkovsky, asking me to be ready by 10 a.m. the next day to travel to the Cultural Centre to meet a former soloist from Perm Theatre. She was looking for a job teaching Classical dance to children. They were expecting us. In the car on the way to the regional Cultural Centre, Sasha drove me around the architectural monuments of the old town, and named the main streets and squares. The director of the regional Cultural Centre gave us a friendly welcome and introduced Zoya Spitsina from Perm. Her husband was a construction engineer and had got a transfer to work at GAZ. So she had had to retire from ballet at the age of thirty-eight. She didn't have any children of her own, but was desperate to work with other people's. I asked Zoya if she had ever given classes to little ones of five to six years old.

"In Perm I often saw the elderly teachers in the ballet school, who had settled in our town when the Kirov Ballet was evacuated in the war. I studied Classical dance with them myself for eight years. They promised to put in a good word for me."

"There's no need for that. But your diploma from ballet school . . ."

"Here it is: my documents, including roles I've performed in programmes of various shows. I'm ready to give a trial class with children or adults."

"Could you come with us now for discussions with the director of the GAZ Palace of Culture?"

"Of course. I've even brought my employment log with me just in case."

At this point Sasha telephoned the Cultural Centre and confirmed a meeting with the Director for 12 noon.

While we were making our way back to the Cultural Centre, Lieberman negotiated the necessary replacement of Yana Volgina with the Factory Committee chairman. She had long indicated her wish to retire as soon as a possible new studio leader was appointed. After half an hour's discussion with Zoya Spitsina, the Director and I unanimously agreed her appointment. The secretary took the happy new addition off to complete the contractual agreement and also to prepare the procedures for the former ballet-studio teacher to take up the retirement she was due. In this way, all three production teams in the different Cultural Centre groups were more or less stable. I was conscious that for the initial period I would have to support Zoya in working with children: offer hands-on assistance to her as with any new recruit, as well as in reorganising the groups. Only under these conditions would it be possible to put together a team to perform extracts from *The Nutcracker*: 'Waltz of the Snowflakes' for forty-eight girls and 'Dance of the Mice' for six boys. Now the mothers were sure to be content. The Factory Committee allocated the funds for costumes and decoration. Zoya promised to rehearse both productions on her own.

I rang Mum and told her that the management had authorised her visit. At the same time I wished her a happy birthday for 6th November. Imagine my surprise when she announced that after meeting her sisters she had decided to come not for New Year, but in a week's time, the sooner the better. I tried to dissuade her, but our Panther had a strong maternal instinct.

She stated categorically: "Any mother should always be with whichever child of hers needs her help and care more than the others at that moment. That's a law of nature."

"All right! Then write down my address and the telephone number for the GAZ Palace of Culture. Telephone or send a telegram once you get to Gorky. Don't forget your passport!"

I arranged with my landlady to pay a bit extra towards communal expenses, and reorganised my office into a bedroom for my guest. Dudkovsky brought a firm mattress with screw-in legs from somewhere and two sets of bedding with a warm blanket. I was touched by how attentive he was.

"Mikhail, relax! It's not a gift, it's coming out of your Centre salary! Ha ha!"

My mother quite naturally spotted me before I saw her, and waved her scarf.

"Misha, Mishenka! My son, I'd already started to think that I'd never see you again." She cried tears of sorrow and joy at having her child back from another world.

"Mum, this is Sasha Dudkovsky – my friend, colleague and fine sponsor."

"It's a pleasure to meet you; my son told me about you on the telephone. Thank you for all your help!"

"Anna Davidovna, welcome! I hope you haven't had too bad a journey."

"Not at all. Some good people were kind enough to help me on the train and when I had to change."

Mum liked her room on the upper floor of the two-storey house, with its toilet/shower room in the flat. After a cup of tea we went to the nearest shops with a large bag on wheels and did some shopping together. Having just turned sixty-seven, the Commander was still mobile, but I was only too aware of all her physical problems from the war. Mum promised not to lift anything heavy and to leave the empty trolley on the ground floor under the stairs, not to wear herself out, to rest in the afternoon, and watch films and shows in the evenings at the Cultural Centre (opposite the house). From this moment my everyday problems almost evaporated. I couldn't recall having experienced this kind of domestic bliss in the last twenty years.

The Police Club constituted an unusual page in my creative programme at the car factory. It was easy to envisage the physical structure of guards, who spent all day or night in charge of the many areas within the closed zone, ready to get into a fight at any moment with thieves of car parts or saboteurs. Art lovers like these would come before or after their shift. Without changing their special clothes, they would sing, dance or play musical instruments for a few hours, just for their own enjoyment, and not for the public. A 'home-made' amateur production of this nature was not worthy of being entered in the festival. I had to seek my chief's advice. Artyom Nikolayevich explained the situation to the manager of the regional Ministry of Internal Affairs. The Colonel listened attentively, making shorthand notes of my report for the minimum essential conditions for classes in the club to be successful.

"Artyom, get me the club deputy. Let's sort all these problems out now, while Berkut's here!"

"Mikhail, what else do we need to organise for our artistes in the club?"

"A tight timetable of their classes with me on Mondays (my day off). Most of the guards work four shifts of six hours. I suggest taking them in two sessions for two hours at a time: in the mornings with the second and third shift, and after 5 p.m. with the fourth and first shift. This way we'll get everyone who's interested and will have more chance of selecting talent for the competition in one or another genre."

Once the club deputy arrived, the Colonel filled him in on my requests. This member of staff rang the factory manager's office and asked them to set up two toilets with showers and a dressing room for the club as soon as possible. No one dared to say no to the manager of the regional Ministry of Internal affairs (MIA). The club deputy obtained from the Colonel the relevant instruction to set up an adjustable timetable of classes, and promised that the artistes would attend regularly. Most likely the police chief realised at this point why his famous club had been unsuccessful in previous shows.

After the first week in the club, getting to know the future performers of the show programmes, I presented to them the forthcoming repertoire for the different work shifts.

1. 'Tennis Quartet' – a sports pantomime – four men with racquets.
2. 'Lyrical Duet' – a masquerade – a pair of young male dancers.
3. 'Singing Hands' – excerpts from popular fiction – four humorous girls' mimes.
4. 'Dancing Musicians' – instrumental divertimenti – a sextet of six men.

It took eight months of serious preparation to devise this complex programme, and demanded a high level of creative discipline. The problem was that these young people were used to having a lot of freedom during their time at the club, and I had to teach them how to conduct themselves to reach a professional standard onstage. It was one thing to expect discipline from staff in the workplace, and quite another to manage their leisure time to master skills in stagecraft.

Mum found plenty to do in Gorky. During the day she was busy with housework. Almost every evening she attended the eight o'clock film or concert at the Cultural Centre. All the usherettes knew her and extended their hospitality by inviting her to cultural events. After this, she would happily cross the square and go back up to her room. Usually when I got back from rehearsals, Mum would already be asleep, and was up before me in the mornings. She often dashed off a letter to Odessa and heard the latest from her sisters. When preparing her famous pirozhki and borscht for New Year, she insisted that I invite Sasha and his wife to a pre-New Year's lunch on Saturday. I was concerned that Dudkovsky would be too busy, but he was happy to accept the invitation, and the four of us really enjoyed our midday time together. Then we all went off to the show at the Centre Theatre.

At the beginning of January we were stunned by a bolt out of the blue. There was a sudden knock on the door one midnight. I thought that someone had got the wrong address and didn't answer. The landlady's flat below was uninhabited.

"Berkut, open up! It's the police. We've got your son Dmitri with us."

I had just about got the front door open when a familiar mug poked through the crack and began shouting: "Daddy, open the door! It's me. They held me at the station as if I was some kind of thief."

"Sonny, looking at you now, I would think the same. You've pitched up like a storm in a teacup and you're all wound up. You should apologise for troubling people, and not make so much noise."

While I was clearing things up with the policemen, my mother had woken up and was looking out on to the stairwell. As soon as he saw her, Dmitri bounded into his grandmother's embrace.

"Mikhail Semyonovich, we found you quickly because of your work at the club with our colleagues. They told us at the station to bring your son straight to you. He has no documents on him whatsoever, and the dog's eaten all his money. Judging by the way he looks, he's run away from home in Moscow."

"Thanks for delivering him safely. I'll deal with him myself, don't worry. Goodnight! Mummy, go back to bed. Things will look better in the morning. Your grandson will sleep with me."

I twigged that the Moscow flat had been the scene of tempestuous family events, but didn't want to upset the boy's grandmother at night. So I asked my son not to talk about it until after breakfast when I would go and buy him a fold-up bed and some personal items. I promised Mum an update on the Moscow situation after lunch, when I'd clarify with the police the legal ramifications of having Dmitri with me, given my parole status. And in the car factory's prohibited zone to boot.

"Right, come on, son, out with it! Who hit who and how many teeth did you knock out with your boot?"

"How do you know that she and I had a fight? Have they told you already?"

"No, my darling. I know you and your mother only too well. Let's cut to the chase."

"After you were arrested, Mum and Tanya turned our home into a brothel. The cooperative chairman gave her several warnings, but it was no good."

"You shouldn't tell me lies like you normally do. You're fourteen now, not four. Why have you run away?"

"On 1st January a few boys and girls were round at our place, getting ready to see in the New Year. Suddenly Mum and Tanya brought in two men and told us to scram. She and I had a tussle. She scratched my neck and I gave her a bloody nose. Tanya called the police and they took us both off to the station. They warned us that if this uproar occurred again, they would take action against both of us for antisocial behaviour in a communal property. A few days later they brought their fuck-buddies back again in the evening. . . ."

"Their who?" I frowned, looking threatening.

"Sorry, Dad! Their men friends. And they started brawling again. Both sisters tied my hands behind my back. I kicked out and got Tanya in the head. She passed out. While Mum was calling an ambulance, I grabbed her purse from her bag and slipped out. I bought a ticket at Kazan Station and caught the first train to you."

"What were the men doing while the fight was going on?"

"Drinking vodka in the sitting room and laughing."

"Let's get this fold-up bed home and you can have a shower and get changed. After lunch we'll go to the police station. I'm obliged to inform the management about these goings-on and seek their advice. The Colonel is the only person here with the authority to decide what happens to you."

"Dad, do we really have to go to the police? Why can't I live with my own dad?"

"Because, as I say, I'm serving my sentence in Gorky. As an exception, they've given permission for Grandma to live with her son. As a minor, you are not permitted to live in close quarters with the criminals here, especially without an identity card."

My son helped me to rearrange Mum's room to make space for the camp bed at night (opposite her mattress) on the other side of the table. The main work was done. Now Mum and her favourite grandson could wish each other 'goodnight'.

Misha, a naïve dad, was one of life's incorrigible idealists. Over lunch, Mum was persistent in her efforts to extract the reasons for her grandson's unexpected visit.

"Mum, people don't run away when things are going well. He had a fight with Milia's sister Tanya and made his escape."

"Exactly like his dad a quarter of a century ago. He fell out with his brother and ran off to live in a children's home where he was working as a musician. 'The apple never falls far from the tree.'"

I laughed, and my son's eyes nearly popped out of his head in surprise. Mum was ladling borscht on to our plates and adding fat to the fire at the same time.

Firstly I called on my supervisor at the police station. He explained that the problem with my son was not his concern. I would have to refer to the Colonel.

Half an hour later I brought the boss up to date with the situation and asked his advice. The Colonel stared straight at the fugitive. He was making notes during my report. He asked Dmitri a series of questions about school, his friends, his younger brother and his relationship with his mother.

"Wait in reception. Your dad and I will discuss the most appropriate way to help you."

"I'm sorry for causing you extra work. My son's arrival was a complete bolt from the blue."

"Mikhail, we all have children: some are easy, some are hard work. Unfortunately, Dmitri falls into the second category. He's been neglected, abandoned and backed into a corner by both his parents. He can't go back to his depraved mother in Moscow, and he is not permitted to stay in Gorky with his convicted father. Either we'll have to get him into a boarding school here, or he'll have to return to his mother, even if we have to send an escort with him. Alternatively, he will roam around with the street children until, in the worst-case scenario, he ends up in a young people's institution."

"Are there any day schools or a children's home in the area for young people like him?"

"In our region there is only one sports boarding school of any note, where experts from Moscow enforce a strict regime and coach future international champions. If you could get to speak to the Director, Shapovalov, then this would be your son's ideal way out of the critical situation he's put the two of you in. I'm obliged to inform the Moscow MIA of Dmitri's whereabouts right away, and give them the address where's he's staying with his grandmother. Your mother is registered for a year here, but you are officially listed at your former barracks. If Dmitri's mother refuses to send him his birth certificate, his grandmother can order a copy from the archive in our station. The main thing is to find him a school of some sort."

I relayed all the information from the MIA manager to my son and advised him to give serious consideration to attending the sports boarding school in the car-factory region, which seemed to be the best available option.

"In general, at your age you won't be able to live anywhere in our country without going to school. I'm sorry, it's time for me to go to work, so you go five or six blocks in this direction and have a look round that unique sports boarding complex. You'll have supper with Granny at 7 p.m. and go with her to the eight o'clock film at the Cultural Centre. Don't say anything to her for now about our plans, or about Milia either."

After the rehearsal I visited Dudkovsky in his administrator's office.

"Misha, are you planning to move your whole family from Odessa and Moscow? The usherette told me that your mother came with her good-looking grandson today."

We both laughed and I updated my friend on the problem that had landed on me. He shook his head in concern and asked a few clarifying questions on the topic.

"I'm good friends with Shapovalov. He's harsh but fair. He doesn't mince his words. He often rents our theatre for his events. I'll have a word with him."

"Sasha, I had to work with the Central School of Athletics in Moscow, preparing programmes for national competitions with artistic gymnasts and figure skaters. Is it possible that the Director might be interested in my help, free of charge, in exchange for accommodating my son? Artyom Nikolayevich would not object to this social commitment on an occasional basis."

"Good! Come in at 9 a.m. I'll call the Director."

In the morning, on the way to Dudkovsky's, I got my son to reflect on his problem.

"Are you sure that you want to live here for the moment or would you rather go back to Moscow? You can see how my bosses are trying to help you, thanks to me. In a month or two you'll have sorted yourself out and will run off somewhere else, without saying goodbye to your granny. You'll let everyone down without a word of thanks or paying your way. I won't get over the shame."

"Dad, do you remember when I used to do swimming at your Cultural Centre in Leningrad? If they accept me at the sports school I saw yesterday, then I'll definitely stay here."

"It's nice to hear that. But you're so out of the habit of sticking to a routine and discipline that you're going to find it hard to adapt quickly at the beginning. Do you have enough patience and willpower to impose self-discipline on yourself, which you're going to need to be successful in sport? We're not talking about playground games with kids here."

"I promise to try my utmost, to prove to you what your eldest is capable of."

"OK, I believe you and ask one thing of you: whatever happens, stay until June."

"Dad, you have Berkut's word of honour. Let's shake on it! Don't worry, I won't let you down."

"Aha, so you're here already? I rang Shapovalov from home this morning; otherwise you can never get him at work. He's expecting us at nine thirty. I also put our director in the picture regarding this unusual project, just in case he has to address the Factory Committee or management. The school is within the grounds of GAZ and is dependent on the landlords in many ways. The boarding-school director is expecting us."

Sasha introduced my son and me to him and rushed off to work.

"My name is Gleb Zakharovich Pinchuk. Dudkovsky told me your story. Our sports school provides specialist education and in principle doesn't take casual students, and in the middle of the academic year either. But there are exceptions to every rule. What are you called?"

"Dmitri Berkut."

"How old are you?"

"Fourteen and a half."

"What's your Dad's name?"

"Mikhail Semyonovich."

"What about your mother?"

"Emilia Sergeyevna."

"Where were you born?"

"In Slavyansk, Krasnodar region."

"What school did you attend, and what class were you in before the New Year?"

"Seventh grade at secondary school No. 139 in Moscow."

"What type of sports do you like?"

"Swimming."

"Since when?"

"From the age of eight."

"Can you list any physical defects?"

"I don't have any."

"What's your height and weight?"

"I don't know."

"Our doctor is waiting for you in reception. Come back here once he's finished examining you."

"Yes, sir!"

"Mikhail, can I speak frankly?"

"Yes, Comrade Director, please do."

"I know all I need to know about you and your son for school purposes. In principle I don't have any objections to this application. I only asked Dmitri those questions, as you'll be aware from teaching, to determine his communication skills. He seems physically strong for his age and to have stamina. Even so, I picked up a couple of hints of insincerity in his eyes and a lack of purpose in his character. Despite all his physical abilities, he likes being horizontal, that is, he has a lazy disposition. Similarly, he's sharp in conversation, but uncommitted in his work. We can take him for a trial period up to the summer holidays and regrettably – and unpleasantly for you – only as a compromise. Everyone's aware that we are making a special exception for you, as the leadership of GAZ, the Cultural Centre and MIA (Ministry of Internal Affairs) are pulling out all the stops to make use of your talent for successful participation in the competition. When we opened here three years ago, the Ministry of Physical Culture and Sport, who rent this place from GAZ, didn't include payment for electricity in the contract, and today we are in debt to the factory to the tune of 11,000 roubles. This management team is threatening to switch off our electricity substation in the next summer holidays, unless we settle our debt by 1st August. I'll personally take on the administrative risk of enrolling your son, without having the proper authority for this, on condition that GAZ write off this debt for us."

Naturally I was shocked at this ultimatum. But I promised Shapovalov that I would forward his conditions for registering my son at the boarding school.

Dudkovsky composed a heart-rending letter to the Factory Committee chairman outlining the complex, risky situation in my family, which meant that I would not be in a fit state to ensure the Cultural Centre groups' creative success at the competition. Lieberman, the Director, called the police chief, and between them they came up with a joint strategy to influence the GAZ leadership. In the meantime, Shapovalov for his part sent the general director a no less sensitive query about writing off the boarding school's historic debt, and enclosing relevant documents. Following rambunctious debates at a meeting of the powers that be, the action was decided in favour of the sports school, on condition that they complied with their obligation to make regular electricity payments from 1st January that year. As a result, 'The sheep were safe while the wolves were full.' Fortune had been more than generous to me this time. I never expected such a gift from her. Worried that she might change her mind, I began preparing my 'sapling' for his prestigious educational establishment. The various special uniform items were being provided by the school, as well as the necessary school equipment. I had only to supply the schoolboy sportsman's personal bits and pieces and psychological, supervisory input for this spiritually neglected lad. Dmitri resisted, considering himself suitably well educated for such a 'provincial' school. I needed to bring him down to earth.

Finally he stood before Shapovalov: clean, with a new haircut and sporting a new coat.

The Director looked the novice up and down sternly. He called in his senior trainer and director of studies. He gave them 'a future champion' and in front of all of us, gave a stark warning: "You do not skip school when you feel like it! Not ever, for any reason!"

Dmitri waved goodbye to me.

I approached the Director with a request: "Gleb Zakharovich, please accept my apologies in advance, if my son fails to adjust to the general routine right from the start. Please take into account that he has lived without his father for the last three years, under the shameful influence of an unhinged mother leading an amoral lifestyle. With your permission, I would like to visit Dmitri every Monday and check on his progress with his trainer and tutor. In an emergency, please ring Dudkovsky at the Cultural Centre, who has the most contact with me at work. Thank you in anticipation."

"Good! I hope this won't be necessary. But who knows?"

It was completely obvious to both Shapovalov and me that Dmitri, with his damaged upbringing, would not endure this test of self-discipline and subjugation to the sports-school regime. It would not be possible in such a short period of time, at the age of fourteen, to break his already formed spiritual and psychological make up, with its attendant outlook on life and habits. The question was, how long would he last in this weightless state of having his time organised for him, without his anarchic impulses, in order to give me the opportunity to finish preparing my artistes for the competition?

After lunch at 2 p.m. every Monday, I visited the school. First I'd get the latest from the director of studies and the trainer. Both stated unanimously that Dmitri was a bright lad with excellent physical attributes for sport, but absolutely unmanageable in group classes/training sessions and particularly in the sleeping quarters, where he completely ignored the rules of communal living.

"For example, every Saturday after supper the kids are happy to watch a new film in the club. The girls and boys are required to sit in different halves of the auditorium, separated by a central passageway. During the screening, Dmitri moved seats in the dark to be with the senior girls and started pestering them. First he was taken out of the auditorium. The next time the teacher gave him a serious reprimand. Last Saturday in the middle of the night, influenced by the film he'd just seen, Dmitri went up to the sleeping girls on the second floor in his swimming trunks with a white sheet wrapped around his head. This area is out of bounds to boys. The wonder boy started whistling, jumping from bed to bed and undoing the sheet from his head, imitating an evil demon. It's not hard to imagine the consequences of this. If I may say so, it's no joking matter. The Director has given a warning: if he does anything like this again, he will be expelled and sent to the police station."

Talking to my eldest in a quiet corner of the school after hearing this news about his latest adventures, I asked him calmly: "Dmitri, what are you trying to achieve?"

He leaped like someone who'd been bitten on the arse. He ran rings around me in a frenzy and yelled, "What are you all having a go at me for? I behave the same way here as I've always done: in Odessa, in Leningrad and in all the other cities. Why should I do things any differently here?"

"Surely you didn't behave like this in your Moscow school?"

My son opened and closed his mouth twice, unsure of the best way of answering.

"Were you a bad student there too, bothering girls, ruining teachers' lessons with your constant messing about, fighting with boys during lesson change, etc., etc.?"

"Where did you get all this from? From your personal experience? Grandma was right when she said, 'The apple never falls far from the tree.' She's your mother, so she should know. So for all the things I've done wrong, you are the guilty one, and can't blame me for anything! I'm leaving."

"If you go now, you needn't bother coming to my home any more. Sit down and stop mucking about. You were the one who said that you wanted to come to this school if they would take you. You swore that you wouldn't let me down with your out-of-control behaviour. You've dumped everything on me after running away from your mother, as if you were unbalanced too. You are jeopardising my parole, forcing me to take urgent precautionary measures and isolate myself from you as the one bringing trouble to my door. Think about everything you've heard me say and make your mind up. I'm going now. Don't expect me next Monday. I won't bother you any more."

How I was able to return to Terpsichore after these rows, God only knows. I would be correcting the artistes, when my eldest would flash before my eyes in his swimming trunks, a sheet wrapped around his head. This tested me to the limit.

Over lunch, Mum asked about Dmitri. Her wise eyes were watering. I passed on the trainer's and director of studies' thoughts without going into detail. Bagheera admitted that she was missing her grandson and felt that he wasn't having a great time there. We talked through this problem from every angle and came to a unanimous conclusion. The longer Dmitri remained among well-behaved children and under the watchful eye of educationalists, the better it would be for all of us. Nevertheless, the boy's grandmother pined for her favourite grandson, who was not allowed to come home even at weekends until the summer holidays.

In mid-March during a stage rehearsal for 'Russian Easter', the usherette came over to me and told me that my mother was in the foyer, asking me to come urgently. I apologised, and asked her to let my mother know that I couldn't get away.

"Please sit her in the lobby and ask her to wait until the break in half an hour's time. Or she could have a cuppa in the café. Thank you for looking after her."

At the end of the rehearsal onstage with the Ballet studio, I found Mum in Dudkovsky's office. She had already told Sasha the unpleasant news about her grandson's return home, with his face all beaten up and covered in bruises. Sasha had telephoned the sports school and clarified what had happened. Dmitri had been rude and decided that he could get away with pawing one of his female peers with impunity, as the director of studies didn't know how to respond to their complaints in the absence of the Principal, who was on a business trip to Moscow. The girls resolved to stop the hooligan by themselves. They ambushed him in a dark spot. Working as a team, they tied his hands behind his back, then bound him and wrapped a bundle around his head, as they do in films about revolutionaries. Kicking him wherever their sporty legs landed, the 'Hollywood hero' eventually lost consciousness. The duty guard happened to come across him on his rounds and took him to the medical room. There the sex maniac was brought back to his senses with a couple of needles in the bottom. The cuts and bruises all over his angelic body were plastered over, and the following day he was pronounced to be in full health and sent to his teacher. He didn't get the chance to prove himself as a swimming champion. Expelled instead, he stuffed his things into a rucksack and left the school in disgrace.

Having dragged himself home, covered in plasters, the 'prodigal grandson' didn't even greet his grandmother, not due to loutish tendencies, but because during the beating, someone's heel had kicked his teeth in. He couldn't even eat properly, let alone talk. The patient lay down on my sofa in the sitting room and looked down listlessly. There was nothing for my mother to do but raise the alarm in the Cultural Centre. Should she call the emergency doctor, or order her beloved grandson's coffin. The Panther couldn't understand it at all: why were Sasha and I laughing, making light of this near-fatal event. The Cultural Centre administrator rang the car-factory hospital and called an ambulance to my address. Mum and I hurried home. The emergency first-aid service arrived at the same time. On the way upstairs, I told the paramedic about the fight that had led to my son's injuries. I woke Dmitri up and helped him to get undressed. The nurse disinfected the open wounds on his back and legs, applied fresh dressings and left some cream for his swollen bruises. She gave him a tetanus injection just to be on the safe side and advised him to spend the next two or three days in bed at home. I suggested that my son rest for today. Tomorrow he could let me know when he would be ready for a serious conversation. I asked him not to bother his grandmother and to remember that she was already sixty-seven years old.

"She's got enough problems to worry about in her life without your antics. Mum, if Dmitri starts getting on your nerves, shove him with the rocking chair in the kitchen."

"Can I give him something to eat? The poor thing hasn't eaten since yesterday."

"That's his bad luck! After this stunt, he only deserves to eat cockroaches and flies."

The Police Club deputy asked me what had happened to my son at school. In response I waved and started perfecting the police programme on the Cultural Centre stage. This was the first allocation of spacing, positions, intervals and directions on the full stage. The dancing 'tennis players' and 'musicians' had to completely reorientate themselves after the small stage in their club: getting used to the new scale of stage to be used, psychologically and intuitively determining the line and spacing/proximity adjustments between partners and opponents, increasing the trajectory envisaged for the tennis ball or length of one's steps and jumps accordingly with the new floor-space dimensions.

None of this would have come that easily even to a professional, but for the adult performers – physically trained MIA staff – it wasn't that complicated. In an hour we succeeded in familiarising ourselves and getting accustomed to the new parameters of the large stage. At the general rehearsal the following Saturday, we would reinforce the new details from today regarding the spacing and movement. The regional Cultural Centre jury would arrive on Sunday to select the best car-factory numbers for the gala festival concert on 8th May, Victory in Europe Day.

Inevitably, in the penultimate week before the competition, I was immersed in the Cultural Centre for days at a time. From 8 a.m. to 12 noon I managed the lighting and staging or audio-recording of the music. After lunch it was individual or group rehearsals in the Police Club with participants from different work shifts and departments. I would usually get home around 10 p.m., but Dmitri would not be there. Mum said that every day he left the house after lunch and came home at midnight when she was already asleep. Over a late supper his grandmother and I discussed a strategy for sending her grandson back to Moscow. Clearly my son was avoiding me, as he didn't want to leave Gorky for home. My artistes from the MIA club reported that during their staff rounds of the car-factory zone they often saw Dmitri in a group of local yobs and petty thieves. They weren't causing any trouble, just peacefully playing cards, drinking beer and smoking. Still, this was extremely damaging to my reputation. During my next review, the department leader requested my chief paid him an urgent visit to discuss the issue of my son's presence in the GAZ zone without a permit.

"Mikhail, we can't go on like this. Dmitri has got in with a gang of undesirables and can really mess up your parole. The week after the show, either willingly or forcibly, we will have to send him back to his mother in Moscow. You and his grandmother need to give your written consent, and because he's a minor, we will organise everything without you being involved."

The day before the show, Dmitri didn't come home for the night. It transpired that he'd been arrested with his 'mates' who'd broken into a beer kiosk and stolen a crate of beer. The police chief handed my son a written warning that he had to sign: he had forty-eight hours to leave the prohibited zone of the car factory for not possessing a permit. Otherwise he would be sent to the Youth Detention Centre for breaching passport rules.

"We would have done this to you long ago, had it not been for your father, who, I'm sorry to say, is far too good for you. With your disgraceful behaviour you have not only demonstrated your arrogant stupidity, but brought shame to the person closest to you. Here is a copy of your birth certificate, ordered by your granny two months ago. If you've got any sense, go and get ready to leave. Remember: forty-eight hours, no longer!"

Once I'd belted home for lunch on the day of the general rehearsal, I heard some good news from Mum. Wiping away tears, she brought me up to date with a jolt.

"The policeman brought my beloved grandson home dirty, reeking of cigarettes and fierce as a dog. I made him take a shower, gave him something to eat and put him to bed. Here are the papers from the police station. He's got to go back to Moscow by Monday at the latest. I washed his clothes and cleaned his boots. Talk to him!"

"Mum, I'm sorry. I don't have time for him right now. It's the Cultural Centre competition tomorrow. They're expecting me at rehearsal. When he wakes up, he can come to the Centre to watch the final run-through onstage. I'll ask Dudkovsky to book a ticket by telephone for Dmitri on Monday's evening express train. Don't worry about your grandson. He'll sleep like a baby all night on the top bunk in the carriage. By late morning he'll already be back in his dear mother's arms."

I led the rehearsal from the production desk in the auditorium. At the final rehearsal the director and cultural organiser of the Factory Committee came to cast a fresh eye over our work before tomorrow's show, so that when it was finished, they could pass on their comments to the group leaders. I invited them to sit next to me and share their opinions as the rehearsal was in progress. All of a sudden, the dishevelled figure of Dmitri appeared before us, taking a seat in the centre of one of the empty rows in the front. I gestured to the usherette to ask my son to move to the rear half of the stalls. He responded by throwing me a dirty look and made a great show of leaving the auditorium. Externally, I made no reaction to his move. But inside I was seething at such a display of insolence.

Dudkovsky willingly carried out my request regarding the railway ticket, and promised to take us to the station on Monday. On my return home, I was astonished to find my son sitting at the table, chatting calmly with his grandmother. He had suddenly remembered that his 'unfortunate friends' should still be at the police station Pretrial Detention Centre, and he had no one else to hang out with. With a smile, Mum handed me a plateful of borscht.

"Enjoy your meal, son!"

"Thanks."

"Cheers."

There was an unusual sense of peace and calm in this house. I wondered what had brought this about. Most likely Mum and her grandson were plotting against me. But what?

"Misha, what time is the competition tomorrow? Could you get us two tickets?"

"It starts at 3 p.m. Here are two complimentary tickets for you, by the aisle in the seventh row."

"Dad, I'm sorry for being so thoughtless at the dress rehearsal today. Grandma has explained to me where I went wrong. You are right to call me an 'uncouth numskull'. I promise from here on to become 'couth'."

Mum and I almost spilt our borscht laughing.

Mum summed up again: "Mishenka, I've told you time and again, that Dmitri was following in your footsteps, but you didn't believe me."

The senior group from the ballet studio opened the show with 'Dancing Dolls': six miniatures to music by Shostakovich in concert-form suites – sixteen minutes long. After that came the 'Fledglings Ballet' to music by Ravel, performed by the little ones – four minutes. The first half closed with artistes from the variety review's 'Satirical Kaleidoscope' – twenty-three minutes. Artistes from the MIA club opened the second half with my repertoire: four miniatures – eighteen minutes. The local show concluded with the Russian Folk Choir's rendition of 'Russian Easter' – twenty-seven minutes. The auditorium was filled with the artistes' families and theatre lovers. They gave it a rapturous reception, even more so when they saw performers they already knew. Once the show was in full swing, they were transfixed until the final chord. It was lovely to experience this theatrical etiquette with representatives of the working class in the auditorium. The regional jury was headed up by the artistic director from the Gorky Drama Theatre, who selected most of the numbers he'd seen for the festival Gala concert in May. He only left out the 'Fledglings Ballet' and 'Masquerade Surprise' by the MIA club. But they accepted the humorous ditty 'Singing Hands' as a piece of mime acting in front of the final curtain while the finale set was being changed.

During discussion of the programme in the conference room the show's chief producer and the director of the regional Cultural Centre expressed their compliments to me and were interested to know how long I would be working at the Cultural Centre. I shrugged my shoulders in answer.

Dudkovsky came to my rescue: "Probably up to the end of next season. But we won't let anyone else have him."

Everyone laughed.

My director explained something to the visitors. I just picked up my chief's name and realised why they were interested in me. I confess, I was so tired after turning my hand to so many different things at the same time in the car factory, that at that moment I didn't relish the thought of going anywhere else straight after the competition. On the contrary, I was much more tempted by the possibility of resuming my project for the textbook on Character dance in the summer. Under my Mum's wing, and without my dear, wayward son.

Could it be that my supervisor will strongly advise me not to spoil relations with the city authorities? They are all exploiting my dependability.

When the local heat was over, Lieberman invited the jury members and group leaders to a traditional banquet, organised by trade-union officials. I gave my apologies as I needed to get my son ready to leave for Moscow. Everyone knew that this was just an excuse for me to avoid getting involved in any social or civic activity due to my status. As we took our leave, Dudkovsky reminded me that he would be coming at 5 p.m. tomorrow to take us to the station.

At home, Mum was cooking up a sumptuous farewell feast to mark her grandson's departure. We even 'divvied up' a litre bottle of kvas (non-alcoholic beverage made from fermented rye bread) between the three of us to toast 'the prodigal son's noble return to his home'. Somewhere along the way, Mum had baked her grandson some of her celebrated potato and cabbage pirozhki for the journey, just to please him.

The 'man of the moment' stumbled up from the table (instead of saying 'thank you'!) and with an unceremonious belch, declared: "I'm going to say goodbye to my mates and will be back in a couple of hours."

Mum and I were open-mouthed in shock, not knowing whether he was joking or not.

"Son, you know you can't do this, and that it's not fair on us."

"Daddy, it's not fair that you're always putting pressure on everyone in the family and taking away their basic freedom of movement. That's why my mother hates you so much."

"My darling grandson, I beg you, spend your last evening at home! You promised me after all."

"God! You're so fussy with your endless demands! I can't stand it. . . ."

Screwing his face up in disgust, the eldest slammed the door and charged down the stairs, whistling.

"Mum, don't get upset! Give him an inch and he'll take a mile."

I escorted the sobbing grandmother into her bedroom, and got stuck into the washing-up.

As expected, after an hour of searching avidly for his mates, my son pitched up in an evil mood, and went straight to bed to avoid our next 'round'. While Dmitri was asleep, Mum and I agreed not to pay him any attention until it was time to leave, so that he wouldn't have any opportunity to create havoc. I took Mum's purse and valuables for safekeeping that night.

"If he asks you to lend him some money, tell him that you don't get your pension here. Every morning I give you the amount you need for household expenses from my account."

"Surely my grandson is not capable of stealing from his grandmother? You're doing him down."

"If he can do what he did with his own mother before running off here, then why wouldn't he do the same the other way round? In any case, be on your guard! Call me if you need anything."

After waking at the usual time of 7 a.m., Mum came into my room instead of the kitchen, where I was already doing my morning exercises.

Looks like something's happened, I thought.

"Misha, pop into my room for a minute and see what Dmitri gets up to at night."

Standing outside my eldest's door and hearing his familiar heavy breathing, I opened it and went in to see my son. On the edge of the table, on Mum's side of the couch lay two large kitchen knives, their blades pointing towards her pillow. In silence I placed both weapons on the sleeping boy's side and pointed them towards his head. Then without a sound I went out into the kitchen, closing both doors behind me. I decided to get to the bottom of this and take precautionary measures.

"Mum, tell me everything! What went on in your room before you went to sleep?"

"When I was getting into bed, exactly as you predicted, Dmitri asked me to lend him 100 roubles. I answered following your instructions and advised him to direct this request to his father. He announced that if I didn't give him the money willingly, he would be driven to take it from me by force and that this would be my fault. What was I to do?"

"Don't worry, just get breakfast ready calmly. I'll deal with him in my own way."

At 8 a.m. I knocked on his door as usual, shouting: "Dmitri, breakfast is on the table!"

Naturally he didn't respond. I went over to his camp bed and knocked on that.

"Son, explain to me why these knives are lying here? Were you dreaming about pirates last night?"

Without answering the question, he pointedly turned to face the wall, covering his head.

"Fine, let's go and explain to your grandmother what happened in my house last night."

I picked the knives up off the table and took them into the kitchen. A moment later I went back into the bedroom.

"Is it true that you tried to extort money from your grandmother and threatened her with knives? 'If you don't come clean willingly, I'll have to use force with you.' I quoted his night-time threat to his grandmother and decided to teach my son a fatherly lesson.

He remained silent. I shook the fold-up bed with both hands. It collapsed flat and 'Sleeping Beauty' tipped on to the floor. At this point my enraged son went for me with his fists, but then remembered a previous incident. Then, naked, he had attacked me from behind in the bathroom, jumping on my back and suffocating me with his elbows because I'd stopped his depraved mother from washing the thirteen-year-old beanpole's (forgive me) penis and balls with both hands. My young son couldn't straighten his back for a long time after this duel with his father. Now he appreciated the difference in our weight.

"What are you waiting for? Let's test our strength again, like we did in the bathroom. For threatening your grandmother with knives you will get a minimum of five years. Is this what your new pals have taught you? I knew that my son was unbalanced like his mother, but a thug? You have exceeded my expectations. Now you need to beg me to pack you, you little mugger, off to Moscow as soon as possible, before I press criminal charges against you. Despite all of this, I'll give you some money to buy a present for your little brother, once you're already in the carriage. For now, go and calm down, and ask your grandmother to forgive you, otherwise you and I will be saying our goodbyes today for a lot longer than you had in mind."

Dmitri sat in the car sulking all the way to the station, not responding to any of Dudkovsky's jokes which were intended to cheer him up. I couldn't look at my son. Mum said that her grandson apologised before leaving and thanked her for the pirozhki. On the platform the porter, who was a friend of Sasha's, asked why his guest was so down in the dumps today.

"He really doesn't want to leave his friends and those beautiful Gorky girls."

"Dmitri, here is an envelope for you. There's fifty roubles exactly for you and your brother. Give him my love. And here's a bottle of kvas that Granny forgot to put in your rucksack."

My son got up into the carriage without saying goodbye to me. Sasha saw him to the compartment and showed him his seat number. We waited by the carriage until the train pulled out, and only then left the station. It felt like a huge weight off my shoulders.

"Mikhail, congratulations on regaining your creative freedom. You've a huge amount of work ahead in April to fine-tune and perfect all the programmes for next year's competition in May. Every cloud has a silver lining!"

The Second World War victory salutes boomed on 8th May, orchestrating the successful end of the car-factory workers' performance in the festival Gala concert. At the celebratory banquet, the city mayor presented the competition prizewinners with honorary certificates and pronounced a toast to mark the victory festival. For ethical considerations, I requested my chief's permission to sit next to him in the MIA (Ministry of Internal Affairs) staff group. I felt like showing people around me that I didn't 'touch a drop of spirits', and that if anyone should attempt to slip me some, it would be under the supervisor's watchful eye. As I expected, in the gap between courses, the director of the regional Cultural Centre and the artistic director of the Drama Theatre came to sit near us.

Apologising for the interruption, they asked: "Mikhail Semyonovich, can we talk to you about doing some work next season?"

"I'm sorry, you're probably better off speaking to my boss, if he doesn't mind."

At a meeting in the MIA department, the chief passed me an urgent request from the mayor to help the city Drama Theatre and regional Cultural Centre the following season.

"Artyom, won't this have a negative impact on my parole?"

"In connection with that the mayor has promised to enquire with the manager of the car factory MIA, with a copy to the GAZ general director. If they come to a positive agreement on this issue, you will receive written instructions from me, setting out the days and hours of work in the theatre and the regional Cultural Centre. In this way, if there are any claims from Moscow, they will be resolved by the leaders of the car factory and the city. Taking precautions like this is in my interests as well."

"If the current project comes out of the Cultural Centre's budget, then what will happen to my salary?"

"We're only talking about three months, June to August, during which you will continue to be paid your current salary in the Centre, where you will only begin the new season after two weeks' leave, on 16th September. That's reasonable, if you are interested in this project."

"Could you give me written notice of the temporary change in my place of work?"

"I don't have the authority to do that, but the manager of the local MIA will do that for you no problem."

"What will my duties be in the new structure?"

"Wait for instructions."

At the end of that week the chief took me to the regional Cultural Centre in the morning. The Director, Yeryomov, welcomed us with emphatic courtesy and introduced his department deputy, Yelizavyeta Stolnikova. While the officials were drawing up the necessary paperwork, Liza and I discussed a three-month programme of seminars on 'European Folk Stage Dance'. The head of department chose Poland, Hungary and Spain. One month for each nationality. The second half of May was taken up with organisation and preparations. The courses were planned to take place twice a week, Mondays and Fridays, from 10 a.m. to 1 p.m. in the regional Cultural Centre. In the last class every month, the seminar participants would be tested by the regional Dance Council on their mastery of technical skills and character presentations from the repertoire of the relevant nationality. I asked Yelizavyeta how quickly we'd be able to set up a meeting with their pianist in the GAZ Cultural Centre to determine the musical accompaniment for exercises and studies.

At midday they were already expecting us in the Drama Theatre. Gavrilov, chief producer, made no effort to conceal his delight that his choreographic dilemma had been resolved with the new repertoire.

"Comrade Berkut, there is no professional ballet master in the whole of Gorky. I had a glowing telephone reference for you from Boris Chirtkov and a pressing recommendation to make use of your talent in our next production. Our actors are impatient to meet you. I suggest we meet in the College of Performing Arts. Their director and I have organised an impressive group of senior students from among the best ones for a dance and mime entourage over the three summer months. Their teacher Valeriya will be only too pleased to work as your assistant for this period. We are planning meetings with the practitioners three mornings per week – Tuesday, Thursday and Saturday. On the remaining three days, Valeriya will work on the new material with them herself. In the afternoons on those same days, we will work together with the actors on body language, imagery and stage movements. Our next show, aimed at a young audience, is *The Three Musketeers*, based on the novel by Alexandre Dumas. Now I hope you understand why we are in such need of a choreographer?"

"When do I need to start work, and who will provide the accompaniment at rehearsals?"

"Hopefully on 1st June. My production assistant will organise everything, including the pianist."

"I'm unable to use public transport. Who will give me a lift?"

"We'll arrange this with our chauffeur. If it comes to the worst, you'll have to take a taxi." On hearing from Valeriya that there was a new choreographer in town, the director of the College of Performing Arts stated that he remembered only too well my vivid presentations at the national seminar in Leningrad and wished to invite me to join an examination committee for students graduating from the college at the end of July.

The chief said, agitated, "Mikhail, we have to satisfy the appetites of Gorky ballet enthusiasts with this."

"I agree and will leave this to your judgement. 'Everything in moderation.' Artyom Nikolayevich, in each separate case where I am employed on the black market, please remind the commissioners to provide transport to get me there and back."

"Of course, Mikhail. By the way, here is a typed-up version of the days of the week, dates and times for both jobs for the three summer months, so that you don't get in a muddle: what, where, when and with whom."

We both had a friendly chuckle at such a sad joke about my cheerful role of Figaro. This probably meant our Great Leader, when he was writing about man's exploitation of man in the socio-economic formation of capitalist society.

It goes without saying that the most appealing theme in the summer repertoire was the choreography for *The Three Musketeers* in the Drama Theatre. This fable had piqued my interest over many years. It was ironic that an opportunity like this was offered to me here in exile, essentially to popularise foreign art and literature on the Soviet stage. No doubt it was one of the Devil's little jokes. Nevertheless, after a sober appraisal of my creative abilities, I asked the theatre's artistic director to invite a fencing consultant/trainer from the sports school, to give the actors some professional training.

"My dear colleague, he's already been working with our lot for two months. I'll definitely get you together for mutual consultation on the military and dance scenes. I'm certain that you'll hit it off. The whole sense of dramatising this novel lies not in naturalising the way the musketeers' exploits are portrayed, but in the playful, pretentious bravado of the battling cavaliers in a grotesque, at times humorous manner, with plenty of dance and acrobatic elements and the odd feat to dazzle a young audience."

One of my tasks as choreographer was to define the individual character traits of each musketeer. I was searching for a fitting form of movement for them, taking into account the specific, personal nuances of one hero or the other. As soon as Athos, Porthos, Aramis or d'Artagnan made their next appearance in masks, any type of audience had to be able to pick out the central characters immediately, by their gait or comportment, customary mannerisms or pose, dance style or fighting technique, particular to the individual in question, etc. This was no easy task, for the producers or performers alike. However, we spent so many happy minutes trying things out, when suddenly eureka! – we struck lucky, and found a successful complicated technical move with a sword in a dance movement.

Following Dmitri's departure, my mother started to miss Odessa. I suggested that she went home. But she was worried about my health and decided to wait until the show was ready for the next festival Gala concert at the beginning of May. During this period we didn't once discuss my future, following my release from exile. I clarified the judge's decision, which essentially blocked me from further creative work in my field in Russia and probably all the other republics too. This had already happened in Central Asia after my graduation from MTA.

"Mishenka, in the six months that I've been here, I've lost a lot of sleep trying to secure a better lot for my 'happy medium'. At first, as you know, I thought that you brought problems on yourself, because of your bullish nature. But living here and seeing how hard you work, how your colleagues relate to you, the success you enjoy with the public, etc., I've realised that I was wrong to think that your profession was too frivolous for a man. The usherettes in the Cultural Centre speak so highly of you and don't have a bad word to say about you. You have to earn that kind of recognition. Unfortunately, I have come to the conclusion that you won't be able to survive here after your release; you should follow your nose and escape to somewhere where you'll be able to show your talent in all its glory. Luckily for you, lots of our people are leaving Odessa, Lvov, Riga and Bessarabia [part of Moldova] now, and going to Israel. I heard from people in the bodega about various ways of emigrating, and consulted my sisters. They are all of the opinion that after your exile there'll be nothing for you here, and promised to make enquiries in the official office for Jewish emigration to Israel. Once I get back to Odessa, I'll get on to this straight away, but only on one condition. You must not, under any circumstances, 'let the cat out of the bag', right up to the moment you return. Otherwise they will destroy you before you get the call to go."

I invited Lieberman and Dudkovsky (without their wives) on Sunday for my mother's farewell lunch. The hostess had prepared her favourite Odessan dishes. Glass in hand, she didn't forget to thank the Cultural Centre leaders for helping her son at a difficult time.

The following day Sasha and I took the 'globetrotter' to the station and sent her off to Odessa via Moscow in a fast sleeper train. Naturally she was in tears, but was happy to be going home to Moldavanka where she belonged.

On the way back, Dudkovsky confessed, with feeling: "Misha, to have a mother like Anna Davidovna, is an enormous gift, which we don't value enough in our self-centred lives. To leave everything behind: her home, family, work, and come to her son at the other end of the world, to share in his woe and loneliness in exile in a foreign land. Losing everything and everyone simultaneously in the process, including her own personal freedom. Not every parent would be up to that by a long shot. I take my hat off to her!"

During the short break after supper I usually signed in at the MIA department, and after taking a walk for half an hour in the fresh air, I would pop in to the Cultural Centre for the 8 p.m. film show. It hurt my eyes to write by the electric light in the evenings. To kill time before going to sleep, I would watch old films and concerts in the Cultural Centre. On one of those evenings, before the start of the film in the semi-darkness, a woman sat down next to me, and seemingly accidentally brushed my side with her elbow. Without turning or tilting my head, I moved to the next free seat. The unknown woman then copied my move. I was already preparing to move to another row, when I suddenly realised that this giggling stalker was Marina, the nurse. It wasn't the first time I'd been similarly confused and previously this had happened due to my poor eyesight or being constantly preoccupied with my next choreography. Obviously I joined in with her laughter and automatically greeted her with a kiss, as if I'd always done that. She in turn also went into autopilot and returned the kiss, but her eyes were wide with fear or surprise. Apologising, I returned to my former seat and took her hand as I sat down. We watched the film cosily together, not letting go of each other's warm palms. I felt her fingers tremble occasionally in mine. But she didn't try to withdraw her hand. On the contrary, she relaxed again and in the dramatic parts of the film she sometimes even leaned against my shoulder. I felt like a schoolboy; I'd been without a woman for a year and a half, I gave in to the attraction, not knowing whether I had the legal right to do so.

Naturally, I saw Marina home after the film, not far from the Cultural Centre. She lived in a workers' settlement within the car-factory zone, on the ground floor of a communal detached house. When her mother died, the flat was left to her, which was her right as a member of the GAZ staff. I started to say goodnight, but the young woman held me back by the gate and invited me in for a cup of tea. I lingered, worried about my status in law, but the nurse took this as unnecessary bashfulness from her former patient and, laughing, pulled me through her front garden towards her front door. I surrendered to my mischievous fate, following her blindly under the moonlight.

"This is our old cat, Vaska. He sleeps in the day, and guards the house. At night he goes hunting for squirrels and rabbits."

While Marina was making the tea, I had a look around. The modest accommodation consisted of a large sitting room, tiny bedroom, kitchen and toilet with shower. Eminently suitable for a couple with no children. It was old-fashioned but cosy. The lady of the house offered apple pie with the tea, and old cherry liqueur which her mother had made. We drank to our meeting, which made me catch my breath. It turned out that you were only supposed to sip this 60% proof liqueur, as per the nurse's example, and not knock it back in one go, which is what this uninitiated guest did. I tried carefully to put out the fire in my stomach with the pie. Marina brought me a glass of cold water, apologising for not having warned me about the drink's inherent danger.

"Sorry, love, you're not getting away with that. You're going to have a pay a fine to get out of this."

I pulled the smiling young lass towards me, sat her on my lap and touched her lips gently. At that moment the cat started meowing at my feet. I jumped.

"What's up with you, Ginger? Get on your way."

"Vaska is jealous of us. I'd better put him outside, then I'll pay my fine. Otherwise we won't get anywhere."

When she got back, Marina sat in her previous spot and hugged me. I was in no hurry, and waited for her to 'warm up' to the right temperature for intimacy.

"Misha, after you'd left the department, I thought about you a lot and wanted to visit my patient. But I changed my mind when I heard that you were living with your mother. There are hundreds of men and women prisoners working at the factory, but you are not like any of them. Everyone in the Cultural Centre and the hospital is amazed, and doesn't understand what's brought you to our part of the world. Over the year I've attended all the concerts and shows you've produced. As someone who admires your talent, I will not only pay the fine for my mistake, but show you how much I like this person who's stolen my heart."

Eventually, when I'd almost given up hope, the mellowing woman pressed against me in a long kiss. Feeling her body against mine was intoxicating, even more so than her mother's old liqueur. I would never have thought that such passion and voluptuousness could be lurking in this modest young woman. We carried on kissing, undressing each other as we did so, until we were both completely naked. Marina dragged me into the shower room and after washing each other for some time, I carried her in my arms into the love torture chamber. This woman (luckily quite small) was laughing like a child on the way to the long-anticipated bed. I have to confess that I was worried about my masculine prowess after a year and a half of sexual abstinence, but fortunately, the nurse was conscious of this and was more than patient in reactivating my natural potential. Marina stood out among my partners as exceptionally loving in intimate relations. She had her own unusual techniques in the sexual act, which drove me out of my mind. And she too got fired up, moving from one orgasm into another. Trembling and lying spent, I suddenly felt someone scratching my heels. Coming to, I saw the cat standing on its back legs behind the lattice bedstead. His whole mouth was open in a wicked smile (or so it seemed to me in my drowsy state). I tried to put my heel on his nose to move him, but managed to hit the grille instead, and squealed with pain. My hostess roused herself. She kissed my screwed-up face 'good morning' and disappeared into the toilet. I then gave full rein to my feelings and told the shaggy Vaska exactly what I thought about his face at that moment. The cat listened to me attentively and replied, "Meow, meow," which in cat language means: you're an idiot too. This was a direct personal insult. Marina bounded naked into the bedroom, all freshened up and ready to get dressed. Sensing me looking at her, like a cat who'd got the cream, she halted my sexual impulse in time:

"Mishanya, breakfast is ready. Don't worry about the cat [as if!]. He can get out of the kitchen to the yard and there's water in his saucer. When you leave, slam the front door without the key. We'll see each other this evening at the Cultural Centre. Be a good boy and don't upset Vaska!" (Ha ha!)

The hostess blurted all this out in one breath. She planted another kiss on my forehead, and flew off to work, leaving a trail of fragrant aromas. After a shower I made the bed, had breakfast, did the washing-up, etc. i.e. did what I would do at my place, so comfortable did I feel in this unfamiliar but hospitable den.

I remembered to sign in at the MIA department on my way home. The duty guard handed me a note from the chief. I thought that this would be about my night-time escapade. After all, 'If the cap fits, wear it.' In his letter, the supervisor asked me to bring the new annual contract for the following season from the Cultural Centre and the timetable of my classes in all four Cultural Centre and club groups.

At home, I flopped down on the trestle bed and slept until lunchtime; I felt so worn out after 'working so hard on the night shift'. Having had such a significant break in the practice of love, my equipment naturally ached a little, and I was walking a bit unsteadily as if on a ship in a storm.

I wrote down all the leaders' wishes for the new season. To start off with, I promised to set out my creative proposals the following Monday after clarifying the final make-up of the groups on the open day, 13th September. The Director asked Zoya (artistic director of the ballet studio) to stay behind for five minutes.

"Mikhail, thanks to last year's success, a whole crowd of children of various ages, including fourteen boys, have already signed up for the ballet. Zoya can't physically manage all of them and persuaded me to give you the disruptive ones twice a week. I've spoken to the Factory Committee chairman, and he's come up with a compromise to remunerate you, if you take on the burden of the boys."

"Fourteen lads plus the six we had already – that's definitely a sign of success. My compliments, madam! But it won't be possible to teach them all in one group. On my free Monday I can train the seniors and juniors separately for an hour and a half, one after the other, from 3 p.m. to 6 p.m., plus, separately, one group on Thursdays and the other on Fridays, to fit in with the general timetable. On Sundays there are production rehearsals on top, as necessary. It follows that we're going to need a pianist and some mums to cover the dressing rooms."

Spitsina thanked me touchingly for taking an interest in the ballet studio. She didn't fathom that my interest in this project was driven by professional ambition, and nothing more.

Once Zoya had gone, Lieberman, in confidence, took me through the compromise they'd been forced to make.

"Berkut, on the question of suitable remuneration: naturally we are not authorised to pay you any more than one and a half times the going rate. For this reason, the Factory Committee chairman is agreeing a contract with the landlady of your flat for the next season, up to September, which compensates for the additional workload as choreographer at the Cultural Centre. Your name won't feature in any of the documents, as this accommodation is rented to factory guests."

"Thank you! This arrangement suits me perfectly. Only please put my bosses at MIA in the picture about this. I hope they won't have any objection."

"This does not concern them."

"What you're contemplating now with the trade union, it's – excuse me – the same criminal act that led to me being sent here from Moscow. So I would prefer to keep everything completely out in the open. In the rental agreement we will have to introduce a compulsory point regarding direct contact between the landlady and the factory on all accommodation and communal issues. I am formally registered as living in the barracks."

"Mishenka, hello! You've caught up on your sleep I daresay, but I've been going around in a fug all day."

"So where's my kiss for completing your chores at home? Ah, that's better!"

"So, what are we going to see today in your wonderful Cultural Centre?"

"A concert by the Academic Choir with the Philharmonic Chamber Orchestra."

"Oh la la!"

"Marina, I'm sorry. It's dangerous for me in my position to spend the night anywhere other than at home."

"Whenever you get the urge to see your Vaska, that is to say, Mishka, you are always welcome! Don't hesitate!"

"But what if I wanted to be with you all the time. What then?"

"Move in with me part-time."

"Are you serious or joking?"

"Here are the keys to my heart. I really like you."

"But Vaska will not put up with this. He's already seventeen – 110 in human years."

"He's so used to me."

"Unfortunately, I'm not allowed to take in a cat. Divide your time between the two males."

"The best way would be for me to stay at yours Tuesdays, Thursdays and Saturdays if that suited you?"

"I'm bursting with happiness at the thought of being with my fairy in a day's time, and sharing my bread, salt and bed with her."

I could never understand why I was so lucky with lovers and yet spectacularly unlucky with my wife. Rather, it was the other way round. They were lucky with me. But my wife wasn't! One way or another, Marina was a co-pilot in my bachelor's life. She was an organised, sincere, and conscientious woman of rare decency. Of course, a professional nurse has to be like that. We enjoyed an easy understanding of each other, despite working in different specialist fields. She helped me around the house, and I helped her with housekeeping. On my day off I chopped wood for the winter in the mornings. In the autumn I tidied up the garden and watered the flowers. Later, I cleared the snow around the house and so on. My friend never asked me to do this. Then on Sunday afternoons she would clean my flat while I was shopping at the market. She earned a lot less than I did, so I didn't allow her to spend any of her money on my flat. Marina appreciated this. Nevertheless our intimate relations suited both duet participants perfectly. We celebrated New Year together with Dudkovsky and his family. After this, our ladies became close friends and we would meet up as a foursome.

As before, I worked hard at the Cultural Centre on the new programme with the Russian Folk Choir and the variety review. But my main focus during this period was Spitsina's ballet studio. Over three months of classes with the boys I 'crammed' them to such an extent that by Christmas, to everyone's amazement, they had managed to learn:

1. 'Dance of the Sabres' (from the ballet *Gayaneh* – music by Khachaturian) for the seniors with plastic blades.
2. 'March of the Gnomes' (music by Grieg) – with antique lamps, for the young lads.

On the parents' insistence, Zoya and I repeated last year's 'Waltz of the Snowflakes' from *The Nutcracker* with double the number of young ballerinas and in a more complex choreographic arrangement for the senior girl soloists. This was a safe bet to make an impact and tug at the mothers' heartstrings. I worked like a dog. As a result of stupendous success at the children's matinees, the Snow Maiden (Zoya) and your humble servant playing the part of Ded Moroz around the Christmas tree, the Factory Committee rewarded both of us with two trips to the government's Winter Holiday Home, for a week. Marina happily organised the paperwork in her name for our trip, making the most of some leftover leave. The management turned a blind eye to our private union. Both adults were single, and working in different departments of the factory. The holiday zone was in Gorky region. I left Artyom a note letting him know when I'd be back.

For me, these were unforgettable days of long-lost human happiness with a woman I felt psychologically and physically close to, in a tranquil corner of picturesque countryside. The four of us (with Zoya and her husband) went on skiing outings and got out into the country on a troika with little bells to watch the mummers' winter celebrations. After supper we alternated between dancing and imbibing decadent drinks in the club. We returned to the car factory refreshed and full of energy to create new work. Levanov was happy to take up my idea for a dance group with the Russian Folk Choir, 'Suburban Mummers'. I continued on the variety review with Dudkovsky, working on a satirical compilation based on Latin-American rhythms, 'Back to our Roots'. Under this guise I could sneak in forms of so-called flamboyance and hippy styles through Rock 'n' Roll dances, the twist, shake and other hits. I warned Sasha about my past failures in this arena. But conversely, he asked me to include as many character qualities of these 'negative' representations of bourgeois culture as possible, which he ridiculed in his couplets, as a corrosion of Marxist–Leninist aesthetics in our Soviet reality. Naturally the choreographer was 'holding all the cards'. For Zoya, I decided to produce 'Pioneers' Summer' for the whole ballet group towards the end of the season: a one-act ballet to music by Soviet composers in a sporty, Character genre.

As the New Year approached, I rang Mum at the bodega. I wished everyone season's greetings and promised to celebrate it with the whole clan next time. Mother reported that there was some positive news on finding a job in Odessa. I understood her coded information about emigration and thanked her for the good news. I reminded her that in the best-case scenario I was planning to return to my home territory by September, to complete my six-month 'criminal education' in Moldavanka. Then I rang my cousin in Leningrad to wish her a happy New Year. She invited me and my sons for the following winter holidays, as she had done in the past. She was very upset to hear that I was forbidden to live in Moscow and Leningrad. I reassured Sofia that we would meet up in Odessa in the summer, in Bugaz. With this, she sensibly wound up the conversation. Finally, I telephoned Pina in Moscow and wished her whole household a happy New Year. She said that my call was the best New Year's present she could wish for. She asked for a telephone number to ring me on. But I apologised, explaining that I didn't want to complicate her life by making the authorities suspicious. I promised to stay a few days at her mother's place at the end of August, on my way to Odessa via Moscow. My friend burst into tears, and said that she would look forward to this.

At the end of April a report was handed over to the Cultural Centre Artistic Council and the Factory Committee Trade Union regarding May's amateur concert in honour of the thirtieth anniversary of the liberation of the motherland from the fascist aggressors in 1944. This was a red-letter day for the car factory with military importance. After the triumphant GAZ leadership meeting, a one-and-a-half-hour concert took place incorporating the three major groups from the Cultural Centre. The ballet studio opened the programme with the children's composition 'Pioneers' Summer'. They were followed by the variety review, including a satirical choreography on 'Back to our Roots'. Traditionally, the Russian Folk Choir would end the concert with a premiere of a vocal, dance piece, 'Suburban Mummers'. This was the pinnacle of my two years of creative endeavours at the Cultural Centre. But it still didn't mean the end of my exile. After the concert the supervisor approached me. He congratulated me on my success and asked me to pop in and see him for a chat on Monday morning. The Director and group leaders congratulated me and thanked me for my assistance. The Factory Committee chairman spoke in the presence of all the amateur participants, to express his gratitude to me for the high-calibre production in creative activity at the Cultural Centre. I gave a deep, Russian style bow, without saying a word.

In the MIA department, the Chief told me about preparing documents to present to the Judicial Committee concerning parole for GAZ workers, serving their corrective working sentences here. At the beginning of every month, on the basis of information presented by the factory administration and local MIA, members of the committee decided the fate of the candidates brought before them.

"Mikhail, for this privilege to result in a positive outcome, you must work out your sentence without interruption (excluding leave) by the beginning of August this year, as per last year. Four months ago we received another enquiry for your help from the Artistic Director of the Drama Theatre and the Director of the regional Cultural Centre, but decided not to bother you, as we knew that you were working at the GAZ Cultural Centre without any days off. Last Saturday at your concert these cultural leaders repeated their request to us: even to allow you to work there on a new repertoire for just two of the summer months, June and July, as we did at the end of last season. You know that our management thinks extremely highly of you and doesn't want to encroach on your interests without good cause. It stands to reason that it's better for you to work these two months until possible parole in your specialist field, than return to some kind of goods-production department. On the other hand, it's not very nice for us to take responsibility once more for breaching an official sentence from Moscow Civil Court. A reference from the mayor referring to your professional service is currently in the hands of the GAZ general director."

"Artyom Nikolayevich, thank you for treating me so courteously. I agree to all of it."

In the middle of May I discussed my production plan for the next show with the artistic director of the Drama Theatre and the director of the regional Cultural Centre – it was a new programme of folk stage (character) dances. Also, as last summer, I worked as intensively with actors in the theatre as with the dance teachers at the seminar, trying my best to satisfy the demands of the stage director for the drama production as well as the appetites of the amateur leaders. By the end of July all the society receptions had taken place successfully in both cultural institutions. Their directors handed me envelopes containing testimonials about the choreography for me to pass on to the bosses of the local MIA. My colleagues and I bade each other warm goodbyes, wishing each other well in our creative endeavours.

Dudkovsky, who attended both viewings that day, observed sadly on the way home: "Misha, it's difficult to overstate just how much valuable knowledge your student actors and dancers have absorbed from you in the last two years. This will stand them in good stead for a long time to come."

The MIA Chief completed my personal file with great satisfaction and announced when the Parole Board was due to meet. He gave me detailed instructions on how to handle myself with the court bureaucrats.

"The main thing is: don't rush your answers and don't say too much. Don't show any emotion! Even if you don't like something or they have a go at you. These officials are past masters at playing on people's weak heartstrings, while they decide to mess up a candidate. Be careful!"

To my great surprise and joy, the interview with the Board went more smoothly than I had anticipated. The main accompanying document (written by the supervisor) outlined the essential reasons for my transfer from the wheel department to the Cultural Centre. This decision, signed by three of the largest car-manufacturing plants in the country, was not open to question. I answered all the questions calmly, although inside I was a nervous wreck. The chairman of the board congratulated me on a positive result and declared that I had authorisation to leave Gorky from 13th August this year. I bowed in gratitude and left the room step by step with my head held high.

Sasha and Marina were waiting for me outside. When Marina heard the good news she burst into tears, kissed me and rushed back to work. Because of me, Dudkovsky and his wife had not gone away on their holiday, as he had wanted to know the board's decision with regard to my future status. He then ordered me a ticket for 17th August which would get me to Moscow on a Sunday, as otherwise no one would be able to meet me. Sasha promised to be back in a week from Ufa, where his wife's parents lived. He asked me not to confirm all my arrangements until they got back. I gave him my word, on 'pioneer's' honour.

My friend shook my hand firmly: "I'm really happy for you."

In the break between the following candidates the Chief came out into the corridor. He too offered me his congratulations and arranged a meeting to draw up the paperwork for my parole. I charged off to the local post office and rang all my nearest and dearest to update them with the great news and approximate time of arrival in Moscow and then Odessa.

I had a week at my disposal. I asked Marina to arrange for the cat to be looked after, so that we could spend the rest of my time together. She was happy to comply. My chief and Marina attended a farewell lunch to mark the end of my exile, in addition to the Director and Cultural Centre group leaders. Everyone was laid-back, cultivating their best anecdotes.

My most serious rival was Sasha. But even he couldn't outwit the competition after the Prince of Odessa's joke, referring to my conviction: "It's generally known that in all Moscow and Gorky trams under the window it says 'Don't lean out!' But in Odessa trams it says something else under the windows: 'Hang out! Hang out!' Let's see what you hang out tomorrow!"

No one laughed. I realised that even making fun of yourself didn't elicit people's humour or goodwill.

"Dear friends, allow me to repent. In the Bolshoi Theatre affiliate at Moscow People's Opera and Ballet Theatre within the ZIL Cultural Centre, I completed a serious administrative error, for which I have been severely punished. But I'm not sorry about that, as thanks to this very event, I have had the good fortune to meet all of you. Thank you for everything – with my deepest gratitude."

After a protracted pause the room burst into tumultuous, sustained applause.

Sasha and Marina saw their exiled ballet master off with warm wishes at the station. I left a little piece of my heart with each of them in Gorky. I have always treasured the GAZ images of a truly like-minded person and tender friend.

Just before the train was due to leave, Dudkovsky embraced me and whispered: "My uncle lives in Detroit (my father's brother). If you see him, give him my love!"

Once settled in my seat in the carriage, I tried to make sense of Sasha's final comment.

The train picked up speed. I realised only then that it was transporting me away from my past placid life and sweet peace, never to return. I was heading for a storm cloud, presaging an ongoing battle for my spiritual ideals and creative principles.

CHAPTER 6 FAREWELL AGONY

Once again the conductor was announcing our imminent arrival in Moscow.

To ensure Agrippina's safety as far as possible, I had telephoned her from Gorky the night before my arrival, and asked her not to meet me at the station, but to wait for me at her mother's house in the morning.

It's not always possible to express emotions in words when meeting close ones after being tragically parted for a long period of time. All day Sunday she and I shared key events from our last few years apart, and delighted desperately in our new-found intimacy. Conscious that I was not permitted to stay long in Moscow, she tried to help me in any way she could in my unexpectedly interrupted dealings with Mosfilm and the ZIL Cultural Centre. She hand-delivered a letter to Isabella Sviderskaya at the regional Cultural Centre, and organised a meeting with my youngest son, Alexander. Essentially, she gave up a full week of her summer holiday for me as she was worried about letting me out on my own in Moscow, to avoid any possible repercussions or 'chance encounters' in the street.

In the three years since I'd seen my son, he had changed markedly. In addition to his physical development as he became more of a young man, he had matured significantly. The youngest had completed junior school this year (fourth grade), and was due to go up to secondary, but didn't want to live in this 'bedlam' (his word) any longer. He asked me to get him a place in a special boarding-school, where all the teaching was in English with a view to a future career abroad or in foreign organisations within the Soviet Union. The three of us went to have a look at this school. The Director explained the admission requirements, programme of study, and students' living arrangements. He gave us an official application form to be completed by Alexander's mother, and emphasised that once the applicant was accepted, tuition fees would need to be paid for ten months annually in advance, amounting to 500 roubles. Registration would have to be completed by 20th August. I guaranteed the financial contribution to Sasha. He would have to sort out the registration documents with his mother by himself. I was pleasantly surprised that my youngest was better organised at the age of eleven than my eldest was at sixteen.

Pina and I went to collect him from Rechnoi Vokzal, kitted him out from head to toe at Children's World department store, and took him off to the English school.

I cautioned my son that he would need to make radical changes to the daily routines in his former home once he was a special boarding-school resident. 'They're chalk and cheese.' My youngest assured me that he understood perfectly well the difference between an education here and in an ordinary school, as well as the demands of discipline and ethical conduct. I wanted so much for one of my sons at least to 'turn out well' as a member of society. But under Dmitri's and his mother's influence at weekends, when Sasha wasn't at boarding school, this was a real problem. I had to negotiate with the management that he would be in the group of children from outside the area who remained in lodgings on Saturdays and Sundays. Pina promised to take the boy home on high days and holidays, and provide diversionary activities for him along with her eighteen-year-old daughter, at my expense, using a fund to which she still had access. My friend was very attached to my son, who in turn felt completely at home with her.

I didn't alert my mother as to the time of my arrival as naturally I didn't want any pomp or ceremony when she met the 'hero home from exile' or 'former legal criminal'. I made my way from the station in a humble taxi with a small suitcase. We stopped a little way from the house, so as not to attract attention from curious neighbours and gapers.

Quietly approaching the sunflower-seed seller seated, as always, by the gates, I asked shyly: "How much for a glassful?"

"Fifteen kopecks. They're very tasty, I roasted them myself. Shall I load you up?" the old woman spoke up.

Raising her grey-white head, Nanny Sasha sighed and was speechless, the glass shaking in her hand. I sat down close to her, kissed her throbbing temples, and hugged her tight.

461

"Nanny Sasha, I'm not a figment of your imagination, I'm still very much alive, despite going to Hell and back."

The glass dropped out of her hands straight back into the sack of seeds. She was dumbfounded, and just felt my face and hair with trembling fingers, convincing herself that I was real. Leaning on my shoulders, she got up without a word, beckoning me upstairs. I gathered up her sack, shoved the folding seat under my arm, and made my way after Nanny, suitcase in hand. She went slowly up to the first floor. She kept glancing around, as if to check that I was still there. As soon as we were indoors, Nanny collapsed on to her knees and began prostrating herself before the Lord God, thanking Him for saving my life and giving her another chance to see her grandson, an errant victim of misfortune, alive and well. I stood stock-still in the doorway with the sack and case in my hands, waiting for Nanny to get up off her knees and invite me in.

I didn't want to cause a fuss at the bodega either. I stole into the manager Fedya's office behind clients' backs, and asked him to take over from Mum on the till for a moment. The counter assistant had already guessed that I was visiting as she had been expecting me any moment. Nevertheless, she was still overcome, and couldn't hold back a mother's tears. She congratulated me on my release. Despite being on parole, I was nonetheless home, among friends and family. We didn't hang about, but went our separate ways, postponing a more in-depth conversation until the evening at Nanny Sasha's, without the risk of my elder brother, Yosif, and his family hearing us. I then hurried to the local MIA office to register my parole documents at my mother's address for the next six months, up to the end of February 1975. On receipt of a temporary document in place of a passport, I was obliged to sign in weekly at the police station, to confirm my presence at the address in question. Mum was allowed to leave work early that evening, and after supper we called in to see Nanny.

The first thing Mum and I had to sort out was the issue of my accommodation for the coming year. It was made more complicated by the fact that Mum's granddaughter Oksana, Roman's daughter, was sharing her small room during this time as her parents were away working in Kamchatka. With two people there, this space was already tight, so there was no way it could accommodate a third. The only solution to this situation was to ask Mum's sister Faina to let me one of her two rooms, where her son Viktor and his wife were staying prior to moving into their own flat. Other than that, if I were to be in close quarters with my hostile, moody brother Yosif, I faced the constant threat of provocation from him, with its potential to affect my parole conditions. By the same token, if I found temporary work in my field, I would need my own space to choreograph using audio equipment, as well as a certain amount of space to move around physically, to test out dance moves.

"All right, sonny. I'll sort this problem out myself. Naturally she won't expect any payment from you. But we'll find another way to contribute to her costs in having you there. Secondly, a no less important issue: your emigration. We have lodged an enquiry with a private overseas office (in strict secrecy) regarding your invitation to Ben Shuster, your cousin's grandfather in Israel. The document is expected at the beginning of next year. You will receive it through the Odessa agency, but can only present it at the police station with a passport. So you will have to complete your sentence before you can start the emigration process, which won't be easy, especially with Milia, Dmitri and Yosif weighing you down. You will have to get written confirmation from them stating that you don't owe them anything (money, valuables, alimony, etc.). In this kind of situation, the people closest to you can often turn into savages, extracting every last penny from those who are leaving. The agency advised me to warn you about these hurdles, and that you should play your cards close to your chest. Finally, what's your financial situation at the moment?"

"I've got over 3,000 roubles in a savings account with my cousin Lina (who was the bank manager). And I've got roughly the same amount on me now. If I manage to find work straight away, I'll be able to double this amount in six months. That's all in Odessa. In Moscow I've left sufficient funds in the bank for the boys' keep until they're eighteen and should receive a few more thousand through the court for the cooperative flat."

"Here, before you leave the country, the state will expect you to repay the cost of your education: 3,000 roubles for secondary school, 5,000 for higher education at MTA. So you're probably going to need another few thousand for all this compensation, including any unforeseen extortion by the state and your nearest and dearest."

"That's daylight robbery! It's hard to get your head around this happening in the world today."

Setting up a place for me to sleep on the floor, Mum advised me not to unpack, as tomorrow evening Aunty Faina would probably be picking me up to take me to her place. The thin walls meant that we could hear my elder brother making threats to his wife in one of their regular arguments.

"I'll be straight down to the police station about these two residents living illegally in a tiny space with a communal kitchen."

Mum didn't react to Yosif's histrionics, but was visibly on edge in her conversation with her thirteen-year-old granddaughter, who couldn't understand why her uncle was so wound up. Evidently the Panther had forgotten her eldest cub's loathsome nature.

In the morning, before Mum started work, we went to the hospital together in the next street, where Aunty Faina worked. Mum knew the security guards from the bodega and they immediately let her through, but giving me the once-over suspiciously, they politely asked me to wait outside. Fifteen minutes later someone in a white coat grabbed me from behind and started to squeeze me like someone who knew me really well. Scarcely recognising my beloved aunt, I then embraced her, picked her up and spun her around in front of the stunned guards. They were at a loss, unsure how to respond.

"Faina Davidovna, do you need us to remove your assailant, or are you . . .?"

"What are you talking about? This is my favourite nephew. He's just come back from . . . the army."

"I'll come and get you at 6 p.m. in an ambulance. They'll take us all the way home."

Now I could get down to business. First of all I decided to visit my former boss Lyuftgarten at the regional Cultural Centre. However, he'd already been reassigned to the role of artistic director of television. A lot of water had flowed under the bridge since my departure to Moscow eight years earlier. I introduced myself to the new director, Zotov, and he gave me his card. I showed him printed programmes of my seminars and courses on Stage Folk dance composition: posters from the gala festivals and amateur artistic competitive shows. Gennady Arsenyevich was clearly impressed by my creative track record and practical experience. He advised that the regional Cultural Centre usually offered seminars during winter and summer holidays.

"If you could give an intensive course on composition in the first week of January, that would be ideal for us. At the moment I can postpone the scheduled programme to the next holidays. When are you planning to go back to Moscow?"

"I have to wrap up my duties in Odessa by the end of May."

"From September to May (inclusive) we'll have a gala festival show on, commemorating the thirtieth anniversary of victory over fascist Germany. Lyuftgarten, whom you know, is the festival's artistic and musical director. I'm sure he's going to need a choreographer of your calibre on his production team. If you wish, I'll get the two of you together. Here's his direct line. Give him a call in the morning before 10 a.m.

"In addition to the Regional Cultural Centre, the regional Teachers' Professional Development Institute is very active in the arena of cultural education. The Department of Stage Arts (music, drama, and dance) is headed up by Anatoly Ivanov, a musician by profession. He will work in parallel with you to lead the children's competition and festival of schoolchildren from the Odessa region, to be held on the same date as the anniversary, but he will be concluding with the May Day celebrations. Here is his telephone number as well. When you speak to him, mention our conversation. We often collaborate on projects and help each other out. As you can see, there is plenty for you to do next season."

"Gennady Arsenyevich, thank you so much for your time and interest. I can give you a 'yes' right now for undertaking the composition course in the first week of January. Your dance specialist and I will have to work out a programme and timetable, find a space and accompanist, and agree the format for testing the course participants on their last day of classes. Here is my mother's work number. Leave me a message whenever you need to. Her name is Anna Davidovna."

"Mikhail, since we've established contact so quickly and easily, let's finish off with calls at the same time: you leave a message for Lyuftgarten from the general line in reception, and I'll use the direct line to give Ivanov my recommendation. After this I'll come out to you in reception and we can compare notes."

I gave Lyuftgarten's secretary my name and asked her to find out urgently from her boss when I would be able to meet him on important business. I had arrived from Moscow yesterday and would soon be returning there. I was calling from the Regional Cultural Centre, and would be there for another five minutes. I left my mother's telephone number as well. The Director rushed out of his office and asked his secretary to give me the second handset for the direct line so that three of us could have a conversation.

"Misha, is that you?"

"Exactly so, Yurgen Karlovich!"

"Are you here for long?"

"Until the end of May."

"Gennady, thank you for putting me in touch with this 'migratory bird'."

"Misha, apologies but I'm busy at the moment. Come by tomorrow at 9 a.m. We'll have a chat about everything then."

Zotov, the Director, stood in the doorway of his office, inviting me in. Everything was happening around me as if in a film: one surprise after another.

With a smile, Gennady observed: "Lucky days like this don't come about that often."

"Yes, it's rare for me too. Most likely it's Taurus's positive influence."

"Ivanov is expecting you tomorrow at midday in the institute. Here's his address. Good luck!"

"Listen, Mikhail, it's absolutely no concern of mine to know which wind has carried you here, and what your plans might be for the future. Zotov has already filled you in on our anniversary competition project and the creative festival in May. Judging by your posters and programmes for various festivals, I can see that you have acquired considerable experience in this field and could be extremely useful to us. The production team for the gala festival concert show is due to be confirmed by the regional Cultural Committee by 1st September this year, i.e. sometime next week. I have my eye on the ballet master, who has too much on in the theatre, and lacks your experience in working with non-professional groups. You are familiar with our creative resources in the area. How do you think you could help us?"

"a) Selection of groups across the area, and practical consultancy to them on site;

"b) staging of the whole prologue and finale for the best dance and choir groups, plus (if appropriate), sporting groups from the city;

"c) body motion training for the Gala Festival concert programme under your patronage."

"And how much (if you don't mind me asking) would such pleasure cost poor Odessa?"

"Here are copies of my similar contracts with Moscow, Leningrad and Ulan-Ude. For eight months' work (allowing 500 roubles per month), it comes to a total of 4,000 roubles, including my assistance in the various districts."

"Well, that's marvellous! You have a firm grasp of all this, and deserve our respect. Leave your promotional material with me. It will help me to persuade the Executive Party Committee leadership."

At twelve thirty I had only just entered the hall at the regional Teachers' Professional Development Institute when an imposing young man called out to me and came to greet me with open arms.

"Mikhail Semyonovich, welcome to our teachers' professional development centre!"

"Anatoly Nikolayevich, I really appreciate such a hospitable welcome from a colleague."

We both smiled and shook hands warmly and went up to the first floor. In Ivanov's office several musical instruments stood outside their cases.

I remarked, "You seem to be a Renaissance man of many talents. It was my dream to become a musician when I was a boy."

"So what stopped you?"

"My sight deteriorated during the war, and I can't read sheet music."

"Isn't that what glasses are for?"

"They don't help in the case of trauma. Let's move on to a more optimistic subject. How does your festival run in principle?"

"In essence, it works in the same way as an adult show, except in miniature. At the institute, the following departments make up the Faculty of Aesthetic Education: Instrumental/Choir and Dance/Drama. Their deans and I lead all stages of the Festival, right up to the Gala Festival concert in May."

"Then why do you need me, if you are in a position to organise it all yourselves?"

"Unfortunately, we are not professional producers, and don't know how to show off our prizewinners to the required artistic level, like the regional Cultural Centre does. Apollo himself has sent you to us, to celebrate the thirtieth anniversary of the great victory just as successfully as the adults."

"It's a huge honour for me, and I'm happy and ready to help you. However, as a professional, I do make a charge for my work I'm afraid. Who will be paying for my time?"

"How much would your expenses come to, roughly, for making the said project happen?"

"As it's for children, it will be less than at the regional Cultural Centre. Working to my existing scale of 400 roubles a month, for eight months in all, this comes to 3,200 roubles, including: selection of items, staging and stage management of the gala festival concert. Naturally this is contingent on you covering the trips, transport and similar contractual items. My promotional materials are with Lyuftgarten. I permit you to take them from him to show the institute management team. We only have a week left to formalise arrangements between us. We need to clarify these fundamental issues."

"How do you propose to combine our regional festivals with the regional Cultural Centre shows?"

"On my days off every other week, I'll either be with you or with them. There's also another possibility: I could do the children's programme on Saturdays and the adults' on Sundays. After the creative meeting in May I could bring both projects together into a united presentation, for an hour and a half each time: Section 1 with the children and Section 2 with the adults."

I set myself up comfortably enough at Aunty Faina's flat. In general, everything had come together suspiciously easily, and much better than I'd expected. 'Once bitten, twice shy.' I decided that my next move would be the ballet school. My former boss Georgi Rels had retired, to be replaced by a former premier dancer with the Odessa Ballet, Anatoly Sereda. He knew me well from the Theatre, but I was a completely different quantity in terms of my Artistic activity. I didn't dare show my face at the Mariners' Centre because of the vow I'd made to a once beloved female work colleague: to disappear from her life forever. I left the Opera Theatre, where my former classmates used to dance in the ballet. But this was dishonourable on my part: reviving friendly relations with them with my status prior to going abroad, risked exposing them to potential complications in future. With this in mind, I was forced to isolate myself from all my former friends and actual family members and bury myself in the godforsaken lair of solitude; maintaining connections only with Mum and Aunty Faina, the landlady of the flat I was occupying. At this stage, this was the best course of action for everyone.

I dashed in to see Mum at the bodega at 5 p.m. every day to find out if there had been any calls for me. Eventually, the third time that I appeared in the doorway, my mother waved me into Fedya's office. The boss gave me a telephone message, but as a prelude, made me promise him two tickets to my concert in May. I couldn't refuse him. In his message, Lyuftgarten asked me to pay a visit to the deputy chairman of the regional Executive Party Committee, Moskalenko, at 10 a.m. tomorrow, where he too would be present with Ivanov (from the teaching institute).

The deputy chairman gave us a dry, officious welcome and remarked: "Mikhail Semyonovich, I have acquainted myself with your file and am happy to have the opportunity to work with a highly qualified master of popular entertainment. However, please take into account that we do not have the budget for cultural enterprise that capital cities enjoy – 7,200 roubles for both projects (not for you, but for us) is rather tight. If possible, could you give freely of yourself as a native Odessan, as an honour to your home hero-city."

All three of us laughed and applauded the speaker. I hesitated.

"How can I refuse such an appeal? I will have to give you a reduction – 3,000 for the regional Cultural Centre, and 2,000 for the regional Teachers' Professional Development Institute. That makes 5,000 roubles in total for both projects. This is my minimum fee for eight months' work."

"Thank you, Maestro. Let's shake on it! Yurgen Karlovich, please organise the necessary paperwork for contracts with the choreographer with both departments and put together a combined schedule of trips to the districts with Ivanov. Let's go!"

"Misha, as far as directing the first section goes, everything is clear there. We've got films of the military parade on Red Square and night bombardments on peaceful cities in our studio archives. Your idea for the composition of the second section using soldiers' reminiscences really impressed me, but will the audience get it? I mean, what exactly are the soldiers seeing in their thoughts, and what is actually going on around them? I'm not sure about this. Also the part with 'a minute's silence' at the end of the show brings to a halt the dynamic development of the monumental static drama of war in the symbolic sculpture of a dead soldier."

"My dear colleague, you are the stage manager and producer. You hold all the cards. As choreographer, I just have to follow your interpretation of any subject. You tell me!"

"OK, I will find some people for 'statues with grieving mothers' and will have a think about which part of the programme would be the most appropriate to use them in. I like the idea of a grand finale with the children. You and I will bring the house down with our finale: 'The sky's the limit.' Using the Pioneers' Palace and the Railway Workers' Cultural Centre, their artistic directors want to meet you on your own at their place tomorrow, at 10 a.m. and 12 noon. Does that work for you?"

"Absolutely."

My domestic arrangements had become a serious problem in my personal life. I had absolutely nowhere to spend time alone, do any cooking or washing, etc. This was in spite of the fresh-produce market being next door, the flat having all mod cons and my having an adequate reserve of spare clothes. I really missed having a partner like Agrippina in my day-to-day life. It was only at this point that I fully appreciated the full worth of her indirect contribution to my creative success. I had naïvely assumed that somehow I would manage the four months until New Year. I was wrong.

One way or another, I would have to rent a room somewhere in the town centre. When I got the green light to go to Israel, I didn't want to bring shame to Aunty Faina's door through residing at her address. This would be taking egoism to an extreme as far as both she and my mother were concerned. Incidentally, Mum came to see me every morning she had a day off. She went shopping at Privoz (at my expense), cleaned the flat, and washed my dance clothes. However hard I tried to dissuade her from taking on this load, she just closed her ears to it all the more and continued to fulfil her parental mission. This was untenable. I decided to rent a bedsit as soon as I could.

I saw in the New Year with Mum at the bodega. The day before, she had asked me to bring my accordion as a way of saying thank you to Fedya for allowing us constant use of his telephone – essentially, my only way of communicating with the outside world. Both dining rooms were jam-packed with single men and widows. They drank and sang their hearts out. After midnight my cousins arrived with their wives or husbands. The party got into its second wave. Just like the old days, the festivities took place outside. Thanks to the mild Odessan winters and drunken conviviality, everyone felt completely relaxed. I sat by the main door to the bodega and drew in those who enjoyed light music with my accordion playing. I started to feel sad.

I lowered my head on my instrument. Bitter tears of ennui dripped on to the keyboard below. The New Year's cries and laughter showed no sign of abating in the centre of Moldavanka for a long time yet. My cousins David and Lina embraced me silently, not wanting to say goodbye, sensing that we would probably not be celebrating together like this again.

At the end of January I received an invitation to Israel in my name from the Immigration Office by diplomatic post. But I knew that I wouldn't be able to take it up without a passport, which would be assigned to me at the police station once I'd completed my parole period at the beginning of March. Even though I'd received this invitation, I was forced to postpone acting on it until the end of May, because of my contractual agreements with the regional Executive Party Committee. I was caught in a trap.

If the KGB found out about my proposed exit, they could force the local officials to cancel my contracts and not let me near my production for the time being.

Ivanov and Zotov looked pleased with their respective cohorts of participants, who had brought about this unprecedented success. Lyuftgarten, who had worked on directing the show during his free time, was the only one to cast a wary glance my way. He probably knew more than all the other production team members, but gave nothing away, and carried on in his creative endeavours as though nothing had happened. This silence amplified the situation for me too. On 3rd May, Yurgen took over the reins of stage management. With the help of my assistants, I corrected staging errors following his direction, or inaccuracies in dancers' performances and the vocalists' expressiveness through their body positions. On 5th May we ran through the whole show twice (up to and after lunch) in the Railway Workers' Cultural Centre, with full costume and props but without the stage lighting and backdrops. The first run-through was chaos, the second went better. The children made lots of noise in the wings and stamped around the stage. I had to appoint four mums for duty at the stage doors while we were rehearsing, and during the show in the opera house Lyuftgarten monitored the theatre from a central panel in the box. I helped him with technical management by the theatre stage panel behind the stage portal. My assistants supervised the changeover of performers from the slips at the side. It seemed that we had covered everything. I had banged my head against the wall so many times in my practice that I decided under no circumstances would I allow a banal or stupid blunder to be my parting shot this time. I negotiated fifty complimentary concert tickets. I took them to Mum for all the relatives including my brother Yosif and his wife, Polina. Their fifteen-year-old daughter, Faina, was playing violin in the string trio. I came across her by chance during a children's rehearsal, while adjusting their positions so that they presented as well as possible to the audience. My niece shot me a frightened look, thinking that I was going to throw her into the orchestra pit. And then I paid them all a compliment within earshot of everyone around.

"Girls, you're playing well. Move your bodies a bit more and look a bit livelier."

The auditorium was full to bursting. The central box was occupied by all the hero-city's bigwigs. The three-hour sound and light set-up went off smoothly in the morning. The ceremonial part was at midday, then after an hour's break, the three associate leaders and I showcased my last show on the Soviet stage. I enjoyed warm accolades from my colleagues and managers, the press and my relations. Nevertheless, feeling professionally satisfied with my creative triumph was a crucial factor for me, plus the fact that I hadn't tarnished the memory of my late father, to whom I had dedicated my farewell anthem.

Initially I decided not to stay for the traditional meal in the next-door restaurant at Red Hotel, but at the last minute I changed my mind and not without reason:

a) this would have been dismissive of everyone who'd played a part in creating the show with me;

b) this could be offensive to the spirit of the person to whom I'd dedicated my last work in my home country;

c) why give my enemies something they could use against me, when this was avoidable?

I sat at the table between Lyuftgarten and Ivanov, enjoying their company.

The next morning I went to the regional Executive Party Committee to collect my fee. I was given a financial requisition in the Accounts Office, and asked to sign it with the executive committee deputy chairman.

Moskalenko congratulated me on my achievement, and asked, "Mikhail, forgive me, but is it true that you intend to forsake the Black Sea jewel of Odessa for a small Asiatic land on the shores of the Dead Sea?"

"Allow me to put you right: this is never going to happen."

"I'm happy to hear that. Good luck!"

"Thanks very much. The same to you."

I had absolutely no intention of living in Israel. So I had answered my boss's bold question with complete sincerity and conviction.

Once finished at the regional Executive Party Committee, I made my way straight to Lina at the savings bank, and put my earnings into my account. My cousin told me that it would take three days at the most for the money to clear. I had enough time.

Next, I went to the Emigration Office, where I presented my passport, birth certificate, divorce certificate and change of surname. They promptly printed out copies and handed me a permit for indefinite leave to remain in Israel with my cousin's grandfather. They made a few copies of this document too, so that I could show it to the police, the Visa and Registration Office and wherever else it would be required. I sped off to the local passport desk with the permit and duly submitted my application requesting authorisation to leave.

The clerk had a look at my documents: "You've only just been released, now you're making a dash for it right away. Do you have any idea how much this is going to cost you? In time and money, not to mention your health? Later you'll be slashing your wrists in regret, but there's no way back. Think about it before it's too late."

"I need an official receipt for giving my passport to you."

"My secretary will issue you a document in place of your Soviet passport. I'm curious, how far will it take you? Come on. You're an educated fellow, if looks are anything to go by."

The woman in reception gave me a receipt and advised me to present myself at the City Passport Department, within the Committee for Foreign Affairs, where the exit papers would be drawn up by the Visa and Registration Office.

The officer at the City Police Station accepted my documents and stated, "You're free to go."

"Can I have a receipt, please?"

"What? What on earth do you need another receipt for?"

"The Emigration Office told me to get a receipt from every place I give in my documents."

"Hold on, let me be clear. They've dumped all this hassle on us?" he yelled.

A few minutes later the officer returned with an official receipt on police-headed paper. I thanked him and rushed off to enrol on an English language course at Mechnikov University. On 3rd May they were starting a new four-month group on a conversational programme for students who were ready to progress from elementary level. When I confirmed that I had studied English for two years at a Moscow institute, they made an exception and admitted me as a latecomer.

The course was delivered by an intellectual woman of around my age, who was very patient and mild-mannered, with piercing eyes. She was the archetypal teacher, and the polar opposite to me, both in personality and star sign. Nonetheless, Svetlana Vasilyevna and I soon found general conversation topics for the interval between the two one-and-a-half-hour lessons. In the first one we learned about spellings and phonetics, idioms and expressions. The second focused on practical conversation on any cultural or everyday subject, excluding the professional or political. Classes took place daily between 6 p.m. and 9.30 p.m. during the week. Exams were scheduled for mid-August.

'The truth will out.' Somehow, word got around really quickly that I was leaving for Israel. I wasn't inclined to divulge my plans for the future to everyone; I would just answer affirmatively when asked. If people tried to dig deeper, I suggested they read the papers or listened to the radio.

In the office I was given four forms for my close family to complete: my mother, two brothers and my ex-wife. My mother wasted no time in setting out that I didn't owe her anything and that she had no need of any assistance from me. She handed the form to her son Yosif in person, and heard him badmouth me to his wife:

"This fucking master will be dancing around me now!"

Roman would sign the consent on his return from Kamchatka with his wife in a month's time. That just left the hardest part: my ex-wife, Milia. She wouldn't pass up the chance to suck me dry before giving her agreement for me to leave the country.

The deputy in the office recommended a lawyer in the Legal Department who specialised in legal matters pertinent to departing Jews. During our consultation, Greenstein filled me in on my rights and obligations. He explained that there were criminal cases concerning the relatives of those leaving, and that there were legal requirements in line with the Ukrainian Soviet Socialist Republic's Criminal Code. In my case, I had to leave enough in my bank account where I lived to cover the children's maintenance until they turned eighteen. More precisely, one more year for my seventeen-year-old son, Dmitri, at fifty roubles a month amounted to around 600 roubles. Alexander was twelve, so it was plus or minus 3,600 roubles for the next six years. In total, for both of them I had to get ready (no doubt it would be a bit more) approximately 4,200 roubles. On top of this, if my wife were to lend me the necessary amount, and this receipt were witnessed by two people, I would be obliged to reimburse the whole debt to her before leaving.

"My youngest son is a permanent boarder in a school where I (let's say) have already paid 3,000 roubles in advance for five years. How would this work with his maintenance? Paying for the remaining year until he's eighteen would be another 600 roubles. Despite all the compensation, what if my ex-wife were to renege on her consent for my departure in an act of malice, just to stir things up or for some other reason?"

"Take her to court on her home turf. If you don't owe her, or your children, anything, the judge himself can authorise your exit visa. Send the form to the mother of your children to sign straight away, and outline what you need from her."

The only person I could confide in at that time regarding all my personal problems was my mother. After she'd finished work, we went across the road to a little garden and I updated her following the news from the lawyer. The Wise One was an expert on the questions of life. That's why all family members came to her for advice on personal matters. She confirmed once again that she would put pressure on Yosif through her sisters and their children, as the eldest was not speaking to her, although he was living under the same roof as his mother, and sharing the kitchen. What can you do? 'There is a black sheep in every family.' He'd been a parasite all his adult life and will be one until he's on his deathbed: a leopard can't change its spots. I found it galling to waste any emotion on him. Most of all, I was worried that he would delay or destroy my mail, as my mother was at work all day and I was living elsewhere, despite being registered here. There had already been more than one occasion when letters addressed to me had not reached me, although the postman, whom we'd known for a long time, swore that he had posted a letter to me the day before through the letter box in the shared front door. The day after, the wise Panther rummaged through the waste bucket in the kitchen and unearthed an empty envelope addressed to me. To avoid bloodshed, she told me about this immediately, but warned Yosif that he would have to face the music with me unless he returned the stolen letter. My conversations with the eldest were always brief. After he had raised his hand to Mum, he was caught red-handed – in the face. Yosif didn't understand any other language. But now I couldn't allow myself this 'luxury', and he exploited this, for the time being. Such as now: arriving at the office for the latest news, the secretary informed me that three days ago she had forwarded me a letter from my wife in Moscow.

I exclaimed in annoyance.

"Don't worry, Mikhail! We always take copies of any correspondence we send to the Visa and Registration Office. You're not the first person to have relatives trying various ways to prevent someone leaving for Israel. Here's a new copy of the missing form."

"Thanks, love! You've saved me from having a heart attack and a family row to boot."

"There's no need to thank me. This is all part of our service to emigrants."

In a handwritten letter, Milia stated officially that I hadn't paid any maintenance for the children since our divorce in 1972, and for this reason, she didn't feel it necessary to give her consent for my departure. I informed the secretary that I was getting ready to go to Moscow to resolve some family issues. I left her my mother's telephone number at work so that she could update her regarding my emigration.

I paid another visit to the lawyer.

Greenstein read what my wife had sent and asked: "What do you intend to do now, and how will you pay your dues?"

"My eldest son lives in my cooperative flat in Moscow, where I have personal savings amounting to 38,000 roubles. I want to withdraw my 25% and use this to pay my historic and future maintenance, including the court and legal costs. Is that feasible?"

"In principle, yes. But it's complicated in your situation, having been exiled, divorced and experienced a gap in payments."

"Leonid, how much would it cost me for you to come to Moscow with me for a few days to meet with the judge and settle the division of assets and obtain his approval for emigration? My lady friend has a flat available where you would be able to stay for this period."

"Mikhail, a nephew of mine lives in the capital, who would love it if I came to visit. You can see how busy I am. However, if I can come to an arrangement with the judge for this district over the telephone to deal with a minor lawsuit on a one-off basis, then we can fit this into one day. We can go to Moscow and back on the fast train in two and a half days. In total, let's say that six working days of my time will cost you 300 roubles. I'll cover the travel expenses myself as I'll make use of the two weeks' leave I've put off from June at the same time, to see my nephew in Moscow. It will be a combination of business and pleasure. The client will pay for the telephone discussions with Moscow and the postal expenses."

As I listened to the lawyer I smiled at my good fortune while he was making some notes.

"Don't feel too pleased with yourself; here is your first bill. For the moment, there's just an advance of 100 roubles for telephone and telegram costs as a guarantee that you won't 'do a runner'. Come in at 4 p.m. tomorrow."

My mother was happy to hear my news regarding the lawyer and emphasised that I would be safe with him alongside as I only had a temporary identity document instead of a passport, in case I encountered any provocation by enemies in the street, on public transport and other public places. I couldn't understand how Mum knew about emigration in such specific detail. Most likely from overhearing clients' conversations at the bodega because at that time this was the most popular topic of discussion for all Odessans. The Panther was worried about me going to sort out matters with Yosif regarding the stolen letter.

"My son, he's just waiting for the chance to send you back to where you've come from. Come round at 11 a.m. when the postman's usually due. Give him ten roubles and ask him to leave your post downstairs by Nanny Sasha's gates (with the seeds). That will be safer. When my sisters, grandchildren and your friends come and visit me, I showed them all the envelope addressed to you in the bin. It will take your brother a long time to clean up his act. This lesson will hit him where it hurts much more than a fight will."

"I'm sorry to say that you are right, Mum. He's actually not worth getting my hands dirty for. If you get a call from the Emigration Office or Visa and Registration Office about anything important in my absence, please call me on this number in Moscow, that's where I'll be staying. Don't tell anyone about my trip – not a word! Tell everyone that I'm in Karolino Bugaz."

As promised, Greenstein found a district judge through his Moscow contacts and arranged for her to hear my case the following Monday at 3 p.m. She promised to call Emilia S. Platonova (formerly Berkut) before then.

The lawyer laid out the invoices and a copy of the initial account on the desk and snapped his fingers, saying, "payment on the nail".

I was happy to pay him everything and asked him anxiously: "What sort of safety precautions should I take for the journey, given that I only have a temporary six-months ID card in place of a passport?"

"You won't need anything extra with me there. If you're travelling by yourself, that's another matter. The main thing is to have on you your birth certificate, divorce certificate, change-of-surname paperwork. And also a piece of paper from the police confirming that you have completed your sentence and a slip from your place of residence. If anyone checks our documents on the way, and starts to give you a hard time, just keep quiet. I'll deal with them in legal language. During the journey we will need to go through the content of the case in detail, to look at all possible ways she can attack you. I must know the reasons for your arguments, the children's part in these, situations where the police were involved, the names of circumstantial intermediaries on both sides, etc. She will probably bring out all her dirty laundry to wash in public. Be ready for this and don't stray outside the realms of decency in your arguments. She is a lawyer herself and doesn't need an advocate. Let me go through everything with her. By the way, don't forget to pick up all the materials on the cooperative from your Moscow lawyer."

After lunch on Friday, we were already seated in the carriage and (thank God) the seats around us were empty. We had more than enough time to prepare for the case. Leonid posed me a series of questions. I described in detail the facts and events that were of interest to him. The lawyer made shorthand notes of the basic ideas and arguments in his notebook. On the second day of the trip, Greenstein asked me not to disturb him as he had to devise an effective plan of attack against a professional adversary the following day.

Agrippina met us at the station at seven thirty, bounding into my arms with unfettered joy. In the taxi she assured Leonid that there was a typewriter at home, which he would be able to use for urgent work on his free days. Immediately after breakfast we left the lawyer to type up his materials, and went by ourselves to reconnect on a bench in the nearest park. My friend was on cloud nine to have me in my former home for a week after the court case, until such time as I had completed the cooperative litigation and seen my sons. The following weekend Sasha was planning to be here, so that we could go with Pina and her daughter Natasha to Serebryanny Bor to tend the grave of her cousin and my close friend.

During my monthly calls from Odessa before the New Year, the director of studies at the boarding school told me that Shurik was adjusting slowly to the internal regime for study and accommodation, due to his reserved nature and habitual solitude. At Christmas time he had won a knockout chess tournament and gained second place in a crossword competition. This elevated his status with his fellow students and teachers, all the more so because he was also one of the best students in English language. These achievements afforded him greater self-confidence and put him on a par with students in the general stream. I asked Pina not to talk to the youngest about my arrival so as not to disrupt his daily routine.

My friend told me about an incident that had happened in the winter holidays. On 30th December, at his mother's request, she had taken Sasha home to Rechnoi Vokzal, where he was forced to celebrate the festivities with his family. A scene between Dmitri and his mother took place during the night of New Year's Eve. The following morning, Shurik ran off to Pina's with his things and stayed there until the end of the holidays. His mother found out where he was from a note on the table and didn't make the slightest attempt to express any remorse about what had happened. My lady friend couldn't understand by what miracle this eleven-year-old boy had found her address and made two changes on public transport.

At 4 p.m. Greenstein and I were summoned by the judge. Milia was already seated there, apparently invited by Morozova in advance of us, for a two-way familiarisation session with the case. The lawyer presented our identity documents and the folder of printed materials. The case content was already familiar to the judge (through the telephone conversation), and leafing through, she noted down information in her notebook. Briefly, she reminded us of both parties' rights and obligations. She expressed her hope that, as former spouses, we would reach a palce of mutual understanding and tolerance in the interests of our children and parents.

Morozova addressed the mother: "I have just outlined the situation to you regarding the petitioner's contribution to the cooperative, and his wish to compensate you for the unpaid maintenance for the children dating back to 1972. This concerns the share due to him for his contribution over six years (a total of 38,000 roubles), 25% of which amounts to 9,500 roubles. The earlier mentioned maintenance will be deducted from this total, minus the period that your son Alexander has been at boarding school, which Mr Berkut is funding, and which comes to 500 roubles per year and is payable for six years. I'll ask you again: are you in agreement with this decision?"

"Not at all. Because he gave up on us long before 1972."

My lawyer, who had been sitting quietly thus far, finally got into his stride at this point.

"Yes, he wasn't living with you for understandable reasons, as recorded on several occasions by police officers. But he continued to pay regular instalments to the cooperative and give you funds for the children, which you and your sister drank away in the company of men whom you brought to the home or saw elsewhere. The Residents' Committee has responded on numerous occasions to indictments following your debauchery in the house, and your neighbours' complaints. There is also the fact that your sister is living there illegally, without a permit. Meanwhile, at the time of your husband's arrest you unilaterally divorced him and changed your surname from Berkut to Platonova without informing him."

Milia opened her mouth a few times to interrupt the lawyer. But she didn't. He left her 'on the ropes', listing one after another the details of her amoral behaviour: her drunkenness, in the presence of her own children, resulting in her punching her eldest son in the face and being taken to the police station.

"Shall I continue, or do we have enough evidence?"

The judge signalled to the speaker to stop, writing down new information in her file. "Mrs Platonova, if you continue to refuse to repay your husband's share of the cooperative investment for the children's maintenance payments, I will be forced to issue an official order to the cooperative chairman to rehouse you in a smaller two-room flat. From the difference in its value with the current flat, deduct the agreed share of the investment (up to 1972) to the father of your children in the interests of the latter. I will expect both of you as parents to come in to sign the agreement on Wednesday, the day after tomorrow. If you should fail to attend the next meeting, we will take a unilateral decision forcing you, Emilia, regrettably, to move into smaller accommodation, assisted by the police and removal men at your own cost. I am counting on your legal training and powers of reason as a mother."

As expected, Milia did not show up to the next meeting with the judge. The guardian of the law acted on her commitment. She passed a resolution forcing Platonova to move into a cheaper flat and reimburse me 9,500 roubles through the cooperative over the course of the following week. So Greenstein and I promptly took one copy to the chairman of the cooperative and the other Leonid was intending to present to Milia. However, she was not at home. Dmitri was amazed to see me with an unknown man. I introduced the lawyer to him and explained the reason for my visit. Tanya came out of the kitchen to see what the noise was, and presented herself as the sister of the mistress of the house.

"Forgive me, are you registered here?" asked Greenstein.

"Yes, and . . .?"

"I must leave you a package from the District Civil Court for Emilia Sergeyevna. It is vitally important that she is notified of this. Please sign to confirm receipt."

Like a robot, Tanya signed, not realising the responsibility this conferred on her.

I asked: "Dmitri, can I have a look in my office?"

"Your former office, you mean – yes, you can. Ha ha!"

"What's happened to my collection of books and artists' reproductions?"

"Everything was auctioned off while you were in . . . Gorky."

"It looks as if someone else lives here in addition to the three of you. Whose are these men's things everywhere?"

"After your divorce, Mum rented out your room to a bloke who paid a monthly sum to the cooperative and gave the sisters 'personal service'. Ha ha!"

"Mikhail, what's the matter? You've gone pale," the lawyer remarked anxiously.

Briefly, I told him about the loss of my professional book and record libraries. And about the lodger. We were already on our way out of the building, when he did an about-turn of 180 degrees and pulled me back to the cooperative chairman, having gained some useful information from me.

"Did you know that a room in my client's flat is being sublet illegally to a lodger?"

"Emilia explained that her relative is helping her with the children."

"Can you tell us his name, and whether he is registered at this address? If yes, then since when?"

"I'll just have a look. Unfortunately there is no information about him in our list of residents for this flat. I expect that's because he's only here on a temporary basis."

The chairman was clearly upset. The lawyer was playing a game with him that I didn't understand.

"Forgive me, do you wish to report this unknown person's extended stay under your roof without a permit and without any details of his identity, or would you prefer me to do it? I'd be happy to help you with this delicate problem."

The chairman was shocked at such deceit by a member of his cooperative and at his own blind trust. He promptly telephoned the local department of the Committee for Internal Affairs and filed an official report about Platonova's illegal subletting of part of the accommodation to an unknown individual, without his, the chairman's, permission and without a permit to stay any length of time.

"Now, my dear Mikhail, let's head for the boarding school to confirm that your youngest is still there. In all probability, his mother will try to collect him from there in order to save herself 3,000 roubles of your alimony, which the judge counted in your favour."

We got to the school in time.

The agitated director informed us: "Alexander Berkut's mother, going by the surname Platonova, came in to remove her son completely from the school, without even giving him the chance to sit his last exams before the holidays, and this aroused our suspicions. I said to her: 'Madam, we will see you first. Your son has told us that he doesn't want to go anywhere with you and is hiding somewhere. You don't even have photographic ID on you. Come back tomorrow with your documents, including your divorce certificate, proving that Alexander is your legal dependent or under your care. His father, Mikhail Berkut, brought your son to us and paid for a year of his education and his maintenance up front. As a lawyer, you will be aware that we cannot entrust a school pupil in our care, to any person off the street without confirming their identity.'"

"What you told her was correct and you have acted prudently. Excuse me, I am legally representing Mikhail in his case against his former wife. Here are my details. We are currently in legal proceedings with Mrs Platonova. She is losing her sense of reason now and did not appear in court today. Please keep Alexander in your school pending the court's decision about his future. Give me your contact details and Judge Morozova will instruct you by telephone as to the next course of action concerning the boy and his mother."

"Mikhail, you need to decide what to do with your son from this point. Children can't be traumatised like this!"

"Zakhar Petrovich, we have agreed the following: on 1st July (after completing his exams) Shurik will come on holiday with me for two months in the south. At the end of August I will take him to start his classes and on the same day I will pay for the next academic year. This Friday afternoon I will take my son to my place for the holidays. That will be easier for everyone."

"OK. When Platonova comes to pick up her son tomorrow, I will advise her to consult with Morozova."

"Thank you, Comrade Director. Here are the telephone numbers for the District Court and my place in Moscow."

At 4 p.m. we were at the Civil Court. With the secretary's permission, my lawyer quickly typed out the vital report for the chairman from Morozova relating to the news from the cooperative and recent events at the boarding school. He asked the judge to exercise extraordinary measures to ensure my son Alexander's safety. I too signed this declaration and thanked the secretary for her help. We left her our temporary telephone numbers.

Greenstein and I arranged to meet the day after tomorrow (Friday) at the cooperative chairman's office, to sort out the flat exchange. We decided to have a break on Thursday, so that our hosts could spend some time with their guests. On the way home I dived into the supermarket, and bought some wine and a few goodies. Moscow offered significantly superior items compared with other cities.

Pina was ready and waiting for me after work and we enjoyed a wonderful evening of love together. The only thing spoiling it was my update to her regarding Sasha at boarding school. She started to cry when she heard that he had hidden from his birth mother, and didn't want to leave this school. But she soon cheered up when I told her that I was taking her to Odessa for two months on 1st July. We checked the funds we had available for the boy's long-term education. I had to come clean with her about my potential departure to take up permanent residence in another country. To my surprise, she took this news more calmly than expected.

"Mishanya, I have given a lot of thought to your future and always end up coming to the same conclusion. To work more effectively in your creative field, you need to live in a less restrictive country. I will really miss you. However, you'll survive without me, but without your creative work, you would die.

The following morning the secretary from the Civil Court rang to say that they were expecting my lawyer and me at 2 p.m., and that he was in the loop about this. I then telephoned Greenstein and we arranged to meet in advance at the cooperative. The chairman brightened on seeing us.

"On Wednesday evening a police officer and I paid a visit to Mrs Platonova and handed her an official letter proposing that she moves swiftly into an available two-bedroom flat one floor below, as per the District Civil Court ruling. Naturally, the woman went into hysterics, insulting the officials for fulfilling the obligations of their job. The officer reminded her about the two occasions she had already been summoned to the department of the Committee for Internal Affairs, and warned her that if she didn't calm down, then this time they would keep her longer. I expressed my regret", continued the chairman, "at having allowed her to sign her sister up in this accommodation, which today formally belongs to Mikhail Berkut. But Mrs Platonova didn't back down, even when I drew her attention to complaints from neighbours about the ongoing debauchery in the flat, and established her part in deception about the lodger/relative, who turned out to be a businessman from the Caucasus, who didn't have a Moscow permit. The woman didn't even know his full name and permanent address. She was just using his money to settle her debts. I told her: just this lack of concern alone, which poses a risk to the residents' security, has resulted in her being excluded from the cooperative membership. The police officers put all the lodger's things into his bag and told her to tell him to come and collect them from the station. Mrs Platonova threatened to complain to her friend, the Moscow state prosecutor, about the police force's illegal behaviour. As they were leaving, the police officers warned her that if she didn't move willingly within the next three days, then the police would come and help her to do so on Monday, assisted by hired removal men for whom she would bear the cost."

In connection with my summons to the Civil Court at 2 p.m., Pina promised to collect Shurik from boarding school on Friday, after obtaining permission to leave work after lunch. This was one of life's paradoxes: someone else's mother selflessly coming to the aid of another's child in his hour of need, while his biological mother paid no consideration whatsoever to her own child.

I was indebted to my lady friend, and felt the need to reward her genuine conscientiousness. I decided to invite Agrippina and her daughter to spend their summer holiday in Odessa, and stay in Aunty Faina's flat in Privoz, or with me in Bugaz.

Morozova met us with a sardonic smile and graciously invited us to sit down at the table.

"I've already heard from the police about Mrs Platonova's response to my ruling. In twenty-something years of practice, this is the first time I've come across a double masters [law and art history] graduate with a total lack of understanding of thought and any method of applying her knowledge to her practical life. What a lot of wasted years and state resources! Forgive me. It's simply unacceptable! On the basis of your report about your son's mother disrupting his education, I have instructed the boarding-school director not to return the boy to his mother pending the court's decision on her amoral conduct both in the family and in the communal cooperative accommodation at the address indicated. I have sent an official letter to the special English school to this effect. As far as the accommodation is concerned, our inspector will be here on Monday with a camera during the potentially forcible operation to ensure that the legal and ethical rules of this unusual case are adhered to. The cooperative chairman has also promised to provide two witnesses from his committee members. If they put up any resistance about moving, they will be taken to the police station and detained until the exercise has been completed."

But all the preparations made by the powers of the land just served essentially as a warning shot to the obstinate 'lawyer'. According to the latest from Dmitri, the more reasonable and practically minded sister persuaded Milia not to get into an argument with the cooperative chairman, as the sale of any flat would hinge on him. Last weekend the three of them had carried everything they could to the lower floor and arranged it to suit them in the smaller flat. They shoved everything that was left into my former office, hoping for a buyer. On Sunday evening the lady of the house returned the keys to the chairman and demanded a receipt from him for returning her former accommodation in acceptable condition. The chairman called off the police and Civil Court inspector, but he retained the removal men to move the heavy furniture into the other flat or out of the way.

At the end of the telephone conversation my eldest asked me for my help urgently: "Dad, in August I'm planning to go on a walking holiday with friends, which costs 120 roubles all in: transport, food, board, trips and so on."

"At noon tomorrow I must go and see the chairman. Bring me the tour company's contact details and I'll pay for your trip. Get some spending money from your mum. By the way, what has she decided re Sasha and the boarding school?"

"She's already forgotten about that. It's just that at that moment she's off the leash. That's everything!"

"It's rude to talk about your mother in that way."

"Well, I can't divorce her like you can."

"Tell your mum that I'm taking Sasha to Odessa for two months on 1st July. She shouldn't get upset."

"Ha ha! It's just the opposite: she'll be delighted to be free. 'No woman, no cry!'"

I wondered where he had got these expressions from, but thought better of asking.

"You're going into tenth grade at school this year if I'm not mistaken?"

"Dad, don't take the mickey out of me! Since I got back from Gorky I haven't been to school at all. I am now a free artist, following in my mother's footsteps."

"The only difference being that she's had an education, whereas you haven't. See you tomorrow."

The cooperative chairman issued me an order for the agreed sum minus the financial payments for both flats. Dmitri didn't show up. I wasn't too worried.

I put 9,500 roubles into my bank account, and asked the manager: "What system is there for making monthly maintenance payments to the mother of my children?"

"Do you have a slip confirming the relevant ruling of the Civil Court or district council?"

I showed her the document and my report, which had been dictated by my lawyer.

"For the past three years as specified, up to the end of the current month, she may receive the appropriate sum immediately. From 1st July your declaration comes into force, based on the court ruling about future alimony payments until the children reach maturity."

I suspected that Dmitri was pulling a fast one regarding the holiday with friends. The canny sisters had probably taught him how to extort money from his father. And the latter had requested the tour company's address. Three of society's parasites were united in their criminal goal: how to profit from others without giving anything. I had lost my eldest to the influence of his disgraceful mother.

From the bank I made my way to the Civil Court. I made three copies of each of the invoices for my monthly maintenance payments from 1st July and about relinquishing my part in the accommodation cooperative. In this way (as I naïvely thought), I was protecting myself from my ex-wife's attacks relating to my emigration. Greenstein completed a new form with me for the Visa and Registration Office, referring to her agreement to my emigration, and took it to Milia for her signature. But she refused, telling him that she needed to check how much I still owed her for the children's additional expenses, and the move to another flat. She promised my lawyer that she would send the document to him within the month. He had to come away empty-handed. I didn't want to upset the person who'd helped me above and beyond what was set out in our agreement.

I telephoned his nephew's flat and asked Greenstein, "How much extra do I owe you for the additional days you've worked with me?"

"I'll leave that to your discretion. I trust your judgement as to the costs incurred."

I informed him that I was taking Sasha with me to Odessa on 30th June. My lawyer was pleased that my son was getting the opportunity to have a holiday with his father before we parted for a long time, if not forever.

The last weekend, while my family was moving, we had an excellent time at Serebryanny Bor. Pina had rented a two-bedroom cottage in the government village through an old acquaintance, where we had once seen in the New Year with Nikolai. On Saturday we went to visit and tidy up his grave first. Then we went for a boat trip.

After supper that evening, we danced contemporary ballroom dances in the club: tango, waltz, foxtrot or rumba, twist and cha-cha-cha. Sasha delighted me with a pleasant surprise. Not only did he possess excellent technique and style in this repertoire, he also expressed himself convincingly in the male role. Of course I was loving being with Agrippina, while my son danced with her daughter, who was seven years older than him. But as they were both virtually the same height, they looked splendid from the side. The young girl felt uplifted by such an exceptional partner. All became clear later: in Sasha's special boarding school a professional teacher couple gave ballroom dancing lessons twice a week, as this formed part of the curriculum of aesthetic education for future 'English citizens'. If Pina's daughter had been in any doubt prior to coming to Serebryanny Bor about whether she would have a good time there, then now she could not get enough of her lucky dance mania that Saturday night, much to her mother's delight.

I took the opportunity to invite Pina and her daughter to visit Odessa during the holidays, promising them a separate flat and a fabulous summer vacation. But Natasha immediately gave her apologies, saying that she had already made other plans for the holidays. Her mother was about to object, but catching my expression, stopped herself in time. While the youngsters were enjoying themselves dancing, my lady friend and I cemented our plans for the summer. I told her that Shurik would probably attend two sessions at the pioneer camp by the sea. I would be taking English classes at the university in the evenings, but could take a break from these at any time during her stay.

"If you're coming without your daughter you will stay at my place, 'like a pig in clover!' My landlady knows about you."

"Mishanya, I was planning to invite myself to yours before you leave, but you've beaten me to it. I usually take my holiday in the second half of August."

"Well, that's great then! I was thinking that I could put my son on the train and you could meet him in Moscow. Now all that remains is for me to send my 'sapling' from Odessa with you, as your bodyguard. When you get to Moscow you can return him to the boarding school and at the same time pay 550 roubles for the next academic year (going on fifty roubles a month), which includes an extra 10% for the music-and-dance courses given by the faculty/external providers, etc."

"Mishenka, I'm as familiar with all of this as you are, and will gladly do what you ask. Thank you so much from Natasha and me for these two magical days in Serebryanny Bor. Don't worry about Sasha. He's my adopted son."

I was speechless, and just spread my hands. For the first time, I kissed my true friend in public.

At Kievsky Station it was easy to punch our tickets to Odessa in the expensive carriage. Shurik's ticket was half-price as he was under thirteen. I called Greenstein and informed him of our arrival time on 30th June. He then told me that the Civil Court chairman had telephoned about Platonova's act of sabotage in signing the consent for my emigration. Morozova proposed that he should wait the thirty days allowed. If a negative response was received, i.e. without confirming facts, or if no response was received at all, then she would face a civil case for breaching the law regarding the exit or repatriation of former Soviet citizens (as prescribed by clause No. X in the Ukrainian Soviet Socialist Republic's Criminal Code). During those last days in the capital, I purchased gifts for my family as usual and got myself ready to leave.

On 29th June Pina and I went to see Sasha in his creative award ceremony to mark the end of the academic year. He was one of the top-achieving pupils, and had come first in the ballroom dancing competition with his partner from the same class. This was validation of my appraisal of his talents. My lady friend asserted that this was down to his father's genes. It was gratifying to hear this. After the concert we thanked the director of studies and the senior teacher. Shurik was already waiting for us at the gates with his suitcase. On the way home we popped into the pelmeni (ravioli) bar quickly and were home by 10 p.m. Pina promised to come to the station in the morning, and gave Sasha a kiss (instead of me).

In the morning, my son and I spent all morning rushing around Moscow. We had his hair cut, kitted him out with new clothes and shoes, and bought him all the personal items he would need for the next school year. Back home, we took our seats and set off for the station. Greenstein and his nephew, and Pina and her daughter, were already waiting for us by the carriage. I apologised for being late and invited them into the carriage. I pulled a bottle of champagne out of my briefcase, and asked the conductor for some glasses with a nudge and a wink. We laughed as we drank toasts until the bottle was empty. Everyone kissed several times until it was time to go. From the open carriage window we could hear the merry cries and laughter of those seeing us off. Eventually everything calmed down and only now, after the champagne-infused chaos, did I introduce my red-faced son to Leonid, 'Better late than never.' They laughed as they shook hands. My son leaped on to the higher bunk and five minutes later, was breathing heavily. My lawyer and I were up late going through all the detail of our trip to the capital, and the various scenarios that our opponent could potentially think up from different angles. I settled up with Greenstein, paying him 100 roubles extra for the extra work. Leonid's analysis was that Dmitri was not as straightforward as he appeared.

"He's playing the two of you off against each other, but he's got his own interests at heart all the time. He's different from his mum in that he has intelligent eyes and the ability to weigh up a situation quickly, fast reactions and reasonable acting ability. He is capable of insolence and lies, and is even starting to believe his own deception."

It took Shurik and me ten minutes to get from the station to my flat. Thankfully, the suitcases had wheels, but then the bags on our shoulders soon let us know about them. At almost twelve years old, my son had much more stamina than I had supposed. With his tall, slim build and auburn hair, he attracted the young Odessa girls' attention. Making a fuss of him, my landlady was happy to see us, and proudly stated that she now had one and a half men in her home.

While she was making tea, I telephoned the director of the pioneer camp at the twelfth metro station, 'Fountain', whom I'd known for a long time, and where my sons had already spent their holidays a few years earlier.

Shurik shouted out: "Dad, I remember this place on the cliff by the sea. I was only seven last time. That's great!"

Yasha Trifonov and I arranged that I would work for him in the morning and afternoon every Saturday and Sunday. I would put on dances and sporty, derivative numbers separately in sections for the Gala concert around the celebratory campfire, at the end of each cohort's stay. In exchange, he would set Sasha up in the second stream, for the older children: eleven-to-twelve-year-olds. I had to let the manager in on my secret emigration plan to avoid letting him down.

He said: "Jews are leaving in droves from our radial machine-tool factory. This comes as no surprise to any of us."

"All the more reason for us to organise things on a four-weekly basis for each separate intake. I don't want to leave you in the lurch through leaving the country unexpectedly."

"Good! Bring your youngest in as soon as you can as the first group of children has already arrived."

Shurik laughed. He hadn't even opened his case after the journey. He quickly transferred the most essential items and suitable clothes into a rucksack, and ten minutes later we were already on our way by tram. My son relished the opportunity to revisit the beautiful views and half-forgotten Odessa slang. I added that his grandmother hadn't seen her youngest grandson in three years, so this would be a fantastic surprise for her.

"It would be best to give her some advance notice, to avoid any unpleasant shock when you meet up."

They were already waiting for us in the camp.

The doctor gave the patient a quick once-over and concluded positively:

"He's in good health, in excellent shape and clean-living."

"Just like his dad," I announced confidently.

"I remember his dad from twenty-five years ago, when he first came here with his accordion."

"Margarita Valeryanovna, you've got it wrong. I can't have aged that much."

"I'm the one who's aged, Mishenka, but you can't have been more than sixteen in 1948."

"Dad, did you really work here at that age? How come we didn't know about this? Mum and Tanya always told us such horrible things about you. Why do they hate you so much?"

"Sonny, I started doing physical work in the allotment and selling potatoes at the market when the war was still going on, during the evacuation when I was ten years old, so that I could stay alive and be laughing today: ha ha ha ha ha!"

On Monday mornings, Mum usually cleaned the house, went to the bathhouse and did her housework. I greeted Nanny Sasha by the gates as always and asked if there was any post. I kissed Nanny as she gave me the letters from my mother.

When she noticed me, my mum shouted in the doorway: "Where have you been, my migratory bird? I've been looking for you everywhere. Here's your post."

Over tea, I recounted in detail the news from Moscow, and passed on my eldest's regards.

"Why only from Dmitri? What about Shurik? What's happened to him? Tell me!"

"My youngest is alive and well. He's staying at the pioneer camp for the holidays from today."

The cup of tea shook in her hand. I went round the table and hugged my mother's shoulders from behind.

"Don't worry! You'll see him soon. I had to prepare you for this news."

"My poor grandson. I've spent so many nights crying about him. You're right: it's best that Sasha and I come and see your concert at the end of the session. After this we can take him home with us. You can both spend the night at Nanny Sasha's and go back to camp for the second session the next morning."

"No wonder everyone in our family calls you the wise old woman."

Once back at my place, I opened both the envelopes I'd received. The first contained news from the Odessa Visa and Registration Office: based on written confirmation from your former wife relating to 'unpaid alimony from 1970', your exit visa has been delayed until such time as the above-mentioned circumstances in the family are rectified. The second letter was from the Emigration Office, requesting me to call in to clarify the situation in Moscow.

I rushed off to my English class, which I'd missed the last two weeks, worried that they would have given me up for dead. But my good-natured teacher knew that I was sorting out crucial issues for my future in the capital, and simply smiled, saying: "Oh! Today a little bright ray of sunshine has risen over the horizon. Welcome to our class!"

I apologised, swearing that all this time I had been thinking in English, despite conversing in Russian. I promised to catch up with the other group members as fast as I could (my classmates groaned in unison). I had brought the teacher a special edition of Shakespeare published by Oxford University

Press, which I'd purchased by chance in a bookshop, when I'd been on the hunt for an English–Russian dictionary for myself. After lessons I took my gift up to her as an apology for missing lectures. Initially, Svetlana was speechless with delight, and then in a gesture of thanks, planted a kiss on my cheek. I immediately grabbed this kiss from my cheek and put it on my chest, pressing it to my heart. She laughed so loudly that students walking past us in the corridor turned to look.

Svetlana pulled me by the arm towards the exit: "Misha, you have brought me a priceless gift. Allow me at the very least to offer you some tea and cake. I live just around the corner here, surrounded by my books and records."

"This is my home and my castle. I'm on the fifth floor with a balcony, and have lived here more than twenty years."

"Have you really lived here all that time in a literary union with your books?" I flirted.

"Not entirely. I was married to a professor of philosophy for seventeen years, but he died of cancer not long ago. He was in agony for the last two years, and passed on to the other world in complete consciousness. I can't complain. I adore this collection of sculptures and paintings. Please have a look through them while I make the tea."

During the refreshments, I tried to demonstrate my knowledge of English, acquired thanks to my hostess. But she stopped me with an apology, and remarked politely: "Misha, your Odessan pronunciation makes me feel like something stronger than tea, if you don't mind."

Fortunately, all that remained was for me to agree to this decree. We drank to the usual clichés: friendship, success in language learning, for people to understand and respect each other; a few more toasts, until I was completely free of tension. Suddenly the whole sitting room was filled with the sound of gentle Oriental music, emanating from God knows where. An iridescent, pastel light bounded mystically around the ceiling.

"After a long day at university, my late husband and I took pleasure in the comforts and contrasting emotional sensations at home. In the last years of his life, as his illness became more acute, we stopped creating any kind of atmosphere."

"But some time after his departure, given that you are still young and attractive, you could easily find yourself another partner. What has stopped you?"

"There are plenty of guys around. The university is out of bounds for professional reasons. Outside of that, there are sadly few who I find aesthetically pleasing, and almost all of those are married or too old. I've already made one mistake in life: getting married as a twenty-three-year-old student to a thirty-eight-year-old doctor of philosophy. As a result, I have been widowed young (to use your words) 'at my peak'. And to sum up, let's dance a Japanese dance if you don't mind. Looking into your eyes, I see that your personal life hasn't worked out very well either. Only before I dance with the ballet master, let's drink to 'brotherhood' to give me a bit of Dutch courage, otherwise I'll damage your equipment. I mean your legs."

At first, observing good manners, we kept our bodies at an acceptable distance.

I asked: "Why doesn't the music stop once the next item is over?"

"Because these audio cassettes are automatically set to play the other side and we can only stop them completely using the remote control on the table there."

"So if someone wants to change this cassette for another one, what does he have to do?"

"If that's the case, you need to open the music cabinet with the sound system and record player behind that picture by Vrubel, and choose whatever music there is that appeals to you."

The gap between our bodies was gradually closing. My partner's bare shoulders and enticing décolletage were drawing me ever closer towards the ultimate male temptation.

"Last question: what has inspired you to call this a Japanese dance?"

"Perhaps I could answer this delicate question with actions rather than words?"

"Of course, as long as they don't put me in danger."

"As you wish, sir."

With a mysterious smile, Svetlana slowly squeezed her frame against mine. I encouraged her Japanese presentation with my actions in response. In the half-light of the sitting room her whole face was ablaze with the passion and lust of a sex-starved woman. Finally our trembling lips came together in a long kiss. The lady embraced my shoulders with both arms and took a large stride between my legs, pressing against my hot love tool. Continuing to move with our legs entwined, in time to the same music and changing light, the shaman was gradually leading me into her bedchamber.

The lady began unhurriedly removing my sleeveless summer shirt, from the bottom up. I worked the other way round: undoing her tunic fastenings from behind, and lowering it from top to bottom. I removed her bra in this way, while she took down my trousers and pants during a deep Japanese bow. I completed the two-way striptease in a full balletic squat, removing the goddess's delicate panties. At that moment, the sorceress leaned over me, lowering her breasts and hands on to my back, lightly touching it with her cheek, almost like the sculpture *Amour and Psyche*. We enjoyed washing together (in the shower) to the same adagio tempo. The nymph rubbed shower gel on to her intriguing 'rosebud' and wiped the leftover cream on my protruding pistol. Then, just like classical Japanese theatre, she led me by the hand to the sacred bed in slow motion. All that was needed to complete the Adam and Eve pairing was an apple. My head was spinning from this music, the lights and the smell of the cream. Everything that happened next was like a dream. Just like a true shaman, Sveta directed the sexual ritual over my shaking body. She indulged me generously, sexily kissing my chest and stomach. She was taking slow sips from the cup of love nectar. With a light touch of my palm I tenderly stroked her velvet down, worried that I might scare off the ritual's magic moment.

Aphrodite eventually straightened up, sitting on top of me and froze for an instant in a magical position. She carefully steered the fertile love weapon into the right channel and with a deep sigh, lowered all of her considerable weight on to me at the same time, completing the long-awaited rendezvous of two bewitched beings. Her cry of triumph and pain echoed around the whole house. The woman's tears of joy dropped on to her breast and trickled down on to my stomach. I manfully tolerated this nonsense, waiting for the poor devil to come to her senses after the shock of contact. I wanted so much to reassure my friend and stroke her extremely appetising bum in sympathy. But I knew that this would be too much at such a dramatic moment. Finally my partner in the love duet started to pull herself free and breathe deeply. I accompanied her with my own delicate movement. The young woman was clearly about to come, with bulging eyes and her mouth half open. I was plateauing, probably due to the magical influence of the act. The poor 'rider' was roaring like an enraged tigress from one orgasm to another, not wishing to interrupt the long-awaited sexual satisfaction. In conclusion, I too started to moan at the same time as my partner, from the fullest, deepest orgasm.

She collapsed on to my chest as if felled, and simply whispered, "Oh, Mishanya, Mishanya. Where have you been all this time? A union like this will never happen again!"

Svetlana awoke the wild animal in me with her lover's ecstasy. I couldn't stop kissing her, weaving my tongue with hers, kissing her nipples, bringing the Madonna to a frenzy, and continually finding myself inside her hungry sex. We both dived into the abyss of oblivion until morning came.

I awoke to the hot sensation of her lips and hands. Lying behind me, she was kissing my neck and shoulders, and caressing my chest and stomach simultaneously in front. This was a terrific way to say, "Good morning"! I turned over to face the sorceress and was met by this unforgettable look of moist, shiny eyes and a dazzling smile on the face of Aphrodite.

"I won't let you out of here until you go abroad. After that, as I've waited for you for three years, pined for you madly for the last two weeks and been drugged today by your love potion, you, my dear, will be my prisoner and I will be your eternal slave."

"My wonderful enchantress, don't get angry! Your no less eternal servant has to be at the Visa and Registration Office in three hours' time, at 10 a.m. From there I have to run to the Emigration Office. After lunch I'm expected at work at the Fountain pioneer camp, where I left my youngest son from Moscow in their care yesterday, and so on. You see, I don't have any time to myself. The most I can do to make you happy at the moment is to exchange caresses and kisses once a week. Let's say on Wednesday and even then not every week. Forgive me, my good lady. Have pity and be kind to your slave Mikhail."

"How can I refuse my favourite man after such sweet words?"

At the Visa and Registration Office I presented the ruling of the Moscow District Court regarding my full payment of maintenance from the time of our divorce in 1972 until both children reached the age of eighteen. The document was attached to my file, together with their mother's consent for my departure. The two forms still needed to be completed by my brothers. I could receive consent from the youngest in a month's time. The eldest had decided to sabotage the Visa and Registration Office form, provoking me in a scene.

When my mother reminded him about the form, he said: "Your stinking choreographer can kiss my arse, then I'll sign his document."

I got in touch with Senia, a friend of Yosif's from work. I outlined the situation to him and asked him to pass this message on to Yosif: if he has reasons to refuse, then he should set them out in the form and send it back to the Visa and Registration Office. Otherwise I would have to go to court, and would rather avoid bringing any shame to the family."

"Misha, I don't wish to interfere between brothers."

"But you are his oldest friend and because of this you should help him by passing on this message. You know very well that since he drove Mum out of the shared kitchen, Yosif and I are not on speaking terms. For this reason I can't have any relationship with him, let alone any financial dealings. Apart from the fact that he owes me a quarter of the floorspace that he occupies, my legal share of the whole flat and 1,000 roubles on top, which I paid to Roma on his behalf to compensate for his share of the living accommodation, also used by him. This was my wedding present to him, which I regret deeply now. Now he wants to get revenge on me for all this."

"All right, I'll pass on your request, but I doubt he'll help you. You know what he's like."

At the Emigration Office I updated them on the events in Moscow and also left a copy of the court ruling on my financial accounts with my former wife. In addition, I told them about the problem with my eldest brother.

On the first point the manager took pains to warn me: "Don't get your hopes up with your ex-wife. In cases like these, once you get one problem sorted, your adversary will think of something else at the very last minute, and mount a direct protest to the central Visa and Registration Office. You'll probably have to go to court more than once before getting your visa. So exercise patience."

"That's easier said than done. Where do I get this patience, especially with Taurus as my star sign?"

"You don't have a choice. Even if Milia and Yosif dig the knife in, just hold your tongue!"

I decided to do some English study to distract myself from these inane thoughts and banish my anxiety. For days at a time I annotated the dictionary with pronunciation from the tape I'd got in Moscow. I learned everyday phrases and conversations from the phrase book. I had no intention of looking foolish in front of Svetlana or on the other side of the border. I gradually got a feel for it and started to move my tongue and lips more boldly, mimicking not only the sound of isolated words on the tape, but also the intonation of whole sentences in dialogues.

While the children were taking their afternoon nap in the pioneer camp, the manager got all the leaders and teachers together. He introduced me and went about his business. Going by the bewildered looks around the room, I realised that as I had started working in this camp twenty-five years earlier, I knew all the ins and outs, even the hush-hush ones, and didn't need to worry about anything as I was 'one of us' at the Fountain.

"My dear colleagues, joking aside, I will be teaching you a certain programme of Stage Folk dances and mime excerpts for the end-of-term campfire concert, just as your accordionist will put together a musical/vocal repertoire with young instrumentalists and singers. The only difference is that he will be doing this as part of his regular hours, whereas I'll be working at weekends (initially) with the help of the group leaders. What I envisage is this: I'll model part of the Dance composition on Friday afternoon and all day Saturday/Sunday, following a timetable allowing for one and a half hours with each group. Their leaders will train their dancers themselves over the other four days of the week. Using this conveyor system for production and rehearsals I promise you this: together we will produce a worthwhile programme in this very short timescale. Today we must meet with each group just for half an hour to determine the maximum number of participants willing to be involved in this Artistic activity. I would request that while the children are resting, the leaders should reorganise the programme planned for today, so that we can gather together all Dance enthusiasts by group. Please forgive me for disrupting your plans and be aware that I am just a paid visiting teacher rather than a member of staff in this establishment, but am ready to invest my energy in organising the best possible time for our children.

The camp manager was back now, and seeing the worried faces all around him, asked: "So how's it going, Mikhail? I hope your good-natured colleagues haven't torn you to shreds?"

"On the contrary! We've have a nice chat and unanimously agreed to work together."

The senior leader, who seemed to have been in situations like this before, was interrupted by general mirth.

"I know that Mikhail has a wealth of experience in working with children, and we will do everything we can to make use of his talent as a choreographer in our holidaying children's Aesthetic education. By the way, your son Alexander is coaching his partner in his own Ballroom dance repertoire after supper today. Now give us half an hour to get on with reorganising the programme."

I made a conscious decision not to pop in on Sasha's dance practice on my first Friday in the camp, so that he could establish his own teaching principles and tastes without my input. I promised to visit him the next time, as long as my presence wasn't going to put him off, and warned Shurik that his grandmother would be coming to the concert with Oksana and would take him back to hers for three days afterwards for a change of scene, to wander around Odessa and visit family.

"Then I'll take you back to the camp for the second term, and you'll head back to Moscow with Agrippina on 31st August. She's coming here for two weeks' holiday. I don't know where I'm going to be at that time: whether I'll be here or there."

"Dad, can I come and stay with you in Karolino Bugaz for a couple of days? We could go fishing like we did before."

"If you'd enjoy that, then I'm always willing! This will be my birthday present to you for 4th August. You deserve it for doing so well at boarding school and camp. You'll be with Grandma tomorrow as it's her day off. In the morning you'll go to the bank with her, then you'll spend the day with your cousins. In the evening, some of the relatives are coming to the bodega to see you. There'll be enough food to feed an army."

"Daddy, thank you so much! It's a pity Dmitri's not here with us. It would be good for us all to be together."

"Sonny! Your brother's not on our team just now. He's dropped out of school and God knows what he gets up to. He's going downhill and who knows where he'll end up with your mum's influence."

I was called to the camp gates to welcome my guests. I took them into my room and asked Mum to psych herself up to meet her grandson. I asked my niece to fetch a glass of water for her grandmother. A few minutes later I came back with Shurik, who was almost as tall as me, and beaming like a newly polished teapot. He launched himself at his grandmother in her chair, falling on his knees before her. The Panther pressed her grandson's head to her breast, leaking tears of happiness on to him – seeing her long-suffering youngest grandson, who was one step away from the other world on the day he was born, surviving through Nanny's miraculous healing hands. Twelve years had shot by with meteoric speed.

"Up you get, my darling grandson!" my parent commanded. "Good gracious, I can't believe it!" she concluded.

'Mum, I'm sorry. Sasha and I need to go and get ready for the performance now. You'll see him later onstage."

Mum couldn't believe that this half-dead little bundle, who'd been brought home from the maternity ward, had transformed into a young man like this, with good manners acquired in the boarding school in Moscow.

"Mummy, you shouldn't be so surprised. This English special school is for children who are going places."

"And this, excuse the expression, tart tried to take her own son away from there against his will?"

"Yes, but let's get into celebration mode for today's pioneer concert."

Once the triumphal camp line had lowered the camp flag in honour of the end of the first cohort, the closing children's concert began around a hot fire. One after another, the groups performed in a steady stream, each with their own thirty-minute programme. At first Shurik danced a slow foxtrot with his partner and immediately after, a cha-cha-cha (two minutes). The astounded parents went mad, shouting, "Encore!" The senior leader asked the soloists to do another dance, the Finnish 'Cross step Polka' (which was now already in my comic version for the stage). The audience laughed non-stop and as the three-minute number came to an end, they gave the youngsters a standing ovation. At the end of the second section's programme, Shurik also took part in the 'Sailors' Dance' for young boys, even performing a solo as one of the sailors.

We arrived home in a taxi at around 10 p.m. Nanny Sasha was sitting on the veranda, trembling in anticipation of the visitors. Shurik gently approached the sleeping old lady, and squatted down in front of her. He gently took her hands from her knees and placed them on his head.

"Nanny! It's your next-door neighbour, Shurik. I'm not speaking to you in your dream, I'm really here."

Nanny Sasha gave him a startled look, assuming that he was a continuation of her dream.

"Is it really you, Shurik? The same little boy that I saved from the Devil?"

My son stood up, lifting the ninety-year-old great-grandmother up from her chair by the hand. She carefully stroked his head, face, shoulders, as usual, wanting to reassure herself that this vision was real. Then she embraced her former patient, pressing his cheek to her breast and as always, thanking and praying to God for saving the boy's soul and flesh. We waited patiently for the devout woman to finish her prayer and then went into her house. Nanny took us into her grandsons', the musketeers', room, who came to visit only occasionally now, as they generally spent their holidays at their country house in Karolino Bugaz. Mum and Oksana said their goodbyes to us quickly, so as not to delay the elderly hostess.

The Panther couldn't take her eyes off her youngest grandson. She kept showing off the tolerant, smiling Shurik to all the neighbours until I took him away.

After lunch Oksana went with her youngest cousin into town to have a look round, and I rushed into the Visa and Registration Office, where my next surprise was already waiting for me. Yosif had returned his form just inside the thirty-day deadline, saying that eight years ago he had lent me 3,000 roubles to buy a cooperative flat in Moscow, which I still hadn't repaid. The manager had then requested that he sent in a copy of my receipt of this credit from him or two witnesses with their passport details and addresses. I sent a copy of this form to my lawyer. They reminded me that unfortunately my brother now had another thirty days from receipt of the last letter, in which to confirm my debt. Yosif was winning, and I was defenceless in the face of his taunts. The bureaucratic machine was working in his favour.

At the bodega in the evening, when Shurik met up with family members, David asked how I was getting on with leaving. I showed him a copy of the form that Yosif had lodged regarding my debt to him of 3,000 roubles.

"Right, we won't spoil the atmosphere of the occasion. In the next few days I'll notify all the family who know the opposite to be the case: how you contributed during his marriage eighteen years ago. I'll warn him that if he doesn't change his position in relation to you, we will cut him off, just as his brothers did, a long time ago."

We had a good time at Mum's, and in the morning, Shurik and I hurried off to go fishing in Bugaz. We enjoyed two magical days: we went to the beach, caught goby and plaice, baked them in the hot sun and drank kvas like we used to in 'the good old days', when Dmitri was with us. I made the most of the closeness and related (in strict confidence) my plans for the future in Europe and America: working with him in pantomime, dance and contemporary ballet.

"Dad, I can't see it happening, although I would really love to work with you in the ballet."

"Yes, you're right. 'Don't run before you can walk,' as your grandmother would say."

We were back at Nanny Sasha's after lunch, and the next morning, we raced back to the pioneer camp.

For the second term, I put in Dance classes with the group leaders four times a week, including Sundays, in readiness for the production of a whole camp dance procession (concert finale) to mark the end of the summer season. The senior leader was alarmed at this idea. She promised to invite the party Komsomol (young persons' communist society) leadership.

On Wednesday, I walked my teacher home as usual after English lessons. Svetlana seemed sad. Walking with her hand in mine, she squeezed her shoulder up against me.

"Svetik, I get the feeling you're saying goodbye to me today. Have you had enough of me already?"

"On the contrary, my knight in shining armour. We have English tests on Friday, as you know. On Saturday I go away to my parents in Sochi for a month as is our tradition, and I would love it so much if you came with me. But I understand that this is complicated for you because of the uncertain situation you're in. I hope I can bear being apart from you till September."

"In August I will be really busy with my son and work in the pioneer camp, let alone all the bother with my family enemies concerning my departure. The paperwork and formalities look like they're going to keep me here for another couple of months."

My lady friend and I shared a night of passion, Japanese-style, before we parted.

Roman and his wife had finally returned from Kamchatka and collected their daughter from Mum. He and I met up at the bodega, and he filled in my exit form without any fuss. He confirmed in writing that I didn't owe him any money. Roman had a look at the copy of Yosif's famous form and started to laugh at the eldest's vulgar lie about my debt.

"Look, he's fine, Misha, you have to factor in that he's always like that. I would have been amazed if he had given you his consent that easily. You'd think it would be the other way round: if the eldest hates the middle one that much, then it's in his interest to get rid of his adversary as soon as possible. But it would be more enjoyable to suck the blood out of you first, given the opportunity. Though Yosif knows very well that even without his cooperation, you could get the OK from the court."

"Taking my own brother to court is not my style, but maybe that's precisely what he's aiming at."

"Don't worry! David and I will spread the word around Odessa about him, and he won't be able to shake that off for a long time: at the factory, in the chess club, at evening classes, where he teaches maths, and with the family."

"Roma, it won't make things any easier for me. But you're right. I need to beat Yosif at his own game."

I received a letter from the Emigration Office with a reminder about the thirty-day deadline from my wife's receipt of the second form relating to my departure in Moscow. They advised me to contact her lawyer again regarding the case against her, otherwise I would never receive the document I needed for my visa. I quickly called in on Greenstein at his legal consultancy office to discuss this question. First he called the Odessa Visa and Registration Office to be sure that they definitely hadn't got my ex-wife's consent for my departure. Then he got through to the judge he already knew in Moscow and informed Morozova about the delay in emigration forms from his client's ex-wife. The chairman of the District Court promised to send Platonova an official warning, threatening to give M. Berkut permission to leave without her agreement, if she didn't return her form on time to the Visa and Registration Office at the return address. At the same time I recounted to my lawyer the situation with my brother Yosif, who had falsified information in his form about my owing him 3,000 roubles, for which he had no official proof whatsoever. The deadline for him to present this last information to the Visa and Registration Office was 31st August. Would I have to take him to court?"

"The problem with your brother is a lot more straightforward. He can be fined for giving false information. But with your ex-wife it's a lot more serious because of the children. All the same, she can only drag out the process of you getting a visa, she can't actually stop it. You'll probably have to go to Moscow again soon, but on your own this time. Keep me as your trump card for when you've come out on top in all the court proceedings, but the central Visa and Registration Office delays your visa for no reason."

On 3rd September, all our relatives (apart from Mum and Roman) usually met up at Yosif's to celebrate his birthday. In mid-August, David handed him a personally written ultimatum, signed by over forty members of the extended family on both Mum's and Dad's sides:

Dear Yosef,

   If you don't stop blackmailing your brother Mikhail, and don't return the legal form to the appointed office by 1st September, we, the undersigned, will cut off all relations with you and your family from that day forward. Hoping that your dark mind will see the light.

   Your (possibly former) generally loving . . . [signatures]

"Well, David, you're really telling him! You're not pulling any punches. But is he really going to take any notice of that? My ex in Moscow didn't take it lying down either. The chairman of the District Court in her area has, via the Odessa lawyer, called the two spouses to a meeting on 2nd September in her office, with all the pertinent documents for 'malicious delay to emigration'."

As time went on, everything started to fall into place. Pina was due to arrive in Odessa on 17th August.

I was on time to meet my lady friend from Moscow. She was ecstatic at meeting again, and realising her long-held dream of spending time on my home turf, in the 'Black Sea jewel', Odessa. On Mondays, Wednesdays and Fridays, I was entirely at her disposal, and on the other days I was free in the evenings after work at the camp. In the mornings, we went down to the beach at Lonzheron or Otrada; we had lunch at a pasty stall, relaxed under the acacia in the heat, and after supper, visited the theatres, cinemas and even dance floors in the park. In her free time away from me, my guest swanned around the museums, department stores and the famous Privoz market.

One Sunday morning, I took Pina to the pioneer camp. While I rehearsed, she enjoyed the beach. The manager invited her to his country house, just below the camp, right on the seashore, for lunch with his family. By 3 p.m. we were already rushing off to Karolino Bugaz. Two hours before sunset, we caught a fish from my boat in the estuary. My lady friend giggled and squealed like a child, enjoying her first experience of catching a live fish. We boiled up our fresh catch with potato, onion and tomato. Naturally we washed down our 'lovers' feast' with a little vodka from the cellar, and were on cloud nine.

"Mishanya, I can't recall ever being this happy. Thank you very much for such a lovely relaxing outdoor break."

The next day we hiked 3 km around the head of the sea and estuary in to Belgorod-Dnestrovskiy. We caught the bus from there to Odessa and hastily went our separate ways: she to the zoo, and I to the pioneer camp.

On Saturday evening I took my friend to Mum's and introduced her to the relatives, who were paying her their customary visit that day.

"Dear lady, Misha has told me so many good things about you that I even began to envy him you. Thank you for the particular attention you have shown his son and my grandson. I hope everything works out for you."

Shurik and his partner weren't taking part in the finale, as their three-minute ballroom-suite performance had paved the way for the rest of the participants to prepare for a general grand finale to finish the season.

On Sunday, after a combined rehearsal for four sections, which my son observed from the side, the twelve-year-old dancer, who was catching me up fast, paid me a compliment: "Dad, I've never seen you so excited. You're riding the crest of your creative wave. Why are you trying so hard? You're not even getting paid for this. I'm sorry, but no one here is able to fully appreciate your work."

"Firstly, true artists create not only for monetary purposes, but also in the name of art. Secondly, my work here is in payment for you having a comfortable stay in the camp. And thirdly, I don't want to leave the country like a rat deserting a sinking ship. I'll feel better spiritually there if I have a positive memory of leaving behind me here something of myself and my creative work."

"Now I understand your enthusiasm and in your shoes, I would act in exactly the same way."

"Sonny, it's not as easy as people may think for me to leave this place. Your home country is not only the place where you were born and grew up. My spiritual roots will remain here, juices that I've drunk over more than forty years in various corners of the Soviet Union and which will always have an influence on my career, wherever I may be in the world, until the end of my days."

I invited Roman and Pina to the closing festivities of the camp season. When he caught sight of my brother that morning, Yakov Aronovich embraced him like a son and introduced to everyone there his chess trainer from twenty-five years ago when Roman was thirteen. Now he was an international master.

"Today, my friends, as a surprise, I've organised for you not twelve as before, but twenty-four boards to play simultaneously at 12 noon. The young chess players are expecting you."

For an hour and a half straight after breakfast, I worked on the evening programme for the concert, assisted by the group leaders to accompaniment provided by the accordionist. The guests began to assemble at 11 a.m.: representatives of the District Komsomol Committee, the management from the radial tools factory, and parents of the camp children. There was an air of celebration. Chess players were preparing for their synchronised battle with a master of the sport at the P-shaped arrangement of tables on the volleyball pitch. Trifonov (the Director) had to borrow more boards from nearby camps, sometimes bringing players back as well. The mass combat got under way to the beat of the drum. Roman quickly strode through the tables, making his first opening moves. The guests stood behind the players were open-mouthed, intrigued to observe such an unusual phenomenon. Before the session, the physical-instruction leader asked the audience to remain silent and not to distract the players with suggestions or sharing homemade cakes or pickles. In under an hour, Roman won twenty-three games and drew one, to tumultuous applause. The camp manager presented him with a souvenir to remember it by.

After an early supper, the pioneers were ready to bring the season to a close with their creative endeavours, and formed a line to lower the flag of friendship. There was also an announcement about the group and solo winners of a range of competitions. Then the concert got going by firelight. Particularly successful was that part of the finale which had begun with a grand procession with battery-operated torches made by the participants themselves. Later, there were acrobatic performances and series of group pyramids, put together by the physical-instruction leader. To round it all off, a group of multinational dancers demonstrated their most impressive figures and movements, completing the concert in the universal code of farandole-style, along with sports groups and the inclusion of a choir made up of all sections, performing the composer Isakovky's patriotic song about how wonderful life was in the Soviet Union. The parents, unable to contain their emotions, picked up the tune and words of this popular song, concluding the celebration jointly with their offspring. Universal rejoicing by adults and children alike resounded through the entire Fountain, in honour of the end of the camp season.

While Shurik was getting changed, Roman, Pina and I said our goodbyes to the management team. We apologised for making a quick getaway, due to Shurik's departure to Moscow on the night train. Trifonov hugged Roman and me in gratitude, expressing the hope that we would meet again in another twenty-five years' time. The taxi was waiting for us at the exit. I assumed that we were going home. Imagine my surprise when Roman took us to Mum's at the bodega for a farewell supper. Poor Shurik: his eyes were popping out of his head and his jaw had dropped.

"What about the train?"

"Whose?"

"Mine."

"Our train leaves for Moscow at 11 p.m. tomorrow."

"Daddy, what have you done?"

"I haven't done anything, anywhere. That's just how it seems, sonny."

"I mean, I didn't even have time to say a proper goodbye to my partner."

"Shurik, please forgive me for this little white lie in the camp. We didn't have time for niceties. Take a look at these poor hungry and thirsty blighters. They've been waiting for you since nine."

"In the morning or evening?"

"Nine in the evening, of course!"

"Yesterday," added David.

All the aunts, cousins and their wives and children cheered so much that I couldn't hear myself. I had to whistle like a thief, like I used to do as a child. Everyone quietened down immediately.

"Dear citizens of Odessa! Allow me to present to you my closest lady friend from Moscow, Agrippina. Sasha has found a surrogate mother in her, and an elder sister in her eighteen-year-old daughter, Natasha. Pina helps my son and looks after him outside boarding school better than his own mother does. I propose a toast to her."

And the fun continued. Luckily I had my accordion with me. My son's farewell party came to an end at midnight. Everyone squeezed him and wished him well, only too aware that they would not be seeing him in his home town for a long time to come.

We returned home tired and happy. I managed to whisper to Mum before we left, that I would be back from Moscow in a few days' time, following the court hearing with Milia. My mother told me that as a result of the ultimatum Yosif had received from the family, he and his family were experiencing constant problems behind closed doors. His wife and daughter were demanding that he sign the Visa and Registration Office form, and he was digging his heels in like a stubborn mule.

On our last day in Odessa, we packed our cases and went down to the sea. We spent time on the beach, ate meat pasties and bought gifts for ourselves and others in the shops. In the evening we made our way to the station, happy to be together. Boarding the train, we flopped down on our bunks without a backward glance.

Pina and I went our separate ways in Moscow: she went home, and Shurik and I headed straight from the station to the boarding school. The doctor examined the 'beach bum'. The leader took in Sasha's winning awards and prizes for the school exhibition of its students' achievements during the summer. I paid for the next school year in the accounts office, and asked the secretary if the Director wished to speak to me. The latter came into reception and all he was interested in was whether my son was here, and whether his education had been paid for. I confirmed that I had returned my 'sapling' safe and sound, and settled up. We shook hands to conclude our official business. I had the feeling that there was something the Director was not telling me, but decided it was just my cursed sensitivity making me unnecessarily suspicious about our interaction.

I returned to Agrippina's mother's home feeling slightly perturbed by the school director's behaviour. I packed my case and took a shower while I waited for my lady friend. But that heavy foreboding of impending doom did not leave me. I started to play mental patience.

My lady friend turned up in an unbuttoned sarafan (tunic dress), bronzed and smiling, and with home-made supper to boot in a pan and jars. I began to feel a little uneasy.

"My mum has made this specially for you from the fresh vegetables that Natasha brought back from the market. They just couldn't believe that this was my natural tan and were trying to wash it off. My daughter was envious, and wished that she had gone to Odessa with us."

"I hope they liked our gifts from the Black Sea coast."

"They told me to say thank you from them and sent you some kisses. Like these! Thank you, my dear friend! You have spoilt us all with your presents. That deserves a drink!"

After supper Pina sat on my knees and as she hugged me, asked tenderly: "Mishanya, what's on your mind? Has something happened at school? I can see it in your eyes." When she heard about the Director's strange behaviour, and how he was hiding something, she said: "Whatever happens, they have taken Sasha in. They've received payment and his prizes. That means that at least for this academic year, the boy is safe both here and there. Relax!"

"In chess, the most important thing is to know how to factor in and anticipate your opponent's next moves. The biggest risk for any man comes in overestimating one's own capabilities and underestimating one's opponent. Just as, after the court had decided in my favour, Milia dumped some shit on me again. I should work out where she's going to target next, so as to protect myself and my son from any potential harm. It's the same with obtaining the visa."

"You won't be able to find out anything today now. Sleep on it. Go to the cooperative tomorrow to give Dmitri the gift from his brother, and try to dig up the evidence you need. As you said yourself, he's playing the two of you off against each other. It's worth a try – you're not going to torture him."

"Pinochka, you are spot on. Let's not waste any more of our precious time chatting. That sarafan is really flattering, but I really don't think you need it on."

My lover giggled loudly, and I carried on doggedly uncovering my Danae until Rembrandt's picture was revealed on my lap. In the morning, my radiant lady friend dashed off to work, while the worried father headed to see his eldest son.

Tanya flung open the door when I rang at the cooperative.

I asked: "Can I see Dmitri?"

"He's still asleep."

"Wake him up. I've got a package for him from Shurik."

Inside, my eldest could be heard driving the courier out of his room. I rang the doorbell again. Finally, my son emerged, looking rather unprepossessing, and instead of "Hello", yelled: "What do you want?"

"We need to have a serious conversation, and here's a present from Odessa from your brother."

"Hang on five minutes. I'll get myself washed and dressed. We can talk in the café downstairs. Take a seat, make yourself comfortable."

I sat on the bench by the door, wondering if I'd done the right thing in coming.

Over a cup of tea and a sandwich, Dmitri softened, and shielding his puffy, hangover face, asked: "How was your holiday? That melting pot of Odessa is still standing then? Ha ha!"

"Did you transfer your telephone number, or have you changed it in the new flat?"

"Mum has kept the old number for now, as she's been thinking of exchanging this cooperative for another district, and then we'd probably get a new one. She thinks every day's Christmas. She just doesn't know what she wants. Now her main preoccupation is to give you a load of crap."

"But why? I left her money in the bank for you and Shurik's keep until you both turn eighteen. And after this I plan to help you personally as much as I can, wherever I am. I don't understand what she needs from me."

"First of all, Mother blames you for all the failures in her life, and for ruining her career. Secondly, she wants to fight you for the 3,000 roubles you left for Sasha's education. Thirdly, that pseudo-lawyer can't forgive you for losing the previous flat. And in general, our mum is psychologically unstable. You can expect her to do what suits her, even if this damages those close to her, or herself. That's what everyone says. Late at night in my room, I often hear the sisters drinking in the kitchen and bad-mouthing me, you and all your Jewish relatives from Odessa. But I pretend I'm asleep and don't rise to it. I need to keep abreast of what they're thinking and plotting against their own family. Sometimes my hair stands on end with the things I hear. But I made a deal with myself to keep quiet for the time being. So, for example, on 4th August, they took a present to Shurik on his birthday: together they wrote a letter to the boarding-school director about you. It's better if I don't quote their expressions and my mother's demands to protect her son from a father like you."

"Right! Why didn't you go to the bank then and pay for your trip?"

"I changed my mind, cos I was so scared that Mother might do irreparable damage without me here. You can't imagine how many times I've stopped her getting into trouble."

"Sonny, you have my deepest sympathy, but unfortunately, I can't help you at all."

I got home feeling even more stressed than when I'd set out. For the whole of the rest of the day, I went through my possible means of attack and defence for tomorrow's meeting with Milia and the judge. I wrote an official statement about the systematic malicious slur on the father as witnessed by my youngest son and the director of the school which Alexander would continue to attend for the following academic year. I asked for protection from Mrs Emilia Platonova's victimisation, through sending that letter to the school which slandered me and my son.

As predicted, Milia did not appear in court. The judge rang her at home and to my surprise, she picked up the telephone. I was sorry that I could only hear one side of the conversation that followed. But even this was sufficient to get the gist of the situation.

"By training, you are a lawyer with a masters degree, and this is the second time you have ignored an official court summons, for which you were given ample notice. I am recording in your file that you have breached professional ethics and the Russian Federation civil proceedings code [date, number]. As a result:

"a) your former spouse Mikhail Semyonovich Berkut will receive a positive outcome to his application today;

"b) you are criminally responsible for falsifying a document in your case;

"c) you have incurred a fine of 200 roubles for failing to appear in court more than once without prior notice.

"If you fail to pay the fine within thirty days, you will be sentenced to forced labour cleaning the capital for a week, and this fact will be noted in your file. You will be notified of all this in writing."

"Excuse me, madam! There is one further statement addressed to Emilia S. Platonova concerning her conduct."

The judge read through the document carefully, stopping to underline in places. She asked a few clarifying questions and then rang the boarding school. Just as I had last time, I left the office, in the interests of basic courtesy. About ten minutes later, the judge appeared in reception and told the secretary to type up an instruction to the boarding-school director regarding Emilia S. Platonova's emotional victimisation of members of her own family, and to send it off urgently to the given address. Also, to make a photocopy of the last court ruling denying Mikhail Semyonovich Berkut's debts to his former wife.

"Mikhail, I hope that these measures will protect you and your youngest son's interests and civil rights, and that Mrs Platonova will leave you in peace. If she doesn't, then I'll be seeing you again!"

I signed to confirm receipt of the document giving me permission to leave on the part of my wife. I thanked the chairman and secretary of the Civil Court. I rang Mum and Greenstein straight away to tell them the latest.

Once I'd punched my return ticket to Odessa the next day, I did my customary dash to buy presents for my loved ones, otherwise they would push me down the famous 200-odd steps of the Potemkin Stairs on the Primorsky shore. In the evening, I invited Pina and her family for meat pasties to celebrate my victory in court, assuming that we wouldn't get the opportunity to meet up again so soon. Although I internalised my feelings, my intuition told me just the opposite in defiance.

I'll probably have to come back to Moscow another time, despite not wanting to.

Just in case, we said definitive goodbyes to Agrippina's family. She herself preferred to stay with me, possibly for our last evening together. My friend didn't want to believe that it was our farewell night. I reassured her, being sarcastic and making fun of myself.

"My darling, I don't believe the authorities will let me go just like that. They'll come up with something else to catch me out, to fray my nerves until the very end. Otherwise they would swap their principles of proletariat dictatorship for bayonets and bullets.

My woman slept in my arms all night, fearful that I would slip quietly away from her forever.

On the train I analysed the 'military operation' involved in obtaining my exit documents.

I heaved my suitcase home from the station on Proletarsky Boulevard, and transferred the presents into my bag. I hadn't forgotten my landlady; she humbly accepted her gift. I hurried off to see Mum, impatient for news of Yosif.

I had scarcely got through the snack-bar door, when my mother shouted to me above the din and over her customers' heads: "Misha, everything's fine! Knock on Fedya's door: get him to cover for me for five minutes. Welcome home, my son!

"Here's what happened: Yosif started to laugh as he was reading the family ultimatum. Your brother assumed that they were all bluffing or that it was a joke. Then, the day before yesterday, when none of the signatories turned up for his birthday, he and his friend Senia marked the quietest birthday he'd ever celebrated in his whole life. The next day, bowing to pressure from his furious wife and daughter, he signed his consent for your departure and immediately forwarded the document as required. Better late than never!"

When I presented the Moscow Civil Court's positive ruling on my debts in the Odessa Visa and Registration Office, I was interested to know whether they'd received my eldest brother's form. The secretary confirmed receipt, and as before, made the necessary photocopies. So now I had in my hot little hands all four pieces of evidence confirming that I did not owe any money to any of my relatives. After five months' wait, the Visa and Registration Office manager then collected up copies of all the necessary enclosures and dispatched them in a precious pack to the central branch in Moscow. For the umpteenth time I would have to wait thirty days before receiving my visa for Israel.

The Emigration Office again commented on my get up and go: "You're not done with this ordeal yet. We have a long list of 'refuseniks' [those denied permission to emigrate], whose visas have been delayed by Moscow for one reason or another. Let's wait and see what they come up with in your case. One way or another, don't make any promises to anyone about leaving the country quickly. This stage of emigration is the most complicated and painful. If, at any time, you have upset the authorities and particularly if you have any convictions, get ready to fight for your rights as far as (if it comes to it) requesting assistance from the relevant international organisations for the protection of human rights."

"If I don't receive my visa within the designated time frame, what other options do I have to be sure of getting it in Moscow?"

"There is a central Emigration Office in the capital, with its own lawyers. If your visa is delayed, you will have to go back to Moscow with someone in a month's time to draw up power of attorney with their lawyer, who will fight your case on receiving your visa with the central Visa and Registration Office at the Ministry of Foreign Affairs. You would enter into an official contract with them to do this, and wait for the outcome in Odessa."

September 1975 was the longest month of my life. It is torture for a genuine warrior to endure an uncertain wait, while his fate is decided by a battle taking place elsewhere. It's much harder to find yourself inactive than to suffer defeat in war, surrendering temporarily and continuing to fight, hoping for victory in the next battle. I decided to adhere to my Zodiac sign. After all, 'Attack is the best form of defence.' On 1st October the Odessa office chief (at my request) rang the lawyer at Moscow Emigration Office. Mark Schwartz asked us to send him a copy of my file in the diplomatic bag, and in exchange, he would forward her a contractual document in my name by telegram. I signed both documents in the office (agreement and guarantee), which went back to the lawyer in Moscow by the same means. This day marked the beginning of the legal battle regarding the illegal hold-up of my visa between the central Visa and Registration Office in the Ministry of Foreign Affairs, and the Emigration Agency at the Israeli Embassy. I got myself ready for a 'prolonged parachute jump out of a plane about to make a crash landing'. Every working day I would be on duty in a corner of the Odessa office reception for several hours at a time, in case a call came in from Moscow to confirm details of my life, family, education, and so on. This wasn't a complete waste of time – I read English literature and newspapers with the help of a dictionary.

Schwartz, the lawyer, reported back on Emilia Platonova's written statement to the central Visa and Registration Office, in which her former husband, Mikhail Berkut, accused her of attempting to avoid her maternal obligations in caring for her children.

'He abandoned them in 1970, and paid no maintenance from that time until our divorce in 1972. Now he is refusing to compensate the children's expenses for the above-indicated period (two years). The Chairman of the District Court illegally gave this traitor of the homeland permission to leave and insulted me professionally as a lawyer (in a telephone conversation). I wonder: how many former prisoners have paid the judge for a privilege of this sort?'

Currently, this case had been transferred to court so that the facts set out could be investigated and sentence could be passed.

Naturally, Emilia's statement fell into the hands of people who were looking for reasons to withhold my visa. They knew perfectly well that this was slanderous both to me and to Judge Morozova. But then it was such an extraordinary case, with convincing grounds for defending the interests of a mother of two children, a member of the Soviet Communist Party, a PhD, of pure Russian nationality, etc. The whole of October was swallowed up by this nonsense. Fortunately, the judge, who had been accused of bribery, had been around the block a bit and had not been born yesterday. Being related to the Minister of Justice, she insisted on bringing a case against Milia for slander and deliberately breaking the Russian Criminal Code by ignoring the court summons. This case acquired an undesirable spin for the authorities.

Schwartz, the lawyer, explained: "The top brass have advised your ex to retract her statement against the judge if she doesn't want to end up behind bars herself. But the lawyer's frustrated ambition overwhelmed the Cossack woman to such an extent that she went too far, and decided to call one of her old classmates from Moscow State University, Sergei Prokhorov, who is today the chief prosecutor in the Moscow region. And he (according to Dmitri) delicately cautioned her to withdraw her suit against his colleague."

My eldest son burst out laughing, demonstrating to me how his mother, after this telephone conversation, ran around the table and tore her hair out because of this failure to put her plan into action.

Schwartz, the lawyer, and the long-suffering Judge Morozova now forced my visa through, permission for which lay in the hands of the top director of the central Visa and Registration Office himself, on Dzerzhinsky Square. At the end of October the lawyer rang the Odessa office to confess that it was futile to expect anything from Moscow. I would have to send a letter to the Ministry of Foreign Affairs Committee who control the operational and administrative functions of foreign departments in the service, and make a complaint about the malicious withholding of my visa by the central Visa and Registration Office within the Ministry of Foreign Affairs. I was despairing and frightened that I would lose all self-control. At this point I cooled myself down with a glass of cold water. I asked for a sheet of paper from the secretary and sat down to write my next statement.

For the attention of the Head of the Directorate at the Ministry of Foreign Affairs charged with . . .
From M. S. Berkut . . . [date]

Over the last six months your Emigration Services, in a malicious, premeditated act, have delayed my departure to Israel using various spurious excuses. I take this to be a deliberate breach of the International Agreement (which includes the USSR) regarding the free exodus of Jewish nationals to their historic Promised Land, Israel. If I do not hear from you within the next week regarding my agreed visa, you will force me (though it goes against my wishes) to apply to the relevant committee of the United Nations to protect my human rights, with all the attendant consequences both here and abroad. I remain hopeful of your sound reason and respect.

The office secretary typed up my letter and I signed it. My letter made its way to Moscow that same day in the diplomatic bag. The chief warned me not to go out alone (without someone with me), to avoid any potential provocation, which had already befallen other refuseniks in similar situations on many occasions.

"Best to avoid any unnecessary complications!" she advised.

I asked her whether there was any way of safeguarding my archive without any potential risk for my education, work in print and academic research.

"As in any international port," the office chief informed me, "there are foreign consulates operating in Odessa. Through negotiation with Israel, the Dutch Consul takes possession (on a legal basis) of any personal documents, paintings, published work and so on, from emigrants to the Promised Land as part of our official application. Give me a list of contents in numbered files. I'll translate it into English and confirm your emigration. The consul will give you an appointment time and you (accompanied by your two brothers) will personally give him your materials. You need to pay the postal costs in advance here, which come to ten roubles per kilogramme. When you arrive at your emigration point, send in your application to the local Dutch Embassy/Consulate and within a month your personal pack will be returned to you at the address given in your application, with a personalised certificate and copies of the dispatch invoices received by the consul in Odessa."

I quickly assembled my entire body of work and set off with Roman, suitcase in hand, to the customs office at the port. The consul examined the content. He weighed the lot wholesale and issued an invoice for eighty-five roubles.

Mum was waiting for an update from me. I told her about the goings-on in Moscow, my statement to the Ministry of Foreign Affairs, sending my archive through the Dutch Consul, the office manager's warning about my safety out on my own in the street. To my astonishment, the Panther didn't panic. The reverse was true: she acknowledged that she had already heard of many such situations.

"Misha, don't worry! Just as we did in the war, we will find a way through this dangerous time. We'll put together a duty rota of your cousins and friends, who will take it in turns to accompany you according to your needs and their availability."

"Mum, I will never cease to be amazed by your organisational and practical skills in life. You'll be seventy soon, and you think and act just like a young woman. Where do you get this from?"

"From the bumps and bruises of life on the old body of any mother who's had a few children."

Something kind of wonderful was happening with my eldest brother. He had suddenly started to pass the time of day with Mum in the communal kitchen. Someone or something had obviously exerted an influence on his thirty-year antagonism towards his mother and brothers. He even asked his parent, "How is Misha getting on with leaving?"

"Why don't you ask your brother yourself?"

Yosif just shrugged his shoulders and went off in silence. Personally, I don't believe in transformative miracles among living beings. Most likely someone had convinced him that it was in his interests to have a loving brother abroad. I didn't want to leave as enemies with anyone of my close family. I always remembered my father's parting words about blood ties.

"To hell with them! Of course I can't forget our differences, but for Mum's sake I'll try to forgive."

As usual in recent times, I was sitting in the corridor at the office holding an English newspaper, waiting for news from Moscow. Suddenly the secretary called me to the telephone urgently. I flew up to the first floor and impatiently grabbed the handset:

"Hello!"

"Is that Mikhail Semyonovich Berkut?"

"Yes, this is he." I was trying to get my breath back.

"You need to meet the head of the Ministry of Foreign Affairs directorate as soon as possible, following your letter to him. When can you be in Moscow?"

"Today is 6th November. Tomorrow morning I'll catch the fast train. I will be with you after lunch on the 9th."

"Good – 4 p.m. on the 9th, with all your documents. Entrance 12, third floor, room 43. Don't be late!"

I was petrified. The secretary removed the beeping receiver from my insensible hands. The manager had overheard the conversation from her office. She came into the reception:

"Mikhail, it's too risky for you to travel alone. Anything could happen on the way."

"Thank you. Don't worry. I will pay the conductors and they will keep me safe. Could you please call Schwartz, the lawyer, and arrange for him to attend the appointment with me at the Ministry of Foreign Affairs on 9th November at 4 p.m., entrance 12. Can he come half an hour early and bring my file? I will settle up with him and pay your telephone costs. Excuse me, I need to go and buy a ticket for the morning train, which will get me to Moscow at 1.30 p.m. on the 9th."

As I left, the office manager chipped in: "Keep your eyes peeled!"

What a mess! The longer this goes on, the worse it gets.

I asked the cashier for a compartment next to the conductor's, as I had a valuable film camera.

"Oh, are you a film-maker?"

"Yes, a cameraman. It's heavy and expensive. Thank you."

I only remembered as I was packing my case for Moscow, that both sides of the family were getting together that evening at the bodega to celebrate Mum's seventieth birthday. It had to fall on the same day! Fedya had put up a notice even yesterday to say that the bodega was closed from 4 p.m. to midnight on 6th November. In my shock after the Moscow telephone call, I'd forgotten all about it, although only yesterday I'd given him 100 roubles towards the costs, as my birthday present to my mother. I decided to tell the birthday girl about my trip to the capital at midnight, once all the guests had left. Danya and I took turns on the accordion, but we didn't carry on our high spirits outside, so as not to attract attention unnecessarily.

Once all the guests had gone, and my brothers and their families were restoring the bodega to some semblance of order, I got Mum on her own in Fedya's office for an urgent one-to-one. I asked her not to get emotional. But as soon as she heard that I was off to Moscow tomorrow morning, she put her head in her hands.

"Misha, going by yourself is very risky. They won't let you out of the KGB prison!"

"Mum, all your sons are well versed in chess. My opponents are moving their knight against me. If I don't go, my opponents will say later that they wanted to hand authorisation for my visa to me in person. But, it will look as if I don't really need it, if I don't consider it necessary to go and get it. I have nothing to lose apart from my shackles. We've talked about this many times. I have to prove to the KGB men that I'm not afraid of them, as I'm open with them and with myself."

"Just be careful with your fellow passengers in the compartment and especially at night, when you're asleep."

"Don't worry, I'll be sleeping both nights in the conductors' quarters, when one of them is resting in my seat. They will be rewarded with a generous tip.

Don't tell anyone that I'm going. As far as everyone except you and Roma are concerned, I'm having a break in Bugaz."

I dialled Agrippina's number right then from Fedya's and told her daughter about my trip to the capital. I asked her to keep the evening of 10th November free for a joint farewell supper at Russian Souvenir. First, Roman dropped his wife and daughter home in the car and then took me and my accordion to my place near Lonzheron. When we were alone together, I told my little brother about the latest events. In contrast to my mother, he took this as a positive sign, although he also cautioned me about the danger on the journey and in public places in Moscow. He promised to give me a lift to the station in the morning.

Once the train had set off, I complained to the conductors that as a musician, I suffered from oversensitive hearing. I couldn't sleep all night because of the din my neighbours were making. For fifty roubles (the value of a ticket), they agreed to rest in my berth in the nearest compartment during their night duties. One of them was dubious about their two-berth sleeping cabin (which was only 1 × 2 m) being comfortable enough for passengers. But I stated that I always got a better night's sleep in these conditions than in a four-person compartment. As usual, I spent the whole journey going through all possible reasons for my invitation to the KGB correction facility, without coming up with any conclusions.

My Moscow lawyer, Schwartz, was waiting for me on the platform.

"How did you know which carriage I was in?"

"I didn't. I just decided to wait by the front of the train, as obviously standing by the entrance to Dzerzhinsky Palace would have aroused the guards' suspicions."

"Forgive me, I was in shock from the telephone call in Odessa about this establishment and gave you the wrong instructions for our meeting in Moscow. Let's go and talk things through over lunch."

"So, troublemaker, what have they summoned you to discuss?"

I gave the lawyer a summary of my disagreement with the Theatre Committee of the Russian Federation Ministry of Culture at Moscow Theatre Academy, and the Tadzhik and Buryat difficulties in the period of ideological repression after the Soviet Communist Party Central Committee plenum in June 1962. I quickly described my arrest, the court and work in Gorky. In some detail, I went through my take on the conflict between Platonova and Morozova, chairman of the Civil Court, and referred to my creative relationship with the current Moscow state prosecutor, Prokhorov, in my student years. All this was aimed at giving the lawyer a broader background into the intention behind my summons.

"I'll come into the palace building with you to confirm your identity, but I won't be allowed into the head of the directorate's office to witness your conversation. From everything you've told me, I can only see one triangular argument, that would interest top officials. The chief prosecutor of Moscow, chairman of the District Court and Mrs Platonova, who has been slandered by the judge, as a public servant. I agreed with Morozova concerning the action she took against your (now) mutual opponent on the question of your obtaining your visa for Israel. I assume that the upper echelons are now trying to bring this case to a close, as it's discrediting the channels of justice. It's critical that they defuse the situation inflamed by your ex, and get you to keep quiet, as the main, dangerous witness to this legal mess, silencing your (forgive me) venomous tongue with your ill-fated visa."

On the way into the Dzerzhinsky building, Schwartz showed his identity document, and I proffered a paper from the police in place of my passport. Mark clarified that he was accompanying me and that we had been summoned to office No. 43. The duty officer telephoned someone to confirm the meeting and called a security guard. I got my head in gear and put myself on my guard.

"Take them to office 43 and come straight back! Look, you can see how many people are still waiting for their appointments," ordered the officer.

In the head's reception area, we were met by his adjutant bearing the rank of lieutenant. He checked our identity documents again and disappeared into the boss's office.

Coming out a moment later, he said: "Mr Schwartz, wait here, please, as this is a personal summons. Come in, Mr Berkut!"

I entered the spacious office. A long table with a dozen chairs down each side extended into the distance as far as a writing desk arranged at right angles, where a grey-haired colonel in glasses was sitting and leafing through a yellow folder on the desk. That was all I could take in during my first minute in there. The bearer of three large stars on his epaulettes, his eyes not leaving the papers, he waved to the Lieutenant and the manager left the room. I continued to stand to attention by the door, anticipating the moment when the boss would finally raise his noble head from the papers and smile at me in greeting:

"Oh, dear Mikhail! Forgive me, I was so distracted by your colourful biography, that I entirely forgot about our meeting. Sit down, please. Would you like some tea?"

But it wasn't quite like that. The experienced official took his time, keeping me dangling. His first task in dealing with his prospective enemy was to take this dissident down a peg. Make him respect authority, and law and order.

He said: "There are too many of you educated anarchists here. You can't just get on with your physics, chemistry or (forgive the expression) ballet quietly. You want to poke your nose into politics as well. Fight for your personal freedom and democracy. You've ended up here after all. It's a pity that we've forgotten how to put the screws on freethinkers like these in . . .."

I was so carried away by my imagination that I forgot where I was. The sound of a pencil tapping on the desk hurled me back to harsh reality. The Colonel was staring straight at me over the top of his glasses, taking some time to study my features.

Eventually he declared in a monotonous voice: "What strikes me is that you've enjoyed life, Mikhail. You've been to lots of places and seen a lot of things. You've managed to hurt everyone to such a degree that your transgressions will not be forgotten quickly here."

"From what I can see, you are an educated, skilled man. Our country gave you all the conditions you needed to realise your dream: of being a qualified specialist who is privileged to work in the capital's theatres. However, none of this has any value to you. The result is that all the state funds that have been spent on you have vanished into thin air. There has been absolutely no return on such a large investment. In fact it's the other way round."

Still standing, I listened to his ten-minute moralising without rising to the bait.

"What surprises me most is that you completed your secondary education with distinction in a Soviet school. You had Stalin's grants in a Soviet institute, produced Gala concerts in Moscow and Leningrad in honour of the fiftieth anniversary of the October Revolution, Soviet Army and Soviet car manufacturing, and also, the twentieth and thirtieth anniversaries of the victory over fascist Germany. All this (according to the reviews) was executed to superior ideological and artistic standards. How do you explain the fact that you have written off your creative credits in your homeland and turned your attention to another country, where you will have to start all over again as a complete unknown, without knowing the language or local culture?"

I listened attentively to the agitator's monologue and was shocked at his capacity for propaganda.

"Why aren't you answering my question? It's discourteous for a refined person."

"I'm sorry, that's how it happened."

"Is that all you've got to say for yourself?"

"Unfortunately, yes!"

"Let's come to the next topic. How do you know Sergei Prokhorov, the chief prosecutor?"

"Eighteen years ago he was my student in the Moscow State University Club ensemble and actually wasn't bad."

"What is the nature of your personal relationship with Mrs Morozova, chairman of the District Civil Court?"

"None whatsoever, it's a business relationship. She summoned me to two court hearings."

"Your former wife asserts that you bribed the judge in return for permission to obtain a visa."

"She'll say the same thing about you tomorrow, only on a larger scale."

"Did you really refuse to pay maintenance for your children?"

"Excuse me, it is so loathsome and humiliating to prove to you that I am not a camel or something that I am obviously not."

"In that case, you are free to go."

The Colonel pressed a button to call his assistant.

"Forgive me, you haven't said anything about my statement regarding the withholding of my visa for Israel."

"Your statement is written in the style of a gangster: 'Pay up or get a bullet in the head.' I'm referring to your threat about protection of your human rights from the United Nations. Three years in prison hasn't taught you to appreciate what you have around you. You will receive a response to your letter in a few days' time. Goodbye!"

Without another word, I bowed and went out into reception, accompanied by the Lieutenant.

"Well, Mikhail! I was starting to get worried. What did you talk about for fifteen minutes?"

"It wasn't a conversation, it was a moral and psychological duel. The Colonel's no fool."

"Is everything OK? You've gone very pale and your hands are shaking. Take a deep breath!"

I asked the accompanying sergeant if I could go to the toilet. He led us there and came inside with us. While Mark was having a pee, I splashed some cold water on my face. The guard waited patiently by the door. I thanked him and we went downstairs.

In the metro, I asked Schwartz: "How much do I owe you for your troubles?" and got out my wallet.

He laughed: "Put that away! My services today are part of the fee from last time. Let's pop into a café. I'll buy you a cuppa, and in return you can tell me what went on between you in there. The professional interest is more important to me than the money."

I relayed to the lawyer the substance and style of my meeting.

Mark paid close attention, occasionally checking the nuances in the singular dialogue, and concluded: "I am absolutely convinced that he will give the go-ahead for your visa or – for your arrest."

We both laughed long and hard at this harsh humour. It was laughter through tears. But that notwithstanding, Mark saw me all the way to Agrippina's house, and waited until her mother opened the door. We parted with genuine warmth, like brothers. He asked me to say hi to Jerusalem. I rang Odessa straight away to let them know that I would be back on the 14th at 8.30 a.m. We booked 15th November for my farewell party.

On her return from work, my lady friend threw herself into my arms as she usually did.

Her mother shouted from the kitchen: "That's enough snogging! Wash your hands and come and sit down. We'll eat without Natasha as she's going to be back late."

We loosened up with a drink as we waited for our tasty cabbage soup. I began to unwind straight away. I cheered up the elderly cook with a series of Odessa jokes and Pina and I went out for a walk. I was inclined to visit some of the capital's famous spots to mark our goodbye, but she declined for safety reasons at evening time, because of my persona non grata status.

"I've requested time off work so that we can spend your last two days together, and I can see you on to the train the day after tomorrow. We have a lot to talk about, and need to visit Sasha at school."

I recalled Larisa's words in Leningrad the last time we met: "Why do couples take so long to find each other, only to part so quickly once they do?"

"Mishanya, don't be sad. Fate gave you to me, and even when you've gone, I will be grateful that I was happy with you for so long. Alas, everything comes to an end."

We made the most of our intimacy deep into the night, as if it were the first time. We reminisced about all the chapters of our travels and of course our late friend and cousin Nikolai. We drank to his soul and memory, and that they would never leave our hearts. We fantasised about the possibility of meeting again in future overseas.

In the morning, we spent half the day rushing around the shops, buying New Year's presents in advance. We reserved a little table in the restaurant Russian Souvenir.

After lunch we went to the school. First of all I called in on the Director. I apologised for the additional trouble caused by Mrs Platonova with her acerbic letters. He reassured me that Shurik's mother was neither the only, nor the worst, in their list of divorced parents. The Director asked if it was true that I was leaving for Israel, and when this was likely to be.

"It's uncertain at the moment, but that's my intention. Agrippina Vasilyevna is Shurik's surrogate mother, with whom he spends time when he's not at school. She has the funds available to cover the costs of his education in your school until it finishes. If necessary, I can pay you an advance."

"Mikhail, there's no issue with payment, but your leaving the Soviet Union could have a negative impact on the relationship between the departmental leaders and the son of a 'traitor of the homeland', as Shurik's mother labels you. In any case, he will remain here up to the end of this academic year. From there, this will depend on the Ministry of Education's position regarding children of émigrés. Sasha is one of our best students and social activists. Everyone here loves him and will be sorry if he doesn't return after the summer holidays."

We found my son in the school library. Initially, he was happy to see us, but quickly became distressed on hearing about my possible imminent departure from the country for good. I reminded him of our conversation in the Odessa pioneer camp and promised to send an invitation to him via Agrippina's address if the situation called for it. Once again, I insisted that he must not under any circumstances breathe a word to anyone about my going or about our plans for the future. He repeated his promise in Pina's presence. She reminded the boy about the winter holidays, which they had long since decided to spend in Serebryanny Bor with all the family. I had paid in advance for a two-room cottage for a week, where Shurik promised to teach Natasha ballroom dancing. Pina was scared that these magical plans could soon come crashing down because of me. I guaranteed her that nothing would happen before New Year. My son walked us to the gates. He said goodbye to Pina, having promised to come and see her on Friday. My youngest hugged me and didn't want to let go.

Sensing that he was losing his father, he whispered: "Dad, can it be that I'm never going to see you again? It's so unfair!"

And suddenly he started to sob on my chest, like a small child. I thought that my heart would break. My lady friend went up behind my son and tried to console him. She had difficulty prising the boy off me. She gave him a big cuddle and kissed his head. She promptly moved over to the father, who could not move, and dragged him by the hand to the bus stop.

"Bye, Dad! Good luck, Dad!"

This cry from the heart resounded in my ears for a long time to come.

As a rule, I'm not that partial to a drink. But that evening, in the restaurant with Agrippina's family, I ignored my principles. It was only after three glasses of vodka that I began to feel normal after the stress of saying goodbye to my son. All 'Three Graces': grandmother, daughter and granddaughter, worked hard to lift my spirits. Accompanied by a local accordionist, we sang humorous little ditties, and gradually we got into party mood. At 8 p.m. the Russian Souvenir Ensemble began their programme of singing and dancing. By this time I was feeling quite sleepy. During the artistes' break, the accordionist came over to our table again and started to play 'Dark Eyes', a popular Russian folk song. The women started singing to the lyrics, and I joined in, harmonising in a lower register. The restaurant fell silent, listening to our singing.

Suddenly my fellow drinking companions started to chant: "Da-ance! Da-ance! Da-ance!" The tables nearest to us followed suit.

I called the smiling accordionist over. I shoved a three-rouble note into his hand and asked him to play 'Serbian Gypsy', starting seven bars before the slow part with a continuous increase in tempo until the fast coda. I took off my jacket. From this point on, I had the time of my life. As the music started up, I got up onstage and with a triple step and a clap, began my farewell rhapsody. At first, the public just regarded me with their mouths open. Then they gradually started to clap, scream, whistle, egging the musician and me on. I was in a frenzy, performing one dance figure after another: tap-dancing, leaps and spins, just as I had done in my youth. For the coda: I did a spin in the air and landed on my knee in a deep bow. The audience roared. Picking myself up, half dead at the ripe old age of forty-three, I noticed only then that the ensemble artistes were applauding all around the stage. I gave a huge bow to everyone. I shook the accordionist's hand and rushed to the toilet to collect myself after my theatrical ecstasy.

On the way home in the taxi, the women complimented me, and I them in return.

"It's all thanks to you 'Three Graces', that your Apollo was able to recall his past life."

First we dropped off the grandmother and her granddaughter. We kissed each other goodbye and Pina and I continued on to my place. When we got home, she ran me a hot bath then undressed the invalid and dragged him off for some restoring aqua-therapy. After a healing massage, forgetting about her bra and knickers, I pulled the nymph in with me to keep me company. Like children, we romped and fooled around, splashing water out of the bath. Her surplus garments flew in the direction of the door. In some strange way, we ended up inside each other. By some miracle, half an hour later we were sitting in our dressing gowns at the table with tea and cake. A short while later still, we were on the bed, moaning in delight. And these wonderful demonstrations were how we spent the whole of our last night together. It was morning before we fell asleep in each other's arms. Pina did not cry at the station. We parted as if we would be seeing each other again tomorrow.

My lady friend took my hands and tenderly placed them on her face. "Good luck, and be happy!"

It was beyond my expectations to find Roman there to meet me on the platform in Odessa, as I had planned to take a taxi.

"Hey, why are you walking on by? Don't you recognise your nearest and dearest, or what?" My brother smiled.

"Well, in the first place, my eyesight's not very good. Secondly, I didn't realise that the youngest had such respect for the middle one."

"How was your journey?"

"I'll tell you later."

"What's in this huge suitcase?"

"Presents from Father Christmas."

"Why so early?"

"Better early than never. Who knows where I'll be by New Year."

"Listen, Misha! We've changed our plans here as far as your safety's concerned. Mum and I have decided that instead of playing leapfrog with lots of cousins and friends, David will accompany you everywhere after work, and I'll transport the dissident around by car in the mornings."

"When did you become a taxi driver? You haven't even got your driving licence."

"In August, when you and Shurik were at pioneer camp. As usual, Sofia came from Leningrad for a holiday with her family in the car. Something went wrong with the engine near Odessa, and the breakdown company dragged the old Volga car to her mother's house. Boris [Sofia's husband] refused to return to Leningrad in that old banger, so they decided to give it to me for my birthday on 11th August. In Kamchatka, I earned enough money to buy a Moskvich car. But to take advantage of the opportunity, I made up my mind to practise in the old car first. I've repaired it, and here it is at your service, Mr Itchy Feet."

"Look, Chessy, you've got to cut your coat according to your cloth. I'm talking about your licence."

"I passed my test in September, so I've already been driving around town for two months now."

"If that's the case, then I will entrust my young life and these presents to you. Where are we going?"

"Mother asked me to bring you to her for an important conversation."

I confess, my personal problems had got so tangled that I didn't know which end to unravel first. My parent came to my aid as always.

"From what I've heard about your latest trip to the chief in Moscow, they have obviously made up their minds to dispose of you one way or another. You're just a thorn in their side now. Due to infighting and external politics, they are forced either to swallow this thorn, or to pull it out. In the first option, the thorn will still bother them in the stomach. In the second, the authorities will always dodge any unnecessary trouble with you."

"Mum, logically you're right. But they often decide to do damage because of their ambition."

"Then we will prepare one small bag for when they arrest you, and three large suitcases for when you emigrate. Now you'd be better off moving in with me. Yosif and I have made our peace. We should be together in these last days, just in case."

"Mum, I have brought everyone New Year's gifts in this suitcase. I wrote my New Year's cards on the train, and have attached them to each parcel. Don't forget to give them out!"

Roman drove me to my temporary home. I quickly gathered up my pitiful belongings. On the way to our former flat, my little brother confirmed that my farewell gathering, whichever side of the border I ended up, would be tomorrow at Yosif's at 7 p.m. Real Odessans never shy away from humour. My family tried to cheer me up with cutting jokes to preserve my fighting spirit. They considered that preferable to letting me snivel at the critical moment. Those close to me were clearly more worried about what had happened than I was. You see, they didn't know how hardened I'd become in the six months following my arrest spent in three Moscow prisons. I reckoned that over the last almost thirty-five years since the fascist occupation, both sides of our family had met up twice in one week for the first time, which included Mum's seventieth birthday. This kind of family activity was understandably due to the growing interest towards someone leaving for Israel.

David spent the whole evening with me and Mum at the bodega. With his experience of managing a factory for over twenty years, he too thought that if they were intending to arrest me, then they would have done so there and then. On the other hand, it was easier for them to justify an arrest in the eyes of the public, if there was the slightest excuse for so doing on public transport, in public toilets, holiday zones or car parks, as had happened with Valery Panov, a refusenik I knew, who was a soloist from the Kirov Ballet Theatre in Leningrad. This scandalous situation was written about in the press the whole world over.

Members of both sides of my parents' families got together again on the veranda of Mum's flat on 14th November. Nanny Sasha was the only one of our neighbours who knew the real reason for this gathering. All the guests knew about my cause, but my mother asked us not to talk about this for the moment. Two accordion players, one inside, the other outside, played popular songs and dances non-stop. Young and old enjoyed themselves in equal measure, had a bite to eat, and resumed their entertainment. They demonstrated an indomitable spirit and belief in a better future for their children.

By 11 p.m. the only people left in Mum's flat were her relatives and my close friends from the Opera theatre. Suddenly there was a loud knock at the door. The room suddenly went dead. I took off my accordion and went to meet the nocturnal visitor. Through the first glass door, in the half-gloom of the veranda, I could make out a male figure in a special uniform, sporting a regulation cap on his head.

"So now, 'You've come with a scythe wanting to chop off my head,'" I sang, opening the door.

"Mikhail Berkut?"

"That's me."

"Please sign here!" the officer ordered, handing me a pen and pad.

He shone his torch at me while I was writing on his briefcase. The courier bade me goodnight and sped off down the stairs.

I wanted to ask him, "Where are the handcuffs?" But first I decided to read the content of the communication. I went over to the kitchen window, which gave out sufficient light, and read the letters in the telegram beneath:

' . . . must leave the borders of the USSR no later than 48 hours . . .'

As if delirious, I staggered back into the party room. All the guests remained in their previous poses, anticipating fateful news. I passed the piece of paper to David.

He read out:

For the attention of the Manager of the Odessa Visa and Registration Office.

Without delay, please draw up the necessary documents for Mr M. S. Berkut's emigration to Israel. He must leave the borders of the USSR no later than 48 hours from receipt of this authorisation.
      Directorate of Ministry of Foreign Affairs.

An excited "Hurrah" echoed through the house. The congratulatory toasts began in earnest, 'in honour of the great man', preparing to set off for the riddles and mania of another world. My mother apologised to the guests for the need to quieten down after midnight, so as not to disturb the neighbours. Everyone went on their way, promising to come to the station at 10 p.m. tomorrow. My mother sat on her sofa and cried bitter tears that God had returned her son to her, only to take him away again a short time later, and for good this time.

On 16th November, Roman took me first to the Visa and Registration Office, where I was issued with permission to leave for Israel, with a special condition: within the next forty-eight hours. They handed me a list: rules, instructions and obligations concerning luggage, documents required, payment, etc. Then we went to the Emigration Office. There, my Visa and Registration Office document had an Israeli visa stamped in it, and I was given 125 dollars for the journey. Next we raced off to the station to buy a ticket, which turned out to have been paid for already, in line with the documents presented by the office. All that remained was for me to punch in my departure date and seat number. We just managed to get everything done by lunchtime. On the way home we bought three strong suitcases and a large leather bag with a shoulder strap. David got permission to leave work early and helped me to pack. While he was packing books into one case, and records and tapes into another, I arranged my things in the third case and food items in the bag, including a 1 kg tin of red caviar from Roman and all my papers.

At 10 p.m. the train at Odessa was heading to Chop Station for the border crossing, and the platform was packed with hundreds of people saying their goodbyes. My brothers and I forced our way through the noisy crowd with our luggage. Roman gave the conductor five roubles, and the latter not only let my capable little brother through with two cases on wheels, but also helped us to get to my seat and stow my baggage in the third berth. I kept my bag on me with all the commotion around me. This picture reminded me of our evacuation during the war. Mum's sisters stood close by her, worrying about how she was bearing up. I didn't leave her side until the guard's last warning, that the 'train will be leaving in five minutes'. The Panther gave me a hug and kissed me.

"Mummy, I'm not saying goodbye to you. We'll all get to meet up again, believe me!"

The train moved. The shouting and crying wafted over the platform and hung in the air for a long time.

Suddenly, everything came to an abrupt halt in a dark, silent tunnel, leaving me in a vacuum, detached.

None of the adult passengers were asleep as we would be nearing the border in a few hours' time. They just chatted about the forthcoming customs check at the border control; and individual emigrants returning to Odessa and even troublemakers being arrested, not wishing to part with their precious jewels from the list of items that we were not allowed to transport. This didn't pose me any problems as my most valuable belongings were my books and recordings. The Emigration Office had given me the range of items allowable by law in as far as exporting the material accessories pertaining to my profession.

We arrived at Chop Station at 3.30 a.m. A dozen men with barrows were loading luggage into four tiers, fastened with cord. They fleeced the last Soviet roubles from the emigrants and took their riches off them in an act of official robbery. In some of the buildings here, they not only inspected all the suitcases and bags simultaneously, but sometimes forced men and women to undress in different cabins and often found the diamonds and gold they were looking for in the innermost reaches of the human body. I was fifth in line in my group. A deep, square-shaped counter fixed to the floor extended into a huge hall, at which three customs officials were working, one in each section. Each individual traveller's luggage had to be placed on the counter in front of an officer. While the contents of the next unpacked item were being inspected, the permitted things moved further along the counter. Those prohibited, i.e. higher-value goods: crystal, porcelain, jewellery and so on, were put carefully into an internal container under the counter. You should have seen the owners losing it while the marauders smiled spiteful smiles. I had never encountered such open vulgarity and cynical theft, even in old films about bandits and pogroms in the time of invasions or revolutions. One old woman, with her head in her hands, cried out at the sight of this vandalism.

"Granny, one more word from you, and you'll be going back where you came from! Ha ha ha!"

People queuing next to her caught the woman as she fainted, and carried her into the centre of the hall.

Eventually it was my turn. I opened my three cases, forgetting about my bag over my shoulder/back. A young soldier, looking through the unusual contents of my luggage, gave me a startled look.

"What on earth is this?"

"Personal effects, books and audio-recordings."

"What?"

"Records, U-matic tapes and cine films."

"They're not allowed!"

I laid my papers out in front of him and pointed to the official permission. The customs officer's eyes darted from one suitcase to another, not knowing what to do.

"Please call your senior officer. He'll confirm that this luggage is authorised."

"Vasya!" he called to his colleague on another counter. "Take a look at this junk. Is that OK?"

"Young man, Tchaikovsky and Shostakovich are not 'junk', but great Russian composers. Don't dishonour Soviet patriots! You should be proud of them!"

The customs official froze at my impudence.

With all the commotion in the hall, the Captain emerged and asked: "What's the problem? Why are you making so much noise? Sidorov, tell me what's going on."

The latter held out his hands in a gesture of helplessness.

"Your officer has rubbished the names of Russia's universally acclaimed writers and composers, branding their works of genius 'junk'."

"I want to know the name of this ignoramus."

The soldier tried to justify himself, but the Captain ordered him to take himself off and send Ivashchenko.

"As a professional musician/choreographer, I have permission to take out these specialist resources for my work. Here is a document confirming this. You can see for yourself."

First the officer scanned through the literary titles on the spines of the books inside the case, then, selected labels on the records and film boxes. He set aside *Lenin's Speech on the Armoured Car* and other dubious titles.

He commanded the soldier: "Ivashchenko, have a look through the case of personal things. I will check the sound recordings." A few minutes later, the Captain reappeared and ordered the customs officer: "Let him through!"

In turn, I carried my cases to the other side of the robbers' den, where the porters were waiting for 'plucked chickens', supplied by the trainload. Suddenly I remembered that in this theatre of acquisition by the customs officials, I had forgotten to show the thieves my bag. In the name of fairness, I was poised to nip straight back with my tin of caviar, but a sobering, inner voice stopped me from acting on my civil impulse for some reason. We waited for a long time still in the carriage, until finally the steam engine sounded its departing whistle and at 10 a.m. on 17th November 1975, the train moved smoothly over the ill-won border between East and West.

I had so many hopes and expectations! But when they came to pass, the flight reflex and thoughts about suffering suddenly disappeared. I was left to grieve for the separation and loss, which eclipsed all the goodness and happiness of the recent past.

What does tomorrow have in store for me?

VOLUME III

WESTERN LIGHTS:

GREATER ORBIT

STAGE I: PURSUING THE DREAM

CHAPTER 1 PRELIMINARY LOTTERY

An hour over the border between East and West, I still could not shake off the feeling of utter exhaustion as we crossed the Siberian tundra. I kept glancing to either side or eavesdropping suspiciously on my fellow travellers' whispered conversations. I felt constantly that someone was following me. Lying on my bunk in the creaking carriage, I started at the slightest sound, and woke up in a cold sweat from a nightmare, in which my old Soviet enemies were chasing me with evil looks on their ugly mugs, and shaming me: "You are a traitor to your homeland, running into bushes full of shit like a downtrodden dog. You've abandoned your nearest and dearest: your children, mother, and friends. You're a base coward! You will never be forgiven for this!"

Panic-stricken, I tried to brush off these gloomy visions. I took a cold shower in the dirty toilet, and breathed in some fresh air on the platform between carriages. Feeling a bit calmer, I resolved to distract myself from unpleasant thoughts about the past.

During our brief time in Prague, we were all transferred to a civilised European train bound for Vienna. The porters 'relieved' every traveller of a quarter of a litre of vodka each in exchange for Czechoslovakian currency. Luckily, Jewish agents in departure points had warned their refugees about this in good time. It was amazing that the Soviet customs officials in Chop had not removed jewellery from the emigrants in similar fashion. As we waited for the Austrian train, a strange individual 'attached' himself to me. Clearly not of European origin, and carrying a large briefcase rather than a suitcase, he instantly began firing a series of questions at me: Where was I from? Where was I going? Why? And so on. It became obvious that this young state security agent was inexperienced in his field. To avoid any trouble, I didn't answer any of his questions, and turned my back on him. But it wasn't that simple. The KGB agent walked around my suitcases and sidled up to me, preparing to say something. This got my 'bull's blood' boiling.

Reminding myself that I was safe among emigrants, I yelled: "Piss off, you piece of shit, before it's too late! You are absolute scum."

Naturally, everyone on the platform looked in our direction, wondering what was going on. My vulgar adversary just disappeared into the crowd of waiting refugees, with a broad grin on his face. It took me ages to relax. But the train's arrival absorbed my attention as I loaded my luggage and settled into a separate compartment with another couple of emigrants. Looking placidly out of the window, I feasted my eyes on the cupolas of passing cathedrals, while the man in the seat next to me asked cautious questions about my religious beliefs. I answered him in the same tranquil tone, that I was not inclined towards any religion, but as someone working in the creative arts, took pleasure in acquainting myself with the portfolio of ancient architecture. I hoped that here, in the free and democratic world, this would not be considered defective.

"Why are you going to Israel if you don't subscribe to Judaism?"

"My dear fellow! You remind me of the KGB guy on the platform in Prague."

"I expect you're thinking of our chaperone from the Czechoslovakian Agency for Jews emigrating to their Promised Land? He's travelling as far as the Austrian border with us, where he will hand our group – more than 100 families – over to his Hungarian emigration counterparts. When we were chatting to him, he warned us that things might get complicated, because of international terrorist acts by Palestinian extremists against Jews throughout the world."

I listened to my elderly travelling companion and felt my ears burning with shame for mistaking the Czech protector for an enemy. The bull had slipped his leash again. Clambering on to the upper bunk, I turned to face the wall.

Vienna greeted us with a triumphant display of gendarmes on the platform, extending down the whole length of the train, with two officers to each carriage. At first the emigrants took fright, expecting everyone to be arrested. But seeing a civilian woman waving folders of papers, they realised that the police had come to protect them from the threat of possible terrorist action by Muslim extremists. The Austrian Jewish Agency for Israel (JAI) staff gave the refugees a warm welcome. After disembarking, we were all divided up into families in one line along the platform, all holding our documents. Out of a hundred and something families, six (including me) were separated out into a special group of renegades. The police accompanied the remaining mass, destined for Israel, to the station exit. There, buses were waiting to take them out of the city into a special zone for Israeli immigrants. As for us, we remained on the platform, and were led into the customs hall, where officials checked our documents and the contents of our luggage, with emphatic – and most unfamiliar – respect from the staff.

We gawped out of the minibus windows as we made our way across the city to the hotel, stunned at the colourful kaleidoscope of changing urban scenery in one of Europe's most beautiful cities. The immigration staff and interpreters quickly and efficiently allocated us to our rooms in the boarding house. They explained the rules of hotel life to the pseudo-Jewish refugees, and instructed them in the standards of behaviour expected in the city's social spots, which were significantly different from those of the Soviet Union. They gave us a modest cash allowance in Austrian currency, and advised us against walking around alone. They informed us that we would be detained in Vienna for two weeks, while our documents were being verified and our transfer to Rome organised. Once in Rome, our eventual immigration destination would be determined.

The next morning, taking my theatre posters and programmes with me just in case, I set off for the famous opera and ballet theatre, which, incidentally, was built by the same architect as the Odessa Opera Theatre, and was essentially a duplicate of the original. Feasting my eyes on this artistic masterpiece, I couldn't help sticking my nose in the air with pride. Five years of scant German lessons in school (1943–48) had left me with a limited vocabulary, just about sufficient for inadequate communication. I found the stage door relatively easily, and showed the doorman my hotel card with my name on and a colourful programme from the Moscow Ballet studio. I asked him to ring the troupe leader. But the latter popped down and took me up to his office. By way of introduction, I told him my tale of woe, and confided that I was looking for work from next season either in one of Europe's Opera houses or a Ballet school. The administrator promised to pass my details on to the Chief ballet master, and suggested that he introduce me to the school's management. I nodded in willing agreement.

The ex-Prima ballerina Terri gave this uninvited guest a cordial welcome. She advised me to have a look at the senior ballet classes – young men and girls were taught separately – to assess their technical level. The Character dance and 'Pas de deux' were the items that interested her out of my teaching experience. We arranged that I would lead these two sample classes during the following week. If the result was positive, we would discuss further opportunities for working in the school, with choreography included. At my request, the Director then arranged a two-week theatre pass for me, so that I could observe shows and stage rehearsals in the current repertoire. I was over the moon at such generosity and kindness. It had been a long time since I'd felt the respect I deserved from theatre management and professional colleagues.

All my time in Vienna was now accounted for; I merely ate breakfast and supper in the guest house. I'd almost forgotten how it felt to experience emotional and creative satisfaction, and was happy to enjoy it again. I spent the mornings observing ballet classes in the school. In the afternoons I visited museums, bookshops or interesting churches. Evenings were for acquainting myself with the repertoire of a leading European theatre, or looking through the ballet literature I had bought, which had cost me the remainder of my Austrian schillings. I had finished my Odessan packet soups. I had nothing left to eat apart from the red caviar which had been Roman's leaving present to me. I put the 2 kg tin of caviar in the middle of the table in an isolated hotel hall where the emigrants were having supper, and announced a swap for packets of soup. My fellow-travellers laughed as they joined in with this unusual sideshow. In total, I acquired twenty-seven packets of soup, more than sufficient for the days we had left.

My taster lessons with Terri in the Ballet school went better than I'd expected. I was terrified because of my poor knowledge of German, especially when I had to give stage explanations or technical comments. But the students were so engrossed in the national forms in Character dance and sets of partnering moves in the 'Pas de deux' that they didn't notice – or at least tolerated – the confused linguistics of my instructions, as I vacillated wildly between German, English and French. Terri smiled understandingly, and had a discussion with the presiding schoolteachers, while the pianist chuckled into her instrument without saying a word. Nevertheless, at the end of the demonstration of both genres, there was tumultuous applause from the students for both teacher and pianist. In her office, the Director confirmed that it would be possible for me to work there during the next academic year, undertaking future productions for school concerts. I would need to let her know regarding my immigration plans no later than May 1975.

I gained a wealth of very valuable information from books purchased on Western choreography in Vienna. Before leaving Austria, I committed a 'moral crime'. I spent half of the emergency US-dollar funds I'd received from the JAI on dance literature. These photographic books went a long way to help fill in the gaps in my knowledge of the repertoire of movements in modern and jazz choreography. At that time, such dance forms were categorically forbidden in the Soviet Union by decrees of the Soviet Union Communist Party, as evil propaganda of Bourgeois ideology against Marxist–Leninist Aesthetics. It's easy to picture me on the way to Italy, drinking my fill from the precious spring of new information, which had been missing from my creative work, and which would feed my fantasy for many years to come. It was offensive to all Soviet ballet proponents and lovers, deprived of such riches in the art of dance. I couldn't help feeling annoyed that members of the Soviet Union Communist Party's Central Committee had spiritually robbed us all.

It's not without reason that they say, 'All roads lead to Rome.' Italy may be Austria's neighbour, but it is so different. At the border, the chaperone accompanying us from Vienna handed over to the JAI officer a folder containing our documents, tickets, and temporary identity papers in place of the usual passports. The elegantly dressed Giovanni gathered the heads of the six families into one carriage and in the time it took to travel from the border to Rome, patiently outlined to us how to conduct ourselves while on the platform at Termini Station, en route in the bus, and in a crowd of passengers. We should not take our eyes off our luggage on the baggage trolleys! It felt like he was talking about Odessa Station and its notorious pickpockets.

"Mikhail, there's no point in smiling. When you get to the hotel with nothing but the clothes on your back, you'll be laughing on the other side of your face. So keep your wits about you! Take your valuables out of your pockets and put your expensive ornaments in well-sealed bags. Don't stop for a moment. Stay close to other people and shout if you have any bother!"

"Forgive me, sir, but you remind me so much of my home town in Ukraine, it's ridiculous!"

The hotel welcomed us very hospitably. Everyone spoke Russian, Giovanni included. He advised that we would be picked up at 9 a.m. to go to the agency. If anyone was late, they would be left behind.

The Rome Emigration Agency was a huge, international organisation involved in resettling Jews in Israel on a global scale. They also provided assistance to persecuted Jews from the USSR and Eastern-bloc countries, helping them to find refuge in the USA, Canada, Australia and New Zealand. Each family or separate individual from our group was attached to a designated leader, who took charge of their safety and security in Rome for the period necessary to complete the emigration process – about three to six months. Our living allowance and rental payments were set out for us. On Monday mornings we were obliged to attend the Emigration Agency to obtain our weekly schedule of meetings with agency staff or embassy consuls on immigration issues relating to this or that country.

The delicate business of deciding people's fate demanded a great deal of patience from both sides. On more than one occasion at the JAI I witnessed tumultuous scenes between family members or serious arguments with their leader regarding problems with their emigration. I, too, did not escape conflict with my guardian, Rita. I had a clear goal: Canada, for various personal reasons. For some reason, the agency decided that, as a single person and an atheist to boot, they would send me to Australia, without first seeking my agreement. When I refused to attend the scheduled meeting with the consul, Rita almost had a heart attack at my impertinence. After this they left me to my own devices for over a month. Making the most of this hiatus, I got on with my personal affairs. Before leaving Moscow, I had found out that my former classmate at MTA from the Teaching Department, Zharko Prebil (a Yugoslav by birth), had been Artistic Director of the Academia Nazionale di Danza in Rome for several years already. I went to visit my old friend, just to see. *Who knows?*

Mussolini's former palace on Aventine Hill was now home to the National Academy of Dance, founded after the war by a Russian prima donna. I waited in the lobby for Prebil to finish his morning professional class for local ballet artistes and teachers. Once they had gone, I popped into the classroom. Zharko was chatting to the pianist Anna-Maria Orlandi, and had his back to me.

Glancing round, he exclaimed: "Misha Berkut? Here, in Rome? I can't believe my eyes. Let me touch my old friend."

We spun around as we hugged, to raucous laughter from the pianist, watching two grown men taking such childish pleasure at seeing each other. Wondering what the noise was, students came into the studio and started to clap. Zharko introduced me to them and led me in to the dressing room. I brought him briefly up to speed on my emigration, and about wanting to make a name for myself in Rome. Taking a united stance, we went up to see the Director. Giuliana Penzi already knew of the Moscow colleagues' reunion and gave a warm welcome to her chance guest. Prebil spoke to his boss in Italian. With my friend's help, I answered a string of questions from the curious director.

Hearing that I would probably have to stay here for six or seven months while waiting for my Canadian visa, Zharko proposed that I took over his morning classes with the professionals at the academy, as in January he would be starting work at the opera theatre. Giuliana gave this idea her full support as none of the Italian masters was interested in temporary work, especially using a Russian classical teaching system. And there was no point in changing the school's methodology for six months. I admitted that due to my immigrant status, I was not permitted to undertake paid work in Italy, as otherwise I would lose my allowance from the JAI and there could be other unpleasant repercussions.

"There's one rule for them, and another for you!" Giuliana Penzi stated. "We are offering you the opportunity to cover for Maestro Prebil on a temporary basis with permission from the Ministry of Culture, and will pay for your work on completion of the agreed period, less tax. Welcome to our academy!"

Zharko proposed that I started lessons in mid-December with the men's classes (a couple of young men), so that I could work my way gently into the Italian rhythm of teaching, given my lack of ability in the language, and could call on him for help in communicating with the pupils if necessary. So that's what we decided. My colleague invited me to his place for lunch, where he was living with his mother in the former mansion of the Academy's founder, Madame Russkaya.

Mussolini's former residence was a private shrine to Italian Ballet. All the walls and shelves in the chambers and corridors of the two-storey detached house were covered with priceless portraits, pictures and other exhibits. Zharko's mother, Signora Maria, a silver-haired beauty, looked every inch the elegant lady from the era of Catherine de' Medici, as if she had just stepped out of the painting in its gilded frame on to our corrupt earth. On making her acquaintance, I kissed her hand, which was a pleasant surprise to the mistress of the house.

She smiled kindly at me and asked Zharko: "My dear son, are all your Moscow classmates as gallant and chivalrous as this?"

"No, Mama. In contrast to the other students, Misha immersed himself in Historical dance at MTA and helped his professor Margarita Rozhdestvenskaya to publish her textbook on this subject. He also assisted her in classes."

"That's extremely commendable for a Soviet student who is not from a noble background."

From that day on, I called in to see Signora Maria once a week, as she reminded me of my own mother. Over tea, I would tell her about the latest happenings at the National Academy of Dance. I asked if she needed anything urgent from the grocer's. During this period, Prebil was establishing a Classical ballet repertoire in Rome's Opera theatre, and was so busy that he didn't have time to come home for lunch, as he went straight from the theatre to teach at the academy. I felt for my friend, and even more so for his mother, who was always on her own.

Not far from Zharko's house was a picturesque public garden adjoining a busy avenue. Half a dozen painted girls were always on duty there, waiting for clients. For a refugee from the Soviet Union, where prostitution carried a prison sentence, this kind of sexual freedom looked criminally depraved. Running past, I often saw drivers negotiating with a girl without getting out of the car, and then driving off with her. On my visits to Signora Maria, I was stopped many a time by one of these streetwalkers, offering her services. I would just smile, spread my hands wide and make my way around the crafty seductress in silence.

"Hey, Mr Cavalier! What's wrong, don't you like my curves?"

"Oh yes! But unfortunately I'm impotent."

She laughed in response, making a vulgar gesticulation relating to my refusal.

After the daily ballet class with the young men in the academy, at the Director's request, I worked with them and one talented girl from the senior *pas de trois* course to put together a concert for New Year. Naturally the first week was swallowed up with learning elementary partnering technique, which was completely new to all three performers. In my free time I studied a lot in the school library. This is where I met the Italian Ballet historian and critic, Albert Testa. I sought his advice regarding music for my trio. He recommended an extract from Vivaldi's symphony for 'solo mandolin and orchestra'. As it happened, this was a fantastic idea for the *pas de trois*: a harmony of rich instrumental sounds and contrasting tempos/rhythms: adagio, andante, allegro with variations and a climactic coda. Success for the performers of the miniature went hand in hand with my choreographic debut in the Academy. Giuliana and Zharko thanked me for my New Year's gift to the school. I signed a contract to lead the professionals' class for four months, starting in January 1976.

With Prebil's permission, I occasionally observed his rehearsals in the theatre with leading soloists Margarita Parilla and Salvatore Pozzo. During these visits I learned Italian turns of phrase from the ballet master's work with his performers. Without this support and help, I couldn't see how I would be able to address the class of professionals in the New Year. For this reason I attended many of Zharko's lessons throughout December. After classes I hammered out this or that expression in Italian. I was constantly astonished by how well he tolerated my curious enquiries. But then he seemed to be impressed with my role as a charitable sponsor. For my part, I was taking advantage of his ambition for my own ends.

One day a friend took me to see Lydia Joffe, a well-known historian and critic of Soviet ballet. Following a heart attack at the beginning of December, she had been confined to bed, frightened by any unnecessary movement. She and I soon discovered a common interest in conversation about different choreographic styles and genres. She enthusiastically leafed through my printed publications from Moscow, with recordings of my own Classical and

Character compositions. I managed to persuade the elderly patient to get out of bed and encouraged her to take a little walk around the house with my help. By the end of the week, Lydia was already trying to move very carefully without my support. We were both pleased with the progress she made in walking unaided and in her increased self-confidence. During one of my visits, Lydia introduced me to her future flatmates; a couple of old-age pensioners from Moscow, who had emigrated for the same reasons as me. Volodya Keen was in fact a reputed conductor and former Artistic Director of the Leningrad Regional Philharmonic Orchestra. His wife Nina was the library manager. They had been waiting for their visas to the USA for about six months. During conversation with them, it became clear that Lydia was moving to take up permanent residence in Paris in three days' time. I was speechless.

"Madam, who is packing up your vast library, not to mention your personal effects?"

"Mishenka, don't worry! I booked a special removal service. Come for a goodbye dinner with Zharko on Saturday. Then we can go off to the station together. I'd like to give you this small statue of Vaslav Nijinsky for taking such good care of me. Be careful with it, it's one of a kind."

Lydia's close friends and admirers gathered to see her off. There I met her daughter Diana, a former soloist with the Riga Ballet, now a teacher of Classical dance at the Mara Fusco Academy in Naples. Most of the guests were Soviet immigrants, but there was one English lady, a beautiful woman called Penelope, from the FAO: the United Nations Food and Agriculture Organisation. It was Christmas Eve, so we drank toasts both to Lydia and Jesus. My 'hungry' eyes came to rest on the British woman, chatting animatedly with the instigator of the celebrations. In a quiet word to the hostess, I asked if Penelope was married. Lydia smiled and passed my question on to the said friend, who raised her eyebrow intriguingly, while looking at me conspiratorially and shaking her head in the negative. I wasted no time in conveying through my intermediary that I wanted to get to know this woman better, seeing as I too was a free agent, and desperate for the heat of love. Everyone laughed as after a dozen or so toasts, we were all feeling much merrier. Penny wrote her telephone number down on a scrap of paper.

"I'm flying to London for Christmas tomorrow, and will be back in Rome on 3rd January. Give me a call at home after work, OK?" the fascinating creature said slowly.

"Thank you very much!" I showed off my English to great applause.

"And thank you for that!"

Hearing that I was doing some temporary teaching in the Rome academy, Diana Joffe asked if I would be interested in giving a sample lesson on Character dance at the Mara Fusco Academy in Naples, which followed Vaganova's Leningrad method and now had its own professional ballet and small dance troupe. Feeling wary, I kept quiet, giving my friend Lydia a meaningful look.

"I too studied under Natalya Dudinskaya in Leningrad, though I was actually born in Riga. Following my retirement, I came here with my family to be with my mother. This is my telephone number in Naples. Mara will be interested in getting to know your method of Character dance."

I asked Zharko what he thought about this, and whether it was worth my while following up this opportunity.

"Mara is certainly a professional teacher with a huge portfolio. But there are lots of schools like this in Italy. You'd be better not to spread yourself too thin, but to concentrate on us in the academy, developing your skills in the culture and relations employed by Western ballet staff and students."

My supervisor at the immigration agency was interested to know whether I had any relatives in the USA. I said that I wasn't aware of any, but was ignorant about my father's side of the family. Rita reported that two of my cousins and their families lived in Los Angeles and that logically it made sense for me to emigrate there, where my family would probably be very attentive and support me initially, if I needed them to.

"Here is their telephone number for you to contact them. After Christmas you will have to start preparing your documents to obtain your visa to the USA."

"I'll have a think about it and let you know next time we meet. Happy New Year!"

"Mikhail, you are not permitted to decline an opportunity offered to you for a second time!"

"Rita, you don't have the right to force a free man to go there, where there are no job opportunities that correspond with his vocation or education."

I went to seek Prebil's advice. The theatre did not open on Mondays. I found my friend in the Academy and told him about my emigration problem.

"Misha, over the last twenty years in the USA, traditional, Classical ballet in the Opera-theatre repertoires has been superseded by Modern shows. Only *Coppélia* and *The Nutcracker* have retained their place in the children's Christmas holidays. In Canada it's the other way round: it's classical ballet that's gathering momentum. So naturally, specialists like us are worth their weight in gold there at the moment. Moreover, you are not just a teacher and répétiteur but a qualified choreographer and producer as well. In order for you to bring your artistic plans to fruition, you need room to move creatively speaking, and for local authorities to be enthusiastic. If you get any choice at all, take Canada by storm. It's still a relatively young culture there, and they are looking for their own theatrical arts specialists in all the pertinent genres. If I were you, I would rather go for virgin territory. But let's get off home now. Mum is expecting us for Christmas lunch and will be pleased to see you."

I felt much more relaxed after speaking to my friend. At the very least, I became more certain of my choice. Now everything depended on the Canadian Consul.

On 8th January I telephoned Penelope. She invited me round the following day. I couldn't believe that Fortune was smiling on me yet again after my failures in the Soviet Union. I feared that I would frighten her off with my impetuous nature. So quietly and carefully, I got myself together. With my last 10,000 lira, I bought a bouquet of red roses near her home and with great ceremony, rang the doorbell of the old six-storey building. I repeated over and over in my head some of the English greetings I had learned. My heart was in my mouth. The lift door opened with a bang on the sixth floor. The graceful figure of Penelope appeared on the landing, the door to her home wide open in welcome. This woman whom I found so intriguing, wore a fulsome smile on her beautiful face. The pitiful Odysseus (or rather Odessan) knelt before the goddess and presented her with a symbolic bouquet of love. Struggling to get up off his knees, the Greek wanderer kept kissing her fingertips, to which the mythological spouse of popular wanderings – Penelope – responded in twentieth-century style.

What happened next complied with the international norms of lovers' encounters. I got to see the layout of her well-presented, earthly abode, which, by the way, was finished in immaculate taste. We ate a magnificent supper, with Italian delicacies and wine, which the hostess drank in preference to water. The conversation at the table was one of few words, using a pocket dictionary. A magical tango made our interaction easier and more enjoyable. The tipsy Penelope pressed against her Odysseus so passionately with her legs entwined in mine, that the latter lost his cool and kissed her hand. Not encountering any desperate resistance from the lady, the cavalier continued his seducer's kisses at reducing intervals on her shoulders, neck, breast . . . At first his partner smiled knowingly, maintaining her Argentinian tango. Then she giggled, revelling in the passion of close contact with a real-life lover. Eventually, after an extended kiss on the lips, the victim of temptation dragged her mate into the bedroom. He resisted, sang out, but quickly moved in on his seductress.

Instead of flinging off our clothes with wild abandon, we curiously and slowly undressed each other to the music, continuing to kiss, until we were groaning with laughter on the bed of love. Penny lay trembling on top of me in the driving seat, but I was holding back. I wanted so badly to feel pleasure once more in the half-forgotten scent and closeness of a woman's body. It was agony, the way she was kissing my chest, rubbing her body against mine, stirring our fiery lust for intimate union. Carefully but confidently, I entered the 'inner sanctum'. She cried out, then held her breath. Every mature man has his own methods for achieving mutual sexual orgasm. If the anatomical morphology of the couple's organs is compatible, then both partners should easily attain mutual satisfaction in the act. When you add more spiritual and lyrical strings to this duet, the physical orgasm turns into a moral, carnal triumph of existence. I didn't view Penny as a receptacle in which to release my sperm. She touched in me some long-forgotten chords, which I had always treasured. That is why I hadn't wanted to rush into my first intimate contact with her. What I wanted was to receive something from her that would endure forever in my memory.

We repeated our lovers' sessions many times that evening. Every time she was about to have another orgasm, she would shout, "Fuck me! Fuck me!"

Unfortunately, I didn't know what that meant in English. Nevertheless, I sustained my sexual marathon until we both collapsed exhausted. In the gaps between love-making we would return naked to the table. She drank some wine, while I drank juice. Then we would dance our impassioned tango again. We had already lost any inhibitions about pressing our naked bodies against each other. And we returned again and again to the bed of carnal desire. It was morning before we fell asleep in each other's embrace. Luckily it was a Sunday, and we came to at midday. Penny reminded me that Maurice Béjart's Paris-based company was beginning their tour with *Notre Faust* at the opera theatre that evening. All of Italy's ballet élite were certain to be there. I was happy to hear this, though my legs were giving way. I felt better after a hot bath.

During the interval at the theatre, Prebil introduced me to Béjart, giving him a brief summary of my specialist profile as a Choreographer of miniatures and Teacher of Character dance. Maurice invited me to visit his Modern Ballet studio in Paris, and teach a sample class. With Zharko's help, I replied that unfortunately, not having a passport, I was unable to travel. At this point,

Béjart told his assistant to make a note of my personal details. He promised to send me an official invitation care of the National Academy of Dance, via the French Consul in Rome, to come for a week to discuss terms of work. I would have to give two demonstrations: Character and 'Pas de deux'. I merely nodded my agreement, not having much faith in this proposal. Again, Prebil whispered something to Maurice, but all I could decipher was 'Bolshoi School'. Apparently he was telling him about my productions with Sofia Golovkina at the Bolshoi Theatre School and the displays at MTA.

In the early days of my emigration, Zharko was not only a true friend and sponsor to his colleague in a strange land, but also an exemplary model of a universal institute colleague, who had adapted professionally to Italian Ballet's Cecchetti method, without losing our common grounding in Vaganova and Tarasov in the process. This was a successful merging of the ballet techniques and styles of three great masters of Classical dance in Europe. That is how Prebil won over the local fickle and stubborn ballet artistes in their class and rehearsal in the opera theatre and academy. He was not a choreographer, nor did he create new works, but he had in-depth knowledge of the traditional ballet repertoire, which elevated him to a high professional level. Zharko undoubtedly possessed talent as a leading soloist with the Belgrade Ballet. This specialist was the best man for the job of Artistic Director in the Rome Ballet troupe. During that period, and in my frequent visits to Italy thereafter, I learned a great deal from him in relation to dancers, colleagues and the management of theatres in the West.

Béjart's *Notre Faust* was the first modern ballet I had seen live. Over the course of the week when I was visiting the Theatre, I learned principles of style and particular technique of what was, for me, a new form of choreography in the way it was transferred to the stage. This is not so much about the choreographer's specific language, as his individual take and transformation of the environment through the contemporary prism of the audience's emotions – into a spectacle expressing movement through Artistic, theatrical art – in all aspects, including costumes, make-up, props, staging, scenery and lighting. In this regard, *Notre Faust* struck me as revolutionary and progressive in Ballet. I have to admit that after the aesthetic vacuum of the Soviet Union, it was a hopeless dream of mine to think that I could use the opportunity of a week's trip to France to broaden my contemporary and historical outlook in modern ballet, assisted by Lydia Joffe. She agreed to take her lost friend from Italy under her wing in Paris while he was visiting Béjart's studio.

At my next meeting with the emigration agency supervisor in Rome, I declined a visa for the USA. In a letter, I set out my professional reasons and personal convictions supporting my preference for emigrating to Canada rather than the United States, where there were already plenty of people with the same skills as me.

"Mikhail, visas to this country are drawn up for emigrants exclusively through invitation from direct relatives, marriage to a Canadian woman or through workplace agreement."

"Nevertheless, I insist on meeting the Canadian Consul and am certain that he will listen to my arguments as a theatre arts specialist, which may be just what they need in that particular country."

"Your naïve stubbornness won't do you any favours. It's a complete waste of time."

"But all the same, Rita, please leave the Consul to decide my fate."

With a heavy sigh, the manager got me to fill in a form, in which I answered in the negative to all the essential questions about relatives, assets or sponsors. Sadly, it did in fact look fairly grim.

"You'll receive a response to your futile request in a week or two's time."

My romance with Penelope was gathering pace. On her insistence, I moved in with her lock, stock and barrel. We split the costs of the household and food. On almost all of her free days, my girlfriend organised trips to Assisi, Capri, Sardinia and other fabulous parts of Italy. This heavenly life lasted four months. After classes at the academy I often went to see her at work in the FAO. Penny introduced me to her boss, Arthur Sager, and two close friends: Valerie and Helen. Both were beautiful single women in their thirties. Now, Apollo Berkut had Three Graces to dance with and kiss in turn during the constant stream of conversations and parties.

Sometimes I even went to watch my girlfriend's stage rehearsals at her drama club, and shows in the local theatre of the huge United Nations complex. I have to say, my beloved was by nature a beautiful and talented individual. She had been dancing and singing from a young age, done modelling and painting, and acted in amateur productions. But unfortunately, because of her innate idleness, she didn't know how to bring her God-given gift to life in artistic creativity. We were frequent visitors to Rome's opera and ballet productions, orchestral concerts, museum exhibitions and other cultural offerings. Thanks to her, I acquired a wealth of new information about Western art over a relatively short period of time, which was essential to me in forging a career for the future. My girlfriend didn't realise how much I was obliged to her for my increasing fluency in Italian and English – both at the same time. The language barrier was actually coming down. I started to chat with friends at the FAO, making them laugh with my ridiculous combinations of words from different languages in unique sentences of my particular brand of Esperanto. But this didn't stop me.

During my fourth month of waiting around in Rome I received an invitation to the French Embassy, where I was given a short-term visa for a trip to Paris to discuss working in the Maurice Béjart Theatre and Ballet Studio. I was met at the station by the Director's assistant, whom I'd already got to know from their Roman tours. He led the dumbstruck visitor through the capital's sights to the well-known twentieth-century avant-garde ballet factory of Western Europe. The manager of the school section, Misha Van-Horn, gave me a friendly welcome in broken Russian. The school made a huge impact on me. Classes of young men and women (sixteen to eighteen) were taking place simultaneously in several studios. Through the glass doors I observed at my leisure over several hours the dance-and-movement curriculum of the school syllabus: Classical, Modern, Jazz, Pantomime, Acrobatics, everything except technique for Character and Duet dances, so essential to future artistes on the professional stage. I realised then why they had been so keen for me to apply as a specialist of both creative disciplines that were lacking in their curriculum, which could only enhance my chances.

Following my taster training session on Folk Stage dance and demonstration of the syllabus for Partnering technique, I received enthusiastic compliments from the students and teachers. Unarguably, this was a tempting opportunity for an emigrant to get a foothold in Europe. But the management only offered me the opportunity to run two of the presented Dance programmes. My fundamental profession as choreographer was understandably of no interest to them. I had come to a crossroads. Back home with the generous hostess, Lydia Joffe insisted that I should accept the Béjart studio proposal. Nevertheless, I decided to hold back. Lydia was astonished. In fact I was quite terrified, because of my past experience of jumping at the first opportunity in the USSR.

Intuitively, I believed that in Canada I would find more creative satisfaction in terms of establishing and developing the Art of professional ballet. It was not without reason that sages prophesied that it made much more sense to move new equipment into an empty space than renovate an old building. Still, I was far from confident that I was doing the right thing. My French colleagues were already very warm towards me. Once I was back in Rome, it made me sad to hear Penny call Paris and tell Misha Van-Horn that I had decided not to accept. For all that, dipping my toe in the Parisian waters had given me much food for thought. First and foremost, moving away from my fundamental vocation as a choreographer to take up a teaching career was not what I wanted to do. I preferred to chance my luck in unfamiliar avenues in Canada. There were only four professional state companies there: the National Ballet in Toronto; Les Grands Ballets Canadiens in Montreal; the Royal Winnipeg Ballet in Manitoba and the Alberta Ballet in Edmonton. All of them were based on Classical dance.

At one of the concerts in Rome, Penelope introduced me to her friend Anna Davidovna, a Russian singer working for Radio Vatican. She and I got on straight away when it came to music. I really needed an accordion for my work. Anna recommended the best shop and offered her services as an interpreter, so that I wouldn't get fleeced by those canny Italians. Naturally I tried out a few instruments and settled for one made by Soprano. Fortunately, this turned out to be a lucky choice.

I didn't know how to thank my new acquaintance, and she said: "Misha, I have close connections with the Russian church near Termini Station and in my role as treasurer, take an active role in organising and running Orthodox celebrations. Next week, as you probably know, we are celebrating our Easter. You are welcome at our holy festivities! Once we're finished at the church, I'm doing supper for friends at my place. You can have the chance to try out your accordion in a joint performance of the Russian repertoire with me. How would you feel about this?"

"That's more than a yes! But you and I will need at least one rehearsal to check our tuning, tempos and dynamics for the singer."

"You're right. Can you make tomorrow at 6 p.m.?"

Anna and I soon established the musical parameters for our performance together at the Easter soirée. Then over tea and cake, we swapped life stories and I got on my way before anything developed. On principle, we didn't want to spoil our purely platonic friendship by getting intimate, although we both felt the tug of attraction. It was more important for me to keep this woman as my spiritual friend and creative partner. It's not always that easy. As a rule, ladies in such situations don't forgive cavaliers who remain indifferent to their sexual potential. But in this exceptional case we both preferred to preserve our friendship for each other. The Easter Mass inside the church was fascinating and I took part in the Orthodox procession around it. It made a huge impression on me and was totally inspiring. During the service, Davidovna conducted the church choir and sang the lead soprano. She had earned the respect and recognition of the local congregation. After supper at her house, she and I put on a concert of Russian folk songs, old-fashioned romances and dances too.

Back home, Penny reported that the Emigration Agency had telephoned. I had to present myself with my documents without delay, in smart attire, to the Canadian Consul.

In the morning Rita spent ages boring me with instructions on how to behave with a man of such high office, as if I had emerged only yesterday from the jungle. She instructed me as to what answers to give to his formal questions, what I should keep quiet about, etc. I just nodded in agreement, impatiently squeezing my underwear through my trouser pocket.

"Mikhail, you don't seem to be listening to my advice, which is based on my long experience here!"

"I'm sorry, madam. I studied basic etiquette a quarter of a century ago at ballet school. I'm more worried about which language I'll use to address the Consul. How much time are we given for our conversation and what additional documents are required?"

"For being such a snob you will get an important official to deal with you."

I greeted the Consul with a bow of the head. My form was in front of him.

"Mr Berkut, why are you so keen to come to Canada in particular?" he asked in English.

"Because I can find work more quickly there in my unusual specialist field and be of use to your country by using my skills as a teacher/ballet master."

I found it difficult to answer in English, even though I had learned some sentences beforehand with Penny with which to answer standard questions. Rita informed the Consul that I had declined her offer to interpret.

He raised an eyebrow, and kept quiet, flicking through my Soviet choreographic/producer's materials, and summed up with interest: "We only have a few opera/ballet companies in the whole country. If there isn't any work for you in any of those in your professional area, what will you do then?"

"Play the accordion for a while wherever I have to and carry on looking for work in my field."

At that moment, Rita gave me a warning kick under the table. I ignored her, continuing my main topic of conversation.

"What if you can't make a living through your music, what will you do then?"

"I'll go and do the washing-up in a restaurant until I find what I'm looking for."

"According to your form, you don't have any relatives or particular friends in Canada. You don't have any cash savings either. Of course, what you have in abundance is professional ambition. This is not sufficient to start a career in a foreign country, although there are exceptions. Which ballet companies do you know, and where would you choose to try your creative hand in line with your choreographic abilities?"

I listed all the possibilities in Canada and added that I would be happy to work with any of these companies.

"I'm certain that none of them would be disappointed with my track record."

"OK, I'm clear on your general stance as an immigrant. The Emigration Agency will get back to you in a couple of months. I can't promise you anything else."

As we came out of the embassy, Rita laughed wickedly, saying: "Well, are you pleased with yourself? You won't set eyes on a Canadian visa. You're too self-opinionated."

After the Easter holidays, the Director of the National Academy of Dance asked me to choreograph several miniatures with the youngest students for a concert to mark the end of the academic year. I realised that Zharko had set me up, after telling Giuliana about my productions in the Bolshoi School. Giuliana Penzi promised to rehearse my choreographic compositions with the course teachers in their own time. I didn't hassle her for payment as I was sure that she would add something to my allowance. I chose the most upbeat dances from my repertoire to music by Shostakovich and Khachaturian. The participants worked with customary Italian enthusiasm and often made fun of each other during rehearsals. I gave this programme to the class teachers before 1st May so that they could refine it at rehearsals and get the individual costumes prepared.

Immediately after the May Day celebrations I was summoned to the agency. I wasn't expecting any good news from the Canadian Embassy. Nevertheless, somewhere deep down I had a sense of foreboding. Recalling our conversation, I was keenly aware of the positive, intriguing expression on the Consul's face, but for now any reassuring chinks of hope were tossed aside. Repeated, critical self-analysis confirmed my supervisor's opinion about the pitiful immigrant's surfeit of ambition. I met Rita for a dry, official meeting, anticipating her next body blow.

"Mikhail, you must have been born with a silver spoon in your mouth. The Canadian Consul has sent us a visa for Canada in your name, with a direct appointment for an interview regarding work at the Royal Winnipeg Ballet, with their director, Arnold Spohr. I just can't understand how you managed to charm the Consul. Here is your flight ticket to Winnipeg for 20th May, your visa, and the other documents you need. I wish you well and safe journey!"

Penelope was happy about my conquest in the consulate, but at the same time, sorry that we would be parting soon. She suggested celebrating my birthday on 7th May, the coming Saturday, with a farewell lunch with close friends. I spent all of the day before hosing down the vast terrace on the roof of our house. I hired enough folding tables and chairs, umbrellas and crockery from the nearest restaurant for thirty people. Penny ordered appetisers from there too. In short, there was enough to feed an army.

I showed off my English as I greeted our guests in the doorway. Collecting their coats, I insisted, with the refined manners of a true aristocrat: "Please take off your dress! Don't be shy!" by which I meant "Let me take your coat! Make yourself at home!"

The men smiled ironically at this, while the ladies flirted: "Oh, right now? Isn't it a bit early for that?"

"What, already? Isn't it a bit soon?"

Everyone fell about. I continued with sincere hospitality, thinking, *What are these Westerners going so wild about? Perhaps they'd prefer to keep their dirty, outdoor clothes on at the table?*

After several toasts and nibbles, we moved the tables aside and started the dancing. Anna Davidovna led the group singing as I accompanied them on the accordion. Then I taught the guests 'Korobushka', a Russian round dance. We concluded the festivities with a chorus of 'Kalinka'.

The next day, Penny and I went to Sicily for a week. This was the finale of our life together in Italy. Neither of us knew when we would see each other again. So once again, we enjoyed our fill of intimacy and the surrounding delights of the beautiful countryside. I invited my girlfriend to come and spend her annual leave in Canada. She was no doubt hoping for a more serious proposal from me. But in my heart of hearts, I couldn't take on any burdensome obligations while I was an immigrant.

During my goodbye visit to the academy, the Director gave me a substantial allowance and changed some currency with me in the bank herself as I didn't have my passport. She thanked me for my excellent work in the school, and was sorry that it was not possible for us to continue working together.

"Misha, our door is always open to you. Here is our testimonial regarding your productive activity and a recommendation as a teacher/ballet master. Good luck and thank you!"

I acknowledged sadly that I was leaving a little piece of my heart in Rome.

The airport was chaotic. I wasn't allowed to take my accordion on board as hand luggage. Even Penelope, who had come to see me off, with the authority she had as someone working at the United Nations, was unable to convince the bureaucrats at the check-in desk. I had to check the huge instrument into the hold, knowing in advance that they only took small items for Canada.

My girlfriend comforted me with her kisses: "Dear Mishutka! I will give you a new instrument for your birthday next year. Don't forget me over there, when you're with all those beautiful ballerinas!"

I couldn't speak.

I repeated a kind of prayer: "Come over in the summer!"

She cried on my shoulder, promising to fly over for a month in July.

Going up the gangway to the plane, I was happy to be fulfilling my dream of Canada, and yet, upset to be losing my beloved girlfriend. I felt a strange, churned, bittersweet sensation inside. I settled in my seat in a trance, and dreamed of the past and future. Again I wondered what fate had in store for me next.

CHAPTER 2 IF AT FIRST YOU DON'T SUCCEED . . .

I spent the seven-hour flight contemplating my new life, and made the following resolutions:

a) to throw myself into everyday life and the customs of the local diverse national and social culture;

b) not to try to revolutionise the Canadian system of theatrical education or practice;

c) to be prepared to adapt my Artistic principles to fit in.

I undertook to abide by this oath for my time as an immigrant in Canada, knowing full well how many undercurrents and thresholds I would have to overcome on my path to self-improvement at the ripe old age of forty-four. But I had no choice after what I'd been through in the Soviet Union, thanks to the impatient 'bull' in me. Most likely, all immigrants go through similar problems of integration. The only difference is that most of them do not go on to work as public servants, which requires them to speak the language to avoid dependency on others. You have to get used to this kind of compromise. Alas, it all requires a lot of time and patience in particular, neither of which I possessed.

I was so engrossed in my musings on life that I barely noticed the plane landing in Montreal, where I had to change planes for Winnipeg. It was hard to believe that spread out before me was that same magical Canada which I had dreamed about from the other side of the earth. With a courteous smile, I asked the airline attendant confidently in English where I needed to go next. She muttered something in French without smiling and took herself off. I would have given chase to rebuke her for her rudeness, but remembered my oath just in time, and smiled serenely at everyone as I went in search of the information desk. Kindly folks helped me – in English – to find my gate in time and complete my transfer. At Manitoba's provincial airport, Linda Isit, a representative of the Immigration Department from Manpower, drew up the documents I needed and helped me to retrieve my luggage. There was no sign of my accordion on the carousel. Linda put everyone on full alert until it was reported that the instrument had been sent to Ottawa by mistake. But keeping to my signed oath, I just kept on smiling, grimacing from the pain in my trouser pocket, where I was squeezing my attributes tightly so that Taurus didn't break free of his chains. For some reason, Canada's pink glow turned to brown before my very eyes. Apparently the Canadians had decided to check whether any prohibited musical enclosures were concealed in the accordion.

I was put up in the same hotel where Misha Baryshnikov had once stayed in hiding, after his escape from his Soviet benefactors on his return journey via Montreal Airport. Thank the Lord! I had no need to hide myself away. Nevertheless, journalists pounced on me in the lobby with questions: why had I left the USSR? And why had I emigrated to Canada? Again, with a dutiful smile, I explained that I had left my children behind in Moscow, and was not in a position to reveal the truth, and didn't want to lie about anything. Apologising, I promised to be more compliant once I was reunited with my family in Canada.

After unpacking in my hotel room, I headed straight off to the Royal Winnipeg Ballet. And here I encountered another fiasco! The whole troupe with their director in tow, were on tour in Europe. They would be back at the end of June. For all that, the school director, David Moroni, greeted me respectfully like an old friend, as he had heard about my arrival from Manpower. At the time the school was hosting an international course on Classical, Modern and Jazz dance, with students from Western and South America. The Director was very interested in my duet and Character dance. He offered me the opportunity to deliver two trial classes in both subjects. As for Classical, it would be better for me to show the Director, Arnold Spohr, and his ballet artistes once they were back from their tour. I agreed to this.

The Director's large office contained a wide one-way window overlooking the ballet studio and dancers. While I was observing a modern dance class, David allocated me two days the following week to present Character dance with students and 'Pas de deux' with professionals. I arranged a meeting with the pianist to agree the musical accompaniment. The administrator José Carmen showed me the workspace and additional premises in the new building, specially equipped for the school and troupe, which was extremely impressive. He boasted about having received a special grant from the British Queen no less, in addition to the usual federal and provincial funding. The number of staff there exceeded the size of the ballet troupe. I just spread my hands and shrugged my shoulders, my smile growing wider all the time. José couldn't help smiling either, taking my mimicking as a compliment.

I prepared for my imminent showcase classes more scrupulously than usual, factoring in the physical, morphological specifics of the students from Mexico, Argentina and Brazil, and their naturally superior emotional awareness. I was less worried about the language in my dealings with them, given the similarity of Spanish to Italian. I didn't show off unnecessarily in these trials. I simply made sure to follow professional methodology in both demonstrations, in line with the students' technical capabilities on the one hand, and their competitive fervour on the other. In the Character class everything went really smoothly. In the duet dance the attendees' excessive temperament hindered rather than helped the artistes' attention and concentration in the finer points of their pairings in upper lifts. This can lead to accidents, so now and again I had to put the brakes on the men's ambition and demonstrate the correct application of the technique myself for the move in question, rather than forcing and straining. This helped them with the lifts and avoided causing their partners any trauma.

With my permission, David invited some retired company members to both demonstrations, while Linda brought along silver-haired representatives of the Ministry of Culture and Sport (no doubt in the interests of my future career). Naturally this diminished the students' confidence, but conversely, heightened their sense of discipline and responsibility. In spite of the language barrier, both displays produced a rapturous response from the guests observing for the first time. I realised that for a provincial backwater this opened the door to the secret, mysterious world of choreography and the mystique of 'moulding' the dancers. I responded to compliments with a modest smile and bow, trying to give the audience a good impression of myself. Linda said that the official for local native peoples pronounced me a shaman. That was the only explanation for the fact that I had pulled off such a wonderful show in two hours.

"You've obviously impressed your students and guests alike. The sports officer has invited us to his board meeting tomorrow at 10 a.m. for discussions."

"Mikhail, it says in your CV that in Moscow you trained young gymnasts and figure skaters for national competitions, where they won top prizes. Our ice-skating champions urgently need your professional help as we approach the next Olympic Games. We'll sign a contract with you for the month of June, prior to the ballet troupe's return from their tour, so as not to disturb your plans with Linda. This idea came to me during your display. What are your thoughts?"

"Thank you for your confidence in me. As a rule, I'd rather be occupied than sit and watch paint dry. But who would I actually be working with, and how often?"

"I expect you've heard of the Canadian figure-skating champion Toller Cranston, and the famous Winnipeg hockey team? You'd have to work with them for an hour each per day, fitting in with their training schedule. Would you be interested in this kind of work?"

"I'm willing, as long as there are wooden handrails in the studio, like the ones you saw yesterday in the ballet school, and lino flooring rather than ice."

"OK, we accept your terms. Your fee will be 250 dollars per week for five days a week."

Linda drew up a new working agreement for me. I just signed at the bottom. What used to take a week in the Soviet Union was wrapped up in half an hour here, with no delays whatsoever.

As always in such situations where I'd had a taste of success, I had an uneasy premonition that I was heading for a fall. The only question was when and where.

I asked Linda Isit to move me from the hotel into private rented accommodation. From her list, I chose the one nearest the city centre, and moved in right away. The ground floor had a spacious veranda overlooking a garden, where I had room to do my exercises in comfort. The downside was that I would have to try and manage on my own now, which made my daily routine extremely complicated. However, I had underestimated my good fairy from Manpower.

After moving in the next day, there was a knock at the door. A beautiful young woman was poised on the step, wearing a figure-hugging knitted suit, carrying bags full of various food items.

I drew near her and sighed deeply: "Excuse me, Mademoiselle, unfortunately I think you've got the wrong address."

"I don't think so. Luckily there is no mistaking the well-known Mikhail Berkut! Isn't that right?"

"Looks like God himself sent you to his hungry servant."

"No, your goddess Linda actually."

We both laughed as we unpacked the bags in the kitchen.

"Are you my guardian angel now?"

"On a temporary basis, just for three months until September. Then I'm going back to Toronto University. My name is Aida Volsh. I help immigrants to get settled in their first few weeks in Winnipeg. Linda Isit included you on my list of deserving subjects. That's if you don't have any objection."

"Aida, forgive my professional curiosity. How did you get such a charming figure like Aphrodite? You must be a ballerina or gymnast."

"You've got it wrong, maestro. I just ride horses. I do equestrian sports."

"My dear girl, it's one and the same: galloping horses or dancing ballerinas, don't you think?"

Aida's laugh was so shrill that even the windowpanes shook. And so did I.

I only had three days available to prepare a programme for practical consultations with the sports champions. First of all I met with Toller Cranston at his training session for the new figure-skating programme that he had devised himself. Without a doubt, the performer's advanced technique and rich range of movements was really impressive to the spectator, but the poor-quality choreography didn't always match the figure skater's capabilities and his expressive abilities in the chosen genre. There were also many compositional errors in the stage presentation as a whole. Becoming a distinguished figure skater doesn't mean that you are an eminent choreographer as well.

I was lucky enough to come across the team coach on the stadium's hockey pitch, who was only too willing to introduce his charges to me. I observed their routine exercises and pair work for about an hour. When the training finished, the boss invited me to the cafeteria and highlighted all the team's weak points in their day-to-day practice. The balance and coordination during an acute change of body position, reaction to being tackled, fall technique and other physical problems led to trauma, which, as well as putting an individual player out of action, can have a negative impact on the whole team's success in this game.

"If you can suggest any specific exercises and give valuable advice to reduce the impact of these problems, the guys will have more chance of winning the hockey at the Olympics."

I needed to recall my old working method from my ten years' experience in the Moscow sports school to provide the players with the appropriate technical skills in body action. To this end, I needed to determine the best exercises and routines to support their training:

a) to strengthen their balance with a hockey stick while turning sharply on one leg;

b) to change coordination of body parts suddenly, when in conflict with another player;

c) to transfer weight as a reflex from one group of muscles to another when falling, doing a head over heels forwards/backwards, high leaps or jumping over opponents, etc.

Toller had his own programme of instruction. What he needed most from me was the methodology I used in choreographic compositions, bearing in mind the audience's perception of them not just from one vantage point (as in a theatre), but from each part of the semicircular stadium. In these conditions 'the foreshortening' of the performer (positioning his body relative to the spectator's eyes) is accounted for by the choreographer in deciding the Artistic form using completely different parameters of stage interpretation. I taught Cranston the basics of Dance composition to music:

a) visual artistic definition of the completed form or subject of the picture;

b) relevant choice and detailed analysis of musical accompaniment;

c) designation of genre characteristics (tragedy, lyricism, comedy, drama, grotesque, etc.);

d) use of sporting elements, manoeuvres, moves in their logical sequence of development through the audience's emotional response to the impact of figure skating;

e) refining the performers' facial expression and artistic body motion.

As a result of our efforts, Toller and I were duly praised by the leadership team.

On Sundays, Winnipeg was deserted. I usually went for a walk for a couple of hours after lunch, getting to know the picturesque suburban surroundings. There were no passers-by, nor any public transport – just dogs and squirrels. I would go as far as the river and walk along the bank, enjoying the abundance of nature. The same elderly Native American man was almost always sitting on the cliff edge, lost in thought and watching the river. When he learned that I was from the USSR, he was only too willing to satisfy my curiosity, and told me local stories about the river, wild animals and popular heroes, who had fought to protect the Native Americans' independence. He sometimes sang local romantic songs, slapping his thighs, trying to impress me with his knowledge of native folklore. He clearly missed his old life on the prairies. I asked Linda to put me in touch with the representative of the indigenous population at Manpower.

As it happened, this was the same civil servant who, with a number of other officials, had come to watch my sample class in the Ballet school, and had referred to me as a Shaman. I asked him if he could take me to the nearest native reservation so that I could familiarise myself with their traditional dances for my own interest and education. In return, I would show them some East European examples of Slav and Caucasian ethnography, and more. If a piano or accordion were available, I would even accompany those wishing to dance myself. The officer was thrilled at this idea. He obtained an instrument for me from somewhere, along with various rattles, pipes, tambourines, etc. I was nervous about meeting real shamans, known to me hitherto only from pictures in books. On the way to the reservation, the boss told me about his authority at Manpower, and the nature of native reservations in Canada and the USA.

As Manpower's elected delegate, the Native Americans welcomed the civil servant with great ceremony. For the Manitoba natives he was part of the highest authority and jurisdiction in the province. I was introduced to the elders' council as a Russian Shaman from Siberia. I found it hard to keep a straight face at this point and keep my eyes focused on my accordion playing. Teaching the young enthusiasts the distinct movements of folk dances from Russia, Ukraine, Moldova and Georgia made me look like a natural Shaman: with long hair, lively eyes and a loud voice, I ran backwards and forwards between the accordion and the wooden dance floor. Instead of applauding, the audience members simply watched me weave my magic in an atmosphere of goodwill. They just accompanied the dancing members of their clan to my music on tambourines. Then the host invited me to join in a ceremonial song and dance with them. To the audience's surprise, I naturally grasped the primitive movements of the arms and legs on the hoof. I even tried to sing in unison with them. This cemented our creative exchange of spiritual riches between two great peoples. The meeting concluded with a celebratory supper around the campfires, with the exchanging of symbolic gifts between the civil servant and overseas visitor, to the backdrop of cries of praise from the sworn brothers. From that day on, my nickname of 'Russian Shaman' became embedded in the province. When Linda and I next met, she asked if it were true that I had brought about a cultural revolution on the reservation.

On one of my visits to Manpower, I met the Riga artist Semyon Shegelman. He too had emigrated here on his own via Rome, a few months before me. He had managed to put on two exhibitions of his work in Italy, while awaiting his visa for Canada. Now he was exhibiting in Winnipeg, where I was lucky enough to see his exhibition of avant-garde drawings and watercolours. We hit it off straight away on the topics of theatre and decorative art. The drama and dynamism of the precise silhouettes in his miniature drawings evoked conflicting emotions in the viewer. The angular contours of his compositions, and contrasting light and shade, the varied range of colours – all this was a lush reflection of the artist's mood in the fettered Soviet censorship of that era. Judging by photos of his previous work, the hand of an exceptional master was evident from his repertoire of paintings.

He had received harsh treatment at home in Riga for deviating from Marxist–Leninist Aesthetic principles. At his last exhibitions in city galleries local police tore his pictures off the walls and stamped on them in a frenzy. Naturally, despite his love for his homeland, the genuine Artist was not in a position to continue to work productively in ideological decay and physical oppression. Semyon and I were closely aligned in the reasons for our creative dissatisfaction in the Soviet Union, although we came from different sectors of the arts world. I was convinced that our paths would definitely cross again in future, either in Toronto or Montreal. So as we said goodbye at his home, I pronounced a toast: "See you soon"! From an aesthetic perspective, getting to know Shegelman turned out to be the only chink of light in my six-week stay in Manitoba. I really wanted this artist and humanist in my treasure chest of close friends, with his rich fantasy world and style of his compositions.

The ballet company returned from their European tour at the end of June. A day later, the Director, Spohr, invited me for an interview. This stocky man with a touch of grey on his temples, looked very imposing. As expected, he proposed that I took the morning class with the artistes, and then we would have a chat. We went down to the studio. The dancers got up from the floor, where they had been warming up sluggishly and lethargically, and said hello to us. Arnold made the introductions and asked me not to work the travellers too hard because of the nine-hour time difference with Europe. I nodded, and went over to the pianist. I determined the tempo for the exercises with him and calmly and confidently started the class. I had to give the tired dancers credit for their high level of discipline and well-maintained self-control. No idle chat, or cutting questions to test my English. We kept to a slow tempo at the barre, and refrained from large leaps or too much stretching in the centre of the studio.

At the end of the class I received grateful applause. I saluted the pianist and went upstairs to see the Director. When I arrived, José Carmen, the administrator, left us alone.

Spohr asked me a range of questions about the Bolshoi and Mariinsky Theatres. My file was out on his desk with posters and programmes from the Soviet Union. He was looking through them as he listened to me. He was clearly interested in whether I knew Sergeyev, Grigorovich, Yakobson, Chabukiani and other ballet masters apart from my institute teachers from the Bolshoi. Or was I just a peripheral specialist in this field?

"Forgive me, sir. May I ask what you thought of my class with the tired artistes?"

"You have satisfied both the dancers' and my professional requirements in this situation."

"What sort of future career could I enjoy as a teacher/choreographer in your company?"

"Oh, we'll talk about that later. Do you know these ballerinas personally?"

Spohr took a large photo album from his bookshelf and came up close behind me. On the desk, he opened the book at group photos of famous ballet artistes. I named all the well-known ballet stars, realising that the Director was checking out my credentials most thoroughly. Suddenly I felt him stroking my hair. Quick as lightning, this action forced me to take charge of the situation. Continuing to go through popular Soviet dancers as if nothing had happened, I carefully removed his hand from my head at the same time. Arnold returned to his chair at this point. He rang someone, speaking in French. I shut the album and stared intently at the Director. He put the receiver down abruptly and apologised that he needed to leave urgently. This brought to a close my conversation with the Artistic Director of the Royal Winnipeg Ballet.

The following morning Arnold was not in his office. I asked the administrator, Carmen: "Where can I find the Director, to sort out my work situation?"

"I don't know where Mr Spohr is, and haven't received any instructions from him regarding you."

"So will I get the opportunity to say goodbye to him? Could you give me back my file, please?"

I had the feeling that he was starting to 'back me into a corner' and I had to stop him at once. I started seething inside. I didn't want to believe what was happening. On the way home I asked myself the same question over and over again, but found no explanation.

As soon as she saw me at Manpower, Linda was alarmed, and looking worried, asked me: "Mikhail, what's happened? You look terrible. Have a drink of water first."

"I think it's better that you don't know the finer points of what's going on at the ballet."

"Why's that? Even if I'm not in a position to sort out what's happened, I need to advise the management regarding what's taken place, and consider your future work plans."

"Linda, I'm genuinely grateful to you for your help and concern for me. But what happened has nothing to do with my professional qualification. It's purely a personal faux pas by Arnold who made an error of judgement regarding my sexual orientation. If you report this through official channels, my theatrical career in Canada will be over before it's begun."

"Surely this homosexual didn't make advances towards you? I can't imagine that."

I told the agent what had happened and the ballet's director's reaction to his false move.

"I beg you to keep quiet about this sordid incident: it will give Dr Spohr and his management reason not to take me on 'due to the choreographer's professional role being incompatible with the artistic profile of the Royal Winnipeg Ballet's repertoire'. If you want to help me, please can you rearrange my immigration to Toronto or Montreal? I beg you!"

"Mikhail, you're not the first one to suffer this fiasco with Arnold. His scandalous escapades with dancers from the troupe have even been published in the local papers. It's very sad. Our ballet-school students and sportsmen were counting on you so badly! Here is a letter from the dean of Manitoba University too, requesting an audience with you to discuss setting up a dance department in the Faculty of Theatre and Sport. Alas! Because of this bastard the province is losing a much needed specialist in the arts. Please accept my sympathy, and don't worry. I'll do everything in my power to get you an urgent transfer to Ontario or Quebec."

A telegram from Penelope was waiting for me at home; she wanted to fly over in mid-July, and asked me to let her know where I would be at that time. I smiled at her naïvety. At the same time, I started packing up my things, getting ready for the journey. At Manpower, Linda gave me a folder of documents which I signed for. I was off to Montreal with a recommendation to talk to the founder and director of Les Grands Ballets Canadiens, Ludmilla Chiriaeff. I read through the document several times.

The plane ticket was for 3rd July, so I sent a telegram to Penny in Rome. 'I'm looking forward to seeing you in Montreal, my new home. Love, Misha.'

Linda took me to the airport well in advance of departure. She explained in detail who would be meeting me on arrival to take me to the hotel. She advised me not to worry if the Québecois addressed me only in French, and ignored my pidgin English.

"The main thing is, don't miss your new agent from the Manpower office, who will be waiting for you next to the gangway after you land. Her name is Elvira. She's a hot brunette."

"Ah! If that's the case, then I'll fly there immediately on my own Berkut wings!"

"After the critical incident with Dr Spohr, I understand only too well," Linda smiled sadly.

She checked that I had my ticket and documents once again, and gave me her card and contact telephone numbers. She asked me to call her from Montreal once I was set up. I took with me the fondest memories of my Manitoba patroness, and her sensitivity towards helpless immigrants.

During the three-hour flight, in keeping with tradition, I decided to go over my doubts.

I was preparing myself, and really looking forward to meeting my second chosen homeland – what a knockout. In Rome the Consul had organised my professional interview with the Royal Winnipeg Ballet with some difficulty through the Manitoba office of Manpower. Linda Isit had gone all out to 'sell' my qualifications to the departmental managers of theatre and sport. David Moroni had reorganised the order of summer courses at the Ballet school, so as to incorporate my taster classes in the timetable. Aida Volsh had looked after me, investing her energy and time as a useful member of society to clean my flat, do my shopping, etc. All this just so that some low-down letch could rubbish my students' endeavours and practically outrage me. That said, I have never had anything against homosexuals. On the contrary, I have always defended them from negative public opinion.

If Dr Spohr could act that way with me, then what value did he attach to his dancers? Were they simply the next object of homosexual satisfaction? How morally low would this leader of the Royal Winnipeg Ballet (the most romantic of all theatre arts) have to go, before he trampled the unearned 'crown of the British Empire' in the mud?

I was very hurt by such an inauspicious start to my emigration to Canada. It felt like a certain fate was hanging over me, but once seated in the plane, my mood changed. I took a deep breath, exhaled all the negative thoughts and evil stench of 'social and public shit'. I tossed my curly, shit-streaked (forgive me) Pegasus mane in the air and stepped proudly towards the exit at Montreal Airport.

CHAPTER 3 CANADIAN ROULETTE

I was met at Montreal Airport by a representative from the local branch of Manpower. When she heard about my missing accordion, she took me straight to the manager of the Baggage Department. At first, this chap refused to get involved. But Madame Grippone kicked up such a fuss that staff and security guards came running as if the place were on fire. Five minutes later a trolley arrived carrying my familiar black case, tightly bound with sticky tape in the shape of a cross. I opened the lid. Inside was my smashed instrument, with deep cracks in several places. Madame Grippone put in a damages claim for 3,000 dollars and made the airport manager sign to confirm liability for his staff's negligence. She also highlighted the point in the transport regulations, which allows passengers to take portable musical instruments with them on board as hand luggage. She threatened to take Air Canada to court for infringing the luggage transportation rules. I just stood modestly to one side, staggered by my chaperone's aggressive stance.

My new carer brought me to the city's immigration centre. Kind-hearted members of staff in the cultural section took me under their wing. One of them sorted me out with a monthly allowance; another booked me a place at the YMCA hostel; yet a third took care of finding me some work. The deputy manager, Madame Grippone, completed forms in French confirming my status as a citizen of Quebec province. I complimented her on how well organised and cooperative her staff were. I asked her how to go about sending an immigration invitation to my closest relatives in the Soviet Union. She explained in some detail, and advised me to do this once I'd received my residence permit. She loaded me up with brochures about social and medical assistance, learning the language, joining religious or social activities, etc. I had never felt so indulged.

During my three days at the YMCA, I found and rented a one-room flat with a kitchen and shower/toilet on the thirty-first floor of a high-rise block, by Guy metro station, right in the city centre. Manpower supplied me with all the furniture I needed and day-to-day items as required. They issued me food coupons and a travel card, organised me a temporary passport, and helped me to open a bank account. In short, they virtually set me up as a fully fledged Canadian citizen. After the rows about my accordion at the airport, I finally felt confident and was now ready to go out into the world. When I was still in Winnipeg, I had noticed with some surprise that in contrast to Europe, American Opera/Ballet theatres as a rule didn't have their own stages. They just rented them as necessary in special performance venues. I confirmed the address of a ballet company I was interested in. To make the best possible impression, I bought some 'special occasion' toiletries and headed out to face judge and jury.

A typically Russian-looking girl was sitting at the secretary's desk in the lobby at Les Grands Ballets Canadiens; she was even called Nastya, and later I discovered her to be Chiriaeff's daughter. I introduced myself timidly. She greeted me cheerfully in Russian and called into the Director's office. A moment later, Ludmilla appeared, her hand outstretched in greeting. I kissed her hand and followed the Director into her office. Nastya offered us tea, in a display of pure Russian hospitality.

"Thank you, I won't be long. Ludmilla Aleksandrovna, here is my file. If you are interested . . ."

"OK, Mikhail, just leave it on the desk. This is a letter from Linda Isit in Winnipeg. She was very impressed by your taster classes and regrets that it was not possible to use you in your main profession as a choreographer. As you know, it's the summer holidays here now. On 16th July, for a whole month, we traditionally run general intensive courses in various genres for Americans, and would like to watch your classical ballet lesson for senior students. I'm also interested in your Character course. When would you prefer to give these presentation classes as part of our curriculum? I hope you are not offended by such a familiar approach?"

"I suggest it would be best to teach Classical in the first week of the international course, and do Character in the second one."

"How does 20th July sound? We can sort out the next programme later, with your agreement."

"All right. I will be in Montreal and at your service until 1st August. After this my lady friend is flying over from Rome, and we are planning to visit my relatives in Los Angeles."

"Just out of interest, Mikhail, do you deliver your 'Pas de deux' course on pointes or some other way?"

"In general I've devised a methodology for three programmes of duet dance:

"a) standard Classical on pointes – for the traditional ballet repertoire;

"b) Contemporary technique on demi-pointes (*Spartacus, Scheherazade, Shurale*, and so on);

"c) Character technique in hard shoes (*Stone Flower, Laurencia, Gayaneh*, etc).

"I'll gladly show you any of these as long as I have some young men and the chance to go through the musical accompaniment first with a pianist."

"Excuse me, maestro! They say, 'The proof of the pudding is in the eating.' That's how I work too."

"What do you mean, Madame? The better I come across to you, the more chance I'll have of securing work in your company."

"In that case, let's start the senior ballet course with Classical. Then Modern 'Pas de deux' on demi-pointes with the middle/senior group. We will end your presentation with Character dance with students from different groups. We'll supply skirts and hard shoes from our wardrobe. Thank you for your interest in our academy. Please don't hesitate to call if you have any questions about this project."

"Thank *you*, Madame, for taking such a professional interest in my teaching repertoire."

"I'll return your file to you the next time we meet, in a week's time."

"Fine, no problem."

As I left, Nastya handed me a business card and a folder of ballet programmes. Looking through these, I realised that half of their repertoire consisted of contemporary ballet.

That's why Madame Chiriaeff was so interested in my 'Pas de deux' on demi-pointes. So what can I do? I will have to get my head around these new Western trends.

I met my Penelope at the airport, full of amorous agitation. With a sunny smile, she was carrying a huge suitcase, probably heavier than she was. Women always take twice as many things with them as they actually need. The elderly taxi driver almost did himself in as he loaded this 'light luggage' into the boot. Penny was anxious about ascending to the thirty-first floor in the lift. But she was rewarded with a fantastic vista of the city from the broad window. My girlfriend was impressed, but didn't leave my shoulder for a long time. Once she'd had time to make herself up, I took her for supper at Troika, a nearby restaurant. This Englishwoman loved French wine and Russian cuisine. Montreal is the most European city in Canada, almost a miniature Paris. There was a five-hour time difference with Italy, so we went home to bed early, naturally checking first that we hadn't forgotten our former intimate relationship. The contented pair fell asleep in their lovers' tender embrace, as in the recent past. But jet lag woke my companion at 5 a.m. She couldn't think of anything better to do than indulge in the sweet, passionate duet again, rather than doing her morning exercise. Only after this and taking a shower, did she return to her usual self.

I told Penny about presenting my teaching programmes at Les Grands Ballets Canadiens on 1st August, and that I needed to give further demonstrations of my capabilities to three ballet companies: Toronto, Edmonton and Vancouver, so I could make the correct choice regarding permanent employment, and not repeat the Royal Winnipeg Ballet fiasco. She reluctantly agreed to write a speculative letter to various places, proposing my professional services and requesting a trial class with ballet artistes or students, to check out my credentials. I took this letter to the work section at Manpower. The member of staff responsible was pleased to see a ready-made proposal, and promised not only to send it out straight away by telegram, but also to make follow-up telephone calls to all three companies to see if there was any mileage in this project. I left with her all the approximate dates of our movements in August. The agency boss was impressed by my level of activity and promised to do everything she could not to let me down. I gave her my new telephone number and asked her to agree any adjustments to my timetable with me if necessary.

The three sample classes at Les Grands Ballets Canadiens absorbed a lot more of my energy and time than I had anticipated. I could not afford to make an ass of myself. And Penny was demanding attention for her holiday diversions at the same time. We went together to see Opera and Ballet performances and Symphony concerts at the Place-des-Arts, but during the day, she visited museums, galleries and shops on her own. Everything turned out well. Madame Chiriaeff offered me the opportunity to take a Pre-professionals' class in her academy in September from 9.30 a.m. to 4.30 p.m. including breaks. There would be a daily Ballet class in the mornings, then every other day, 'Pas de deux' or Character dance. After lunch I would put on a Choreographic Miniature for the show. This seemed to be the best possible arrangement. But I was worried about the difference in the Vaganova/Tarasov teaching systems of Classical dance and the local, unspecified method of preparing my future students used in the past over a number of years. As is well known, it's harder for anyone to relearn something than to learn something from scratch.

Eventually my good fairy from Manpower proudly informed me by telephone that she had secured a schedule for my three demonstrations at the National Ballet (Toronto), Alberta Ballet (Edmonton) and Anna Wyman Dance Theatre (Vancouver). I would spend two days in each city, including an overnight stay in a hotel. Naturally, Penny would have to pay for her own travel and accommodation and she gratefully reimbursed the agency for her portion of the costs to avoid wasting precious time queuing at the station. I imagined it had been quite a gamble for my link worker to coordinate three Ballet companies into a tour of this nature. It helped that at this time they were all running their intensive summer courses, with the aim of recruiting more dancers. It made more sense for any school management to introduce something innovative during the holidays than in the middle of the academic year. With a smile, the manager handed me railway tickets to Vancouver, which just had to be punched in each new place, covering letters to the management regarding my employment, copies of hotel reservations for each night, my allowance for August, with the hope that it would be the last one, and a wealth of advice on the diplomatic handling of directors.

Unfortunately, I couldn't deliver the same set of exercises and sequences in each place, as the participants' technical level and stage experience generally varied from one province to another. I had to get the measure of their abilities on the first day, then concoct something to suit the performers' standard and deliver my hour-and-a-half-long demonstration class accordingly the following day. Fortunately, a different set of questions arose with each different demonstration. In Toronto they were interested in Character dance, in Edmonton the classical Vaganova system, while in Vancouver they liked the modern-style duet. Penny nicknamed me 'Jack of all Trades'. With this compliment, I took my leave. She was delighted to be setting off on what was a bit of a honeymoon. She had friends in Toronto and California, whom she'd worked with previously in Rome. She really wanted to meet up with them after not seeing them for a long time and they in turn, were keen to have her to stay. This was great for me as it didn't impinge on my plans. I must admit that after chasing around the world, I too had no objection to a bit of distraction from the perpetual nervous tension of the last few months. She had earned this relaxation through her patience and help. I hoped that this would not interrupt my programme of demonstrations.

In the train, Penny highlighted the places in the Toronto brochure that she was interested in visiting. As always before a demonstration, I was checking through my notes. As we left the platform, Penny's old friend Joanna called out to her. We dropped our luggage off at our hotel, before I was given a lift to the National Ballet and she and her old workmate went back to her place.

The Director, Betty Oliphant, welcomed me drily with an official smile. She offered me a coffee and read carefully through the information from Manpower, then leafed through my file with its posters, programmes and CV. After asking me a few standard questions, she went on to tell me that at 11 a.m. tomorrow morning, after her ballet class, I would give my trial Character dance class with intermediate-level students. Skirts and hard shoes would be provided.

"The pianist is expecting you in the ballet studio to agree the musical accompaniment."

"Would you allow me to watch the students from my group at their class beforehand?"

"Of course. You are welcome to come at 9 a.m. I'll let the ballet teacher know. Here's your file. You'll receive a written evaluation of your trial tomorrow afternoon, with the outcome of your enquiry regarding work."

The next morning, Penelope went off to Niagara with Joanna, while I set off to take the National Ballet by storm. During my initial observation of the ballet class, I realised that I was dealing with students professionally trained in the Cecchetti method. I mentally reorganised my initial positions, after deciding to retain the Russian exercises at the barre and to give Italian sequences of Furlana and Tarantella in the centre. This was the right decision. I managed to cement the change before my class with the pianist, and order tambourines for everyone from the Wardrobe Department. My Italian excerpts with the tambourine on a classical basis, went down a treat. The students were fascinated to learn really ornate combinations of arm and leg movements. Their eyes were shining. The Director was looking very pleased.

After the class she made no effort to conceal her curiosity, asking: "Maestro, what other nationalities do you include in your Character programme?"

"All European and Asian from the traditional opera/ballet repertoire."

"And how does Historical dance fit in with this? What eras do you cover in the syllabus?"

"Early and late eras of Court dances: Medieval, Renaissance and Baroque."

"Who taught you at MTA?"

"Margarita Rozhdestvenskaya."

"Yes, I know this name from her book. Remember to collect our feedback on your taster from the secretary. Thank you for the class. Good luck!"

I bowed and went proudly out of the office with my head held high.

Penny read out an invitation from the National Ballet, addressed to Manpower, offering me the opportunity to lead Character dance from September with all the youngest groups, as well as Historical dance with the middle/senior classes. A full workload: six days a week, four classes a day. I had to give them my answer within the next ten days. There was no mention of choreography. The salary was in line with qualifications of the highest category of teaching staff.

"Misha, you now have two offers: Les Grands Ballets and the National. Perhaps you could afford to relax a bit now? It might be best to spend longer relaxing at Tony's, by the ocean in Monterey."
    "Penny darling, of course that's better than leaping over youngsters like a goat in this heat. But . . .'
    "OK! Don't lecture me. Let's get off to the station before we miss our train talking."

I lay down on the seat all the way to Edmonton, while Penny slept sitting up. From the station, we took a taxi to the hotel then I sped off in the same car to Alberta Ballet, where the manager was already waiting for me. He explained where and when I would give my class the following day to a mixed-ability group of students. Every now and again he would glance at his watch, letting me know that his working day was coming to an end. It was obvious that they needed me like a hole in the head. Nevertheless, I didn't want to let down my sponsor from Manpower.
    In the morning, the school Director apologised for not having met me yesterday evening, for family reasons. She explained that generally their Intensive Course consisted of students who were not professionally trained, as unfortunately the best students and dancers in the province were now attending summer courses at Banff (with Arnold Spohr directing).
    "Our school desperately needs a qualified Ballet Teacher and we have funds available for this. These students from the nearby schools are not typical of Alberta Ballet. Here is your pianist. You have fifteen minutes with her. Please try to keep to time."
    During this introduction, the ballet director, Brydon Paige, was leading a rehearsal on the top floor and had sent his assistant in his place. While I was sorting out the accompaniment, he and the school director were having a look at my file. Students were limbering up on the floor in the studio. Once I'd finished specifying the finer points of the music with the pianist, I turned to face the students. The Director introduced me, and I nodded to the accompanist. It was hot and stuffy in the studio. I decided to make the class light and entertaining: half an hour at the barre on basic stretching and simple combinations of well-known elements. In the centre, we would do short études in adagio or andante tempos, with the necessary port de bras for the students, plenty of dance sequences and small jumps. I alternated between the young men and girls without any long pauses, not giving them the chance to lose focus during my demonstration of the next combinations. I took serious note of their movements without paying attention to their trivial errors. They didn't even notice the hour and a half passing, and were amazed when I announced the final curtsey. The troupe manager and Director were smiling, united in their applause for the students.
    Ten minutes later, I was up on the second floor, from where music from *The Nutcracker* was wafting down. I watched the rehearsal through open doors, until the ballet manager spotted me and invited me in. Apologising, I explained that the school director was waiting for me, and continued to

observe the rehearsal from the corridor for a little while longer. I was really interested in pinpointing the degree of professional preparation for the Character dancers in this ballet. Eventually I made my way downstairs to the waiting Director. I justified my lateness by being distracted by the beautiful dancers at the rehearsal. Character dance clearly did not command respect in this establishment.

"Mikhail, thank you very much for the class. This was pitched at exactly the right level for students of this calibre. Here is your file and our letter. If the enclosed proposals are of interest to you, then we'd be delighted to welcome you to Alberta Ballet in September."

I bowed in gratitude and hurried back to the hotel, where Penelope would no doubt be looking anxiously at her watch, as we had just forty-five minutes left to catch our train to Vancouver. I hailed a taxi in the square, and loaded the suitcases in silence, not responding to my lady friend's entirely justified reproaches. I just apologised with a kiss and gave her the latest envelope.

We were the only ones in our carriage. To assuage my guilt, I asked my upset travelling companion how she had spent her last solitary day in a strange city.

"I bought a multi-journey ticket on a tour bus and from ten until three, I rode in and around the city with an elderly couple from England. The most impressive sights in the province belong to the local Indians or immigrant communities from Hungary, Ukraine, Poland and other countries, who have kept up their social and cultural traditions."

"Yes, I've heard that there is a really strong Ukrainian community with a National school, church services and folk traditions in applied Decorative arts. There are three generations of immigrants from Ukraine: from the time of the revolution; after the Second World War and nowadays – unfortunately they are at each other's throats for religious reasons. The Catholics from Western Ukraine and the Orthodox from the East and atheists on both sides are all unable to make peace with each other. Extremists sometimes go to the extremes of burning down their adversaries' churches, as did actually happen in Montreal, Toronto, and other Canadian cities. I am very disappointed by this. Although I'm not religious, wherever I've been in Europe or America I am never indifferent as I pass by a church or cathedral. I often pop in even if only for ten minutes, as a mark of respect. I love architecture, and enjoy the peaceful silence and spiritual atmosphere of a holy building. I show sincere respect to Church priests."

Our hotel in Vancouver was in the Old Town, not far from bright reservoirs surrounded by greenery. We both fell in love with this city and decided to stay a day longer after my presentation at the Anna Wyman Dance Theatre. The Director/founder greeted me rather cautiously at first. But after looking through my file, her eyes lit up. Anna invited me to have a look at her senior students in the Ballet school she sponsored in the neighbourhood and I stayed there until the lesson finished, fascinated by the unfamiliar Modern style of body movements and their performance technique. Disconcerted, I asked innocently if they could put me in touch with the pianist, but it turned out that apart from production rehearsals for new choreography (and even then, not always), as a rule, all classes took place with accompaniment on small percussion instruments. Still, I needed to get to grips with this accompaniment, which was quite alien to me.

"Mikhail, don't worry! You are not the first, and certainly won't be the last, Soviet teacher to be shocked by this. Modern dance not only has its own language in terms of movement, but can also take place without any accompaniment. It is performed on the basis of the dancer's internal tempo and rhythm and his spiritual and emotional richness."

As I play a musical instrument myself, within the hour I had succeeded in cobbling together a soundtrack for tomorrow's demonstration with the percussionist. Once again, I recalled the partnering technique that I'd learned with a trainer in stage movement at the Odessa Ballet School a quarter of a century earlier, with his fusion of acrobatic elements and natural body movements. In addition, I drew on my own neoclassical vocabulary in the 'Polovtsian Dances' in *Prince Igor* and contemporary, space-themed miniatures 'Martians' World', 'Lunar Scherzo' and so on. This gave me sufficient material for the duet dance in modern style: extremities not turned out, natural forms of movement, acrobatic moves, etc. My accompanist carefully recorded the order of exercises and études with individual, character parameters in the music: size, tempo, rhythm, dynamics, structure, etc. Now I was ready for my demonstration.

In addition to the dance theatre director, the teachers/répétiteurs and the troupe's leading soloists also attended the contemporary duet-technique demonstration. After Anna had introduced me as her guest, I gave a few warm-up exercises at the barre, also on tiptoe to stretch/loosen up the dancers' musculoskeletal equipment. Next, I took the whole course carefully and meticulously at a moderate tempo/rhythm. I have to admit, it was lovely to complete the last session in my series of trials with disciplined students and in a creative, professional environment. The guests nodded their heads good-naturedly from time to time as pairs executed successful, intricate sequences of movements in the centre, including partnering in aerial supports, sometimes even applauding their approval. The accompanying percussionist quickly got the hang of my instructions and keenly observed the varying tempos of separate pairs in alternate double work, where one partner is on the other's shoulder or lifted over the supporting dancer's head, travelling in a circle or diagonally across the studio. The cascade of elementary lifts and uncomplicated moves impressed even the most seasoned spectators, although there was nothing out of the ordinary about the partners' tactile contact and their sustained self-control.

Once the taster had concluded successfully, the troupe soloists said how sorry they were not to have taken part in this demonstration. I expressed my heartfelt thanks to the musician, redirecting the students' applause towards him. Anna realised that just one training session on Dance Partnering would not be enough to keep me in Winnipeg. While I was getting myself together in the dressing room, she, just as the other directors had done, typed out an official offer to my sponsors in Montreal. Anna Wyman taught Modern dance at the Faculty of Theatre Arts in the local university, and guaranteed me a full timetable there: Classical, Historical and Character, but without any choreography, as in the other locations.

"Mikhail, the Dean is looking for a specialist of your calibre to open a separate Department of Dance in the Faculty of Theatre Arts, which includes a range of diverse facilities."

My colleagues tried to convince me of the long-term benefit to my professional profile in British Columbia, where at one time there were even private ballet schools, as well as a small company. But they had given way to the growing interest in contemporary dance. I kept quiet while I analysed the situation.

I promised Anna that I would think about it, list all the pros and cons, and get back to her with my decision once I was back in Montreal. I gave my colleague a goodbye hug, feeling a warm bond of friendship between us.

Penelope was delighted at finally having the chance to use her leave for its intended purpose. In the evening we went to see the touring opera in the city auditorium. In the morning we took a sea cruise to Victoria, the provincial capital. After lunch, we sat on the bus, racing along the shores of the Pacific Ocean. Penny really loved the picturesque changes of scene flying past. She refused to talk about work, just blissfully sipped wine, tenderly snuggling up against her worn-out dancer. She hummed a few lines from the opera.

We were met in Monterey by Tony, Penny's former boss at FAO, and his wife Christina. They took us to their luxurious villa close to the Pacific Ocean, where a large number of guests from their extended family were already waiting to enjoy a late supper.

Tony had headed up a large and important department at the FAO. When he retired, he became leader of the local Italian community, a highly revered person in a small town. For three days, members of his family made a fuss of us, taking us out to the fairy-tale environs in an effort to indulge their chief's friends from Rome. Penny boasted about my four job offers and drew on the old man's wisdom: in his opinion, where would be the best place to start a creative career in Canada? After reading through all the letters, Tony reflected for a moment. He clarified some of the details, and without further ado, concluded: in his view, out of the four cities and provinces Montreal was the most European cultural centre, with the most potential for foreigners starting out in the arts. In this respect, the Québecois are more flexible than others, although they take pride in their Francophone chauvinism. After the visit to Monterey, Tony's home became a favourite refuge on Pacific shores.

Our next overnight stop on our Californian odyssey was San Francisco. A unique city of people of different races and civilisations from all around the world. You hear all tongues known to man on the streets. Goods from almost every continent brighten the huge open markets, transported from the furthest reaches of our planet. Penny didn't know where to look. She had spent two years in Asia working with the United Nations, on agricultural aid to underdeveloped countries, and was familiar with their range of products. She tasted a few things and licked her lips with pleasure, at the same time as I was recoiling in disgust. As a punishment, Penny kissed me on the lips as the traders laughed, forcing me also to swallow the samples from her mouth. After supper the two of us went to a strip club. Inside, they split us up. The usherettes sent Penny off into the left-hand auditorium to watch naked men dancing onstage, while I was directed to the right-hand side to enjoy the nude female dancers. You can imagine how shocked I was after the Soviet Union's 'dry law'. To start with, I turned around shamefaced, naturally sneaking the odd peek at the stage. Nevertheless, a few minutes later I couldn't tear my eyes away from such gratuitous nudity and sat through the remaining half-hour with my mouth open, occasionally licking my lips, which had dried out in my state of agitation. It was enough to make you weep, that this magical show was over so quickly. I would have liked to repeat my inquisitive study of the female anatomy, but Penny dragged me back to the hotel.

Before we left the next morning, I rang my cousin in Los Angeles and confirmed our arrival time at the central bus station. All the way south, Penny and I discussed my work choices and unanimously decided in favour of Montreal. At the terminus, my older cousin Musya met us with her husband from Odessa.

While he was loading our luggage into the boot of his car, the latter asked: "Have you got bricks or gold in your cases, or something?"

"No, no, just bottles."

Both cousins lived with their families in separate halves of a large detached house. There was such a din as we arrived that their neighbours almost called the fire brigade. My younger cousin Dora squeezed me so close that my brittle bones almost cracked. Eventually, the whole clan was seated around a long table in the garden, stuffing themselves from early till late. The hosts probably thought that we had come from a country where people were hungry. They fed us tasty dishes as if we were starting a two-week fast the next day. Everyone spoke fluent English so Penny didn't miss out on any gossip. I asked the children to fetch a map of the city and tourist brochures. In addition to Hollywood, there were all sorts of attractions in LA: the zoo, aquarium, museums, theatres, markets and so on. We dashed around for four days of tourist hell, visiting all the sights on offer, returning home dead on our feet. After supper, my cousins and I caught up on the last few years. Their husbands and Penelope got to know each other over Californian wine in the garden, pinpointing how it differed from Italian wine.

We returned to Montreal by a magical route. During the last three days of her leave, Penny had charged around the shops, buying gifts for herself and friends in Rome. I drew up my immigration work permit at Manpower for Les Grands Ballets Canadiens as a teacher/choreographer on the pre-professionals' course, comprising: five young men and nine girls, plus Character dance twice a week with the younger students on Wednesdays and Saturdays from 2 p.m. My fate was finally decided.

Before her departure, Penny kept asking me: "When will we see each other next?"

It was just like when I left Rome: she was clearly longing for a decisive statement from me in our relationship. But again, it was beyond my control to make a premature decision and get her hopes up, without knowing how I would be received in a school with a different teaching methodology for Classical dance: or how I would survive in a French province without knowing the language. And just as in Italy, Penny cried on my shoulder as we said goodbye.

Gradually, I took up my usual hands-on Teaching method. I got the students moving around the entire studio from one corner to another over a five-hour period with breaks. After the daily Classical dance I taught Duet or Historical dance on alternate days. The lunch break was filled with two hours of choreography again, but with less physical exertion. And it was like this five days a week. The students moaned that they weren't used to wearing themselves out with such hard work.

I reassured them: "The harder the lesson, the easier the battle," and carried on steadfastly with the regime I had established.

A couple of weeks later, Ludmilla Chiriaeff dropped into the studio. As the next exercise at the barre came to an end, I nodded to the pianist. We carried on with the class in the usual way. Peter, one of the young men, made a serious technical error. Before the following exercise I corrected him tactfully and politely asked him to repeat the corrected part of the sequence. He responded rudely to my comments. I pretended that nothing had happened and continued the class. During the transition from barre to centre, Chiriaeff nodded to me and then addressed Peter, asking him to come and see her in the lunch break. As we started on composition work the rule-breaker apologised to the group for his undignified behaviour at the previous lesson and promised that it wouldn't happen again.

I don't know what Ludmilla said to poor Peter, but after this incident not only he, but all the remaining pre-professionals, behaved impeccably in my classes in their dealings with the teacher and pianist. I was very pleased with the younger groups in the Character class. Getting stuck in with their French emotional excitement, they completed routines at the barre and in the centre, trying to outdo each other. Chiriaeff popped in to these classes too. She couldn't help but smile as she watched her young charges, for the most part Québecois, performing Russian tap-dancing or Ukrainian 'doves' (cabrioles). Every time the Director appeared, we saluted her as a group, but now we did it the Ukrainian way. By the end of term I had prepared a Christmas programme with the children to perform at the traditional parents' evening. Chiriaeff and her colleagues were very complimentary about this.

I had almost no free time in the week. I didn't receive any compensation for my smashed accordion, and had to have it repaired in a workshop at my own expense. The Dutch Embassy finally returned the box with my documents and author's publications, which I'd left with them in Odessa before emigrating. On Saturdays, after Les Grands Ballets Canadiens, I did some shopping and housework and enjoyed some time to myself. In the evenings I would go to see Opera/Ballet performances and touring Modern dance companies in the Place-des-Arts. Luckily, Chiriaeff organised a season ticket for me there, as compensation for my unpaid additional hours on productions in the academy. The school budget did not stretch to choreography. In my first month of working there, I was so busy that I didn't notice the eager looks from all the single women in the ballet company and the Academy. But nature always finds a way. After missing my beloved Penelope for a month, the unhappy Odysseus began casting his eye over all the captivating sirens. At first he was worried about the risk to his personal reputation as a ballet master, but soon he realised his mistake.

I chose the lesser of two evils, in keeping with my nature. Alas! I used typical male thinking to justify my natural urges.

Claudette, a teacher of the younger classes sat next to me at one of the teachers' meetings. She was about twenty years younger than me. Unlike other locals, she had an excellent command of English. She and I discussed school issues, separate from personal matters. She asked if she could observe one of my morning classes as a learning point for herself. I answered affirmatively, advising that it was best to come to the open assessment in mid-December, when the students would feel more confident in presenting their programme from that term. A week after we had met, I was rushing around doing my shopping in the local shops after finishing classes on Saturday. There, completely out of the blue, I bumped into Claudette. We both expressed delight at meeting up, and carried on buying what we needed together.

My companion stopped at the bus stop and announced with a kind smile: "This is where I live. I'm on the third floor. If you have time, you're welcome to pop up for a coffee."

"Fortunately I am free this evening. I'd love to, if that's OK."

"Oh you are a one!" laughed Claudette. "Always grabbing the bull by the horns."

"What do you mean? I'm just trying to help a young woman carry her heavy bag up to the third floor like a real gentleman. Is there anything wrong in that? If there is, then please forgive me."

"Maybe not. I appreciate your chivalry and selfless assistance. Thank you!"

Over a delicious cup of coffee we initially chatted about nothing in particular. I told amusing ballet stories.

The hostess laughed and suddenly asked, curious: "Mikhail, would you like something stronger? It's Sunday tomorrow, so school's out."

I smiled. All this was reminiscent of banal scenes from films.

"Madame, in spite of my modesty, I can't refuse."

The young woman laughed again. "Tell me, are you always this compliant, or just with women? I have heard that you are much more demanding of your students than all the other teachers at the academy."

"That's a fact. That's why the Russian ballet school is so highly regarded in the West."

We hadn't noticed that we had got through nearly a litre of wine and were getting a bit drowsy. I moved to sit next to my friend on the settee, and proposed a final toast in Russian–French style to German brotherhood. Our symbolic kiss somehow became sexual, and lasted a long time. We nearly broke our empty glasses, and couldn't leave each other alone.

From this point on, the outcome was predictable. We kissed hungrily, got undressed and quickly established the right mood for love-making. Sitting on my lap, the half-naked girl whispered apologetically that she needed to take a shower. After several hours of moving around in the studio, I usually washed at the academy. While Claudette was showering, I removed all my unnecessary garments and stood in front of the bathroom like a satyr, in anticipation of the duet with *l'amour*. The blushing Venus came out in an open gown, fiddling with her untied hair. I scooped the laughing Amazon up in my arms, and staggering around the furniture, carried her into the bedroom. That's when my 'Pas de deux' technique came in useful with a partner who was a bit on the heavy side. Carefully depositing the young woman on the bed of love, I threw off my last bodily burden quick as a flash and pressed myself against the charming seductress. A strange feeling took hold of us, as if we had already known each other intimately for a long time. Without any awkwardness about being naked together, we rubbed and caressed each other's sexual organs until Claudette could not bear the torture of any more foreplay before the approaching union.

With each new technique in the sexual act we reached greater and deeper sexual satisfaction in the final orgasm. She cried out and I moaned. I had never experienced being engulfed like this before. I was also insatiable, as my organ firmed up without the customary break. Only now did I understand why Frenchwomen are so celebrated in the love act. Claudette made such intricate movements above and below me, that she would have been the envy of any high-wire circus acrobats. Eventually, we both collapsed from exhaustion and lay still for a while. Throughout the stormy night we returned several times to our bacchanalia of rolling around together, and it was morning before we moved away from each other and fell asleep.

I awoke to the aroma of fresh coffee. I kissed my hostess 'good morning' on the nape of her neck. I took her by surprise and she jumped, turning around sharply and pressing up against me: "Thank you, darling! I had such a good time with you in our intimate 'Pas de deux'."

"No, my dear. Thank *you* for that St Bartholomew's Night with satyr and nymph."

"Tell me, Michel, are all Russian men Casanovas like you?"

"Claudette, I'm not a man, I'm a choreographer. All women are Terpsichore to me!"

"You're full of jokes, but I'm genuinely curious to know where you learned the art of sex and the ability to make your partner so happy both physically and spiritually."

"My dear girl, it's impossible to learn this. It comes naturally or never – it's the same for women, as far as I understand them."

From that day on, Claudette came over to Guy Street every Saturday, to my pigeon loft on the thirty-first floor, where we took pleasure in each other's company. First we would have supper downstairs in a nearby cafeteria. Then we'd satisfy our mutual earthly needs. Both of us were happy in our unambiguous sexual relationship, and were not interested in any wider commitment as partners. A significant gap in our education, individual views and general interests prevented us from having a future together. I was convinced then and since that I needed more than one sexual partner to be truly happy. I thought about Penelope more and more. When I compared her to Claudette, I realised what I was losing.

Finally I took the plunge, and sent a telegram to Penny in Rome: 'My beloved, on bended knee, I am asking for your hand. If your answer is yes, I am willing to fly to London to marry you in the New Year. Love, Misha.'

I was not certain that Penny would give up her job at the UN and abandon Italy in favour of Canada for my sake. I imagined the girly fuss that would ensue on receipt of this telegram. I waited nervously for an answer from her. By all logic, she should have refused me (except perhaps for her parents' dream of having grandchildren in their old age). I had given up hope, when finally the telegram came. Hooray!

'Darling, please take my hand and my heart! I'll be waiting for you in London on 27th December. Love, Penny.'

When I first read it, I was petrified in shock. Then I started to jump in such a frenzy that I almost fell off the balcony. Coming to my senses on the settee, I put together an action plan for my visit to England to claim my future wife:

a) go urgently to Ottawa to obtain a visa and temporary passport;

b) buy a plane ticket to London and back for a week after the wedding;

c) remember to buy gifts for your bride and her parents, plus an engagement ring in London;

d) inform Chiriaeff of your leave during the winter holidays;

e) seek assistance from Manpower in drawing up the documentation in Ottawa for marriage.

I was passed from one department to another in the capital's passport office; no one knew how to help me. My travel document only allowed me to travel to America. To go to Europe, I needed a visa, which I could only get with a standard passport. I could be issued with the latter once I'd been in Canada for three years, and had become an official Canadian citizen. This is where the bureaucratic circle closed, but not for the loved-up Odysseus. I bent everyone's ear. I got to speak to the department manager. I showed him the telegram from Penny and my contract with Les Grands Ballets Canadiens, and made him ring Chiriaeff. She promised to telex over a personal reference for my week-long trip to England within the hour. The manager told me to come back after lunch.

Two hours later, with his approval on my declaration, with a copy of the reference from the director of Les Grands Ballets Canadiens and Penny's telegram, I was standing to attention before the consul at the British Embassy in Ottawa.

"Mr Berkut, why are you in such a hurry? Haven't you been married before?"

"Actually I have. And I don't want to lose my chance of happiness again. Please help me!"

"Is this actually an event in your life, or are you acting out a wedding scene from one of Shakespeare's tragedies? OK, OK! I can see that you're serious. Please accept this as a wedding gift."

Back in Montreal with my British visa, I booked a plane ticket to London and confirmed my arrival time to Penny by telegram. I couldn't get out of it now.

Following a successful assessment/demonstration of all the academy groups, the Director outlined a fruitful start to new disciplines in the school's curriculum at the teachers' meeting. She reminded everyone that when we came back from the winter holidays we would be starting production rehearsals well in advance for the Gala concert at the end of the academic year. I was pleased about this.

After the teachers' meeting, I thanked Chiriaeff for her help with my visa, and gave her the dates of my trip to Europe.

"Say hi to Penelope! I hope you'll both be very happy together!"

On the last Saturday before I left, I let Claudette know that I would be away in London for the holidays, and that I was planning to marry my English girlfriend from Italy.

"You can see how difficult it is for me on my own, and I hope you can understand my reasons."

"I've told you, I'm not planning to get married any time soon. So I wish you the very best!"

This was a heartbreaking situation. But Claudette was not surprised at my news and took it fairly coolly. Even so, I felt a bit out of sorts. In the plane, I counted up my successes and failures over the past year, and formulated plans for the year ahead. Naturally I was worried that my everyday life with Penny would get in the way of my creative plans. From past experience, it's completely different from having fun as a couple and sleeping with your lover.

At passport control in London Airport I was detained for having a British visa in an unorthodox travel document. But after checking the authenticity of the stamp and signature of the English Consul in Ottawa, and many personal questions, they reluctantly allowed this sleepy person into the UK. Penelope and her father met me at the exit. I apologised for keeping them. As it transpired, this powerful and impatient retired major had already elicited from the information desk that my documents looked a bit dodgy. My future father-in-law, Geoffrey, took the sleep-deprived groom to the most enormous house in the small town of Purley, in the London suburbs. Penny's petite mother gave her future son-in-law a cheery welcome. They allocated me one of the five bedrooms on the first floor. Penny and Rena then put me to bed. Seven hours of night flight plus five hours' time difference had naturally finished me off. I dreamed that I was still flying and unable to land.

Over lunch and with huge effort from all parties, I chatted to Penny's parents in English. The housekeeper, Rena, Penny's nanny, had always lived in this house, taking care of the whole family. I was used to looking after myself, so had to adjust to being waited on, otherwise she would have been offended, taking my independence as a lack of trust in her. After lunch we all had some quiet time. But with the aim of gaining information, I chatted to Rena in the kitchen while she did the washing-up.

The next day, Penny and I took the train to Croydon, a good shopping centre. I committed my first faux pas, as I had forgotten to change Canadian dollars into British sterling in Montreal. The bride chose for her husband an elegant suit, shirt and tie, shoes and even a raincoat. She didn't want to hear about my money, saying that it was a wedding present. I just accepted it all and bowed. I spent my last savings on an engagement ring, with three stones of my bride's choice.

We were married in the register office at noon on 31st December, and then went to a restaurant to celebrate. Penny's friends Maggie and Earl from the USA gave us a night in a Central London hotel as their gift. For four days, my new wife took me to theatres, museums, and other sights in the capital. My heavenly holidays concluded with a cosy family supper. The whole week in England had been like a delicious dream. After the wedding I vowed to get myself castrated if I were ever unfaithful to Penelope in future.

The happy couple returned to Montreal. I introduced my new spouse to the staff at Manpower. They issued me a one-off allowance for a dependant and handed me vouchers for postnuptial purchases in the food shop, so that the newly-weds didn't die of hunger in Quebec. With a chuckle, my partner stated that it was the first time in her life that she had ever received any handouts. But she didn't decline, on the principle 'Don't look a gift horse in the mouth!' Penny had brought a recommendation from the FAO in Rome addressed to the Civil Aviation Authority (CAA) in Montreal. Following an interview there, she was given a three-month trial, from 1st March 1977. Before starting work, my wife found us a stylish apartment on the top floor in the city centre on the corner of Dr Penfield and Drummond Streets. This painted house reminded us of our home in Rome on Piazza Rondonini. Throughout February, Penelope kept herself busy getting the flat ready and helping her Odysseus to perfect his English. For my part, from mid-January I immersed myself once more in my hectic routine of teaching and choreography at the academy, so as to do as good a job as possible in finishing my first, and possibly last, year with the pre-professional group and the little ones.

I was determined to open my own ballet school next season, and to form my own dance ensemble in time using the most talented students. Without telling my wife, I began scouring Montreal for a suitable space near our place to bring this project to fruition. It could either be in a new venue or by arrangement with the proprietor of one of the private city-centre schools. I made Chiriaeff aware of my plans beforehand, and sought her advice on selecting a prospective path for creative collaboration in the private sector of Montreal's ballet education.

"Misha, I have my eye on one suitable candidate for your project. But I have a request to make of you. Whatever happens, please keep doing your Character classes with the little ones. It's important to the Academy and for the art of Ballet in general."

"Ludmilla Aleksandrovna, I would love to! I wanted to ask you about this anyway, but didn't like to, given this situation. I could give two classes a day in the afternoons on two or even three days a week, if that works for you, plus choreographic projects with the youngest and the seniors too, as you see fit."

"So, right in the centre of town, on Rue St Catherine by the corner with

Drummond Street, is a small dance studio belonging to the former ballerina Camilla Malashenko. They just give adult keep-fit classes. She's not doing that well and there's a good chance that she'd be interested in a joint business venture or selling it to someone who can build on what she's been doing."

That same evening I paid a visit to Malashenko and introduced myself after her lesson. She offered me the opportunity to deliver a ballet class the next day. During the second senior class I managed to determine the students' levels. Mainly these were people just having a go at ballet: students from other institutes or people working in nearby organisations. All in all, their artistic level was low and amateur. There was one classroom of average size, with huge windows, on the first floor, a dressing room with toilet, but no shower. It was a very lively area with a lot of potential. After my mixed-genre trial class: classical, Historical and Character dance, the students not only stretched their hardened muscles and bones, but also enjoyed performing light dance sequences of diverse genres. Camilla invited me to a neighbouring taverna for a cup of coffee and recounted her sorry story.

She had been a dancer in various companies in America over seventeen years. During one of their performances, her partner had dropped her from a high lift over his back. Sustaining a cracked spine, she stopped dancing and decided to take up teaching, more for her well-being than commercial gain.

"Mikhail, I opened this studio three years ago with my husband's help. But alas! I've now realised that I can't do this by myself. In addition, the rents in this area are high and go up by 8 to 10% every year. I've decided to sell my business for the modest amount that I've invested in equipping the studio and advertising. Let's say 1,500 dollars. My contract terms oblige me to give the landlord of this building three months' notice, i.e. no later than 31st March. As far as I understand, judging by your credentials, you're not entirely set on working at the academy with Chiriaeff, and are looking for an opportunity to open your own school? Well? Put your cards on the table. You won't find a better deal in the centre of town."

"Camilla, I've listened carefully to what you've got to say and sympathise with your tragic accident. You're right about the reason for my visit and I hope you also appreciate my caution in the delicate matter of purchasing a business that's already set up, but is not very successful. You only have a total of seventeen students in both groups: beginners and intermediate. As you know, selling or renting even a small studio with real people is impossible on an informal basis. I propose going about it in two stages:

a) For the whole of March I will work for free with the seniors or young ones (alternately) four evenings a week after I've finished at Les Grands Ballets. You and I will get the measure of each other, and I'll get to know the students better. At the end of this trial period we'll meet up here again and decide whether to go for it or not. If we sign a rental agreement for the studio, I'll pay you an agreed sum against your receipt. We'll do all of this in the presence of your husband and my wife acting as witnesses to our deal.

b) On 1st April we meet in the administration office of your building and give the landlord a copy of our agreement. We'll transfer the rental contract into my name from 1st July. You will stay on as studio director and pay the rent in accordance with the contract. At that stage you will gradually hand over your authority to the new school director, who will take over rental payments on the space from you from 1st July. All of these details will be set out in our agreement. Here is my professional CV and promotional file. Have a look with your husband at home and talk through the proposed terms. If you decide not to go ahead with this project, let me know tomorrow after your classes. There won't be any repercussions. In any case, we'll maintain a good working relationship."

Penny did not settle in at the CAA. She had got used to the relaxed and flexible Italian work climate during her thirteen years in Rome.

There was a group of representatives from the Soviet aviation industry within the CAA. On the eve of 1st May (a red-letter day for communists), they gave a party in the reception hall, to which the husbands or wives of their colleagues were invited. After a celebratory toast, the guests drank and ate canapés as they mingled and chatted with each other. Penelope dragged me off to meet her hosts to wish them a happy May Day and thank them for their hospitality. One of them unexpectedly came up to me and introduced himself in Russian: "I'm Petrosyan, and you are . . .?"

"I'm the husband of that lady over there, next to your manager."

"From which department?"

"From the Brainwashing Department."

"Ah, I see. You are one of the ones who fled his homeland in a wave of emigration."

"No, highly respected Comrade Dickhead! I fled from fucking scum like you."

At the sound of my angry voice, Penny appeared quickly and asked: "What's going on?"

"Sorry, darling. Time for us to leave. Tell you later, OK?"

Bewildered, she fixed her gaze on little Petrosyan, who gave a nasty smile as he spread his hands to both sides. I headed for the exit without a word and waited by the door for my wife, who was saying her goodbyes.

On the way home I was angry with myself for rising to the bait, and breaking my oath. I asked my wife to forgive my tactless conduct.

"Don't worry about it! It doesn't matter any more now. I resigned yesterday. Today my boss signed me off as of Monday – a month before the end of my probationary period."

"In that case, I can offer you an administrator's position from 1st June in our academy 'Les Ballets Russes de Montréal', paying the same as the CAA."

STAGE II: FORTUNE'S SMILE

CHAPTER 4 TERPSICHORE REBORN

As I was renting Malashenko's former studio, I also negotiated with the building managers to convert the space next door into a large ballet studio, adding a dressing room and shower room and toilet. When Penny and I discussed how the ballet studio would operate from 1st July, I felt that she was not very optimistic about investing money in this project, with no guarantee of commercial success.

My wife was worried: "What makes you think that you'll attract more students to the studio than Camilla did?"

"Because I'm not Camilla, and I know how to appeal to ballet fans, how to make amateurs feel like ballet dancers and how to help women keep their beautiful figures, teach people how to move well, so that they're attractive to others and in their own eyes."

"OK, I agree to help you achieve your dream. But if in a year's time, I find a job that suits me better, promise me that you won't hold me back."

Penny and I spent all of May producing promotional material: posters, flyers, radio and newspapers ads, etc., proclaiming, that from 1st June we would be registering students for professional classes and dance-therapy courses in the new studio 'Les Ballets Russes de Montréal'. We emphasised that classes would be led by specialists in two languages (French and English), but could also be offered in Italian and Russian if necessary. Group sizes would be limited.

The last phrase elicited a negative response from my naïve administrator: "How can you write that when you haven't signed anyone up yet?"

"My dear, I am sufficiently confident in my abilities and my project's success that . . ."

"This is pure speculation. It's not like Russia here, where corruption is probably allowed."

"Penny, calm down. No one's going to send you to prison for this. And I don't want to get into the habit of it either."

With Camilla's consent, we had the telephone transferred into my name well in advance. I set up a registration desk in the studio hallway. The owner of the building gave permission for me to put up some posters outside next to the entrance, and I left some flyers around the hallway. Camilla smiled benevolently at my activity, while my wife responded to clients' enquiries on the telephone in a gloomy voice.

On 1st June I was working at Les Grands Ballets Canadiens as usual in the morning. I was preparing a programme with my ballet charges for the Gala concert to mark the end of the school year at the Place-des-Arts. In keeping with what we'd advertised, Penelope had gone (as she told me) 'to get a numb bum for no good reason, just to satisfy your whim'. By the studio entrance, a group of would-be dancers waited in the stairwell. Once they'd said hello to the lady in charge, the young women and girls pushed through behind her into the hallway. The administrator's eyes nearly popped out of her head and on to the registration desk. When I hurtled in after lunch, over forty people had already signed up for the different sections advertised in the brochure. Camilla, assisted by two of her students, collected her personal things in bags, freeing up space in a large cupboard, where she had kept all the stage costumes for students' concert appearances. Before she left with the luggage, I asked my colleague if she could leave one of her assistants to help register the newcomers alongside Penny for a fixed payment, but in a separate section of the school. Camilla gladly recommended her student Louisa (whom I knew) from the senior group, who was looking to earn a bit of money. Following this collaboration, there was a much more positive atmosphere to registering the newcomers.

That very same day, by pure coincidence, refurbishment started on the neighbouring building to turn it into a large ballet studio. I was worried that this would make a bad impression on the people enrolling. As it turned out, it had completely the opposite effect. They were impressed with its wide windows that looked out over Rue St Catherine, and the unique, vast space for future classes. I pulled a small cupboard out of the storeroom and put it next to Penny to make things more comfortable for her and her assistant. Now my wife was enrolling students in both groups of the dance-therapy section: beginners and experienced. Louisa followed the same principle in enrolling for the professional section, taking their word regarding their level of training. She advised them that the Director/Ballet master would have the final say on 1st July before classes began. Inevitably, there were fewer signed up for this section due to the exams currently taking place in the academic and educational establishments combined with the low profile of the new Ballet studio. Nevertheless, I was confident of success, thanks to my specially promoted summer courses, presenting the famous Russian ballet school, the only one in Canada at that time.

Now I could make arrangements with the teachers put forward by Chiriaeff: Mary Abdel Malek for students with some experience, and Zhenya Bonzulo for beginners. One of the former pianists was staying on, the other, Valentina, from Les Grands Ballets Canadiens, had been offered evening classes at Les Ballets Russes de Montréal. In order to monitor attendance at paid classes and register new students, I took on a dedicated manageress, Natasha, and a daily cleaner on a part-time basis (7 to 10 a.m.). For one month before the summer courses I enrolled around seventy students in four groups, plus sixteen from Camilla's previous groups. This wasn't bad for starters. But we needed as many students again by the beginning of the academic year, to keep the business on track in the first season.

Penny and I had to overcome a multitude of hurdles along the way that summer while I was trying to get my project off the ground. We barely managed to plug one hole before the next one appeared. Student numbers increased, and with them administrative and organisational problems; until then, we had had no experience in running a commercial business. In order to set the studio up as a 'non-profit-making enterprise', we had to hire a full-time experienced bookkeeper, Jean, and draw up a contract with a lawyer and tax accountant to establish the ballet studio's non-commercial status officially. Penny went into panic mode and ranted and raved. I patiently filled out and signed all the paper instructions, revealing my total ignorance as a businessman. On top of all my creative workload, I tried my best to get to grips with all the business relationships in Quebec's government bodies, so as to avoid getting anything wrong.

To bring in as many permanent students as possible for both sections by 1st September, I had to take four classes a day with Mary on the summer courses. We both had the knack of hooking new clients in. Partly we played on the girls' or boys' natural flirtatiousness. Sometimes we even flirted with them a little ourselves. Both sides understood this game perfectly well and took such nuances with a pinch of salt during classes. As a result, Terpsichore heard my prayers. By the beginning of the academic year, people had returned from their holidays and the influx of new students in the studio reached almost 200. My wife had to go to the bank with the bookkeeper every day to deposit cheques and cash payments, as the elderly Jean was nervous about making the 150-metre walk down the street by herself. Penelope was happy to oversee a solid injection of funds into the account to support the functioning of a start-up business comprising nine members of staff, which was a positive indication of future financial potential.

The administrator and bookkeeper shared a separate office. I had my own equipped ballet master's office where I prepared my courses and held meetings with teachers. As an experiment, we began with two genres of work in the studio: Classical ballet and Dance Therapy. But in the second six months we broadened the curriculum to include two further class subjects: Ballet-jazz with Michele-France Clotier and Flamenco with Sonia Del-Rio. We also had to train up our own young teachers urgently from the best ballet students in the intermediate group and work with the young beginners on the Russian Vaganova method of Classical dance. We enrolled so many beginner girls (aged sixteen to twenty) in the ballet section that we were forced to open two more beginners' groups after the Christmas holidays. In line with such great progress, I was forced to rent additional premises for a third classroom. Penny was frightened by the scale of the operation and the increased workload for her as the administrator. She tried to stop me, but the studio's growing success eclipsed my sensible commercial judgement (which, I have to admit, was zero). I was thinking more about how to create a Ballet company or international Folk stage Dance ensemble in the year to come, using the dancers I had trained. After all, that was the point of opening the school in the first place.

I continued to lead Character dance with intermediate groups at Les Grands Ballets Canadiens three times a week at this time. It was a creative outlet for me during the heavy demands in getting my new studio up and running. Every time Chiriaeff bumped into me in the evenings, she would ask about my 'baby', and give me some useful advice. Despite being much more overworked in her own academy than I was in mine, she still found the time and remembered to take an interest in how other people's ventures were doing. I was in awe of this noble lady and indomitable person of action.

My final graduates' performances in the Academy on Place-des-Arts that last summer were a resounding success. The Director paid tribute to me in public. She promised that she would pass on and recommend our studio to anyone who didn't get through the auditions for the Les Grands Ballets Canadiens. I really wanted to maintain my warm relationship with Chiriaeff. In spite of my reduced working hours with her, Ludmilla continued to invite me to her place. She sought my opinion on administrative and financial issues and internal staff relations. She was not an official trustee of Les Ballets Russes de Montréal, but regularly attended all the displays and meetings even so, and later the Ensemble premieres and Festival evenings. She was a genuine patron.

At the end of the first academic year, my teachers and I ran a series of open classes for our students' parents and children. We held a banquet to celebrate our first anniversary, inviting Federal and Provincial officials in the dance/ballet arena, including the management and stars of Les Grands Ballets Canadiens, the press/television etc. We demonstrated a specially devised half-hour programme of exercises and sequences from both sections of the studio. After this the guests moved into the other studio, where Penelope served them cakes and non-alcoholic drinks. To round things off, everyone learned Russian round dances accompanied by the accordion, sensitively directed by yours truly.

In the second half of July we opened our first summer course of intensive classes with international Masters experienced in European ballet: Classical dance (Vladimir Ukhtomsky, Les Ballets Russes de Monte Carlo); Ballet-jazz (Eva Von Genscy – founder of Les Ballets Jazz de Montréal); and Character dance (Mikhail Berkut, Les Ballets Russes de Montréal).

Thanks to the huge amount of publicity we had circulated in North and South America, many more delegates than expected signed up. Some probably came out of curiosity, as this was the first large-scale course of its kind in Montreal situated in a friendly, city-centre environment with excellent learning facilities. It was immaterial that even with two weeks of full classes we barely broke even. This helped us to show off big time our professional potential and the course delegates' creative spirit. It was, in fact, an excellent way to introduce our traditional international summer courses in future.

The studio's teaching and training programme, the staff's work regime and the organised structure of the enterprise, which were all established in the first year of business, had a lasting impact on the way Les Ballets Russes de Montréal operated later on. With increasing student numbers (over 400) we engaged proportionately more teachers, expanded the usable space through additional studios and extra premises, and improved the sound accompaniment for classes in contemporary technique, thereby enhancing the curriculum of studies with new vocal and instrumental interests. The school gradually became a Dance factory like the one I had seen in Paris with Maurice Béjart, the National Academy of Dance in Rome and other Ballet Centres. I invited the pre-eminent Masters from Europe and America to the traditional summer courses. Only Penny and I knew what all this cost us both physically and materially. Our reward was great spiritual satisfaction in our tangible, successful work together. Guest teachers included: classical, Andrei Kramarevsky, Bolshoi/New York City Ballet; modern, Edvard di Soto (Limon technique), professor at Boston Conservatoire; and tap, John Stanzel, Montreal Dance Company, director/ choreographer.

Progressive advances such as these required the management to be extremely well organised. It soon became clear that Penelope was overwhelmed by it. At the beginning, she had tried really hard, and was satisfied with what she achieved with her small workload. But as the business grew, the administration became too much for her. I realised that I wouldn't be able to put up with a critical gap like this for long.

I was losing patience. Moreover, my wife clearly had no interest in my creative dream to establish even a small Dance ensemble.

On the contrary, she asserted, "It's a complete waste of money, energy and time. Enjoy life, while you have the chance!"

In adopting this attitude, Penelope was effectively demonstrating our utter incompatibility as life partners working on the same team. In other words: we were at odds with each other. When she learned that I was renting additional premises for a third studio from the following season, she went into hysterics in the accounts office while other people were present, completely losing control of herself.

"Penny, calm down! I decided to hire you an assistant to deal with all these administrative and organisational issues. You will retain financial responsibility only and oversee all monies that are paid into the bank by the bookkeeper. Everything else will be done for you by your future assistant. All you have to do is to give her instructions accordingly.

"Misha, you're not being fair. Stop now before it's too late!"

This is how our professional, critical debates ended. I was in a hole and didn't know how to get out of it. I too was up to my ears in work. It was complete bedlam at home. I asked the school cleaner to clean our flat just once a week for extra cash. Penny had never done this in her life, as she had grown up in the care of a nanny. Neither of us had time to go shopping either. It was becoming all too clear that my wife was fed up with this chaotic life and was looking for a way to release herself from such hard labour. Our colleagues and students felt the lack of care/ managerial oversight and as always in these situations, discipline broke down.

Four candidates responded to the advertisement for an administrative assistant. My wife chose Caroline, who had some experience, and went through her duties with her. Caroline started work two months earlier than I had planned, purely to defuse the tension in the management team. Now Penny had more time for marketing, and correspondence with clients and agents. I asked her not to entrust financial control to Caroline under any circumstances, particularly where cash was concerned. My wife accused me of being insulting and suspicious of someone I didn't know, reminding me once again that we were not in Russia. Fortunately, in the mornings I led dance therapy at the same time as Mary: she worked with the intermediate students, while I worked with the beginners. Through the wide observational window in the corridor for visitors, I could also see (if I wanted to) what was going on in enrolment. I only trusted Penelope and Jean to receive cash payments when Zina, the registrar, was at lunch. But my wife overruled me and in the lunch hour, without telling her husband, she put Caroline in charge of registration. I was working at Les Grands Ballets Canadiens on these days, and was unaware of this.

We had visitors' books in all our classrooms, which were signed after each lesson by the teachers and their students. On the days I was not present, Penny would go to lunch with Zina and leave her assistant to collect the students' cash payments. I found out about this six months later, when Jean, while doing a financial report, picked up a discrepancy in the total payment for a class and the number of students attending, based on their signatures in the book. This was happening consistently at exactly the same time that Zina took her lunch break, on the days I was not around. The shortfall came to around 700 dollars, hardly enough to kick up a fuss. The main issue was the breakdown in trust between Penny and me, and Penny and Caroline. My wife was shocked and disappointed because it was now out in the open. Of course I sacked the unlucky assistant at this point. I had to talk to the administrator about this, and let her know how disappointed I was. I told Jean to deduct the sum missing from Caroline's final payment and return it to the studio's account.

At the beginning of the third season, as I had assumed, many new students signed up for different groups. So we had to engage further teachers/instructors: Helen and Daniel in classical and Pierre in jazz beginners. The last two had been pupils of ours, and had shown serious interest and exceptional teaching ability. In two years of regular instruction from Masters in the studio, they had achieved outstanding results, earning them respect as teachers of beginner students. However strange it may seem, it was more complicated to find someone to take my place for the morning dance-therapy classes. What was needed here was a particular training method in therapeutic movement for a wide range of older people and occasionally eccentric types from neighbouring institutions. There were also housewives who popped in for an hour to work on their figure or escape the chaos at home. Every day, including Saturdays, six groups, each with twenty to twenty-five students, ran in three studios from morning on. Remuneration from these classes made up 70% of the studio's income. One of these was a specialist class, which I had to run myself, not that I minded in the least.

Rue St Catherine was lined with numerous strip clubs, bars and restaurants. A few of them were opposite our building or next door. Girls there usually worked from 12 p.m. to 4 a.m. It was crucial for them to keep in good shape for their kind of work. The first season they came to us one by one to work out before their shift. Then the strippers formed a group and asked me to devise a bespoke programme for them, with more challenging exercises and a more intensive tempo/rhythm, every day (apart from Sundays) at 10 a.m. But they insisted that the course had to be delivered by a man, as lots of women with families and clients were hostile because of their profession. I was only too happy to agree to this 'punishment'. Meanwhile, in the evenings, while I was taking the men's class or rehearsing with male dancers, they would often hang around by the huge studio windows and take turns to stare through the windows of the building opposite at my morning students, showing off their naked bodies on the dining tables. Sometimes I had a job to tear my dancers away from the riveting, free floor show. Should they concentrate on my 'boring' displays or their, alas, clothed partners? I didn't get angry with the young men, as I could relate to their healthy male interest.

When we opened the third studio, students in the morning dance-therapy classes numbered over 450, all of whom had enrolled for two to three classes a week. Now they had three instructors, not counting me filling in as necessary. Keeping to our agreement, I carried on teaching one course for the strippers at 10 a.m. which was purely a kind of morning workout. Once I'd sacked the thieving assistant, I took on a professional administrator, Claudia, on a full-time basis. She turned out to be really experienced and skilled in business, including credit control. At her insistence I had to hire an additional registrar for the morning classes from 9 a.m. to 3 p.m. (without a lunch break) and move Zina from 3 p.m. to 9 p.m. to cover the evening classes and forthcoming productions and rehearsals in the dance ensembles. Penny got a promotion, becoming deputy studio director, with responsibility for monitoring the timetable of classes and her colleagues' work schedules.

As owner/president of a non-profit-making social enterprise, I was not entitled to receive a salary from the studio. On the advice of a private financial adviser, I had to register my own commercial company 'Berkut Dance Enterprises Inc.' in parallel with the school in 1977, which encompassed all my creative activity in Canada and the USA. Out of this I also paid all expenses for the studio: advertising, the flat, housekeeping, food, etc. Three years after starting the business, this came to a sizeable amount. I wondered if I should purchase a property or organise my trained artistes into an ensemble of European dance. Naturally I preferred the second option. I didn't say anything about this to my wife yet, as I knew how she would react. I opened a personal account in New York City Bank and transferred into it all my fees from the intensive courses and choreography I had done in USA universities and ballet schools. My financial adviser advised me to keep these earnings separate from the not-for-profit business in Montreal. I was obliged to register my teaching activity in the USA separately with the local tax inspectorate, to avoid any confusion in future.

In line with the creative aims of Les Ballets Russes de Montréal, laid down when the company was established, Caucasian students had to wait until the end of the second season to join the professional ensemble of Folk Stage Dance.

I was always careful never to promise future success to students as this depended mostly on their own abilities and dedication. Because of the acute shortage of male dancers of the right age and standard, I had to advertise a free course for young men of sixteen years and over, with secondary-level physical and musical skills for possible inclusion in a newly formed variety group. This brought in a few more candidates, but mostly of an older age group, twenty to twenty-five years old. I decided to name the future ensemble 'Kalinka' in honour of the universally popular Russian folk song, symbolising beauty, love and fertility.

Strange as it may seem, defining the Ensemble's dance component was easier with the male performers than the women. The publicity in the press for auditions had generated more young men than women. Nevertheless, by the end of the second season I had settled on the final version of the group:

Men's group: three Ukrainians, two Québecois, a Pole, a Georgian and an Armenian.

Girls' group: four Québecoises, two Ukrainians, a Russian and a Serb.

Two Russian folk singers: Alexander Zelkin (with a guitar) and Ludmilla Monina.

Compère: (singer and dancer) Michel Gravelin, Québecois.

Instrumental Sextet: two balalaikas, two accordions, a violin and a bass.

In this way, I achieved an international array of performers, who, on top of their basic professions, were also willing to take part in complex stage genres, performing harmoniously together.

Using this principle, each artiste in the ensemble effectively performed both as soloist and group member. In addition to singing to their own accompaniment on the guitar, like Sasha Zelkin did, the vocalists moved around the stage surrounded by dancing girls. Ludmilla performed poems in a duet with the compère, Michel, who would be playing on the bass balalaika at the same time, etc. The dancers moved swiftly from duets to trios to quartets and quintets. It was important and difficult not only to perform these complex, technical movements and patterns effectively, but to convey the particular authentic folk style of the relevant European nation. But the main thing I got out of my 'green' artists was this: emotional expression and acting ability in all their performances.

As soon as I had determined the final repertoire for the first programme, I signed a year's contract with a professional dressmaker to make multinational stage costumes for the dancers, and a regular uniform for the singers and musicians. I ordered clogs and dance shoes in different colours and shapes for the whole Kalinka group from a local shoe factory. Jean just about managed to pay the bills that came in for headdresses, body adornments, outfits, etc. Penny was still worried when she saw thousands of dollars leaving my bank account. But our costs on Kalinka did not end there. I wasn't able to accompany my own choreography on the accordion at all production rehearsals. I had to hire a permanent accordionist to provide musical accompaniment for the technical performance practice: Mary Abdel Malek and Pierre Hardy. They danced the leading parts from the repertoire themselves and taught Classical and Jazz in our studio. I was lucky that there was such a wealth of talent and devoted colleagues in Les Ballets Russes de Montréal among staff and students alike.

The Ensemble's musical director was Aurel Monolesko: a Romanian professor from Bucharest Conservatoire, and former dean of the Faculty of Folk Instruments. He was a fantastic musician, of Russian descent. He orchestrated Kalinka's whole programme for our instrumental sextet and played the first balalaika in it himself, as well as performing solos from the classical repertoire in the concert. Everyone in the ensemble worshipped this seventy-year-old musician for his purity of tone, expert professionalism, enormous patience with his (not always accurate) instrumentalists, and his personal good nature. The conductor and accordionist were part of the staff. The rest of the musicians, singers and répétiteurs worked on a sessional basis. The dancers received payment only for concert performances, as I was teaching them Folk Stage Dance technique and putting on productions for free. They could see for themselves where all the Ensemble's costs were going, and tried to complete the first programme as quickly and productively as possible.

Kalinka's repertoire in the main consisted of melodies from the Slav nations: Russia, Ukraine, Belarus, Poland, etc. But to make a stronger audio and visual impact on the audience, I also incorporated Gypsy and Moldovan motifs as a finishing touch. I even put in four pairs of comic 'Quebec Quadrilles' as an acknowledgement to my second homeland. Unexpectedly for the choreographer, this dance enjoyed huge success with local audiences, as it incorporated French folklore and factored in the specific characteristics of the Québecois. A musician sat at the edge of the proscenium arch. He played dance motifs on a mouth organ while simultaneously tapping out rhythms in the style of gigs on wooden clogs. The audience was in raptures of delight as this continued for five minutes. We often had to repeat this dance. The press was fulsome in its praise of Kalinka's premiere at the Centaur Theatre in old Montreal.

Linde Howe-Beck from *The Gazette* raved about our achievement, calling Kalinka the 'Mini Moiseyev Ballet'. This made happy reading, but we didn't actually deserve such plaudits. Naturally, compared to the primitive, amateur offerings in various municipal and national Canadian cities, we scored highly. But compared with artistic standards of ensembles in the Soviet Union, we had a long way to go. As we embarked on our creative development, it was crucial that we were potentially on the right path, and to believe that we had a future as a group. I persisted in rolling out the first programme all year in Ottawa, Quebec City, Toronto and other places on the tour. All free of charge, for publicity purposes. This took a lot out of me, understandably. Penny made no secret of her concern at the expenditure on costumes and shoes, travel and advertising. My financial adviser tried to explain to her that all of the ensemble's expenses, such as the stage practice for students from Les Ballets Russes de Montréal, were deducted from the general amount of income tax at the end of the financial year for non-profit-making organisations. Nevertheless, my wife felt that her husband was stealing from her. She made an official request to the province's Ministry of Culture, for a grant (subsidy) for Kalinka, in view of the young body of dancers from Quebec and the studio's non-profit-making status, but without success.

For those Kalinka artistes from other cities, I had to rent a large two-storey house (a former boarding house), not far from the studio, with eight individual rooms, four on each floor. There were two showers/toilets (separate for men and women). Everything was paid for by Les Ballets Russes de Montréal, because the one-off payments to artistes for rehearsals and performances at occasional concerts could not cover people's daily living expenses. Three months later, after sending another letter to the Quebec Government, Penny telephoned the Minister of Culture's office and asked for the outcome of her application for a grant for the Kalinka ensemble. A week later the response arrived with an attached copy of the letter she had sent, in which one word with an incorrect acute accent was underlined in red. 'Dear Mme. Berkut, prior to addressing the Province Governors to request a subsidy, please learn how to write properly in French.' My wife took this personal slap in the face very badly.

At the beginning of the 1980s, the Quebec separatists' activities were coming to a head. As a result of the outburst of chauvinistic activity of the francophones, a mass of English-speaking organisations, business and inhabitants moved to Ontario. I had no intention of leaving Montreal and tried my best to adapt to local national and political conditions. I paid special attention to my Quebec students and teachers. But I didn't consider it fair to discriminate against representatives of other nationalities or races. As a rule I related equally to all the studio's students and without exception, allocated their dance parts in composition strictly in line with their individual capabilities and physical attributes.

Kalinka extended its repertoire and gained more concert practice. It became too much for Mary, the répétiteur, to accommodate this work with teaching classical in the studio, as well as dancing solo miniatures in the ensemble herself: the Mazurka, Gypsy, Swan, etc. I personally was so wrapped up in my new choreography and growing business in my school, that to my great chagrin, I had to leave Les Grands Ballets Canadiens completely at the end of that season. Much more enjoyable were my creative trips to universities and ballet academies in the USA, the list of which had got significantly longer over the past year. Nevertheless, the situation in Kalinka forced me to recruit some help for Mary, in the shape of Sasha Kalinin, a former soloist from the Moscow ensemble Beryozka. He was extremely experienced as a Folk Stage Dance specialist and brought a wealth of expertise in strengthening the men in Kalinka. This enabled me to start work on a new programme for the Euro-Slavic repertoire: Bulgaria, Poland and Czechoslovakia. I had to enlarge the vocal-instrumental group accordingly with additional musicians and singers.

Now I could afford a professional impresario to organise more regular tours. Ludmilla Chiriaeff's husband, Juriel Liufft, agreed to take us into his family of ballet/dance companies touring North and South America. He signed a contract with us for a year. The impresario made a point of advising us for a third time to apply to the Quebec Government using his written recommendation, for a grant for the Kalinka ensemble, which comprised twenty-eight artistes. In anticipation of this grant, we performed free of charge at almost all social enterprises and festivals in the province throughout the following season. We were counting on the Ministry of Culture granting us the minimum possible subsidy at least this time. But our hopes were in vain. Liufft explained that this fiasco was due to a new wave of separatists, fighting for Quebec to separate from Canada and form a self-sufficient republic. For all the positive reviews of Kalinka's performances, the revenue from ticket sales did not cover the ensemble's touring costs. I plugged all the financial holes using the school's resources. Unfortunately I had to put our concert activity on hold temporarily and take care of producing the ensemble's new repertoire until I got some new funds into the studio's bank account.

In a year, our new administrator, Claudia, managed to increase the teaching and training organisation of both sections to such an extent that by the end of the season I was forced to rent and kit out a fourth studio on the same floor for 100-plus new students. With this came the need for a qualified teacher from the Russian School of Classical dance. All the more so because I had already selected candidates for the professional section of a future ballet miniatures ensemble. These six pairs of students had studied with us for four to five years and were sufficiently well trained for a contemporary choreographic repertoire: 'Mini Ballets Russes'. We couldn't find a suitable teacher/répétiteur for this project either in Toronto or in New York. I had to seek assistance from my old friend Lydia Joffe in Paris.

Lydia, having been involved with Soviet immigrants in Israel, knew everyone in the Tolstoy Foundation in Europe (whose original purpose was to help Russian refugees from Europe and the Soviet Union and, later, played an important role in helping Soviet displaced persons, dissidents and former Soviet citizens to settle in the West). After sampling Zionist charms, many of them tried to move to Western Europe or America. But the Jewish Agency for Israel, because of their 'betrayal', refused to help these people, and stuck the renegades in Italy (a staging post) without any prospects. Lydia, who was very well connected, helped ballet specialists to emigrate through personal invitations or contracts from official companies for work, even if they didn't have a passport, just using their birth certificates.

My first experience with Lydia in this regard came to a scandalous conclusion. Three years previously, when I had been looking for a teacher/répétiteur for Kalinka, she recommended to me over the telephone her Riga compatriot Bella Kovarskaya, who had fled from Jerusalem to Paris. With complete trust in Joffe's integrity, I drew up a work invitation through the Montreal branch of Manpower for her to come over, to work full-time at Les Ballets Russes de Montréal. I was forming a new company with a new group of semi-professional students, including a women's group from my future ballet miniatures ensemble. As it happened, Bella had previously taught Misha Baryshnikov in the Riga Ballet School. Using this to my advantage, I publicised her widely in both languages in the city's leading newspapers. I thanked the local Manpower agency for their help, and went to the airport with Penny to welcome our honoured guest with flowers. After waiting for an hour at the passengers' exit, Penny found out at the information desk that a female passenger from Paris, Kovarskaya, had arrived in Montreal fifty minutes earlier and without getting off the plane after landing, had continued her intended journey to Toronto, as per her ticket. Naturally I was shocked, but my wife simply laughed hysterically at my blunder.

When Lydia heard about the vulgar deceit perpetrated by her close friend and Latvian compatriot, she was really upset. She apologised, begging me over the telephone to give her another chance to find me a worthwhile candidate. But I reassured her, promising that I would take her up on her kind offer another time. Three years later Joffe was happy to make amends for this cock-up by recommending a ballet teacher. Hearing that I needed a men's specialist to rehearse choreographic miniatures in Montreal, she got in touch with the Tolstoy and Catholic Foundations in Rome. Both of these were social organisations who differed from Manpower in that they helped Soviet refugees of any nationality to emigrate to Australia or America. I received from them the personal files of several candidates for the post of men's ballet teacher in my studio.

Having studied the information carefully, I settled on Victor Litvinov from the Odessa Opera Theatre. I telephoned Silve Valter, and Natasha Karabach, famous ballerinas in Odessa, who were classmates of mine from thirty years previously. I got all the personal and professional details that I needed from them. I then telephoned Anna Davidovna in Rome and asked her to make enquiries in the Tolstoy Foundation about Victor and his family. It soon became apparent that, like many others trying to escape the Soviet straitjacket, he, as a Russian, had married a Jewish woman in a sham wedding. As you can expect, on his way to the wonderful West, his travelling companion fell pregnant. Now in her seventh month of pregnancy, Dora was having to fly halfway across the planet. All the reports from Odessa confirmed Victor as a talented and competent dancer, a sharp and persistent character. He occasionally assisted répétiteurs, and stood in for the troupe's teacher. He had carved a good living for himself in private ballet schools in Italy.

After the incident with Bella Kovarskaya, I met Litvinov and his wife at the airport, without any flowers this time. Yes! Once bitten, twice shy. We went with an emigration official to the hotel and leaving the tired Dora there, then paid a visit to the Manpower agency. I signed all the necessary documents for Victor to work and hurried back to the studio. This time there was no publicity or fuss. The next day I introduced Litvinov to his new colleagues at Les Ballets Russes de Montréal. I went through his conditions of employment and salary. Keeping things on a business footing, we signed a contract for the current season. I explained that I was not in a position to offer him a full timetable at my place. However, if he settled in well and took up my help in adding to his knowledge on methodology for teaching Contemporary Classical dance in school, as well as acting as professional répétiteur for the Ballet miniatures, I would be happy to recommend him for work with my colleague Ludmilla Chiriaeff, director of Les Grand Ballets Canadiens.

Victor was seriously impressed with the scale of Les Ballets Russes de Montréal, but understood perfectly well that he was dealing with non-professionals. Still, I had to put the reins on his ambition in the intermediate classes, as he wanted to show off his skills. I have to admit that he did take heed of my comments as a more experienced teacher, and repeatedly affirmed in his practice the value of the advice he'd received. Dora was an intelligent mother-to-be and a good-natured woman. She realised that sooner or later her husband would lose interest in her, surrounded by young ballerinas. He was not yet thirty when he became father to a beautiful baby boy. Dora's sister and her family lived in New York, and invited her to stay. She went to visit her sister with her Canadian travel document, and never returned to Montreal.

As promised, I set Victor up in Les Grands Ballets Canadiens to teach morning classes in the troupe. Chiriaeff visited to watch his class with my semi-professionals. Once this was finished, she invited the candidate to give a trial class with her ballet artistes. As a result she offered Litvinov a short-term trial contract for six months in the New Year. Ludmilla was treading carefully in view of the language barrier. If they could overcome the communication difficulties, the Director promised a longer engagement with a full schedule, including rehearsals for the traditional repertoire. My protégé was satisfied with his workload at this stage. He would be with Chiriaeff in the mornings, and with me after lunch. He established a good working relationship with Mary Abdel Malek, through sharing responsibility for senior-group students and evening Choreographic Miniature rehearsals.

Once I'd come through the creative process of setting up Kalinka, I turned my anxious sights and thoughts to staging a Contemporary Mini Ballets Russes. I knew full well that this idea was much more involved than creating a Folk Stage Dance Ensemble. It would take considerably more time and energy to pull it off in a non-professional school setting, teaching Contemporary ballet dancers with varying standards of physical capabilities and musicality and level of technical training using unspecified teaching systems in the past. Even though I wasn't planning to include female performers on pointes in my choreography, Mary and I had to spend a long time patiently selecting nine girls, no older than twenty, from the top students in her class. They had to work with guys in close physical contact during Partnering training practice. *Dancing Dolls* to music by Shostakovich, Prokofiev, Debussy, Villa-Lobos and other 'avant-garde' composers from that period required contrasting qualities from performers in 'free motion', expressing 'extravagant adagio' or 'grotesque allegro' moods. Four years of intensive classes with Mary and me, even with all the progress made by the Intermediate students, was not enough to bring it off successfully and secure the Mini Ballets Russes project. I had to postpone *Dancing Dolls* for another year because of the need to find a male teacher/répétiteur for both ensembles and a further men's section.

With Litvinov's arrival, both specialists perfected their Contemporary dance technique for performers in the choreographic miniatures during classes and rehearsals. For my part, as well as teaching them how to master 'Pas de deux' in my Partnering classes on Sundays, I also gradually introduced future artistes to their role and the proposed repertoire's inherent character, to avoid shocking the novices with the strange 'neoclassical' style of free movement, which was in stark contrast to traditional ballet-course exercises. All seven young men (twenty to twenty-three years of age) took regular classical lessons: the first years were with me, then with Litvinov, and they made fairly successful progress. But two of them were gay and unwilling to work with girls in my Partnering classes. Initially I directed a look of consternation in their direction. Learning that this was part of their natural make-up and principal position in the studio, I warned them both: "Either you . . . or . . . !" The guys got my drift and totally changed their attitude towards their female partners. I didn't want to give them a lecture on morals or highlight their sexual orientation. The girls were much stronger than the boys, both technically and emotionally. Although they were younger than the lads, they were intelligent and sufficiently sexually mature to handle them. This made it easy for all of us. In two years of practice with them, they became so physically strong and got so used to each other that I had absolutely no doubts about the work in future.

In the ballet concert *Dancing Dolls*, each performer is a soloist in line with their own ability, taking part in three or four miniature compositions: solo, duet, trio, etc. This kind of stage work was much more complex and carried more responsibility than dancing in several group appearances in a full three-act ballet, where the audience's attention is dissipated by easily replaceable characters in multidimensional action. Moreover, in *Dancing Dolls*, most of the costumes were close-fitting tights/leotards, with different coverings depending on the character. This kind of attire makes it impossible to conceal inaccuracies in body motion and poses or errors in movement, which are covered by character costumes. So Mary and Victor had to repeat the fundamental details and complex sequences over and over with the artistes in their solo/duet performances, to build their confidence and make them physically secure in more precise delivery of the miniatures' spiritual and graphic content. We were happy to see these charges improving their technical competence and artistry before our very eyes. I noticed more than once how difficult it was in those final minutes to change outfits and make the transformation from a Cat to a Prince or from a Princess to an Ugly Duckling and so on. Nevertheless, thanks to the répétiteurs, the results of their efforts looked promising.

The music for *Dancing Dolls* by genial composers such as Dmitri Shostakovich and Claude Debussy naturally enough demanded particular attention from the choreographer in terms of tempo/rhythm and dynamics as well as meter and phrasing. It was crucial for the choreography to reflect accurately the genre and style of the musical work, and to follow precisely the composer's direction in the main and supporting leitmotif, so as not to offend the memory of these great musicians through lack of professional courtesy. Putting together the entire choreographic outline for the given subject or episode in keeping with the composition's musical structure was extremely complex. It goes without saying that it's difficult to teach inexperienced performers quickly to capture the subtle rhythms and sounds of Contemporary symphonic music, and to convey these to the audience through their personal prism of emotion, using expressive choreographic movement. But they were so enthusiastic about the instruction I gave them on infusing their stage interpretation with everyday feelings and emotions to produce an interactive art form, that I was pleasantly surprised at every production rehearsal. By the same token, they forced the choreographer to sharpen up his creative criteria in appraising his continual corrections and wishes.

We celebrated the studio's fifth season with the premiere of *Dancing Dolls* in the European Drama Theatre, in honour of the company's New Year run. The show ran for children twice a day all through the Christmas holiday week. The press and public gave the fledgling Mini Ballets Russes a warm reception. Ludmilla Chiriaeff congratulated all the artistes in the Contemporary Ballet on their successful debut and invited me to lunch at her house on Sunday. There, with some distress, she told me that she and Juriel Liufft were getting divorced, which meant that both ensembles would be losing their impresario, as he was involved with Kalinka and Mini Ballets Russes at his former wife's insistence. Still, I persisted in expanding the repertoire of Choreographic Miniatures, now based on Rakkmaninor's 'Musical Moments'. I tried to keep the dancers in top ballet shape and maintain their creative enthusiasm at production rehearsals for the new programme: twelve miniatures on motifs from international popular tales and *bylinas* (Russian traditional heroic poems). Fortunately, the costumes were relatively inexpensive.

Litvinov did not last at Les Grands Ballets Canadiens. He had clearly overestimated the professional level of their Classical dancers, who had been trained in unspecified/mixed methods of Cecchetti and Vaganova and were unaccustomed to the Russian regime of work both in class and at rehearsals.

I advised him: "Less is more! It'll be easier for everyone this way."

The early days as an immigrant drained my energy and patience too as I adapted to local customs and requirements at the ballet. I would often remark: "When in Rome, do as the Romans do. Even more so when it comes to the arts."

In the aim of keeping Victor on for his evening classes and rehearsals with the young men, I recommended him to Eva Von Genscy, my jazz ballet teacher (she actually founded the Canadian Ballet Jazz Troupe) on the next floor up in our building. Victor worked there in the mornings and adjusted really well to their simple requirements in classical form.

Keeping things simple with my Kalinka singers and dancers, I also didn't want to lose any dancers. So on my free days I continued to put onstage folk compositions with them from the East European Slav nations: Bulgaria, Poland, Czechoslovakia and others. My creative choreography was a powerful distraction from the studio's commercial affairs. Claudia, the administrator, who worked mornings, frequently warned her relief worker, Zina, about delays or missing payments for classes. 'While the cat's away, the mice will play,' as the wise folk saying goes. As studio Director, I should have been, but was unable, to keep a constant watch on the business because of my frequent trips away on seminars. Penny generally took a 'devil may care' view of her business obligations in her capacity as deputy director. I had to ask the administrator and bookkeeper to check that student payments were up to date for classes in both sections of the studio.

There was a massive shortfall in our income. Roughly twenty students were in the class, but only about half of them were listed as having paid for this lesson. It turned out that apart from those who paid monthly, the cash in the till at the end of the day came to a lot less than the amount invoiced. The bookkeeper calculated the daily losses as averaging 35% of the cash in the till, which happened only during the afternoon classes. Zina, the administrator, was in her early twenties, and in her youthful inexperience had become overfamiliar with clients of her age in Les Ballets Russes de Montréal, mixing business with pleasure. Inevitably, dishonourable course attendees took advantage of the lack of control in the system and breached payment regulations unimpeded. I had a serious conversation with Zina. I warned her that if there were any further infringements of discipline in the workplace, she would face dismissal, irrespective of my long-standing friendship with her father (the owner of the Moscow Restaurant). I was a useless businessman.

It was as if Fortune had turned her back (and possibly her nether regions too) on me. Litvinov advised me that at the end of the season he would be moving to New York to be with his family. So I started looking in various places for a suitable replacement. The best prospects seemed to be in Toronto. I got in touch with Mary Aslamazovaya, a compatriot from Odessa Ballet School, who'd opened her own studio in the city centre a few years earlier. She told me about two possible candidates from 'Peter' (Leningrad), and invited me to come and stay at her place. Mary's husband ran a huge factory/bakery, supplying Canada and the USA with several varieties of fresh and frozen bread. At my request Otto took me to his business to demonstrate to the choreographer how to set up and run a successful private business. I was impressed, and very grateful to Otto for his useful advice on managing a production run. He suggested that even if I had complete faith in my staff, I should double-check their work as a matter of course, to avoid any surprise losses.

Unfortunately, neither candidate met the specific requirements of Les Ballets Russes de Montréal. But then I was lucky enough to meet Shegelman in Toronto. Semyon showed me his new canvases, which were really impressive. Just like the first time we had met in Winnipeg, I felt great respect for this great artist. I invited him to visit me when he came to Montreal, where he would enjoy greater recognition as an avant-garde artist among aficionados of fine art. I promised to promote him to the exhibition organisers at the European Cultural Centre within the drama theatre. He furnished me with some brochures about his exhibitions, photo albums and printed reviews.

On my return to Montreal, I resolved that come what may, I would regain control over my business. I held a formal meeting with my financial and administrative staff. Penny refused to attend, so as not to get into an argument with me in public. One way or another, I got across to Zina that I was unhappy with her negligence in the workplace, and needed all three of them to maintain formal relations with the students on studio premises in particular, with the exception of national festivals and special work-related celebrations.

The bookkeeper smiled: "Misha, are you thinking of turning Ballets Russes into Gulag Russe?"

"No, Jean. I just want there to be professional relationships between staff and clients, as you would find in any establishment worth its salt. I'm really sorry that the Deputy Director is not present."

In actual fact, Penny had down-tooled, and didn't want to do anything at home or at school. She considered, with some justification, that I was throwing all the profits from the business with my dance ensembles to the wind, and she didn't want any part in this. Her attitude towards me had repercussions both at home and at work. She felt justified in going off to Ottawa by herself for a week, or not coming home at night in Montreal. She had clearly had enough of marriage in general, and of our business in particular. My wife made this obvious wherever and whenever she could. I realised that she was provoking me to react like a bull, so that we would split up. But at that time, in mid-season, I didn't see this as viable. Playing the patience card, I decided to distract her from her constant nihilism with something that would be of interest to her. She had often mentioned how unhappy she was at not having her own car, like other respectable people, as it was essential in her personal life as well as work. My short-sightedness meant that I was not fit to drive, and Penny was frightened of the speed on the motorways. Nevertheless, I persuaded her to take her driving test so that she too could become a 'respectable person'.

My deputy committee chairman at Les Ballets Russes de Montréal, Sergei Kozlovsky, offered me his services in selecting and purchasing a car. He had his own real-estate business and was a brilliant negotiator. On his recommendation, we bought a Chevrolet station wagon: a ten-seater minibus, which was even suitable for sleeping in and for transporting stage costumes, props and so on. Once my wife had got her driving licence, Kozlovsky took charge of her driving practice. I must confess that I was a little worried by this development, as my friend Sergei was a notorious ladies' man in the city, and very popular with women.

Having an extremely jealous nature, I made a point of warning my love consultant: "If you sleep with Penelope in my new car, I'll cut your balls off and let the dogs eat them and force you to take her into your harem forever."

My 'knight's move' worked. The deputy director of Les Ballets Russes de Montréal relished her new role as chauffeur and resumed her office duties on a temporary basis.

I was forced to take the night train to New York in my urgent search for a male teacher/répétiteur. I stayed at Nina and Volodya Keen's (friends from Rome) in a huge residential complex for people working in the arts, right in the centre of Manhattan. I visited Andrei Kramarevsky, my regular teacher for summer courses at Les Ballets Russes de Montréal. Of all the Russian colleagues he knew in New York, he recommended Anatoly Aristov in the first instance, a former dancer with a branch of the Bolshoi Theatre. Andrei's protégé made a positive impression on me. He had recently emigrated to the USA in the middle of the theatre season, and urgently needed a job.

It was a risk, taking him to Montreal without checking him out first. In the morning, I left Tolya relaxing in the lodgings and by the evening I was waiting for the outcome of his taster class with artistes from Mini Ballets Russes. He appeared looking very arty with a claret, satin gown draped over his shoulders, which he threw theatrically on to his chair while bowing to the expectant dancers. Without any prompting from me, they responded with a classical group curtsey. Aristov was, in fact, an experienced teacher.

I introduced him to my colleagues, showed him around the studio and signed a six-month trial contract with him, to include the traditional summer courses. The last ones had been hugely successful as always, thanks to widespread marketing and a really well-organised teaching system, with diligent leadership from the management. Having burned my fingers in the past, when guest teachers took up sexual relationships with sixteen-year-old students, I gave the school visitors a severe warning about this kind of criminal behaviour, which would result in instant dismissal. I didn't fancy having to deal with the Quebec police and wanton girls' furious parents.

The sixth season of Les Ballets Russes de Montréal took off on a massive wave of learning and creativity. Twelve teachers were working full- or part-time on a range of genres. Students in four classrooms generally exceeded 700. A team of five administrative staff looked after the various courses. The financial return was correspondingly positive. I continued, assisted by Kalinin as répétiteur, on my East European programme of national dances for the Kalinka ensemble, and on the new contemporary classical range of international subjects in the mini ballet company, with Anatoly Aristov as my assistant. I made Mary chief répétiteur of both groups and the studio's deputy artistic director during my frequent business trips to American courses and choreographic productions.

Every day apart from Sunday, Mary and Anatoly alternately gave a general class for professional dancers at 10 a.m. During the winter holidays these teachers were overwhelmed with matinee performances, but they were still duty-bound to give the morning class to keep the dancers in physical shape.

The day after the traditional Christmas celebrations, Aristov was due to give the lesson in keeping with the timetable. That morning, Valya, the pianist, telephoned from the studio to report that he had not arrived. Concerned about Anatoly's health, I popped into his place on my way to school. But he wasn't answering the doorbell. Recognising me, the warden went to fetch the keys, to find out what had happened to his tenant. Aristov had not bargained for this. Opening the door to his rented flat, we found the greatly respected teacher in bed with one of his students from the studio – who must have been seventeen at the most.

To my mind, no further comment was needed other than: "What the hell are you doing? How are we going to get through this?"

I hurtled off to school to cover for Anatoly, to find Mary already leading the artistes on behalf of her wayward colleague. Aristov was sacked that same day, and given a bus ticket back to New York with no payment in lieu of notice for breach of contract. Still, Jean gave him his final December salary with a note from me as to the reason: 'Dismissed for amoral conduct, i.e. sexual relations with an underage student from the school.' By her own choice, his young partner withdrew from the course she had paid for, without any fuss, to spare herself negative moral judgment from her classmates. I got one more lesson out of my former townsman from the Soviet Union, and fortunately there were no criminal repercussions or scandal on the part of the girl's parents. Yet again I found myself without a men's teacher/répétiteur at the height of the season. I had to ask Mary to split the dismissed assistant's duties with me to cover the New Year's shows and rehearsals with Mini Ballets Russes artistes. Fortunately, she knew the whole repertoire and never let me down. Our friendship continued within the boundaries of our work at the studio.

Penny's next phase of depression and drinking had taken hold. In winter she couldn't use the car in Montreal due to the abundant snow and ice on the roads. Our relationship was stretched to breaking point again. Once more, I started searching for another diversion for her, to relieve the loneliness she felt at not having her husband to go for walks with, or see shows or symphony concerts. I'd saved a substantial amount of money in my New York bank account from my university courses in the USA. For a long time, I'd dreamed of buying a holiday apartment in Florida for Penny and me to use in the winter and summer holidays. After completing the next intensive course in Birmingham, Alabama, I went to Florida to check out flats for sale near St Petersburg beach. They were in a luxury, gated complex, with a yacht and tennis club on the waterfront. The apartments were on the fifth and sixth floors in that block, about forty metres from the water. The luxurious interior comprised two bedrooms, a sitting room, dining room, up-to-date kitchen, separate toilet and bathroom with shower. A balcony encircled the entire apartment, which occupied the whole floor. There were four separate blocks, each with its own swimming pool, jacuzzi, and tennis court. The club restaurant was housed in a further block. There were two volleyball and basketball courts, a fully equipped gym and so on. A collection of yachts belonging to various people was moored by the estuary. In other words, it was a veritable holiday paradise.

The agent persuaded me to buy both flats with the aim of letting one long-term to cover the costs for both. The initial instalment for each flat was 175,000 dollars, plus payments totalling 350,000 dollars over five years. In total it came to 525,000 dollars for each apartment. My head was spinning from these kinds of figures. Still, I didn't want to lose such an opportunity and signed up for both apartments there and then. I hoped that a surprise like this would make Penny happy on her birthday, and reignite her interest in our business. I signed an apartment over to each son in my will.

CHAPTER 5 PEDAGOGICAL HIGHS

Once the American students had returned home from their first summer course at Les Ballets Russes de Montréal, news of its success soon spread throughout North America. Penny started getting calls and letters enquiring about the possibility of my coming to deliver two week-long courses in dance education. Basically, there were three different types of institution which wanted intensive, experimental programmes:

1. Private dance studios and professional schools attached to Ballet companies.
2. Semi-professional Folk Stage Dance ensembles of different nationalities.
3. Dance departments in Performing Arts Faculties in colleges/universities.

Each of these made different demands of their guest master in line with their students' requirements, depending on their spiritual and physical interests in dance, elementary musical and technical training, and innate abilities in movement.

Out of the five teaching disciplines within my gift, the most popular in the USA and Canada were: Character, Partnering and Methodology in Choreographic Composition. Historical dance (Court dancing) formed part of the production cycle of theatre repertoire in opera/ballet and drama performances with a court component. I only gave classical lessons in ballet schools, and even that was a compromise, as American dancers were generally schooled in the Cecchetti system rather than Vaganova. So it stood to reason that the Americans had their own classical teachers and did not need me for this. Character and Duet technique were the most popular subjects on all my courses. Here I was universally regarded as something of an expert, as there were simply no other method specialists in these 'pearls' of Terpsichore. Qualified partners from ballet companies were usually invited to the 'Pas de deux' course, and they were only too happy to enhance their technique during my choreography workshop.

The initial format of my intensive courses in North America as guest teacher/choreographer of various genres, was a mix of disadvantaged permanent students from ballet schools and private studios. Dancers both young and not so young would start learning or perfecting their standard in the duet and Character syllabus in the mornings (after a Classical lesson/warm-up). In the second half of the day, they worked with me on choreography for Contemporary miniatures or Folk Stage compositions. Each session was four hours long including fifteen-minute breaks. In the evenings, I would plan the morning session with the eager students. To round off the intensive course, we showed off our achievements to the management in an open performance. By repeating this annually, we systematically improved the standard of performance within the given time in both genres of dance art, i.e. technique as well as artistic expression. The best examples of these courses were at: Boston Ballet School, Perry Dance Studios (New York), Quaint Dance Centre (Toronto), Les Sortilèges (Montreal) and the like.

Other creative activity outside of Les Ballets Russes de Montréal included production and rehearsal sessions with Folk Stage Dance ensembles and drama theatres. Naturally, before starting the choreographic process in both cases I first had to prepare the dancers for technical/stylistic performance of this or that national folklore, as well as preparing the actors to express the spiritual form through rhythmic body pliability that corresponded to the specifics of the dramatic scene and theatre director's production. The more initial preparation I did with the dancers and actors, the better they – and my chances of success on the stage – were all together. Among the talented and successful theatre groups with which

I enjoyed real creative satisfaction were: Seagal Drama Theatre (Canada) and the Neva Dance Ensemble, as well as Tamburiza Dance (USA), Mazeppa and Kasatka Cossacks (UK).

However, the trips to the USA on intensive two-to-three-week courses in universities and colleges held the greatest interest and significance for me. Here, in contrast with other courses, I not only shared the secrets of dance pedagogy and choreographic composition with students, but gained useful academic learning myself for my future research in the field of social and cultural anthropology. Students in these educational establishments learned their craft at the highest professional level: teacher, art historian, dance-therapy instructor, and choreographer were further course options. For students like these, I had devised a teaching programme to suit their dance profile while still in the Soviet Union. Over twelve days, the course delegates attended daily six-hour intensive classes, gaining general knowledge and basic skills in the aesthetic nature of dance, performance technique, prompts for emotional expression and general methods and principles for choreographic composition in the children's repertoire. The following year we moved on to a more complicated programme of theoretical and practical classes with the same group, including principles of analysis in assimilating new material. Then I repeated the same two-year cycle with the next third-year students from the same universities/colleges such as: Northern Illinois University, Bay San Francisco, Birmingham Southern, and Hamilton New York.

A large number of those who attended my touring courses came annually to the summer courses at Les Ballets Russes de Montréal. We maintained our creative links over many years, which was a great honour for me in my quest to educate young dancers and teachers in aesthetics. At those same regular courses in America I had the good fortune to come into contact with several leaders of ballet schools and university dance departments. In turn, I invited them to deliver summer courses in Montreal, returning their hospitality in my own home. Mira Popovich, Marian Roth and Andrei Kramarevsky all occupied a special place in my creative life. Mira ran the Dance Department at Birmingham University, and was Yugoslavian by birth. The former prima ballerina with Belgrade Opera had the rare gift of being both a talented performer and a competent teacher. Her innate wisdom, decisiveness and patience helped the immigrant from the European socialist bloc to reach exceptional heights in the professional education of capitalist America's future dance luminaries.

I knew that most of Alabama's inhabitants were black people who had emigrated from Africa eons ago. I was used to being with Negroes as in Moscow I had often visited the Patrice Lumumba University, where thousands of black African students studied Russian for one to two years initially, before enrolling in the capital's higher-educational establishments. The purpose of my visits and getting acquainted with them, as an MTA student, was to gather information on the folk dances from different nations of Africa. These visits were strictly managed by the Moscow Centre of International Friendship, and the Specialist Department within MTA. In the Soviet Union I had heard and read a great deal about racial discrimination in the USA, but didn't believe Soviet propaganda about the vices of the capitalist world. Still, when I decided, as I always did when visiting other states, to go for a walk around Birmingham town after work, to check out the local architecture and how people lived, Mira cautioned me that I'd be better off staying at home.

On Sunday, a colleague took me into the city centre to show me the sights. I expected the streets to be full of tourists at the weekend, but there were only a few people out in the state capital. There were no white faces to be seen apart from Mira's and mine, and a few of Asian descent. At a car park near the hotel, cars with their windows smashed caught our eye. I was shocked.

"Misha, 90% of the population of Alabama is black, including the government, police, etc. In their eyes, any white visitor from elsewhere, is a racist in disguise. The cars with smashed windows have number plates from out of the area. Don't worry, your life is not in danger while you are with me, as I have a special badge on my coat, indicating that I am not an outsider, and have a position in this state."

"But, darling, this is the same kind of discrimination, just the other way round."

"There are lots of white professors in our university who have acclimatised to these unusual conditions, and don't consider themselves either morally or physically restricted."

"I have never encountered any problems with Negroes previously either. On the contrary, I always use them as examples of the most capable people in music, dance and sport. But to accuse all whites universally of racism, and take revenge on them for what's happened in the past – this is inherently incorrect, and means that they have become blatant racists themselves. The more they drum it into the innocent party, that he is a thief and a bandit, the more they will leave him no other option in the final account, than to start thieving and robbing, i.e. to become the person they take him for."

"I agree. Any extremism on both sides just snowballs. That's how all our problems and wars begin. Unfortunately, it's virtually impossible to put a stop to this antagonism."

The discussion with Mira Popovich left an indelible memory in my creative life.

I got to know Marian Roth at my summer courses in Montreal. She stood head and shoulders above the other course delegates, due to her exceptional talents. An undergraduate student at Northern Illinois University, she offered me her services on a voluntary basis as my assistant with the beginners' character course, in the interests of gaining some teaching practice. Once she was back in Chicago, Marian was one of the first to organise an invitation for me from her university to deliver an intensive course in the Methodology of Choreography. From then on, I worked successfully in the Theatre Faculty there for several years to come. When she had completed her higher education, Marian took up a post as teacher/répétiteur in the Neva Dance Ensemble in San Francisco. A short while later I received an invitation from them to choreograph a dance programme from my character repertoire. A small group of eighteen dancers had formed a semi-professional group of performers of assorted ages and qualification levels. With Marian's help, I managed to satisfy the creative requirements of a broad range of choreographic compositions and receive compliments from the ensemble management and artistes at the final demonstration.

I felt that my younger colleague was dissatisfied with her work in the ensemble, and I advised her to set up her own studio, as I had done in Montreal. She told me about her long-held dream of opening a children's studio, but didn't know where to start. I gave her a detailed consultation, to thank her for her selfless support as my assistant. In reciprocal gratitude, she planted a kiss on my cheek. I removed her kiss from my cheek and placed it on my chest. It was lovely to hear the sound of a young woman's laughter. To tell you the truth, I was very fond of Marian and often sensed that she had feelings for me. But my principal role as her personal patron prevented me from entering into an intimate relationship, taking advantage of human weaknesses on both sides. I was genuinely happy that we were able to maintain a warm, platonic friendship.

I have to confess to being favoured by Fortune, who, during the time I was emigrating to North America, had given me a true friend and companion in Andrei Kramarevsky, an artiste and teacher at New York City Ballet. Of course, I knew him by sight from the stage back in Moscow in the 1950s, as one of the Bolshoi's leading soloists, and then, after his retirement as a teacher/répétiteur of touring dancers with Russian Concerto (the republic's Philharmonic Society). But he and I only got to know each other on a personal level in Rome when we were emigrating. Like me, he was waiting for his visa to America, and working temporarily in private schools in Italy.

I was astonished at how extremely modest this specialist was, and asked him:

"Andrei, why didn't you apply to the Rome Opera Theatre?"

"I didn't want to give them false hope, as New York City Ballet were already expecting me."

I thought he was joking: "Didn't Balanchine have enough of his own staff then?"

"Of course not, there are lots of specialists in America, but not like there are in Russia."

"In that case, I wish you all the best from the bottom of my heart. See you again on the other side of the world!"

A year later I visited New York, met up with Kramarevsky, and invited him to my summer course at Les Ballets Russes de Montréal. I promoted the famous master widely, and had him to stay with me. Every holiday he came to teach the advanced ballet class, which was always phenomenally successful. Professionals came on Kramarevsky's course from Ottawa, Toronto and other nearby cities. As a rule, dancers would give him a standing ovation at the end of every lesson.

Andrei and I enjoyed an easy understanding with each other. We each had a handle on the other's capabilities and shortcomings, and were never conceited or disdainful about them. For many years to come, we retained our respect and trust in each other, despite the repeated attempts of schemers in the ballet world to drive a wedge between us out of envy with their sordid tittle-tattle and slander. But we never gave in to their provocation.

"Misha, don't take it to heart! Just hang in there!" my senior colleague liked to say.

Kramar (as he was known in the United States), still taught and continued to dance mime roles aged eighty in the New Year's performances for children: Dr Coppélius in the Delibes ballet *Coppélia*, or the Master of Ceremony in Tchaikovsky's *The Nutcracker*. George Balanchine had studied with Andrei's father in the Bolshoi Theatre's ballet class. When he heard that his oldest friend's son had emigrated, he sent a secret invitation to Moscow for Kramar to visit New York City Ballet once he got to the United States. When he met Balanchine (*the* Balanchivadze himself, brother of the famous Georgian composer), he offered the new immigrant the opportunity to give a trial class for the troupe's soloists.

After tumultuous applause from the artistes at the end of the lesson, the New York City Ballet's Artistic Director announced happily: "Andryusha, I've been waiting for you for fifty years. Say thank you to your father for the recommendation."

This was no hyperbole, but rather, the great choreographer acknowledging sadly how much he missed Russian style and technique in Classical dance. Andrei soon established his reputation as a master with the school's intermediate classes and professional lessons for the troupe's soloists before the start of the working day in the theatre. He was a man of incredible willpower and self-control, with good judgement, a high level of optimism, and decency in his dealings with people which disarmed his main enemies in the bohemian world of the theatre. I learned a great deal from him in the early days while I was establishing myself. He was an immigrant/teacher with a different approach to teaching in a foreign country; leader of a large-scale Ballet establishment; a consummate diplomat with regard to envious detractors from the Soviet Union and local chauvinists. I am really proud of my creative collaboration with Andrei and our genuine friendship over more than forty years.

As I leaf through the pages in my head of all the courses and productions I delivered in the United States, I smile when I recall the funniest situations which happened to me as I began my ascent of any unfamiliar, steep incline of knowledge. These were all just light-hearted tragicomic impromptus, many of which took place during my initial trips to new places of work in American locations. I got my first invitation for a tour from the managers of Boston Ballet School, to run a two-week course in the first half of August 1977, covering Classical and Character dance. There were four courses of each in a day. They put me up in the apartment belonging to Violetta Verdi (the ballet's artistic director), who was away on holiday in Paris at the time.

On the first day, I got home late from the theatre after the show, and went straight to bed. Early the next morning, following my customary exercises in my underpants on the balcony, I decided to check whether there was anything to eat in the kitchen. Opening the door, I saw three Siamese cats in three wicker baskets on three small cupboards by the wall.

Naturally I was surprised, but greeted them courteously. They responded as one, lazily raising their beautiful heads and staring at me with contempt: 'What kind of hairless animal is this, with his primitive pants on but no bra?'

I trod carefully but kept my eyes fixed on them. I opened the door of the fridge alongside and pulled out a bottle of milk and a piece of bread. I had just turned around to leave, when, *oh, mamma mia!*

The three cats were standing in a semicircle before me, baring their teeth, their backs arched threateningly, and making evil growling noises, ready to attack the solitary, almost naked mouse. I admit that my hairs were standing on end all over my body. The hunk of bread and bottle of milk were shaking feverishly in my hands. *They're thinking that I've invaded their territory and nicked their beloved milk.* The thought struck me at lightning speed, but the beautiful creatures took their squealing and growling up a tone, waiting for me to react. Then it dawned on me! Once upon a time I used to do a good impersonation of various bird and animal sounds. I growled back at the attacking monsters, gnashing my teeth in exactly the same way, which then caught *them* off guard, pricking up their ears and not understanding who this person in front of them was with two trembling extremities. This one-second pause was enough for me to jump through the doorway and slam it shut with my foot. It's a miracle I didn't soil my pants in a situation this stressful.

Then at school, when I explained why I was late to the Director at the morning meeting, the teachers inexplicably burst into hysterical laughter, almost wetting themselves.

From the day after for the next two weeks, every morning different colleagues would ask me, while trying not to laugh: "Maestro, what did you do last night? Did you get the better of those Siamese beauties this time?"

I decided to wipe the slate clean after this shameful event, and after the final course assessment, I invited my good-humoured colleagues to a farewell lunch at the steak house, to celebrate my debut. I also brought along Penny, and my close friend, the deputy chairman of Les Ballets Russes de Montréal, Sergei Kozlovsky, so that I could flaunt my latest achievements. We were given such enormous chop cuts that the modest ballet appetites couldn't manage even half of the standard amount of food. The young waitress offered me a 'doggy bag'. I automatically shook my head, not realising what she meant.

Handing me a huge parcel, the sweet waitress asked me politely: "Excuse me, sir, what breed of dog do you have, if you don't mind me asking?"

At first I was a bit taken aback, but then got the question and answered proudly: "An Alsatian."

The naïve and trusting Penelope was sitting at the other end of the table. Eavesdropping jealously on my conversation with the waitress, she suddenly shouted right across the table: "My husband is lying. We don't have any such dog at home. He's going to eat these leftovers himself for breakfast."

Half the guests were choking with laughter, while the others collapsed under the table. A little tipsy, my straight-talking wife embarrassed me more than the Siamese Three Graces.

Seriously speaking, apart from fame and money, the courses and productions afforded me endless opportunities to study choreographic genres that I didn't know much about: contemporary, modern, jazz and square dance. To this end, I attended lectures given by friendly university colleagues. I bought books and recordings; watched shows and ceremonial folk celebrations. After each trip I brought back new information and systematically applied this to enhance my standing in Montreal. Over the last few years I had amassed a unique collection of music and dance examples of national folklore and literary descriptions of the roots of Native American traditional rituals. I also dipped into published notation systems for conventional recordings of choreography by Laban and Benesh. It was difficult to overplay the significance of these acquisitions for a specialist of my calibre in the free Western World of the arts, who'd come from such an alien, ideological straitjacket. I fully intended to take up academic research in future on the theory of choreography and mime, and their anthropological, sociocultural sources. Colleagues and students often asked me if they could buy any of my published books or videotapes anywhere on the method/syllabus of historical or Character dance. I promised to plug this gap one day in my retirement.

My invitations to universities and Ballet schools came thick and fast to such an extent that I had to be selective in prioritising the most prestigious locations so as not to lose control of Les Ballets Russes de Montréal, or interest in my own 'baby', including the dancers in both ensembles. Fortune was apparently accompanying me on my creative career and business path during this period. But from past experience I was afraid that this could not last, and kept my ambition in check.

CHAPTER 6 IRONY OF MISCHIEVOUS FATE

I was feeling more confident both creatively and financially, as I recalled my promise to my youngest son Alexander in the Moscow special boarding school, prior to emigrating from the Soviet Union. That day I had handed to the Director at his request 5,500 roubles to cover the last five years of Sasha's schooling, until he had completed his education at the English school. I'd been given an official receipt bearing a circular stamp, but all the same, I suspected that I had made a basic error. But at that time I just didn't have the energy to take on the emotional responsibility for my youngest's future in the boarding school without paying in advance.

So I sent him an official invitation to come and live with his father in Canada on a permanent basis. Direct relatives were permitted under an international United Nations charter. I dispatched similar invitations to Mum and younger brother, Roman, together with his wife and daughter in Odessa. Now everything depended on them – and on the authorities. I didn't expect to hear anything for at least six months, but to my astonishment I received a letter from my ex-wife (Sasha's mother) after just one month.

'Unlike some others I could mention, my son is no traitor to the Motherland, and will never leave here!'

I confess, it was no surprise to receive a nasty letter from St Emilia to her ex. It just reinforced my feeling that it was a waste of my time and emotional energy. I didn't send my eldest son, Dmitri, a personal invitation because of my certainty that he would only bring me a load of grief, as he had done several times already. It was difficult to turn down the opportunity to fulfil yet another naïve ambition: to set up a family business with my sons. Fortune was obviously protecting me from any potential risk vis-à-vis my ex-wife and close family. But my horoscope sign, Taurus, stubbornly refused to heed the voice of experience and I was inclined to follow my natural instinct to repeat the errors of my ways.

At my invitation, my younger brother, Roman, and his wife and daughter were the first to emigrate from Odessa to Canada in autumn 1978. Following the required quarantine period in Italy, and without notifying their host, they landed not in Montreal, where I was waiting for them at the airport, but at the plane's next stop in Toronto. I swallowed this bitter pill without making a fuss, knowing that Roman's weak character had made him give in to his wife's power-hungry will. But he could still have let me know about this change of plan, before letting his kind-hearted brother look like a complete idiot with Manpower, Penny, and others who were looking forward to meeting the chess grand master.

Chess was not a popular sport in Canada and there was little call for paid trainers. Having enjoyed a successful career for so many years as a chess trainer in the Soviet Union, Roman was suddenly in a dilemma. Like me, he didn't want to give up his vocation and experience. Because of this, my little brother suffered acutely, and caused his family a lot of trauma. In a telephone conversation, instead of expressing gratitude for my invitation to Canada, he reproached me for the fact that his profession was of no use to anyone there. I felt dispirited. As if I didn't have enough problems of my own!

The upshot was that I needn't have bothered to send my brother an invitation as he hadn't requested it. Once again, I had taken the initiative to offer help which was not valued by others. After giving it some thought, I decided all the same to try to rectify my mistake. One room right inside our studio had previously housed Camilla's show costumes, and it might be possible to organise something if Roman didn't mind such modest facilities for a chess club. This was a feasible idea long-term, as the small classroom opposite his office could be used for group sessions with the trainer playing games simultaneously, when the studio was closed at weekends.

Without mentioning this project to Penny, I invited my brother over on Saturday to discuss his work plans. I showed him around our school and put forward in detail my idea for chess and ballet to run side by side, promising to buy him folding tables and chairs, games clocks and twelve chess sets, a display scoreboard and other necessary items, on condition that he paid me back once he became successful. I showed him a sample contract for a trial one-year period and the fine print of terms for working together in the same confined space. I asked him to go through every point in the agreement, to avoid any potential arguments between us.

"On Sunday we'll chat through any adjustments we need to make, and either sign an agreement, or forget it. Sorry, Roma, that's all I can do for you just now."

My little brother promised to think about it, discuss the long-term future of chess in Quebec (as opposed to Ontario) on the telephone with his wife, and get back to me on Monday before returning to Toronto. The youngest agreed to all the fundamental conditions. He expressed a preference to start his business by setting up a mini chess club starting the following week. We said friendly goodbyes on the platform. I got home to find Penny in state of inebriation, and when she heard about our project, she threw her glass in my face.

"Misha, you have completely lost the plot. It's taken us so much effort to set up an excellent school and business that are doing well. Now you will destroy your own child with your own hands. Any old tramps will now roll in off the street, scaring the young girls and rubbing shoulders with respectable ballet-studio clients in the various departments."

Roman signed up a dozen members for his chess club. In the main, they were adults with some experience, who wanted to gain more knowledge of the theory. Three months later, without a word to me, he started to hold simultaneous games sessions with his students and various guests on Sundays. The morning after the first of these weekends, the small classroom was scattered with cigarette butts, spilt wine, rubbish everywhere and tables and chairs littered with debris. My regular cleaner, who worked from 7 a.m., refused to clean the room. Rolling my sleeves up, I cleared everything away myself, and washed the floor in readiness for the class due to start there in an hour's time. My brother didn't accept for one moment that we needed to agree how we were going to work together. Smoking and drinking were pretty much prohibited in the studio, as well as in my contract with him. I warned Roman that if this happened again, he would have to find himself another venue.

I realised that for his students chess was a form of entertainment, like dominoes or cards in a bar. Still, one half of a joint business can't be allowed to ruin the other. I had to bring in a total ban on smoking and alcohol in the studio in spite of my brother's protestations.

The chess school grew and Sundays alone were not sufficient for tournaments. Roman asked if he could use the small classroom on Saturdays as well. In an effort to avoid any further confrontation, I moved my rehearsal from 6 p.m. to another time which was not convenient for me. This did not suit him and he insisted on using the small classroom on both days of the weekend. I realised that my brother was taking advantage of my good nature, and said 'no' to him. 'Everything in moderation.' After this, the youngest began to behave aggressively in the studio. The teachers had complained before, that he often interrupted their dance lessons, without apologising, insisting that they turned the volume down on their audio systems as they were disturbing the chess players' concentration during practice. I tried to reason with Roman, but he announced that his contract with me ran till 1st July, and he had no intention of losing any clients. This meant that I had to stand by and watch him ruin my business in the name of his own interests. Luckily there were only two to three months left to the end of the period covered by our agreement.

Now if teachers ignored my brother's requests to turn the music down during a lesson, he burst rudely into the classroom. Stepping over the students as they worked on the floor, he made straight for the sound equipment and turned the music off completely. This was the last straw.

Once his training session had finished, I invited my brother into the office and without going into detail about relationships, politely told him: "If you display any further loutish behaviour to my dance teachers, that will be the end of your mini club on my premises for good and I will change the locks on the doors. My advice to you is: look for another base for your business before it's too late, with private accommodation thrown in, so that you can be independent. If you leave without a fuss, I'll let you take with you all the chess paraphernalia I've bought you, which comes to more than 3,000 dollars in total. If there is any trouble, I will have you forcibly removed and you'll leave with nothing."

In the summer of 1979 (again, at my personal invitation), my mother emigrated to Canada. It's understandable that with two of her sons gone, and left with her hostile, third son, Yosif, there was no reason for her to stay, despite her six sisters and numerous relatives. At seventy-four years old, she endured all the pre-departure problems regarding emigration formalities with considerable courage, as well as the three-month quarantine period in Rome and seven-hour flight to Montreal. It goes without saying that she received a warm welcome from Manpower and my family alike, although Penny was slightly worried about her mother-in-law's reaction to her. But she was delighted from the outset, seeing my mother rolling her sleeves up straight away and taking over responsibility for all the household tasks and cooking. By contrast, this did not particularly suit me, as it allowed my dear wife a lot more free time to go out, indulge in secret drinking, spending time with her old friends from Europe, etc. Nevertheless, she and Mum rubbed along well together.

The Panther was happy to live alongside her two sons. She would make her famous Ukrainian borscht for everyone and update us on the latest from Odessa over a late supper. After hearing about the cleaning problem in the small classroom at the studio following Roman's Sunday tournaments, my mother volunteered her services for a couple of hours on Mondays to put the chess club area back in order. This was to be unpaid, in the interests of keeping peace between the brothers. I reluctantly agreed to this compromise, fearing that people around us would get the wrong idea about our family. That's why I insisted on putting my mother on the payroll for her work and giving her fifty dollars every Monday. Like all women from Odessa, she couldn't really turn this down, as she had undertaken to send this money to each of her sisters in turn in Odessa every month. Penny didn't approve of the idea of her mother-in-law cleaning the premises of Les Ballets Russes de Montréal, as she considered it more sensible to spend this money on additional work for the permanent cleaner.

After my refusal to make the small classroom available for additional chess sessions due to my Saturday classes, relations between my brother and me became hopelessly strained. Once my mother found out about this, she got into quite a state, and begged me not to damage his business, by giving him Saturday and extending his contract for another year. I tried in vain to convince Bagheera that two such contrasting enterprises were incompatible. As always in such situations, my mother sprang to the defence of her youngest child, the victim. She didn't want to hear the detail of how our business links had been set up, and the potential consequences of any conflict. When she found out that my brother now had to pay his rent somewhere else off his own bat, out of his Toronto allowance, the Panther voted with her feet. While I was at work in the studio, Mum packed her bags, said goodbye to Penny, and announced that she was moving in with Roman. She left her new address so that we could forward her mail. I wasn't in the least surprised at my brother's behaviour or Bagheera's reaction. I blamed myself more than anyone for this sorry state of affairs.

'Don't do anyone too many favours, if you don't want to acquire sworn enemies.'

As Roman was officially registered as an immigrant in Ontario province, he was not supposed to be receiving any type of financial aid in Quebec. For this reason, Mum now had to pay the chess-club rent for the rest of the year's contract out of her own allowance. As a result, the youngest had to move her to Toronto, where he set her up in a retirement home not far from his place. The Panther refused outright to share a flat with his wife and daughter, so my brother had to take on a new job as a school bus driver. Still, he carried on giving private chess lessons from home. Mother settled fantastically well in a luxurious, health-conscious complex for the elderly. All the same, she and I had no contact for the next ten years. Roman and I are still not on speaking terms to this day. To everyone's satisfaction, I restored the previous creative atmosphere in the group to enable the smooth running of the studio.

Six months after my mother had arrived in Montreal and established herself in our family, I had a call at the studio from the immigration agency in Rome. The supervisor asked me to send through them a personal invitation addressed to my eldest son, Dmitri Berkut, and his pregnant wife, Polina, so that they could emigrate to Canada. I responded that I knew nothing about any invitation either for him or his wife. I was completely unaware of the enquiry through Italy.

The next day Dr Cage, chairman of the Canadian branch of Manpower, telephoned me and unsettled me with a disturbing question: "Mr Berkut, why are you refusing to invite your son to emigrate here after inviting so many others?"

"Excuse me, sir! May I know how they came to be in Italy? And how come I didn't know about it?"

"So. They left the Soviet Union on an invitation from her father in New York. Polina became pregnant in Rome. During an examination by an American doctor, she was diagnosed with syphilis. Because of this, she was refused an immigration visa by the USA. The immigration agency in Rome, who knew you personally, recommended that they reissue their invitation to Canada with your help, where this problem will not be a factor, as today syphilis can generally be cured, although it is passed down through the mother. And if necessary, it would be better to perform an abortion here rather than there."

"As you know, I'm currently sponsoring my brother and mother. I need to think about this. My son won't live here in any case. His arrival here will just put paid to my career in Canada."

Mum and Penny launched a two-pronged attack on me when they heard that I was having doubts about inviting my son.

"That was all a long time ago, when he was a youngster in the Soviet Union. He's a grown man now."

"He's a twenty-two-year-old scrounger with no particular profession or qualifications. He has an aversion to work. . . ."

"What will people say about you? First you abandoned your son to his fate in the Soviet Union. Then you refused to give him and his pregnant wife shelter in Canada. Everyone you know will think you're a monster."

"All right, don't get hysterical! I will do this for you, not for him. Mark my words: as soon as Dmitri gets here, he'll start wangling money out of me, or borrowing from family and friends on my account. His mother and his mates from the street have damaged him. He's beyond repair."

The following day, I visited Manpower in Montreal and drew up an invitation for my son and his wife. I warned the Quebec supervisor that the consequences of this action were on her head.

I rented a two-bedroom flat in plenty of time for the youngsters, not far from the studio, so that I could keep an eye on them. With all the communal services, it came to around 300 dollars a month on top of their regular allowance. Plus there were clothes, food, travel and other essential relocation costs for both of them. Polina had a late private abortion and took a course of treatment for syphilis. Naturally, I paid for everything: the surgeon, drugs and a doctor's home visits, etc. I was happy to help them both to get on their feet and adapt to local life, as all immigrants have to do.

I suggested to my son that he took up study in a line of work that interested him, at the government's expense. He couldn't believe my naïvety, and he and his wife continued to live it up on a daily basis at the Moscow Restaurant, where the manager was well known to me as Zina's father. Noting how negative they were about work, I advised them instead to take a three-month course together in French, funded again from the province's coffers, and explained that this would help them to find a more suitable job. They took an interest in this and from the beginning of the month, they attended a course for four hours every morning. No doubt someone had persuaded them to endure this 'humiliation'.

I understood perfectly well that, like any young man, Dmitri needed some money for out-of-pocket expenses. When he came to me for help, I offered him a proper job as promoter at the studio, on too high a salary. For two hours a day after French lessons he would distribute printed flyers advertising Les Ballets Russes de Montréal around town in various public places, educational institutions, and street stalls. He received a comprehensive package from me in return: a pension for the future, sick pay, federal and government income tax registration, etc.

"Daddy dear, I'm not a slave at your beck and call; I'm a free Canadian citizen," my son declared disdainfully, and turned away.

I stood there, open-mouthed in shock. His insolence was the turning point which made me change my position as his parent once and for all. At the end of the annual rental contract on his flat, I stopped paying. I told the newly pregnant Polina to apply to Manpower for support and to tell her husband that he could not depend on me any longer.

Penelope was now furious at the way my brother and son were behaving: impinging on our business and family interests. Once the conflict between Roman and me was in full swing, she often saw him with Dmitri, and warned me that they were obviously plotting against me.

"Misha, you were right not to want to bring your son over here. I was wrong to persuade you, I was influenced by Mummikins [as she called her mother-in-law]. Please forgive me."

"Penny, this is just the beginning. The worst is yet to come. Be ready for anything!"

"I won't be able to put up with this shit. Everyone at the studio is amazed at how blind and patient you've been. Let me and Jean go away to Florida for a week while you're working in Montreal with your Ensembles."

My frequent trips to deliver courses in the United States definitely made it more complicated to keep control of business. In my absence, Jean and Claudia (the administrator) were my stalwart staff. Zina was now working on two fronts: our side and theirs, as she was as thick as thieves with my son. I couldn't rely on Penny because of her weakness for the bottle; her support was symbolic in nature.

I alerted my close dancers and the men, whose loyalty was not in question: "Keep your wits about you with those two! If you notice anything suspicious, please let Jean or Claudia know rather than Penny. They will safeguard the students and the studio itself."

When Dmitri's son Richard was born, my mother persuaded me to help her grandson find a suitable job so that he didn't get in with filthy drug addicts or sharks. I reminded her that he and I had fallen out. The great-grandmother started to cry, assuring me that the man had expressed a wish to work in a photo studio. She asserted that this would be her last attempt at setting Dmitri up in a career, and promised to call it a day this time if it didn't work out. A well-known, local photo lab occupied part of the building that housed Les Ballets Russes de Montréal. I knew the owner, of course, and he was persuaded to take on my son as an apprentice if I subsidised half of his wages with a monthly advance. I put my neighbour in the picture regarding the young father's family situation, and he agreed to a month's trial period. Dmitri was not used to having to clock in and out, and walked out after a month, without even saying goodbye to his boss. Once again he had embarrassed me in my neighbour's eyes. I knew that Mum's mission would end here, but it was still important for me to show her how things really were.

It was pointless to keep badgering Manpower and the welfare services. My eldest sponger would rather do the washing-up in the restaurant next door than fulfil a marketing role in his father's school or the photo studio. With one term's experience as a drama institute student, Dmitri considered himself the Great Producer of his own family saga. Friends in misfortune quickly found common ground, using his grandmother and the chess master's mother (one and the same) against her other son only to make the latter stop giving any more encouragement to scroungers, and those who enjoyed getting something out of his family.

"Let everyone see", the untrained actor shouted from the kitchen sink, "how mean my father is! Thanks to him I've sunk to the depths of civilisation. Damn him forever!"

Every time, Penny would tearfully update me with the latest muck my son had flung our way, blaming all his misfortune and failures on his beloved Uncle Roma.

By this time my brother had already moved his chess club. Mum, under pressure from her youngest son and eldest grandson, had abandoned Penny and me in an act of revenge for disobeying our clan's Almighty Parent. However strange it may seem, the talented chess player and cheap dilettante/dramatist genially concocted a court case against their own brother and father, who had apparently exploited their mother/grandmother, and forced her to clean up the ballerinas' daily sweat and dirt in the ballet studio. He had refused to pay her a maintenance allowance (which was so necessary to pay the chess club rent). He had driven her out of her home and on to the street in winter, and there her good-natured grandson had picked up the unfortunate victim and taken her off, not to a retirement home, but to the chess club to be his cleaner/caretaker. Being subjected to libel such as this makes one's hair stand on end! The son's unprecedented cruelty towards his mother! With exquisite skill, Dmitri devised and spread such a cock-and-bull story to everyone we knew, that many of them believed the pitiful schemer and had grave doubts about how morally decent and humane Penny and I actually were.

Thanks to the initiative of the kind and warm staff at Manpower, Dmitri got a job as general manager of a large residential complex, in exchange for a semi-basement two-bedroom flat with all mod cons. As part of his contract, he was responsible for making everything ready for new residents; maintaining the cleanliness of the lobby, corridors and other communal areas; and ensuring the residents' safety. The Panther stopped worrying about her grandson's family and often came from Toronto with Roman to visit them at weekends. But Dmitri's reign as general manager at the residential complex didn't last long. It was like asking a fox to take care of a herd of sheep. In the process of being recruited to this responsible position, my son hid from the organisation his parasitical philosophy about the enslavement of the communist proletariat: 'Work is not like a wolf – it would not run in the forest' or 'Don't put off till tomorrow what you can do the day after tomorrow,' etc. But when the super-parasite had a daughter, Regina, he then demanded a three-bedroom flat from the owner. Inevitably, the shocked boss refused the supervisor who had then overstepped the mark.

However, the would-be anarchist, and magnanimous super-warrior for the trampled rights of the free man did not really mind too much, as, a week after my granddaughter's birth, Dmitri's neighbour got fed up with the constant crying through the wall from two children, and fled lock, stock and barrel to a new complex. The genial super-burglar had been waiting for this opportunity. Hiding the keys from the newly vacated one-bedroom flat, he then cut a door into it from his kitchen, and rearranged things quite comfortably, having created a three-bedroom dwelling without any thought of the repercussions. When the owner of the building sent Dmitri a new tenant for the stolen flat, the new chap tried the lock and returned to the dismayed proprietor. It was as laughable as it was desperate. The perplexed police didn't know whether to send this bandit to prison or a psychiatric unit. It was only then, at the request of a lawyer from Manpower, that the law enforcers released this emotionally unwell father to his two young children following a guilty plea, requiring him first to pay 3,000 dollars in damages. Manpower were soft-hearted enough to cancel the debt for the super-bandit they had backed. They moved his family into a private house where they covered all his needs, politely requesting the criminal to find himself a job.

In response to this request, Dmitri found a unique opportunity to gain a new professional profile. He had overstepped the mark to such an extent in slandering Penny and me, that even the residents ceased to have any trust in him. His career as a general manager, with its opportunities for 'poisoning' the residents' brains and landing them up to their ears in trouble, finished up with a criminal record on police files. Immigrant circles in the Moscow Restaurant drunkenly boasted about his swindling and thieving operations with fridges, washing machines and other high-end electrical appliances from large, corporate shops. My eldest was interested in the possibilities in making a quick buck. His drinking buddies suggested that he needed his own minivan.

"Where will I find a vehicle like that?" asked the bewildered super-dealer, scratching his head.

"Thanks to your Jewish immigrant status, Manpower will just give you the money to buy it for 16,000 dollars."

"I wonder why they would do that? And when would I be able to repay the loan?"

"They'll let you off all of it if you agree to a bar mitzvah in synagogue [a ritual of the Jewish faith]. You have nothing to lose by doing this, apart from the skin of your sexual organ."

My son thought his friends were making fun of him. But after checking this story with a well-known rabbi, and without blinking, he completed the sacred ceremony, and obtained the promised credit in return. Armed with the keys to a deluxe minivan, 'for a pile of skin', these mates welcomed the lost sheep into their midst: a notorious den of thieves of other people's property. To achieve total victory, Dmitri just had to sit an exam to get his driving licence. It followed that with his outstanding talents, he managed this easily. He promised Manpower that he would find a job more quickly with the van. However, it was a blessing in disguise. While the chauffeur-to-be was sitting his exam, his mates were caught on their latest operation in a shop, and were all sent to prison. On the one hand, the super-wheeler-dealer was born with a silver spoon in his mouth, and escaped arrest. On the other, he'd lost his job again. Various firms offered him contracts several times as a delivery driver. But my son was certain that he was not created to be a slave and drive a lorry. He just wanted to be his own boss.

The deputy manager of Manpower rang and asked nervously: "Mikhail, why are you refusing to help your son's family? This is unlike you!"

He didn't want to believe that following his arrival in Montreal, Dmitri had abandoned his advertising duties at my studio on grounds of 'exploitation of his human rights'. I reminded the deputy that I had forewarned him about Dmitri's behaviour, and all the trouble there had been about him emigrating to Canada with his pregnant wife. But Dr Cage didn't know whether he could trust me. I didn't feel I needed to justify myself to him, but explained the internal family ramifications of this conflict. I didn't want to damage relations with Manpower. Nevertheless, I was, and remain convinced that excessive support to people like my son often does a lot of damage to humanitarian ideals. It makes parasites of them, destroying personal initiative and the wish to overcome life's challenges. It sometimes leads to tragic consequences.

By this time, Roman and Mum were already living in Toronto. Zina, the studio administrator, who was friends with Dmitri, told Penny all the latest news about my family. Mum really missed her grandson and great-grandson. Every weekend she came to Montreal by train, to catch up with her 'poor and abandoned' children. At seventy-six, she cleaned their filthy flat, washed the dirty clothes and bathed the foul-smelling children. She listened to her grandson's latest claptrap about his painstaking search for work, about the financial difficulties caused by his bloodsucking father, who wouldn't hear of helping his own flesh and blood. Well, how was a good-hearted grandmother expected to respond? Oh yes! The young man, already practised in the art of scheming from Soviet times, knew perfectly well how to play the sympathy card with his soft grandmother, who would readily sacrifice the last dollars of her pension to her favourite, 'starving' grandchildren, while their father, Dmitri, shedding a crocodile tear, would squander his grandmother's 'help' an hour later in the nearest strip joint. This floor show went on every weekend between Dmitri and his grandmother on various stage settings. The wise old Panther realised that she had fallen victim to her grandson's swindling, but didn't have the heart to put a stop to this outrage. This would mean acknowledging her own mistake and losing her last chance to spend time with her direct descendants.

Driving his family around in his own luxury van cost money. The unemployed waster's expenses were clearly higher than his income from social benefits and occasional handouts from Manpower or his grandmother. The idea of going back to wash dishes at the restaurant made the owner of this trendy vehicle feel sick. No one was lending him any more money, as they couldn't expect it ever to be repaid. The only option left for survival was to steal from his own father, on the principle that 'When you take a little from many, it's not stealing, it's sharing.' But to do this expediently with others, you wouldn't find a safer pair of hands than Mum's. Getting together in a threesome with Roman, they went through all possible family gambits on how to extract money from me for Dmitri and his family. My brother didn't need my money, but was only too happy to get his own back on me for 'dishonouring the chess player'. From the day she left Penny and me, my mother received the equivalent from me of her state pension in cash every month, which came to 350 dollars a month at that time. On the first of every month, Penny took her my allowance, which her mother-in-law signed for in a notebook. Once she left her with bags full of items from the supermarket. This support served as a cause for systematic, organised extortion of money by the almost 'Holy Trinity'.

Dmitri gave me such a bad name at the respected Manpower agency that they engaged Segal, one of the best Jewish defence lawyers, for my mother. The very same man whose services I had declined when officially incorporating Les Ballets Russes de Montréal. Now, the offended lawyer had the chance 'to show me what's what', assisted by my son. My lawyer, Greenberg, called me in and showed me a statement from my mother, in which she was asking for 500 dollars, rather than 350 dollars in maintenance, to allow for inflation over the last year. I was wary, but without any negotiation, wrote out twelve cheques for 500 dollars a month in advance, and asked my lawyer to send Mum one cheque a month with a signed receipt by return, and I would cover any postal and other costs. He was astonished by this unnecessary formality. I had to tell him about my family dilemmas and my mother's attempt to extort money from me. He announced that this was not the Soviet Union, and that I had no reason to fear the Canadian justice system as I had not done anything illegal.

Two months later Penny received a second letter from Mum, penned by Segal, in which she now demanded 850 dollars a month to pay for the costly medication that she needed from the United States. I explained to my lawyer that this was premeditated extortion on the part of my 'family threesome' and decided to ignore it. Greenberg persisted in trying to convince me that it was better to forfeit the difference than go through a court case, which would ruin my personal reputation in Canada, and have a negative impact on the business.

I disagreed. "This 'Tale of the Golden Goose' will run and run. They'll be blackmailing me forever."

"Mikhail, Canadian legal proceedings won't allow this. I'll negotiate with my colleague Segal in writing to confirm that this will be the final increase in financial support, and sort everything out."

"But what if they don't stop there and demand 1,000 dollars in their next statement? What then?"

"Then we'll go back to court. But I'm sure it won't come to that, you mark my words."

Nevertheless, I was certain that money was not the only basis of their desire for revenge. They needed the court to discredit me publicly and force me out of Quebec. It was as plain as the nose on my face.

Returning from my next course in America, I found my infuriated wife with a third letter, in which my mother, as dictated to by her grandson, was demanding 1,100 dollars a month to cover her costs adequately. I placated Penny by promising to suspend support payments to Mum pending the court's decision. But this upset her even more. She loved her mother-in-law, and felt sorry for the old woman. Still, she couldn't understand how any mother could consciously ruin her own son. I'm sure that the Panther was unaware of the content of the document that she had signed, as in the third statement she itemised her monthly outgoings, which included seventy-five dollars on newspapers and magazines every month. My mother had absolutely no knowledge of either English or French, and all the periodicals were available free of charge in Russian. Doubts aside, this was inflammatory. My mother had got in with two complete scumbags and was hopelessly entrenched in a mire of lies and loathing from which she couldn't seem to extricate herself.

The first court summons arrived while I was working in one of the United States universities. The hearing was adjourned for six months. I purposely delayed the legal encounter with my mother, to give me more time to organise my financial affairs. It was in my interest to keep the maximum amount in both banks to keep the business going, pay for the flat and Penny's and my general day-to-day outgoings. Jean helped me to produce budgets for Les Ballets Russes de Montréal and Berkut Dance Enterprises. The two Florida apartments were a real stumbling block. At that point, half of the bank loan had been paid off. Over the previous two years the price of each had increased by 50%, i.e. up to 525,000 dollars, less the remaining loan in the bank. The actual value of one flat worked out to approximately 400,000 dollars. I decided to sell both at a lower price as a matter of urgency, but realistically, I could only get shot of one as the other was rented out at the time and it was illegal to sever the contract midterm. There was nothing for it other than to immediately suspend repayments to the bank, continuing to receive rental payments from the tenant for as long as possible to compensate for my enormous financial loss. Penny's parents in England were fairly well off. As their sole legatee, she was more than adequately provided for, for the rest of her days. But when she heard that we had to forgo the opportunity to holiday with friends in the decadent surroundings of St Petersburg beach, my wife cried like a baby. She was upset that she'd wasted so much time and energy on furnishing and setting up the living space, only for my nearest and dearest to outrage her endeavours to make all our guests happy, including the very people who were destroying it. Sadly, there was nothing else for it.

The second court summons came when Penny and I were busy arranging to sell the now vacated Florida flat and its relatively expensive furniture. My lawyer in Montreal asked me to postpone the case again due to our being away from Canada. The furious Segal obtained a court ruling on the basis of our 'sabotage' of the legal proceedings, to allow the court hearing to go ahead without us. Greenberg warned me that on this occasion, I, as the defendant, and Penny as the key witness, would be obliged to attend court. In the previous six months, I had succeeded in selling the flat and furniture in Florida, and transferred all the money into my personal account in New York City Bank, which no one in Montreal knew about, apart from my devoted bookkeeper, Jean. My will, in which I had signed over both flats to my two sons, was nullified. The monies from the sale of the apartment were allocated to developing Kalinka and Mini Ballets Russes, which I had set up by then and which were being rehearsed by my assistants as much as possible.

Of course I didn't relish the prospect of facing my mother in court. I asked my administrator, Zina, who was in the know regarding our family conflict, to organise a meeting on one of Mum's weekend visits to Dmitri, for all parties to get together in Montreal to discuss a way forward. She took me to my son's place, where my mother was already waiting for me at the 'round table'. She explained to the head of the household that neither he, nor Zina, had the right to participate in this exclusive personal debate between his father and grandmother, i.e. they were only attending as witnesses. The super-troublemaker muttered a bit, but the Panther gave him a meaningful look and her discontented grandson went off into the kitchen. I explained to my mother that it was in both our interests to resolve our disagreement peacefully, as following the court case, all the English and Russian newspapers would drag us into the mud, which we would never manage to clean off. Agreeing to retract my statement to the court, I guaranteed her a monthly allowance of 500 dollars, with an annual increase of 5% for inflation, for the rest of her life. In the worst-case scenario, I would move to Europe and she would never get a bean from me. She would lose her 'happy medium' for good.

At these words, Dmitri bounded out of the kitchen brandishing a large knife.

Running around the table like a rabid dog, he howled: "Grandma, don't listen to him! He's just feeding you a load of lies to keep you quiet. If you do a deal with him, I'll stab him right in front of you and it'll be your fault that I end up in prison. Granny, don't do this!"

My mother sat there with hot red cheeks, looking fiercely right into my eyes. Zina was nodding at me in fear. We hurried out to avoid a tragedy. Once outside, the young girl heaved a sigh of relief.

"Mikhail, why did you drag me into this? Now they'll blame me for your wrongdoings."

"I'm sorry, Zina. I never expected Dmitri to react like this. Even though he's a brilliant Shakespearean actor, if he wasn't my son, he'd be in prison for threatening me with that knife."

"It turns out that I was just there to witness the crap between you and your son, is that it?"

"Why exaggerate? You know that's not how it is. Again, please accept my apologies."

As I hadn't paid off my debt to the bank by the deadline, my remaining personal property in Florida was confiscated after a lengthy lawsuit, which came as no surprise to me. On the contrary, it was timely in returning me from a successful capitalist to my original status as a theatrical entrepreneur, who had invested money in art as fast as he was earning. However paradoxical it may seem, in spite of everything that was going on, the latest season at the studio had been extremely successful. The total number of students had risen to 850 following the liquidation of the chess club. I made and purchased complete sets of costumes and footwear for both ensembles, and signed new contracts with the singers and musicians for the year ahead. The concert agency arranged weekly performances for Mini Ballets Russes and Kalinka, in exchange for a steep commission. Everyone was happy, apart from Penny and me. She was unable to deal with the Florida disgrace and material losses. She had made up her mind to leave Montreal after the court case, which she was obliged to attend as she had been summoned as a witness. She had never been in a courtroom before and was in a complete panic about this impending disaster.

Dmitri didn't expect the court case to last six months, due to my occasional work in the USA. The lawyer promised that my son and his grandmother would receive substantial compensation for their patience, on account of the defendant's confiscated private property in America. But my son's frequent visits to strip joints required additional funds, and there simply wasn't enough money to provide for the unemployed man's family. The impatient super-fraudster turned to crime. He stole two Ballets Russes chequebooks from the bookkeeper, containing my sole, authorised signature, which he forged to pay for his strip entertainment. Jean confided this to Penny. The studio's deputy director decided to conceal this criminal activity from me and persuaded the bookkeeper not to tell me, so that no blood would be spilt. Fortunately, there were only twenty-five cheques in the book, limited to 50 dollars a piece, totalling 1,250 dollars.

When the second series of strip cheques with a counterfeit signature started coming into the accounts office, Jean went behind Penny's back, asking: "Misha, when did you turn into a sex maniac despite having such a beautiful wife?"

I summoned Zina to my office, and showed her copies of the stolen cheques and their forged signatures.

"What do you think? Who could have stolen our chequebooks and forged my signature so crudely?"

"Are you pointing the finger at me?"

"Not at all. You wouldn't be that stupid."

"Then why are you asking me about this? What has this got to do with me?"

"In the evenings, once Jean and Claudia (the administrator) have left, you are the only person with access to the accounts office, apart from Penny and me. If I were to call the police right now, the first person they'd want to interview would be you, followed swiftly by the rest of the studio employees."

"How can I help you in this matter, if you think I'm not implicated in the theft?"

"Please tell Dmitri that the next time he forges my signature, I'm calling the police."

Analysing what had happened, it was obvious that Dmitri could not have stolen the cheques without help. When Zina was registering new students in the evenings, she often left the accounts office open. The thief must have known where the chequebooks were kept, and stolen them while classes were going on, when there was no one around in the corridors and Zina was on her own in the registration spot next to the studio entrance. It was a smooth operation.

When I asked my wife why she had concealed the theft of the chequebooks from me, Penny got into a state again, declaring that she hadn't wanted to wash her dirty linen in public. Instead of being grateful to Jean for her vigilance in looking after the studio's interests, the Deputy Director reproached her for disloyalty and for reneging on her promise not to divulge the crime. I threatened to deduct the amount of fraudulent cheques from Penny's salary, to punish her for her negligence. I just wanted to give her a fright, so that she wouldn't ever again turn a blind eye to employee theft. I realised that my son had lost all sense of danger and had been driven into a hole in his search for a way out of his material difficulties. Not wishing to deny his parasitic principles, Dmitri wanted to enjoy all the riches of life around him at the same time. He was so spoilt by the good natures of his father, grandmother, Manpower and unemployment benefit, that psychologically he was not in the right place to refuse this manna from heaven and re-establish himself in line with socialist doctrine: "from each according to his abilities, to each according to his needs'. My son sincerely believed that everyone owed him. I decided, whatever happened, to prove that the contrary was true. But it was disheartening when he took to crime, not to provide food or clothes for his children, but to satisfy his wretched, philistine instincts, using his natural talents to negative ends.

The first court session lasted an hour rather than the allotted thirty minutes. Mum's lawyer naturally presented me (in line with my son's testimony) as a monster, who had driven my mother out of her home and forced her to seek shelter with Roman and his family. During the recess, Penny couldn't help herself, shouting out indignantly, "That's a lie!"

The judge silenced the witness sternly, warning her that she would have the opportunity to refute any untrue statements later. The judge went on to accuse me of exploiting my mother, saying that I had brought her over from Ukraine to use her as an unpaid servant and cleaner in my home. The seventy-three-year-old woman spent days on her own without any attention from the accused or his wife. Six months ago the defendant had stopped paying the plaintiff any allowance on the basis of goodwill.

With the judge's permission, I set out in detail the reasons behind the conflict with my mother and my suspending payment of her monthly keep. I presented the three different demands for support from me at two-month intervals: 500, 850 and 1,100 dollars. I admitted that after the third demand for money I had stopped support payments altogether pending the court's decision. I specified that my mother had not been financially dependent on me since emigrating, as she also received a substantial state pension. After she moved in with my brother, my wife and I had continued to help her with money and food as necessary. At the present time she was living in a Toronto retirement home on full board, and didn't need any additional financial assistance. Irrespective of this, I still sent her a specific amount. She required the above-mentioned allowance to pay the costs of her grandson and youngest son, Roman, who were out for anything they could get. I considered this to be wrong and refused to pay it.

The judge asked whether I had any money invested in the United States, and if so, how much.

My reply: "Before, I owned two cooperative flats on St Petersburg beach. But last year, following the Quebec Government's third refusal to award my two dance ensembles a grant, I had to sell both properties to meet my contractual obligations to my artistes and musicians regarding payment."

I gave the judge copies of documents relating to the sale of one of the apartments and the confiscation by the bank of the other. You should have seen the looks on my adversaries' faces at that point.

When it was Penny's turn to speak, she got upset, citing the unreasonableness of the accusations levelled at us.

"I have been very attentive and loving to my mother-in-law and was really sorry when she decided to leave us. When his mother was preparing to leave, my husband was virtually absent all day. He would never have thrown out his own mother, who is more precious to him than his wife. I officially insist that Dmitri Berkut be held criminally responsible for arranging to extort money from his father and for bringing false testimony into the court against us."

Both defence lawyers were locked in a verbal skirmish of arguments. The judge only managed to stop their noisy round by threatening to fine them both.

Lots of spectators continued to stream into the courtroom, ready for the next cross-examination. They would applaud this or that case or laugh as our hearing unfolded, just as in popular comedy films. The French can be very humorous as well as highly emotional. It was hard for the judge to manage his auditorium. The public approved of Penny's court performance, giving her a thunderous ovation, all the more so as half of her indignation was expressed in French. Following his interaction with her, the judge rather strangely turned his attention to me. Cross-examining the three people related to me, he highlighted the fact that I had invited them here from the USSR and taken care of all their needs for nothing during a protracted period, contributing to helping my brother to set up a chess club in my studio without asking him to pay any rent for use of the premises. The judge required an explanation from all three:

"What has caused you to take such an aggressive stance against your generous sponsor? What harm has he actually done you since you've been living in Canada?"

The room was buzzing with excitement. The arbiter of the law obviously hadn't noticed that he had gradually turned prosecutor/accuser, so indignant was he at the perverse conduct of the ill-advised immigrants, with their cruelty, avarice and parasitic attitude.

In conclusion, the judge pronounced his verdict, which compelled me to pay my mother an allowance of 500 dollars, in line with Quebec provincial law.

In my last few words, I thanked the servant of the law for his patient examination and resolving matters objectively. But I also apologised as I declared: "My Lord, in spite of all the respect I have for the legal system, I consider it essential to put you and my notorious relatives in the picture regarding your decision on this case. In relation to the scandalous, hostile deeds of my family members against me, I swear before all here present: I will never, in any circumstances, offer them any kind of help, financial included. I would rather give all my savings to the Red Cross or other charities. My wife and I have decided, with enormous regret, to close our studio and leave this country for the time being. I wish my relatives health and happiness!"

A week later, to my great surprise, I received a personal letter from the judge. He expressed sympathy for my family disaster. He apologised for the fact that although it was very unpleasant for him, he was obliged to find in favour of my elderly mother, and explained the legal position regarding the Federal Code, which allows Dmitri's witness statements more legal weight as a direct relative of the defendant, than my wife Penelope's. I had the legal right to appeal against his ruling during the next ten days.

Having read his letter, Penny summarised: "Thank God that all Québecois are not chauvinists. But even so, it's better back home in England."

After this whole shameful affair, I didn't dare to contradict her. I was still licking my wounds. My wife announced that she would be returning to Europe in a month's time at the end of the season.

"Misha, if you want to hang on to your family, you should close your studio and move to London with me on one condition: you're not having your own business! There are lots of ballet schools and companies available to you in the British capital, who won't give you any unnecessary bother."

I delivered my final course for teachers at the University of Illinois in Chicago in March 1983. In April I perfected a new repertoire for both ensembles with my assistants. In spite of my negative frame of mind following the court case, the two premieres of Mini Ballets Russes and Kalinka were a great success. My charges probably decided to give it their all for our farewell performance, to show what they were capable of and how professional the studio leadership was. I tried my best to remain upbeat and not to lose heart. Immediately after the season's final shows and the students' last evening, Penny gathered up all her chattels and flew to London. I made a promise to join her in a month's time. It was absolutely vital for me to find a worthy successor to take over the ballet studio, and fulfil the creative contracts with all the artistes and musicians on 30th June, before they all went off on leave and summer holidays. I also needed to pack up all the theatre costumes, folk-orchestra instruments, audio equipment and similar theatre accessories for both ensembles, so that I could continue my creative work in Europe, forwarding everything to London in containers. There was also the business of redoing all the documentation with my lawyer Tobolyevsky, to transfer Les Ballets Russes de Montréal into his wife's name, an ex-ballerina with the Warsaw Opera Company.

I spent all month agonising about leaving, and having everything completed in time by 1st July. It was spiritually and physically tough to part with my seven-year-old child. My name was mud among my colleagues and friends after the court commentaries in the press. This caused me serious mental and material hardship, inflicted by my nearest family members – which was exactly what they had hoped to achieve with such persistence in Montreal. Dmitri, who had not been awarded any compensation by his grandmother's lawyer, was in despair. His creditors were on his back, so he had to give up the strip clubs. As luck would have it, the Soviet Embassy put an advertisement in the papers offering support to immigrants wishing to return home. Without stopping to think, my son got in touch with the consul in Montreal, a Mr Kuznetsov, and requested his assistance in helping him and his family to return to Moscow. Kuznetsov was happy to take on the prodigal son, even promising to help the super-renegade to settle in the Soviet capital, if he agreed to write about the downsides of Canadian life and its social welfare system in the National press.

Dmitri had not anticipated getting such a lucky break and becoming a popular hero instead of a loser. I kept cuttings from French and English newspapers in which my son denigrated the country that had given him a home. He lied about starving citizens sleeping rough on the streets and the suffering endured by his own family at the hands of his father, who had summoned him and his wife to Montreal and refused to help his grandsons; there was a photo of the happy family returning to their homeland. The articles by Manpower, published in the local press, were laughable. Their super-liar protégé had firstly cheated his sponsors, and slandered his father, who had so often helped this dependable agency for Jews fleeing Israel and emigrating to Canada. Next, Dmitri made a fool of them by obtaining credit to buy an expensive van, in exchange for adopting the Jewish faith. Finally, through their blind and overly charitable philosophy, Manpower let this sponger/parasite loose in civilised society, only for him to shit on them in his parting press article. Well done to the president of this respectable organisation, for his contribution to the destruction of my business in Quebec and the breakdown of my family in Canada! The Moscow newspapers, too, were packed with stories of dying immigrants on Montreal streets, and the happy homecomers, including my son, with the same sunny-coloured photo of his family. Before I left Montreal I received an unexpected telephone call from Dmitri, telling me that they were back in Moscow. He was clearly anticipating a violent reaction from me. But I just wished him a safe journey and happy homecoming to the stall he deserved. 'What must be, must be.'

I had to vacate my luxurious flat on 1st July. I put out a call to my colleagues and friends that I needed a place to stay for a month and would pay rent and running costs. Eva Von Genscy (Les Ballets Jazz de Montréal) was going to be working in Vancouver all summer and offered me the use of her home.

She gave me the keys at the studio, saying: "Misha, don't be shocked by the mess in my flat and the fact that the Soviet Consulate is a close neighbour of mine."

"Don't worry, Eva. I'm used to living in all sorts of places. I'll manage my loneliness somehow."

At these words my colleague gave an intriguing smile. I thought that she had a cat at home, and didn't attach any particular meaning to this. When I struggled through her door with my suitcases the next day, I was greeted by a student of Eva's from the jazz group in my studio, Christina Corso, who was smiling broadly.

"Excuse me, I must have got the wrong address."

"No, you haven't. This is your room, and that one's mine."

I started to babble, stuttering from embarrassment, but Christina put her hand over my mouth.

"Calm down, Mr Berkut! I promise not to do anything nasty to you. Lunch is ready, go and wash your hands!"

In the toilet, I tried to make out whether the cheerful Eva was trying to provoke me, or just having a little joke. How should I behave with this young, attractive woman? I had no doubt that my friend had set me up with a pleasant goodbye surprise. Over lunch we enjoyed analysing Eva's joke. In the evening we went to Place-des-Arts to see a show by a touring company. At night, Christina slipped under the covers with me, saying that she was scared to sleep next to the Soviet Consulate. There was only one thing for it: to shield her from the threat of the enemy with my 'manly protection' all night. In between, she told me about her ballet school in the town of Corte on Corsica.

The bittersweet two weeks with the girl from Corsica flew past in an ironic whirlwind as we approached the moment when the founder of Les Ballets Russes de Montréal was tragically parted from his charges. Christina invited me to visit her on Napoleon's island. When I rang London, Penny's mother answered that she had gone to visit friends in Italy, and would be back in a week's time.

I couldn't sleep at all during the night flight to London. As always, I was going over the last seven years of activity in Canada, along with the family rows. There was more disappointment than joy, and yet more progress than failure. It felt like a tragic ending.

My heart began to ache as I thought about this. The conclusions of my self-analysis were gloomy. This meant that I should never help my loved ones in future. Then how would I be able to ask my friends for help? My musings were cut short by the Captain's voice, announcing that the plane would shortly be landing in London. With a heavy sigh, I wished myself patience and prudence in my dealings with Penny and her entourage. In spite of all our free relations with the opposite sex, I didn't want to lose her completely, although I didn't hold out much hope that we would be able to make this kind of compromise work.

STAGE III: LAUNCHING THE NEXT DREAM

CHAPTER 7 BRITISH EXPERIMENT

Penelope, who had forsaken Canada for England and her parents, came to meet her errant husband early in 1983. There were no flowers or fanfare. Reconnecting with my wife who'd fled Montreal six months earlier, was an arid, cool affair. Nevertheless, my father-in-law gave his Odessan son-in-law from Canada a fairly warm welcome and without further ado, took us to his substantial house with its large, well-maintained garden in Croydon, just outside London. My petite, fragile mother-in-law, who had always been very indulgent of me, began making a fuss of me, inviting the frozen guest to take a seat at the table. Over lunch I told my relatives of my creative plans for the near future. I found out from Penny at this point that she had got a job as manager of the sponsorship department with the international oil company, Phillips Petroleum, through Earl, an old family friend.

A week later my costumes, footwear, sets of orchestral folk instruments and props arrived in a container from Montreal. My first task was to draw up a professional CV and, with Penny's help, I wrote letters to various ballet organisations, schools and theatres, proposing my services as a teacher and choreographer. I spent the first few days exploring the job market in London and England's other cultural centres. Naturally, for a little-known artiste, the prospects for work were better in provincial areas. From a long list of Theatres, Schools and Ensembles, I chose to start with the residential Nikolai Legat Russian Ballet School in Tunbridge Wells and the Doreen Bird College of Performing Arts in Sidcup. I also advised the director of the Kasatka Cossacks ensemble of my new place of residence; I had met him during their tour to Canada two years earlier, when I'd staged a Pair dance. In addition, I circulated my printed programmes and posters from seminars I'd delivered in North America to a range of European opera/ballet theatres.

Of course, before anything else, I re-established contact with the professional Ballet academies in Rome, Paris and Vienna, which I knew from when I had first emigrated from the Soviet Union eight years previously. This time I was not impeded by the language barrier, and had amassed a solid track record of hands-on work with stars of the Western ballet scene, which gave me more hope of running intensive courses in my unique genres of Historical and Character dance. Plus, it gave me broader opportunities to achieve my choreography projects on the professional stage. In European dance magazines, I spotted a range of tempting possibilities in Germany, Norway, Switzerland, Israel and other countries where ballet was well developed. It was absolutely clear that at this stage of its historical and cultural development, America still lagged a long way behind Europe in all respects, although it was taking steps in the right direction. Nevertheless, despite the conservative attitudes in European ballet, my specialist skills piqued the interest of local dance professionals. Invitations to interviews or to give trial classes attested to their interest in these genres.

As a result of my presentations in July I was invited to take up a full-time position with the Legat school (Classical, Historical, and Character dance) six days a week, with an overnight stay on full board. The boarding-school director, Eunice Bartell, permitted me to work at the Doreen Bird College at the same time, on two afternoons a week (Character dance and Partnering). I only got to spend Monday evenings (my free day) with Penny, which essentially estranged her from me further. I had absolutely no intention of losing my wife, so in the New Year we rented a separate flat in the Primrose Hill area, and after work at the Doreen Bird College, I met up with Penny for two additional evenings during the week. We would go to the theatre, eat out, and enjoy our time together as husband and wife. In the mornings, at first light, I would rush back to the Legat boarding school just in time, and teach my classes as timetabled. I was charging around like a hamster on a wheel, though my teaching in both institutions generated really satisfying results.

The students at the Legat ballet school were seventeen to eighteen years old, and had been through general secondary-school education. The fairly robust teaching base of Legat's classical system allowed me to make swift progress in helping them to master the techniques in Character dance and the stylistic manner of the Historical repertoire. With both groups in turn (beginners and intermediate) I worked on training in the mornings and dance production in the afternoons. Before turning in at night, I checked through the old programme and prepared lesson plans and choreography for the next day. At the end of the academic year, the Director invited representatives from various ballet organisations in England to a final Gala concert. She organised the stage costumes and set up a small performing space on her premises. The guests included: Dame Beryl Gray, president of ISTD (Imperial Society of Teachers of Dancing), Steven Rayner, a lawyer, (later to become my lawyer), the film director Andrew Winstone, and many other well-known names in local cultural bodies. After the show, Dame Beryl was very complimentary and invited me to give a trial lesson in Character dance at a teachers' seminar in London, which I was delighted to accept.

However strange it may seem, my successful presentation at the final Legat concert, had a negative effect on my relationship with Eunice Bartell, the Director. She suddenly announced that she could not allow me to continue my work at the Doreen Bird College at the same time, for employment-regulation reasons. I would have to choose between the two by the summer holidays, in one week's time. I was so shocked by this unexpected ultimatum that I left her office in silence. I decided to analyse the whole situation before making a decision.

I was sorry to leave the Legat school. During a year of intensive work I had got used to my students and colleagues, and invested considerable energy and patience in developing a range of skills in my audience. As a result, after achieving positive results, I had no choice but to call it a day. Our mother would often say, "Whatever happens, happens for the best. Don't take it to heart, boys!" In actual fact, for my new career in England and being middle-aged, it didn't make sense to work outside London. All the more so, since thanks to Dame Beryl, after the Gala concert at the Legat school, I had received several invitations from London ballet schools to give trial classes with a view to future work. Out of these, the Central School of Ballet held particular interest for me as it was a professional school and had a ballet troupe in Central London.

Following a demonstration and class in Character dance, the Director, Christopher Gable, offered me the opportunity to teach this subject to intermediate groups twice a week, and to choreograph concert work as directed by him. I signed a contract on 1st September. This change in workplace not only restored my professional status as a specialist, but also reduced my precious time spent on lengthy train journeys to the Legat school and back to London three times a week. My mother was right.

In spite of everything, I maintained business and friendly relations over the years with my lawyer Steven Rayner, who was president of the board of directors, and owned the Legat Estate on a cooperative basis (extensive grounds, teaching and accommodation blocks, school equipment and so on). Thanks to Eunice Bartell, I also gained a friend and creative colleague in the shape of Andrew Winstone (editor/film director) for years to come. In addition, I recommended the following Legat school graduates to the Doreen Bird College: Charlotte Bell, Alistair White and Brady Weaddon, as promising dancers with great potential, who went on to become keen proponents of my method of teaching Character dance in school. I must say, that the Legat boarding school proved to be a good springboard for my subsequent teaching success in England.

Getting to know Andrew Winstone brought about a revolution in my creative and academic research projects. Suddenly I saw an opportunity to put my choreography courses on film. I'm not talking about straightforward, complete compositions or shows as filmed for many years by cinematographers in the past, but rather, a visual method for teaching elements of time and space in stage movement and presentation for any genre of dance or pantomime, circus or sport. I popped in to the Ballet Bookshop in Covent Garden, and asked the manager, David Leppard, whether there were any video courses on teaching Dance or Mime, to which the answer was no. Only one of the many bookshelves featured a few filmed Ballets produced by various European Film studios.

"David, in a year's time I'll bring you a dance syllabus on video to sell."

"Misha, I'm not certain that my clients will know how to make use of that in practice," he replied.

"I assure you: in the near future, all annotated Dance textbooks will be replaced by video courses."

"Alright!" David agreed. "Bring in your version and we'll see who's right."

I shared with Andrew my idea for a 'teach yourself' video programme using my pupils from various schools to demonstrate character-genre methods. He approved of this project but regrettably, didn't have the means to achieve it at that moment.

"Misha, you'll need to budget for at least 15,000 pounds to include the production team, rent of premises, montage of tapes and preparing the wording for instructions; plus training costumes and footwear, accompanist and sound engineer, printing of the video covers and promotional brochures, making copies to sell, etc. Do you have the finances to cover all the production costs for a complete video course in three parts, each lasting sixty minutes: beginners, intermediate and advanced? Ha ha!"

"Andrew, I have a sponsor. I am ready to sign a contract with someone for this amount, if you will guarantee to produce this video series within twelve months. Ha ha!"

At this, we laughed entirely naturally, without a hint of sarcasm, slapping each other on the back.

During one of my summer courses in Genoa, Italy, the mother of an exceptionally talented, seventeen-year-old student, Angela Cavagna, approached me to ask if I could get her into a professional school in London where I was teaching and give her some personal guidance. I was shocked by such a naïve and risky request from a well-grounded woman: trusting a fifty-year-old man (and a foreigner at that!) whom she barely knew, with her only daughter, who happened to be a beauty.

"Maestro, don't be so surprised, and don't worry! I will cover all the costs. Angela is without a father and she worships you. Yesterday my daughter announced that if I don't arrange for her to go to an English ballet school, she will commit suicide. I implore you, please have mercy on us and help us."

I stood there dumbfounded, not knowing how to react to this more than strange request.

My thoughts and feelings were racing chaotically between pluses and minuses, yes and no, when suddenly I recalled my three Legat school protégés, whom I'd recommended to the Doreen Bird College: Charlotte, Alistair and Brady.

Angela could complete this group and make up two couples for my video demonstrations.

My mind was made up. I suggested to the distraught signora that we continue our conversation about the private English college in a nearby cafeteria, along with Angela. The mother and daughter listened attentively to all the detailed information about the conditions for learning and accommodation. I emphasised that she must observe discipline unconditionally and submit to my tutelage. In an outpouring of gratitude, Angie threw herself at me and kissed me, tears running down her face. Her mother, muttering a prayer, crossed herself and her daughter and me while she was at it.

After a thorough meeting with the Italian candidate, Doreen Bird was only too happy to take her into the second grade at her college, alongside my trinity from the Legat school. Everyone was happy.

On our days off, Penny and I usually ate at a local Greek restaurant, revelling in our rare evenings out together. We even attempted to dance, Zorba-style, to romantic strains on the bouzouki.

One day, we had just got home a bit worse for wear from all the retsina, when my wife suddenly cried out from the kitchen while I was liberating a fountain in the toilet: "Look, Misha! There's a poor man outside who looks like he's dying of a heart attack."

In a panic, I ran in and seeing what was going on, tried to reassure my wife: "Darling, that's not a heart attack, he's just had a skinful. He's just trying to get up off the ground by holding on to the electricity pole." He would pull himself up using his arms, but then slip back down on to his back.

"That's not true! You've got such a massive ego, you just don't want to help a dying man."

I didn't even have time to open my mouth to respond, before my wife had run down from the second floor to save the dying man. From the window, I watched as Penny, who was quite drunk herself, struggled to get the drunken man on his feet, while he crawled over to kiss her, pawing his rescuer all over her tasty, appetising body. The soft-hearted saviour extricated herself from the 'dying' man's sexual advances, and slammed the front door in his face at the last minute. Deep into the night the 'miserable heart-attack victim' played football against our entrance portal, preventing his poor neighbours from sleeping until the police eventually showed up. So in the end, our evening out was ruined.

After this I started to worry about my lonely wife's well-being during my late rehearsals, and couldn't see a palatable solution to this risky situation. I begged her not to let anyone into our house in the evenings, as homeless wasters and boozers usually got together opposite us on Primrose Hill, to engage in 'philosophical debate'. But all the same, trouble soon came knocking when I was delivering my next seminar in Italy during the winter holidays. Penny didn't want to worry me in Rome, and only told me what had happened when I got back to London and noticed that the door had been broken into.

"Misha, you were right about the potential risk to our quiet street with its expensive houses, a long way from the city centre and police surveillance.

"The morning after you'd left, I was in a hurry for work and left some important documents behind in the house so I decided to fetch them in my lunch hour. As I neared the house, I noticed a strange person standing at the roadside opposite our closed front door. He was looking into our kitchen window, which for some reason was slightly ajar, even though it was still winter. I realised that something wasn't right, and proceeded with care. Slamming the front door shut behind me, I heard a whistle outside that sounded like someone giving a warning signal. This alarmed me even more. I made my way slowly up the stairs to the first floor and all of a sudden came face to face with a man rushing down, carrying a large package in a black bin bag in his left hand, and a short metal crowbar in his right. He threatened me, smiling nastily as he elbowed his way past me on the narrow stairs. I yelled in shock and pushed him away from me. In a panic I ran up to the second floor and heard the front door bang and the noise of a car engine starting up. The door to our home along with its main frame had been ripped out of the wall and stood to one side. Your new tape recorder (with its spools) was sitting on the sofa, covered with a tablecloth. My unexpected arrival saved your precious equipment. The landlady quickly called in some workmen to put the door back on."

"I hope you called the police and they wrote up a file on the burglary and damaged door."

"Unfortunately, the police who came to inspect the crime scene behaved strangely. When they heard that my family jewellery had been stolen, they were surprised that it wasn't insured. Enquiring about my husband, the officers of the law initially suspected you of masterminding the robbery and getting away from England. I tried to explain to them that you didn't need to wait ten years to do this. But they responded by saying that they would need to take your fingerprints as soon as you returned to London, if indeed you were coming back at all."

So I paid a visit to the nearest police station. I gave my prints as requested and took an interest in the findings of the investigation. The police acted out a cheap farce, surprised at my naïvety and wounded pride due to the lack of grounds for their suspicions.

"In our district," they declared, "there are about twenty burglaries a day. We can't waste our valuable time. We have much more serious crimes to deal with than the possible theft of uninsured jewellery."

It felt like Moscow in Soviet times, rather than the capital of Great Britain. "Professional bureaucrats are exactly the same from one country to another!" I concluded.

Still, on the advice of my lawyer Steven Rayner, I requested the landlady of our house, who had insured the property for a huge sum, to compensate us for our material damages, as we now had to move to another address following the break-in.

After the events at Primrose Hill, Penny refused to live with me in a new, small flat on Gray's Inn Road, between the British Museum and St Pancras Station. She preferred to move back in with her parents in Croydon rather than vegetate in the role of 'grass widow'. I understood how she felt and did not censure my wife's latest flight, as she abandoned me once more to the vagaries of fate. We rarely met up now, as after work she usually stayed in London, where she spent the evenings with friends and drinking companions. In the early stages, I just visited my wife and her parents in Croydon on my days off, painfully aware that this was the beginning of the end for us.

My new home was called Trinity Court. Originally a Catholic monastery, it had been converted into residential accommodation after the Second World War, preserving the inner garden with its antique sculptures adorning several priests' tombs. There was a wonderful view from my balcony on the sixth floor. I transformed my bedroom into a tiny rehearsal studio. I installed a double bed that folded out from one wall on springs and an enormous, decadent mirror on another, with a ballet barre in front of it. Now I was free to prepare my dance and choreography exercise programmes. The Tube and main-line railway stations were within five minutes' walk, as was my new place of work, the Central School of Ballet. On top of this, I was given another opportunity to visit new shows and exhibitions, and take full advantage of the capital's cultural life. I was really lucky to find this latest accommodation which was so suited to bachelor life. By the beginning of the academic year I had managed to get everything ready by the time I started work.

A friendly welcome awaited me at the Central School of Ballet. Both second- and third-year intermediate pupils had been thoroughly schooled in Classical dance to their own particular standard. The students embraced my Character dance syllabus wholeheartedly and displayed exemplary discipline in class. As far as I could see, Christopher Gable, artistic director, and Ann Stannard, administrator, did a professional job in managing both school and troupe administration and teaching. The main specialism for students there was Contemporary dance. Modern and Character dance were the key training subjects for performers of this genre. There were several ballet classrooms/studios and many additional spaces within the school. The most talented graduates were selected for a small Central School of Ballet troupe under Christopher Gable's leadership, which was grant-funded by British Gas. At that time this company was just starting out, but it had great potential for creative success in the future. After the Legat school, this organisation, without a doubt, restored me to the professional level of work that I was used to in the theatre. My next challenge would be to get in with the Royal Ballet.

The Doreen Bird College of Performing Arts was one of the leading theatrical teaching establishments in England. Its curriculum included singing, acting and dancing, and specialised in professional musical comedy and operetta. This is why, wherever possible, all students also took up opportunities in the above-mentioned combined forms of stage art on top of their basic profession. Pat Izen was head of the Singing Department, and Sue Passmore ran the Drama Department. The Dance Faculty programme consisted of: Classical, Modern, Jazz and Character dance and Partnering. I took the last two teaching subjects at first twice and then later three times a week after I had left the Legat school. All dance teachers were engaged in choreography during their working hours.

Doreen, the director/founder of the college, was an experienced Modern-dance teacher who had taught the course for many years. She was an excellent organiser with highly developed people skills. Working with her was interesting and enjoyable. My first season at the Doreen Bird College concluded with the students' inspiring demonstration of their achievements in the Character dance and Duet courses during their assessment classes and final concert of the academic year onstage in the local theatre. In discussing the results of the past year with the leadership team, Doreen picked up on the positive outcomes from my dance courses and referred to this with a view to possible plans during the next school year for productions of vocal and drama suites from popular Anglo-American variety shows with a choreographed component.

My Character dance courses at the Doreen Bird College were so manifestly successful that Dame Beryl Gray offered me the chance to give a demonstration class with my students from the Doreen Bird College at the next seminar in the Euston Concert Hall, in London. We removed the seats from the central stalls and installed temporary ballet barres. Seated on the stage in the presiding council were Ninette de Valois, Beryl Gray and other stars. Several dozen seminar attendees were dotted around the semicircular amphitheatre. Four pairs of college students and I greeted the audience with a Character dance curtsey, and were welcomed with applause. The youngsters and I demonstrated forms of barre exercises for ten minutes and then several centre studio études (five minutes each) to a lively tempo. After this, the seminar leader invited the dance and pantomime teachers/instructors to leave their seats and come down to the barres and say hello to me. But none of them made a move from their allotted seats.

I then addressed the seminar attendees: "Dear colleagues, please come down from your seats to the barre and try out the Russian School of Character dance! As you can see, down from your seats, I am a modest (almost) man, and promise not to bite or pinch anyone (well, only sometimes). Please make your way downstairs carefully. Just not all at once – one at a time!"

General laughter ensued, then after a pregnant pause, a few middle-aged women carefully picked their way through to me. Once we'd introduced ourselves, we worked on three exercises at the barre and one étude in the centre. I thanked these brave heroines for their display and presented each of them with a video for bravery, featuring my Canadian ensemble Kalinka, made by the Quebec film maker Bernard Piccard. The demonstration was a huge success. Both of the famous, esteemed ladies on the presiding council wanted to be photographed with me in a cute trio, to record this historic cooperation between nations. A few days later I received an official letter of thanks from the ISTD president, full of genuine praise for the professionalism I brought to my teaching.

The growing interest in my Character dance gave me sufficient courage to sign a deal with film producer Andrew Winstone, for an initial work on this genre in a series of three sequential demonstrations of teaching methods:

a) training course (three hour-long cassettes, beginners, intermediate and advanced levels);

b) 'Methodology of Dance Composition' (one cassette lasting two hours, ethnographic material);

c) 'Concert and Theatre Repertoire for Character Dance' on four hour-long cassettes.

All in all: eight cassettes, lasting nine hours in total. It would take ten months to produce, i.e. completion due in May 1985.

It's not for no reason that my close friends and acquaintances think me a gambler. In the positive sense of the word, this trait is an inalienable factor in any creative endeavour, to a greater or lesser extent. If an artist has confidence in his creative capabilities and conviction in his ideas, then as long as he has the means to realise these things, the greater are his chances of success.

I hammered out the directorial scripts for the video course at home, constantly picking Andrew's brains on the telephone regarding the staging and lighting. I worked out the choreography for the trial études and sequences with the students in both schools: Bird, for two hours after our classes; Central, on free days for four hours in the mornings. My demonstrator pairs: Alistair with Charlie and Brady with Angie, physically and in terms of personality, were compatible and looked great together in their performances. Crystal-clear technique, precise expression, absolute musicality and most importantly, impeccable creative discipline. I was genuinely proud of these products of my teaching, as in forty years of school-based theatre practice, they were some of the best jewels in my Character dance crown. Without them I would not have been able to pull off such a complex project.

I signed an official year-long employment contract with each performer in my quartet. I explained to them their professional obligations and the serious nature of the undertaking, which included many other specialists in addition, who made a living from this work all year round. There was no going back. It seemed to me that everyone involved in such a small-scale project bore responsibility not just for themselves and their partner, but for all the other team members too, united in their common goal both onstage and behind the scenes. Self-control during filming was crucial: the quality of film and safety during movements in poor light behind the filming platform; care over costume and shoes; concentrating on the Director's cues, etc. The film editor could easily erase any unnecessary sound when putting the film together, but inaccuracies in movement technique or an inappropriate facial expression, or someone stumbling accidentally while changing places – these could not be removed, and the Director would then be forced to re-record the ruined tape over and over. Every such repeat would use up everyone's valuable time, energy and consequently reduce the overall quality of the film – not to mention my financial losses.

For group video illustrations of Composition methods in Character dance, for études I used the intermediate students from the Central School of Ballet, who had a good foundation in Classical and some stage experience. It was easier to develop the choreography with them, but more challenging to keep control of their creative discipline. For all their solid classical background, they clearly lacked a sense of performance as an Ensemble and ability to work in harmony with the music, as well as motion and acting skills. They were more concerned with the technical impact of performing sequences than in the artistic presentation of the stage form. The students were not to blame; they had simply never been taught the art of drama. After all, in the rehearsal studio, with full lighting and no theatre wings, it was difficult for the non-professional dancers to transform themselves from ballet students into fearless Cossacks with sabres or into fiery-tempered Neapolitans with tambourines. All the more so in the training format, without stage costumes to distract audience attention from the performers' uneven body shapes and errors.

We started rehearsing and filming the Character dance video course in the Christmas holidays, in a room I had rented at the ISTD theatre, where my teachers' seminar had taken place. Students from both schools were now working separately on a daily basis before or after lunch, to complete the programme for all three videos on schedule: beginners, intermediate and advanced. Our production and camera crew were working round the clock, so we did complete all the final film reels on schedule. I paid everyone the balance of their fee before Easter and couldn't wait to see myself on screen. Andrew and I continued to work together on the text of my instruction for the musical/voice notation, as well as the content and cover design for the cassette sleeve. The editor and I were both pleased with the result of filming. In addition, I was getting ready for celebratory concerts to mark the end of the academic year in both places of work, and choreographing the Kasatka ensemble's summer tours. It was hard not to feel overwhelmed by this amount of pressure. I sought my wife's help in reprinting the design of my manuscript for the brochure insert for the videocassette. She kindly agreed to get in touch with Andrew.

Pat and Sue, my colleagues at Doreen Bird College, devised some musical and dramatic scripts resembling a type of operetta or review, where the majority of the cast acted, sang and danced all at once. The first (for me) concrete piece of work in this genre was the stage version of the Musical Comedy *The Jolly Cruise*. Tourists of various nationalities danced to my choreography for 'Russian Matryoshkas', 'Italian Tarantella', 'Gypsy Rhapsody', 'Sailors' Dance' and so on. The second, more serious production, was a dance adaptation of *Fiddler on the Roof* from the show of the same name by Sholem Aleichem. Here, as well as choreography with the dancers, I had to work with actors/vocalists on their stage presentation. After the huge success of the American film on this theme, thanks to Jerome Robbins' wonderful choreography, I didn't want to come a cropper in front of my students. So I tried my damnedest, if not to outdo my rival, then at least to equal his level of theatricality through physical expression of Jewish morphology. The college students were fortunate to perform such an exotic repertoire in England's associate local theatres, gaining vast stage experience. I made use of a few such episodes to illustrate my video demonstrations.

To be honest, this college was more than just another workplace: it was my family. I related to many of my charges quite honestly as if they were my own children, flaws and talents alike. In twelve years of excellent work, the teachers and other staff became very dear to me – probably because I was living alone at that time, far from those close to me. In no other school in England have I ever felt, either before or since, such a personal affinity with my colleagues or students. I found it really painful when any of them left. It always seemed to me that I in turn benefited hugely from my attachment to and trust in them too.

One day, while returning from Sidcup by train after a full day's work at Doreen Bird College, I found myself in the middle of a fire at King's Cross Underground Station. As we stepped out of the train on to the platform, we were engulfed in columns of poisonous smoke. All the passengers made a rush for the exit. The escalator, overloaded with people and luggage, suddenly stopped, propelling passengers into one another. I even thought, *Thank God we're going up rather than down!* Eye-watering smoke seeped out through the steps with a foul smell of burning machine oil. Up above people were indicating that the exit had been closed off. Terrible panic ensued. Just as during the bombing of Stalingrad, I didn't stop to think; I just jumped over the panel on to the empty escalator handrail, which was still descending. Luckily, I had my work bag over one shoulder so my hands were free. I hurtled down, leaping down the steps two or three at a time at breakneck speed, trying to avoid colliding with others who had crawled on to this escalator from the other side. Inevitably, I flew over someone; was kicked by another, and landed head over heels on the final steps. That's when my falling technique came in handy, learned from a stage-movement teacher at Odessa Ballet School forty years previously.

Let's just check: are all your vital signs working, your bones intact, no bleeding from the nose or ears? On you go!

A crowd of young passengers for some reason carried me in a wave towards the passage to the Victoria line. I realised that this would be a mistake. If the stupid staff up top were sealing off the main exit to King's Cross from us, then they would have done it first, down here, where passengers were changing lines, so as not to get people piling up in the depths of the station. I tried to go back, but this proved impossible due to the general panic. I shouted out to the people nearest me that we should return to the main platform and get on a train to another station from there. But everyone carried on yelling and no one was listening to anyone. I struggled to squeeze myself up against the corridor wall and slowly slid my back along the marble, starting to make headway in the opposite direction towards the place where I'd flown off the escalator. Voicing obscenities, men punched me in the skull, but I stoically endured all of this until I was halfway back to a familiar place, where there were now far fewer people. Scratching the blisters on my head and gulping from the smoke, I rushed back to the place where I'd got out of the train. Eventually I saw a policeman I recognised, who a few minutes earlier, had mistakenly been directing the panicking passengers the wrong way. There was less smoke here due to the tunnels on both sides. I had to get my breath back from the ash, check my head wounds after the punches, and weigh up the situation which had become more complicated on the single, functioning platform.

That idiot policeman is not making any decisions or using his radio to report the situation on the platform to his superiors. All the trains are passing straight through in both directions without stopping. This means they're giving safety announcements to those in them, but how will they deal with those of us trapped here, condemned to death, unless they get us out of here fast? Why isn't this man of the law stopping a half-empty train and getting people out of the fire?

A moment later, passengers flooded on to the platform from various directions. A new wave of panic erupted. Old men were sitting next to the columns, exhausted. The young were yelling and waving on the platform edges, trying carefully to halt the train as it passed through, and attempting to pull passengers off the rails, who'd been knocked down by the surging crowd. A few brave souls started heading off into the tunnel with the aim of getting to the next station. This looked like suicide to me. I needed to think of something, but I was paralysed and unable to move an inch. Eventually, the Taurus in me came to life. I took a determined step towards the policeman.

I grabbed the giant's arms and began screeching hysterically for everyone around to listen, "Officer! Stop the train and get the people out! Stop the train! Stop . . ."

Naturally, he flung me off a few metres like a puppy, knocking over the people nearest him. Contorted with pain in my elbow from the concrete floor, I observed with satisfaction as the infuriated crowd, after hearing the appeal in my voice, formed a tight circle around the officer. I caught fleeting glimpses of mens' fists and womens' heels threatening him right in the face. They were all starting to chant as one ever more loudly: "Train! Train! Train!" The hair all over my body was standing on end. The policeman once more dictated something on his radio to his boss, who this time got to hear personally about the events on the ill-fated platform. Finally the official strode decisively through the baying throng and headed towards the spot on the platform which marked the front of the train.

This is where the real pandemonium starts, I thought. *How many elderly people will be run over in this chaos?! It reminds me so much of Mum with the three of us in the war. She too could have ended up in the same situation as that old lady over there with a walking stick next to the column.* I dragged myself over to her, and helped her up to her feet.

She regarded me with astonishment, saying. "What are you doing? Look after yourself! My life's over, but yours is still ahead of you."

I made my way around the crowd with her and made a point of moving her in front of the policeman. Along the way, men in the crowd swore at me, and furious girls elbowed me. I 'accidentally' stamped on the feet of those who didn't want to let us through. Of course, curses resounded in my wake, but my 'partner' and I managed to reach the officer in time. He understood my request, and stepped forwards to take the old lady from me, while I receded into the crowd. The old woman looked around and waved to me, shaking her head. This was the best reward from someone who reminded me so strongly of my mother. The approaching train hooted like mad. Over the tannoy, we could hear the driver constantly urging us to stay calm. The policeman gave a whistle of warning, but the poor passengers were not easily reassured. The empty train picked everyone up apart from the officer, who remained on the platform to watch out for 'lost sheep'. I was in shock but at the same time felt a sense of moral satisfaction at having managed to help an ill, elderly woman.

All of us fire victims had to get out at the next station. We were all shaking from shock, not so much for own safety now but for the old and infirm, and women with children. Without wishing to generalise, you could see by what had happened that things weren't right in the authority responsible for safety on the Underground. Thirty-eight people died in the fire at King's Cross Underground Station. As reported in the press, the fire started with cigarettes discarded on the escalator. These fell into the workings and ignited machine oil that was spilt on the floor, which had been collecting there for half a century, since the station was built – and the accumulated rubbish had never once been cleared up. What more can one say? When I got home, before doing anything else I packed all my clothes into a bin bag as they reeked of smoke. I spent ages in the shower, but my long, shoulder-length hair continued to stink of burning oil. The following day I cut it off completely, so that I wouldn't be reminded of the trauma I'd been through. Colleagues from college were ringing me all night long, knowing that I could have been caught up in the fire around the time I left them. When they heard what had happened, they calmed me down and congratulated me on receiving this gift from Fortune. Penelope was the only one who took no interest in the fate of her still lawfully wedded husband. I was not surprised as I realised that her busy social life with her old friends after work had so distracted the 'free woman' that she was probably quite unaware of my traumatic experience.

In addition to working in two different schools for two to three days a week each, I was sometimes invited to various productions in theatres and ensembles throughout England. One such creative project was with London's famous professional song and dance ensemble Kasatka Cossacks led by Goggi Bestavachvili, with a Russian/Georgian repertoire. I had got to know them back in Montreal while they were touring Canada, and had done some temporary work with their dancers to produce a Character Miniature. On arrival in London I had been in contact to resume our creative relations. Almost the entire group (singers, musicians and dancers) had emigrated from the former Soviet Union, or were children of post-war immigrants. They were extremely talented and enthusiastic, and desperate to make it on stage.

In one of our rehearsals together in 1985, we had an unexpected visit from my young colleague Sasha Agadzhanov whom I had met during my emigration hiatus in Rome. I was delighted to see him. During the lunch break, we sat in a cafeteria and he told me about his dilemma. Alexander, who had been dancing with the Royal Ballet for several years, had decided to requalify as a teacher. He had been offered a post teaching Classical and Character dance in the Children's Department of the Royal Ballet School. He had to agree though, that as far as Character dance was concerned, he only knew what he'd learned some time ago in his schooldays. When he found out from the Director, Barbara Fewster, that Berkut had arrived in London from Canada, Sasha heartily recommended me as an expert in the Character genre, making no secret of his personal connection. Barbara decided to send him out on a solo reconnaissance mission first. My videocassettes were not yet ready at the time. Fortunately, at one of Goggi's Ensemble's concerts, Agadzhanov had spotted my name in Kasatka's printed programme and resolved to seek me out. I asked how I could help him.

He answered: "The new Director of the Royal Ballet School and the Head of studies would like to observe your rehearsal. Would that be possible?"

"They're more than welcome to watch Kasatka next Saturday from 10 a.m. to 1 p.m." In my haste to reply, I forgot to ask Goggi's permission for their visit, hoping that meeting these people would flatter his ego.

I enjoyed close professional and personal relationships with the people running the Central School of Ballet. The previous year they had been only too happy to rent me space after 7 p.m. to work on my video courses with students from the school. The management considered this good advertising for their business and extra rental income for the school. But once they discovered that I preferred to use other students from Doreen Bird College as leading video demonstrators, they took serious umbrage at my choice. I tried to explain that I had trained these students for a whole year at the Legat boarding school and then at Doreen Bird College, prior to coming here to the Central School of Ballet. Nevertheless, Gable and Stannard could not forgive me for this.

At the end of the academic year I found out by chance that some dancer from the Maly Theatre, Leningrad, was visiting, and looking for teaching work. After watching his class, Gable recommended that he got in touch with ISTD. When the Soviet refugee discovered that I worked there, the visitor dropped me in it from head to toe. This came as no surprise to me, as I was used to Soviet scum 'dancing on graves', even those of their parents. It seems that I underestimated the Central School of Ballet management's reaction to my video course, as I promptly felt a kind of undercurrent against me.

I really valued this school, and derived genuine professional satisfaction there, so it was a pity to lose the respect of my colleagues and students for no valid reason. At this point, Gable found out that the Royal Ballet School had offered me work next season.

"Here or there!" the Director declared unequivocally. "We don't want other schools poaching our best students. You've got until the summer holidays to make up your mind!" I hadn't realised that the Royal Ballet School and Central School of Ballet were such fierce rivals.

CHAPTER 8 BALLET CORONATION

In spring 1986 the senior Royal Ballet School (RBS) was still located in its former studio next to Barons Court Underground Station. After observing my rehearsal with the Kasatka Cossacks ensemble, the Director, Merle Park, asked me to give a demonstration class with undergraduate classes of boys and girls together in an hour-long presentation. She had probably decided to frighten me, by putting me in the main rehearsal studio's amphitheatre with its ten rows of seats and vast windows along the sides to give the best possible view of students taking exams or ballet artistes in their run-throughs. Dame Merle didn't know then that I was accustomed to giving Character dance displays. I decided to make the most of this opportunity to promote this little-known genre and my own popularity. Agadzhanov had no doubt spread so many rumours about me to his colleagues, as, in addition to the dozens of teachers seated in the amphitheatre, a complete kaleidoscope of curious faces was pressed up against the windows outside.

Judging by what I'd seen, previously there hadn't been any professional teachers or choreographers with specialist qualifications in the Character genre. A few Classical Masters, such as Maria Fay, occasionally gave introductory Character lessons as and when demand dictated, to fill gaps in the course/seminar curriculum. But without following up with a disciplined technical syllabus or training method, such practice was not only ineffectual in developing performance skills, but also disorienting to devotees of Terpsichore in relation to this genre's role in opera, drama, musical comedy and other forms of Dramatic art.

I understood how important my demonstration was for RBS's prestige as well as my future creative career in Europe. For this reason, I put serious preparation into the crucial event. I met up with the pianist in advance and provided the musical accompaniment for the demonstration lesson. This time I decided not to give the intermediate students involved complicated barre exercises or centre sequences. I chose instead to play on the effect of motion in the pattern of legs and arms, which Maria Fay was not familiar with, but which used amusing graphic figures to excite the youngsters' enthusiasm for these charades. Similarly, with the young men clapping and girls tapping their heels in intricate, syncopated rhythm. I finished the taster with an étude in pairs, incorporating an ornate movement together, without them letting go of each other's hands. While the lad was in motion, he grabbed his partner below the knee, spun around with her and effectively lowered her to a sitting position on his knee. There was wholehearted acclaim for the demonstration. Neither the performers nor the audience could believe it when the hour was up.

Dame Merle thanked me for my presentation and invited me into her office. In front of the director of studies, she offered me three intermediate groups twice a week. The director of studies noted down the details of the training attire I requested. She handed me a class timetable from 1st September, and invited me to the forthcoming classical exams to have a look at my future students' technical abilities. When the Director and I were alone, I asked about the possibility of choreographing the graduate concert from the opera/ballet repertoire, or some other symphonic music.

"Mikhail, give us your list of suggestions and we will discuss them at the Artistic Committee in October. Tomorrow we'll send you our official offer letter confirming all the terms discussed. Please return one copy to us with your signature and photograph."

As usual, on the way home I mulled over my triumphs and defeats during my recent years in England. For all the reasons I've explained, I was shocked by the antagonism between ballet schools. Rivalry between theatres or companies was understandable. But teaching establishments? I found it hard to accept this. I had always considered education to be beyond deviousness.

I had to promise Doreen that I would keep one of my free days clear for her college.

I began my course with the intermediate groups at RBS in the usual way by teaching the students about Character dance through a short historical excursion back to its origins, specifics of the genre and dramatic roles in ballet. The beginners were usually surprised to hear that this well-known form of choreography dated back 300 years to Louis XIV. It seems that when visiting teachers or casual staff with the Russian Ballet School gave a Character dance lesson in the professional institution, they didn't find time to explain in advance what went with what. For this reason, the RBS students absorbed this detail on the movements as if it were something exotic or (worse still) the opposite of Classical dance. So I was surprised that even in the Royal Ballet, right from the outset, pupils viewed this important academic subject as a pleasant diversion and light relief after the repetitive daily grind of classical training. I had to lay down the law with some of them. To this end, I would use a particularly aggressive 'upstart' to demonstrate a complicated barre exercise or sequence in the centre, which he couldn't grasp immediately, provoking laughter from everyone around us. As a rule, this was more effective than censuring or reprimanding him.

The students from all three courses at Barons Court understood that there was never any point or right time to play the fool in Character dance lessons. Not because I was too good or nasty, but because they were constantly saturated with new material to learn, which they had to work on for an hour and a half at each of my classes. I never displayed any antagonism or partiality towards anyone in school. I treated all pupils equally, and the youngsters knew and respected this. My first season at RBS was so successful that the day after the final concert,

Dame Merle called me to her office and offered me Character dance classes in the beginners' school at White Lodge (near Richmond) from third grade (eleven to twelve-year-olds). But I assured the Director that it would be better to start teaching the little ones Historical dance as a ballet genre in the theatre programme, which she had observed in the Bolshoi School during a visit to Moscow. Court dance is used more to train children physically in a style bordering on classical, and instils a more refined manner in them. It also helps to overcome the psychosexual barrier between young partners when they first come into physical contact with each other. The aim of beginning Character dance at White Lodge in the fourth year of the ballet course, was to develop the students' muscular strength, and give them some experience in performing the Great British folk repertoire with RBS teachers. Dame Merle confirmed this project for the beginning of the academic year and swiftly ordered the necessary clothing for both genres. Patrizia Linton, head of studies at White Lodge, gave me my class timetable for the following term and wished me well.

Commercial advertising on video was fast becoming popular in Europe. The RBS administrator decided to shoot a film featuring the school's diverse activities, and sell it for £9.50 to people wishing to register for performance exams. Character dance was also included in the video programme illustrating the teaching process. Without any advance warning, a camera crew appeared out of the blue one morning in my lesson with intermediate students at Barons Court, and after lunch with the beginners at White Lodge near Richmond. Apparently they managed to give the later ones some notice about the visitors. They weren't worried about them being there as the children boarded for five days a week and only went home at the weekends. I decided to keep quiet about my author's rights while being filmed with my students for commercial purposes. Neither was any financial remuneration for the teacher or pianist discussed, which wasn't exactly fair. Nevertheless, it suited me for the time being, as otherwise RBS could present me with a bill or claim for using their students in my own commercial video business.

May 1985 saw the whole world celebrating forty years since the defeat of fascism. I flinched as I recalled that time. The memories suddenly came flooding back to me: war, bloodshed, death . . .

How are my sons and grandchildren doing in Moscow? Are our aunts in Odessa still alive?

I decided to ring my cousin Sofia in St Petersburg as she'd probably have the latest on everyone, and more.

"Hi there, my dear cousin!"

"Misha, is that you?"

"Who else would ring once in five years?"

"Well, good for you, you knock-kneed bear! Where are you calling from? And who are you living with now, you rolling stone?"

"Sofia, I'm calling from London, I'm living in England."

"And who is she then? Have you got a new woman now?"

"Just my wife. She filled my life and there's no time for anyone else."

"Really? I don't believe you!"

"Come over and see for yourself, Sofia! I'll send you an invitation for a visa and pay for your flight."

"OK, don't put ideas in my head. Tell me, what's the news from your lot in Moscow?"

"No idea."

"Mine have moved to Berlin with all the kids. They've got a flat there, they're living the life of Riley."

Once I'd got the information out of my cousin, I spent all of Sunday ringing around my family. I wished them a happy Victory Day, using this as a pretext for re-establishing contact with them. They explained that my cousin David from Odessa had also moved to Germany with his family some time ago. But my eldest brother, Yosif, was still making plans to leave his home town. My aunts were still with us, thank God. Penny and I were invited to go for a beach holiday with them on the Black Sea. My eldest son, Dmitri, had developed a large business in Moscow. He had converted the old tsarist villas and stables in Kuzminki into school buildings with extra accommodation. The condensed secondary education comprised seven courses, and all charges were paid in dollars. Business was booming. My grandson, Richard, attended his father's school. Thanks to the improvement in the family's fortune, my youngest son, Sasha (on his mother's insistence), had abandoned his three children in Novosibirsk and returned to Moscow, but he was unable to stay clear of drugs. He wasn't allowed to live with his brother in the school, so he became permanently homeless. This intelligent, talented man was in his prime. He blamed his mother for everything and cursed her for refusing to allow him to emigrate to Canada.

On Saturdays I usually undertook extra choreography at the senior RBS premises with a fixed group working on a specific production. Svetlana Beryozova gave a general warm-up class at 9.30 a.m. and it was only after this that various teachers/répétiteurs started practical work with the warmed-up performers in the free classrooms. Svetlana's father, Nikolai Beryozov, was a famous figure in the ballet world and it was no accident that the maestro's daughter had followed in his footsteps. A leading soloist with the Royal Ballet, and teacher with ballet master credentials, she enjoyed tremendous success in many European companies. The elderly Nikolai missed the theatre and was in the habit of popping in to watch separate rehearsals or productions on Saturdays. It was on one such occasion that he and I first met. Beryozov was clearly keen on the Character genre, so we shared many mutual interests, and occasionally called on each other at home. We ate out in restaurants together with Russian and other Soviet artistes, and formed a close friendship. I would sometimes put myself in his shoes a quarter of a century later and wonder wistfully if I would live as long as he did.

An equally legendary figure in England's theatre world was Dame Ninette de Valois. She was considered the matriarch of the Royal Ballet. I had read a great deal about her creative achievements and had heard her lecture at MTA when I was a student there. Unfortunately, in my student days, Russian leading lights abroad such as Simyon Troyanov and Nikolai Beryozov, were not mentioned in lectures on the history of ballet by Professor Elyazh for political reasons. Nevertheless, I considered myself very fortunate to come into such close contact with these experts, debate essential problems in the art of ballet, and listen to their fascinating stories. I met Dame Ninette in London at an ISTD seminar, where I had demonstrated my method of teaching Character dance to teachers and, incidentally, received a very positive response from her. From then on, when she came to see how 'her protégée', Dame Merle, was getting on, Dame Ninette would always drop in (accompanied by the Director) to my class to observe her young charges performing Russian Gypsy or Italian rhapsodies. She really enjoyed this. Sometimes, caught up in the emotion of the dance, she would even get up from her chair and address a pertinent remark to one of the participants on their musicality or expression of movement. I was touched by

Dame Ninette's concern, and always made a point of thanking her for this in public.

At the end of the first season at RBS, following successful exam results in all my courses, Merle Park introduced me to Valerie Adams, her head at the Teacher Training Course (TTC), and invited me to teach my method of Character dance there from September, twice a week: two classes each day from 3 p.m. to 6 p.m. The first course was for beginners, and the second for those completing their studies. Both groups were headed for a future career with a ballet school or company. I specified the time I had available: Tuesday and Thursday afternoons. Mrs Adams invited me to visit her, promising to formalise all the details of my employment without further ado. She told me about my predecessor at RBS, Maria Fay, who would often cancel classes due to her extremely busy workload, without having a suitable cover teacher in place. Valerie and I went through the detail of the academic programme for these teachers-to-be, opportunities for practice at our lessons with children at White Lodge, and agreed that it was crucial to put on choreographic productions for the final concert of the year on the summer stage at Holland Park, etc. This is how my sphere of activity at RBS came to include all three departments: those enrolled at White Lodge and Barons Court, plus the TTC. On the one hand, being so popular fuelled my self-esteem. On the other, it worried me: I had too many eggs in one basket. I had to tread a fine line most of the time, i.e. manoeuvre my way diplomatically between the heads of department, who were always rivals for attention from the multitasker on production.

There were eight to nine adult learners aged in their early thirties from different continents in both groups on the TTC. All of them had already undergone specialist training in dance and were experienced performers, but in a range of styles within their local cultures: Japanese and Chinese or European classics, American or Australian modern, etc. As you would expect, devising a uniform, methodical approach to stage art from such a diverse range of backgrounds, was (to put it mildly) quite a complex task. Even taking into account that the students were physically and musically competent to master the Character method, the most difficult thing for all of them was overcoming their own personal limitations, i.e. those heterogeneous movement skills of the muscular and nervous system as well as psychological and spiritual principles of aesthetic education which had become ingrained over many years in the past. Nevertheless, I must admit that though it was not straightforward for everyone, in general, both groups studied the method and repertoire of European Character dance with great enthusiasm and a high degree of success. In view of the small number of male students (one or two in each group), I often had to demonstrate and work out duet sequences with different partners. One of these, Kafuyu Shintani, a thirty-six-year-old Japanese teacher from Osaka, stood out from the others. She had resolved that on completing the course she would teach classical (Cecchetti) and my Character syllabus in a school back home. To this end, she collected relevant materials, and observed my production rehearsals with RBS delegates on Saturdays and in the city's professional ensembles. Now and again, she would even assist as my partner on her own initiative. I was impressed by this, within limits.

In September 1987, ex-soloists from the Mariinsky Theatre began to teach Classical in the senior RBS: Valentina Mukhanova (girls) and German Zamuel (boys). After they had emigrated to the USA, both had been invited in by the Royal Ballet management because of their impressive qualifications from the Vaganova school in Leningrad. They were fantastic friends as well as intellectual specialists. Along with Anatoly Grigoryevich, who for many years had taught boys Classical dance at White Lodge, and Alexander Agadzhanov, who worked as a teacher of the Royal Ballet troupe at that time, we made up a group of five Russian professionals in all. Out of jealousy, detractors branded the Royal Ballet 'a branch of the Bolshoi'. And this was no accident, as many ballet stars at Covent Garden over the last century had taken private lessons or partnered such masters as Nikolai Legat, Konstantin Myasin, Nikolai Beryozov, Rudolf Nureyev and others. It was not without reason that Dame Ninette de Valois, Margot Fontaine, and Merle Park were in sympathy with the Russian ballet style. This was indeed a fruitful union of two great cultures.

Valentina, German and I frequently dropped in on each other's classes to enhance our teaching practice and gain greater insight into what made our shared students successful in the various dance genres. We discussed their individual abilities and realistic chances of a future career. In addition to our hands-on work in the school, German and I both spent time at home researching our academic projects on pedagogy and choreography, although he was writing a literary work, and I was using the cinematic medium. The three of us enjoyed warm personal relationships and often met up in each other's homes. In contrast to many Soviet immigrants, who badmouthed each other as soon as they landed on foreign soil, Zamuel, Mukhanova and I operated in reverse fashion: we gave each other moral support, and helped one another physically as required, along the lines of 'You scratch my back, I'll scratch yours'; not only because our theatre genres in the ballet school were different, but on the strength of our professional status as teachers/ballet masters with postgraduate education. German had graduated from the Leningrad Conservatoire, and I was a graduate of MTA. Plus we both had more than twenty years of experience in the theatre. Many dancers arriving from Russia, even the talented and celebrated ones, have little understanding of Pedagogy or Choreography and were therefore never in competition with us. But for all that, it's not always pleasant to wash off the mud that's stuck and prove your worth to those around you.

Having taken up the RBS management's offer to teach a full timetable of Historical dance at White Lodge, I took on a massive workload in preparing the course content:

a) resurrecting information thirty years on from my personal archive and Soviet textbooks about periods of European social history, comprising the Middle Ages, Renaissance and baroque;

b) adding to this knowledge in the British Library, with the help of printed works by Western authors from the twelfth to nineteenth centuries;

c) devising an academic programme over three years on the basis of six dances for each era, i.e. two examples each per term (in total; eighteen typical pair compositions over nine terms);

d) putting down musical accompaniment for a whole course from audio-recordings of dance arrangements in classical composers' symphonies, to match the chosen historical periods;

e) composing my unique forms of choreography based on the original sources of steps, pauses, mimicry, gesticulations, ornaments in spatial patterns;

f) drawing up a syllabus of exercises and sequences for children to train foot and arm technique, mimicry (facial expression), symbolic gestures and Partnering supports (including lifts).

I had to carry out this additional workload without it infringing on my day-to-day work, over the course of the next six months. *Well, what of it? In for a penny, in for a pound.*

I was pleasantly surprised at the positive reception granted me by Patrizia Linton, head of studies at White Lodge. She was, in fact, a qualified teacher and manager, who managed the learning and discipline in the school with ease, and had published a book about RBS. The children took to both of my subjects, Historical and Character dance, with rare inquisitiveness. An atmosphere of creativity and respect for the master always pervaded the lessons. For this reason I allowed children to address me as Misha (the diminutive form of my name). But when anyone crossed the line of decency, I immediately demanded an apology from the guilty party. If anyone refused, I asked them to refer to me henceforth only by my official title: Mr Berkut or sir. This was the worst possible punishment for intransigent individuals. More often than not, this happened during observations by my students from the TTC. The children would sometimes meet them in their Classical lessons and various popular entertainments at White Lodge. It was probably because of this that they didn't accept those on the teaching course as fully fledged masters, and were too familiar with them. Nevertheless, this teaching practice for teachers-to-be was invaluable as, on the one hand, it gave us the opportunity to analyse and evaluate our TTC, and on the other, it stimulated young students to work harder on the programme of Character or Historical dance in front of senior colleagues. Patrizia seemed pleased with our results at the termly assessed demonstrations.

The adult students in the RBS Teaching Department spoke a variety of languages between them, and required a lot of individual attention and patience. Although I could explain poorly in four European languages excluding the Slav ones, my reserve of foreign vocabulary was still not up to the task of presenting the academic historical detail of the multinational world of Character dance. The TTC students always wanted answers to the essential questions in their eyes: the origins of various dances; the method of choreographic composition; technical principles of performance for original movements with objects (tambourines, castanets, sables, etc.); the logic behind a Character dance lesson and the phrasing of sequences, and how these are combined with elements or component parts. And the main thing was the secret of stylising folk movements into Classical form for Character dance stage performance, while preserving the roots and flavour of the original in the process. This was the 'stumbling block' for an ignorant audience or critic, who didn't appreciate the essential difference between the visual perception of the *natural* everyday Folk dances and their *artistic* interpretation in Character dances onstage. This form of stylised everyday body motions has existed in Ballet art for over 300 years, the original proponents being classics from the eighteenth- and nineteenth-century world of choreography: Jean-Georges Noverre, August Bournonville, Jean Dauberval, and other great Ballet luminaries. However, many contemporaries are unaware of the history of dance and theatre. Therefore they often castigated me for denigrating my nation's sacred heritage, forgetting about stylisation in Classical music, opera and pantomime.

A similar situation arose with Historical dance too. Over three centuries, both of these genres (Character dance included) constitute an outstanding stage form of dramatic action, emotional expression and the performers socio-ethnic characteristics in ballet performance. Nevertheless, the public and critics alike have unfortunately never taken these into account or simply brushed them aside – not because of the quality, but because ballet aficionados lack sufficient understanding of the essence and role of these channels of expression in performance. From time immemorial, even ballet artistes themselves regard these allied genres of Classical dance with a certain amount of snobbery, viewing them arrogantly as 'lower caste'. This lack of understanding that is present in

Character dance, also applies to Historical dance. Many participating pairs (even instructors) in social and society Ballroom dances (*Danza di corte*) confuse these understandings with Historical dance in ballet performance. They simply don't factor in that people wishing to take part in these entertaining aspects of dance, are motivated by personal satisfaction in their interaction with their companions. While in Historical dance on the theatre stage (as with Character dance), the performers work the public, not just for their own enjoyment, but also to fulfil the supplementary functions of playwright, director and artistic expression of the show. It's just a pity that this aesthetic knowledge is not cultivated in theatregoers from an early age.

From March 1989 I had guests coming to see me every term for the half-term holidays from the Soviet Union, Europe and Canada. The 'first swallow' was my cousin Sofia from Leningrad. I gave her a royal welcome, not just because I was indebted to her for helping me in my youth, but also thanks to my sentimental feelings towards my family and nostalgia for Odessa. Then Semyon Shegelman visited me from Canada, my friend and idol who was also a well-known artist in North America. He came for a week and to my delight, stuck around for two years! He painted a series of rich canvases here which I bought. Along with a dozen paintings that he'd brought with him to England, I organised a wonderful exhibition of his fabulous work at Islington Cultural Centre in London, which was hugely successful. After him, various dear friends continued to visit every three months, a constant reminder of my estranged, worldly life in my fanatical passion for work, learning and creativity.

In spite of our cool marital relations, I had promised to take Penny to visit my home country. But I must admit that I feared my former enemies all the more now as they had been disgraced since Perestroika. Thinking about it logically, with a British wife in tow, most ringleaders would not dare to attack someone who'd caused them trouble in the past. My eldest son, Dmitri, was happy to see us. He kindly drove us around Moscow, and took great pride in demonstrating his showcase school. Sofia was especially honoured by a visit from these precious visitors from England. At some point she had brought her son (Arkady) back a good camera as a gift from London during one of her stays with me. Now, as a sign of gratitude, my nephew took photos of Penny and me on every corner of our tour of St Petersburg, as Leningrad was renamed. Penelope was bowled over by this city of museums, theatres, palaces and cathedrals, such that she didn't want to leave. But Mum was expecting us in Odessa. The other issue was that we were carrying a huge suitcase full of presents for the family the whole time from one city to another, which was really irksome. Still, it was a happy burden, bringing pleasure to those who had been deprived of any attention or generosity from me for far too long. I introduced my spouse to my bosom pals: Syoma Kogan: now concert master/second violinist in the Opera Theatre orchestra; Sasha Sandler: ballet soloist with the Operetta Theatre and other former colleagues from Odessa's cultural centres. Before we left, I organised a huge meal for everyone in a waterfront restaurant, to mark the occasion as something to remember in our separate countries. To Penny's surprise, a cheery throng of friends and relations came to see us off at the station.

Back in Moscow, after rushing about between St Petersburg and Odessa, Penny finally immersed herself in her comfort zone of theatre and music. In our last few days, thanks to my son, we went to the Opera at the Bolshoi and saw a new ballet in the Nimerovich-Danchenko Theatre. After the shows we dined right in the city centre in exotic Caucasus restaurants. My wife was on cloud nine. I had to give my son credit. He knew how to look after a spoiled British tourist. I just smiled ironically, realising that my eldest had proved to be an even bigger show-off than his father. By midnight, Penny was dead on her feet and had fallen into a deep sleep. My son and I had a heart-to-heart, and went through everything that had happened in our family over the last few years. Since his return to Moscow after emigrating to Canada, our relationship had broken down completely.

Without a doubt, his business was flourishing. He had escaped the clutches of his unhinged mother by buying her a small house with a garden in Kislovodsk in the Northern Caucasus. But even from there she still managed to get at him. Still, the school director managed to keep a handle on his mother's strange ways. People persist in saying that: 'Children can't teach their elders anything.' Well, actually, sometimes they can. My youngest was still living the life of a tramp in Moscow's drug scene. He sucked money out of his brother, gave him a load of grief and brought shame on his benefactor. Every time he turned up my eldest made him take a shower, gave him clean clothes, fed him and offered him a bed for the night. But once he'd got his next handout, the youngest would disappear again for another week or two. To this day, this miserable, irreparable state of affairs continues to haunt our broken family like a curse.

After the series of three video courses in Character dance had come out, I immediately took on my next video project in Historical dance (Court dancing). Initial preparation to bring the latter to fruition required significantly more time. I was spending all my free time in the academic and history department of the British Library, studying the history of European social culture from the twelfth to the nineteenth centuries. It was one thing to reanimate choreography of the original forms of Branle, Sarabande or Minuet from Italian and French books, but quite another to recall the real underlying historical basis, and describe it succinctly in the brochures to insert in the videocassettes. Now it was possible to get on with the bits describing the historical eras of European culture. I decided to present this in the form of a live interview with Liz Ferguson, a famous dancer working at RBS at that time. In parallel with our live dialogue, she and I presented practical illustrations of the poses and choreography for the specific dance being discussed in a progressive, sequential content in the interest of a more conducive teaching process. Winstone and his camera crew assured me that our video course was a totally unique format in the expanding and fast-growing film industry of self-instruction programmes in dance, pantomime, sport, games, etc. But there were some with conservative views who held that learning from a screen in school could never replace direct contact between teacher and student and therefore there was no place for indirect methods like video to encourage adolescents, adults, the elderly and disabled people to maintain or develop their physical education and good spirits through body motion.

As far as the direct Art of dance was concerned, this screen version of the teaching process for performing choreographic composition opened up infinite possibilities for both teachers and dancers to perfect their work. In contrast to work in class or onstage, people watching a video course, show, or sporting game could go back again and again on their tape to the position they needed on the screen, checking how well they had assimilated the material or information. In broad terms, the advent of video production played a revolutionary role in the aesthetic education of a whole generation and improved the qualifications of professional performers once and for all. When I showed David, the owner of the Ballet Bookshop in London, a demonstration cassette of the Character dance video course as a set of three, he was only too happy to sell them. Naturally, this led me to believe that my Historical dance video course would enjoy similar success in future.

Over the previous three years at White Lodge, I had succeeded in delivering a complete course to the children on Historical dance covering seven centuries of European civilisation: the Middle Ages, Renaissance and baroque. By this time, Andrew had finished the preparatory drafts of printed materials, illustrating social and cultural conditions in major European countries, including colourful episodes at balls in imperial palaces and squares. All the youngest groups at RBS gave excellent demonstrations of their programmes in their final assessment for the term, and were curious to see themselves on the television screen. After selecting the most talented and effective students from each course, I took the list of candidates to Dame Merle for permission to undertake a day of video recording Historical dance onstage in the school's theatre that coming Friday evening and Saturday during the day. I promised to show her the working version before it went to the studio for editing.

The Director then called Patrizia Linton, head of studies at the beginners' school, White Lodge, and asked her to ensure that the theatre stage, the students taking part and supervisory staff were available at the weekend. She would advise the kitchen and dormitory staff. I tried to make sure everything was covered. The week before filming Historical dance, I instructed all participants in each group: to be as well disciplined and organised as they could, if they didn't want to look like complete idiots on screen. They should shower beforehand and cut their hair and nails, bring a spare clean outfit, and advise their parents that they would be home on Saturday rather than Friday evening. I did my best to answer all their work-related and silly questions.

On Friday afternoon we got everyone onstage under the lights and dressed to represent all three eras. On Saturday we managed to record the whole programme without any hiccups. As the shoot came to an end, I confirmed to the parents waiting in the foyer that I would be giving each of them a complete set of the Historical dance video course. Without a doubt, the children had earned this, as they had worked two days without a single break. Is there a mother anywhere who would not want to see her child dancing on the stage of an imperial palace in court dress? Of course not! This tapped straight into parental ambitions. 'You have to make sacrifices for your Art.' We had managed to record eighteen dances in one day, even including some repeats. So we had plenty to choose from in putting together the best performances. No one believed that we would fit everything in by the end of the working day. We all applauded each other, glowing with pride.

While Andrew was putting the film together, I checked the content of the video course's Historical introduction in the literary, artistic format of the material and cassette inserts. This was the last chance for any corrections before typesetting. All the informative dialogues with my partner Liz for the eighteen examples of 'danza di corte Europea' were scrupulously completed and included in the accompanying brochures. There was no room for errors or lack of clarity here. With my lack of specialist education in history, critics could eat me alive, which I did not relish in the slightest. So (I emphasise) I spent twice as much time preparing the Historical dance video course as I did on the Character dance course. A series of illustrations and photographs from ancient literature imparted a distinctive flavour to the Historical introduction of this journey into past aristocratic society on imperial estates. It took 700 years to democratise social relations between city inhabitants through this genre of dance.

In May 1992 I decided to celebrate my sixtieth birthday and the universal success of the Character dance video course in a large restaurant. I booked an instrumental quartet with a singer from the Kasatka Cossacks ensemble, where occasionally I still produced dances for their repertoire. Penelope came to my big event with her new partner, Peter (a museum restorer), signalling a lack of respect for the birthday boy. The place set for her next to me, remained empty. I didn't know what to say to my guests' puzzled looks, and carried on playing the happy party host. But inside I was hurt by my ex's cynical conduct. I would never have acted in such a way towards her, in spite of my lowly upbringing. Clearly there was something I didn't get about relations between people in civilised society. Couples get together and split up, stay friends or become enemies – this is all understandable. But why make fun of a once-close partner, embarrassing him in front of friends and colleagues? Something inside me broke in relation to my former beloved wife. Nevertheless, I played my role of hospitable host until the very end, and didn't unleash the zodiac bull. Now, I knew where I stood: I was morally free to enter into new romances and distractions.

In 1992 I made a proposal to Dame Merle to put on the 'Polish Ball' from Glinka's opera *Ivan Susanin* for the final Gala concert in Holland Park, which would include all RBS departments and the TTC. The beginners from White Lodge opened with a group Polonaise, followed by a Mazurka performed by students from the TTC. The ball closed with the intermediate students from Barons Court performing the 'Cracovienne' Character dance. The summer audience at the theatre in the park responded rapturously to the thirteen-minute-long 'Polish Ball' with thunderous applause. I received many compliments, but sensed storm clouds in the air at the same time. Understandably the presidents of the Royal Academy of Dance (RAD) and ISTD attended. I was not a member of either. Most likely of all, my Historical dance course at White Lodge, which wasn't part of their programme, had irritated them as far as their judgement of my work was concerned, on the principle that 'Whoever is not for us is against us.' I was actually so overwhelmed by my teaching work that I had absolutely no time or inclination to be a member of any party or association whatsoever. I wanted to be free creatively from any kind of obligation, following my experience of Soviet ideological constraints. I naïvely assumed that the British inquisitors would simply have a bit of a moan and leave me in peace after a while.

But this was not the case. My ignorance of the accepted views within the ISTD regarding Historical dance (Court dancing) and Character dance (Folk Stage dancing) obviously provoked the conservative purists into protesting their chauvinistic nature against 'foreign upstarts' who showed no respect for established traditions in British culture. Doreen Bird, an experienced Modern dance teacher as well as an ISTD committee member, had already defended me to the hilt with her colleagues for several years. The Royal Ballet only came under the umbrella of RAD within the sphere of Classical dance, which I was not teaching during that period. Its director, Merle Park, was generally sympathetic to Russian specialists at RBS, and kept my modern methods/styles of Historical and Character dance close to her ample chest. It wouldn't have surprised me if ISTD had criticised my choreography of Scottish or Irish folk dancing. But I had studied Slav folk traditions for over fifty years to such a degree that even their own Folk and Character dance specialists: Robert Harold and Maria Fay respectively, could still learn something from me.

Everyone knows that homosexuality is widespread in the Ballet world. I personally don't belong to this group of men, but I have no objection to this form of intimacy. However, both Royal Ballet schools (beginners and intermediate) exercised tight control to limit its influence on relationships with students and teachers. Before I arrived, the RBS management had gone so far as sacking the director of their beginners' school at White Lodge for 'playing these kind of games' with his boys. Monitoring the sexual behaviour of both students and staff occasionally reached excessive proportions. One day this happened to me too. At RBS, the children's dressing rooms and toilets for boys and girls were separate, as you'd expect. Teachers of both genders changed in the same large area and shared the toilet.

When I asked naïvely why female teachers didn't change in the same room as the girls, like the men did with the boys, as is the case in many ballet schools across Europe and America, my colleagues responded, "It's precisely this mishap that forced the Director of the beginners' school out."

I made a mental note of this and decided not to give anyone cause for unnecessary suspicion.

All the corners of the communal teachers' dressing room were fitted with little curtains. One of them was designated for men, and all the rest were for female teachers, who made up the greater number. On one of the days I was working, after two hour-and-a-half-long classes in the senior school I flopped down exhausted behind the men's curtain to catch my breath. As everyone does in moments of solitude, I was muttering something to myself. I had only just got my pants off ready to change into clean ones, when suddenly someone tore at the curtain from the other side, exposing the handsome naked specimen to the whole world with his mouth open wide.

"Oh, it's you!" shouted the Director. "We thought that a couple of people were up to mischief in here."

In shock, my first reflex was to cover my equipment with my palms, but then I came to my senses and started waving in alarm to the hysterical laughter of women behind Dame Merle. "So be it! Let these ladies fall for my charms, it might come in handy one day."

I admit that at that time my male prowess was something I took pride in vis-à-vis the ever eager female sex. I don't know what happened to me, but I was in good form. Passing up such a great opportunity to teach the management a lesson in tactlessness without it becoming farcical was beyond me. The Director, no doubt sensing my tactic, drew the curtain.

I carried on shouting: "Dear Merle, in the land of my fathers there's an unshakeable law that's been passed down through the ages: if a woman sees a man in the nude, she has to become his lover."

"Thank God", explained the Director, "that we find ourselves in the land of my fathers rather than yours!"

The fallout from this chaos resonated through the building of the ballet troupe and school for a long time to come.

I was meticulous in my preparation for the TTC graduate examination. Here, face-to-face with the examiner from RAD and ISTD, students could affirm my teaching method for training Character dancers and their instructors, or disgrace me with their ignorance of ethnography and performance techniques. I must pay tribute to the high level of professionalism shown by Valerie Adams, head of the RBS Teaching Department. Everything – organisation, creative discipline, enthusiasm, mutual support for students and a sense of responsibility – were inculcated in the graduates by the TTC leader over a two-year period.

At the 'Character exam', each student demonstrated to the rest their combination of barre exercises and sequence from a specific nationality in the centre. Then by ticket (as was customary in most institutes) the ones who stood out gave oral responses to questions on ethnography and methods of teaching Choreographic composition. It was not only the European students, but natives also of Turkey, Japan, Finland and other commonwealth countries who did well to endure the first test of their professional status as instructors and aesthetes in the art of Character dance. As per the programme for the training syllabus or ethnographical vocabulary, so it was for the acting skills or emotional expression. This was the norm for the scheme of elementary foundation in the given dance genre. I presented to all the graduates the recently published video course on Character dance, which would help them to perfect and expand their knowledge among devotees of dance art on the spot. We swapped addresses and said goodbye for now.

Kafuyu caught up with me in the lobby and asked if it were true that I was looking for a partner to demonstrate programmes for my courses in England and Europe. She had heard Liz Ferguson talking to someone about this and was trying her luck.

"Kafuyu, aren't you going back to Osaka to work in your mum's school?"

"No, Mr Berkut. I've decided to look for a job in London and gain some experience over the next few years."

"Do you mean dancing or teaching others to dance?" I enquired.

"It's a bit late to be dancing as I'm thirty-seven now. But I would gladly assist someone else. All the more so because you already know me and I would learn a lot from you. If you can, please outline my duties and I'll give you a 'yes' or 'no' right away."

As we headed out into the street, Kafuyu tendered her hand before we got to the crossroads.

"I'm renting a flat with a girlfriend in that yellow building over there. Why don't you come up and we can have a chat."

"I'm a bit uncomfortable about visiting a student of mine at home. It's not what teachers do."

"In the first place, I'm an ex-student of yours. Secondly, I trust you. I hope that you trust me too."

Over tea, I went through the detail with Kafuyu of what I needed an assistant to do in terms of organising and delivering international courses: producing video materials and related advertising; setting up tours for creative groups from Russia and Ukraine.

"I can pay twenty pounds a day in cash, as well as related expenses. Two regular days off in the week or time off in lieu during overseas courses."

"When are you looking for someone to start?"

"Monday, if that suits you."

"Could I work till Saturday free of charge, just to familiarise myself with the material? That way I can get my head around what you need, and understand your current priorities."

I smiled, transfixed by her open gaze and those strikingly curious eyes.

"OK. I'll have a reciprocal cup of tea ready for you at 9 a.m. Here's my card just in case."

Kafuyu arrived on time, and even brought some Japanese biscuits and a laptop. After a brief cuppa, I showed my assistant where everything was in the cupboards and storage areas. I discussed with her a more practical system for setting out the promotional materials and where she would sit with her computer. I then went into my bedroom/studio, where I had a folding table next to the window for correspondence and phototypesetting. We worked for three hours before enjoying a light snack and then did another three hours of sorting all the video/audio project explanatory texts into packs on the shelves and in the cassette brochures. Finally, at 5 p.m., I suggested going for something to eat somewhere. Kafuyu proposed buying a few things in the supermarket and preparing supper at my place. The canny Japanese woman quickly checked the contents of my kitchen cupboards and fridge. She made a list of the additional essential items, and ordered me out. I froze, trying to guess what was going on in this woman's mind: was she a good fairy or just another witch? That's what I often used to call Penelope as her birthday was on 31st October: Halloween.

Before supper I timidly suggested a drink. My guest stated that she did not drink, but would allow me to drink to her health. I made a pleading face.

Then Kafuyu poured a little vodka into a glass of orange juice and made a toast: "Here's to our creative friendship!" and made a show of drinking down half a glass.

We repeated this 'game' a few times, confessing our sins to each other as we did so. Eventually I suggested (as I usually did in such situations) drinking to *Brüderschaft* – friendship. The lady opened her astonished eyes wide, seeking to decipher this unfamiliar social code.

Confused, the old musketeer shrugged, saying, "There are no words to explain it."

My guest smiled curiously as she came around the table and tentatively sat herself down on my lap. Repeating the motion of her glass behind me, this beautiful, tipsy woman had worked things out; she put down her glass, and went for my lips. I hadn't yet revealed any spark of interest towards the lady, as I wasn't sure whether this situation was real or just a wind-up. The woman gave in all too quickly and easily to my seduction, as if she had been waiting for this for a long time.

Coming up for air after a protracted kiss, Kafuyu asked flirtatiously, and somewhat embarrassed: "Mikhail, how many more times can we do that last *Brüderschaft* ritual?"

Rather than giving her an answer, I laughed as I embraced the wanton woman, this time kissing her with all the pent-up passion inside me. We started to undress each other, kissed some more, then undressed completely until we ended up in the shower. Kafuyu was an experienced woman, and took the lead in our intimate relations with natural tact and patience.

The two of us were like hungry travellers in the desert, relishing every drop of love, unable to leave each other alone all night long. My partner was so businesslike in her every approach to the sexual act, that I lost all sense of romance in our love-making. I had to give her credit: she was an expert rider. Her galloping nearly made my eyes pop out of my head with each orgasm. I was amazed: where do people get so much energy? Initially I couldn't understand why Kafuyu was always so keen to be on top during the act. But one day, holding her close, I discovered her secret. The 'winter beauty' (this is what 'Kafuyu' means in Japanese) had a stunning figure, with very small, but bouncy, breasts. When she was underneath during love-making, she bucked her jockey so vigorously that he could end up under the bed at any moment, as holding on to the single-minded filly from on top was no easy matter. Joking aside, my lady friend was a wonderful girl, who gave me back a normal sex life.

Right from the following week, Kafuyu took responsibility for advertising courses, tours, video promotions, etc. Of course I provided her with all the essential information in the first place. She got the hang of everything really quickly and took charge of all the arrangements so conscientiously that she would have been the envy of even the most experienced secretaries. Once she discovered that I, too, had now found myself a regular partner, Penny came to visit one Sunday. Seeing how Kafuyu was working and managing affairs, she was only too willing to give her some professional advice in dealing with English apathy and bureaucracy.

My ex had tears in her eyes as she was leaving, and remarked that my assistant and I were really compatible, and that I should hang on to her at all costs. "You won't get another opportunity like this!"

Kafuyu's next task was to prepare for the urgent print run of the folded brochures/inserts for the Historical dance video course. I had produced an outline of Court dancing in English the year before, then had it professionally translated into French, Italian and German. Now this brochure in its four languages urgently needed to have photographs inserted into it before going to print, while we produced copies of the video master at the same time. By September 1993, everything was ready for publication. The commissioned samples were dispatched to sales points alongside the previously supplied Character dance video course. At the beginning of the school year I presented the RBS management and each participating student with a Historical dance video course, a complete set as a token of the author's gratitude. But there was no peace for the wicked. A month later, representatives from RAD, ISTD and other societies started to stick the knife in. Storm clouds were gathering above me.

CHAPTER 9 INTERNATIONAL KALEIDOSCOPE

Over fifty years of creative output, my main mission was to develop the Character genre in the art of dance using universal moves to express natural human emotions and movements in an artistic way. Literary descriptions or video demonstrations can never replace direct contact between teachers/ choreographers and performers – either to master the style and technique of a specific composition as effectively as possible, or to tease out the deepest spiritual content of the work and the intense relationship between partners. This is why I consistently devoted so much time and attention to practical courses in various countries in Europe, America, Asia and even the Far East, including choreographic productions in theatre performances, films and review concerts.

In the twentieth century, England replaced France as the front runner in theatre culture. After spending time in America, where anything new is welcomed with enthusiasm, I was on guard in my, let's say, 'progressive', intensive courses, which were not well-known in Europe at that time. For these reasons I decided not to take a risk but to conduct the first experimental 'UK Summer Dance' at Doreen Bird College in Sidcup, and just for one week rather than the usual fortnight. In any case, I had to cover my own costs for rent of the hall, advertising in dance magazines, printing flyers, etc.

My fears were well founded, as it turned out. Even my solid track record in organising and running similar projects was no protection against failure. The college management ignored most of my enquiries. My classical partner, Margaret Field, gave her usual class for students at various levels of development rather than her specialist, intensive method for teaching course participants. She paid more attention to her own students from the local college than those who had come from other areas. The latter were also unhappy about the half-hour train journey to London, where there was more to do after classes than in a small provincial town. In short, I made a strategic mistake, which taught me some useful lessons for subsequent courses. 'There's no point reinventing the wheel,' as all the old wisdom confirms.

One year later, in the first half of August, I organised another international UK Summer Dance course. This time I rented a ballet studio in the centre of London next to the Royal Opera House in Covent Garden. I invited Diana Joffe from Paris, who in previous years had come from New York to work on my Montreal courses. She had danced many roles in the traditional Classical ballet repertoire in Riga Ballet (Latvia) and more recently had been working as a teacher/répétiteur in professional companies in Europe and America. Most significantly, she could not be dictated to by the British associations RAD or ISTD. There were many more attending the course than I'd anticipated – both local and from overseas. By all accounts, the course couldn't fail, thanks to the presence of Madame Joffe, and the prestigious venue. In the mornings, Diana gave a general ballet class, and then I took 'Pas de deux'. In the afternoons we ran parallel classes in two studios: she worked with the girls on variations, while I did Character dance training with the men. Then we swapped them over. In the evenings we went to see shows or met up with Masters of the stage in the Covent Garden Theatre Club. To round off the course, Diana and I produced a final, assessed concert, featuring the Classical and Character dance repertoires. I ran the same course in the same venue every other year with an updated programme.

Last time, as Diana and I were saying goodbye at London Airport, she asked me: "Mishenka, why haven't you taken me back to your place, like a proper woman? You've lost out, my dear!"

I was dumbstruck. So in a swift riposte to her challenge, I cracked a stupid joke: "Forgive me, darling. As a man, I was worried that I wouldn't be able to satisfy a stunner of your calibre."

I was unaware that she and her husband (whom I'd known for many years) were having problems. He was the one who would tell me about my friend and colleague's fatal illness that would bring her life to a premature end.

I usually planned all my courses to run in the long holidays to fit in with the British education system; these generally lasted a minimum of sixteen weeks a year, including three half-terms plus four weeks for Christmas and Easter and nine for the summer holidays. This allowed me to make concrete plans for scheduled trips and have time to prepare programmes that tied in with these. The categories for these courses were the same as the American ones, with the exception of the universities. In Europe these had been replaced by teaching institutes in ballet academies such as RBS or regular seminars by teaching associations similar to RAD and ISTD. I worked on the remaining categories: ballet schools, short-term intensive courses, productions in theatres and ensembles in line with the format already approved in Canada and the USA. My choreographic resources never ran out as I was always devising and putting on new compositions at the RBS and Doreen Bird College. I would usually give an annual one- or two-week course in each establishment. The exceptions to this were the professional academies in Rome, Oslo, Jerusalem and other such cities. At first, Penny had helped me to organise intensive courses by dealing with the international registration, advertising, etc., but as the network of European courses grew, she got fed up with it and dropped out. On my own, I was unable to shoulder the entire load I'd taken on, and was on the verge of a nervous and physical breakdown. Fortunately, with Kafuyu coming into my life as a qualified assistant and faithful friend, all aspects of my creative and business life gradually fell into place. I was just sorry that I had not been blessed by such fortune earlier.

During my transitory emigration stay in Rome in 1975, Zharko Prebil, my friend/classmate from MTA, had helped me to become a teacher in the National Academy of Dance, pending receipt of my visa to Canada. Six months later, as we were saying goodbye, Giuliana Penzi stated that the doors of her academy were always open to me. When she heard that I had returned to Europe and was working at RBS in London, she invited me to run a Character dance course the following July, and at the same time, to put together something concrete for the final Gala concert to mark the end of the academic year. I was delighted to take up her invitation and from then on, made regular repeat visits over many years to the National Academy of Dance in Italy, and created various dance productions for the end of the academic year. For me, this was a rare opportunity to maintain my professional status as a choreographer of mass compositions, working on projects involving qualified dancers. From one year to the next, I presented the Italian audience with my premieres of suites from the opera/ballet repertoire or those set to symphony music by classical composers: Vivaldi's 'Concerto for Mandolin and Orchestra'; Tchaikovsky's 'Suite from the opera *The Queen of Spades*'; 'Lisztiana' ('Hungarian Wedding' by Liszt); the 'Polish Ball' from Glinka's opera *Ivan Susanin*; 'Polovtsian Camp' from Borodin's opera *Prince Igor*, and other choreographic works. The National Academy of Dance in Rome was a wonderful sanctuary for an itinerant creator.

My professional head was also turned in Europe by the Norwegian Advanced Ballet School in Oslo. The Performance Department, in which I regularly gave Character courses, was headed up by Jurine Kirkenaer, the founder of this dance institute. The Teaching Faculty was supervised by her former pupil Elisabeth Frich. Now an experienced tutor, she was an astute leader and the author of several ballet biographies. I particularly enjoyed working here, imparting my experience of Character dance training (barre and centre) to eager dancers. I shared my secrets of Choreographic composition: from subject conception, through musical structure and choice of body motion, to performance style, dance technique and stage expression. I was amazed by Norwegian enthusiasm and the curiosity displayed by these future teachers. They were hungry to learn, and devoured the theoretical and practical knowledge I offered them. We had to make time to summarise this in the notes for further self-study. They would come to the next lesson having swotted up, word-perfect as the course developed. With them, I didn't have to mark time, waiting for them to pick up either with brains or feet the basics of complex sequences or composition structure either in the configuration of motion, or in the way the performers used the space. I remained good friends with Elisabeth and her family for many years to come, making exchange visits between London and Oslo. We never lost touch.

Jurine Kirkenaer was famous in Norway's theatre circles as a veteran of contemporary ballet, with a wide range of creative interests spanning Folk dance to Modern/Jazz forms of choreography. Many of today's professional dancers in theatres and private companies around the country started out in her children's classes. Jurine had a deeply artistic nature and (strange though it seems) stood out due to her ability to bring off new progressive projects. It was no coincidence that the Ministry of Culture entrusted her with opening a teaching department within her facility. During my first Character dance course, she asked me to give her senior students a ballet class in the Vaganova style, so that she could compare notes and define how it differed from the Cecchetti system, which was the one mainly used in Norway. In my lessons, she sought to combine methods from both syllabi to achieve greater expression in Contemporary dance. This fusion in training future Modern dancers produced really good results and was popular in America. But there was no accurate description for this method of training. Jurine Kirkenaer asked if I could arrange for her to observe a one-off ballet class at RBS and Doreen Bird College. After getting the go-ahead from both directors, I invited Jurine and her husband to come and stay with me in London. By way of thanks for my hospitality, she drew an allegorical portrait of me as a charging bull. Regrettably, that's how she saw me during my demonstrations in class.

Ever since my youth, Greece had fuelled my creative imagination with its rich mythology and depictions of the gods, nymphs and other romantic characters in museum collections. It's no coincidence that in my earlier choreography of the 1950s, I celebrated their beauty and poetry in my ballet miniatures: 'Amour and Psyche', 'Satyr and Nymphs', 'Three Graces', etc. Unfortunately, as a result of this, Soviet critics attacked me without mercy in the 1960s, accusing me of breaking the Marxist–Leninist code of aesthetics. I had transgressed Communist Party censorship on propaganda of bourgeois ideology by using the impressionistic music of Debussy, Massenet, Ravel and other avant-garde Western composers; offended conservative Eastern balletophiles by the neoclassical style of my choreographic language, and Asian religious fundamentalists by refusing to replace the performers' close-fitting, suggestive garments and traditional tutus with wide trousers. It goes without saying that I was more than happy to accept an invitation from the Greek Dance Research Institute to deliver a seminar in Athens on Historical and Character dance. My long-held dream of visiting the birthplace of my creative idols was a real prospect at last. And this was thanks to that same freedom which I had fought for in Beethoven's 'Appassionata' and for which I'd been exiled to the back of beyond for three awful years by those 'humanitarian' ideologists.

Sophia Smailow, institute director, was genuinely amazed by my syllabus for Character dance training and the impact of combining conventional ballet choreography with ethnographic elements in the stage repertoire she offered her students. She suddenly asked whether I had previously studied ancient Greek Classical choreography. I apologised, explaining that this was a clear gap in my advanced ballet education from MTA, and I would be extremely grateful to my colleague for helping me to fill in this missing piece of the jigsaw.

"Mikhail, it's very kind of you to have presented me with your unique Character dance video-course series, which my teachers and students have been following with great interest. It's down to them that you are here. Allow me to reciprocate by giving you my course on Classical Greek dance, and you will see how close our choreographic styles are in terms of musical and motion expression, and the spiritual content of artistic forms in Contemporary classical compositions."

I awaited this demonstration with some trepidation. After my Saturday classes, three students directed by Sophia and accompanied by two musicians, showed me a twenty-minute programme of Greek classics dating back 1,000 years, taken from a vast series of illustrations from wall and vase paintings. Without any particular analysis, it was clear that the roots of body motion as interpreted by modern masters, lay in Classical Greek dance. Nevertheless, from the photo albums I had bought in museums, constant reference was made to man's artistic motions, which naturally carried through into choreography.

617

Through repeating my courses at Sophia's place, I was always enriched by new aesthetic knowledge of Greece, this ancient cradle of the arts.

Israel was a very dramatic place during the years I was giving Choreographic training courses there. In one visit during the winter holidays, I spent the last week of December in Tel Aviv delivering a dance-composition seminar for provincial ensemble directors who had come to the main cultural centre, Bikurei Haitim from all areas of the country. Then I set off for Jerusalem on 1st January, where I gave my methodology course in the Rubin Academy of Music at Givatram University to students in the Education Department, who were learning to teach Classical and Character dance as part of the school curriculum. From there, I returned to my usual job in London. The choreographers' seminar in Tel Aviv was coordinated by Uzi Adoram, a representative from the Ministry of Culture. An able manager, he was an intelligent man with a good background. He didn't know much about the art of dance, but this in no way hampered his ability to organise the event.

By the beginning of the 1990s, a huge number of people had emigrated to Israel from various parts of Europe and Asia. Inevitably they brought with them particular cultural customs from different national and ethnic minorities. It's easy to imagine the 'cocktail' resulting from such a mix of often contrasting folk elements into a single choreography on heterogeneous motifs and rhythms. This came to the fore now with my students for Israeli dance. I realised that I had put my foot in it with amateurs like these, and didn't even try to persuade them that they were deluding themselves. I just asked Uzi to get hold of an accordion as quickly as he could, and invite an experienced local dancer who had a handle on genuine Israeli folk traditions. After Character dance training at our next class, the guest dancer and klezmer musician (fiddler) demonstrated to us typical forms of national choreography stemming from ancient Israel. Next, I played some popular tunes from Soviet republics on the accordion. The more I played, the more the surprised the faces in the audience, convinced that the music familiar to them as 'some Israeli dance' had originally belonged to various European or Asian nations.

After this demonstration, I suggested that the course delegates put aside their erroneous forms in their (forgive me) 'cacophony' of music and motion, and instead get down to the professional study of production methods in dance composition that were common to all nationalities, which they had nearly all represented in the past. As a result, everyone did their own thing: either to preserve their pre-immigration native culture in dance, or, irrespective of this, to practise original, traditional, Israel choreography, or develop contemporary forms of dance art: Ballroom, Modern, Jazz, Tap, Break dance and so on. We agreed that on the basis of the composition methods and principles I suggested, by the end of the week each of the delegates would present a two-minute étude for two performers chosen from their colleagues and after joint corrections, would repeat it at the assessment concert on Sunday. This idea appealed to everyone and they all got down to work with renewed vigour. The manager of the Cultural Committee was pleased with the outcome of the seminar and expressed his hope that it would continue to run for a long time to come.

Hasia Levi was principal of the Rubin Academy of Music at Givatram University, Jerusalem, and a veteran of the theatre. Her managerial skills left a lot to be desired, but aesthetically speaking, she was a deeply discerning specialist in analysis/criticism of artistic riches; educationally, she had masses of experience in training professional personnel. Her students consisted primarily of young women, half of whom had completed secondary school at eighteen and then had served two years in the army, before entering higher education. It's hard to imagine their physically exhausted bodies and square shoulders (from constantly carrying weapons) at the Faculty of Music and Dance; their 'rock-hard' limbs and permanently 'severe' facial expressions. Those poor girls! Recalling my own difficult childhood during the Second World War, I found it painful to look at these brave female soldiers, who had lost their natural grace in army service, trying in agony to beat their swords into ploughshares. I was flummoxed at first, not knowing how to help them. Overnight I redesigned the structure and method of my usual training into a special set of exercises within the syllabus, to soften the whole musculoskeletal system of these modern Amazons. I needed them to change their military bearing and become civilians, otherwise I would be frightened to correct them. The young ladies rewarded me with kind smiles.

I gave a general ballet class at 9 a.m. Hardened bodies warmed up at the barre. In the centre, three young guys and twelve girls swapped places non-stop. Character training followed after a thirty-minute break. In the afternoon we studied composition methodology. I got three men to do the 'Soldiers' Dance', and spun the women around in the Tarantella. In their excitement, they gave the tambourines such a beating that they broke some of the leather straps. I had to remind them that the drums were not their enemies' heads on the front line. Nevertheless, Hasia commented on the damage to state property. The final assessment concert at the university theatre was a resounding success. The Dean invited me to run a two-week course in the summer in the Be'er Sheva Conservatoire, which was supported by them. One of my students was from this town. I decided to find out a bit more from her about the establishment mentioned by the Dean. She told me that as there was no Choreography Department in this conservatoire, she had to live in Jerusalem during term time. I asked the student whether there were any Russian specialists in her town, and she could only name Kanterman, a choirmaster from Moscow. I let out a cry on hearing the name of my old friend and colleague. The young woman suggested that I ask the Dean for his contact details, and his secretary promptly noted down my compatriot's address and telephone number. She even dialled the number, to witness the impact of this surprise.

Misha recognised my voice straight away and yelled down the telephone like a market trader: "Is that you, 'Itchy Feet'? Are you in Israel already? What are you waiting for – no excuses, just get yourself down here!"

My namesake was disappointed to hear that I was flying straight back to England the next day, but I extended the invitation to my friend and his charming wife to visit me in London. Kanterman gave me a quick rundown of his duties as leader of the Vocal and Choral Department. He confirmed that there was no permanent Dance Department in the Conservatoire, and that was why they ran intensive summer courses at the local sports centre, in conjunction with Rubin Academy of Music in Jerusalem. He made me promise to stay with him rather than in a hotel for the two weeks in August.

On my return to London, an invitation had already arrived by telegram for me to deliver the course to the Be'er Sheva Conservatoire students. Two months later Kanterman rang to tell me that his wife Sheryl had been made a professor in the local branch of the Academy of Science for significant discoveries in the field of chemistry. The following week she was due to give a lecture on this subject at London University. I was delighted to give them the use of my spare room and treated them like royalty for five days. With permission from management, I invited them to my class at RBS, and Penny took them to the British Museum. Sheryl's lecture was well received by her London colleagues. Misha got to hear the celebrated Westminster Abbey Boys' Choir. My guests were happy with their trip to London and threatened to do the same for me when I visited Israel.

That summer, I just couldn't think of a suitable gift to take to my Israeli friends on my way to the Be'er Sheva Conservatoire course. I settled for a kilogram of red caviar from a Russian shop. The first week of my exotic business trip went brilliantly both on the intensive course in the sports centre, and at home with the Kantermans. Their sons were in Jerusalem. The eldest was a member of the armed guard for government ministers; the youngest was studying in a religious seminary in Jerusalem and was, unbeknown to me, a religious extremist. Arriving home for the weekend one Friday, he spotted the jar of caviar in the fridge and threw it in the rubbish, declaring it too decadent for the righteous.

Over a family supper that evening, I asked the troubled hostess: "Sheryl, what's happened to the caviar? Have you given it to a neighbour or have the infidels stolen it?"

Furious with me, the young fundamentalist began foaming at the mouth, demanding respect for the traditions of the house. His father cut him dead, demanding that he in turn showed me respect as their guest. His mother rushed over to her son and told him off in Hebrew. The son dropped the bad language and started filling everyone's glasses with sweet red wine, which I had declined earlier in the week. Then he stuck his two dirty, smelly fingers into each glass in turn as a sign of God's blessing and began reading a prayer. To avoid any further outbursts, I raised my glass too and instead of drinking, carefully put it back down on the table. The deranged seminarist was shaking with rage. Kanterman ran over to him, dragged his son away from the table and into the kitchen, slammed the door and ripped into him with as much force as his voice allowed. The son, who was still screeching like a half-slaughtered pig, stormed off up to his room. Supper was ruined. Even a shot of vodka could not save me from shame.

Early on Saturday morning Penny rang from London to update me on urgent matters from the past week. My 'moral guardian' ran downstairs with a huge commotion and cut us off by pressing the receiver down. Sheryl darted out of the kitchen to stop her son, but he was already halfway back up the stairs to his room. The lady of the house apologised. Thanks to this religious fanatic, it turned out that during the Sabbath, we were not allowed to listen to music or put on the radio, answer the telephone or use any other kind of equipment.

I asked, "Why didn't you warn me about this? I would have been happy to go to a hotel."

"My son and I had agreed that he would spend the weekend at his elder brother's but the latter changed his mind."

My host returned home from work at that moment. When he heard what had happened, he apologised profusely. We ate breakfast in silence and set off for the Conservatoire together. He headed off to his choir rehearsal, and I to my course programme. I felt so uncomfortable all day that I couldn't concentrate on the production process in the hall. At the end of classes, the students invited me to a local club, which in the main was full of young people. But what interested me most were their social dances and other contemporary forms of entertainment in their society.

The concluding course concert elicited an emotional response from the management and esteemed guests. I have to pay tribute to the students from the Israeli learning institutions who worked with me. In two weeks they had taken up Character dance training with great enthusiasm, and performed dances from diverse nationalities for assessment with a temperament rarely found in the provinces. However, for all my professional satisfaction, I was left with the lasting, unpleasant aftertaste of religious bigotry and pressure on the artist, reminiscent of what I'd experienced thirty years earlier in Tadzhikistan. I hadn't felt this in Jerusalem or Tel Aviv, probably because most of my students consisted of immigrants from Slav and Western European countries. Although I was a non believer myself, I had great respect for others' religious beliefs, as long as they did not use them in the name of death and violence. No doubt the Communist dictatorship had left me with a heightened reaction against any form of aggression that threatened my spiritual freedom, moral code and professional credo in Art.

I continued to work with choreographers and dance teachers in Tel Aviv and Jerusalem respectively during the Christmas holidays for several years, and gained a good reputation in this country. I taught summer courses every year at various private schools in Israel, and my dance composition methods became very popular. I occasionally added new material to my syllabus and repertoire at the following studios, which were particularly significant for me: ballet, Jenny Ordman; Modern, Shucki Hoifman; Jazz, Barry Avidan. These courses were satisfying creatively and quite well paid. In addition, they gave me the chance to get to see this ancient land's historical monuments and main sights. In the Soviet Union it was out of the question even to dream (before Perestroika) about buying books on the history of the Jewish state and its cultural heritage. To my great shame, I was totally ignorant in this area.

During this period, Valery Panov (Shulman), a former leading soloist with the Mariinsky Theatre, was living in Jerusalem with his wife Galina Rogozinaya (also a ballet soloist) and their son Petrusha. I had known Valery since 1963 when I produced my miniatures for the troupe's USA tour: Zubkovskaya and Kuznetsov, and Fedicheva and Budarin. I had planned to include a solo with Panov, 'Song of the Falcon', but at that time he was very busy launching his new ballet and unfortunately couldn't take up my proposal. After emigrating to Israel, Valery and Galya toured extensively throughout the Western World. Whenever they came to Montreal, they would perfect their repertoire in my ballet studio. In turn, I would visit them in their temporary residence in Bonn, West Germany, and of course, in Jerusalem. Although Valery and I specialised in different areas of ballet, what we had in common was suffering political persecution at the hands of the Soviet authorities. Summing up Panov's professional profile, I always believed that if he had emigrated ten or fifteen years earlier, he could have created as good a career in Europe as other Soviet artistes, and possibly been even more successful. He was just unlucky with timing.

On one of my visits, Valery introduced me to Yuri Lyubimov, the famous producer from Moscow's Taganka Theatre. He had married a Jewish woman and defected to Israel because of that same ideological oppression. Russia had lost yet another champion of creative freedom in art. By this time he was getting on a bit, and his sad yearning for his motherland never left his sorrowful eyes, even when he was smiling. I turned my attention to the problem he was having with his back. Apologising, I asked my compatriot why he was physically incapacitated. When I learned that he had a slipped disc just like me, I offered my colleague professional help from a self-employed therapist, guaranteed to help him feel better.

Lyubimov asked sarcastically: "How much will this set a poor immigrant back?"

"Three bottles of vodka for three therapy sessions."

The patient laughed, but agreed to give it a try. We arranged it for the following Sunday, when I would be free from teaching. Ida, Lyubimov's wife, greeted me with suspicion, asking what kind of quackery this was. Where had this self-taught charlatan popped up from? However, she was reassured as she observed my healing process at work. She wrote down the order of physical manipulations needed to restore the slipped discs to their original position, and promised to complete the procedure accurately. Yuri Petrovich announced that we had to drink to this, otherwise it would never happen. The lady of the house insisted that I stayed for lunch. I declined out of politeness, but rather half-heartedly, as I didn't want to pass up the opportunity to try a tasty-looking goulash. With two hours to go until lunchtime, Lyubimov and I had downed half a litre of vodka, and swapped all our best stories. My patient stated that he felt less pain in his back and thanked me for my help. In my opinion, this in itself justified a second bottle over lunch, even if I could not take the credit.

After lunch the three of us went to a government reception marking some kind of festival. Lyubimov advised the guards that I was there as his guest. The producer and his wife had official invitations, whereas I had to wait for the security guards to check my passport. As we were standing around with glasses of wine in the lively throng, an official I didn't recognise came over to me. My colleague introduced me to him, explaining that I was currently delivering a seminar for teachers at the university.

"Ah! So you are Berkut, the famous ballet master," he declared, "who fled to Canada on his way to Israel from the USSR, and then moved to England instead emigrating as per the invitation to our country. You really are a prodigal son! Ha ha!"

"First off, I didn't flee, but emigrated officially to Canada, and secondly, you have no right to—"

"Secondly," my official interrupted, "the government here regards you as a double traitor."

The blood drained from my face. Yuri squeezed my elbow sharply, to stop me rising to the bait, and pre-empt a scene. I took my leave and hurried back to the hotel, as the next day I was due back in London for the new academic year at RBS.

On the plane I couldn't stop thinking about being insulted at the government reception, and couldn't work out why he chose to punish me in public.

But mischievous Fate has her own way of dealing with things. The week before I was due to fly out to Israel for my next seminar, war broke out in Kuwait. Flights to this area were temporarily suspended.

I sent an urgent telex both to Tel Aviv and Jerusalem: "Due to military strikes in the airspace, I request that we postpone our seminar to a later date."

Neither Tel Aviv nor Jerusalem could forgive me for breaching our contract at such an inopportune moment. In their eyes, they were right. From my perspective, war had made the decision for me: 'to be or not to be'. From that moment I sacrificed my most treasured colleagues and protégés in this country of continuing conflict. I alone know the real extent of the disappointment and shame this loss brought me.

As is widely known, France has been the cradle of European Classical ballet from the time of Louis XIV, so it's no accident that both my specialist genres of Historical and Classical dance gained most recognition in the homeland of Jean-Georges Noverre, Arthur Saint-Léon, Marius Petipa and other great French choreographers, following their conception in Italy. Thanks to these Masters, for over three centuries these genres burst into the repertoire of European opera/ ballet theatres, and the Russian tsar's palace in particular, in the Mariinsky and the Bolshoi. I assume that it was largely owing to past popularity that the intensive courses and Character dance choreography I was offering, resonated so strongly with French ballet schools and theatres. Completely out of the blue, a broad field of creative activity opened up before me in this largely forgotten sphere of ballet art. Thankfully, the fundamental terminology had survived in French or Italian till the present day, plus my experience of communicating in Quebec undoubtedly facilitated my interactions with French students in the initial stages.

My first visit to this country came about with an invitation from the Société de la Danse. Their board used to hold an annual seminar in the spring holidays for teachers of various genres of dance in the outskirts of Paris. Before I arrived, Character dance was run by a certain Irina Grzhebina, who had taught this discipline for many years in the school of Le Grand Opéra. She was nationally regarded as the only recognised specialist in this genre and even opened her own private school in the city centre. When she heard that her English rival from the Royal Ballet had arrived in Paris, Irina was naturally curious, and flouting theatre etiquette, showed up at our assessed seminar concert without an invitation. Knowing full well the aggressive nature of the uninvited guest, the seminar director warned me as we met before the concert, not to get into discussion with her because of her obstreperous character. I promised to be the consummate gentleman.

The young course participants gave a brilliant demonstration, reflecting the positive outcome of their week-long course in a practical display of compositions from various genres of choreography. As Grzhebina and I got acquainted, she began to ask leading questions. I smiled as I asked her permission to visit her school, which I'd heard a lot about, and ventured that I would consider it a great honour to give a taster lesson for her, if she had nothing against it. Initially, Irina's jaw dropped in surprise at my impertinence, before she went quiet for a while. Then she gave me her business card with an insincere smile, and asked me to call her and set up a meeting. I thanked her with exaggerated politeness for her interest, and went as far as to kiss her hand.

At the next teachers' seminar I received invitations from several delegates to run a Character dance course at their schools. It was obvious to me that, commercially speaking, it was difficult for any ballet school director to retain the interest of their impatient young clients through monotonous Classical training alone. They desperately needed some other appealing course in the curriculum to achieve 'emotional' and 'technical' balance in their learning. For this reason, I maintained a strong reputation in my specialist subject. At the seminar, Louise De La Place from Aix-en-Provence was one of the most interested in this genre. She set out there and then the terms of a week's contract: three classes a day, plus choreography for the students' final concert. But of course, I was more interested in the ballet school at Le Grand Opéra, where Grzhebina was still teaching the intermediate classes. When I met Claude Bessi, the school director explained that the octogenarian Irina was terribly jealous of all Russian colleagues from Moscow and St Petersburg. Consequently, the management would never invite any of these to their summer courses until Grzhebina retired. So for the moment, any real prospects at Le Grand Opéra were unfortunately zero. I could only hope that one of my employers would take such care of me at the finale of my creative career.

I went to work in Aix-en-Provence during the next holidays. Louise De La Place greeted me like family. Despite its small size, her school was well organised. It comprised one single studio accommodating about fifty pupils, with a huge six- or seven-room flat on the second floor of the building, which housed the accounts office, Wardrobe Department and other work areas. In addition to the Director, the staff included four other women: an assistant/ teacher of children's classes, pianist, secretary and cleaner. It all reminded me of my first steps as a ballet master in the Mariners' Cultural Centre in Odessa.

The best surprise came on that very first evening, when after a long day at work, supper and a refreshing shower I finally dragged my worn-out body to its sleeping quarters, only to find a brightly smiling Venus in the bed. Her classically appealing body was half obscured by her long blond hair. In my astonished eyes, her graceful, outstretched hand was an invitation for love. I swear! Forget Rembrandt. No one can know what secrets nature harbours. How I mustered the energy to throw myself over and over again into the depths of passion and agonising ecstasy, God alone knows. Nevertheless, at midnight I begged for mercy, reminding her that I was working tomorrow. Lingering on my dry lips after such a marathon, Venus said goodbye, wished me a good sleep, and promptly slipped away. I had enjoyed French novels in the past, but this was the first time I had experienced such natural, immediate intimacy and release. 'God works in mysterious ways.'

These amorous midnight distractions probably inspired both of us in our creative endeavours the following day. So it was that in the first week, I produced and Louise rehearsed around a dozen dances with all the groups, which the school showcased on the town's central square. The entire staff worked their socks off to pull off a real blinder. To some extent this was down to the locals' fiery, French character. The performers reprised a few dances at the concert at the excited audience's request.

The town mayor thanked us for the concert and cheekily asked Louise: "Forgive me, Madame. Your colleague must be one of Napoleon's descendants, isn't he?"

"My Lord Mayor, what makes you say that?"

"Because, just like Bonaparte and Julius Caesar before him, 'He came, he saw, he conquered.'"

Everyone was congratulating us. Never in my life: neither before, nor since, have I enjoyed such acclaim. Unfortunately, I was so engrossed in my globetrotting that even Venus in Aix-en-Provence was just a distraction on my life path at that point.

In the dim and distant past, I used to give regular courses in Paris with top ballet studio leaders, Solonge Golovin and Ivone Goubé. Both their institutions were highly esteemed and universally acclaimed by critics and the capital's official circles. I was convinced on many occasions that people here understood and valued Character dance, despite its fundamental difference from Traditional or Contemporary styles, as offered by both studios. In contrast to Ivone's place, the atmosphere at Solonge's was much more homely. I was always amused by Solonge Golovin's little dog, Zhuchka (meaning 'pet dog'). During the ballet class she would sit and quiver in the armchair next to the teacher's chair. Every time one of the students got it wrong, and Solonge pulled them up, Zhuchka would wake up and bark at the culprit, echoing her mistress's tone of voice. After a 'verdict' of this nature, Zhuchka would close her eyes again. It was impossible to watch this scene without smiling. But everyone there was so used to this eccentricity in class that they simply didn't react to it any more.

As well as her ballet studio, Ivone Goubé taught Classical dance for many years in the school of Le Grand Opéra, where she often rubbed shoulders with Irina Grzhebina. In one of our courses Ivone handed me an invitation from Grzhebina to give a demonstration lesson in her Parisian school for the next seminar on Character genre. I was wary at first, in case I roused her aggressive side which I'd already witnessed. But Ivone assured me that Irina would be retiring soon and was planning to sell her school to a suitable buyer. At this, I sensed something else was going on, but if I were to decline, this could be interpreted as fear of her advantage in our shared credentials. I agreed to do it, as long as Ivone attended this demonstration. She laughed, but gave her word, realising that I needed a neutral witness in case of any conflict. As the current seminar at Goubé's Parisian base came to an end, we went together to see Grzhebina's school and I gave my promised demonstration lesson on Character dance with her intermediate group. As always, I taught them several Italian and Russian sequences in the centre. After the final bow, the students stood stock-still, watching as their leader chatted with the pianist. Ivone, who was seated next to them, looked at me quizzically as she started to clap. The students also picked up on her approval of me, chanting my name to show their appreciation.

Grzhebina cut short the applause, gesturing to everyone to form a circle in pairs.

"Dear Maestro, would you allow us to dance a farewell Mazurka for you?"

The students looked on in astonishment at their leader, who was behaving so strangely.

"Ladies and gentlemen, I will remind you at this point of a few steps from last year's dance and we will show our guest from England's Royal Ballet, what you are capable of."

Naturally, I picked up on the devious woman's tactic: to portray me as incapable of grasping dance sequences 'on the hoof' and one of the most complicated styles of Mazurka in European national choreography at that. Poor Irina had decided to show me up in front of her charges, not realising that I was like a terrier with this Polish material. Goubé was white-faced with shock at her friend and colleague's scheming. Once Irina had reminded her students of the basic Mazurka movements, I made a big show of approaching Grzhebina with a smile as I made a nineteenth-century 'reverence' (bow) and invited her to dance at the imperial ball of the King of Europe.

Without responding to my bow, Irina took my hand and led (rather than the other way round) her cavalier to the circle. Luckily I hadn't had time to change after my demonstration, and felt really up for this. I was also at least fifteen years younger than my partner, which gave me some advantage in performing the Mazurka's intricate technique. I made up my mind to teach my hostess a lesson in manners and hospitality. Once they'd finished performing the sequences they knew, Grzhebina's students lost their way, and stopped. I signalled to the pianist to carry on playing. My partner tried to cut short our dance, but I continued to spin Irina around.

Completing sequences that were unfamiliar to her, I called out, "Don't be shy, Madame! Please carry on dancing your beloved Mazurka with me!"

Eventually, during a partner turn with me, she broke free and teetered back towards her studio chair. I overtook my partner in one leap. I grabbed her hand and chivalrously walked her to her seat. I thanked the lady once more with a traditional bow, took my leave of the students and went off to get changed.

It's possible that some of the students thought badly of me. But at that moment I considered it a base act on my hostess's part, to invite a foreign colleague to give a free class to students he didn't know, then to try to humiliate him professionally before those same performers rather than express her thanks to her guest. Forgive me, but 'If you're going to run with wolves, you have to hunt like a wolf.'

On the way back to my hotel, Ivone Goubé apologised for her colleague's disappointing, tactless behaviour, remarking that it was not the first time she had acted so shamelessly in the theatre out of professional jealously. This was why Le Grand Opéra were respectfully advising her to retire, before it was too late. The only thing was – she was refusing to retire!

"Ivone, I feel really sorry for this elderly woman, a ballet veteran. But nonetheless, I'm certain that Irina has an inferiority complex about her own lack of knowledge of contemporary choreography, and continues to work sixty years on with the artistic and technical level of the 1930s. Please pass on my apologies to her for reacting inappropriately to her aggressive behaviour towards me."

I often stayed with my old friends Diana Joffe or her mother Lydia during my courses in Paris. Both of these ballet specialists told me as one voice not to get involved with this unbalanced person, who for some reason hated Soviet ballet contemporary professionals more than anyone else, and was out to get them as soon as she could in France, especially in Paris. She always thought that visitors from the Soviet Union wanted to invade her 'turf', so she defended herself aggressively against potential competitors from the outset.

"Forget about her, Misha!" cautioned the faithful Lydia, a well-known former ballet critic from Riga. "Irina will drag your name through the mud throughout France and even further afield now. I think it would be a good idea for me to recommend you to Rosella Hightower, and suggest that you deliver your Character dance course in the south of France. Her advanced school trains professional dancers in a range of genres and categories. It would be in both your creative interests to work together, combining your choreography with her prowess as a répétiteur."

Lydia was right. After the first course, Rosella subsequently used me several times as a teacher and choreographer in her school and troupe.

Maria Gorkin's Ballett-Akademie was a close neighbour of France's in Basle, Switzerland. This was the best dance school in the country for the prevailing Contemporary style in Ballet. The Director was impressed by the 'spiritual' and 'physical' basis of my stage technique and 'emotional' expression, which fitted in with her personal approach to 'Contemporary' Classical. We never had any difficulties in our professional or personal dealings with each other, so Madame Gorkin used to invite me from one year to the next and I would willingly go and work there with three groups: junior, secondary and advanced from sixteen to eighteen years of age. I boarded on the second floor in the same building, preparing my lessons and productions there in the evenings. Most of the students spoke fluent French, Italian and German. Everything seemed to be really well set up with one exception. After the last lesson on the first day of classes, the Director and I went through the next day's plans. I got my notes together and headed upstairs to my room. As I left the classroom, I had to pass through the lobby, where some parents were sitting waiting to collect their children.

After a few steps, I suddenly found myself in the middle of a group of my students, who were completely naked following their showers, as they sorted themselves out. These young lads and girls didn't give me a second glance, and just carried on chatting about their last lesson. Body parts flapped about all over the place, as they displayed their delightful physiques without any embarrassment, as if they were in their own homes. Naturally, I froze on one leg in shock, not knowing how to proceed: should I go back to the ballet studio or make a run for the stairs in the opposite corner, weaving between these disrobed satyrs and nymphs? The parents cottoned on and could see why I was embarrassed; they started to laugh, pointing me towards the exit. I bent down, covered my head with my bag and made a dash for the stairs to everyone's great amusement.

The next morning, Maria apologised for neglecting to warn me in advance: "Mikhail, you're not the first to have experienced this situation. Don't worry about it. The education authorities in our country are battling with pornography and unhealthy, premature sexual interest. They are trying to deal with this problem by censoring the natural facts about how people use their bodies in sexual relations."

From then on, I was obliged to go through the throng of (forgive me) bare-arsed youngsters every time after lessons, pretending to be busy with my notes so I didn't notice anything.

The next French-speaking venue for my courses in Europe was Académie Princesse Grace in Monte Carlo. I would have said that this was the most established ballet institution after Le Grand Opéra in francophone Europe. Both the troupe and school were small in numbers, but equal in stature to many Western ballet companies. Marika Besobrasova, the Academy's director, had based her school of Classical dance on the Russian Vaganova school in St Petersburg, so she was enthusiastic and had great hopes for my Character dance and 'Pas de deux' training method as they were based on the classical system akin to hers. All lessons followed the same progressive regime used by RBS. In the main, I put on productions that she selected from the Russian ballet repertoire. Within two weeks I managed to prepare a broad programme for an assessed lesson and concert, attended by Princess Grace herself, the academy's generous sponsor. Besobrasova kindly honoured my work and we agreed that I would run a course annually in the summer holidays. But even here, a 'nice' surprise was in store for me.

The Academy was closed on Sundays, for religious reasons. In the height of summer I decided to go and relax on a nearby beach. Snug in my training hoodie, I encountered many sun worshippers on the beach already at 8 a.m., but found an uncrowded spot in the middle, next to the volleyball court and lay down for some happy and peaceful relaxation. Wearing sunglasses, and being short-sighted to boot, I didn't notice all the half-naked women around me. Not trusting my shades, I took them off and wiped the lenses, thinking, *I'm starting to hallucinate.* Initially, as at Maria Gorkin's in Switzerland, paralysis set in, but then I got a grip on myself and pretended that female nudity was of no interest to me.

In the process of lying down and philosophising, I was getting a good tan, and a large circle of new neighbours had moved in around me.

Raising my head and looking around, I couldn't believe my half-blind eyes. Even through sunglasses, I observed at close quarters entirely naked people of both genders, sunbathing and chatting away to each other without a care in the world. I almost shouted out: "Hey, you good people! Have you gone sex mad? Aren't you ashamed of being so insolent?"

Don't be hysterical, Mishenka! When in Rome, do as the Romans do.

I turned over, hoping to escape these immoral, naked bodies at such close proximity. But this time, the sight of naked men and women leaping as they played volleyball over the net stopped me in my tracks. Thinking this a delusion or nightmare at first, I slapped myself on the ear, realising that this was 'healthy' reality for everyone relaxing around me. I felt like an ignorant savage, watching these volleyball players with women's breasts and men's tackle bouncing up and down. This went beyond my limit of moral tolerance. I ran into the sea to cool down my racing brain. Swimming a long way out from the shore, it dawned on me how far removed I had become from contemporary civilisation in terms of sexual morality.

I gave my last seminar in France at the Perpignan Conservatoire, which was run by my old friend Vladimir Ukhtomsky. He had flown to Montreal several times to teach on summer courses at Les Ballets Russes de Montréal, and given Classical lessons to my senior students. My colleague led the Ballet Department in the local Conservatoire and invited me for a week every year to present Russian technique in Character dance and choreography from European nations, which appealed both to him personally as well as to his students. The town was also home to Matt Mattox and his family, a celebrated European Jazz master, whose biography had been written by Elisabeth Frich, my friend and colleague from the Norwegian Teaching Institute. Ukhtomsky had danced with Tamara Karsavina, and was her partner in the Monte Carlo Ballet even in Myasin's time. Unfortunately, due to his advanced years, he was no longer able to come and teach on my UK Summer Dance course in London, as he used to. I asked him about Spanish Classical.

Volodya explained in layman's terms that Spanish dance history boasts its own Classical culture. For this reason, European ballet did not take root there, and coupled with that, my Character dance method did not work in the Barcelona Conservatoire. In Spain, local specialists prefer to teach national folk or Classical dances, such as: the Aragon Jota, Gypsy Flamenco, Classical Seguidilla, and other similar choreographic gems. Anthropologically speaking, Spain's entire dance repertoire is an assimilation of motions rooted in local ethnography, informed by other overseas cultures during 1,000 years of occupation or battles with conquistadors from other settled, social groups. That's why Spanish choreography stands apart from European Classical choreography in all genres.

During our evening get-togethers, Matt Mattox was always very interested in my method of stylising Folk dance in Character genre and he himself (at my request) outlined the sources for interpreting his method of Ballet-jazz based on Contemporary dance.

Thanks to my colleagues I acquired a great deal of new knowledge in the development and transformation of twentieth-century European dance culture. During our frequent trips to international seminars, I enjoyed satisfying conversations with great masters in Perpignan: a precious gift from Fortune, who had not always been very well disposed towards me. Unlike Grzhebina, not all famous masters harbour hostility/jealously towards their colleagues. The more talent an artiste or artist has, the more likely he is to excel and share the fruits of his labours with others, and this is where you'll find a real gift from nature.

STAGE IV: COSMIC STORMS

CHAPTER 10 FALLEN IDOLS

My experience with Character dance had shown me that misunderstandings could also arise in teaching Historical dance at RBS White Lodge. In an exam class with second-year students at the end of the first academic year, they expressed their wish to bring in representatives from ISTD, RAD and other English dance-related organisations. Dame Merle warned me that they were very negative about my unconventional way of presenting this genre. She asked the head of White Lodge if we could use the school theatre stage for the exam rather than a ballet classroom, given that we were expecting a lot of visitors. We spent the last lesson before the exam on the stage. Patrizia Linton (principal) gave the children a pep talk and asked them to make sure their uniforms were looking spic and span. At the exam before the display I gave everyone present a brief run-down on society dances from the Middle Ages that we had learned in our syllabus, and emphasised that the academic programme had been adapted for the stage to be used in future opera-ballet performances, to match their historical era and theatrical producer.

Miss Linton gave everyone a list of the dances that would be performed and answered their questions about the dancers in the group (boys and girls).

We kicked off the demonstration with a cheery Farandole from Greece, in which all the dancers joined hands in a chain, and leaped neatly across the stage for two minutes in an intricate design of spatial patterns, or galloped off in opposite directions, hand in hand and facing each other in a double circle (boys and girls separately). Next they spun around in pairs holding hands. To finish off, they took hands again and formed a chain that snaked decoratively across the stage, until they all disappeared into the wings with a shriek. The RBS teachers and Merle were beaming widely. The official guests frowned and pursed their lips in disgust. In contrast, the participants performed the next four slow and graceful dances – Branle (France), Estampida (Italy), Allemande (Germany) and Sarabande (Spain) – with real emotion, in keeping with the character of the music and style of the times: featuring low curtseys or graceful ports de bras, promenades in pairs or do-si-dos and other traditional, formal sequences. They concluded their exam review with a lively Saltarello dance, which was the first to include more complicated dance elements in Classical ballet (*balance, pas de basque, satte, pas de bourré, temps levé*, etc.). One of my objectives was to develop the historical vocabulary of the *danza di corte* into a contemporary, stage performance.

The performance ended with a group curtain call in front of the assembled guests. I congratulated the performers onstage for passing their exams and wished them a happy holiday. They responded with a collective cheer, which was cut short by the RBS management. Dame Merle thanked the children for their excellent display, and invited me down into the studio. She introduced all the officials from ISTD and RAD, and asked me to stay behind for half an hour to have a chat over a cup of tea. I had to extend my thanks and apologies as my classes at Doreen Bird College in Sidcup were starting in two hours' time. I assumed that the dignitaries wanted to give me a grilling after the exam, which I was ill-prepared for. I promised to come and see the Director for a chat in the morning. Grabbing a few lavishly illustrated books on Italian and Soviet authors of court dances from the twelfth to nineteenth centuries, I headed for my meeting with Merle.

"Misha, I'm not interested in your excuses as I'm of the same mind as my teachers, i.e. we are giving our children a professional education in theatre arts, rather than teaching them disco dancing. What you showed us yesterday evening at White Lodge is just what we need right now. Keep up the good work! But please remember that you've blocked the way for lots of your rivals, and they're out to get you."

England has boasted about her giants of musical theatre and fine art for centuries. Nevertheless, being geographically separate from mainland Europe, Great Britain had for too long been spiritually and aesthetically isolated from revolutionary changes taking part in the social and cultural life of progressive European countries: Italy, France, Germany, Spain, etc. Inevitably, this affected the growth of British conservatism in all spheres of social activity in high society, including Court dancing (historical social dances). While Catherine de' Medici was creating the *danza di corte* repertoire in her Italian court, Henry VIII was making do with masquerades and grotesque comedies and country-dancing events in London. There was nothing to be ashamed of in either case: fashioning Italian ethnography into a court-style repertoire as enjoyed in imperial balls or transforming British folklore into a more progressive type of country dance, which in essence is a Historical (social) dance.

England also boasts an abundance of critics/historians in the art of dance.

The best known in my specialist field are Melusine Wood, former head of ISTD, Julia Sutton, now an American author, and Mary Clark, the editor of the English magazine *Dancing Times*. All three of them wrote seminal works on the history of social culture, ballet theatre and Historical dance in particular. To be honest, I gleaned a lot of useful information for my own purposes from these sources. But London was also full of self-proclaimed critics claiming to be 'historians', who had their own agenda, and lacked any specialist knowledge of art history or appreciation, but just had experience in amateur circles (companies) of Historical dance (Court dancing) as a form of entertainment, of course, under ISTD supervision. These included particularly fierce proponents of the officially established standard of Historical dance at ISTD such as Belinda Quirey and her former pupil Richard Glaston (he was actually the ex-principal of RBS White Lodge). Of course with my foreign style of teaching Historical dance at White Lodge I was a thorn in the side of these predators. They were just waiting for their alma mater to give them the green light to tear this foreign interloper to shreds for encroaching upon their long-standing falsification of the original. Gracing my bookshelves were unique books by eighteenth-century Italian authors and choreographers Corozo and Ebreo, with annotations of their very first repertoire of *danza di corte*, dating back three centuries. I had bought them in Rome and referred to them as my bibles.

In the interests of professional curiosity I checked out the performances of a few Court dance groups in the capital and provincial areas. These were clearly amateur displays of European Historical social dances to recordings of the original music. But the original source choreography had been perverted in a conventional assortment of heavyweight long costumes and flat, contemporary jazz slippers through lack of funds. All of this could have been forgiven with the exception of one thing: completely careless handling of the traditional Partner dance. It's not just a matter of capturing the medieval style of interaction between male and female partners, or the style of hand and foot movements; it's more about preserving the atmosphere of the Court dance with the inherently prim and affected style that prevailed during the Renaissance. The dancers (elderly couples in the main) clearly didn't appreciate that dancing for your own pleasure in private was an entirely different matter from performing the same routine in public, and showing an audience the social and sociological bases of a specific historical era through the artistic medium of dance. In addition, the age-old subjective interpretation of original choreography from the *danza di corte* repertoire, was the reason that composition had become so multifaceted. The performers (through no fault of their own) had almost completely lost their sense of contrast in their interpretation of essential Character dance and diverse forms of basic music. As a result, they could not convey the social and cultural idiosyncrasies of society life in bygone eras in an authentic way, thanks to their arbitrary rendition of Historical dance.

For all my negativity towards these fake displays of the social and ethical anthropology of human interactions from a specific period, I didn't judge the dancers, and when their leaders asked my opinion, I summarised: "This is a great pastime for amateurs. Making an effort to preserve historic cultural traditions on the one hand, and enjoying moving to music instead of spending hours in front of the TV on the other."

The leaders would smile sarcastically in response. In these situations, I avoided any unnecessary complications in my life, which was already pressured enough. At least that's how it seemed to me. But it was naïve of me to underestimate British chauvinism. A year and a half later, following the successful publication of my Historical dance video course and its unexpected sales in Europe, Mary

Clark, editor of *Dancing Times*, wrote to warn me officially that Richard Glaston's damning article about my presentation of Historical dance would be coming out in the next issue.

Mary Clark's warning about the impending attack was not a matter of chance. Over the previous eight years she had published regular advertisements in her magazine for all my audiovisual productions and sold them by mail order on a commission basis. She needed to maintain her professional credibility as editor and her commercial interest in my business. One way or another, this helped me to equip myself to protect my own interests and be ready for a potential counter-attack from my adversaries. After several readings of Richard's lambasting of Historical dance at White Lodge in the next issue of the magazine, I was reassured, as I was expecting a much more serious dialectical analysis of the subject through an official argument in the pages of this prestigious magazine. As it turned out, they were the third-rate ramblings of, in my opinion, an uneducated man, unversed both in critical analysis and his chosen method of public flogging.

I felt it was beneath my dignity to enter into an academic and historical polemic with him. After consulting Andrew Winstone, I decided to write a satirical article as a rejoinder to Richard. Andrew corrected this letter to Mary Clark, but warned that she would not publish it free of charge, because it made my well-known opponent look too stupid, and discredited him for introducing a platform for discussion in which he was so lacking in knowledge. I explained to the *Dancing Times* editor Glaston's error in choosing to rally the ISTD troops against me. But in the course of discussion I realised that they had used a fall guy on purpose with the aim of discrediting me, as there was no other reason to do this. It was a typical dirty trick used by the weak in face of a threat by the strong to expose one's own shortcomings.

In response to Richard's attack on my Historical dance video I received many private letters from the magazine's readers (without signatures and return addresses) accusing me of maligning the history of British culture, and using personal insults and demands in places to 'stop perverting our children'. It was clear to me that these elderly performers from amateur dance groups had no direct link to the *Dancing Times*, which had unintentionally become an indirect propaganda vehicle for national chauvinism. Moreover, Mary refused to print my article in response to the unfounded criticism of the video Andrew and I had made. However, following Andrew's protestations about discrimination, she placed several positive articles from British dance teachers in the following issue attesting to the positive qualities in the form and content of the course in question, and praising the highly qualified Russian dancers and teachers in ballet (teaching and theatre) establishments from Moscow and St Petersburg, especially highlighting the system of Classical, Historical and Character dance training perfected and developed in Russia, for which a wealth of information was available in print.

Imagine my surprise when, after all this, I received official notice from Mary Clark, that she was withdrawing my regular advertisement for my Historical video in her publication. I was fully aware of her invidious position. Nevertheless, I found it hard to take such a public slap in the face. ISTD's strategy was obvious. After several attempts to stop me teaching Historical dance at White Lodge, they had decided to change their plan of attack and use Richard as a buffer in the press. Astute board members didn't dare to speak out publicly against an RBS teacher on their own initiative. They preferred to put their wounded member in this role, and he was only too happy to take up the opportunity to seek revenge against RBS after being sacked from White Lodge. Now that my name was mud, no one wanted to deal with a discredited specialist, even one with higher qualifications. I imagined the elevated debates going on in ISTD and RBS concerning my future Historical dance practice. What I couldn't understand was why the British Association of Teachers so fiercely defended the shared English origin of some Court dancing, when it had been proved, as I had demonstrated in the family tree of Court dancing that I had published after much research, that Court dancing didn't include a single dance of English origin. Undoubtedly this helped to ensure that the odds were stacked against me.

The only positive element in this scandal was the unintentional promotion for my video and the resulting sudden increase in sales of *Dancing Times*. I must admit that production and advertising for the six Historical dance cassettes on VHS had set me back over 26,000 pounds. Inevitably, I had had to borrow a substantial amount from Penny again at a high interest rate to cover production costs.

When she heard about the negative press reaction to my latest video project, she shouted in panic: "That's my money down the drain! I should never have subsidised your fanciful ideas!"

But only three months later after Glaston's stinking article, just one shop, Dance Book Ltd sold more than 600 copies (100 sets of six videos) in England and Europe. With the help of my assistant Kafuyu, I just managed to scrape together the shop's next orders, and get the Director, David Leppard, to write out a cheque to Penny. This was how (thanks to Richard Glaston) I paid Penny back almost everything she'd lent me, much earlier than planned. It was a blessing in disguise.

It was no secret who was galvanising an aggressive group of people against my creative presence in England. My local friends and colleagues had warned me repeatedly about this. Standing up to ISTD on my own was like spitting in the wind. Sooner or later they would stop me from working in England, one way or another. Having worked for more than ten years at Doreen Bird College prior to the scandal in the press, I had had the opportunity to examine the structure of that association, where one of the committee members was the college director herself in the Modern dance section. Three times a year, every dance school or theatre college in England was obliged to invite ISTD specialists to sit on their exam board at the end of term. Conversely, when these schools applied for state subsidies for disadvantaged students, the ISTD board refused to give the necessary references in support of the applicants. To cut a long story short: 'If you want more state-funded students in your school, invite our specialists on a regular basis and don't forget to pay for this through the ISTD bank account.' This collective guarantee was understandable as the exam board was often made up of qualified teachers and experienced masters from a range of dance genres. Their top-notch professional credentials no doubt justified their fee.

But ISTD had gambled with ballet enthusiasts' ambitions quite happily for many years. At one of my Character dance courses in Malta I came across a well-known British teacher (now retired) from ISTD in a ballet school. Along with other association members, she visited other islands or countries in Europe twice a year, with the aim of passing young ballerinas (aged five to fifteen) in the Cecchetti method of Classical dance at various levels: preparatory I, II and III, and the same with beginners, intermediate and advanced. As they completed each test to pinpoint their technical level, the ballet school pupils were given official certificates with the ISTD stamp, confirming their achievements over the previous six months with their local dance teacher. The certificates were framed and hung in an empty space in private homes and lists of the best in each subgroup were published regularly in the local press. Congratulations ISTD! It was buffoonery of the highest order, or to be exact, a dazzling, contrived profanity of the art of Classical dance, shamelessly exploiting children's competitive drive, most of whom lacked the natural physical attributes to be born ballerinas. Year in, year out, ISTD staff conscientiously and systematically infected these children – who were simply not capable of Classical ballet – with the star-struck disease's deceitful poison, for their own personal gain.

Of course it would be beneficial for all adolescents to dance from a young age so that they develop well physically, move smoothly, enjoy positive relationships with each other, and acquire an ear for music and self-discipline. But to instil in young children a false sense of their own spiritual and physical abilities, and disorient them in their personal plans for the future, flies in the face of all the methodology in teaching and educating children, and is morally reprehensible.

Back in London (a long time before Glaston's attack in the press), I had put a naïve question to Doreen Bird in the break between lessons at college: "To what end is the ISTD examining young children in Malta on the Cecchetti standards in ballet?"

She was so shocked that she nearly fell off her chair, almost spilling her tea in the process: "Misha, how can you suspect my colleagues of lacking any moral scruples?"

"Forgive me, madam! I just wanted to know why a bow-legged young boy would need to pass a Cecchetti-method ballet certificate on a faraway island in the middle of the ocean."

Doreen was silent, shook her head, and retreated to her office without finishing her tea. I realised at this point that I had stuck my nose in where it wasn't wanted, and put my faithful sponsor in an awkward position, as she, too, was one of the ISTD examiners in modern dance.

You should have kept your mouth shut. Why do you always have to poke your nose into other people's business? Haven't you got enough problems of your own? You've been an idiot again.

Yes, you're right. I've lost the plot a bit with this historical dance video. I'll go and apologise.

Not under any circumstances! Better not to highlight your faux pas. Let Doreen think that you've already forgotten your flippant remarks.

All through April and May of 1995 I was anticipating the reaction from RBS and Doreen Bird College to the damaging reviews in the press. Doreen was the first to respond. I received an official letter from her, advising that in future, she was forbidding her students to take part in my public displays of Historical dances. At the same time, she stated how much she valued my work in the college as a Character and Partnering dance teacher. It was a veritable judgement of Solomon. I admit, I had assumed that the Director was giving me notice to complete my contract at the end of the current season, in three months' time. But judging from her letter, she had no intention of letting me go just yet, in spite of pressure from ISTD and my provocative questions about the said organisation during our most recent meeting in the cafeteria.

Don't jump to conclusions. It won't be long before Doreen too will get fed up with the pressure from ISTD. One way or another, these Mafiosi will force her to get rid of you. Charity begins at home.

I was continually tortured by the question: what actual, serious reasons did ISTD have to take such an aggressive stand against my presentation of twelfth-to-fifteenth-century Historical dance? In search of an answer to this capricious question, I decided to look again at the printed materials on European Court dances in three main source languages of Italian, French and English. I put aside the Russian publications by Soviet and pre-revolutionary writers on this subject as they had been called into question by Western critics. In painstaking detail, I went through original publications over three eras to verify the times and places the partner compositions I had used at balls had been performed. Naturally I had included these details in the audio and visual inserts in three languages. As a result of my own research, I unearthed four dances which could have antagonised ISTD.

Over seven centuries of historical development, the Imperial Court dance (which had originated in Italy and developed in France) was disseminated by troubadours through various European countries, who obviously made a few adaptations and changes here and there. These social innovations arrived much later in England, not only because of its relative geographical isolation, but also due to the British monarchy's conservative nature. A few dances were immediately dismissed by public censorship. Others were included in the repertoire for a while, but some, like the Pavane and Galliard, became the number one favourites at the court of Queen Elizabeth I. Moreover, both these dances became such a part of English social life over the years, that it never occurred to any of the performers that they might have originated in Italy and Spain. Local composers included them in classical suites within their symphonies, and painters in their monumental portraits of the dancing queen.

The documented roots of the Historical Gigue were even more complex. From ancient times, as confirmed by musicologists, folk violinists in Italian provinces named it the *Gigolo* because they usually accompanied traditional dances at festivals, where one of the most popular dances was the Gigue. During the Roman Empire, this lively sailors' dance spread throughout Europe and settled in Ireland, where it became their folk masterpiece, the Jig, exactly as the Gypsy flamenco from India became a symbol of Spanish choreography in the migration process. During the baroque period, the Italian *Gigga* had its place in the *danza di corte* repertoire. Nevertheless, to this day, the Irish and English consider this dance to be their national property with the sole right to adapt it.

Contredanse provided another long-standing international genetic dilemma in terms of its provenance. The French branded it a stylised version of the Quadrille, their national dance. The English disputed this by adapting their 'Country dance' from national folklore. In actual fact, both of these dances, though close in name, differ essentially in content and performance style. I myself have often danced French versions of Contredanse both in Moscow and subsequently in Europe, as well as choreographing my stage compositions in various American schools and theatres. At the same time, I have observed many rehearsals and performances of English Country dance programmes as presented by my colleagues. I can state with professional confidence that these two social dances are not identical in style or character and it is nonsense to mix the two. For this reason I chose to use the French Contredanse in my historical repertoire, as performed at fashionable balls during the Baroque, but not the Medieval, period.

By the time I had finished my analysis, I understood why ISTD had been unable to accept my objective presentation of European Historical dance, which conflicted with their long-standing falsification of the heritage and consequent evolution of Court ballroom dances of the twelfth to fifteenth centuries. They did not have absolute proof that I had distorted history and made Great Britain look bad. On the contrary, they understood that essentially I was right, but they were not in a position to change their stated positions, as this would have meant admitting they were wrong. I didn't teach Historical dance at Doreen Bird

College, as I did at RBS White Lodge, where I taught children Court dances outside of ISTD control. So to preserve their age-old prestige, the society had no choice but to remove the element of danger (whether willingly or not), which threatened to contradict their authority. It became abundantly clear that my career in England was doomed. I began to consider how best to protect myself from the imminent attacks and shocks which would surely follow.

I didn't have to wait long for the next blow. Prior to the final Gala concert of the academic year in May, I was summoned to see the RBS governor (administrative director).

In the presence of two people whom I had not seen before, he opened our conversation: "Mr Berkut, please excuse these personal questions in connection with White Lodge students, and the Royal Ballet's legal interests."

"Please continue."

"To our knowledge, you have made a video recording of our children during a Historical dance lesson, and this is on sale to the public."

"Yes, that's right."

"Who gave you permission to make these films for your own private business on our premises?"

"I obtained official authorisation for this video recording from the Director, Merle Park."

"Do you have her written confirmation of this agreement?"

"No."

"Then it is not official, just a personal favour."

"Whatever it was, all the White Lodge staff knew about it and helped as much as they could."

"Exactly! They were employed to work for us! You used our premises, not to mention the children. Now you are selling these videos without reimbursing anyone for their labour or time."

I felt my face flush, but kept myself in check.

"Sir, you may be right in making these claims. But this is a somewhat belated reaction and I'm amazed: why didn't you put a stop to this, as I recall in your words 'illegal operation' while it was happening? I had permission from the RBS director a month before we started filming so that I could organise the cameramen, director, costumes, etc."

"Mr Berkut, I can assure you that those who have overstepped the mark with your video film will have to answer to the board of directors of the Royal Ballet and will be punished accordingly. At the same time, in accordance with the law on authors' rights, you must stop selling the Historical video as neither I, as RBS governor, nor the parents of the children gave you written consent for a commercial video film."

Shocked, I paused for a moment: 'to be or not to be', and decided to go for broke.

"Excuse me, sir. When you made a promotional video film seven years ago to attract talented children to your school, you breached authors' rights in exactly the same way. Without my written agreement, not to mention the other teachers, pianists and parents of the children, you recorded excerpts of all dance genres in the school's curriculum, including my Character dance class with my own demonstration. You have been selling this marketing material throughout Europe for seven years at £9.50 apiece, and have never 'reimbursed anyone for their labour or time', let alone author's royalties. For this reason I do not accept your accusation, as I have just completed my work following your example, and have no intention of withdrawing my Historical video from sale. This series of six cassettes has cost me more than 26,000 pounds in loans, which I need to repay. These videos promote our school everywhere so much better than your film does."

By the end of my tirade, the two officials who up to then had remained silent while making notes in their notepads, got up from their seats, and with a nod to the Director, left the office.

The Director sighed heavily: "Mikhail, do you have any idea what position you've put us and yourself in, with your tough-guy act in front of these officials? Surely you value your work at the Royal Ballet? You are respected by everyone here and the children love you. Merle and I went as far as we could to back you and your Historical dance course at White Lodge. But there are limits to our authority."

"Thank you for your kind words, sir. I completely understand your and Merle's position and in the circumstances, regretfully, I'll go quietly at the end of the academic season. I deeply sympathise with your having to work under the control of organisations such as ISTD and RAD."

A week after my chat with the RBS governor, David Leppard rang me and invited me to drop into Dance Book Ltd to familiarise myself with the newly published video course 'European Court Dances', produced by ISTD. I realised that this was not good news and queried our commercial status with the shop with Kafuyu. She reported that they still had a few copies of the Historical video. When I met David, I asked him to show me the new video. This was a home-produced recording with a typed inscription on the label and the list of contents. The Director kindly allowed me to watch some extracts of all three cassettes behind the shop counter. These were the same amateur groups that I had seen previously, wearing scruffy costumes in a gloomy hall in one of London's ballet studios, using a squeaky sound system. David was walking past while serving customers, and smiling ironically:

"What's the matter, Mikhail? I don't think you'll be able to match competition of this calibre. The quality is not important, but it's a quarter of the price of your cassettes. And you don't notice the mistakes in the darkness. That's what you need to do. You've set the bar really high and now you have to make way for them."

"I'm sorry, David. I accept your opinion, but have no wish to pave the way for anyone."

"Unfortunately, my dear Berkut, others have already made the decision for you. I've received strict instructions to withdraw your Historical video from sale due to a breach of author's rights in their internal performers, starting next month. Forgive me, my friend."

I then rang my lawyer Steven Rayner and briefly outlined my business dilemma to him. He promised to make enquiries in a telephone call to the RBS lawyer and bookshop owner. We arranged to meet in a few days' time. I had to know my position so that I could find another job as soon as possible. Several enticing possibilities were open to me in Europe, thanks to my ongoing intensive courses there. On meeting the lawyer, I brought him fully up to speed with the Historical dance video, showing my various printed materials and photos. I also gave him a Historical dance demonstration video as a souvenir, which included the whole series on one cassette, to give him an idea of the issue under dispute just in case.

Steven asked for my full attention. "Mikhail, I had a brief telephone conversation with the RBS governor and shop owner. I've also read through all the letters and promotional materials that were faxed to me. I've drawn up a pretty clear picture of your problem with the video and complications with regular terms of business in London. This is not a pleasant matter, but it is retrievable.

"a) As regards author's rights to stage performance, RBS has legal grounds to withdraw your Historical dance video from sale until this issue has been resolved with the participants' parents. But in view of the fact that RBS itself has 'a finger in the pie', because of your participation in their commercial marketing film without consideration for your author's rights, they are prepared to drop the court case on both points.

"b) The remaining two companies: the magazine *Dancing Times* and the Dance Bookshop are obliged not to advertise your Historical dance video in future under pressure from society organisations. Nevertheless, they are extremely keen to continue professional and business relations with you by employing you in other genres of choreography. It's not as bad as you imagine."

"From a legal perspective, I agree with you. But there's also a moral dimension to this case. In art, if an artist or actor has suffered a public fiasco (as in my situation), all his colleagues and friends inevitably change their opinion of him and react to his public downfall with either pity or contempt. Neither one of those is acceptable to me."

"But, Misha, you must understand that all your directors, partners, colleagues and friends were born here. They have frequently had to compromise in situations that were unfair in order to keep their jobs and live in their home country. It doesn't make any difference to you where your next career move takes you, as long as you are able to satisfy your professional requirements. Most people here can't live as birds of passage."

"Again, I agree with you, Steve. But you must understand me properly. I have been discredited here, and had my creative wings clipped. Without these I am spiritually empty. This is what marks me out psychologically as an individual. I can't help it, and I don't want to. I understand perfectly well that ISTD does not represent all of England, and have great sympathy for my colleagues, friends and students. But staying here would be torture for me, at least for the next few years. I'm sure you won't condemn me for speaking so frankly. Thank you for everything you've done for me."

"I understand how you feel, Mikhail, and wish you all the best!"

As I was talking to my lawyer, I finally realised that my creative activity in England was coming to an end, in both organisational and personal terms. I'd be better leaving with my head held high than waiting for them to kick me out like a mangy dog. With a month to go before the end of the school year, I gave formal notice to both directors, at RBS and Doreen Bird College, of my intention to leave their employment at the end of the current season, without elaborating on the reasons. They fully understood the complexities of the situation, and expressed warmth and gratitude as we said our goodbyes. I was so upset at losing the creative fruits of my labours (twelve years in the college and eight years at RBS) that on leaving I decided to publish my materials about corruption at ISTD in their international activities. I sent a covering letter with exposing documents to Mary Clark at *Dancing Times* and to editors of all the leading English newspapers. I was convinced that they would not print this sensationalist, devastating scandal. But I really had to find an outlet for the bitter taste of this injustice, and expose the real character behind the prestigious organisation which went by the imperial title of ISTD, proving to them that even in the face of their might, there are dance specialists who won't resort to dirty tricks and persecution in pursuit of the real story behind European culture.

I realised that from my point of view this was the hysterical, mindless cry of a wounded bird in a stormy sky. Some of the newspaper editors rang to try and get the finer points of my exposé of ISTD's shameful actions. But the press reaction stopped at this, and I expected nothing else. All I wanted was to rid myself of this suppurating pus. Thirty-five years ago I had been arrested in the Soviet Union for a letter of this nature to the Central Communist Party Ideology Department, and exiled to the back of beyond for three years. The English (thank God) turned out to be more humane and democratic. Kafuyu, my faithful assistant, had passed on all the telephone messages from colleagues and friends in the last few months, each offering support, sympathy and good wishes. From time to time, my lady friend would travel with me to various courses.

My assistant continued to take charge of organising my video and audio cassette sales in Europe, Australia and other countries that used the VHS or SECAM formats. She also managed my (much fuller) schedule of European courses/seminars. Kafuyu persuaded me to accept my son's invitation to Moscow, and was delighted to spend a month in Russia. Dmitri kindly drove us around the capital's main sights and St Petersburg, as he had on my last visit with Penelope. We also visited my friend/colleague Tolya Shikero, chief ballet master at the Kiev Opera Theatre, for his sixtieth anniversary gala evening. I paid a sad visit to the grave of my beloved teacher, Ludmilla Tzhomelidze, former répétiteur at this theatre. Enjoying a sightseeing trip with my friend restored me to my normal creative state and brought us closer than I had ever felt to any woman. This genuinely helped me to get through the British ballet quake.

CHAPTER 11 MUSES IN CONFLICT

Returning to Canada for a protracted period meant, at the very least, losing my flat in the centre of London, all my courses/seminars in Europe and England, proximity to Moscow and my faithful colleague, Kafuyu. This was a great deal to lose. On top of this, at sixty-three years old, following fifty years in the business (honest!), it would be a challenge to carry on working at this pace: twelve hours a day in schools and at home on my own projects. But there's a reason for the expression 'Every cloud has a silver lining.' As a result of lengthy discussions, Kafuyu and I agreed to focus our attention on our two main areas of business which were already established in England and Europe:

a) international courses for performers and seminars for teachers on Character dance;

b) production of new videos based on my creative repertoire, with a clearance sale of the old ones.

We did the housework together on Saturday mornings, and went to the theatre in the evening. On Sundays, she got on with her own affairs, and I spent time on academic research. This suited us both really well at that stage of our lives together.

As a matter of priority Kafuyu and I decided to widen the net of courses to make use of my increased availability now that I was no longer working at RBS and Doreen Bird College, and to visit committed institutions in Europe more often, so that I generally had half of every month in London to complete new video projects as a secondary objective.

As you can imagine, 1996 just flew by in this way. During this time I wrote two cultural and historical articles on Character dance and Court dancing in

Europe from the Medieval to Baroque periods. I decided to place them in one of the English or American dance magazines. At this time, *Dancing Times* was still carrying advertisements for my international summer courses, UK Summer Dance, in London. Naturally, I made contact initially with their editor, Mary Clark, proposing that she printed my work on Historical and Character dance with colour illustrations on a monthly basis over a six-month period. Unsurprisingly, she refused outright: quod erat demonstrandum. Ethically speaking, I was now within my rights to find another publisher.

My business plans with Kafuyu gradually solidified, and we were more than happy in our personal relationship. We seemed to have the ideal set-up, and had no need to fantasise about how things might be. Prior to my next course in London, she suggested that we reorganise it to bring in Japanese amateurs in European ballet over the summer holidays. At first I was lukewarm about her idea, well aware that the Japanese have their own traditional Classical dance and are rather sceptical about our Classical style. But she argued that I was just jaded. A European-style ballet company had existed in Tokyo for twenty years, and many private ballet schools operated in Japan nowadays, including her own family's Classical dance studio in Osaka, where she had studied from a young age under her mother's leadership. My girlfriend guaranteed to sign up at least twenty students, as long as we taught them in a separate group because of the language problem, which she was prepared to run herself. Kafuyu also promised to organise a course for me in one of Tokyo's foremost schools, to include my air ticket and hotel accommodation. I appreciated her ambition, and had no valid reason to say no to such an optimistic plan. Now that she had the green light from me, my assistant enthusiastically set about making this exciting project happen.

One Saturday evening on our way home from the ballet *Othello* in the Kremlin Palace, Kafuyu suddenly smiled mysteriously, and asked: "Misha, we've been living together for almost two years now. Were you thinking of offering me your hand and heart any time soon?"

She put her question in a very flirtatious way, so I thought she was joking, and replied in a similar vein: "Darling, you already have both my hands and my three hearts. Isn't that enough for you?"

"You're making a joke of it as usual, but seriously, I want to know, would I not make a suitable wife for you?"

I was stunned, and gazed searchingly into her unfathomable eyes for a while.

"I'm sorry, Kafuyu, I'd assumed that we were both happy to be close but free. You know how much I value our friendship and your enormous help with my work. Of course I would be happy to marry you, despite the almost thirty-year age gap between us. But having been married twice already, I'm not really inclined to destroy another person's life again. Sadly, I belong entirely to Terpsichore and will never trade her in, come what may. Any woman will always come second to her. In spite of the professional interests you and I share, you would quite reasonably want special attention for yourself, a child, your family. I'm sorry, I'm just not capable of this. On top of this, your parents, as far as I know, would never sanction you marrying a European, flouting the ancient Japanese customs of family life."

"Everything you've said is true, Misha. But you don't realise how much my parents and brothers love me, and want me to be happy. I'm sure that I'll be able to bring them round to my way of thinking, considering our shared business interests and the fact that I'm already thirty-seven years old."

"All right, Kafuyu, I'll give it some thought, while you check out how your mother would feel about it. I suspect that nothing will come of it, but I'm happy to be proved wrong."

She hugged me in a surge of emotion, and kissed me so passionately that my whole body was tingling. I was convinced that I was right, but couldn't refuse her definitively while she was making a brave attempt to secure her future options. It would be best if she came by herself to the realisation of how misguided this idea was, than for me to wound her feelings of self-worth with my refusal. Perhaps this would enable me to keep her as my assistant. One way or another, I was all on edge after our conversation about marriage.

The flight to Japan took over ten hours. This gave us plenty of time to discuss in detail our work schedule and the various repercussions of the wedding project. I reminded her again how sensitive this was and asked her not to put too much pressure on her mother, otherwise we could lose each other for good. She just smiled in reply.

"Maestro, we're not in England now. This is my home, and I know how to manage my family. Please don't worry about it. The last thing we need is your nerves getting in the way."

We landed in Tokyo on schedule, and a few hours later we were in Osaka. Kafuyu took me to the hotel by taxi, having stowed the suitcase of videocassettes in the boot, asked me to remember which room I was in, and took my passport. She gave instructions about me to the receptionist to show that she was in charge, and that I was just her appendage. This suited me down to the ground. I was so tired that I collapsed on to the bed as soon as I got into my room. Waking up a couple of hours later, I switched on the television to watch the news and froze in shock: naked couples were engaged in group sex of various descriptions. I tried the other channels, but got exactly the same result, only these solitary couples were mastering such sexual feats that I immediately wanted to take photos of them for my forthcoming choreography 'Walpurgis Night' from the opera *Faust*. I hopped through twelve channels and finding nothing but filthy pornography, went down to reception for help.

In the gloom it was difficult to make out the duty receptionist who was chatting on the telephone. While I was waiting, I thought, *I've probably been asleep for a long time and now it's already night-time. I'm such a brainless idiot, I forgot to change my watch.*

As if reading my mind, the receptionist put the lights on in the lobby. Behind him I saw half a dozen girls in flimsy, virtually see-through gowns with belts. They were all the same height, with identical haircuts and saccharine smiles.

Eventually, the receptionist addressed me in Japanese. I showed him my hotel card and explained the problem with my television. He rattled off something else in Japanese while I repeated, "News, BBC, CNN, RAI1, Novosti!"

He kept going, gesturing towards the girls standing behind him. As if obeying his command, the girls undid their belts to reveal their gorgeous bodies. Once more, I was dumbfounded by this unprecedented spectacle. They turned first one leg then the other towards me, moving in perfect time to the same cloying music, drawing back the flaps of their gowns.

The receptionist realised that I was 'biting' on his 'bait', and buried himself in the papers on his desk. I stood there in a trance, unable to tear my half-blind eyes away from the tantalising temptresses, and felt some movement in my trousers. I decided to head for home before it was too late and I disgraced myself. Being a Taurean, another minute and I could quite simply have leaped over the registrar's desk and got down to group sex with these sirens in one fell swoop. Or so it seemed as I was going up to my room in the lift.

Kafuyu rang from her place to wake me in the morning. She arranged for us to meet at midday downstairs in the lobby, and enquired how I had settled in at the hotel. In my innocence, I recounted the story of my evening surprises with the television. At the last minute I curtailed my report about the beautiful nymphs, unsure how she would react. This was the right decision. A few hours later, as I was coming out of the lift, I heard Kafuyu wailing hysterically. She was lambasting the hotel manager because I hadn't been able to switch off the pornography to watch the news. I understood just two words of my Japanese lady friend's tirade at the poor manager: sex and police. It was a job tearing her away from the registration desk. Apologising to the manager, I explained that I hadn't factored in my lady friend's jealous nature after telling her about the problem with the television programmes yesterday. He accepted my apology with a nod. This scandalous scene left me with an unpleasant aftertaste.

As we went up to my hotel room, Kafuyu elaborated on yesterday's television issue. I should have changed the sex channel – which is on automatically during the night – to the usual Central Television one, as she then showed me. We confirmed our plans for the next three days in Osaka and set off for the Travel Express Agency. Kawasaki received us extremely cordially, in keeping with Japanese custom. Kafuyu clarified all the terms for booking transport and accommodation for her group of sixteen-year-old students' three-week stay in London: they would spend two weeks with me on the course, and the third would be for trips, shows and similar distractions. Next, Kafuyu hurried off to give classes in her mother's studio. I presented Kawasaki with a few of my videocassettes. In exchange, he offered me a look around his collection of paintings in his second-floor gallery, Casa del Arte. Semyon Shegelman's pictures that had once belonged to me were still on display in one of the rooms of Russian artists. Two years previously in London, I had instructed the gallery owner not to sell Semyon's work, as I needed it to promote him internationally rather than for any commercial purpose.

Kawasaki invited me to lunch. I wasn't used to Japanese food, but put a brave face on it. Over the meal I asked my acquaintance why he had reserved this particular hotel/bordello in Osaka.

The jocular travel agent laughed as he replied: "Dear Mikhail, you asked for something as lively as possible. They charge less for a night here than for one hour with a girl of your choice. You saw those beauties. That's right, isn't it?"

"Dear Yoshiyuki, thank you for being so thoughtful. Those sirens are certainly beautiful. But I'm here as Kafuyu's guest, and she is my girlfriend. Like all Japanese women, she is dangerously jealous. Please don't refer to these concubines in front of her, otherwise I'm finished."

Kawasaki laughed loudly and promptly suggested that we visit a famous temple on the way back to the hotel.

"Thank you, that would be great. I love ancient sacred buildings, despite the fact that I'm not religious."

"Mikhail, it's a special temple, which accurately predicts the future of those who come to visit."

"I'll say it again, Yoshiyuki, I don't believe in mysticism. Why spend time and money on nothing?"

Nevertheless, my companion stopped in front of the sacred temple and insisted that I went inside. Complying with etiquette, I followed him obediently.

While Kawasaki was completing his customary ritual, I stood by the wall next to the exit, awestruck as I studied the temple's fantastic frescoes and unusual sculptures. Eventually, Yoshiyuki went over to some kind of idol, and threw a few coins into a machine. First we could hear something in it squeaking as it turned and next a tiny envelope popped out of the slot. We went outside and stopped at the end of the square. In keeping with tradition I was supposed to take the prediction out of the envelope and read it with my own eyes. I did so, but as it was, of course, in Japanese I had to ask my friend to read it for me. He scanned the text without saying anything, then froze open-mouthed. I was convinced that Kawasaki was playing a joke on me now and was preparing a comic response to his English translation. But for some reason he kept quiet for some time, without looking my way. Finally I gave in and as we drew near the hotel I asked him what the prediction had said, as he seemed determined to keep it from me.

"Mikhail, you told me that you don't believe in mysticism. So it's better for you not to know what it says here."

I gathered that it was some evil prophesy.

Saying a cheerful goodbye to him, I thanked him for lunch. Once inside the hotel I asked the now familiar manager to give me the English translation of the oracle.

The latter proclaimed in a clear voice: "In the near future your friend and helper will let you down through no fault of his/her own." And he added, in an effort to reassure me, "Don't believe these sayings. They're just for Japanese people."

Once back in my room, I lay on the bed and lost myself in deep thought.

So! You can't seriously believe in this rubbish? I'd suggest you get on with something more useful.

You're right. But still, 'God helps those who help themselves.' Didn't they brainwash you enough in the Soviet Union? You'd be better off calling Kawasaki and checking how accurate the manager's translation is.

OK, but one way or another, you need to prepare for the worst because Kafuyu is being a bit emotional, and not taking into consideration that the school business still belongs to her mother.

In spite of that, she is not sufficiently experienced to conceive of the amount of responsibility she will have to take on with a group of twenty girls overseas, even with two assistants/mothers there to help.

I listed all the points to discuss in our meeting with the parents that evening after observing Kafuyu's ballet class with her own students.

Kawasaki rang: "Yoshiyuki, is it true that the temple prophesy predicted that my secretary would let me down?"

"Yes, Mikhail, I'm afraid that is the case. But it only applies to people who believe in our religion."

Kawasaki's answer just gave me more cause for concern, and forced me to steel myself for the project's possible failure, in order to protect my personal and commercial interests.

The following morning, Kafuyu came to collect me in her school administrator's car. She introduced me to her mother's assistant and asked me to bring a few video/audio cassettes with me to give to the Parents' Committee to promote Berkut Dance International (BDI). I asked her if I would have the opportunity to meet the Director herself.

"Mum has promised to attend the parents' meeting, but she's very shy with men, especially foreign ones. I have brought her up to speed on our relationship."

"I hope you told her that I'm wearing a tie for the first time ever today in her honour," I quipped.

"Mum doesn't really get the European sense of humour, Misha. Try not to joke with her."

The school was bright and clean and in the central district of the provincial town. Two groups totalling approximately fifty participants were running in the studio. Three subjects were covered on the curriculum: European ballet, American modern dance and Japanese Classical dance. One large classroom was full of children from noon till 7 p.m., and was hired out in the evenings for various corporate show rehearsals.

The girls greeted us with a ballet curtsey. Kafuyu delivered an entire lesson to show her students in the best possible light for the London course. I was scared to ask any additional questions, hoping that the school director would definitely be at the parents' meeting. Thankfully, it was the weekend, and the mothers had no problem staying on for an extra hour with the children. But the school owner did not appear. After the girls had got changed, Kafuyu invited them into the classroom with their mothers. Apart from the two of us, everyone sat on the floor in a semicircle.

My girlfriend introduced me to the group, and gave a summary of the planned UK Summer Dance course in London and the various tourist excursions that would follow the intensive course with the two of us and a third person in the form of a Jazz teacher. The girls fidgeted with excitement on the floor as they heard more about the tempting opportunity to visit London and experience new pleasures in dance classes with European masters. Kafuyu had her work cut out to keep up with the questions coming at her thick and fast from the bunch. Seated at the piano, the secretary took endless notes on the matter being discussed, no doubt so that she could report back to the Director. I kept quiet at first, as I observed this discussion in its alien format. Judging by their excited expressions, there was unanimous interest in the London course from the girls and their mothers. They directed some questions direct to me in English or through my partner. It seemed that the project was destined to be a success, but for some reason I was plagued with doubt. Everything was coming together almost too easily.

At the meeting, Kafuyu registered twenty-three people interested in attending the course in London. She decided to call in at the Travel Express Agency and reserved twenty-five tickets to London, to include two mothers from the Parents' Committee. On the train into Osaka, I asked her why her mother had not attended the meeting.

"I can't talk about this now, Misha. As you know, Mum is not in favour of the London project. Even after I showed her posters and brochures from the last few years of UK Summer Dance, she is convinced that this is a scam to fleece her clients, and doesn't want any part in it. Mum was in school all morning, and made a point of leaving before we got there as she had no wish to meet you."

"Darling, these are her students. You can't ignore the Director's opinion!"

"The school always closes in August. The students are free to go where they want. That's their right."

"I agree with you, Kafuyu. But it's not appropriate for the Director and her daughter, and their staff to air their differences of opinion in public. Sorry if you feel I'm interfering."

Kawasaki noted all the details of the group trip to England and started ringing round the airlines and London hotels straight away to get something booked for this large number as soon as possible for the peak summer season. We went out and sat on a bench by the entrance. I didn't say anything. Kafuyu sighed heavily.

"Misha, I understand your concerns about the course project and my mother's behaviour. I'm sorry; her aggressive stance against me has taken me by surprise too. She was hoping that when I completed my course at the Royal Ballet, I would come back here and take over from her in the school, allowing her to retire at seventy-five. But I stayed on in London for two more years with you, and she can't forgive me for this. This is without me even mentioning the possibility of us getting married."

"My darling colleague, I understand all of that, but I honestly don't know how I can help you."

"That's just it. I don't need your help. You'll be off to Tokyo tomorrow, to start your course in the ballet studio the following day. Just focus on that and forget about everything else for a week. When you get back from Tokyo we'll sort it all out. I promise!"

The agency secretary invited us in to see the Director. Within half an hour, Kawasaki had managed to reserve flight tickets and rooms in boarding houses in London's King's Cross for the entire group. Kafuyu thanked him and wrote out a cheque to 'Travel Express' for 1,000 yen in advance.

Back at the hotel I gave her the suitcase with my videocassettes and helped her to carry it to the nearest railway station. As were walking, I was weighed down by the feeling that she wasn't telling me the whole story.

Noticing my despondent look, she kept assuring me: "Don't worry, sweetheart. Everything's going to be all right. We'll see each other next week. I hope it goes well!"

I decided to make a list of pros and cons in my hotel room. There's nothing worse than uncertainty.

Why didn't Kafuyu's mother want to see me? Why has she taken against her daughter's partner so strongly?

Most likely your girlfriend told the aging director that she wanted to marry you. To all intents and purposes, this meant losing her daughter forever, and it was for her that she established the ballet studio in the first place. She's paid five years' rent on her London flat, and was dreaming of looking after her Japanese grandchildren in her latter years.

And then her beloved daughter brings home a sixty-three-year-old European out of the blue, to carry on the family line! Ha ha! She can't put up with that – she has to make a stand!

Mishenka, don't you think that you might be exaggerating the risk? As they say: once bitten, twice shy. It's understandable – in your past life you have been so put upon that now you think everyone around you poses a threat to you at every turn.

Yes, unfortunately that's how it is. You need to get a grip before panic sets in. Go and take Tokyo by storm!

Having calmed down a bit, I busied myself checking through my forthcoming course materials, and packing for the journey. But all night long my head was spinning with a heavy foreboding of imminent attack, which I was powerless to dispel.

Micki, the Ballet School administrator, was waiting for me at Tokyo's central bus station as arranged in advance with Kafuyu. He asked in good English, "How was your journey?"

"Excellent, thanks."

"Then let's go."

Micki swiftly settled me into a small, cosy hotel without any concubines on display. I just had time to grab my work bag from my suitcase. We enjoyed a light snack in the canteen and set off promptly for the studio, as there was only an hour to go before my class began. Fortunately, the hotel was only two blocks from the school, where the Director, Sonni, was waiting for me with her staff team. The classes in all three studios started at 2 p.m. and changed around without stopping until 10 p.m. Sonni and her colleagues came out of the Director's office into the hall the moment I arrived, and welcomed their guests with applause. I bowed as a sign of gratitude, which prompted a deeper, universal bow from my hosts. Sonni invited me into her office to discuss the course programme and timetable based on three classes a day: Character dance, Partnering and Choreography. On Sunday morning there would be an assessed concert for parents and then a farewell lunch with the teachers. Micki and Sonni had agreed the commercial aspect of the contract with Kafuyu on the telephone. I just signed the document and asked to meet the pianist for ten minutes prior to the lesson. The Director informed me that they often welcomed guest teachers of Classical dance from Russia and Modern dance from the USA. But this was the first time they were including my disciplines, and they were a little nervous. I reassured her, promising to be gentle and patient.

Sonni laughed and shook her head. "That's unlikely with Russian teachers. Although the fact that you speak English will make it easier for you to build a rapport with the Japanese students, as most of them are proficient in this language."

The following morning, I visited the Tokyo Ballet, again as per Kafuyu's arrangements with the company director. She had forwarded my CV in advance, along with a few programmes/librettos of my choreographic miniatures from the Soviet Union and Canada. The artistic director gave me a traditionally cordial welcome. He showed me some brochures from their repertoire, which attested to the troupe's Contemporary Classical form (not traditional ballet). As far as I could tell, they were working to Goleizovsky's style. Yakobson and even Grigorovich to some extent were quite close to my genres in Contemporary Choreography. The ballet master invited me to watch the dancers in a warm-up class that had just got under way, and their subsequent rehearsal for the current repertoire. If I was willing to consider their performance for use in my own productions, we would discuss the possibility of using me as a choreographer in future. I studied the poster advertising Saturday evening's Tokyo Ballet show. The Director then made a telephone call, and a moment later, his secretary brought me a complimentary ticket for their ballet triptych (three one-act compositions).

As we said our goodbyes, the artistic director asked me to deliver a parcel of their posters and programmes to Kafuyu. We agreed to stay in touch through her, as I was always coming and going. I left him a few of my videocassettes to give him a more comprehensive picture of my work. This potential opportunity was of great interest to me.

As was to be expected, the first day of the course with the Japanese students in school was quite stressful. At the beginning of the Character dance class they were clearly very shy, and apologised continually for any errors they made. But once they understood that I was not angry with them, they started to laugh at each other instead of apologising. This lightened the atmosphere in the studio. Thanks to their enthusiasm and concentration, I succeeded in teaching them the beginners' programme both at the barre and in the centre in a week. I had never managed this before. By the end of the week, the students were performing 'Russian Dance' and 'Neapolitan Tarantella' quite happily. The Director dropped into the studio from time to time and couldn't suppress a smile. To be honest, it was tough for me to deal with anyone who didn't speak English without Kafuyu there. I had to ask the

Director to assign a fluent English speaker in the group to help me communicate with her monolingual colleagues.

The Partnering course gave rise to a significant problem in body contact between students. I felt that the girls must have been more awkward with me than with their regular male course mates. The ratio in the group was nine young men to twenty-three girls. Luckily, the latter were as light as feathers, short in stature and confident on pointes. The girls related to me as if I were a doctor. They allowed me to hold them by the legs, waist, lean on their shoulders, etc. without embarrassment. But when they came into contact with the young men, it was a case of 'laughter and tears'. The Director had to come to my rescue once again. I spent one half of the lesson in one corner with the lads while Sonni worked on the girls in the other for five minutes of instruction. After this, both camps were much more relaxed in the Director's presence. The girls stopped flirting and the young men took a more confident approach in supporting their partners by the arms or legs, lifting them by the waist above their heads in jumps, etc. By the end of the week even the course delegates themselves were amazed at what they'd achieved in such a short time. Sonni said everyone had me down as a wizard. I took this as a compliment and stated that it was all thanks to her input.

It was obvious that the Director had been talking to the Tokyo ballet master about me when she invited him to our assessment concert, and he asked her to pass on a request for me to meet him backstage on Saturday after the show. In all probability he couldn't accept Sonni's invitation because he was putting on a matinee at the Tokyo Ballet on Sunday. I twigged that the artistic director wanted to make me a proposal. We were rehearsing with the groups on Saturday morning, and in the afternoon did a final run-through separately for the Partnering and Character dance genres. The Director and I gave the performers our final feedback and wished them luck for the next day.

I relaxed in the hotel after a hard day's work, and spruced myself up to look presentable for the beautiful Japanese women in the theatre foyer. The ballet triptych to classical music by local composers quite simply dazzled me from the off in the first act. In the second, I grew accustomed to the unusual style of choreography and musical orchestration. Then I was totally enthralled by the harmonious blend of dance motion and symphony music in the third act. Of course the way the Japanese went about putting a ballet together was a unique experience for me. The auditorium was sighing with rapture one minute, and reacting in a united show of emotional astonishment the next, watching the dramatic scenes of these unfamiliar legends.

When the ballet master asked my opinion of the show backstage, I answered: "It's absolutely amazing! I am completely bowled over by a style of ballet that I've never seen before. Such a combination of original classical movements in a contemporary form of artistic expression, with a high level of performance technique and acting skills that were unreservedly worthy of the audience's attention."

"Mikhail, I've had rave reviews about your work in the studio from my colleague Sonni. Can you stay another week in Tokyo at the company's expense, to lead a workshop with our dancers on Partnering technique at a professional level?"

"Unfortunately, this won't be possible as I have an engagement next month in Italy. I'm planning to come back in the autumn and if that time of year suits you, then we can sort out a course that's convenient to us both."

"OK, maestro, I'll check our plans for the autumn and let your assistant know."

Back at the hotel, I tried unsuccessfully to get through to Kafuyu. Anxious thoughts began to play on my mind again, with a sense of impending doom. I took charge of myself, forcing myself to focus on preparing tomorrow's studio assessment which would have a direct bearing on my future career in Japan.

The school director decided to make maximum use of our assessed display as a way of promoting her business. She had rented a small amphitheatre next door, where all the final concerts were held at the end of the school year. Sonni couldn't pass up such a brilliant opportunity to upset her competitors in the town and in view of this, she laid out her own money. She invited the press and television to a demonstration of the unusual – for the local audience – genre of Partnering technique. To her delight, the mini auditorium was available in the afternoon and Sonni reserved the space right there and then. I was the last to know about it at the final assessment programme run-through on Saturday. Naturally I put in a request to the Director for a stage rehearsal at 9 a.m. to confirm the positioning of the ballet barres and piano on the stage. At 10 a.m. an hour in separate groups by genre at half strength, i.e. marching; at 12 noon: snack and break; and at 2 p.m., the assessment performance.

The Director noted all my requirements and guaranteed that they would all be put in place. I admit, I did have my doubts about whether she would be able to reorganise all of this at the last minute. But hey, I had most definitely underestimated the Japanese work ethic. As I came into the performance space at 9 a.m., I noticed all the items I had asked for were on the stage. Moreover, on both sides of the metallic moveable barres, everyone who was taking part in the display was warming up with a Classical training routine led by the Director to musical accompaniment provided by the smiling pianist. As the exercises ended, they all turned towards me and greeted me with a ballet curtsey. I applauded instinctively and blew Sonni a kiss. The students giggled in unison, but on the teacher's command, turned promptly to face the barre. While the young men were completing their warm-up, the manager and I marked out on the floor the exact positions for the musical instrument and ballet barres during the show. I wrote down in my pad all the young men's and girls' entrances and exits from different sides of the arena, gave this information to the manager and asked him to take care of the usual lighting sequence for scene changes during the two-hour rehearsal. It was essential to check out how each lighting change fitted in with the next numbers, so that the dancers got used to strong lighting.

I was pleasantly surprised to see how well organised it all was: the staging, rehearsal, and students' relaxation and refreshments during their break time. I couldn't fault the Director for the way she had organised everything, and she put my mind to rest in a short space of time. The Japanese gave a dazzling display of their amazing business skills. With an hour to go before the demonstration, the Director entreated me as to whether I would be willing to give a five-minute interview to journalists. I wasn't keen on seeing myself on local television or in the press, but it would have been unethical to decline Sonni in these circumstances. I agreed to give them five minutes of my time.

1. "Mr Berkut, this being your first visit to Japan, what have you been most impressed by here?"

"You are extremely welcoming of tourists, you have an excellent public transport system and other public services, and the Japanese are enthusiastic and proactive by nature."

2. "Has there been anything negative about the city environment or where you're staying?"

"The streets are incredibly dirty and the noise is deafening."

3. "What's your opinion of Japanese dramatic arts, and stage dance in particular?

"Classical Japanese dramatic arts speak for themselves. I'm delighted to see that European Classical ballet and Modern dance have a place in Japanese contemporary culture."

4. "What do you think your students have achieved in their week's work with you?"

"You will see a display of the students' achievements over the next two hours. May I just express my great satisfaction with the professional training they have received from their studio teachers, the students' creative interest in new genres and forms of choreography, and this ballet studio management's high standard of organisation in the learning process and practice. I'd just like to use this opportunity to ask you not to use flash photography when taking pictures during the demonstration, as this disturbs the dancers and can put them off."

The assessment demonstration went smoothly and was of an advanced artistic and technical level. During the farewell lunch I received many compliments, half of which fell on the ears of the school's leadership team. Sonni asked me to commit at least two weeks for an autumn course with a production from their repertoire. Micki, the administrator, proposed a toast in my honour to thunderous applause from everyone present. I thanked them all for their interest and attention in my creative endeavours. Micki first took me to the hotel and settled up with them and with me. He delivered me to the central bus station just in time for the bus to Osaka. We said goodbye until the autumn and embraced like old friends. I was touched by his attentiveness and gratitude.

Once I was on the road, I analysed the latest events as always, counting up all the pluses and minuses. To sum up, I felt positive about the opportunities ahead.

The bus arrived in Osaka late at night. The English-speaking manager in my previous hotel was not on duty, but the night receptionist was expecting me. He handed me my room key and instinctively gestured in the direction of the row of those same girls behind him. Once they noticed me they turned on sweet smiles initially, but recognising that this client was a lost cause, they promptly resumed their business masks. A knock on the door woke me up at 8 a.m.

Holding an envelope, the manager excused himself, saying: "Mr Berkut, this is for you from Miss Shintani. Please sign to confirm receipt."

I didn't get round to opening the bulky envelope as I was desperate for the toilet. Once I got back to the room, I forgot all about it, busy with my morning routine. I suddenly remembered after my shave, and decided to check the good news from my lady friend. Inside were 5,000 yen and a short note.

'Forgive me, Misha, you were right. This is to reimburse you for your travel expenses. Goodbye.'

I was paralysed by this news. Despite several readings, there was no changing the statement. I went to the bathroom again, dunked my head under a stream of cold water (so as not to get a shock) and slowly lay down on the bed, trying not to go to pieces.

So, first things first, I must call Kawasaki urgently and tell him that the UK trip is off.

Don't forget to pick up Shegelman's pictures from him, as you're unlikely to come back here.

I went down for breakfast and asked the manager who had given him the envelope for me.

"Two men from Tokyo. They introduced themselves as your partner Miss Shintani's brothers."

"Thanks for letting me know. I would like to settle up with you now as I'm flying back to England tomorrow."

Back in my room, I called Kawasaki and asked if we could meet up as a matter of urgency.

"What's happened, Mikhail?"

"Yoshiyuki, I can't tell you over the telephone."

"OK, see you soon."

After reading Kafuyu's note, he more or less leaped out of his seat at the impertinence.

"I warned you. The prophets never get it wrong! Now you can see that for yourself."

I stared at him in silence, not knowing what to say to this. He read my mind.

"Fine. Don't let a woman into your heart. All of them just play on your emotions in business. Don't worry about me. I'll cancel all the group's travel and accommodation in London."

"May I take Shegelman's paintings please, Yoshiyuki? I promised to get them into an exhibition in Paris for him. I must take the chance to get them back to Europe while I'm here."

"OK. I'll get some guys to pack them up for you in two secure packages. It'll be easier to transport them unframed. I'll bring the pictures over to your hotel tomorrow morning."

I got a trolley at Tokyo Airport and checked in my items without any problems. Once seated on the plane, I unwound a little with a shot of vodka, and began my customary self-analysis.

STAGE V: OUT OF ORBIT

CHAPTER 12 ONE STEP BACK, TWO STEPS FORWARD

The failure of the Japanese project didn't impact hugely on my emotional well-being as a choreographer, as in my heart of hearts I had never believed that the Far Eastern peoples, with their ancient culture and natural morphology (thickset build, bow legs, etc.) were physically equipped for the aesthetic demands of European Classical dance. Making a European perform a traditional role from the ancient Classical repertoire of Japanese, Chinese and Korean theatre would have the same end result. But it's a different matter when individuals from these countries come to study European art in Italy, France, England, or vice versa. Flouting the laws of nature is not always a good thing. One way or another, I had paid a high price, as usual, for my Japanese mistake. Now, licking my fresh wounds, I decided to take advantage of some rare free time to sort out my private pensions in Canada and England, and to consider my future creative career. I wasn't thinking of courses/seminars, which I'd enjoyed doing for more than twenty years as a fun sideline to my main profession as a ballet master. To be specific, I was studying the anthropology of dance for a book I was working on in my spare time. In my current circumstances, it was a matter of finding opportunities to continue working in a prestigious ballet school for the foreseeable future. Penny was aware of all my physical problems caused by professional traumas over the last fifty years, and was seriously worried about my prospects.

"Misha, don't you think it's time for a career change, now that you are of pensionable age?" she insisted.

"Darling, everything I do will always involve some form of physical work."

"But lots of your colleagues and ballet stars have become 'ballet boutique' shopkeepers in their retirement. Their girlfriends/wives do the actual selling, while the men source the goods. You are a professional director by nature and training. You hold all the cards."

Initially I thought that my ex-wife was making fun of me, and took no notice of her remarks. Nevertheless, it inspired me to try my hand at being an impresario. I was no stranger to this role. The more I thought about it, the more I wanted to follow in the footsteps of Diaghilev. Kafuyu was the only one who had been party to this idea in her time, and had helped me to set up a project to organise a touring exhibition of Russian artists and small song-and-dance ensembles from Moscow, St Petersburg and former Soviet republics touring Europe. Changing my professional profile in this way seemed a realistic option given my physical limitations. It follows that concrete funds were needed to pull off this project. I had a couple of hundred thousand in New York City Bank from the sale of my Florida flat, and some savings in London from sales of my various videocassettes. It was more than enough to start a small new business. I hoped to secure long-term financial success for these Russian artistes and painters, once they'd become known in Europe.

I met up with lots of artists at their Moscow and St Petersburg exhibitions during my travels around Russia. After comparing the selected candidates, I settled on three painters with diverse styles and genres who all offered something different:

1. Edward Ulan (Moscow): decorative art; religious, literary and theatrical pieces.
2. Yevgeni Goryainov (Moscow): monumental painting on historical themes in classical style.
3. Mikhail Shcheglov (St Petersburg): cityscapes and everyday scenes in pastel.

All three masters were highly accomplished with distinct individual styles in painting on canvas. I signed a year's agreement with them, and confirmed which works I was interested in before scheduling a time and place for the first exhibition in London. Our long-term business relations between producers and clients would hinge on this test run. What appeals to the domestic market may not work for foreign buyers, and vice versa.

I really needed to find someone to represent my company BDI. My cousin Sofia in St Petersburg strongly recommended her brother-in-law who lived in Moscow. Mark Feferman worked in administration at an engineering institute and came across as a sound, trustworthy person. At a meeting in his flat, we discussed the financial and operational terms in detail and signed an official agreement to cement these. He dealt with all stages of accepting and registering new artists, which I would confirm on receiving photos of their work which he would send to London. Feferman would then forward large packages of canvases (unframed, just on stretchers) to my address via Aeroflot freight services. I stored them in a basement cupboard at my home. This system worked very well while it lasted and suited both parties.

Things were more difficult with the song-and-dance ensembles. After Perestroika, as is commonly known, ex-Soviet citizens without any basic understanding of commercial affairs (just like yours truly, overseas), made fatal errors, wasting time, money and energy in the process. All of us were of the impression that making money didn't require any specialist economic knowledge or training, experience or patience. So whether you were stealing or trading on the open market, you bought for three and sold for five. For this reason, after looking at the programmes offered by former Soviet dance ensembles, talking to their leaders brought me into contact with vile, ignorant counterparts involved in commercially focused tours, not on the state's behalf, as previously, but for multiple mutual interests: creative as well as financial, including a business budget for incomings and outgoings. They drew up a balance sheet for each concert without factoring in my realistic costs, which included travel, accommodation, advertising, insurance, etc. My son only explained to me afterwards that ensembles were obliged to hand over 25% of their revenue to their sponsors/promoters. I had to narrow my sights regarding the number of members in each group: from nine down to six music ensembles, and twenty-four down to sixteen dance-group performers (including the accompanists). Despite these compromises, it was impossible to find a suitable dance ensemble option in Russia.

Then I had a stroke of luck with 'Terem' (Doll's House) a balalaika quartet. This unusual music ensemble consisted of two mandolins, an accordion and bass/balalaika, and featured Conservatoire graduates – qualified musicians of a very high standard. Each of them was a professional virtuoso on their chosen instrument. Their repertoire comprised classical, folk and popular items which had been sympathetically orchestrated specifically for their unique quartet by their leader. I was astonished that they accepted my terms unreservedly and signed a contract with me without haggling over any of the details. On the surface it probably looked like small beer in Russia for such a seemingly well-established impresario. But to my mind they suited my taste and my budget too. Naturally I played my cards close to my chest. Exactly as they did, as their slow-witted administrator Katya entered into a clear compromise arrangement with me, with these high-calibre instrumentalists who were too good for me. They desperately needed help from this inexperienced entrepreneur to promote themselves more actively and break into the overseas circuit to get themselves noticed in the hope of securing more suitable engagements. What they didn't know was that I had the same goal (in reverse) to take advantage of their qualifications to establish my own fledgling business in this field.

The next stop on my journey through the former Soviet republics was Kiev (capital of Ukraine), where I spent some time at the invitation of Anatoly Shikero, chief ballet master at the Opera Theatre, (once my classmate in MTA) for his sixtieth birthday. After the celebration I stayed with him for a few days while looking for a dance ensemble. Anatoly recommended me several potential candidates. But my forays turned out to be fruitless, for the same reasons I'd come across in

Moscow. The last resort, and the slimmest hope, was Uzbekistan. Bernara Karieva was ready and waiting for me there, eager to discuss a scheduled production of 'Polovtsian Dances' from Borodin's opera *Prince Igor* in her Opera Theatre. When she first heard about my new line as an entrepreneur and my search for a dance ensemble, Bernara recommended a small, contemporary group of professionals who, following Perestroika, no longer benefited from financial support from the Ministry of Culture for their troupe's regular tours. My colleague introduced me to the Ensemble director and wished me luck.

Takhir led his foreign guest in to meet his group, and showed me a half-hour programme: six pairs of dancers with three musicians/accompanists was exactly the kind of grouping that I was looking for. But the performers were all qualified at different levels. After the display, I asked the Director if this was all of the group's performers or whether there were any female dancers.

"We have a younger group which we usually take with us on tours around Uzbekistan, but no further. Most of them are senior students from the local ballet school."

"Takhir, in principal, I'm interested in your Ensemble and could invite them for a two-week European tour, but not in their current format. Having half the women and two of the men of pensionable age will not work – you will have to replace them with young, energetic performers. Then we can sign a contract for regular overseas trips; initially two to three times a year. I'd like to see your full touring programme again in a few days' time if possible, with the new configuration of dancers. Let me know your decision via Madame Karieva. Thanks for the demonstration."

Three days later, Bernara reported that the Ensemble was ready for me. At the agreed time I turned up again to watch the troupe in its revised format. Karieva was already there, having spent three hours that morning refining the repertoire with the young artistes. It definitely looked more saleable to the European market now. I presented them with the contract terms in Russian to sign.

Terem, the instrumental quartet, was the first to come on tour in England. They enjoyed a successful debut in music festivals and concerts in church halls. A week later, they were joined by the Uzbek Dance Ensemble in the second half. Both groups performed an hour-long programme of their unique numbers, astounding the audience. They showed themselves in an excellent light onstage in later excerpts of the concert at Queen Elizabeth Hall and the Barbican Centre, even when the auditoriums were only half full. My aim was to use these prestigious concert venues as advertising to the attendant press and television representatives. The expectant audience gave a warm welcome to the diverse artistes in both sections during their first London performance. They saw this as a uniquely exotic act from the former Soviet Union. All subsequent concerts in various towns around England were warmly received by audiences, and the spirited artistes in both ensembles lapped up the compliments. I invariably saw my guests off with individual gifts as a souvenir of England, and a token of thanks for their performances. My twelve-month trial contracts with the two groups were coming to an end. In spite of the positive conclusion of this experience, I was far from convinced that my new business would last.

The problem was that in the preparatory stage of this project, I had initially enjoyed administrative support from Kafuyu. Once I took on full responsibility for this enterprise, the whole workload was too much for me to cope with when I was so busy. Still, everything went a lot more smoothly with the artists in that first year than with the ensembles, as it was easier to resolve any organisational matters with four clients rather than twenty. In addition, Mark, my representative in Moscow, had helped me to a greater or lesser degree. This enabled me to focus on preparing and setting up English exhibitions on a higher level. It became clear that I couldn't keep both parts of the Russian enterprise going by myself. Based on her understanding of the project, and her experience of charitable work in the Arts, Penny refused point-blank to have any part in it. I had to choose the lesser of two evils: to withdraw from both the instrumental and dance ensembles as the contract ended, while persisting with the touring exhibitions of Russian artists in Europe with a view to them making it big.

Of course, Semyon Shegelman had continued to be a priority over the previous twenty years and here, too, in my new enterprise with artists from Moscow and St Petersburg. Semyon's avant-garde paintings could not take pride of place over contrasting work by the first members of our artists' corporation at joint exhibitions in London (Islington Cultural Centre, Folkestone Pavilion, etc.), Berlin (Russian House and City Art Centre), Sorrento (history museum), Osaka (art gallery), San Francisco (Bay Pavilion), and Montreal (Bronfman Centre), etc. In line with our agreement, individual artists from Russia could fly over for one of our exhibitions with a stock of new paintings at my expense, and stay with me for this period. It was helpful to have the artist present to drum up sales of his work at particularly important viewings at the opening of the next exhibition in the various venues.

I was fully aware that my enthusiasm for touring exhibitions would not last forever. In essence, this was more of a charitable than commercial exercise, which required substantial funding, i.e. it was completely non-profit-making. The commercial drawback lay in the fact that I was unable to sell the best works as I then risked ending up without sufficient reserves of paintings for the next exhibition. I couldn't not sell them either, as my financial resources were gradually dwindling away, threatening to bankrupt me. Moreover, the artists from Russia were no longer topping up their picture stocks for some reason. As I discovered from my discussions with them, Mark Feferman, my Moscow representative, was in fact an archetypal 'jack the lad', demanding 10% of my payment to them as commission for buying their latest pieces. This was on top of the sum he received from me for his work as outlined in our signed agreement. Naturally, the Russian artists lost interest in our enterprise and were scared to tell me about it until I got it out of them.

So my attempt to make a fundamental career change came to a sorry end – I was certainly no Diaghilev. I made a gift of the remaining Russian artists' works to Russian House at the final exhibition in Germany, for the Russian Embassy to use at some point in setting up artistic and cultural enterprises in Berlin. The other part of my collection remained with friends in San Francisco for safekeeping. Let's be honest, Mark was not the first or last of my close friends or relations with the chutzpah and cynicism to take from me in our commercial dealings. Even my nephew Boris, whom I had supported financially while he was emigrating to the USA with his family, had sold my videocassettes with his notorious wife behind my back, hiding it from me for a long time.

However, one Igor Braverman outdid all my personal so-called friends; both his daughters aged nine and twelve had studied in my dance class at some point in the Vancouver Ballet School. Their mother, who worked like a Trojan, carried virtually the entire family's load on her shoulders as her husband hardly ever did any work. At her insistence, I foolishly trusted him to sell my videocassettes for a generous commission only because my former pupils were short of material possessions. Once again, I was severely punished for my kind-heartedness. In a colossal error of judgement and naïvety, I trusted him with a copy of my bank card, which he then used to take funds from my BDI bank account over a long period of time. My experience with this underlined my lack of ability in commercial business affairs. I made a decision to return to my academic project on the origin of mime and dance, where I would be mingling with other members of the animal kingdom rather than untrustworthy human beings.

Two months later after finishing at RBS and Doreen Bird College, I started to feel rheumatic pain in my joints along with grinding, a bit like toothache at times. The doctor said it looked like arthritis and prescribed suitable medication. Some time ago I'd heard that carrying extreme physical loads over a long period without a break can cause serious damage to the way your musculoskeletal equipment continues to work. In particular this relates to joints in the extremities, all vertebrae and your hip joints. Not wishing to panic about it, I read up a load of medical advice on how to stay mobile as you age while enhancing your ability to undertake physical tasks. I decided to keep my arthritis to myself for the time being. But with each teaching course I suffered acute pain more frequently, and the worst of it was the sympathetic looks from those around me. This reinforced my choice of lifestyle from that point on. I would eradicate the arthritis, or at least stall its destructive process at any cost. The question was: how? Strong drugs don't help, they just numb the brain. Going swimming at the pool, as recommended, takes up too much time just getting there. The doctors don't know of any therapeutic exercises I can do myself. How can this be?

The answer was straightforward enough. After my August course, I would move to Vancouver for a while, to allow myself time to recover my physical strength.

Nevertheless, I began whizzing around London as a matter of urgency. I let my flat on a long-term basis, and covered my monthly bills. I said goodbye to Penny and landed in Vancouver at the end of August to raise the almost 'saintly' Mikhail from the dead. London didn't miss me at all. Even the dogs carried on placidly pissing on building corners and howling at the moon. Fourteen years in England had just flown by.

From Vancouver I took myself off to Victoria, the capital of British Columbia. I had been awarded a modest pension, just sixty-five dollars a month. For this reason, being a free artist/entrepreneur, I had paid an annual standard pension contribution of just twenty-five dollars a month, among other taxes. You reap what you sow. But I had to live off my two private pensions, which I'd wisely cobbled together over twenty years in Canada and England. In any case, my old age was taken care of. I could happily undertake my academic research programme in the university libraries of British Columbia and lick my spiritual wounds after the Japanese carnage.

I soon found a suitable flat in central Victoria, and went for a medical and general well-being check-up. My doctor said that apart from the arthritis tablets I was already aware of, nothing else would be effective for now. All the remaining homeopathic treatments from Oriental charlatans were a complete waste of time and money. The increasing momentum of my paradoxical situation was seriously dispiriting. On the one hand, the tablets had a detrimental effect on the brain of an author at work, and on the other, sooner or later I would be paralysed by progressive arthritis if I didn't stop its destructive advance. You didn't have to be a doctor to realise this. I was already using crutches to go out, and was going at snail's pace.

In addition to studying general human anatomy at school, any professional teacher or choreographer has to know how to administer first aid to his/her pupils/

dancers in case of accident in class or onstage. For this reason I always carry with me a small medical reference book of physical traumas and musculoskeletal chronic conditions. Just to be on the safe side, I decided to check if this offered any advice or preventative measures for arthritis. Unfortunately, it recommended nothing other than the familiar tablets and swimming. I decided to go to the library. In a special leaflet on arthritis I studied the photos and illustrations where the physiotherapist was treating a group of patients in a swimming pool using underwater leg exercises. Like an electric shock, I was struck by the idea of working out my own physiotherapy system to combat arthritis using specific, tailored exercises for each individual joint of the body and for a combination of movements in connection with each other (wrists, feet, hip joint and so on). I could base all of this on my own personal experience.

"Eureka!" I exclaimed, unable to contain my excitement.

My neighbours in the university reading room turned suddenly towards me and smiled in solidarity.

Apologising, I put my head down and asked the librarian for a detailed diagram of the human skeleton and nervous/muscular system. Having photocopied all the materials, I skipped happily home on my uncontrollable legs. *There is a glimmer of light on the horizon.*

Half a century on from my schooldays, I retrieved my memory of the first complete picture of man's physical anatomy. Next I drew out all his connecting joints and tendons, beginning with the vertebrae in the neck and finishing with the big toe. I tried out on myself the feeling of motion, confirming the old wisdom that the weakest link in the dancing machine's movement is the legs, and the feet in particular. This is hardly surprising in that they have a starring role to perform in the instrumental ensemble that is the human body. That is why they are the first part of the ballerina's arsenal to go. After spending a week analysing my illness and its therapeutic programmes in meticulous detail, I:

a) observed and tested out on myself how comfortable it was to perform a series of exercise movements for my upper and lower limbs, head and vertebrae with my torso;

b) devised for each of these a separate breathing system in line with the tempo and rhythm of movements I was performing, and my body's general position;

c) coordinated and performed a balance of routines using different parts of my upper and lower body at the same time, as well as my head and torso, etc., throughout the programme;

d) established a specific sequence of exercises with commensurate weight distribution;

e) combined, tried and tested or my own original elements of physiotherapy with great care, performing them with increasing strength and speed.

This resulted in forty different exercises lasting roughly twenty minutes in total. There was no musical accompaniment, just my free internal count beating out a work regime.

I had already spent the whole of last year regularly researching courses of arthritis and ways of combating it in London's libraries, and came back to this time and again as the disease took hold.

In just one day, I had checked out the opportunities for Chinese medicine, as recommended in Vancouver. Sorting out my physiotherapy programme for arthritis wasted a whole week in Victoria. Mastering my own programme (without help from any other source), completing my own therapy consistently every morning and comparing the results of my daily hour-long walks (initially with crutches, later without) kept me busy for a month.

But the most pressing problem in adapting my body to this complicated set of somatic physiotherapy exercises was staying focused, not just on the order of exercises or how many times I was repeating them. Rather, it was the specific concentration required to complete them while keeping my breathing at a steady rhythm. Failing to adhere to the regime's latter conditions could result in negative side effects rather than the anticipated benefits.

In the second month of treatment I repeated my morning half-hour therapy session before supper. I moved my hour's walk to the afternoon as my mornings were taken up researching the anthropology of dance in the university library. Three times a day, I found time to prioritise getting my mobility back like this without exerting myself too much.

I finally got rid of the crutches during my afternoon walks by the beginning of the third month of treatment, and started to visit the nearest swimming pool on Saturday mornings, which had a Jacuzzi that I used for hydrotherapy as well. It was crucial for me to get back into my previous shape as a dancer as soon as possible, and at the same time to force my body to banish the arthritis. My family doctor warned me not to overdo it, and to be as patient as I could with my own treatment. I assured him that I would achieve my ambition. Nevertheless, to my amazement, by the end of the fourth month I had decided to bring in reinforcements, and jumped on a boat to Vancouver.

This time, I visited Anna Wyman, my colleague of twenty years, and the director of Modern Dance Theatre – pain-free. I wished her a happy New Year and made her a present of my Kalinka video. She confessed that she had heard about my success in Montreal and London. I asked what was new in the ballet world here over the last few years. Anna cited 'Goh Academy', a private school with a small ballet troupe of semi-professional standing. It was run by a couple, both retired from Beijing Opera. It was the crème de la crème in Vancouver today. Anna gave me their telephone number and I hurried home, musing that this was more than enough for this arthritic's first sortie beyond Victoria.

After seeing in the New Year, I took off to Vancouver again for a whole day, and went to visit Goh Academy. I presented my CV to both directors along with video brochures and posters from Les Ballets Russes de Montréal. They told me they knew more about me than I did about them, and would be happy to welcome me into their fold with the 'Russian Classical School' on 10th January, after the Christmas holidays. I would have a full teaching load of four classes a day: 'Partnering Dance' with the troupe in the mornings and three classes with various students in the dance academy in the afternoons. Also, a competition/festival of dance art for adults and children would be starting in Vancouver after the holidays. The school was in desperate need of a choreographer. I could devise solo or duet miniatures for their students on a private basis at weekends, which would be paid for (cash in hand) by the parents. This would be exclusively for their clients. In addition to this, the management was planning ballet performances from the Russian imperial repertoire and if I could lend a hand, they would be happy to pay me extra for these productions. It all sounded too good to be true, as I hadn't expected much from Goh Academy. I had the feeling they'd known I was coming beforehand. Anna Wyman had probably told them that we'd met up before New Year. One way or another, Fortune was clearly smiling on me.

I rang Vancouver a week before I was due to start work, having got everything together by the skin of my teeth in Victoria.

"Mr Goh, I'm wondering if you know a few places with flats to let near the academy?"

656

"Firstly, Misha, please call me Chiat, not Mr Goh. Secondly, come straight over. You can stay with us until you find somewhere suitable."

"I'm not really comfortable with that, Chiat."

"Sleeping on the ceiling is what you call uncomfortable 'cos the blanket falls off. See you when you get here."

The next day I said goodbye to my beloved Victoria, and moved to Vancouver.

It only took me three or four days to find a good flat nearby. In the meantime, I got stuck in to classes at Goh Academy. This was a well-established organisation, with a load of teenagers ranging from ten to twenty years old. Half of them were from the local Chinese community, half a dozen were Russian immigrants, and the rest were English-speaking Canadians. The mix of nationalities made for quite a potent cocktail. The three levels comprised: beginners, intermediate and advanced, and there was also a semi-professional group of five men and seven women with a solid repertoire of Classical and Contemporary ballet. The Goh spouses worked mainly with the latter, while I taught them two classes a week each: 'Pas de deux' and Character dance. The rest of my lessons were split between the intermediate and advanced students. A photo of me and my CV were displayed on the teachers' noticeboard in the school reception area. Next to this was a numbered sheet listing the names of students wishing to learn dances designed to suit their individual character, for the forthcoming arts-festival competition at the end of March. Candidates had to pay the choreographer forty dollars an hour at weekends for the pertinent production, ten dollars of which was deducted for the ballet studio hire. I found this cold, commercial way of doing things somewhat distasteful, but you get used to anything in time.

What appealed to me most at Goh Academy was the opportunity to restore my creative potential and courage in stage management following the Japanese disaster and, significantly, without shouting about it or having pressure from above. Moreover, I could use it as a test bed for experimental choreography with non-professional performers who were still young. My Character dance classes, as always, were hands-on and productive, and engaged the students well. It's true that my once arthritic legs still made themselves known to me at times, but 'Rome was not built in a day.'

A month later, about thirty students had signed up for my Choreographic Miniatures as part of the competition. In the main, these were children and adolescents from seven to thirteen years of age, and almost exclusively girls. The advanced students were offered various options for the competition by their regular teachers, taken from the classical European ballet repertoire in the original version. But not many of them possessed the necessary natural talent or technique for this, especially where dancing on pointes was concerned. Only three Chinese youths (aged fourteen to fifteen) registered with me out of the advanced students. Without giving it much thought, I decided to set the 'Squabblers' dance to Shostakovich's Polka and Scherzo music. All of them were of stocky build, but strong and light on their feet in acrobatics. For the girls, I organised a solo and duets suitable for their physique, drawing from my choreography tool kit of comprehensive themes and forms: flowers, animals or human characters: capricious child, gossips (duet), figure skater, tennis match, matryoshka (nesting dolls), 'Ganzya', 'Lyana', 'Katyusha', 'Neapolitana' (various choreographed folk songs, the last with tambourine), 'Gypsy Rhapsody', etc.

It took at least three hours for the students to pick up each Miniature. Next, I put my clients into pairs, then groups of four for an hour. This was a considerable financial saving for them and more efficient use of my time working at the weekend. When the parents settled up with me I gave them an audio cassette of the music for their dance so that their daughter could practice with her regular teacher or with other professionals by private arrangement. I explained to the mothers that the quality of performance was the main criterion any competition jury would use in judging.

Using this conveyor-belt system, I managed to deliver and refine all the compositions by the beginning of April. Credit must go to the young dancers and their parents. They were so well organised, that they never allowed me a free minute between sessions even to spend a penny. Our school resembled a dance factory over the three months we spent preparing for the competition. Only the Chinese could set up and manage a production line like this. No one else could match the energy and patience of these fanatics. The festival competition concluded with the British Columbia provincial panel awarding most of the prizes to dancers from Goh Academy. It goes without saying that this was the best form of advertising to attract new students, and it didn't cost the management a cent.

As the academic year drew to an end, the school management organised their traditional students' concert in a concert hall in the city centre. The first half included a demonstration of all the recent prizewinners, and the second, a presentation of new group productions incorporating all genres on the academy curriculum: Classical, Modern, Character and Jazz. Attending the concert was just like being in Beijing.

I said goodbye to everyone quite happily until September, as the last six months of creative agony required me to switch to a completely different type of activity for the summer. With so much going on, I had almost forgotten about my arthritis. They say that 'Like cures like.' Nevertheless, as I left, I was happy to accept a video copy of the *Fairy Doll* ballet as a goodbye gift, from the imperial theatre repertoire (in the pre-revolution era), performed by the Mariinsky Theatre School. Chiat advised me to watch this ballet very attentively with a view to possibly producing it next season with the academy to my own choreography. I thanked him for his faith in me and undertook to give him an answer in a month. The Director was fully aware that if he didn't entice me with some kind of offer before the holidays, I would be trying to find myself a more prestigious position for the autumn.

I spent the whole of July studying anthropology in the university library on a daily basis from dawn till dusk, absorbing new information on the social and everyday life of various animals, starting with insects and finishing with primates. I was particularly impressed with the work and films of the naturalist David Attenborough, concerning the behaviour and mutual relations between the sexes of one species of animal: the way they communicated through moving their limbs and bodies, and the way they seduce potential sexual partners with fascinating body motions in their own unique form of mime and dance. At times I couldn't believe my eyes: birds and snakes spinning around several times in these lyrical duets, insects in dialogue using their antennae and feet, mammals' emotional expression through their heads, ears, tails, etc. Owing to the generalisations in the source materials I'd looked at, it struck me that I could put down my thoughts in the form of a new book about the origin of mime and dance from my own natural primary source. It was perfectly clear to me that before putting pen to paper, I would need to add to my knowledge in many areas, but still, I decided 'It's worth a try'!

After learning the hard way through being inactive in the past, I resumed my half-hour physiotherapy sessions from the very first morning to keep on top of my arthritis. In the evenings, after the library, I would have something to eat near home after doing an hour's walk around a large reservoir in the south of the city. I managed to distribute the weight on my legs in this way over the summer break. Once I got home, I would watch the *Fairy Doll* ballet over and over before bed, imagining my own version on this theme to Bayer's same music with a few additions from the composer's collection of pieces. The libretto for *Fairy Doll* was too similar to the old, well-known ballet *Coppélia*. The only difference between them was that Coppélius made his own dolls in his workshop, where they came to life in his hands. In *Fairy Doll* one of the dolls in the shop possessed the ability to come to life unbeknownst to the other dolls around her. My task as choreographer was not only to devise and produce an interesting ballet for children; I also had to involve as many academy students as possible in this performance, of whom only a small number of advanced youngsters could dance on pointes. This made the St Petersburg company's video version impossible for the students. Otherwise, Mr and Mrs Goh could have lifted this from the video without any help from me.

On numerous occasions in my creative life, I have produced *Dancing Dolls*, my own one-act ballet-concert to Shostakovich's music in a range of theatres and schools in the Soviet Union, Canada, England, Italy, etc. So, by this stage, I had amassed a suitable track record in this genre both with adults and children. There is nothing more demanding than depicting everyday human characters onstage, as in choreographing – and acting out – the doll part (either with or without pointes). It is more about acting skills than any inherent challenges in performance technique. The young, beginner ballerinas had to employ artistic, mechanical movements and expressions to convey the dying doll, whereas they much preferred to dance a living character. This is a tough call even for adult professional dancers. You can imagine how much work, patience and persistence were involved on the part of the children/teenagers in meeting these challenges. I'm certain that ambition and a sense of healthy creative competition worked in my young artistes' favour. Surely herein lies the heart of the all-pervading power of the art displayed by those both onstage and behind the scenes, who are blessed with the talent and intelligence to put this magic to good use in their work.

At the beginning of August 1996 I paid a visit to Mr Goh, and went through the detail of my project to produce the ballet he had put forward. I supplied the Director with a contract, my general production costs and a list of the academy groups involved in different dances, mime and crowd scenes. He agreed to discuss it all with his wife and call me in a couple of days. At our next meeting in the academy, Chiat introduced me to the academy's patron, Irina Rid: a Russian millionairess who was sponsoring this show. A designer by profession, Irina was only too happy to take responsibility for the decorative content of the ballet – costumes and stage design. She played the piano competently, and even offered her services to produce and record the Bayer music I needed for *Fairy Doll* in a professional sound studio. I had a month to complete the main choreography before the start of the school year. After signing the contract with Goh, I soared skywards on my Pegasus and immersed myself in deepest heaven to revel in the pink clouds of creative fantasy. In this short period I needed to:

a) set out clearly in writing (for children) a simple storyline for the ballet libretto;

b) arrange a combination of Bayer's musical plays in harmony, for a two-act show;

c) make a final decision on the main configuration of performers (soloists and groups, in keeping with their level of training, age, height, outer appearance and inner nature).

With the aim of keeping in touch with the young ballerinas' parents, Chiat allocated two hands-on mothers, who supervised round the clock, swapping stints at my rehearsals. I had never encountered such attention to organisational detail in my entire, long career. To be honest, had it not been for this, I would not have been able to deal with all the issues that arose constantly in amateur settings and even more so with a mixed bag of children. It was obviously no coincidence that the Director often got worked up and told his clients off in Chinese. By some amazing miracle we completed the first stage of preparation by the New Year. The selected parents/actors were hugely enthusiastic and I had no real problem in getting all the mass scenes done according to plan (shop, square, etc.). Beyond my wildest dreams, we completed the whole ballet on schedule, including costumes, staging and props. The dress rehearsal was intense, but went without any hitches or nasty surprises. In spite of all my worries, the show came together and surpassed everyone's expectations in its standard.

Our *Fairy Doll* received a warm reception from young Vancouverites. Chiat invited his colleagues from nearby cities to the premiere. They were unanimous in asserting that this staged production for children was of an exceptionally high standard, given the working conditions in the school. My contract with Goh Academy was due to finish at the end of June. I had two more shows to rehearse on my last weekend. Out of the blue I bumped into the Rogers company cameramen in the theatre on Saturday, who were getting ready to film a video (so they explained) of my whole ballet production. Initially I felt like asking Chiat Goh why they hadn't sought my permission for this as the author. But the stop sign of reason halted my heady Taurean hot-headedness. I decided to give them the opportunity to make a quality film and produce a master copy over two performances, and then we would see what was what. As he said goodbye to me, Chiat made a guilty promise to send me a copy of the video in London.

I had more or less almost completely got rid of my arthritis during my two years in Victoria and Vancouver by religiously completing my morning physiotherapy sessions. I got back into creative shape as a teacher/ballet master at Goh Academy, and cemented the content of my academic research project on the origin of mime and dance. There was no change on the personal front though.

Dmitri telephoned from Moscow and told me that he was flying to Montreal on business for a month in July. In fifteen years, his private school in Russia's capital city had flourished, allowing him to amass a considerable sum which he'd decided to invest in Quebec. Last summer during his holidays in Montreal, the great businessman had invested 100,000 Canadian dollars in the construction of a new international airport. He had bought a huge, luxurious flat in the city centre. Now he was flying over to check on his property, and asked me to meet him in Montreal, after having no contact for many years. In any case I had been planning to stop over in Toronto – where my mother was in a nursing home – for a couple of days on my way to London. She was now ninety-three years old. I tried to see her once a year if possible, as I never knew if I would see her the next time I visited North America.

Dmitri greeted me with great ceremony at the airport in his swanky car and whisked me stylishly off to his fashionable home, next to Atwater metro station. My son had plenty to boast about. But I was more interested to hear about his capital investment. It turned out that following last year's investment in a sham project, this firm had gone bankrupt and Dmitri had lost all his money. My Quebec lawyers and old friends had tried to help him, but all their efforts came to nothing. My son sent his car to Moscow and engaged Sergei Kozlovsky (an agent) to sell his plush apartment.

Before his return to Moscow, I persuaded Dmitri to drop in on his grandmother in Toronto. Mum burst into tears on seeing her beloved grandson. She looked very frail. The doctor said she only had a few months left. On the way back to Montreal I shared this news with my son, along with my decision to remain in Montreal for another five months until the New Year.

"I'll stay at your place until the flat is sold, at which time I'll move into a boarding house. I'll give Sergei a hand with prospective buyers of your mansion, and will keep you posted."

Dmitri was physically much stronger than me. At forty-four, he was a very imposing man. As for women, he was a real ladykiller. In his two weeks in Montreal, he brought home a different woman in her thirties every night, introducing them as friends he'd known for fifteen years. This wouldn't have bothered me unduly, had my eldest not tried to indulge his father (as he explained) after losing Kafuyu, whom my son had known. He and I had separate bedrooms and I usually went to bed at 11 p.m., before he got home from the restaurant. Somewhere around midnight the Moscow sex maniac's girlfriends always seemed curiously to lose their way on the way back from the lavatory, and would end up in my room where they slipped deftly under my duvet.

Having learned from pleasurable experience, I didn't shout or kick out, merely made a polite announcement every time in my smooth baritone: "Excuse me, Madam! You are in the wrong place. Your compartment is in the next carriage."

"Oh! Misha darling, why are you making such a song and dance about it? Wouldn't you like some pleasure for yourself?"

"Alas! Unfortunately I'm suffering with arthritis."

"Forgive me, but what does arthritis have to do with sex?"

"It has a direct bearing, Madam. This ailment strikes the extremities first of all." With some such excuse I dispatched the lady to her more deserving partner.

In the morning I would hear the taxi ferrying away my son's latest nymph. He and I never referred to it. It was only when Dmitri was saying goodbye to me at the airport that he remarked, "Dad, I'm sorry about the sexual shenanigans at night. I was curious to hear the ever inventive reasons you gave my women friends for declining their services. It made us laugh all night long."

"I hope that giggling didn't get any of your mistresses pregnant. Have a good flight, son!"

CHAPTER 13 ALL ROADS LEAD TO ROME

It took me a year to find somewhere to call home during my various courses and seminars in Europe after twelve years of professional peaks and troughs in the UK and EU ballet worlds. Having thought long and hard, I plumped for Italy, the place closest to my heart in terms of the poetic life of the soul that it offered. Despite all its sociopolitical problems, this country had dazzled me with her artistic riches from the moment I first emigrated in 1975. From then on, wherever my travels across the world took me, I always had a soft spot for my second homeland. I thanked Fortune for such a generous gift after surviving the Soviet Union during the thirty years following the Second World War.

While working on summer courses in Italy, I devoted all my spare time to hunting for a modest house on the Gulf of Gaeta between Rome and Naples, those cities being my principal areas of work. Fortunately, in 1996, I managed to find a fairy-tale cottage in the old town of Gaeta in the hills overlooking the gulf, thirty metres from the sea. It was roughly fifty metres to the water from the main street, which was about four metres wide. Eighty rickety steps climbed up to my house, between the attached houses either side. It was a fabulously romantic place, but more suited to young inhabitants with marathon-fit legs. The house was arranged on three floors with a large balcony just below the roof; flowerpots adorned a paved terrace by the front door. On the boundary of my property was an antique metal gate spanning the metre-wide stone corridor, which snaked its way down to the gulf. My balcony looked out on to a beautiful vista of fishing vessels and passing cruise ships.

My creative contacts with many ballet companies and schools in Italy's various provinces had become regular over the previous twenty years, both in the state and private sectors of education and entertainment. In terms of practice and substance, my entire professional teaching portfolio (Character, Historical, and Classical dance) originated and developed here. It took some time before these choreographic genres, which evolved artistically in the French court of Louis XIV, were successfully adopted through European culture and later spread throughout the civilised world. That's why I'd dreamed of living and working in this country for fifty years, as I felt in tune with the place spiritually and professionally. If the Italians couldn't understand and appreciate my creativity, then who could?

When Giuliana Penzi retired as director of the National Academy of Dance in Rome, she was succeeded in the post by Margarita Parilla, a leading soloist from the Rome Opera Ballet. I had known her well since 1975 when Zharko Prebil, my friend and colleague from MTA in Moscow, introduced the young ballerina and her partner Salvatore Pozzo to the theatre's ballet repertoire. At that time, Jarko was chief ballet master at the Rome Opera Ballet and artistic director of the National Academy of Dance. Margarita quickly blossomed in her new role as director, and tried her hardest to expand the curriculum of Italy's most prestigious ballet school. Once a week I taught Character all day to intermediate students here, and went through basic 'Pas de deux' technique with those about to graduate. As always, by the end of the season, I had prepared my own version of Character dance excerpts from the opera/ballet repertoire, or unique productions to symphony music by popular classical composers from a range of periods.

Elisabetta Terabust was artistic director of the Rome Opera Theatre Ballet School at that time. She knew me from the academy, where she had watched many of my classes and production rehearsals. The children in her school were mainly of secondary-school age. Paola Yorio, the school director, offered me groups of thirteen-to-fifteen-year-olds for a Character dance course with the European repertoire. They were more interested in meticulous technique in Character dance performance based on Classical dance, than choreography for a specific programme. Because of this, I was very happy to put on études in the centre with them using various accessories: tambourines or shawls for the girls and mandolins or sabres for the boys. The patriotic spirit and competitive nature inherent in the Italian character enabled me to incorporate a series of acrobatic devices in individual versions and complex spatial patterns in groups of boys and girls.

Balleto di Roma was a professional troupe dancing in Contemporary Classical ballet style. Volter Zappollini, the Director and founder, invited me to teach universal Partnering technique for *passo due* in freestyle human motion to his pre-professional group and his main ensemble corps. This was my favourite genre, the one I'd used previously in my earlier ballet miniatures in the Soviet Union in the 1950s. So I wholeheartedly embraced both groups: sharing my wealth of experience in this field of choreography with both novice and experienced students according to their physical level. I demonstrated and trained them in unconventional methods of Partnering technique and body contact in contemporary duets, using music by contemporary neoclassicists. I used examples from my own repertoire and also occasionally improvised sequences of elements from classical 'Pas de deux' with a light and experienced ballerina, supported by a mature partner. Twice a month, at the end of each course, students from the next workshop and I would perform a demonstration of our latest achievements to the Director, which Zappollini recorded on video and used to great effect in his future productions. As did I.

I had started to run Character dance courses in the Alla Scala Ballet School a long time before coming to live in Italy. A few students from my Milan courses came to my intensive UK Summer Dance courses. Anna-Maria Prina, school director, was a highly qualified Classical dance teacher of the Cecchetti method. In addition, she had attended a year-long course at the Bolshoi Teaching Faculty and used to dance onstage with my former student, Alexander Khmelnitsky as her partner, who had been the first in the establishment to perform Choreographic Miniatures. Anna-Maria was acquainted with many Soviet ballet artistes.

It's quite normal for dancers to do a bit of mud-slinging – especially those who have been successful overseas or kept their marriage together. The theatre world is well-known for being bohemian. And I did not escape vicious gossip just because I'd emigrated. But I never paid any attention to this and continued to work like a dog and study like a schoolboy. Nevertheless, Anna-Maria Prina was suspicious of me right from the start and asked lots of questions about my past life. During this period, Italy was a pro-communist country and the Director's cautious approach came as no surprise to me. She was satisfied with my work and continued to use me as a specialist. One day the theatre secretary forwarded me a request to call on the ballet director. I had received an invitation to take part in running auditions to find replacement dancers for those leaving or retiring after over twenty years on the stage. Character dance solo or duet, which I'd prepared with my candidates, was included in the audition programme. On completion of the work, the Alla Scala management handed me written thanks and a substantial fee, which my modest nature could not refuse.

The work I felt most spiritually and professionally at home with in Italy was the Lyceum Danza de Mara Fusco and her small Balletto di Napoli troupe. Mara had first seen my Character dance class at the National Academy of Dance in Rome in 1985, and invited me to run a course in Naples. From that day until I retired more than twenty years later, the school and Fusco's home were my natural learning centre, creative lab and inclusive shelter. Mara had trained as a teacher at the Mariinsky Ballet's Vaganova school in St Petersburg. She had attained an excellent qualification as a top-rank teacher in Natalya Dudinskaya's class. On her return to Naples, Fusco had taken over her mother's family business and using her school as a base, created the best private studio in Italy in the style of the Mariinsky School. It had always amazed me how this petite ballerina could single-handedly manage eight consecutive groups of students in two sections (children and adults), the hundreds of parents, troupe dancers, all the staff: teachers, pianists and administrative personnel. I was in awe of this professional working woman who was mother to a stubborn daughter, Giovanna, while successfully running a large house. Mara also played an active part in the social side of ballet associations, and published a book about Classical dance technique.

The people who ran Teatro Nuovo Torino held annual European ballet courses at their theatre as well as national auditions for a range of dance genres. In the summer of 1985, at the request of Jan Mesturino, theatre director, I brought my young male students over from England (Doreen Bird College and Central

Ballet School) for a course in Turin. The deal was that my guests just paid for their travel and food. The rest – courses, accommodation, trips – were provided free of charge for the lads. The point was that the local men were very sceptical about ballet. Having a dancer for a son was a matter of shame for a father then. Nevertheless, girls need partners for duets, and these boys being here resulted in double the amount of girls registering; even if they weren't dancing duets with the male partners, they still flirted with them in the meantime. That is nature's way! I usually brought over fifteen to twenty guys who were already reasonably experienced in both Character dance and Partnering. Of course they also had a strong foundation in Classical dance for the other subjects. So the two-week course covered all parts of this project equally satisfactorily.

The Italian ballet auditions for young talent under the UNESCO banner was another international event of note in Turin. Jan Mesturino organised this as well. He invited me on to the jury for three days. Ballet academies and schools from around Italy sent their top students to this public exam in national culture. Imagine the local participants' surprise on seeing Cuban Ballet School competitors from Havana in the mix. Teachers from the Bolshoi had worked there for many years at this time and, naturally, thanks to their Russian experience, were successfully turning out strong performers in the Vaganova classical style. Everyone assumed that they were not actually auditioning, but just showing off how good they were to encourage local candidates to try and beat them. The panel were perplexed, and expected Mesturino to offer some sort of explanation regarding competition rules, but sadly, these were not forthcoming. They were obviously making a specific political point, which was lost on me; I'd got out of the habit during the previous twenty-five years and did not want to be party to it in any way. For this reason, I decided to give Mesturino a good reason not to invite me to any more fake auditions in future. Without offering any justification, I upped the scores for all the Italians and marked the Cubans down. In response to my fellow jury members' astonished faces, I simply smiled sympathetically and shrugged. After this incident, Jan stopped inviting me to his audition panels, and I hung on to more friends in Italian ballet.

Dmitri flew over to Italy for a holiday with his new girlfriend and Richard in the summer of 1997, while I was running one of my courses in Rome. I was really struck by how good-looking my fourteen-year-old grandson was, and how ill-mannered into the bargain. Clearly, his father was much too busy with his big business in Moscow, not to mention his women. I made no criticism of Dmitri, as I figured that 'A leopard can't change his spots.'

Still, on the subject of Ricky, I remarked to my son over supper in a restaurant with his girlfriend in tow: "The lad has intelligent eyes, a remarkable physique and is completely ignorant as far as education goes. You are obviously spoiling him materially, trying to compensate for not being around for the guy when he desperately needs a father, who is making exactly the same mistake that I made with you. 'History is repeating itself like a spiral staircase,' as the Great Leader of the revolution declared.

"By the way, I've decided to move to Italy and am looking for a house by the sea. I've got a proposal for you: let me bring up my grandson for a few years and by the time I return him to you, you won't recognise him. This'll free you up to manage your business and all your other interests. You can pay for your son's keep, but my work in raising him is free of charge. You've got twenty-four hours to give me your decision!"

Everyone around overheard my quick-fire tirade and looked on in shock.

"Dad, you can't be serious . . .? You have to know the language to be able to attend school in another country."

"There are English schools for children of army personnel on American bases here. I've made some enquiries. It'll be very straightforward for Ricky with a Canadian passport. The only thing stopping him is you."

Dmitri and his girlfriend exchanged glances.

The woman just smiled sarcastically, then remarked, "Darling, your father doesn't realise what he's taking on. But this is a fantastic opportunity for Ricky."

"Daddy, thanks for thinking of us all. We'll talk about this and let you know tomorrow."

"Granddad, have I got this right – you want me to come and live with you in Italy for a while?"

"That's right, yes. But your father will go through it all with you in more detail after supper. Don't worry."

"Granddad, I beg you, please take me away from there. Dad is very preoccupied with his business and doesn't have time for me."

"Ricky, you're a bright lad so you must understand that your dad's the only one who can decide what's best for you."

On a visit to Anna Davidovna's, where I usually stayed during my trips to Rome, I told my old and faithful friend of Dmitri's success in Moscow, and our plans for Richard.

"Do you really need to do this, Misha? What with all your creative commitments in Italian theatres and schools. And the fact that you have no personal life of your own. Why don't you let your son deal with him?"

"Annushka, I expect you're right. I want to make up for neglecting my sons in the past, by helping to raise my grandson in the present. Although I'd like to have had more input earlier on. In a few years' time it'll be too late to reshape him."

"You never give up, do you, Maestro! I hope to God it works out for you both, though I very much doubt it!"

"You're probably right about that too, my darling Anyuta. But still, I have to try and clear my conscience as a parent; otherwise it'll eat me up as long as I live."

The next day Dmitri confirmed his intention to leave Richard with me until he finished secondary school – three years at the most – on the understanding that he could go back to Moscow at any time if either party broke the terms of the agreement.

My grandson was on cloud nine. He and I promptly set off for Gaeta to buy furniture for the house and to register him at the American school on the local military base on a mountain plateau, half a kilometre from our home. The house urgently needed kitting out before the beginning of the academic year. My grandson and I charged around the shops and markets like bulls in a china shop. Passers-by on the streets moved aside to let us through, yelling expletives after us. Nevertheless, we got the house set up in the space of two weeks, registered at the police station and even got the television and telephone installed. Ricky was on great form, and willingly helped me with everything. His face glowed from the sense of equality with me and freedom of movement, and the satisfaction of his own hard work and optimistic future.

When we met the school director, Ricky impressed everyone there with his youthful, inquisitive spirit, and immediately signed up for the 'sports and leisure' section he'd selected. He started his long school day from 8.30 a.m. to 5.30 p.m. in the second week of September, with lunch included in the cost. At weekends, he came with me on my regular dance courses in ballet schools throughout the Rome and Naples areas. Sometimes he sat in on my classes. He would often chat up his female peers in the waiting room, or amuse himself in the Internet café. In the school holidays, we would travel to my week-long courses and seminars in far-flung parts of Northern or Southern Italy. He would bring along his laptop, on which he never tired of dressing and undressing beautiful women of all shapes and sizes. I had nothing against his healthy interest in sex, figuring that this was better than taking drugs.

Occasionally there were downsides to life with Richard too: when he was engrossed in his computer and wouldn't pop out for bread or milk, pizza or juice. I didn't give him a hard time. I simply didn't make his favourite spaghetti bolognese that night. When he asked, "Granddad, what time is supper?" I replied, "We are fasting today in honour of all the lazybones and stay-in-beds, so we won't be having supper because of them. Bite your nails and chew your fists. That's how it is, mate!" The hungry young man would grab some change and with a hop, skip and jump, leg it down to the nearest pizzeria. Five minutes later he would return with steaming pepperoni and Coca Cola or lemonade. I used the same parenting technique when my dear grandson refused to clean his teeth after a meal, take a shower before bed, change his socks and pants every day, polish his shoes, cut his nails, and so on. Ricky got the hump with me at first. But gradually he got into the habit of doing all of the above on his own initiative and boasted to everyone that he had got used to this.

One of the teaching establishments and directors that was closest to my heart was Scuola Danza Classica e Moderna, run by Patty Scisa in Sorrento. It specialised in Character and Historical dance. After retiring as a dancer, this flame-haired beauty opened a small but fantastically well-organised ballet school for children and adult dance enthusiasts, with support from the local authorities. She taught there herself and was not lacking in funds to attract qualified teachers from elsewhere. Taking an interest in choreographic productions of diverse genres, she played an active part in the concert scene in the Naples area, seeking to improve the aesthetic knowledge of the local population by providing accompanying explanations. She also managed to give birth to and bring up two daughters to take on the family business. Once a year Patty ran a summer course on Modern/Jazz dance and my two dance genres. She organised a wonderful art exhibition featuring the famous North American painter from Riga: Semyon Shegelman, my friend and colleague from our emigration to Canada in 1975, with her friend and partner, Valery (a member of the town council), in the historic Sorrento district. We often saw how exceptionally learned Patty Scisa was, and what exquisite taste she had in all aspects of stage and fine art. It was a joy to work with her and be in her orbit during our courses in Sorrento.

In addition to its regular courses, Teatro Balletto Marinella Santini at Grosseto, stood out from other Italian ballet schools thanks to an extremely busy concert schedule in the north of the country and across the border. As Marinella was completing her intensive courses in Historical and Character dance during my first visit, she proposed that I put on completely separate concert programmes for both genres, of an hour's duration each with handmade costumes and footwear. What self-respecting choreographer could turn down such good fortune? Besides, this was a real opportunity to broaden my video repertoire in terms of pictorial material for my teaching seminars for group leaders who had limited resources for stage work. Each programme comprised fourteen to sixteen compositions in the first half: stage adaptations of *danze storiche* or *danze carattere*. The dancers took to their home stages with great enthusiasm, and travelled abroad with my programme fairly frequently: to Spain, France, Germany, and elsewhere. They presented the Historical dance repertoire in the first half and Character dance in the second. The audience was always interested to see the stage interpretation of these little-known choreographic genres. I was so overwhelmed by the community's positive regard for my work that I decided to give them my entire private collection of dance costumes and shoes (more than 100 sets) from different nationalities and eras, which I'd accumulated in Montreal for my Kalinka ensemble and Les Ballets Russes de Montréal. The managers and dancers at Teatro Balletto Marinella Santini remained the most expressive advocates of my choreographic ideas in performance genres for many years of my creative career.

The base for the European course in Northern Italy was the extraordinary 'Vacanza con la Danza', run by Doriana Comar in Trieste. For four weeks in the height of summer, local dancers and overseas guests perfected their skills in the choreographic genres available, and took an active part in various entertainment programmes. The private-school directors frequently brought their own students to these intensive courses and got to practise themselves alongside them at seminars for teachers/choreographers on teaching methods for dance and composition production. I was busy every day from dawn till dusk and would get back to my tiny room somewhere around midnight, dead on my feet. One day, having only just collapsed into bed, I heard a cautious knock at the door. I thought something had happened at home and leaped out into the corridor, half naked in my pyjamas, almost knocking a young woman in a nightdress off her feet. I apologised, but she pushed me inside and slammed the door behind her. As I was edging around her to turn on the light, she got hold of my arm:

"Excuse me, Maestro, I'm a student on your teaching seminar. I want to get to know you better."

I thought: *Excellent, Misha! A tipsy nymph is just what you need right now. I wish she would let go of my arm.*

"Please don't turn on the light. We can see our way by moonlight. I can see that my unseemly invasion has disturbed you. But if we start to get closer gradually, our seminar will culminate in me being able to show you how much I adore you."

While she was gabbling on without pausing for breath, I was trying to divine her real reason for being here. *A madwoman in a drunken state tries to entice me to have sex with her and disgrace me in public.*

"Maestro, I'm in awe of your talent as a teacher/choreographer and noble . . ."

I had a job to stop her verbal diarrhoea, pressing my palm over her lips.

"What's your name?"

"Stefania."

"Where are you from?"

"Rome."

"Who sent you to see me?"

"No one."

"You reek of wine, my dear. You've probably got a bet with someone that you can crack your Maestro just like that. Go back to your room and take a cold shower!"

Gently but firmly, I directed the disheartened maiden into the corridor and locked the door behind her. I was all too familiar with these kinds of pranks and they simply didn't faze me any more.

I met the ballet teacher Ricardo Nunez for the first time at this course. The famous Alicia Alonso and her male entourage from Havana were on tour in Paris, when part of her troupe hid in the French capital before returning to Cuba. Ricardo was one of them. From that day forward, he enjoyed a successful career, first dancing and then working as a teacher/répétiteur in various opera and ballet theatres around Europe, and occasionally he would teach ballet at international courses. Here in Trieste, he and I became friends and in the years that followed to the present day, we have maintained warm relations as colleagues and 'friends through misfortune' by being immigrants. We spent long evenings swapping stories about the way the Cuban and Soviet authorities had perverted aesthetic ideology in art, and the sacrifices made in the name of the theoretical communist regimes. At the end of the Vacanza con la Danza course I found out by chance that the management had no plans to pay the teachers, due to a lack of funds. Anything can happen in Italy. Naturally I was disappointed, but decided not to mount a third Russian revolution about it. I just shared this with Ricardo. Instead of replying, he headed off to senior management to clarify what he'd heard. I have no idea what went on between them there. It would appear that the uncouth Italian shyster unexpectedly rubbed the Hispanic Cuban Character up the wrong way. Consequently, all the teachers were invited into the accounts office after supper and given their fee as per the contract. It pays to 'play people at their own game'.

In the winter holidays, the provincial ballet school Centro Arti del Movimento ran 'Stage Danza Carattere e Passo Due' with great ceremony under the leadership of Alessandra Matarrelli, a former student of mine. Naples Town Council made substantial funds available for this project, as well as half a pitch and available time in an enormous sports centre. On top of this, they provided organisational support to secure the most productive results from the young people's creative learning institution. I ran this course over two weeks for the men's ballet corps from the San Carlo Opera Theatre, Naples. Their work in partnering girls from the advanced group and individual professionals was paid for by the council, who wanted to avoid any accidents in class during overhead lifts. As always, I put on a public display at the end of the course to showcase the learning in both genres from the course on Sunday. Local councillors obviously made the most of the opportunity to celebrate the course's success with a sumptuous banquet, and exploited their political capital in the next day's press to ensure a win at the next elections. Alexandra and I also used a similar strategy to promote ourselves, and with this, the Matarrelli enterprise grew every year, and strengthened its links with the opera theatre.

I also had the idea to organise a joint course with the Scuola di Ballo Eliana Lo Bue in Sicily with the male ballet corps from the Massimo Opera Theatre in Palermo, led by Jack Bertran. The inclusion of Contemporary (rather than Classical) Partner dance constituted a marked difference from the other course in Trieste. The style and technique of this genre in Partnering is divided into three categories of stage expression, which differ from each other both in content and form:

a) contemporary ballet to classical music, interpreted using free body motion;

b) contemporary Character choreography, to light operetta music, with elements of ballroom dance;

c) street dance to jazz music, with a host of acrobatic moves and flamboyant displays.

Over the years I had gradually developed a syllabus for unique sequences in free improvisations involving lifts (excluding classical canons). My ambition was to release a series of videos at some point.

One day after finishing the next course at Eliana Lo Bue's in Palermo, Jack and I agreed to follow other people's example and organise a course the following year for advanced students, who had already been through the general Partnering class with the male ballet dancers from the Massimo Opera Theatre. We said our goodbyes and went our separate ways. Crossing the square around the theatre, I was deep in thought, and didn't notice the little cars suddenly dart out from nowhere. With a screech, they followed each other around the square garden to form a circle and engaged in a continuous exchange of gunfire. I froze, watching panic-stricken pedestrians who just happened to be passing, prostrating themselves on the ground, shielding their heads with their hands. A young woman standing near to me shouted something to me hysterically. When I didn't react, she slithered up like a snake and pulled me down by my bag with such force that I fell on her, apologising as I did so. All this happened in about ten seconds. The cars, done with their shoot-out, turned 180 degrees and took off again. My saviour yelled something after them, waving her fists.

In shock, I picked myself up, dusted myself down, and repeated like a madman: *"Grazie, Signora, molto grazie!"*

"Prego, niente!" she replied, wringing her hands.

I never returned to Sicily. The damage was done.

The payment delay in Trieste and the street shooting in Palermo made me exercise greater caution in drawing up contracts and travelling around Italian cities. 'Once bitten, twice shy.' Still, I couldn't avoid personal problems in some private schools, even those which were meticulously organised with flawless credentials.

At Liliana Merlo's school in Teramo, I stayed at her flat for the duration of the course, on another floor in the same building where classes were taking place. On the second day at work there, my bag containing all my personal documents: two passports (UK and Canadian), credit cards, etc., was stolen from my room.

The first two weeks at Lia Madrigala's ballet school in Pescara went really well. I was fêted by the parents and my colleagues at the end of the course. As the traditional student display came to an end, the Director announced that she couldn't pay my agreed fee or travel expenses because her husband, the provincial prosecutor, was away on business and wouldn't be back for a week.

"We have your address, Maestro. We'll send you a cheque as soon as he gets back."

I listened to her without blinking, and just smiled sweetly as if I'd been expecting this from them. "Don't worry, Signora, I'll wait here until your husband returns to settle up with me."

An hour later some men came to the house and handed me a load of cash instead of a cheque. I left a receipt on the desk and went down to leave. Lia didn't even come out to say goodbye.

The directors from both the Teramo and Pescara schools were absolute professionals. They were intelligent women, neither of them ever had any issue with my work or conduct. On the contrary: they always told me how satisfied they were with the course outcomes and were already negotiating terms for next time: the programme, repertoire, costs, etc. What possible reasons could they have to stoop so low as to treat me so badly in Teramo and refuse to pay for my work in Pescara?

However, the establishments I'd worked in continued to engage me, and

I was still being invited to new places. I had to postpone my acceptance to the latter to the end of my second season in Italy, pending clarification of my position.

During my seminars and courses in Europe, teachers and school directors often asked me if I could design a course on Methodology in Choreographic Composition. On my return to Italy, I learned that Giuliana Penzi had retired from the National Academy of Dance, and went to visit her at home. Over tea, I asked if she was willing to be the *madrina di onore* (patron) of the regular course for ballet teachers on methods of dance composition in diverse genres. Giuliana agreed in principal, on condition that the project was properly organised and consisted of students from professional backgrounds. To further this plan, she recommended that I enlisted the help of CADC-AICS di Grazia Casu in Rome, the secretary of the Association of Italian Dance Teachers. I was well acquainted with Grazia, as I had occasionally presented my Character and even more occasionally, my Historical genre (*di corte*) at her seminars. She liked the idea of a seminar that would run consistently throughout the year on the first Sunday of every month. Grazia Casu's husband, Jan Carlo (an accountant by profession) looked after the finances in their private school as well as the association. Both dance enterprises looked extremely well organised to me, and I had no reason to doubt their commercial diligence. In view of this, I gladly signed a contract with them for a new two-year project, on condition that I would present my programme for the proposed teachers' seminar for approval by the association's board over the next week, and before the end of the month.

My unpublished dissertation on the Methodology of Choreographic Composition and production enabled me to quickly transfer its fundamental points into the format needed for the current situation.

1. Concept: idea, theme, subject; style, genre, form; make-up of performers, their age and standard, etc.
2. Music: the process of composing or compiling the programme, with key and time signatures, dynamics, analysis, instruments, etc.
3. Dance movements, poses, mime: spatial patterns in available time and setting.

I had to impart these and many other theoretical considerations to the students and teachers in the first year of intensive classes on the following lines: on the first Sunday I presented a new theme with a demonstration (on the board) and then outlined the content in person. I delivered my entire two-year programme using this two-pronged principle of exposition and interpretation on the composition course. Professor Giuliana Penzi, *madrina di onore*, approved it and in August 1998, we began to put this project into practice in Grazia Casu's school. She even took me to Sardinia to meet local dance teachers to encourage them to attend our seminar. Grazia had established a branch of her Rome school in Sássari, where I worked from time to time.

Both sides were exceptionally enthusiastic and engaged throughout the whole of the first year of teachers' seminars. Following the students' successful assessment and presentation of their creative projects to the association's main board, chaired by Giuliana Penzi, I got wind of some worrying rumours among the delegates and visitors. I was perturbed by this, of course, but pretended that it was nothing to do with me. A banquet had been arranged for the following Sunday to celebrate completing the first composition course. I decided to try and resolve any issues before then, as by then I already had first-hand experience of the supposed 'strength' of Italian work contracts.

Eventually the truth will out. Backing our administrator Jan Carlo into a corner, I found out about a unilateral change of financial management regarding the agreement with me and the seminar delegates. In the absence of the obligatory 'insurance', the teachers/delegates were having to pay 25% more for the course to continue from the start of the academic year, and 20% of my fee would be deducted as well for my own so-called 'insurance'. This was a completely unprecedented action, but I was powerless to fight it in any way. At the banquet, I congratulated my colleagues on successfully completing the composition course as if everything was as it should be. On behalf of everyone, I thanked Professor Penzi for her magnanimous contribution to Italy's dance culture. Giving my apologies, I advised that I would have to postpone the composition methodology programme for a year due to health reasons, and expressed my deepest regret in this regard. The seminar delegates were understandably disappointed to hear this, and wished me a speedy recovery. To my great astonishment, everyone present (completely spontaneously) played out a classical melodrama using the whole gamut of Shakespearean devices most professionally.

I had serious doubts about staying on in my second homeland after the Palermo car shoot-out and the underhand dealings with my professional fee to make it look like 20% 'insurance'. On top of this, Dmitri telephoned from Moscow asking me to return Ricky to him forthwith so that he could continue his education at home with his father. The latter event prompted my decision to sell my wonderful house in Gaeta and move to Canada. There I hoped to cure my arthritis once and for all, write my academic work on the origin of dance and be closer to my mother, whose health was seriously deteriorating according to reports from my cousin in St Petersburg. I would be able to avail myself of my Canadian pension and social benefits. Continuing to work full-time was becoming untenable too. But I should still be able to run occasional seminars and courses in North America with an assistant (one of my former students).

While Ricky was coming to the end of his academic year, I drew up the documents for the sale of the house with the nearest estate agent. In 1999 Italy began to make the transition from lira to euro, which slowed down house sales and purchases along with everything else. Ricky really didn't want to leave Italy. I was in no hurry as I had courses and seminars all over Italy for the whole of the summer, which had been organised way before I'd decided to leave. My grandson graduated from the American base school with flying colours. But we had serious problems with the Soviet visa in his Canadian passport, despite his father's application to the Italian Embassy in Moscow. There was no alternative: Ricky would have to fly to Canada with me. Dmitri could retrieve his son there the next time he visited Montreal in a couple of months' time. My grandson travelled with me to all my work engagements that summer, revelling in the opportunity to meet real girls instead of computer imitations, and gradually catching the dance bug.

A buyer for my fairy-tale house in Gaeta came forward in early September. As soon as we'd signed the contract I booked two flight tickets to Montreal for 13th November. I let my friend Kozlovsky know that we would be coming, and asked him to find a one-room flat in the city centre as a permanent bachelor pad.

Sergei promised to meet us at the airport, and as usual, said that Richard and I could stay at his home on a temporary basis. Once I'd confirmed that monies from the property sale had gone into my account, I wired the whole amount to my New York City Bank account. While I was waiting for my intercontinental transaction to go through, I was distracted by a dramatic clip from some blockbuster film on the television in the corner of the banking hall. One after another, all of us there were shocked to see planes attacking both twin towers of the World Trade Centre in New York right in front of our eyes.

I asked a security guard next to me: "What's the name of this film?"

"That's no film, this is something really happening in the news."

I was outside in a flash and ringing our friend Nina Keen in New York on my mobile. She gave me a quick update on this act of terrorism and said that all American airspace had been closed. I took this as a sign that the Third World War had started. Rushing back into the bank in a panic, I asked them to stop the transfer of money to the USA.

The response was: "We can't do that. The money has already been received there and transferred to your business account."

I was given a printout confirming the transfer and sat down on a bench outside, churning.

I telephoned Davidovna in Rome straight away and asked if I could come and see her tomorrow to talk things through. She and her Italian husband would probably know more about what had happened and could explain better in Russian what the impact on world affairs was likely to be.

Anything could happen on the flight there in this climate, and you are responsible for your grandson.

Anna and George explained the massive repercussions of this terrorist act as clearly as possible, which reassured me sufficiently to get moving and prepare for our departure. After saying goodbye to our friends, my grandson and I bravely made our way to Fiumicino Airport, where we endured the shocking, torturous process of passenger checks and landed in Montreal, relieved. Here we went through further extreme security checks and eventually met up with Sergei Kozlovsky. I had a tad too much to drink that evening to celebrate our safe arrival.

STAGE VI: SACRIFICES FOR ART

CHAPTER 14 THROUGH THREE GENERATIONS

My first task once we arrived in Quebec the following day, was to find us somewhere to live. It had to be somewhere near medical institutions in view of my worsening arthritis and other aches and pains. From Sergei's list of available rental properties, I chose a two-room flat with a large kitchen and all mod cons on the third and last floor, near Queen Mary Hospital, next to the metro station in the medical district of Montreal. Best not to think about it. Peaceful and leafy, Rue Lavoie was close to the park, sports and leisure centre and other facilities. It was a mere ten-minute metro ride to the Old Town and the new library, and suited me down to the ground. I retained this flat as my Canadian base while I was travelling around the world until 2010, when the state of my health put an end to my frequent long-haul flights between Europe and America. This was a popular stop-off point for my colleagues, friends, family and former students.

On this occasion too, Ricky helped me to get set up in the new flat, and was happy to get to know his birthplace, having left it at the age of two. On our second day there, I took him to the Ballet Divertimento studio, where my old colleague Brydon Paige was still in post as artistic director. I asked him to assess my grandson's ability in Modern/Jazz dance genres.

The ballet master was only too happy to declare: "This young man has an excellent physique and a great ear for rhythm and music. But eighteen is the upper age limit to start professional dance classes. As an exception we can enrol him in our preparatory youth group once the course has started, on the understanding that Richard quickly joins the beginners. We will need a medical certificate and photograph. You can purchase the uniform he needs in our school shop. Please sort out the application forms and payment with Suzanne Alexander, our director. We look forward to seeing him tomorrow."

I duly completed the paperwork in the administrative office and paid for a month on a trial basis, then kitted the lad out with clothing and footwear. He was flabbergasted at his quick-fire introduction to the art of dance. The Director showed us the studios and similar spaces in the relatively new building. The impatient Ricky fired endless, tricky questions at me, but I urged him to be quiet after each one, whispering that I would explain everything once we were outside. Losing his temper, he tugged at my sleeve, wanting to understand what was going on and what my thoughts were.

So I repeated, "Smile, you idiot! You could at least look happy that your dream has come true! That's the truth of it." I made a face.

My grandson sniggered at this, but from then on, he put his hand over his mouth every time he felt like laughing. It was only then, when we got outside that Ricky's nervous laughter about his new-found status as a ballet student was given free rein.

I waited for him to calm down and over lunch in a health-food cafeteria, explained in detail: "My dear grandson, you must understand that recruiting new students and forming groups usually takes place at the end of October. We are at least two weeks late. It's not clear when your dad will get here due to the terrorist act in New York. I don't want you hanging around here while you wait for him to take you back to Moscow. It makes sense for you to try your luck at Jazz/Modern dance first on a month's trial period. This will give you time to consider whether you want to look for another option or profession. If you wish, you could try to get into the Dawson College Theatre Faculty in the summer. By the way, you'd be able to combine your classes with a dance course at Ballet Divertimento there. If you refuse to study anywhere, I'll put you straight on a plane and send you back to Daddy in Moscow. It's your future so you need to make up your mind."

Fortunately, Ricky loved the course and his teachers were pleased with him.

The next item on my list after sorting out my grandson and our accommodation was to visit Mum in hospital and give her some support before she passed on. By first light the following day, I was already en route for Toronto. While my mother was having a rest in the afternoon, I asked to meet the administrator. Realising how concerned I was, the duty sister suggested I'd be better off speaking to Janine, the permanent social worker in their department, and pointed out her office door in the hall.

The grey-haired lady asked: "What's brought you to see me, sir?"

"I'm Anna Pelts' son – she's in Ward 3."

"I've met her son Roma."

"Oh, he's my younger brother. I've flown over from England to see how my mother is, and just want her to be as comfortable as possible in her last few months."

"What did you have in mind?"

"I'd like to move her into a separate ward for the critically ill and pay for her to have her own telephone."

"Technically, your brother should be dealing with this, as her official carer."

"Roma is really tied up with his chess. He doesn't have time for his dying mother, though he's quite happy to spend her pension. My brother doesn't even consider that she needs her own telephone to keep in touch with her other sons who live in Europe. That's why I've come. Don't you take note of these issues in your duty of care for patients at the end of their lives? I'm sorry, have I come to the wrong place?"

"OK, fine. Leave me your instructions in writing, with your contact details, and I'll need a cheque to pay for the telephone installation and any calls your mother makes. I'll try to do whatever I can for Annushka. But it'll take at least a week to sort this out. Please be patient!"

Mum was thrilled to be able to keep in touch with her loved ones, and thanked me.

Once I'd sorted out the hospital matter, I got down to work on my book. I spent days on end in the new public library, built recently by the Americans in the centre of Montreal, and the last word in architecture and technology. Whatever I couldn't find in the archives, the librarians would order for me from Toronto, Ottawa and even New York's Library of Stage Arts. Over the previous three months I had made considerable progress in contributing to the little I knew about: the biophysical nature of animals' morphology, the nervous and physiological reactions of primates according to Darwin's theory on 'expression of emotions' and the original sociocultural survival instincts of primitive people. At my ripe old age, it was no mean feat to sit at a desk again and chip away at the coalface of research, though, I found it very spiritually satisfying to educate myself about connections and occurrences in natural phenomena, and Darwin's theories on the evolutionary laws of the animal kingdom. My private collection of books looked like a miniature version of New York Library.

A week after I'd been to visit my mother, Janine (the social worker) rang from Toronto to tell me that they had moved Annushka into her own room on the ward for the seriously ill, and that she now had her own telephone line. She dictated the number to me and I promised to come and settle my account at the end of September.

I then telephoned the hospital to check and heard Bagheera's rasping voice: "Mishenka, when are you coming?"

"I'm going to come every week, Mummy."

"I've got Rivka coming to look after me every day now – she's a carer from Social Services. She takes me to the park in a wheelchair and treats me like a child."

My heart turned over, but I reminded her breezily that her birthday was coming up on 6th November, and promised to take her for lunch with Rivka that day in the hospital visitors' cafeteria.

"Let's wait and see, Mishutka. I'm looking forward to seeing you. Give my love to Dima!"

This is what Mum used to call Dmitri when he was five. She thought that he was still living with me. She was confusing time, events and places, now. At least I'd given her the means to keep in touch with everyone. Every single morning she would get a call from me after breakfast in the hospital so that she wouldn't feel alone. I updated her with news of friends and family, and didn't divulge her telephone number to anyone except Dmitri, not even to Yosif, my elder brother in Germany. I didn't want anyone to give her any more hassle in her frail state. At the same time, I promised Janine that we would keep Mum's incoming calls to a minimum.

At 12 noon on 6th November, I arrived with flowers and her favourite treats: lemonade and fruit drops. I gave her some photos that Dmitri had sent from Moscow. Quite naturally, she was a bit tearful as she ran her fingers over colour prints of her great-grandchildren, whom she hadn't seen for fifteen years. Roman appeared in the doorway at that moment with a bouquet of flowers. Without a second glance, he made straight for Mum and leaned over the bed to wish her a happy birthday. As he straightened up, my brother suddenly noticed me at the back of the room and froze on the spot. Rivka carefully relieved him of the flowers. My brother and I hadn't seen each other for twenty-odd years, and hadn't spoken to each other since Roman had left Mum in Montreal and gone to Toronto. The incapacitated Panther's frightened eyes darted from one son to the other, anticipating a scene. My brother made to leave, but I stopped him in his tracks: "Don't rush off! It's Mum's birthday today. I'll wait outside while you have a chat."

I exited the room and returned half an hour later once Roman had left. Rivka was getting my mother into the wheelchair for our celebration lunch in the cafeteria. Before tucking in, the three of us clinked glasses of lemonade and then we sang the traditional 'Happy Birthday to Mum'!

People at nearby tables joined in with the familiar refrain. Everyone visiting the café finished the song's final phrase and applauded the star of the show. Mum was amazed:

"Misha, how did they know it was my birthday? Did you tell them? Own up!"

"No, Mum, they announced it on the radio today."

"Mishutka, you still like to have your little joke, even though you're an old man now."

We said goodbye by the lift in the hall. Rivka settled Mum into bed, and I set off for Montreal.

I had planned to start writing the actual text of the book in December. But I was stuck on a few points which could only be cleared up definitively in the New York Library of Stage Arts. The only thing for it was to ring Nina Keen, an old friend of Penny's and mine, and ask if she could accommodate her prodigal son for a couple of weeks while he completed his preparatory work on the book project. I decided to go to Manhattan by train via Toronto, so that I could visit Mum in hospital both ends of the journey. When I got to Toronto, Mum was in a sorry state. She hardly ever took off the oxygen mask and her visits to the park with Rivka were happening less often too. I left my New York telephone number in the registrar's office in case of emergency. Mum's doctor advised that she wouldn't make it past New Year. You can imagine how I felt as I headed off to the United States. I tried to justify my trip by telling myself that there was nothing more I could do for Mum, but this didn't make it any easier for either of us.

Nina gave me a terrific welcome, and wanted to hear all about Penny, Dmitri and Mum. She had known about all our family's ins and outs since we'd emigrated together via Rome. She was very upset to hear that Penny and I had split up, and of the tragic situation with Mum too. My friend did a great job of making me feel better, topping me up with a glass of vodka or bowl of borscht until I had got everything off my chest.

"Mishanya, you know that nothing lasts forever in this life. It's inevitable that we'll all go there in the end."

Her husband, Volodya, a famous conductor and close friend of ours, had died in New York recently. Nina and I drank to his memory too. My hostess continued to soothe me with drink.

"You've got to make the most of what you've got here on this earth, my dear. Enjoy what life has to offer. Live your dreams!"

I'd had such a skinful I couldn't recall getting into the warm bed.

I found it hard to concentrate in the library at first. Pictures of my mother kept swirling around in front of me. Scenes from before the war in Odessa merged with trains full of evacuated refugees, Stalingrad bombings and a huge fire that had broken out during the Zhigulyovksy starvation and then Mum's illness in hospital. . . . My mother had always protected her sons from the risk of dying, shielding us with her battered body wherever we were. Now she was fading away in front of her own children whom she'd saved so many times, and they were powerless to stop it. I settled down to work and finished the New York part of the work in December, on schedule. In trepidation, I called Toronto a few times. Mum didn't answer at first, probably because of her oxygen mask. They must have disconnected her telephone altogether as there was no dialling tone even. I left a message in the hospital office for Janine to give me a call in New York.

Nina received a telephone message from the hospital that my mother's condition was continuing to deteriorate. My friend invited me to stay and see in the New Year with friends. This was a tempting offer. But all my senses were telling me the opposite: go and see Mum without delay. Shoving my things into my case without another thought, I raced off to the railway station, much to Nina's surprise. I was a bag of nerves in the train all the way there, sensing that Mum was in a bad way. Panicking now, I grabbed the first available taxi from Toronto Station and tore off to the hospital. At 2.30 p.m. the duty doctor informed me that my mother was in a critical condition. They had been feeding her through a tube in the last few days so that food did not go into her lungs instead of her stomach. At night she could only get to sleep with morphine now because of the acute pain she was experiencing.

"It's best not to disturb her for long now. Leave your suitcase here. You've got about half an hour."

Rivka was very pleased to see me when she came back from her lunch. Apparently Mum was always asking after me. She gave me a white gown and took me into another ward, more fully equipped with modern medical equipment. There was just the one bed in the centre of the room, and no telephone.

Going over to Mum, I smiled cheerily and kissed her forehead. The Panther's dark eyes sparkled with happiness. I perched on the edge of the bed (in breach of clinic rules) and began to reminisce, telling funny stories about our family before and after the war, the family's red-letter days (weddings, birthdays, etc.), when Daniel and I had played our accordions and how my cousin and I had given a rendition of amusing sketches or sung popular hit songs.

After half an hour, the duty sister asked me to bring my visit to a close. I kissed my mother again and pressed my head to her chest as I used to as a boy. With a spasm, she hugged my shoulders and began to groan through the mask. My mother was trying to tell me something using her eyebrows.

Rivka steered me towards the door and then into the registrar's office, keeping a firm hold of my elbow. In a state of shock, I picked up my suitcase and pressed the button to call the lift without thinking. Just then I realised what my mother had been asking me through facial gestures.

Flinging my suitcase and bag against the wall, I sped back to the room where my mother lay. I dropped to my knees in front of her, took her trembling hand in both of mine, and sobbed like a child: "Mummy, forgive me for all the grief and fuss I've given you my whole life. Thank you for your patience, love and care. Please don't blame yourself for the conflict between Roma and me; I forgave you a long time ago for getting it wrong as a mother and favouring one child over another. You dropped lots of hints to me about the serious error you'd made in Montreal. It doesn't matter – I still love you very much!"

I kissed her hand, drenching it in tears. Rivka and a nurse pulled me up off my knees and led me back. My mother was squeezing my fingers, not letting go of her 'happy medium' (as I used to joke). We both knew that we would never see each other again. Finally, she raised her feeble hand and nodded in a farewell gesture. I couldn't stop myself from crying before leaving the hospital. I took a taxi to Central Station, then rang Kozlovsky to ask him to meet me the other end and got the first train to Montreal, hoping to avoid a heart attack.

I had trouble finding Sergei's car in the station forecourt.

He asked: "What's the matter, Berkut? You don't look yourself at all."

"I'll tell you later, Seryozha. Let's go!"

On the way to his place I told my friend in two words why I was so upset. At that moment I couldn't even speak as I was crying so much. My friend understood completely, and without any superfluous pleasantries, he put me to bed after supper.

"Try to get some sleep, Misha. 'An hour before midnight is worth two after twelve.' You're going to need all your strength and wits about you tomorrow."

He must have read my mind. I was tossing and turning all night, unable to sleep a wink. I rang the hospital at 7 a.m.

"It's Mikhail, Anna Pelts' son, she's in intensive care. I'm calling from Montreal. Is my mother still with us?"

"Just a moment," the nurse replied, "our instruments show positive readings. The duty doctor will be doing his rounds with the seriously ill patients, including your mother. Please ring again later."

Sergei appeared from his bedroom at the sound of my voice. I started shivering again as if I had a fever.

"Misha, it's time to let your mother die in peace. Her time has come. Don't make a fuss at the end for someone so close."

"You're right, Sergei. I can't control myself. I expect something's gone wrong there. I can definitely hear my mother calling."

"OK, OK! Go and splash some cold water on your face and these hallucinations will pass. I'll make some tea in the meantime."

I called the hospital again at nine o'clock. Rivka happened to be in the registrar's office, and picked up the telephone.

"Misha, your mum got worse before bedtime yesterday, the doctor prescribed a double dose of morphine and now she is in a coma. It's unlikely that she'll regain consciousness. I'm sorry to be the bearer of bad news."

"Do you mean that the decision was made to put her to sleep? Who gave them the right to cut her life short?"

"They had a discussion with Roma, her official next of kin within the family. He gave his consent for this. In Canada, it is legal to do this when there is no hope, and the decision is taken to put an end to the patient's extreme physical suffering, from a humanitarian point of view. . . ."

Rivka was still speaking, but I didn't hear anything else above the banging of my heart. Something snapped inside me. I didn't notice Sergei sitting me down in the armchair or dousing me with water. I only came to my senses as he splashed the rest of the cold liquid in my face and stated: "Misha, you're frightening me! I don't have time for this now. I have to be at work in an hour."

Kozlovsky lay me down on the settee, stuffed a pillow under my head and charged off to work.

I don't know how long I'd been lying flat out before the man of the house brought me something hot to eat. I asked him to book me a ticket to London on the overnight flight as soon as he could. Once it was confirmed, Sergei helped me to pack my case and gave me a lift to the airport. I didn't say a word all the way there, and felt like the stuffing had been knocked out of me. I thanked my friend for his help and hospitality. On the one-hour flight, I just couldn't understand how Roman could make a unilateral decision to end Mum's life, knowing that I was close at hand in Montreal. At the very least, he could have given me some warning via Dmitri if he'd wanted to.

CHAPTER 15 THE SONATA'S LAST CHORD

During our trip to the former Soviet Union in autumn 1995, Kafuyu and I had visited Tashkent straight from Kiev. We were guests of Bernara Karieva, artistic director of the Uzbek Theatre of Opera and Ballet, who had been a colleague of mine when I was chief ballet master at a neighbouring theatre in Dushanbe, Tadzhikistan, in 1959. After thirty-five years of contributing to the world of theatrical arts, Bernara had garnered a plethora of esteemed titles: 'People's Artist of the USSR', 'Lenin Prizewinner', 'Deputy of the USSR Supreme Soviet', and other honours. Two figures were mentioned in the Uzbek republic's entry in the *Soviet Encyclopaedia*: Islam Karimov, head of the government and Karieva, national ballerina. Bernara received Kafuyu and me with customary, unbeatable Asiatic hospitality. It transpired that along with others from the ballet world, she too had followed in my footsteps and enjoyed a career overseas in America and Europe. Karieva invited me to produce my version of 'Polovtsian Camp' from the opera *Prince Igor* at some point, having seen it in the Buryat Theatre in Ulan-Ude. I agreed to do this, on receipt of an official invitation/contract from her theatre detailing all the terms of engagement.

Two years later in 1997, while I was living in Italy, I received an invitation from Bernara to produce the performance we'd discussed previously, which would involve: opera soloists, a choir, and mime artistes. This was a serious challenge for me, if my last three productions of this work were anything to go by in theatres and the National Academy of Dance in Rome where I was dealing only with ballet performers. In the end, I'd been given the chance to reach a broad, mass audience in the foremost theatre in all of the former Soviet Union's Asiatic republics. Fortune was smiling brightly on her prodigal son.

Once I'd received the relevant details on the dimensions of troupe and stage, I quickly set about tweaking my earlier choreography; working out the musical and theatrical stage positions for the choir and the solo singers with the mime artistes: updating the stage presentation (costumes, decor, lighting, etc.) The week before I left for Asia I was well prepared for creative battle with the former producer of Borodin's opera fifty years ago on the Uzbek stage.

Bernara put me up in her elderly mother's flat in Tashkent; the latter still worked as a senior nurse in the Central Children's Hospital. Karieva's husband was the republic's Minister of Health. My colleague introduced me to him at a government reception and we exchanged business cards. I got to meet the theatre's leadership team over the course of a week. The chief ballet master was Ibrahim Yusupov, my younger classmate from MTA forty years earlier. I felt a distinct lack of warmth from him right from the start. Still, I maintained an emphatically respectful attitude towards him in recognition of his senior position in the ballet, as in his place I too would have been only too aware of a sense of professional rivalry. As you'd expect, when I got to the theatre in the mornings I attended rehearsals for the theatre's various creative groups, and in the evenings I went to see shows to absorb any material that could be used in my forthcoming production. It wasn't an easy task, but there was lots of scope. To this day I still bear the scars from religious opposition to ballet art in neighbouring Tadzhikistan. Karieva guaranteed me creative freedom as a choreographer using her authority as artistic director of the theatre.

At the beginning of the season, Bernara gave her overseas visitor a quick introduction to the group, highlighting my Soviet grounding in professional education at MTA. I gave a brief summary of my modern take on the well-known opera. I asked both ballet répétiteurs to stay on afterwards, and explained my method of working on the production with the male and female corps in parallel fashion, in separate studios.

Seeing their puzzled expressions, Karieva clarified: "Don't look so surprised, folks. Mikhail is well-known for his multitasking as far back as the 1950s in Dushanbe."

The répétiteurs laughed and, taking the words right out of my mouth, began demonstrating stylised movements from Mongolian folklore for the men's or women's repertoire. They worked at such a frenetic pace with the 'corps de ballet' that it was as much as I could do to run from one studio to the other to demonstrate new elements of dance or sequences. Nevertheless, by the end of the first stage of rehearsals, they'd managed to liven up the artistes just back from their annual leave and long drinking binges. Despite being weary, everyone teased the indefatigable choreographer and each other at the end of the working day. As a rule, the répétiteurs agreed to learn new production material beforehand in their own time (without music, but with lights) so as to feel more confident with the dancers at rehearsals and achieve a better result.

It was not so straightforward with the mime artistes. They were old-age pensioners in the main, able to pose or move carefully around the stage in mass scenes. But what I needed were some young and energetic mime artistes who could imitate galloping horses or the hand-to-hand combat employed by the Mongolian horde. I had to ask Karieva to arrange for students from the local ballet and theatre schools to take part in our mass scenes under my direction as part of their studio practice. These young men and women were really enthusiastic about working with me on tableaux of Mongolian warriors or prisoners of various nationalities they'd captured for slave labour.

I couldn't work with the choir members until they'd memorised their singing parts. Their cavalier attitude was a serious concern to me.

For reasons of sensitivity, the most complex task was working with the opera's leading singers in the main roles in Borodin's score: Prince Igor and his wife Yaroslavna; Khan Konchak and his daughter Konchakovna. These venerable, lauded artistes demanded respect and required an appropriately tailored approach in changing the traditional interpretation of their stage characters, and the subtle gestures during their singing in particular. The latter was essential to achieve the clearest and fullest theatrical insight into the action taking place in the performance. The main problem was in the long-held tradition that opera singers and the choir should stand still onstage. I heard it said that 'The public is coming to these shows to hear singing and music.' The rest of the action onstage is of no interest to them, in fact they find it distracting and bothersome. This can be so, if the stage manager and actors do not observe a sensible, artistic balance between a representation's internal content and its external, emotional form in the fluid expression of mime, gestures and movement. So, as we finished working on the next episode with the vocalists (Yaroslavna's weeping, the dialogue between Igor and Konchak, etc.) I asked Bernara to invite the chief producer to my rehearsal to cast a fresh eye over the danger of overenthusiastic acting skills. Of course, afterwards, in Karieva's office, we discussed how to get the right balance of visual content and expressiveness. I insisted on staging classical operas in contemporary style, as this was the current trend worldwide. Usually, thanks to Bernara's clout, we managed to get our way in these arguments.

Rehearsals were always much more productive with the group of ballet soloists. In the first week I taught them a technique for Character dance lifts, unfamiliar to them up to that point. Next I trained them to do partner sequences in Modern style (as opposed to the traditionally Classical), which were included in the choreography of those or other operatic extracts with soloists and singers. These were generally helpful expressive devices, illustrating in artistic form the chorus singers supporting solo arias which told of yearning for their homeland or their husband in prison, the Prince's seduction scenes or the Khan at leisure, skirmishes between Russian and Mongolian fighters, etc. As far as the composition was concerned, it was always just duets. Sometimes group technique in body contact was called for – when the Prince was seduced by three dancing beauties or when Konchakovna was being fêted by her posse of bodyguards. Both of the soloist contingents (male and female) worked tirelessly to synchronise the partner compositions for the final performance, occasionally using acrobatic flight in partnering techniques, where the professionals had to assume a great deal of responsibility for their partners.

As expected, I had to address some challenging issues with the choir. Three-quarters of this group were women, and almost all of them were plump and ungainly from a life of inactivity. The musical director advised me only to work on stage movement with them when Karieva was present, to avoid any potential misunderstandings. Unfortunately, I had to abandon the idea of the Russian choir comprising a vocal group made up from a number of young choir members around the 'weeping' Yaroslavna. In a banal compromise, I used artistes from the 'corps de ballet' in this scene instead, dancing in the background while the choir stood still. The opera singers sabotaged all my production ideas: to move their arms or heads during gaps between songs, but in time to the orchestral music. Bernara was in constant battle with them over each individual move, but to no avail. I had to change half of my stage effects because of the leaden religious limitations imposed on Muslim women in everyday life. Karieva persuaded me to compromise, otherwise their husbands would stop them working in the theatre for good.

"Bernara, as you know, thousands of years ago our Greek forefathers introduced mixed choirs who sang and moved together in the space and recited poetry to music in their open-air amphitheatres. They presented the audience with a huge range of topics or historical events in artistic and graphic format, without any problems whatsoever. Through all the wars there have been up to today, performing arts have been preserved in the folklore of underdeveloped African countries and the cultures of civilised European nations. Only in the higher sphere of operatic and conservatoire (allow me to say) 'art' of the twentieth century, are such frozen canons of imitation folk and historical subjects permitted."

"You know that I'm in complete agreement with you on this, Mikhail. You are also aware of the critical situation our theatre faces currently in terms of its future. You can see the effort I am having to put in to ease your communication problem with the choir singers. In the interests of successfully completing the production, you and I will have to cut a few sharp corners at this stage. I implore you; please don't get the wrong idea. I'm counting on you."

We concluded our conversation with a handshake.

Ibrahim Yusupov, the ballet master, was also responsible for the artistic and production contribution that guest choreographers made to new productions. Where I was concerned, he just helped his counterpart at the opera with the dance costumes. In our discussions with the artistic director about the sketches for a lightweight costume option for the 'corps de ballet' and mime artistes, Ibrahim gave me some friendly advice: not to get too wound up in my eagerness to present Borodin's pre-revolutionary opera in contemporary styles.

He was sympathetic, acknowledging: "Misha, these modern reforms in Classical Opera have not yet reached us from the West. A lot of people in the theatre are not happy about the way you have brought in innovations in such aggressive fashion. 'One man's pleasure is another man's poison.'"

I thanked him for the tip and ventured that it was a bit late to be talking about this now, as we had already adjusted everything that could be changed in this regard.

"As you know, with Ramadan coming up, the management has asked me to fly to London for a few days to purchase some fabric needed for the opera and ballet costumes. May I request that you kindly keep an eye on my production rehearsals in case I get held up for a couple of days? If you need me to bring anything back for you, just say. I'd be happy to do so."

"Thanks, I don't need anything. Don't worry about the rehearsals. This is part of my job."

Karieva handed me a folder of official, blank theatre forms which just had the stamp and director's signature on them to enable me to purchase the required fabrics and ready-made garments. She told me about the critical shortage of medical syringes in the republic's hospitals, leading to many patients dying of post-operative infection. She gave me three copies of an authorised letter in my name, addressed to the British and Russian customs officials, signed by the Uzbek Minister of Health. I was apprehensive, but didn't see how I could refuse this humanitarian request. Still, I had my doubts and was slightly perturbed. When I got home, I asked Bernara's mother if it were true that there was a shortage of syringes for immunisations that children needed, in the hospital where she worked.

The first thing I did in London was to meet up with Penny at her late parents' house in Croydon. In the morning I ordered the necessary fabrics in a central department store and arranged for them to be dispatched to Tashkent as soon as possible. Next I paid a visit to a pharmacy in the city. They kept me waiting a long time for two boxes, each containing 500 syringes. They took 950 pounds from my bank account and asked for a copy of my passport details. I already felt like a hardened criminal as all the staff were treating me so suspiciously. They probably thought I was a drug smuggler. But at the same time, they couldn't refuse a request from the Minister of Health. His Uzbek signature on the English translation of the order was particularly dubious. Anyway, an hour and a half later the manager called a taxi. Two women accompanied me down to the car. They loaded both boxes of syringes into the boot of the taxi and wished me a safe journey. Exceptional politeness has always been the downfall of the English. No doubt I was blacklisted by MI5.

Nevertheless, I sent off a fax straight away from Croydon to Karieva in the theatre: 'Everything's going to plan! One consignment is on its way by air, and I'll bring the other one with me.'

I devoted my third day in London to my own affairs. I topped up the stock of my Character dance videocassettes in the Ballet Bookshop, where I bought newly published books that were of interest to me and souvenir books of photographs for Bernara, Ibrahim and the directors of the ballet and theatre schools. Back home I started to pack for the return journey. Thankfully both boxes of syringes were labelled 'Medical Accessories'. Early next morning I called a taxi and spent a long time at the airport before the flight. I promptly made my way to the customs office, where I advised an official of the contents of my cargo and showed him the relevant documentation. At a sign from him, two customs officers came over with a dog, who didn't react to my boxes, suitcase or bag in the slightest. They also scanned me, before inviting me into a neighbouring room. They asked lots of questions which were recorded. They issued an official receipt for the luggage and said that I would need it at the customs office in Tashkent Airport. I couldn't believe they were letting me through without any fuss.

During the long flight I asked myself the same questions over and over again.

"Mr Berkut?"

"Yes."

"Follow us."

"With great pleasure."

After subjecting me to all the usual routine checks, they led me into the customs centre, where I presented the documents along with Kanayev's business card, a member of the presidium of the Uzbek Parliament. You should have seen the flabbergasted look on the official's face as his shaky hands held the papers.

I reminded him: "Madame Karieva is waiting for me right now in the deputies' lounge in your airport. Please don't cause her to worry when I fail to appear with the consignment for the Ministry of Health."

As soon as she saw me, Bernara rushed over to meet her English guest with an official handshake. She showed her deputy's credentials to the men accompanying me, and asked them to escort us safely to the waiting car. My colleague conducted herself in such a way that all the stern officials around quaked before her, as if she were the British Queen no less. I too colluded in this game, trailing obediently after her in the role of lackey. The only thing missing was for me to be holding the train of Her Majesty's dress.

In the car I described the fabrics I'd bought the chief, but forgot to mention that I'd paid out of my own money. Throughout the entire journey we discussed the state of the *Polovtsian Camp* production process and problems that could arise in producing a contemporary performance with the opera/ballet troupe.

I asked the artistic director if he could drop in on the joint rehearsals of the choir, ballet and mime artistes during the second half of my directorial exercise, to check on the performers' discipline in the theatre to avoid any subtle undermining of the contemporary flavour of stage expression by conservative factions within the local troupe.

The troupe's artistic spirits got a considerable lift in the run-up to the forthcoming premiere with news of the fabrics from London and accessories for *Polovtsian Camp*'s new costumes, plus celebrities from Russian Opera. The more vivid the dramatic impact of the scenes combining the choir and ballet or solo singers and mime artistes, the greater the performers' creative enthusiasm in the second act's lyrical, dramatic episodes. As stage rehearsals went on, the whole show was gradually taking shape, coming together in a beautiful blend of costumes, decoration and light. All the artistes, répétiteurs and stagehands worked flat out for the week leading up to the premiere. None of us wanted to get it wrong on the night. Without Bernara to coordinate the many-layered process of bringing the show to the stage, I could not have coped with this motley crew of performers and technicians. I still don't understand how all of us involved in this theatrical adventure succeeded in getting such a complex opera/ballet production off the ground in such a short time.

Karieva explained the secret of this theatre in one of our tea breaks.

"Misha, with your indomitable energy as producer, you have lit the creative spark in most of our artistes, which has carried them to glory on Pegasus wings in your wake!"

The dress rehearsal, complete with full artistic staging, went unexpectedly well and was of a high standard. Two scenes were particularly engaging: Igor's aria, reminiscing about his homeland in front of a picturesque backdrop featuring the choir of Russian women, symbolising his motherland, and Yaroslavna's weeping – yearning for her captured husband, as a couple performed a lyrical ballet duet behind a veil at the back of the stage. Naturally, the dancers performed the dramatic Tatars' invasion and their battles with their enemies with great artistry, etc. The choreography for the latter was created not in a naturalistic, technical style of sporting combat or pursuits, but in an artistic, graphic method of freestyle dance composition incorporating universal symbolism, and adapted for theatre using moving silhouettes of actual dancers, lit behind a semi-transparent backdrop on the stage. Even the mass scenes by mime artistes were delivered in this unusual, fluid, pantomime style. They injected dynamics and drama into the various episodes through their sculptural groupings and movements around the stage in harmony with the music. By the same token, they reinforced the overall emotional impact on the public. Sadly, I had to put up with a fiasco with the choir. I had trouble getting them to rock their bodies even slightly without moving from their spot, or even shaking their hands or heads in particular places or lining up holding hands in their choir positions. The most interesting part for me as a stage producer was working with the singers in their solos and duets. I was looking for minimal body motion here in their vocal delivery of an image, to achieve optimum stage expression and at the same time avoid disturbing the artistes either in their spiritual, musical interaction with their partner or their solo performance. They were fascinated by this innovation and willing to try various options to perfect their artistic harmony.

The premiere of *Polovtsian Camp* coincided with the republic's anniversary. In actual fact, the entire government attended our debut after their ceremonial meeting. Bernara was very anxious. The problem was that as a result of Perestroika, when the Soviet Union disintegrated, opera theatres in the other Asiatic republics were destroyed. Following internal reconstruction, their buildings were converted into mosques. They had tried to make similar changes in Tashkent too. Karieva had to be prepared to fight to the bitter end to preserve the only remaining monument to opera/ballet art in Central Asia. Breaching state etiquette at meetings with foreign diplomats at government receptions, she asked for their support in preserving the Uzbek Theatre of Opera and Ballet. Both the local and international press ran stories about this spiritual tragedy in the national culture of Central Asian countries. It's a miracle that Bernara survived, testament to her personal endeavours and reputation. 'It's one rule for some, and another for everyone else.' In view of her popularity, the authorities decided to withstand pressure from local religious fanatics until after the republic's anniversary celebrations. *Polovtsian Camp*'s theatre production should have marked a turning point in the question of whether there was a place for classical art in Uzbekistan. For an unbiased and creative outcome in the embodiment of the conceptualised historic episode, as sung in Borodin's opera, the artistic director was seeking (politically and religiously speaking) a neutral choreographer to produce the second act of *Prince Igor*. These reasons made me the best candidate for the job. Karieva was au fait with my creative track record, and had no concerns regarding my suitability.

The Tashkent Opera and Ballet Theatre was sponsored by the American company Coca Cola. By all accounts, it was the government leader's son who had brought this firm into Uzbekistan. They were the ones who signed the contract with me for the *Polovtsian Camp* production and paid for my work in dollars, including the flight tickets to and from Rome. When I asked them to reimburse me for the syringes for local hospitals, they replied that they knew nothing about this. So I turned to Karieva to help me out.

She was very surprised and remarked in overtly farcical fashion: "We all thought that this was a gift from you to our children as a charitable act."

Back home, I asked Bernara's mother once more whether the syringes from London had arrived at her hospital.

"I enquired specially with the management. No one there has heard anything about any English syringes."

As I said goodbye to my MTA colleague, I told Ibrahim the story of the syringes and sought his advice.

"I tried to drill it into you, Misha, that Asia is different to Europe. We have our own way of responding to world events. Forget about the syringes and think about the good things in life, otherwise you're going to have trouble at the airport."

Yusupov had warned me. Before my flight out, I placed my dollars in a plastic bag and hid this in my swimming trucks which I had on. I put my usual underpants over the top to camouflage them. As expected, I was stopped at customs in the airport. They searched my pockets and asked me to open my case and bag.

After they had rummaged around for some time without finding anything incriminating, I decided to ask them: "Excuse me, what are you looking for? Perhaps I can help you?"

"We are looking for foreign currency and syringes."

"I spent the dollars from Coca Cola on gifts for my friends and family in Europe. You will find the syringes with your Minister of Health. Here is his business card."

At this, the customs officers let me go, warning me not to talk to anyone in the airport before my flight. Amazingly, I wasn't in the least bit worried as I'd heard so many stories about the workings of the Mafia in the former Soviet republics – a natural consequence of Perestroika.

What hurt me personally about the Uzbek story with the syringes was not losing the cash, as money comes and goes. Rather, it was the cynical attitude and apparent duplicity from such high-ranking figures as a star from the world of ballet or a government minister. It makes me wonder what kind of sorry excuse for society we have where it is possible for individuals to line their own pockets at the expense of charitable aid for sick children? Stealing syringes intended for them in the aim of selling them on to drug addicts, without any pangs of conscience or fear of the judicial system. *These are people I'm close to, whom I've known and respected for so many years. Everyone in the area talks about this and plays out a cheap farce, turning a blind eye to crimes committed by their superiors, because if the situation were reversed, they too could be castigated both on paper and physically. Of course, this is not the first or last case of its kind, and it would be stupid for a mere mortal to try and fight against such modern vices. However, it's painful to witness talented stage luminaries stooping so morally low as to corrupt themselves.*

It's not without reason that the ancient philosophers affirm the paradox in all areas of Mother Nature's functions, including human ones. Such a natural blend of endless contradictions between strong and weak, wise and naïve, gifted and untalented, etc., no doubt houses the secret of human society's existence, and likewise the entire animal kingdom. Sociologists naturally divide people of any race and nationality or belief systems into three main social types: creators, users and destroyers. From the earliest civilisations, representatives of these groups have tolerated each other or fought among themselves for their rights as unwitting users (children, the elderly, the disabled) or conscious destroyers (murderers, thieves, terrorists) against creators of material and cultural treasures, not wishing to support the latter to their cost. But there are no winners or losers in this internal, political conflict, as in a united society, all three contrasting groups are closely bound through blood and territory. These members, depending on their age, physical condition or social class, cross regularly from one group into another, thereby maintaining the sum of all three sociological categories in the remaining, defined system of government. That is why all members of such a large family, even with the deficiencies in our individual characters, material wealth and social position, must be tolerant of one another, and acknowledge personal differences between us from a humanitarian perspective, taking into account the multifaceted nature of man. We must be guided by a sense of spiritual harmony in the way we are and natural balance in the global environment we share with others.

STAGE VII: BACK TO EARTH

CHAPTER 16 BRAND-NEW CENTURY, SAME OLD PROBLEMS

"Hello! Happy new millennium, Mikhail Semyonovich! May it bring you health and success!"

"Thanks, David, and the same to you!"

"That would be good."

"Are you on your own at the moment?"

"Yes, I don't feel like seeing anyone. I keep picturing my mother lying there just before she passed away. I've been all over the place in the last two weeks."

"This is no good, Misha. You're a strong chap and need to pull yourself together!"

"You're right, my friend. I'll do my best."

"It's always a shock, losing people we love. Hang on in there!"

My cousin in Berlin was the only person to offer me any sympathy while I was going through such a hard time emotionally. None of my children or grandchildren even called me to talk about their grandmother. They were too wrapped up in their everyday lives. I spent the first few days of the New Year in a state of depression, recalling my successes and failures in the West over the last quarter of a century, as was my wont. All in all, this established ballet master had quite a lot to show for his creative work between the ages of forty-five and seventy. I was convinced that I would have achieved more and better creative work if I hadn't got involved in family squabbles and factions.

Ah well! There's no point in locking the stable door after the horse has bolted. You should get on with your theory of Origins of Dance and Mime *and that'll take your mind off your emotional trauma.*

I found it difficult to get on with things. But once I was back in the library, I soon rekindled my interest in the topic of study and resumed my work routine in researching my academic project.

I had kept on my old flat in Montreal's hospital district. The city's new Federal Library housed a rich collection of printed matter on the cultural anthropology of North and South America. I shuttled between England and Canada every three or four weeks, slowly but surely moving forwards in my research. I bought a desktop PC and printer in London, and a laptop with accessories in Montreal. Having learned my way around the electronic technology, I found that the first six months of actually using it made my eye problems significantly worse. Both the hospital and private opticians were unanimous in advising me to stop using the computer altogether with my chronically bad eyesight, a legacy of the Second World War, otherwise I was likely to go blind. I'm afraid I had to decline the treatment on offer and speed up the process to complete the writing of my *Origins* project using technology.

The fact that I was often away from Canada prompted me to hand over the commercial activities of Berkut Dance International (BDI) to Pierre Hardy, my former Kalinka soloist from Les Ballets Russes de Montréal, who by this time had already become an experienced Jazz dance teacher. He'd set up his own private studio and acquired significant commercial experience.

Pierre happily took over sales of my fifteen videocassettes and six audio tapes, both privately and wholesale. He also managed the accounts and earned commission. I was more interested in getting my work out there than making money out of it. His input freed me up to work on the book and stopped me worrying so much about the business while I was abroad. Hardy proved to be a solid partner.

Visiting Africa was absolutely crucial in gaining a deeper insight into primeval ethnography than could be acquired from library materials. Primitive tribal dances to the sound of drums or maracas transported me back to the long-lost past. Ritual, flexible forms of different types and species of animals (from insects to mammals) challenged my hypothesis as an author, which was close to the silhouettes in prehistoric paintings and incised drawings. I got so wrapped up in collecting copies of these samples and placing them in Darwin's evolutionary system that I decided to create a specially illustrated reference book on the anthropology of mime and dance. My pupils – children and adults alike – were forever asking me: "Where did dance and mime come from?" To my great shame, I couldn't give them an intelligent answer, in spite of my excellent education at MTA. It wasn't so much about the history of theatre and dance, but rather their social, everyday origin in the animal kingdom in terms of the original means of interacting and expressing emotions.

The Ethnographic Museum in Palermo provided a wealth of information for my project. My research involved me spending hours at work in Italy (Sicily, Calabria and Sardinia), so it was absolutely vital for me to have a permanent home-study base here. Hearing about this problem, Mara Fusco, director of Balletto di Napoli, my closest friend and colleague at the time, and her husband Marcello di Vincenzo, offered me a cosy peid-à-terre at their home during my visits to Italy. I grew so close to them that to all intents and purposes, I became another member of this big-hearted family. In practical terms, I completed *Origins of Mime and Dance* here.

I wrote the book in English, and obviously needed to transcribe my stilted text into academic language. I remembered my old friend and production director/editor on my video courses in London. I wouldn't find a better proofreader for *Origins*. Andrew Winstone took on this painstaking task with great enthusiasm, patiently converting my raw literary product into print-ready perfection over the course of three years. I doubt that I will ever be able to thank my friend/colleague enough for his enormous contribution to my *Origins of Dance and Mime* project, undertaken in the spirit of friendship rather than any commercial basis. I knew Winstone's family very well. I was always round at their place in connection with work, and found his children Milo and Heloise utterly delightful; he had brought them up single-handedly in a harmonious, conducive learning environment.

All things considered, I have to acknowledge that the richest seam of information on the origin of mime and dance was David Attenborough's unique collection of films and work in print on the individual behaviour and mating rituals of a huge variety of creatures; their reactions and relationships through flexible body movements, rhythmic sounds and facial expressions. When I complimented him warmly in conversation, he expressed regret that he hadn't managed to devote sufficient time in his studies to dance and mime, as being the most expressive device used by all types of animals to convey their emotional states and relationships.

As dance and mime are visual forms of interaction and expression, illustration had a particularly important role to play in my forthcoming book. There is plenty of material in print on this theme. But, for me, what was missing was the bridge between behaviour in the natural world and its artificial stylisation in body motion for communication and performance. I had to enlist the support of a specialist animation artist from Vancouver. Jeffrey Antonio was wholeheartedly recommended by my surrogate daughter Elena Lidina, who had sent me samples of his fascinating work. Antonio stayed with me in Montreal for six months, investing huge imagination and finesse in this singular commission.

In 2005 I completed a mock-up of the illustrations and text based on my collections of dance annotations. Now I could present my project to a publisher. But it wasn't as simple as that! As a rule, higher-education establishments publish academic works by authors of their own. Even glowing references and random recommendations from England did not get me anywhere. I had to look elsewhere for a publisher. I sought Mara Fusco's help, remembering that her new book had been printed in Italy. Her husband Marcello was very enthusiastic about helping me to get published. He and I went to meet Pronto Stampa, a publishing company he knew of in Naples. Acting as my authorised representative, Marcello guaranteed that the author would pay Renato, the Director, as agreed, and we signed a contract. In my thirty-five years of dealing with Italians, I had heard a lot about underhand skulduggery in this fabulously beautiful country. Nevertheless, with Marcello as my front man, I felt totally secure. Mara invited me to stay with her while the book was being published.

From then on, I spent a few months with my colleagues in Naples at various times throughout the year. I would go to Pronto Stampa every morning and work there for five or six hours with Poseidon, the editor, formatting the text and setting it with the illustrations that had been chosen for print. This was genuinely laborious and meticulous work, which brought the eccentric editor and me into constant conflict. I insisted on a smaller book size overall, with lighter-weight paper. But no one paid any heed to the mere author. On top of this, Marcello (my friend and broker) turned traitor. Not wanting to damage his personal relationships with his fellow countrymen, he was agreeing to all their subterfuge so as to extract as much money as he could from me for something he knew to be unachievable. So in his presence, Renato demanded an extra 1,000 euros for the publication, to pay for a special lining to strengthen the overly heavy book. On Marcello's advice, I agreed. When I checked the quality of the binding at the end of the printing process, it turned out to be completely unfit for practical handling of the book. Naturally I refused to accept work like this. It was only after I kicked up a fuss with Pronto Stampa's director that they strengthened the existing lining – in a pathetic attempt at a compromise – in such a way that the book fell apart as soon as it was moved. As a result of this fiasco I fell out with my close friend Mara and her celebrated husband Marcello. What I gained was disgrace as an author on the world stage.

In spite of this, I decided to hold a proper event to launch my ten-year project on the *Origins of Dance and Mime*. I timed this momentous occasion to coincide with my seventy-fifth birthday. Penny did a great job of organising the double celebration in a London restaurant. Our colleagues and old friends flew in for this bash from all over Europe. Hot on England's heels, we repeated the celebrations in Montreal for our American associates. My writing received a generally positive reception, which went some way to compensating for the many years of hard slog and complexities of searching for a new career, and masked the unpleasant aftertaste of the book-publishing process.

Now, when my charges ask me, "Maestro, how did mime and dance first appear in the world?" I magnanimously offer them a copy of my 'unique' work. Every individual has to find their niche in life: something they can be genuinely proud of and share with others. Otherwise, what's the point of life? As the last toasts in honour of the aged birthday boy's book launch faded away, so began the dreary rounds to medical establishments: time to atone for ignoring my health while the book was being published. Still, I just considered all these physical complications and failings as temporary issues, as I fervently believed that the experience of writing a piece of research was worthwhile. My work was well received in the dance world as an academic, historical reference book. During the first three to four years, professionals and enthusiasts of mime and dance purchased the book avidly, and academic institutions in particular. Later, in view of its narrow field of interest, demand for this niche work naturally decreased. My ambition is to republish it in a small-scale version.

In addition to this, my poor anxious brain was already formulating a new lyrical, dramatic plan for my autobiographical epic. I had lived through so many events and eras in different countries over eighty-plus years that I could have filled several books. I decided that the three war years when we were evacuated (1941–44) could be added into the completed ode to my mother, *Beam of Hope*. I could divide the rest of my autobiography into two main periods: Soviet (1945–75) and Emigration (1976–2012). I conditioned myself to write less about life's irritations and more about my creative encounters with Masters of the Arts; my personal theatre and artistic preferences and actions; romantic distractions and moral principles. I looked objectively at my professional highs and lows (this was the hardest part), judging fairly without being unduly critical of others. I exposed the evils of the dictatorial Soviet regime and the cruel acts committed by individual advocates.

Progress on the detailed programme of memoirs was sluggish, partly due to my state of health, and also the fact that part of my personal archive was in Canada, and part in England. I had to make frequent trips between Montreal and London before making a final decision on how to structure my account. In the beginning, I gave it the provisional title *Eternity (Perpetual Motion)*, which really captures the essence of my daily life. In contrast to *Origins*, this time I decided to write in Russian, because of the challenge of converting my common, everyday English into literary style. But I realised immediately that I wouldn't be able to manage with my failing eyesight, and would need a permanent assistant with a computer to help me. After searching long and hard for a suitable candidate, I was lucky enough to find Natalya Savitskaya, a former school teacher from Moscow. A young mother to two young girls, she proved to be an exceptionally well-organised student, who had no hesitation in entrusting me with details of her personal life, which was full of dubious liaisons and upheavals. Her husband Evgeny, an academic, was happy that his wife was engaged in intellectual pursuits in addition to being a mother or doing occasional work for him in the lab. Natalya completely took over as typist for the half-blind author for the five years it took him to finish the book.

CHAPTER 17 IN THE EYE OF THE HURRICANE

In spite of my best efforts, my health (hopeless eyes, rotten back and cancer of the prostate) was deteriorating. My long-standing, chronic defects made me aware of their presence with increasing frequency from all angles, regardless of what the doctors did for me. They affected my state of mind, preventing me from concentrating on my memoirs. The tablets my doctor had prescribed dulled my brain to such an extent that I had to stop taking them, moving on to homeopathic treatment, a strict diet and physiotherapy. This helped a little, but not straight away. I drummed it into my head that from now on, I would just have to keep up with my failings to the bitter end, and this suddenly made it easier to accept the gloomy platitude: 'what's to be will be'.

At the next appointment for my latest test results, the Quebec doctor asked me: "What's happened, Mikhail, have you won the lottery?"

"No, Doctor! I've just got rid of my emotional and psychological problems."

"Is that so?"

"You can put your faith in your doctor but can't give up on yourself! Ha ha!"

Nevertheless, mischievous fate wouldn't leave me alone. After seven comfortable years in my Montreal flat on Rue Lavoie, the city's quietest and greenest street, there was a sudden bolt out of the blue. My peaceful neighbour from the next floor down moved into a retirement home, to be replaced by a twenty-three-year-old waster. As the manager of our building put it: this good for nothing's parents had rented this flat for their sponger of a son, to get some peace and quiet for themselves after this idiot had terrorised his whole family. He and his partner in crime of the same age slept till lunchtime to the neighbours' relief. Then they would turn their so-called 'music' on so loudly that the glass in the windows of the building would shake as if there were an earthquake. From 5 p.m. they would disappear off for a couple of hours (thank God), before returning to start up their cacophony again. In an attempt to get some respite from the trouble-maker, I would go to a nearby library from 9 a.m. to 8 p.m., where I wrote this book, only breaking for lunch. After supper I would go to bed, hoping, like all normal people, to get a good night's kip, as the police are the guardians of sleep at this time.

It didn't turn out like that. Full-blown fights were in full swing below my flat from midnight to 3 a.m. Broken furniture reverberated, saucepan lids rang, buckets and boxes clattered, the floor shook with the thud of bodies and inanimate objects. Naturally, the first night it happened I called the police and led them to the ill-fated flat downstairs. Silence: there was no response to our knock at the door. The police officers looked suspiciously at this elderly schizophrenic in his pyjamas. After knocking for some time, the policemen quite reasonably stated that they had no right to disturb the neighbours any further in the middle of the night, and advised me to seek psychiatric help. I realised that I couldn't prove anything, but promised to come back the next night with a witness of a similar age to me, who lived another floor down underneath the 'entertainers'. Of course this was quite risky: what if she suddenly got cold feet at the idea of observing such blatant troublemakers at her age? But after two further occurrences of the nocturnal goings-on, my neighbour downstairs came to me herself and asked me to come down to her as soon as the next chaotic scene got under way.

The next time there was no answer when the police knocked on the perpetrators' door, the police officers fetched the manager with the keys at 2 a.m. Imagine our surprise on finding the flat empty. All the flats above the first floor in our old blocks had an emergency fire escape down a separate staircase, through the garage on to the street. This safety door into the lobby was ajar, and could only be locked from the inside. One of the police officers went down and returned through the front entrance. He suggested that my neighbour and I wrote and complained to the building proprietor and wished us well. There was nothing more to discuss.

A day later, in response to the threat of a police fine, Leon, the landlord of the residential block, turned up and explained: "The youngsters living downstairs are having fun playing simulated fights with objects and knives on the Internet. This is the 'in thing' with young people all over the world just now."

The bewildered youths agreed to keep the noise down at night. Leon advised us residents to put in our earplugs before retiring to bed. This triggered the zodiac bull in me. It was as much as I could do to restrain my animal instinct to pick up this piece of pond life and hurl him into the dustbin from the third-floor window. I decided instead to enlist the help of local social services. They advised me to move into one of the nearby old people's homes for disabled pensioners of over seventy. That was exactly what I needed! My support worker during my time at 5700 Westbury Avenue, Montreal, was Stephanie Geer. But she was evasive about giving me a reference in support of my registration with the regional old people's home, and even refused to give me their contact details for reasons that were not clear to me. She probably didn't accept that I had a problem in my current accommodation just a few streets away. And I didn't blame her. No one believed my 'stories' about the bandit Internet games. I had to apply to community and social services for assistance, where Sasha Vigent gave me a warm welcome.

Sasha took me to see that very same old people's home, where they put my name down immediately without any fuss. I dropped in there every week to check if a room had become available. Every evening I would return home from the library to my hateful abode. I started sleeping in the kitchen on a fold-up bed, to be further away from the noise of the gaming boys downstairs. I couldn't wait to move out. Eventually, thanks to a worker from community and social services, I was called in to see Anthony, director of the old people's complex, to talk about moving in there soon. The Director went through a list of formal questions in French and concluded by asking if I had any personal preferences regarding my accommodation. I replied in the same courteous manner, that I would find it hard to tolerate loud noise and people smoking nearby, quite genuinely not suspecting that he was trying to catch me out.

At this point, Anthony started as if he'd had an electric shock. "This means that every time your neighbours smoke or put some loud music on, you're going to be running in here to complain. Thanks, but we have enough of that already without you adding to it!"

With these parting words, the Director left the office, leaving me open-mouthed in shock.

I didn't understand the retirement home director's reaction, and sought assistance from community and social services. Sasha Vigent confirmed that Anthony had decided not to give me a place in their complex. Any fool could see that the Director had used 'noise and smoking' as a pretext to refuse me. I asked my friend/assistant Pierre Hardy to find out the real reason for Anthony's antagonistic stance towards me. I really didn't understand how my behaviour or comments sometimes irritated petty bureaucrats such as Stephanie and Anthony. I had made a concerted effort over many years to adapt to life in Canada, forgetting about the preference for French over English in official Quebec institutions. After speaking to the home's director in his first language, my local assistant Pierre advised me to prioritise my health and forget about this unlucky establishment. I should find a flat that met my needs better in the south of the city, and he would help me to move in and get settled as comfortably as possible, without any problems of this kind.

It didn't take me long to find a place back on Rue Maison Neuve, next to Guy metro station, where I had lived in May 1976, during my first visit to Montreal as an immigrant. I liked the flat on the twelfth floor with its balcony and south-facing view. It was compact, cosy, and quiet, and smoking was officially prohibited in communal areas. On the day of the move, Pierre was happy to help me get set up and I had a good laugh joking around with him. Suddenly (just like a cheap blockbuster movie) a shot rang out in the corridor on the other side of my door. Bounding out, I almost crashed into an injured girl, covered in blood in the doorway. A guy with a revolver in his hand was making off down the corridor towards the exit. Pierre called the police on his mobile, while trying to help the girl at the same time. Once more I was in shock, not knowing how to handle any of this.

Welcome to your new home, Mishenka! That's what they call 'out of the frying pan, into the fire'. Youthful neighbours ran out at the sound of the shooting, whispering feverishly about drugs. Pierre clearly didn't want me to suffer any further difficulties, and dragged this newcomer into the 'front-line apartment headquarters'. He tried his utmost to distract me from the events going on around us by planning where to put my furniture and household objects, etc., but my triumphant, happy move had already turned into 'Well, I'll be damned.' I was beginning to feel overwhelmed by gloomy thoughts: I felt a hopeless failure, something I'd never been.

Surely this isn't happening to me again? It's as if evil Fate is stalking me.
Wait a minute, don't panic too soon! This is just a Saturday-night coincidence. That's why no one from the staff is here now. None of them are working today.

Hearing the din of a commotion in the corridor, I opened the door. The cleaners were pushing the wounded woman into the lift in a wheelchair. The remaining policeman was standing guard over the bloodstains on the carpet by my doorway, bearing witness to the scene of the crime. Two eyewitnesses in the flat opposite were turning the contents upside down, searching for evidence. Pierre pulled me inside, forcing me away from the unpleasant spectacle, as he was aware of my extremely impressionable nature. Towards midnight we finally found a home for all my bits and pieces in the cupboards and went our separate ways. All night long I dreamed of shootings, burglaries, muggings and similar nightmare scenarios.

When I registered for my new accommodation at Chateau Tower, Cristiano, the manager, persuaded me to pay double the rent in the first and last months, promising to give the entire flat a prompt clean-up, repair the communication devices that didn't work, and replace broken glass in the window. He did not fulfil any of his undertakings. *That's just what you need, you fool!* Then on my second day as a resident in this highly prestigious building I noticed a foul smell from the corridor. It wasn't cigarettes or marijuana, but something more toxic. I called down to the manager and assured him that if he didn't sort out this poisonous odour I would call the police.

He gave a nasty laugh in response: "Welcome! We wish you well!"

I realised that I was in deep shit and was forced to call on my assistant again, as I couldn't get to sleep a few nights running because of the stifling smell emanating from the corridor and nearby flats. I was well aware that this all seemed so far-fetched that no one would ever believe what was going on.

I felt awful about bothering Pierre again, and was worried that he would also regard me as mentally unwell or someone with social problems. But tolerating these night trials any longer was beyond me now. Visiting me before bedtime, my rescuer first knocked on my neighbours' doors on either side of me. He had to establish for himself whether the origin of this odour came from their flats. He repeated this process with many occupants upstairs and downstairs, apologising for disturbing them at such a late hour. Each time, Pierre asked the residents where they thought the smell came from. As if scripted, all of them named that same flat opposite mine, the one from which they had taken the injured girl to hospital on the day I'd moved in. I couldn't understand how I'd got into such a predicament and thought I must be hallucinating. The manager had clearly been economical with the truth when he explained to residents that this smell was just the natural smell of the varnish on the parquet flooring or DIY activity in the flats. But no one was having any work done on our floor at that time, as none of the flats were vacant.

When I asked Pierre if he could write a formal complaint to the police in French, he stated: "There's no point! It's not a criminal offence in Quebec to smoke marijuana or sniff aerosols."

In actual fact, at the entrance to our building, and indeed at the front door of each large residential or office block on Rue Maison Neuve, young people openly offered a range of tobacco and solvent-based drugs to people going in and out at any time of night or day. These also included those same aerosol chemicals which made me feel nauseous and physically sick at night, and had me waking up with a headache in the mornings.

I decided that I couldn't and shouldn't put up with one misfortune after another. I was pushing my destiny to its limits again. Ironically, my experience as a child in Stalingrad during the Second World War had produced a strong and acute instinct in me when it came to fighting for my own survival, a characteristic common to all species in the animal kingdom. Sometimes I couldn't even find any logic to explain this internal drive for physical survival and action based on pure instinct. That is how it was during the war and it was happening to me again now. First it was triggered by the simulated Internet night battles below my flat on Rue Lavoie; next, in-house bigots in the retirement home off Côte Ste Catherine and finally, by the glut of drug addicts in the neighbouring flat on the same floor as me at Chateau Tower on Rue Maison Neuve. Isn't that rather a lot for a solitary, elderly disabled man? When a situation becomes especially dramatic at a certain stage of life, there comes a moment when each of us has to decide whether it's worth going deeper into battle for your own miserable (at that moment) existence, or better to avoid these chronic situations which threaten your peace of mind and even your life itself at times. 'Letting go doesn't have to mean giving up.'

I called my assistant Hardy and my old friend Sergei Onikichuk to come and see me urgently, and advised them that due to unforeseen circumstances I was moving to England on a permanent basis, but retaining my Canadian citizenship. I would come to Montreal regularly to see my close friends, along with New York, Vancouver and other North American cities. I asked them to help me pack and divide up between them all the items in the flat apart from my personal belongings. After this shock news, they completed the arrangements for the immigrant's unexpected evacuation to Europe over the following weekend. By Monday morning the fugitive was already in London, but there was no welcome party or flowers. Penny had agreed beforehand that I could stay in Croydon for a while, in the house her late parents had left her, while I looked for suitable accommodation. You can imagine how I felt about fleeing Canada, the place I'd dreamed about for so many years before leaving the Soviet Union for the first time. Sadly, I had to choose the lesser of two evils.

After I left, Pierre Hardy sent off a barrage of indignant protests to the provincial social-welfare authorities, police departments and human-rights bodies. The telephone rang non-stop during my first week in London, with officials from various Quebec organisations enquiring about the reasons for my sudden departure. I wasn't inclined to jump on the political bandwagon regarding the particular circumstances of their lack of care for the moral and physical condition of an elderly disabled man. But not to say anything would also have been unconscionable. So I gave everyone the same response: I spared myself social discrimination and corruption in the province's care services. I had emigrated to my beloved Canada thirty-five years earlier: the land of my hopes and future creative career. I had been happy there, acquiring many good friends. I never thought that dedicating so many years to Canada's cultural scene and my beloved pupils would lead to being bankrupted by that same country. In actual fact, the social departments personified by Stephanie, Anthony and similar bureaucrats had outraged not only me, but humanity itself.

EPILOGUE

At the end of one's journey through life, any intelligent person looks back in an attempt to define what motivated them to act as they did in both positive and negative contexts, and to re-evaluate anything that remains unresolved: actions undertaken without sober judgement but driven by emotional impulse or physiological shutdown of the brain's workings. No one has yet succeeded in changing their own core nature. Generally man, like any animal, enters and leaves the world with the same genes passed down through the generations. But just like all his zoological brothers, linked by the aim of surviving biophysically or conditioned by reflex, he is able to tolerate many changes in atmosphere, geography and social settings. Everything depends on the nuances of the said individual's character, and the motor and psychological memory of cells in his muscular and nervous systems or instinct, as to whether he risks repeating the negative effects from the world around him, or continues using its positive sources to ensure long-term survival. Our planet's entire animal kingdom has been founded on this kind of primitive principle of survival of generations over several million years. And there is nothing wrong in that, it's just the laws of nature.

Man is the only inspired creature capable of logical thought, scientific discovery, space exploration, and so on. At the same time, no other animal on the globe would set out to kill their young or fellow tribesmen for no reason, destroy their own creations and objects of spiritual value in the name of racial, ideological and religious convictions. Clearly, something pathological has happened to man in the process of his cultural anthropology. The human conscience of the most superior representative of zoological species has overcome fear of conquering space, instead of fighting for proper release from incurable diseases. The extreme preoccupation with electronic technology has caused sedentary members of our society to become unnecessarily obese and lose the ability of independent, analytical thought if there is no screen in front of them. Children from the age of three sit in front of computers for hours instead of engaging in the physical activity that is so essential to their health: dancing, sport, energetic play, etc. If this process of man's self-destruction does not stop now, the next century could be our last on this planet.

People, get your heads out of the clouds and back down to Mother Earth on your own two feet, before it's too late. You've got to move your body regularly, even if only to do some physical activity on the spot – this is crucial to Man's continued biophysical existence!

MY PROFESSIONAL CAREER

Musician/accordionist for the Lilliputian Circus, Odessa Philharmonic	1948
Dancing in Odessa Opera Theatre Corps de Ballet	1950
Ballet Master/Choreography Faculty, Moscow Theatre Academy	1956
Artistic Director of Ballet, Tadzhik Opera Theatre, Dushanbe	1959
Artistic Director of Ballet, Buryat Opera Theatre, Ulan-Ude	1961
Artistic Director of Song and Dance Ensemble, Leningrad Philharmonic	1963
Artistic Director, 'Sputnik' – Bolshoi Satellite, Moscow	1967

Producer/Choreographer of commemorative concerts/festivals:

40th Anniversary of Buryat-Mongolian Autonomous Republic, former USSR	1962
20th Anniversary of Victory over Germany, Leningrad	1965
50th Anniversary of October Revolution, with I. Toumanoff, Moscow Kremlin	1967
100th Anniversary of birth of Lenin, the Columned Hall, Moscow	1971
30th Anniversary of Victory over Germany, Odessa Opera Theatre	1975

Author of libretto and choreography for own ballet repertoire, including:

Dancing Dolls to music by Shostakovich, Tadzhik Ballet, Dushanbe	1960
Poem of Man to music by various composers, Buryat Ballet, Ulan-Ude	1962
Appassionata to music by Beethoven, Bolshoi 'Sputnik', Moscow	1971
Class Concert, Les Ballet Russes de Montréal, Canada	1979
Lisztiana to music by F. Liszt: Academia Nazionale di Danza, Rome	1996

Own versions of classical opera/ballet repertoire:

Polish Act from *Ivan Susanin* by Glinka, Tadzhik Opera House	1959
'Fairy Doll' by Bayer (from Imperial repertoire) with 'Goh Ballet', Vancouver	1994
'Polovtsian Camp' from the opera *Prince Igor* by Borodin, with Uzbek Ballet	1995
Act III of *Swan Lake* Ballet by Tchaikovsky, with Balletto di Napoli	2003

Over 250 choreographic compositions in dramas, operas, shows, festivals, etc.

Arrest and exile to Gorky Automobile Plant, the Urals, for three years 1972

Emigration from Ukraine. Teaching at Academia Nazionale di Danza, Rome	1975

Settled in Montreal. Teaching in École Supérieure de Grands Ballets
    Canadiens   1976
Founded Dance School 'Les Ballets Russes de Montréal'   1977
Created Folk Dance Ensemble 'Kalinka' with European repertoire   1979
Created contemporary Dance Ensemble 'Mini Ballets Russes'   1981
Teacher/choreographer at The Royal Ballet School, London, UK   1984
Periodic seminars and stages for teachers and dancers in Europe and USA   1992

Production:

Fifteen video courses for Historical (Court) and Character (Theatre) dancing   1985
Six audio cassettes of musical accompaniment for Character/Historical
    repertoire   1986
Piano scores of accompaniment for dance classes   1987
'60 Plus' somatic physiotherapy video course (to combat arthritis):
    in production   2016

Publication of various dance textbooks and choreographic notation:

Heroism Through the Generations (Revolution, War and Space), Iskusstvo,
    Moscow   1967
Dancing Girls (Russian, Ukrainian and Moldovan), Sovietskaya
    Rossiya, Moscow   1970
Origin of Mime and Dance: Ten years of anthropological research,
    'Prontoprint', Italy   2007
Historical articles and critical reviews in European and American
    dance magazines   2013
Beam of Hope (an ode to my mother), Pegasus Elliot Mackenzie
    Publishers, UK   2015
Perpetual Motion: autobiographical work about my creative life,
    Arthur H. Stockwell Ltd, UK   2016